Econometrics

Econometrics

FUMIO HAYASHI

PRINCETON UNIVERSITY PRESS
PRINCETON AND OXFORD

Published by Princeton University Press
41 William Street, Princeton, New Jersey 08540

In the United Kingdom: Princeton University Press, 3 Market Place,
Woodstock, OX20 1SY

Library of Congress Cataloging-in-Publication Data
Hayashi, Fumio.
Econometrics / Fumio Hayashi.
p. cm.
Includes bibliographical references and index.
ISBN 0-691-01018-8 (alk. paper)
1. Econometrics. I. Title.

HB139.H39 2000
330′.01′5195—dc21 00–034665

This book has been composed in Times Roman and Helvetica

The paper used in this publication meets the minimum requirements of
ANSI/NISO Z39.48-1992 (R 1997)
(Permanence of Paper)

www.pup.princeton.edu

Printed in the United States of America

10 9 8 7 6 5 4 3 2 1

Contents

List of Figures

Preface

This book is designed to serve as the textbook for a first-year graduate course in econometrics. It has two distinguishing features. First, it covers a full range of techniques with the estimation method called the Generalized Method of Moments (GMM) as the organizing principle. I believe this unified approach is the most efficient way to cover the first-year materials in an accessible yet rigorous manner. Second, most chapters include a section examining in detail original applied articles from such diverse fields in economics as industrial organization, labor, finance, international, and macroeconomics. So the reader will know how to *use* the techniques covered in the chapter and under what conditions they are applicable.

Over the last several years, the lecture notes on which this book is based have been used at the University of Pennsylvania, Columbia University, Princeton University, the University of Tokyo, Boston College, Harvard University, and Ohio State University. Students seem to like the book a lot. My own experience from teaching out of the book is that students think the book is better than the instructor.

Prerequisites

The reader of this book is assumed to have a working knowledge of the basics of calculus, probability theory, and linear algebra. An understanding of the following concepts is taken for granted: functions of several variables, partial derivatives, integrals, random variables, joint distributions, independence, unconditional and conditional expectations, variances and covariances of vector random variables, normal distributions, chi-square distributions, matrix multiplication, inverses of matrices, the rank of a matrix, determinants, and positive definite matrices. Any relevant concepts above this level will be introduced as the discussion progresses. Results on partitioned matrices and Kronecker products are collected in the appendix. Prior exposure to undergraduate econometrics is not required.

Organization of the Book

To understand how the book is organized, it is useful to distinguish between a *model* and an *estimation procedure*. The basic premise of econometrics is that economic data (such as postwar U.S. GDP) are random variables. A *model* is a family of probability distributions that could possibly have generated the economic data. An *estimation procedure* is a data-based protocol for choosing from the model a particular distribution that is likely to have generated the data. Most estimation procedures in econometrics are a specialization of the GMM estimation principle. For example, when GMM is applied to a model called the classical linear regression model, the resulting estimation procedure is Ordinary Least Squares (OLS), the most basic estimation procedure in econometrics. This viewpoint is the organizing principle in the first six chapters of the book, where most of the standard estimation procedures are presented.

The book could have presented GMM in the first chapter, but that would deprive the reader of the option to follow a series of topics specific to OLS without getting distracted by GMM. For this reason I chose to use the first two chapters to present the finite-sample and large-sample theory of OLS. GMM is presented in Chapter 3 as a generalization of OLS.

A major expositional innovation of the book is to treat multiple-equation estimation procedures — such as Seemingly Unrelated Regressions (SUR), Three-Stage Least Squares (3SLS), the Random-Effects method, covered in Chapter 4, and the Fixed-Effects method covered in Chapter 5 — as special cases of the single-equation GMM of Chapter 3. This makes it possible to derive the statistical properties of those advanced techniques merely by suitably specializing the results about single-equation GMM developed in Chapter 3. Chapter 6 completes the book's discussion of GMM by indicating how serial dependence in the error term can be incorporated in GMM.

For some models in econometrics, Maximum Likelihood (ML) is the more natural estimation principle than GMM. ML is covered in Chapters 7 and 8. To make clear the relationship between GMM and ML, the book's discussion of ML starts out in Chapter 7 with an estimation principle called Extremum Estimators, which includes both ML and GMM as special cases. Applications of ML to various models are covered in Chapter 8.

The book also includes an extensive treatment of time-series analysis. Basic time-series topics are covered in Section 2.2 and in the first half of Chapter 6. That is enough of a prerequisite for the important recent advances in nonstationary time-series analysis, which are covered in the last two chapters of the book.

Designing a Course Out of the Book

Several different courses can be designed based on the book.

- Assuming that the course meets twice for an hour and a half, eight weeks should be enough to cover core theory, which is Chapters 1–4 and 6 (excluding those sections on specific economic applications), Chapter 7 (with proofs and examples skipped), and Chapter 8.

- A twelve-week semester course can cover, in addition to the core theory, Chapter 5 and the economic applications included in Chapters 1–6.
- A short (say, six-week) course specializing in GMM estimation in cross-section and panel data would cover Chapters 1–5 (excluding Sections 2.10–2.12 but including Section 2.2). Chapters 7 and 8 (excluding Section 8.7) would add the ML component to the course.
- A short time-series course covering recent developments with economic applications would consist of Chapter 1 (excluding Section 1.7), Chapter 2, parts of Chapters 6 and 7 (Sections 6.1–6.5, 6.8, and 7.1), and Chapters 9 and 10. The applications sections in Chapters 2, 6, 9, and 10 can be dropped if the course focuses on just theory.

Review Questions and Analytical Exercises

The book includes a number of short questions for review at the end of each chapter, with lots of hints (and even answers). They can be used to check whether the reader actually understood the materials of the section. On the second reading, if not the first, readers should try to answer them before proceeding. Answers to selected review questions are available from the book's website, http://pup.princeton.edu/titles/6946.html.

There are several analytical exercises at the end of each chapter that ask the reader to prove results left unproved in the text or supplementary results that are useful for their own sake. Unless otherwise indicated, analytical exercises can be skipped without loss of continuity.

Empirical Exercises

Each chapter usually has one big empirical exercise. It asks for a replication of the empirical results of the original article discussed in the applications section of the chapter and an estimation of the various extensions of the article's model using the estimation procedures presented in the chapter. The dataset for estimation, which usually is the same as the one used by the original article, can be downloaded from the book's website mentioned above.

To implement the estimation procedure on the dataset, readers should run a statistical package on a computer. There are many statistical packages that are widely used in econometrics. They include GAUSS (www.aptech.com), MATLAB (www.mathworks.com), Eviews (www.eviews.com), LIMDEP (www.limdep.com),

RATS (www.estima.com), SAS (www.sas.com), Stata (www.stata.com), and TSP (www.tsp.com). GAUSS and MATLAB are different from the rest in that they are matrix-based languages rather than a collection of procedures. Consider, for example, carrying out OLS with GAUSS or MATLAB. After loading the dataset into the computer's workspace, it takes several lines reflecting the matrix operations of OLS to calculate the OLS estimate and associated statistics (such as R^2). With the other packages, which are procedure-driven and sometimes called "canned packages," those several lines can be replaced by a one-line command invoking the OLS procedure. For example, TSP's OLS command is `OLSQ`.

There are advantages and disadvantages with canned packages. Obviously, it takes far fewer lines to accomplish the same thing, so one can spend less time on programming. On the other hand, procedures in a canned package, which accept data and spit out point estimates and associated statistics, are essentially a black box. Sometimes it is not clear from the documentation of the package how certain statistics are calculated. Although those canned packages mentioned above regularly incorporate new developments in econometrics, the estimation procedure desired may not be currently supported by the package, in which case it will be necessary to write one's own procedures in GAUSS or MATLAB. But it may be a blessing in disguise; actually writing down the underlying matrix operations provides you with an excellent chance to understand the estimation procedure.

With only a few exceptions, all the calculations needed for the empirical exercises of the book can be carried out with any of the canned packages mentioned above. My recommendation, therefore, is for economics Ph.D. students who are planning to write an applied thesis using state-of-the-art estimation procedures or a theoretical thesis proposing new ones, to use GAUSS or MATLAB. Otherwise, students should use any of the canned packages mentioned above.

Mathematical Notation

There is no single mathematical notation used by everyone in econometrics. The book's notation follows the most standard, if not universal, practice. Vectors are treated as column vectors and written in bold lowercase letters. Matrices are in bold uppercase letters. The transpose of the matrix $\mathbf{A}$ is denoted by $\mathbf{A}'$. Scalar variables are (mostly lowercase) letters in italics.

Acknowledgments

I acknowledge with gratitude help from the following individuals and institutions. Mark Watson, Dale Jorgenson, Bo Honore, Serena Ng, Masao Ogaki, and Jushan Bai were kind and courageous enough to use early versions of the book as the textbook for their econometrics courses. Comments made by them and their students have been incorporated in this final version. Yuzo Honda read the manuscript and offered helpful suggestions. Naoto Kunitomo, Whitney Newey, Serena Ng, Pierre Perron, Jim Stock, Katsuto Tanaka, Mark Watson, Hal White, and Yoshihiro Yajima took time out to answer my questions and enquiries. Two graduate students at University of Tokyo, Mari Sakudo and Naoki Shimoi, read the entire manuscript to weed out typos. Their effort was underwritten by a grant-in-aid from the Zengin Foundation for Studies on Economics and Finance. Peter Dougherty, my editor at Princeton University Press, provided enthusiasm and just the right amount of pressure. Stephanie Hogue was a versatile enough LaTeX expert to accommodate my formatting whims. Ellen Foos supervised production of the book. Last but not least, Jessica Helfand agreed, probably out of friendship, to do the cover design.

For more than five years all my free time went into writing this book. Now, having completed the book, I feel like someone who has just been released from prison. My research suffered, but hopefully the profession has not noticed.

Econometrics

CHAPTER 1

Finite-Sample Properties of OLS

ABSTRACT

The **Ordinary Least Squares** (OLS) estimator is the most basic estimation procedure in econometrics. This chapter covers the **finite-** or **small-sample properties** of the OLS estimator, that is, the statistical properties of the OLS estimator that are valid for any given sample size. The materials covered in this chapter are entirely standard. The exposition here differs from that of most other textbooks in its emphasis on the role played by the assumption that the regressors are "strictly exogenous."

In the final section, we apply the finite-sample theory to the estimation of the cost function using cross-section data on individual firms. The question posed in Nerlove's (1963) study is of great practical importance: are there increasing returns to scale in electricity supply? If yes, microeconomics tells us that the industry should be regulated. Besides providing you with a hands-on experience of using the techniques to test interesting hypotheses, Nerlove's paper has a careful discussion of why the OLS is an appropriate estimation procedure in this particular application.

1.1 The Classical Linear Regression Model

In this section we present the assumptions that comprise the classical linear regression model. In the model, the variable in question (called the **dependent variable**, the **regressand**, or more generically the **left-hand [-side] variable**) is related to several other variables (called the **regressors**, the **explanatory variables**, or the **right-hand [-side] variables**). Suppose we observe n values for those variables. Let y_i be the i-th observation of the dependent variable in question and let $(x_{i1}, x_{i2}, \ldots, x_{iK})$ be the i-th observation of the K regressors. The **sample** or **data** is a collection of those n observations.

The data in economics cannot be generated by experiments (except in experimental economics), so both the dependent and independent variables have to be treated as random variables, variables whose values are subject to chance. A **model** is a set of restrictions on the joint distribution of the dependent and independent variables. That is, a model is a set of joint distributions satisfying a set of assumptions. The classical regression model is a set of joint distributions satisfying Assumptions 1.1–1.4 stated below.

The Linearity Assumption

The first assumption is that the relationship between the dependent variable and the regressors is linear.

Assumption 1.1 (linearity):

$$y_i = \beta_1 x_{i1} + \beta_2 x_{i2} + \cdots + \beta_K x_{iK} + \varepsilon_i \quad (i = 1, 2, \ldots, n), \tag{1.1.1}$$

where β*'s are unknown parameters to be estimated, and* ε_i *is the unobserved error term with certain properties to be specified below.*

The part of the right-hand side involving the regressors, $\beta_1 x_{i1} + \beta_2 x_{i2} + \cdots + \beta_K x_{iK}$, is called the **regression** or the **regression function**, and the coefficients (β's) are called the **regression coefficients**. They represent the marginal and separate effects of the regressors. For example, β_2 represents the change in the dependent variable when the second regressor increases by one unit while other regressors are held constant. In the language of calculus, this can be expressed as $\partial y_i / \partial x_{i2} = \beta_2$. The linearity implies that the marginal effect does not depend on the level of regressors. The error term represents the part of the dependent variable left unexplained by the regressors.

Example 1.1 (consumption function): The simple consumption function familiar from introductory economics is

$$CON_i = \beta_1 + \beta_2 YD_i + \varepsilon_i, \tag{1.1.2}$$

where *CON* is consumption and *YD* is disposable income. If the data are annual aggregate time-series, CON_i and YD_i are aggregate consumption and disposable income for year i. If the data come from a survey of individual households, CON_i is consumption by the i-th household in the cross-section sample of n households. The consumption function can be written as (1.1.1) by setting $y_i = CON_i$, $x_{i1} = 1$ (a constant), and $x_{i2} = YD_i$. The error term ε_i represents other variables besides disposable income that influence consumption. They include those variables — such as financial assets — that might be observable but the researcher decided not to include as regressors, as well as those variables — such as the "mood" of the consumer — that are hard to measure. When the equation has only one nonconstant regressor, as here, it is called the **simple regression model**.

The linearity assumption is not as restrictive as it might first seem, because the dependent variable and the regressors can be transformations of the variables in question. Consider

Example 1.2 (wage equation): A simplified version of the wage equation routinely estimated in labor economics is

$$\log(WAGE_i) = \beta_1 + \beta_2 S_i + \beta_3 TENURE_i + \beta_4 EXPR_i + \varepsilon_i, \qquad (1.1.3)$$

where $WAGE$ = the wage rate for the individual, S = education in years, $TENURE$ = years on the current job, and $EXPR$ = experience in the labor force (i.e., total number of years to date on all the jobs held currently or previously by the individual). The wage equation fits the generic format (1.1.1) with $y_i = \log(WAGE_i)$. The equation is said to be in the **semi-log** form because only the dependent variable is in logs. The equation is derived from the following nonlinear relationship between the level of the wage rate and the regressors:

$$WAGE_i = \exp(\beta_1)\exp(\beta_2 S_i)\exp(\beta_3 TENURE_i)\exp(\beta_4 EXPR_i)\exp(\varepsilon_i). \qquad (1.1.4)$$

By taking logs of both sides of (1.1.4) and noting that $\log[\exp(x)] = x$, one obtains (1.1.3). The coefficients in the semi-log form have the interpretation of *percentage changes*, not changes in levels. For example, a value of 0.05 for β_2 implies that an additional year of education has the effect of raising the wage rate by 5 percent. The difference in the interpretation comes about because the dependent variable is the log wage rate, not the wage rate itself, and the change in logs equals the percentage change in levels.

Certain other forms of nonlinearities can also be accommodated. Suppose, for example, the marginal effect of education tapers off as the level of education gets higher. This can be captured by including in the wage equation the squared term S^2 as an additional regressor in the wage equation. If the coefficient of the squared term is β_5, the marginal effect of education is

$$\beta_2 + 2\beta_5 S \quad (= \partial \log(WAGE)/\partial S).$$

If β_5 is negative, the marginal effect of education declines with the level of education.

There are, of course, cases of genuine nonlinearity. For example, the relationship (1.1.4) could not have been made linear if the error term entered additively rather than multiplicatively:

$$WAGE_i = \exp(\beta_1)\exp(\beta_2 S_i)\exp(\beta_3 TENURE_i)\exp(\beta_4 EXPR_i) + \varepsilon_i.$$

Estimation of nonlinear regression equations such as this will be discussed in Chapter 7.

Matrix Notation

Before stating other assumptions of the classical model, we introduce the vector and matrix notation. The notation will prove useful for stating other assumptions precisely and also for deriving the OLS estimator of $\boldsymbol{\beta}$. Define K-dimensional (column) vectors $\mathbf{x}_i$ and $\boldsymbol{\beta}$ as

$$\underset{(K\times 1)}{\mathbf{x}_i} = \begin{bmatrix} x_{i1} \\ x_{i2} \\ \vdots \\ x_{iK} \end{bmatrix}, \quad \underset{(K\times 1)}{\boldsymbol{\beta}} = \begin{bmatrix} \beta_1 \\ \beta_2 \\ \vdots \\ \beta_K \end{bmatrix}. \tag{1.1.5}$$

By the definition of vector inner products, $\mathbf{x}_i'\boldsymbol{\beta} = \beta_1 x_{i1} + \beta_2 x_{i2} + \cdots + \beta_K x_{iK}$. So the equations in Assumption 1.1 can be written as

$$y_i = \mathbf{x}_i'\boldsymbol{\beta} + \varepsilon_i \quad (i = 1, 2, \ldots, n). \tag{1.1.1$'$}$$

Also define

$$\underset{(n\times 1)}{\mathbf{y}} = \begin{bmatrix} y_1 \\ \vdots \\ y_n \end{bmatrix}, \quad \underset{(n\times 1)}{\boldsymbol{\varepsilon}} = \begin{bmatrix} \varepsilon_1 \\ \vdots \\ \varepsilon_n \end{bmatrix}, \quad \underset{(n\times K)}{\mathbf{X}} = \begin{bmatrix} \mathbf{x}_1' \\ \vdots \\ \mathbf{x}_n' \end{bmatrix} = \begin{bmatrix} x_{11} & \ldots & x_{1K} \\ \vdots & \ldots & \vdots \\ x_{n1} & \ldots & x_{nK} \end{bmatrix}. \tag{1.1.6}$$

In the vectors and matrices in (1.1.6), there are as many rows as there are observations, with the rows corresponding to the observations. For this reason $\mathbf{y}$ and $\mathbf{X}$ are sometimes called the **data vector** and the **data matrix**. Since the number of columns of $\mathbf{X}$ equals the number of rows of $\boldsymbol{\beta}$, $\mathbf{X}$ and $\boldsymbol{\beta}$ are conformable and $\mathbf{X}\boldsymbol{\beta}$ is an $n\times 1$ vector. Its i-th element is $\mathbf{x}_i'\boldsymbol{\beta}$. Therefore, Assumption 1.1 can be written compactly as

$$\underset{(n\times 1)}{\mathbf{y}} = \underbrace{\underset{(n\times K)}{\mathbf{X}}\underset{(K\times 1)}{\boldsymbol{\beta}}}_{(n\times 1)} + \underset{(n\times 1)}{\boldsymbol{\varepsilon}}.$$

The Strict Exogeneity Assumption

The next assumption of the classical regression model is

Assumption 1.2 (strict exogeneity):

$$\mathrm{E}(\varepsilon_i \mid \mathbf{X}) = 0 \quad (i = 1, 2, \ldots, n). \tag{1.1.7}$$

Here, the expectation (mean) is conditional on the regressors for *all* observations. This point may be made more apparent by writing the assumption without using the data matrix as

$$\mathrm{E}(\varepsilon_i \mid \mathbf{x}_1, \ldots, \mathbf{x}_n) = 0 \quad (i = 1, 2, \ldots, n).$$

To state the assumption differently, take, for any given observation i, the joint distribution of the $nK + 1$ random variables, $f(\varepsilon_i, \mathbf{x}_1, \ldots, \mathbf{x}_n)$, and consider the conditional distribution, $f(\varepsilon_i \mid \mathbf{x}_1, \ldots, \mathbf{x}_n)$. The conditional mean $\mathrm{E}(\varepsilon_i \mid \mathbf{x}_1, \ldots, \mathbf{x}_n)$ is in general a nonlinear function of $(\mathbf{x}_1, \ldots, \mathbf{x}_n)$. The strict exogeneity assumption says that this function is a constant of value zero.[1]

Assuming this constant to be zero is not restrictive if the regressors include a constant, because the equation can be rewritten so that the conditional mean of the error term is zero. To see this, suppose that $\mathrm{E}(\varepsilon_i \mid \mathbf{X})$ is μ and $x_{i1} = 1$. The equation can be written as

$$\begin{aligned} y_i &= \beta_1 + \beta_2 x_{i2} + \cdots + \beta_K x_{iK} + \varepsilon_i \\ &= (\beta_1 + \mu) + \beta_2 x_{i2} + \cdots + \beta_K x_{iK} + (\varepsilon_i - \mu). \end{aligned}$$

If we redefine β_1 to be $\beta_1 + \mu$ and ε_i to be $\varepsilon_i - \mu$, the conditional mean of the new error term is zero. In virtually all applications, the regressors include a constant term.

[1] Some authors define the term "strict exogeneity" somewhat differently. For example, in Koopmans and Hood (1953) and Engle, Hendry, and Richards (1983), the regressors are strictly exogenous if $\mathbf{x}_i$ is independent of ε_j for all i, j. This definition is stronger than, but not inconsistent with, our definition of strict exogeneity.

Example 1.3 (continuation of Example 1.1): For the simple regression model of Example 1.1, the strict exogeneity assumption can be written as

$$\mathrm{E}(\varepsilon_i \mid YD_1, YD_2, \dots, YD_n) = 0.$$

Since $\mathbf{x}_i = (1, YD_i)'$, you might wish to write the strict exogeneity assumption as

$$\mathrm{E}(\varepsilon_i \mid 1, YD_1, 1, YD_2, \dots, 1, YD_n) = 0.$$

But since a constant provides no information, the expectation conditional on

$$(1, YD_1, 1, YD_2, \dots, 1, YD_n)$$

is the same as the expectation conditional on

$$(YD_1, YD_2, \dots, YD_n).$$

Implications of Strict Exogeneity

The strict exogeneity assumption has several implications.

- The *un*conditional mean of the error term is zero, i.e.,

$$\mathrm{E}(\varepsilon_i) = 0 \quad (i = 1, 2, \dots, n). \tag{1.1.8}$$

  This is because, by the Law of Total Expectations from basic probability theory,[2] $\mathrm{E}[\mathrm{E}(\varepsilon_i \mid \mathbf{X})] = \mathrm{E}(\varepsilon_i)$.

- If the cross moment $\mathrm{E}(xy)$ of two random variables x and y is zero, then we say that x is **orthogonal** to y (or y is orthogonal to x). Under strict exogeneity, the regressors are orthogonal to the error term for *all* observations, i.e.,

$$\mathrm{E}(x_{jk}\varepsilon_i) = 0 \quad (i, j = 1, \dots, n; k = 1, \dots, K)$$

  or

$$\mathrm{E}(\mathbf{x}_j \cdot \varepsilon_i) = \begin{bmatrix} \mathrm{E}(x_{j1}\,\varepsilon_i) \\ \mathrm{E}(x_{j2}\,\varepsilon_i) \\ \vdots \\ \mathrm{E}(x_{jK}\,\varepsilon_i) \end{bmatrix} = \underset{(K\times 1)}{\mathbf{0}} \quad \text{(for all } i, j\text{)}. \tag{1.1.9}$$

[2] The Law of Total Expectations states that $\mathrm{E}[\mathrm{E}(y \mid \mathbf{x})] = \mathrm{E}(y)$.

The proof is a good illustration of the use of properties of conditional expectations and goes as follows.

PROOF. Since x_{jk} is an element of $\mathbf{X}$, strict exogeneity implies

$$\mathrm{E}(\varepsilon_i \mid x_{jk}) = \mathrm{E}[\mathrm{E}(\varepsilon_i \mid \mathbf{X}) \mid x_{jk}] = 0 \tag{1.1.10}$$

by the Law of Iterated Expectations from probability theory.[3] It follows from this that

$$\begin{aligned}\mathrm{E}(x_{jk}\varepsilon_i) &= \mathrm{E}[\mathrm{E}(x_{jk}\varepsilon_i \mid x_{jk})] \quad \text{(by the Law of Total Expectations)}\\ &= \mathrm{E}[x_{jk}\,\mathrm{E}(\varepsilon_i \mid x_{jk})] \quad \text{(by the linearity of conditional expectations}^4\text{)}\\ &= 0.\end{aligned}$$

■

The point here is that strict exogeneity requires the regressors be orthogonal not only to the error term from the same observation (i.e., $\mathrm{E}(x_{ik}\varepsilon_i) = 0$ for all k), but also to the error term from the other observations (i.e., $\mathrm{E}(x_{jk}\varepsilon_i) = 0$ for all k and for $j \neq i$).

- Because the mean of the error term is zero, the orthogonality conditions (1.1.9) are equivalent to zero-correlation conditions. This is because

$$\begin{aligned}\mathrm{Cov}(\varepsilon_i, x_{jk}) &= \mathrm{E}(x_{jk}\varepsilon_i) - \mathrm{E}(x_{jk})\,\mathrm{E}(\varepsilon_i) \quad \text{(by definition of covariance)}\\ &= \mathrm{E}(x_{jk}\varepsilon_i) \quad \text{(since } \mathrm{E}(\varepsilon_i) = 0\text{, see (1.1.8))}\\ &= 0 \quad \text{(by the orthogonality conditions (1.1.9)).}\end{aligned}$$

In particular, for $i = j$, $\mathrm{Cov}(x_{ik}, \varepsilon_i) = 0$. Therefore, strict exogeneity implies the requirement (familiar to those who have studied econometrics before) that the regressors be contemporaneously uncorrelated with the error term.

Strict Exogeneity in Time-Series Models

For time-series models where i is time, the implication (1.1.9) of strict exogeneity can be rephrased as: the regressors are orthogonal to the past, current, and future error terms (or equivalently, the error term is orthogonal to the past, current, and future regressors). But for most time-series models, this condition (and *a fortiori* strict exogeneity) is not satisfied, so the finite-sample theory based on strict exogeneity to be developed in this section is rarely applicable in time-series con-

[3]The Law of Iterated Expectations states that $\mathrm{E}[\mathrm{E}(y \mid \mathbf{x}, \mathbf{z}) \mid \mathbf{x}] = \mathrm{E}(y \mid \mathbf{x})$.
[4]The linearity of conditional expectations states that $\mathrm{E}[f(\mathbf{x})y \mid \mathbf{x}] = f(\mathbf{x})\,\mathrm{E}(y \mid \mathbf{x})$.

texts. However, as will be shown in the next chapter, the estimator possesses good large-sample properties without strict exogeneity.

The clearest example of a failure of strict exogeneity is a model where the regressor includes the **lagged dependent variable**. Consider the simplest such model:

$$y_i = \beta y_{i-1} + \varepsilon_i \quad (i = 1, 2, \dots, n). \tag{1.1.11}$$

This is called the **first-order autoregressive model** (AR(1)). (We will study this model more fully in Chapter 6.) Suppose, consistent with the spirit of the strict exogeneity assumption, that the regressor for observation i, y_{i-1}, is orthogonal to the error term for i so $\mathrm{E}(y_{i-1}\varepsilon_i) = 0$. Then

$$\begin{aligned} \mathrm{E}(y_i\varepsilon_i) &= \mathrm{E}[(\beta y_{i-1} + \varepsilon_i)\varepsilon_i] \quad \text{(by (1.1.11))} \\ &= \beta\,\mathrm{E}(y_{i-1}\varepsilon_i) + \mathrm{E}(\varepsilon_i^2) \\ &= \mathrm{E}(\varepsilon_i^2) \quad (\text{since } \mathrm{E}(y_{i-1}\varepsilon_i) = 0 \text{ by hypothesis}). \end{aligned}$$

Therefore, unless the error term is always zero, $\mathrm{E}(y_i\varepsilon_i)$ is not zero. But y_i is the regressor for observation $i+1$. Thus, the regressor is not orthogonal to the past error term, which is a violation of strict exogeneity.

Other Assumptions of the Model

The remaining assumptions comprising the classical regression model are the following.

Assumption 1.3 (no multicollinearity): *The rank of the $n \times K$ data matrix, $\mathbf{X}$, is K with probability 1.*

Assumption 1.4 (spherical error variance):

$$\textit{(homoskedasticity)} \quad \mathrm{E}(\varepsilon_i^2 \mid \mathbf{X}) = \sigma^2 > 0 \quad (i = 1, 2, \dots, n),^5 \tag{1.1.12}$$

(no correlation between observations)

$$\mathrm{E}(\varepsilon_i\varepsilon_j \mid \mathbf{X}) = 0 \quad (i, j = 1, 2, \dots, n;\ i \neq j). \tag{1.1.13}$$

[5]When a symbol (which here is σ^2) is given to a moment (which here is the second moment $\mathrm{E}(\varepsilon_i^2 \mid \mathbf{X})$), by implication the moment is assumed to exist and is finite. We will follow this convention for the rest of this book.

To understand Assumption 1.3, recall from matrix algebra that the rank of a matrix equals the number of linearly independent columns of the matrix. The assumption says that none of the K columns of the data matrix $\mathbf{X}$ can be expressed as a linear combination of the other columns of $\mathbf{X}$. That is, $\mathbf{X}$ is of **full column rank**. Since the K columns cannot be linearly independent if their dimension is less than K, the assumption implies that $n \geq K$, i.e., there must be at least as many observations as there are regressors. The regressors are said to be **(perfectly) multicollinear** if the assumption is not satisfied. It is easy to see in specific applications when the regressors are multicollinear and what problems arise.

Example 1.4 (continuation of Example 1.2): If no individuals in the sample ever changed jobs, then $TENURE_i = EXPR_i$ for all i, in violation of the no multicollinearity assumption. There is evidently no way to distinguish the tenure effect on the wage rate from the experience effect. If we substitute this equality into the wage equation to eliminate $TENURE_i$, the wage equation becomes

$$\log(WAGE_i) = \beta_1 + \beta_2 S_i + (\beta_3 + \beta_4) EXPR_i + \varepsilon_i,$$

which shows that only the sum $\beta_3 + \beta_4$, but not β_3 and β_4 separately, can be estimated.

The homoskedasticity assumption (1.1.12) says that the conditional second moment, which in general is a nonlinear function of $\mathbf{X}$, is a constant. Thanks to strict exogeneity, this condition can be stated equivalently in more familiar terms. Consider the conditional variance $\text{Var}(\varepsilon_i \mid \mathbf{X})$. It equals the same constant because

$$\begin{aligned} \text{Var}(\varepsilon_i \mid \mathbf{X}) &\equiv \text{E}(\varepsilon_i^2 \mid \mathbf{X}) - \text{E}(\varepsilon_i \mid \mathbf{X})^2 \quad \text{(by definition of conditional variance)} \\ &= \text{E}(\varepsilon_i^2 \mid \mathbf{X}) \quad (\text{since } \text{E}(\varepsilon_i \mid \mathbf{X}) = 0 \text{ by strict exogeneity}). \end{aligned}$$

Similarly, (1.1.13) is equivalent to the requirement that

$$\text{Cov}(\varepsilon_i, \varepsilon_j \mid \mathbf{X}) = 0 \quad (i, j = 1, 2, \ldots, n;\ i \neq j).$$

That is, in the joint distribution of $(\varepsilon_i, \varepsilon_j)$ conditional on $\mathbf{X}$, the covariance is zero. In the context of time-series models, (1.1.13) states that there is no **serial correlation** in the error term.

Since the (i, j) element of the $n \times n$ matrix $\boldsymbol{\varepsilon\varepsilon}'$ is $\varepsilon_i \varepsilon_j$, Assumption 1.4 can be written compactly as

$$\mathrm{E}(\boldsymbol{\varepsilon\varepsilon}' \mid \mathbf{X}) = \sigma^2 \mathbf{I}_n. \tag{1.1.14}$$

The discussion of the previous paragraph shows that the assumption can also be written as

$$\mathrm{Var}(\boldsymbol{\varepsilon} \mid \mathbf{X}) = \sigma^2 \mathbf{I}_n.$$

However, (1.1.14) is the preferred expression, because the more convenient measure of variability is second moments (such as $\mathrm{E}(\varepsilon_i^2 \mid \mathbf{X})$) rather than variances. This point will become clearer when we deal with the large sample theory in the next chapter. Assumption 1.4 is sometimes called the **spherical** error variance assumption because the $n \times n$ matrix of second moments (which are also variances and covariances) is proportional to the identity matrix $\mathbf{I}_n$. This assumption will be relaxed later in this chapter.

The Classical Regression Model for Random Samples

The sample $(\mathbf{y}, \mathbf{X})$ is a **random sample** if $\{y_i, \mathbf{x}_i\}$ is i.i.d. (independently and identically distributed) across observations. Since by Assumption 1.1 ε_i is a function of $(y_i, \mathbf{x}_i)$ and since $(y_i, \mathbf{x}_i)$ is independent of $(y_j, \mathbf{x}_j)$ for $j \neq i$, $(\varepsilon_i, \mathbf{x}_i)$ is independent of $\mathbf{x}_j$ for $j \neq i$. So

$$\begin{aligned}
\mathrm{E}(\varepsilon_i \mid \mathbf{X}) &= \mathrm{E}(\varepsilon_i \mid \mathbf{x}_i), \\
\mathrm{E}(\varepsilon_i^2 \mid \mathbf{X}) &= \mathrm{E}(\varepsilon_i^2 \mid \mathbf{x}_i), \\
\text{and } \mathrm{E}(\varepsilon_i \varepsilon_j \mid \mathbf{X}) &= \mathrm{E}(\varepsilon_i \mid \mathbf{x}_i)\,\mathrm{E}(\varepsilon_j \mid \mathbf{x}_j) \quad (\text{for } i \neq j).
\end{aligned} \tag{1.1.15}$$

(Proving the last equality in (1.1.15) is a review question.) Therefore, Assumptions 1.2 and 1.4 reduce to

$$\text{Assumption 1.2:} \quad \mathrm{E}(\varepsilon_i \mid \mathbf{x}_i) = 0 \quad (i = 1, 2, \ldots, n), \tag{1.1.16}$$

$$\text{Assumption 1.4:} \quad \mathrm{E}(\varepsilon_i^2 \mid \mathbf{x}_i) = \sigma^2 > 0 \quad (i = 1, 2, \ldots, n). \tag{1.1.17}$$

The implication of the identical distribution aspect of a random sample is that the joint distribution of $(\varepsilon_i, \mathbf{x}_i)$ does not depend on i. So the *un*conditional second moment $\mathrm{E}(\varepsilon_i^2)$ is constant across i (this is referred to as **unconditional homoskedasticity**) and the functional form of the conditional second moment $\mathrm{E}(\varepsilon_i^2 \mid \mathbf{x}_i)$ is the same across i. However, Assumption 1.4—that the *value* of the conditional second moment is the same across i — does not follow. Therefore, Assumption 1.4 remains restrictive for the case of a random sample; without it, the conditional second moment $\mathrm{E}(\varepsilon_i^2 \mid \mathbf{x}_i)$ can differ across i through its possible dependence on $\mathbf{x}_i$. To emphasize the distinction, the restrictions on the conditional second moments, (1.1.12) and (1.1.17), are referred to as **conditional homoskedasticity**.

"Fixed" Regressors

We have presented the classical linear regression model, treating the regressors as random. This is in contrast to the treatment in most textbooks, where $\mathbf{X}$ is assumed to be "fixed" or deterministic. If $\mathbf{X}$ is fixed, then there is no need to distinguish between the conditional distribution of the error term, $f(\varepsilon_i \mid \mathbf{x}_1, \dots, \mathbf{x}_n)$, and the unconditional distribution, $f(\varepsilon_i)$, so that Assumptions 1.2 and 1.4 can be written as

$$\text{Assumption 1.2:}\quad \mathrm{E}(\varepsilon_i) = 0 \quad (i = 1, \dots, n), \tag{1.1.18}$$

$$\text{Assumption 1.4:}\quad \mathrm{E}(\varepsilon_i^2) = \sigma^2 \quad (i = 1, \dots, n);$$

$$\mathrm{E}(\varepsilon_i \varepsilon_j) = 0 \quad (i, j = 1, \dots, n; i \neq j). \tag{1.1.19}$$

Although it is clearly inappropriate for a nonexperimental science like econometrics, the assumption of fixed regressors remains popular because the regression model with fixed $\mathbf{X}$ can be interpreted as a set of statements conditional on $\mathbf{X}$, allowing us to dispense with "$\mid \mathbf{X}$" from the statements such as Assumptions 1.2 and 1.4 of the model.

However, the economy in the notation comes at a price. It is very easy to miss the point that the error term is being assumed to be uncorrelated with current, past, and future regressors. Also, the distinction between the unconditional and conditional homoskedasticity gets lost if the regressors are deterministic. Throughout this book, the regressors are treated as random, and, unless otherwise noted, statements conditional on $\mathbf{X}$ are made explicit by inserting "$\mid \mathbf{X}$."

QUESTIONS FOR REVIEW

1. (Change in units in the semi-log form) In the wage equation, (1.1.3), of Example 1.2, if *WAGE* is measured in cents rather than in dollars, what difference does it make to the equation? **Hint:** $\log(x\,y) = \log(x) + \log(y)$.

2. Prove the last equality in (1.1.15). **Hint:** $\mathrm{E}(\varepsilon_i \varepsilon_j \mid \mathbf{X}) = \mathrm{E}[\varepsilon_j\, \mathrm{E}(\varepsilon_i \mid \mathbf{X}, \varepsilon_j) \mid \mathbf{X}]$. $(\varepsilon_i, \mathbf{x}_i)$ is independent of $(\varepsilon_j, \mathbf{x}_1, \dots, \mathbf{x}_{i-1}, \mathbf{x}_{i+1}, \dots, \mathbf{x}_n)$ for $i \neq j$.

3. (Combining linearity and strict exogeneity) Show that Assumptions 1.1 and 1.2 imply

$$\mathrm{E}(y_i \mid \mathbf{X}) = \mathbf{x}_i'\boldsymbol{\beta} \quad (i = 1, 2, \ldots, n). \tag{1.1.20}$$

Conversely, show that this assumption implies that there exist error terms that satisfy those two assumptions.

4. (Normally distributed random sample) Consider a random sample on consumption and disposable income, (CON_i, YD_i) $(i = 1, 2, \ldots, n)$. Suppose the joint distribution of (CON_i, YD_i) (which is the same across i because of the random sample assumption) is normal. Clearly, Assumption 1.3 is satisfied; the rank of $\mathbf{X}$ would be less than K only by pure accident. Show that the other assumptions, Assumptions 1.1, 1.2, and 1.4, are satisfied. **Hint:** If two random variables, y and x, are jointly normally distributed, then the conditional expectation is linear in x, i.e.,

$$\mathrm{E}(y \mid x) = \beta_1 + \beta_2 x,$$

and the conditional variance, $\mathrm{Var}(y \mid x)$, does not depend on x. Here, the fact that the distribution is the same across i is important; if the distribution differed across i, β_1 and β_2 could vary across i.

5. (Multicollinearity for the simple regression model) Show that Assumption 1.3 for the simple regression model is that the nonconstant regressor (x_{i2}) is really nonconstant (i.e., $x_{i2} \neq x_{j2}$ for some pairs of $(i, j), i \neq j$, with probability one).

6. (An exercise in conditional and unconditional expectations) Show that Assumptions 1.2 and 1.4 imply

$$\begin{aligned} &\mathrm{Var}(\varepsilon_i) = \sigma^2 \quad (i = 1, 2, \ldots, n) \\ \text{and } &\mathrm{Cov}(\varepsilon_i, \varepsilon_j) = 0 \quad (i \neq j; i, j = 1, 2, \ldots n). \end{aligned} \tag{$*$}$$

Hint: Strict exogeneity implies $\mathrm{E}(\varepsilon_i) = 0$. So $(*)$ is equivalent to

$$\begin{aligned} &\mathrm{E}(\varepsilon_i^2) = \sigma^2 \quad (i = 1, 2, \ldots, n) \\ \text{and } &\mathrm{E}(\varepsilon_i \varepsilon_j) = 0 \quad (i \neq j; i, j = 1, 2, \ldots, n). \end{aligned}$$

1.2 The Algebra of Least Squares

This section describes the computational procedure for obtaining the OLS estimate, $\mathbf{b}$, of the unknown coefficient vector $\boldsymbol{\beta}$ and introduces a few concepts that derive from $\mathbf{b}$.

OLS Minimizes the Sum of Squared Residuals

Although we do not observe the error term, we can calculate the value implied by a hypothetical value, $\widetilde{\boldsymbol{\beta}}$, of $\boldsymbol{\beta}$ as

$$y_i - \mathbf{x}_i'\widetilde{\boldsymbol{\beta}}.$$

This is called the **residual** for observation i. From this, form the **sum of squared residuals (SSR)**:

$$SSR(\widetilde{\boldsymbol{\beta}}) \equiv \sum_{i=1}^{n}(y_i - \mathbf{x}_i'\widetilde{\boldsymbol{\beta}})^2 = (\mathbf{y} - \mathbf{X}\widetilde{\boldsymbol{\beta}})'(\mathbf{y} - \mathbf{X}\widetilde{\boldsymbol{\beta}}).$$

This sum is also called the **error sum of squares (ESS)** or the **residual sum of squares (RSS)**. It is a function of $\widetilde{\boldsymbol{\beta}}$ because the residual depends on it. The **OLS estimate**, $\mathbf{b}$, of $\boldsymbol{\beta}$ is the $\widetilde{\boldsymbol{\beta}}$ that minimizes this function:

$$\mathbf{b} \equiv \underset{\widetilde{\boldsymbol{\beta}}}{\operatorname{argmin}}\, SSR(\widetilde{\boldsymbol{\beta}}). \tag{1.2.1}$$

The relationship among $\boldsymbol{\beta}$ (the unknown coefficient vector), $\mathbf{b}$ (the OLS estimate of it), and $\widetilde{\boldsymbol{\beta}}$ (a hypothetical value of $\boldsymbol{\beta}$) is illustrated in Figure 1.1 for $K = 1$. Because $SSR(\widetilde{\boldsymbol{\beta}})$ is quadratic in $\widetilde{\boldsymbol{\beta}}$, its graph has the U shape. The value of $\widetilde{\boldsymbol{\beta}}$ corresponding to the bottom is $\mathbf{b}$, the OLS estimate. Since it depends on the sample $(\mathbf{y}, \mathbf{X})$, the OLS estimate $\mathbf{b}$ is in general different from the true value $\boldsymbol{\beta}$; if $\mathbf{b}$ equals $\boldsymbol{\beta}$, it is by sheer accident.

By having squared residuals in the objective function, this method imposes a heavy penalty on large residuals; the OLS estimate is chosen to prevent large residuals for a few observations at the expense of tolerating relatively small residuals for many other observations. We will see in the next section that this particular criterion brings about some desirable properties for the estimate.

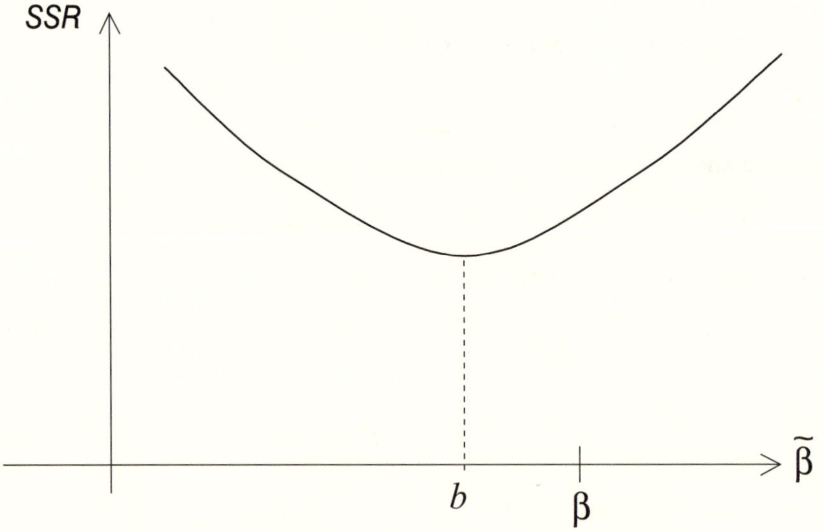

Figure 1.1: Hypothetical, True, and Estimated Values

Normal Equations

A sure-fire way of solving the minimization problem is to derive the first-order conditions by setting the partial derivatives equal to zero. To this end we seek a K-dimensional vector of partial derivatives, $\partial SSR(\widetilde{\boldsymbol{\beta}})/\partial\widetilde{\boldsymbol{\beta}}$.[6] The task is facilitated by writing $SSR(\widetilde{\boldsymbol{\beta}})$ as

$$\begin{aligned}
SSR(\widetilde{\boldsymbol{\beta}}) &= (\mathbf{y}-\mathbf{X}\widetilde{\boldsymbol{\beta}})'(\mathbf{y}-\mathbf{X}\widetilde{\boldsymbol{\beta}}) \quad (\text{since the } i\text{-th element of } \mathbf{y}-\mathbf{X}\widetilde{\boldsymbol{\beta}} \text{ is } y_i - \mathbf{x}_i'\widetilde{\boldsymbol{\beta}})\\
&= (\mathbf{y}' - \widetilde{\boldsymbol{\beta}}'\mathbf{X}')(\mathbf{y}-\mathbf{X}\widetilde{\boldsymbol{\beta}}) \quad (\text{since } (\mathbf{X}\widetilde{\boldsymbol{\beta}})' = \widetilde{\boldsymbol{\beta}}'\mathbf{X}')\\
&= \mathbf{y}'\mathbf{y} - \widetilde{\boldsymbol{\beta}}'\mathbf{X}'\mathbf{y} - \mathbf{y}'\mathbf{X}\widetilde{\boldsymbol{\beta}} + \widetilde{\boldsymbol{\beta}}'\mathbf{X}'\mathbf{X}\widetilde{\boldsymbol{\beta}}\\
&= \mathbf{y}'\mathbf{y} - 2\mathbf{y}'\mathbf{X}\widetilde{\boldsymbol{\beta}} + \widetilde{\boldsymbol{\beta}}'\mathbf{X}'\mathbf{X}\widetilde{\boldsymbol{\beta}}\\
&\qquad (\text{since the scalar } \widetilde{\boldsymbol{\beta}}'\mathbf{X}'\mathbf{y} \text{ equals its transpose } \mathbf{y}'\mathbf{X}\widetilde{\boldsymbol{\beta}})\\
&\equiv \mathbf{y}'\mathbf{y} - 2\mathbf{a}'\widetilde{\boldsymbol{\beta}} + \widetilde{\boldsymbol{\beta}}'\mathbf{A}\widetilde{\boldsymbol{\beta}} \quad \text{with } \mathbf{a} \equiv \mathbf{X}'\mathbf{y} \text{ and } \mathbf{A} \equiv \mathbf{X}'\mathbf{X}. \qquad (1.2.2)
\end{aligned}$$

The term $\mathbf{y}'\mathbf{y}$ does not depend on $\widetilde{\boldsymbol{\beta}}$ and so can be ignored in the differentiation of $SSR(\widetilde{\boldsymbol{\beta}})$. Recalling from matrix algebra that

$$\frac{\partial(\mathbf{a}'\widetilde{\boldsymbol{\beta}})}{\partial\widetilde{\boldsymbol{\beta}}} = \mathbf{a} \quad \text{and} \quad \frac{\partial(\widetilde{\boldsymbol{\beta}}'\mathbf{A}\widetilde{\boldsymbol{\beta}})}{\partial\widetilde{\boldsymbol{\beta}}} = 2\mathbf{A}\widetilde{\boldsymbol{\beta}} \quad \text{for } \mathbf{A} \text{ symmetric,}$$

[6]If $h\colon \mathbb{R}^K \to \mathbb{R}$ is a scalar-valued function of a K-dimensional vector $\mathbf{x}$, the derivative of h with respect to $\mathbf{x}$ is a K-dimensional vector whose k-th element is $\partial h(\mathbf{x})/\partial x_k$ where x_k is the k-th element of $\mathbf{x}$. (This K-dimensional vector is called the **gradient**.) Here, the $\mathbf{x}$ is $\widetilde{\boldsymbol{\beta}}$ and the function $h(\mathbf{x})$ is $SSR(\widetilde{\boldsymbol{\beta}})$.

the K-dimensional vector of partial derivatives is

$$\frac{\partial SSR(\widetilde{\boldsymbol{\beta}})}{\partial \widetilde{\boldsymbol{\beta}}} = -2\mathbf{a} + 2\mathbf{A}\widetilde{\boldsymbol{\beta}}.$$

The first-order conditions are obtained by setting this equal to zero. Recalling from (1.2.2) that $\mathbf{a}$ here is $\mathbf{X}'\mathbf{y}$ and $\mathbf{A}$ is $\mathbf{X}'\mathbf{X}$ and rearranging, we can write the first-order conditions as

$$\underset{(K\times K)(K\times 1)}{\mathbf{X}'\mathbf{X}\ \ \mathbf{b}} = \mathbf{X}'\mathbf{y}. \tag{1.2.3}$$

Here, we have replaced $\widetilde{\boldsymbol{\beta}}$ by $\mathbf{b}$ because the OLS estimate $\mathbf{b}$ is the $\widetilde{\boldsymbol{\beta}}$ that satisfies the first-order conditions. These K equations are called the **normal equations**.

The vector of residuals evaluated at $\widetilde{\boldsymbol{\beta}} = \mathbf{b}$,

$$\underset{(n\times 1)}{\mathbf{e}} \equiv \mathbf{y} - \mathbf{X}\mathbf{b}, \tag{1.2.4}$$

is called the vector of **OLS residuals**. Its i-th element is $e_i \equiv y_i - \mathbf{x}_i'\mathbf{b}$. Rearranging (1.2.3) gives

$$\mathbf{X}'(\mathbf{y} - \mathbf{X}\mathbf{b}) = \mathbf{0} \text{ or } \mathbf{X}'\mathbf{e} = \mathbf{0} \text{ or}$$

$$\frac{1}{n}\sum_{i=1}^{n} \mathbf{x}_i \cdot e_i = \mathbf{0} \text{ or } \frac{1}{n}\sum_{i=1}^{n} \mathbf{x}_i \cdot (y_i - \mathbf{x}_i'\mathbf{b}) = \mathbf{0}, \tag{1.2.3$'$}$$

which shows that the normal equations can be interpreted as the sample analogue of the orthogonality conditions $\mathrm{E}(\mathbf{x}_i \cdot \varepsilon_i) = \mathbf{0}$. This point will be pursued more fully in subsequent chapters.

To be sure, the first-order conditions are just a necessary condition for minimization, and we have to check the second-order condition to make sure that $\mathbf{b}$ achieves the minimum, not the maximum. Those who are familiar with the Hessian of a function of several variables[7] can immediately recognize that the second-order condition is satisfied because (as noted below) $\mathbf{X}'\mathbf{X}$ is positive definite. There is, however, a more direct way to show that $\mathbf{b}$ indeed achieves the minimum. It utilizes the "add-and-subtract" strategy, which is effective when the objective function is quadratic, as here. Application of the strategy to the algebra of least squares is left to you as an analytical exercise.

[7] The **Hessian** of $h(\mathbf{x})$ is a square matrix whose (k, ℓ) element is $\partial^2 h(\mathbf{x})/\partial x_k\, \partial x_\ell$.

Two Expressions for the OLS Estimator

Thus, we have obtained a system of K linear simultaneous equations in K unknowns in $\mathbf{b}$. By Assumption 1.3 (no multicollinearity), the coefficient matrix $\mathbf{X}'\mathbf{X}$ is positive definite (see review question 1 below for a proof) and hence nonsingular. So the normal equations can be solved uniquely for $\mathbf{b}$ by premultiplying both sides of (1.2.3) by $(\mathbf{X}'\mathbf{X})^{-1}$:

$$\mathbf{b} = (\mathbf{X}'\mathbf{X})^{-1}\mathbf{X}'\mathbf{y}. \tag{1.2.5}$$

Viewed as a function of the sample $(\mathbf{y}, \mathbf{X})$, (1.2.5) is sometimes called the **OLS estimator**. For any given sample $(\mathbf{y}, \mathbf{X})$, the value of this function is the **OLS estimate**. In this book, as in most other textbooks, the two terms will be used almost interchangeably.

Since $(\mathbf{X}'\mathbf{X})^{-1}\mathbf{X}'\mathbf{y} = (\mathbf{X}'\mathbf{X}/n)^{-1}\mathbf{X}'\mathbf{y}/n$, the OLS estimator can also be rewritten as

$$\mathbf{b} = \mathbf{S}_{\mathbf{xx}}^{-1}\,\mathbf{s}_{\mathbf{xy}}, \tag{1.2.5$'$}$$

where

$$\mathbf{S}_{\mathbf{xx}} = \frac{1}{n}\mathbf{X}'\mathbf{X} = \frac{1}{n}\sum_{i=1}^{n}\mathbf{x}_i\mathbf{x}_i' \quad \text{(sample average of } \mathbf{x}_i\mathbf{x}_i'\text{)}, \tag{1.2.6a}$$

$$\mathbf{s}_{\mathbf{xy}} = \frac{1}{n}\mathbf{X}'\mathbf{y} = \frac{1}{n}\sum_{i=1}^{n}\mathbf{x}_i \cdot y_i \quad \text{(sample average of } \mathbf{x}_i \cdot y_i\text{)}. \tag{1.2.6b}$$

The data matrix form (1.2.5) is more convenient for developing the finite-sample results, while the sample average form (1.2.5$'$) is the form to be utilized for large-sample theory.

More Concepts and Algebra

Having derived the OLS estimator of the coefficient vector, we can define a few related concepts.

- The **fitted value** for observation i is defined as $\hat{y}_i \equiv \mathbf{x}_i'\mathbf{b}$. The vector of fitted value, $\hat{\mathbf{y}}$, equals $\mathbf{X}\mathbf{b}$. Thus, the vector of OLS residuals can be written as $\mathbf{e} = \mathbf{y} - \hat{\mathbf{y}}$.

- The **projection matrix P** and the **annihilator M** are defined as

$$\underset{(n\times n)}{\mathbf{P}} \equiv \mathbf{X}(\mathbf{X}'\mathbf{X})^{-1}\mathbf{X}', \tag{1.2.7}$$

$$\underset{(n\times n)}{\mathbf{M}} \equiv \mathbf{I}_n - \mathbf{P}. \tag{1.2.8}$$

They have the following nifty properties (proving them is a review question):

$$\text{Both } \mathbf{P} \text{ and } \mathbf{M} \text{ are symmetric and idempotent,}^{8} \tag{1.2.9}$$

$$\mathbf{PX} = \mathbf{X} \quad \text{(hence the term \textbf{projection} matrix)}, \tag{1.2.10}$$

$$\mathbf{MX} = \mathbf{0} \quad \text{(hence the term \textbf{annihilator})}. \tag{1.2.11}$$

Since $\mathbf{e}$ is the residual vector at $\tilde{\boldsymbol{\beta}} = \mathbf{b}$, the sum of squared OLS residuals, *SSR*, equals $\mathbf{e}'\mathbf{e}$. It can further be written as

$$SSR = \mathbf{e}'\mathbf{e} = \boldsymbol{\varepsilon}'\mathbf{M}\boldsymbol{\varepsilon}. \tag{1.2.12}$$

(Proving this is a review question.) This expression, relating *SSR* to the true error term $\boldsymbol{\varepsilon}$, will be useful later on.

- The OLS estimate of σ^2 (the variance of the error term), denoted s^2, is the sum of squared residuals divided by $n - K$:

$$s^2 \equiv \frac{SSR}{n-K} = \frac{\mathbf{e}'\mathbf{e}}{n-K}. \tag{1.2.13}$$

(The definition presumes that $n > K$; otherwise s^2 is not well-defined.) As will be shown in Proposition 1.2 below, dividing the sum of squared residuals by $n - K$ (called the **degrees of freedom**) rather than by n (the sample size) makes this estimate unbiased for σ^2. The intuitive reason is that K parameters ($\boldsymbol{\beta}$) have to be estimated before obtaining the residual vector $\mathbf{e}$ used to calculate s^2. More specifically, $\mathbf{e}$ has to satisfy the K normal equations (1.2.3′), which limits the variability of the residual.

- The square root of s^2, s, is called the **standard error of the regression (SER)** or **standard error of the equation (SEE)**. It is an estimate of the standard deviation of the error term.

- The **sampling error** is defined as $\mathbf{b} - \boldsymbol{\beta}$. It too can be related to $\boldsymbol{\varepsilon}$ as follows.

$$\begin{aligned}
\mathbf{b} - \boldsymbol{\beta} &= (\mathbf{X}'\mathbf{X})^{-1}\mathbf{X}'\mathbf{y} - \boldsymbol{\beta} \quad \text{(by (1.2.5))} \\
&= (\mathbf{X}'\mathbf{X})^{-1}\mathbf{X}'(\mathbf{X}\boldsymbol{\beta} + \boldsymbol{\varepsilon}) - \boldsymbol{\beta} \quad \text{(since } \mathbf{y} = \mathbf{X}\boldsymbol{\beta} + \boldsymbol{\varepsilon} \text{ by Assumption 1.1)} \\
&= (\mathbf{X}'\mathbf{X})^{-1}(\mathbf{X}'\mathbf{X})\boldsymbol{\beta} + (\mathbf{X}'\mathbf{X})^{-1}\mathbf{X}'\boldsymbol{\varepsilon} - \boldsymbol{\beta} \\
&= \boldsymbol{\beta} + (\mathbf{X}'\mathbf{X})^{-1}\mathbf{X}'\boldsymbol{\varepsilon} - \boldsymbol{\beta} = (\mathbf{X}'\mathbf{X})^{-1}\mathbf{X}'\boldsymbol{\varepsilon}.
\end{aligned} \tag{1.2.14}$$

[8] A square matrix $\mathbf{A}$ is said to be **idempotent** if $\mathbf{A} = \mathbf{A}^2$.

- **Uncentered R^2.** One measure of the variability of the dependent variable is the sum of squares, $\sum y_i^2 = \mathbf{y}'\mathbf{y}$. Because the OLS residual is chosen to satisfy the normal equations, we have the following decomposition of $\mathbf{y}'\mathbf{y}$:

$$\begin{aligned}\mathbf{y}'\mathbf{y} &= (\hat{\mathbf{y}} + \mathbf{e})'(\hat{\mathbf{y}} + \mathbf{e}) \quad (\text{since } \mathbf{e} = \mathbf{y} - \hat{\mathbf{y}}) \\ &= \hat{\mathbf{y}}'\hat{\mathbf{y}} + 2\hat{\mathbf{y}}'\mathbf{e} + \mathbf{e}'\mathbf{e} \\ &= \hat{\mathbf{y}}'\hat{\mathbf{y}} + 2\mathbf{b}'\mathbf{X}'\mathbf{e} + \mathbf{e}'\mathbf{e} \quad (\text{since } \hat{\mathbf{y}} \equiv \mathbf{X}\mathbf{b}) \\ &= \hat{\mathbf{y}}'\hat{\mathbf{y}} + \mathbf{e}'\mathbf{e} \quad (\text{since } \mathbf{X}'\mathbf{e} = \mathbf{0} \text{ by the normal equations; see (1.2.3}')). \end{aligned} \tag{1.2.15}$$

The **uncentered R^2** is defined as

$$R_{uc}^2 \equiv 1 - \frac{\mathbf{e}'\mathbf{e}}{\mathbf{y}'\mathbf{y}}. \tag{1.2.16}$$

Because of the decomposition (1.2.15), this equals

$$\frac{\hat{\mathbf{y}}'\hat{\mathbf{y}}}{\mathbf{y}'\mathbf{y}}.$$

Since both $\hat{\mathbf{y}}'\hat{\mathbf{y}}$ and $\mathbf{e}'\mathbf{e}$ are nonnegative, $0 \leq R_{uc}^2 \leq 1$. Thus, the uncentered R^2 has the interpretation of the fraction of the variation of the dependent variable that is attributable to the variation in the explanatory variables. The closer the fitted value tracks the dependent variable, the closer is the uncentered R^2 to one.

- **(Centered) R^2, the coefficient of determination.** If the only regressor is a constant (so that $K = 1$ and $x_{i1} = 1$), then it is easy to see from (1.2.5) that $\mathbf{b}$ equals $\bar{y}$, the sample mean of the dependent variable, which means that $\hat{y}_i = \bar{y}$ for all i, $\hat{\mathbf{y}}'\hat{\mathbf{y}}$ in (1.2.15) equals $n\bar{y}^2$, and $\mathbf{e}'\mathbf{e}$ equals $\sum_i (y_i - \bar{y})^2$. If the regressors also include nonconstant variables, then it can be shown (the proof is left as an analytical exercise) that $\sum_i (y_i - \bar{y})^2$ is decomposed as

$$\sum_{i=1}^{n} (y_i - \bar{y})^2 = \sum_{i=1}^{n} (\hat{y}_i - \bar{y})^2 + \sum_{i=1}^{n} e_i^2 \text{ with } \bar{y} \equiv \frac{1}{n}\sum_{i=1}^{n} y_i. \tag{1.2.17}$$

The **coefficient of determination**, R^2, is defined as

$$R^2 \equiv 1 - \frac{\sum_{i=1}^{n} e_i^2}{\sum_{i=1}^{n} (y_i - \bar{y})^2}. \tag{1.2.18}$$

Because of the decomposition (1.2.17), this R^2 equals

$$\frac{\sum_{i=1}^{n}(\hat{y}_i - \bar{y})^2}{\sum_{i=1}^{n}(y_i - \bar{y})^2}.$$

Therefore, provided that the regressors include a constant so that the decomposition (1.2.17) is valid, $0 \leq R^2 \leq 1$. Thus, this R^2 as defined in (1.2.18) is a measure of the explanatory power of the nonconstant regressors.

If the regressors do not include a constant but (as some regression software packages do) you nevertheless calculate R^2 by the formula (1.2.18), then the R^2 can be negative. This is because, without the benefit of an intercept, the regression could do worse than the sample mean in terms of tracking the dependent variable. On the other hand, some other regression packages (notably STATA) switch to the formula (1.2.16) for the R^2 when a constant is not included, in order to avoid negative values for the R^2. This is a mixed blessing. Suppose that the regressors do not include a constant but that a linear combination of the regressors equals a constant. This occurs if, for example, the intercept is replaced by seasonal dummies.[9] The regression is essentially the same when one of the regressors in the linear combination is replaced by a constant. Indeed, one should obtain the same vector of fitted values. But if the formula for the R^2 is (1.2.16) for regressions without a constant and (1.2.18) for those with a constant, the calculated R^2 declines (see Review Question 7 below) after the replacement by a constant.

Influential Analysis (optional)

Since the method of least squares seeks to prevent a few large residuals at the expense of incurring many relatively small residuals, only a few observations can be extremely influential in the sense that dropping them from the sample changes some elements of $\mathbf{b}$ substantially. There is a systematic way to find those **influential observations.**[10] Let $\mathbf{b}^{(i)}$ be the OLS estimate of $\boldsymbol{\beta}$ that would be obtained if OLS were used on a sample from which the i-th observation was omitted. The key equation is

$$\mathbf{b}^{(i)} - \mathbf{b} = -\Big(\frac{1}{1 - p_i}\Big)(\mathbf{X}'\mathbf{X})^{-1}\mathbf{x}_i \cdot e_i, \tag{1.2.19}$$

[9]Dummy variables will be introduced in the empirical exercise for this chapter.

[10]See Krasker, Kuh, and Welsch (1983) for more details.

where $\mathbf{x}_i$ as before is the i-th row of $\mathbf{X}$, e_i is the OLS residual for observation i, and p_i is defined as

$$p_i \equiv \mathbf{x}_i'(\mathbf{X}'\mathbf{X})^{-1}\mathbf{x}_i, \tag{1.2.20}$$

which is the i-th diagonal element of the projection matrix $\mathbf{P}$. (Proving (1.2.19) would be a good exercise in matrix algebra, but we will not do it here.) It is easy to show (see Review Question 7 of Section 1.3) that

$$0 \le p_i \le 1 \text{ and } \sum_{i=1}^{n} p_i = K. \tag{1.2.21}$$

So p_i equals K/n on average.

To illustrate the use of (1.2.19) in a specific example, consider the relationship between equipment investment and economic growth for the world's poorest countries between 1960 and 1985. Figure 1.2 plots the average annual GDP-per-worker growth between 1960 and 1985 against the ratio of equipment investment to GDP over the same period for thirteen countries whose GDP per worker in 1965 was less than 10 percent of that of the United States.[11] It is clear visually from the plot that the position of the estimated regression line would depend very much on the single outlier (Botswana). Indeed, if Botswana is dropped from the sample, the estimated slope coefficient drops from 0.37 to 0.058. In the present case of simple regression, it is easy to spot outliers by visually inspecting the plot such as Figure 1.2. This strategy would not work if there were more than one nonconstant regressor. Analysis based on formula (1.2.19) is not restricted to simple regressions. Table 1.1 displays the data along with the OLS residuals, the values of p_i, and (1.2.19) for each observation. Botswana's p_i of 0.7196 is well above the average of 0.154 ($= K/n = 2/13$) and is highly **influential**, as the last two columns of the table indicate. Note that we could not have detected the influential observation by looking at the residuals, which is not surprising because the algebra of least squares is designed to avoid large residuals at the expense of many small residuals for other observations.

What should be done with influential observations? It depends. If the influential observations satisfy the regression model, they provide valuable information about the regression function unavailable from the rest of the sample and should definitely be kept in the sample. But more probable is that the influential observations are atypical of the rest of the sample because they do not satisfy the model.

[11]The data are from the Penn World Table, reprinted in DeLong and Summers (1991). To their credit, their analysis is based on the whole sample of sixty-one countries.

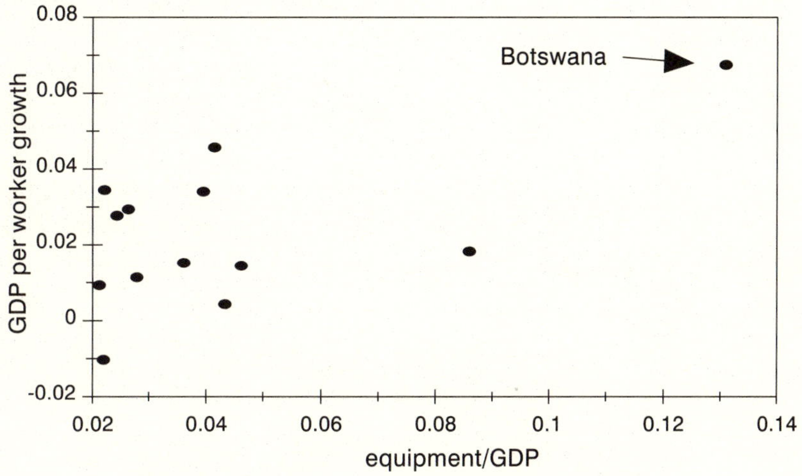

Figure 1.2: Equipment Investment and Growth

In this case they should definitely be dropped from the sample. For the example just examined, there was a worldwide growth in the demand for diamonds, Botswana's main export, and production of diamonds requires heavy investment in drilling equipment. If the reason to expect an association between growth and equipment investment is the beneficial effect on productivity of the introduction of new technologies through equipment, then Botswana, whose high GDP growth is demand-driven, should be dropped from the sample.

A Note on the Computation of OLS Estimates[12]

So far, we have focused on the conceptual aspects of the algebra of least squares. But for applied researchers who actually calculate OLS estimates using digital computers, it is important to be aware of a certain aspect of digital computing in order to avoid the risk of obtaining unreliable estimates without knowing it. The source of a potential problem is that the computer approximates real numbers by so-called **floating-point numbers**. When an arithmetic operation involves both very large numbers and very small numbers, floating-point calculation can produce inaccurate results. This is relevant in the computation of OLS estimates when the regressors greatly differ in magnitude. For example, one of the regressors may be the interest rate stated as a fraction, and another may be U.S. GDP in dollars. The matrix $\mathbf{X}'\mathbf{X}$ will then contain both very small and very large numbers, and the arithmetic operation of inverting this matrix by the digital computer will produce unreliable results.

[12] A fuller treatment of this topic can be found in Section 1.5 of Davidson and MacKinnon (1993).

Table 1.1: Influential Analysis

Country	GDP/worker growth	Equipment/ GDP	Residual	p_i	(1.2.19) for β_1	(1.2.19) for β_2
Botswana	0.0676	0.1310	0.0119	0.7196	0.0104	−0.3124
Cameroon	0.0458	0.0415	0.0233	0.0773	−0.0021	0.0045
Ethiopia	0.0094	0.0212	−0.0056	0.1193	0.0010	−0.0119
India	0.0115	0.0278	−0.0059	0.0980	0.0009	−0.0087
Indonesia	0.0345	0.0221	0.0192	0.1160	−0.0034	0.0394
Ivory Coast	0.0278	0.0243	0.0117	0.1084	−0.0019	0.0213
Kenya	0.0146	0.0462	−0.0096	0.0775	0.0007	0.0023
Madagascar	−0.0102	0.0219	−0.0254	0.1167	0.0045	−0.0527
Malawi	0.0153	0.0361	−0.0052	0.0817	0.0006	−0.0036
Mali	0.0044	0.0433	−0.0188	0.0769	0.0016	−0.0006
Pakistan	0.0295	0.0263	0.0126	0.1022	−0.0020	0.0205
Tanzania	0.0184	0.0860	−0.0206	0.2281	−0.0021	0.0952
Thailand	0.0341	0.0395	0.0123	0.0784	−0.0012	0.0047

A simple solution to this problem is to choose the units of measurement so that the regressors are similar in magnitude. For example, state the interest rate in percents and U.S. GDP in trillion dollars. This sort of care would prevent the problem most of the time. A more systematic transformation of the $\mathbf{X}$ matrix is to subtract the sample means of all regressors and divide by the sample standard deviations before forming $\mathbf{X}'\mathbf{X}$ (and adjust the OLS estimates to undo the transformation). Most OLS programs (such as TSP) take a more sophisticated transformation of the $\mathbf{X}$ matrix (called the **QR decomposition**) to produce accurate results.

QUESTIONS FOR REVIEW

1. Prove that $\mathbf{X}'\mathbf{X}$ is positive definite if $\mathbf{X}$ is of full column rank. **Hint:** What needs to be shown is that $\mathbf{c}'\mathbf{X}'\mathbf{X}\mathbf{c} > 0$ for $\mathbf{c} \neq \mathbf{0}$. Define $\mathbf{z} \equiv \mathbf{X}\mathbf{c}$. Then $\mathbf{c}'\mathbf{X}'\mathbf{X}\mathbf{c} = \mathbf{z}'\mathbf{z} = \sum_{k=1}^{K} z_i^2$. If $\mathbf{X}$ is of full column rank, then $\mathbf{z} \neq \mathbf{0}$ for any $\mathbf{c} \neq \mathbf{0}$.

2. Verify that $\mathbf{X}'\mathbf{X}/n = \frac{1}{n}\sum_i \mathbf{x}_i\mathbf{x}_i'$ and $\mathbf{X}'\mathbf{y}/n = \frac{1}{n}\sum_i \mathbf{x}_i \cdot y_i$ as in (1.2.6). **Hint:** The (k, ℓ) element of $\mathbf{X}'\mathbf{X}$ is $\sum_i x_{ik}x_{i\ell}$.

3. (OLS estimator for the simple regression model) In the simple regression model, $K = 2$ and $x_{i1} = 1$. Show that

$$\mathbf{S_{xx}} = \begin{bmatrix} 1 & \bar{x}_2 \\ \bar{x}_2 & \frac{1}{n}\sum_{i=1}^{n} x_{i2}^2 \end{bmatrix}, \quad \mathbf{s_{xy}} = \begin{bmatrix} \bar{y} \\ \frac{1}{n}\sum_{i=1}^{n} x_{i2}y_i \end{bmatrix}$$

where

$$\bar{y} \equiv \frac{1}{n}\sum_{i=1}^{n} y_i \quad \text{and} \quad \bar{x}_2 \equiv \frac{1}{n}\sum_{i=1}^{n} x_{i2}.$$

Show that

$$b_2 = \frac{\frac{1}{n}\sum_{i=1}^{n}(x_{i2} - \bar{x}_2)(y_i - \bar{y})}{\frac{1}{n}\sum_{i=1}^{n}(x_{i2} - \bar{x}_2)^2} \quad \text{and} \quad b_1 = \bar{y} - \bar{x}_2 b_2.$$

(You may recognize the denominator of the expression for b_2 as the sample variance of the nonconstant regressor and the numerator as the sample covariance between the nonconstant regressor and the dependent variable.) **Hint:**

$$\frac{1}{n}\sum_{i=1}^{n} x_{i2}^2 - (\bar{x}_2)^2 = \frac{1}{n}\sum_{i=1}^{n}(x_{i2} - \bar{x}_2)^2$$

and

$$\frac{1}{n}\sum_{i=1}^{n} x_{i2}\, y_i - \bar{x}_2\, \bar{y} = \frac{1}{n}\sum_{i=1}^{n}(x_{i2} - \bar{x}_2)(y_i - \bar{y}).$$

You can take (1.2.5′) and use the brute force of matrix inversion. Alternatively, write down the two normal equations. The first normal equation is $b_1 = \bar{y} - \bar{x}_2 b_2$. Substitute this into the second normal equation to eliminate b_1 and then solve for b_2.

4. Prove (1.2.9)–(1.2.11). **Hint:** They should easily follow from the definition of $\mathbf{P}$ and $\mathbf{M}$.

5. (Matrix algebra of fitted values and residuals) Show the following:

   (a) $\hat{\mathbf{y}} = \mathbf{Py}$, $\mathbf{e} = \mathbf{My} = \mathbf{M}\boldsymbol{\varepsilon}$. **Hint:** Use (1.2.5).

   (b) (1.2.12), namely, $SSR = \boldsymbol{\varepsilon}'\mathbf{M}\boldsymbol{\varepsilon}$.

6. (Change in units and R^2) Does a change in the unit of measurement for the dependent variable change R^2? A change in the unit of measurement for the regressors? **Hint:** Check whether the change affects the denominator and the numerator in the definition for R^2.

7. (Relation between R^2_{uc} and R^2) Show that

$$1 - R^2 = \left(1 + \frac{n \cdot \bar{y}^2}{\sum_{i=1}^{n}(y_i - \bar{y})^2}\right)(1 - R^2_{uc}).$$

   Hint: Use (1.2.16), (1.2.18), and the identity $\sum_i (y_i - \bar{y})^2 = \sum_i y_i^2 - n \cdot \bar{y}^2$.

8. Show that

$$R^2_{uc} = \frac{\mathbf{y}'\mathbf{P}\mathbf{y}}{\mathbf{y}'\mathbf{y}}.$$

9. (Computation of the statistics) Verify that $\mathbf{b}$, SSR, s^2, and R^2 can be calculated from the following sample averages: $\mathbf{S_{xx}}$, $\mathbf{s_{xy}}$, $\mathbf{y}'\mathbf{y}/n$, and $\bar{y}$. (If the regressors include a constant, then $\bar{y}$ is the element of $\mathbf{s_{xy}}$ corresponding to the constant.) Therefore, those sample averages need to be computed just once in order to obtain the regression coefficients and related statistics.

1.3 Finite-Sample Properties of OLS

Having derived the OLS estimator, we now examine its finite-sample properties, namely, the characteristics of the distribution of the estimator that are valid for any given sample size n.

Finite-Sample Distribution of $\mathbf{b}$

Proposition 1.1 (finite-sample properties of the OLS estimator of $\boldsymbol{\beta}$):

(a) (unbiasedness) Under Assumptions 1.1–1.3, $\mathrm{E}(\mathbf{b} \mid \mathbf{X}) = \boldsymbol{\beta}$.

(b) (expression for the variance) Under Assumptions 1.1–1.4, $\mathrm{Var}(\mathbf{b} \mid \mathbf{X}) = \sigma^2 \cdot (\mathbf{X}'\mathbf{X})^{-1}$.

(c) (Gauss-Markov Theorem) Under Assumptions 1.1–1.4, the OLS estimator is ***efficient*** *in the class of linear unbiased estimators. That is, for any unbiased estimator* $\widehat{\boldsymbol{\beta}}$ *that is linear in* $\mathbf{y}$, $\mathrm{Var}(\widehat{\boldsymbol{\beta}} \mid \mathbf{X}) \geq \mathrm{Var}(\mathbf{b} \mid \mathbf{X})$ *in the matrix sense.*[13]

(d) Under Assumptions 1.1–1.4, $\mathrm{Cov}(\mathbf{b}, \mathbf{e} \mid \mathbf{X}) = \mathbf{0}$, *where* $\mathbf{e} \equiv \mathbf{y} - \mathbf{X}\mathbf{b}$.

Before plunging into the proof, let us be clear about what this proposition means.

- The matrix inequality in part (c) says that the $K \times K$ matrix $\mathrm{Var}(\widehat{\boldsymbol{\beta}} \mid \mathbf{X}) - \mathrm{Var}(\mathbf{b} \mid \mathbf{X})$ is positive semidefinite, so

$$\mathbf{a}'[\mathrm{Var}(\widehat{\boldsymbol{\beta}} \mid \mathbf{X}) - \mathrm{Var}(\mathbf{b} \mid \mathbf{X})]\mathbf{a} \geq 0 \quad \text{or} \quad \mathbf{a}' \mathrm{Var}(\widehat{\boldsymbol{\beta}} \mid \mathbf{X})\mathbf{a} \geq \mathbf{a}' \mathrm{Var}(\mathbf{b} \mid \mathbf{X})\mathbf{a}$$

for any K-dimensional vector $\mathbf{a}$. In particular, consider a special vector whose elements are all 0 except for the k-th element, which is 1. For this particular $\mathbf{a}$, the quadratic form $\mathbf{a}'\mathbf{A}\mathbf{a}$ picks up the (k, k) element of $\mathbf{A}$. But the (k, k) element of $\mathrm{Var}(\widehat{\boldsymbol{\beta}} \mid \mathbf{X})$, for example, is $\mathrm{Var}(\widehat{\beta}_k \mid \mathbf{X})$ where $\widehat{\beta}_k$ is the k-th element of $\widehat{\boldsymbol{\beta}}$. Thus the matrix inequality in (c) implies

$$\mathrm{Var}(\widehat{\beta}_k \mid \mathbf{X}) \geq \mathrm{Var}(b_k \mid \mathbf{X}) \quad (k = 1, 2, \ldots, K). \tag{1.3.1}$$

That is, for any regression coefficient, the variance of the OLS estimator is no larger than that of any other linear unbiased estimator.

[13]Let $\mathbf{A}$ and $\mathbf{B}$ be two square matrices of the same size. We say that $\mathbf{A} \geq \mathbf{B}$ if $\mathbf{A} - \mathbf{B}$ is positive semidefinite. A $K \times K$ matrix $\mathbf{C}$ is said to be positive semidefinite (or nonnegative definite) if $\mathbf{x}'\mathbf{C}\mathbf{x} \geq 0$ for all K-dimensional vectors $\mathbf{x}$.

- As clear from (1.2.5), the OLS estimator is linear in $\mathbf{y}$. There are many other estimators of $\boldsymbol{\beta}$ that are linear and unbiased (you will be asked to provide one in a review question below). The Gauss-Markov Theorem says that the OLS estimator is **efficient** in the sense that its conditional variance matrix $\text{Var}(\mathbf{b} \mid \mathbf{X})$ is smallest among linear unbiased estimators. For this reason the OLS estimator is called the Best Linear Unbiased Estimator (**BLUE**).

- The OLS estimator $\mathbf{b}$ is a function of the sample $(\mathbf{y}, \mathbf{X})$. Since $(\mathbf{y}, \mathbf{X})$ are random, so is $\mathbf{b}$. Now imagine that we fix $\mathbf{X}$ at some given value, calculate $\mathbf{b}$ for all samples corresponding to all possible realizations of $\mathbf{y}$, and take the average of $\mathbf{b}$ (the Monte Carlo exercise to this chapter will ask you to do this). This average is the (population) conditional mean $\text{E}(\mathbf{b} \mid \mathbf{X})$. Part (a) (unbiasedness) says that this average equals the true value $\boldsymbol{\beta}$.

- There is another notion of unbiasedness that is weaker than the unbiasedness of part (a). By the Law of Total Expectations, $\text{E}[\text{E}(\mathbf{b} \mid \mathbf{X})] = \text{E}(\mathbf{b})$. So (a) implies

$$\text{E}(\mathbf{b}) = \boldsymbol{\beta}. \tag{1.3.2}$$

  This says: if we calculated $\mathbf{b}$ for all possible different samples, differing not only in $\mathbf{y}$ but also in $\mathbf{X}$, the average would be the true value. This unconditional statement is probably more relevant in economics because samples do differ in both $\mathbf{y}$ and $\mathbf{X}$. The import of the conditional statement (a) is that it implies the unconditional statement (1.3.2), which is more relevant.

- The same holds for the conditional statement (c) about the variance. A review question below asks you to show that statements (a) and (b) imply

$$\text{Var}(\widehat{\boldsymbol{\beta}}) \geq \text{Var}(\mathbf{b}) \tag{1.3.3}$$

  where $\widehat{\boldsymbol{\beta}}$ is any linear unbiased estimator (so that $\text{E}(\widehat{\boldsymbol{\beta}} \mid \mathbf{X}) = \boldsymbol{\beta}$).

We will now go through the proof of this important result. The proof may look lengthy; if so, it is only because it records every step, however easy. In the first reading, you can skip the proof of part (c). Proof of (d) is a review question.

PROOF.

(a) (Proof that $\text{E}(\mathbf{b} \mid \mathbf{X}) = \boldsymbol{\beta}$) $\text{E}(\mathbf{b} - \boldsymbol{\beta} \mid \mathbf{X}) = \mathbf{0}$ whenever $\text{E}(\mathbf{b} \mid \mathbf{X}) = \boldsymbol{\beta}$. So we prove the former. By the expression for the sampling error (1.2.14),

$\mathbf{b} - \boldsymbol{\beta} = \mathbf{A}\boldsymbol{\varepsilon}$ where $\mathbf{A}$ here is $(\mathbf{X}'\mathbf{X})^{-1}\mathbf{X}'$. So

$$\mathrm{E}(\mathbf{b} - \boldsymbol{\beta} \mid \mathbf{X}) = \mathrm{E}(\mathbf{A}\boldsymbol{\varepsilon} \mid \mathbf{X}) = \mathbf{A}\,\mathrm{E}(\boldsymbol{\varepsilon} \mid \mathbf{X}).$$

Here, the second equality holds by the linearity of conditional expectations; $\mathbf{A}$ is a function of $\mathbf{X}$ and so can be treated as if nonrandom. Since $\mathrm{E}(\boldsymbol{\varepsilon} \mid \mathbf{X}) = \mathbf{0}$, the last expression is zero.

(b) (Proof that $\mathrm{Var}(\mathbf{b} \mid \mathbf{X}) = \sigma^2 \cdot (\mathbf{X}'\mathbf{X})^{-1}$)

$$\begin{aligned}
\mathrm{Var}(\mathbf{b} \mid \mathbf{X}) &= \mathrm{Var}(\mathbf{b} - \boldsymbol{\beta} \mid \mathbf{X}) \quad (\text{since } \boldsymbol{\beta} \text{ is not random}) \\
&= \mathrm{Var}(\mathbf{A}\boldsymbol{\varepsilon} \mid \mathbf{X}) \quad (\text{by (1.2.14) and } \mathbf{A} \equiv (\mathbf{X}'\mathbf{X})^{-1}\mathbf{X}') \\
&= \mathbf{A}\,\mathrm{Var}(\boldsymbol{\varepsilon} \mid \mathbf{X})\mathbf{A}' \quad (\text{since } \mathbf{A} \text{ is a function of } \mathbf{X}) \\
&= \mathbf{A}\,\mathrm{E}(\boldsymbol{\varepsilon}\boldsymbol{\varepsilon}' \mid \mathbf{X})\mathbf{A}' \quad (\text{by Assumption 1.2}) \\
&= \mathbf{A}(\sigma^2\mathbf{I}_n)\mathbf{A}' \quad (\text{by Assumption 1.4, see (1.1.14)}) \\
&= \sigma^2\mathbf{A}\mathbf{A}' \\
&= \sigma^2 \cdot (\mathbf{X}'\mathbf{X})^{-1} \quad (\text{since } \mathbf{A}\mathbf{A}' = (\mathbf{X}'\mathbf{X})^{-1}\mathbf{X}'\mathbf{X}(\mathbf{X}'\mathbf{X})^{-1} = (\mathbf{X}'\mathbf{X})^{-1}).
\end{aligned}$$

(c) (Gauss-Markov) Since $\widehat{\boldsymbol{\beta}}$ is linear in $\mathbf{y}$, it can be written as $\widehat{\boldsymbol{\beta}} = \mathbf{C}\mathbf{y}$ for some matrix $\mathbf{C}$, which possibly is a function of $\mathbf{X}$. Let $\mathbf{D} \equiv \mathbf{C} - \mathbf{A}$ or $\mathbf{C} = \mathbf{D} + \mathbf{A}$ where $\mathbf{A} \equiv (\mathbf{X}'\mathbf{X})^{-1}\mathbf{X}'$. Then

$$\begin{aligned}
\widehat{\boldsymbol{\beta}} &= (\mathbf{D} + \mathbf{A})\mathbf{y} \\
&= \mathbf{D}\mathbf{y} + \mathbf{A}\mathbf{y} \\
&= \mathbf{D}(\mathbf{X}\boldsymbol{\beta} + \boldsymbol{\varepsilon}) + \mathbf{b} \quad (\text{since } \mathbf{y} = \mathbf{X}\boldsymbol{\beta} + \boldsymbol{\varepsilon} \text{ and } \mathbf{A}\mathbf{y} = (\mathbf{X}'\mathbf{X})^{-1}\mathbf{X}'\mathbf{y} = \mathbf{b}) \\
&= \mathbf{D}\mathbf{X}\boldsymbol{\beta} + \mathbf{D}\boldsymbol{\varepsilon} + \mathbf{b}.
\end{aligned}$$

Taking the conditional expectation of both sides, we obtain

$$\mathrm{E}(\widehat{\boldsymbol{\beta}} \mid \mathbf{X}) = \mathbf{D}\mathbf{X}\boldsymbol{\beta} + \mathrm{E}(\mathbf{D}\boldsymbol{\varepsilon} \mid \mathbf{X}) + \mathrm{E}(\mathbf{b} \mid \mathbf{X}).$$

Since both $\mathbf{b}$ and $\widehat{\boldsymbol{\beta}}$ are unbiased and since $\mathrm{E}(\mathbf{D}\boldsymbol{\varepsilon} \mid \mathbf{X}) = \mathbf{D}\,\mathrm{E}(\boldsymbol{\varepsilon} \mid \mathbf{X}) = \mathbf{0}$, it follows that $\mathbf{D}\mathbf{X}\boldsymbol{\beta} = \mathbf{0}$. For this to be true for any given $\boldsymbol{\beta}$, it is necessary that $\mathbf{D}\mathbf{X} = \mathbf{0}$. So $\widehat{\boldsymbol{\beta}} = \mathbf{D}\boldsymbol{\varepsilon} + \mathbf{b}$ and

$$\begin{aligned}
\widehat{\boldsymbol{\beta}} - \boldsymbol{\beta} &= \mathbf{D}\boldsymbol{\varepsilon} + (\mathbf{b} - \boldsymbol{\beta}) \\
&= (\mathbf{D} + \mathbf{A})\boldsymbol{\varepsilon} \quad (\text{by (1.2.14)}).
\end{aligned}$$

So

$$\begin{aligned}
\text{Var}(\widehat{\boldsymbol{\beta}} \mid \mathbf{X}) &= \text{Var}(\widehat{\boldsymbol{\beta}} - \boldsymbol{\beta} \mid \mathbf{X}) \\
&= \text{Var}[(\mathbf{D} + \mathbf{A})\boldsymbol{\varepsilon} \mid \mathbf{X}] \\
&= (\mathbf{D} + \mathbf{A}) \, \text{Var}(\boldsymbol{\varepsilon} \mid \mathbf{X})(\mathbf{D}' + \mathbf{A}') \\
&\qquad \text{(since both } \mathbf{D} \text{ and } \mathbf{A} \text{ are functions of } \mathbf{X}) \\
&= \sigma^2 \cdot (\mathbf{D} + \mathbf{A})(\mathbf{D}' + \mathbf{A}') \quad (\text{since } \text{Var}(\boldsymbol{\varepsilon} \mid \mathbf{X}) = \sigma^2 \mathbf{I}_n) \\
&= \sigma^2 \cdot (\mathbf{D}\mathbf{D}' + \mathbf{A}\mathbf{D}' + \mathbf{D}\mathbf{A}' + \mathbf{A}\mathbf{A}').
\end{aligned}$$

But $\mathbf{DA}' = \mathbf{DX}(\mathbf{X}'\mathbf{X})^{-1} = \mathbf{0}$ since $\mathbf{DX} = \mathbf{0}$. Also, $\mathbf{AA}' = (\mathbf{X}'\mathbf{X})^{-1}$ as shown in (b). So

$$\begin{aligned}
\text{Var}(\widehat{\boldsymbol{\beta}} \mid \mathbf{X}) &= \sigma^2 \cdot [\mathbf{D}\mathbf{D}' + (\mathbf{X}'\mathbf{X})^{-1}] \\
&\geq \sigma^2 \cdot (\mathbf{X}'\mathbf{X})^{-1} \quad (\text{since } \mathbf{D}\mathbf{D}' \text{ is positive semidefinite}) \\
&= \text{Var}(\mathbf{b} \mid \mathbf{X}) \quad (\text{by (b)}). \qquad \blacksquare
\end{aligned}$$

It should be emphasized that the strict exogeneity assumption (Assumption 1.2) is critical for proving unbiasedness. Anything short of strict exogeneity will not do. For example, it is not enough to assume that $\text{E}(\varepsilon_i \mid \mathbf{x}_i) = 0$ for all i or that $\text{E}(\mathbf{x}_i \cdot \varepsilon_i) = \mathbf{0}$ for all i. We noted in Section 1.1 that most time-series models do not satisfy strict exogeneity even if they satisfy weaker conditions such as the orthogonality condition $\text{E}(\mathbf{x}_i \cdot \varepsilon_i) = \mathbf{0}$. It follows that for those models the OLS estimator is not unbiased.

Finite-Sample Properties of s^2

We defined the OLS estimator of σ^2 in (1.2.13). It, too, is unbiased.

Proposition 1.2 (Unbiasedness of s^2): *Under Assumptions 1.1–1.4,* $\text{E}(s^2 \mid \mathbf{X}) = \sigma^2$ *(and hence* $\text{E}(s^2) = \sigma^2$*), provided* $n > K$ *(so that* s^2 *is well-defined).*

We can prove this proposition easily by the use of the trace operator.[14]

PROOF. Since $s^2 = \mathbf{e}'\mathbf{e}/(n - K)$, the proof amounts to showing that $\text{E}(\mathbf{e}'\mathbf{e} \mid \mathbf{X}) = (n - K)\sigma^2$. As shown in (1.2.12), $\mathbf{e}'\mathbf{e} = \boldsymbol{\varepsilon}'\mathbf{M}\boldsymbol{\varepsilon}$ where $\mathbf{M}$ is the annihilator. The proof consists of proving two properties: (1) $\text{E}(\boldsymbol{\varepsilon}'\mathbf{M}\boldsymbol{\varepsilon} \mid \mathbf{X}) = \sigma^2 \cdot \text{trace}(\mathbf{M})$, and (2) $\text{trace}(\mathbf{M}) = n - K$.

[14] The **trace** of a square matrix $\mathbf{A}$ is the sum of the diagonal elements of $\mathbf{A}$: $\text{trace}(\mathbf{A}) = \sum_i a_{ii}$.

(1) (Proof that $\mathrm{E}(\boldsymbol{\varepsilon}'\mathbf{M}\boldsymbol{\varepsilon} \mid \mathbf{X}) = \sigma^2 \cdot \operatorname{trace}(\mathbf{M})$) Since $\boldsymbol{\varepsilon}'\mathbf{M}\boldsymbol{\varepsilon} = \sum_{i=1}^n \sum_{j=1}^n m_{ij}\, \varepsilon_i\, \varepsilon_j$ (this is just writing out the quadratic form $\boldsymbol{\varepsilon}'\mathbf{M}\boldsymbol{\varepsilon}$), we have

$$\begin{aligned}
\mathrm{E}(\boldsymbol{\varepsilon}'\mathbf{M}\boldsymbol{\varepsilon} \mid \mathbf{X}) &= \sum_{i=1}^{n}\sum_{j=1}^{n} m_{ij}\ \mathrm{E}(\varepsilon_i\, \varepsilon_j \mid \mathbf{X}) \text{ (because } m_{ij}\text{'s are functions of } \mathbf{X}, \\
&\qquad\qquad \mathrm{E}(m_{ij}\, \varepsilon_i\, \varepsilon_j \mid \mathbf{X}) = m_{ij}\ \mathrm{E}(\varepsilon_i\, \varepsilon_j \mid \mathbf{X})) \\
&= \sum_{i=1}^{n} m_{ii}\, \sigma^2 \\
&\qquad\qquad \text{(since } \mathrm{E}(\varepsilon_i\, \varepsilon_j \mid \mathbf{X}) = 0 \text{ for } i \neq j \text{ by Assumption 1.4)} \\
&= \sigma^2 \sum_{i=1}^{n} m_{ii} \\
&= \sigma^2 \cdot \operatorname{trace}(\mathbf{M}).
\end{aligned}$$

(2) (Proof that $\operatorname{trace}(\mathbf{M}) = n - K$)

$$\begin{aligned}
\operatorname{trace}(\mathbf{M}) &= \operatorname{trace}(\mathbf{I}_n - \mathbf{P}) \quad (\text{since } \mathbf{M} \equiv \mathbf{I}_n - \mathbf{P}\text{; see (1.2.8)}) \\
&= \operatorname{trace}(\mathbf{I}_n) - \operatorname{trace}(\mathbf{P}) \quad (\text{fact: the trace operator is linear}) \\
&= n - \operatorname{trace}(\mathbf{P}),
\end{aligned}$$

and

$$\begin{aligned}
\operatorname{trace}(\mathbf{P}) &= \operatorname{trace}[\mathbf{X}(\mathbf{X}'\mathbf{X})^{-1}\mathbf{X}'] \quad (\text{since } \mathbf{P} \equiv \mathbf{X}(\mathbf{X}'\mathbf{X})^{-1}\mathbf{X}'\text{; see (1.2.7)}) \\
&= \operatorname{trace}[(\mathbf{X}'\mathbf{X})^{-1}\mathbf{X}'\mathbf{X}] \quad (\text{fact: } \operatorname{trace}(\mathbf{AB}) = \operatorname{trace}(\mathbf{BA})) \\
&= \operatorname{trace}(\mathbf{I}_K) = K.
\end{aligned}$$

So $\operatorname{trace}(\mathbf{M}) = n - K$. ■

Estimate of Var(b | X)

If s^2 is the estimate of σ^2, a natural estimate of $\operatorname{Var}(\mathbf{b} \mid \mathbf{X}) = \sigma^2 \cdot (\mathbf{X}'\mathbf{X})^{-1}$ is

$$\widehat{\operatorname{Var}(\mathbf{b} \mid \mathbf{X})} \equiv s^2 \cdot (\mathbf{X}'\mathbf{X})^{-1}. \tag{1.3.4}$$

This is one of the statistics included in the computer printout of any OLS software package.

QUESTIONS FOR REVIEW

1. (Role of the no-multicollinearity assumption) In Propositions 1.1 and 1.2, where did we use Assumption 1.3 that $\operatorname{rank}(\mathbf{X}) = K$? **Hint:** We need the no-multicollinearity condition to make sure $\mathbf{X}'\mathbf{X}$ is invertible.

2. (Example of a linear estimator) For the consumption function example in Example 1.1, propose a linear and unbiased estimator of β_2 that is different from the OLS estimator. **Hint:** How about $\widehat{\beta}_2 = (CON_2 - CON_1)/(YD_2 - YD_1)$? Is it linear in $(CON_1, \ldots, CON_n)$? Is it unbiased in the sense that $\mathrm{E}(\widehat{\beta}_2 \mid YD_1, \ldots, YD_n) = \beta_2$?

3. (What Gauss-Markov does not mean) Under Assumptions 1.1–1.4, does there exist a linear, but not necessarily unbiased, estimator of $\boldsymbol{\beta}$ that has a variance smaller than that of the OLS estimator? If so, how small can the variance be? **Hint:** If an estimator of $\boldsymbol{\beta}$ is a constant, then the estimator is trivially linear in $\mathbf{y}$.

4. (Gauss-Markov for Unconditional Variance)

   (a) Prove: $\mathrm{Var}(\widehat{\boldsymbol{\beta}}) = \mathrm{E}[\mathrm{Var}(\widehat{\boldsymbol{\beta}} \mid \mathbf{X})] + \mathrm{Var}[\mathrm{E}(\widehat{\boldsymbol{\beta}} \mid \mathbf{X})]$. **Hint:** By definition,

   $$\mathrm{Var}(\widehat{\boldsymbol{\beta}} \mid \mathbf{X}) \equiv \mathrm{E}\big[\big(\widehat{\boldsymbol{\beta}} - \mathrm{E}(\widehat{\boldsymbol{\beta}} \mid \mathbf{X})\big)\big(\widehat{\boldsymbol{\beta}} - \mathrm{E}(\widehat{\boldsymbol{\beta}} \mid \mathbf{X})\big)' \mid \mathbf{X}\big]$$

   and

   $$\mathrm{Var}[\mathrm{E}(\widehat{\boldsymbol{\beta}} \mid \mathbf{X})] \equiv \mathrm{E}\big\{[\mathrm{E}(\widehat{\boldsymbol{\beta}} \mid \mathbf{X}) - \mathrm{E}(\widehat{\boldsymbol{\beta}})][\mathrm{E}(\widehat{\boldsymbol{\beta}} \mid \mathbf{X}) - \mathrm{E}(\widehat{\boldsymbol{\beta}})]'\big\}.$$

   Use the add-and-subtract strategy: take $\widehat{\boldsymbol{\beta}} - \mathrm{E}(\widehat{\boldsymbol{\beta}} \mid \mathbf{X})$ and add and subtract $\mathrm{E}(\widehat{\boldsymbol{\beta}})$.

   (b) Prove (1.3.3). **Hint:** If $\mathrm{Var}(\widehat{\boldsymbol{\beta}} \mid \mathbf{X}) \geq \mathrm{Var}(\mathbf{b} \mid \mathbf{X})$, then $\mathrm{E}[\mathrm{Var}(\widehat{\boldsymbol{\beta}} \mid \mathbf{X})] \geq \mathrm{E}[\mathrm{Var}(\mathbf{b} \mid \mathbf{X})]$

5. Propose an unbiased estimator of σ^2 if you had data on $\boldsymbol{\varepsilon}$. **Hint:** How about $\boldsymbol{\varepsilon}'\boldsymbol{\varepsilon}/n$? Is it unbiased?

6. Prove part (d) of Proposition 1.1. **Hint:** By definition,

   $$\mathrm{Cov}(\mathbf{b}, \mathbf{e} \mid \mathbf{X}) \equiv \mathrm{E}\Big\{[\mathbf{b} - \mathrm{E}(\mathbf{b} \mid \mathbf{X})][\mathbf{e} - \mathrm{E}(\mathbf{e} \mid \mathbf{X})]' \;\Big|\; \mathbf{X}\Big\}.$$

   Since $\mathrm{E}(\mathbf{b} \mid \mathbf{X}) = \boldsymbol{\beta}$, we have $\mathbf{b} - \mathrm{E}(\mathbf{b} \mid \mathbf{X}) = \mathbf{A}\boldsymbol{\varepsilon}$ where $\mathbf{A}$ here is $(\mathbf{X}'\mathbf{X})^{-1}\mathbf{X}'$. Use $\mathbf{M}\boldsymbol{\varepsilon} = \mathbf{e}$ (see Review Question 5 to Section 1.2) to show that $\mathbf{e} - \mathrm{E}(\mathbf{e} \mid \mathbf{X}) = \mathbf{M}\boldsymbol{\varepsilon}$. $\mathrm{E}(\mathbf{A}\boldsymbol{\varepsilon}\boldsymbol{\varepsilon}'\mathbf{M} \mid \mathbf{X}) = \mathbf{A}\,\mathrm{E}(\boldsymbol{\varepsilon}\boldsymbol{\varepsilon}' \mid \mathbf{X})\mathbf{M}$ since both $\mathbf{A}$ and $\mathbf{M}$ are functions of $\mathbf{X}$. Finally, use $\mathbf{M}\mathbf{X} = \mathbf{0}$ (see (1.2.11)).

7. Prove (1.2.21). **Hint:** Since $\mathbf{P}$ is positive semidefinite, its diagonal elements are nonnegative. Note that $\sum_{i=1}^{n} p_i = \mathrm{trace}(\mathbf{P})$.

1.4 Hypothesis Testing under Normality

Very often, the economic theory that motivated the regression equation also specifies the values that the regression coefficients should take. Suppose that the underlying theory implies the restriction that β_2 equals 1. Although Proposition 1.1 guarantees that, on average, b_2 (the OLS estimate of β_2) equals 1 if the restriction is true, b_2 may not be exactly equal to 1 for a particular sample at hand. Obviously, we cannot conclude that the restriction is false just because the estimate b_2 differs from 1. In order for us to decide whether the sampling error $b_2 - 1$ is "too large" for the restriction to be true, we need to construct from the sampling error some test statistic whose probability distribution is known given the truth of the hypothesis. It might appear that doing so requires one to specify the joint distribution of $(\mathbf{X}, \boldsymbol{\varepsilon})$ because, as is clear from (1.2.14), the sampling error is a function of $(\mathbf{X}, \boldsymbol{\varepsilon})$. A surprising fact about the theory of hypothesis testing to be presented in this section is that the distribution can be derived without specifying the joint distribution when the conditional distribution of $\boldsymbol{\varepsilon}$ conditional on $\mathbf{X}$ is normal; there is no need to specify the distribution of $\mathbf{X}$.

In the language of hypothesis testing, the restriction to be tested (such as "$\beta_2 = 1$") is called the **null hypothesis** (or simply the **null**). It is a restriction on the **maintained hypothesis**, a set of assumptions which, combined with the null, produces some test statistic with a known distribution. For the present case of testing hypothesis about regression coefficients, only the normality assumption about the conditional distribution of $\boldsymbol{\varepsilon}$ needs to be added to the classical regression model (Assumptions 1.1–1.4) to form the maintained hypothesis (as just noted, there is no need to specify the joint distribution of $(\mathbf{X}, \boldsymbol{\varepsilon})$). Sometimes the maintained hypothesis is somewhat loosely referred to as "the model." We say that the model is **correctly specified** if the maintained hypothesis is true. Although too large a value of the test statistic is interpreted as a failure of the null, the interpretation is valid only as long as the model is correctly specified. It is possible that the test statistic does not have the supposed distribution when the null is true but the model is false.

Normally Distributed Error Terms

In many applications, the error term consists of many miscellaneous factors not captured by the regressors. The Central Limit Theorem suggests that the error term has a normal distribution. In other applications, the error term is due to errors in measuring the dependent variable. It is known that very often measurement errors are normally distributed (in fact, the normal distribution was originally developed for measurement errors). It is therefore worth entertaining the normality assumption:

Assumption 1.5 (normality of the error term): *The distribution of* $\boldsymbol{\varepsilon}$ *conditional on* $\mathbf{X}$ *is jointly normal.*

Recall from probability theory that the normal distribution has several convenient features:

- The distribution depends only on the mean and the variance. Thus, once the mean and the variance are known, you can write down the density function. If the distribution conditional on $\mathbf{X}$ is normal, the mean and the variance can depend on $\mathbf{X}$. It follows that, if the distribution conditional on $\mathbf{X}$ is normal and if neither the conditional mean nor the conditional variance depends on $\mathbf{X}$, then the marginal (i.e., unconditional) distribution is the same normal distribution.
- In general, if two random variables are independent, then they are uncorrelated, but the converse is not true. However, if two random variables are joint normal, the converse is also true, so that independence and a lack of correlation are equivalent. This carries over to conditional distributions: if two random variables are joint normal and uncorrelated conditional on $\mathbf{X}$, then they are independent conditional on $\mathbf{X}$.
- A linear function of random variables that are jointly normally distributed is itself normally distributed. This also carries over to conditional distributions. If the distribution of $\boldsymbol{\varepsilon}$ conditional on $\mathbf{X}$ is normal, then $\mathbf{A}\boldsymbol{\varepsilon}$, where the elements of matrix $\mathbf{A}$ are functions of $\mathbf{X}$, is normal conditional on $\mathbf{X}$.

It is thanks to these features of normality that Assumption 1.5 delivers the following properties to be exploited in the derivation of test statistics:

- The mean and the variance of the distribution of $\boldsymbol{\varepsilon}$ conditional on $\mathbf{X}$ are already specified in Assumptions 1.2 and 1.4. Therefore, Assumption 1.5 together with Assumptions 1.2 and 1.4 implies that the distribution of $\boldsymbol{\varepsilon}$ conditional on $\mathbf{X}$ is $N(\mathbf{0}, \sigma^2 \mathbf{I}_n)$:

  $$\boldsymbol{\varepsilon} \mid \mathbf{X} \sim N(\mathbf{0}, \sigma^2 \mathbf{I}_n). \tag{1.4.1}$$

  Thus, the distribution of $\boldsymbol{\varepsilon}$ conditional on $\mathbf{X}$ does not depend on $\mathbf{X}$. It then follows that $\boldsymbol{\varepsilon}$ and $\mathbf{X}$ are *independent*. Therefore, in particular, the marginal or unconditional distribution of $\boldsymbol{\varepsilon}$ is $N(\mathbf{0}, \sigma^2 \mathbf{I}_n)$.

- We know from (1.2.14) that the sampling error $\mathbf{b} - \boldsymbol{\beta}$ is linear in $\boldsymbol{\varepsilon}$ given $\mathbf{X}$. Since $\boldsymbol{\varepsilon}$ is normal given $\mathbf{X}$, so is the sampling error. Its mean and variance are given by parts (a) and (b) of Proposition 1.1. Thus, under Assumptions 1.1–1.5,

$$(\mathbf{b} - \boldsymbol{\beta}) \mid \mathbf{X} \sim N(\mathbf{0}, \sigma^2 \cdot (\mathbf{X}'\mathbf{X})^{-1}). \tag{1.4.2}$$

Testing Hypotheses about Individual Regression Coefficients

The type of hypothesis we first consider is about the k-th coefficient

$$\text{H}_0\colon \beta_k = \overline{\beta}_k.$$

Here, $\overline{\beta}_k$ is some known value specified by the null hypothesis. We wish to test this null against the alternative hypothesis $\text{H}_1\colon \beta_k \neq \overline{\beta}_k$, at a significance level of α. Looking at the k-th component of (1.4.2) and imposing the restriction of the null, we obtain

$$(b_k - \overline{\beta}_k) \mid \mathbf{X} \sim N\Big(0, \sigma^2 \cdot \big((\mathbf{X}'\mathbf{X})^{-1}\big)_{kk}\Big),$$

where $\big((\mathbf{X}'\mathbf{X})^{-1}\big)_{kk}$ is the (k, k) element of $(\mathbf{X}'\mathbf{X})^{-1}$. So if we define the ratio z_k by dividing $b_k - \overline{\beta}_k$ by its standard deviation

$$z_k \equiv \frac{b_k - \overline{\beta}_k}{\sqrt{\sigma^2 \cdot \big((\mathbf{X}'\mathbf{X})^{-1}\big)_{kk}}}, \tag{1.4.3}$$

then the distribution of z_k is $N(0, 1)$ (the standard normal distribution).

Suppose for a second that σ^2 is known. Then the statistic z_k has some desirable properties as a test statistic. First, its value can be calculated from the sample. Second, its distribution conditional on $\mathbf{X}$ does not depend on $\mathbf{X}$ (which should not be confused with the fact that the *value* of z_k depends on $\mathbf{X}$). So z_k and $\mathbf{X}$ are independently distributed, and, regardless of the value of $\mathbf{X}$, the distribution of z_k is the same as its unconditional distribution. This is convenient because different samples differ not only in $\mathbf{y}$ but also in $\mathbf{X}$. Third, the distribution is known. In particular, it does not depend on unknown parameters (such as $\boldsymbol{\beta}$). (If the distribution of a statistic depends on unknown parameters, those parameters are called **nuisance parameters**.) Using this statistic, we can determine whether or not the sampling error $b_k - \overline{\beta}_k$ is too large: it is too large if the test statistic takes on a value that is surprising for a realization from the distribution.

If we do not know the true value of σ^2, a natural idea is to replace the nuisance parameter σ^2 by its OLS estimate s^2. The statistic after the substitution of s^2 for

σ^2 is called the ***t*-ratio** or the ***t*-value**. The denominator of this statistic is called the **standard error** of the OLS estimate of β_k and is sometimes written as $SE(b_k)$:

$$SE(b_k) \equiv \sqrt{s^2 \cdot \left((\mathbf{X}'\mathbf{X})^{-1}\right)_{kk}} = \sqrt{(k,k) \text{ element of } \widehat{\text{Var}(\mathbf{b} \mid \mathbf{X})} \text{ in (1.3.4)}}. \quad (1.4.4)$$

Since s^2, being a function of the sample, is a random variable, this substitution changes the distribution of the statistic, but fortunately the changed distribution, too, is known and depends on neither nuisance parameters nor $\mathbf{X}$.

Proposition 1.3 (distribution of the *t*-ratio): *Suppose Assumptions 1.1–1.5 hold. Under the null hypothesis* $\text{H}_0\colon \beta_k = \overline{\beta}_k$, *the t-ratio defined as*

$$t_k \equiv \frac{b_k - \overline{\beta}_k}{SE(b_k)} \equiv \frac{b_k - \overline{\beta}_k}{\sqrt{s^2 \cdot \left((\mathbf{X}'\mathbf{X})^{-1}\right)_{kk}}} \quad (1.4.5)$$

is distributed as $t(n-K)$ *(the t distribution with* $n-K$ *degrees of freedom).*

PROOF. We can write

$$t_k = \frac{b_k - \overline{\beta}_k}{\sqrt{\sigma^2 \cdot \left((\mathbf{X}'\mathbf{X})^{-1}\right)_{kk}}} \cdot \sqrt{\frac{\sigma^2}{s^2}} = \frac{z_k}{\sqrt{s^2/\sigma^2}}$$
$$= \frac{z_k}{\sqrt{\frac{\mathbf{e}'\mathbf{e}/(n-K)}{\sigma^2}}} = \frac{z_k}{\sqrt{\frac{q}{n-K}}},$$

where $q \equiv \mathbf{e}'\mathbf{e}/\sigma^2$ to reflect the substitution of s^2 for σ^2. We have already shown that z_k is $N(0,1)$. We will show:

(1) $q \mid \mathbf{X} \sim \chi^2(n-K)$,

(2) two random variables z_k and q are independent conditional on $\mathbf{X}$.

Then, by the definition of the t distribution, the ratio of z_k to $\sqrt{q/(n-K)}$ is distributed as t with $n-K$ degrees of freedom,[15] and we are done.

(1) Since $\mathbf{e}'\mathbf{e} = \boldsymbol{\varepsilon}'\mathbf{M}\boldsymbol{\varepsilon}$ from (1.2.12), we have

$$q = \frac{\mathbf{e}'\mathbf{e}}{\sigma^2} = \frac{\boldsymbol{\varepsilon}'}{\sigma}\mathbf{M}\frac{\boldsymbol{\varepsilon}}{\sigma}.$$

[15] Fact: If $x \sim N(0,1)$, $y \sim \chi^2(m)$ and if x and y are independent, then the ratio $x/\sqrt{y/m}$ has the t distribution with m degrees of freedom.

The middle matrix $\mathbf{M}$, being the annihilator, is idempotent. Also, $\boldsymbol{\varepsilon}/\sigma \mid \mathbf{X} \sim N(\mathbf{0}, \mathbf{I}_n)$ by (1.4.1). Therefore, this quadratic form is distributed as χ^2 with degrees of freedom equal to rank$(\mathbf{M})$.[16] But rank$(\mathbf{M})$ = trace$(\mathbf{M})$, because $\mathbf{M}$ is idempotent.[17] We have already shown in the proof of Proposition 1.2 that trace$(\mathbf{M}) = n - K$. So $q \mid \mathbf{X} \sim \chi^2(n-K)$.

(2) Both $\mathbf{b}$ and $\mathbf{e}$ are linear functions of $\boldsymbol{\varepsilon}$ (by (1.2.14) and the fact that $\mathbf{e} = \mathbf{M}\boldsymbol{\varepsilon}$), so they are jointly normal conditional on $\mathbf{X}$. Also, they are uncorrelated conditional on $\mathbf{X}$ (see part (d) of Proposition 1.1). So $\mathbf{b}$ and $\mathbf{e}$ are independently distributed conditional on $\mathbf{X}$. But z_k is a function of $\mathbf{b}$ and q is a function of $\mathbf{e}$. So z_k and q are independently distributed conditional on $\mathbf{X}$.[18] ■

Decision Rule for the t-Test

The test of the null hypothesis based on the t-ratio is called the t-test and proceeds as follows:

Step 1: Given the hypothesized value, $\overline{\beta}_k$, of β_k, form the t-ratio as in (1.4.5). Too large a deviation of t_k from 0 is a sign of the failure of the null hypothesis. The next step specifies how large is too large.

Step 2: Go to the t-table (most statistics and econometrics textbooks include the t-table) and look up the entry for $n-K$ degrees of freedom. Find the **critical value**, $t_{\alpha/2}(n-K)$, such that the area in the t distribution to the right of $t_{\alpha/2}(n-K)$ is $\alpha/2$, as illustrated in Figure 1.3. (If $n-K = 30$ and $\alpha = 5\%$, for example, $t_{\alpha/2}(n-K) = 2.042$.) Then, since the t distribution is symmetric around 0,

$$\text{Prob}\big(-t_{\alpha/2}(n-K) < t < t_{\alpha/2}(n-K)\big) = 1 - \alpha.$$

Step 3: Accept H_0 if $-t_{\alpha/2}(n-K) < t_k < t_{\alpha/2}(n-K)$ (that is, if $|t_k| < t_{\alpha/2}(n-K)$), where t_k is the t-ratio from *Step 1*. Reject H_0 otherwise. Since $t_k \sim t(n-K)$ under H_0, the probability of rejecting H_0 when H_0 is true is α. So the size (significance level) of the test is indeed α.

A convenient feature of the t-test is that the critical value does not depend on $\mathbf{X}$; there is no need to calculate critical values for each sample.

[16] Fact: If $\mathbf{x} \sim N(\mathbf{0}, \mathbf{I}_n)$ and $\mathbf{A}$ is idempotent, then $\mathbf{x}'\mathbf{A}\mathbf{x}$ has a chi-squared distribution with degrees of freedom equal to the rank of $\mathbf{A}$.

[17] Fact: If $\mathbf{A}$ is idempotent, then rank$(\mathbf{A})$ = trace$(\mathbf{A})$.

[18] Fact: If $\mathbf{x}$ and $\mathbf{y}$ are independently distributed, then so are $f(\mathbf{x})$ and $g(\mathbf{y})$.

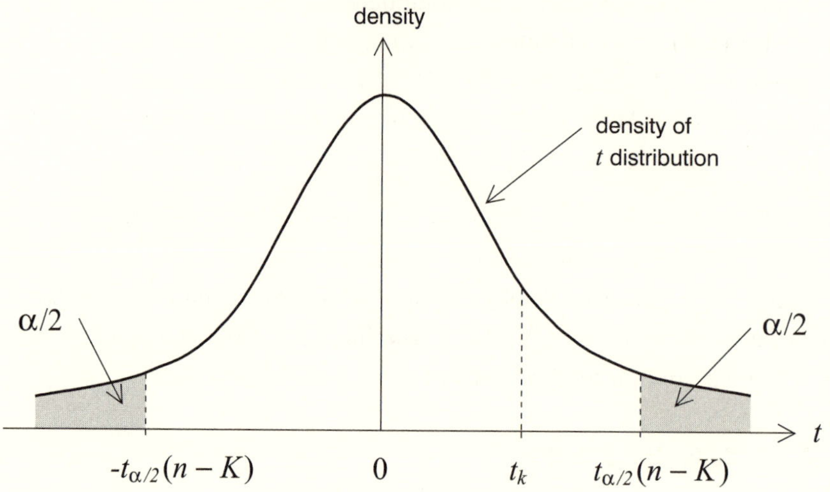

Figure 1.3: t Distribution

Confidence Interval

Step 3 can also be stated in terms of b_k and $SE(b_k)$. Since t_k is as in (1.4.5), you accept H_0 whenever

$$-t_{\alpha/2}(n-K) < \frac{b_k - \overline{\beta}_k}{SE(b_k)} < t_{\alpha/2}(n-K)$$

or

$$b_k - SE(b_k)\cdot t_{\alpha/2}(n-K) < \overline{\beta}_k < b_k + SE(b_k)\cdot t_{\alpha/2}(n-K).$$

Therefore, we accept if and only if the hypothesized value $\overline{\beta}_k$ falls in the interval:

$$[b_k - SE(b_k)\cdot t_{\alpha/2}(n-K),\, b_k + SE(b_k)\cdot t_{\alpha/2}(n-K)]. \qquad (1.4.6)$$

This interval is called the **level $1-\alpha$ confidence interval**. It is narrower the smaller the standard error. Thus, the smallness of the standard error is a measure of the estimator's precision.

***p*-Value**

The decision rule of the t-test can also be stated using the ***p*-value**.

Step 1: Same as above.

Step 2: Rather than finding the critical value $t_{\alpha/2}(n-K)$, calculate

$$p = \text{Prob}(t > |t_k|) \times 2.$$

Since the t distribution is symmetric around 0, $\text{Prob}(t > |t_k|) = \text{Prob}(t < -|t_k|)$, so

$$\text{Prob}(-|t_k| < t < |t_k|) = 1 - p. \tag{1.4.7}$$

Step 3: Accept H_0 if $p > \alpha$. Reject otherwise.

To see the equivalence of the two decision rules, one based on the critical values such as $t_{\alpha/2}(n - K)$ and the other based on the p-value, refer to Figure 1.3. If $\text{Prob}(t > |t_k|)$ is greater than $\alpha/2$ (as in the figure), that is, if the p-value is more than α, then $|t_k|$ must be to the left of $t_{\alpha/2}(n - K)$. This means from *Step 3* that the null hypothesis is not rejected. Thus, when p is small, the t-ratio is surprisingly large for a random variable from the t distribution. The smaller the p, the stronger the rejection.

Examples of the t-test can be found in Section 1.7.

Linear Hypotheses

The null hypothesis we wish to test may not be a restriction about individual regression coefficients of the maintained hypothesis; it is often about linear combinations of them written as a system of linear equations:

$$H_0\colon \mathbf{R}\boldsymbol{\beta} = \mathbf{r}, \tag{1.4.8}$$

where values of $\mathbf{R}$ and $\mathbf{r}$ are known and specified by the hypothesis. We denote the number of equations, which is the dimension of $\mathbf{r}$, by $\#\mathbf{r}$. So $\mathbf{R}$ is $\#\mathbf{r} \times K$. These $\#\mathbf{r}$ equations are restrictions on the coefficients in the maintained hypothesis. It is called a linear hypothesis because each equation is linear. To make sure that there are no redundant equations and that the equations are consistent with each other, we require that $\text{rank}(\mathbf{R}) = \#\mathbf{r}$ (i.e., $\mathbf{R}$ is of full *row* rank with its rank equaling the number of rows). But do not be too conscious about the rank condition; in specific applications, it is very easy to spot a failure of the rank condition if there is one.

Example 1.5 (continuation of Example 1.2): Consider the wage equation of Example 1.2 where $K = 4$. We might wish to test the hypothesis that education and tenure have equal impact on the wage rate and that there is no experience effect. The hypothesis is two equations (so $\#\mathbf{r} = 2$):

$$\beta_2 = \beta_3 \text{ and } \beta_4 = 0.$$

This can be cast in the format $\mathbf{R}\boldsymbol{\beta} = \mathbf{r}$ if $\mathbf{R}$ and $\mathbf{r}$ are defined as

$$\mathbf{R} = \begin{bmatrix} 0 & 1 & -1 & 0 \\ 0 & 0 & 0 & 1 \end{bmatrix}, \quad \mathbf{r} = \begin{bmatrix} 0 \\ 0 \end{bmatrix}.$$

Because the two rows of this $\mathbf{R}$ are linearly independent, the rank condition is satisfied.

But suppose we require additionally that

$$\beta_2 - \beta_3 = \beta_4.$$

This is redundant because it holds whenever the first two equations do. With these three equations, $\#\mathbf{r} = 3$ and

$$\mathbf{R} = \begin{bmatrix} 0 & 1 & -1 & 0 \\ 0 & 0 & 0 & 1 \\ 0 & 1 & -1 & -1 \end{bmatrix}, \quad \mathbf{r} = \begin{bmatrix} 0 \\ 0 \\ 0 \end{bmatrix}.$$

Since the third row of $\mathbf{R}$ is the difference between the first two, $\mathbf{R}$ is not of full row rank. The consequence of adding redundant equations is that $\mathbf{R}$ no longer meets the full row rank condition.

As an example of inconsistent equations, consider adding to the first two equations the third equation $\beta_4 = 0.5$. Evidently, β_4 cannot be 0 and 0.5 at the same time. The hypothesis is inconsistent because there is no $\boldsymbol{\beta}$ that satisfies the three equations simultaneously. If we nevertheless included this equation, then $\mathbf{R}$ and $\mathbf{r}$ would become

$$\mathbf{R} = \begin{bmatrix} 0 & 1 & -1 & 0 \\ 0 & 0 & 0 & 1 \\ 0 & 0 & 0 & 1 \end{bmatrix}, \quad \mathbf{r} = \begin{bmatrix} 0 \\ 0 \\ 0.5 \end{bmatrix}.$$

Again, the full row rank condition is not satisfied because the rank of $\mathbf{R}$ is 2 while $\#\mathbf{r} = 3$.

The F-Test

To test linear hypotheses, we look for a test statistic that has a known distribution under the null hypothesis.

Proposition 1.4 (distribution of the F-ratio): *Suppose Assumptions 1.1–1.5 hold. Under the null hypothesis* $\text{H}_0\colon \mathbf{R}\boldsymbol{\beta} = \mathbf{r}$, *where* $\mathbf{R}$ *is* $\#\mathbf{r} \times K$ *with* $\text{rank}(\mathbf{R}) = \#\mathbf{r}$, *the* ***F*-ratio** *defined as*

$$F \equiv \frac{(\mathbf{Rb}-\mathbf{r})'\left[\mathbf{R}(\mathbf{X}'\mathbf{X})^{-1}\mathbf{R}'\right]^{-1}(\mathbf{Rb}-\mathbf{r})/\#\mathbf{r}}{s^2}$$

$$= (\mathbf{Rb}-\mathbf{r})'[\mathbf{R}\widehat{\mathrm{Var}(\mathbf{b} \mid \mathbf{X})}\mathbf{R}']^{-1}(\mathbf{Rb}-\mathbf{r})/\#\mathbf{r} \quad \textit{(by (1.3.4))} \tag{1.4.9}$$

is distributed as $F(\#\mathbf{r}, n-K)$ (the F distribution with $\#\mathbf{r}$ and $n-K$ degrees of freedom).

As in Proposition 1.3, it suffices to show that the distribution conditional on $\mathbf{X}$ is $F(\#\mathbf{r}, n-K)$; because the F distribution does not depend on $\mathbf{X}$, it is also the unconditional distribution of the statistic.

PROOF. Since $s^2 = \mathbf{e}'\mathbf{e}/(n-K)$, we can write

$$F = \frac{w/\#\mathbf{r}}{q/(n-K)}$$

where

$$w \equiv (\mathbf{Rb}-\mathbf{r})'[\sigma^2 \cdot \mathbf{R}(\mathbf{X}'\mathbf{X})^{-1}\mathbf{R}']^{-1}(\mathbf{Rb}-\mathbf{r}) \quad \text{and} \quad q \equiv \frac{\mathbf{e}'\mathbf{e}}{\sigma^2}.$$

We need to show

(1) $w \mid \mathbf{X} \sim \chi^2(\#\mathbf{r})$,

(2) $q \mid \mathbf{X} \sim \chi^2(n-K)$ (this is part (1) in the proof of Proposition 1.3),

(3) w and q are independently distributed conditional on $\mathbf{X}$.

Then, by the definition of the F distribution, the F-ratio $\sim F(\#\mathbf{r}, n-K)$.

(1) Let $\mathbf{v} \equiv \mathbf{Rb}-\mathbf{r}$. Under H_0, $\mathbf{Rb}-\mathbf{r} = \mathbf{R}(\mathbf{b}-\boldsymbol{\beta})$. So by (1.4.2), conditional on $\mathbf{X}$, $\mathbf{v}$ is normal with mean $\mathbf{0}$, and its variance is given by

$$\mathrm{Var}(\mathbf{v} \mid \mathbf{X}) = \mathrm{Var}(\mathbf{R}(\mathbf{b}-\boldsymbol{\beta}) \mid \mathbf{X}) = \mathbf{R}\,\mathrm{Var}(\mathbf{b}-\boldsymbol{\beta} \mid \mathbf{X})\mathbf{R}' = \sigma^2 \cdot \mathbf{R}(\mathbf{X}'\mathbf{X})^{-1}\mathbf{R}',$$

which is none other than the inverse of the middle matrix in the quadratic form for w. Hence, w can be written as $\mathbf{v}'\,\mathrm{Var}(\mathbf{v} \mid \mathbf{X})^{-1}\mathbf{v}$. Since $\mathbf{R}$ is of full row rank and $\mathbf{X}'\mathbf{X}$ is nonsingular, $\sigma^2 \cdot \mathbf{R}(\mathbf{X}'\mathbf{X})^{-1}\mathbf{R}'$ is nonsingular (why? Showing this is a review question). Therefore, by the definition of the χ^2 distribution, $w \mid \mathbf{X} \sim \chi^2(\#\mathbf{r})$.[19]

[19]Fact: Let $\mathbf{x}$ be an m dimensional random vector. If $\mathbf{x} \sim N(\boldsymbol{\mu}, \boldsymbol{\Sigma})$ with $\boldsymbol{\Sigma}$ nonsingular, then $(\mathbf{x}-\boldsymbol{\mu})'\boldsymbol{\Sigma}^{-1}(\mathbf{x}-\boldsymbol{\mu}) \sim \chi^2(m)$.

(3) w is a function of **b** and q is a function of **e**. But **b** and **e** are independently distributed conditional on **X**, as shown in part (2) of the proof of Proposition 1.3. So w and q are independently distributed conditional on **X**. ■

If the null hypothesis $\mathbf{R}\boldsymbol{\beta} = \mathbf{r}$ is true, we expect $\mathbf{Rb} - \mathbf{r}$ to be small, so large values of F should be taken as evidence for a failure of the null. This means that we look at only the upper tail of the distribution in the F-statistic. The decision rule of the F-test at the significance level of α is as follows.

Step 1: Calculate the F-ratio by the formula (1.4.9).

Step 2: Go to the table of F distribution and look up the entry for $\#\mathbf{r}$ (the numerator degrees of freedom) and $n - K$ (the denominator degrees of freedom). Find the critical value $F_\alpha(\#\mathbf{r}, n - K)$ that leaves α for the upper tail of the F distribution, as illustrated in Figure 1.4. For example, when $\#\mathbf{r} = 3$, $n - K = 30$, and $\alpha = 5\%$, the critical value $F_{.05}(3, 30)$ is 2.92.

Step 3: Accept the null if the F-ratio from *Step 1* is less than $F_\alpha(\#\mathbf{r}, n - K)$. Reject otherwise.

This decision rule can also be described in terms of the p-value:

Step 1: Same as above.

Step 2: Calculate

$$p = \text{area of the upper tail of the } F \text{ distribution to the right of the } F\text{-ratio.}$$

Step 3: Accept the null if $p > \alpha$; reject otherwise.

Thus, a *small* p-value is a signal of the failure of the null.

A More Convenient Expression for F

The above derivation of the F-ratio is by the **Wald principle**, because it is based on the unrestricted estimator, which is not constrained to satisfy the restrictions of the null hypothesis. Calculating the F-ratio by the formula (1.4.9) requires matrix inversion and multiplication. Fortunately, there is a convenient alternative formula involving two different sum of squared residuals: one is *SSR*, the minimized sum of squared residuals obtained from (1.2.1) now denoted as SSR_U, and the other is the restricted sum of squared residuals, denoted SSR_R, obtained from

$$\min_{\widetilde{\boldsymbol{\beta}}} SSR(\widetilde{\boldsymbol{\beta}}) \quad \text{s.t. } \mathbf{R}\widetilde{\boldsymbol{\beta}} = \mathbf{r}. \tag{1.4.10}$$

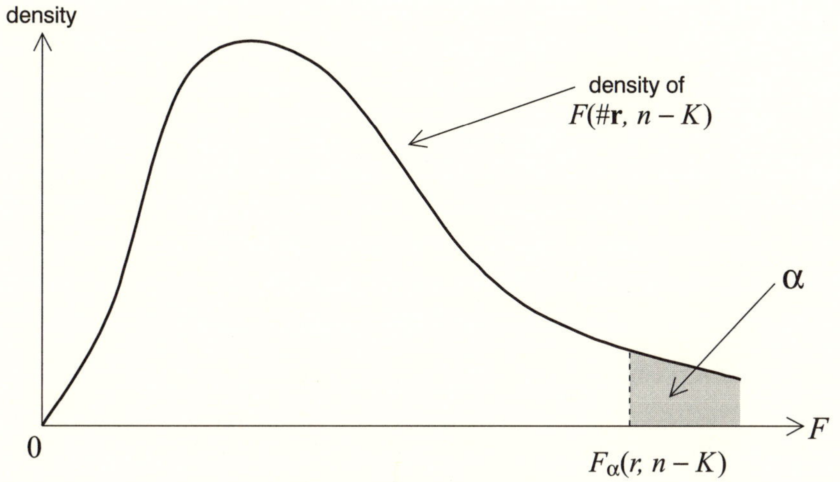

Figure 1.4: F Distribution

Finding the $\tilde{\boldsymbol{\beta}}$ that achieves this constrained minimization is called the **restricted regression** or **restricted least squares**. It is left as an analytical exercise to show that the F-ratio equals

$$F = \frac{(SSR_R - SSR_U)/\#\mathbf{r}}{SSR_U/(n-K)}, \tag{1.4.11}$$

which is the difference in the objective function deflated by the estimate of the error variance. This derivation of the F-ratio is analogous to how the likelihood-ratio statistic is derived in maximum likelihood estimation as the difference in log likelihood with and without the imposition of the null hypothesis. For this reason, this second derivation of the F-ratio is said to be by the **Likelihood-Ratio principle**. There is a closed-form expression for the restricted least squares estimator of $\boldsymbol{\beta}$. Deriving the expression is left as an analytical exercise. The computation of restricted least squares will be explained in the context of the empirical example in Section 1.7.

t versus *F*

Because hypotheses about individual coefficients are linear hypotheses, the t-test of $\text{H}_0\colon \beta_k = \overline{\beta}_k$ is a special case of the F-test. To see this, note that the hypothesis can be written as $\mathbf{R}\boldsymbol{\beta} = \mathbf{r}$ with

$$\underset{(1\times K)}{\mathbf{R}} = \begin{bmatrix} 0 & \cdots & 0 & \underset{(k)}{1} & 0 & \cdots & 0 \end{bmatrix}, \quad \mathbf{r} = \overline{\beta}_k.$$

So by (1.4.9) the F-ratio is

$$F = (b_k - \overline{\beta}_k)\big[s^2 \cdot (k,k) \text{ element of } (\mathbf{X}'\mathbf{X})^{-1}\big]^{-1}(b_k - \overline{\beta}_k),$$

which is the square of the t-ratio in (1.4.5). Since a random variable distributed as $F(1, n-K)$ is the square of a random variable distributed as $t(n-K)$, the t- and F-tests give the same test result.

Sometimes, the null is that a set of individual regression coefficients equal certain values. For example, assume $K = 2$ and consider

$$\text{H}_0\colon \beta_1 = 1 \text{ and } \beta_2 = 0.$$

This can be written as a linear hypothesis $\mathbf{R}\boldsymbol{\beta} = \mathbf{r}$ for $\mathbf{R} = \mathbf{I}_2$ and $\mathbf{r} = (1,0)'$. So the F-test can be used. It is tempting, however, to conduct the t-test separately for each individual coefficient of the hypothesis. We might accept H_0 if both restrictions $\beta_1 = 1$ and $\beta_2 = 0$ pass the t-test. This amounts to using the confidence region of

$$\big\{(\beta_1, \beta_2) \mid b_1 - SE(b_1)\cdot t_{\alpha/2}(n-K) < \beta_1 < b_1 + SE(b_1)\cdot t_{\alpha/2}(n-K),$$
$$b_2 - SE(b_2)\cdot t_{\alpha/2}(n-K) < \beta_2 < b_2 + SE(b_2)\cdot t_{\alpha/2}(n-K)\big\},$$

which is a rectangular region in the (β_1, β_2) plane, as illustrated in Figure 1.5. If $(1,0)$, the point in the (β_1, β_2) plane specified by the null, falls in this region, one would accept the null. On the other hand, the confidence region for the F-test is

$$\left\{(\beta_1, \beta_2) \mid (b_1 - \beta_1, b_2 - \beta_2)\big(\widehat{\text{Var}(\mathbf{b} \mid \mathbf{X})}\big)^{-1}\begin{bmatrix} b_1 - \beta_1 \\ b_2 - \beta_2 \end{bmatrix} < 2F_\alpha(\#\mathbf{r}, n-K)\right\}.$$

Since $\widehat{\text{Var}(\mathbf{b} \mid \mathbf{X})}$ is positive definite, the F-test acceptance region is an ellipse in the (β_1, β_2) plane. The two confidence regions look typically like Figure 1.5.

The F-test should be preferred to the test using two t-ratios for two reasons. First, if the size (significance level) in each of the two t-tests is α, then the overall size (the probability that $(1,0)$ is outside the rectangular region) is not α. Second, as will be noted in the next section (see (1.5.19)), the F-test is a likelihood ratio test and likelihood-ratio tests have certain desirable properties. So even if the significance level in each t-test is controlled so that the overall size is α, the test is less desirable than the F-test.[20]

[20]For more details on the relationship between the t-test and the F-tests, see Scheffe (1959, p. 46).

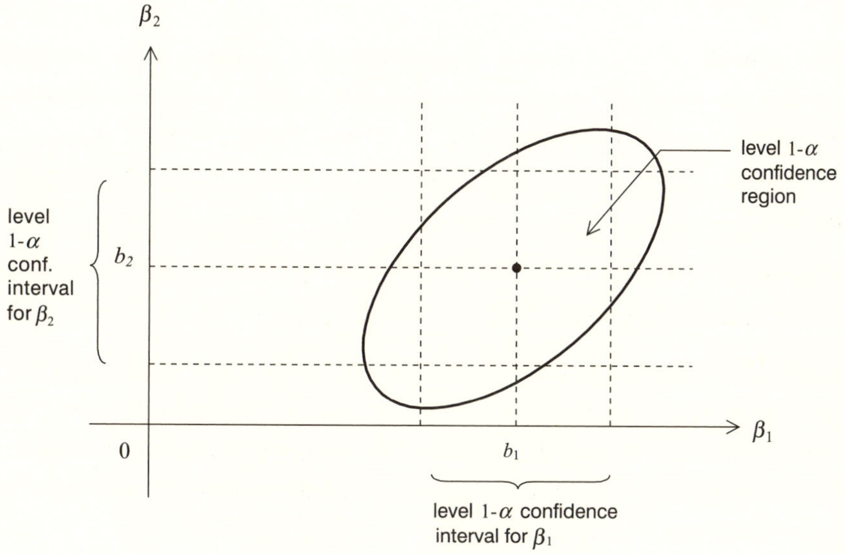

Figure 1.5: t- versus F-Tests

An Example of a Test Statistic Whose Distribution Depends on X

To place the discussion of this section in a proper perspective, it may be useful to note that there are some statistics whose conditional distribution depends on **X**. Consider the celebrated **Durbin-Watson statistic**:

$$\frac{\sum_{i=2}^{n}(e_i - e_{i-1})^2}{\sum_{i=1}^{n} e_i^2}.$$

The conditional distribution, and hence the critical values, of this statistic depend on **X**, but J. Durbin and G. S. Watson have shown that the critical values fall between two bounds (which depends on the sample size, the number of regressors, and whether the regressor includes a constant). Therefore, the critical values for the unconditional distribution, too, fall between these bounds.

The statistic is designed for testing whether there is no serial correlation in the error term. Thus, the null hypothesis is Assumption 1.4, while the maintained hypothesis is the other assumptions of the classical regression model (including the strict exogeneity assumption) and the normality assumption. But, as emphasized in Section 1.1, the strict exogeneity assumption is not satisfied in time-series models typically encountered in econometrics, and serial correlation is an issue that arises only in time-series models. Thus, the Durbin-Watson statistic is not useful in econometrics. More useful tests for serial correlation, which are all based on large-sample theory, will be covered in the next chapter.

QUESTIONS FOR REVIEW

1. (Conditional vs. unconditional distribution) Do we know from Assumptions 1.1–1.5 that the marginal (unconditional) distribution of $\mathbf{b}$ is normal? [Answer: No.] Are the statistics z_k (see (1.4.3)), t_k, and F distributed independently of $\mathbf{X}$? [Answer: Yes, because their distributions conditional on $\mathbf{X}$ don't depend on $\mathbf{X}$.]

2. (Computation of test statistics) Verify that $SE(b_k)$ as well as $\mathbf{b}$, SSR, s^2, and R^2 can be calculated from the following sample averages: $\mathbf{S_{xx}}$, $\mathbf{s_{xy}}$, $\mathbf{y}'\mathbf{y}/n$, and $\bar{y}$.

3. For the formula (1.4.9) for the F to be well-defined, the matrix $\mathbf{R}(\mathbf{X}'\mathbf{X})^{-1}\mathbf{R}'$ must be nonsingular. Prove the stronger result that the matrix is positive definite. **Hint:** $\mathbf{X}'\mathbf{X}$ is positive definite. The inverse of a positive definite matrix is positive definite. Since $\mathbf{R}$ ($\#\mathbf{r} \times K$) is of full row rank, for any nonzero $\#\mathbf{r}$ dimensional vector $\mathbf{z}$, $\mathbf{R}'\mathbf{z} \neq \mathbf{0}$.

4. (One-tailed t-test) The t-test described in the text is the **two-tailed *t*-test** because the significance α is equally distributed between both tails of the t distribution. Suppose the alternative is one-sided and written as $\text{H}_1: \beta_k > \overline{\beta}_k$. Consider the following modification of the decision rule of the t-test.

   Step 1: Same as above.
   Step 2: Find the critical value t_α such that the area in the t distribution to the right of t_α is α. Note the difference from the two-tailed test: the left tail is ignored and the area of α is assigned to the upper tail only.
   Step 3: Accept if $t_k < t_\alpha$; reject otherwise.

   Show that the size (significance level) of this **one-tailed *t*-test** is α.

5. (Relation between $F(1, n-K)$ and $t(n-K)$) Look up the t and F distribution tables to verify that $F_\alpha(1, n-K) = (t_{\alpha/2}(n-K))^2$ for degrees of freedom and significance levels of your choice.

6. (t vs. F) "It is nonsense to test a hypothesis consisting of a large number of equality restrictions, because the t-test will most likely reject at least some of the restrictions." Criticize this statement.

7. (Variance of s^2) Show that, under Assumptions 1.1–1.5,

$$\text{Var}(s^2 \mid \mathbf{X}) = \frac{2\sigma^4}{n-K}.$$

   Hint: If a random variable is distributed as $\chi^2(m)$, then its mean is m and variance $2m$.

1.5 Relation to Maximum Likelihood

Having specified the distribution of the error vector $\boldsymbol{\varepsilon}$, we can use the **maximum likelihood (ML) principle** to estimate the model parameters $(\boldsymbol{\beta}, \sigma^2)$.[21] In this section, we will show that $\mathbf{b}$, the OLS estimator of $\boldsymbol{\beta}$, is also the ML estimator, and the OLS estimator of σ^2 differs only slightly from the ML counterpart, when the error is normally distributed. We will also show that $\mathbf{b}$ achieves the **Cramer-Rao lower bound**.

The Maximum Likelihood Principle

As you might recall from elementary statistics, the basic idea of the ML principle is to choose the parameter estimates to maximize the probability of obtaining the observed sample. To be more precise, we assume that the probability density of the sample $(\mathbf{y}, \mathbf{X})$ is a member of a family of functions indexed by a finite-dimensional parameter vector $\tilde{\boldsymbol{\zeta}}$: $f(\mathbf{y}, \mathbf{X}; \tilde{\boldsymbol{\zeta}})$. (This is described as **parameterizing** the density function.) This function, viewed as a function of the hypothetical parameter vector $\tilde{\boldsymbol{\zeta}}$, is called the **likelihood function**. At the true parameter vector $\boldsymbol{\zeta}$, the density of $(\mathbf{y}, \mathbf{X})$ is $f(\mathbf{y}, \mathbf{X}; \boldsymbol{\zeta})$. The ML estimate of the true parameter vector $\boldsymbol{\zeta}$ is the $\tilde{\boldsymbol{\zeta}}$ that maximizes the likelihood function given the data $(\mathbf{y}, \mathbf{X})$.

Conditional versus Unconditional Likelihood

Since a (joint) density is the product of a marginal density and a conditional density, the density of $(\mathbf{y}, \mathbf{X})$ can be written as

$$f(\mathbf{y}, \mathbf{X}; \boldsymbol{\zeta}) = f(\mathbf{y} \mid \mathbf{X}; \boldsymbol{\theta}) \cdot f(\mathbf{X}; \boldsymbol{\psi}), \tag{1.5.1}$$

where $\boldsymbol{\theta}$ is the subset of the parameter vector $\boldsymbol{\zeta}$ that determines the conditional density function and $\boldsymbol{\psi}$ is the subset determining the marginal density function. The parameter vector of interest is $\boldsymbol{\theta}$; for the linear regression model with normal errors, $\boldsymbol{\theta} = (\boldsymbol{\beta}', \sigma^2)'$ and $f(\mathbf{y} \mid \mathbf{X}; \boldsymbol{\theta})$ is given by (1.5.4) below.

Let $\tilde{\boldsymbol{\zeta}} \equiv (\tilde{\boldsymbol{\theta}}', \tilde{\boldsymbol{\psi}}')'$ be a hypothetical value of $\boldsymbol{\zeta} = (\boldsymbol{\theta}', \boldsymbol{\psi}')'$. Then the (unconditional or joint) likelihood function is

$$f(\mathbf{y}, \mathbf{X}; \tilde{\boldsymbol{\zeta}}) = f(\mathbf{y} \mid \mathbf{X}; \tilde{\boldsymbol{\theta}}) \cdot f(\mathbf{X}; \tilde{\boldsymbol{\psi}}). \tag{1.5.2}$$

If we knew the parametric form of $f(\mathbf{X}; \tilde{\boldsymbol{\psi}})$, then we could maximize this joint

[21] For a fuller treatment of maximum likelihood, see Chapter 7.

likelihood function over the entire hypothetical parameter vector $\tilde{\boldsymbol{\zeta}}$, and the ML estimate of $\boldsymbol{\theta}$ would be the elements of the ML estimate of $\boldsymbol{\zeta}$. We cannot do this for the classical regression model because the model does not specify $f(\mathbf{X}; \tilde{\boldsymbol{\psi}})$. However, if there is no functional relationship between $\tilde{\boldsymbol{\theta}}$ and $\tilde{\boldsymbol{\psi}}$ (such as a subset of $\tilde{\boldsymbol{\psi}}$ being a function of $\tilde{\boldsymbol{\theta}}$), then maximizing (1.5.2) with respect to $\tilde{\boldsymbol{\zeta}}$ is achieved by separately maximizing $f(\mathbf{y} \mid \mathbf{X}; \tilde{\boldsymbol{\theta}})$ with respect to $\tilde{\boldsymbol{\theta}}$ and maximizing $f(\mathbf{X}; \tilde{\boldsymbol{\psi}})$ with respect to $\tilde{\boldsymbol{\psi}}$. Thus the ML estimate of $\boldsymbol{\theta}$ also maximizes the **conditional likelihood** $f(\mathbf{y} \mid \mathbf{X}; \tilde{\boldsymbol{\theta}})$.

The Log Likelihood for the Regression Model

As already observed, Assumption 1.5 (the normality assumption) together with Assumptions 1.2 and 1.4 imply that the distribution of $\boldsymbol{\varepsilon}$ conditional on $\mathbf{X}$ is $N(\mathbf{0}, \sigma^2 \mathbf{I}_n)$ (see (1.4.1)). But since $\mathbf{y} = \mathbf{X}\boldsymbol{\beta} + \boldsymbol{\varepsilon}$ by Assumption 1.1, we have

$$\mathbf{y} \mid \mathbf{X} \sim N(\mathbf{X}\boldsymbol{\beta}, \sigma^2 \mathbf{I}_n). \tag{1.5.3}$$

Thus, the conditional density of $\mathbf{y}$ given $\mathbf{X}$ is[22]

$$f(\mathbf{y} \mid \mathbf{X}) = (2\pi\sigma^2)^{-n/2} \exp\left[-\frac{1}{2\sigma^2}(\mathbf{y} - \mathbf{X}\boldsymbol{\beta})'(\mathbf{y} - \mathbf{X}\boldsymbol{\beta})\right]. \tag{1.5.4}$$

Replacing the true parameters $(\boldsymbol{\beta}, \sigma^2)$ by their hypothetical values $(\tilde{\boldsymbol{\beta}}, \tilde{\sigma}^2)$ and taking logs, we obtain the **log likelihood function**:

$$\log L(\tilde{\boldsymbol{\beta}}, \tilde{\sigma}^2) = -\frac{n}{2}\log(2\pi) - \frac{n}{2}\log(\tilde{\sigma}^2) - \frac{1}{2\tilde{\sigma}^2}(\mathbf{y} - \mathbf{X}\tilde{\boldsymbol{\beta}})'(\mathbf{y} - \mathbf{X}\tilde{\boldsymbol{\beta}}). \tag{1.5.5}$$

Since the log transformation is a monotone transformation, the ML estimator of $(\boldsymbol{\beta}, \sigma^2)$ is the $(\tilde{\boldsymbol{\beta}}, \tilde{\sigma}^2)$ that maximizes this log likelihood.

ML via Concentrated Likelihood

It is instructive to maximize the log likelihood in two stages. First, maximize over $\tilde{\boldsymbol{\beta}}$ for any given $\tilde{\sigma}^2$. The $\tilde{\boldsymbol{\beta}}$ that maximizes the objective function could (but does not, in the present case of Assumptions 1.1–1.5) depend on $\tilde{\sigma}^2$. Second, maximize over $\tilde{\sigma}^2$ taking into account that the $\tilde{\boldsymbol{\beta}}$ obtained in the first stage could depend on $\tilde{\sigma}^2$. The log likelihood function in which $\tilde{\boldsymbol{\beta}}$ is constrained to be the value from

[22]Recall from basic probability theory that the density function for an n-variate normal distribution with mean $\boldsymbol{\mu}$ and variance matrix $\boldsymbol{\Sigma}$ is

$$(2\pi)^{-n/2} |\boldsymbol{\Sigma}|^{-1/2} \exp\left[-\frac{1}{2}(\mathbf{y} - \boldsymbol{\mu})'\boldsymbol{\Sigma}^{-1}(\mathbf{y} - \boldsymbol{\mu})\right].$$

To derive (1.5.4), just set $\boldsymbol{\mu} = \mathbf{X}\boldsymbol{\beta}$ and $\boldsymbol{\Sigma} = \sigma^2\mathbf{I}_n$.

the first stage is called the **concentrated log likelihood function** (concentrated with respect to $\widetilde{\beta}$). For the normal log likelihood (1.5.5), the first stage amounts to minimizing the sum of squares $(\mathbf{y} - \mathbf{X}\widetilde{\boldsymbol{\beta}})'(\mathbf{y} - \mathbf{X}\widetilde{\boldsymbol{\beta}})$. The $\widetilde{\boldsymbol{\beta}}$ that does it is none other than the OLS estimator $\mathbf{b}$, and the minimized sum of squares is $\mathbf{e}'\mathbf{e}$. Thus, the concentrated log likelihood is

$$\text{concentrated log likelihood} = -\frac{n}{2}\log(2\pi) - \frac{n}{2}\log(\tilde{\sigma}^2) - \frac{1}{2\tilde{\sigma}^2}\mathbf{e}'\mathbf{e}. \quad (1.5.6)$$

This is a function of $\tilde{\sigma}^2$ alone, and the $\tilde{\sigma}^2$ that maximizes the concentrated likelihood is the ML estimate of σ^2. The maximization is straightforward for the present case of the classical regression model, because $\mathbf{e}'\mathbf{e}$ is not a function of $\tilde{\sigma}^2$ and so can be taken as a constant. Still, taking the derivative with respect to $\tilde{\sigma}^2$, rather than with respect to $\tilde{\sigma}$, can be tricky. This can be avoided by denoting $\tilde{\sigma}^2$ by $\tilde{\gamma}$. Taking the derivative of (1.5.6) with respect to $\tilde{\gamma}$ ($\equiv \tilde{\sigma}^2$) and setting it to zero, we obtain the following result.

Proposition 1.5 (ML Estimator of $(\boldsymbol{\beta}, \sigma^2)$): *Suppose Assumptions 1.1–1.5 hold. Then the ML estimator of $\boldsymbol{\beta}$ is the OLS estimator* $\mathbf{b}$ *and*

$$\textit{ML estimator of } \sigma^2 = \frac{1}{n}\mathbf{e}'\mathbf{e} = \frac{SSR}{n} = \frac{n-K}{n}s^2. \quad (1.5.7)$$

We know from Proposition 1.2 that s^2 is unbiased. Since s^2 is multiplied by a factor $(n-K)/n$ which is different from 1, the ML estimator of σ^2 is biased, although the bias becomes arbitrarily small as the sample size n increases for any given fixed K.

For later use, we calculate the maximized value of the likelihood function. Substituting (1.5.7) into (1.5.6), we obtain

$$\text{maximized log likelihood} = -\frac{n}{2}\log\left(\frac{2\pi}{n}\right) - \frac{n}{2} - \frac{n}{2}\log(SSR),$$

so that the maximized likelihood is

$$\max_{\widetilde{\boldsymbol{\beta}}, \tilde{\sigma}^2} L(\widetilde{\boldsymbol{\beta}}, \tilde{\sigma}^2) = \left(\frac{2\pi}{n}\right)^{-n/2} \cdot \exp\left(-\frac{n}{2}\right) \cdot (SSR)^{-n/2}. \quad (1.5.8)$$

Cramer-Rao Bound for the Classical Regression Model

Just to refresh your memory of basic statistics, we temporarily step outside the classical regression model and present without proof the Cramer-Rao inequality for the variance-covariance matrix of any unbiased estimator. For this purpose, define the **score vector** at a hypothetical parameter value $\tilde{\boldsymbol{\theta}}$ to be the gradient (vector of partial derivatives) of log likelihood:

$$\text{score: } \mathbf{s}(\tilde{\boldsymbol{\theta}}) \equiv \frac{\partial \log L(\tilde{\boldsymbol{\theta}})}{\partial \tilde{\boldsymbol{\theta}}}. \tag{1.5.9}$$

Cramer-Rao Inequality: *Let* $\mathbf{z}$ *be a vector of random variables (not necessarily independent) the joint density of which is given by* $f(\mathbf{z}; \boldsymbol{\theta})$, *where* $\boldsymbol{\theta}$ *is an* m-*dimensional vector of parameters in some parameter space* Θ. *Let* $L(\tilde{\boldsymbol{\theta}}) \equiv f(\mathbf{z}; \tilde{\boldsymbol{\theta}})$ *be the likelihood function, and let* $\hat{\boldsymbol{\theta}}(\mathbf{z})$ *be an unbiased estimator of* $\boldsymbol{\theta}$ *with a finite variance-covariance matrix. Then, under some regularity conditions on* $f(\mathbf{z}; \boldsymbol{\theta})$ *(not stated here),*

$$\text{Var}[\hat{\boldsymbol{\theta}}(\mathbf{z})] \geq \underset{(m\times m)}{\mathbf{I}(\boldsymbol{\theta})^{-1}} \quad (\equiv \textit{Cramer-Rao Lower Bound}),$$

where $\mathbf{I}(\boldsymbol{\theta})$ *is the* ***information matrix*** *defined by*

$$\mathbf{I}(\boldsymbol{\theta}) \equiv \text{E}[\mathbf{s}(\boldsymbol{\theta})\,\mathbf{s}(\boldsymbol{\theta})']. \tag{1.5.10}$$

(Note well that the score is evaluated at the true parameter value $\boldsymbol{\theta}$.*) Also under the regularity conditions, the information matrix equals the negative of the expected value of the Hessian (matrix of second partial derivatives) of the log likelihood:*

$$\mathbf{I}(\boldsymbol{\theta}) = -\,\text{E}\left[\frac{\partial^2 \log L(\boldsymbol{\theta})}{\partial \tilde{\boldsymbol{\theta}}\, \partial \tilde{\boldsymbol{\theta}}'}\right]. \tag{1.5.11}$$

This is called the ***information matrix equality***.

See, e.g., Amemiya (1985, Theorem 1.3.1) for a proof and a statement of the regularity conditions. Those conditions guarantee that the operations of differentiation and taking expectations can be interchanged. Thus, for example,

$$\text{E}[\partial L(\boldsymbol{\theta})/\partial \tilde{\boldsymbol{\theta}}] = \partial\, \text{E}[L(\boldsymbol{\theta})]/\partial \tilde{\boldsymbol{\theta}}.$$

Now, for the classical regression model (of Assumptions 1.1–1.5), the likelihood function $L(\tilde{\boldsymbol{\theta}})$ in the Cramer-Rao inequality is the conditional density (1.5.4), so the variance in the inequality is the variance conditional on $\mathbf{X}$. It can be shown that those regularity conditions are satisfied for the normal density (1.5.4) (see, e.g., Amemiya, 1985, Sections 1.3.2 and 1.3.3). In the rest of this subsection, we calculate the information matrix for (1.5.4). The parameter vector $\boldsymbol{\theta}$ is $(\boldsymbol{\beta}', \sigma^2)'$.

So $\tilde{\boldsymbol{\theta}} = (\tilde{\boldsymbol{\beta}}', \tilde{\gamma})'$ and the matrix of second derivatives we seek to calculate is

$$\underset{((K+1)\times(K+1))}{\frac{\partial^2 \log L(\boldsymbol{\theta})}{\partial \tilde{\boldsymbol{\theta}}\, \partial \tilde{\boldsymbol{\theta}}'}} = \begin{bmatrix} \underset{(K\times K)}{\frac{\partial^2 \log L(\boldsymbol{\theta})}{\partial \tilde{\boldsymbol{\beta}}\, \partial \tilde{\boldsymbol{\beta}}'}} & \underset{(K\times 1)}{\frac{\partial^2 \log L(\boldsymbol{\theta})}{\partial \tilde{\boldsymbol{\beta}}\, \partial \tilde{\gamma}}} \\ \underset{(1\times K)}{\frac{\partial^2 \log L(\boldsymbol{\theta})}{\partial \tilde{\gamma}\, \partial \tilde{\boldsymbol{\beta}}'}} & \underset{(1\times 1)}{\frac{\partial^2 \log L(\boldsymbol{\theta})}{\partial^2 \tilde{\gamma}}} \end{bmatrix}. \tag{1.5.12}$$

The first and second derivatives of the log likelihood (1.5.5) with respect to $\tilde{\boldsymbol{\theta}}$, evaluated at the true parameter vector $\boldsymbol{\theta}$, are

$$\frac{\partial \log L(\boldsymbol{\theta})}{\partial \tilde{\boldsymbol{\beta}}} = \frac{1}{\gamma}\mathbf{X}'(\mathbf{y} - \mathbf{X}\boldsymbol{\beta}), \tag{1.5.13a}$$

$$\frac{\partial \log L(\boldsymbol{\theta})}{\partial \tilde{\gamma}} = -\frac{n}{2\gamma} + \frac{1}{2\gamma^2}(\mathbf{y} - \mathbf{X}\boldsymbol{\beta})'(\mathbf{y} - \mathbf{X}\boldsymbol{\beta}). \tag{1.5.13b}$$

$$\frac{\partial^2 \log L(\boldsymbol{\theta})}{\partial \tilde{\boldsymbol{\beta}}\, \partial \tilde{\boldsymbol{\beta}}'} = -\frac{1}{\gamma}\mathbf{X}'\mathbf{X}, \tag{1.5.14a}$$

$$\frac{\partial^2 \log L(\boldsymbol{\theta})}{\partial^2 \tilde{\gamma}} = \frac{n}{2\gamma^2} - \frac{1}{\gamma^3}(\mathbf{y} - \mathbf{X}\boldsymbol{\beta})'(\mathbf{y} - \mathbf{X}\boldsymbol{\beta}), \tag{1.5.14b}$$

$$\frac{\partial^2 \log L(\boldsymbol{\theta})}{\partial \tilde{\boldsymbol{\beta}}\, \partial \tilde{\gamma}} = -\frac{1}{\gamma^2}\mathbf{X}'(\mathbf{y} - \mathbf{X}\boldsymbol{\beta}). \tag{1.5.14c}$$

Since the derivatives are evaluated at the true parameter value, $\mathbf{y} - \mathbf{X}\boldsymbol{\beta} = \boldsymbol{\varepsilon}$ in these expressions. Substituting (1.5.14) into (1.5.12) and using $\mathrm{E}(\boldsymbol{\varepsilon} \mid \mathbf{X}) = \mathbf{0}$ (Assumption 1.2), $\mathrm{E}(\boldsymbol{\varepsilon}'\boldsymbol{\varepsilon} \mid \mathbf{X}) = n\sigma^2$ (implication of Assumption 1.4), and recalling $\gamma = \sigma^2$, we can easily derive

$$\mathbf{I}(\boldsymbol{\theta}) = \begin{bmatrix} \frac{1}{\sigma^2}\mathbf{X}'\mathbf{X} & \mathbf{0} \\ \mathbf{0}' & \frac{n}{2\sigma^4} \end{bmatrix}. \tag{1.5.15}$$

Here, the expectation is conditional on $\mathbf{X}$ because the likelihood function (1.5.4) is a conditional density conditional on $\mathbf{X}$. This block diagonal matrix can be inverted to obtain the Cramer-Rao bound:

$$\text{Cramer-Rao bound} \equiv \mathbf{I}(\boldsymbol{\theta})^{-1} = \begin{bmatrix} \sigma^2 \cdot (\mathbf{X}'\mathbf{X})^{-1} & \mathbf{0} \\ \mathbf{0}' & \frac{2\sigma^4}{n} \end{bmatrix}. \tag{1.5.16}$$

Therefore, the unbiased estimator $\mathbf{b}$, whose variance is $\sigma^2 \cdot (\mathbf{X}'\mathbf{X})^{-1}$ by Proposition 1.1, attains the Cramer-Rao bound. We have thus proved

Proposition 1.6 (b is the Best Unbiased Estimator (BUE)): *Under Assumptions 1.1–1.5, the OLS estimator* $\mathbf{b}$ *of* $\boldsymbol{\beta}$ *is BUE in that any other unbiased (but not necessarily linear) estimator has larger conditional variance in the matrix sense.*

This result should be distinguished from the Gauss-Markov Theorem that $\mathbf{b}$ is minimum variance among those estimators that are unbiased *and* linear in $\mathbf{y}$. Proposition 1.6 says that $\mathbf{b}$ is minimum variance in a larger class of estimators that includes nonlinear unbiased estimators. This stronger statement is obtained under the normality assumption (Assumption 1.5) which is not assumed in the Gauss-Markov Theorem. Put differently, the Gauss-Markov Theorem does not exclude the possibility of some nonlinear estimator beating OLS, but this possibility is ruled out by the normality assumption.

As was already seen, the ML estimator of σ^2 is biased, so the Cramer-Rao bound does not apply. But the OLS estimator s^2 of σ^2 is unbiased. Does it achieve the bound? We have shown in a review question to the previous section that

$$\mathrm{Var}(s^2 \mid \mathbf{X}) = \frac{2\sigma^4}{n-K}$$

under the same set of assumptions as in Proposition 1.6. Therefore, s^2 does not attain the Cramer-Rao bound $2\sigma^4/n$. However, it can be shown that an unbiased estimator of σ^2 with variance lower than $2\sigma^4/(n-K)$ does not exist (see, e.g., Rao, 1973, p. 319).

The F-Test as a Likelihood Ratio Test

The **likelihood ratio test** of the null hypothesis compares L_U, the maximized likelihood without the imposition of the restriction specified in the null hypothesis, with L_R, the likelihood maximized subject to the restriction. If the likelihood ratio $\lambda \equiv L_U/L_R$ is too large, it should be a sign that the null is false. The F-test of the null hypothesis H_0: $\mathbf{R}\boldsymbol{\beta} = \mathbf{r}$ considered in the previous section is a likelihood ratio test because the F-ratio is a monotone transformation of the likelihood ratio λ. For the present model, L_U is given by (1.5.8) where the *SSR*, the sum of squared residuals minimized without the constraint H_0, is the SSR_U in (1.4.11). The restricted likelihood L_R is given by replacing this *SSR* by the restricted sum of squared residuals, SSR_R. So

$$L_R = \max_{\tilde{\boldsymbol{\beta}}, \tilde{\sigma}^2 \text{ s.t. } \mathrm{H}_0} L(\tilde{\boldsymbol{\beta}}, \tilde{\sigma}^2) = \left(\frac{2\pi}{n}\right)^{-n/2} \cdot \exp\left(-\frac{n}{2}\right) \cdot (SSR_R)^{-n/2}, \tag{1.5.17}$$

and the likelihood ratio is

$$\lambda \equiv \frac{L_U}{L_R} = \left(\frac{SSR_U}{SSR_R}\right)^{-n/2}. \tag{1.5.18}$$

Comparing this with the formula (1.4.11) for the F-ratio, we see that the F-ratio is a monotone transformation of the likelihood ratio λ:

$$F = \frac{n-K}{\#\mathbf{r}}(\lambda^{2/n} - 1), \tag{1.5.19}$$

so that the two tests are the same.

Quasi-Maximum Likelihood

All these results assume the normality of the error term. Without normality, there is no guarantee that the ML estimator of $\boldsymbol{\beta}$ is OLS (Proposition 1.5) or that the OLS estimator **b** achieves the Cramer-Rao bound (Proposition 1.6). However, Proposition 1.5 does imply that **b** is a **quasi-** (or **pseudo-**) **maximum likelihood estimator**, an estimator that maximizes a misspecified likelihood function. The misspecified likelihood function we have considered is the normal likelihood. The results of Section 1.3 can then be interpreted as providing the finite-sample properties of the quasi-ML estimator when the error is incorrectly specified to be normal.

QUESTIONS FOR REVIEW

1. (Use of regularity conditions) Assuming that taking expectations (i.e., taking integrals) and differentiation can be interchanged, prove that the expected value of the score vector given in (1.5.9), if evaluated at the true parameter value $\boldsymbol{\theta}$, is zero. **Hint:** What needs to be shown is that

$$\int \frac{\partial \log f(\mathbf{z}; \boldsymbol{\theta})}{\partial \tilde{\boldsymbol{\theta}}} f(\mathbf{z}; \boldsymbol{\theta})\, d\mathbf{z} = \mathbf{0}.$$

Since $f(\mathbf{z}; \tilde{\boldsymbol{\theta}})$ is a density, $\int f(\mathbf{z}, \tilde{\boldsymbol{\theta}})\, d\mathbf{z} = 1$ for any $\tilde{\boldsymbol{\theta}}$. Differentiate both sides with respect to $\tilde{\boldsymbol{\theta}}$ and use the regularity conditions, which allows us to change the order of integration and differentiation, to obtain $\int [\partial f(\mathbf{z}; \boldsymbol{\theta})/\partial \tilde{\boldsymbol{\theta}}]\, d\mathbf{z} = \mathbf{0}$. Also, from basic calculus,

$$\frac{\partial \log f(\mathbf{z}; \boldsymbol{\theta})}{\partial \tilde{\boldsymbol{\theta}}} = \frac{1}{f(\mathbf{z}; \boldsymbol{\theta})} \frac{\partial f(\mathbf{z}; \boldsymbol{\theta})}{\partial \tilde{\boldsymbol{\theta}}}.$$

2. (Maximizing joint log likelihood) Consider maximizing (the log of) the joint likelihood (1.5.2) for the classical regression model, where $\tilde{\boldsymbol{\theta}} = (\tilde{\boldsymbol{\beta}}', \tilde{\sigma}^2)'$ and $\log f(\mathbf{y} \mid \mathbf{X}; \tilde{\boldsymbol{\theta}})$ is given by (1.5.5). You would parameterize the marginal like-

lihood $f(\mathbf{X}; \tilde{\boldsymbol{\psi}})$ and take the log of (1.5.2) to obtain the objective function to be maximized over $\boldsymbol{\zeta} \equiv (\boldsymbol{\theta}', \boldsymbol{\psi}')'$. What is the ML estimator of $\boldsymbol{\theta} \equiv (\boldsymbol{\beta}', \sigma^2)'$? [Answer: It should be the same as that in Proposition 1.5.] Derive the Cramer-Rao bound for $\boldsymbol{\beta}$. **Hint:** By the information matrix equality,

$$\mathbf{I}(\boldsymbol{\zeta}) = -\mathrm{E}\left[\frac{\partial^2 \log L(\boldsymbol{\zeta})}{\partial \tilde{\boldsymbol{\zeta}}\, \partial \tilde{\boldsymbol{\zeta}}'}\right].$$

Also, $\partial^2 \log L(\boldsymbol{\zeta})/(\partial \tilde{\boldsymbol{\theta}}\, \partial \tilde{\boldsymbol{\psi}}') = \mathbf{0}$.

3. (Concentrated log likelihood with respect to $\tilde{\sigma}^2$) Writing $\tilde{\sigma}^2$ as $\tilde{\gamma}$, the log likelihood function for the classical regression model is

$$\log L(\widetilde{\boldsymbol{\beta}}, \tilde{\gamma}) = -\frac{n}{2}\log(2\pi) - \frac{n}{2}\log(\tilde{\gamma}) - \frac{1}{2\tilde{\gamma}}(\mathbf{y} - \mathbf{X}\widetilde{\boldsymbol{\beta}})'(\mathbf{y} - \mathbf{X}\widetilde{\boldsymbol{\beta}}).$$

In the two-step maximization procedure described in the text, we first maximized this function with respect to $\widetilde{\boldsymbol{\beta}}$. Instead, first maximize with respect to $\tilde{\gamma}$ given $\widetilde{\boldsymbol{\beta}}$. Show that the concentrated log likelihood (concentrated with respect to $\tilde{\gamma} \equiv \tilde{\sigma}^2$) is

$$-\frac{n}{2}[1 + \log(2\pi)] - \frac{n}{2}\log\left(\frac{(\mathbf{y} - \mathbf{X}\widetilde{\boldsymbol{\beta}})'(\mathbf{y} - \mathbf{X}\widetilde{\boldsymbol{\beta}})}{n}\right).$$

4. (Information matrix equality for classical regression model) Verify (1.5.11) for the linear regression model.

5. (Likelihood equations for classical regression model) We used the two-step procedure to derive the ML estimate for the classical regression model. An alternative way to find the ML estimator is to solve for the first-order conditions that set (1.5.13) equal to zero (the first-order conditions for the log likelihood is called the **likelihood equations**). Verify that the ML estimator given in Proposition 1.5 solves the likelihood equations.

1.6 Generalized Least Squares (GLS)

Assumption 1.4 states that the $n \times n$ matrix of conditional second moments $\mathrm{E}(\boldsymbol{\varepsilon}\boldsymbol{\varepsilon}' \mid \mathbf{X})$ $(= \mathrm{Var}(\boldsymbol{\varepsilon} \mid \mathbf{X}))$ is spherical, that is, proportional to the identity matrix. Without the assumption, each element of the $n \times n$ matrix is in general a nonlinear function of $\mathbf{X}$. If the error is not (conditionally) homoskedastic, the values of the diagonal elements of $\mathrm{E}(\boldsymbol{\varepsilon}\boldsymbol{\varepsilon}' \mid \mathbf{X})$ are not the same, and if there is correlation in the error term between observations (the case of serial correlation for time-series models), the values of the off-diagonal elements are not zero. For any given positive scalar σ^2, define $\mathbf{V}(\mathbf{X}) \equiv \mathrm{E}(\boldsymbol{\varepsilon}\boldsymbol{\varepsilon}' \mid \mathbf{X})/\sigma^2$ and assume $\mathbf{V}(\mathbf{X})$ is nonsingular and known. That is,

$$\mathrm{E}(\boldsymbol{\varepsilon}\boldsymbol{\varepsilon}' \mid \mathbf{X}) = \sigma^2 \underset{(n \times n)}{\mathbf{V}(\mathbf{X})}, \quad \mathbf{V}(\mathbf{X}) \text{ nonsingular and known.} \tag{1.6.1}$$

The reason we decompose $\mathrm{E}(\boldsymbol{\varepsilon}\boldsymbol{\varepsilon}' \mid \mathbf{X})$ into the component σ^2 that is common to all elements of the matrix $\mathrm{E}(\boldsymbol{\varepsilon}\boldsymbol{\varepsilon}' \mid \mathbf{X})$ and the remaining component $\mathbf{V}(\mathbf{X})$ is that we do not need to know the value of σ^2 for efficient estimation. The model that results when Assumption 1.4 is replaced by (1.6.1), which merely assumes that the conditional second moment $\mathrm{E}(\boldsymbol{\varepsilon}\boldsymbol{\varepsilon}' \mid \mathbf{X})$ is nonsingular, is called the **generalized regression model**.

Consequence of Relaxing Assumption 1.4

Of the results derived in the previous sections, those that assume Assumption 1.4 are no longer valid for the generalized regression model. More specifically,

- The Gauss-Markov Theorem no longer holds for the OLS estimator

  $$\mathbf{b} \equiv (\mathbf{X}'\mathbf{X})^{-1}\mathbf{X}'\mathbf{y}.$$

  The BLUE is some other estimator.

- The t-ratio is not distributed as the t distribution. Thus, the t-test is no longer valid. The same comments apply to the F-test.

- However, the OLS estimator *is* still unbiased, because the unbiasedness result (Proposition 1.1(a)) does not require Assumption 1.4.

Efficient Estimation with Known V

If the value of the matrix function $\mathbf{V}(\mathbf{X})$ is known, does there exist a BLUE for the generalized regression model? The answer is yes, and the estimator is called the **generalized least squares (GLS) estimator**, which we now derive. The basic idea of the derivation is to transform the generalized regression model, which consists of Assumptions 1.1–1.3 and (1.6.1), into a model that satisfies all the assumptions, including Assumption 1.4, of the classical regression model.

For economy of notation, we use $\mathbf{V}$ for the value $\mathbf{V}(\mathbf{X})$. Since $\mathbf{V}$ is by construction symmetric and positive definite, there exists a nonsingular $n \times n$ matrix $\mathbf{C}$ such that

$$\mathbf{V}^{-1} = \mathbf{C}'\mathbf{C}. \tag{1.6.2}$$

This decomposition is not unique, with more than one choice for $\mathbf{C}$, but, as is clear from the discussion below, the choice of $\mathbf{C}$ doesn't matter. Now consider creating a new regression model by transforming $(\mathbf{y}, \mathbf{X}, \boldsymbol{\varepsilon})$ by $\mathbf{C}$ as

$$\tilde{\mathbf{y}} \equiv \mathbf{C}\mathbf{y}, \quad \widetilde{\mathbf{X}} \equiv \mathbf{C}\mathbf{X}, \quad \tilde{\boldsymbol{\varepsilon}} \equiv \mathbf{C}\boldsymbol{\varepsilon}. \tag{1.6.3}$$

Then Assumption 1.1 for $(\mathbf{y}, \mathbf{X}, \boldsymbol{\varepsilon})$ implies that $(\tilde{\mathbf{y}}, \widetilde{\mathbf{X}}, \tilde{\boldsymbol{\varepsilon}})$ too satisfies linearity:

$$\tilde{\mathbf{y}} = \widetilde{\mathbf{X}}\boldsymbol{\beta} + \tilde{\boldsymbol{\varepsilon}}. \tag{1.6.4}$$

The transformed model satisfies the other assumptions of the classical linear regression model. Strict exogeneity is satisfied because

$$\begin{aligned}
\mathrm{E}(\tilde{\boldsymbol{\varepsilon}} \mid \widetilde{\mathbf{X}}) &= \mathrm{E}(\tilde{\boldsymbol{\varepsilon}} \mid \mathbf{X}) \\
&\qquad \text{(since } \mathbf{C} \text{ is nonsingular, } \mathbf{X} \text{ and } \widetilde{\mathbf{X}} \text{ contain the same information)} \\
&= \mathrm{E}(\mathbf{C}\boldsymbol{\varepsilon} \mid \mathbf{X}) \\
&= \mathbf{C}\,\mathrm{E}(\boldsymbol{\varepsilon} \mid \mathbf{X}) \quad \text{(by the linearity of conditional expectations)} \\
&= \mathbf{0} \quad (\text{since } \mathrm{E}(\boldsymbol{\varepsilon} \mid \mathbf{X}) = \mathbf{0} \text{ by Assumption 1.2}).
\end{aligned}$$

Because $\mathbf{V}$ is positive definite, the no-multicollinearity assumption is also satisfied (see a review question below for a proof). Assumption 1.4 is satisfied for the transformed model because

$$\begin{aligned}
\mathrm{E}(\tilde{\boldsymbol{\varepsilon}}\tilde{\boldsymbol{\varepsilon}}' \mid \widetilde{\mathbf{X}}) &= \mathrm{E}(\tilde{\boldsymbol{\varepsilon}}\tilde{\boldsymbol{\varepsilon}}' \mid \mathbf{X}) \quad \text{(since } \widetilde{\mathbf{X}} \text{ and } \mathbf{X} \text{ contain the same information)} \\
&= \mathbf{C}\ \mathrm{E}(\boldsymbol{\varepsilon}\boldsymbol{\varepsilon}' \mid \mathbf{X})\mathbf{C}' \quad (\text{since } \tilde{\boldsymbol{\varepsilon}}\tilde{\boldsymbol{\varepsilon}}' = \mathbf{C}\boldsymbol{\varepsilon}\boldsymbol{\varepsilon}'\mathbf{C}') \\
&= \mathbf{C} \cdot \sigma^2 \cdot \mathbf{V}\mathbf{C}' \quad \text{(by (1.6.1))} \\
&= \sigma^2 \mathbf{C}\mathbf{V}\mathbf{C}' \\
&= \sigma^2 \mathbf{I}_n \quad (\text{since } (\mathbf{C}')^{-1}\mathbf{V}^{-1}\mathbf{C}^{-1} = \mathbf{I}_n \text{ or } \mathbf{C}\mathbf{V}\mathbf{C}' = \mathbf{I}_n \text{ by (1.6.2)}).
\end{aligned}$$

So indeed the variance of the transformed error vector $\tilde{\boldsymbol{\varepsilon}}$ is spherical. Finally, $\tilde{\boldsymbol{\varepsilon}} \mid \widetilde{\mathbf{X}}$ is normal because the distribution of $\tilde{\boldsymbol{\varepsilon}} \mid \widetilde{\mathbf{X}}$ is the same as $\tilde{\boldsymbol{\varepsilon}} \mid \mathbf{X}$ and $\tilde{\boldsymbol{\varepsilon}}$ is a linear transformation of $\boldsymbol{\varepsilon}$. This completes the verification of Assumptions 1.1–1.5 for the transformed model.

The Gauss-Markov Theorem for the transformed model implies that the BLUE of $\boldsymbol{\beta}$ for the generalized regression model is the OLS estimator applied to (1.6.4):

$$\begin{aligned}\widehat{\boldsymbol{\beta}}_{\text{GLS}} &= (\widetilde{\mathbf{X}}'\widetilde{\mathbf{X}})^{-1}\widetilde{\mathbf{X}}'\tilde{\mathbf{y}} \\ &= [(\mathbf{CX})'(\mathbf{CX})]^{-1}(\mathbf{CX})'\mathbf{Cy} \\ &= (\mathbf{X}'\mathbf{C}'\mathbf{CX})^{-1}(\mathbf{X}'\mathbf{C}'\mathbf{Cy}) \\ &= (\mathbf{X}'\mathbf{V}^{-1}\mathbf{X})^{-1}\mathbf{X}'\mathbf{V}^{-1}\mathbf{y} \quad \text{(by (1.6.2))}. \qquad (1.6.5)\end{aligned}$$

This is the GLS estimator. Its conditional variance is

$$\begin{aligned}&\text{Var}(\widehat{\boldsymbol{\beta}}_{\text{GLS}} \mid \mathbf{X}) \\ &= (\mathbf{X}'\mathbf{V}^{-1}\mathbf{X})^{-1}\mathbf{X}'\mathbf{V}^{-1}\,\text{Var}(\mathbf{y} \mid \mathbf{X})\mathbf{V}^{-1}\mathbf{X}(\mathbf{X}'\mathbf{V}^{-1}\mathbf{X})^{-1} \\ &= (\mathbf{X}'\mathbf{V}^{-1}\mathbf{X})^{-1}\mathbf{X}'\mathbf{V}^{-1}(\sigma^2\mathbf{V})\mathbf{V}^{-1}\mathbf{X}(\mathbf{X}'\mathbf{V}^{-1}\mathbf{X})^{-1} \quad (\text{since Var}(\mathbf{y} \mid \mathbf{X}) = \text{Var}(\boldsymbol{\varepsilon} \mid \mathbf{X})) \\ &= \sigma^2 \cdot (\mathbf{X}'\mathbf{V}^{-1}\mathbf{X})^{-1}. \qquad (1.6.6)\end{aligned}$$

Since replacing $\mathbf{V}$ by $\sigma^2 \cdot \mathbf{V}$ ($=$ Var($\boldsymbol{\varepsilon} \mid \mathbf{X}$)) in (1.6.5) does not change the numerical value, the GLS estimator can also be written as

$$\widehat{\boldsymbol{\beta}}_{\text{GLS}} = \left[\mathbf{X}'\,\text{Var}(\boldsymbol{\varepsilon} \mid \mathbf{X})^{-1}\mathbf{X}\right]^{-1}\mathbf{X}'\,\text{Var}(\boldsymbol{\varepsilon} \mid \mathbf{X})^{-1}\mathbf{y}.$$

As noted above, the OLS estimator $(\mathbf{X}'\mathbf{X})^{-1}\mathbf{X}'\mathbf{y}$ too is unbiased without Assumption 1.4, but nevertheless the GLS estimator should be preferred (provided $\mathbf{V}$ is known) because the latter is more efficient in that the variance is smaller in the matrix sense. The gain in efficiency is achieved by exploiting the heteroskedasticity and correlation between observations in the error term, which, operationally, is to insert the inverse of (a matrix proportional to) Var($\boldsymbol{\varepsilon} \mid \mathbf{X}$) in the OLS formula, as in (1.6.5). The discussion so far can be summarized as

Proposition 1.7 (finite-sample properties of GLS):

(a) (unbiasedness) Under Assumption 1.1–1.3, $\text{E}(\widehat{\boldsymbol{\beta}}_{\text{GLS}} \mid \mathbf{X}) = \boldsymbol{\beta}$.

(b) (expression for the variance) Under Assumptions 1.1–1.3 and the assumption (1.6.1) that the conditional second moment is proportional to $\mathbf{V}(\mathbf{X})$,

$$\text{Var}(\widehat{\boldsymbol{\beta}}_{\text{GLS}} \mid \mathbf{X}) = \sigma^2 \cdot (\mathbf{X}'\mathbf{V}(\mathbf{X})^{-1}\mathbf{X})^{-1}.$$

(c) (efficiency of GLS) Under the same set of assumptions as in (b), the GLS estimator is efficient in that the conditional variance of any unbiased estimator that is linear in $\mathbf{y}$ *is greater than or equal to* $\text{Var}(\widehat{\boldsymbol{\beta}}_{\text{GLS}} \mid \mathbf{X})$ *in the matrix sense.*

A Special Case: Weighted Least Squares (WLS)

The idea of adjusting for the error variance matrix becomes more transparent when there is no correlation in the error term between observations so that the matrix $\mathbf{V}$ is diagonal. Let $v_i(\mathbf{X})$ be the i-th diagonal element of $\mathbf{V}(\mathbf{X})$. So

$$\mathrm{E}(\varepsilon_i^2 \mid \mathbf{X}) \; (= \mathrm{Var}(\varepsilon_i \mid \mathbf{X})) = \sigma^2 \cdot v_i(\mathbf{X}).$$

It is easy to see that $\mathbf{C}$ is also diagonal, with the square root of $1/v_i(\mathbf{X})$ in the i-th diagonal. Thus, $(\tilde{\mathbf{y}}, \widetilde{\mathbf{X}})$ is given by

$$\tilde{y}_i = \frac{y_i}{\sqrt{v_i(\mathbf{X})}}, \quad \tilde{\mathbf{x}}_i = \frac{\mathbf{x}_i}{\sqrt{v_i(\mathbf{X})}} \quad (i = 1, 2, \ldots, n).$$

Therefore, efficient estimation under a known form of heteroskedasticity is first to weight each observation by the reciprocal of the square root of the variance $v_i(\mathbf{X})$ and then apply OLS. This is called the **weighted regression** (or the **weighted least squares (WLS)**).

An important further special case is the case of a random sample where $\{y_i, \mathbf{x}_i\}$ is i.i.d. across i. As was noted in Section 1.1, the error is unconditionally homoskedastic (i.e., $\mathrm{E}(\varepsilon_i^2)$ does not depend on i), but still GLS can be used to increase efficiency because the error can be conditionally heteroskedastic. The conditional second moment $\mathrm{E}(\varepsilon_i^2 \mid \mathbf{X})$ for the case of random samples depends only on $\mathbf{x}_i$, and the functional form of $\mathrm{E}(\varepsilon_i^2 \mid \mathbf{x}_i)$ is the same across i. Thus

$$v_i(\mathbf{X}) = v(\mathbf{x}_i) \quad \text{for random samples.} \tag{1.6.7}$$

So the knowledge of $\mathbf{V}(\cdot)$ comes down to a single function of K variables, $v(\cdot)$.

Limiting Nature of GLS

All these sanguine conclusions about the finite-sample properties of GLS rest on the assumption that the regressors in the generalized regression model are strictly exogenous ($\mathrm{E}(\tilde{\boldsymbol{\varepsilon}} \mid \widetilde{\mathbf{X}}) = \mathbf{0}$). This fact limits the usefulness of the GLS procedure. Suppose, as is often the case with time-series models, that the regressors are not strictly exogenous and the error is serially correlated. So neither OLS nor GLS has those good finite-sample properties such as unbiasedness. Nevertheless, as will be shown in the next chapter, the OLS estimator, which ignores serial correlation in the error, will have some good large sample properties (such as "consistency" and "asymptotic normality"), provided that the regressors are "predetermined" (which is weaker than strict exogeneity). The GLS estimator, in contrast, does not have that redeeming feature. That is, if the error is not strictly exogenous but is merely predetermined, the GLS procedure to correct for serial correlation can make the estimator inconsistent (see Section 6.7). A procedure for explicitly taking serial correlation into account while maintaining consistency will be presented in Chapter 6.

If it is not appropriate for correcting for serial correlation, the GLS procedure can still be used to correct for heteroskedasticity when the error is not serially correlated with diagonal $\mathbf{V}(\mathbf{X})$, in the form of WLS. But that is provided that the matrix function $\mathbf{V}(\mathbf{X})$ is known. Very rarely do we have *a priori* information specifying the values of the diagonal elements of $\mathbf{V}(\mathbf{X})$, which is necessary to weight observations. In the case of a random sample where serial correlation is guaranteed not to arise, the knowledge of $\mathbf{V}(\mathbf{X})$ boils down to a single function of K variables, $v(\mathbf{x}_i)$, as we have just seen, but even for this case the knowledge of such a function is unavailable in most applications.

If we do not know the function $\mathbf{V}(\mathbf{X})$, we can estimate its functional form from the sample. This approach is called the **Feasible Generalized Least Squares (FGLS)**. But if the function $\mathbf{V}(\mathbf{X})$ is estimated from the sample, its value $\mathbf{V}$ becomes a random variable, which affects the distribution of the GLS estimator. Very little is known about the finite-sample properties of the FGLS estimator. We will cover the large-sample properties of the FGLS estimator in the context of heteroskedasticity correction in the next chapter.

Before closing, one positive side of GLS should be noted: most linear estimation techniques—including the 2SLS, 3SLS, and the random effects estimators to be introduced later—can be expressed as a GLS estimator, with some liberal definition of data matrices. However, those estimators and OLS can also be interpreted as a GMM (generalized method of moments) estimator, and the GMM interpretation is more useful for developing large-sample results.

QUESTIONS FOR REVIEW

1. (The no-multicollinearity assumption for the transformed model) Assumption 1.3 for the transformed model is that $\text{rank}(\mathbf{CX}) = K$. This is satisfied since $\mathbf{C}$ is nonsingular and $\mathbf{X}$ is of full column rank. Show this. **Hint:** Since $\mathbf{X}$ is of full column rank, for any K-dimensional vector $\mathbf{c} \neq \mathbf{0}$, $\mathbf{Xc} \neq \mathbf{0}$.

2. (Generalized *SSR*) Show that $\widehat{\boldsymbol{\beta}}_{\text{GLS}}$ minimizes $(\mathbf{y} - \mathbf{X}\widetilde{\boldsymbol{\beta}})'\mathbf{V}^{-1}(\mathbf{y} - \mathbf{X}\widetilde{\boldsymbol{\beta}})$.

3. Derive the expression for $\text{Var}(\mathbf{b} \mid \mathbf{X})$ for the generalized regression model. What is the relation of it to $\text{Var}(\widehat{\boldsymbol{\beta}}_{\text{GLS}} \mid \mathbf{X})$? Verify that Proposition 1.7(c) implies

$$(\mathbf{X}'\mathbf{X})^{-1}\mathbf{X}'\mathbf{V}\mathbf{X}(\mathbf{X}'\mathbf{X})^{-1} \geq (\mathbf{X}'\mathbf{V}^{-1}\mathbf{X})^{-1}.$$

4. (Sampling error of GLS) Show: $\widehat{\boldsymbol{\beta}}_{\text{GLS}} - \boldsymbol{\beta} = (\mathbf{X}'\mathbf{V}^{-1}\mathbf{X})^{-1}\mathbf{X}'\mathbf{V}^{-1}\boldsymbol{\varepsilon}$.

1.7 Application: Returns to Scale in Electricity Supply

Nerlove's 1963 paper is a classic study of returns to scale in a regulated industry. It also is excellent material for illustrating the techniques of this chapter and presenting a few more not yet covered.

The Electricity Supply Industry

At the time of Nerlove's writing, the U.S. electric power supply industry had the following features:

(1) Privately owned local monopolies supply power on demand.

(2) Rates (electricity prices) are set by the utility commission.

(3) Factor prices (e.g., the wage rate) are given to the firm, either because of perfect competition in the market for factor inputs or through long-term contracts with labor unions.

These institutional features will be relevant when we examine whether the OLS is an appropriate estimation procedure.[23]

The Data

Nerlove assembled a cross-section data set on 145 firms in 44 states in the year 1955 for which data on all the relevant variables were available. The variables in the data are total costs, factor prices (the wage rate, the price of fuel, and the rental price of capital), and output. Although firms own capital (such as power plants, equipment, and structures), the standard investment theory of Jorgenson (1963) tells us that (as long as there are no costs in changing the capital stock) the firm should behave as if it rents capital on a period-to-period basis from itself at a rental price called the "user cost of capital," which is defined as $(r+\delta)\cdot p_I$, where r here is the real interest rate (below we will use r for the degree of returns to scale), δ is the depreciation rate, and p_I is the price of capital goods. For this reason capital

[23]Thanks to the deregulation of the industry since the time of Nerlove's writing, multiple firms are now allowed to compete in the same local market, and the strict price control has been lifted in many states. So the first two features no longer characterize the industry.

input can be treated as if it is a variable factor of production, just like labor and fuel inputs.

Appendix B of Nerlove (1963) contains a careful and honest discussion of how the data were constructed. Data on output, fuel, and labor costs (which, along with capital costs, make up total costs) were obtained from the Federal Power Commission (1956). For the wage rate, Nerlove used statewide average wages for utility workers. Ideally, one would calculate capital costs as the reproduction cost of capital times the user cost of capital. Due to data limitation, Nerlove instead used interest and depreciation charges available from the firm's books.

Why Do We Need Econometrics?

Why do we need a fancy econometric technique like OLS to determine returns to scale? Why can't we be simple-minded and plot the average cost (which can be easily calculated from the data as the ratio of total costs to output) against output and see whether the AC (average cost) curve is downward sloping? The reason is that each firm can have a different AC curve. If firms face different factor prices, then the average cost is less for firms facing lower factor prices. That cross-section units at a given moment face the same prices is usually a good assumption to make, but not for the U.S. electricity industry with substantial regional differences in factor prices. The effect of factor prices on the AC curve has to be isolated somehow. The approach taken by Nerlove, which became a standard econometric practice, is to estimate a parameterized cost function.

Another factor that shifts the individual AC curve is the level of production efficiency. If more efficient firms produce more output, then it is possible that the individual AC curve is upward sloping but the line connecting the observed combination of the average cost and output is downward sloping. To illustrate, consider a competitive industry described in Figure 1.6, where the AC and MC (marginal cost) curves are drawn for two firms competing in the same market. To focus on the connection between production efficiency and output, assume that all firms face the same factor prices so that the only reason the AC and MC curves differ between firms is the difference in production efficiency. The AC and MC curves are upward sloping to reflect decreasing returns to scale. The AC and MC curves for firm A lie above those for firm B because firm A is less efficient than B. Because the industry is competitive, both firms face the same price p. Since output is determined at the intersection of the MC curve and the market price, the combinations of output and the average cost for two firms are points A and B in the figure. The curve obtained from connecting these two points can be downward sloping, giving a false impression of *increasing* returns to scale.

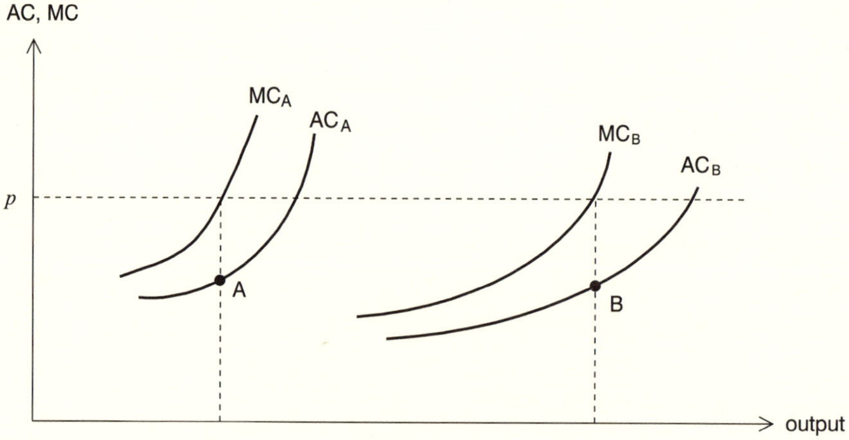

Figure 1.6: Output Determination

The Cobb-Douglas Technology

To derive a parameterized cost function, we start with the Cobb-Douglas production function

$$Q_i = A_i \, x_{i1}^{\alpha_1} \, x_{i2}^{\alpha_2} \, x_{i3}^{\alpha_3}, \tag{1.7.1}$$

where Q_i is firm i's output, x_{i1} is labor input for firm i, x_{i2} is capital input, and x_{i3} is fuel. A_i captures unobservable differences in production efficiency (this term is often called **firm heterogeneity**). The sum $\alpha_1 + \alpha_2 + \alpha_3 \equiv r$ is the degree of returns to scale. Thus, it is assumed *a priori* that the degree of returns to scale is constant (this should not be confused with constant returns to scale, which is that $r = 1$). Since the electric utilities in the sample are privately owned, it is reasonable to suppose that they are engaged in cost minimization (see, however, the discussion at the end of this section). We know from microeconomics that the cost function associated with the Cobb-Douglas production function is Cobb-Douglas:

$$TC_i = r \cdot (A_i \, \alpha_1^{\alpha_1} \, \alpha_2^{\alpha_2} \, \alpha_3^{\alpha_3})^{-1/r} \, Q_i^{1/r} \, p_{i1}^{\alpha_1/r} \, p_{i2}^{\alpha_2/r} \, p_{i3}^{\alpha_3/r}, \tag{1.7.2}$$

where TC_i is total costs for firm i. Taking logs, we obtain the following log-linear relationship:

$$\log(TC_i) = \mu_i + \frac{1}{r}\log(Q_i) + \frac{\alpha_1}{r}\log(p_{i1}) + \frac{\alpha_2}{r}\log(p_{i2}) + \frac{\alpha_3}{r}\log(p_{i3}), \tag{1.7.3}$$

where $\mu_i = \log[r \cdot (A_i \, \alpha_1^{\alpha_1} \, \alpha_2^{\alpha_2} \, \alpha_3^{\alpha_3})^{-1/r}]$. The equation is said to be **log-linear** because both the dependent variable and the regressors are logs. Coefficients in log-linear equations are **elasticities**. The $\log(p_{i1})$ coefficient, for example, is the elasticity of total costs with respect to the wage rate, i.e., the percentage change in total costs when the wage rate changes by 1 percent. The degree of returns to scale, which in (1.7.3) is the reciprocal of the output elasticity of total costs, is independent of the level of output.

Now let $\mu \equiv \mathrm{E}(\mu_i)$ and define $\varepsilon_i \equiv \mu_i - \mu$ so that $\mathrm{E}(\varepsilon_i) = 0$. This ε_i represents the inverse of the firm's production efficiency relative to the industry's average efficiency; firms with positive ε_i are high-cost firms. With this notation, (1.7.3) becomes

$$\log(TC_i) = \beta_1 + \beta_2 \log(Q_i) + \beta_3 \log(p_{i1}) + \beta_4 \log(p_{i2}) + \beta_5 \log(p_{i3}) + \varepsilon_i, \tag{1.7.4}$$

where

$$\beta_1 = \mu, \ \ \beta_2 = \frac{1}{r}, \ \ \beta_3 = \frac{\alpha_1}{r}, \ \ \beta_4 = \frac{\alpha_2}{r}, \ \text{ and } \ \beta_5 = \frac{\alpha_3}{r}. \tag{1.7.5}$$

Thus, the cost function has been cast in the regression format of Assumption 1.1 with $K = 5$. We noted a moment ago that the simple-minded approach of plotting the average cost against output cannot account for the factor price effect. What we have shown is that under the Cobb-Douglas technology the factor price effect is controlled for by the inclusion in the cost function of the logs of factor prices. Because the equation is derived from an explicit description of the firm's technology, the error term as well as the regression coefficients have clear interpretations.

How Do We Know Things Are Cobb-Douglas?

The Cobb-Douglas functional form is certainly a very convenient parameterization of technology. But how do we know that the true production function is Cobb-Douglas? The Cobb-Douglas form satisfies the properties, such as diminishing marginal productivities, that we normally require for the production function, but the Cobb-Douglas form is certainly not the only functional form with those desirable properties. A number of more general functional forms have been proposed in the literature, but the Cobb-Douglas form, despite its simplicity, has proved to be a surprisingly good description of technology. Nerlove's paper is one of the relatively few studies in which the Cobb-Douglas (log-linear) form is found to be inadequate, but it only underscores the importance of the Cobb-Douglas functional form as the benchmark from which one can usefully contemplate generalizations.

Are the OLS Assumptions Satisfied?

To justify the use of least squares, we need to make sure that Assumptions 1.1–1.4 are satisfied for the equation (1.7.4). Evidently, Assumption 1.1 (linearity) is satisfied with

$$y_i = \log(TC_i), \mathbf{x}_i = (1, \log(Q_i), \log(p_{i1}), \log(p_{i2}), \log(p_{i3}))'.$$

There is no reason to expect that the regressors in (1.7.4) are perfectly multicollinear. Indeed, in Nerlove's data set, $\text{rank}(\mathbf{X}) = 5$ and $n = 145$, so Assumption 1.3 (no multicollinearity) is satisfied as well.

In verifying the strict exogeneity assumption (Assumption 1.2), the features of the electricity industry mentioned above are relevant. It is reasonable to assume, as in most cross-section data, that $\mathbf{x}_i$ is independent of ε_j for $i \neq j$. So the question is whether $\mathbf{x}_i$ is independent of ε_i. If it is, then $\text{E}(\boldsymbol{\varepsilon} \mid \mathbf{X}) = \mathbf{0}$. According to the third feature of the industry, factor prices are given to the firm with no regard for the firm's efficiency, so it is eminently reasonable to assume that factor prices are independent of ε_i.

What about output? Since the firm's output is supplied on demand (the first feature of the industry), output depends on the price of electricity set by the utility commission (the second feature). If the regulatory scheme is such that the price is determined regardless of the firm's efficiency, then $\log(Q_i)$ and ε_i are independently distributed. On the other hand, if the price is set to cover the average cost, then the firm's efficiency affects output through the effect of the electricity price on demand and output in this case is **endogenous**, being correlated with the error term. We will very briefly come back to this point at the end, but until then we will ignore the possible endogeneity of output. This certainly would not do if we were dealing with a competitive industry. Since high-cost firms tend to produce less, there would be a *negative* correlation between $\log(Q_i)$ and ε_i, making OLS an inappropriate estimation procedure.

Regarding Assumption 1.4, the assumption of no correlation in the error term between firms (observations) would be suspect if, for example, there were technology spillovers running from one firm to other closely located firms. For the industry under study, this is probably not the case.

There is no *a priori* reason to suppose that homoskedasticity is satisfied. Indeed, the plot of residuals to be shown shortly suggests a failure of this condition. The main part of Nerlove's paper is exploring ways to deal with this problem.

Restricted Least Squares

The equation (1.7.4) is **overidentified** in that its five coefficients, being functions of the four technology parameters (which are α_1, α_2, α_3, and μ), are not free parameters. We can easily see that from (1.7.5): $\beta_3+\beta_4+\beta_5 = 1$ (recall: $r \equiv \alpha_1+\alpha_2+\alpha_3$). This is a reflection of the generic property of the cost function that it is linearly homogeneous in factor prices. Indeed, multiplying total costs TC_i and all factor prices (p_{i1}, p_{i2}, p_{i3}) by a common factor leaves the cost function (1.7.4) intact if and only if $\beta_3 + \beta_4 + \beta_5 = 1$.

Estimating the equation by least squares while imposing *a priori* restrictions on the coefficient vector is the restricted least squares. It can be done easily by deriving from the original regression a separate regression that embodies the restrictions. In the present example, to impose the homogeneity restriction $\beta_3 + \beta_4 + \beta_5 = 1$ on the cost function, we take any one of the factor prices, say p_{i3}, and subtract $\log(p_{i3})$ from both sides of (1.7.4) to obtain

$$\log\left(\frac{TC_i}{p_{i3}}\right) = \beta_1 + \beta_2 \log(Q_i) + \beta_3 \log\left(\frac{p_{i1}}{p_{i3}}\right) + \beta_4 \log\left(\frac{p_{i2}}{p_{i3}}\right) + \varepsilon_i. \quad (1.7.6)$$

There are now four coefficients in the regression, from which unique values of the four technology parameters can be determined. The restricted least squares estimate of $(\beta_1, \ldots, \beta_4)$ is simply the OLS estimate of the coefficients in (1.7.6). The restricted least squares estimate of β_5 is the value implied by the estimate of $(\beta_1, \ldots, \beta_4)$ and the restriction.

Testing the Homogeneity of the Cost Function

Before proceeding to the estimation of the restricted model (1.7.6), in order to test the homogeneity restriction $\beta_3+\beta_4+\beta_5 = 1$, we will first estimate the unrestricted model (1.7.4). If one uses the data available in printed form in Nerlove's paper, the OLS estimate of the equation is:

$$\begin{aligned}
\log(TC_i) = \; & \underset{(1.8)}{-3.5} \; + \; \underset{(0.017)}{0.72} \log(Q_i) \; + \; \underset{(0.29)}{0.44} \log(p_{i1}) \\
& - \underset{(0.34)}{0.22} \log(p_{i2}) \; + \; \underset{(0.10)}{0.43} \log(p_{i3}) \\
& R^2 = 0.926, \text{ mean of dep. variable} = 1.72, \\
& SER = 0.392, \; SSR = 21.552, \; n = 145. \qquad (1.7.7)
\end{aligned}$$

Here, numbers in parentheses are the standard errors of the OLS coefficient estimates. Since $\beta_2 = 1/r$, the estimate of the degree of returns to scale implied by the OLS coefficient estimates is about 1.4 (= 1/0.72). The OLS estimate of $\beta_4 = \alpha_2/r$ has the wrong sign. As noted by Nerlove, there are reasons to believe that p_{i2}, the rental price of capital, is poorly measured. This may explain why b_4 is so imprecisely determined (i.e., the standard error is large relative to the size of the coefficient estimate) that one cannot reject the hypothesis that $\beta_4 = 0$ with a t-ratio of -0.65 (= $-0.22/0.34$).[24]

To test the homogeneity restriction $\text{H}_0\colon \beta_3 + \beta_4 + \beta_5 = 1$, we could write the hypothesis in the form $\mathbf{R}\boldsymbol{\beta} = \mathbf{r}$ with $\mathbf{R} = (0, 0, 1, 1, 1)$ and $\mathbf{r} = 1$ and use the formula (1.4.9) to calculate the F-ratio. The maintained hypothesis is the unrestricted model (1.7.4) (that is, Assumptions 1.1–1.5 where the equation in Assumption 1.1 is (1.7.4)), so the $\mathbf{b}$ and the estimated variance of $\mathbf{b}$ in the F-ratio formula should come from the OLS estimation of (1.7.4). Alternatively, we can use the F-ratio formula (1.4.11). The unrestricted model producing SSR_U is (1.7.4) and the restricted model producing SSR_R is (1.7.6), which superimposes the null hypothesis on the unrestricted model. The OLS estimate of (1.7.6) is

$$\begin{aligned}\log\left(\frac{TC_i}{p_{i3}}\right) &= \underset{(0.88)}{-4.7} + \underset{(0.017)}{0.72}\log(Q_i) \\ &\quad + \underset{(0.20)}{0.59}\log(p_{i1}/p_{i3}) - \underset{(0.19)}{0.007}\log(p_{i2}/p_{i3}) \\ &R^2 = 0.932,\ \text{mean of dep. var.} = -1.48, \\ &SER = 0.39,\ SSR = 21.640,\ n = 145. \end{aligned} \tag{1.7.8}$$

The F test of the homogeneity restriction proceeds as follows.

Step 1: Using (1.4.11), the F-ratio can be calculated as

$$\frac{(21.640 - 21.552)/1}{21.552/(145 - 5)} = 0.57.$$

Step 2: Find the critical value. The number of restrictions (equations) in the null hypothesis is 1, and K (the number of coefficients) in the unrestricted model (which is the maintained hypothesis) is 5. So the degrees of freedom are 1 and 140 (= 145 − 5). From the table of F distributions, the critical value is about 3.9.

Step 3: Thus, we can easily accept the homogeneity restriction, a very comforting conclusion for those who take microeconomics seriously (like us).

[24]The consequence of measurement error is not just that the coefficient of the variable measured with error is poorly determined; it could also contaminate the coefficient estimates for all other regressors. The appropriate context to address this problem is the large sample theory for endogeneous regressors in Chapter 3.

Detour: A Cautionary Note on R^2

The R^2 of 0.926 is surprisingly high for cross-section estimates, but some of the explanatory power of the regression comes from the scale effect that total costs increase with firm size. To gauge the contribution of the scale effect on the R^2, subtract $\log(Q_i)$ from both sides of (1.7.4) to obtain an equivalent cost function:

$$\log\left(\frac{TC_i}{Q_i}\right) = \beta_1 + (\beta_2 - 1)\log(Q_i) + \beta_3 \log(p_{i1}) + \beta_4 \log(p_{i2}) + \beta_5 \log(p_{i3}) + \varepsilon_i. \qquad (1.7.4')$$

Here, the dependent variable is the average cost rather than total costs. Application of the OLS to (1.7.4′) using the same data yields

$$\log\left(\frac{TC_i}{Q_i}\right) = \underset{(1.8)}{-3.5} - \underset{(0.017)}{0.28}\log(Q_i) + \underset{(0.29)}{0.44}\log(p_{i1}) - \underset{(0.34)}{0.22}\log(p_{i2}) + \underset{(0.10)}{0.43}\log(p_{i3})$$

$$R^2 = 0.695,\ \text{mean of dep. var.} = -4.83,$$

$$SER = 0.392,\ SSR = 21.552,\ n = 145. \qquad (1.7.9)$$

As you no doubt have anticipated, the output coefficient is now -0.28 ($= 0.72 - 1$) with the standard errors and the other coefficient estimates unchanged. The R^2 changes only because the dependent variable is different. It is nonsense to say that the higher R^2 makes (1.7.4) preferable to (1.7.4′), because the two equations represent the same model. The point is: when comparing equations on the basis of the fit, the equations must share the same dependent variable.

Testing Constant Returns to Scale

As an application of the t-test, consider testing whether returns to scale are constant ($r = 1$). We take the maintained hypothesis to be the restricted model (1.7.6). Because β_2 (the log output coefficient) equals 1 if and only if $r = 1$, the null hypothesis is that $H_0\colon \beta_2 = 1$. The t-test of constant returns to scale proceeds as follows.

Step 1: Calculate the t-ratio for the hypothesis. From the estimation of the restricted model, we have $b_2 = 0.72$ with a standard error of 0.017, so

$$t\text{-ratio} = \frac{0.72 - 1}{0.017} = -16.$$

Because the maintained hypothesis here is the restricted model (1.7.6), K (the number of coefficients) = 4.

Step 2: Look for the critical value in the $t(141)$ distribution. If the size of the test is 5 percent, the critical value is 1.98.

Step 3: Since the absolute value of the t-ratio is far greater than the critical value, we reject the hypothesis of constant returns to scale.

Importance of Plotting Residuals

The regression has a problem that cannot be seen from the estimated coefficients and their standard errors. Figure 1.7 plots the residuals against $\log(Q_i)$. Notice two things from the plot. First, as output increases, the residuals first tend to be positive, then negative, and again positive. This strongly suggests that the degree of returns to scale (r) is not constant as assumed in the log-linear specification. Second, the residuals are more widely scattered for lower outputs, which is a sign of a failure of the homoskedasticity assumption that the error variance does not depend on the regressors. To deal with these problems, Nerlove divided the sample of 145 firms into five groups of 29, ordered by output, and estimated the model (1.7.6) separately for each group. This amounts to allowing all the coefficients (including $\beta_2 = 1/r$) *and* the error variance to differ across the five groups differing in size. Nerlove finds that returns to scale diminish steadily, from a high of well over 2 to a low of slightly below 1, over the output range of the data. In the empirical exercise of this chapter, the reader is asked to replicate this finding and do some further analysis using **dummy variables** and the weighted least squares.

Subsequent Developments

One strand of the subsequent literature is concerned about generalizing the Cobb-Douglas technology while maintaining the assumption of cost minimization. An obvious alternative to Cobb-Douglas is the Constant Elasticity of Substitution (CES) production function, but it has two problems. First, the cost function implied by the CES production function is highly nonlinear (which, though, could be overcome by the use of nonlinear least squares to be covered in Chapter 7). Second, the CES technology implies a constant degree of returns to scale. One of Nerlove's main findings is that the degree varies with output. Christensen and Greene (1976) are probably the first to estimate the technology parameters allowing for variable degrees of returns to scale. Using the **translog cost function** introduced by Christensen, Jorgenson, and Lau (1973), they find that the significant scale economies evident in the 1955 data were mostly exhausted by 1970, with most firms operating at much higher output levels where the AC curve is essentially flat. Their work will be examined in detail in Chapter 4.

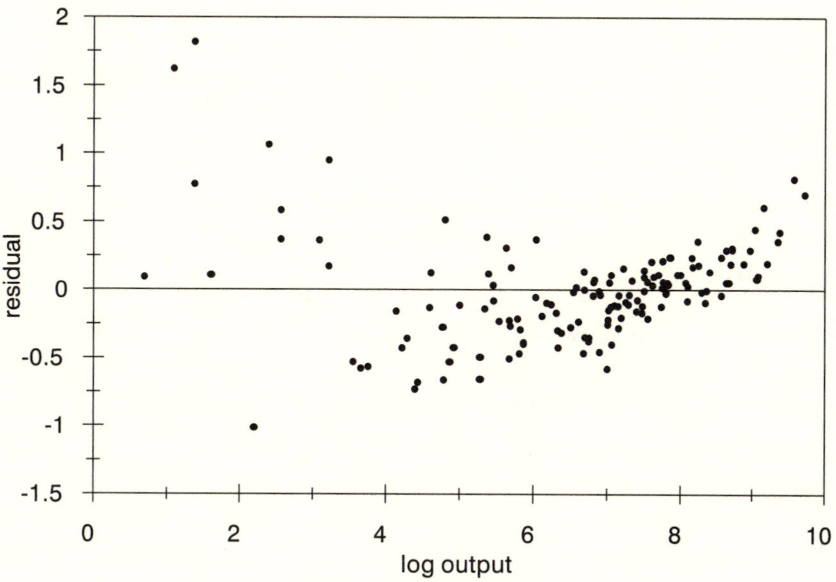

Figure 1.7: Plot of Residuals against Log Output

Another issue is whether regulated firms minimize costs. The influential paper by Averch and Johnson (1962) argues that the practice by regulators to guarantee utilities a "fair rate of return" on their capital stock distorts the choice of input levels. Since the fair rate of return is usually higher than the interest rate, utilities have an incentive to overinvest. That is, they minimize costs, but the relevant rate of return in the definition of the user cost of capital is the fair rate of return. Consequently, unless the fair rate of return is used in the calculation of p_{i2}, the true technology parameters cannot be estimated from the cost function. The fair-rate-of-return regulation creates another econometric problem: to guarantee utilities a fair rate of return, the price of electricity must be kept relatively high in markets served by high-cost utilities. Thus output will be endogenous.

A more recent issue is whether the regulator has enough information to bring about cost minimization. If the utility has more information about costs, it has an incentive to misreport to the regulator the true value of the efficiency parameter. Schemes to be adopted by the regulator to take into account this incentive problem may not lead to cost minimization. Wolak's (1994) empirical results for California's water utility industry indicate that the observed level of costs and output is better modeled as the outcome of a regulator-utility interaction under asymmetric information. Wolak resolves the problem of the endogeneity of output by estimating the demand function along with the cost function. Doing so, however, requires an estimation technique more sophisticated than the OLS.

QUESTIONS FOR REVIEW

1. (Review of duality theory) Consult your favorite microeconomic textbook to remember how to derive the Cobb-Douglas cost function from the Cobb-Douglas production function.

2. (Change of units) In Nerlove's data, output is measured in kilowatt hours. If output were measured in megawatt hours, how would the estimated restricted regression change?

3. (Recovering technology parameters from regression coefficients) Show that the technology parameters $(\mu, \alpha_1, \alpha_2, \alpha_3)$ can be determined uniquely from the first four equations in (1.7.5) and the definition $r \equiv \alpha_1 + \alpha_2 + \alpha_3$. (Do not use the fifth equation $\beta_5 = \alpha_3/r$.)

4. (Recovering left-out coefficients from restricted OLS) Calculate the restricted OLS estimate of β_5 from (1.7.8). How do you calculate the standard error of b_5 from the printout of the restricted OLS? **Hint:** Write $b_5 = a + \mathbf{c}'\mathbf{b}$ for suitably chosen a and $\mathbf{c}$ where $\mathbf{b}$ here is $(b_1, \ldots, b_4)'$. So $\text{Var}(b_5 \mid \mathbf{X}) = \mathbf{c}' \text{Var}(\mathbf{b} \mid \mathbf{X})\mathbf{c}$. The printout from the restricted OLS should include $\widehat{\text{Var}(\mathbf{b} \mid \mathbf{X})}$.

5. If you take p_{i2} instead of p_{i3} and subtract $\log(p_{i2})$ from both sides of (1.7.4), how does the restricted regression look? Without actually estimating it on Nerlove's data, can you tell from the estimated restricted regression in the text what the restricted OLS estimate of $(\beta_1, \ldots, \beta_5)$ will be? Their standard errors? The *SSR*? What about the R^2?

6. Why is the R^2 of 0.926 from the unrestricted model (1.7.7) *lower* than the R^2 of 0.932 from the restricted model (1.7.8)?

7. A more realistic assumption about the rental price of capital may be that there is an economy-wide capital market so p_{i2} is the same across firms. In this case,

   (a) Can we estimate the technology parameters? **Hint:** The answer is yes, but why? When p_{i2} is constant, (1.7.4) will have the perfect multicollinearity problem. But recall that $(\beta_1, \ldots, \beta_5)$ are not free parameters.

   (b) Can we test homogeneity of the cost function in factor prices?

8. Taking logs of both sides of the production function (1.7.1), one can derive the log-linear relationship:

$$\log(Q_i) = \alpha_0 + \alpha_1 \log(x_{i1}) + \alpha_2 \log(x_{i2}) + \alpha_3 \log(x_{i3}) + \varepsilon_i,$$

where ε_i here is defined as $\log(A_i) - \mathrm{E}[\log(A_i)]$ and $\alpha_0 = \mathrm{E}[\log(A_i)]$. Suppose, in addition to total costs, output, and factor prices, we had data on factor inputs. Can we estimate α's by applying OLS to this log-linear relationship? Why or why not? **Hint:** Do input levels depend on ε_i? Suggest a different way to estimate α's. **Hint:** Look at input shares.

PROBLEM SET FOR CHAPTER 1

ANALYTICAL EXERCISES

1. (Proof that **b** minimizes *SSR*) Let **b** be the OLS estimator of $\boldsymbol{\beta}$. Prove that, for any hypothetical estimate, $\widetilde{\boldsymbol{\beta}}$, of $\boldsymbol{\beta}$,

$$(\mathbf{y} - \mathbf{X}\widetilde{\boldsymbol{\beta}})'(\mathbf{y} - \mathbf{X}\widetilde{\boldsymbol{\beta}}) \geq (\mathbf{y} - \mathbf{X}\mathbf{b})'(\mathbf{y} - \mathbf{X}\mathbf{b}).$$

In your proof, use the add-and-subtract strategy: take $\mathbf{y} - \mathbf{X}\widetilde{\boldsymbol{\beta}}$, add $\mathbf{X}\mathbf{b}$ to it and then subtract the same from it. It produces the decomposition of $\mathbf{y} - \mathbf{X}\widetilde{\boldsymbol{\beta}}$:

$$\mathbf{y} - \mathbf{X}\widetilde{\boldsymbol{\beta}} = (\mathbf{y} - \mathbf{X}\mathbf{b}) + (\mathbf{X}\mathbf{b} - \mathbf{X}\widetilde{\boldsymbol{\beta}}).$$

Hint: $(\mathbf{y} - \mathbf{X}\widetilde{\boldsymbol{\beta}})'(\mathbf{y} - \mathbf{X}\widetilde{\boldsymbol{\beta}}) = [(\mathbf{y} - \mathbf{X}\mathbf{b}) + \mathbf{X}(\mathbf{b} - \widetilde{\boldsymbol{\beta}})]'[(\mathbf{y} - \mathbf{X}\mathbf{b}) + \mathbf{X}(\mathbf{b} - \widetilde{\boldsymbol{\beta}})]$. Using the normal equations, show that this equals

$$(\mathbf{y} - \mathbf{X}\mathbf{b})'(\mathbf{y} - \mathbf{X}\mathbf{b}) + (\mathbf{b} - \widetilde{\boldsymbol{\beta}})'\mathbf{X}'\mathbf{X}(\mathbf{b} - \widetilde{\boldsymbol{\beta}}).$$

2. (The annihilator associated with the vector of ones) Let $\mathbf{1}$ be the n-dimensional column vector of ones, and let $\mathbf{M}_1 \equiv \mathbf{I}_n - \mathbf{1}(\mathbf{1}'\mathbf{1})^{-1}\mathbf{1}'$. That is, $\mathbf{M}_1$ is the annihilator associated with $\mathbf{1}$. Prove the following:

   (a) $\mathbf{M}_1$ is symmetric and idempotent.

   (b) $\mathbf{M}_1\mathbf{1} = \mathbf{0}$.

   (c) $\mathbf{M}_1\mathbf{y} = \mathbf{y} - \bar{y} \cdot \mathbf{1}$ where

$$\bar{y} = \frac{1}{n}\sum_{i=1}^{n} y_i.$$

   $\mathbf{M}_1\mathbf{y}$ is the vector of **deviations from the mean**.

   (d) $\mathbf{M}_1\mathbf{X} = \mathbf{X} - \mathbf{1}\bar{\mathbf{x}}'$ where $\bar{\mathbf{x}} = \mathbf{X}'\mathbf{1}/n$. The k-th element of the $K \times 1$ vector $\bar{\mathbf{x}}$ is $\frac{1}{n}\sum_{i=1}^{n} x_{ik}$.

3. (Deviation-from-the-mean regression) Consider a regression model with a constant. Let $\mathbf{X}$ be partitioned as

$$\underset{(n\times K)}{\mathbf{X}} = \left[\underset{n\times 1}{\mathbf{1}} \;\vdots\; \underset{n\times(K-1)}{\mathbf{X}_2}\right]$$

so the first regressor is a constant. Partition $\boldsymbol{\beta}$ and $\mathbf{b}$ accordingly:

$$\boldsymbol{\beta} = \begin{bmatrix} \beta_1 \\ \boldsymbol{\beta}_2 \end{bmatrix} \begin{matrix} \leftarrow \text{scalar} \\ \leftarrow (K-1)\times 1 \end{matrix}, \quad \mathbf{b} = \begin{bmatrix} b_1 \\ \mathbf{b}_2 \end{bmatrix}.$$

Also let $\widetilde{\mathbf{X}}_2 \equiv \mathbf{M}_1\mathbf{X}_2$ and $\tilde{\mathbf{y}} \equiv \mathbf{M}_1\mathbf{y}$. They are the deviations from the mean for the nonconstant regressors and the dependent variable. Prove the following:

(a) The K normal equations are

$$\bar{y} - b_1 - \bar{\mathbf{x}}_2'\mathbf{b}_2 = 0$$

where $\bar{\mathbf{x}}_2 = \mathbf{X}_2'\mathbf{1}/n$,

$$\mathbf{X}_2'\mathbf{y} - n \cdot b_1 \cdot \bar{\mathbf{x}}_2 - \mathbf{X}_2'\mathbf{X}_2\mathbf{b}_2 = \underset{((K-1)\times 1)}{\mathbf{0}}.$$

(b) $\mathbf{b}_2 = (\widetilde{\mathbf{X}}_2'\widetilde{\mathbf{X}}_2)^{-1}\widetilde{\mathbf{X}}_2'\tilde{\mathbf{y}}$. **Hint:** Substitute the first normal equation into the other $K-1$ equations to eliminate b_1 and solve for $\mathbf{b}_2$. This is a generalization of the result you proved in Review Question 3 in Section 1.2.

4. (Partitioned regression, generalization of Exercise 3) Let $\mathbf{X}$ be partitioned as

$$\underset{(n\times K)}{\mathbf{X}} = \left[\underset{(n\times K_1)}{\mathbf{X}_1} \;\vdots\; \underset{(n\times K_2)}{\mathbf{X}_2}\right].$$

Partition $\boldsymbol{\beta}$ accordingly:

$$\boldsymbol{\beta} = \begin{bmatrix} \boldsymbol{\beta}_1 \\ \boldsymbol{\beta}_2 \end{bmatrix} \begin{matrix} \leftarrow K_1\times 1 \\ \leftarrow K_2\times 1 \end{matrix}.$$

Thus, the regression can be written as

$$\mathbf{y} = \mathbf{X}_1\boldsymbol{\beta}_1 + \mathbf{X}_2\boldsymbol{\beta}_2 + \boldsymbol{\varepsilon}.$$

Let $\mathbf{P}_1 \equiv \mathbf{X}_1(\mathbf{X}_1'\mathbf{X}_1)^{-1}\mathbf{X}_1'$, $\mathbf{M}_1 \equiv \mathbf{I} - \mathbf{P}_1$, $\widetilde{\mathbf{X}}_2 \equiv \mathbf{M}_1\mathbf{X}_2$ and $\tilde{\mathbf{y}} \equiv \mathbf{M}_1\mathbf{y}$. Thus, $\tilde{\mathbf{y}}$ is the residual vector from the regression of $\mathbf{y}$ on $\mathbf{X}_1$, and the k-th column of $\widetilde{\mathbf{X}}_2$ is the residual vector from the regression of the corresponding k-th column of

$\mathbf{X}_2$ on $\mathbf{X}_1$. Prove the following:

(a) The normal equations are

$$\mathbf{X}_1'\mathbf{X}_1\mathbf{b}_1 + \mathbf{X}_1'\mathbf{X}_2\mathbf{b}_2 = \mathbf{X}_1'\mathbf{y}, \qquad (*)$$

$$\mathbf{X}_2'\mathbf{X}_1\mathbf{b}_1 + \mathbf{X}_2'\mathbf{X}_2\mathbf{b}_2 = \mathbf{X}_2'\mathbf{y}. \qquad (**)$$

(b) $\mathbf{b}_2 = (\widetilde{\mathbf{X}}_2'\widetilde{\mathbf{X}}_2)^{-1}\widetilde{\mathbf{X}}_2'\tilde{\mathbf{y}}$. That is, $\mathbf{b}_2$ can be obtained by regressing the residuals $\tilde{\mathbf{y}}$ on the matrix of residuals $\widetilde{\mathbf{X}}_2$. **Hint:** Derive $\mathbf{X}_1\boldsymbol{\beta}_1 = -\mathbf{P}_1\mathbf{X}_2\boldsymbol{\beta}_2 + \mathbf{P}_1\mathbf{y}$ from $(*)$. Substitute this into $(**)$ to obtain $\mathbf{X}_2'\mathbf{M}_1\mathbf{X}_2\boldsymbol{\beta}_2 = \mathbf{X}_2'\mathbf{M}_1\mathbf{y}$. Then use the fact that $\mathbf{M}_1$ is symmetric and idempotent. Or, if you wish, you can apply the brute force of the partitioned inverse formula (A.10) of Appendix A to the coefficient matrix

$$\mathbf{X}'\mathbf{X} = \begin{bmatrix} \mathbf{X}_1'\mathbf{X}_1 & \mathbf{X}_1'\mathbf{X}_2 \\ \mathbf{X}_2'\mathbf{X}_1 & \mathbf{X}_2'\mathbf{X}_2 \end{bmatrix}.$$

Show that the second diagonal block of $(\mathbf{X}'\mathbf{X})^{-1}$ is $(\widetilde{\mathbf{X}}_2'\widetilde{\mathbf{X}}_2)^{-1}$.

(c) The residuals from the regression of $\tilde{\mathbf{y}}$ on $\widetilde{\mathbf{X}}_2$ numerically equals $\mathbf{e}$, the residuals from the regression of $\mathbf{y}$ on $\mathbf{X}$ $(\equiv (\mathbf{X}_1 \vdots \mathbf{X}_2))$. **Hint:** If $\mathbf{e}$ is the residual from the regression of $\mathbf{y}$ on $\mathbf{X}$,

$$\mathbf{y} = \mathbf{X}_1\mathbf{b}_1 + \mathbf{X}_2\mathbf{b}_2 + \mathbf{e}.$$

Premultiplying both sides by $\mathbf{M}_1$ and using $\mathbf{M}_1\mathbf{X}_1 = \mathbf{0}$, we obtain

$$\tilde{\mathbf{y}} = \widetilde{\mathbf{X}}_2\mathbf{b}_2 + \mathbf{M}_1\mathbf{e}.$$

Show that $\mathbf{M}_1\mathbf{e} = \mathbf{e}$ and observe that $\mathbf{b}_2$ equals the OLS coefficient estimate in the regression of $\tilde{\mathbf{y}}$ on $\widetilde{\mathbf{X}}_2$.

(d) $\mathbf{b}_2 = (\widetilde{\mathbf{X}}_2'\widetilde{\mathbf{X}}_2)^{-1}\widetilde{\mathbf{X}}_2'\mathbf{y}$. Note the difference from (b). Here, the vector of dependent variable is $\mathbf{y}$, not $\tilde{\mathbf{y}}$. Are the residuals from the regression of $\mathbf{y}$ on $\widetilde{\mathbf{X}}_2$ numerically the same as $\mathbf{e}$? [Answer: No.] Is the *SSR* from the regression of $\mathbf{y}$ on $\widetilde{\mathbf{X}}_2$ the same as the *SSR* from the regression of $\tilde{\mathbf{y}}$ on $\widetilde{\mathbf{X}}_2$? [Answer: No.]

The results in (b)–(d) are known as the **Frisch-Waugh Theorem**.

(e) Show:

$$\tilde{\mathbf{y}}'\tilde{\mathbf{y}} - \mathbf{e}'\mathbf{e} = \tilde{\mathbf{y}}'\mathbf{X}_2(\mathbf{X}_2'\mathbf{M}_1\mathbf{X}_2)^{-1}\mathbf{X}_2'\tilde{\mathbf{y}}.$$

Hint: Apply the general decomposition formula (1.2.15) to the regression in (c) to derive

$$\tilde{\mathbf{y}}'\tilde{\mathbf{y}} = \mathbf{b}_2'\widetilde{\mathbf{X}}_2'\widetilde{\mathbf{X}}_2\mathbf{b}_2 + \mathbf{e}'\mathbf{e}.$$

Then use (b).

(f) Consider the following four regressions:

(1) regress $\tilde{\mathbf{y}}$ on $\mathbf{X}_1$.

(2) regress $\tilde{\mathbf{y}}$ on $\widetilde{\mathbf{X}}_2$.

(3) regress $\tilde{\mathbf{y}}$ on $\mathbf{X}_1$ and $\mathbf{X}_2$.

(4) regress $\tilde{\mathbf{y}}$ on $\mathbf{X}_2$.

Let SSR_j be the sum of squared residuals from regression j. Show:

(i) $SSR_1 = \tilde{\mathbf{y}}'\tilde{\mathbf{y}}$. **Hint:** $\tilde{\mathbf{y}}$ is constructed so that $\mathbf{X}_1'\tilde{\mathbf{y}} = \mathbf{0}$, so $\mathbf{X}_1$ should have no explanatory power.

(ii) $SSR_2 = \mathbf{e}'\mathbf{e}$. **Hint:** Use (c).

(iii) $SSR_3 = \mathbf{e}'\mathbf{e}$. **Hint:** Apply the Frisch-Waugh Theorem on regression (3). $\mathbf{M}_1\tilde{\mathbf{y}} = \tilde{\mathbf{y}}$.

(iv) Verify by numerical example that SSR_4 is not necessarily equal to $\mathbf{e}'\mathbf{e}$.

5. (Restricted regression and F) In the restricted least squares, the sum of squared residuals is minimized subject to the constraint implied by the null hypothesis $\mathbf{R}\boldsymbol{\beta} = \mathbf{r}$. Form the Lagrangian as

$$\mathcal{L} = \frac{1}{2}(\mathbf{y} - \mathbf{X}\widetilde{\boldsymbol{\beta}})'(\mathbf{y} - \mathbf{X}\widetilde{\boldsymbol{\beta}}) + \boldsymbol{\lambda}'(\mathbf{R}\widetilde{\boldsymbol{\beta}} - \mathbf{r}),$$

where $\boldsymbol{\lambda}$ here is the #$\mathbf{r}$-dimensional vector of Lagrange multipliers (recall: $\mathbf{R}$ is #$\mathbf{r} \times K$, $\widetilde{\boldsymbol{\beta}}$ is $K \times 1$, and $\mathbf{r}$ is #$\mathbf{r} \times 1$). Let $\widehat{\boldsymbol{\beta}}$ be the restricted least squares estimator of $\boldsymbol{\beta}$. It is the solution to the constrained minimization problem.

(a) Let $\mathbf{b}$ be the unrestricted OLS estimator. Show:

$$\widehat{\boldsymbol{\beta}} = \mathbf{b} - (\mathbf{X}'\mathbf{X})^{-1}\mathbf{R}'[\mathbf{R}(\mathbf{X}'\mathbf{X})^{-1}\mathbf{R}']^{-1}(\mathbf{R}\mathbf{b} - \mathbf{r}),$$
$$\boldsymbol{\lambda} = [\mathbf{R}(\mathbf{X}'\mathbf{X})^{-1}\mathbf{R}']^{-1}(\mathbf{R}\mathbf{b} - \mathbf{r}).$$

Hint: The first-order conditions are $\mathbf{X}'\mathbf{y} - (\mathbf{X}'\mathbf{X})\widehat{\boldsymbol{\beta}} = \mathbf{R}'\boldsymbol{\lambda}$ or $\mathbf{X}'(\mathbf{y} - \mathbf{X}\widehat{\boldsymbol{\beta}}) = \mathbf{R}'\boldsymbol{\lambda}$. Combine this with the constraint $\mathbf{R}\widehat{\boldsymbol{\beta}} = \mathbf{r}$ to solve for $\boldsymbol{\lambda}$ and $\widehat{\boldsymbol{\beta}}$.

(b) Let $\hat{\boldsymbol{\varepsilon}} \equiv \mathbf{y} - \mathbf{X}\widehat{\boldsymbol{\beta}}$, the residuals from the restricted regression. Show:

$$\begin{aligned} SSR_R - SSR_U &= (\mathbf{b} - \widehat{\boldsymbol{\beta}})'(\mathbf{X}'\mathbf{X})(\mathbf{b} - \widehat{\boldsymbol{\beta}}) \\ &= (\mathbf{Rb} - \mathbf{r})'[\mathbf{R}(\mathbf{X}'\mathbf{X})^{-1}\mathbf{R}']^{-1}(\mathbf{Rb} - \mathbf{r}) \\ &= \boldsymbol{\lambda}'\mathbf{R}(\mathbf{X}'\mathbf{X})^{-1}\mathbf{R}'\boldsymbol{\lambda} \\ &= \hat{\boldsymbol{\varepsilon}}'\mathbf{P}\hat{\boldsymbol{\varepsilon}}, \end{aligned}$$

where $\mathbf{P}$ is the projection matrix. **Hint:** For the first equality, use the add-and-subtract strategy:

$$\begin{aligned} SSR_R &= (\mathbf{y} - \mathbf{X}\widehat{\boldsymbol{\beta}})'(\mathbf{y} - \mathbf{X}\widehat{\boldsymbol{\beta}}) \\ &= [(\mathbf{y} - \mathbf{Xb}) + \mathbf{X}(\mathbf{b} - \widehat{\boldsymbol{\beta}})]'[(\mathbf{y} - \mathbf{Xb}) + \mathbf{X}(\mathbf{b} - \widehat{\boldsymbol{\beta}})]. \end{aligned}$$

Use the normal equations $\mathbf{X}'(\mathbf{y} - \mathbf{Xb}) = \mathbf{0}$. For the second and third equalities, use (a). To prove the fourth equality, the easiest way is to use the first-order condition mentioned in (a) that $\mathbf{R}'\boldsymbol{\lambda} = \mathbf{X}'\hat{\boldsymbol{\varepsilon}}$.

(c) Verify that you have proved in (b) that (1.4.9) = (1.4.11).

6. (Proof of the decomposition (1.2.17)) Take the unrestricted model to be a regression where one of the regressors is a constant, and the restricted model to be a regression where the only regressor is a constant.

(a) Show that (b) in the previous exercise is the decomposition (1.2.17) for this case. **Hint:** What is $\widehat{\boldsymbol{\beta}}$ for this case? Show that $SSR_R = \sum_i (y_i - \bar{y})^2$ and $(\mathbf{b} - \widehat{\boldsymbol{\beta}})'(\mathbf{X}'\mathbf{X})(\mathbf{b} - \widehat{\boldsymbol{\beta}}) = \sum_i (\hat{y} - \bar{y})^2$.

(b) (R^2 as an F-ratio) For a regression where one of the regressors is a constant, prove that

$$F = \frac{R^2/(K-1)}{(1-R^2)/(n-K)}.$$

7. (Hausman principle in finite samples) For the generalized regression model, prove the following. Here, it is understood that the expectations, variances, and covariances are all conditional on $\mathbf{X}$.

(a) $\mathrm{Cov}(\widehat{\boldsymbol{\beta}}_{\mathrm{GLS}}, \mathbf{b} - \widehat{\boldsymbol{\beta}}_{\mathrm{GLS}}) = \mathbf{0}$. **Hint:** Recall that, for any two random vectors $\mathbf{x}$ and $\mathbf{y}$,

$$\mathrm{Cov}(\mathbf{x}, \mathbf{y}) \equiv \mathrm{E}\big[\big(\mathbf{x} - \mathrm{E}(\mathbf{x})\big)\big(\mathbf{y} - \mathrm{E}(\mathbf{y})\big)'\big].$$

So

$$\text{Cov}(\mathbf{Ax}, \mathbf{By}) = \mathbf{A}\,\text{Cov}(\mathbf{x}, \mathbf{y})\mathbf{B}'.$$

Also, since $\boldsymbol{\beta}$ is nonrandom,

$$\text{Cov}(\widehat{\boldsymbol{\beta}}_{\text{GLS}}, \mathbf{b} - \widehat{\boldsymbol{\beta}}_{\text{GLS}}) = \text{Cov}(\widehat{\boldsymbol{\beta}}_{\text{GLS}} - \boldsymbol{\beta}, \mathbf{b} - \widehat{\boldsymbol{\beta}}_{\text{GLS}}).$$

(b) Let $\widetilde{\boldsymbol{\beta}}$ be any unbiased estimator and define $\mathbf{q} \equiv \widetilde{\boldsymbol{\beta}} - \widehat{\boldsymbol{\beta}}_{\text{GLS}}$. Assume $\widetilde{\boldsymbol{\beta}}$ is such that $\mathbf{V_q} \equiv \text{Var}(\mathbf{q})$ is nonsingular. Prove: $\text{Cov}(\widehat{\boldsymbol{\beta}}_{\text{GLS}}, \mathbf{q}) = \mathbf{0}$. (If we set $\widetilde{\boldsymbol{\beta}} = \mathbf{b}$, we are back to (a).) **Hint:** Define: $\widehat{\boldsymbol{\beta}} \equiv \widehat{\boldsymbol{\beta}}_{\text{GLS}} + \mathbf{Hq}$ for some $\mathbf{H}$. Show:

$$\text{Var}(\widehat{\boldsymbol{\beta}}) = \text{Var}(\widehat{\boldsymbol{\beta}}_{\text{GLS}}) + \mathbf{CH}' + \mathbf{HC}' + \mathbf{HV_q H}',$$

where $\mathbf{C} \equiv \text{Cov}(\widehat{\boldsymbol{\beta}}_{\text{GLS}}, \mathbf{q})$. Show that, if $\mathbf{C} \neq \mathbf{0}$ then $\text{Var}(\widehat{\boldsymbol{\beta}})$ can be made smaller than $\text{Var}(\widehat{\boldsymbol{\beta}}_{\text{GLS}})$ by setting $\mathbf{H} = -\mathbf{CV_q^{-1}}$. Argue that this is in contradiction to Proposition 1.7(c).

(c) (Optional, only for those who are proficient in linear algebra) Prove: if the K columns of $\mathbf{X}$ are characteristic vectors of $\mathbf{V}$, then $\mathbf{b} = \widehat{\boldsymbol{\beta}}_{\text{GLS}}$, where $\mathbf{V}$ is the $n \times n$ variance-covariance matrix of the n-dimensional error vector $\boldsymbol{\varepsilon}$. (So not all unbiased estimators satisfy the requirement in (b) that $\text{Var}(\widetilde{\boldsymbol{\beta}} - \widehat{\boldsymbol{\beta}}_{\text{GLS}})$ be nonsingular.) **Hint:** For any $n \times n$ symmetric matrix $\mathbf{V}$, there exists an $n \times n$ matrix $\mathbf{H}$ such that $\mathbf{H}'\mathbf{H} = \mathbf{I}_n$ (so $\mathbf{H}$ is an orthogonal matrix) and $\mathbf{H}'\mathbf{VH} = \boldsymbol{\Lambda}$, where $\boldsymbol{\Lambda}$ is a diagonal matrix with the characteristic roots (which are real since $\mathbf{V}$ is symmetric) of $\mathbf{V}$ in the diagonal. The columns of $\mathbf{H}$ are called the characteristic vectors of $\mathbf{V}$. Show that

$$\mathbf{H}^{-1} = \mathbf{H}', \;\; \mathbf{H}'\mathbf{V}^{-1}\mathbf{H} = \boldsymbol{\Lambda}^{-1}, \;\; \mathbf{H}'\mathbf{V}^{-1} = \boldsymbol{\Lambda}^{-1}\mathbf{H}'.$$

Without loss of generality, $\mathbf{X}$ can be taken to be the first K columns of $\mathbf{H}$. So $\mathbf{X} = \mathbf{HF}$, where

$$\underset{(n\times K)}{\mathbf{F}} = \begin{bmatrix} \mathbf{I}_K \\ \mathbf{0} \end{bmatrix}.$$

EMPIRICAL EXERCISES

Read Marc Nerlove, "Returns to Scale in Electricity Supply" (except paragraphs of equations (6)–(9), the part of section 2 from p. 184 on, and Appendix A and

C) before doing this exercise. For 145 electric utility companies in 1955, the file NERLOVE.ASC has data on the following:

Column 1: total costs (call it TC) in millions of dollars
Column 2: output (Q) in billions of kilowatt hours
Column 3: price of labor (PL)
Column 4: price of fuels (PF)
Column 5: price of capital (PK).

They are from the data appendix of his article. There are 145 observations, and the observations are ordered in size, observation 1 being the smallest company and observation 145 the largest. Using the data transformation facilities of your computer software, generate for each of the 145 firms the variables required for estimation. To estimate (1.7.4), for example, you need to generate $\log(TC)$, a constant, $\log(Q)$, $\log(PL)$, $\log(PK)$, and $\log(PF)$, for each of the 145 firms.

(a) (Data question) Does Nerlove's construction of the price of capital conform to the definition of the user cost of capital? **Hint:** Read Nerlove's Appendix B.4.

(b) Estimate the unrestricted model (1.7.4) by OLS. Can you replicate the estimates in the text?

(c) (Restricted least squares) Estimate the restricted model (1.7.6) by OLS. To do this, you need to generate a new set of variables for each of the 145 firms. For example, the dependent variable is $\log(TC/PF)$, not $\log(TC)$. Can you replicate the estimates in the text? Can you replicate Nerlove's results? Nerlove's estimate of β_2, for example, is 0.721 with a standard error of 0.0174 (the standard error in his paper is 0.175, but it is probably a typographical error). Where in Nerlove's paper can you find this estimate? What about the other coefficients? (Warning: You will not be able to replicate Nerlove's results precisely. One reason is that he used common rather than natural logarithms; however, this should affect only the estimated intercept term. The other reason: the data set used for his results is a corrected version of the data set published with his article.)

As mentioned in the text, the plot of residuals suggests a nonlinear relationship between $\log(TC)$ and $\log(Q)$. Nerlove hypothesized that estimated returns to scale varied with the level of output. Following Nerlove, divide the sample of 145 firms into five subsamples or groups, each having 29 firms. (Recall that since the data are ordered by level of output, the first 29 observations will have the smallest output levels, whereas the last 29 observations will have the largest output levels.) Consider the following three generalizations of the model (1.7.6):

Model 1: Both the coefficients (β's) and the error variance in (1.7.6) differ across groups.

Model 2: The coefficients are different, but the error variance is the same across groups.

Model 3: While each group has common coefficients for β_3 and β_4 (price elasticities) and common error variance, it has a different intercept term and a different β_2. Model 3 is what Nerlove called the hypothesis of neutral variations in returns to scale.

For Model 1, the coefficients and error variances specific to groups can be estimated from

$$\mathbf{y}^{(j)} = \mathbf{X}^{(j)}\boldsymbol{\beta}^{(j)} + \boldsymbol{\varepsilon}^{(j)} \quad (j = 1, \ldots, 5),$$

where $\mathbf{y}^{(j)}$ (29×1) is the vector of the values of the dependent variable for group j, $\mathbf{X}^{(j)}$ (29×4) is the matrix of the values of the four regressors for group j, $\boldsymbol{\beta}^{(j)}$ (4×1) is the coefficient vector for group j, and $\boldsymbol{\varepsilon}^{(j)}$ (29×1) is the error vector. The second column of $\mathbf{X}^{(5)}$, for example, is $\log(Q)$ for $i = 117, \ldots, 145$. Model 1 assumes conditional homoskedasticity $\mathrm{E}(\boldsymbol{\varepsilon}^{(j)}\boldsymbol{\varepsilon}^{(j)\prime} \mid \mathbf{X}^{(j)}) = \sigma_j^2\mathbf{I}_{29}$ within (but not necessarily across) groups.

(d) Estimate Model 1 by OLS. How well can you replicate Nerlove's reported results? On the basis of your estimates of β_2, compute the point estimates of returns to scale in each of the five groups. What is the general pattern of estimated scale economies as the level of output increases? What is the general pattern of the estimated error variance as output increases?

Model 2 assumes for Model 1 that $\sigma_j^2 = \sigma^2$ for all j. This equivariance restriction can be incorporated by stacking vectors and matrices as follows:

$$\mathbf{y} = \mathbf{X}\boldsymbol{\beta} + \boldsymbol{\varepsilon},$$

where

$$\underset{(145\times 1)}{\mathbf{y}} = \begin{bmatrix} \mathbf{y}^{(1)} \\ \vdots \\ \mathbf{y}^{(5)} \end{bmatrix}, \quad \underset{(145\times 20)}{\mathbf{X}} = \begin{bmatrix} \mathbf{X}^{(1)} & & \\ & \ddots & \\ & & \mathbf{X}^{(5)} \end{bmatrix}, \quad \underset{(145\times 1)}{\boldsymbol{\varepsilon}} = \begin{bmatrix} \boldsymbol{\varepsilon}^{(1)} \\ \vdots \\ \boldsymbol{\varepsilon}^{(5)} \end{bmatrix}. \qquad (*)$$

In particular, $\mathbf{X}$ is now a block-diagonal matrix. The equivariance restriction can be expressed as $\mathrm{E}(\boldsymbol{\varepsilon}\boldsymbol{\varepsilon}' \mid \mathbf{X}) = \sigma^2\mathbf{I}_{145}$. There are now 20 variables derived from the original four regressors. The 145 dimensional vector corresponding to the second variable, for example, has $\log(Q_1), \ldots, \log(Q_{29})$ as the first 29 elements and zeros elsewhere. The vector corresponding to the 6th variable, which represents log output for the second group of firms, has $\log(Q_{30}), \ldots, \log(Q_{58})$ for the 30th through 58th elements and zeros elsewhere, and so on.

The stacking operation needed to form the $\mathbf{y}$ and $\mathbf{X}$ in $(*)$ can be done easily if your computer software is matrix-based. Otherwise, you trick your software into accomplishing the same thing by the use of dummy variables. Define the j-th dummy variable as

$$D_{ji} = \begin{cases} 1 & \text{if firm } i \text{ belongs to the } j\text{-th group,} \\ 0 & \text{otherwise,} \end{cases} \qquad (i = 1, \ldots, 145).$$

Then the second regressor is $D_{1i} \cdot \log(Q_i)$. The 6th variable is $D_{2i} \cdot \log(Q_i)$, and so forth.

(e) Estimate Model 2 by OLS. Verify that the OLS coefficient estimates here are the same as those in (d). Also verify that

$$\sum_{j=1}^{5} SSR_j = SSR,$$

where SSR_j is the SSR from the j-th group in your estimation of Model 1 in (d) and SSR is the SSR from Model 2. This agreement is not by accident, i.e., not specific to the present data set. Prove that this agreement for the coefficients and the SSR holds in general, temporarily assuming just two groups without loss of generality. **Hint:** First show that the coefficient estimate is the same between Model 1 and Model 2. Use formulas (A.4), (A.5), and (A.9) of Appendix A.

(f) (Chow test) Model 2 is more general than Model (1.7.6) because the coefficients can differ across groups. Test the null hypothesis that the coefficients are the same across groups. How many equations (restrictions) are in the null hypothesis? This test is sometimes called the **Chow test for structural change**. Calculate the p-value of the F-ratio. **Hint:** This is a linear hypothesis about the coefficients of Model 2. So take Model 2 to be the maintained hypothesis and (1.7.6) to be the restricted model. Use the formula (1.4.11) for the F-ratio.

Gauss Tip: If x is the F-ratio, the Gauss command `cdffc(x,df1,df2)` gives the area to the right of F for the F distribution with $df1$ and $df2$ degrees of freedom.

TSP Tip: The TSP command to do the same is `cdf(f, df1=df1, df2=df2) x`. An output of TSP's OLS command, `OLSQ`, is `@SSR`, which is the *SSR* for the regression.

RATS Tip: The RATS command is `cdf ftest x df1 df2`. An output of RATS's OLS command, `LINREG`, is `%RSS`, which is the *SSR* for the regression.

The restriction in Model 3 that the price elasticities are the same across firm groups can be imposed on Model 2 by applying the dummy variable transformation only to the constant and log output. Thus, there are 12 $(= 2 \times 5 + 2)$ variables in $\mathbf{X}$. Now $\mathbf{X}$ looks like

$$\mathbf{X} = \begin{bmatrix} 1 & \log(Q_1) & & 0 & 0 & \log(PL_1/PF_1) & \log(PK_1/PF_1) \\ \vdots & \vdots & & \vdots & \vdots & \vdots & \vdots \\ 1 & \log(Q_{29}) & & 0 & 0 & \log(PL_{29}/PF_{29}) & \log(PK_{29}/PF_{29}) \\ & & \ddots & & & \vdots & \vdots \\ 0 & 0 & & 1 & \log(Q_{117}) & \log(PL_{117}/PF_{117}) & \log(PK_{117}/PF_{117}) \\ \vdots & \vdots & & \vdots & \vdots & \vdots & \vdots \\ 0 & 0 & & 1 & \log(Q_{145}) & \log(PL_{145}/PF_{145}) & \log(PK_{145}/PF_{145}) \end{bmatrix} \tag{**}$$

(g) Estimate Model 3. The model is a special case of Model 2, with the hypothesis that the two price elasticities are the same across the five groups. Test the hypothesis at a significance level of 5 percent, assuming normality. (Note: Nerlove's F-ratio on p. 183 is wrong.)

As has become clear from the plot of residuals in Figure 1.7, the conditional second moment $\mathrm{E}(\varepsilon_i^2 \mid \mathbf{X})$ is likely to depend on log output, which is a violation of the conditional homoskedasticity assumption. This time we do not attempt to test conditional homoskedasticity, because to do so requires large sample theory and is postponed until the next chapter. Instead, we pretend to know the form of the function linking the conditional second moment to log output. The function, specified below, implies that the conditional second moment varies continuously with output, contrary to the three models we have considered above. Also contrary to those models, we assume that the degree of returns to scale varies continuously with output by including the square of log output.[25] Model 4 is

Model 4:

$$\log\left(\frac{TC_i}{p_{i3}}\right) = \beta_1 + \beta_2 \log(Q_i) + \beta_3 [\log(Q_i)]^2$$
$$+ \beta_4 \log\left(\frac{p_{i1}}{p_{i3}}\right) + \beta_5 \log\left(\frac{p_{i2}}{p_{i3}}\right) + \varepsilon_i$$
$$\mathrm{E}(\varepsilon_i^2 \mid \mathbf{X}) = \sigma^2 \cdot \left(0.0565 + \frac{2.1377}{Q_i}\right) \quad (i = 1, 2, \dots, 145)$$

for some unknown σ^2.

(h) Estimate Model 4 by weighted least squares on the whole sample of 145 firms. (Be careful about the treatment of the intercept; in the equation after weighting, none of the regressors is a constant.) Plot the residuals. Is there still evidence for conditional homoskedasticity or further nonlinearities?

MONTE CARLO EXERCISES

Monte Carlo analysis simulates a large number of samples from the model to study the finite-sample distribution of estimators. In this exercise, we use the technique to confirm the two finite-sample results of the text: the unbiasedness of the OLS coefficient estimator and the distribution of the t-ratio. The model is the following simple regression model satisfying Assumptions 1.1–1.5 with $n = 32$. The regression equation is

$$y_i = \beta_1 + \beta_2 x_i + \varepsilon_i \quad (i = 1, 2, \dots, n)$$
$$\text{or } \mathbf{y} = \mathbf{1} \cdot \beta_1 + \mathbf{x} \cdot \beta_2 + \boldsymbol{\varepsilon} = \mathbf{X}\boldsymbol{\beta} + \boldsymbol{\varepsilon}, \qquad (*)$$

where $\mathbf{X} = (\mathbf{1} \vdots \mathbf{x})$ and $\boldsymbol{\beta} = (\beta_1, \beta_2)'$. The model parameters are $(\beta_1, \beta_2, \sigma^2)$.

As mentioned in the text, a model is a set of joint distributions of $(\mathbf{y}, \mathbf{X})$. We pick a particular joint distribution by specifying the regression model as follows. Set $\beta_1 = 1$, $\beta_2 = 0.5$, and $\sigma^2 = 1$. The distribution of $\mathbf{x} = (x_1, x_2, \dots, x_n)'$ is specified by the following AR(1) process:

$$x_i = c + \phi x_{i-1} + \eta_i \quad (i = 1, 2, \dots, n), \qquad (**)$$

[25] We have derived the log-linear cost function from the Cobb-Douglas production function. Does there exist a production function from which this generalized cost function with a quadratic term in log output can be derived? This is a question of the "integrability" of cost functions and is discussed in detail in Christensen et al. (1973).

where $\{\eta_i\}$ is i.i.d. $N(0, 1)$ and

$$x_0 \sim N\Big(\frac{c}{1-\phi}, \frac{1}{1-\phi^2}\Big), \quad c = 2, \quad \phi = 0.6.$$

This fixes the joint distribution of $(\mathbf{y}, \mathbf{X})$. From this distribution, a large number of samples will be drawn.

In programming the simulation, the following expression for $\mathbf{x}$ will be useful. Solve the first-order difference equation $(**)$ to obtain

$$\begin{aligned} x_i = \phi^i x_0 &+ (1 + \phi + \phi^2 + \cdots + \phi^{i-1})c \\ &+ (\eta_i + \phi\eta_{i-1} + \phi^2\eta_{i-2} + \cdots + \phi^{i-1}\eta_1), \end{aligned}$$

or, in matrix notation,

$$\underset{(n\times 1)}{\mathbf{x}} = \underset{(n\times 1)}{\mathbf{r}} \cdot x_0 + \underset{(n\times 1)}{\mathbf{d}} + \underset{(n\times n)}{\mathbf{A}}\underset{(n\times 1)}{\boldsymbol{\eta}}, \qquad (***)$$

where $\mathbf{d} = (d_1, d_2, \ldots, d_n)'$ and

$$d_1 = c, \quad d_2 = (1+\phi)c, \ldots, \quad d_i = (1 + \phi + \phi^2 + \cdots + \phi^{i-1})c, \ldots,$$

$$\mathbf{r} = \begin{bmatrix} \phi \\ \phi^2 \\ \vdots \\ \phi^n \end{bmatrix}, \quad \mathbf{A} = \begin{bmatrix} 1 & 0 & \cdots & \cdots & 0 \\ \phi & 1 & 0 & \cdots & 0 \\ \phi^2 & \phi & 1 & \ddots & 0 \\ \vdots & \vdots & \ddots & \ddots & \vdots \\ \phi^{n-1} & \phi^{n-2} & \cdots & \phi & 1 \end{bmatrix}, \quad \boldsymbol{\eta} = \begin{bmatrix} \eta_1 \\ \eta_2 \\ \vdots \\ \eta_n \end{bmatrix}.$$

Gauss Tip: To form the $\mathbf{r}$ matrix, use `seqm`. To form the $\mathbf{A}$ matrix, use `toeplitz` and `lowmat`.

(a) Run two Monte Carlo simulations. The first simulation calculates $\mathrm{E}(\mathbf{b} \mid \mathbf{x})$ and the distribution of the t-ratio as a distribution conditional on $\mathbf{x}$. A computer program for the first simulation should consist of the following steps.

(1) (Generate $\mathbf{x}$ just once) Using the random number generator, draw a vector $\boldsymbol{\eta}$ of n i.i.d. random variables from $N(0, 1)$ and x_0 from $N(c/(1-\phi), 1/(1-\phi^2))$, and calculate $\mathbf{x}$ by $(***)$. (Calculation of $\mathbf{x}$ can also be accomplished recursively by $(**)$ with a do loop, but vector operations such as $(***)$ consume less CPU time than do loops. This becomes a consideration in the second simulation, where $\mathbf{x}$ has to be generated in each replication.)

(2) Set a counter to zero. The counter will record the incidence that $|t| > t_{0.025}(n-2)$. Also, set a two-dimensional vector at zero; this vector will be used for calculating the mean of the OLS estimator **b** of $(\beta_1, \beta_2)'$.

(3) Start a do loop of a large number of replications (1 million, say). In each replication, do the following.

(i) (Generate **y**) Draw an n dimensional vector $\boldsymbol{\varepsilon}$ of n i.i.d. random variables from $N(0, 1)$, and calculate $\mathbf{y} = (y_1, \ldots, y_n)'$ by (*). This **y** is paired with the same **x** from step (1) to form a sample (**y**, **x**).

(ii) From the sample, calculate the OLS estimator **b** and the t-value for $\text{H}_0\colon \beta_2 = 0.5$.

(iii) Increase the counter by one if $|t| > t_{0.025}(n-2)$. Also, add **b** to the two-dimensional vector.

(4) After the do loop, divide the counter by the number of replications to calculate the frequency of rejecting the null. Also, divide the two-dimensional vector that has accumulated **b** by the number of replications. It should equal $\text{E}(\mathbf{b} \mid \mathbf{x})$ if the number of replications is infinite.

Note that in this first simulation, **x** is *fixed* throughout the do loop for **y**. The second simulation calculates the *un*conditional distribution of the t-ratio. It should consist of the following steps.

(1) Set the counter to zero.

(2) Start a do loop of a large number of replications. In each replication, do the following.

(i) (Generate **x**) Draw a vector $\boldsymbol{\eta}$ of n i.i.d. random variables from $N(0, 1)$ and x_0 from $N(c/(1-\phi), 1/(1-\phi^2))$, and calculate **x** by (***).

(ii) (Generate **y**) Draw a vector $\boldsymbol{\varepsilon}$ of n i.i.d. random variables from $N(0, 1)$, and calculate $\mathbf{y} = (y_1, \ldots, y_n)'$ by (*).

(iii) From a sample (**y**, **x**) thus generated, calculate the t-value for $\text{H}_0\colon \beta = 0.5$ from the sample (**y**, **x**).

(iv) Increase the counter by one if $|t| > t_{0.025}(n-2)$.

(3) After the do loop, divide the counter by the number of replications.

For the two simulations, verify that, for a sufficiently large number of replications,

1. the mean of $\mathbf{b}$ from the first simulation is arbitrarily close to the true value $(1, 0.5)$;

2. the frequency of rejecting the true hypothesis H_0 (the type I error) is arbitrarily close to 5 percent in either simulation.

(b) In those two simulations, is the (nonconstant) regressor strictly exogenous? Is the error conditionally homoskedastic?

ANSWERS TO SELECTED QUESTIONS

ANALYTICAL EXERCISES

1. $$\begin{aligned}
&(\mathbf{y} - \mathbf{X}\widetilde{\boldsymbol{\beta}})'(\mathbf{y} - \mathbf{X}\widetilde{\boldsymbol{\beta}})\\
&= [(\mathbf{y} - \mathbf{X}\mathbf{b}) + \mathbf{X}(\mathbf{b} - \widetilde{\boldsymbol{\beta}})]'[(\mathbf{y} - \mathbf{X}\mathbf{b}) + \mathbf{X}(\mathbf{b} - \widetilde{\boldsymbol{\beta}})]\\
&\qquad \text{(by the add-and-subtract strategy)}\\
&= [(\mathbf{y} - \mathbf{X}\mathbf{b})' + (\mathbf{b} - \widetilde{\boldsymbol{\beta}})'\mathbf{X}'][(\mathbf{y} - \mathbf{X}\mathbf{b}) + \mathbf{X}(\mathbf{b} - \widetilde{\boldsymbol{\beta}})]\\
&= (\mathbf{y} - \mathbf{X}\mathbf{b})'(\mathbf{y} - \mathbf{X}\mathbf{b}) + (\mathbf{b} - \widetilde{\boldsymbol{\beta}})'\mathbf{X}'(\mathbf{y} - \mathbf{X}\mathbf{b})\\
&\qquad + (\mathbf{y} - \mathbf{X}\mathbf{b})'\mathbf{X}(\mathbf{b} - \widetilde{\boldsymbol{\beta}}) + (\mathbf{b} - \widetilde{\boldsymbol{\beta}})'\mathbf{X}'\mathbf{X}(\mathbf{b} - \widetilde{\boldsymbol{\beta}})\\
&= (\mathbf{y} - \mathbf{X}\mathbf{b})'(\mathbf{y} - \mathbf{X}\mathbf{b}) + 2(\mathbf{b} - \widetilde{\boldsymbol{\beta}})'\mathbf{X}'(\mathbf{y} - \mathbf{X}\mathbf{b}) + (\mathbf{b} - \widetilde{\boldsymbol{\beta}})'\mathbf{X}'\mathbf{X}(\mathbf{b} - \widetilde{\boldsymbol{\beta}})\\
&\qquad \text{(since } (\mathbf{b} - \widetilde{\boldsymbol{\beta}})'\mathbf{X}'(\mathbf{y} - \mathbf{X}\mathbf{b}) = (\mathbf{y} - \mathbf{X}\mathbf{b})'\mathbf{X}(\mathbf{b} - \widetilde{\boldsymbol{\beta}})\text{)}\\
&= (\mathbf{y} - \mathbf{X}\mathbf{b})'(\mathbf{y} - \mathbf{X}\mathbf{b}) + (\mathbf{b} - \widetilde{\boldsymbol{\beta}})'\mathbf{X}'\mathbf{X}(\mathbf{b} - \widetilde{\boldsymbol{\beta}})\\
&\qquad \text{(since } \mathbf{X}'(\mathbf{y} - \mathbf{X}\mathbf{b}) = \mathbf{0} \text{ by the normal equations)}\\
&\geq (\mathbf{y} - \mathbf{X}\mathbf{b})'(\mathbf{y} - \mathbf{X}\mathbf{b})\\
&\qquad \text{(since } (\mathbf{b} - \widetilde{\boldsymbol{\beta}})'\mathbf{X}'\mathbf{X}(\mathbf{b} - \widetilde{\boldsymbol{\beta}}) = \mathbf{z}'\mathbf{z} = \sum_{i=1}^{n} z_i^2 \geq 0 \text{ where } \mathbf{z} \equiv \mathbf{X}(\mathbf{b} - \widetilde{\boldsymbol{\beta}})\text{).}
\end{aligned}$$

7a. $\widehat{\boldsymbol{\beta}}_{\text{GLS}} - \boldsymbol{\beta} = \mathbf{A}\boldsymbol{\varepsilon}$ where $\mathbf{A} \equiv (\mathbf{X}'\mathbf{V}^{-1}\mathbf{X})^{-1}\mathbf{X}'\mathbf{V}^{-1}$ and $\mathbf{b} - \widehat{\boldsymbol{\beta}}_{\text{GLS}} = \mathbf{B}\boldsymbol{\varepsilon}$ where $\mathbf{B} \equiv (\mathbf{X}'\mathbf{X})^{-1}\mathbf{X}' - (\mathbf{X}'\mathbf{V}^{-1}\mathbf{X})^{-1}\mathbf{X}'\mathbf{V}^{-1}$. So

$$\begin{aligned}
&\text{Cov}(\widehat{\boldsymbol{\beta}}_{\text{GLS}} - \boldsymbol{\beta}, \mathbf{b} - \widehat{\boldsymbol{\beta}}_{\text{GLS}})\\
&= \text{Cov}(\mathbf{A}\boldsymbol{\varepsilon}, \mathbf{B}\boldsymbol{\varepsilon})\\
&= \mathbf{A}\,\text{Var}(\boldsymbol{\varepsilon})\mathbf{B}'\\
&= \sigma^2\mathbf{A}\mathbf{V}\mathbf{B}'.
\end{aligned}$$

It is straightforward to show that $\mathbf{A}\mathbf{V}\mathbf{B}' = \mathbf{0}$.

7b. For the choice of **H** indicated in the hint,

$$\text{Var}(\widehat{\boldsymbol{\beta}}) - \text{Var}(\widehat{\boldsymbol{\beta}}_{\text{GLS}}) = -\mathbf{C}\mathbf{V}_q^{-1}\mathbf{C}'.$$

If $\mathbf{C} \neq \mathbf{0}$, then there exists a nonzero vector $\mathbf{z}$ such that $\mathbf{C}'\mathbf{z} \equiv \mathbf{v} \neq \mathbf{0}$. For such $\mathbf{z}$,

$$\mathbf{z}'[\text{Var}(\widehat{\boldsymbol{\beta}}) - \text{Var}(\widehat{\boldsymbol{\beta}}_{\text{GLS}})]\mathbf{z} = -\mathbf{v}'\mathbf{V}_q^{-1}\mathbf{v} < 0 \quad (\text{since } \mathbf{V}_q \text{ is positive definite}),$$

which is a contradiction because $\widehat{\boldsymbol{\beta}}_{\text{GLS}}$ is efficient.

EMPIRICAL EXERCISES

(a) Nerlove's description in Appendix B.4 leads one to believe that he did not include the depreciation rate δ in his construction of the price of capital.

(b) Your estimates should agree with (1.7.7).

(c) Our estimates differ from Nerlove's slightly. This would happen even if the data used by Nerlove were the same as those provided to you, because computers in his age were much less precise and had more frequent rounding errors.

(d) How well can you replicate Nerlove's reported results? Fairly well. The point estimates of returns to scale in each of the five subsamples are 2.5, 1.5, 1.1, 1.1, and .96. As the level of output increases, the returns to scale decline.

(e) Model 2 can be written as $\mathbf{y} = \mathbf{X}\boldsymbol{\beta} + \boldsymbol{\varepsilon}$, where $\mathbf{y}$, $\mathbf{X}$, and $\boldsymbol{\varepsilon}$ are as in (∗). So (setting $j = 2$),

$$\mathbf{X}'\mathbf{X} = \begin{bmatrix} \mathbf{X}^{(1)\prime}\mathbf{X}^{(1)} & \mathbf{0} \\ \mathbf{0} & \mathbf{X}^{(2)\prime}\mathbf{X}^{(2)} \end{bmatrix},$$

which means

$$(\mathbf{X}'\mathbf{X})^{-1} = \begin{bmatrix} \left(\mathbf{X}^{(1)\prime}\mathbf{X}^{(1)}\right)^{-1} & \mathbf{0} \\ \mathbf{0} & \left(\mathbf{X}^{(2)\prime}\mathbf{X}^{(2)}\right)^{-1} \end{bmatrix}.$$

And

$$\mathbf{X}'\mathbf{y} = \begin{bmatrix} \mathbf{X}^{(1)\prime}\mathbf{y}^{(1)} \\ \mathbf{X}^{(2)\prime}\mathbf{y}^{(2)} \end{bmatrix}.$$

Therefore,

$$(\mathbf{X}'\mathbf{X})^{-1}\mathbf{X}'\mathbf{y} = \begin{bmatrix} (\mathbf{X}^{(1)\prime}\mathbf{X}^{(1)})^{-1}\mathbf{X}^{(1)\prime}\mathbf{y}^{(1)} \\ (\mathbf{X}^{(2)\prime}\mathbf{X}^{(2)})^{-1}\mathbf{X}^{(2)\prime}\mathbf{y}^{(2)} \end{bmatrix}.$$

Thus, the OLS estimate of the coefficient vector for Model 2 is the same as that for Model 1. Since the estimate of the coefficient vector is the same, the sum of squared residuals, too, is the same.

(f) The number of restrictions is 16. K = #coefficients in Model 2 = 20. So the two degrees of freedom should be (16, 125). $SSR_U = 12.262$ and $SSR_R = 21.640$. F-ratio = 5.97 with a p-value of 0.0000. So this can be rejected at any reasonable significance level.

(g) $SSR_U = 12.262$ and $SSR_R = 12.577$. So $F = .40$ with 8 and 125 degrees of freedom. Its p-value is 0.92. So the restrictions can be accepted at any reasonable significance level. Nerlove's F-ratio (see p. 183, 8th line from bottom) is 1.576.

(h) The plot still shows that the conditional second moment is somewhat larger for smaller firms, but now there is no evidence for possible nonlinearities.

References

Amemiya, T., 1985, *Advanced Econometrics*, Cambridge: Harvard University Press.

Averch, H., and L. Johnson, 1962, "Behavior of the Firm under Regulatory Constraint," *American Economic Review*, 52, 1052–1069.

Christensen, L., and W. Greene, 1976, "Economies of Scale in US Electric Power Generation," *Journal of Political Economy*, 84, 655–676.

Christensen, L., D. Jorgenson, and L. Lau, 1973, "Transcendental Logarithmic Production Frontiers," *Review of Economics and Statistics*, 55, 28–45.

Davidson, R., and J. MacKinnon, 1993, *Estimation and Inference in Econometrics*, Oxford: Oxford University Press.

DeLong, B., and L. Summers, 1991, "Equipment Investment and Growth," *Quarterly Journal of Economics*, 99, 28–45.

Engle, R., D. Hendry, and J.-F. Richards, 1983, "Exogeneity," *Econometrica*, 51, 277–304.

Federal Power Commission, 1956, *Statistics of Electric Utilities in the United States, 1955, Class A and B Privately Owned Companies*, Washington, D.C.

Jorgenson, D., 1963, "Capital Theory and Investment Behavior," *American Economic Review*, 53, 247–259.

Koopmans, T., and W. Hood, 1953, "The Estimation of Simultaneous Linear Economic Relationships," in W. Hood, and T. Koopmans (eds.), *Studies in Econometric Method*, New Haven: Yale University Press.

Krasker, W., E. Kuh, and R. Welsch, 1983, "Estimation for Dirty Data and Flawed Models," Chapter 11 in Z. Griliches, and M. Intriligator (eds.), *Handbook of Econometrics*, Volume 1, Amsterdam: North-Holland.

Nerlove, M., 1963, "Returns to Scale in Electricity Supply," in C. Christ (ed.), *Measurement in Economics: Studies in Mathematical Economics and Econometrics in Memory of Yehuda Grunfeld*, Stanford: Stanford University Press.

Rao, C. R., 1973, *Linear Satistical Inference and Its Applications* (2d ed.), New York: Wiley.

Scheffe, H., 1959, *The Analysis of Variance*, New York: Wiley.

Wolak, F., 1994, "An Econometric Analysis of the Asymmetric Information, Regulator-Utility Interaction," *Annales D'Economie et de Statistique*, 34, 13–69.

CHAPTER 2

Large-Sample Theory

ABSTRACT

In the previous chapter, we derived the exact- or finite-sample distribution of the OLS estimator and its associated test statistics. However, not very often in economics are the assumptions of the exact distribution satisfied. The finite-sample theory breaks down if one of the following three assumptions is violated: (1) the exogeneity of regressors, (2) the normality of the error term, and (3) the linearity of the regression equation. This chapter develops an alternative approach, retaining only the third assumption. The approach, called **asymptotic** or **large-sample theory**, derives an approximation to the distribution of the estimator and its associated statistics assuming that the sample size is sufficiently large.

Rather than making assumptions on the sample of a given size, large-sample theory makes assumptions on the stochastic process that generates the sample. The first two sections of this chapter provide the necessary language for describing stochastic processes.

The concepts introduced in this chapter are essential for rational expectations econometrics, as illustrated in Fama's classic paper on the Fisher Hypothesis that the real interest rate is constant. The hypothesis has a very strong policy implication: monetary and fiscal policies cannot influence aggregate demand through the real interest rate. Very surprisingly, one cannot reject the hypothesis for the United States (at least if the sample period ends in the early 1970s).

2.1 Review of Limit Theorems for Sequences of Random Variables

The material of this section concerns the limiting behavior of a sequence of random variables, $(z_1, z_2, \dots)$. Since the material may already be familiar to you, we present it rather formally, in a series of definitions and theorems. An authoritative source is Rao (1973, Chapter 2c) which gives proofs of all the theorems included in this section. In this section and the rest of this book, a sequence $(z_1, z_2, \dots)$ will be denoted by $\{z_n\}$.

Various Modes of Convergence

Convergence in Probability

A sequence of random scalars $\{z_n\}$ **converges in probability** to a constant (nonrandom) α if, for any $\varepsilon > 0$,

$$\lim_{n\to\infty} \text{Prob}(|z_n - \alpha| > \varepsilon) = 0. \tag{2.1.1}$$

The constant α is called the **probability limit** of z_n and is written as "$\text{plim}_{n\to\infty} z_n = \alpha$" or "$z_n \to_{\text{p}} \alpha$". Evidently,

$$\text{“}z_n \underset{\text{p}}{\to} \alpha\text{”} \quad \text{is the same as} \quad \text{“}z_n - \alpha \underset{\text{p}}{\to} 0.\text{”}$$

This definition of convergence in probability is extended to a sequence of random vectors or random matrices (by viewing a matrix as a vector whose elements have been rearranged) by requiring element-by-element convergence in probability. That is, a sequence of K-dimensional random vectors $\{\mathbf{z}_n\}$ converges in probability to a K-dimensional vector of constants $\boldsymbol{\alpha}$ if, for any $\varepsilon > 0$,

$$\lim_{n\to\infty} \text{Prob}(|z_{nk} - \alpha_k| > \varepsilon) = 0 \quad \text{for all } k \ (= 1, 2, \ldots, K), \tag{2.1.2}$$

where z_{nk} is the k-th element of $\mathbf{z}_n$ and α_k the k-th element of $\boldsymbol{\alpha}$.

Almost Sure Convergence

A sequence of random scalars $\{z_n\}$ **converges almost surely** to a constant α if

$$\text{Prob}\Big(\lim_{n\to\infty} z_n = \alpha\Big) = 1. \tag{2.1.3}$$

We write this as "$z_n \to_{\text{a.s.}} \alpha$." The extension to random vectors is analogous to that for convergence in probability. As will be mentioned below, this concept of convergence is stronger than convergence in probability; that is, if a sequence converges almost surely, then it converges in probability. The concept involved in (2.1.3) is harder to grasp because the probability is about an event concerning an infinite sequence $(z_1, z_2, \ldots)$. For our purposes, however, all that matters is that almost sure convergence is stronger than convergence in probability. If we can show that a sequence converges almost surely, that is one way to prove the sequence converges in probability.

Convergence in Mean Square

A sequence of random scalars $\{z_n\}$ **converges in mean square** (or **in quadratic mean**) to α (written as "$z_n \to_{\text{m.s.}} \alpha$") if

$$\lim_{n\to\infty} \mathrm{E}[(z_n - \alpha)^2] = 0. \tag{2.1.4}$$

The extension to random vectors is analogous to that for convergence in probability: $\mathbf{z}_n \to_{\text{m.s.}} \boldsymbol{\alpha}$ if each element of $\mathbf{z}_n$ converges in mean square to the corresponding component of $\boldsymbol{\alpha}$.

Convergence to a Random Variable

In these definitions of convergence, the limit is a constant (i.e., a real number). The limit can be a random variable. We say that a sequence of K-dimensional random variables $\{\mathbf{z}_n\}$ converges to a K-dimensional random variable $\mathbf{z}$ and write $\mathbf{z}_n \to_{\text{p}} \mathbf{z}$ if $\{\mathbf{z}_n - \mathbf{z}\}$ converges to $\mathbf{0}$:

$$\text{“}\mathbf{z}_n \underset{\text{p}}{\to} \mathbf{z}\text{”} \quad \text{is the same as} \quad \text{“}\mathbf{z}_n - \mathbf{z} \underset{\text{p}}{\to} \mathbf{0}.\text{”} \tag{2.1.5a}$$

Similarly,

$$\text{“}\mathbf{z}_n \underset{\text{a.s.}}{\to} \mathbf{z}\text{”} \quad \text{is the same as} \quad \text{“}\mathbf{z}_n - \mathbf{z} \underset{\text{a.s.}}{\to} \mathbf{0},\text{”} \tag{2.1.5b}$$

$$\text{“}\mathbf{z}_n \underset{\text{m.s.}}{\to} \mathbf{z}\text{”} \quad \text{is the same as} \quad \text{“}\mathbf{z}_n - \mathbf{z} \underset{\text{m.s.}}{\to} \mathbf{0}.\text{”} \tag{2.1.5c}$$

Convergence in Distribution

Let $\{z_n\}$ be a sequence of random scalars and F_n be the cumulative distribution function (c.d.f.) of z_n. We say that $\{z_n\}$ **converges in distribution** to a random scalar z if the c.d.f. F_n of z_n converges to the c.d.f. F of z at every continuity point of F.[1] We write "$z_n \to_{\text{d}} z$" or "$z_n \to_{\text{L}} z$" and call F the **asymptotic** (or **limit** or **limiting**) **distribution** of z_n. Sometimes we write "$z_n \to_{\text{d}} F$," when the distribution F is well-known. For example, "$z_n \to_{\text{d}} N(0, 1)$" should read "$z_n \to_{\text{d}} z$ and the distribution of z is $N(0, 1)$ (normal distribution with mean 0 and variance 1)." It can be shown from the definition that convergence in probability is stronger than convergence in distribution, that is,

$$\text{“}\mathbf{z}_n \underset{\text{p}}{\to} \mathbf{z}\text{”} \Rightarrow \text{“}\mathbf{z}_n \underset{\text{d}}{\to} \mathbf{z}.\text{”} \tag{2.1.6}$$

[1] Do not be concerned about the qualifier "at every continuity point of F." For the most part, except possibly for the chapters on the discrete or limited dependent variable, the relevant distribution is continuous, and the distribution function is continuous at all points.

A special case of convergence in distribution is that z is a constant (a trivial random variable).

The extension to a sequence of random vectors is immediate: $\mathbf{z}_n \to_{\text{d}} \mathbf{z}$ if the joint c.d.f. F_n of the random vector $\mathbf{z}_n$ converges to the joint c.d.f. F of $\mathbf{z}$ at every continuity point of F. Note, however, that, unlike the other concepts of convergence, for convergence in distribution, element-by-element convergence does not necessarily mean convergence for the vector sequence. That is, "each element of $\mathbf{z}_n \to_{\text{d}}$ corresponding element of $\mathbf{z}$" does not necessarily imply "$\mathbf{z}_n \to_{\text{d}} \mathbf{z}$." A common way to establish the connection between scalar convergence and vector convergence in distribution is

Multivariate Convergence in Distribution Theorem: *(stated in Rao, 1973, p. 128) Let $\{\mathbf{z}_n\}$ be a sequence of K-dimensional random vectors. Then:*

$$\text{“}\mathbf{z}_n \underset{\text{d}}{\to} \mathbf{z}\text{”} \Leftrightarrow \text{“}\boldsymbol{\lambda}'\mathbf{z}_n \underset{\text{d}}{\to} \boldsymbol{\lambda}'\mathbf{z} \textit{ for any } K\textit{-dimensional vector of real numbers.”}$$

Convergence in Distribution vs. Convergence in Moments

It is worth emphasizing that the moments of the limit distribution of z_n are not necessarily equal to the limits of the moments of z_n. For example, "$z_n \to_{\text{d}} z$" does not necessarily imply "$\lim_{n\to\infty} \text{E}(z_n) = \text{E}(z)$." However,

Lemma 2.1 (convergence in distribution and in moments): *Let α_{sn} be the s-th moment of z_n and $\lim_{n\to\infty} \alpha_{sn} = \alpha_s$ where α_s is finite (i.e., a real number). Then:*

$$\text{“}z_n \underset{\text{d}}{\to} z\text{”} \Rightarrow \text{“}\alpha_s \textit{ is the } s\textit{-th moment of } z.\text{”}$$

Thus, for example, if the variance of a sequence of random variables converging in distribution converges to some *finite* number, then that number is the variance of the limiting distribution.

Relation among Modes of Convergence

Some modes of convergence are weaker than others. The following theorem establishes the relationship between the four modes of convergence.

Lemma 2.2 (relationship among the four modes of convergence):

(a) "$\mathbf{z}_n \to_{\text{m.s.}} \boldsymbol{\alpha}$" $\Rightarrow$ "$\mathbf{z}_n \to_{\text{p}} \boldsymbol{\alpha}$." *So* "$\mathbf{z}_n \to_{\text{m.s.}} \mathbf{z}$" $\Rightarrow$ "$\mathbf{z}_n \to_{\text{p}} \mathbf{z}$."

(b) "$\mathbf{z}_n \to_{\text{a.s.}} \boldsymbol{\alpha}$" $\Rightarrow$ "$\mathbf{z}_n \to_{\text{p}} \boldsymbol{\alpha}$." *So* "$\mathbf{z}_n \to_{\text{a.s.}} \mathbf{z}$" $\Rightarrow$ "$\mathbf{z}_n \to_{\text{p}} \mathbf{z}$."

(c) "$\mathbf{z}_n \to_{\text{p}} \boldsymbol{\alpha}$" $\Leftrightarrow$ "$\mathbf{z}_n \to_{\text{d}} \boldsymbol{\alpha}$." *(That is, if the limiting random variable is a constant [a trivial random variable], convergence in distribution is the same as convergence in probability.)*

Three Useful Results

Having defined the modes of convergence, we can state three results essential for developing large-sample theory.

Lemma 2.3 (preservation of convergence for continuous transformation): *Suppose* $\mathbf{a}(\cdot)$ *is a vector-valued continuous function that does not depend on* n.

(a) "$\mathbf{z}_n \to_{\text{p}} \boldsymbol{\alpha}$" $\Rightarrow$ "$\mathbf{a}(\mathbf{z}_n) \to_{\text{p}} \mathbf{a}(\boldsymbol{\alpha})$." *Stated differently,*

$$\operatorname*{plim}_{n\to\infty} \mathbf{a}(\mathbf{z}_n) = \mathbf{a}(\operatorname*{plim}_{n\to\infty} \mathbf{z}_n)$$

provided the plim *exists.*

(b) "$\mathbf{z}_n \to_{\text{d}} \mathbf{z}$" $\Rightarrow$ "$\mathbf{a}(\mathbf{z}_n) \to_{\text{d}} \mathbf{a}(\mathbf{z})$."

An immediate implication of Lemma 2.3(a) is that the usual arithmetic operations preserve convergence in probability. For example:

$$\text{“}x_n \underset{\text{p}}{\to} \beta,\ y_n \underset{\text{p}}{\to} \gamma\text{”} \Rightarrow \text{“}x_n + y_n \underset{\text{p}}{\to} \beta + \gamma\text{”}$$

$$\text{“}x_n \underset{\text{p}}{\to} \beta,\ y_n \underset{\text{p}}{\to} \gamma\text{”} \Rightarrow \text{“}x_n y_n \underset{\text{p}}{\to} \beta\gamma.\text{”}$$

$$\text{“}x_n \underset{\text{p}}{\to} \beta,\ y_n \underset{\text{p}}{\to} \gamma\text{”} \Rightarrow \text{“}x_n / y_n \underset{\text{p}}{\to} \beta/\gamma,\text{” provided that } \gamma \neq 0.$$

$$\text{“}\mathbf{Y}_n \underset{\text{p}}{\to} \boldsymbol{\Gamma}\text{”} \Rightarrow \text{“}\mathbf{Y}_n^{-1} \underset{\text{p}}{\to} \boldsymbol{\Gamma}^{-1},\text{” provided that } \boldsymbol{\Gamma} \text{ is invertible.}$$

The next result about combinations of convergence in probability and in distribution will be used repeatedly to derive the asymptotic distribution of the estimator.

Lemma 2.4:

(a) "$\mathbf{x}_n \to_{\text{d}} \mathbf{x},\ \mathbf{y}_n \to_{\text{p}} \boldsymbol{\alpha}$" $\Rightarrow$ "$\mathbf{x}_n + \mathbf{y}_n \to_{\text{d}} \mathbf{x} + \boldsymbol{\alpha}$."

(b) "$\mathbf{x}_n \to_{\text{d}} \mathbf{x},\ \mathbf{y}_n \to_{\text{p}} \mathbf{0}$" $\Rightarrow$ "$\mathbf{y}_n'\mathbf{x}_n \to_{\text{p}} 0$."

(c) "$\mathbf{x}_n \to_{\text{d}} \mathbf{x},\ \mathbf{A}_n \to_{\text{p}} \mathbf{A}$" $\Rightarrow$ "$\mathbf{A}_n\mathbf{x}_n \to_{\text{d}} \mathbf{A}\mathbf{x}$," *provided that* $\mathbf{A}_n$ *and* $\mathbf{x}_n$ *are conformable. In particular, if* $\mathbf{x} \sim N(\mathbf{0}, \boldsymbol{\Sigma})$, *then* $\mathbf{A}_n\mathbf{x}_n \to_{\text{d}} N(\mathbf{0}, \mathbf{A}\boldsymbol{\Sigma}\mathbf{A}')$.

(d) "$\mathbf{x}_n \to_{\text{d}} \mathbf{x},\ \mathbf{A}_n \to_{\text{p}} \mathbf{A}$" $\Rightarrow$ "$\mathbf{x}_n' \mathbf{A}_n^{-1} \mathbf{x}_n \to_{\text{d}} \mathbf{x}' \mathbf{A}^{-1} \mathbf{x}$," *provided that* $\mathbf{A}_n$ *and* $\mathbf{x}_n$ *are conformable and* $\mathbf{A}$ *is nonsingular.*

Parts (a) and (c) are sometimes called **Slutzky's Theorem**. By setting $\boldsymbol{\alpha} = \mathbf{0}$, part (a) implies:

$$\text{“}\mathbf{x}_n \underset{\text{d}}{\to} \mathbf{x},\ \mathbf{y}_n \underset{\text{p}}{\to} \mathbf{0}\text{”} \Rightarrow \text{“}\mathbf{x}_n + \mathbf{y}_n \underset{\text{d}}{\to} \mathbf{x}.\text{”} \tag{2.1.7}$$

That is, if $\mathbf{z}_n = \mathbf{x}_n + \mathbf{y}_n$ and $\mathbf{y}_n \to_{\text{p}} \mathbf{0}$ (i.e., if $\mathbf{z}_n - \mathbf{x}_n \to_{\text{p}} \mathbf{0}$), then the asymptotic distribution of $\mathbf{z}_n$ is the same as that of $\mathbf{x}_n$. When $\mathbf{z}_n - \mathbf{x}_n \to_{\text{p}} \mathbf{0}$, we sometimes (but not always) say that the two sequences are **asymptotically equivalent** and write it as

$$\text{“}\mathbf{z}_n \underset{\text{a}}{\sim} \mathbf{x}_n\text{” or “}\mathbf{z}_n = \mathbf{x}_n + o_p,\text{”}$$

where o_p is some suitable random variable ($\mathbf{y}_n$ here) that converges to zero in probability.

A standard trick in deriving the asymptotic distribution of a sequence of random variables is to find an asymptotically equivalent sequence whose asymptotic distribution is easier to derive. In particular, by replacing $\mathbf{y}_n$ by $\mathbf{y}_n - \boldsymbol{\alpha}$ in part (b) of the lemma, we obtain

$$\text{“}\mathbf{x}_n \underset{\text{d}}{\to} \mathbf{x},\ \mathbf{y}_n \underset{\text{p}}{\to} \boldsymbol{\alpha}\text{”} \Rightarrow \text{“}\mathbf{y}_n'\mathbf{x}_n \underset{\text{a}}{\sim} \boldsymbol{\alpha}'\mathbf{x}_n\text{” or “}\mathbf{y}_n'\mathbf{x}_n = \boldsymbol{\alpha}'\mathbf{x}_n + o_p.\text{”} \tag{2.1.8}$$

The o_p here is $(\mathbf{y}_n - \boldsymbol{\alpha})'\mathbf{x}_n$. Therefore, replacing $\mathbf{y}_n$ by its probability limit does not change the asymptotic distribution of $\mathbf{y}_n'\mathbf{x}_n$, *provided* $\mathbf{x}_n$ converges in distribution to some random variable.

The third result will allow us to test nonlinear hypotheses given the asymptotic distribution of the estimator.

Lemma 2.5 (the "delta method"): *Suppose* $\{\mathbf{x}_n\}$ *is a sequence of* K*-dimensional random vectors such that* $\mathbf{x}_n \to_{\text{p}} \boldsymbol{\beta}$ *and*

$$\sqrt{n}(\mathbf{x}_n - \boldsymbol{\beta}) \underset{\text{d}}{\to} \mathbf{z},$$

and suppose $\mathbf{a}(\cdot): \mathbb{R}^K \to \mathbb{R}^r$ *has continuous first derivatives with* $\mathbf{A}(\boldsymbol{\beta})$ *denoting the* $r \times K$ *matrix of first derivatives evaluated at* $\boldsymbol{\beta}$*:*

$$\underset{(r\times K)}{\mathbf{A}(\boldsymbol{\beta})} \equiv \frac{\partial \mathbf{a}(\boldsymbol{\beta})}{\partial \boldsymbol{\beta}'}.$$

Then

$$\sqrt{n}[\mathbf{a}(\mathbf{x}_n) - \mathbf{a}(\boldsymbol{\beta})] \underset{d}{\rightarrow} \mathbf{A}(\boldsymbol{\beta})\mathbf{z}.$$

In particular:

$$\text{“}\sqrt{n}(\mathbf{x}_n - \boldsymbol{\beta}) \underset{d}{\rightarrow} N(\mathbf{0}, \boldsymbol{\Sigma})\text{”} \Rightarrow \text{“}\sqrt{n}[\mathbf{a}(\mathbf{x}_n) - \mathbf{a}(\boldsymbol{\beta})] \underset{d}{\rightarrow} N\big(\mathbf{0}, \mathbf{A}(\boldsymbol{\beta})\boldsymbol{\Sigma}\mathbf{A}(\boldsymbol{\beta})'\big).\text{”}$$

Proving this is a good way to learn how to use the results covered so far.

PROOF. By the mean-value theorem from calculus (see Section 7.3 for a statement of the theorem), there exists a K-dimensional vector $\mathbf{y}_n$ between $\mathbf{x}_n$ and $\boldsymbol{\beta}$ such that

$$\mathbf{a}(\mathbf{x}_n) - \mathbf{a}(\boldsymbol{\beta}) = \underset{(r\times K)}{\mathbf{A}(\mathbf{y}_n)} \underset{(K\times 1)}{(\mathbf{x}_n - \boldsymbol{\beta})}.$$

Multiplying both sides by $\sqrt{n}$, we obtain

$$\sqrt{n}[\mathbf{a}(\mathbf{x}_n) - \mathbf{a}(\boldsymbol{\beta})] = \mathbf{A}(\mathbf{y}_n)\sqrt{n}(\mathbf{x}_n - \boldsymbol{\beta}).$$

Since $\mathbf{y}_n$ is between $\mathbf{x}_n$ and $\boldsymbol{\beta}$ and since $\mathbf{x}_n \rightarrow_{\mathrm{p}} \boldsymbol{\beta}$, we know that $\mathbf{y}_n \rightarrow_{\mathrm{p}} \boldsymbol{\beta}$. Moreover, the first derivative $\mathbf{A}(\cdot)$ is continuous by assumption. So by Lemma 2.3(a),

$$\mathbf{A}(\mathbf{y}_n) \underset{p}{\rightarrow} \mathbf{A}(\boldsymbol{\beta}).$$

By Lemma 2.4(c), this and the hypothesis that $\sqrt{n}(\mathbf{x}_n - \boldsymbol{\beta}) \rightarrow_{\mathrm{d}} \mathbf{z}$ imply that

$$\mathbf{A}(\mathbf{y}_n)\sqrt{n}(\mathbf{x}_n - \boldsymbol{\beta}) \big(= \sqrt{n}[\mathbf{a}(\mathbf{x}_n) - \mathbf{a}(\boldsymbol{\beta})]\big) \underset{d}{\rightarrow} \mathbf{A}(\boldsymbol{\beta})\mathbf{z}. \qquad \blacksquare$$

Viewing Estimators as Sequences of Random Variables

Let $\hat{\boldsymbol{\theta}}_n$ be an estimator of a parameter vector $\boldsymbol{\theta}$ based on a sample of size n. The sequence $\{\hat{\boldsymbol{\theta}}_n\}$ is an example of a sequence of random variables, so the concepts introduced in this section for sequences of random variables are applicable to $\{\hat{\boldsymbol{\theta}}_n\}$. We say that an estimator $\hat{\boldsymbol{\theta}}_n$ is **consistent for $\boldsymbol{\theta}$** if

$$\underset{n\to\infty}{\text{plim}}\, \hat{\boldsymbol{\theta}}_n = \boldsymbol{\theta} \quad \text{or} \quad \hat{\boldsymbol{\theta}}_n \underset{p}{\rightarrow} \boldsymbol{\theta}.$$

The **asymptotic bias** of $\hat{\boldsymbol{\theta}}_n$ is defined as $\text{plim}_{n\to\infty} \hat{\boldsymbol{\theta}}_n - \boldsymbol{\theta}$.[2] So if the estimator is consistent, its asymptotic bias is zero. A consistent estimator $\hat{\boldsymbol{\theta}}_n$ is **asymptotically normal** if

$$\sqrt{n}(\hat{\boldsymbol{\theta}}_n - \boldsymbol{\theta}) \underset{\mathrm{d}}{\to} N(\mathbf{0}, \boldsymbol{\Sigma}).$$

Such an estimator is called **$\sqrt{n}$-consistent**. The acronym sometimes used for "consistent and asymptotically normal" is **CAN**. The variance matrix $\boldsymbol{\Sigma}$ is called the **asymptotic variance** and is denoted $\text{Avar}(\hat{\boldsymbol{\theta}}_n)$. Some authors use the notation $\text{Avar}(\hat{\boldsymbol{\theta}}_n)$ to mean $\boldsymbol{\Sigma}/n$ (which is zero in the limit). In this book, $\text{Avar}(\hat{\boldsymbol{\theta}}_n)$ is the variance of the limiting distribution of $\sqrt{n}(\hat{\boldsymbol{\theta}}_n - \boldsymbol{\theta})$.

Laws of Large Numbers and Central Limit Theorems

For a sequence of random scalars $\{z_i\}$, the **sample mean** $\bar{z}_n$ is defined as

$$\bar{z}_n \equiv \frac{1}{n}\sum_{i=1}^{n} z_i.$$

Consider the sequence $\{\bar{z}_n\}$. Laws of large numbers (LLNs) concern conditions under which $\{\bar{z}_n\}$ converges either in probability or almost surely. An LLN is called strong if the convergence is almost surely and weak if the convergence is in probability. We can derive the following weak LLN easily from Part (a) of Lemma 2.2.

A Version of Chebychev's Weak LLN:

$$\text{“}\lim_{n\to\infty} \mathrm{E}(\bar{z}_n) = \mu,\ \lim_{n\to\infty} \mathrm{Var}(\bar{z}_n) = 0\text{”} \Rightarrow \text{“}\bar{z}_n \underset{\mathrm{p}}{\to} \mu.\text{”}$$

This holds because, under the condition specified, it is easy to prove (see an analytical question) that $\bar{z}_n \to_{\text{m.s.}} \mu$. The following strong LLN assumes that $\{z_i\}$ is i.i.d. (independently and identically distributed), but the variance does not need to be finite.

Kolmogorov's Second Strong Law of Large Numbers: *Let $\{z_i\}$ be i.i.d. with $\mathrm{E}(z_i) = \mu$.*[3] *Then $\bar{z}_n \to_{\text{a.s.}} \mu$.*

[2]Some authors use the term "asymptotic bias" differently. Amemiya (1985), for example, defines it to mean $\lim_{n\to\infty} \mathrm{E}(\hat{\boldsymbol{\theta}}_n) - \boldsymbol{\theta}$.

[3]So the mean exists and is finite (a real number). When a moment (e.g., the mean) is indicated, as here, then by implication the moment is assumed to exist and is finite.

These LLNs extend readily to random vectors by requiring element-by-element convergence.

Central Limit Theorems (CLTs) are about the limiting behavior of the difference between $\bar{z}_n$ and $E(\bar{z}_n)$ (which equals $E(z_i)$ if $\{z_i\}$ is i.i.d.) blown up by $\sqrt{n}$. The only Central Limit Theorem we need for the case of i.i.d. sequences is:

Lindeberg-Levy CLT: *Let* $\{\mathbf{z}_i\}$ *be i.i.d. with* $E(\mathbf{z}_i) = \boldsymbol{\mu}$ *and* $\text{Var}(\mathbf{z}_i) = \boldsymbol{\Sigma}$. *Then*

$$\sqrt{n}(\bar{\mathbf{z}}_n - \boldsymbol{\mu}) = \frac{1}{\sqrt{n}} \sum_{i=1}^{n} (\mathbf{z}_i - \boldsymbol{\mu}) \underset{\text{d}}{\rightarrow} N(\mathbf{0}, \boldsymbol{\Sigma}).$$

This reads: a sequence of random vectors $\{\sqrt{n}(\bar{\mathbf{z}}_n - \boldsymbol{\mu})\}$ converges in distribution to a random vector whose distribution is $N(\mathbf{0}, \boldsymbol{\Sigma})$. (Usually, the Lindeberg-Levy CLT is for a sequence of *scalar* random variables. The vector version displayed above is derived from the scalar version as follows. Let $\{\mathbf{z}_i\}$ be i.i.d. with $E(\mathbf{z}_i) = \boldsymbol{\mu}$ and $\text{Var}(\mathbf{z}_i) = \boldsymbol{\Sigma}$, and let $\boldsymbol{\lambda}$ be any vector of real numbers of the same dimension. Then $\{\boldsymbol{\lambda}'\mathbf{z}_n\}$ is a sequence of scalar random variables with $E(\boldsymbol{\lambda}'\mathbf{z}_n) = \boldsymbol{\lambda}'\boldsymbol{\mu}$ and $\text{Var}(\boldsymbol{\lambda}'\mathbf{z}_n) = \boldsymbol{\lambda}'\boldsymbol{\Sigma}\boldsymbol{\lambda}$. The scalar version of Linderberg-Levy then implies that

$$\sqrt{n}(\boldsymbol{\lambda}'\bar{\mathbf{z}}_n - \boldsymbol{\lambda}'\boldsymbol{\mu}) = \boldsymbol{\lambda}'\sqrt{n}(\bar{\mathbf{z}}_n - \boldsymbol{\mu}) \underset{\text{d}}{\rightarrow} N(0, \boldsymbol{\lambda}'\boldsymbol{\Sigma}\boldsymbol{\lambda}).$$

But this limit distribution is the distribution of $\boldsymbol{\lambda}'\mathbf{x}$ where $\mathbf{x} \sim N(\mathbf{0}, \boldsymbol{\Sigma})$. So by the Multivariate Convergence in Distribution Theorem stated a few pages back, $\{\sqrt{n}(\bar{\mathbf{z}}_n - \boldsymbol{\mu})\} \rightarrow_{\text{d}} \mathbf{x}$, which is the claim of the vector version of Lindeberg-Levy.)

QUESTIONS FOR REVIEW

1. (Usual convergence vs. convergence in probability) A sequence of real numbers is a trivial example of a sequence of random variables. Is it true that "$\lim_{n\to\infty} z_n = \alpha$" $\Rightarrow$ "$\text{plim}_{n\to\infty} z_n = \alpha$"? **Hint:** Look at the definition of plim. Since $\lim_{n\to\infty} z_n = \alpha$, $|z_n - \alpha| < \varepsilon$ for n sufficiently large.

2. (Alternative definition of convergence for vector sequences) Verify that the definition in the text of "$\mathbf{z}_n \rightarrow_{\text{m.s.}} \mathbf{z}$" is equivalent to

$$\lim_{n\to\infty} E[(\mathbf{z}_n - \mathbf{z})'(\mathbf{z}_n - \mathbf{z})] = 0.$$

Hint: $E[(\mathbf{z}_n - \mathbf{z})'(\mathbf{z}_n - \mathbf{z})] = E[(z_{n1} - z_1)^2] + \cdots + E[(z_{nK} - z_K)^2]$, where K is the dimension of $\mathbf{z}$. Similarly, verify that the definition in the text of

"$\mathbf{z}_n \to_p \boldsymbol{\alpha}$" is equivalent to

$$\lim_{n\to\infty} \text{Prob}\big((\mathbf{z}_n - \boldsymbol{\alpha})'(\mathbf{z}_n - \boldsymbol{\alpha}) > \varepsilon\big) = 0 \text{ for any } \varepsilon > 0.$$

3. Prove Lemma 2.4(c) from Lemma 2.4(a) and (b). **Hint:** $\mathbf{A}_n\mathbf{x}_n = (\mathbf{A}_n - \mathbf{A})\mathbf{x}_n + \mathbf{A}\mathbf{x}_n$. By (b), $(\mathbf{A}_n - \mathbf{A})\mathbf{x}_n \to_p \mathbf{0}$.

4. Suppose $\sqrt{n}(\hat{\theta}_n - \theta) \to_d N(0, \sigma^2)$. Does it follow that $\hat{\theta}_n \to_p \theta$? **Hint:**

$$\hat{\theta}_n - \theta = \frac{1}{\sqrt{n}} \cdot \sqrt{n}(\hat{\theta}_n - \theta), \quad \underset{n\to\infty}{\text{plim}} \frac{1}{\sqrt{n}} = 0.$$

5. (Combine Delta method with Lindeberg-Levy) Let $\{z_i\}$ be a sequence of i.i.d. (independently and identically distributed) random variables with $\text{E}(z_i) = \mu \neq 0$ and $\text{Var}(z_i) = \sigma^2$, and let $\bar{z}_n$ be the sample mean. Show that

$$\sqrt{n}\left(\frac{1}{\bar{z}_n} - \frac{1}{\mu}\right) \underset{d}{\to} N\left(0, \frac{\sigma^2}{\mu^4}\right).$$

Hint: In Lemma 2.5, set $\boldsymbol{\beta} = \mu$, $\mathbf{a}(\boldsymbol{\beta}) = 1/\mu$, $\mathbf{x}_n = \bar{z}_n$.

2.2 Fundamental Concepts in Time-Series Analysis

In this section, we define the very basic concepts in time-series analysis that will form an integral part of our language. The key concept is a **stochastic process**, which is just a fancy name for a sequence of random variables. If the index for the random variables is interpreted as representing time, the stochastic process is called a **time series**. If $\{z_i\}$ $(i = 1, 2, \dots)$ is a stochastic process, its **realization** or a **sample path** is an assignment to each i of a possible value of z_i. So a realization of $\{z_i\}$ is a sequence of real numbers. We will frequently use the term time series to mean both the realization and the process of which it is a realization.

Need for Ergodic Stationarity

The fundamental problem in time-series analysis is that we can observe the realization of the process only once. For example, the sample on the U.S. annual inflation rate for the period from 1946 to 1995 is a string of 50 particular numbers, which is just one possible outcome of the underlying stochastic process for the inflation rate; if history took a different course, we could have obtained a different sample.

If we could observe the history many times over, we could assemble many samples, each containing a possibly different string of 50 numbers. The mean inflation rate for, say, 1995 can then be estimated by taking the average of the 1995 inflation rate (the 50th element of the string) across those samples. The population mean thus estimated is sometimes called the **ensemble mean**. In the language of general equilibrium theory in economics, the ensemble mean is the average across all the possible different states of nature at any given calendar time.

Of course, it is not feasible to observe many different alternative histories. But if the distribution of the inflation rate remains unchanged (this property will be referred to as **stationarity**), the particular string of 50 numbers we do observe can be viewed as 50 different values from the *same* distribution. Furthermore, if the process is not too persistent (what's called **ergodicity** has this property), each element of the string will contain some information not available from the other elements, and, as shown below, the time average over the elements of the single string will be consistent for the ensemble mean.

Various Classes of Stochastic Processes[4]

Stationary Processes

A stochastic process $\{\mathbf{z}_i\}$ $(i = 1, 2, \ldots)$ is (strictly) stationary if, for any given finite integer r and for any set of subscripts, $i_1, i_2, \ldots, i_r$, the joint distribution of $(\mathbf{z}_i, \mathbf{z}_{i_1}, \mathbf{z}_{i_2}, \ldots, \mathbf{z}_{i_r})$ depends only on $i_1 - i, i_2 - i, i_3 - i, \ldots, i_r - i$ but not on i. For example, the joint distribution of $(\mathbf{z}_1, \mathbf{z}_5)$ is the same as that of $(\mathbf{z}_{12}, \mathbf{z}_{16})$. What matters for the distribution is the relative position in the sequence. In particular, the distribution of $\mathbf{z}_i$ does not depend on the absolute position, i, of $\mathbf{z}_i$, so the mean, variance, and other higher moments, if they exist, remain the same across i. The definition also implies that any transformation (function) of a stationary process is itself stationary, that is, if $\{\mathbf{z}_i\}$ is stationary, then $\{f(\mathbf{z}_i)\}$ is.[5] For example, $\{\mathbf{z}_i\mathbf{z}_i'\}$ is stationary if $\{\mathbf{z}_i\}$ is.

> **Example 2.1 (i.i.d. sequences):** A sequence of independent and identically distributed random variables is a stationary process that exhibits no serial dependence.

[4]Many of the concepts collected in this subsection can also be found in Section 4.7 of Davidson and MacKinnon (1993).

[5]The function $f(\cdot)$ needs to be "measurable" so that $f(\mathbf{z}_i)$ is a well-defined random variable. Any continuous function is measurable. In what follows, we won't bother to add the qualifier "measurable" when a function f of a random variable is understood to be a random variable.

Example 2.2 (constant series): Draw z_1 from some distribution and then set $z_i = z_1$ $(i = 2, 3, \dots)$. So the value of the process is frozen at the initial date. The process $\{z_i\}$ thus created is a stationary process that exhibits maximum serial dependence.

Evidently, if a vector process $\{\mathbf{z}_i\}$ is stationary, then each element of the vector forms a univariate stationary process. The converse, however, is not true.

Example 2.3 (element-wise vs. joint stationarity): Let $\{\varepsilon_i\}$ $(i = 1, 2, \dots)$ be a scalar i.i.d. process. Create a two-dimensional process $\{\mathbf{z}_i\}$ from it by defining $z_{i1} = \varepsilon_i$ and $z_{i2} = \varepsilon_1$ The scalar process $\{z_{i1}\}$ is stationary (this is the process of Example 2.1). The scalar process $\{z_{i2}\}$, too, is stationary (the Example 2.2 process). The vector process $\{\mathbf{z}_i\}$, however, is not (jointly) stationary, because the (joint) distribution of $\mathbf{z}_1$ $(= (\varepsilon_1, \varepsilon_1)')$ differs from that of $\mathbf{z}_2$ $(= (\varepsilon_2, \varepsilon_1)')$.

Most aggregate time series such as GDP are not stationary because they exhibit time trends. A less obvious example of nonstationarity is international exchange rates, which are alleged to have increasing variance. But many time series with trend can be reduced to stationary processes. A process is called **trend stationary** if it is stationary after subtracting from it a (usually linear) function of time (which is the index i). If a process is not stationary but its first difference, $z_i - z_{i-1}$, is stationary, $\{z_i\}$ is called **difference stationary**. Trend-stationary processes and difference-stationary processes will be studied in Chapter 9.

Covariance Stationary Processes

A stochastic process $\{\mathbf{z}_i\}$ is **weakly** (or **covariance**) **stationary** if:

(i) $\mathrm{E}(\mathbf{z}_i)$ does not depend on i, and

(ii) $\mathrm{Cov}(\mathbf{z}_i, \mathbf{z}_{i-j})$ exists, is finite, and depends only on j but not on i (for example, $\mathrm{Cov}(\mathbf{z}_1, \mathbf{z}_5)$ equals $\mathrm{Cov}(\mathbf{z}_{12}, \mathbf{z}_{16})$).

The relative, not absolute, position in the sequence matters for the mean and covariance of a covariance-stationary process. Evidently, if a sequence is (strictly) stationary *and* if the variance and covariances are finite, then the sequence is weakly stationary (hence the term "strict"). An example of a covariance-stationary but not strictly stationary process will be given in Example 2.4 below.

The **j-th order autocovariance**, denoted $\mathbf{\Gamma}_j$, is defined as

$$\mathbf{\Gamma}_j \equiv \text{Cov}(\mathbf{z}_i, \mathbf{z}_{i-j}) \quad (j = 0, 1, 2, \dots).$$

The term "auto" comes about because the two random variables are taken from the same process. $\mathbf{\Gamma}_j$ does not depend on i because of covariance-stationarity. Also by covariance stationarity, $\mathbf{\Gamma}_j$ satisfies

$$\mathbf{\Gamma}_j = \mathbf{\Gamma}'_{-j}. \tag{2.2.1}$$

(Showing this is a review question below.) The 0-th order autocovariance is the variance $\mathbf{\Gamma}_0 = \text{Var}(\mathbf{z}_i)$. The processes in Examples 2.1 and 2.2 are covariance stationary if the variance exists and is finite. For the process of Example 2.1, $\mathbf{\Gamma}_0$ is the variance of the distribution and $\mathbf{\Gamma}_j = \mathbf{0}$ for $j \geq 1$. For the process of Example 2.2, $\mathbf{\Gamma}_j = \mathbf{\Gamma}_0$.

For a scalar covariance stationary process $\{z_i\}$, the j-th order autocovariance is now a scalar. If γ_j is this autocovariance, it satisfies

$$\gamma_j = \gamma_{-j}. \tag{2.2.2}$$

Take a string of n successive values, $(z_i, z_{i+1}, \dots, z_{i+n-1})$, from a scalar process. By covariance stationarity, its $n \times n$ variance-covariance matrix is the same as that of $(z_1, z_2, \dots z_n)$ and is a band spectrum matrix:

$$\text{Var}(z_i, z_{i+1}, \dots z_{i+n-1}) = \begin{bmatrix} \gamma_0 & \gamma_1 & \gamma_2 & \cdots & \gamma_{n-1} \\ \gamma_1 & \gamma_0 & \gamma_1 & \cdots & \gamma_{n-2} \\ \vdots & \ddots & \ddots & \ddots & \vdots \\ \gamma_{n-2} & \cdots & \gamma_1 & \gamma_0 & \gamma_1 \\ \gamma_{n-1} & \cdots & \gamma_2 & \gamma_1 & \gamma_0 \end{bmatrix}.$$

This is called the **autocovariance matrix** of the process. The **j-th order autocorrelation coefficient**, ρ_j, is defined as

$$j\text{-th order autocorrelation coefficient} \equiv$$
$$\rho_j \equiv \frac{\gamma_j}{\gamma_0} = \frac{\text{Cov}(z_i, z_{i-j})}{\text{Var}(z_i)} \quad (j = 1, 2, \dots). \tag{2.2.3}$$

For $j = 0$, $\rho_j = 1$. The plot of $\{\rho_j\}$ against $j = 0, 1, 2, \dots$ is called the **correlogram**.

White Noise Processes

A very important class of weakly stationary processes is a **white noise process**, a process with zero mean and no serial correlation:

a covariance-stationary process $\{\mathbf{z}_i\}$ is **white noise** if

$$\mathrm{E}(\mathbf{z}_i) = \mathbf{0} \text{ and } \mathrm{Cov}(\mathbf{z}_i, \mathbf{z}_{i-j}) = \mathbf{0} \text{ for } j \neq 0.$$

Clearly, an independently and identically distributed (i.i.d.) sequence with mean zero and finite variance is a special case of a white noise process. For this reason, it is called an **independent white noise process**.

Example 2.4 (a white noise process that is not strictly stationary[6]): Let w be a random variable uniformly distributed in the interval $(0, 2\pi)$, and define

$$z_i = \cos(iw) \quad (i = 1, 2, \dots).$$

It can be shown that $\mathrm{E}(z_i) = 0$, $\mathrm{Var}(z_i) = 1/2$, and $\mathrm{Cov}(z_i, z_j) = 0$ for $i \neq j$. So $\{z_i\}$ is white noise. However, clearly, it is not an independent white noise process. It is not even strictly stationary.

Ergodicity

A stationary process $\{z_i\}$ is said to be **ergodic** if, for any two bounded functions $f : \mathbb{R}^k \to \mathbb{R}$ and $g : \mathbb{R}^\ell \to \mathbb{R}$,

$$\begin{aligned}\lim_{n\to\infty} \left| \mathrm{E}[f(z_i, \dots, z_{i+k}) g(z_{i+n}, \dots, z_{i+n+\ell})] \right| \\ = \left| \mathrm{E}[f(z_i, \dots, z_{i+k})] \right| \left| \mathrm{E}[g(z_{i+n}, \dots, z_{i+n+\ell})] \right|.\end{aligned}$$

Heuristically, a stationary process is ergodic if it is asymptotically independent, that is, if any two random variables positioned far apart in the sequence are almost independently distributed. A stationary process that is ergodic will be called **ergodic stationary**. Ergodic stationarity will be an integral ingredient in developing large-sample theory because of the following property.

Ergodic Theorem: *(See, e.g., Theorem 9.5.5 of Karlin and Taylor (1975).) Let $\{\mathbf{z}_i\}$ be a stationary and ergodic process with $\mathrm{E}(\mathbf{z}_i) = \boldsymbol{\mu}$.*[7] *Then*

[6] Drawn from Example 7.8 of Anderson (1971, p. 379).

[7] So the mean is assumed to exist and is finite.

$$\bar{\mathbf{z}}_n \equiv \frac{1}{n}\sum_{i=1}^{n} \mathbf{z}_i \underset{\text{a.s.}}{\rightarrow} \boldsymbol{\mu}.$$

The Ergodic Theorem, therefore, is a substantial generalization of Kolmogorov's LLN. Serial dependence, which is ruled out by the i.i.d. assumption in Kolmogorov's LLN, is allowed in the Ergodic Theorem, provided that it disappears in the long run. Since, for any (measurable) function $f(\cdot)$, $\{f(\mathbf{z}_i)\}$ is ergodic stationary whenever $\{\mathbf{z}_i\}$ is, this theorem implies that any moment of a stationary and ergodic process (if it exists and is finite) is consistently estimated by the sample moment. For example, suppose $\{\mathbf{z}_i\}$ is stationary and ergodic and $\mathrm{E}(\mathbf{z}_i\mathbf{z}_i')$ exists and is finite. Then, $\frac{1}{n}\sum_i \mathbf{z}_i\mathbf{z}_i'$ is consistent for $\mathrm{E}(\mathbf{z}_i\mathbf{z}_i')$.

The simplest example of ergodic stationary processes is independent white noise processes. (White noise processes where independence is weakened to no serial correlation are not necessarily ergodic; Example 2.4 above is an example.) Another important example is the AR(1) process satisfying

$$z_i = c + \rho z_{i-1} + \varepsilon_i, \quad |\rho| < 1,$$

where $\{\varepsilon_i\}$ is independent white noise.

Martingales

Let x_i be an element of $\mathbf{z}_i$. The scalar process $\{x_i\}$ is called a **martingale with respect to** $\{\mathbf{z}_i\}$ if

$$\mathrm{E}(x_i \mid \mathbf{z}_{i-1}, \mathbf{z}_{i-2}, \ldots, \mathbf{z}_1) = x_{i-1} \text{ for } i \geq 2.^8 \tag{2.2.4}$$

The conditioning set $(\mathbf{z}_{i-1}, \mathbf{z}_{i-2}, \ldots, \mathbf{z}_1)$ is often called the **information set** at point (date) $i-1$. $\{x_i\}$ is called simply a **martingale** if the information set is its own past values $(x_{i-1}, x_{i-2}, \ldots, x_1)$. If $\mathbf{z}_i$ includes x_i, then $\{x_i\}$ is a martingale, because

$$\begin{aligned}
&\mathrm{E}(x_i \mid x_{i-1}, x_{i-2}, \ldots, x_1)\\
&= \mathrm{E}[\mathrm{E}(x_i \mid \mathbf{z}_{i-1}, \mathbf{z}_{i-2}, \ldots, \mathbf{z}_1) \mid x_{i-1}, x_{i-2}, \ldots, x_1]\\
&\qquad \text{(Law of Iterated Expectations)}\\
&= \mathrm{E}(x_{i-1} \mid x_{i-1}, x_{i-2}, \ldots, x_1) = x_{i-1}.
\end{aligned}$$

[8]If the process started in the infinite past so that i runs from $-\infty$ to $+\infty$, the definition is $\mathrm{E}(x_i \mid \mathbf{z}_{i-1}, \mathbf{z}_{i-2}, \ldots) = x_{i-1}$, and the qualifier "$i \geq 2$" is not needed. Whether the process started in the infinite past or in date $i = 1$ is not important for large-sample theory to be developed below. What will matter is that the process starts before the sample period.

A vector process $\{\mathbf{z}_i\}$ is called a **martingale** if

$$\mathrm{E}(\mathbf{z}_i \mid \mathbf{z}_{i-1}, \dots, \mathbf{z}_1) = \mathbf{z}_{i-1} \text{ for } i \geq 2. \tag{2.2.5}$$

Example 2.5 (Hall's Martingale Hypothesis): Let $\mathbf{z}_i$ be a vector containing a set of macroeconomic variables (such as the money supply or GDP) including aggregate consumption c_i for period i. Hall's (1978) martingale hypothesis is that consumption is a martingale with respect to $\{\mathbf{z}_i\}$:

$$\mathrm{E}(c_i \mid \mathbf{z}_{i-1}, \mathbf{z}_{i-2}, \dots, \mathbf{z}_1) = c_{i-1}.$$

This formalizes the notion in consumption theory called "consumption smoothing": the consumer, wishing to avoid fluctuations in the standard of living, adjusts consumption in date $i-1$ to the level such that no change in subsequent consumption is anticipated.

Random Walks

An important example of martingales is a **random walk**. Let $\{\mathbf{g}_i\}$ be a vector independent white noise process (so it is i.i.d. with mean $\mathbf{0}$ and finite variance matrix). A random walk, $\{\mathbf{z}_i\}$, is a sequence of cumulative sums:

$$\mathbf{z}_1 = \mathbf{g}_1,\ \mathbf{z}_2 = \mathbf{g}_1 + \mathbf{g}_2, \dots,\ \mathbf{z}_i = \mathbf{g}_1 + \mathbf{g}_2 + \cdots + \mathbf{g}_i, \cdots. \tag{2.2.6}$$

Given the sequence $\{\mathbf{z}_i\}$, the underlying independent white noise sequence, $\{\mathbf{g}_i\}$, can be backed out by taking first differences:

$$\mathbf{g}_1 = \mathbf{z}_1,\ \mathbf{g}_2 = \mathbf{z}_2 - \mathbf{z}_1, \dots,\ \mathbf{g}_i = \mathbf{z}_i - \mathbf{z}_{i-1}, \dots. \tag{2.2.7}$$

So the first difference of a random walk is independent white noise. A random walk is a martingale because

$$\begin{aligned}
\mathrm{E}(\mathbf{z}_i \mid \mathbf{z}_{i-1}, \dots, \mathbf{z}_1) &= \mathrm{E}(\mathbf{z}_i \mid \mathbf{g}_{i-1}, \dots, \mathbf{g}_1) \quad \text{(since } (\mathbf{z}_{i-1}, \dots, \mathbf{z}_1) \text{ and} \\
&\qquad (\mathbf{g}_{i-1}, \dots, \mathbf{g}_1) \text{ have the same information, as just seen)} \\
&= \mathrm{E}(\mathbf{g}_1 + \mathbf{g}_2 + \cdots + \mathbf{g}_i \mid \mathbf{g}_{i-1}, \dots, \mathbf{g}_1) \\
&= \mathrm{E}(\mathbf{g}_i \mid \mathbf{g}_{i-1}, \dots, \mathbf{g}_1) + (\mathbf{g}_1 + \cdots + \mathbf{g}_{i-1}) \\
&= \mathbf{g}_1 + \cdots + \mathbf{g}_{i-1} \quad (\mathrm{E}(\mathbf{g}_i \mid \mathbf{g}_{i-1}, \dots, \mathbf{g}_1) = \mathbf{0} \text{ as } \{\mathbf{g}_i\} \text{ is independent white noise)} \\
&= \mathbf{z}_{i-1} \quad \text{(by the definition of } \mathbf{z}_{i-1}\text{)}.
\end{aligned} \tag{2.2.8}$$

Martingale Difference Sequences

A vector process $\{\mathbf{g}_i\}$ with $\mathrm{E}(\mathbf{g}_i) = \mathbf{0}$ is called a **martingale difference sequence (m.d.s.)** or **martingale differences** if the expectation conditional on its past values, too, is zero:

$$\mathrm{E}(\mathbf{g}_i \mid \mathbf{g}_{i-1}, \mathbf{g}_{i-2}, \ldots, \mathbf{g}_1) = \mathbf{0} \quad \text{for} \quad i \geq 2. \tag{2.2.9}$$

The process is so called because the cumulative sum $\{\mathbf{z}_i\}$ created from a martingale difference sequence $\{\mathbf{g}_i\}$ is a martingale; the proof is the same as in (2.2.8). Conversely, if $\{\mathbf{z}_i\}$ is martingale, the first differences created as in (2.2.7) are a martingale difference sequence.

A martingale difference sequence has no serial correlation (i.e., $\mathrm{Cov}(\mathbf{g}_i, \mathbf{g}_{i-j}) = \mathbf{0}$ for all i and $j \neq 0$). A proof of this claim is as follows.

PROOF. First note that we can assume, without loss of generality, that $j \geq 1$. Since the mean is zero, it suffices to show that $\mathrm{E}(\mathbf{g}_i \mathbf{g}'_{i-j}) = \mathbf{0}$. So consider rewriting it as follows.

$$\begin{aligned}
&\mathrm{E}(\mathbf{g}_i \mathbf{g}'_{i-j}) \\
&= \mathrm{E}[\mathrm{E}(\mathbf{g}_i \mathbf{g}'_{i-j} \mid \mathbf{g}_{i-j})] \quad \text{(by the Law of Total Expectations)} \\
&= \mathrm{E}[\mathrm{E}(\mathbf{g}_i \mid \mathbf{g}_{i-j})\mathbf{g}'_{i-j}] \quad \text{(by the linearity of conditional expectations).}
\end{aligned}$$

Now, since $j \geq 1$, $(\mathbf{g}_{i-1}, \ldots, \mathbf{g}_{i-j}, \ldots, \mathbf{g}_1)$ includes $\mathbf{g}_{i-j}$. Therefore,

$$\begin{aligned}
&\mathrm{E}(\mathbf{g}_i \mid \mathbf{g}_{i-j}) \\
&= \mathrm{E}[\mathrm{E}(\mathbf{g}_i \mid \mathbf{g}_{i-1}, \ldots, \mathbf{g}_{i-j}, \ldots, \mathbf{g}_1) \mid \mathbf{g}_{i-j}] \quad \text{(by the Law of Iterated Expectations)} \\
&= \mathbf{0}.
\end{aligned}$$

The last equality holds because $\mathrm{E}(\mathbf{g}_i \mid \mathbf{g}_{i-1}, \ldots, \mathbf{g}_{i-j}, \ldots, \mathbf{g}_1) = \mathbf{0}$. ■

ARCH Processes

An example of martingale differences, frequently used in analyzing asset returns, is an autoregressive conditional heteroskedastic (**ARCH**) process introduced by Engle (1982). A process $\{g_i\}$ is said to be an **ARCH process of order 1 (ARCH(1))** if it can be written as

$$g_i = \sqrt{\zeta + \alpha g_{i-1}^2} \cdot \varepsilon_i, \tag{2.2.10}$$

where $\{\varepsilon_i\}$ is i.i.d. with mean zero and unit variance. If g_1 is the initial value of the process, we can use (2.2.10) to calculate subsequent values of g_i. For example,

$$g_2 = \sqrt{\zeta + \alpha g_1^2} \cdot \varepsilon_2.$$

More generally, g_i $(i \geq 2)$ is a function of g_1 and $(\varepsilon_2, \varepsilon_3, \ldots, \varepsilon_i)$. Therefore, ε_i is independent of $(g_1, g_2, \ldots, g_{i-1})$. It is then easy to show that $\{g_i\}$ is an m.d.s. because

$$\begin{aligned}
&\mathrm{E}(g_i \mid g_{i-1}, g_{i-2}, \ldots, g_1) && (2.2.11)\\
&= \mathrm{E}\big(\sqrt{\zeta + \alpha g_{i-1}^2} \cdot \varepsilon_i \mid g_{i-1}, g_{i-2}, \ldots, g_1\big)\\
&= \sqrt{\zeta + \alpha g_{i-1}^2}\, \mathrm{E}(\varepsilon_i \mid g_{i-1}, g_{i-2}, \ldots, g_1)\\
&= \sqrt{\zeta + \alpha g_{i-1}^2}\, \mathrm{E}(\varepsilon_i) \quad (\text{since } \varepsilon_i \text{ is independent of } (g_1, g_2, \ldots, g_{i-1}))\\
&= 0 \quad (\text{since } \mathrm{E}(\varepsilon_i) = 0). && (2.2.12)
\end{aligned}$$

By a similar argument, it follows that

$$\mathrm{E}(g_i^2 \mid g_{i-1}, g_{i-2}, \ldots, g_1) = \zeta + \alpha g_{i-1}^2. \tag{2.2.13}$$

So the conditional second moment (which equals the conditional variance since $\mathrm{E}(g_i \mid g_1, g_2, \ldots, g_{i-1}) = 0$) is a function of its own history of the process. In this sense the process exhibits **own conditional heteroskedasticity**. It can be shown (see, e.g., Engle, 1982) that the process is strictly stationary and ergodic if $|\alpha| < 1$, provided that g_1 is a draw from an appropriate distribution or provided that the process started in the infinite past. If g_i is stationary, the *un*conditional second moment is easy to obtain. Taking the unconditional expectation of both sides of (2.2.13) and noting that

$$\mathrm{E}[\mathrm{E}(g_i^2 \mid g_{i-1}, g_{i-2}, \ldots, g_1)] = \mathrm{E}(g_i^2) \quad \text{and} \quad \mathrm{E}(g_i^2) = \mathrm{E}(g_{i-1}^2) \text{ if } g_i \text{ is stationary},$$

we obtain

$$\mathrm{E}(g_i^2) = \zeta + \alpha\, \mathrm{E}(g_i^2) \quad \text{or} \quad \mathrm{E}(g_i^2) = \frac{\zeta}{1-\alpha}. \tag{2.2.14}$$

If $\alpha > 0$, this model captures the characteristic found for asset returns that large values tend to be followed by large values. (For more details of ARCH processes, see, e.g., Hamilton, 1994, Section 21.1.)

Different Formulation of Lack of Serial Dependence

Evidently, an independent white noise process is a stationary martingale difference sequence with finite variance. And, as just seen, a martingale difference sequence has no serial correlation. Thus, we have three formulations of a lack of serial dependence for zero-mean covariance stationary processes. They are, in the order of strength,

$$\begin{aligned} &(1)\ \text{“}\{\mathbf{g}_i\}\text{ is independent white noise.”} \\ \Rightarrow\ &(2)\ \text{“}\{\mathbf{g}_i\}\text{ is stationary m.d.s. with finite variance.”} \\ \Rightarrow\ &(3)\ \text{“}\{\mathbf{g}_i\}\text{ is white noise.”} \end{aligned} \tag{2.2.15}$$

Condition (1) is stronger than (2) because there are processes satisfying (2) but not (1). An ARCH(1) process (2.2.10) with $|\alpha| < 1$ is an example. Figure 2.1 shows how a realization of a process satisfying (1) typically differs from that satisfying (2). Figure 2.1, Panel (a), plots a realization of a sequence of independent and normally distributed random variables with mean 0 and unit variance. Panel (b) plots an ARCH(1) process (2.2.10) with $\zeta = 0.2$ and $\alpha = 0.8$ (so that the unconditional variance, $\zeta/(1-\alpha)$, is unity as in panel (a)), where the value of the i.i.d. sequence ε_i in (2.2.10) is taken from Figure 2.1, Panel (a), so that the sign in both panels is the same at all points. The series in Panel (b) is generally less volatile than in Panel (a), but at some points it is much more volatile. Nevertheless, the series is stationary.

Condition (2) is stronger than (3); the process in Example 2.4 is white noise, but (as you will show in a review question) it does not satisfy (2).

The CLT for Ergodic Stationary Martingale Differences Sequences

The following CLT extends the Lindeberg-Levy CLT to stationary and ergodic m.d.s.

Ergodic Stationary Martingale Differences CLT (Billingsley, 1961): *Let* $\{\mathbf{g}_i\}$ *be a vector martingale difference sequence that is stationary and ergodic with* $\mathrm{E}(\mathbf{g}_i\mathbf{g}_i') = \boldsymbol{\Sigma}$,[9] *and let* $\bar{\mathbf{g}} \equiv \frac{1}{n}\sum_{i=1}^{n}\mathbf{g}_i$. *Then*

$$\sqrt{n}\,\bar{\mathbf{g}} = \frac{1}{\sqrt{n}}\sum_{i=1}^{n}\mathbf{g}_i \underset{d}{\rightarrow} N(\mathbf{0}, \boldsymbol{\Sigma}).$$

[9] Since $\{\mathbf{g}_i\}$ is stationary, this matrix of cross moments does not depend on i. Also, since a cross moment matrix is indicated, it is implicitly assumed that all the cross moments exist and are finite.

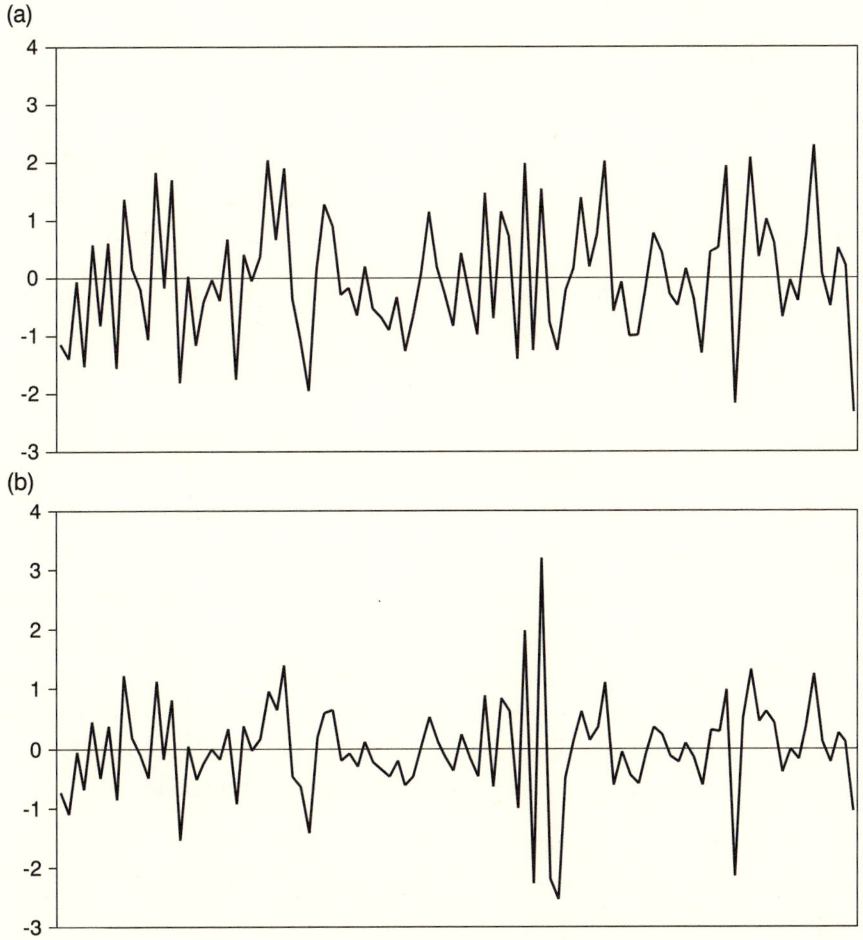

Figure 2.1: Plots of Serially Uncorrelated Time Series: (a) An i.i.d. $N(0, 1)$ sequence. (b) ARCH(1) with shocks taken from panel (a)

Unlike in the Lindeberg-Levy CLT, there is no need to subtract the mean from $\mathbf{g}_i$ because the unconditional mean of an m.d.s. is by definition zero. For the same reason, $\mathbf{\Sigma}$ also equals $\text{Var}(\mathbf{g}_i)$. This CLT, being applicable not just to i.i.d. sequences but also to stationary martingale differences such as ARCH(1) processes, is more general than Lindeberg-Levy.

We have presented an LLN for serially correlated processes in the form of the Ergodic Theorem. A central limit theorem for serially correlated processes will be presented in Chapter 6.

QUESTIONS FOR REVIEW

1. Prove that $\mathbf{\Gamma}_{-j} = \mathbf{\Gamma}'_j$. **Hint:** $\text{Cov}(\mathbf{z}_i, \mathbf{z}_{i-j}) = \text{E}[(\mathbf{z}_i - \boldsymbol{\mu})(\mathbf{z}_{i-j} - \boldsymbol{\mu})']$ where $\boldsymbol{\mu} = \text{E}(\mathbf{z}_i)$. By covariance-stationarity, $\text{Cov}(\mathbf{z}_i, \mathbf{z}_{i-j}) = \text{Cov}(\mathbf{z}_{i+j}, \mathbf{z}_i)$.

2. (Forecasting white noise) For the white noise process of Example 2.4, $\text{E}(z_i) = 0$. What is $\text{E}(z_i \mid z_1)$ for $i \geq 2$? **Hint:** You should be able to forecast the future exactly if you know the value of z_1. Is the process an m.d.s? [Answer: No.]

3. (No anticipated changes in martingales) Suppose $\{x_i\}$ is a martingale with respect to $\{\mathbf{z}_i\}$. Show that $\text{E}(x_{i+j} \mid \mathbf{z}_{i-1}, \mathbf{z}_{i-2}, \dots, \mathbf{z}_1) = x_{i-1}$ and $\text{E}(x_{i+j+1} - x_{i+j} \mid \mathbf{z}_{i-1}, \mathbf{z}_{i-2}, \dots, \mathbf{z}_1) = 0$ for $j = 0, 1, \dots$. **Hint:** Use the Law of Iterated Expectations.

4. Let $\{x_i\}$ be a sequence of real numbers that change with i and $\{\varepsilon_i\}$ be a sequence of i.i.d. random variables with mean 0 and finite variance. Is $\{x_i \cdot \varepsilon_i\}$ i.i.d.? [Answer: No.] Is it serially independent? [Answer: Yes.] An m.d.s? [Answer: Yes.] Stationary? [Answer: No.]

5. Show that a random walk is nonstationary. **Hint:** Check the variance.

6. (The first difference of a martingale is a martingale difference sequence) Let $\{\mathbf{z}_i\}$ be a martingale. Show that the process $\{\mathbf{g}_i\}$ created by (2.2.7) is an m.d.s. **Hint:** $(\mathbf{g}_1, \dots, \mathbf{g}_i)$ and $(\mathbf{z}_1, \dots, \mathbf{z}_i)$ share the same information.

7. (An m.d.s. that is not independent white noise) Let $g_i = \varepsilon_i \cdot \varepsilon_{i-1}$, where $\{\varepsilon_i\}$ is an independent white noise process. Evidently, $\{g_i\}$ is not i.i.d. Verify that $\{g_i\}$ $(i = 2, 3, \dots)$ is an m.d.s. **Hint:** $\text{E}(g_i \mid g_{i-1}, \dots, g_2) = \text{E}[\text{E}(\varepsilon_i \cdot \varepsilon_{i-1} \mid \varepsilon_{i-1}, \dots, \varepsilon_1) \mid \varepsilon_{i-1}\cdot\varepsilon_{i-2}, \varepsilon_{i-2}\cdot\varepsilon_{i-3}, \dots, \varepsilon_2\cdot\varepsilon_1]$.

8. (Revision of expectations is m.d.s.) Let $\{y_i\}$ be a process such that $\text{E}(y_i \mid y_{i-1}, y_{i-2}, \dots, y_1)$ exists and is finite, and define $r_{i1} \equiv \text{E}(y_i \mid y_{i-1}, y_{i-2}, \dots, y_1) - \text{E}(y_i \mid y_{i-2}, y_{i-3}, \dots, y_1)$. So r_{i1} is the change in the expectation as one more observation is added to the information set. Show that $\{r_{i1}\}$ $(i \geq 2)$ is an m.d.s. with respect to $\{y_i\}$.

9. (Billingsley is stronger than Lindeberg-Levy) Let $\{\mathbf{z}_i\}$ be an i.i.d. sequence with $\text{E}(\mathbf{z}_i) = \boldsymbol{\mu}$ and $\text{Var}(\mathbf{z}_i) = \mathbf{\Sigma}$, as in the Lindeberg-Levy CLT. Use the Martingale Differences CLT to prove the claim of the Lindeberg-Levy CLT, namely, that $\sqrt{n}(\bar{\mathbf{z}}_n - \boldsymbol{\mu}) \to_{\text{d}} N(\mathbf{0}, \mathbf{\Sigma})$. **Hint:** $\{\mathbf{z}_i - \boldsymbol{\mu}\}$ is an independent white noise process and hence is an ergodic stationary m.d.s.

2.3 Large-Sample Distribution of the OLS Estimator

The importance in econometrics of the OLS procedure, originally developed for the classical regression model of Chapter 1, lies in the fact that it has good asymptotic properties for a class of models, different from the classical model, that are useful in economics. Of those models, the model presented in this section has probably the widest range of economic applications. No specific distributional assumption (such as the normality of the error term) is required to derive the asymptotic distribution of the OLS estimator. The requirement in finite-sample theory that the regressors be strictly exogenous or "fixed" is replaced by a much weaker requirement that they be "predetermined." (For the sake of completeness, the appendix develops the parallel asymptotic theory for a model with "fixed" regressors.)

The Model

We use the term the **data generating process** (**DGP**) for the stochastic process that generated the finite sample $(\mathbf{y}, \mathbf{X})$. Therefore, if we specify the DGP, the joint distribution of the finite sample $(\mathbf{y}, \mathbf{X})$ can be determined. In finite-sample theory, where the sample size is fixed and finite, we defined a model as a set of the joint distributions of $(\mathbf{y}, \mathbf{X})$. In large-sample theory, a model is stated as a set of DGPs. The model we study is the set of DGPs satisfying the following set of assumptions.

Assumption 2.1 (linearity):

$$y_i = \mathbf{x}_i'\boldsymbol{\beta} + \varepsilon_i \quad (i = 1, 2, \ldots, n)$$

where $\mathbf{x}_i$ is a K-dimensional vector of explanatory variables (regressors), $\boldsymbol{\beta}$ is a K-dimensional coefficient vector, and ε_i is the unobservable error term.

Assumption 2.2 (ergodic stationarity): *The $(K+1)$-dimensional vector stochastic process $\{y_i, \mathbf{x}_i\}$ is jointly stationary and ergodic.*

Assumption 2.3 (predetermined regressors): *All the regressors are* ***predetermined*** *in the sense that they are orthogonal to the* contemporaneous *error term:* $\mathrm{E}(x_{ik}\varepsilon_i) = 0$ *for all i and k $(= 1, 2, \ldots, K)$.*[10] *This can be written as*

[10]Our definition of the term *predetermined* is not universal. Some authors say that the regressors are predetermined if $\mathrm{E}(\mathbf{x}_{i-j} \cdot \varepsilon_i) = \mathbf{0}$ for all $j \geq 0$, not just for $j = 0$. That is, the error term is orthogonal not only to the contemporaneous but also the past regressors. In Koopmans and Hood (1953), the regressors are said to be predetermined if ε_i is independent of $\mathbf{x}_{i-j}$ for all $j \geq 0$. Our definition is the same as Hamilton's (1994).

$$\mathrm{E}[\mathbf{x}_i \cdot (y_i - \mathbf{x}_i'\boldsymbol{\beta})] = \mathbf{0} \quad \textit{or equivalently} \quad \mathrm{E}(\mathbf{g}_i) = \mathbf{0}$$

where $\mathbf{g}_i \equiv \mathbf{x}_i \cdot \varepsilon_i$.

Assumption 2.4 (rank condition): *The* $K \times K$ *matrix* $\mathrm{E}(\mathbf{x}_i\mathbf{x}_i')$ *is nonsingular (and hence finite). We denote this matrix by* $\boldsymbol{\Sigma}_{\mathbf{xx}}$.

Assumption 2.5 ($\mathbf{g}_i$ is a martingale difference sequence with finite second moments): $\{\mathbf{g}_i\}$ *is a martingale difference sequence (so* a fortiori $\mathrm{E}(\mathbf{g}_i) = \mathbf{0}$*). The* $K \times K$ *matrix of cross moments,* $\mathrm{E}(\mathbf{g}_i\mathbf{g}_i')$*, is nonsingular. We use* $\mathbf{S}$ *for* $\mathrm{Avar}(\bar{\mathbf{g}})$ *(the variance of the asymptotic distribution of* $\sqrt{n}\,\bar{\mathbf{g}}$*, where* $\bar{\mathbf{g}} \equiv \frac{1}{n}\sum_i \mathbf{g}_i$*). By Assumption 2.2 and the ergodic stationary Martingale Differences CLT,* $\mathbf{S} = \mathrm{E}(\mathbf{g}_i\mathbf{g}_i')$.

The first assumption is just reproducing Assumption 1.1. The rest of the assumptions require some lengthy comments.

- (Ergodic stationarity) A trivial but important special case of ergodic stationarity is that $\{y_i, \mathbf{x}_i\}$ is i.i.d., that is, the sample is a random sample.[11] Most existing microdata on households are random samples, with observations randomly drawn from a population of a nation's households. Thus, we are in no way ruling out models that use cross-section data.

- (The model accommodates conditional heteroskedasticity) If $\{y_i, \mathbf{x}_i\}$ is stationary, then the error term $\varepsilon_i = y_i - \mathbf{x}_i'\boldsymbol{\beta}$ is also stationary. Thus, Assumption 2.2 implies that the unconditional second moment $\mathrm{E}(\varepsilon_i^2)$—if it exists and is finite—is constant across i. That is, the error term is unconditionally homoskedastic. Yet the error can be conditionally heteroskedastic in that the conditional second moment, $\mathrm{E}(\varepsilon_i^2 \mid \mathbf{x}_i)$, can depend on $\mathbf{x}_i$. An example in which the error is homoskedastic unconditionally but not conditionally is included in Section 2.6, where the consequence of superimposing conditional homoskedasticity (that $\mathrm{E}(\varepsilon_i^2 \mid \mathbf{x}_i) = \sigma^2$) on the model will be explored.

- ($\mathrm{E}(\mathbf{x}_i \cdot \varepsilon_i) = \mathbf{0}$ vs. $\mathrm{E}(\varepsilon_i \mid \mathbf{x}_i) = 0$) Sometimes, instead of the orthogonality condition $\mathrm{E}(\mathbf{x}_i \cdot \varepsilon_i) = \mathbf{0}$, it is assumed that the error is unrelated in the sense that $\mathrm{E}(\varepsilon_i \mid \mathbf{x}_i) = 0$. This is stronger than the orthogonality condition because it

[11] Actually, once the independence assumption is made, the same large-sample results can be proved for the more general case where $\{y_i, \mathbf{x}_i\}$ is independently but not identically distributed (i.n.i.d.), provided that some conditions on higher moments of the joint distribution of $(\varepsilon_i, \mathbf{x}_i)$ are satisfied. We will not entertain this generalization because the i.i.d. assumption is satisfied in most microdata sets.

implies that, for any (measurable) function f of $\mathbf{x}_i$, $f(\mathbf{x}_i)$ is orthogonal to ε_i:

$$\mathrm{E}[f(\mathbf{x}_i)\varepsilon_i] = \mathrm{E}[\mathrm{E}(f(\mathbf{x}_i)\varepsilon_i \mid \mathbf{x}_i)] = \mathrm{E}[f(\mathbf{x}_i)\,\mathrm{E}(\varepsilon_i \mid \mathbf{x}_i)] = 0.$$

In rational expectations models, this stronger condition is satisfied, but for the purpose of developing asymptotic theory, we need only the weaker assumption of the orthogonality condition.

- (Predetermined vs. strictly exogenous regressors) The regressors are *not* required to be strictly exogenous. As we noted in Section 1.2, the exogeneity assumption (Assumption 1.2) implies that, for any regressor k, $\mathrm{E}(x_{jk}\varepsilon_i) = 0$ for all i and j, not just for $i = j$, which rules out the possibility that the current error term, ε_i, is correlated with future regressors, $\mathbf{x}_{i+j}$ for $j \geq 1$. Assumption 2.3, restricting only the *contemporaneous* relationship between the error term and the regressors, does not rule out that possibility. For example, the AR(1) process, which does not satisfy the exogeneity assumption of the classical regression model, can be accommodated in the model of this chapter. This weaker assumption of predetermined regressors will be further relaxed in the next chapter.

- (Rank condition as no multicollinearity in the limit) Since $\mathrm{E}(\mathbf{x}_i\mathbf{x}_i')$ is finite by Assumption 2.4, $\lim_{n\to\infty} \mathbf{S_{xx}} = \mathbf{\Sigma_{xx}}$ (where $\mathbf{S_{xx}} \equiv \frac{1}{n}\sum_{i=1}^{n} \mathbf{x}_i\mathbf{x}_i'$) with probability one by the Ergodic Theorem. So, for n sufficiently large, the sample cross moment of the regressors $\mathbf{S_{xx}}$, which can be written as $\frac{1}{n}\mathbf{X}'\mathbf{X}$, is nonsingular by Assumptions 2.2 and 2.4. Since $\frac{1}{n}\mathbf{X}'\mathbf{X}$ is nonsingular if and only if $\mathrm{rank}(\mathbf{X}) = K$, Assumption 1.3 (no multicollinearity) is satisfied with probability one for sufficiently large n. In the OLS formula $\mathbf{b} = \mathbf{S}_{\mathbf{xx}}^{-1}\mathbf{s_{xy}}$ (where $\mathbf{s_{xy}} \equiv \frac{1}{n}\sum_{i=1}^{n} \mathbf{x}_i \cdot y_i$), $\mathbf{S_{xx}}$ needs to be inverted. If $\mathbf{S_{xx}}$ is singular in a finite sample (so it cannot be inverted), we just assign an arbitrary value to $\mathbf{b}$ so that the OLS estimator is well-defined for any sample.

- (A sufficient condition for $\{\mathbf{g}_i\}$ to be an m.d.s.) Since an m.d.s. (martingale difference sequence) is zero-mean by definition, Assumption 2.5 is stronger than Assumption 2.3. We will need Assumption 2.5 to prove the asymptotic normality of the OLS estimator. The assumption, about the product of the regressors and the error term, may be hard to interpret. A sufficient condition that is easier to interpret is

$$\mathrm{E}(\varepsilon_i \mid \varepsilon_{i-1}, \varepsilon_{i-2}, \ldots, \varepsilon_1, \mathbf{x}_i, \mathbf{x}_{i-1}, \ldots, \mathbf{x}_1) = 0. \tag{2.3.1}$$

Note that the *current* as well as lagged regressors is included in the information set. This condition implies that the error term is serially uncorrelated and also is uncorrelated with the current and past regressors (the proof is much like the proof in the previous section that an m.d.s. is serially uncorrelated). That (2.3.1) is sufficient for $\{\mathbf{g}_i\}$ to be an m.d.s. can be seen as follows. We have

$$
\begin{aligned}
&\mathrm{E}(\mathbf{g}_i \mid \mathbf{g}_{i-1}, \dots, \mathbf{g}_1) \\
&= \mathrm{E}[\mathrm{E}(\mathbf{g}_i \mid \varepsilon_{i-1}, \varepsilon_{i-2}, \dots, \varepsilon_1, \mathbf{x}_i, \mathbf{x}_{i-1}, \dots, \mathbf{x}_1) \mid \mathbf{g}_{i-1}, \dots, \mathbf{g}_1].
\end{aligned}
$$

This holds by the Law of Iterated Expectations because there is more information in the "inside" information set $(\varepsilon_{i-1}, \varepsilon_{i-2}, \dots, \varepsilon_1, \mathbf{x}_i, \mathbf{x}_{i-1}, \dots, \mathbf{x}_1)$ than in the "outside" information set $(\mathbf{g}_{i-1}, \dots, \mathbf{g}_1)$. Therefore,

$$
\begin{aligned}
&\mathrm{E}(\mathbf{g}_i \mid \mathbf{g}_{i-1}, \dots, \mathbf{g}_1) \\
&= \mathrm{E}[\mathbf{x}_i\, \mathrm{E}(\varepsilon_i \mid \varepsilon_{i-1}, \varepsilon_{i-2}, \dots, \varepsilon_1, \mathbf{x}_i, \mathbf{x}_{i-1}, \dots, \mathbf{x}_1) \mid \mathbf{g}_{i-1}, \dots, \mathbf{g}_1] \\
&\qquad \text{(by the linearity of conditional expectations)} \\
&= \mathbf{0} \quad \text{(by (2.3.1))}. \qquad (2.3.2)
\end{aligned}
$$

- (When the regressors include a constant) In virtually all applications, the regressors include a constant. If the regressors include a constant so that $x_{i1} = 1$ for all i, then Assumption 2.3 of predetermined regressors can be stated in more familiar terms: the mean of the error term is zero (which is implied by $\mathrm{E}(x_{ik}\varepsilon_i) = 0$ for $k = 1$), and the contemporaneous correlation between the error term and the regressors is zero (which is implied by $\mathrm{E}(x_{ik}\varepsilon_i)$ for $k \neq 1$ and $\mathrm{E}(\varepsilon_i) = 0$). Also, since the first element of the K-dimensional vector $\mathbf{g}_i$ $(\equiv \mathbf{x}_i \cdot \varepsilon_i)$ is ε_i, Assumption 2.5 implies

$$\mathrm{E}(\varepsilon_i \mid \mathbf{g}_{i-1}, \mathbf{g}_{i-2}, \dots, \mathbf{g}_1) = 0.$$

Then, by the Law of Iterated Expectations, $\{\varepsilon_i\}$ is a scalar m.d.s:

$$\mathrm{E}(\varepsilon_i \mid \varepsilon_{i-1}, \varepsilon_{i-2}, \dots, \varepsilon_1) = 0. \qquad (2.3.3)$$

Therefore, Assumption 2.5 implies that the error term itself is an m.d.s. and hence is serially uncorrelated.

- (**S** is a matrix of fourth moments) Since $\mathbf{g}_i \equiv \mathbf{x}_i \cdot \varepsilon_i$, the **S** in Assumption 2.5 can be written as $\mathrm{E}(\varepsilon_i^2 \mathbf{x}_i \mathbf{x}_i')$. Its (k, j) element is $\mathrm{E}(\varepsilon_i^2 x_{ik} x_{ij})$. So **S** is a matrix of fourth moments (the expectation of products of four different variables). Consistent estimation of **S** will require an additional assumption to be specified in Section 2.5.

- ($\mathbf{S}$ will take a different expression without Assumption 2.5) Thanks to the assumption that $\{\mathbf{g}_i\}$ is an m.d.s., $\mathbf{S}$ ($\equiv$ Avar($\bar{\mathbf{g}}$)) is equal to $\mathrm{E}(\mathbf{g}_i\mathbf{g}_i')$. Without the assumption, as we will see in Chapter 6, the expression for $\mathbf{S}$ is more complicated and involves autocovariances of $\mathbf{g}_i$.

Asymptotic Distribution of the OLS Estimator

We now prove that the OLS estimator is consistent and asymptotically normal. It should be kept in mind throughout the rest of this chapter that the OLS estimator $\mathbf{b}$ depends on the sample size n (although the dependence is not made explicit by our choice of not to subscript $\mathbf{b}$ by n) and that K, the number of regressors, is held fixed when we track the sequence of OLS estimators indexed by n. For the time being, we presume that there is available some consistent estimator, denoted $\widehat{\mathbf{S}}$, of $\mathbf{S}$ ($\equiv \mathrm{Avar}(\bar{\mathbf{g}}) = \mathrm{E}(\mathbf{g}_i\mathbf{g}_i') = \mathrm{E}(\varepsilon_i^2\mathbf{x}_i\mathbf{x}_i')$). The issue of estimating $\mathbf{S}$ consistently will be taken up later.

Proposition 2.1 (asymptotic distribution of the OLS Estimator):

(a) *(Consistency of* $\mathbf{b}$ *for* $\boldsymbol{\beta}$*) Under Assumptions 2.1–2.4,* $\mathrm{plim}_{n\to\infty}\,\mathbf{b} = \boldsymbol{\beta}$. *(So Assumption 2.5 is not needed for consistency.)*

(b) *(Asymptotic Normality of* $\mathbf{b}$*) If Assumption 2.3 is strengthened as Assumption 2.5, then*

$$\sqrt{n}(\mathbf{b} - \boldsymbol{\beta}) \underset{\mathrm{d}}{\to} N(\mathbf{0}, \mathrm{Avar}(\mathbf{b})) \quad as \quad n \to \infty,$$

where

$$\mathrm{Avar}(\mathbf{b}) = \boldsymbol{\Sigma}_{\mathbf{xx}}^{-1}\, \mathbf{S}\, \boldsymbol{\Sigma}_{\mathbf{xx}}^{-1}. \tag{2.3.4}$$

(Recall: $\boldsymbol{\Sigma}_{\mathbf{xx}} \equiv \mathrm{E}(\mathbf{x}_i\mathbf{x}_i')$, $\mathbf{S} = \mathrm{E}(\mathbf{g}_i\mathbf{g}_i')$, $\mathbf{g}_i \equiv \mathbf{x}_i \cdot \varepsilon_i$.*)*

(c) *(Consistent Estimate of* Avar($\mathbf{b}$)*) Suppose there is available a consistent estimator,* $\widehat{\mathbf{S}}$, *of* $\mathbf{S}$ $(K \times K)$. *Then, under Assumption 2.2,* Avar($\mathbf{b}$) *is consistently estimated by*

$$\widehat{\mathrm{Avar}(\mathbf{b})} = \mathbf{S}_{\mathbf{xx}}^{-1}\, \widehat{\mathbf{S}}\, \mathbf{S}_{\mathbf{xx}}^{-1}, \tag{2.3.5}$$

where $\mathbf{S}_{\mathbf{xx}}$ *is the sample mean of* $\mathbf{x}_i\mathbf{x}_i'$*:*

$$\underset{(K\times K)}{\mathbf{S}_{\mathbf{xx}}} \equiv \frac{1}{n}\sum_{i=1}^{n}\mathbf{x}_i\mathbf{x}_i' = \frac{1}{n}\mathbf{X}'\mathbf{X}. \tag{2.3.6}$$

The proof is a showcase of all the standard tricks in asymptotics. For proving (a) and (b), three tricks will be employed: (1) write the object in question in terms of sample means, (2) apply the relevant LLN (the Ergodic Theorem in the present context) and CLT (the ergodic stationary Martingale Differences CLT) to sample means, and (3) use Lemma 2.4(c) to derive the asymptotic distribution. Proof of (c) will not be given because it is an immediate implication of ergodic stationarity.

PROOF (Parts (a) and (b)).

(1) We first write the sampling error $\mathbf{b} - \boldsymbol{\beta}$ in terms of sample means.

$$\begin{aligned}\mathbf{b} - \boldsymbol{\beta} &= (\mathbf{X}'\mathbf{X})^{-1}\mathbf{X}'\boldsymbol{\varepsilon} \\ &= \left(\frac{1}{n}\mathbf{X}'\mathbf{X}\right)^{-1}\left(\frac{1}{n}\mathbf{X}'\boldsymbol{\varepsilon}\right) \\ &= \left(\frac{1}{n}\sum_{i=1}^{n}\mathbf{x}_i\mathbf{x}_i'\right)^{-1}\left(\frac{1}{n}\sum_{i=1}^{n}\mathbf{x}_i\cdot\varepsilon_i\right) \\ &\equiv \mathbf{S}_{\mathbf{xx}}^{-1}\,\bar{\mathbf{g}},\end{aligned} \tag{2.3.7}$$

where

$$\bar{\mathbf{g}} \equiv \frac{1}{n}\sum_{i=1}^{n}\mathbf{g}_i, \quad \mathbf{g}_i \equiv \mathbf{x}_i\cdot\varepsilon_i.$$

The sample means $\mathbf{S}_{\mathbf{xx}}$ and $\bar{\mathbf{g}}$ depend on the sample size n, although the notation does not make it explicit.

(2) (Consistency) Since by Assumption 2.2 $\{\mathbf{x}_i\mathbf{x}_i'\}$ is ergodic stationary, $\mathbf{S}_{\mathbf{xx}} \to_{\text{p}} \boldsymbol{\Sigma}_{\mathbf{xx}}$. (The convergence is actually almost surely, but almost sure convergence implies convergence in probability.) Since $\boldsymbol{\Sigma}_{\mathbf{xx}}$ is invertible by Assumption 2.4, $\mathbf{S}_{\mathbf{xx}}^{-1} \to_{\text{p}} \boldsymbol{\Sigma}_{\mathbf{xx}}^{-1}$ by Lemma 2.3(a). Similarly, $\bar{\mathbf{g}} \to_{\text{p}} \text{E}(\mathbf{g}_i)$ which by Assumption 2.3 is $\mathbf{0}$. So by Lemma 2.3(a), $\mathbf{S}_{\mathbf{xx}}^{-1}\bar{\mathbf{g}} \to_{\text{p}} \boldsymbol{\Sigma}_{\mathbf{xx}}^{-1}\mathbf{0} = \mathbf{0}$. Therefore, $\text{plim}_{n\to\infty}(\mathbf{b} - \boldsymbol{\beta}) = \mathbf{0}$, which implies $\text{plim}_{n\to\infty}\,\mathbf{b} = \boldsymbol{\beta}$.

(3) (Asymptotic normality) Rewrite (2.3.7) as

$$\sqrt{n}(\mathbf{b} - \boldsymbol{\beta}) = \mathbf{S}_{\mathbf{xx}}^{-1}(\sqrt{n}\,\bar{\mathbf{g}}). \tag{2.3.8}$$

As mentioned in the statement of Assumption 2.5, $\sqrt{n}\,\bar{\mathbf{g}} \to_{\text{d}} N(\mathbf{0}, \mathbf{S})$. So, by Lemma 2.4(c), $\sqrt{n}(\mathbf{b} - \boldsymbol{\beta})$ converges to a normal distribution with mean $\mathbf{0}$ and variance $\boldsymbol{\Sigma}_{\mathbf{xx}}^{-1}\mathbf{S}(\boldsymbol{\Sigma}_{\mathbf{xx}}^{-1})'$. But since $\boldsymbol{\Sigma}_{\mathbf{xx}}$ is symmetric, this expression equals (2.3.4). ■

This result says that the distribution of $\sqrt{n}$ times the sampling error is approximated arbitrarily well by a normal distribution when the sample size is sufficiently large. The natural question is how large is "large": how large must the sample size be for the asymptotic approximation to be valid? The asymptotic result we just derived holds for all the DGPs satisfying the model assumptions. However, the sample size needed to achieve a given measure of proximity to the asymptotic distribution depends on the DGP. We will partially address this issue in the Monte Carlo experiment of this chapter.

s^2 Is Consistent

We now turn to the OLS estimator, s^2, of the error variance.

Proposition 2.2 (consistent estimation of error variance): *Let $e_i \equiv y_i - \mathbf{x}_i'\mathbf{b}$ be the OLS residual for observation i. Under Assumptions 2.1–2.4,*

$$s^2 \equiv \frac{1}{n-K}\sum_{i=1}^{n} e_i^2 \underset{\text{p}}{\rightarrow} \mathrm{E}(\varepsilon_i^2),$$

provided $\mathrm{E}(\varepsilon_i^2)$ exists and is finite.

If we could observe the error term ε_i, then the obvious estimator would be the sample mean of ε_i^2. It is consistent by ergodic stationarity. The message of Proposition 2.2 is that the substitution of the OLS residual e_i for the true error term ε_i does not impair consistency. Let us go through a sketch of the proof, because knowing how to handle the discrepancy between ε_i and its estimate e_i will be useful in other contexts as well. Since

$$s^2 = \frac{n}{n-K}\left(\frac{1}{n}\sum_{i=1}^{n} e_i^2\right),$$

it suffices to prove that the sample mean of e_i^2, $\frac{1}{n}\sum_i e_i^2$, converges in probability to $\mathrm{E}(\varepsilon_i^2)$. The relationship between e_i and ε_i is given by

$$\begin{aligned} e_i &\equiv y_i - \mathbf{x}_i'\mathbf{b} \\ &= y_i - \mathbf{x}_i'\boldsymbol{\beta} - \mathbf{x}_i'(\mathbf{b}-\boldsymbol{\beta}) \quad \text{(by adding and subtracting } \mathbf{x}_i'\boldsymbol{\beta}) \\ &= \varepsilon_i - \mathbf{x}_i'(\mathbf{b}-\boldsymbol{\beta}), \end{aligned} \tag{2.3.9}$$

so that

$$e_i^2 = \varepsilon_i^2 - 2(\mathbf{b}-\boldsymbol{\beta})'\mathbf{x}_i \cdot \varepsilon_i + (\mathbf{b}-\boldsymbol{\beta})'\mathbf{x}_i\mathbf{x}_i'(\mathbf{b}-\boldsymbol{\beta}). \tag{2.3.10}$$

Summing over i, we obtain

$$\frac{1}{n}\sum_{i=1}^{n} e_i^2 = \frac{1}{n}\sum_{i=1}^{n} \varepsilon_i^2 - 2(\mathbf{b}-\boldsymbol{\beta})'\frac{1}{n}\sum_{i=1}^{n} \mathbf{x}_i \cdot \varepsilon_i + (\mathbf{b}-\boldsymbol{\beta})'\Big(\frac{1}{n}\sum_{i=1}^{n} \mathbf{x}_i\mathbf{x}_i'\Big)(\mathbf{b}-\boldsymbol{\beta})$$

$$= \frac{1}{n}\sum_{i=1}^{n} \varepsilon_i^2 - 2(\mathbf{b}-\boldsymbol{\beta})'\bar{\mathbf{g}} + (\mathbf{b}-\boldsymbol{\beta})'\mathbf{S_{xx}}(\mathbf{b}-\boldsymbol{\beta}). \tag{2.3.11}$$

The rest of the proof, which is to show that the plims of the last two terms are zero so that $\text{plim}\,\frac{1}{n}\sum_i \varepsilon_i^2 = \text{plim}\,\frac{1}{n}\sum_i e_i^2$, is left as a review question. If you do the review question, it should be clear to you that all that is required for the coefficient estimator is consistency; if some consistent estimator, rather than the OLS estimator $\mathbf{b}$, is used to form the residuals, the error variance estimator is still consistent for $\text{E}(\varepsilon_i^2)$.

QUESTIONS FOR REVIEW

1. Suppose $\text{E}(y_i \mid \mathbf{x}_i) = \mathbf{x}_i'\boldsymbol{\beta}$, that is, suppose the regression of y_i on $\mathbf{x}_i$ is a linear function of $\mathbf{x}_i$. Define $\varepsilon_i \equiv y_i - \mathbf{x}_i'\boldsymbol{\beta}$. Show that $\mathbf{x}_i$ is orthogonal to ε_i. **Hint:** First show that $\text{E}(\varepsilon_i \mid \mathbf{x}_i) = 0$.

2. (Is $\text{E}(\varepsilon_i^2)$ assumed to be finite?)

   (a) Do Assumptions 2.1–2.5 imply that $\text{E}(\varepsilon_i^2)$ exists and is finite? **Hint:** A strictly stationary process may not have finite second moments.

   (b) If one of the regressors is a constant in our model, then the variance of the error term is finite. Prove this. **Hint:** If $x_{i1} = 1$, the (1, 1) element of $\text{E}(\mathbf{g}_i\mathbf{g}_i')$ is ε_i^2.

3. (Alternative expression for $\mathbf{S}$) Let $f(\mathbf{x}_i) \equiv \text{E}(\varepsilon_i^2 \mid \mathbf{x}_i)$. Show that $\mathbf{S}$ ($\equiv \text{E}(\varepsilon_i^2\mathbf{x}_i\mathbf{x}_i')$) can be written as

$$\mathbf{S} = \text{E}[f(\mathbf{x}_i)\mathbf{x}_i\mathbf{x}_i'].$$

   Hint: Law of Total Expectations.

4. Complete the proof of Proposition 2.2. **Hint:** We have already proved for Proposition 2.1 that $\text{plim}\,\bar{\mathbf{g}} = \mathbf{0}$, $\text{plim}\,\mathbf{S_{xx}} = \boldsymbol{\Sigma}_{\mathbf{xx}}$, and $\text{plim}(\mathbf{b}-\boldsymbol{\beta}) = \mathbf{0}$ under Assumptions 2.1–2.4. Use Lemma 2.3(a) to show that $\text{plim}(\mathbf{b}-\boldsymbol{\beta})'\bar{\mathbf{g}} = 0$ and $\text{plim}(\mathbf{b}-\boldsymbol{\beta})'\mathbf{S_{xx}}(\mathbf{b}-\boldsymbol{\beta}) = 0$.

5. (Proposition 2.2 with consistent $\widehat{\boldsymbol{\beta}}$) Prove the following generalization of Proposition 2.2:

Let $\hat{\varepsilon}_i \equiv y_i - \mathbf{x}_i'\widehat{\boldsymbol{\beta}}$ where $\widehat{\boldsymbol{\beta}}$ is any consistent estimator of $\boldsymbol{\beta}$. Under Assumptions 2.1, 2.2, and the assumption that $\mathrm{E}(\mathbf{x}_i \cdot \varepsilon_i)$ and $\mathrm{E}(\mathbf{x}_i\mathbf{x}_i')$ are finite, $\frac{1}{n}\sum_i \hat{\varepsilon}_i^2 \to_{\mathrm{p}} \mathrm{E}(\varepsilon_i^2)$.

So the regressors do not have to be orthogonal to the error term.

2.4 Hypothesis Testing

Statistical inference in large-sample theory is based on test statistics whose asymptotic distributions are known under the truth of the null hypothesis. Derivation of the distribution of test statistics is easier than in finite-sample theory because we are only concerned about the large-sample *approximation* to the exact distribution. In this section we derive test statistics, assuming throughout that a consistent estimator, $\widehat{\mathbf{S}}$, of $\mathbf{S}$ $(\equiv \mathrm{E}(\mathbf{g}_i\mathbf{g}_i'))$ is available. The issue of consistent estimation of $\mathbf{S}$ will be taken up in the next section.

Testing Linear Hypotheses

Consider testing a hypothesis about the k-th coefficient β_k. Proposition 2.1 implies that under the H_0: $\beta_k = \overline{\beta}_k$,

$$\sqrt{n}(b_k - \overline{\beta}_k) \underset{\mathrm{d}}{\to} N\big(0, \mathrm{Avar}(b_k)\big) \quad \text{and} \quad \widehat{\mathrm{Avar}(b_k)} \underset{\mathrm{p}}{\to} \mathrm{Avar}(b_k),$$

where b_k is the k-th element of $\mathbf{b}$ and $\mathrm{Avar}(b_k)$ is the (k, k) element of the $K \times K$ matrix $\mathrm{Avar}(\mathbf{b})$. So Lemma 2.4(c) guarantees that

$$t_k \equiv \frac{\sqrt{n}(b_k - \overline{\beta}_k)}{\sqrt{\widehat{\mathrm{Avar}(b_k)}}} = \frac{b_k - \overline{\beta}_k}{SE^*(b_k)} \underset{\mathrm{d}}{\to} N(0, 1), \tag{2.4.1}$$

where

$$SE^*(b_k) \equiv \sqrt{\tfrac{1}{n} \cdot \widehat{\mathrm{Avar}(b_k)}} \equiv \sqrt{\tfrac{1}{n} \cdot \big(\mathbf{S}_{\mathbf{xx}}^{-1}\widehat{\mathbf{S}}\mathbf{S}_{\mathbf{xx}}^{-1}\big)_{kk}}.$$

The denominator in this t-ratio, $SE^*(b_k)$, is called the **heteroskedasticity-consistent standard error**, **(heteroskedasticity-)robust standard error**, or **White's standard error**. The reason for this terminology is that the error term can be conditionally heteroskedastic; recall that we have not assumed conditional homoskedasticity (that $\mathrm{E}(\varepsilon_i^2 \mid \mathbf{x}_i)$ does not depend on $\mathbf{x}_i$) to derive the asymptotic distribution of t_k. This t-ratio is called the **robust** t-ratio, to distinguish it from the

t-ratio of Chapter 1. The relationship between these two sorts of t-ratio will be discussed in Section 2.6.

Given this t-ratio, testing the null hypothesis H_0: $\beta_k = \overline{\beta}_k$ at a significance level of α proceeds as follows:

Step 1: Calculate t_k by the formula (2.4.1).

Step 2: Look up the table of $N(0, 1)$ to find the critical value $t_{\alpha/2}$ which leaves $\alpha/2$ to the upper tail of the standard normal distribution. (example: if $\alpha = 5\%$, $t_{\alpha/2} = 1.96$.)

Step 3: Accept the hypothesis if $|t_k| < t_{\alpha/2}$; otherwise reject.

The differences from the finite-sample t-test are: (1) the way the standard error is calculated is different, (2) we use the table of $N(0, 1)$ rather than that of $t(n - K)$, and (3) the **actual size** or **exact size** of the test (the probability of Type I error given the sample size) equals the **nominal size** (i.e., the desired significance level α) only approximately, although the approximation becomes arbitrarily good as the sample size increases. The difference between the exact size and the nominal size of a test is called the **size distortion**. Since t_k is asymptotically standard normal, the size distortion of the t-test converges to zero as the sample size n goes to infinity.

Thus, we have proved the first half of

Proposition 2.3 (robust *t*-ratio and Wald statistic): *Suppose Assumptions 2.1–2.5 hold, and suppose there is available a consistent estimate* $\widehat{\mathbf{S}}$ *of* $\mathbf{S}$ $(= \mathrm{E}(\mathbf{g}_i\mathbf{g}_i'))$. *As before, let*

$$\widehat{\mathrm{Avar}(\mathbf{b})} \equiv \mathbf{S}_{\mathbf{xx}}^{-1}\,\widehat{\mathbf{S}}\,\mathbf{S}_{\mathbf{xx}}^{-1}.$$

Then

(a) Under the null hypothesis H_0*:* $\beta_k = \overline{\beta}_k$, t_k *defined in (2.4.1)* $\to_d N(0, 1)$.

(b) Under the null hypothesis H_0*:* $\mathbf{R}\boldsymbol{\beta} = \mathbf{r}$, *where* $\mathbf{R}$ *is an* $\#\mathbf{r} \times K$ *matrix (where* $\#\mathbf{r}$, *the dimension of* $\mathbf{r}$, *is the number of restrictions) of full row rank,*

$$W \equiv n \cdot (\mathbf{Rb} - \mathbf{r})'\{\mathbf{R}[\widehat{\mathrm{Avar}(\mathbf{b})}]\mathbf{R}'\}^{-1}(\mathbf{Rb} - \mathbf{r}) \underset{d}{\to} \chi^2(\#\mathbf{r}). \tag{2.4.2}$$

What remains to be shown is that $W \to_d \chi^2(\#\mathbf{r})$, which is a straightforward application of Lemma 2.4(d).

PROOF (continued). Write W as

$$W = \mathbf{c}_n' \mathbf{Q}_n^{-1} \mathbf{c}_n \quad \text{where} \quad \mathbf{c}_n \equiv \sqrt{n}(\mathbf{Rb} - \mathbf{r}) \text{ and } \mathbf{Q}_n \equiv \mathbf{R}\widehat{\text{Avar}(\mathbf{b})}\mathbf{R}'.$$

Under H_0, $\mathbf{c}_n = \mathbf{R}\sqrt{n}(\mathbf{b} - \boldsymbol{\beta})$. So by Proposition 2.1,

$$\mathbf{c}_n \underset{\text{d}}{\to} \mathbf{c} \quad \text{where} \quad \mathbf{c} \sim N(\mathbf{0}, \mathbf{R}\,\text{Avar}(\mathbf{b})\mathbf{R}').$$

Also by Proposition 2.1,

$$\mathbf{Q}_n \underset{\text{p}}{\to} \mathbf{Q} \quad \text{where} \quad \mathbf{Q} \equiv \mathbf{R}\,\text{Avar}(\mathbf{b})\mathbf{R}'.$$

Because $\mathbf{R}$ is of full row rank and Avar($\mathbf{b}$) is positive definite, $\mathbf{Q}$ is invertible. Therefore, by Lemma 2.4(d),

$$W \underset{\text{d}}{\to} \mathbf{c}'\mathbf{Q}^{-1}\mathbf{c}.$$

Since the $\#\mathbf{r}$-dimensional random vector $\mathbf{c}$ is normally distributed and since $\mathbf{Q}$ equals Var($\mathbf{c}$), $\mathbf{c}'\mathbf{Q}^{-1}\mathbf{c} \sim \chi^2(\#\mathbf{r})$. ■

This chi-square statistic W is a Wald statistic because it is based on unrestricted estimates ($\mathbf{b}$ and $\widehat{\text{Avar}(\mathbf{b})}$ here) not constrained by the null hypothesis H_0. Testing H_0 at a significance level of α proceeds as follows.

Step 1: Calculate the W statistic by the formula (2.4.2).

Step 2: Look up the table of $\chi^2(\#\mathbf{r})$ distribution to find the critical value $\chi^2_\alpha(\#\mathbf{r})$ that gives α to the upper tail of the $\chi^2(\#\mathbf{r})$ distribution.

Step 3: If $W < \chi^2_\alpha(\#\mathbf{r})$, then accept H_0; otherwise reject.

The probability of Type I error approaches α as the sample becomes larger. As will be made clear in Section 2.6, this Wald statistic is closely related to the familiar F-test under conditional homoskedasticity.

The Test Is Consistent

Recall from basic statistics that the (finite-sample) **power** of a test is the probability of rejecting the null hypothesis when it is false given a sample of finite size (that is, the power is 1 minus the probability of Type II error). Power will obviously depend on the DGP (i.e., how the data were actually generated) considered as the alternative as well as on the size (significance level) of the test. For example, consider any DGP $\{y_i, \mathbf{x}_i\}$ satisfying Assumptions 2.1–2.5 but *not* the null hypothesis

H_0: $\beta_k = \overline{\beta}_k$. The power of the t-test of size α against this alternative is

$$\text{power} = \text{Prob}(|t_k| > t_{\alpha/2}),$$

which depends on the DGP in question because the DGP controls the distribution of t_k. We say that a test is **consistent** against a set of DGPs, none of which satisfies the null, if the power against any particular member of the set approaches unity as $n \to \infty$ for any assumed significance level.

That the t-test is consistent against the set of alternatives (DGPs) satisfying Assumptions 2.1–2.5 can be seen as follows. Look at the expression (2.4.1) for the t-ratio, reproduced here:

$$t_k \equiv \frac{\sqrt{n}(b_k - \overline{\beta}_k)}{\sqrt{\widehat{\text{Avar}(b_k)}}}.$$

The denominator converges to $\sqrt{\text{Avar}(b_k)}$ despite the fact that the DGP does not satisfy the null (recall that all parts of Proposition 2.1 hold regardless of the truth of the null, provided Assumptions 2.1–2.5 are satisfied). On the other hand, the numerator tends to $+\infty$ or $-\infty$ because b_k converges in probability to the DGP's β_k, which is different from $\overline{\beta}_k$. So the power tends to unity as the sample size n tends to infinity, implying that the t-test of Proposition 2.3 is consistent against those alternatives, the DGPs that do not satisfy the null. The same is true for the Wald test.

Asymptotic Power

For later use in the next chapter, we define here the **asymptotic power** of a consistent test. As noted above, the power of the t-test approaches to unity as the sample size increases while the DGP taken as the alternative is held fixed. But if the DGP gets closer and closer to the null as the sample size increases, the power may not converge to unity. A sequence of such DGPs is called a **sequence of local alternatives**. For the regression model and for the null of H_0: $\beta_k = \overline{\beta}_k$, it is a sequence of DGPs such that (i) the n-th DGP, $\{y_i^{(n)}, \mathbf{x}_i^{(n)}\}$ $(i = 1, 2, \ldots)$, satisfies Assumptions 2.1–2.5 and converges in a certain sense to a fixed DGP $\{y_i, \mathbf{x}_i\}$,[12] and (ii) the value of β_k of the n-th DGP, $\beta_k^{(n)}$, converges to $\overline{\beta}_k$. Suppose, further, that $\beta_k^{(n)}$ satisfies

$$\beta_k^{(n)} = \overline{\beta}_k + \frac{\gamma}{\sqrt{n}} \tag{2.4.3}$$

[12]See, e.g., Assumption 1 of Newey (1985) for a precise statement.

for some given $\gamma \neq 0$. So $\beta_k^{(n)}$ approaches to $\overline{\beta}_k$ at a rate proportional to $1/\sqrt{n}$. This special sequence of local alternatives is called a **Pitman drift** or a **Pitman sequence**. Substituting (2.4.3) into (2.4.1), the t-ratio above can be rewritten as

$$t_k = \frac{\sqrt{n}(b_k - \beta_k^{(n)})}{\sqrt{\widehat{\text{Avar}(b_k)}}} + \frac{\gamma}{\sqrt{\widehat{\text{Avar}(b_k)}}}. \tag{2.4.4}$$

If the sample of size n is generated by the n-th DGP of a Pitman drift, does t_k converge to a nontrivial distribution? Since the n-th DGP satisfies Assumptions 2.1–2.5, the first term on the right hand side of (2.4.4) converges in distribution to $N(0, 1)$ by parts (b) and (c) of Proposition 2.1. By part (c) of Proposition 2.1 and the fact that $\{y_i^{(n)}, \mathbf{x}_i^{(n)}\}$ "converges" to a fixed DGP, the second term converges in probability to

$$\mu \equiv \frac{\gamma}{\sqrt{\text{Avar}(b_k)}}, \tag{2.4.5}$$

where $\text{Avar}(b_k)$ is evaluated at the fixed DGP. Therefore, $t_k \to_{\text{d}} N(\mu, 1)$ along this sequence of local alternatives. If the significance level is α, the power converges to

$$\text{Prob}(|x| > t_{\alpha/2}) \tag{2.4.6}$$

where $x \sim N(\mu, 1)$ and $t_{\alpha/2}$ is the level-α critical value. This probability is called the **asymptotic power**. It is a measure of the ability of the test to detect small deviations of the model from the null hypothesis. Evidently, the larger is $|\mu|$, the higher is the asymptotic power for any given size α. By a similar argument, it is easy to show that the Wald statistic converges to a distribution called **noncentral chi-squared**.

Testing Nonlinear Hypotheses

The Wald statistic can be generalized to a test of a set of nonlinear restrictions on $\boldsymbol{\beta}$. Consider a null hypothesis of the form

$$\text{H}_0\colon \mathbf{a}(\boldsymbol{\beta}) = \mathbf{0}.$$

Here, $\mathbf{a}$ is a vector-valued function with continuous first derivatives. Let $\#\mathbf{a}$ be the dimension of $\mathbf{a}(\boldsymbol{\beta})$ (so the null hypothesis has $\#\mathbf{a}$ restrictions), and let $\mathbf{A}(\boldsymbol{\beta})$ be the $\#\mathbf{a} \times K$ matrix of first derivatives evaluated at $\boldsymbol{\beta}$: $\mathbf{A}(\boldsymbol{\beta}) = \partial \mathbf{a}(\boldsymbol{\beta})/\partial \boldsymbol{\beta}'$. For the hypothesis to be well-defined, we assume that $\mathbf{A}(\boldsymbol{\beta})$ is of full row rank (this is the generalization of the requirement for linear hypothesis $\mathbf{R}\boldsymbol{\beta} = \mathbf{r}$ that $\mathbf{R}$ is of full row rank). Lemma 2.5 of Section 2.1 and Proposition 2.1(b) imply that

$$\sqrt{n}[\mathbf{a}(\mathbf{b}) - \mathbf{a}(\boldsymbol{\beta})] \underset{d}{\rightarrow} \mathbf{c}, \ \mathbf{c} \sim N\big(\mathbf{0}, \mathbf{A}(\boldsymbol{\beta})\,\mathrm{Avar}(\mathbf{b})\,\mathbf{A}(\boldsymbol{\beta})'\big). \tag{2.4.7}$$

Since $\mathbf{a}(\boldsymbol{\beta}) = \mathbf{0}$ under H_0, (2.4.7) becomes

$$\sqrt{n}\mathbf{a}(\mathbf{b}) \underset{d}{\rightarrow} \mathbf{c}, \ \mathbf{c} \sim N\big(\mathbf{0}, \mathbf{A}(\boldsymbol{\beta})\,\mathrm{Avar}(\mathbf{b})\,\mathbf{A}(\boldsymbol{\beta})'\big). \tag{2.4.8}$$

Since $\mathbf{b} \rightarrow_{\mathrm{p}} \boldsymbol{\beta}$ by Proposition 2.1(a), Lemma 2.3(a) implies that $\mathbf{A}(\mathbf{b}) \rightarrow_{\mathrm{p}} \mathbf{A}(\boldsymbol{\beta})$. By Proposition 2.1(c), $\widehat{\mathrm{Avar}(\mathbf{b})} \rightarrow_{\mathrm{p}} \mathrm{Avar}(\mathbf{b})$. So by Lemma 2.3(a),

$$\mathbf{A}(\mathbf{b})\widehat{\mathrm{Avar}(\mathbf{b})}\,\mathbf{A}(\mathbf{b})' \underset{\mathrm{p}}{\rightarrow} \mathbf{A}(\boldsymbol{\beta})\,\mathrm{Avar}(\mathbf{b})\,\mathbf{A}(\boldsymbol{\beta})' = \mathrm{Var}(\mathbf{c}). \tag{2.4.9}$$

Because $\mathbf{A}(\boldsymbol{\beta})$ is of full row rank and $\mathrm{Avar}(\mathbf{b})$ is positive definite, $\mathrm{Var}(\mathbf{c})$ is invertible. Then Lemma 2.4(d), (2.4.8), and (2.4.9) imply

$$\sqrt{n}\,\mathbf{a}(\mathbf{b})'\{\mathbf{A}(\mathbf{b})\widehat{\mathrm{Avar}(\mathbf{b})}\mathbf{A}(\mathbf{b})'\}^{-1}\sqrt{n}\,\mathbf{a}(\mathbf{b}) \underset{d}{\rightarrow} \mathbf{c}'\,\mathrm{Var}(\mathbf{c})^{-1}\mathbf{c} \sim \chi^2(\#\mathbf{a}). \tag{2.4.10}$$

Combining two $\sqrt{n}$'s in (2.4.10) into one n, we have proved

Proposition 2.3 (continued):

(c) Under the null hypothesis with #$\mathbf{a}$ *restrictions* H_0: $\mathbf{a}(\boldsymbol{\beta}) = \mathbf{0}$ *such that* $\mathbf{A}(\boldsymbol{\beta})$, *the #*$\mathbf{a} \times K$ *matrix of continuous first derivatives of* $\mathbf{a}(\boldsymbol{\beta})$, *is of full row rank, we have*

$$W \equiv n \cdot \mathbf{a}(\mathbf{b})'\{\mathbf{A}(\mathbf{b})\widehat{\mathrm{Avar}(\mathbf{b})}\,\mathbf{A}(\mathbf{b})'\}^{-1}\mathbf{a}(\mathbf{b}) \underset{d}{\rightarrow} \chi^2(\#\mathbf{a}). \tag{2.4.11}$$

Part (c) is a generalization of (b); by setting $\mathbf{a}(\boldsymbol{\beta}) = \mathbf{R}\boldsymbol{\beta} - \mathbf{r}$, (2.4.11) reduces to (2.4.2), the Wald statistic for linear restrictions.

The choice of $\mathbf{a}(\cdot)$ for representing a given set of restrictions is not unique. For example, $\beta_1\beta_2 = 1$ can be written as $a(\boldsymbol{\beta}) = 0$ with $a(\boldsymbol{\beta}) = \beta_1\beta_2 - 1$ or with $a(\boldsymbol{\beta}) = \beta_1 - 1/\beta_2$. While part (c) of the proposition guarantees that in large samples the outcome of the Wald test is the same regardless of the choice of the function $\mathbf{a}$, the numerical value of the Wald statistic W does depend on the representation, and the test outcome can be different in finite samples. In the above example, the second representation, $a(\boldsymbol{\beta}) = \beta_1 - 1/\beta_2$, does not satisfy the requirement of continuous derivatives at $\beta_2 = 0$. Indeed, a Monte Carlo study by Gregory and Veall (1985) reports that, when β_2 is close to zero, the Wald test based on the second representation rejects the null too often in small samples.

QUESTIONS FOR REVIEW

1. Does $SE^*(b_k) \to_p 0$ as $n \to \infty$?

2. (Standard error of a nonlinear function) For simplicity let $K = 1$ and let b be the OLS estimate of β. The standard error of b is $\sqrt{\widehat{\text{Avar}(b)}/n}$. Suppose $\lambda = -\log(\beta)$. The estimate of λ implied by the OLS estimate of β is $\hat{\lambda} = -\log(b)$. Verify that the standard error of $\hat{\lambda}$ is $(1/b) \cdot \sqrt{\widehat{\text{Avar}(b)}/n}$.

3. (Invariance [or lack thereof] of the Wald statistic) There is no unique way to write the linear hypothesis $\mathbf{R}\boldsymbol{\beta} = \mathbf{r}$, because for any $\#\mathbf{r} \times \#\mathbf{r}$ nonsingular matrix $\mathbf{F}$, the same set of restrictions can be represented as $\widetilde{\mathbf{R}}\boldsymbol{\beta} = \widetilde{\mathbf{r}}$ with $\widetilde{\mathbf{R}} \equiv \mathbf{FR}$ and $\widetilde{\mathbf{r}} \equiv \mathbf{Fr}$. Does a different choice of $\mathbf{R}$ and $\mathbf{r}$ affect the asymptotic distribution of W? The finite-sample distribution? The numerical value?

2.5 Estimating $\text{E}(\varepsilon_i^2 \mathbf{x}_i \mathbf{x}_i')$ Consistently

The theory developed so far presumes that there is available a consistent estimator, $\widehat{\mathbf{S}}$, of $\mathbf{S}$ $(= \text{E}(\mathbf{g}_i \mathbf{g}_i') \equiv \text{E}(\varepsilon_i^2 \mathbf{x}_i \mathbf{x}_i'))$ to be used to calculate the estimated asymptotic variance, $\widehat{\text{Avar}(\mathbf{b})}$. This section explains how to obtain $\widehat{\mathbf{S}}$ from the sample $(\mathbf{y}, \mathbf{X})$.

Using Residuals for the Errors

If the error were observable, then the sample mean of $\varepsilon_i^2 \mathbf{x}_i \mathbf{x}_i'$ is obviously consistent by ergodic stationarity. But we do not observe the error term, and the substitution of some consistent estimate of it results in

$$\widehat{\mathbf{S}} \equiv \frac{1}{n} \sum_{i=1}^{n} \hat{\varepsilon}_i^2 \mathbf{x}_i \mathbf{x}_i', \tag{2.5.1}$$

where $\hat{\varepsilon}_i \equiv y_i - \mathbf{x}_i' \widehat{\boldsymbol{\beta}}$, and $\widehat{\boldsymbol{\beta}}$ is some consistent estimator of $\boldsymbol{\beta}$. (Although the obvious candidate for the consistent estimator $\widehat{\boldsymbol{\beta}}$ is the OLS estimator $\mathbf{b}$, we use $\widehat{\boldsymbol{\beta}}$ rather than $\mathbf{b}$ here, in order to make the point that the results of this section hold for any consistent estimator.) For this estimator to be consistent for $\mathbf{S}$, we need to make a fourth-moment assumption about the regressors.

Assumption 2.6 (finite fourth moments for regressors): $\text{E}[(x_{ik} x_{ij})^2]$ *exists and is finite for all* k, j $(= 1, 2, \ldots, K)$.

Proposition 2.4 (consistent estimation of S): *Suppose the coefficient estimate $\widehat{\boldsymbol{\beta}}$ used for calculating the residual $\hat{\varepsilon}_i$ for $\widehat{\mathbf{S}}$ in (2.5.1) is consistent, and suppose $\mathbf{S} = \mathrm{E}(\mathbf{g}_i\mathbf{g}_i')$ exists and is finite. Then, under Assumptions 2.1, 2.2, and 2.6, $\widehat{\mathbf{S}}$ given in (2.5.1) is consistent for* $\mathbf{S}$.

To indicate why the fourth-moment assumption is needed for the regressors, we provide a sketch of the proof for the special case of $K = 1$ (only one regressor). So $\mathbf{x}_i$ is now a scalar x_i, $\mathbf{g}_i$ is a scalar $g_i = x_i\varepsilon_i$, and (2.3.10) (with $\mathbf{b} = \widehat{\boldsymbol{\beta}}$ and $e_i = \hat{\varepsilon}_i$) simplifies to

$$\hat{\varepsilon}_i^2 = \varepsilon_i^2 - 2(\widehat{\beta} - \beta)x_i\varepsilon_i + (\widehat{\beta} - \beta)^2 x_i^2. \tag{2.5.2}$$

By multiplying both sides by x_i^2 and summing over i,

$$\frac{1}{n}\sum_{i=1}^{n}\hat{\varepsilon}_i^2 x_i^2 - \frac{1}{n}\sum_{i=1}^{n}\varepsilon_i^2 x_i^2 = -2(\widehat{\beta} - \beta)\frac{1}{n}\sum_{i=1}^{n}\varepsilon_i x_i^3 + (\widehat{\beta} - \beta)^2\frac{1}{n}\sum_{i=1}^{n}x_i^4. \tag{2.5.3}$$

Now we can see why the finite fourth-moment assumption on x_i is required: if the fourth moment $\mathrm{E}(x_i^4)$ is finite, then by ergodic stationarity the sample average of x_i^4 converges in probability to some finite number, so that the last term in (2.5.3) vanishes (converges to 0 in probability) if $\widehat{\beta}$ is consistent for β. It can also be shown (see Analytical Exercise 4 for proof) that, by combining the same fourth-moment assumption about the regressors and the fourth-moment assumption that $\mathrm{E}(\mathbf{g}_i\mathbf{g}_i')$ ($= \mathrm{E}(\varepsilon_i^2\mathbf{x}_i\mathbf{x}_i')$) is finite, the sample average of $x_i^3\varepsilon_i$ converges in probability to some finite number, so that the other term on the RHS of (2.5.3), too, vanishes.

According to Proposition 2.1(a), the assumptions made in Proposition 2.3 are sufficient to guarantee that $\mathbf{b}$ is consistent, so we can set $\mathbf{b} = \widehat{\boldsymbol{\beta}}$ in (2.5.1) and use the OLS residual to calculate $\widehat{\mathbf{S}}$. Also, the assumption made in Proposition 2.4 that $\mathrm{E}(\mathbf{g}_i\mathbf{g}_i')$ is finite is part of Assumption 2.5, which is assumed in Proposition 2.3. Therefore, the import of Proposition 2.4 is:

> If Assumption 2.6 is added to the hypothesis in Proposition 2.3, then the $\widehat{\mathbf{S}}$ given in (2.5.1) with $\mathbf{b} = \widehat{\boldsymbol{\beta}}$ (so $\hat{\varepsilon}_i$ is the OLS residual e_i) can be used in (2.3.5) to calculate the estimated asymptotic variance:
>
> $$\widehat{\mathrm{Avar}(\mathbf{b})} = \mathbf{S}_{\mathbf{xx}}^{-1}\Big(\frac{1}{n}\sum_{i=1}^{n}e_i^2\mathbf{x}_i\mathbf{x}_i'\Big)\mathbf{S}_{\mathbf{xx}}^{-1}, \tag{2.5.4}$$
>
> which is consistent for $\mathrm{Avar}(\mathbf{b})$.

Data Matrix Representation of S

If $\mathbf{B}$ is the $n \times n$ diagonal matrix whose i-th diagonal element is $\hat{\varepsilon}_i^2$, then the $\widehat{\mathbf{S}}$ in (2.5.1) can be represented in terms of data matrices as

$$\widehat{\mathbf{S}} = \frac{\mathbf{X}'\mathbf{B}\mathbf{X}}{n} \tag{2.5.1$'$}$$

with

$$\mathbf{B} = \begin{bmatrix} \hat{\varepsilon}_1^2 & & \\ & \ddots & \\ & & \hat{\varepsilon}_n^2 \end{bmatrix}.$$

So (2.5.4) can be rewritten (with $\hat{\varepsilon}_i$ in $\mathbf{B}$ set to e_i) as

$$\widehat{\text{Avar}(\mathbf{b})} = n \cdot (\mathbf{X}'\mathbf{X})^{-1}(\mathbf{X}'\mathbf{B}\mathbf{X})(\mathbf{X}'\mathbf{X})^{-1}. \tag{2.5.4$'$}$$

These expressions, although useful for some purposes, should not be used for computation purposes, because the $n \times n$ matrix $\mathbf{B}$ will take up too much of the computer's working memory, particularly when the sample size is large. To compute $\widehat{\mathbf{S}}$ from the sample, the formula (2.5.1) is more useful than (2.5.1$'$).

Finite-Sample Considerations

Of course, in finite samples, the power may well be far below one against certain alternatives. Also, the probability of rejecting the null when the DGP does satisfy the null (the Type I error) may be very different from the assumed significance level. Davidson and MacKinnon (1993, Section 16.3) report that, at least for the Monte Carlo simulations they have seen, the robust t-ratio based on (2.5.1) rejects the null too often and that simply replacing the denominator n in (2.5.1) by the degrees of freedom $n - K$ or equivalently multiplying (2.5.1) by $n/(n-K)$ (this is a **degrees of freedom correction**) mitigates the problem of overrejecting. They also report that the robust t-ratios based on the following adjustments on $\widehat{\mathbf{S}}$ perform even better:

$$\widehat{\mathbf{S}} = \frac{1}{n}\sum_{i=1}^{n} \frac{e_i^2}{(1-p_i)^d}\mathbf{x}_i\mathbf{x}_i', \quad d = 1 \text{ or } 2, \tag{2.5.5}$$

where p_i is the p_i defined in the context of the influential analysis in Chapter 1: it is the i-th diagonal element of the projection matrix $\mathbf{P}$, that is,

$$p_i \equiv \mathbf{x}_i'(\mathbf{X}'\mathbf{X})^{-1}\mathbf{x}_i = \frac{\mathbf{x}_i'\mathbf{S}_{\mathbf{xx}}^{-1}\mathbf{x}_i}{n}.$$

QUESTIONS FOR REVIEW

1. (Computation of robust standard errors) In Review Question 9 of Section 1.2, we observed that the standard errors of the OLS coefficient estimates can be calculated from $\mathbf{S_{xx}}$, $\mathbf{s_{xy}}$ (the sample mean of $\mathbf{x}_i \cdot y_i$), $\mathbf{y}'\mathbf{y}/n$, and $\bar{y}$, so the sample moments need to be computed just once. Is the same true for the robust standard errors where the $\widehat{\mathbf{S}}$ is calculated according to the formula (2.5.1) with $\hat{\varepsilon}_i = e_i$?

2. The finite-sample variance of the OLS estimator in the generalized regression model of Chapter 1 is $\text{Var}(\mathbf{b} \mid \mathbf{X}) = (\mathbf{X}'\mathbf{X})^{-1}\mathbf{X}'(\sigma^2\mathbf{V})\mathbf{X}(\mathbf{X}'\mathbf{X})^{-1}$. Compare this to (2.5.4′). What are the differences?

2.6 Implications of Conditional Homoskedasticity

The test statistics developed in Sections 2.4 and 2.5 are different from the finite-sample counterparts of Section 1.4 designed for testing the same null hypothesis. How are they related? What is the asymptotic distribution of the t and F statistics of Chapter 1? This section answers these questions.

It turns out that the robust t-ratio is numerically equal to the t-ratio of Section 1.4, for a particular choice of $\widehat{\mathbf{S}}$. Therefore, the asymptotic distribution of the t-ratio of Section 1.4 is the same as that of the robust t-ratio, if that particular choice is consistent for $\mathbf{S}$. The same relationship holds between the F-ratio of Section 1.4 and the Wald statistic W of this chapter. Under the conditional homoskedasticity assumption stated below, that particular choice is indeed consistent.

Conditional versus Unconditional Homoskedasticity

The conditional homoskedasticity assumption is:

Assumption 2.7 (conditional homoskedasticity):

$$\text{E}(\varepsilon_i^2 \mid \mathbf{x}_i) = \sigma^2 > 0. \tag{2.6.1}$$

This assumption implies that the unconditional second moment $\text{E}(\varepsilon_i^2)$ equals σ^2 by the Law of Total Expectations. To be clear about the distinction between unconditional and conditional homoskedasticity, consider the following example.

Example 2.6 (unconditionally homoskedastic but conditionally heteroskedastic errors): As already observed, if $\{y_i, \mathbf{x}_i\}$ is stationary, so is $\{\varepsilon_i\}$, and the error is *un*conditionally homoskedastic in that $\mathrm{E}(\varepsilon_i^2)$ does not depend on i. To illustrate that the error can nevertheless be conditionally heteroskedastic, suppose that ε_i is written as $\varepsilon_i \equiv \eta_i f(\mathbf{x}_i)$, where $\{\eta_i\}$ is zero-mean $\mathrm{E}(\eta_i) = 0$ and is independent of $\mathbf{x}_i$. The conditional second moment of ε_i depends on $\mathbf{x}_i$ because

$$\begin{aligned}\mathrm{E}(\varepsilon_i^2 \mid \mathbf{x}_i) &= \mathrm{E}(\eta_i^2 f(\mathbf{x}_i)^2 \mid \mathbf{x}_i) \quad (\text{since } \varepsilon_i \equiv \eta_i f(\mathbf{x}_i))\\ &= f(\mathbf{x}_i)^2\,\mathrm{E}(\eta_i^2 \mid \mathbf{x}_i) \qquad (\text{by the linearity of conditional expectations})\\ &= f(\mathbf{x}_i)^2\,\mathrm{E}(\eta_i^2) \quad (\text{since } \eta_i \text{ is independent of } \mathbf{x}_i \text{ by assumption}),\end{aligned}$$

which varies across i because of the variation in $f(\mathbf{x}_i)$ across i.

Reduction to Finite-Sample Formulas

To examine the large-sample distribution of the t and F statistics of Chapter 1 under the additional Assumption 2.7, we first examine the *algebraic* relationship to their robust counterparts. Consider the following choice for the estimate of $\mathbf{S}$:

$$\widehat{\mathbf{S}} = s^2 \mathbf{S}_{\mathbf{xx}},$$

where s^2 is the OLS estimate of σ^2. (We will show in a moment that this estimator is consistent under conditional homoskedasticity.) Then the expression (2.3.5) for $\widehat{\mathrm{Avar}(\mathbf{b})}$ becomes

$$\widehat{\mathrm{Avar}(\mathbf{b})} = s^2 \mathbf{S}_{\mathbf{xx}}^{-1} = n \cdot s^2 \cdot (\mathbf{X}'\mathbf{X})^{-1}. \tag{2.6.2}$$

Substituting this expression into (2.4.1), we see that the robust standard error becomes

$$\sqrt{s^2 \text{ times } (k, k) \text{ element of } (\mathbf{X}'\mathbf{X})^{-1}}, \tag{2.6.3}$$

which is the usual standard error in finite-sample theory. So the robust t-ratio is numerically identical to the usual finite-sample t-ratio when we set $\widehat{\mathbf{S}} = s^2\,\mathbf{S}_{\mathbf{xx}}$. Similarly, substituting (2.6.2) into the expression for the Wald statistic (2.4.2), we obtain

$$
\begin{aligned}
W &= n \cdot (\mathbf{Rb} - \mathbf{r})'\{\mathbf{R}[n \cdot s^2 \cdot (\mathbf{X}'\mathbf{X})^{-1}]\mathbf{R}'\}^{-1}(\mathbf{Rb} - \mathbf{r}) \\
&= (\mathbf{Rb} - \mathbf{r})'\{\mathbf{R}[s^2 \cdot (\mathbf{X}'\mathbf{X})^{-1}]\mathbf{R}'\}^{-1}(\mathbf{Rb} - \mathbf{r}) \quad \text{(the two } n\text{'s cancel)} \\
&= (\mathbf{Rb} - \mathbf{r})'\left\{\mathbf{R}[(\mathbf{X}'\mathbf{X})^{-1}]\mathbf{R}'\right\}^{-1}(\mathbf{Rb} - \mathbf{r})/s^2 \\
&= r \cdot F \quad \text{(by the definition of (1.4.9) of the } F\text{-ratio)} \\
&= (SSR_R - SSR_U)/s^2 \quad \text{(by (1.4.11)).}
\end{aligned}
$$

Thus, when we set $\widehat{\mathbf{S}} = s^2\, \mathbf{S_{xx}}$, the Wald statistic W is numerically identical to $\#\mathbf{r} \cdot F$ (where $\#\mathbf{r}$ is the number of restrictions in the null hypothesis).

Large-Sample Distribution of t and F Statistics

It then follows from Proposition 2.3 that the t-ratio (2.4.1) is asymptotically $N(0, 1)$ and $\#\mathbf{r} \cdot F$ asymptotically $\chi^2(\#\mathbf{r})$, if $s^2\, \mathbf{S_{xx}}$ is consistent for $\mathbf{S}$. That $s^2\, \mathbf{S_{xx}}$ is consistent for $\mathbf{S}$ can be seen as follows. Under conditional homoskedasticity, the matrix of fourth moments $\mathbf{S}$ can be expressed as a product of second moments:

$$
\begin{aligned}
\mathbf{S} = \mathrm{E}(\mathbf{g}_i\mathbf{g}_i') &= \mathrm{E}(\mathbf{x}_i\mathbf{x}_i'\varepsilon_i^2) \quad (\text{since } \mathbf{g}_i \equiv \mathbf{x}_i \cdot \varepsilon_i) \\
&= \mathrm{E}[\mathrm{E}(\mathbf{x}_i\mathbf{x}_i'\varepsilon_i^2 \mid \mathbf{x}_i)] \quad \text{(by the Law of Total Expectations)} \\
&= \mathrm{E}[\mathbf{x}_i\mathbf{x}_i'\, \mathrm{E}(\varepsilon_i^2 \mid \mathbf{x}_i)] \quad \text{(by the linearity of conditional expectations)} \\
&= \mathrm{E}(\mathbf{x}_i\mathbf{x}'\sigma^2) \quad \text{(by Assumption 2.7)} \\
&= \sigma^2\, \mathrm{E}(\mathbf{x}_i\mathbf{x}_i') = \sigma^2 \mathbf{\Sigma_{xx}}. \qquad (2.6.4)
\end{aligned}
$$

This decomposition has several implications.

- ($\mathbf{\Sigma_{xx}}$ is nonsingular) Since by Assumption 2.5 $\mathbf{S}$ is nonsingular, this decomposition of $\mathbf{S}$ implies that $\sigma^2 > 0$ and $\mathbf{\Sigma_{xx}}$ is nonsingular. Hence, Assumption 2.4 (rank condition) is implied.

- (No need for fourth-moment assumption) By ergodic stationarity $\mathbf{S_{xx}} \to_{\mathrm{p}} \mathbf{\Sigma_{xx}}$. By Proposition 2.2, s^2 is consistent for σ^2 under Assumptions 2.1–2.4. Thus, $s^2\, \mathbf{S_{xx}} \to_{\mathrm{p}} \sigma^2\mathbf{\Sigma_{xx}} = \mathbf{S}$. We do not need the fourth-moment assumption (Assumption 2.6) for consistency.

As another implication of (2.6.4), the expression for Avar($\mathbf{b}$) can be simplified: inserting (2.6.4) into (2.3.4) of Proposition 2.1, the expression for Avar($\mathbf{b}$) becomes

$$
\mathrm{Avar}(\mathbf{b}) = \sigma^2 \mathbf{\Sigma_{xx}^{-1}}. \qquad (2.6.5)
$$

Thus, we have proved

Proposition 2.5 (large-sample properties of b, t, and F under conditional homoskedasticity): *Suppose Assumptions 2.1–2.5 and 2.7 are satisfied. Then*

(a) *(Asymptotic distribution of* $\mathbf{b}$*) The OLS estimator* $\mathbf{b}$ *of* $\boldsymbol{\beta}$ *is consistent and asymptotically normal with* $\text{Avar}(\mathbf{b}) = \sigma^2 \boldsymbol{\Sigma}_{\mathbf{xx}}^{-1}$.

(b) *(Consistent estimation of asymptotic variance) Under the same set of assumptions,* $\text{Avar}(\mathbf{b})$ *is consistently estimated by* $\widehat{\text{Avar}(\mathbf{b})} = s^2\, \mathbf{S}_{\mathbf{xx}}^{-1} = n \cdot s^2 \cdot (\mathbf{X}'\mathbf{X})^{-1}$.

(c) *(Asymptotic distribution of the t and F statistics of the finite-sample theory) Under* H_0*:* $\beta_k = \overline{\beta}_k$*, the usual t-ratio (1.4.5) is asymptotically distributed as* $N(0, 1)$*. Under* H_0*:* $\mathbf{R}\boldsymbol{\beta} = \mathbf{r}$*,* $\#\mathbf{r} \cdot F$ *is asymptotically* $\chi^2(\#\mathbf{r})$*, where F is the F statistic from (1.4.9) and* $\#\mathbf{r}$ *is the number of restrictions in* H_0.

Variations of Asymptotic Tests under Conditional Homoskedasticity

According to this result, you should look up the $N(0, 1)$ table to find the critical value to be compared with the t-ratio (1.4.5) and the χ^2 table for the statistic $\#\mathbf{r} \cdot F$ derived from (1.4.9). Some researchers replace the s^2 in (1.4.5) and (1.4.9) by $\frac{1}{n}\sum_i e_i^2$. That is, the degrees of freedom $n - K$ is replaced by n, or the degrees of freedom adjustment implicit in s^2 is removed. The difference this substitution makes vanishes in large samples, because $\lim_{n\to\infty}[n/(n - K)] = 1$. Therefore, regardless of which test to use, the outcome of the test will be the same if the sample size is sufficiently large.

Another variation is to retain the degrees of freedom $n - K$ but use the $t(n - K)$ table for the t ratio and the $F(\#\mathbf{r}, n - K)$ table for F, which is *exactly* the prescription of finite-sample theory. This, too, is asymptotically valid because, as $n - K$ tends to infinity (which is what happens when $n \to \infty$ with K fixed), the $t(n - K)$ distribution converges to $N(0, 1)$ (just compare the t table for large degrees of freedom with the standard normal table) and $F(\#\mathbf{r}, n-K)$ to $\chi^2(\#\mathbf{r})/\#\mathbf{r}$. Put differently, even if the error is not normally distributed and the regressors are merely predetermined (orthogonal to the error term) and not strictly exogenous, the distribution of the t-ratio (1.4.5) is well approximated by $t(n - K)$, and the distribution of the F ratio by $F(\#\mathbf{r}, n - K)$.

These variations are all asymptotically equivalent in that the differences in the values vanishes in large samples and hence (by Lemma 2.4(a)) their asymptotic distributions are the same. However, when the sample size is only moderately large, the approximation to the finite-sample or exact distribution of test statistics may be better with $t(n-K)$ and $F(\#\mathbf{r}, n-K)$, rather than with $N(0, 1)$ and $\chi^2(\#\mathbf{r})$. Because the exact distribution depends on the DGP, there is no simple guide as to which variation works better in finite samples. This issue of which table — $N(0, 1)$

or $t(n-K)$—should be used for moderate sample sizes will be taken up in the Monte Carlo exercise of this chapter.

QUESTIONS FOR REVIEW

1. (Inconsistency of finite sample-formulas without conditional homoskedasticity) Without Assumption 2.7, Avar($\mathbf{b}$) is given by (2.3.4) in Proposition 2.1. Is it consistently estimated by (2.6.2) without Assumption 2.7? [The answer is no. Why?] Is the t-ratio (1.4.5) asymptotically standard normal without the assumption? [Answer: No.]

2. (Advantage of finite-sample formulas under conditional homoskedasticity) Conversely, under Assumption 2.7, Avar($\mathbf{b}$) is given by (2.6.5). Is it consistently estimated by (2.3.5) under Assumption 2.7? If Assumption 2.7 holds, what do you think is the advantage of using (2.6.2) over (2.3.5) to estimate the asymptotic variance? [**Note:** The finite-sample properties of an estimator are generally better, the fewer the number of population parameters estimated to form the estimator. How many population parameters need to be estimated to form (2.3.5)? (2.6.2)?]

3. (Relation of F to χ^2) Find the 5 percent critical value of $F(10, \infty)$ and compare it to the 5 percent critical value of $\chi^2(10)$. What is the relationship between the two?

4. Without conditional homoskedasticity, is $(SSR_R - SSR_U)/s^2$ asymptotically $\chi^2(\#\mathbf{r})$? [Answer: No.]

5. (nR^2 test) For a regression with a constant, consider the null hypothesis that the coefficients of the $K-1$ nonconstant regressors are all zero. Show that $nR^2 \to_{\text{d}} \chi^2(K-1)$ under the hypothesis of Proposition 2.5. **Hint:** You have proved for a Chapter 1 analytical exercise that the algebraic relationship between the F-ratio for the null and R^2 is

$$F = \frac{R^2/(K-1)}{(1-R^2)/(n-K)}.$$

Can you use the nR^2 statistic when the error is not conditionally homoskedastic? [Answer: No.]

2.7 Testing Conditional Homoskedasticity

With the advent of robust standard errors allowing us to do inference without specifying the conditional second moment $\mathrm{E}(\varepsilon_i^2 \mid \mathbf{x}_i)$, testing conditional homoskedasticity is not as important as it used to be. This section presents only the most popular test due to White (1980) for the case of random samples.[13]

Recall that $\widehat{\mathbf{S}}$ given in (2.5.1) (with $\hat{\varepsilon}_i = e_i$) is consistent for $\mathbf{S}$ (Proposition 2.4), and $s^2\,\mathbf{S_{xx}}$ is consistent for $\sigma^2\boldsymbol{\Sigma}_{\mathbf{xx}}$ (an implication of Proposition 2.2). But under conditional homoskedasticity, $\mathbf{S} = \sigma^2\boldsymbol{\Sigma}_{\mathbf{xx}}$ (see (2.6.4)), so the difference between the two consistent estimators should vanish:

$$\begin{aligned}\widehat{\mathbf{S}} - s^2\,\mathbf{S_{xx}} &= \frac{1}{n}\sum_{i=1}^{n} e_i^2\mathbf{x}_i\mathbf{x}_i' - s^2\frac{1}{n}\sum_{i=1}^{n}\mathbf{x}_i\mathbf{x}_i' \\ &= \frac{1}{n}\sum_{i=1}^{n}(e_i^2 - s^2)\mathbf{x}_i\mathbf{x}_i' \underset{\mathrm{p}}{\to} \mathbf{0}.\end{aligned} \tag{2.7.1}$$

Let $\boldsymbol{\psi}_i$ be a vector collecting unique and nonconstant elements of the $K \times K$ symmetric matrix $\mathbf{x}_i\mathbf{x}_i'$. (Construction of $\boldsymbol{\psi}_i$ from $\mathbf{x}_i\mathbf{x}_i'$ will be illustrated in Example 2.7 below.) Then (2.7.1) implies

$$\mathbf{c}_n \equiv \frac{1}{n}\sum_{i=1}^{n}(e_i^2 - s^2)\boldsymbol{\psi}_i \underset{\mathrm{p}}{\to} \mathbf{0}. \tag{2.7.2}$$

This $\mathbf{c}_n$ is a sample mean converging to zero. Under some conditions appropriate for a Central Limit Theorem to be applicable, we would expect $\sqrt{n}\,\mathbf{c}_n$ to converge in probability to a normal distribution with mean zero and some asymptotic variance $\mathbf{B}$, so for any consistent estimator $\widehat{\mathbf{B}}$ of $\mathbf{B}$,

$$n \cdot \mathbf{c}_n'\widehat{\mathbf{B}}^{-1}\mathbf{c}_n \underset{\mathrm{d}}{\to} \chi^2(m), \tag{2.7.3}$$

where m is the dimension of $\mathbf{c}_n$. For a certain choice of $\widehat{\mathbf{B}}$, this statistic can be computed as nR^2 from the following auxiliary regression:

$$\text{regress } e_i^2 \text{ on a constant and } \boldsymbol{\psi}_i. \tag{2.7.4}$$

[13]See, e.g., Judge et al. (1985, Section 11.3) or Greene (1997, Section 12.3) for other tests.

White (1980) rigorously developed this argument[14] to prove

Proposition 2.6 (White's Test for Conditional Heteroskedasticity): *In addition to Assumptions 2.1 and 2.4, suppose that (a)* $\{y_i, \mathbf{x}_i\}$ *is i.i.d. with finite* $\mathrm{E}(\varepsilon_i^2 \mathbf{x}_i \mathbf{x}_i')$ *(thus strengthening Assumptions 2.2 and 2.5), (b)* ε_i *is independent of* $\mathbf{x}_i$ *(thus strengthening Assumption 2.3 and conditional homoskedasticity), and (c) a certain condition holds on the moments of* ε_i *and* $\mathbf{x}_i$*. Then,*

$$nR^2 \underset{\mathrm{d}}{\rightarrow} \chi^2(m),$$

where R^2 *is the* R^2 *from the auxiliary regression (2.7.4), and* m *is the dimension of* $\boldsymbol{\psi}_i$*.*

Example 2.7 (regressors in White's nR^2 test): Consider the Cobb-Douglas cost function of Section 1.7:

$$\log\left(\frac{TC_i}{p_{i3}}\right) = \beta_1 + \beta_2 \log(Q_i) + \beta_3 \log\left(\frac{p_{i1}}{p_{i3}}\right) + \beta_4 \log\left(\frac{p_{i2}}{p_{i3}}\right) + \varepsilon_i.$$

Here, $\mathbf{x}_i' = (1, \log(Q_i), \log(p_{i1}/p_{i3}), \log(p_{i2}/p_{i3}))$, a four-dimensional vector. There are 10 $(= 4 \cdot 5/2)$ unique elements in $\mathbf{x}_i \mathbf{x}_i'$:

$$1,\ \log(Q_i),\ \log\left(\frac{p_{i1}}{p_{i3}}\right),\ \log\left(\frac{p_{i2}}{p_{i3}}\right),$$
$$[\log(Q_i)]^2,\ \log(Q_i)\cdot\log\left(\frac{p_{i1}}{p_{i3}}\right),\ \log(Q_i)\cdot\log\left(\frac{p_{i2}}{p_{i3}}\right),$$
$$\left[\log\left(\frac{p_{i1}}{p_{i3}}\right)\right]^2,\ \log\left(\frac{p_{i1}}{p_{i3}}\right)\cdot\log\left(\frac{p_{i2}}{p_{i3}}\right),\ \left[\log\left(\frac{p_{i2}}{p_{i3}}\right)\right]^2.$$

$\boldsymbol{\psi}_i$ is a nine-dimensional vector excluding a constant from this list. So the m in Proposition 2.6 is 9.

If White's test accepts the null of conditional homoskedasticity, then the results of Section 2.6 apply, and statistical inference can be based on the t- and F-ratios from Chapter 1. Otherwise inference should be based on the robust t and Wald statistics of Proposition 2.3.

Because the regressors $\boldsymbol{\psi}_i$ in the auxiliary regression have many elements consisting of squares and cross-products of the elements of $\mathbf{x}_i$, the test should be consistent (i.e., the power approaches unity as $n \to \infty$) against most heteroskedas-

[14]The original statement of White's theorem is more general as it covers the case where $\{y_i, \mathbf{x}_i\}$ is independent, but not identically distributed (i.n.i.d.).

tic alternatives but may require a fairly large sample to have power close to unity. If the researcher knows that some of the elements of $\boldsymbol{\psi}_i$ do not affect the conditional second moment, then they can be dropped from the auxiliary regression and the power might be increased in finite samples. The downside of it, of course, is that if such knowledge is false, the test will have no power against heteroskedastic alternatives that relate the conditional second moment to those elements that are excluded from the auxiliary regression.

QUESTION FOR REVIEW

1. (Dimension of $\boldsymbol{\psi}_i$) Suppose $\mathbf{x}_i = (1, q_i, q_i^2, p_i)'$, a four-dimensional vector. How many nonconstant and unique elements are there in $\mathbf{x}_i\mathbf{x}_i'$? [Answer: 8.]

2.8 Estimation with Parameterized Conditional Heteroskedasticity (optional)

Even when the error is found to be conditionally heteroskedastic, the OLS estimator is still consistent and asymptotically normal, and valid statistical inference can be conducted with robust standard errors and robust Wald statistics. However, in the (somewhat unlikely) case of *a priori* knowledge of the functional form of the conditional second moment $\mathrm{E}(\varepsilon_i^2 \mid \mathbf{x}_i)$, it should be possible to obtain sharper estimates with smaller asymptotic variance. Indeed, in finite-sample theory, the WLS (weighted least squares) can incorporate such knowledge for increased efficiency in the sense of smaller finite-sample variance. Does this finite-sample result carry over to large-sample theory? This section deals with the large-sample properties of the WLS estimator. To simplify the discussion, throughout this section we strengthen Assumptions 2.2 and 2.5 by assuming that $\{y_i, \mathbf{x}_i\}$ is i.i.d. This is a natural assumption to make, because it is usually in cross-section contexts where WLS is invoked.

The Functional Form

The parametric functional form for the conditional second moment we consider is

$$\mathrm{E}(\varepsilon_i^2 \mid \mathbf{x}_i) = \mathbf{z}_i'\boldsymbol{\alpha}, \tag{2.8.1}$$

where $\mathbf{z}_i$ is a function of $\mathbf{x}_i$.

Example 2.8 (parametric form of the conditional second moment): The functional form used in the WLS estimation in the empirical exercise to Chapter 1 was

$$\mathrm{E}\Big(\varepsilon_i^2 \mid \log(Q_i), \log(Q_i)^2, \log\Big(\frac{p_{i1}}{p_{i3}}\Big), \log\Big(\frac{p_{i2}}{p_{i3}}\Big)\Big) = \alpha_1 + \alpha_2 \cdot \Big(\frac{1}{Q_i}\Big).$$

Since the elements of $\mathbf{z}_i$ can be nonlinear functions of $\mathbf{x}_i$, this specification is more flexible than it might first look, but still it rules out some nonlinearities. For example, the functional form

$$\mathrm{E}(\varepsilon_i^2 \mid \mathbf{x}_i) = \exp(\mathbf{z}_i'\boldsymbol{\alpha}) \tag{2.8.2}$$

might be more attractive because its value is guaranteed to be positive. We consider the linear specification (2.8.1) only because estimating parameters in nonlinear specifications such as (2.8.2) requires the use of nonlinear least squares.

WLS with Known $\boldsymbol{\alpha}$

To isolate the complication arising from the fact that the unknown parameter vector $\boldsymbol{\alpha}$ must be estimated, we first examine the large-sample distribution of the WLS estimator with known $\boldsymbol{\alpha}$. If $\boldsymbol{\alpha}$ is known, the conditional second moment can be calculated from data as $\mathbf{z}_i'\boldsymbol{\alpha}$, and WLS proceeds exactly as in Section 1.6: dividing both sides of the estimation equation $y_i = \mathbf{x}_i'\boldsymbol{\beta} + \varepsilon_i$ by the square root of $\mathbf{z}_i'\boldsymbol{\alpha}$, to obtain

$$\tilde{y}_i = \tilde{\mathbf{x}}_i'\boldsymbol{\beta} + \tilde{\varepsilon}_i, \tag{2.8.3}$$

where

$$\tilde{y}_i \equiv \frac{y_i}{\sqrt{\mathbf{z}_i'\boldsymbol{\alpha}}}, \quad \tilde{\mathbf{x}}_i \equiv \frac{\mathbf{x}_i}{\sqrt{\mathbf{z}_i'\boldsymbol{\alpha}}}, \quad \tilde{\varepsilon}_i \equiv \frac{\varepsilon_i}{\sqrt{\mathbf{z}_i'\boldsymbol{\alpha}}},$$

and then apply OLS. For later reference, write the resulting WLS estimator as $\widehat{\boldsymbol{\beta}}(\mathbf{V})$. It is given by

$$\begin{aligned}
\widehat{\boldsymbol{\beta}}(\mathbf{V}) &\equiv \Big(\frac{1}{n}\sum_{i=1}^{n}\tilde{\mathbf{x}}_i\tilde{\mathbf{x}}_i'\Big)^{-1}\frac{1}{n}\sum_{i=1}^{n}\tilde{\mathbf{x}}_i \cdot \tilde{y}_i \\
&= \Big(\frac{1}{n}\sum_{i=1}^{n}\frac{1}{\mathbf{z}_i'\boldsymbol{\alpha}}\mathbf{x}_i\mathbf{x}_i'\Big)^{-1}\frac{1}{n}\sum_{i=1}^{n}\frac{1}{\mathbf{z}_i'\boldsymbol{\alpha}}\mathbf{x}_i \cdot y_i \\
&= (\mathbf{X}'\mathbf{V}^{-1}\mathbf{X})^{-1}\mathbf{X}'\mathbf{V}^{-1}\mathbf{y},
\end{aligned} \tag{2.8.4}$$

with

$$\mathbf{V} \equiv \begin{bmatrix} \mathbf{z}_1'\boldsymbol{\alpha} & & \\ & \ddots & \\ & & \mathbf{z}_n'\boldsymbol{\alpha} \end{bmatrix}.$$

If Assumption 2.3 is strengthened by the condition that

$$\mathrm{E}(\varepsilon_i \mid \mathbf{x}_i) = 0, \tag{2.8.5}$$

then $\mathrm{E}(\tilde{\varepsilon}_i \mid \tilde{\mathbf{x}}_i) = 0$. To see this, note first that, because $\mathbf{z}_i$ is a function of $\mathbf{x}_i$,

$$\mathrm{E}(\tilde{\varepsilon}_i \mid \mathbf{x}_i) = \mathrm{E}\biggl(\frac{\varepsilon_i}{\sqrt{\mathbf{z}_i'\boldsymbol{\alpha}}} \;\Big|\; \mathbf{x}_i\biggr) = \frac{1}{\sqrt{\mathbf{z}_i'\boldsymbol{\alpha}}}\,\mathrm{E}\,(\varepsilon_i \mid \mathbf{x}_i) = 0. \tag{2.8.6}$$

Second, because $\tilde{\mathbf{x}}_i$ is a function of $\mathbf{x}_i$, there is no more information in $\tilde{\mathbf{x}}_i$ than in $\mathbf{x}_i$. So by the Law of Iterated Expectations we have

$$\mathrm{E}(\tilde{\varepsilon}_i \mid \tilde{\mathbf{x}}_i) = \mathrm{E}[\mathrm{E}(\tilde{\varepsilon}_i \mid \mathbf{x}_i) \mid \tilde{\mathbf{x}}_i] = 0.$$

Therefore, provided that $\mathrm{E}(\tilde{\mathbf{x}}_i\tilde{\mathbf{x}}_i')$ is nonsingular, Assumptions 2.1–2.5 are satisfied for equation (2.8.3). Furthermore, by construction, the error $\tilde{\varepsilon}_i$ is conditionally homoskedastic: $\mathrm{E}(\tilde{\varepsilon}_i^2 \mid \tilde{\mathbf{x}}_i) = 1$. So Proposition 2.5 applies with $\sigma^2 = 1$: the WLS estimator is consistent and asymptotically normal, and the asymptotic variance is

$$\begin{aligned}
\mathrm{Avar}(\widehat{\boldsymbol{\beta}}(\mathbf{V})) &= \mathrm{E}(\tilde{\mathbf{x}}_i\tilde{\mathbf{x}}_i')^{-1} \quad \text{(since the error variance is 1)} \\
&= \operatorname{plim}\Bigl(\frac{1}{n}\sum_{i=1}^{n}\tilde{\mathbf{x}}_i\tilde{\mathbf{x}}_i'\Bigr)^{-1} \quad \text{(by ergodic stationarity)} \\
&= \operatorname{plim}\Bigl(\frac{1}{n}\sum_{i=1}^{n}\frac{1}{\mathbf{z}_i'\boldsymbol{\alpha}}\mathbf{x}_i\mathbf{x}_i'\Bigr)^{-1} \quad \Bigl(\text{since } \tilde{\mathbf{x}}_i = \mathbf{x}_i/\sqrt{\mathbf{z}_i'\boldsymbol{\alpha}}\Bigr) \\
&= \operatorname{plim}\Bigl(\frac{1}{n}\mathbf{X}'\mathbf{V}^{-1}\mathbf{X}\Bigr)^{-1}.
\end{aligned} \tag{2.8.7}$$

So $(\frac{1}{n}\mathbf{X}'\mathbf{V}^{-1}\mathbf{X})^{-1}$ is a consistent estimator of $\mathrm{Avar}(\widehat{\boldsymbol{\beta}}(\mathbf{V}))$.

Regression of e_i^2 on $\mathbf{z}_i$ Provides a Consistent Estimate of $\boldsymbol{\alpha}$

If $\boldsymbol{\alpha}$ is unknown, it can be estimated by running a separate regression. (2.8.1) says that $\mathbf{z}_i'\boldsymbol{\alpha}$ is a regression of ε_i^2. If we define $\eta_i \equiv \varepsilon_i^2 - \mathrm{E}(\varepsilon_i^2 \mid \mathbf{x}_i)$, then (2.8.1) can be written as a regression equation:

$$\varepsilon_i^2 = \mathbf{z}_i'\boldsymbol{\alpha} + \eta_i. \tag{2.8.8}$$

By construction, $\mathrm{E}(\eta_i \mid \mathbf{x}_i) = 0$, which, together with the fact that $\mathbf{z}_i$ is a function of $\mathbf{x}_i$, implies that the regressors $\mathbf{z}_i$ are orthogonal to the error term η_i. Hence, provided that $\mathrm{E}(\mathbf{z}_i\mathbf{z}_i')$ is nonsingular, Proposition 2.1 is applicable to this auxiliary regression (2.8.8): the OLS estimator of $\boldsymbol{\alpha}$ is consistent and asymptotically normal.

Of course, this we cannot do because we don't observe the error term. However, since the OLS estimator $\mathbf{b}$ for the original regression $y_i = \mathbf{x}_i'\boldsymbol{\beta} + \varepsilon_i$ is consistent despite the presence of conditional heteroskedasticity, the OLS residual e_i provides a consistent estimate of ε_i. It is left to you as an analytical exercise to show that, when ε_i is replaced by e_i in the regression (2.8.8), the OLS estimator, call it $\hat{\boldsymbol{\alpha}}$, is consistent for $\boldsymbol{\alpha}$.

WLS with Estimated $\boldsymbol{\alpha}$

The WLS estimation of the original equation $y_i = \mathbf{x}_i'\boldsymbol{\beta} + \varepsilon_i$ with estimated $\boldsymbol{\alpha}$ is $\widehat{\boldsymbol{\beta}}(\widehat{\mathbf{V}})$, where $\widehat{\mathbf{V}}$ is the $n \times n$ diagonal matrix whose i-th diagonal is $\mathbf{z}_i'\hat{\boldsymbol{\alpha}}$. Under suitable additional conditions (see, e.g., Amemiya (1977) for an explicit statement of such conditions), it can be shown that

(a) $\sqrt{n}\,(\widehat{\boldsymbol{\beta}}(\mathbf{V}) - \boldsymbol{\beta})$ and $\sqrt{n}\,(\widehat{\boldsymbol{\beta}}(\widehat{\mathbf{V}}) - \boldsymbol{\beta})$ are asymptotically equivalent in that the difference converges to zero in probability as $n \to \infty$. Therefore, by Lemma 2.4(a), the asymptotic distribution of $\sqrt{n}\,(\widehat{\boldsymbol{\beta}}(\widehat{\mathbf{V}}) - \boldsymbol{\beta})$ is the same as that of $\sqrt{n}\,(\widehat{\boldsymbol{\beta}}(\mathbf{V}) - \boldsymbol{\beta})$. So $\mathrm{Avar}(\widehat{\boldsymbol{\beta}}(\widehat{\mathbf{V}}))$ equals $\mathrm{Avar}(\widehat{\boldsymbol{\beta}}(\mathbf{V}))$, which in turn is given by (2.8.7);

(b) $\operatorname{plim} \frac{1}{n}\mathbf{X}'\widehat{\mathbf{V}}^{-1}\mathbf{X} = \operatorname{plim} \frac{1}{n}\mathbf{X}'\mathbf{V}^{-1}\mathbf{X}$.
So $(\frac{1}{n}\mathbf{X}'\widehat{\mathbf{V}}^{-1}\mathbf{X})^{-1}$ is consistent for $\mathrm{Avar}(\widehat{\boldsymbol{\beta}}(\widehat{\mathbf{V}}))$.

All this may sound complicated, but the operational implication for the WLS estimation of the equation $y_i = \mathbf{x}_i'\boldsymbol{\beta} + \varepsilon_i$ is very clear:

Step 1: Estimate the equation $y_i = \mathbf{x}_i'\boldsymbol{\beta} + \varepsilon_i$ by OLS and compute the OLS residuals e_i.

Step 2: Regress e_i^2 on $\mathbf{z}_i$, to obtain the OLS coefficient estimate $\hat{\boldsymbol{\alpha}}$.

Step 3: Re-estimate the equation $y_i = \mathbf{x}_i'\boldsymbol{\beta} + \varepsilon_i$ by WLS, using $1/\sqrt{\mathbf{z}_i'\hat{\boldsymbol{\alpha}}}$ as the weight for observation i.

Since the correct estimate of the asymptotic variance, $(\frac{1}{n}\mathbf{X}'\widehat{\mathbf{V}}^{-1}\mathbf{X})^{-1}$ in (b), is (n times) the estimated variance matrix routinely printed out by standard regression packages for the *Step 3* regression, calculating appropriate test statistics is quite straightforward: the standard t- and F-ratios from *Step 3* regression can be used to do statistical inference.

OLS versus WLS

Thus we have two consistent and asymptotically normal estimators, the OLS and WLS estimators. We say that a consistently and asymptotically normal estimator is **asymptotically more efficient** than another consistent and asymptotically normal estimator of the same parameter if the asymptotic variance of the former is no larger than that of the latter. It is left to you as an analytical exercise to show that the WLS estimator is asymptotically more efficient than the OLS estimator.

The superiority of WLS over OLS, however, rests on the premise that the sample size is sufficiently large *and* the functional form of the conditional second moment is correctly specified. If the functional form is misspecified, the WLS estimator would still be consistent, but its asymptotic variance may or may not be smaller than Avar($\mathbf{b}$). In finite samples, even if the functional form is correctly specified, the large-sample approximation will probably work less well for the WLS estimator than for OLS because of the estimation of extra parameters ($\boldsymbol{\alpha}$) involved in the WLS procedure.

QUESTIONS FOR REVIEW

1. Prove: "$\text{E}(\eta_i \mid \mathbf{x}_i) = 0$, $\mathbf{z}_i$ is a function of $\mathbf{x}_i$" $\Rightarrow$ "$\text{E}(\mathbf{z}_i \cdot \eta_i) = \mathbf{0}$." **Hint:** Law of Total Expectations.

2. Is the error conditionally homoskedastic in the auxiliary regression (2.8.8)? If so, does it matter for the asymptotic distribution of the WLS estimator?

2.9 Least Squares Projection

What if the assumptions justifying the large-sample properties of the OLS estimator (except for ergodic stationarity) are not satisfied but we nevertheless go ahead and apply OLS to the sample? What is it that we estimate? The answer is in this section. OLS provides an estimate of the best way linearly to combine the explanatory variables to predict the dependent variable. The linear combination is called the **least squares projection**.

Optimally Predicting the Value of the Dependent Variable

We have been concerned about estimating unknown parameters from a sample. Let us temporarily suspend the role of econometrician and put ourselves in the following situation. There is a random scalar y and a random vector $\mathbf{x}$. We know the joint distribution of $(y, \mathbf{x})$ and the value of $\mathbf{x}$. On the basis of this knowledge we wish to predict y. So a predictor is a function $f(\mathbf{x})$ of $\mathbf{x}$ with the functional form $f(\cdot)$ determined by the joint distribution of $(y, \mathbf{x})$. Naturally, we choose the function $f(\cdot)$ so as to minimize some index that is a function of the **forecast error** $y - f(\mathbf{x})$. We take the loss function to be the **mean squared error** $\mathrm{E}[(y - f(\mathbf{x}))^2]$ because it seems as reasonable a loss function as any other and, more importantly, because it produces the following convenient result:

Proposition 2.7: $\mathrm{E}(y \mid \mathbf{x})$ *is the best predictor of* y *in that it minimizes the mean squared error.*

We have seen in Chapter 1 that the add-and-subtract strategy is effective in showing that the candidate solution minimizes a quadratic function. Let us apply the strategy to the squared error here. Let $f(\mathbf{x})$ be any forecast. Add $\mathrm{E}(y \mid \mathbf{x})$ to the forecast error $y - f(\mathbf{x})$ and then subtract it to obtain the decomposition

$$y - f(\mathbf{x}) = (y - \mathrm{E}(y \mid \mathbf{x})) + (\mathrm{E}(y \mid \mathbf{x}) - f(\mathbf{x})). \tag{2.9.1}$$

So the squared forecast error is

$$\begin{aligned}(y - f(\mathbf{x}))^2 = (y - \mathrm{E}(y \mid \mathbf{x}))^2 &+ 2(y - \mathrm{E}(y \mid \mathbf{x}))(\mathrm{E}(y \mid \mathbf{x}) - f(\mathbf{x})) \\ &+ (\mathrm{E}(y \mid \mathbf{x}) - f(\mathbf{x}))^2.\end{aligned} \tag{2.9.2}$$

Take the expectation of both sides to obtain

$$\begin{aligned}&\text{mean squared error} \equiv \mathrm{E}\big[(y - f(\mathbf{x}))^2\big] \\ &= \mathrm{E}\big[(y - \mathrm{E}(y \mid \mathbf{x}))^2\big] + 2\,\mathrm{E}\big[(y - \mathrm{E}(y \mid \mathbf{x}))(\mathrm{E}(y \mid \mathbf{x}) - f(\mathbf{x}))\big] \\ &\quad + \mathrm{E}\big[(\mathrm{E}(y \mid \mathbf{x}) - f(\mathbf{x}))^2\big].\end{aligned} \tag{2.9.3}$$

It is a straightforward application of the Law of Total Expectations to show that the middle term, which is the covariance between the optimal forecast error and the difference in forecasts, is zero (a review question). Therefore,

$$\begin{aligned}&\text{mean squared error} = \mathrm{E}\big[(y - \mathrm{E}(y \mid \mathbf{x}))^2\big] + \mathrm{E}\big[(\mathrm{E}(y \mid \mathbf{x}) - f(\mathbf{x}))^2\big] \\ &\geq \mathrm{E}\big[(y - \mathrm{E}(y \mid \mathbf{x}))^2\big],\end{aligned} \tag{2.9.4}$$

which shows that the mean squared error is bounded from below by $\mathrm{E}\big[(y - \mathrm{E}(y \mid \mathbf{x}))^2\big]$, and this lower bound is achieved by the conditional expectation.

Best Linear Predictor

It requires the knowledge of the joint distribution of $(y, \mathbf{x})$ to calculate $\mathrm{E}(y \mid \mathbf{x})$, which may be highly nonlinear. We now restrict the predictor to being a linear function of $\mathbf{x}$ and ask: what is the best (in the sense of minimizing the mean squared error) linear predictor of y based on $\mathbf{x}$? For this purpose, consider $\boldsymbol{\beta}^*$ that satisfies the orthogonality condition

$$\mathrm{E}[\mathbf{x} \cdot (y - \mathbf{x}'\boldsymbol{\beta}^*)] = \mathbf{0} \quad \text{or} \quad \mathrm{E}(\mathbf{x}\mathbf{x}')\boldsymbol{\beta}^* = \mathrm{E}(\mathbf{x} \cdot y). \tag{2.9.5}$$

The idea is to choose $\boldsymbol{\beta}^*$ so that the forecast error $y - \mathbf{x}'\boldsymbol{\beta}^*$ is orthogonal to $\mathbf{x}$. If $\mathrm{E}(\mathbf{x}\mathbf{x}')$ is nonsingular, the orthogonality condition can be solved for $\boldsymbol{\beta}^*$:

$$\boldsymbol{\beta}^* = [\mathrm{E}(\mathbf{x}\mathbf{x}')]^{-1}\,\mathrm{E}(\mathbf{x} \cdot y). \tag{2.9.6}$$

The **least squares** (or **linear**) **projection** of y on $\mathbf{x}$, denoted $\widehat{\mathrm{E}}^*(y \mid \mathbf{x})$, is defined as $\mathbf{x}'\boldsymbol{\beta}^*$, where $\boldsymbol{\beta}^*$ satisfies (2.9.5) and is called the **least squares projection coefficients**.

Proposition 2.8: *The least squares projection* $\widehat{\mathrm{E}}^*(y \mid \mathbf{x})$ *is the best linear predictor of* y *in that it minimizes the mean squared error.*

The add-and-subtract strategy also works here.

PROOF. For any linear predictor $\mathbf{x}'\widetilde{\boldsymbol{\beta}}$,

$$\begin{aligned}
\text{mean squared error} &\equiv \mathrm{E}\big[(y - \mathbf{x}'\widetilde{\boldsymbol{\beta}})^2\big] \\
&= \mathrm{E}\big\{\big[(y - \mathbf{x}'\boldsymbol{\beta}^*) + \mathbf{x}'(\boldsymbol{\beta}^* - \widetilde{\boldsymbol{\beta}})\big]^2\big\} \quad \text{(by the add-and-subtract strategy)} \\
&= \mathrm{E}\big[(y - \mathbf{x}'\boldsymbol{\beta}^*)^2\big] + 2(\boldsymbol{\beta}^* - \widetilde{\boldsymbol{\beta}})'\,\mathrm{E}\big[\mathbf{x} \cdot (y - \mathbf{x}'\boldsymbol{\beta}^*)\big] + \mathrm{E}\big[(\mathbf{x}'(\boldsymbol{\beta}^* - \widetilde{\boldsymbol{\beta}}))^2\big] \\
&= \mathrm{E}\big[(y - \mathbf{x}'\boldsymbol{\beta}^*)^2\big] + \mathrm{E}\big[(\mathbf{x}'(\widetilde{\boldsymbol{\beta}} - \boldsymbol{\beta}^*))^2\big] \\
&\qquad \text{(by the orthogonality condition (2.9.5))} \\
&\geq \mathrm{E}\big[(y - \mathbf{x}'\boldsymbol{\beta}^*)^2\big].
\end{aligned}$$

■

In contrast to the best predictor, which is the conditional expectation, the best linear predictor requires only the knowledge of the second moments of the joint distribution of $(y, \mathbf{x})$ to calculate (see (2.9.6)).

If one of the regressors $\mathbf{x}$ is a constant, the least squares projection coefficients can be written in terms of variances and covariances. Let $\tilde{\mathbf{x}}$ be the vector of non-constant regressors so that

$$\mathbf{x} = \begin{bmatrix} 1 \\ \tilde{\mathbf{x}} \end{bmatrix}.$$

An analytical exercise to this chapter asks you to prove that

$$\widehat{\mathrm{E}}^*(y \mid \mathbf{x}) \equiv \widehat{\mathrm{E}}^*(y \mid 1, \tilde{\mathbf{x}}) = \mu + \boldsymbol{\gamma}'\tilde{\mathbf{x}}, \tag{2.9.7}$$

where

$$\boldsymbol{\gamma} = \mathrm{Var}(\tilde{\mathbf{x}})^{-1}\,\mathrm{Cov}(\tilde{\mathbf{x}}, y), \;\; \mu = \mathrm{E}(y) - \boldsymbol{\gamma}'\,\mathrm{E}(\tilde{\mathbf{x}}).$$

This formula is the population analogue of the "deviations-from-the-mean regression" formula of Chapter 1 (Analytical Exercise 3).

OLS Consistently Estimates the Projection Coefficients

Now let us put the econometrician's hat back on and consider estimating $\boldsymbol{\beta}^*$. Suppose we have a sample of size n drawn from an ergodic stationary stochastic process $\{y_i, \mathbf{x}_i\}$ with the joint distribution $(y_i, \mathbf{x}_i)$ (which does not depend on i because of stationarity) identical to that of $(y, \mathbf{x})$ above. So, for example, $\mathrm{E}(\mathbf{x}_i\mathbf{x}_i') = \mathrm{E}(\mathbf{x}\mathbf{x}')$. By the Ergodic Theorem the second moments in (2.9.6) can be consistently estimated by the corresponding sample second moments. Thus a consistent estimator of the projection coefficients $\boldsymbol{\beta}^*$ is

$$\Big(\frac{1}{n}\sum_{i=1}^{n}\mathbf{x}_i\mathbf{x}_i'\Big)^{-1}\Big(\frac{1}{n}\sum_{i=1}^{n}\mathbf{x}_i \cdot y_i\Big) = (\mathbf{X}'\mathbf{X})^{-1}\mathbf{X}'\mathbf{y},$$

which is none other than the OLS estimator $\mathbf{b}$. That is, under Assumption 2.2 (ergodic stationarity) and Assumption 2.4 guaranteeing the nonsingularity of $\mathrm{E}(\mathbf{x}\mathbf{x}')$, the OLS estimator is always consistent for the projection coefficient vector, the $\boldsymbol{\beta}^*$ that satisfies the orthogonality condition (2.9.5).

QUESTIONS FOR REVIEW

1. (Unforecastability of forecast error) For the minimum mean square error forecast $\mathrm{E}(y \mid \mathbf{x})$, the forecast error is orthogonal to any function $\phi(\mathbf{x})$ of $\mathbf{x}$. That is, $\mathrm{E}[\eta\phi(\mathbf{x})] = 0$ where $\eta \equiv y - \mathrm{E}(y \mid \mathbf{x})$. Prove this. **Hint:** The Law of Total Expectations. Show that the middle term on the RHS of (2.9.3) is zero by setting $\phi(\mathbf{x}) = \mathrm{E}(y \mid \mathbf{x}) - f(\mathbf{x})$.

2. (Forecasting white noise) Suppose $\{\varepsilon_i\}$ is white noise. What is $\widehat{\mathrm{E}}^*(\varepsilon_i \mid \varepsilon_{i-1}, \varepsilon_{i-2}, \dots, \varepsilon_{i-m})$? What is $\widehat{\mathrm{E}}^*(\varepsilon_i \mid 1, \varepsilon_{i-1}, \varepsilon_{i-2}, \dots, \varepsilon_{i-m})$? Is it true that $\mathrm{E}(\varepsilon_i \mid \varepsilon_{i-1}, \varepsilon_{i-2}, \dots, \varepsilon_{i-m}) = 0$? **Hint:** Is it zero for the process of Example 2.4?

3. (Conditional expectations that are linear) Suppose $\mathrm{E}(y \mid \tilde{\mathbf{x}}) = \mu + \boldsymbol{\gamma}'\tilde{\mathbf{x}}$. Show: $\widehat{\mathrm{E}}^*(y \mid 1, \tilde{\mathbf{x}}) = \mathrm{E}(y \mid \tilde{\mathbf{x}})$.

4. (Partitioned projection) Consider the model $y_i = \mathbf{x}_i'\boldsymbol{\beta} + \mathbf{z}_i'\boldsymbol{\delta} + \varepsilon_i$ with $\mathrm{E}(\mathbf{x}_i \cdot \varepsilon_i) = \mathbf{0}$, $\mathrm{E}(\mathbf{z}_i \cdot \varepsilon_i) \neq \mathbf{0}$, and $\mathrm{E}(\mathbf{z}_i\mathbf{x}_i') = \mathbf{0}$. Thus, $\mathbf{z}_i$ is not predetermined (i.e., not orthogonal to the error term), but it is unrelated to the predetermined regressor $\mathbf{x}_i$ in that the cross moments are zero.

   (a) Show that the least squares projection coefficient of $\mathbf{x}_i$ in the projection of y_i on $\mathbf{x}_i$ and $\mathbf{z}_i$ is $\boldsymbol{\beta}$. **Hint:** Calculate $\widehat{\mathrm{E}}^*(\varepsilon_i \mid \mathbf{x}_i, \mathbf{z}_i)$.

   (b) What is the least squares projection coefficient of $\mathbf{x}_i$ in the least squares projection of y_i on $\mathbf{x}_i$? **Hint:** Treat $\mathbf{z}_i'\boldsymbol{\delta} + \varepsilon_i$ as the error term.

   (c) Which projection would you use for estimating $\boldsymbol{\beta}$? **Hint:** You want the error variance to be smaller.

2.10 Testing for Serial Correlation

As remarked in Section 2.3 (see (2.3.3)), when the regressors include a constant (true in virtually all known applications), Assumption 2.5 implies that the error term is a scalar martingale difference sequence (m.d.s.), so if the error is found to be serially correlated, that is an indication of a failure of Assumption 2.5. Serial correlation has traditionally been an important subject in econometrics, and there are available a number of tests for serial correlation (i.e., tests of the null of no serial correlation in the error term). Some of them, however, require that the regressors be strictly exogenous. The test to be presented in this section does not require strict exogeneity. Because the issue of serial correlation arises only in time-series models, we use the subscript "t" instead of "i" in this section (and the next). Throughout this section we assume that the regressors include a constant.

It would be nice to have those tests extended to cover serial correlation in $\mathbf{g}_t$ $(\equiv \mathbf{x}_t \cdot \varepsilon_t)$, but no such tests have been proposed to gain acceptance. This is a gap in the literature, but not a serious one, because nowadays researchers know how to live with serial correlation in $\mathbf{g}_t$. That is, as will be shown in Chapter 6, there is available a method to do inference in the presence of serial correlation in $\mathbf{g}_t$.

Earlier in this chapter we learned how to calculate standard errors that are robust to conditional heteroskedasticity. In Chapter 6, those standard errors will be made robust to serial correlation as well.

Box-Pierce and Ljung-Box

Before turning to the tests for serial correlation in the error term, we temporarily step outside the regression framework and consider serial correlation in a univariate time series. Suppose we have a sample of size n, $\{z_1, \ldots, z_n\}$, drawn from a scalar covariance-stationary process. In Section 2.2 we defined the (population) j-th order autocovariance γ_j. The **sample j-th order autocovariance** is

$$\hat{\gamma}_j \equiv \frac{1}{n} \sum_{t=j+1}^{n} (z_t - \bar{z}_n)(z_{t-j} - \bar{z}_n) \quad (j = 0, 1, \ldots), \tag{2.10.1}$$

where

$$\bar{z}_n \equiv \frac{1}{n} \sum_{t=1}^{n} z_t.$$

(If the population mean $\mathrm{E}(z_t)$ is known, it can replace the sample mean $\bar{z}_n$; doing so would improve the small sample property.) Here, even though only $n - j$ terms are in the sum, the denominator is n rather than $n - j$. Whether the sum of $n - j$ terms is divided by n or by $n - j$ does not affect large-sample results. For moderate sample sizes, however, the numerical difference can be substantial, and you should always be explicit about which is used as the denominator. The **sample j-th order autocorrelation coefficient**, $\hat{\rho}_j$, is defined as

$$\hat{\rho}_j \equiv \frac{\hat{\gamma}_j}{\hat{\gamma}_0} \quad (j = 1, 2, \ldots). \tag{2.10.2}$$

If $\{z_t\}$ is ergodic stationary, then it is easy to show (see a review question) that $\hat{\gamma}_j$ is consistent for γ_j $(j = 0, 1, 2, \ldots)$. Hence, by Lemma 2.3(a), $\hat{\rho}_j$ is consistent for ρ_j $(j = 1, 2, \ldots)$. In particular, if $\{z_t\}$ is serially uncorrelated, then all the sample autocorrelation coefficients converge to 0 in probability. To test for serial correlation, however, we need to know the asymptotic distribution of $\sqrt{n}\hat{\rho}_j$. It is provided by

Proposition 2.9 (special case of Theorem 6.7 of Hall and Heyde (1980)): *Suppose $\{z_t\}$ can be written as $\mu + \varepsilon_t$, where ε_t is a stationary martingale difference sequence with "own" conditional homoskedasticity:*

$$\textit{(own conditional homoskedasticity)} \quad \mathrm{E}(\varepsilon_t^2 \mid \varepsilon_{t-1}, \varepsilon_{t-2}, \ldots) = \sigma^2, \; \sigma^2 > 0.$$

Let the sample autocorrelation $\hat{\rho}_j$ be defined as in (2.10.1) and (2.10.2). Then

$$\sqrt{n}\hat{\boldsymbol{\gamma}} \underset{d}{\to} N(\mathbf{0}, \sigma^4 \mathbf{I}_p) \quad \text{and} \quad \sqrt{n}\hat{\boldsymbol{\rho}} \underset{d}{\to} N(\mathbf{0}, \mathbf{I}_p),$$

where $\hat{\boldsymbol{\gamma}} = (\hat{\gamma}_1, \hat{\gamma}_2, \ldots, \hat{\gamma}_p)'$ and $\hat{\boldsymbol{\rho}} = (\hat{\rho}_1, \hat{\rho}_2, \ldots, \hat{\rho}_p)'$.

Here, the process ε_t is not required to be ergodic. Proving this under the additional condition of ergodicity is left as an analytical exercise. Thus, asymptotically, ($\sqrt{n}$ times) the autocorrelations are i.i.d. and the distribution is $N(0, 1)$. The process $\{\varepsilon_t\}$ assumed here is more general than independent white noise processes, but the conditional second moment has to be constant, so this result does not cover ARCH processes, for example.

One way to test for serial correlation in the series is to check whether the first-order autocorrelation, ρ_1, is 0. Proposition 2.9 implies that

$$\sqrt{n}\hat{\rho}_1 = \frac{\hat{\rho}_1}{1/\sqrt{n}} \underset{d}{\to} N(0, 1). \tag{2.10.3}$$

So the t-statistic formed as the ratio of $\hat{\rho}_1$ to a "standard error" of $1/\sqrt{n}$ is asymptotically standard normal.

We can also test whether a group of autocorrelations are simultaneously zero. Let $\hat{\boldsymbol{\rho}} = (\hat{\rho}_1, \ldots, \hat{\rho}_p)'$ be the p-dimensional vector collecting the first p sample autocorrelations. Since the elements of $\sqrt{n}\hat{\boldsymbol{\rho}}$ are asymptotically independent and individually distributed as standard normal, their squared sum, called the **Box-Pierce Q** because it was first considered by Box and Pierce (1970), is asymptotically chi-squared:

$$\text{Box-Pierce } Q \text{ statistic} \equiv n \sum_{j=1}^{p} \hat{\rho}_j^2 = \sum_{j=1}^{p} \left(\sqrt{n}\hat{\rho}_j\right)^2 \underset{d}{\to} \chi^2(p). \tag{2.10.4}$$

It is easy to show (see a review question) that the following modification, called the **Ljung-Box Q**, is asymptotically equivalent in that its difference from the Box-Pierce Q vanishes in large samples. So by Lemma 2.4(a) it, too, is asymptotically chi-squared:

$$\text{Ljung-Box } Q \text{ statistic} \equiv n \cdot (n+2) \sum_{j=1}^{p} \frac{\hat{\rho}_j^2}{n-j} = \sum_{j=1}^{p} \frac{n+2}{n-j} \left(\sqrt{n}\hat{\rho}_j\right)^2 \underset{d}{\to} \chi^2(p). \tag{2.10.5}$$

This modification often provides a better approximation to the chi-square distribution for moderate sample sizes (you will be asked to verify this in a Monte Carlo exercise). For either statistic, there is no clear guide to the choice of p. If p is too small, there is a danger of missing the existence of higher-order autocorrelations, but if p is too large relative to the sample size, its finite-sample distribution is likely to deteriorate, diverging greatly from the chi-square distribution.

Sample Autocorrelations Calculated from Residuals

Now go back to the regression model described by Assumptions 2.1–2.5. If the error term ε_t were observable, we would calculate the sample autocorrelations as

$$\tilde{\rho}_j \equiv \frac{\tilde{\gamma}_j}{\tilde{\gamma}_0} \quad (j = 1, 2, \dots), \tag{2.10.6}$$

where

$$\tilde{\gamma}_j \equiv \frac{1}{n} \sum_{t=j+1}^{n} \varepsilon_t \, \varepsilon_{t-j} \quad (j = 0, 1, 2, \dots). \tag{2.10.7}$$

(There is no need to subtract the sample mean because the population mean is zero, an implication of the inclusion of a constant in the regressors.) Since $\{\varepsilon_t \varepsilon_{t-j}\}$ is ergodic stationary by Assumption 2.2, $\tilde{\gamma}_j$ converges in probability to the corresponding population mean, $\mathrm{E}(\varepsilon_t \varepsilon_{t-j})$, for all j, and $\tilde{\rho}_j$ is consistent for the population j-th autocorrelation coefficient of ε_t.

Next consider the more realistic case where we do not observe the error term. We can replace ε_t in the above formula by the OLS estimate e_t and calculate the sample autocorrelations as

$$\hat{\rho}_j \equiv \frac{\hat{\gamma}_j}{\hat{\gamma}_0} \quad (j = 1, 2, \dots), \tag{2.10.8}$$

where

$$\hat{\gamma}_j \equiv \frac{1}{n} \sum_{t=j+1}^{n} e_t \, e_{t-j} \quad (j = 0, 1, 2, \dots). \tag{2.10.9}$$

(Because the regressors include a constant, the normal equation corresponding to the constant ensures that the sample mean of e_t is zero. So there is no need to subtract the sample mean.) Is it all right to use $\hat{\rho}_j$ (calculated from the residuals) instead of $\tilde{\rho}_j$ and the residual-based Q statistics derived from $\{\hat{\rho}_j\}$ for testing for serial correlation? The answer is yes, but only if the regressors are strictly exogenous.

Recall that the expression linking the residual e_t to the true error term ε_t was given in (2.3.9). Using this, the difference between $\tilde{\gamma}_j$ and $\hat{\gamma}_j$ can be written as

$$\begin{aligned}\hat{\gamma}_j &\equiv \frac{1}{n}\sum_{t=j+1}^{n} e_t\, e_{t-j} \\ &= \frac{1}{n}\sum_{t=j+1}^{n} [\varepsilon_t - \mathbf{x}_t'(\mathbf{b}-\boldsymbol{\beta})][\varepsilon_{t-j} - \mathbf{x}_{t-j}'(\mathbf{b}-\boldsymbol{\beta})] \\ &= \tilde{\gamma}_j - \frac{1}{n}\sum_{t=j+1}^{n} (\mathbf{x}_{t-j}\cdot\varepsilon_t + \mathbf{x}_t\cdot\varepsilon_{t-j})'(\mathbf{b}-\boldsymbol{\beta}) \\ &\quad + (\mathbf{b}-\boldsymbol{\beta})'\Big(\frac{1}{n}\sum_{t=j+1}^{n} \mathbf{x}_t\,\mathbf{x}_{t-j}'\Big)(\mathbf{b}-\boldsymbol{\beta}). \end{aligned} \tag{2.10.10}$$

If $\mathrm{E}(\mathbf{x}_t\cdot\varepsilon_{t-j})$, $\mathrm{E}(\mathbf{x}_{t-j}\cdot\varepsilon_t)$, and $\mathrm{E}(\mathbf{x}_t\mathbf{x}_{t-j}')$ are all finite, then the second and the third terms vanish (converges to zero in probability) because $\mathbf{b}-\boldsymbol{\beta} \to_{\mathrm{p}} \mathbf{0}$. Therefore,

$$\hat{\gamma}_j - \tilde{\gamma}_j \underset{\mathrm{p}}{\to} 0 \quad (j = 0, 1, 2, \dots),$$

and thus the difference between $\tilde{\rho}_j$ and $\hat{\rho}_j$, too, vanishes in large samples.

However, $\sqrt{n}$ times the difference does not. $\sqrt{n}\tilde{\rho}_j$ and $\sqrt{n}\hat{\rho}_j$ can be written as

$$\sqrt{n}\tilde{\rho}_j = \frac{\sqrt{n}\tilde{\gamma}_j}{\tilde{\gamma}_0} \quad \text{and} \quad \sqrt{n}\hat{\rho}_j = \frac{\sqrt{n}\hat{\gamma}_j}{\hat{\gamma}_0}. \tag{2.10.11}$$

We have just seen that, for both $\sqrt{n}\tilde{\rho}_j$ and $\sqrt{n}\hat{\rho}_j$, the denominator $\to_{\mathrm{p}} \sigma^2$. So the difference between $\sqrt{n}\tilde{\rho}_j$ and $\sqrt{n}\hat{\rho}_j$ will vanish if the difference between $\sqrt{n}\tilde{\gamma}_j$ and $\sqrt{n}\hat{\gamma}_j$ does (if you are not convinced, see Review Question 3 below). Now, by multiplying both sides of (2.10.10) by $\sqrt{n}$, we obtain

$$\begin{aligned}\sqrt{n}\hat{\gamma}_j &= \sqrt{n}\tilde{\gamma}_j - \frac{1}{n}\sum_{t=j+1}^{n} (\mathbf{x}_{t-j}\cdot\varepsilon_t + \mathbf{x}_t\cdot\varepsilon_{t-j})'\sqrt{n}\,(\mathbf{b}-\boldsymbol{\beta}) \\ &\quad + \sqrt{n}\,(\mathbf{b}-\boldsymbol{\beta})'\Big(\frac{1}{n}\sum_{t=j+1}^{n} \mathbf{x}_t\,\mathbf{x}_{t-j}'\Big)(\mathbf{b}-\boldsymbol{\beta}). \end{aligned} \tag{2.10.12}$$

Because $\sqrt{n}\,(\mathbf{b}-\boldsymbol{\beta})$ converges to a random variable (whose distribution is normal), the third term on the RHS vanishes by Lemma 2.4(b). Regarding the second term, we have

$$\frac{1}{n}\sum_{t=j+1}^{n}(\mathbf{x}_{t-j}\cdot\varepsilon_t+\mathbf{x}_t\cdot\varepsilon_{t-j})\underset{p}{\rightarrow}\mathrm{E}(\mathbf{x}_{t-j}\cdot\varepsilon_t)+\mathrm{E}(\mathbf{x}_t\cdot\varepsilon_{t-j}). \tag{2.10.13}$$

If the regressors are strictly exogenous in the sense that $\mathrm{E}(\mathbf{x}_t \cdot \varepsilon_s) = \mathbf{0}$ for all t, s, then

$$\mathrm{E}(\mathbf{x}_{t-j}\cdot\varepsilon_t)+\mathrm{E}(\mathbf{x}_t\cdot\varepsilon_{t-j})=\mathbf{0}, \tag{2.10.14}$$

and by Lemma 2.4(b) the second term converges to zero in probability. So the difference between $\sqrt{n}\tilde{\rho}_j$ and $\sqrt{n}\hat{\rho}_j$ vanishes, which means that the Q statistic calculated from the regression residuals $\{e_t\}$, too, is asymptotically chi-squared, and we can use this residual-based Q to test for serial correlation. If, on the other hand, the regressors are not strictly exogenous, then there is no guarantee that (2.10.14) holds. Consequently, the residual-based Q statistic may not be asymptotically chi-squared.

Testing with Predetermined, but Not Strictly Exogenous, Regressors

Therefore, when the regressors are not strictly exogenous, we need to modify the Q statistic to restore its asymptotic distribution. For this purpose, consider two restrictions:

$$\text{(stronger form of predeterminedness)}\quad \mathrm{E}(\varepsilon_t \mid \varepsilon_{t-1},\varepsilon_{t-2},\dots,\mathbf{x}_t,\mathbf{x}_{t-1},\dots)=0, \tag{2.10.15}$$

(stronger form of conditional homoskedasticity)

$$\mathrm{E}(\varepsilon_t^2 \mid \varepsilon_{t-1},\varepsilon_{t-2},\dots,\mathbf{x}_t,\mathbf{x}_{t-1},\dots)=\sigma^2>0. \tag{2.10.16}$$

The first condition is just reproducing (2.3.1) (with "t" now being used as the subscript). As was shown in Section 2.3, this is stronger than Assumption 2.3 and implies that $\mathbf{g}_t$ ($\equiv \mathbf{x}_t \cdot \varepsilon_t$) is an m.d.s. Condition (2.10.16), with the conditioning set including $\mathbf{x}_t$, is obviously stronger than Assumption 2.7 (conditional homoskedasticity). It also is stronger than the own conditional homoskedasticity assumption in Proposition 2.9 because the conditioning set includes current and past $\mathbf{x}$ as well as past ε. The next result shows that under these additional conditions there is an appropriate modification of the Q statistic.

Proposition 2.10 (testing for serial correlation with predetermined regressors): *Suppose that Assumptions 2.1, 2.2, 2.4, (2.10.15), and (2.10.16) are satisfied. Let the sample autocorrelation of the OLS residuals, $\hat{\rho}_j$, be defined as in (2.10.8). Then,*

$$\sqrt{n}\hat{\boldsymbol{\gamma}} \underset{\text{d}}{\rightarrow} N(\mathbf{0}, \sigma^4 \cdot (\mathbf{I}_p - \mathbf{\Phi})) \text{ and } \sqrt{n}\hat{\boldsymbol{\rho}} \underset{\text{d}}{\rightarrow} N(\mathbf{0}, \mathbf{I}_p - \mathbf{\Phi}), \tag{2.10.17}$$

where $\hat{\boldsymbol{\gamma}} = (\hat{\gamma}_1, \hat{\gamma}_2, \ldots, \hat{\gamma}_p)'$, $\hat{\boldsymbol{\rho}} = (\hat{\rho}_1, \hat{\rho}_2, \ldots, \hat{\rho}_p)'$, *and* ϕ_{jk} *(≡* (j, k) *element of the* $p \times p$ *matrix* $\mathbf{\Phi}$*) is given by*

$$\phi_{jk} = \text{E}(\mathbf{x}_t \cdot \varepsilon_{t-j})' \, \text{E}(\mathbf{x}_t\mathbf{x}_t')^{-1} \, \text{E}(\mathbf{x}_t \cdot \varepsilon_{t-k})/\sigma^2. \tag{2.10.18}$$

The proof, though not very difficult, is relegated to Appendix 2.B. By the Ergodic Theorem, matrix $\mathbf{\Phi}$ is consistently estimated by its sample counterpart:

$$\widehat{\mathbf{\Phi}} \equiv (\hat{\phi}_{jk}), \ \hat{\phi}_{jk} \equiv \bar{\boldsymbol{\mu}}_j' \mathbf{S}_{\mathbf{xx}}^{-1} \bar{\boldsymbol{\mu}}_k / s^2 \quad (j, k = 1, 2, \ldots, p), \tag{2.10.19}$$

where

$$s^2 \equiv \frac{1}{n-K} \sum_{t=1}^{n} e_t^2, \ \bar{\boldsymbol{\mu}}_j \equiv \frac{1}{n} \sum_{t=j+1}^{n} \mathbf{x}_t \cdot e_{t-j}.$$

It follows from this and Proposition 2.10 that

$$\text{modified Box-Pierce } Q \equiv n \cdot \hat{\boldsymbol{\rho}}'(\mathbf{I}_p - \widehat{\mathbf{\Phi}})^{-1}\hat{\boldsymbol{\rho}} \underset{\text{d}}{\rightarrow} \chi^2(p). \tag{2.10.20}$$

As long as the regressors are predetermined and the error is conditionally homoskedastic in the sense of (2.10.15) and (2.10.16), this modified Q statistic can be used even when the regressors are not strictly exogenous.

An Auxiliary Regression-Based Test

Although calculating this modified Q statistic is straightforward with matrix-based software, it is useful to find an asymptotically equivalent statistic that can be calculated from regression packages. For this purpose, consider the following auxiliary regression:

$$\text{regress } e_t \text{ on } \mathbf{x}_t, e_{t-1}, e_{t-2}, \ldots, e_{t-p}. \tag{2.10.21}$$

To run this auxiliary regression for $t = 1, 2, \ldots, n$, we need data on $(e_0, e_{-1}, \ldots, e_{-p+1})$. It does not matter asymptotically which particular numbers to assign to them, but it seems sensible to set them equal to 0, their expected value.[15] From this auxiliary regression, we can calculate the F statistic for the hypothesis that the p coefficients of $e_{t-1}, e_{t-2}, \ldots, e_{t-p}$ are all zero. Given Proposition 2.5(c), it is only natural to wonder whether $p \cdot F$ is asymptotically $\chi^2(p)$. This conjecture is indeed

[15] Another asymptotically equivalent choice is to run the auxiliary regression for $t = p+1, p+2, \ldots, n$.

true: under the hypothesis of Proposition 2.10, the modified Q statistic (2.10.20) is asymptotically equivalent to $p \cdot F$ (i.e., the difference between the two converges to zero in probability as $n \to \infty$), so $p \cdot F$, too, is asymptotically chi-squared (showing this is an analytical exercise).

This $p \cdot F$ statistic, in turn, is asymptotically equivalent to nR^2 from the auxiliary regression. This can be shown as follows. Recall the algebraic result from Chapter 1 that the F-ratio can be calculated from the difference in the sum of squared residuals between the unrestricted and restricted regressions. The unrestricted regression in the present context is (2.10.21) while the restricted regression is

$$\text{regress } e_t \text{ on } \mathbf{x}_t. \tag{2.10.22}$$

Therefore, if SSR_U and SSR_R are SSRs from (2.10.21) and (2.10.22), respectively, we have

$$p \cdot F = \frac{SSR_R - SSR_U}{SSR_U/(n - \#\mathbf{x}_t - p)} = (n - \#\mathbf{x}_t - p)\frac{SSR_R - SSR_U}{SSR_U} \tag{2.10.23}$$

where $\#\mathbf{x}_t$ is the number of variables in $\mathbf{x}_t$. However, since e_t is the residual from the original regression (a regression of y_t on $\mathbf{x}_t$), the regressors $\mathbf{x}_t$ in (2.10.22) have no explanatory power. So $SSR_R = \mathbf{e}'\mathbf{e}$ where $\mathbf{e}$ is the n-dimensional vector of residuals from the original regression, and (2.10.23) is numerically identical to

$$(n - \#\mathbf{x}_t - p)\,\frac{R_{uc}^2}{1 - R_{uc}^2},$$

where R_{uc}^2 is the uncentered R^2 for the auxiliary regression (2.10.21).[16] But since the sample mean of e_t is by construction zero (this is because $\mathbf{x}_t$ includes a constant), R_{uc}^2 is numerically identical to the R^2 for the auxiliary regression. Thus, we have proved the algebraic result that

$$p \cdot F = (n - \#\mathbf{x}_t - p)\,\frac{R^2}{1 - R^2},$$

where R^2 is equal to the R^2 for the auxiliary regression (2.10.21). Solving this equation for R^2 and multiplying both sides by n, we obtain

[16]Recall from (1.2.16) that the uncentered R^2 for a regression of $\mathbf{y}$ on $\mathbf{x}$ is defined as

$$R_{uc}^2 \equiv \frac{\mathbf{y}'\mathbf{y} - \mathbf{e}'\mathbf{e}}{\mathbf{y}'\mathbf{y}}.$$

In the present context, the $\mathbf{y}'\mathbf{y}$ in this formula is $\mathbf{e}'\mathbf{e}$ while the $\mathbf{e}'\mathbf{e}$ in the formula is SSR_U.

$$nR^2 = \frac{n}{n - \#\mathbf{x}_t - p} \cdot \frac{1}{1 + \frac{p \cdot F}{n - \#\mathbf{x}_t - p}} \cdot p \cdot F.$$

Since $\frac{p \cdot F}{n - \#\mathbf{x}_t - p} \to_p 0$ as $n \to \infty$ (an implication of Lemma 2.4(b)), this equation shows that $p \cdot F - nR^2 \to_p 0$. Therefore, nR^2 from the auxiliary regression (2.10.21) is asymptotically $\chi^2(p)$. The test based on nR^2 is called the **Breusch-Godfrey test for serial correlation**. When $p = 1$, the test statistic is asymptotically equivalent to the square of what is known as **Durbin's *h*** statistic.[17]

QUESTIONS FOR REVIEW

1. (Consistency of sample autocovariances) Show: if $\{z_t\}$ is ergodic stationary, then the sample autocovariance $\hat{\gamma}_j$ given in (2.10.1) is consistent for γ_j, the population autocovariance. **Hint:** $\gamma_j = \mathrm{E}(z_t z_{t-j}) - \mathrm{E}(z_t)\,\mathrm{E}(z_{t-j})$. Rewrite $\hat{\gamma}_j$ as

$$\hat{\gamma}_j = \frac{1}{n}\sum_{t=j+1}^{n} z_t\, z_{t-j} - \bar{z}_n \frac{1}{n}\sum_{t=j+1}^{n} z_{t-j} - \bar{z}_n \frac{1}{n}\sum_{t=j+1}^{n} z_t + \frac{n-j}{n}(\bar{z}_n)^2.$$

2. (Asymptotic equivalence of two Q's) Prove that the difference between the Box-Pierce Q and the Ljung-Box Q converges to 0 in probability as $n \to \infty$ (so their asymptotic distributions are the same). **Hint:** Let

$$\mathbf{x}_n \equiv \left((\sqrt{n}\hat{\rho}_1)^2, \ldots, (\sqrt{n}\hat{\rho}_p)^2\right)'.$$

Find a p-dimensional vector $\mathbf{a}_n$ such that the difference between two Q's is $\mathbf{a}_n'\mathbf{x}_n$. Show that $\mathbf{a}_n \to \mathbf{0}$. The asymptotic property to use is Lemma 2.4(b).

3. Consider $\sqrt{n}\tilde{\rho}_j$ and $\sqrt{n}\hat{\rho}_j$ in (2.10.11). We have shown that $\hat{\gamma}_0 \to_p \sigma^2$ and $\tilde{\gamma}_0 \to_p \sigma^2$. By Proposition 2.9, $\sqrt{n}\tilde{\gamma}_j \to_d N(0, \sigma^4)$. Taking these for granted, show that $\sqrt{n}\tilde{\rho}_j - \sqrt{n}\hat{\rho}_j \to_p 0$ if $\sqrt{n}\tilde{\gamma}_j - \sqrt{n}\hat{\gamma}_j \to_p 0$. **Hint:** If $\sqrt{n}\tilde{\gamma}_j - \sqrt{n}\hat{\gamma}_j \to_p 0$, then by Lemma 2.4(a), $\sqrt{n}\hat{\gamma}_j \to_d N(0, \sigma^4)$.

$$\frac{\tilde{\gamma}_j}{\tilde{\gamma}_0} - \frac{\hat{\gamma}_j}{\hat{\gamma}_0} = \tilde{\gamma}_j \cdot \left(\frac{1}{\tilde{\gamma}_0} - \frac{1}{\sigma^2}\right) - \hat{\gamma}_j \cdot \left(\frac{1}{\hat{\gamma}_0} - \frac{1}{\sigma^2}\right) + \frac{1}{\sigma^2} \cdot (\tilde{\gamma}_j - \hat{\gamma}_j).$$

Multiply both sides by $\sqrt{n}$ and apply Lemma 2.4(b).

[17]See Breusch (1978) and Godfrey (1978). The Breusch-Godfrey test was originally derived as a Lagrange Multiplier test for the case where the error is normally distributed and $\mathbf{x}_t$ consists of fixed regressors and the lagged dependent variable. The discussion in the text shows that the test is applicable to the more general case considered in Proposition 2.10.

2.11 Application: Rational Expectations Econometrics

In dynamic economic models and other contexts, expectations about the future naturally play an important role. **Rational expectations econometrics** concerns estimating equations involving expectations. Expectations are usually not observable, but, if we assume that economic agents form expectations rationally, we can overcome the problem of unobservable expectations using the techniques of this chapter. The application we consider is Fama's **efficient market hypothesis**. In his own words, "An efficient capital market is a market that is efficient in processing information.... In an efficient market, prices 'fully reflect' available information" (Fama, 1976, p. 133). The words "fully reflect" can be formalized precisely. We will do so for a particular capital market and test its implication.

The Efficient Market Hypotheses

The capital market studied in Fama (1975) is the market for U.S. Treasury bills. In this section we focus on the one-month Treasury bill rates observed on a monthly basis. (Later in the book we will also consider Treasury bills of different maturities.) To formalize market efficiency for the bills market, we need to introduce a few concepts from macroeconomics and finance. Since in this section we deal exclusively with time-series data, we use "t" rather than "i" for the subscript. Define

$v_t \equiv$ price of a one-month Treasury bill at the beginning of month t,

$R_t \equiv$ one-month nominal interest rate over month t, i.e., nominal return on the bill over the month $= (1 - v_t)/v_t$, so $v_t = 1/(1 + R_t)$,

$P_t \equiv$ value of the Consumer Price Index (CPI), which is our measure of the price level at the beginning of month t,

$\pi_{t+1} \equiv$ inflation rate over month t (i.e., from the beginning of month t to the beginning of month $t+1$) $= (P_{t+1} - P_t)/P_t$,

${}_t\pi_{t+1} \equiv$ expected inflation rate over month t, expectation formed at the beginning of month t,

$\eta_{t+1} \equiv$ inflation forecast error $= \pi_{t+1} - {}_t\pi_{t+1}$,

$$r_{t+1} \equiv \text{ex-post real interest rate over month } t = \frac{1/P_{t+1} - v_t/P_t}{v_t/P_t} = \frac{1+R_t}{1+\pi_{t+1}} - 1 \approx R_t - \pi_{t+1},$$

$${}_tr_{t+1} \equiv \text{ex-ante real interest rate} = \frac{1+R_t}{1+{}_t\pi_{t+1}} - 1 \approx R_t - {}_t\pi_{t+1}.$$

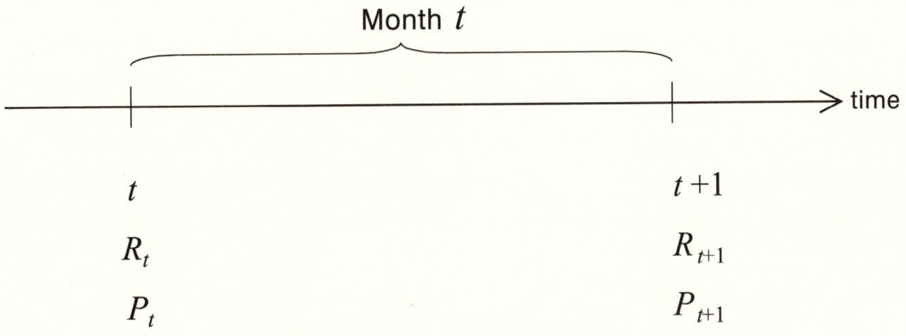

Figure 2.2: What's Observed When

Timing — the value of which variable is observed at what point in time — is very important in rational expectations econometrics. Our rule for dating variables (which is different from Fama's) is that the variable has subscript t if its value is first observed at the beginning of period (month) t.[18] For example, because π_{t+1}, the inflation rate over month t, depends on P_{t+1}, its subscript is $t+1$ rather than t. For the same reason, r_{t+1}, the ex-post real interest rate over month t has subscript $t+1$. In contrast, the nominal interest rate R_t over month t has subscript t, not $t+1$, because it is determined by the price of the Treasury bill at the beginning of month t, v_t. Figure 2.2 shows the value of which variable is observed at what point in time.

We take a period to be a month, only because our data are monthly. Note that the maturity of the security (one month) coincides with the sampling interval (a month). If the sampling interval is finer than the maturity, which is the case if, for example, we have monthly data on the three-month Treasury bill rate, then maturities overlap and we need a more sophisticated technique to be introduced in Chapter 6.

The efficient market hypothesis is a joint hypothesis combining:

Rational Expectations. Inflationary expectations are rational: ${}_t\pi_{t+1} = \mathrm{E}(\pi_{t+1} \mid I_t)$, where I_t is information available at the beginning of month t and includes $\{R_t, R_{t-1}, \ldots, \pi_t, \pi_{t-1}, \ldots\}$. Also, $I_t \supseteq I_{t-1} \supseteq I_{t-2} \ldots$. That is, agents participating in the market do not forget.

Constant Real Rates. The ex-ante real interest rate is constant: ${}_t r_{t+1} = r$.

[18] In Fama's (1975) notation, our π_{t+1} is $-\widetilde{\Delta}_t$, r_{t+1} is $\tilde{r}_{t+1}$, and I_t is ϕ_t.

Testable Implications

We derive two testable implications of the efficient market hypothesis by utilizing the following key observations about the inflation forecast error under rational expectations.

(a) $\mathrm{E}(\eta_{t+1} \mid I_t) = 0$, that is, the inflation forecast error is a martingale difference sequence with respect to the information set.

(b) $\{\eta_t, \eta_{t-1}, \dots\}$ as well as $\{R_t, R_{t-1}, \dots, \pi_t, \pi_{t-1}, \dots\}$ are included in I_t (known at the beginning of month t). That is, agents remember all past mistakes.

(a) makes intuitive sense; if people use all available information to forecast the inflation rate, the forecast error, which is known only after the fact, will not have any systematic relation to what people knew when they formed expectations. It can be proved easily:

$$
\begin{aligned}
&\mathrm{E}(\eta_{t+1} \mid I_t)\\
&= \mathrm{E}(\pi_{t+1} - {}_t\pi_{t+1} \mid I_t) \quad (\text{since } \eta_{t+1} \equiv \pi_{t+1} - {}_t\pi_{t+1})\\
&= \mathrm{E}(\pi_{t+1} \mid I_t) - \mathrm{E}({}_t\pi_{t+1} \mid I_t)\\
&= \mathrm{E}(\pi_{t+1} \mid I_t) - \mathrm{E}[\mathrm{E}(\pi_{t+1} \mid I_t) \mid I_t]\\
&\qquad (\text{since } {}_t\pi_{t+1} = \mathrm{E}(\pi_{t+1} \mid I_t) \text{ by rational expectations})\\
&= \mathrm{E}(\pi_{t+1} \mid I_t) - \mathrm{E}(\pi_{t+1} \mid I_t) = 0.
\end{aligned}
\tag{2.11.1}
$$

(b) follows because agents remember past inflation forecasts. Since ${}_{t-j-1}\pi_{t-j} = \mathrm{E}(\pi_{t-j} \mid I_{t-j-1})$ is a function of I_{t-j-1}, it is included in I_{t-j-1} (i.e., known at the beginning of month $t-j-1$) and hence in I_t (known at the beginning of month t) for $j \geq 0$. Thus $\eta_{t-j} \equiv \pi_{t-j} - {}_{t-j-1}\pi_{t-j}$ is included in I_t for all $j \geq 0$. Observations (a) and (b), together with the Law of Total Expectations, imply

(c) $\{\eta_t\}$ is m.d.s.

So, it is a zero mean and serially uncorrelated process.

These are not testable because expectations are unobservable, but, when combined with the constant-real-rate assumption, they imply two testable implications about the inflation rate and the interest rate which are observable.

Implication 1: The ex-post real interest rate has a constant mean and is serially uncorrelated.

This follows because

$$\begin{aligned} r_{t+1} &\equiv R_t - \pi_{t+1} \\ &= (R_t - {}_t\pi_{t+1}) - (\pi_{t+1} - {}_t\pi_{t+1}) \\ &= {}_tr_{t+1} - \eta_{t+1} \quad \text{(by definition)} \\ &= r - \eta_{t+1} \quad (\text{since } {}_tr_{t+1} = r \text{ by assumption}). \end{aligned} \tag{2.11.2}$$

By (c), $\{r_t\}$ has mean r and is serially uncorrelated.

Implication 2: $\mathrm{E}(\pi_{t+1} \mid I_t) = -r + R_t$.

That is, the best (in the sense of minimum mean squared error) inflation forecast on the basis of all the available information is the nominal interest rate; the nominal rate R_t, which is determined by the price of a Treasury bill v_t, summarizes all the currently available information relevant for predicting future inflation. This is the formalization of asset prices "fully reflecting" available information. This, too, can be derived easily. Solve (2.11.2) for π_{t+1} as $\pi_{t+1} = -r + R_t + \eta_{t+1}$. So

$$\begin{aligned} &\mathrm{E}(\pi_{t+1} \mid I_t) \\ &= \mathrm{E}(-r + R_t + \eta_{t+1} \mid I_t) \\ &= -r + R_t + \mathrm{E}(\eta_{t+1} \mid I_t) \quad (\text{since } r \text{ is a constant and } R_t \text{ is included in } I_t) \\ &= -r + R_t \quad \text{(by (a))}. \end{aligned} \tag{2.11.3}$$

In the rest of this section, we test these two implications of market efficiency.

Testing for Serial Correlation

Consider first the implication that the ex-post real rate has no serial correlation, which Fama tests using the result from Proposition 2.9. We use the monthly data set used by Mishkin (1992) on the one-month T-bill rate and the monthly CPI inflation rate, stated in percent at annual rates.[19] Figure 2.3 plots the data. The ex-post real interest rate, defined as the difference between the T-bill rate and the CPI inflation rate, is plotted in Figure 2.4. To duplicate Fama's results, we take the sample period to be the same as in Fama (1975), which is January 1953 through July 1971. The sample size is thus 223. The time-series properties of the real interest rate are summarized in Table 2.1. In calculating the sample autocorrelations $\hat{\rho}_j = \hat{\gamma}_j / \hat{\gamma}_0$,

[19]The data set is described in some detail in the empirical exercise. Following Fama, the inflation measure used in the text is calculated from the raw CPI numbers. The inflation measure used by Mishkin (1992) treats the housing component of the CPI consistently. See question (k) of Empirical Exercise 1.

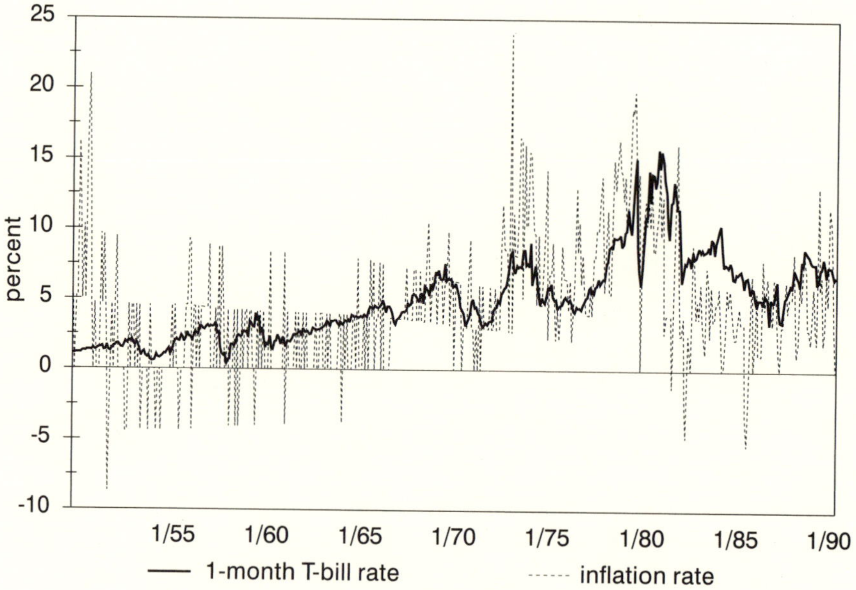

Figure 2.3: Inflation and Interest Rates

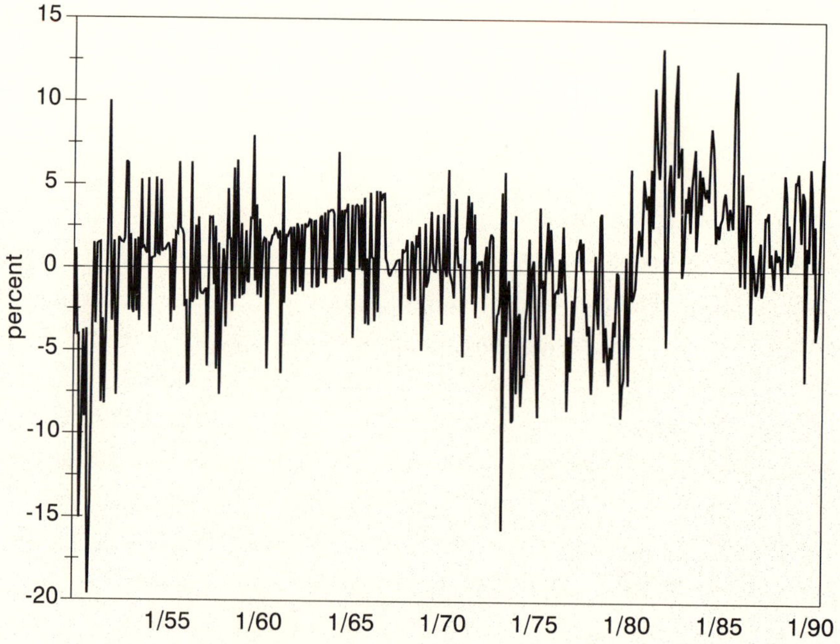

Figure 2.4: Real Interest Rates

Table 2.1: Real Interest Rates, January 1953–July 1971

	mean = 0.82%, standard deviation = 2.847%, sample size = 223											
	$j = 1$	$j = 2$	$j = 3$	$j = 4$	$j = 5$	$j = 6$	$j = 7$	$j = 8$	$j = 9$	$j = 10$	$j = 11$	$j = 12$
$\hat{\rho}_j$	−0.101	0.172	−0.019	−0.004	−0.064	−0.021	−0.092	0.095	0.094	0.019	0.004	0.207
std. error	0.067	0.067	0.067	0.067	0.067	0.067	0.067	0.067	0.067	0.067	0.067	0.067
Ljung-Box Q	2.3	9.1	9.1	9.1	10.1	10.2	12.1	14.2	16.3	16.4	16.4	26.5
p-value (%)	12.8%	1.1%	2.8%	5.8%	7.3%	11.7%	9.6%	7.6%	6.1%	8.9%	12.8%	0.9%

we use the formula (2.10.1) for $\hat{\gamma}_j$ where the denominator is the sample size rather than $n - j$. Similarly, the formula for the standard error of $\hat{\rho}_j$ is $1/\sqrt{n}$ rather than $1/\sqrt{n-j}$ (so the standard error does not depend on j). The Ljung-Box Q statistic in the table for, say, $j = 2$ is (2.10.5) with $p = 2$. The results in the table show that none of the autocorrelations are highly significant individually or as a group, in accordance with the first implication of the efficient market hypothesis.

Is the Nominal Interest Rate the Optimal Predictor?

We can test Implication 2 by estimating an appropriate regression and carrying out the t-test of Proposition 2.3. The remarkable fact about the efficient market hypothesis is that, despite its simplicity, it is specific enough to imply the important parts of the assumptions justifying the t-test.[20] To see this, let $y_t \equiv \pi_{t+1}$, $\mathbf{x}_t \equiv (1, R_t)'$, $\varepsilon_t \equiv \eta_{t+1}$ (the inflation forecast error), and rewrite (2.11.2) as

$$\pi_{t+1} = \beta_1 + \beta_2 R_t + \eta_{t+1} \quad \text{or} \quad y_t = \mathbf{x}_t'\boldsymbol{\beta} + \varepsilon_t, \tag{2.11.4}$$

so Assumption 2.1 is obviously satisfied with

$$\boldsymbol{\beta} = (-r, 1)'. \tag{2.11.5}$$

The other assumptions of the model are verified as follows.

- *Assumption 2.3 (predetermined regressors).* The $\mathbf{g}_t$ ($\equiv \mathbf{x}_t \cdot \varepsilon_t$) in the present context is $(\eta_{t+1}, R_t\eta_{t+1})'$. What we need to show is that $\mathrm{E}(\eta_{t+1}) = 0$ and $\mathrm{E}(R_t\eta_{t+1}) = 0$. The former is implied by (a) and the Law of Total Expectations:

$$\mathrm{E}(\eta_{t+1}) = \mathrm{E}[\mathrm{E}(\eta_{t+1} \mid I_t)] = 0. \tag{2.11.6}$$

  The latter holds because

$$\begin{aligned} &\mathrm{E}(R_t\eta_{t+1}) \\ &= \mathrm{E}[\mathrm{E}(R_t\eta_{t+1} \mid I_t)] \quad \text{(by the Law of Total Expectations)} \\ &= \mathrm{E}[R_t\,\mathrm{E}(\eta_{t+1} \mid I_t)] \quad \text{(by linearity of conditional expectations and } R_t \in I_t) \\ &= 0 \quad \text{(by (a))}. \end{aligned} \tag{2.11.7}$$

- *Assumption 2.5.* By (b), I_t includes $(\varepsilon_{t-1}\ (= \eta_t), \varepsilon_{t-2}, \ldots)$ as well as $(\mathbf{x}_t, \mathbf{x}_{t-1}, \ldots)$. (a) then implies (2.3.1), which is a sufficient condition for $\{\mathbf{g}_t\}$ to be m.d.s.

[20] The technical part—that the fourth-moment matrix $\mathrm{E}(\mathbf{g}_t\mathbf{g}_t')$ exists and is finite and that the regressors have finite fourth moments—is not implied by the efficient market hypothesis and needs to be assumed.

- *Assumption 2.4.* $E(\mathbf{x}_t\mathbf{x}_t')$ here is

$$E(\mathbf{x}_t\mathbf{x}_t') = \begin{bmatrix} 1 & E(R_t) \\ E(R_t) & E(R_t^2) \end{bmatrix}. \tag{2.11.8}$$

  Its determinant is $E(R_t^2) - [E(R_t)]^2 = \text{Var}(R_t)$, which must be positive; if the variance were zero, we would not observe the interest rate R_t fluctuating.

- *Assumption 2.2 (ergodic stationarity).* It requires $\{\pi_{t+1}, R_t\}$ to be ergodic stationary. The plot in Figure 2.3 shows a stretch of upward movements, especially for the nominal interest rate, although the stretch is followed by a reversion to a lower level. Testing stationarity of the series will be covered in Example 9.2 of Chapter 9. For now, despite this rather casual evidence to the contrary, we proceed under the assumption of stationarity (but the implication of having trending series will be touched upon in the final subsection). For ergodicity, we just have to assume it.

What we have shown is that, under the efficient market hypothesis, $\{y_t, \mathbf{x}_t\}$ (where $y_t = \pi_{t+1}$ and $\mathbf{x}_t = (1, R_t)'$) belongs to the set of DGPs satisfying Assumptions 2.1–2.5.

Having verified the required assumptions, we now proceed to estimation. Using our data, the estimated regression is, for $t = 1/53, \ldots, 7/71$,

$$\pi_{t+1} = \underset{(0.431)}{-0.868} + \underset{(0.112)}{1.015}\ R_t,$$

$$R^2 = 0.24,\ \text{mean of dependent variable} = 2.35,\ SER = 2.84\%, n = 223. \tag{2.11.9}$$

The heteroskedasticity-robust standard errors calculated as in (2.4.1) (where $\widehat{\mathbf{S}}$ is given by (2.5.1) with $\hat{\varepsilon}_i = e_i$) are shown in parentheses. As shown in (2.11.5), market efficiency implies that the R_t coefficient equals 1.[21] The robust t-ratio for the null that the R_t coefficient equals 1 is $(1.015 - 1)/0.112 = 0.13$. Its p-value is about 90 percent. Thus, we can easily accept the null hypothesis.

There are other ways to test the implication of the nominal interest rate summarizing all the currently available information. We can bring in more explanatory variables in the regression and see if they have an explanatory power over and above the nominal rate. The additional variables to be brought in, however, must be part of the current information set I_t because, obviously, the efficient market

[21] The intercept is known to be $-r$, but it does not produce a testable restriction since the efficient market hypothesis does not specify the value of r.

hypothesis is consistent with the existence of some variable *not currently available* predicting future inflation better than the current nominal rate. Formally, if $\mathbf{x}_t$ includes variables not included in I_t, the argument we used for verifying Assumption 2.3 is no longer valid.

R_t Is Not Strictly Exogenous

As has been emphasized, one important advantage of large-sample theory over finite-sample theory of Chapter 1 is that the regressors do not have to be strictly exogenous as long as they are orthogonal to the error term. We now show by example that R_t is not strictly exogenous, so finite-sample theory is not applicable to the Fama regression (2.11.4). Suppose that the process for the inflation rate is an AR(1) process:

$$\pi_t = c + \rho\pi_{t-1} + \eta_t, \quad \{\eta_t\} \text{ is independent white noise.}$$

If η_{t+1} is independent of any elements of I_t, then

$$\begin{aligned} &\mathrm{E}(\pi_{t+1} \mid I_t) \\ &= c + \rho\pi_t + \mathrm{E}(\eta_{t+1} \mid I_t) \quad (\text{since } \pi_t \text{ is in } I_t) \\ &= c + \rho\pi_t \quad (\text{since } \mathrm{E}(\eta_{t+1} \mid I_t) = \mathrm{E}(\eta_{t+1}) \text{ and } \mathrm{E}(\eta_{t+1}) = 0 \text{ by assumption}). \end{aligned}$$

So η_{t+1} is indeed the inflation forecast error for π_{t+1} and

$$R_t = r + c + \rho\pi_t$$

(since $R_t = r + \mathrm{E}(\pi_{t+1} \mid I_t)$ under market efficiency). It is then easy to see that the error term ε_t in the Fama regression (of π_{t+1} on a constant and R_t), which is the inflation forecast error η_{t+1}, can be correlated with future regressors. For example,

$$\begin{aligned} &\mathrm{Cov}(\varepsilon_t, R_{t+1}) \\ &= \mathrm{Cov}(\eta_{t+1}, r + c + \rho\pi_{t+1}) \\ &= \rho\,\mathrm{Cov}(\eta_{t+1}, \pi_{t+1}) \\ &= \rho\,\mathrm{Var}(\eta_{t+1}) \quad (\text{since } \pi_{t+1} = c + \rho\pi_t + \eta_{t+1} \text{ and } \mathrm{Cov}(\eta_{t+1}, \pi_t) = 0), \end{aligned}$$

which is not zero.

Although finite-sample theory is not applicable, its prescription for statistical inference is approximately valid, provided that the error is conditionally homoskedastic and the sample size is large enough, which was the message of Section 2.6.

Subsequent Developments

Although Fama's paper represents perhaps the finest example of rational expectations econometrics, events after its publication and a large number of empirical studies it inspired proved that the near one-for-one relation between inflation and interest rates is limited to the postwar period until 1979. Such strong association cannot be found for the prewar period or for many other countries. Furthermore, the increase in the real interest rates after the change in the Fed's operating procedure that took place in October 1979 runs counter to the premise of the Fama regression that the expected real interest rate is constant over time. When the sample is restricted to the post-October 1979 period, the interest rate coefficient in the Fama regression is far below unity.[22]

These findings raise the question of why the strong association occurs only for certain periods but not for others. The explanation by Mishkin (1992) is that the inflation premium gets incorporated into interest rates only gradually. In periods when the inflation rate shows only short-run fluctuations, interest rates are not responsive to inflation. However, sustained movements in inflation will be reflected in interest rates. The period when the strong association is observed (which includes Fama's sample period, see Figure 2.3) is precisely when inflation showed a sustained upward movement.

On January 29, 1997, the U.S. Treasury auctioned \$7 billion in ten-year inflation-indexed bonds, making it possible for researchers to observe the ex-ante real interest rate as the yield on indexed bonds. Evidence from Great Britain, where indexed bonds have been available since the early 1980s, is that the yields on indexed bonds, although much less volatile than the yield on ordinary bonds, are not constant over time. The constant-real-rate assumption that we made was the auxiliary assumption whereby we can test whether bond prices fully reflect available information. Now we can do so without the auxiliary assumption by regressing the actual inflation rate on the yield differential between the conventional and indexed bonds. We can also relax the assumption, made implicitly so far, that the yield differential equals the expected inflation rate. Investors may not be risk-neutral, and the inflation risk premium over and above the expected inflation rate may be needed to induce them to hold ordinary bonds. If so, the expected inflation rate is once again unobservable. Rational expectations econometrics will continue to be a useful tool for dealing with unobservable expectations.

[22] See, for example, Mishkin (1992, Table 1). We will verify this in part (l) of Empirical Exercise 1.

QUESTIONS FOR REVIEW

1. Let $R_t = 5\%$ and $\pi_{t+1} = 2\%$. Calculate r_{t+1} using the two formulas, $(1 + R_t)/(1 + \pi_{t+1}) - 1$ and $R_t - \pi_{t+1}$. Is the difference small? What if $R_t = 20\%$ and $\pi_{t+1} = 17\%$?

2. Show that $\widehat{\mathrm{E}}^*(\pi_{t+1} \mid 1, R_t) = -r + R_t$ under the efficient market hypothesis. **Hint:** Use (2.9.7).

3. If the inflation forecast error η_{t+1} were observable, how would you test market efficiency? Do we need the constant ex-ante real rate assumption?

4. If the inflation rates and the interest rates were measured in fractions rather than percent (e.g., 0.08 instead of 8%), how would the regression result (2.11.9) change? If the inflation rate is in percent but per month and the interest rate is in percent per year? **Hint:** If x is the inflation rate per month and y is its annual rate, then $1 + y = (1 + x)^{12}$ so that $y \approx 12x$.

5. Suppose in (2.11.4) $\mathbf{x}_t$ includes a third variable which is not in I_t. Which part of the argument deriving Assumption 2.3 fails? **Hint:** The third element of $\mathbf{g}_t$ is the third variable times η_{t+1}.

6. Provide an example of market *in*efficiency such that Implication 1 holds but Implication 2 does not. **Hint:** Suppose π_t and R_t are serially independent and mutually independent processes.

2.12 Time Regressions

Throughout this chapter, we have assumed that $\{y_t, \mathbf{x}_t\}$ is stationary. This assumption, however, is not always satisfied in time-series regressions. In this book, we examine two cases where the regressors are not stationary and yet OLS is applicable. The first is examined here, while the other case, called "cointegrating regressions," is covered in Chapter 10.

The regression we consider is written as

$$y_t = \alpha + \delta \cdot t + \varepsilon_t, \tag{2.12.1}$$

where $\{\varepsilon_t\}$ is independent white noise. This regression can be written as $y_t = \mathbf{x}_t'\boldsymbol{\beta} + \varepsilon_t$ with

$$\mathbf{x}_t = (1, t)', \quad \boldsymbol{\beta} = (\alpha, \delta)'. \tag{2.12.2}$$

Clearly, $\mathbf{x}_t$ is not stationary because the mean of the second element is t, which increases with time. Similarly, y_t is not stationary. The linear function, $\alpha + \delta \cdot t$, is called the **time trend** of y_t. We say that a process is **trend stationary** if it can be written as the sum of a time trend and a stationary process. The process $\{y_t\}$ here is a special trend-stationary process where the stationary component is independent white noise.

The Asymptotic Distribution of the OLS Estimator

Let $\mathbf{b}$ be the OLS estimate of $\boldsymbol{\beta}$ based on a sample of size n:

$$\mathbf{b} \equiv \begin{bmatrix} \hat{\alpha} \\ \hat{\delta} \end{bmatrix} = \Big(\sum_{t=1}^{n} \mathbf{x}_t \mathbf{x}_t'\Big)^{-1} \Big(\sum_{t=1}^{n} \mathbf{x}_t \cdot y_t\Big). \tag{2.12.3}$$

The sampling error can be written as

$$\mathbf{b} - \boldsymbol{\beta} = \begin{bmatrix} \hat{\alpha} - \alpha \\ \hat{\delta} - \delta \end{bmatrix} = \Big(\sum_{t=1}^{n} \mathbf{x}_t \mathbf{x}_t'\Big)^{-1} \Big(\sum_{t=1}^{n} \mathbf{x}_t \cdot \varepsilon_t\Big). \tag{2.12.4}$$

Using the algebraic result that $\sum_{t=1}^{n} t = n \cdot (n+1)/2$, $\sum_{t=1}^{n} t^2 = n \cdot (n+1)(2n+1)/6$, it is easy to show

$$\sum_{t=1}^{n} \mathbf{x}_t \mathbf{x}_t' = \begin{bmatrix} n & n \cdot (n+1)/2 \\ n \cdot (n+1)/2 & n \cdot (n+1)(2n+1)/6 \end{bmatrix}. \tag{2.12.5}$$

So, unlike in the stationary case, $\sum_{t=1}^{n} \mathbf{x}_t \mathbf{x}_t'/n$ does not converge in probability to a nonsingular matrix; it actually diverges.

It turns out that the OLS estimates $\hat{\alpha}$ and $\hat{\delta}$ are consistent but have different rates of convergence. As in the stationary case, the rate of convergence for $\hat{\alpha}$ is $\sqrt{n}$. In contrast, the rate for $\hat{\delta}$ is $n^{3/2}$. That is, $n^{3/2}(\hat{\delta} - \delta)$ converges to a nondegenerate distribution (the distribution of a nonconstant random variable). To assign those different rates of convergence to the elements of $\mathbf{b} - \boldsymbol{\beta}$, consider multiplying both sides of (2.12.4) by the matrix

$$\boldsymbol{\Upsilon}_n = \begin{bmatrix} \sqrt{n} & 0 \\ 0 & n^{3/2} \end{bmatrix}. \tag{2.12.6}$$

This produces

$$\begin{aligned}\boldsymbol{\Upsilon}_n(\mathbf{b}-\boldsymbol{\beta}) = \begin{bmatrix}\sqrt{n}(\hat{\alpha}-\alpha)\\ n^{3/2}(\hat{\delta}-\delta)\end{bmatrix} &= \boldsymbol{\Upsilon}_n\Big(\sum_{t=1}^{n}\mathbf{x}_t\mathbf{x}_t'\Big)^{-1}\Big(\sum_{t=1}^{n}\mathbf{x}_t\cdot\varepsilon_t\Big)\\ &= \boldsymbol{\Upsilon}_n\Big(\sum_{t=1}^{n}\mathbf{x}_t\mathbf{x}_t'\Big)^{-1}\boldsymbol{\Upsilon}_n\boldsymbol{\Upsilon}_n^{-1}\Big(\sum_{t=1}^{n}\mathbf{x}_t\cdot\varepsilon_t\Big)\\ &= \Big[\boldsymbol{\Upsilon}_n^{-1}\Big(\sum_{t=1}^{n}\mathbf{x}_t\mathbf{x}_t'\Big)\boldsymbol{\Upsilon}_n^{-1}\Big]^{-1}\Big(\boldsymbol{\Upsilon}_n^{-1}\sum_{t=1}^{n}\mathbf{x}_t\cdot\varepsilon_t\Big)\\ &\equiv \mathbf{Q}_n^{-1}\mathbf{v}_n,\end{aligned} \tag{2.12.7}$$

where

$$\mathbf{Q}_n \equiv \boldsymbol{\Upsilon}_n^{-1}\Big(\sum_{t=1}^{n}\mathbf{x}_t\mathbf{x}_t'\Big)\boldsymbol{\Upsilon}_n^{-1} \quad\text{and}\quad \mathbf{v}_n \equiv \boldsymbol{\Upsilon}_n^{-1}\sum_{t=1}^{n}\mathbf{x}_t\cdot\varepsilon_t. \tag{2.12.8}$$

Substituting (2.12.5) and (2.12.6) into these expressions for $\mathbf{Q}_n$ and $\mathbf{v}_n$, we obtain

$$\mathbf{Q}_n = \begin{bmatrix}1 & (n+1)/(2n)\\ (n+1)/(2n) & (n+1)(2n+1)/(6n^2)\end{bmatrix},$$

$$\mathbf{v}_n = \begin{bmatrix}\frac{1}{\sqrt{n}}\sum_{t=1}^{n}\varepsilon_t\\ \frac{1}{\sqrt{n}}\sum_{t=1}^{n}(t/n)\varepsilon_t\end{bmatrix}. \tag{2.12.9}$$

Clearly, we have

$$\mathbf{Q}_n \to \mathbf{Q} \equiv \begin{bmatrix}1 & 1/2\\ 1/2 & 1/3\end{bmatrix}. \tag{2.12.10}$$

For $\mathbf{v}_n$, it can be shown (see, e.g., Hamilton, 1994, pp. 458–460) that

$$\mathbf{v}_n \underset{d}{\to} N(\mathbf{0}, \sigma^2\mathbf{Q}) \tag{2.12.11}$$

if $\{\varepsilon_t\}$ is independent white noise with $\mathrm{E}(\varepsilon_t^2) = \sigma^2$ and $\mathrm{E}(\varepsilon_t^4) < \infty$. Thus the asymptotic distribution of (2.12.7) is normal with mean $\mathbf{0}$ and variance $\mathbf{Q}^{-1}(\sigma^2\mathbf{Q})\cdot\mathbf{Q}^{-1} = \sigma^2\mathbf{Q}^{-1}$. Summarizing the discussion so far,

Proposition 2.11 (OLS estimation of the time regression): *Consider the time regression (2.12.1) where* ε_t *is independent white noise with* $\mathrm{E}(\varepsilon_t^2) = \sigma^2$ *and*

$\mathrm{E}(\varepsilon_t^4) < \infty$ *and let* $\hat{\alpha}$ *and* $\hat{\delta}$ *be the OLS estimate of* α *and* δ. *Then*

$$\begin{bmatrix} \sqrt{n}(\hat{\alpha} - \alpha) \\ n^{3/2}(\hat{\delta} - \delta) \end{bmatrix} \underset{d}{\to} N\left(\mathbf{0}, \sigma^2 \cdot \begin{bmatrix} 1 & 1/2 \\ 1/2 & 1/3 \end{bmatrix}^{-1}\right).$$

As in the stationary case, $\hat{\alpha}$ is $\sqrt{n}$-consistent because $\sqrt{n}(\hat{\alpha} - \alpha)$ converges to a (normal) random variable. The OLS estimate of the time coefficient, $\hat{\delta}$, too is consistent, but the speed of convergence is faster: it is $n^{3/2}$-consistent in that $n^{3/2}(\hat{\delta} - \delta)$ converge to a random variable. In this sense, $\hat{\delta}$ is **hyperconsistent**.[23]

Hypothesis Testing for Time Regressions

Thus, the OLS coefficient estimates of the time regression are asymptotically normal, provided the sampling error is properly scaled. We now show that the deflation of the sampling error by the standard error provides a scaling that makes the resulting ratio — the t-value — asymptotically standard normal.

First consider the t-value for the null $\alpha = \alpha_0$. Noting that

$$(1, 1) \text{ element of } \left(\sum_{t=1}^{n} \mathbf{x}_t \mathbf{x}_t'\right)^{-1} = [1 \quad 0]\left(\sum_{t=1}^{n} \mathbf{x}_t \mathbf{x}_t'\right)^{-1} \begin{bmatrix} 1 \\ 0 \end{bmatrix}, \qquad (2.12.12)$$

the t-value can be written as

$$\begin{aligned} t &= \frac{\hat{\alpha} - \alpha_0}{\sqrt{s^2 \cdot [1 \quad 0]\left(\sum_{t=1}^{n} \mathbf{x}_t \mathbf{x}_t'\right)^{-1} \left[\begin{smallmatrix} 1 \\ 0 \end{smallmatrix}\right]}} \\ &= \frac{\sqrt{n}(\hat{\alpha} - \alpha_0)}{\sqrt{s^2 \cdot [\sqrt{n} \quad 0]\left(\sum_{t=1}^{n} \mathbf{x}_t \mathbf{x}_t'\right)^{-1} \left[\begin{smallmatrix} \sqrt{n} \\ 0 \end{smallmatrix}\right]}} \\ &= \frac{\sqrt{n}(\hat{\alpha} - \alpha_0)}{\sqrt{s^2 \cdot [1 \quad 0]\mathbf{\Upsilon}_n\left(\sum_{t=1}^{n} \mathbf{x}_t \mathbf{x}_t'\right)^{-1} \mathbf{\Upsilon}_n \left[\begin{smallmatrix} 1 \\ 0 \end{smallmatrix}\right]}} \qquad (\text{since } [\sqrt{n} \quad 0] = [1 \quad 0]\mathbf{\Upsilon}_n) \\ &= \frac{\sqrt{n}(\hat{\alpha} - \alpha_0)}{\sqrt{s^2 \cdot [1 \quad 0]\left\{\mathbf{\Upsilon}_n^{-1}\left(\sum_{t=1}^{n} \mathbf{x}_t \mathbf{x}_t'\right)\mathbf{\Upsilon}_n^{-1}\right\}^{-1} \left[\begin{smallmatrix} 1 \\ 0 \end{smallmatrix}\right]}} \\ &= \frac{\sqrt{n}(\hat{\alpha} - \alpha_0)}{\sqrt{s^2 \cdot [1 \quad 0]\mathbf{Q}_n^{-1} \left[\begin{smallmatrix} 1 \\ 0 \end{smallmatrix}\right]}} \qquad (\text{by } (2.12.8)). \end{aligned} \qquad (2.12.13)$$

[23]Estimators that are n-consistent are usually called **superconsistent**. A prominent example of superconsistent estimators arises in the estimation of unit-root processes; see Chapter 9. Some authors use the term "superconsistent" more broadly, to refer to estimators that are n^{γ}-consistent with $\gamma > \frac{1}{2}$. In their language, $\hat{\delta}$ in the text is superconsistent.

It is straightforward (see review question 1) to show that s^2 is consistent for σ^2. And by (2.12.10), $\mathbf{Q}_n \to_p \mathbf{Q}$. Thus by Lemma 2.4(c) and Proposition 2.11,

$$t\text{-value for the null of } \alpha = \alpha_0 \underset{d}{\to} \frac{\text{1st element of } \mathbf{z}}{\sqrt{\sigma^2 \times (1,1) \text{ element of } \mathbf{Q}^{-1}}} \tag{2.12.14}$$

where $\mathbf{z} \sim N(\mathbf{0}, \sigma^2\mathbf{Q}^{-1})$. So the t-value for α is asymptotically $N(0, 1)$, as in the stationary case.

Using the same trick and noting that $[0 \quad n^{3/2}] = [0 \quad 1]\boldsymbol{\Upsilon}_n$, we can write the t-value for the null of $\delta = \delta_0$ as

$$t = \frac{n^{3/2}(\hat{\delta} - \delta_0)}{\sqrt{s^2 \cdot [0 \quad 1]\mathbf{Q}_n^{-1}\left[\begin{smallmatrix}0\\1\end{smallmatrix}\right]}}. \tag{2.12.15}$$

So the t-value for the coefficient of time, too, is asymptotically $N(0, 1)$! Inference about α or δ can be done exactly as in the stationary case.

QUESTIONS FOR REVIEW

1. (s^2 is consistent for σ^2) Show that $s^2 \to_p \sigma^2$. **Hint:** From (2.3.10), derive

$$e_t^2 = \varepsilon_t^2 - 2(\mathbf{b} - \boldsymbol{\beta})'\boldsymbol{\Upsilon}_n\boldsymbol{\Upsilon}_n^{-1}\mathbf{x}_t \cdot \varepsilon_t + (\mathbf{b} - \boldsymbol{\beta})'\boldsymbol{\Upsilon}_n\boldsymbol{\Upsilon}_n^{-1}\mathbf{x}_t\mathbf{x}_t'\boldsymbol{\Upsilon}_n^{-1}\boldsymbol{\Upsilon}_n(\mathbf{b} - \boldsymbol{\beta}).$$

Sum over t to obtain

$$\frac{1}{n}\sum_{t=1}^{n} e_t^2 = \frac{1}{n}\sum_{t=1}^{n} \varepsilon_t^2 - \frac{2}{n}(\mathbf{b} - \boldsymbol{\beta})'\boldsymbol{\Upsilon}_n\mathbf{v}_n + \frac{1}{n}(\mathbf{b} - \boldsymbol{\beta})'\boldsymbol{\Upsilon}_n\mathbf{Q}_n\boldsymbol{\Upsilon}_n(\mathbf{b} - \boldsymbol{\beta}).$$

2. (Serially uncorrelated errors) Suppose $\{\varepsilon_t\}$ is a general stationary process, rather than an independent white noise process, but suppose that $\mathbf{v}_n \to_d N(\mathbf{0}, \mathbf{V})$ where $\mathbf{V} \neq \sigma^2\mathbf{Q}$. Are the OLS estimators, $\hat{\alpha}$ and $\hat{\delta}$, consistent? Does $\boldsymbol{\Upsilon}_n(\mathbf{b} - \boldsymbol{\beta})$ converge to a normal random vector with mean zero? If so, what is the variance of the normal distribution? [Answer: $\mathbf{Q}^{-1}\mathbf{V}\mathbf{Q}^{-1}$.] Are the t-values asymptotically normal? [Answer: Yes, but the variance will not be unity.]

Appendix 2.A: Asymptotics with Fixed Regressors

To prove results similar in conclusion to Proposition 2.5, we add to Assumption 2.1 the following.

Assumption 2.A.1: $\mathbf{X}$ *is deterministic. As* $n \to \infty$, $\mathbf{S_{xx}} \to \mathbf{\Sigma_{xx}}$, *a nonsingular matrix (conventional convergence here, because* $\mathbf{X}$ *is nonrandom).*

Assumption 2.A.2: $\{\varepsilon_i\}$ *is i.i.d. with* $\mathrm{E}(\varepsilon_i) = 0$ *and* $\mathrm{Var}(\varepsilon_i) = \sigma^2$.

Proposition 2.A.1 (asymptotics with fixed regressors): *Under Assumptions 2.1, 2.A.1, and 2.A.2, plus an assumption called the Lindeberg condition on* $\{\mathbf{g}_i\}$ *(where* $\mathbf{g}_i \equiv \mathbf{x}_i \cdot \varepsilon_i$*), the same conclusions as in Proposition 2.5 hold.*

Rather than stating the Lindeberg condition, we explain why such condition is needed. To prove the asymptotic normality of $\mathbf{b}$, we would take (2.3.8) and show that $\sqrt{n}\,\bar{\mathbf{g}}$ converges to a normal distribution. The technical difficulty is that the sequence $\{\mathbf{g}_i\}$ is not stationary thanks to the assumption that $\{\mathbf{x}_i\}$ is a sequence of nonrandom vectors. For example,

$$\mathrm{Var}(\mathbf{g}_i) = \mathrm{E}(\varepsilon_i^2 \mathbf{x}_i \mathbf{x}_i') = \mathrm{E}(\varepsilon_i^2)\mathbf{x}_i \mathbf{x}_i' = \sigma^2 \mathbf{x}_i \mathbf{x}_i'$$

is not constant across observations. Consequently, neither the Lindeberg-Levy CLT nor the Martingale Differences CLT is applicable. Fortunately, however, there is a generalization of the Lindeberg-Levy CLT to nonstationary processes with nonconstant variance, called the **Lindeberg-Feller CLT**, which places a technical restriction on the tail distribution of $\mathbf{g}_i$ to prevent observations with large $\mathbf{x}_i$ from dominating the distribution of $\sqrt{n}\,\bar{\mathbf{g}}$.

Appendix 2.B: Proof of Proposition 2.10

This appendix provides a proof of Proposition 2.10. We start with the expression for $\hat{\gamma}_j$ given in (2.10.12). The first part of the proof is to find an expression that is asymptotically equivalent.

$$\begin{aligned}
\sqrt{n}\hat{\gamma}_j &= \sqrt{n}\tilde{\gamma}_j - \frac{1}{n}\sum_{t=j+1}^{n} (\mathbf{x}_{t-j} \cdot \varepsilon_t + \mathbf{x}_t \cdot \varepsilon_{t-j})'\sqrt{n}(\mathbf{b} - \boldsymbol{\beta}) \\
&\quad + \sqrt{n}(\mathbf{b} - \boldsymbol{\beta})'\Big(\frac{1}{n}\sum_{t=j+1}^{n} \mathbf{x}_t \mathbf{x}_{t-j}'\Big)(\mathbf{b} - \boldsymbol{\beta}) \\
&\underset{a}{\sim} \sqrt{n}\tilde{\gamma}_j - \frac{1}{n}\sum_{t=j+1}^{n} (\mathbf{x}_{t-j} \cdot \varepsilon_t + \mathbf{x}_t \cdot \varepsilon_{t-j})'\sqrt{n}(\mathbf{b} - \boldsymbol{\beta})
\end{aligned}$$

(since the last term above vanishes)

$$
\begin{aligned}
&\underset{a}{\sim} \sqrt{n}\tilde{\gamma}_j - \mathrm{E}(\mathbf{x}_{t-j} \cdot \varepsilon_t + \mathbf{x}_t \cdot \varepsilon_{t-j})' \sqrt{n}(\mathbf{b} - \boldsymbol{\beta}) \\
&\qquad \Big(\text{since } \frac{1}{n} \sum_{t=j+1}^{n} (\mathbf{x}_{t-j} \cdot \varepsilon_t + \mathbf{x}_t \cdot \varepsilon_{t-j}) \underset{\mathrm{p}}{\to} \mathrm{E}(\mathbf{x}_{t-j} \cdot \varepsilon_t + \mathbf{x}_t \cdot \varepsilon_{t-j})\Big) \\
&= \sqrt{n}\tilde{\gamma}_j - \boldsymbol{\mu}_j' \sqrt{n}(\mathbf{b} - \boldsymbol{\beta}) \quad \text{where } \boldsymbol{\mu}_j \equiv \mathrm{E}(\mathbf{x}_t \cdot \varepsilon_{t-j}) \\
&\qquad (\text{since } \mathrm{E}(\mathbf{x}_{t-j} \cdot \varepsilon_t) = \mathbf{0} \text{ by (2.10.15)}) \\
&= \sqrt{n}\tilde{\gamma}_j - \boldsymbol{\mu}_j' \sqrt{n} \mathbf{S}_{\mathbf{xx}}^{-1} \frac{1}{n} \sum_{t=1}^{n} \mathbf{x}_t \cdot \varepsilon_t \\
&= \sqrt{n} \frac{1}{n} \sum_{t=j+1}^{n} \varepsilon_t \varepsilon_{t-j} - \boldsymbol{\mu}_j' \sqrt{n} \mathbf{S}_{\mathbf{xx}}^{-1} \frac{1}{n} \sum_{t=1}^{n} \mathbf{x}_t \cdot \varepsilon_t \quad \text{(by (2.10.7))} \\
&\underset{a}{\sim} \sqrt{n} \frac{1}{n} \sum_{t=1}^{n} \varepsilon_t \varepsilon_{t-j} - \boldsymbol{\mu}_j' \sqrt{n} \mathbf{S}_{\mathbf{xx}}^{-1} \frac{1}{n} \sum_{t=1}^{n} \mathbf{x}_t \cdot \varepsilon_t \\
&\qquad \Big(\text{since } \sqrt{n} \frac{1}{n} \sum_{t=1}^{n} \varepsilon_t \varepsilon_{t-j} - \sqrt{n} \frac{1}{n} \sum_{t=j+1}^{n} \varepsilon_t \varepsilon_{t-j} \\
&\qquad\qquad = \frac{1}{\sqrt{n}} \sum_{t=1}^{j} \varepsilon_t \varepsilon_{t-j} \underset{\mathrm{p}}{\to} 0 \text{ for each } j\Big) \\
&\underset{a}{\sim} \sqrt{n} \frac{1}{n} \sum_{t=1}^{n} \varepsilon_t \varepsilon_{t-j} - \boldsymbol{\mu}_j' \sqrt{n} \boldsymbol{\Sigma}_{\mathbf{xx}}^{-1} \frac{1}{n} \sum_{t=1}^{n} \mathbf{x}_t \cdot \varepsilon_t \qquad (\text{since } \mathbf{S}_{\mathbf{xx}} \underset{\mathrm{p}}{\to} \boldsymbol{\Sigma}_{\mathbf{xx}}) \\
&= \mathbf{c}_j' \sqrt{n}\, \bar{\mathbf{g}}_j,
\end{aligned}
$$

where

$$
\underset{((K+1)\times 1)}{\mathbf{c}_j} \equiv \begin{bmatrix} 1 \\ -\boldsymbol{\Sigma}_{\mathbf{xx}}^{-1} \boldsymbol{\mu}_j \end{bmatrix}, \quad \underset{((K+1)\times 1)}{\bar{\mathbf{g}}_j} \equiv \frac{1}{n} \sum_{t=1}^{n} \mathbf{g}_{jt}, \quad \underset{((K+1)\times 1)}{\mathbf{g}_{jt}} \equiv \begin{bmatrix} \varepsilon_{t-j}\varepsilon_t \\ \mathbf{x}_t \cdot \varepsilon_t \end{bmatrix}. \tag{2.B.1}
$$

Thus, letting

$$
\underset{(p\times 1)}{\hat{\boldsymbol{\gamma}}} \equiv \begin{bmatrix} \hat{\gamma}_1 \\ \vdots \\ \hat{\gamma}_p \end{bmatrix},
$$

we have proved that

$$
\sqrt{n}\, \hat{\boldsymbol{\gamma}} \underset{a}{\sim} \mathbf{C}' \sqrt{n}\, \bar{\mathbf{g}}
$$

where

$$\underset{(p(K+1)\times p)}{\mathbf{C}} \equiv \begin{bmatrix} \mathbf{c}_1 & & \\ & \ddots & \\ & & \mathbf{c}_p \end{bmatrix},$$

$$\underset{(p(K+1)\times 1)}{\bar{\mathbf{g}}} \equiv \frac{1}{n}\sum_{t=1}^{n} \mathbf{g}_t,$$

$$\underset{(p(K+1)\times 1)}{\mathbf{g}_t} \equiv \begin{bmatrix} \mathbf{g}_{1t} \\ \vdots \\ \mathbf{g}_{pt} \end{bmatrix}.$$

The second part of the proof is to show that $\mathbf{g}_t$ is a martingale difference sequence, namely, that

$$\mathrm{E}(\mathbf{g}_{jt} \mid \mathbf{g}_{t-1}, \mathbf{g}_{t-2}, \dots) = \mathbf{0} \quad (\text{for } j = 1, 2, \dots, p).$$

But this easily follows from the Law of Total Expectations, the fact that $(\mathbf{g}_{t-1}, \mathbf{g}_{t-2}, \dots)$ has less information than $(\mathbf{x}_t, \mathbf{x}_{t-1}, \dots, \varepsilon_{t-1}, \varepsilon_{t-2}, \dots)$, and (2.10.15).

Clearly, $\mathbf{g}_t$ is ergodic stationary. Therefore, by the ergodic stationary Martingale Differences CLT, $\sqrt{n}\,\bar{\mathbf{g}} \to_{\mathrm{d}} N(\mathbf{0}, \mathrm{E}(\mathbf{g}_t\mathbf{g}_t'))$. The next step is to calculate $\mathrm{E}(\mathbf{g}_t\mathbf{g}_t')$. Its (j, k) block is

$$\underset{((K+1)\times(K+1))}{\mathrm{E}(\mathbf{g}_{jt}\mathbf{g}_{kt}')} = \begin{bmatrix} \mathrm{E}(\varepsilon_t^2\varepsilon_{t-j}\varepsilon_{t-k}) & \mathrm{E}(\mathbf{x}_t'\varepsilon_t^2\varepsilon_{t-j}) \\ \mathrm{E}(\mathbf{x}_t\varepsilon_t^2\varepsilon_{t-k}) & \mathrm{E}(\varepsilon_t^2\mathbf{x}_t\mathbf{x}_t') \end{bmatrix}.$$

By using the Law of Total Expectations and (2.10.16), it is easy to show that

$$\underset{((K+1)\times(K+1))}{\mathrm{E}(\mathbf{g}_{jt}\mathbf{g}_{kt}')} = \begin{bmatrix} \sigma^4\delta_{jk} & \sigma^2\boldsymbol{\mu}_j' \\ \sigma^2\boldsymbol{\mu}_k & \sigma^2\boldsymbol{\Sigma}_{\mathbf{xx}} \end{bmatrix}, \tag{2.B.2}$$

where δ_{jk} is "Kronecker's delta," which is 1 if $j = k$ and 0 otherwise.

Since, as shown above, $\sqrt{n}\hat{\boldsymbol{\gamma}} \underset{a}{\sim} \mathbf{C}'\sqrt{n}\,\bar{\mathbf{g}}$ and $\sqrt{n}\,\bar{\mathbf{g}} \to_{\mathrm{d}} N(\mathbf{0}, \mathrm{E}(\mathbf{g}_t\mathbf{g}_t'))$, we have

$$\mathrm{Avar}(\hat{\boldsymbol{\gamma}}) \ (\equiv \text{variance of limiting distribution of } \sqrt{n}\hat{\boldsymbol{\gamma}}) = \mathbf{C}'\,\mathrm{E}(\mathbf{g}_t\mathbf{g}_t')\mathbf{C}.$$

Its (j, k) element is

$$(j, k) \text{ element of } \mathrm{Avar}(\hat{\boldsymbol{\gamma}}) = \mathbf{c}_j'\,\mathrm{E}(\mathbf{g}_{jt}\mathbf{g}_{kt}')\mathbf{c}_k.$$

Substituting (2.B.2) into this and using the definition of $\mathbf{c}_j$ in (2.B.1), we obtain, after some simple calculations,

$$(j, k) \text{ element of } \text{Avar}(\hat{\boldsymbol{\gamma}}) = \sigma^4 \cdot [\delta_{jk} - \boldsymbol{\mu}_j' \boldsymbol{\Sigma}_{\mathbf{xx}}^{-1} \boldsymbol{\mu}_k / \sigma^2].$$

So

$$\sqrt{n}\hat{\boldsymbol{\gamma}} \underset{\text{d}}{\to} N(\mathbf{0}, \sigma^4 \mathbf{I}_p - \sigma^4 \boldsymbol{\Phi}),$$

where $\boldsymbol{\Phi}$ is defined in Proposition 2.10. Since $\sqrt{n}\hat{\boldsymbol{\rho}} \underset{a}{\sim} \sqrt{n}\hat{\boldsymbol{\gamma}}/\sigma^2$, the limiting distribution of $\sqrt{n}\hat{\boldsymbol{\rho}}$ is the same as that of $\sqrt{n}\,\hat{\boldsymbol{\gamma}}/\sigma^2$, which is $N(\mathbf{0}, \mathbf{I}_p - \boldsymbol{\Phi})$. ■

PROBLEM SET FOR CHAPTER 2

ANALYTICAL EXERCISES

1. (Taken from Example 3.4.2 of Amemiya (1985)) Let z_n be defined by

$$z_n = \begin{cases} 0 & \text{with probability } (n-1)/n, \\ n^2 & \text{with probability } 1/n. \end{cases}$$

Show that $\text{plim}_{n\to\infty} z_n = 0$ but $\lim_{n\to\infty} \text{E}(z_n) = \infty$.

2. Prove Chebychev's weak LLN, by showing that $\bar{z}_n \to_{\text{m.s.}} \mu$. **Hint:**

$$\bar{z}_n - \mu = \big(\bar{z}_n - \text{E}(\bar{z}_n)\big) + \big(\text{E}(\bar{z}_n) - \mu\big).$$

So

$$(\bar{z}_n - \mu)^2 = \big(\bar{z}_n - \text{E}(\bar{z}_n)\big)^2 + 2\big(\bar{z}_n - \text{E}(\bar{z}_n)\big)\big(\text{E}(\bar{z}_n) - \mu\big) + \big(\text{E}(\bar{z}_n) - \mu\big)^2.$$

Show that $\text{E}\big[\big(\bar{z}_n - \text{E}(\bar{z}_n)\big)\big(\text{E}(\bar{z}_n) - \mu\big)\big] = 0.$

3. (Consistency and Asymptotic Normality of OLS for Random Samples) Consider replacing Assumption 2.2 by

Assumption 2.2′: $\{y_i, \mathbf{x}_i\}$ *is a random sample.*

and Assumption 2.5 by

Assumption 2.5′: $\mathbf{S} \equiv \text{E}(\mathbf{g}_i \mathbf{g}_i')$ *exists and is finite.*

Prove the following simplified version of Proposition 2.1:

Proposition 2.1 for Random Samples: *Under Assumptions 2.1, 2.3, 2.4, and 2.2′, the OLS estimator* **b** *is consistent. Under the additional assumption of Assumption 2.5′, the OLS estimator* **b** *is asymptotically normal with* Avar(**b**) *given by (2.3.4).*

(a) Show that this is a special case of Proposition 2.1 of the text.

(b) Give a direct proof of this proposition.
Hint: Use Kolmogorov and Linderberg-Levy.

4. (Proof of Proposition 2.4) We wish to prove Proposition 2.4. To avoid inessential complications, we assume as in the text that $K = 1$ (only one regressor). What remains to be shown is that the sample mean of the first term on the RHS of (2.5.3) converges in probability to some finite number. Prove it. **Hint:** Let $f \equiv x_i \varepsilon_i$ and $h \equiv x_i^2$. The **Cauchy-Schwartz inequality** states:

$$\mathrm{E}(|f \cdot h|) \le \sqrt{\mathrm{E}(f^2)\,\mathrm{E}(h^2)}.$$

So

$$\mathrm{E}(|x_i^3 \varepsilon_i|) \le \sqrt{\mathrm{E}(x_i^2 \varepsilon_i^2)\,\mathrm{E}(x_i^4)}.$$

By assumption, $\mathrm{E}(x_i^2 \varepsilon_i^2)$ $(= \mathrm{E}(g_i^2))$ is finite, and by Assumption 2.6 $\mathrm{E}(x_i^4)$ is also finite. So $\mathrm{E}(\varepsilon_i x_i^3)$ is finite and $\frac{1}{n}\sum_i \varepsilon_i x_i^3 \to_{\mathrm{p}}$ some finite number by ergodic stationarity.

5. (Direct proof that the change in *SSR* divided by σ^2 is asymptotically χ^2) In Section 2.6, we proved that

$$(SSR_R - SSR_U)/s^2 \underset{\mathrm{d}}{\to} \chi^2(\#\mathbf{r})$$

as a corollary to Proposition 2.3. Give a direct proof, first by showing that

$$SSR_R - SSR_U = (\sqrt{n}\,\bar{\mathbf{g}})'\mathbf{S}_{\mathbf{xx}}^{-1}\,\mathbf{R}'(\mathbf{R}\,\mathbf{S}_{\mathbf{xx}}^{-1}\,\mathbf{R}')^{-1}\mathbf{R}\,\mathbf{S}_{\mathbf{xx}}^{-1}(\sqrt{n}\,\bar{\mathbf{g}}),$$
$$\bar{\mathbf{g}} \equiv \frac{1}{n}\sum_{i=1}^{n} \mathbf{x}_i \cdot \varepsilon_i.$$

6. (Optional, consistency of $\hat{\boldsymbol{\alpha}}$) In this question we prove the claim made in Section 2.8 that $\hat{\boldsymbol{\alpha}}$, the OLS estimate for the regression of e_i^2 on $\mathbf{z}_i$, is consistent.

Let $\tilde{\boldsymbol{\alpha}}$ be the OLS estimate from

$$\varepsilon_i^2 = \mathbf{z}_i'\boldsymbol{\alpha} + \eta_i, \ \eta_i \equiv \varepsilon_i^2 - \mathrm{E}(\varepsilon_i^2 \mid \mathbf{x}_i). \tag{2.8.8}$$

(a) Make appropriate assumptions in addition to Assumptions 2.1 and 2.2 to show that $\tilde{\boldsymbol{\alpha}}$ is consistent. **Hint:** You need a rank condition for $\mathbf{z}_i$.

(b) Derive:

$$\hat{\boldsymbol{\alpha}} - \tilde{\boldsymbol{\alpha}} = \Big(\frac{1}{n}\sum_{i=1}^{n} \mathbf{z}_i\mathbf{z}_i'\Big)^{-1} \frac{1}{n}\sum_{i=1}^{n} \mathbf{z}_i \cdot v_i \tag{$*$}$$

with $v_i \equiv -2(\mathbf{b}-\boldsymbol{\beta})'\mathbf{x}_i \cdot \varepsilon_i + (\mathbf{b}-\boldsymbol{\beta})'\mathbf{x}_i\mathbf{x}_i'(\mathbf{b}-\boldsymbol{\beta})$. **Hint:** The discrepancy between ε_i^2 and the squared OLS residual e_i^2 from the OLS estimation of the original equation $y_i = \mathbf{x}_i'\boldsymbol{\beta} + \varepsilon_i$ is given by (2.3.10). Substituting it into (2.8.8) gives: $e_i^2 = \mathbf{z}_i'\boldsymbol{\alpha} + (\eta_i + v_i)$.

(c) To avoid inessential complications, suppose that $\mathbf{x}_i$ is a scalar x_i. Then $\frac{1}{n}\sum_i \mathbf{z}_i \cdot v_i$ in ($*$) becomes

$$-2(b-\beta)\frac{1}{n}\sum_{i=1}^{n} x_i\varepsilon_i\mathbf{z}_i + (b-\beta)^2\frac{1}{n}\sum_{i=1}^{n} x_i^2\mathbf{z}_i. \tag{$**$}$$

Show that the plim of the first term is zero. **Hint:**

$$\mathrm{E}(x_i\varepsilon_i\mathbf{z}_i) = \mathrm{E}[\mathbf{z}_i \cdot x_i \cdot \mathrm{E}(\varepsilon_i \mid x_i)].$$

Show that the plim of the second term is zero if $\mathrm{E}(x_i^2\mathbf{z}_i)$ exists and is finite.

(d) Thus we have proved that $\hat{\boldsymbol{\alpha}} - \tilde{\boldsymbol{\alpha}}$ vanishes. Prove the stronger result that $\sqrt{n}(\hat{\boldsymbol{\alpha}} - \tilde{\boldsymbol{\alpha}})$ vanishes. **Hint:** Use Lemma 2.4(b).

7. (Optional, proof that WLS is asymptotically more efficient than OLS) In Section 2.8, the WLS estimator is denoted $\widehat{\boldsymbol{\beta}}(\widehat{\mathbf{V}})$. We wish to prove that it is asymptotically more efficient than OLS, namely,

$$\mathrm{Avar}(\widehat{\boldsymbol{\beta}}(\widehat{\mathbf{V}})) \leq \mathrm{Avar}(\mathbf{b}).$$

But since $\mathrm{Avar}(\widehat{\boldsymbol{\beta}}(\widehat{\mathbf{V}})) = \mathrm{Avar}(\widehat{\boldsymbol{\beta}}(\mathbf{V}))$, it is sufficient to prove that

$$\mathrm{Avar}(\widehat{\boldsymbol{\beta}}(\mathbf{V})) \leq \mathrm{Avar}(\mathbf{b}).$$

Prove this last matrix inequality. **Hint:** In Chapter 1, we proved the algebraic result that

$$(\mathbf{X}'\mathbf{X})^{-1}(\mathbf{X}'\mathbf{V}\mathbf{X})(\mathbf{X}'\mathbf{X})^{-1} \geq (\mathbf{X}'\mathbf{V}^{-1}\mathbf{X})^{-1} \tag{$*$}$$

for any positive definite matrix $\mathbf{V}$. (This follows from the fact that GLS is more efficient than OLS; the LHS is (σ^2 times) the variance of the OLS estimator for the generalized regression model while the RHS is (σ^2 times) the variance of the GLS estimator.) Dividing both sides of ($*$) by n and taking probability limits yields:

$$\big(\text{plim}\,\tfrac{1}{n}\mathbf{X}'\mathbf{X}\big)^{-1}\big(\text{plim}\,\tfrac{1}{n}\mathbf{X}'\mathbf{V}\mathbf{X}\big)\big(\text{plim}\,\tfrac{1}{n}\mathbf{X}'\mathbf{X}\big)^{-1} \geq \text{plim}\big(\tfrac{1}{n}\mathbf{X}'\mathbf{V}^{-1}\mathbf{X}\big)^{-1}. \tag{$**$}$$

The RHS is $\text{Avar}(\widehat{\boldsymbol{\beta}}(\mathbf{V}))$ (see (2.8.7)). Show that the LHS equals $\text{Avar}(\mathbf{b}) = \boldsymbol{\Sigma}_{\mathbf{xx}}^{-1}\,\mathbf{S}\,\boldsymbol{\Sigma}_{\mathbf{xx}}^{-1}$.

8. Prove (2.9.7). **Hint:** If $(\mu, \boldsymbol{\gamma})$ is the least squares projection coefficients, it satisfies

$$\text{E}(\mathbf{x}\mathbf{x}')\begin{bmatrix}\mu\\ \boldsymbol{\gamma}\end{bmatrix} = \text{E}(\mathbf{x}\cdot y), \tag{$*$}$$

or

$$\begin{bmatrix}\mu\\ \boldsymbol{\gamma}\end{bmatrix} = [\text{E}(\mathbf{x}\mathbf{x}')]^{-1}\,\text{E}(\mathbf{x}\cdot y), \tag{$**$}$$

where

$$\text{E}(\mathbf{x}\mathbf{x}') = \begin{bmatrix}1 & \text{E}(\tilde{\mathbf{x}})'\\ \text{E}(\tilde{\mathbf{x}}) & \text{E}(\tilde{\mathbf{x}}\tilde{\mathbf{x}}')\end{bmatrix},\quad \text{E}(\mathbf{x}\cdot y) = \begin{bmatrix}\text{E}(y)\\ \text{E}(\tilde{\mathbf{x}}\cdot y)\end{bmatrix}.$$

The first equation of ($*$) is $\mu + \text{E}(\tilde{\mathbf{x}})'\boldsymbol{\gamma} = \text{E}(y)$. Use this to eliminate μ from the rest of the equations of ($*$) and then solve for $\boldsymbol{\gamma}$. In the process, use $\text{Var}(\tilde{\mathbf{x}}) = \text{E}(\tilde{\mathbf{x}}\tilde{\mathbf{x}}') - \text{E}(\tilde{\mathbf{x}})\,\text{E}(\tilde{\mathbf{x}}')$, $\text{Cov}(\tilde{\mathbf{x}}, y) = \text{E}(\tilde{\mathbf{x}}\cdot y) - \text{E}(\tilde{\mathbf{x}})\,\text{E}(y)$. Alternatively, use the formula for the partitioned inverse (see (A.10) of Appendix A) to obtain

$$\text{E}(\mathbf{x}\mathbf{x}')^{-1} = \begin{bmatrix}1 + \text{E}(\tilde{\mathbf{x}})'\,\text{Var}(\tilde{\mathbf{x}})^{-1}\,\text{E}(\tilde{\mathbf{x}}) & -\text{E}(\tilde{\mathbf{x}})'\,\text{Var}(\tilde{\mathbf{x}})^{-1}\\ -\text{Var}(\tilde{\mathbf{x}})^{-1}\,\text{E}(\tilde{\mathbf{x}}) & \text{Var}(\tilde{\mathbf{x}})^{-1}\end{bmatrix}.$$

Then substitute this into ($**$).

9. (Proof of Proposition 2.9 for $p = 1$) Assume that $\{\varepsilon_t\}$ is an ergodic stationary martingale difference sequence and that $\text{E}(\varepsilon_t^2 \mid \varepsilon_{t-1}, \varepsilon_{t-2}, \ldots, \varepsilon_1) = \sigma^2 < \infty$.

Let $g_t = \varepsilon_t \cdot \varepsilon_{t-1}$ and

$$\hat{\gamma}_j = \frac{1}{n} \sum_{t=j+1}^{n} \varepsilon_t \cdot \varepsilon_{t-j} \quad (j = 0, 1), \ \hat{\rho}_1 = \frac{\hat{\gamma}_1}{\hat{\gamma}_0}.$$

(a) Show that $\{g_t\}$ $(t = 2, 3, \dots)$ is a martingale difference sequence.

(b) Show that $\mathrm{E}(g_t^2) = \sigma^4$.

(c) Show that $\sqrt{n}\,\hat{\gamma}_1 \to_{\mathrm{d}} N(0, \sigma^4)$ as $n \to \infty$.

(d) Show that $\sqrt{n}\,\hat{\rho}_1 \to_{\mathrm{d}} N(0, 1)$. **Hint:** First show that $\sqrt{n}\,\hat{\gamma}_1/\sigma^2 \to_{\mathrm{d}} N(0, 1)$. Then use Lemma 2.4(c).

10. (Asymptotics of sample mean of MA(2)) Let $(\varepsilon_{-1}, \varepsilon_0, \varepsilon_1, \varepsilon_2, \dots)$ be i.i.d. with mean zero and variance σ_ε^2. Consider a process $(y_{-1}, y_0, y_1, y_2, \dots)$ generated by

$$y_{-1} = \varepsilon_{-1}, \ y_0 = \varepsilon_0 + \theta_1 \varepsilon_{-1}, \ y_t = \varepsilon_t + \theta_1 \varepsilon_{t-1} + \theta_2 \varepsilon_{t-2} \quad (t = 1, 2, \dots).$$

(This process is called a second-order moving average process (MA(2)); see Chapter 6.

(a) Show that $(y_1, y_2, \dots)$ is covariance stationary. Derive the expressions for the autocovariances γ_j $(j = 0, 1, 2, \dots)$.

(b) Let

$$\begin{aligned} r_{tj} \equiv\ & \mathrm{E}(y_t \mid y_{t-j}, y_{t-j-1}, \dots, y_0, y_{-1}) \\ & - \mathrm{E}(y_t \mid y_{t-j-1}, y_{t-j-2}, \dots, y_0, y_{-1}) \\ & \qquad (t = j, j+1, \dots; j = 0, 1, 2, \dots). \end{aligned}$$

Show that

$$r_{t0} = \varepsilon_t, \ r_{t1} = \theta_1 \varepsilon_{t-1}, \ r_{t2} = \theta_2 \varepsilon_{t-2}, \ r_{t3} = 0, \ r_{t4} = 0, \dots$$

Hint: There is a one-to-one mapping between $(\varepsilon_{-1}, \varepsilon_0, \varepsilon_1, \dots, \varepsilon_t)$ and $(y_{-1}, y_0, y_1, \dots, y_t)$ so $\mathrm{E}(y_t \mid y_{t-j}, \dots, y_{-1}) = \mathrm{E}(y_t \mid \varepsilon_{t-j}, \dots, \varepsilon_{-1})$.

(c) Let

$$\bar{y}_n \equiv \frac{1}{n}(y_1 + y_2 + \cdots + y_n).$$

Show that

$$\operatorname{Var}(\sqrt{n}\,\bar{y}_n) = \gamma_0 + 2\Big[\Big(1 - \frac{1}{n}\Big)\gamma_1 + \Big(1 - \frac{2}{n}\Big)\gamma_2\Big].$$

(d) Because $\{y_t\}$ is not i.i.d, the Lindeberg-Levy CLT is not applicable. However, it will be shown in Chapter 6 that $\sqrt{n}\,\bar{y}_n$ converges in distribution to a normal random variable. What is the mean of the limiting distribution? What is the variance of the limiting distribution (i.e., $\operatorname{Avar}(\bar{y}_n)$)? **Hint:** In Lemma 2.1, set $z_n = \sqrt{n}\,\bar{y}_n$, and $\lim_{n\to\infty}(1 - q/n) = 1$ for any fixed q.

11. (Optional, Breusch-Godfrey test for serial correlation) In this question, we prove that the modified Box-Pierce Q is asymptotically equivalent to pF from auxiliary regression (2.10.21), where p is the number of lags and F is the F-ratio for the hypothesis that the coefficients of $e_{t-1}, e_{t-2}, \ldots, e_{t-p}$ are all zero. First we establish the notation. Let

$$\underset{(n\times K)}{\mathbf{X}} = \begin{bmatrix} \mathbf{x}_1' \\ \vdots \\ \mathbf{x}_n' \end{bmatrix}, \quad \underset{(n\times p)}{\mathbf{E}} = \begin{bmatrix} 0 & 0 & \cdots & 0 \\ e_1 & 0 & \cdots & \vdots \\ e_2 & e_1 & & 0 \\ e_3 & e_2 & & e_1 \\ \vdots & \vdots & & \vdots \\ e_{n-1} & e_{n-2} & \cdots & e_{n-p} \end{bmatrix}, \quad \underset{(n\times 1)}{\mathbf{e}} = \begin{bmatrix} e_1 \\ \vdots \\ e_n \end{bmatrix},$$

$$\underset{((K+p)\times(K+p))}{\widehat{\mathbf{B}}} = \begin{bmatrix} \frac{1}{n}\mathbf{X}'\mathbf{X} & \frac{1}{n}\mathbf{X}'\mathbf{E} \\ \frac{1}{n}\mathbf{E}'\mathbf{X} & \frac{1}{n}\mathbf{E}'\mathbf{E} \end{bmatrix}, \quad \widehat{\mathbf{B}}^{-1} = \begin{bmatrix} \underset{(K\times K)}{\widehat{\mathbf{B}}^{11}} & \underset{(K\times p)}{\widehat{\mathbf{B}}^{12}} \\ \underset{(p\times K)}{\widehat{\mathbf{B}}^{21}} & \underset{(p\times p)}{\widehat{\mathbf{B}}^{22}} \end{bmatrix}, \quad \underset{(p\times 1)}{\hat{\boldsymbol{\gamma}}} = \begin{bmatrix} \hat{\gamma}_1 \\ \vdots \\ \hat{\gamma}_p \end{bmatrix},$$

where e_t is the residual from the original regression $y_t = \mathbf{x}_t'\boldsymbol{\beta} + \varepsilon_t$ and $\hat{\gamma}_j$ is the sample j-th order autocovariance, defined in (2.10.8), calculated from the residuals.

(a) The auxiliary regression (2.10.21) has $K+p$ regressors. Let $\hat{\boldsymbol{\alpha}}$ be the vector of the $K+p$ coefficients. Show that

$$\hat{\boldsymbol{\alpha}} = \widehat{\mathbf{B}}^{-1} \begin{bmatrix} \underset{(K\times 1)}{\mathbf{0}} \\ \underset{(p\times 1)}{\hat{\boldsymbol{\gamma}}} \end{bmatrix}.$$

Hint: Since $\mathbf{e}$ is the vector of residuals from the original regression with $\mathbf{X}$ as regressors, $\mathbf{X}'\mathbf{e} = \mathbf{0}$.

(b) Show:

$$\widehat{\mathbf{B}} \underset{\mathrm{p}}{\to} \mathbf{B} \equiv \begin{bmatrix} \boldsymbol{\Sigma}_{\mathbf{xx}} & \mathbf{H} \\ \mathbf{H}' & \sigma^2 \mathbf{I}_p \end{bmatrix},$$

where

$$\underset{(K\times p)}{\mathbf{H}} \equiv \begin{bmatrix} \mathrm{E}(\mathbf{x}_t \cdot \varepsilon_{t-1}) & \cdots & \mathrm{E}(\mathbf{x}_t \cdot \varepsilon_{t-p}) \end{bmatrix}.$$

Hint: The j-th column of $\frac{1}{n}\mathbf{X}'\mathbf{E}$ is $\frac{1}{n}\sum_{t=j+1}^{n} \mathbf{x}_t \cdot e_{t-j}$. Use (2.3.9) to show that it converges in probability to $\mathrm{E}(\mathbf{x}_t \cdot \varepsilon_{t-j})$.

(c) (very easy) Show: $\hat{\boldsymbol{\alpha}} \to_{\mathrm{p}} \mathbf{0}$.

(d) Let *SSR* here be the sum of squared residuals from the auxiliary, *not* the original, regression. Show:

$$\frac{SSR}{n-K-p} \underset{\mathrm{p}}{\to} \sigma^2,$$

where σ^2 is the variance of ε_t, the error term from the original regression. **Hint:** $[\mathbf{X} \;\vdots\; \mathbf{E}]\,\hat{\boldsymbol{\alpha}} = \mathbf{E}\,\hat{\boldsymbol{\gamma}}$. So $SSR = (\mathbf{e} - \mathbf{E}\hat{\boldsymbol{\gamma}})'(\mathbf{e} - \mathbf{E}\hat{\boldsymbol{\gamma}})$. $\frac{1}{n}\mathbf{E}'\mathbf{e} = \hat{\boldsymbol{\gamma}}$, $\frac{1}{n}\mathbf{E}'\mathbf{E} \to_{\mathrm{p}} \sigma^2 \mathbf{I}_p$.

(e) Show:

$$pF = \frac{n\hat{\boldsymbol{\gamma}}'\widehat{\mathbf{B}}^{22}\hat{\boldsymbol{\gamma}}}{SSR/(n-K-p)}.$$

Hint: Apply the formula for the F-ratio in (1.4.9) to the auxiliary regression.

(f) Use the formula for the partitioned inverse (see (A.10) of Appendix A) to show

$$\widehat{\mathbf{B}}^{22} = \left[\frac{1}{n}\mathbf{E}'\mathbf{E} - \left(\frac{1}{n}\mathbf{E}'\mathbf{X}\right)\mathbf{S}_{\mathbf{xx}}^{-1}\left(\frac{1}{n}\mathbf{X}'\mathbf{E}\right)\right]^{-1}.$$

(g) Let $\hat{\rho}$ and $\widehat{\boldsymbol{\Phi}}$ be as in (2.10.8) and (2.10.19). Show that the modified Box-Pierce Q defined in (2.10.20) is asymptotically equivalent to pF (i.e., the difference between the two converges to zero in probability). **Hint:** Show that both pF and the modified Q are asymptotically equivalent to

$$n\hat{\boldsymbol{\gamma}}'(\mathbf{I}_p - \boldsymbol{\Phi})^{-1}\hat{\boldsymbol{\gamma}}/\sigma^2,$$

where $\boldsymbol{\Phi}$ is defined in (2.10.18).

12. (Optional, Chow test for structural change in large samples) Consider applying the Chow test for structural change to the regression model with conditional homoskedasticity described in Proposition 2.5. Since the issue of structural change arises mostly in time-series models, we use "t" for the subscript. We generalize Assumption 2.1 by allowing the coefficient vector to change at the break date r:

$$y_t = \begin{cases} \mathbf{x}_t'\boldsymbol{\beta}_1 + \varepsilon_t & \text{for } t = 1, 2, \dots, r, \\ \mathbf{x}_t'\boldsymbol{\beta}_2 + \varepsilon_t & \text{for } t = r+1, r+2, \dots, n. \end{cases}$$

We assume that the break date r is known. (When the break date is unknown, the situation is more complicated and has been an object of recent research. See Stock (1994, Section 5) for a survey.) The null hypothesis to test is that $\boldsymbol{\beta}_1 = \boldsymbol{\beta}_2$. This is a set of K restrictions. Let SSR_1 be the sum of squared residuals from the first period ($t = 1, 2, \dots, r$), SSR_2 be the SSR from the second period ($t = r+1, r+2, \dots, n$), and SSR_R be the SSR from the entire sample under the constraint $\boldsymbol{\beta}_1 = \boldsymbol{\beta}_2$. From Chapter 1, the Chow statistic is defined as

$$F = \frac{[SSR_R - (SSR_1 + SSR_2)]/K}{(SSR_1 + SSR_2)/(n-2K)}.$$

Let $\mathbf{b}_1$ be the OLS estimate of $\boldsymbol{\beta}_1$ obtained from the first period and $\mathbf{b}_2$ be the OLS estimate of $\boldsymbol{\beta}_2$ from the second period.

(a) Show that KF is numerically equal to

$$\sqrt{n}(\mathbf{b}_1 - \mathbf{b}_2)'\left[\left(\frac{\frac{1}{n}\sum_{t=1}^{r}\mathbf{x}_t\mathbf{x}_t'}{s^2}\right)^{-1} + \left(\frac{\frac{1}{n}\sum_{t=r+1}^{n}\mathbf{x}_t\mathbf{x}_t'}{s^2}\right)^{-1}\right]^{-1}\sqrt{n}(\mathbf{b}_1 - \mathbf{b}_2),$$

where $s^2 = (SSR_1 + SSR_2)/(n-2K)$. **Hint:** The n equations can be written in matrix form as $\mathbf{y} = \mathbf{X}\boldsymbol{\beta} + \boldsymbol{\varepsilon}$, where

$$\underset{(n\times 2K)}{\mathbf{X}} = \begin{bmatrix} \mathbf{X}_1 & \mathbf{0} \\ \mathbf{0} & \mathbf{X}_2 \end{bmatrix}, \quad \underset{(r\times K)}{\mathbf{X}_1} = \begin{bmatrix} \mathbf{x}_1' \\ \vdots \\ \mathbf{x}_r' \end{bmatrix},$$

$$\underset{((n-r)\times K)}{\mathbf{X}_2} = \begin{bmatrix} \mathbf{x}_{r+1}' \\ \vdots \\ \mathbf{x}_n' \end{bmatrix}, \quad \underset{(2K\times 1)}{\boldsymbol{\beta}} = \begin{bmatrix} \boldsymbol{\beta}_1 \\ \boldsymbol{\beta}_2 \end{bmatrix}.$$

The null hypothesis that $\boldsymbol{\beta}_1 = \boldsymbol{\beta}_2$ can be written as $\mathbf{R}\boldsymbol{\beta} = \mathbf{r}$ where $\mathbf{R} = [\mathbf{I}_K \vdots -\mathbf{I}_K]$ and $\mathbf{r} = \mathbf{0}$. Use Proposition 1.4.

(b) Let $\lambda \equiv r/n$. Show that, as $n \to \infty$ with λ fixed,

$$\frac{1}{n}\sum_{t=1}^{r} \mathbf{x}_t\mathbf{x}_t' \underset{\mathrm{p}}{\to} \lambda\boldsymbol{\Sigma}_{\mathbf{xx}}, \quad \frac{1}{n}\sum_{t=r+1}^{n} \mathbf{x}_t\mathbf{x}_t' \underset{\mathrm{p}}{\to} (1-\lambda)\boldsymbol{\Sigma}_{\mathbf{xx}},$$

where $\boldsymbol{\Sigma}_{\mathbf{xx}} \equiv \mathrm{E}(\mathbf{x}_t\mathbf{x}_t')$.

(c) Show that, as $n \to \infty$ with λ fixed,

$$\frac{1}{\sqrt{n}}\sum_{t=1}^{r} \mathbf{x}_t\cdot\varepsilon_t \underset{\mathrm{d}}{\to} N(\mathbf{0}, \lambda\sigma^2\boldsymbol{\Sigma}_{\mathbf{xx}}), \quad \frac{1}{\sqrt{n}}\sum_{t=r+1}^{n} \mathbf{x}_t\cdot\varepsilon_t \underset{\mathrm{d}}{\to} N(\mathbf{0}, (1-\lambda)\sigma^2\boldsymbol{\Sigma}_{\mathbf{xx}}).$$

It can be shown (see, e.g., Stock, 1994, Section 5) that $\frac{1}{\sqrt{n}}\sum_{t=1}^{r}\mathbf{x}_t\varepsilon_t$ and $\frac{1}{\sqrt{n}}\sum_{t=r+1}^{n}\mathbf{x}_t\varepsilon_t$ are asymptotically uncorrelated. So

$$\begin{bmatrix} \frac{1}{\sqrt{n}}\sum_{t=1}^{r}\mathbf{x}_t\cdot\varepsilon_t \\ \frac{1}{\sqrt{n}}\sum_{t=r+1}^{n}\mathbf{x}_t\cdot\varepsilon_t \end{bmatrix} \underset{\mathrm{d}}{\to} N\left(\mathbf{0}, \begin{bmatrix} \lambda\sigma^2\boldsymbol{\Sigma}_{\mathbf{xx}} & \mathbf{0} \\ \mathbf{0} & (1-\lambda)\sigma^2\boldsymbol{\Sigma}_{\mathbf{xx}} \end{bmatrix}\right).$$

(d) Show that $\mathrm{Avar}(\mathbf{b}_1 - \mathbf{b}_2) = \lambda^{-1}\sigma^2\boldsymbol{\Sigma}_{\mathbf{xx}}^{-1} + (1-\lambda)^{-1}\sigma^2\boldsymbol{\Sigma}_{\mathbf{xx}}^{-1}$. **Hint:** Let

$$\mathbf{b} \equiv \begin{bmatrix} \mathbf{b}_1 \\ \mathbf{b}_2 \end{bmatrix}.$$

Show that

$$\mathrm{Avar}(\mathbf{b}) = \begin{bmatrix} \lambda^{-1}\sigma^2\boldsymbol{\Sigma}_{\mathbf{xx}}^{-1} & \mathbf{0} \\ \mathbf{0} & (1-\lambda)^{-1}\sigma^2\boldsymbol{\Sigma}_{\mathbf{xx}}^{-1} \end{bmatrix}.$$

$\mathbf{b}_1 - \mathbf{b}_2 = [\mathbf{I}_K \vdots -\mathbf{I}_K]\mathbf{b}$. Use Lemma 2.4(c).

(e) Finally, show that $KF \to_{\mathrm{d}} \chi^2(K)$ as $n \to \infty$ with $\lambda = r/n$ fixed.

EMPIRICAL EXERCISES

1. Read the introduction and Sections I–IV of Fama (1975), before doing this exercise. In the data file MISHKIN.ASC, monthly data are provided on:

Column 1: year
Column 2: month

Column 3: one-month inflation rate (in percent, annual rate; call this *PAI1*)
Column 4: three-month inflation rate (in percent, annual rate; call this *PAI3*)
Column 5: one-month T-bill rate (in percent, annual rate; call this *TB1*)
Column 6: three-month T-bill rate (in percent, annual rate; call this *TB3*)
Column 7: CPI for urban consumers, all items (the 1982–1984 average is set to 100; call this *CPI*).

The sample period is February 1950 to December 1990 (491 observations). The data on *PAI1*, *PAI3*, *TB1*, and *TB3* are the same data used in Mishkin (1992) and were made available to us by him. The T-bill data were obtained from the Center for Research in Security Prices (CRSP) at the University of Chicago. The T-bill rates for the month are as of the last business day of the previous month (and so can be taken for the interest rates at the beginning of the month). The construction of *PAI1* and *PAI3* will be described toward the end of this exercise; for the time being, we will use the inflation derived from *CPI*.

(a) (Library/internet work) To check the accuracy of the data in MISHKIN.ASC, find relevant tables from back issues of *Treasury Bulletin* or *Federal Reserve Bulletin* for hard-copy data on T-bill rates. Or visit the web sites of the Board of Governors (www.bog.frb.fed.us) or the Treasury Department (www.ustreas.gov) to accomplish the same. Can you find one-month T-bill rates? [Answer: Probably not.] Are the rates in MISHKIN.ASC close to those in the relevant tables? Do they appear to be at the beginning of the month?

(b) (Library/internet work) Find relevant tables from back issues of *Monthly Labor Review* (or visit the web site of the Bureau of Labor Statistics, www.bls.gov) to verify that the CPI figures in MISHKIN.ASC are correct. Verify that the timing of the variable is such that a January CPI observation is the CPI for the month. Regarding the definition of the CPI, verify the following. (1) The CPI is for urban consumers, for all items including food and housing, and is not seasonally adjusted. (2) Prices of the component items of the index are sampled throughout the month. When is the CPI for the month announced?

(c) Is the CPI a fixed-weight index or a variable-weight index? **Hint:** Dig up your old intermediate macro textbook; graduate macro textbooks won't do.

The one-month T-bill rate for month t in the data set is for the period from the beginning of month t to the end of the month (as you just verified). Ideally, if we had data on the price level at the beginning of each period, we would calculate the inflation rate for the same period as $(P_{t+1} - P_t)/P_t$, where P_t is the beginning-of-the-period price level. We use CPI for month $t - 1$ for P_t (i.e., set $P_t = CPI_{t-1}$). Since the CPI component items are collected at different times during the month, there arises the inevitable misalignment of the inflation measure and the interest-rate data. Another problem is the timing of the release of the CPI figure. The efficient market theory assumes that P_t is known to the market at the beginning of month t when the T-bill rates for the month are set. However, the CPI for month $t - 1$, which we take to be P_t, is not announced until sometime in the following month (month t). Thus we are assuming that people know the CPI for month $t-1$ at the beginning of month t.

TSP Tip: When reading in the data and calculating the inflation rate, you should exploit TSP's ability to handle calendar dates. The initial part of your TSP program might look like:

```
? The data are monthly, 1950:2 thru 1990:12
freq m;smpl 50:2 90:12;
? Read in the ASCII data
read(file='mishkin.asc') year month pai1 pai3
                                    tb1 tb3 cpi;
? Calculate inflation rate and the real rate
smpl 50:3 90:12;
pai=((cpi/cpi(-1))**12-1)*100;
r = tb1-pai;
```

RATS Tip: Similarly, the initial part of your RATS program might look like:

```
* The data are monthly, 1950:2 thru 1990:12
cal 50 2 12;all 0 90:12
* Read in the ASCII data
open data mishkin.asc
data(org=obs) / year month pai1 pai3 tb1 tb3 cpi
* Calculate inflation rate and real rate
set pai = ((cpi(t)/cpi(t-1))**12-1)*100
set r = tb1(t)-pai(t)
```

(d) Reproduce the results in Table 2.1. Because the T-bill rate is in percent and at an annual rate, the inflation rate must be measured in the same unit. Calculate π_{t+1}, which is to be matched with $TB1_t$ (the one-month T-bill rate for month t), as the continuously compounded rate in percent:

$$\left[\left(\frac{P_{t+1}}{P_t}\right)^{12} - 1\right] \times 100.$$

Gauss Tip: One way to compute the sample autocovariances by formula (2.10.1) and the sample autocorrelations by (2.10.2) is the following. Let z be the n-dimensional vector whose i-th component is z_i and `nobs` be the sample size, n.

```
z=z-meanc(z);     /* de-mean the series */
nlag=12;    /* lag length */
rho=zeros(nlag,1);
j=1;do until j>nlag;
  rho[j]=z'*shiftr(z',j,0)'/nobs;
  /* sample autocovariances */
j=j+1;endo;
rho=rho./(z'*z/nobs);
  /* sample autocorrelations */
```

TSP Tip: Use the `BJIDENT` command. It does not calculate p-values, so (unless you are willing to learn how to use TSP's matrix commands) give up the idea of producing p-values.

RATS Tip: Use `CORRELATE` or `BOXJENK`.

(e) Can you reproduce (2.11.9), which has robust standard errors? What is the interpretation of the intercept?

Gauss Tip: For the heteroskedasticity-robust standard errors, you have to calculate $\widehat{\mathbf{S}}$ by formula (2.5.1) with $\hat{\varepsilon}_i = e_i$ (OLS residual). An example of the Gauss codes is the following. Let `x` be the $n \times K$ data matrix and `ehat` the n-dimensional vector of OLS residuals. If `g` is the $n \times K$ matrix whose i-th row is $\mathbf{x}_i \cdot e_i$, the Gauss code for generating `g` is `g = x.*ehat`. The Gauss code for calculating $\widehat{\mathbf{S}}$ is `g'g/nobs`, where `nobs` is the sample size. This, however, does not exploit the fact that $\widehat{\mathbf{S}}$ is symmetric. The more computationally efficient command is `moment(g,0)/nobs`.

TSP Tip: Use the option `HCTYPE=0` of `OLSQ`.

RATS Tip: Use the `ROBUSTERRORS` option of `LINREG`.

(f) (Davidson-MacKinnon correction of White) The finite-sample properties of the robust t-ratio might be improved by the Davidson-MacKinnon adjustment discussed in the text. Calculate robust standard errors using the three formulas discussed in the text. The first is the degrees of freedom correction of multiplying $\widehat{\mathbf{S}}$ by $n/(n-K)$. The second is to calculate $\widehat{\mathbf{S}}$ by formula (2.5.5) with $d = 1$. The third is (2.5.5) with $d = 2$. These correspond to TSP's OLSQ options `HCTYPE = 1, 2, 3`.

Gauss Tip: Let `p` be the n-dimensional vector to store the p_i's of (2.5.5), `sxxinv` = $\mathbf{S}_{\mathbf{xx}}^{-1}$, `x` = the data matrix $\mathbf{X}$. One way to compute `p` is

```
p=zeros(nobs,1);
i=1;do until i>nobs;
  p[i]=x[i,.]*sxxinv*x[i,.]'/nobs;
i=i+1;endo;
```

(g) (Estimation under conditional homoskedasticity) Test market efficiency by regressing π_{t+1} on a constant and $TB1_t$ *under conditional homoskedasticity* (2.6.1). Compare your results with those in (e) and (f). Which part is different?

(h) (Breusch-Godfrey test) For the specification in (g), conduct the Breusch-Godfrey test for serial correlation with $p = 12$. (The nR^2 statistic should be about 27.0.) Let e_t ($t = 1, 2, \ldots, n$) be the OLS residual from the regression in (g). To perform the Breusch-Godfrey test as described in the text, we need to set e_t ($t = 0, 1, \ldots, -11$) to zero in running the auxiliary regression for $t = 1, 2, \ldots, n$.

TSP Tip: The TSP codes for calculating the nR^2 statistic are the following. `resid` is the OLS residual from the original regression.

```
? Part (h): Breusch-Godfrey
resid=@res;
smpl 52:1 52:12;
resid=0;
smpl 53:1 71:7;
olsq resid c tb1 resid(-1) resid(-2) resid(-3)
                 resid(-4) resid(-5) resid(-6)
                 resid(-7) resid(-8) resid(-9)
                 resid(-10) resid(-11)
                 resid(-12);
set w=@nob*@rsq;cdf(chisq,df=12) w;
```

Here, `w` is the nR^2 statistic.

RATS Tip: The RATS codes for calculating the nR^2 statistic are the following. `resid` is the OLS residual from the original regression.

```
* Part (h): Breusch-Godfrey
set resid 53:1 71:7 = pai-%beta(1)-%beta(2)*tb1
set resid 52:1 52:12 = 0
linreg resid 53:1 71:7;
  # constant tb1 resid{1 to 12}
compute w = %nobs*%rsquared
cdf chisquared w 12
```

Here, `w` is the nR^2 statistic.

Gauss Tip: As in the Gauss codes for (d), the `shiftr` command is useful here. Let `y` (223×1) and `x` (223×2) be the vector of the dependent variable and the matrix of regressors, respectively, from the previous regression. Let `b` (2×1) be the vector of estimated coefficients from the previous regression. Your Gauss program for creating the `y` and `x` for the auxiliary regression might look like:

```
"@ Part (h): Breusch-Godfrey @";
y=y-x*b; /* residual vector from the previous
            regression */
j=1;do until j>12;
 x=x~shiftr(y',j,0)';
j=j+1;endo;
```

(i) (Reconstructing Fama) What are Fama's own point estimate and standard error of the nominal interest rate coefficient? Are they identical to your results? (Fama uses different notation, so you need to translate his results in our notation.) Why is his estimate of the intercept different from yours? (One obvious reason is that our data are different, but there is another reason.) Optional: What are the differences between his data and our data?

(j) (Seasonal dummies) The CPI used to calculate the inflation rate is not seasonally adjusted. To take account of seasonal factors while still using seasonally unadjusted data in the regression, define twelve monthly dummies, $M1, M2, \dots, M12$, and use them in place of a constant in the regression in (g). Does this make any difference to your results? What happens if you include a constant along with the twelve monthly dummies in the regression? Optional: Is there any reason for preferring seasonally unadjusted data to seasonally adjusted?

TSP Tip: Use the DUMMY command to create monthly dummies.

RATS Tip: Use the SEASONAL command to create monthly dummies.

A well-known problem with the CPI series is that its residential housing component is home mortgage interest costs for periods before 1983 and a more appropriate "rental equivalence" measure since 1983. The inflation variables *PAI1* and *PAI3* in MISHKIN.ASC are calculated from a price index that uses the rental-equivalence measure for all periods. For more details on this, see Section II of Huizinga and Mishkin (1984). The timing of the variables is such that a January observation for *PAI1* is calculated from the December and January data on the price index and *PAI3* from the December and March data on the price index. So, under the assumption that the price index is for the end of the month, a January observation for *PAI1* is the inflation rate during the month, and a January observation for *PAI3* is the inflation rate from the beginning of January to the end of March.

(k) Estimate the Fama regression for 1/53–7/71 using this better measure of the one-month inflation rate and compare the results to those you obtained in (e).

(l) Estimate the Fama regression for the post-October 1979 period. Is the nominal interest rate coefficient much lower? (The coefficient should drop to 0.564.)

2. (Continuation of the Nerlove exercise of Chapter 1, p. 76)

   (i) For Model 4, carry out White's nR^2 test for conditional heteroskedasticity. (nR^2 should be 66.546).

   (j) (optional) Estimate Model 4 by OLS. This is *Step 1* of the procedure of Section 2.8. Carry out *Step 2* by estimating the following auxiliary regression: regress e_i^2 on a constant and $1/Q_i$. Verify that *Step 3* is what you did in part (h).

   (k) Calculate White standard errors for Model 4.

MONTE CARLO EXERCISES

1. (Degrees of freedom correction) In the model of the Monte Carlo exercise of Chapter 1, we assumed that the error term was normal. Assume instead that ε_i is uniformly distributed between -0.5 and 0.5.

   (a) Verify that the DGP of the second simulation (where **X** differs across simulated samples) satisfies Assumptions 2.1–2.5 and 2.7. (It can be shown that

Assumption 2.2 [ergodic stationarity] is also satisfied. This is an implication of Proposition 6.1(d).)

(b) Run the second simulation of the Chapter 1 Monte Carlo exercise with the uniformly distributed error term. In each replication, calculate the usual t-ratio, as before, and compare it with two critical values. The first is the same critical value (2.042) implied by the $t(30)$ distribution, and the second is the critical value (1.96) from $N(0, 1)$. Compute the rejection frequency for each critical value. Which one is closer to the nominal size of 5%?

2. (Box-Pierce vs. Ljung-Box) We wish to verify the claim that the small sample properties of the Box-Ljung Q statistic are superior to those of the Box-Pierce Q. Generate a string of 50 i.i.d. random numbers with mean 0. (Choose your favorite distribution.) Taking this string as data, do the following.

   (1) Calculate the Box-Pierce Q and the Ljung-Box Q statistics (see (2.10.4) and (2.10.5)) with $p = 4$. (The ensemble mean is 0 by construction. Nevertheless take the sample mean from the series when you compute the autocorrelations.)

   (2) For each statistic, accept or reject the null of no serial correlation at a significance level of 5%, assuming that the statistic is distributed as $\chi^2(4)$.

   Do this a large number of times, each time using a different string of 50 i.i.d. random numbers generated afresh. For each Q statistic, calculate the frequency of rejecting the null. If the finite-sample distribution of the statistic is well approximated by $\chi^2(4)$, the frequency should be close to 5%. Which statistic gives you the frequency closer to the nominal size of 5%? Do we fail to reject the null too often if we use the Box-Pierce Q?

ANSWERS TO SELECTED QUESTIONS

ANALYTICAL EXERCISES

3. From (2.3.7) of the text, $\mathbf{b} - \boldsymbol{\beta} = \mathbf{S}_{\mathbf{xx}}^{-1}\bar{\mathbf{g}}$. By Kolmogorov, $\mathbf{S}_{\mathbf{xx}} \to_{\text{p}} \text{E}(\mathbf{x}_i\mathbf{x}_i')$ and $\bar{\mathbf{g}} \to_{\text{p}} \mathbf{0}$. So $\mathbf{b}$ is consistent. By the Lindeberg-Levy CLT, $\sqrt{n}\,\bar{\mathbf{g}} \to_{\text{d}} N(\mathbf{0}, \mathbf{S})$. The rest of the proof should now be routine.

7. What remains to be shown is that the LHS of (∗∗) equals $\text{Avar}(\mathbf{b}) = \boldsymbol{\Sigma}_{\mathbf{xx}}^{-1}\mathbf{S}\boldsymbol{\Sigma}_{\mathbf{xx}}^{-1}$.

$$\boldsymbol{\Sigma}_{\mathbf{xx}} = \text{plim}\,\frac{1}{n}\mathbf{X}'\mathbf{X}$$

and

$$
\begin{aligned}
\mathbf{S} &= \mathrm{E}(\varepsilon_i^2 \mathbf{x}_i \mathbf{x}_i') \\
&= \mathrm{E}[\mathrm{E}(\varepsilon_i^2 \mid \mathbf{x}_i)\mathbf{x}_i \mathbf{x}_i'] \\
&= \mathrm{E}[(\mathbf{z}_i'\boldsymbol{\alpha})\mathbf{x}_i \mathbf{x}_i'] \quad \text{(by (2.8.1))} \\
&= \operatorname{plim} \frac{1}{n}\sum_{i=1}^{n}(\mathbf{z}_i'\boldsymbol{\alpha})\mathbf{x}_i \mathbf{x}_i' \quad \text{(by ergodic stationarity)} \\
&= \operatorname{plim} \frac{1}{n}\mathbf{X}'\mathbf{V}\mathbf{X} \quad \text{(by definition (2.8.4) of } \mathbf{V}\text{)}.
\end{aligned}
$$

EMPIRICAL EXERCISES

1c. The CPI is probably the most widely used fixed-weight price index.

1e. The negative of the intercept $= r$ (the constant ex-ante real interest rate).

1g. Point estimates are the same. Only standard errors are different.

1i. Looking at Fama's Table 3, his R_t coefficient when the sample period is 1/53 to 7/71 is 0.98 with a s.e. of 0.10. Very close, but not exactly the same. There are two possible explanations for the difference between our estimates and Fama's. First, in calculating the inflation rate for month t, $\pi_{t+1} = (P_{t+1} - P_t)/P_t$, it is not clear from Fama that CPI_{t-1} rather than CPI_t was used for P_t. Second, the weight for the *CPI* at the time of his writing may be for 1958. The weight for the *CPI* in our data is for 1982–1984. Our estimate of the intercept (−0.868) differs from Fama's (0.00070) because, first, his dependent variable is the negative of the inflation rate and, second, the inflation rate and the T-bill rate are monthly rates in Fama.

1j. The seasonally adjusted series manufactured by the BLS is a sort of two-sided moving average. Thus, for example, seasonally adjusted CPI_t depends on seasonally unadjusted values of *future CPI*, which is not in I_t. Thus if there is no reason to take account of seasonal factors in the relationship between the inflation rate and the nominal interest rate, one should use seasonally unadjusted data. If there is a need to take account of seasonal factors, it is better to include seasonal dummies in the regression rather than use seasonally adjusted data. Inclusion of seasonal dummies does not change results in any important way.

1k. The R_t coefficient drops to 0.807 from 1.014.

References

Amemiya, T., 1977, "A Note on a Heteroscedastic Model," *Journal of Econometrics*, 6, 365–370.

______, 1985, *Advanced Econometrics*, Cambridge: Harvard University Press.

Anderson, T. W., 1971, *The Statistical Analysis of Time Series*, New York: Wiley.

Billingsley, P., 1961, "The Lindeberg-Levy Theorem for Martingales," in *Proceedings of the American Mathematical Society*, Volume 12, 788–792.

Box, G., and D. Pierce, 1970, "Distribution of Residual Autocorrelations in Autoregressive-Integrated Moving Average Time Series Models," *Journal of the American Statistical Association*, 65, 1509–1526.

Breusch, T., 1978, "Testing for Autocorrelation in Dynamic Linear Models," *Australian Economic Papers*, 17, 334–355.

Davidson, R., and J. MacKinnon, 1993, *Estimation and Inference in Econometrics*, Oxford: Oxford University Press.

Durbin, J., 1970, "Testing for Serial Correlation in Least-Squares Regression When Some of the Regressors are Lagged Dependent Variables," *Econometrica*, 38, 410–421.

Engle, R., 1982, "Autoregressive Conditional Heteroscedasticity with Estimates of the Variance of United Kingdom Inflation," *Econometrica*, 50, 987–1007.

Fama, E., 1975, "Short-Term Interest Rates as Predictors of Inflation," *American Economic Review*, 65, 269–282.

______, 1976, *Foundations of Finance*, Basic Books.

Godfrey, L., 1978, "Testing against General Autoregressive and Moving Average Error Models When the Regressors Include Lagged Dependent Variables," *Econometrica*, 46, 1293–1301.

Greene, W., 1997, *Econometric Analysis* (3d ed.), New York: Prentice Hall.

Gregory, A., and M. Veall, 1985, "Formulating Wald Tests of Nonlinear Restrictions," *Econometrica*, 53, 1465–1468.

Hall, P., and C. Heyde, 1980, *Martingale Limit Theory and Its Application*, New York: Academic.

Hall, R., 1978, "Stochastic Implications of the Life Cycle-Permanent Income Hypothesis: Theory and Evidence," *Journal of Political Economy*, 86, 971–987.

Hamilton, J., 1994, *Time Series Analysis*, Princeton: Princeton University Press.

Huizinga, J., and F. Mishkin, 1984, "Inflation and Real Interest Rates on Assets with Different Risk Characteristics," *Journal of Finance*, 39, 699–714.

Judge, G., W. Griffiths, R. Hill, H. Lütkepohl, and T. Lee, 1985, *The Theory and Practice of Econometrics* (2nd ed.), New York: Wiley.

Karlin, S., and H. M. Taylor, 1975, *A First Course in Stochastic Processes* (2d ed.), New York: Academic.

Koopmans, T., and W. Hood, 1953, "The Estimation of Simultaneous Linear Economic Relationships," in W. Hood and T. Koopmans (eds.), *Studies in Econometric Method*, New Haven: Yale University Press.

Mishkin, F., 1992, "Is the Fisher Effect for Real?" *Journal of Monetary Economics*, 30, 195–215.

Newey, W., 1985, "Generalized Method of Moments Specification Testing," *Journal of Econometrics*, 29, 229–256.

Rao, C. R., 1973, *Linear Satistical Inference and Its Applications* (2nd ed.), New York: Wiley.

Stock, J., 1994, "Unit Roots, Structural Breaks and Trends," in R. Engle and D. McFadden (eds.), *Handbook of Econometrics*, Volume IV, New York: North Holland.

White, H., 1980, "A Heteroskedasticity-Consistent Covariance Matrix Estimator and a Direct Test for Heteroskedasticity," *Econometrica*, 48, 817–838.

CHAPTER 3

Single-Equation GMM

ABSTRACT

The most important assumption made for the OLS is the orthogonality between the error term and regressors. Without it, the OLS estimator is not even consistent. Since in many important applications the orthogonality condition is not satisfied, it is imperative to be able to deal with endogenous regressors. The estimation method called the **Generalized Method of Moments (GMM)**, which includes OLS as a special case, provides a solution. This chapter presents GMM for single-equation models, while the next chapter develops its multiple-equation extension. These chapters deal only with linear equations. GMM estimation of nonlinear equations will be covered in Chapter 7. The major alternative to GMM, the maximum likelihood (ML) estimation, will be covered in Chapter 8.

Reflecting the prevalence of endogenous regressors in economics, this chapter starts out with a number of examples. This is followed by a general formulation of endogenous regressors in Section 3.3. Section 3.4 introduces the GMM procedure for the model of Section 3.3. Sections 3.5–3.7 are devoted to developing the large sample properties of the GMM estimator and associated test statistics. Under conditional homoskedasticity, the formulas derived in these sections can be simplified. Section 3.8 collects those simplified formulas. In particular, the two-stage least squares (2SLS), the techniques originally designed for the estimation of simultaneous equations models, is a special case of GMM. The ML counterpart of 2SLS is called limited-information maximum likelihood (LIML), which will be covered in Section 8.6.

The empirical exercise of the chapter takes up the most widely estimated equation in economics, the wage equation. The equation relates the wage rate to the individual's various characteristics such as education and ability. Because education is a choice made by individuals, and also because ability is imperfectly measured in data, the regressors are likely to be endogenous. We apply the estimation techniques introduced in this chapter to the wage equation and verify that the parameter estimates depend on whether we correct for endogeneity.

3.1 Endogeneity Bias: Working's Example

A Simultaneous Equations Model of Market Equilibrium

The classic illustration of biases created by endogenous regressors is Working (1927). Consider the following simple model of demand and supply:

$$q_i^d = \alpha_0 + \alpha_1 p_i + u_i, \quad \text{(demand equation)} \tag{3.1.1a}$$

$$q_i^s = \beta_0 + \beta_1 p_i + v_i, \quad \text{(supply equation)} \tag{3.1.1b}$$

$$q_i^d = q_i^s, \quad \text{(market equilibrium)} \tag{3.1.1c}$$

where q_i^d is the quantity demanded for the commodity in question (coffee, say) in period i, q_i^s is the quantity supplied, and p_i is the price. The error term u_i in the demand equation represents factors that influence coffee demand other than price, such as the public's mood for coffee. Depending on the value of u_i, the demand curve in the price-quantity plane shifts up or down. Similarly, v_i represents supply factors other than price. We assume that $\mathrm{E}(u_i) = 0$ and $\mathrm{E}(v_i) = 0$ (if not, include the nonzero means in the intercepts α_0 and β_0). To avoid inessential complications, we also assume $\mathrm{Cov}(u_i, v_i) = 0$. If we define $q_i = q_i^d = q_i^s$, the three-equation system (3.1.1) can be reduced to a two-equation system:

$$q_i = \alpha_0 + \alpha_1 p_i + u_i, \quad \text{(demand equation)} \tag{3.1.2a}$$

$$q_i = \beta_0 + \beta_1 p_i + v_i. \quad \text{(supply equation)} \tag{3.1.2b}$$

We say that a regressor is **endogenous** if it is not predetermined (i.e., not orthogonal to the error term), that is, if it does not satisfy the orthogonality condition. When the equation includes the intercept, the orthogonality condition is violated and hence the regressor is endogenous, if and only if the regressor is correlated with the error term. In the present example, the regressor p_i is necessarily endogenous in both equations. To see why, treat (3.1.2) as a system of two simultaneous equations and solve for (p_i, q_i) as

$$p_i = \frac{\beta_0 - \alpha_0}{\alpha_1 - \beta_1} + \frac{v_i - u_i}{\alpha_1 - \beta_1} \tag{3.1.3a}$$

$$q_i = \frac{\alpha_1 \beta_0 - \alpha_0 \beta_1}{\alpha_1 - \beta_1} + \frac{\alpha_1 v_i - \beta_1 u_i}{\alpha_1 - \beta_1}. \tag{3.1.3b}$$

So price is a function of the two error terms. From (3.1.3a), we can calculate the covariance of the regressor p_i with the demand shifter u_i and the supply shifter v_i to be

$$\text{Cov}(p_i, u_i) = -\frac{\text{Var}(u_i)}{\alpha_1 - \beta_1}, \quad \text{Cov}(p_i, v_i) = \frac{\text{Var}(v_i)}{\alpha_1 - \beta_1}, \tag{3.1.4}$$

which are not zero (unless $\text{Var}(u_i) = 0$ and $\text{Var}(v_i) = 0$). Therefore, price is correlated positively with the demand shifter and negatively with the supply shifter, if the demand curve is downward-sloping ($\alpha_1 < 0$) and the supply curve upward-sloping ($\beta_1 > 0$). In this example, endogeneity is a result of market equilibrium.

Endogeneity Bias

When quantity is regressed on a constant and price, does it estimate the demand curve or the supply curve? The answer is neither, because price is endogenous in both the demand and supply equations. Recall from Section 2.9 that the OLS estimator is consistent for the least squares projection coefficients. In the least squares projection of q_i on a constant and p_i, the coefficient of p_i is $\text{Cov}(p_i, q_i)/\text{Var}(p_i)$,[1] so,

$$\text{plim of the OLS estimate of the price coefficient} = \frac{\text{Cov}(p_i, q_i)}{\text{Var}(p_i)}. \tag{3.1.5}$$

To rewrite this ratio in relation to the price effect in the demand curve (α_1), use the demand equation (3.1.2a) to calculate $\text{Cov}(p_i, q_i)$ as

$$\text{Cov}(p_i, q_i) = \alpha_1 \text{Var}(p_i) + \text{Cov}(p_i, u_i). \tag{3.1.6}$$

Substituting (3.1.6) into (3.1.5), we obtain the expression for the asymptotic bias for α_1

$$\text{plim of the OLS estimate of the price coefficient} - \alpha_1 = \frac{\text{Cov}(p_i, u_i)}{\text{Var}(p_i)}. \tag{3.1.7}$$

Similarly, the asymptotic bias for β_1, the price effect in the supply curve, is

$$\text{plim of the OLS estimate of the price coefficient} - \beta_1 = \frac{\text{Cov}(p_i, v_i)}{\text{Var}(p_i)}. \tag{3.1.8}$$

But, as seen from (3.1.4), $\text{Cov}(p_i, u_i) \neq 0$ and $\text{Cov}(p_i, v_i) \neq 0$, so the OLS estimate is consistent for neither α_1 nor β_1. This phenomenon is known as the **endogeneity bias**. It is also known as the **simultaneous equations bias** or **simultaneity bias**, because the regressor and the error term are often related to each other through a system of simultaneous equations, as in the present example.

[1]Fact: Let $\boldsymbol{\gamma}$ be the least squares coefficients in $\widehat{\text{E}}^*(y \mid 1, \mathbf{x}) = \alpha + \mathbf{x}'\boldsymbol{\gamma}$. Then $\boldsymbol{\gamma} = \text{Var}(\mathbf{x})^{-1}\,\text{Cov}(\mathbf{x}, y)$. Proving this was an analytical exercise for Chapter 2.

In the extreme case of no demand shifters (so that $u_i = 0$ for all i), we have $\text{Cov}(p_i, u_i) = 0$, and the formula (3.1.7) indicates that the OLS estimate is consistent for the demand parameter α_1. In this case, the demand curve does not shift, and, as illustrated in Figure 3.1(a), all the observed combinations of price and quantity fall on the demand curve as the supply curve shifts. In the other extreme case of no supply shifters, the observed price-quantity pairs trace out the supply curve as the demand curve shifts (see Figure 3.1(b)). In the general case of both curves shifting, the OLS estimate should be consistent for a weighted average of α_1 and β_1. This can be seen analytically by deriving yet another expression for the plim of the OLS estimate:

$$\text{plim of the OLS estimate of the price coefficient} = \frac{\alpha_1 \operatorname{Var}(v_i) + \beta_1 \operatorname{Var}(u_i)}{\operatorname{Var}(v_i) + \operatorname{Var}(u_i)}. \tag{3.1.9}$$

Proving this is a review question.

Observable Supply Shifters

The reason neither the demand curve nor the supply curve is consistently estimated in the general case is that we cannot infer from data whether the change in price and quantity is due to a demand shift or a supply shift. This suggests that it might be possible to estimate the demand curve (resp. the supply curve) if some of the factors that shift the supply curve (resp. the demand curve) are observable. So suppose the supply shifter, v_i, can be divided into an observable factor x_i and an unobservable factor ζ_i uncorrelated with x_i.[2]

$$q_i = \beta_0 + \beta_1 p_i + \beta_2 x_i + \zeta_i \quad \text{with } \beta_2 \neq 0. \quad \text{(supply)} \tag{3.1.2b$'$}$$

Now imagine that this observed supply shifter x_i is predetermined (i.e., uncorrelated with the error term) in the demand equation; think of x_i as the temperature in coffee-growing regions. If the temperature (x_i) is uncorrelated with the unobserved taste for coffee (u_i), it should be possible to extract from price movements a component that is related to the temperature (the observed supply shifter) but uncorrelated with the demand shifter. We can then estimate the demand curve by examining the relationship between coffee consumption and that component of price. Let us formalize this argument.

[2]This decomposition is always possible. If the least squares projection of v_i on a constant and x_i is $\gamma_0 + \beta_2 x_i$, define $\zeta_i \equiv v_i - \gamma_0 - \beta_2 x_i$, so $v_i = \zeta_i + \gamma_0 + \beta_2 x_i$. By definition, ζ_i is uncorrelated with x_i. Substitute this equation into the original supply equation (3.1.2b) and submerge γ_0 in the intercept. This produces (3.1.2b$'$).

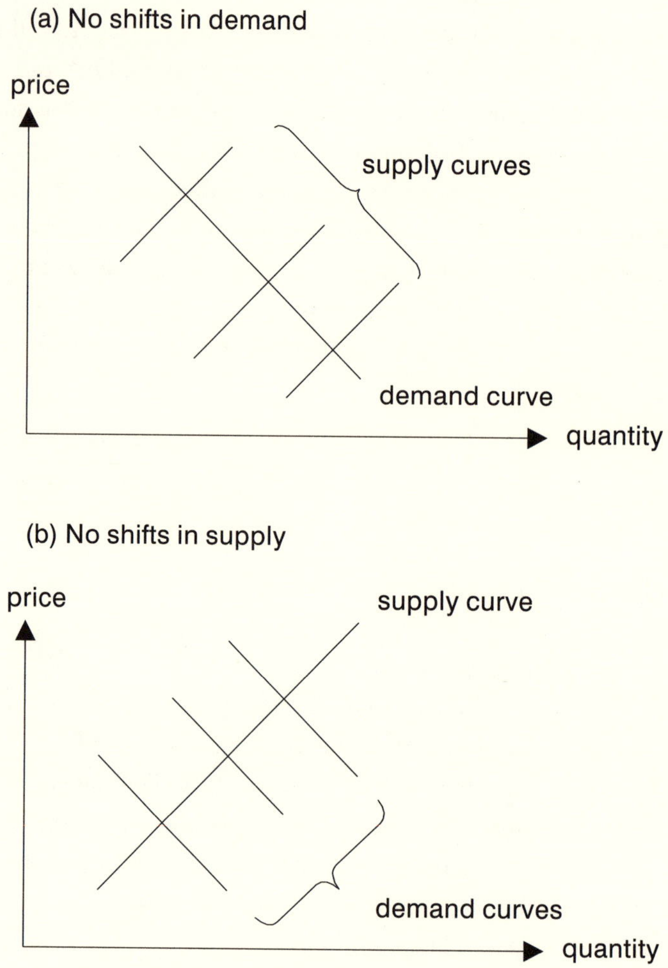

Figure 3.1: Supply and Demand Curves

For the equation in question, a predetermined variable that is correlated with the endogenous regressor is called an **instrumental variable** or an **instrument**. We sometimes call it a **valid instrument** to emphasize that its correlation with the endogenous regressor is not zero. In this example, the observable supply shifter x_i can serve as an instrument for the demand equation. This can be seen easily. Solve the system of two simultaneous equations (3.1.2a) and (3.1.2b$'$) for (p_i, q_i):

$$p_i = \frac{\beta_0 - \alpha_0}{\alpha_1 - \beta_1} + \frac{\beta_2}{\alpha_1 - \beta_1} x_i + \frac{\zeta_i - u_i}{\alpha_1 - \beta_1}, \tag{3.1.10a}$$

$$q_i = \frac{\alpha_1\beta_0 - \alpha_0\beta_1}{\alpha_1 - \beta_1} + \frac{\alpha_1\beta_2}{\alpha_1 - \beta_1} x_i + \frac{\alpha_1\zeta_i - \beta_1 u_i}{\alpha_1 - \beta_1}. \tag{3.1.10b}$$

Since $\text{Cov}(x_i, \zeta_i) = 0$ by construction and $\text{Cov}(x_i, u_i) = 0$ by assumption, it follows from (3.1.10a) that

$$\text{Cov}(x_i, p_i) = \frac{\beta_2}{\alpha_1 - \beta_1} \text{Var}(x_i) \neq 0.$$

So x_i is indeed a valid instrument.

With a valid instrument at hand, we can estimate the price coefficient α_1 of the demand curve consistently. Use the demand equation (3.1.2a) to calculate, not $\text{Cov}(p_i, q_i)$ as in (3.1.6), but $\text{Cov}(x_i, q_i)$:

$$\begin{aligned}\text{Cov}(x_i, q_i) &= \alpha_1 \text{Cov}(x_i, p_i) + \text{Cov}(x_i, u_i)\\ &= \alpha_1 \text{Cov}(x_i, p_i) \quad (\text{Cov}(x_i, u_i) = 0 \text{ by assumption}).\end{aligned}$$

As we just verified, $\text{Cov}(x_i, p_i) \neq 0$. So we can divide both sides by $\text{Cov}(x_i, p_i)$ to obtain

$$\alpha_1 = \frac{\text{Cov}(x_i, q_i)}{\text{Cov}(x_i, p_i)}. \tag{3.1.11}$$

A natural estimator that suggests itself is

$$\hat{\alpha}_{1,\text{IV}} = \frac{\text{sample covariance between } x_i \text{ and } q_i}{\text{sample covariance between } x_i \text{ and } p_i}. \tag{3.1.12}$$

This estimator is called the **instrumental variables (IV) estimator** with x_i as the instrument. We sometimes say "the endogenous regressor p_i is instrumented by x_i."

Another popular procedure for consistently estimating α_1 is the **two-stage least squares (2SLS)**. It is so called because the procedure consists of running two regressions. In the first stage, the endogenous regressor p_i is regressed on a constant and the predetermined variable x_i, to obtain the fitted value, $\hat{p}_i$, of p_i. The second stage is to regress the dependent variable q_i on a constant and $\hat{p}_i$. The use of $\hat{p}_i$ rather than p_i distinguishes 2SLS from the simple-minded application of OLS to the demand equation. The 2SLS estimator of α_1 is the OLS estimate of the $\hat{p}_i$ coefficient in the second-stage regression. So it equals[3]

$$\hat{\alpha}_{1,2\text{SLS}} = \frac{\text{sample covariance between } \hat{p}_i \text{ and } q_i}{\text{sample variance of } \hat{p}_i}. \tag{3.1.13}$$

To relate the regression in the second stage to the demand equation, rewrite (3.1.2a) as

$$q_i = \alpha_0 + \alpha_1 \hat{p}_i + [u_i + \alpha_1(p_i - \hat{p}_i)]. \tag{3.1.14}$$

The second stage regression estimates this equation, treating the bracketed term as the error term. The OLS estimate of α_1 is consistent for the following reason. If the fitted value $\hat{p}_i$ were exactly equal to the least squares projection $\widehat{\mathrm{E}}^*(p_i \mid 1, x_i)$, then neither u_i nor $(p_i - \hat{p}_i)$ would be correlated with $\hat{p}_i$: u_i is uncorrelated because it is uncorrelated with x_i and $\hat{p}_i$ is a linear function of x_i, and $(p_i - \hat{p}_i)$ is uncorrelated because it is a least squares projection error. The fitted value $\hat{p}_i$ is not exactly equal to $\widehat{\mathrm{E}}^*(p_i \mid 1, x_i)$, but the difference between the two vanishes as the sample gets larger. Therefore, asymptotically, $\hat{p}_i$ is uncorrelated with the error term in (3.1.14), making the 2SLS estimator consistent. Furthermore, since the projection is the best linear predictor, the fitted value incorporates all of the effect of the supply shifter on price. This suggests that minimizing the asymptotic variance is minimized for the 2SLS estimator.

In the present example, the IV and 2SLS estimators are numerically the same (we will prove this in a more general context). More generally, the 2SLS estimator can be written as an IV estimator with an appropriate choice of instruments, and the IV estimator, in turn, is a particular GMM estimator.

QUESTIONS FOR REVIEW

1. In the simultaneous equations model (3.1.2), suppose $\mathrm{Cov}(u_i, v_i)$ is not necessarily zero. Is it necessarily true that price and the demand shifter u_i are positively correlated when $\alpha_1 < 0$ and $\beta_1 > 0$? [Answer: No.] Why?

[3]Fact: In the regression of y_i on a constant and x_i, the OLS estimator of the x_i coefficient is the ratio of the sample covariance between x_i and y_i to the sample variance of x_i. Proving this was a review question of Section 1.2.

2. (3.1.7) shows that the OLS estimate of the price coefficient in the regression of quantity on a constant and price is biased for the price coefficient α_1. Is the OLS estimate of the intercept biased for α_0, the intercept in the demand equation? **Hint:** The plim of the OLS estimate of the intercept in the regression is

$$\mathrm{E}(q_i) - \frac{\mathrm{Cov}(p_i, q_i)}{\mathrm{Var}(p_i)}\,\mathrm{E}(p_i).$$

But from (3.1.2a), $\mathrm{E}(q_i) = \alpha_0 + \alpha_1\,\mathrm{E}(p_i)$.

3. Derive (3.1.9). **Hint:** Show:

$$\mathrm{Var}(p_i) = \frac{\mathrm{Var}(v_i) + \mathrm{Var}(u_i)}{(\alpha_1 - \beta_1)^2}, \quad \mathrm{Cov}(p_i, q_i) = \frac{\alpha_1\,\mathrm{Var}(v_i) + \beta_1\,\mathrm{Var}(u_i)}{(\alpha_1 - \beta_1)^2}.$$

4. For the market equilibrium model (3.1.2a), (3.1.2b′) (on page 189) with $\mathrm{Cov}(u_i, \zeta_i) = 0$, $\mathrm{Cov}(x_i, u_i) = 0$, and $\mathrm{Cov}(x_i, \zeta_i) = 0$, verify that price is endogenous in the demand equation. Is it in the supply equation? **Hint:** Look at (3.1.10a). Do we need the assumption that the demand and supply shifters are uncorrelated (i.e., $\mathrm{Cov}(u_i, \zeta_i) = 0$) for $\hat{\alpha}_{1,\mathrm{IV}}$ and $\hat{\alpha}_{1,\mathrm{2SLS}}$ to be consistent? **Hint:** Is x_i a valid instrument without the assumption?

3.2 More Examples

Endogeneity bias arises in a wide variety of situations. We examine a few more examples.

A Simple Macroeconometric Model

Haavelmo's (1943) illustrative model is an extremely simple macroeconometric model:

$$\begin{aligned} &C_i = \alpha_0 + \alpha_1 Y_i + u_i, \quad 0 < \alpha_1 < 1 \quad \text{(consumption function)} \\ &Y_i = C_i + I_i \quad \text{(GNP identity)}, \end{aligned}$$

where C_i is aggregate consumption in year i, Y_i is GNP, I_i is investment, and α_1 is the Marginal Propensity to Consume out of income (the MPC). As is familiar from introductory macroeconomics, GNP in equilibrium is

$$Y_i = \frac{\alpha_0}{1-\alpha_1} + \frac{I_i}{1-\alpha_1} + \frac{u_i}{1-\alpha_1}. \tag{3.2.1}$$

If investment is predetermined in that $\text{Cov}(I_i, u_i) = 0$, it follows from (3.2.1) that

$$\text{Cov}(Y_i, u_i) = \frac{\text{Var}(u_i)}{1-\alpha_1} > 0,$$
$$\text{Cov}(I_i, Y_i) = \frac{\text{Var}(I_i)}{1-\alpha_1} > 0.$$

So income is endogenous in the consumption function, but investment is a valid instrument for the endogenous regressor. A straightforward calculation similar to the one we used to derive (3.1.7) shows that the OLS estimator of the MPC obtained from regressing consumption on a constant and income is asymptotically biased:

$$\text{plim}\,\hat{\alpha}_{1,\text{OLS}} - \alpha_1 = \frac{\text{Cov}(Y_i, u_i)}{\text{Var}(Y_i)} = \frac{1-\alpha_1}{1 + \frac{\text{Var}(I_i)}{\text{Var}(u_i)}} > 0. \tag{3.2.2}$$

This is perhaps the clearest example of simultaneity bias. The difference from Working's example of market equilibrium is that here the second equation is an identity, which only makes it easier to see the endogeneity of the regressor. The asymptotic bias can be corrected for by the use of investment as the instrument for income in the consumption function. The role played by the observable supply shifter in Working's example is played here by investment.

Errors-in-Variables

The term **errors-in-variables** refers to the phenomenon that an otherwise predetermined regressor necessarily becomes endogenous when measured with error. This problem is ubiquitous, particularly in micro data on households. For example, in the Panel Study of Income Dynamics (PSID), information on variables such as food consumption and income is collected over the telephone. It is perhaps too much to hope that the respondent can recall on the spot how much was spent on food over a specified period of time.

The cross-section version of M. Friedman's (1957) Permanent Income Hypothesis can be formulated neatly as an errors-in-variables problem. The hypothesis states that "permanent consumption" C_i^* for household i is proportional to "permanent income" Y_i^*:

$$C_i^* = kY_i^* \quad \text{with } 0 < k < 1. \tag{3.2.3}$$

It is assumed that measured consumption C_i and measured income Y_i are error-ridden measures of permanent consumption and income:

$$C_i = C_i^* + c_i \quad \text{and} \quad Y_i = Y_i^* + y_i. \tag{3.2.4}$$

Measurement errors c_i and y_i are assumed to be zero mean and uncorrelated with permanent consumption and income:

$$\mathrm{E}(c_i) = 0, \;\; \mathrm{E}(y_i) = 0, \;\; \mathrm{E}(c_i y_i) = 0, \tag{3.2.5}$$

$$\mathrm{E}(C_i^* c_i) = 0, \;\; \mathrm{E}(Y_i^* y_i) = 0, \;\; \mathrm{E}(C_i^* y_i) = 0, \;\; \mathrm{E}(Y_i^* c_i) = 0. \tag{3.2.6}$$

Substituting (3.2.4) into (3.2.3), the relationship can be expressed in terms of measured consumption and income:

$$C_i = kY_i + u_i \quad \text{with } u_i \equiv c_i - ky_i. \tag{3.2.7}$$

This example differs from the previous ones in that the equation does not include a constant. So we should examine the cross moment $\mathrm{E}(Y_i u_i)$ rather than the covariance $\mathrm{Cov}(Y_i, u_i)$ to determine whether income is predetermined. It is straightforward to derive from (3.2.4)–(3.2.7) that

$$\mathrm{E}(Y_i u_i) = -k\,\mathrm{E}(y_i^2) < 0.$$

So measured income is endogenous in the consumption function (3.2.7). Unlike in the previous examples, the endogeneity is due to measurement errors. Using the fact that the OLS estimator of the Y_i coefficient in (3.2.7) is consistent for the corresponding least squares projection coefficient $\mathrm{E}(C_i Y_i)/\,\mathrm{E}(Y_i^2)$, we can also derive from (3.2.4)–(3.2.7) that

$$\operatorname{plim} \widehat{k}_{\text{OLS}} = \frac{k\,\mathrm{E}[(Y_i^*)^2]}{\mathrm{E}[(Y_i^*)^2] + \mathrm{E}(y_i^2)} < k. \tag{3.2.8}$$

So the regression of measured consumption on measured income (without the intercept) underestimates k. Friedman used this result to explain why the MPC from the cross-section regression of consumption on income is lower than the MPC estimated from aggregate time-series data.

Let us suppose for a moment that there exists a valid instrument x_i. So $\mathrm{E}(x_i u_i) = 0$ and $\mathrm{E}(x_i Y_i) \neq 0$. A similar argument we used for deriving (3.1.11) establishes that

$$k = \frac{\mathrm{E}(x_i C_i)}{\mathrm{E}(x_i Y_i)}. \tag{3.2.9}$$

So a consistent IV estimator is

$$\widehat{k}_{\text{IV}} = \frac{\text{sample mean of } x_i C_i}{\text{sample mean of } x_i Y_i}. \tag{3.2.10}$$

But is there a valid instrument? Yes, and it is a constant. Substituting $x_i = 1$ into (3.2.10), we obtain a consistent estimator of k which is the ratio of the sample mean of measured consumption to the sample mean of measured income. This is how Friedman estimated k.

Production Function

In many contexts, the error term includes factors that are observable to the economic agent under study but unobservable to the econometrician. Endogeneity arises when regressors are decisions made by the agent on the basis of such factors. Consider a cross-sectional sample of firms choosing labor input to maximize profits. The production function of the i-th firm is

$$Q_i = A_i \cdot (L_i)^{\phi_1} \cdot \exp(v_i), \quad 0 < \phi_1 < 1, \tag{3.2.11}$$

where Q_i is the firm's output, L_i is labor input, A_i is the firm's efficiency level known to the firm, and v_i is the technology shock. In contrast to A_i, v_i is not observable to the firm when it chooses L_i. Neither A_i nor v_i is observable to the econometrician.

Assume that, for each firm i, v_i is serially independent over time. Therefore, $B \equiv \mathrm{E}[\exp(v_i)]$ is the same for all i,[4] and the level of output the firm expects when it chooses L_i is

$$A_i \cdot (L_i)^{\phi_1} \cdot B.$$

Let p be the output price and w the wage rate. For simplicity, assume that all the firms are from the same competitive industry so that p and w are constant across firms. Firm i's objective is to choose L_i to maximize expected profits

$$p \cdot A_i \cdot (L_i)^{\phi_1} \cdot B - w \cdot L_i.$$

Take the derivative of this with respect to L_i, set it equal to zero, and solve it for

[4] If v_i for firm i were correlated over time, the firm would use past values of v_i to forecast the current value of v_i when choosing labor input, and so B would differ across firms. Also, since the expected value of a nonlinear function of a random variable whose mean is zero is not necessarily zero, B is not necessarily zero even if $\mathrm{E}(v_i) = 0$.

L_i, to obtain the profit-maximizing labor input level:

$$L_i = \left(\frac{w}{p}\right)^{\frac{1}{\phi_1 - 1}} (A_i B \phi_1)^{\frac{1}{1-\phi_1}}. \tag{3.2.12}$$

Let u_i be firm i's deviation from the mean log efficiency: $u_i \equiv \log(A_i) - \mathrm{E}[\log(A_i)]$, and let $\phi_0 \equiv \mathrm{E}[\log(A_i)]$ (so $\mathrm{E}(u_i) = 0$ and $A_i = \exp(\phi_0 + u_i)$). Then, the production function (3.2.11) and the labor demand function (3.2.12) in logs can be written as

$$\log(Q_i) = \phi_0 + \phi_1 \log(L_i) + (v_i + u_i), \tag{3.2.13}$$

$$\log(L_i) = \beta_0 + \frac{1}{1 - \phi_1} u_i, \tag{3.2.14}$$

where

$$\beta_0 = \frac{1}{\phi_1 - 1} [\log(w/p) - \phi_0 - \log(\phi_1 B)].$$

Because all firms face the same prices, β_0 is constant across firms. (3.2.14) shows that, in the log-linear production function (3.2.13), $\log(L_i)$ is an endogenous regressor positively correlated with the error term $(v_i + u_i)$ through u_i. Thus, the OLS estimator of ϕ_1 in the estimation of the log-linear production function confounds the contribution to output of u_i with labor's contribution. This example illustrates yet another source of endogeneity: a variable chosen by the agent taking into account some error component unobservable to the econometrician.

QUESTIONS FOR REVIEW

1. In Friedman's Permanent Income Hypothesis, consider the regression of C_i on a constant and Y_i. Derive the plim of the OLS estimator of the Y_i coefficient in this regression with a constant. **Hint:** The plim equals the ratio of $\mathrm{Cov}(C_i, Y_i)$ to $\mathrm{Var}(Y_i)$. Show that it equals

$$\frac{k \, \mathrm{Var}(Y_i^*)}{\mathrm{Var}(Y_i^*) + \mathrm{Var}(y_i)}.$$

2. In the production function example, show that $\mathrm{plim}_{n\to\infty} \hat{\phi}_{1,\mathrm{OLS}} = 1$, where $\hat{\phi}_{1,\mathrm{OLS}}$ is the OLS estimate of ϕ_1 from (3.2.13). **Hint:** Eliminate u_i from the log output equation (3.2.13) by using the labor demand equation (3.2.14).

3. In the production function example, suppose the firm can observe v_i as well as u_i before deciding on labor input. How does the demand equation for labor

(3.2.12) change? Show that $\log(Q_i)$ and $\log(L_i)$ are perfectly correlated. **Hint:** $\log(Q_i)$ will be an exact linear function of $\log(L_i)$ without errors.

3.3 The General Formulation

We now provide a general formulation. It is a model described by the following set of assumptions and is a generalization of the model of Chapter 2.

Regressors and Instruments

Assumption 3.1 (linearity): *The equation to be estimated is linear:*

$$y_i = \mathbf{z}_i'\boldsymbol{\delta} + \varepsilon_i \quad (i = 1, 2, \ldots, n),$$

where $\mathbf{z}_i$ *is an* L*-dimensional vector of regressors,* $\boldsymbol{\delta}$ *is an* L*-dimensional coefficient vector, and* ε_i *is an unobservable error term.*

Assumption 3.2 (ergodic stationarity): *Let* $\mathbf{x}_i$ *be a* K*-dimensional vector to be referred to as the vector of instruments, and let* $\mathbf{w}_i$ *be the unique and nonconstant elements of* $(y_i, \mathbf{z}_i, \mathbf{x}_i)$.[5] $\{\mathbf{w}_i\}$ *is jointly stationary and ergodic.*

Assumption 3.3 (orthogonality conditions): *All the* K *variables in* $\mathbf{x}_i$ *are* ***predetermined*** *in the sense that they are all orthogonal to the current error term:* $\mathrm{E}(x_{ik}\,\varepsilon_i) = 0$ *for all* i *and* k $(k = 1, 2, \ldots, K)$.[6] *This can be written as*

$$\mathrm{E}[\mathbf{x}_i \cdot (y_i - \mathbf{z}_i'\boldsymbol{\delta})] = \mathbf{0} \quad \textit{or} \quad \mathrm{E}(\mathbf{g}_i) = \mathbf{0},$$

where $\mathbf{g}_i \equiv \mathbf{x}_i \cdot \varepsilon_i$.

We remarked in Section 2.3 that, when the regressors include a constant, the orthogonality conditions about the regressors are equivalent to the condition that $\mathrm{E}(\varepsilon_i) = 0$ and that the regressors be uncorrelated with the error term. Here, the orthogonality conditions are about the instrumental variables. So if one of the instruments is

[5] See examples below for illustrations of $\mathbf{w}_i$.

[6] As was noted in Section 2.3, our use of the term *predetermined* may not be standard in some quarters of the profession. All we require for the term is that the current error term be orthogonal to the current regressors. We do not require that the current error term be orthogonal to the past regressors.

a constant, Assumption 3.3 is equivalent to the condition that $\mathrm{E}(\varepsilon_i) = 0$ and that nonconstant instruments be uncorrelated with the error term.

The examples examined in the previous two sections can be written in this general format. For example,

Example 3.1 (Working's example with an observable supply shifter): Consider the market equilibrium model of (3.1.2a) and (3.1.2b′) on page 189. Suppose the equation to be estimated is the demand equation. The example can be cast in the general format by setting

$$y_i = q_i,\ L = 2,\ \boldsymbol{\delta} = \begin{bmatrix} \alpha_0 \\ \alpha_1 \end{bmatrix},\ \mathbf{z}_i = \begin{bmatrix} 1 \\ p_i \end{bmatrix},\ \varepsilon_i = u_i,\ K = 2,\ \mathbf{x}_i = \begin{bmatrix} 1 \\ x_i \end{bmatrix},$$

and $\mathbf{w}_i = (q_i, p_i, x_i)'$. Since the mean of the error term is zero, a constant is orthogonal to the error term and so can be included in $\mathbf{x}_i$. It follows that x_i, which is assumed to be uncorrelated with the error term, satisfies the orthogonality condition $\mathrm{E}(x_i\,\varepsilon_i) = 0$. So it too can be included in $\mathbf{x}_i$.

The other examples of the previous sections can be similarly written as special cases of the general model.

Having two separate symbols, $\mathbf{x}_i$ and $\mathbf{z}_i$, may give you the impression that the regressors and the instruments do not share the same variables, but that is not always the case. Indeed in the above example, $\mathbf{x}_i$ and $\mathbf{z}_i$ share the same variable (a constant). The instruments that are also regressors are called **predetermined regressors**, and the rest of the regressors, those that are not included in $\mathbf{x}_i$, are called **endogenous regressors**. A good example to make the point is

Example 3.2 (wage equation): A simplified version of the wage equation to be estimated later in this chapter is

$$LW_i = \delta_1 + \delta_2 S_i + \delta_3 EXPR_i + \delta_4 IQ_i + \varepsilon_i,$$

where LW_i is the log wage of individual i, S_i is completed years of schooling, $EXPR_i$ is experience in years, IQ_i is IQ, and ε_i is unobservable individual characteristics relevant for the wage rate. We assume $\mathrm{E}(\varepsilon_i) = 0$ (if not, include the mean of ε_i in δ_1). In one of the specifications we estimate later, we assume that S_i is predetermined but that IQ_i, an error-ridden measure of the individual's ability, is endogenous due to the errors-in-variables problem. We also assume that $EXPR_i$, AGE_i (age of the individual), and MED_i (mother's education in years) are predetermined. AGE_i is excluded from the wage equation, reflecting the underlying assumption that, once experience is controlled for, age has no effect on the wage rate. In terms of the general model,

$$y_i = LW_i, \quad L = 4, \quad \mathbf{z}_i = \begin{bmatrix} 1 \\ S_i \\ EXPR_i \\ IQ_i \end{bmatrix}, \quad K = 5, \quad \mathbf{x}_i = \begin{bmatrix} 1 \\ S_i \\ EXPR_i \\ AGE_i \\ MED_i \end{bmatrix},$$

and $\mathbf{w}_i = (LW_i, S_i, EXPR_i, IQ_i, AGE_i, MED_i)'$. As in Example 3.1, we can include a constant in $\mathbf{x}_i$ because $\mathrm{E}(\varepsilon_i) = 0$. In this example, $\mathbf{x}_i$ and $\mathbf{z}_i$ share three variables $(1, S_i, EXPR_i)$. If, for example, S_i were not included in $\mathbf{x}_i$, that would amount to treating S_i as endogenous.

If, as in this example, some of the regressors $\mathbf{z}_i$ are predetermined, those predetermined regressors should be included in the list of instruments $\mathbf{x}_i$. The GMM estimation of the parameter vector is about how to exploit the information afforded by the orthogonality conditions. Not including predetermined regressors as elements of $\mathbf{x}_i$ amounts to throwing away the orthogonality conditions that could have been exploited.

Identification

As seen from the examples of the previous two sections, an instrument must be not only predetermined (i.e., orthogonal to the error term) but also correlated with the regressors. Otherwise, the instrumental variables estimator cannot be defined (see, e.g., (3.1.11)). The generalization to the case with more than one regressor and more than one predetermined variable is

Assumption 3.4 (rank condition for identification): *The $K \times L$ matrix $\mathrm{E}(\mathbf{x}_i\mathbf{z}_i')$ is of full column rank (i.e., its rank equals L, the number of its columns). We denote this matrix by $\mathbf{\Sigma}_{\mathbf{xz}}$.*[7]

To see that this is indeed a generalization, consider Example 3.1. With $\mathbf{z}_i = (1, p_i)'$, $\mathbf{x}_i = (1, x_i)'$, the $\mathbf{\Sigma}_{\mathbf{xz}}$ matrix is

[7] So the cross moment $\mathrm{E}(\mathbf{x}_i\mathbf{z}_i')$ is assumed to exist and is finite. If a moment is indicated, as here, then by implication the moment is assumed to exist and is finite.

$$\boldsymbol{\Sigma}_{\mathbf{xz}} = \begin{bmatrix} 1 & \mathrm{E}(p_i) \\ \mathrm{E}(x_i) & \mathrm{E}(x_i p_i) \end{bmatrix}.$$

The determinant of this matrix is not zero (and hence is of full column rank) if and only if $\mathrm{Cov}(x_i, p_i) = \mathrm{E}(x_i p_i) - \mathrm{E}(x_i)\,\mathrm{E}(p_i) \neq 0$.

Assumption 3.4 is called the **rank condition for identification** for the following reason. To emphasize the dependence of $\mathbf{g}_i$ ($\equiv \mathbf{x}_i \cdot \varepsilon_i$) on the data and the parameter vector, rewrite $\mathbf{g}_i$ as

$$\mathbf{g}_i = \mathbf{g}(\mathbf{w}_i; \boldsymbol{\delta}) \equiv \mathbf{x}_i \cdot (y_i - \mathbf{z}_i'\boldsymbol{\delta}). \tag{3.3.1}$$

So the orthogonality conditions can be rewritten as

$$\mathrm{E}[\mathbf{g}(\mathbf{w}_i; \boldsymbol{\delta})] = \underset{(K\times 1)}{\mathbf{0}}. \tag{3.3.2}$$

Now let $\tilde{\boldsymbol{\delta}}$ $(L \times 1)$ be a hypothetical value of $\boldsymbol{\delta}$ and consider the system of K simultaneous equations in L unknowns (the L elements of $\tilde{\boldsymbol{\delta}}$):

$$\mathrm{E}[\mathbf{g}(\mathbf{w}_i; \tilde{\boldsymbol{\delta}})] = \underset{(K\times 1)}{\mathbf{0}}. \tag{3.3.3}$$

The orthogonality conditions (3.3.2) mean that the true value of the coefficient vector, $\boldsymbol{\delta}$, is *a* solution to this system of K simultaneous equations (3.3.3). So the assumptions we have made so far guarantee that there exists a solution to the simultaneous equations system. We say that the coefficient vector (or the equation) is **identified** if $\tilde{\boldsymbol{\delta}} = \boldsymbol{\delta}$ is the *only* solution.

Because the estimation equation is linear in our model, the function $\mathbf{g}(\mathbf{w}_i; \tilde{\boldsymbol{\delta}})$ is linear in $\tilde{\boldsymbol{\delta}}$, as it can be written as $\mathbf{x}_i \cdot y_i - \mathbf{x}_i\mathbf{z}_i'\tilde{\boldsymbol{\delta}}$. So (3.3.3) is a system of K linear equations:

$$\mathrm{E}(\mathbf{x}_i \cdot y_i) - \mathrm{E}(\mathbf{x}_i\mathbf{z}_i')\tilde{\boldsymbol{\delta}} = \mathbf{0} \quad \text{or} \quad \underset{(K\times L)}{\boldsymbol{\Sigma}_{\mathbf{xz}}}\underset{(L\times 1)}{\tilde{\boldsymbol{\delta}}} = \underset{(K\times 1)}{\boldsymbol{\sigma}_{\mathbf{xy}}}, \tag{3.3.4}$$

where

$$\boldsymbol{\sigma}_{\mathbf{xy}} \equiv \mathrm{E}(\mathbf{x}_i \cdot y_i),\ \boldsymbol{\Sigma}_{\mathbf{xz}} \equiv \mathrm{E}(\mathbf{x}_i\mathbf{z}_i').$$

A necessary and sufficient condition that $\tilde{\boldsymbol{\delta}} = \boldsymbol{\delta}$ is the only solution can be derived from the following result from matrix algebra.[8]

Suppose there exists a solution to a system of linear simultaneous equations

[8] See, e.g., Searle (1982, pp. 233–234).

in $\mathbf{x}$: $\mathbf{Ax} = \mathbf{b}$. A necessary and sufficient condition that it is the only solution is that $\mathbf{A}$ is of full column rank.

Therefore, $\tilde{\boldsymbol{\delta}} = \boldsymbol{\delta}$ is the only solution to (3.3.4) if and only if $\boldsymbol{\Sigma}_{\mathbf{xz}}$ is of full column rank, which is Assumption 3.4.

Order Condition for Identification

Since $\text{rank}(\boldsymbol{\Sigma}_{\mathbf{xz}}) < L$ if $K < L$, a *necessary* condition for identification is that

$$K \text{ (= \#predetermined variables)} \geq L \text{ (= \#regressors)}. \tag{3.3.5a}$$

This is called the **order condition for identification**. It can be stated in different ways. Since K is also the number of orthogonality conditions and L is the number of parameters, the order condition can be stated equivalently as

$$\text{\#orthogonality conditions} \geq \text{\#parameters}. \tag{3.3.5b}$$

By subtracting the number of predetermined regressors from both sides of the inequality, we obtain another equivalent statement:

$$\begin{aligned}&\text{\#predetermined variables excluded from the equation}\\ &\qquad \geq \text{\#endogenous regressors}.\end{aligned} \tag{3.3.5c}$$

Depending on whether the order condition is satisfied, we say that the equation is

- **overidentified** if the rank condition is satisfied and $K > L$,
- **exactly identified** or **just identified** if the rank condition is satisfied and $K = L$,
- **underidentified** (or not identified) if the order condition is not satisfied (i.e., if $K < L$).

Since the order condition is a necessary condition for identification, a failure of the order condition means that the equation is not identified.

The Assumption for Asymptotic Normality

As in Chapter 2, we need to strengthen the orthogonality conditions for the estimator to be asymptotically normal.

Assumption 3.5 ($\mathbf{g}_i$ is a martingale difference sequence with finite second moments): *Let* $\mathbf{g}_i \equiv \mathbf{x}_i \cdot \varepsilon_i$. $\{\mathbf{g}_i\}$ *is a martingale difference sequence (so* a for-

tiori $\text{E}(\mathbf{g}_i) = \mathbf{0}$*). The* $K \times K$ *matrix of cross moments,* $\text{E}(\mathbf{g}_i\mathbf{g}_i')$*, is nonsingular. We use* $\mathbf{S}$ *for* $\text{Avar}(\bar{\mathbf{g}})$ *(i.e., the variance of the limiting distribution of* $\sqrt{n}\,\bar{\mathbf{g}}$*, where* $\bar{\mathbf{g}} \equiv \frac{1}{n}\sum_{i=1}^{n}\mathbf{g}_i$*). By Assumption 3.2 and the ergodic stationary Martingale Differences CLT,* $\mathbf{S} = \text{E}(\mathbf{g}_i\mathbf{g}_i')$.

This is the same as Assumption 2.5, and the same comments apply:

- If the instruments include a constant, then this assumption implies that the error is a martingale difference sequence (and *a fortiori* serially uncorrelated).
- A sufficient and perhaps easier to understand condition for Assumption 3.5 is that

$$\text{E}(\varepsilon_i \mid \varepsilon_{i-1}, \ldots, \varepsilon_1, \mathbf{x}_i, \mathbf{x}_{i-1}, \ldots, \mathbf{x}_1) = 0, \tag{3.3.6}$$

  which means that, besides being a martingale difference sequence, the error term is orthogonal not only to the current but also to the past instruments.
- Since $\mathbf{g}_i\mathbf{g}_i' = \varepsilon_i^2\mathbf{x}_i\mathbf{x}_i'$, $\mathbf{S}$ is a matrix of fourth moments. Consistent estimation of $\mathbf{S}$ will require a fourth-moment assumption to be specified in Assumption 3.6 below.
- If $\{\mathbf{g}_i\}$ is serially correlated, then $\mathbf{S}$ (which is defined to be $\text{Avar}(\bar{\mathbf{g}})$) does not equal $\text{E}(\mathbf{g}_i\mathbf{g}_i')$ and will take a more complicated form, as we will see in Chapter 6.

QUESTIONS FOR REVIEW

1. In the Working example of Example 3.1, is the demand equation identified? Overidentified? Is the supply equation identified?
2. Suppose the rank condition is satisfied for the wage equation of Example 3.2. Is the equation overidentified?
3. In the production function example, no instrument other than a constant is specified. So $K = 1$ and $L = 2$. The order condition informs us that the log output equation (3.2.13) cannot be identified. Write down the orthogonality condition and verify that there are infinitely many combinations of (ϕ_0, ϕ_1) that satisfy the orthogonality condition.
4. Verify that the examples of Section 3.2 are special cases of the model of this section by specifying $(y_i, \mathbf{x}_i, \mathbf{z}_i)$ and writing down the rank condition for each example.

5. Show that the model implies

$$\text{rank}\Big(\underset{(K\times L)}{\boldsymbol{\Sigma}_{\mathbf{xz}}}\Big) = \text{rank}\Big(\underset{(K\times L)}{\boldsymbol{\Sigma}_{\mathbf{xz}}} \ \vdots \ \underset{(K\times 1)}{\boldsymbol{\sigma}_{\mathbf{xy}}}\Big).$$

Hint: $\tilde{\boldsymbol{\delta}} = \boldsymbol{\delta}$ is a solution to (3.3.4). (Some textbooks add this equation to the rank condition for identification, but the equation is implied by the other assumptions of the model.)

6. (Irrelevant instruments) Consider adding another variable, call it ξ_i, to $\mathbf{x}_i$. Although it is predetermined, the variable is unrelated to the regressors in that $\text{E}(\xi_i z_{i\ell}) = 0$ for all ℓ $(= 1, 2, \ldots, L)$. Is the rank condition still satisfied? **Hint:** If a $K \times L$ matrix is of full column rank, then adding any L-dimensional row vector to the rows of the matrix does not alter the rank.

7. (Linearly dependent instruments) In Example 3.2, suppose $AGE_i = EXPR_i + S_i$ for all the individuals in the population. Does that necessarily mean a failure of the rank condition? [Answer: No.] Is the full-rank condition in Assumption 3.5 (that $\text{E}(\mathbf{g}_i\mathbf{g}_i')$ be nonsingular) satisfied? **Hint:** There exists a K-dimensional vector $\boldsymbol{\alpha} \neq \mathbf{0}$ such that $\boldsymbol{\alpha}'\mathbf{x}_i = 0$. Show that $\boldsymbol{\alpha}'\,\text{E}(\mathbf{g}_i\mathbf{g}_i') = \mathbf{0}$.

8. (Linear combinations of instruments) Let $\mathbf{A}$ be a $q \times K$ matrix of full row rank (so $q \leq K$) such that $\mathbf{A}\boldsymbol{\Sigma}_{\mathbf{xz}}$ is of full column rank. Let $\hat{\mathbf{x}}_i \equiv \mathbf{A}\mathbf{x}_i$ (so $\tilde{\mathbf{x}}_i$ is a vector of q transformed instruments). Verify: Assumptions 3.3–3.5 hold for $\hat{\mathbf{x}}_i$ if they do for $\mathbf{x}_i$.

9. Verify that the model, consisting of Assumptions 3.1–3.5, reduces to the regression model of Chapter 2 if $\mathbf{z}_i = \mathbf{x}_i$.

3.4 Generalized Method of Moments Defined

The orthogonality conditions state that a set of population moments are all equal to zero. The basic principle of the **method of moments** is to choose the parameter estimate so that the corresponding sample moments are also equal to zero. The population moments in the orthogonality conditions are $\text{E}[\mathbf{g}(\mathbf{w}_i; \boldsymbol{\delta})]$. Its sample analogue is the sample mean of $\mathbf{g}(\mathbf{w}_i; \boldsymbol{\delta})$ (where $\mathbf{g}(\mathbf{w}_i; \boldsymbol{\delta})$ is defined in (3.3.1)) evaluated at some hypothetical value $\tilde{\boldsymbol{\delta}}$ of $\boldsymbol{\delta}$:

$$\underset{(K\times 1)}{\mathbf{g}_n(\tilde{\boldsymbol{\delta}})} \equiv \frac{1}{n}\sum_{i=1}^{n} \mathbf{g}(\mathbf{w}_i;\tilde{\boldsymbol{\delta}}). \tag{3.4.1}$$

Applying the method of moments principle to our model amounts to choosing a $\tilde{\boldsymbol{\delta}}$ that solves the system of K simultaneous equations in L unknowns: $\mathbf{g}_n(\tilde{\boldsymbol{\delta}}) = \mathbf{0}$, which is the sample analog of (3.3.3). Because the estimation equation is linear, $\mathbf{g}_n(\tilde{\boldsymbol{\delta}})$ can be written as

$$\begin{aligned}\mathbf{g}_n(\tilde{\boldsymbol{\delta}}) &= \frac{1}{n}\sum_{i=1}^{n} \mathbf{x}_i \cdot (y_i - \mathbf{z}_i'\tilde{\boldsymbol{\delta}}) \quad \text{(by definition (3.3.1) of } \mathbf{g}(\mathbf{w}_i;\tilde{\boldsymbol{\delta}})) \\ &= \frac{1}{n}\sum_{i=1}^{n} \mathbf{x}_i \cdot y_i - \Big(\frac{1}{n}\sum_{i=1}^{n} \mathbf{x}_i\mathbf{z}_i'\Big)\tilde{\boldsymbol{\delta}} \equiv \mathbf{s}_{\mathbf{xy}} - \mathbf{S}_{\mathbf{xz}}\tilde{\boldsymbol{\delta}}, \end{aligned} \tag{3.4.2}$$

where $\mathbf{s}_{\mathbf{xy}}$ and $\mathbf{S}_{\mathbf{xz}}$ are the corresponding sample moments of $\boldsymbol{\sigma}_{\mathbf{xy}}$ and $\boldsymbol{\Sigma}_{\mathbf{xz}}$:

$$\underset{(K\times 1)}{\mathbf{s}_{\mathbf{xy}}} \equiv \frac{1}{n}\sum_{i=1}^{n} \mathbf{x}_i \cdot y_i \quad \text{and} \quad \underset{(K\times L)}{\mathbf{S}_{\mathbf{xz}}} \equiv \frac{1}{n}\sum_{i=1}^{n} \mathbf{x}_i\mathbf{z}_i'.$$

So the sample analog $\mathbf{g}_n(\tilde{\boldsymbol{\delta}}) = \mathbf{0}$ is a system of K linear equations in L unknowns:

$$\mathbf{S}_{\mathbf{xz}}\tilde{\boldsymbol{\delta}} = \mathbf{s}_{\mathbf{xy}}. \tag{3.4.3}$$

This is the sample analogue of (3.3.4). If there are more orthogonality conditions than parameters, that is, if $K > L$, then the system may not have a solution. The extension of the method of moments to cover this case as well is the **generalized method of moments (GMM)**.

Method of Moments

If the equation is exactly identified, then $K = L$ and $\boldsymbol{\Sigma}_{\mathbf{xz}}$ is square and invertible. Since under Assumption 3.2 $\mathbf{S}_{\mathbf{xz}}$ converges to $\boldsymbol{\Sigma}_{\mathbf{xz}}$ almost surely, $\mathbf{S}_{\mathbf{xz}}$ is invertible for sufficiently large sample size n with probability one. Thus, when the sample size is large, the system of simultaneous equations (3.4.3) has a unique solution given by

$$\hat{\boldsymbol{\delta}}_{\text{IV}} = \mathbf{S}_{\mathbf{xz}}^{-1}\mathbf{s}_{\mathbf{xy}} = \Big(\frac{1}{n}\sum_{i=1}^{n} \mathbf{x}_i\mathbf{z}_i'\Big)^{-1}\frac{1}{n}\sum_{i=1}^{n} \mathbf{x}_i \cdot y_i. \tag{3.4.4}$$

This estimator is also called the **instrumental variables estimator** with $\mathbf{x}_i$ serving as instruments. Because it is defined for the exactly identified case, the formula assumes that there are as many instruments as regressors. If, moreover, $\mathbf{z}_i = \mathbf{x}_i$ (all the regressors are predetermined or orthogonal to the error term), then $\hat{\boldsymbol{\delta}}_{\text{IV}}$ reduces to the OLS estimator. Thus, the OLS estimator is a method of moments estimator.

Generalized Method of Moments

If the equation is overidentified so that $K > L$, we cannot in general choose an L-dimensional $\tilde{\boldsymbol{\delta}}$ to satisfy the K equations in (3.4.3). If we cannot set $\mathbf{g}_n(\tilde{\boldsymbol{\delta}})$ exactly equal to $\mathbf{0}$, we can at least choose $\tilde{\boldsymbol{\delta}}$ so that $\mathbf{g}_n(\tilde{\boldsymbol{\delta}})$ is as close to $\mathbf{0}$ as possible. To make precise what we mean by "close," we define the distance between any two K-dimensional vectors $\boldsymbol{\xi}$ and $\boldsymbol{\eta}$ by the quadratic form $(\boldsymbol{\xi} - \boldsymbol{\eta})'\widehat{\mathbf{W}}(\boldsymbol{\xi} - \boldsymbol{\eta})$, where $\widehat{\mathbf{W}}$, sometimes called the **weighting matrix**, is a symmetric and positive definite matrix defining the distance.[9]

Definition 3.1 (GMM estimator): Let $\widehat{\mathbf{W}}$ be a $K \times K$ symmetric positive definite matrix, possibly dependent on the sample, such that $\widehat{\mathbf{W}} \to_{\text{p}} \mathbf{W}$ as the sample size n goes to infinity with $\mathbf{W}$ symmetric and positive definite. The **GMM estimator** of $\boldsymbol{\delta}$, denoted $\hat{\boldsymbol{\delta}}(\widehat{\mathbf{W}})$, is

$$\hat{\boldsymbol{\delta}}(\widehat{\mathbf{W}}) \equiv \underset{\tilde{\boldsymbol{\delta}}}{\operatorname{argmin}}\, J(\tilde{\boldsymbol{\delta}}, \widehat{\mathbf{W}}), \tag{3.4.5}$$

where

$$J(\tilde{\boldsymbol{\delta}}, \widehat{\mathbf{W}}) \equiv n \cdot \mathbf{g}_n(\tilde{\boldsymbol{\delta}})'\widehat{\mathbf{W}}\mathbf{g}_n(\tilde{\boldsymbol{\delta}}).$$

(The reason the distance $\mathbf{g}_n(\tilde{\boldsymbol{\delta}})'\widehat{\mathbf{W}}\mathbf{g}_n(\tilde{\boldsymbol{\delta}})$ is multiplied by the sample size (n) becomes clear in Section 3.6.) The weighting matrix is allowed to be random and depend on the sample size, to cover the possibility that the matrix is estimated from the sample. The definition makes clear that the GMM is a special case of **minimum distance estimation**. In minimum distance estimation, $\operatorname{plim} \mathbf{g}_n(\boldsymbol{\delta}) = \mathbf{0}$, as here, but the $\mathbf{g}_n(\cdot)$ function is not necessarily a sample mean.

Since $\mathbf{g}_n(\tilde{\boldsymbol{\delta}})$ is linear in $\tilde{\boldsymbol{\delta}}$ (see (3.4.2)), the objective function is quadratic in $\tilde{\boldsymbol{\delta}}$ when the equation is linear:

$$J(\tilde{\boldsymbol{\delta}}, \widehat{\mathbf{W}}) = n \cdot (\mathbf{s}_{\mathbf{xy}} - \mathbf{S}_{\mathbf{xz}}\tilde{\boldsymbol{\delta}})'\widehat{\mathbf{W}}(\mathbf{s}_{\mathbf{xy}} - \mathbf{S}_{\mathbf{xz}}\tilde{\boldsymbol{\delta}}). \tag{3.4.6}$$

[9]Do not let the word "weight" confuse you between GMM and weighted least squares (WLS). In GMM, the weighting is applied to the sample mean $\bar{\mathbf{g}}$, while in WLS it applies to each observation.

It is left to you to show that the first-order condition for the minimization of this with respect to $\tilde{\boldsymbol{\delta}}$ is

$$\underset{(L\times K)}{\mathbf{S}'_{\mathbf{xz}}}\ \underset{(K\times K)}{\widehat{\mathbf{W}}}\ \underset{(K\times 1)}{\mathbf{s}_{\mathbf{xy}}} = \underset{(L\times K)}{\mathbf{S}'_{\mathbf{xz}}}\ \underset{(K\times K)}{\widehat{\mathbf{W}}}\ \underset{(K\times L)}{\mathbf{S}_{\mathbf{xz}}}\ \underset{(L\times 1)}{\tilde{\boldsymbol{\delta}}}. \tag{3.4.7}$$

If Assumptions 3.2 and 3.4 hold, then $\mathbf{S}_{\mathbf{xz}}$ is of full column rank for sufficiently large n with probability one. Then, since $\widehat{\mathbf{W}}$ is positive definite, the $L \times L$ matrix $\mathbf{S}'_{\mathbf{xz}}\widehat{\mathbf{W}}\mathbf{S}_{\mathbf{xz}}$ is nonsingular. So the unique solution can be obtained by multiplying both sides by the inverse of $\mathbf{S}'_{\mathbf{xz}}\widehat{\mathbf{W}}\mathbf{S}_{\mathbf{xz}}$. That unique solution is the GMM estimator:

$$\text{GMM estimator: } \hat{\boldsymbol{\delta}}(\widehat{\mathbf{W}}) = (\mathbf{S}'_{\mathbf{xz}}\widehat{\mathbf{W}}\mathbf{S}_{\mathbf{xz}})^{-1}\,\mathbf{S}'_{\mathbf{xz}}\widehat{\mathbf{W}}\mathbf{s}_{\mathbf{xy}}. \tag{3.4.8}$$

If $K = L$, then $\mathbf{S}_{\mathbf{xz}}$ is a square matrix and (3.4.8) reduces to the IV estimator (3.4.4). The GMM is indeed a generalization of the method of moments.

Sampling Error

For later use, we derive the expression for the sampling error. Multiplying both sides of the estimation equation $y_i = \mathbf{z}_i'\boldsymbol{\delta} + \varepsilon_i$ from left by $\mathbf{x}_i$ and taking the averages yields

$$\mathbf{s}_{\mathbf{xy}} = \mathbf{S}_{\mathbf{xz}}\boldsymbol{\delta} + \bar{\mathbf{g}}, \tag{3.4.9}$$

where

$$\bar{\mathbf{g}} \equiv \frac{1}{n}\sum_{i=1}^{n}\mathbf{x}_i\cdot\varepsilon_i = \frac{1}{n}\sum_{i=1}^{n}\mathbf{g}(\mathbf{w}_i;\boldsymbol{\delta}) = \mathbf{g}_n(\boldsymbol{\delta}). \tag{3.4.10}$$

Substituting (3.4.9) into (3.4.8), we obtain

$$\hat{\boldsymbol{\delta}}(\widehat{\mathbf{W}}) - \boldsymbol{\delta} = (\mathbf{S}'_{\mathbf{xz}}\widehat{\mathbf{W}}\mathbf{S}_{\mathbf{xz}})^{-1}\,\mathbf{S}'_{\mathbf{xz}}\widehat{\mathbf{W}}\bar{\mathbf{g}}. \tag{3.4.11}$$

QUESTIONS FOR REVIEW

1. Verify that (3.1.12) is the IV estimator of α_1 when the method of moments is applied to the demand equation (3.1.2a) with $(1, x_i)$ as instruments.
2. If the equation is just identified, what is the minimized value of $J(\tilde{\boldsymbol{\delta}}, \widehat{\mathbf{W}})$?
3. Even if the equation is overidentified, the population version, (3.3.4), of the system of K equations (3.4.3) has a solution. Then, why does not the sample version, (3.4.3), have a solution? **Hint:** The population version has a solution

because the $K \times (L+1)$ matrix $[\mathbf{\Sigma_{xz}} \vdots \boldsymbol{\sigma}_{\mathbf{xy}}]$ is of rank L. The rank condition is a set of *equality* conditions on the elements of $\mathbf{\Sigma_{xz}}$ and $\boldsymbol{\sigma}_{\mathbf{xy}}$. Even if $\mathbf{S_{xz}}$ and $\mathbf{s_{xy}}$ converge to $\mathbf{\Sigma_{xz}}$ and $\boldsymbol{\sigma}_{\mathbf{xy}}$, respectively, it does not necessarily follow that $[\mathbf{S_{xz}} \vdots \mathbf{s_{xy}}]$ is of rank L for sufficiently large n. In contrast, $\mathbf{S_{xz}}$ is of full column rank for sufficiently large n when its limit, $\mathbf{\Sigma_{xz}}$ is of full column rank. This is because the full column rank condition for a matrix is a set of *inequality* conditions on the elements of the matrix.

4. What is wrong with the following argument?

   Even if the equation is overidentified, there is no problem finding a solution to (3.4.3). Just premultiply both sides by $\mathbf{S}'_{\mathbf{xz}}$ to obtain

$$\mathbf{S}'_{\mathbf{xz}}\mathbf{S_{xz}}\,\tilde{\boldsymbol{\delta}} = \mathbf{S}'_{\mathbf{xz}}\mathbf{s_{xy}}. \tag{3.4.12}$$

   Since $\mathbf{S_{xz}}$ is of full column rank, $\mathbf{S}'_{\mathbf{xz}}\mathbf{S_{xz}}$ is invertible. So the solution is

$$\tilde{\boldsymbol{\delta}} = (\mathbf{S}'_{\mathbf{xz}}\mathbf{S_{xz}})^{-1}\mathbf{S}'_{\mathbf{xz}}\mathbf{s_{xy}}.$$

   Hint: This $\tilde{\boldsymbol{\delta}}$ certainly solves (3.4.12), but does it solve (3.4.3)?

5. (Singular $\mathbf{W}$) Verify that the GMM estimator (3.4.8) remains well-defined for sufficiently large n even if $\mathbf{W}$ ($\equiv \operatorname{plim} \widehat{\mathbf{W}}$) is singular, as long as $\mathbf{\Sigma}'_{\mathbf{xz}}\mathbf{W}\mathbf{\Sigma_{xz}}$ is nonsingular.

3.5 Large-Sample Properties of GMM

The GMM formula (3.4.8) defines GMM estimators, which are a set of estimators, each indexed by the weighting matrix $\widehat{\mathbf{W}}$. You will be delighted to know that *every* estimator to be introduced in the next few chapters is a GMM estimator for some choice of $\widehat{\mathbf{W}}$. The task of this section is to develop the large-sample theory for the GMM estimator for any given choice of $\widehat{\mathbf{W}}$, which can be carried out quite easily with the techniques of the previous chapter. The first half of this section extends Propositions 2.1–2.4 of Chapter 2 to GMM estimators. One issue that did not arise in those propositions is which GMM estimators should be preferred to other GMM estimators. This is a question of choosing $\widehat{\mathbf{W}}$ optimally and will be taken up in the latter part of this section.

Asymptotic Distribution of the GMM Estimator

The large-sample theory for $\hat{\boldsymbol{\delta}}(\widehat{\mathbf{W}})$ valid for any given choice of $\widehat{\mathbf{W}}$ is

Proposition 3.1 (asymptotic distribution of the GMM estimator):

(a) (Consistency) Under Assumptions 3.1–3.4, $\text{plim}_{n\to\infty}\, \hat{\boldsymbol{\delta}}(\widehat{\mathbf{W}}) = \boldsymbol{\delta}$.

(b) (Asymptotic Normality) If Assumption 3.3 is strengthened as Assumption 3.5, then

$$\sqrt{n}(\hat{\boldsymbol{\delta}}(\widehat{\mathbf{W}}) - \boldsymbol{\delta}) \underset{\text{d}}{\to} N\big(\mathbf{0}, \text{Avar}(\hat{\boldsymbol{\delta}}(\widehat{\mathbf{W}}))\big) \quad \textit{as } n \to \infty,$$

where

$$\text{Avar}(\hat{\boldsymbol{\delta}}(\widehat{\mathbf{W}})) = (\boldsymbol{\Sigma}'_{\mathbf{xz}}\mathbf{W}\boldsymbol{\Sigma}_{\mathbf{xz}})^{-1}\boldsymbol{\Sigma}'_{\mathbf{xz}}\mathbf{WSW}\boldsymbol{\Sigma}_{\mathbf{xz}}(\boldsymbol{\Sigma}'_{\mathbf{xz}}\mathbf{W}\boldsymbol{\Sigma}_{\mathbf{xz}})^{-1}. \tag{3.5.1}$$

(Recall: $\boldsymbol{\Sigma}_{\mathbf{xz}} \equiv \text{E}(\mathbf{x}_i\mathbf{z}'_i)$, $\mathbf{S} = \text{E}(\mathbf{g}_i\mathbf{g}'_i) = \text{E}(\varepsilon_i^2\, \mathbf{x}_i\mathbf{x}'_i)$, $\mathbf{W} \equiv \text{plim}\,\widehat{\mathbf{W}}$.*)*

(c) (Consistent Estimate of $\text{Avar}(\hat{\boldsymbol{\delta}}(\widehat{\mathbf{W}}))$*) Suppose there is available a consistent estimator,* $\widehat{\mathbf{S}}$, *of* $\mathbf{S}$ $(K \times K)$. *Then, under Assumption 3.2,* $\text{Avar}(\hat{\boldsymbol{\delta}}(\widehat{\mathbf{W}}))$ *is consistently estimated by*

$$\widehat{\text{Avar}(\hat{\boldsymbol{\delta}}(\widehat{\mathbf{W}}))} \equiv (\mathbf{S}'_{\mathbf{xz}}\widehat{\mathbf{W}}\mathbf{S}_{\mathbf{xz}})^{-1}\mathbf{S}'_{\mathbf{xz}}\widehat{\mathbf{W}}\widehat{\mathbf{S}}\widehat{\mathbf{W}}\mathbf{S}_{\mathbf{xz}}(\mathbf{S}'_{\mathbf{xz}}\widehat{\mathbf{W}}\mathbf{S}_{\mathbf{xz}})^{-1}, \tag{3.5.2}$$

where $\mathbf{S}_{\mathbf{xz}}$ *is the sample mean of* $\mathbf{x}_i\mathbf{z}'_i$*:*

$$\underset{(K\times L)}{\mathbf{S}_{\mathbf{xz}}} \equiv \frac{1}{n}\sum_{i=1}^{n}\mathbf{x}_i\mathbf{z}'_i.$$

The ugly looking expression for the asymptotic variance will become much prettier when we choose the weighting matrix optimally. If you have gone through the proof of Proposition 2.1, you should find it a breeze to prove Proposition 3.1. The key observations are:

(1) $\mathbf{S}_{\mathbf{xz}} \to_{\text{p}} \boldsymbol{\Sigma}_{\mathbf{xz}}$ (by ergodic stationarity)

(2) $\bar{\mathbf{g}}$ $(\equiv \frac{1}{n}\sum_{i=1}^{n}\mathbf{g}_i) \to_{\text{p}} \mathbf{0}$ (by ergodic stationarity and the orthogonality conditions)

(3) $\sqrt{n}\,\bar{\mathbf{g}} \to_{\text{d}} N(\mathbf{0}, \mathbf{S})$ (by Assumption 3.5).

Consistency immediately follows if you use (1), (2), and Lemma 2.3(a) on the expression for the sampling error (3.4.11). To prove asymptotic normality, multiply both sides of (3.4.11) by $\sqrt{n}$ to obtain

$$\sqrt{n}(\hat{\boldsymbol{\delta}}(\widehat{\mathbf{W}}) - \boldsymbol{\delta}) = (\mathbf{S}'_{\mathbf{xz}}\widehat{\mathbf{W}}\mathbf{S}_{\mathbf{xz}})^{-1}\mathbf{S}'_{\mathbf{xz}}\widehat{\mathbf{W}}\sqrt{n}\,\bar{\mathbf{g}} \tag{3.5.3}$$

and use (3), Lemma 2.3(a), and Lemma 2.4(c). Part (c) of Proposition 3.1 follows immediately from Lemma 2.3(a).

Estimation of Error Variance

In Section 2.3, we proved the consistency of the OLS estimator, s^2, of the error variance. As was noted there, the result holds as long as the residual is from some consistent estimator of the coefficient vector. The same is true here.

Proposition 3.2 (consistent estimation of error variance): *For any consistent estimator, $\hat{\boldsymbol{\delta}}$, of $\boldsymbol{\delta}$, define $\hat{\varepsilon}_i \equiv y_i - \mathbf{z}_i'\hat{\boldsymbol{\delta}}$. Under Assumptions 3.1, 3.2, plus the assumption that $\mathrm{E}(\mathbf{z}_i\mathbf{z}_i')$ (second moments of the regressors) exists and is finite,*

$$\frac{1}{n}\sum_{i=1}^{n}\hat{\varepsilon}_i^2 \underset{\mathrm{p}}{\rightarrow} \mathrm{E}(\varepsilon_i^2),$$

provided $\mathrm{E}(\varepsilon_i^2)$ exists and is finite.

The proof is very similar to the proof of Proposition 2.2. The relationship between $\widehat{\varepsilon_i}$ and ε_i is given by

$$\hat{\varepsilon}_i \equiv y_i - \mathbf{z}_i'\hat{\boldsymbol{\delta}} = \varepsilon_i - \mathbf{z}_i'(\hat{\boldsymbol{\delta}} - \boldsymbol{\delta}), \tag{3.5.4}$$

so that

$$\hat{\varepsilon}_i^2 = \varepsilon_i^2 - 2(\hat{\boldsymbol{\delta}} - \boldsymbol{\delta})'\mathbf{z}_i\cdot\varepsilon_i + (\hat{\boldsymbol{\delta}} - \boldsymbol{\delta})'\mathbf{z}_i\mathbf{z}_i'(\hat{\boldsymbol{\delta}} - \boldsymbol{\delta}). \tag{3.5.5}$$

Summing over i, we obtain

$$\frac{1}{n}\sum_{i=1}^{n}\hat{\varepsilon}_i^2 = \frac{1}{n}\sum_{i=1}^{n}\varepsilon_i^2 - 2(\hat{\boldsymbol{\delta}} - \boldsymbol{\delta})'\frac{1}{n}\sum_{i=1}^{n}\mathbf{z}_i\cdot\varepsilon_i + (\hat{\boldsymbol{\delta}} - \boldsymbol{\delta})'\Big(\frac{1}{n}\sum_{i=1}^{n}\mathbf{z}_i\mathbf{z}_i'\Big)(\hat{\boldsymbol{\delta}} - \boldsymbol{\delta}). \tag{3.5.6}$$

As usual, $\frac{1}{n}\Sigma_i\varepsilon_i^2 \to_{\mathrm{p}} \mathrm{E}(\varepsilon_i^2)$. Since $\hat{\boldsymbol{\delta}}$ is consistent and $\frac{1}{n}\Sigma_i\mathbf{z}_i\mathbf{z}_i'$ converges in probability to some finite matrix by assumption, the last term vanishes. It is easy to show that $\mathrm{E}(\mathbf{z}_i\cdot\varepsilon_i)$ exists and is finite.[10] Then, by ergodic stationarity,

[10]By the Cauchy-Schwartz inequality, $\mathrm{E}(|z_{i\ell}\varepsilon_i|) \le \sqrt{\mathrm{E}(z_{i\ell}^2)\cdot\mathrm{E}(\varepsilon_i^2)}$, where $z_{i\ell}$ is the ℓ-th element of $\mathbf{z}_i$. Both $\mathrm{E}(z_{i\ell}^2)$ and $\mathrm{E}(\varepsilon_i^2)$ are finite by assumption.

$$\frac{1}{n}\Sigma_i \mathbf{z}_i \cdot \varepsilon_i \underset{p}{\to} \text{ some finite vector.}$$

So the second term on the RHS of (3.5.6), too, vanishes.

Hypothesis Testing

It should now be routine to derive from Proposition 3.1(b) and 3.1(c) the following.

Proposition 3.3 (robust t-ratio and Wald statistics): *Suppose Assumptions 3.1–3.5 hold, and suppose there is available a consistent estimate $\widehat{\mathbf{S}}$ of $\mathbf{S}$ ($\equiv \text{Avar}(\bar{\mathbf{g}}) = \text{E}(\mathbf{g}_i\mathbf{g}_i')$). Let*

$$\widehat{\text{Avar}(\hat{\boldsymbol{\delta}}(\widehat{\mathbf{W}}))} \equiv (\mathbf{S}_{\mathbf{xz}}'\widehat{\mathbf{W}}\mathbf{S}_{\mathbf{xz}})^{-1}\mathbf{S}_{\mathbf{xz}}'\widehat{\mathbf{W}}\,\widehat{\mathbf{S}}\,\widehat{\mathbf{W}}\mathbf{S}_{\mathbf{xz}}(\mathbf{S}_{\mathbf{xz}}'\widehat{\mathbf{W}}\mathbf{S}_{\mathbf{xz}})^{-1}.$$

Then:

(a) Under the null hypothesis $\text{H}_0\colon \delta_\ell = \bar{\delta}_\ell$,

$$t_\ell \equiv \frac{\sqrt{n}(\hat{\delta}_\ell(\widehat{\mathbf{W}}) - \bar{\delta}_\ell)}{\sqrt{\left(\widehat{\text{Avar}(\hat{\boldsymbol{\delta}}(\widehat{\mathbf{W}}))}\right)_{\ell\ell}}} = \frac{\hat{\delta}_\ell(\widehat{\mathbf{W}}) - \bar{\delta}_\ell}{SE_\ell^*} \underset{d}{\to} N(0,1),$$

where $\left(\widehat{\text{Avar}(\hat{\boldsymbol{\delta}}(\widehat{\mathbf{W}}))}\right)_{\ell\ell}$ *is the* (ℓ,ℓ) *element of* $\widehat{\text{Avar}(\hat{\boldsymbol{\delta}}(\widehat{\mathbf{W}}))}$ *[which is* $\widehat{\text{Avar}(\hat{\delta}_\ell(\widehat{\mathbf{W}}))}$*] and*

$$SE_\ell^* \text{ (robust standard error)} \equiv \sqrt{\frac{1}{n}\cdot\left(\widehat{\text{Avar}(\hat{\boldsymbol{\delta}}(\widehat{\mathbf{W}}))}\right)_{\ell\ell}}. \tag{3.5.7}$$

(b) Under the null hypothesis $\text{H}_0\colon \mathbf{R}\boldsymbol{\delta} = \mathbf{r}$ *where* $\#\mathbf{r}$ *is the number of restrictions (the dimension of* $\mathbf{r}$*) and* $\mathbf{R}$ $(\#\mathbf{r} \times L)$ *is of full row rank,*

$$W \equiv n\cdot(\mathbf{R}\hat{\boldsymbol{\delta}}(\widehat{\mathbf{W}}) - \mathbf{r})'\left\{\mathbf{R}[\widehat{\text{Avar}(\hat{\boldsymbol{\delta}}(\widehat{\mathbf{W}}))}]\mathbf{R}'\right\}^{-1}(\mathbf{R}\hat{\boldsymbol{\delta}}(\widehat{\mathbf{W}}) - \mathbf{r}) \underset{d}{\to} \chi^2(\#\mathbf{r}). \tag{3.5.8}$$

(c) Under the null hypothesis $\text{H}_0\colon \mathbf{a}(\boldsymbol{\delta}) = \mathbf{0}$ *such that* $\mathbf{A}(\boldsymbol{\delta})$*, the* $\#\mathbf{a} \times L$ *matrix of first derivatives of* $\mathbf{a}(\boldsymbol{\delta})$ *(where* $\#\mathbf{a}$ *is the dimension of* $\mathbf{a}$*), is continuous and of full row rank,*

$$W \equiv n\cdot\mathbf{a}(\hat{\boldsymbol{\delta}}(\widehat{\mathbf{W}}))'\left\{\mathbf{A}(\hat{\boldsymbol{\delta}}(\widehat{\mathbf{W}}))[\widehat{\text{Avar}(\hat{\boldsymbol{\delta}}(\widehat{\mathbf{W}}))}]\mathbf{A}(\hat{\boldsymbol{\delta}}(\widehat{\mathbf{W}}))'\right\}^{-1}\mathbf{a}(\hat{\boldsymbol{\delta}}(\widehat{\mathbf{W}})) \underset{d}{\to} \chi^2(\#\mathbf{a}). \tag{3.5.9}$$

For the Wald statistic for the nonlinear hypothesis, the same comment that we made for Proposition 2.3 applies here: the numerical value of the Wald statistic is not invariant to how the nonlinear restriction is represented by $\mathbf{a}(\cdot)$.

Estimation of S

We have already studied the estimation of $\mathbf{S}$ $(= \mathrm{E}(\mathbf{g}_i\mathbf{g}_i') = \mathrm{E}(\varepsilon_i^2\, \mathbf{x}_i\mathbf{x}_i'))$ in Section 2.5. The proposed estimator was, if adapted to the present estimation equation $y_i = \mathbf{z}_i'\boldsymbol{\delta} + \varepsilon_i$,

$$\widehat{\mathbf{S}} \equiv \frac{1}{n}\sum_{i=1}^{n} \hat{\varepsilon}_i^2\, \mathbf{x}_i\mathbf{x}_i', \tag{3.5.10}$$

where $\hat{\varepsilon}_i \equiv y_i - \mathbf{z}_i'\hat{\boldsymbol{\delta}}$ and $\hat{\boldsymbol{\delta}}$ is consistent for $\boldsymbol{\delta}$. The fourth-moment assumption needed for this to be consistent for $\mathbf{S}$ is a generalization of Assumption 2.6.

Assumption 3.6 (finite fourth moments): $\mathrm{E}[(x_{ik}z_{i\ell})^2]$ *exists and is finite for all* k $(= 1, \ldots, K)$ *and* ℓ $(= 1, \ldots, L)$.

It is left as an analytical exercise to prove

Proposition 3.4 (consistent estimation of S): *Suppose the coefficient estimate* $\hat{\boldsymbol{\delta}}$ *used for calculating the residual* $\hat{\varepsilon}_i$ *for* $\widehat{\mathbf{S}}$ *in (3.5.10) is consistent, and suppose* $\mathbf{S} = \mathrm{E}(\mathbf{g}_i\mathbf{g}_i')$ *exists and is finite. Then, under Assumptions 3.1, 3.2, and 3.6,* $\widehat{\mathbf{S}}$ *given in (3.5.10) is consistent for* $\mathbf{S}$.

Efficient GMM Estimator

Naturally, we wish to choose from the GMM estimators indexed by $\widehat{\mathbf{W}}$ one that has the least asymptotic variance. The next proposition provides a choice of $\mathbf{W}$ that minimizes the asymptotic variance.

Proposition 3.5 (optimal choice of the weighting matrix): *A lower bound for the asymptotic variance of the GMM estimators (3.4.8) indexed by* $\widehat{\mathbf{W}}$ *is given by* $(\boldsymbol{\Sigma}_{\mathbf{xz}}'\mathbf{S}^{-1}\boldsymbol{\Sigma}_{\mathbf{xz}})^{-1}$. *The lower bound is achieved if* $\widehat{\mathbf{W}}$ *is such that* $\mathbf{W}$ $(\equiv \operatorname{plim} \widehat{\mathbf{W}}) = \mathbf{S}^{-1}$.[11]

Because the asymptotic variance for any given $\widehat{\mathbf{W}}$ is (3.5.1), this proposition is proved if we can show that

[11]The condition that $\mathbf{W} = \mathbf{S}^{-1}$ is sufficient but not necessary for efficiency. A necessary and sufficient condition is that there exists a matrix $\mathbf{C}$ such that $\boldsymbol{\Sigma}_{\mathbf{xz}}'\mathbf{W} = \mathbf{C}\,\boldsymbol{\Sigma}_{\mathbf{xz}}'\mathbf{S}^{-1}$. See Newey and McFadden (1994, p. 2165).

$$(\mathbf{\Sigma}'_{\mathbf{xz}}\mathbf{W}\mathbf{\Sigma}_{\mathbf{xz}})^{-1}\mathbf{\Sigma}'_{\mathbf{xz}}\mathbf{WSW}\mathbf{\Sigma}_{\mathbf{xz}}(\mathbf{\Sigma}'_{\mathbf{xz}}\mathbf{W}\mathbf{\Sigma}_{\mathbf{xz}})^{-1} \geq (\mathbf{\Sigma}'_{\mathbf{xz}}\mathbf{S}^{-1}\mathbf{\Sigma}_{\mathbf{xz}})^{-1} \quad (3.5.11)$$

for any symmetric positive definite matrix $\mathbf{W}$. Proving this algebraic result is left as an analytical exercise.

A GMM estimator satisfying the efficiency condition that plim $\widehat{\mathbf{W}} = \mathbf{S}^{-1}$ will be called the **efficient** (or **optimal**) **GMM estimator**. Simply by replacing $\widehat{\mathbf{W}}$ by $\widehat{\mathbf{S}}^{-1}$ (which is consistent for $\mathbf{S}^{-1}$) in the formulas of Proposition 3.1, we obtain

$$\text{Efficient GMM estimator: } \hat{\boldsymbol{\delta}}(\widehat{\mathbf{S}}^{-1}) = (\mathbf{S}'_{\mathbf{xz}}\widehat{\mathbf{S}}^{-1}\mathbf{S}_{\mathbf{xz}})^{-1}\mathbf{S}'_{\mathbf{xz}}\widehat{\mathbf{S}}^{-1}\mathbf{s}_{\mathbf{xy}}, \quad (3.5.12)$$

$$\text{Avar}(\hat{\boldsymbol{\delta}}(\widehat{\mathbf{S}}^{-1})) = (\mathbf{\Sigma}'_{\mathbf{xz}}\mathbf{S}^{-1}\mathbf{\Sigma}_{\mathbf{xz}})^{-1}, \quad (3.5.13)$$

$$\widehat{\text{Avar}(\hat{\boldsymbol{\delta}}(\widehat{\mathbf{S}}^{-1}))} = (\mathbf{S}'_{\mathbf{xz}}\widehat{\mathbf{S}}^{-1}\mathbf{S}_{\mathbf{xz}})^{-1}. \quad (3.5.14)$$

With $\widehat{\mathbf{W}} = \widehat{\mathbf{S}}^{-1}$, the formulas for the robust t and the Wald statistics in Proposition 3.3 become

$$t_\ell = \frac{\hat{\delta}_\ell(\widehat{\mathbf{S}}^{-1}) - \bar{\delta}_\ell}{SE^*_\ell}, \quad (3.5.15)$$

where SE^*_ℓ is the robust standard error given by

$$SE^*_\ell = \sqrt{\frac{1}{n}\cdot\left((\mathbf{S}'_{\mathbf{xz}}\widehat{\mathbf{S}}^{-1}\mathbf{S}_{\mathbf{xz}})^{-1}\right)_{\ell\ell}},$$

and

$$W = n\cdot\mathbf{a}(\hat{\boldsymbol{\delta}}(\widehat{\mathbf{S}}^{-1}))'\left\{\mathbf{A}(\hat{\boldsymbol{\delta}}(\widehat{\mathbf{S}}^{-1}))(\mathbf{S}'_{\mathbf{xz}}\widehat{\mathbf{S}}^{-1}\mathbf{S}_{\mathbf{xz}})^{-1}\mathbf{A}(\hat{\boldsymbol{\delta}}(\widehat{\mathbf{S}}^{-1}))'\right\}^{-1}\mathbf{a}(\hat{\boldsymbol{\delta}}(\widehat{\mathbf{S}}^{-1})). \quad (3.5.16)$$

To calculate the efficient GMM estimator, we need the consistent estimator $\widehat{\mathbf{S}}$. But Proposition 3.4 assures us that the $\widehat{\mathbf{S}}$ based on any consistent estimator of $\boldsymbol{\delta}$ is consistent for $\mathbf{S}$. This leads us to the following **two-step efficient GMM procedure**:

Step 1: Choose a matrix $\widehat{\mathbf{W}}$ that converges in probability to a symmetric and positive definite matrix, and minimize $J(\tilde{\boldsymbol{\delta}}, \widehat{\mathbf{W}})$ over $\tilde{\boldsymbol{\delta}}$ to obtain $\hat{\boldsymbol{\delta}}(\widehat{\mathbf{W}})$. There is no shortage of such matrices $\widehat{\mathbf{W}}$ (e.g., $\widehat{\mathbf{W}} = \mathbf{I}$), but usually we set $\widehat{\mathbf{W}} = \mathbf{S}_{\mathbf{xx}}^{-1}$. The resulting estimator $\hat{\boldsymbol{\delta}}(\mathbf{S}_{\mathbf{xx}}^{-1})$ is the celebrated two-stage least squares (as we will see in Section 3.8). Use this to calculate the residual $\hat{\varepsilon}_i \equiv y_i - \mathbf{z}'_i\hat{\boldsymbol{\delta}}(\widehat{\mathbf{W}})$ and obtain a consistent estimator $\widehat{\mathbf{S}}$ of $\mathbf{S}$ by (3.5.10).

Step 2: Minimize $J(\tilde{\boldsymbol{\delta}}, \widehat{\mathbf{S}}^{-1})$ over $\tilde{\boldsymbol{\delta}}$. The minimizer is the efficient GMM estimator.

Asymptotic Power

Like the coefficient estimator, the t and Wald statistics depend on the choice of $\mathbf{W}$. It seems intuitively obvious that those statistics associated with the efficient GMM estimator should be preferred in large samples. This intuition can be formalized in terms of asymptotic power introduced in Section 2.4. Take, for example, the t-ratio for testing H_0: $\delta_\ell = \bar{\delta}_\ell$. The t-ratio is written (reproducing (3.5.7)) as

$$t_\ell \equiv \frac{\sqrt{n}(\hat{\delta}_\ell(\widehat{\mathbf{W}}) - \bar{\delta}_\ell)}{\sqrt{\left(\widehat{\mathrm{Avar}(\hat{\boldsymbol{\delta}}(\widehat{\mathbf{W}}))}\right)_{\ell\ell}}}. \tag{3.5.17}$$

The denominator converges to some finite number even when the null is false. In contrast, the numerator explodes (its plim is infinite) when the null is false. So the power under any fixed alternative approaches unity. That is, the test is consistent. This is true for any choice of $\mathbf{W}$, so test consistency cannot be a basis for choosing $\mathbf{W}$.

Next, consider a sequence of local alternatives subject to Pitman drift:

$$\delta_\ell^{(n)} = \bar{\delta}_\ell + \frac{\gamma}{\sqrt{n}} \tag{3.5.18}$$

for some given $\gamma \neq 0$. Substituting (3.5.18) into (3.5.17), the t-ratio above can be rewritten as

$$t_\ell = \frac{\sqrt{n}(\hat{\delta}_\ell(\widehat{\mathbf{W}}) - \delta_\ell^{(n)})}{\sqrt{\left(\widehat{\mathrm{Avar}(\hat{\boldsymbol{\delta}}(\widehat{\mathbf{W}}))}\right)_{\ell\ell}}} + \frac{\gamma}{\sqrt{\left(\widehat{\mathrm{Avar}(\hat{\boldsymbol{\delta}}(\widehat{\mathbf{W}}))}\right)_{\ell\ell}}}. \tag{3.5.19}$$

Applying the same argument for deriving the asymptotic distribution of the t-ratio in (2.4.4), we can show that $t_\ell \to_{\mathrm{d}} N(\mu, 1)$, where

$$\mu \equiv \frac{\gamma}{\sqrt{\left(\mathrm{Avar}(\hat{\boldsymbol{\delta}}(\widehat{\mathbf{W}}))\right)_{\ell\ell}}}. \tag{3.5.20}$$

If the significance level is α, the asymptotic power is given by $\mathrm{Prob}(|x| > t_{\alpha/2})$, where $x \sim N(\mu, 1)$ and $t_{\alpha/2}$ is the level-α critical value. Evidently, the larger is $|\mu|$, the higher is the asymptotic power. And $|\mu|$ decreases with the asymptotic variance. Therefore, the asymptotic power against local alternatives is maximized by the efficient GMM estimator.

Small-Sample Properties

Do these desirable asymptotic properties of the efficient GMM estimator and associated test statistics carry over to their finite-sample distributions? The efficient GMM estimator uses $\widehat{\mathbf{S}}^{-1}$, a function of estimated fourth moments, for $\widehat{\mathbf{W}}$. Generally, it takes a substantially larger sample size to estimate fourth moments reliably than to estimate first and second moments. So we would expect the efficient GMM estimator to have poorer small-sample properties than the GMM estimators that do not use fourth moments for $\widehat{\mathbf{W}}$. The July 1996 issue of the *Journal of Business and Economic Statistics* has a number of papers examining the small-sample distribution of GMM estimators and associated test statistics for various DGPs. Their overall conclusion is that the equally weighted GMM estimator with $\widehat{\mathbf{W}} = \mathbf{I}$ generally outperforms the efficient GMM in terms of the bias and variance in finite samples. They also find that the size of the efficient Wald statistic in small samples far exceeds the assumed significance level. That is, if α is the assumed significance level and c_α is the associated critical value so that $\text{Prob}(\chi^2 > c_\alpha) = \alpha$, the probability in finite samples that the Wald statistic is greater than c_α far exceeds α; the test rejects the null too often. Unfortunately, however, like most other small-sample studies, those studies fail to produce clear quantitative guidance which the empirical researcher could follow.

QUESTIONS FOR REVIEW

1. Verify that all the results of Sections 2.3–2.5 are special cases of those of this section. In particular, verify that (3.5.1) reduces to (2.3.4). **Hint:** $\mathbf{\Sigma}_{\mathbf{xz}}$ is square if $\mathbf{z}_i = \mathbf{x}_i$.

2. (Singular $\mathbf{W}$) Suppose $\mathbf{W}$ is singular but $\mathbf{\Sigma}'_{\mathbf{xz}}\mathbf{W}\mathbf{\Sigma}_{\mathbf{xz}}$ is nonsingular. Verify that all the results of this section (except Proposition 3.5) remain valid.

3. (Asymptotically equivalent choice of $\widehat{\mathbf{W}}$) Suppose $\widehat{\mathbf{W}}_1 - \widehat{\mathbf{W}}_2 \to_{\text{p}} \mathbf{0}$. Show that

$$\sqrt{n}\,\hat{\boldsymbol{\delta}}(\widehat{\mathbf{W}}_1) - \sqrt{n}\,\hat{\boldsymbol{\delta}}(\widehat{\mathbf{W}}_2) \underset{\text{p}}{\to} \mathbf{0}.$$

Hint:

$$\begin{aligned}&\sqrt{n}\,\hat{\boldsymbol{\delta}}(\widehat{\mathbf{W}}_1) - \sqrt{n}\,\hat{\boldsymbol{\delta}}(\widehat{\mathbf{W}}_2)\\ &\quad = \left[(\mathbf{S}'_{\mathbf{xz}}\widehat{\mathbf{W}}_1\mathbf{S}_{\mathbf{xz}})^{-1}\mathbf{S}'_{\mathbf{xz}}\widehat{\mathbf{W}}_1 - (\mathbf{S}'_{\mathbf{xz}}\widehat{\mathbf{W}}_2\mathbf{S}_{\mathbf{xz}})^{-1}\mathbf{S}'_{\mathbf{xz}}\widehat{\mathbf{W}}_2\right]\sqrt{n}\,\bar{\mathbf{g}}.\end{aligned}$$

$\sqrt{n}\,\bar{\mathbf{g}}$ converges in distribution to a random variable. Use Lemma 2.4(b).

4. (Three-step GMM) Consider adding to the efficient two-step GMM procedure the following third step: Recompute $\widehat{\mathbf{S}}$ by (3.5.10), but this time using the residual from the second step. Calculate the GMM estimator with this recomputed $\widehat{\mathbf{S}}$. Is this estimator consistent? Asymptotically normal? Efficient? **Hint:** Verify by Proposition 3.4 that the recalculated $\widehat{\mathbf{S}}$ is consistent for $\mathbf{S}$. Does the asymptotic distribution of the GMM estimator depend on the choice of $\widehat{\mathbf{W}}$ if $\text{plim}_{n\to\infty} \widehat{\mathbf{W}}$ is the same?

5. (When $\mathbf{z}_i$ is a strict subset of $\mathbf{x}_i$) Suppose $\mathbf{z}_i$ is a strict subset of $\mathbf{x}_i$. So $\mathbf{x}_i$ includes, in addition to the regressors (which are all predetermined), some other predetermined variables. Are the efficient two-step GMM estimator and the OLS estimator numerically the same? [Answer: No.]

6. (Data matrix representation of efficient GMM) Let $\mathbf{B}$ be the $n \times n$ diagonal matrix whose i-th element is $\hat{\varepsilon}_i^2$, where $\hat{\varepsilon}_i$ is the residual from the first-step consistent estimation. That is,

$$\mathbf{B} \equiv \begin{bmatrix} \hat{\varepsilon}_1^2 & & \\ & \ddots & \\ & & \hat{\varepsilon}_n^2 \end{bmatrix}.$$

Verify that

$$\hat{\boldsymbol{\delta}}(\widehat{\mathbf{S}}^{-1}) = [\mathbf{Z}'\mathbf{X}(\mathbf{X}'\mathbf{B}\mathbf{X})^{-1}\mathbf{X}'\mathbf{Z}]^{-1}\mathbf{Z}'\mathbf{X}(\mathbf{X}'\mathbf{B}\mathbf{X})^{-1}\mathbf{X}'\mathbf{y},$$

where $\mathbf{X}$, $\mathbf{y}$, and $\mathbf{Z}$ are data matrices for the instruments, the dependent variable, and the regressors (they are defined in Section 3.8 below).

7. (GLS interpretation of efficient GMM) Let $\mathbf{X}$, $\mathbf{Z}$, and $\mathbf{y}$ be as in the previous question. Then the estimation equation can be written as $\mathbf{y} = \mathbf{Z}\boldsymbol{\delta} + \boldsymbol{\varepsilon}$. Premultiply both sides by $\mathbf{X}$ to obtain

$$\mathbf{X}'\mathbf{y} = \mathbf{X}'\mathbf{Z}\boldsymbol{\delta} + \mathbf{X}'\boldsymbol{\varepsilon}.$$

Taking $\mathbf{S}$ to be the variance matrix of $\mathbf{X}'\boldsymbol{\varepsilon}$ and $\widehat{\mathbf{S}}$ to be its consistent estimate, apply FGLS. Verify that the FGLS estimator is the efficient GMM estimator (the FGLS estimator was defined in Section 1.6).

8. (Linear combination of orthogonality conditions) Derive the efficient GMM estimator that exploits a linear combination of orthogonality conditions,

$$\mathbf{A}\,\mathrm{E}(\mathbf{g}_i) = \mathbf{0},$$

where $\mathbf{A}$ is a $q \times K$ matrix of full row rank (so $q \leq K$). [Answer: Replace $\mathbf{S_{xz}}$ by $\mathbf{AS_{xy}}$, $\mathbf{s_{xz}}$ by $\mathbf{As_{xy}}$, and $\mathbf{S}$ by $\mathbf{ASA'}$. Formally, the estimator can be written as (3.4.8) with $\widehat{\mathbf{W}} = \mathbf{A}'(\mathbf{A}\widehat{\mathbf{S}}\mathbf{A}')^{-1}\mathbf{A}$.] Verify: If $q = K$ (so that $\mathbf{A}$ is nonsingular), then the efficient GMM estimator is numerically equal to the efficient GMM estimator associated with the orthogonality conditions $\mathrm{E}(\mathbf{g}_i) = \mathbf{0}$.

3.6 Testing Overidentifying Restrictions

If the equation is exactly identified, then it is possible to choose $\tilde{\boldsymbol{\delta}}$ so that all the elements of the sample moments $\mathbf{g}_n(\tilde{\boldsymbol{\delta}})$ are zero and the distance

$$J(\tilde{\boldsymbol{\delta}}, \widehat{\mathbf{W}}) \equiv n \cdot \mathbf{g}_n(\tilde{\boldsymbol{\delta}})' \,\widehat{\mathbf{W}} \mathbf{g}_n(\tilde{\boldsymbol{\delta}})$$

is zero. (The $\tilde{\boldsymbol{\delta}}$ that does it is the IV estimator.) If the equation is overidentified, then the distance cannot be set to zero exactly, but we would expect the minimized distance to be close to zero. It turns out that, if the weighting matrix $\widehat{\mathbf{W}}$ is chosen optimally so that $\operatorname{plim} \widehat{\mathbf{W}} = \mathbf{S}^{-1}$, then the minimized distance is asymptotically chi-squared.

Let $\widehat{\mathbf{S}}$ be a consistent estimator of $\mathbf{S}$, and consider first the case where the distance is evaluated at the true parameter value $\boldsymbol{\delta}$, $J(\boldsymbol{\delta}, \widehat{\mathbf{S}}^{-1})$. Since by definition $\mathbf{g}_n(\tilde{\boldsymbol{\delta}}) = \bar{\mathbf{g}}$ $(\equiv \frac{1}{n}\Sigma_i \mathbf{g}_i)$ for $\tilde{\boldsymbol{\delta}} = \boldsymbol{\delta}$, the distance equals

$$J(\boldsymbol{\delta}, \widehat{\mathbf{S}}^{-1}) = n \cdot \bar{\mathbf{g}}' \widehat{\mathbf{S}}^{-1} \bar{\mathbf{g}} = (\sqrt{n}\, \bar{\mathbf{g}})' \widehat{\mathbf{S}}^{-1} (\sqrt{n}\, \bar{\mathbf{g}}). \tag{3.6.1}$$

Since $\sqrt{n}\, \bar{\mathbf{g}} \to_{\mathrm{d}} N(\mathbf{0}, \mathbf{S})$ and $\widehat{\mathbf{S}} \to_{\mathrm{p}} \mathbf{S}$, its asymptotic distribution is $\chi^2(K)$ by Lemma 2.4(d). Now if $\boldsymbol{\delta}$ is replaced by $\hat{\boldsymbol{\delta}}(\widehat{\mathbf{S}}^{-1})$, then the degrees of freedom change from K to $K - L$. The intuitive reason is that we have to estimate L parameters $\boldsymbol{\delta}$ before forming the sample average of $\mathbf{g}_i$. (We encountered a similar situation in Chapter 1 in the context of the unbiased estimation of σ^2.) We summarize this as

Proposition 3.6 (Hansen's test of overidentifying restrictions (Hansen, 1982)): *Suppose there is available a consistent estimator, $\widehat{\mathbf{S}}$, of $\mathbf{S}$ $(= \mathrm{E}(\mathbf{g}_i \mathbf{g}_i'))$. Under Assumptions 3.1–3.5,*

$$J\big(\hat{\boldsymbol{\delta}}(\widehat{\mathbf{S}}^{-1}), \widehat{\mathbf{S}}^{-1}\big) \; \big(= n \cdot \mathbf{g}_n(\hat{\boldsymbol{\delta}}(\widehat{\mathbf{S}}^{-1}))' \widehat{\mathbf{S}}^{-1} \mathbf{g}_n(\hat{\boldsymbol{\delta}}(\widehat{\mathbf{S}}^{-1}))\big) \underset{\mathrm{d}}{\to} \chi^2(K - L).$$

A formal proof is left as an optional exercise. Because the $\widehat{\mathbf{S}}$ given in (3.5.10) is consistent (under the additional condition of Assumption 3.6), the minimized distance calculated in the second step of the efficient two-step GMM is asymptotically $\chi^2(K - L)$.

Three points on the use and interpretation of the J test are in order.

- This is a **specification test**, testing whether all the restrictions of the model (which are the assumptions maintained in Proposition 3.6) are satisfied. If the J statistic of Proposition 3.6 is surprisingly large, it means that either the orthogonality conditions (Assumption 3.3) or the other assumptions (or both) are likely to be false. Only when we are confident about those other assumptions can we interpret the large J statistic as evidence for the endogeneity of some of the K instruments included in $\mathbf{x}_i$.

- Unlike the tests we have encountered so far, the test is not consistent against some failures of the orthogonality conditions. The essential reason is the loss of degrees of freedom from K to $K - L$. It is easy to show that $\bar{\mathbf{g}}$ is related to its sample counterpart, $\mathbf{g}_n(\hat{\boldsymbol{\delta}}(\widehat{\mathbf{S}}^{-1}))$, as

$$\sqrt{n}\,\mathbf{g}_n(\hat{\boldsymbol{\delta}}(\widehat{\mathbf{S}}^{-1})) = \widehat{\mathbf{B}}\sqrt{n}\,\bar{\mathbf{g}}, \quad \widehat{\mathbf{B}} \equiv \mathbf{I}_K - \mathbf{S}_{\mathbf{xz}}(\mathbf{S}_{\mathbf{xz}}'\widehat{\mathbf{S}}^{-1}\mathbf{S}_{\mathbf{xz}})^{-1}\mathbf{S}_{\mathbf{xz}}'\widehat{\mathbf{S}}^{-1}. \tag{3.6.2}$$

The problem is that, since $\widehat{\mathbf{B}}\mathbf{S}_{\mathbf{xz}} = \mathbf{0}$, this matrix $\widehat{\mathbf{B}}$ is not of full column rank. If the orthogonality conditions fail and $\mathrm{E}(\mathbf{g}_i) \neq \mathbf{0}$, then the elements of $\sqrt{n}\,\bar{\mathbf{g}}$ will diverge to $+\infty$ or $-\infty$. But, since $\widehat{\mathbf{B}}$ is not of full column rank, $\widehat{\mathbf{B}}\sqrt{n}\,\bar{\mathbf{g}}$ and hence $J(\hat{\boldsymbol{\delta}}(\widehat{\mathbf{S}}^{-1}), \widehat{\mathbf{S}}^{-1})$ may remain finite for some pattern of nonzero orthogonalities.[12]

- It is only recently that the small-sample properties of the test became a concern. Several papers in the July 1996 issue of the *Journal of Business and Economic Statistics* report that the finite-sample or actual size of the J test in small samples far exceeds the nominal size (i.e., the test rejects too often).

Testing Subsets of Orthogonality Conditions

Suppose we can divide the K instruments into two groups: the vector $\mathbf{x}_{i1}$ of K_1 variables that are known to satisfy the orthogonality conditions, and the vector $\mathbf{x}_{i2}$ of remaining $K - K_1$ variables that are suspect. Since the ordering of instruments does not change the numerical values of the estimator and test statistics, we can assume without loss of generality that the last $K - K_1$ elements of $\mathbf{x}_i$ are the suspect

[12] See Newey (1985, Section 3) for a thorough treatment of this issue.

instruments:

$$\mathbf{x}_i = \begin{bmatrix} \mathbf{x}_{i1} \\ \mathbf{x}_{i2} \end{bmatrix} \begin{matrix} \} & K_1 \text{ rows,} \\ \} & K - K_1 \text{ rows.} \end{matrix} \tag{3.6.3}$$

The part of the model we wish to test is

$$\mathrm{E}(\mathbf{x}_{i2} \cdot \varepsilon_i) = \mathbf{0}. \tag{3.6.4}$$

This restriction is testable if there are at least as many nonsuspect instruments as there are coefficients so that $K_1 \geq L$. The basic idea is to compare two J statistics from two separate GMM estimators of the same coefficient vector $\boldsymbol{\delta}$, one using only the instruments included in $\mathbf{x}_{i1}$, and the other using also the suspect instruments $\mathbf{x}_{i2}$ in addition to $\mathbf{x}_{i1}$. If the inclusion of the suspect instruments significantly increases the J statistic, that is a good reason for doubting the predeterminedness of $\mathbf{x}_{i2}$.

In accordance with the partition of $\mathbf{x}_i$, the sample orthogonality conditions $\mathbf{g}_n(\tilde{\boldsymbol{\delta}})$ and $\mathbf{S}$ can be written as

$$\underset{(K\times 1)}{\mathbf{g}_n(\tilde{\boldsymbol{\delta}})} \equiv \begin{bmatrix} \underset{(K_1\times 1)}{\mathbf{g}_{1n}(\tilde{\boldsymbol{\delta}})} \\ \underset{((K-K_1)\times 1)}{\mathbf{g}_{2n}(\tilde{\boldsymbol{\delta}})} \end{bmatrix}, \quad \underset{(K\times K)}{\mathbf{S}} \equiv \begin{bmatrix} \mathbf{S}_{11} & \mathbf{S}_{12} \\ \mathbf{S}_{21} & \mathbf{S}_{22} \end{bmatrix}, \tag{3.6.5}$$

where

$$\mathbf{S}_{11} = \mathrm{E}(\varepsilon_i^2 \mathbf{x}_{i1}\mathbf{x}_{i1}'),\ \mathbf{S}_{12} = \mathrm{E}(\varepsilon_i^2 \mathbf{x}_{i1}\mathbf{x}_{i2}'),\ \mathbf{S}_{21} = \mathrm{E}(\varepsilon_i^2 \mathbf{x}_{i2}\mathbf{x}_{i1}'),\ \mathbf{S}_{22} = \mathrm{E}(\varepsilon_i^2 \mathbf{x}_{i2}\mathbf{x}_{i2}').$$

In particular, $\mathbf{g}_{1n}(\tilde{\boldsymbol{\delta}})$ can be written as

$$\mathbf{g}_{1n}(\tilde{\boldsymbol{\delta}}) = \frac{1}{n}\sum_{i=1}^{n} \mathbf{x}_{i1} \cdot (y_i - \mathbf{z}_i'\tilde{\boldsymbol{\delta}}) \equiv \mathbf{s}_{\mathbf{x}_1 y} - \mathbf{S}_{\mathbf{x}_1 \mathbf{z}}\tilde{\boldsymbol{\delta}},$$

where

$$\mathbf{s}_{\mathbf{x}_1 y} \equiv \frac{1}{n}\sum_{i=1}^{n} \mathbf{x}_{i1} \cdot y_i, \quad \mathbf{S}_{\mathbf{x}_1 \mathbf{z}} \equiv \frac{1}{n}\sum_{i=1}^{n} \mathbf{x}_{i1}\mathbf{z}_i'. \tag{3.6.6}$$

For a consistent estimate $\widehat{\mathbf{S}}$ of $\mathbf{S}$, the efficient GMM estimator using all the K instruments and its associated J statistic have already been derived in this and the previous section. Reproducing them,

$$\hat{\delta} = (\mathbf{S}'_{\mathbf{xz}}\widehat{\mathbf{S}}^{-1}\mathbf{S}_{\mathbf{xz}})^{-1}\mathbf{S}'_{\mathbf{xz}}\widehat{\mathbf{S}}^{-1}\mathbf{s}_{\mathbf{xy}}, \tag{3.6.7}$$

$$J = n \cdot \mathbf{g}_n(\hat{\delta})'\widehat{\mathbf{S}}^{-1}\mathbf{g}_n(\hat{\delta}). \tag{3.6.8}$$

The efficient GMM estimator of the *same* coefficient vector $\boldsymbol{\delta}$ using only the first K_1 instruments and its associated J statistic are obtained by replacing $\mathbf{x}_i$ by $\mathbf{x}_{i1}$ in these expressions. So

$$\bar{\delta} = [\mathbf{S}'_{\mathbf{x}_1\mathbf{z}}(\widehat{\mathbf{S}}_{11})^{-1}\mathbf{S}_{\mathbf{x}_1\mathbf{z}}]^{-1}\mathbf{S}'_{\mathbf{x}_1\mathbf{z}}(\widehat{\mathbf{S}}_{11})^{-1}\mathbf{s}_{\mathbf{x}_1\mathbf{y}}, \tag{3.6.9}$$

$$J_1 = n \cdot \mathbf{g}_{1n}(\bar{\delta})'(\widehat{\mathbf{S}}_{11})^{-1}\mathbf{g}_{1n}(\bar{\delta}), \tag{3.6.10}$$

where $\widehat{\mathbf{S}}_{11}$ is a consistent estimate of $\mathbf{S}_{11}$.

The test is based on the following proposition specifying the asymptotic distribution of $J - J_1$ (the proof is left as an optional exercise).

Proposition 3.7 (testing a subset of orthogonality conditions[13]): *Suppose Assumptions 3.1–3.5 hold. Let $\mathbf{x}_{i1}$ be a subvector of $\mathbf{x}_i$, and strengthen Assumption 3.4 by requiring that the rank condition for identification is satisfied for $\mathbf{x}_{i1}$ (so $\mathrm{E}(\mathbf{x}_{i1}\mathbf{z}_i')$ is of full column rank). Then, for any consistent estimators $\widehat{\mathbf{S}}$ of $\mathbf{S}$ and $\widehat{\mathbf{S}}_{11}$ of $\mathbf{S}_{11}$,*

$$C \equiv J - J_1 \underset{d}{\rightarrow} \chi^2(K - K_1),$$

where $K = \#\mathbf{x}_i$ (dimension of $\mathbf{x}_i$), $K_1 = \#\mathbf{x}_{i1}$ (dimension of $\mathbf{x}_{i1}$), and J and J_1 are defined in (3.6.8) and (3.6.10).

Clearly, the choice of $\widehat{\mathbf{S}}$ and $\widehat{\mathbf{S}}_{11}$ does not matter asymptotically as long as they are consistent. But in finite samples, the test statistic C can be negative. This problem can be avoided and C can be made nonnegative in finite samples if the same $\widehat{\mathbf{S}}$ is used throughout, that is, if $\widehat{\mathbf{S}}_{11}$ in (3.6.9) and (3.6.10) is the submatrix of $\widehat{\mathbf{S}}$ in (3.6.7) and (3.6.8). This is accomplished by taking the following steps:

(1) do the efficient two-step GMM with full instruments $\mathbf{x}_i$ to obtain $\widehat{\mathbf{S}}$ from the first step, $\hat{\delta}$ and J from the second step;

(2) extract the submatrix $\widehat{\mathbf{S}}_{11}$ from $\widehat{\mathbf{S}}$ obtained from (1), calculate $\bar{\delta}$ by (3.6.9) using this $\widehat{\mathbf{S}}_{11}$ and J_1 by (3.6.10). Then take the difference in J.

[13] The test was developed in Newey (1985, Section 4) and Eichenbaum, Hansen, and Singleton (1985, Appendix C).

It is left as an optional analytical exercise to prove that C calculated as just described is nonnegative in finite samples.

We can use Proposition 3.7 to test for the endogeneity of a subset of regressors, as the next example illustrates.

Example 3.3 (testing whether schooling is predetermined in the wage equation): In the wage equation of Example 3.2, suppose schooling S_i is suspected to be endogenous. To test for the endogeneity of S_i, partition $\mathbf{x}_i$ as

$$\mathbf{x}_{i1} = \begin{bmatrix} 1 \\ EXPR_i \\ AGE_i \\ MED_i \end{bmatrix}, \quad \mathbf{x}_{i2} = S_i.$$

The vector of regressors, $\mathbf{z}_i$, is the same as in Example 3.2. The first step is to do the efficient two-step GMM estimation of $\boldsymbol{\delta}$ with $\mathbf{x}_i \equiv (1, EXPR_i, AGE_i, MED_i, S_i)'$ as the instruments. This produces J and the 5×5 matrix $\widehat{\mathbf{S}}$. Second, extract the leading 4×4 submatrix $\widehat{\mathbf{S}}_{11}$ corresponding to $\mathbf{x}_{i1}$ from $\widehat{\mathbf{S}}$ and estimate the same coefficients $\boldsymbol{\delta}$ by GMM, this time with the fewer instruments $\mathbf{x}_{i1}$ and using this $\widehat{\mathbf{S}}_{11}$. The difference in the J statistic from the two different GMM estimators of $\boldsymbol{\delta}$ should be asymptotically $\chi^2(1)$.

QUESTIONS FOR REVIEW

1. Does $J(\hat{\boldsymbol{\delta}}(\widehat{\mathbf{S}}^{-1}), \overline{\mathbf{S}}^{-1}) \to_d \chi^2(K - L)$ where $\widehat{\mathbf{S}}$ and $\overline{\mathbf{S}}$ are two different consistent estimators of $\mathbf{S}$?
2. Show: $J(\hat{\boldsymbol{\delta}}(\widehat{\mathbf{S}}^{-1}), \widehat{\mathbf{S}}^{-1}) = n \cdot \mathbf{s}'_{\mathbf{xy}} \widehat{\mathbf{S}}^{-1}(\mathbf{s}_{\mathbf{xy}} - \mathbf{S}_{\mathbf{xz}} \hat{\boldsymbol{\delta}}(\widehat{\mathbf{S}}^{-1}))$.
3. Can the degrees of freedom of the C statistic be greater than $K - L$? [Answer: No.]
4. Suppose $K_1 = L$. Does the numerical value of C depend on the partition of $\mathbf{x}_i$ between $\mathbf{x}_{i1}$ and $\mathbf{x}_{i2}$?

3.7 Hypothesis Testing by the Likelihood-Ratio Principle

We have derived in Section 3.5 the chi-squared test statistics for the null hypothesis H_0: $\mathbf{a}(\boldsymbol{\delta}) = \mathbf{0}$ by the Wald principle. This section does the same by the likelihood-ratio (LR) principle, which is to examine the difference in the objective function with and without the imposition of the null. Derivation of test statistics by the Lagrange Multiplier principle for GMM and extension to nonlinear equations are given in Section 7.4.

In the efficient GMM estimation, the objective function is $J(\tilde{\boldsymbol{\delta}}, \widehat{\mathbf{S}}^{-1})$ for a given consistent estimate $\widehat{\mathbf{S}}$ of $\mathbf{S}$. The **restricted efficient GMM estimator** is defined as

$$\text{restricted efficient GMM: } \bar{\boldsymbol{\delta}}(\widehat{\mathbf{S}}^{-1}) \equiv \underset{\tilde{\boldsymbol{\delta}}}{\operatorname{argmin}}\, J(\tilde{\boldsymbol{\delta}}, \widehat{\mathbf{S}}^{-1}) \quad \text{subject to } H_0. \tag{3.7.1}$$

The LR principle suggests that

$$LR \equiv J(\bar{\boldsymbol{\delta}}(\widehat{\mathbf{S}}^{-1}), \widehat{\mathbf{S}}^{-1}) - J(\hat{\boldsymbol{\delta}}(\widehat{\mathbf{S}}^{-1}), \widehat{\mathbf{S}}^{-1}) \tag{3.7.2}$$

should be asymptotically chi-squared. Indeed it is.

Proposition 3.8 (test statistic by the LR principle): *Suppose Assumptions 3.1–3.5 hold and suppose there is available a consistent estimator, $\widehat{\mathbf{S}}$, of $\mathbf{S}$ $(= \mathrm{E}(\mathbf{g}_i\mathbf{g}_i'))$. Consider the null hypothesis of #$\mathbf{a}$ restrictions H_0: $\mathbf{a}(\boldsymbol{\delta}) = \mathbf{0}$ such that $\mathbf{A}(\boldsymbol{\delta})$, the #$\mathbf{a} \times L$ matrix of first derivatives, is continuous and of full row rank. Define two statistics, W and LR, by (3.5.16) and (3.7.2), respectively. Then, under the null, the following holds:*

(a) The two statistics are asymptotically equivalent in that their asymptotic distributions are the same (namely, $\chi^2(\#\mathbf{a})$).

(b) The two statistics are asymptotically equivalent in the stronger sense that their numerical difference converges in probability to zero: $LR - W \to_{\mathrm{p}} 0$. (By Lemma 2.4(a), this result is stronger than (a).)

(c) Furthermore, if the hypothesis is linear so that the restrictions can be written as $\mathbf{R}\boldsymbol{\delta} = \mathbf{r}$, then the two statistics are numerically equal.

Proving this for the linear case, which is an algebraic result, is left as an analytical exercise. For a full proof, see Section 7.4.

Several comments about Proposition 3.8:

- The advantage of *LR* over *W* is invariance: the numerical value of *LR* does not depend on how the nonlinear restrictions are represented by $\mathbf{a}(\cdot)$. On the other hand, you have to write a nonlinear optimization computer program to find the restricted efficient GMM when the hypothesis is nonlinear.

- Proposition 3.8 requires that the distance matrix $\widehat{\mathbf{W}}$ satisfy the efficiency condition $\text{plim}\,\widehat{\mathbf{W}} = \mathbf{S}^{-1}$. Otherwise *LR* is not asymptotically chi-squared. In contrast, the Wald statistic is asymptotically chi-squared without $\widehat{\mathbf{W}}$ satisfying the efficiency condition.

- The same estimate of $\mathbf{S}$ should be used throughout in the calculation of *LR*. Let $\widetilde{\mathbf{S}}$ and $\overline{\mathbf{S}}$ be two different consistent estimators of $\mathbf{S}$, and consider the statistic

$$J(\bar{\delta}(\overline{\mathbf{S}}^{-1}), \overline{\mathbf{S}}^{-1}) - J(\hat{\delta}(\widetilde{\mathbf{S}}^{-1}), \widetilde{\mathbf{S}}^{-1}).$$

  This statistic is what you end up with if you perform two separate two-step efficient GMMs with and without the constraint of the null; $\overline{\mathbf{S}}$ is the estimate of $\mathbf{S}$ from the first step with the constraint, while $\widetilde{\mathbf{S}}$ is from the first step without the constraint. The statistic is asymptotically equivalent to *LR* (in that the difference between the two converges in probability to zero), but in finite samples it may be negative. Having the same estimate of $\mathbf{S}$ throughout ensures the nonnegativity of the statistic in finite samples. Researchers usually use the estimate from unconstrained estimation ($\widetilde{\mathbf{S}}$) here, but the estimate from constrained estimation is also valid because it is consistent for $\mathbf{S}$ under the null.

- Part (b) of the proposition (the asymptotic equivalence in a stronger sense) means that if the sample size is large enough and the hypothesis is true, then the outcome (not just the probability of rejection or acceptance) of the test based on *LR* will be the same as that based on *W* because the probability that the two statistics differ numerically by an even tiny amount is zero in sufficiently large samples.

- For the numerical equivalence $LR = W$ for the linear case to hold, the same $\widehat{\mathbf{S}}$ must be used throughout to calculate not only *LR* but also the Wald statistic. Otherwise *LR* and *W* are only asymptotically equivalent.

The *LR* Statistic for the Regression Model

Because the regression model of Chapter 2 is a special case of the GMM model of this chapter, it may be useful to know how *LR* would look for that special case.

Because $\mathbf{x}_i = \mathbf{z}_i$ in the regression model, the (unrestricted) efficient GMM estimator is OLS and $J(\hat{\boldsymbol{\delta}}(\widehat{\mathbf{S}}^{-1}), \widehat{\mathbf{S}}^{-1}) = 0$. Therefore,

$$LR = J(\bar{\boldsymbol{\delta}}(\widehat{\mathbf{S}}^{-1}), \widehat{\mathbf{S}}^{-1}), \tag{3.7.3}$$

where $\bar{\boldsymbol{\delta}}(\widehat{\mathbf{S}}^{-1})$ is the restricted efficient GMM estimator. By Proposition 3.8, this statistic is asymptotically chi-squared and is numerically equal to the Wald statistic if the null is linear. As will be shown below, under conditional homoskedasticity, this statistic can be written as the difference in the sum of squared residuals normalized to the error variance.

Variable Addition Test (optional)

In the previous section, we considered a specification test based on the C statistic for the endogeneity of a subset, $\mathbf{x}_{i2}$ of instruments $\mathbf{x}_i$ while assuming that the other instruments $\mathbf{x}_{i1}$ are predetermined. Occasionally, we encounter a special case where $\mathbf{z}_i = \mathbf{x}_{i1}$:

$$y_i = \mathbf{x}_{i1}'\boldsymbol{\delta} + \varepsilon_i. \tag{3.7.4}$$

A popular method to test whether the suspect instruments $\mathbf{x}_{i2}$ are predetermined is to estimate the augmented equation

$$y_i = \mathbf{x}_{i1}'\boldsymbol{\delta} + \mathbf{x}_{i2}'\boldsymbol{\alpha} + \varepsilon_i = \mathbf{x}_i'\boldsymbol{\gamma} + \varepsilon_i \quad \text{with } \boldsymbol{\gamma} = \begin{bmatrix} \boldsymbol{\delta} \\ \boldsymbol{\alpha} \end{bmatrix} \tag{3.7.5}$$

and test the null H_0: $\boldsymbol{\alpha} = \mathbf{0}$. Testing is either by the Wald statistic W or by the LR statistic, which is numerically equal to W. This test is sometimes called the **variable addition test**. How is the test related to the C test of Proposition 3.7?

To calculate LR, we have to calculate two efficient GMM estimators of $\boldsymbol{\gamma}$ with the same instrument set $\mathbf{x}_i$: one with the constraint $\boldsymbol{\alpha} = \mathbf{0}$ and one without. The unrestricted efficient GMM estimator is the OLS estimator on the unconstrained equation (3.7.5). The associated J statistic is zero. Let

$$\widehat{\mathbf{S}} \equiv \frac{1}{n}\sum_{i=1}^{n} e_i^2 \, \mathbf{x}_i\mathbf{x}_i', \tag{3.7.6}$$

where e_i is the OLS residual from the unrestricted regression (3.7.5). If we use this estimate of $\mathbf{S}$, the restricted efficient GMM estimator of $\boldsymbol{\gamma}$ minimizes the J function

$$J(\tilde{\boldsymbol{\gamma}}, \widehat{\mathbf{S}}^{-1}) = n \cdot (\mathbf{s_{xy}} - \mathbf{S_{xx}}\tilde{\boldsymbol{\gamma}})' \widehat{\mathbf{S}}^{-1} (\mathbf{s_{xy}} - \mathbf{S_{xx}}\tilde{\boldsymbol{\gamma}})$$

subject to $\boldsymbol{\alpha} = \mathbf{0}$. Clearly, the restricted estimator can be written as

$$\bar{\boldsymbol{\gamma}} = \begin{bmatrix} \hat{\boldsymbol{\delta}}(\widehat{\mathbf{S}}^{-1}) \\ \mathbf{0} \end{bmatrix},$$

where $\hat{\boldsymbol{\delta}}(\widehat{\mathbf{S}}^{-1})$ is the efficient GMM estimator with $\mathbf{x}_i$ as instruments on the restricted equation (3.7.4). So

$$\begin{aligned} LR &= n \cdot (\mathbf{s_{xy}} - \mathbf{S_{xx}}\bar{\boldsymbol{\gamma}})' \widehat{\mathbf{S}}^{-1} (\mathbf{s_{xy}} - \mathbf{S_{xx}}\bar{\boldsymbol{\gamma}}) \quad \text{(since } J = 0 \text{ for unrestricted GMM)} \\ &= n \cdot (\mathbf{s_{xy}} - \mathbf{S_{xx_1}}\hat{\boldsymbol{\delta}}(\widehat{\mathbf{S}}^{-1}))' \widehat{\mathbf{S}}^{-1} (\mathbf{s_{xy}} - \mathbf{S_{xx_1}}\hat{\boldsymbol{\delta}}(\widehat{\mathbf{S}}^{-1})) \quad \text{(since } \mathbf{S_{xx}}\bar{\boldsymbol{\gamma}} = \mathbf{S_{xx_1}}\hat{\boldsymbol{\delta}}(\widehat{\mathbf{S}}^{-1})). \end{aligned}$$

This is none other than Hansen's J statistic for the restricted equation (3.7.4) when $\mathbf{x}_i$ is the instrument vector. This statistic, in turn, equals the C statistic because the J_1 in Proposition 3.7 is zero in the present case. Therefore, all three statistics, W from the unrestricted regression, LR, and C, are numerically equal to Hansen's J, provided that the same $\widehat{\mathbf{S}}$ is used throughout. That is, the variable addition test is numerically equivalent to Hansen's test for overidentifying restrictions.

QUESTIONS FOR REVIEW

1. (*LR* for the regression model) Verify that, for the regression model where $\mathbf{z}_i = \mathbf{x}_i$,

$$LR = \mathbf{y}'\mathbf{X}(n\widehat{\mathbf{S}})^{-1}\mathbf{X}'\mathbf{y} - 2\mathbf{y}'\mathbf{X}(n\widehat{\mathbf{S}})^{-1}(\mathbf{X}'\mathbf{X})\bar{\boldsymbol{\delta}} + \bar{\boldsymbol{\delta}}'(\mathbf{X}'\mathbf{X})(n\widehat{\mathbf{S}})^{-1}(\mathbf{X}'\mathbf{X})\bar{\boldsymbol{\delta}}.$$

2. (Choice of $\widehat{\mathbf{S}}$ in variable addition test) Suppose you form $\widehat{\mathbf{S}}$ from the residual from the restricted regression (3.7.4) and use it to form W, *LR*, and C. Are they numerically equal? Are they asymptotically chi-squared? **Hint:** Is this $\widehat{\mathbf{S}}$ consistent under the null?

3.8 Implications of Conditional Homoskedasticity

So far, we have not assumed conditional homoskedasticity in developing the asymptotics of the GMM estimator. This section considers the implication of imposing

Assumption 3.7 (conditional homoskedasticity):

$$\mathrm{E}(\varepsilon_i^2 \mid \mathbf{x}_i) = \sigma^2.$$

Under conditional homoskedasticity, the matrix of fourth moments $\mathbf{S}$ $(= \mathrm{E}(\mathbf{g}_i\mathbf{g}_i') = \mathrm{E}(\varepsilon_i^2\,\mathbf{x}_i\mathbf{x}_i'))$ can be written as a product of second moments:

$$\mathbf{S} = \sigma^2 \boldsymbol{\Sigma}_{\mathbf{xx}}, \tag{3.8.1}$$

where $\boldsymbol{\Sigma}_{\mathbf{xx}} = \mathrm{E}(\mathbf{x}_i\mathbf{x}_i')$. As in Chapter 2, this decomposition of $\mathbf{S}$ has several implications.

- Since $\mathbf{S}$ is nonsingular by Assumption 3.5, this decomposition implies that $\sigma^2 > 0$ and $\boldsymbol{\Sigma}_{\mathbf{xx}}$ is nonsingular.
- The estimator exploiting this structure of $\mathbf{S}$ is

$$\widehat{\mathbf{S}} = \hat{\sigma}^2 \frac{1}{n}\sum_{i=1}^{n} \mathbf{x}_i\mathbf{x}_i' = \hat{\sigma}^2\,\mathbf{S}_{\mathbf{xx}}, \tag{3.8.2}$$

  where $\hat{\sigma}^2$ is some consistent estimator to be specified below. By ergodic stationarity, $\mathbf{S}_{\mathbf{xx}} \to_{\text{a.s.}} \boldsymbol{\Sigma}_{\mathbf{xx}}$. Thus, provided that $\hat{\sigma}^2$ is consistent, we do not need the fourth-moment assumption (Assumption 3.6) for $\widehat{\mathbf{S}}$ to be consistent.

Needless to say, all the results presented so far are valid under the extra condition of conditional homoskedasticity. But many of the results and formulas can be simplified substantially under this extra condition, by just replacing $\mathbf{S}$ by $\sigma^2\boldsymbol{\Sigma}_{\mathbf{xx}}$ and the expression (3.5.10) for $\widehat{\mathbf{S}}$ by (3.8.2). This section collects those simplifications.

Efficient GMM Becomes 2SLS

In the efficient GMM estimation, the weighting matrix is $\widehat{\mathbf{S}}^{-1}$. If we set $\widehat{\mathbf{S}}$ to (3.8.2), the GMM estimator becomes

$$\begin{aligned}
\hat{\boldsymbol{\delta}}(\widehat{\mathbf{S}}^{-1}) &= [\mathbf{S}_{\mathbf{xz}}'(\hat{\sigma}^2\,\mathbf{S}_{\mathbf{xx}})^{-1}\,\mathbf{S}_{\mathbf{xz}}]^{-1}\,\mathbf{S}_{\mathbf{xz}}'(\hat{\sigma}^2\,\mathbf{S}_{\mathbf{xx}})^{-1}\,\mathbf{s}_{\mathbf{xy}} \\
&= (\mathbf{S}_{\mathbf{xz}}'\,\mathbf{S}_{\mathbf{xx}}^{-1}\,\mathbf{S}_{\mathbf{xz}})^{-1}\,\mathbf{S}_{\mathbf{xz}}'\,\mathbf{S}_{\mathbf{xx}}^{-1}\,\mathbf{s}_{\mathbf{xy}} \\
&= \hat{\boldsymbol{\delta}}(\mathbf{S}_{\mathbf{xx}}^{-1}) \equiv \hat{\boldsymbol{\delta}}_{\text{2SLS}},
\end{aligned} \tag{3.8.3}$$

which does not depend on $\hat{\sigma}^2$. In the general case, the whole point of the first step in the efficient two-step GMM was to obtain a consistent estimator of $\mathbf{S}$. Under conditional homoskedasticity, there is no need to do the first step because the second-step estimator collapses to the GMM estimator with $\mathbf{S_{xx}}$ used for $\widehat{\mathbf{S}}$, $\hat{\boldsymbol{\delta}}(\mathbf{S}_{\mathbf{xx}}^{-1})$. This estimator, $\hat{\boldsymbol{\delta}}_{2SLS}$, is called the **Two-Stage Least Squares** (2SLS or TSLS).[14] The same equation can be estimated by maximum likelihood. Section 8.6 will cover the ML counterpart of 2SLS, called the "limited-information maximum likelihood estimator."

The expression for $\text{Avar}(\hat{\boldsymbol{\delta}}_{2SLS})$ can be obtained by substituting (3.8.1) into (3.5.13):

$$\text{Avar}(\hat{\boldsymbol{\delta}}_{2SLS}) = \sigma^2 \cdot (\boldsymbol{\Sigma}_{\mathbf{xz}}' \, \boldsymbol{\Sigma}_{\mathbf{xx}}^{-1} \, \boldsymbol{\Sigma}_{\mathbf{xz}})^{-1}. \tag{3.8.4}$$

A natural estimator of this is

$$\widehat{\text{Avar}(\hat{\boldsymbol{\delta}}_{2SLS})} = \hat{\sigma}^2 \cdot (\mathbf{S}_{\mathbf{xz}}' \, \mathbf{S}_{\mathbf{xx}}^{-1} \, \mathbf{S}_{\mathbf{xz}})^{-1}. \tag{3.8.5}$$

For $\hat{\sigma}^2$, consider the sample variance of the 2SLS residuals:

$$\hat{\sigma}^2 \equiv \frac{1}{n} \sum_{i=1}^{n} (y_i - \mathbf{z}_i' \hat{\boldsymbol{\delta}}_{2SLS})^2. \tag{3.8.6}$$

(Some authors divide the sum of squares by $n - L$, not by n, to calculate $\hat{\sigma}^2$.) By Proposition 3.2, (3.8.6) $\to_p \sigma^2$ if $\text{E}(\mathbf{z}_i \mathbf{z}_i')$ exists and is finite. Thus $\widehat{\mathbf{S}}$ defined in (3.8.2) with this $\hat{\sigma}^2$ is consistent for $\mathbf{S}$.

Substituting (3.8.2) into (3.5.15) and (3.5.16), the t-ratio and the Wald statistic become

$$t_\ell = \frac{\hat{\delta}_{2SLS,\ell} - \bar{\delta}_\ell}{SE_\ell} \quad \text{with} \quad SE_\ell = \sqrt{\frac{\hat{\sigma}^2}{n} \cdot \left((\mathbf{S}_{\mathbf{xz}}' \, \mathbf{S}_{\mathbf{xx}}^{-1} \, \mathbf{S}_{\mathbf{xz}})^{-1} \right)_{\ell\ell}}, \tag{3.8.7}$$

$$W = n \cdot \frac{\mathbf{a}(\hat{\boldsymbol{\delta}}_{2SLS})' \left[\mathbf{A}(\hat{\boldsymbol{\delta}}_{2SLS}) (\mathbf{S}_{\mathbf{xz}}' \, \mathbf{S}_{\mathbf{xx}}^{-1} \, \mathbf{S}_{\mathbf{xz}})^{-1} \mathbf{A}(\hat{\boldsymbol{\delta}}_{2SLS})' \right]^{-1} \mathbf{a}(\hat{\boldsymbol{\delta}}_{2SLS})}{\hat{\sigma}^2}. \tag{3.8.8}$$

J Becomes Sargan's Statistic

When $\widehat{\mathbf{W}}$ is set to $(\hat{\sigma}^2 \mathbf{S_{xx}})^{-1}$, the distance defined in (3.4.6) becomes

$$J\left(\tilde{\boldsymbol{\delta}}, (\hat{\sigma}^2 \cdot \mathbf{S_{xx}})^{-1}\right) = n \cdot \frac{(\mathbf{s_{xy}} - \mathbf{S_{xz}} \tilde{\boldsymbol{\delta}})' \mathbf{S}_{\mathbf{xx}}^{-1} (\mathbf{s_{xy}} - \mathbf{S_{xz}} \tilde{\boldsymbol{\delta}})}{\hat{\sigma}^2}. \tag{3.8.9}$$

[14]This estimator was first proposed by Theil (1953).

Proposition 3.6 then implies that the distance evaluated at the efficient GMM estimator under conditional homoskedasticity, $\hat{\boldsymbol{\delta}}_{\text{2SLS}}$, is asymptotically chi-squared. This distance is called **Sargan's statistic** (Sargan, 1958):

$$\text{Sargan's statistic} = n \cdot \frac{(\mathbf{s}_{\mathbf{xy}} - \mathbf{S}_{\mathbf{xz}}\hat{\boldsymbol{\delta}}_{\text{2SLS}})'\mathbf{S}_{\mathbf{xx}}^{-1}(\mathbf{s}_{\mathbf{xy}} - \mathbf{S}_{\mathbf{xz}}\hat{\boldsymbol{\delta}}_{\text{2SLS}})}{\hat{\sigma}^2}. \tag{3.8.10}$$

We summarize our results so far as

Proposition 3.9 (asymptotic properties of 2SLS):

(a) Under Assumptions 3.1–3.4, the 2SLS *estimator (3.8.3) is consistent. If Assumption 3.5 is added, the estimator is asymptotically normal with the asymptotic variance given by (3.5.1) with* $\mathbf{W} = (\sigma^2 \boldsymbol{\Sigma}_{\mathbf{xx}})^{-1}$. *If Assumption 3.7 (conditional homoskedasticity) is added to Assumptions 3.1–3.5, then the estimator is the efficient GMM estimator.*

Furthermore, if $\text{E}(\mathbf{z}_i\mathbf{z}_i')$ *exists and is finite,*[15] *then*

(b) the asymptotic variance is consistently estimated by (3.8.5),

(c) t_ℓ *in (3.8.7)* $\to_{\text{d}} N(0, 1)$, W *in (3.8.8)* $\to_{\text{d}} \chi^2(\#\mathbf{r})$, *and*

(d) the Sargan statistic in (3.8.10) $\to_{\text{d}} \chi^2(K - L)$.

Proposition 3.8 states that the *LR* statistic, which is the difference in J with and without the imposition of the null hypothesis, is asymptotically chi-squared. Since J can be written as (3.8.9), we have

$$LR = n \cdot \frac{(\mathbf{s}_{\mathbf{xy}} - \mathbf{S}_{\mathbf{xz}}\bar{\boldsymbol{\delta}})'\mathbf{S}_{\mathbf{xx}}^{-1}(\mathbf{s}_{\mathbf{xy}} - \mathbf{S}_{\mathbf{xz}}\bar{\boldsymbol{\delta}}) - (\mathbf{s}_{\mathbf{xy}} - \mathbf{S}_{\mathbf{xz}}\hat{\boldsymbol{\delta}}_{\text{2SLS}})'\mathbf{S}_{\mathbf{xx}}^{-1}(\mathbf{s}_{\mathbf{xy}} - \mathbf{S}_{\mathbf{xz}}\hat{\boldsymbol{\delta}}_{\text{2SLS}})}{\hat{\sigma}^2}, \tag{3.8.11}$$

where $\bar{\boldsymbol{\delta}}$ is the restricted 2SLS estimator which minimizes (3.8.9) under the null hypothesis.[16] In Proposition 3.8, the use of the same $\widehat{\mathbf{S}}$ guaranteed the statistic to be nonnegative in finite samples. Here, deflation by the same $\hat{\sigma}^2$ ensures the statistic to be nonnegative. If the hypothesis is linear, then this *LR* is numerically equal to the Wald statistic W.

[15]This additional assumption is needed for the consistency of $\hat{\sigma}^2$; see Proposition 3.2.

[16]This statistic was first derived by Gallant and Jorgenson (1979).

Small-Sample Properties of 2SLS

There is a fairly large literature on the finite-sample distribution of the 2SLS estimator (see, e.g., Judge et al. (1985, Section 15.4) and Staiger and Stock (1997, Section 1)). Some studies manage to derive analytically the exact finite-sample distribution of the estimator, while others are Monte Carlo studies for various DGPs. The analytical results, however, are not useful for empirical researchers, because they are derived under the restrictive assumptions of fixed instruments and normal errors and the analytical expressions for distributions are computationally intractable.

For the case of a single regressor and a single (stochastic) instrument with normal errors, Nelson and Startz (1990) derive the exact finite-sample distribution of the 2SLS estimator that is fairly simple and easy to calculate. They also show that, when the instrument is "weak" in the sense of low explanatory power in the first-stage regression of the regressor on the instrument, a mass of the distribution of the sampling error $\hat{\delta}_{2SLS} - \delta$ remains apart from zero until the sample size gets really large.

Their work illustrates the need for reporting the R^2 for the first-stage regressions; if the R^2 is low, we should suspect the large-sample approximation to the distribution of the 2SLS estimator to be poor (you will see a dramatic example in part (g) of the empirical exercise). Recently, Staiger and Stock (1997) proposed an alternative asymptotic approximation to the finite-sample distribution of the 2SLS and other estimators and associated test statistics, for the case of "weak" instruments. Their device is to look at a sequence of models along which the coefficients of the instruments in the first-stage regressions converge to zero. (Analytical Exercise 10 works out this type of asymptotics for the simple case of one regressor and one instrument.)

Alternative Derivations of 2SLS

If we define data matrices as

$$\underset{(n\times K)}{\mathbf{X}} = \begin{bmatrix} \mathbf{x}_1' \\ \mathbf{x}_2' \\ \vdots \\ \mathbf{x}_n' \end{bmatrix}, \quad \underset{(n\times L)}{\mathbf{Z}} = \begin{bmatrix} \mathbf{z}_1' \\ \mathbf{z}_2' \\ \vdots \\ \mathbf{z}_n' \end{bmatrix}, \quad \underset{(n\times 1)}{\mathbf{y}} = \begin{bmatrix} y_1 \\ y_2 \\ \vdots \\ y_n \end{bmatrix},$$

then it is easy to see that the 2SLS estimator and associated statistics can be written as

$$\hat{\boldsymbol{\delta}}_{\text{2SLS}} = [\mathbf{Z}'\mathbf{X}(\mathbf{X}'\mathbf{X})^{-1}\mathbf{X}'\mathbf{Z}]^{-1}\mathbf{Z}'\mathbf{X}(\mathbf{X}'\mathbf{X})^{-1}\mathbf{X}'\mathbf{y}$$
$$= (\mathbf{Z}'\mathbf{P}\mathbf{Z})^{-1}\mathbf{Z}'\mathbf{P}\mathbf{y}, \tag{3.8.3$'$}$$

where $\mathbf{P} \equiv \mathbf{X}(\mathbf{X}'\mathbf{X})^{-1}\mathbf{X}'$ is the projection matrix,

$$\widehat{\text{Avar}(\hat{\boldsymbol{\delta}}_{\text{2SLS}})} = n \cdot \hat{\sigma}^2 \cdot [\mathbf{Z}'\mathbf{X}(\mathbf{X}'\mathbf{X})^{-1}\mathbf{X}'\mathbf{Z}]^{-1} = n \cdot \hat{\sigma}^2 \cdot (\mathbf{Z}'\mathbf{P}\mathbf{Z})^{-1}. \tag{3.8.5$'$}$$

$$\hat{\sigma}^2 \equiv \frac{\hat{\boldsymbol{\varepsilon}}'\hat{\boldsymbol{\varepsilon}}}{n} \quad \text{where } \hat{\boldsymbol{\varepsilon}} \equiv \mathbf{y} - \mathbf{Z}\hat{\boldsymbol{\delta}}_{\text{2SLS}}. \tag{3.8.6$'$}$$

$$t_\ell = \frac{\hat{\delta}_{\text{2SLS},\ell} - \bar{\delta}_\ell}{\sqrt{\hat{\sigma}^2 \cdot \left([\mathbf{Z}'\mathbf{X}(\mathbf{X}'\mathbf{X})^{-1}\mathbf{X}'\mathbf{Z}]^{-1}\right)_{\ell\ell}}}. \tag{3.8.7$'$}$$

$$W = \frac{\mathbf{a}(\hat{\boldsymbol{\delta}}_{\text{2SLS}})' \left[\mathbf{A}(\hat{\boldsymbol{\delta}}_{\text{2SLS}})(\mathbf{Z}'\mathbf{X}(\mathbf{X}'\mathbf{X})^{-1}\mathbf{X}'\mathbf{Z})^{-1}\mathbf{A}(\hat{\boldsymbol{\delta}}_{\text{2SLS}})'\right]^{-1} \mathbf{a}(\hat{\boldsymbol{\delta}}_{\text{2SLS}})}{\hat{\sigma}^2}. \tag{3.8.8$'$}$$

$$J(\tilde{\boldsymbol{\delta}}, (\hat{\sigma}^2 \cdot \mathbf{S}_{\mathbf{xx}})^{-1}) = \frac{(\mathbf{y} - \mathbf{Z}\tilde{\boldsymbol{\delta}})'\mathbf{P}(\mathbf{y} - \mathbf{Z}\tilde{\boldsymbol{\delta}})}{\hat{\sigma}^2}. \tag{3.8.9$'$}$$

$$\text{Sargan's statistic} = \frac{\hat{\boldsymbol{\varepsilon}}'\mathbf{P}\hat{\boldsymbol{\varepsilon}}}{\hat{\sigma}^2}. \tag{3.8.10$'$}$$

Using this formula, we can provide two other derivations of the 2SLS estimator.

2SLS as an IV Estimator

Let $\hat{\mathbf{z}}_i$ $(L \times 1)$ be the vector of L instruments (which will be generated from $\mathbf{x}_i$ as described below) for the L regressors, and let $\widehat{\mathbf{Z}}$ be the $n \times L$ data matrix of those L instruments. So the i-th row of $\widehat{\mathbf{Z}}$ is $\hat{\mathbf{z}}_i'$. The IV estimator of $\boldsymbol{\delta}$ with $\hat{\mathbf{z}}_i$ serving as instruments is, by (3.4.4),

$$\hat{\boldsymbol{\delta}}_{\text{IV}} = \left(\frac{1}{n}\sum_{i=1}^{n} \hat{\mathbf{z}}_i \mathbf{z}_i'\right)^{-1} \frac{1}{n}\sum_{i=1}^{n} \hat{\mathbf{z}}_i \cdot y_i = (\widehat{\mathbf{Z}}'\mathbf{Z})^{-1}\widehat{\mathbf{Z}}'\mathbf{y}. \tag{3.8.12}$$

Now we generate those L instruments from $\mathbf{x}_i$ as follows. The ℓ-th instrument is the fitted value from regressing $z_{i\ell}$ (the ℓ-th regressor) on $\mathbf{x}_i$. The n-vector of fitted value is $\mathbf{X}(\mathbf{X}'\mathbf{X})^{-1}\mathbf{X}'\mathbf{z}_\ell$, where $\mathbf{z}_\ell$ is the n-vector of the ℓ-th regressor (i.e., the ℓ-th column of $\mathbf{Z}$). Therefore, the $n \times L$ data matrix of instruments is

$$\widehat{\mathbf{Z}} = (\mathbf{X}(\mathbf{X}'\mathbf{X})^{-1}\mathbf{X}'\mathbf{z}_1, \ldots, \mathbf{X}(\mathbf{X}'\mathbf{X})^{-1}\mathbf{X}'\mathbf{z}_L) = \mathbf{X}(\mathbf{X}'\mathbf{X})^{-1}\mathbf{X}'\mathbf{Z} = \mathbf{P}\mathbf{Z}, \tag{3.8.13}$$

where $\mathbf{P}$ is the projection matrix. Substituting this into the IV format (3.8.12) yields the 2SLS estimator (see (3.8.3$'$)).

2SLS as Two Regressions

Instead of substituting the generated instruments $\hat{\mathbf{z}}_i$ into the IV format to estimate the equation $y_i = \mathbf{z}_i'\boldsymbol{\delta} + \varepsilon_i$, consider regressing y_i on $\hat{\mathbf{z}}_i$. The coefficient estimate is

$$\begin{aligned}(\widehat{\mathbf{Z}}'\widehat{\mathbf{Z}})^{-1}\widehat{\mathbf{Z}}'\mathbf{y} &= (\mathbf{Z}'\mathbf{P}'\mathbf{P}\mathbf{Z})^{-1}\mathbf{Z}'\mathbf{P}\mathbf{y}\\ &= (\mathbf{Z}'\mathbf{P}\mathbf{Z})^{-1}\mathbf{Z}'\mathbf{P}\mathbf{y} \quad (\text{since } \mathbf{P} \text{ is symmetric and idempotent}).\end{aligned}$$

This is the 2SLS estimator. So the 2SLS coefficient estimate can be obtained in two stages: the first stage is to regress the L regressors on $\mathbf{x}_i$ and obtain fitted values $\hat{\mathbf{z}}_i$, and the second stage is to regress y_i on those fitted values.

For those regressors that are predetermined and hence included in $\mathbf{x}_i$, there is no need to carry out the first-stage regression because the fitted value is the regressor itself. To see this, if $z_{i\ell}$ is predetermined and included in $\mathbf{x}_i$ as the k-th instrument, the n-vector of fitted values for the ℓ-th regressor is $\mathbf{P}\mathbf{z}_\ell$, where $\mathbf{z}_\ell$ is the n-vector whose i-th element is $z_{i\ell}$. But since $\mathbf{z}_\ell$ is also the k-th column of $\mathbf{X}$, $\mathbf{P}\mathbf{z}_\ell = \mathbf{P}\mathbf{x}_k$. Since $\mathbf{P}$ is the projection matrix, $\mathbf{P}\mathbf{x}_k = \mathbf{x}_k$.

This derivation of the 2SLS is useful as it justifies the naming of the estimator, but there is a pitfall. In the second-stage regression where y_i is regressed on $\hat{\mathbf{z}}_i$, the standard errors routinely calculated by the OLS package are based on the residual vector $\mathbf{y} - \widehat{\mathbf{Z}}\hat{\boldsymbol{\delta}}_{\text{2SLS}}$. This does *not* equal the 2SLS residual $\mathbf{y} - \mathbf{Z}\hat{\boldsymbol{\delta}}_{\text{2SLS}}$. Therefore, the OLS standard errors and estimated asymptotic variance from the second stage cannot be used for statistical inference.

When Regressors Are Predetermined

When all the regressors are predetermined and the errors are conditionally homoskedastic, there is a close connection between the distance function J for efficient GMM and the sum of squared residuals (*SSR*). From (3.8.9′) on page 230,

$$\begin{aligned}J(\tilde{\boldsymbol{\delta}}, (\hat{\sigma}^2\cdot\mathbf{S}_{\mathbf{xx}})^{-1}) &= \frac{(\mathbf{y}-\mathbf{Z}\tilde{\boldsymbol{\delta}})'\mathbf{P}(\mathbf{y}-\mathbf{Z}\tilde{\boldsymbol{\delta}})}{\hat{\sigma}^2}\\ &= \frac{\mathbf{y}'\mathbf{P}\mathbf{y} - 2\mathbf{y}'\mathbf{P}\mathbf{Z}\tilde{\boldsymbol{\delta}} + \tilde{\boldsymbol{\delta}}'\mathbf{Z}'\mathbf{P}\mathbf{Z}\tilde{\boldsymbol{\delta}}}{\hat{\sigma}^2}\\ &= \frac{\mathbf{y}'\mathbf{P}\mathbf{y} - 2\mathbf{y}'\mathbf{Z}\tilde{\boldsymbol{\delta}} + \tilde{\boldsymbol{\delta}}'\mathbf{Z}'\mathbf{Z}\tilde{\boldsymbol{\delta}}}{\hat{\sigma}^2} \quad (\text{since } \mathbf{P}\mathbf{Z} = \mathbf{Z} \text{ when } \mathbf{z}_i \subset \mathbf{x}_i)\\ &= \frac{(\mathbf{y}-\mathbf{Z}\tilde{\boldsymbol{\delta}})'(\mathbf{y}-\mathbf{Z}\tilde{\boldsymbol{\delta}})}{\hat{\sigma}^2} - \frac{\mathbf{y}'\mathbf{y} - \mathbf{y}'\mathbf{P}\mathbf{y}}{\hat{\sigma}^2}\\ &= \frac{(\mathbf{y}-\mathbf{Z}\tilde{\boldsymbol{\delta}})'(\mathbf{y}-\mathbf{Z}\tilde{\boldsymbol{\delta}})}{\hat{\sigma}^2} - \frac{(\mathbf{y}-\hat{\mathbf{y}})(\mathbf{y}-\hat{\mathbf{y}})'}{\hat{\sigma}^2},\end{aligned} \tag{3.8.14}$$

where $\hat{\mathbf{y}} \equiv \mathbf{Py}$ is the vector of fitted values from unrestricted OLS. Since the last term does not depend on $\tilde{\boldsymbol{\delta}}$, minimizing J amounts to minimizing the sum of squared residuals $(\mathbf{y} - \mathbf{Z}\tilde{\boldsymbol{\delta}})'(\mathbf{y} - \mathbf{Z}\tilde{\boldsymbol{\delta}})$. It then follows that (1) the efficient GMM estimator is OLS (which actually is true without conditional homoskedasticity as long as $\mathbf{z}_i = \mathbf{x}_i$), (2) the restricted efficient GMM estimator subject to the constraints of the null hypothesis is the restricted OLS (whose objective function is not J but *SSR*), and (3) the Wald statistic, which is numerically equal to the *LR* statistic, can be calculated as the difference in *SSR* with and without the imposition of the null, normalized to $\hat{\sigma}^2$. This last result confirms the derivation in Section 2.6 of the Wald statistic by the Likelihood Ratio principle.

Testing a Subset of Orthogonality Conditions

In Section 3.6 we introduced the statistic C for testing a subset of orthogonality conditions. It utilizes two efficient GMM estimators of the same equation, one using the full set $\mathbf{x}_i$ of instruments and the other using only a subset, $\mathbf{x}_{i1}$, of $\mathbf{x}_i$. To examine what expression it takes under conditional homoskedasticity, let $\mathbf{X}_1$ $(n \times K_1)$ be the data matrix whose i-th row is $\mathbf{x}'_{i1}$. Because the two-step efficient GMM estimator is the 2SLS estimator under conditional homoskedasticity, the two GMM estimators are given by

$$\hat{\boldsymbol{\delta}} = (\mathbf{Z}'\mathbf{PZ})^{-1}\mathbf{Z}'\mathbf{Py} \quad \text{with} \quad \mathbf{P} = \mathbf{X}(\mathbf{X}'\mathbf{X})^{-1}\mathbf{X}', \tag{3.8.15}$$

$$\bar{\boldsymbol{\delta}} = (\mathbf{Z}'\mathbf{P}_1\mathbf{Z})^{-1}\mathbf{Z}'\mathbf{P}_1\mathbf{y} \quad \text{with} \quad \mathbf{P}_1 = \mathbf{X}_1(\mathbf{X}_1'\mathbf{X}_1)^{-1}\mathbf{X}_1'. \tag{3.8.16}$$

And the C statistic becomes the difference in two Sargan statistics:

$$C = \frac{\hat{\boldsymbol{\varepsilon}}'\mathbf{P}\hat{\boldsymbol{\varepsilon}} - \bar{\boldsymbol{\varepsilon}}'\mathbf{P}_1\bar{\boldsymbol{\varepsilon}}}{\hat{\sigma}^2}, \tag{3.8.17}$$

where

$$\hat{\boldsymbol{\varepsilon}} \equiv \mathbf{y} - \mathbf{Z}\hat{\boldsymbol{\delta}}, \quad \bar{\boldsymbol{\varepsilon}} \equiv \mathbf{y} - \mathbf{Z}\bar{\boldsymbol{\delta}}, \quad \hat{\sigma}^2 \equiv \frac{\hat{\boldsymbol{\varepsilon}}'\hat{\boldsymbol{\varepsilon}}}{n}.$$

As seen for the case without conditional homoskedasticity, C is guaranteed to be nonnegative in finite samples if the same matrix $\widehat{\mathbf{S}}$ is used throughout, which under conditional homoskedasticity amounts to using the same estimate of the error variance, $\hat{\sigma}^2$, to deflate both $\hat{\boldsymbol{\varepsilon}}'\mathbf{P}\hat{\boldsymbol{\varepsilon}}$ and $\bar{\boldsymbol{\varepsilon}}'\mathbf{P}_1\bar{\boldsymbol{\varepsilon}}$, as in (3.8.17). By Proposition 3.7, this C is asymptotically $\chi^2(K - K_1)$.

Perhaps more popular is the test statistic proposed by Hausman and Taylor (1980) and further examined by Newey (1985). $\hat{\boldsymbol{\delta}}$ is asymptotically more efficient than $\bar{\boldsymbol{\delta}}$ because $\hat{\boldsymbol{\delta}}$ exploits more orthogonality conditions. Therefore, $\text{Avar}(\bar{\boldsymbol{\delta}}) \geq$

$\text{Avar}(\hat{\boldsymbol{\delta}})$. Furthermore, as you will be asked to show (Analytical Exercise 9), under the same hypothesis guaranteeing C to be asymptotically chi-squared,

$$\text{Avar}(\bar{\boldsymbol{\delta}} - \hat{\boldsymbol{\delta}}) = \text{Avar}(\bar{\boldsymbol{\delta}}) - \text{Avar}(\hat{\boldsymbol{\delta}}). \tag{3.8.18}$$

(If you have been exposed to the Hausman test in the ML context, you can recognize this as the GMM version of the Hausman principle.) By Proposition 3.9, $\text{Avar}(\hat{\boldsymbol{\delta}})$ is consistently estimated by

$$\widehat{\text{Avar}(\hat{\boldsymbol{\delta}})} \equiv n \cdot \hat{\sigma}^2 \cdot (\mathbf{Z}'\mathbf{P}\mathbf{Z})^{-1}. \tag{3.8.19}$$

Similarly, a consistent estimator of $\text{Avar}(\bar{\boldsymbol{\delta}})$ is

$$\widehat{\text{Avar}(\bar{\boldsymbol{\delta}})} \equiv n \cdot \hat{\sigma}^2 \cdot (\mathbf{Z}'\mathbf{P}_1\mathbf{Z})^{-1}. \tag{3.8.20}$$

Here, as in the calculation of the C statistic, the same estimate, $\hat{\sigma}^2$, is used throughout, in order to guarantee the test statistic below to be nonnegative. The resulting estimator of $\text{Avar}(\bar{\boldsymbol{\delta}} - \hat{\boldsymbol{\delta}})$ is

$$\widehat{\text{Avar}(\bar{\boldsymbol{\delta}} - \hat{\boldsymbol{\delta}})} = \hat{\sigma}^2 \cdot n \cdot \left[(\mathbf{Z}'\mathbf{P}_1\mathbf{Z})^{-1} - (\mathbf{Z}'\mathbf{P}\mathbf{Z})^{-1}\right]. \tag{3.8.21}$$

Hausman and Taylor (1980) have shown that (1) this matrix in finite samples is positive semidefinite (nonnegative definite) but not necessarily nonsingular, but (2) for any generalized inverse[17] of this matrix, the **Hausman statistic**

$$\begin{aligned} H &\equiv \sqrt{n}(\bar{\boldsymbol{\delta}} - \hat{\boldsymbol{\delta}})' \left\{\hat{\sigma}^2 \cdot n \cdot \left[(\mathbf{Z}'\mathbf{P}_1\mathbf{Z})^{-1} - (\mathbf{Z}'\mathbf{P}\mathbf{Z})^{-1}\right]\right\}^{-} \sqrt{n}(\bar{\boldsymbol{\delta}} - \hat{\boldsymbol{\delta}}) \\ &= \frac{(\bar{\boldsymbol{\delta}} - \hat{\boldsymbol{\delta}})' \left[(\mathbf{Z}'\mathbf{P}_1\mathbf{Z})^{-1} - (\mathbf{Z}'\mathbf{P}\mathbf{Z})^{-1}\right]^{-} (\bar{\boldsymbol{\delta}} - \hat{\boldsymbol{\delta}})}{\hat{\sigma}^2} \end{aligned} \tag{3.8.22}$$

is invariant to the choice of the generalized inverse and is asymptotically chi-squared with $\min(K - K_1, L - s)$ degrees of freedom, where

$$s = \#\mathbf{z}_i \cap \mathbf{x}_{i1} = \text{number of regressors which are retained as instruments in } \mathbf{x}_{i1}.$$

What is the relationship between C and H under conditional homoskedasticity? It can be shown (see Newey, 1985) that:

[17] A **generalized inverse**, $\mathbf{A}^-$, of a matrix $\mathbf{A}$ is any matrix satisfying $\mathbf{A}\mathbf{A}^-\mathbf{A} = \mathbf{A}$. If $\mathbf{A}$ is square and nonsingular, then $\mathbf{A}^-$ is unique and equal to $\mathbf{A}^{-1}$.

If $K - K_1 \leq L - s$ so that both H and C have the same degrees of freedom, then $H = C$ (numerically equal). Otherwise, the two statistics are numerically different and have different degrees of freedom.

One frequent case where $K - K_1 \leq L - s$ holds is when $\mathbf{x}_{i2}$ is a subset of $\mathbf{z}_i$, that is, when the suspect instruments are a subset of regressors. In this case, the formulas (3.8.17) and (3.8.22) are two alternative ways of calculating numerically the same statistic. In the case where $K - K_1 > L - s$, the degrees of freedom for H are less than those for the C statistic $(K - K_1)$. For this reason, the Hausman test, unlike the C test, is not consistent against some local alternatives.[18]

Testing Conditional Homoskedasticity

For the OLS case with predetermined regressors, as shown in Section 2.7, there is a convenient nR^2 test of conditional homoskedasticity. In the present case, the nR^2 statistic obtained by regressing the squared 2SLS residuals on a constant and second-order cross products of the instrumental variables turns out *not* to have the desired asymptotic distribution. A test statistic that is asymptotically chi-squared is available but is extremely cumbersome. See White (1982, note 2).

Testing for Serial Correlation

For the OLS case, we developed in Section 2.10 tests for serial correlation in the error term. More specifically, under (2.10.15) (which is stronger than Assumption 2.3 or 3.3) and (2.10.16) (which is stronger than Assumption 2.7 or 3.7 of conditional homoskedasticity), the modified Box-Pierce Q given in (2.10.20) can be used for testing the null of no serial correlation in the error term, and this statistic is asymptotically equivalent (in the stronger sense of the plim of the difference being zero) to the nR^2 statistic from regression (2.10.21). Can this test be extended to the case where the regressors $\mathbf{z}_i$ are endogenous? If the instruments $\mathbf{x}_i$ satisfy (2.10.15) and (2.10.16), then the argument in Appendix 2.B of Chapter 2 can be generalized to produce a modified Q statistic that is asymptotically chi-squared under the null of no serial correlation. However, the expression for the statistic is more complicated than (2.10.20) and so is not presented here. This modified Q statistic for the case of endogenous regressors does not seem to be asymptotically equivalent to the nR^2 statistic from regression (2.10.21).

[18]The Hausman statistic can be generalized to the case of conditional heteroskedasticity, but it is not practical because the degrees of freedom depend on the unknown values of the matrices $\boldsymbol{\Sigma}_{\mathbf{xz}}$ and $\mathbf{S}$. See Newey (1985).

QUESTIONS FOR REVIEW

1. (GMM with conditional homoskedasticity) In efficient two-step GMM estimation, $\widehat{\mathbf{S}}$ in the second step is calculated from the first step by (3.5.10) using the first-step residuals. Under conditional homoskedasticity, derive the asymptotic variance of the two-step estimator. Is it the same as (3.8.4)? **Hint:** Under conditional homoskedasticity, (3.5.10) $\to_{\text{p}} \sigma^2 \boldsymbol{\Sigma}_{\mathbf{xx}}$.

2. (2SLS without conditional homoskedasticity) Is the 2SLS consistent when conditional homoskedasticity does not hold? Derive the plim of (3.8.2) and $\text{Avar}(\hat{\boldsymbol{\delta}}_{2\text{SLS}})$ without assuming conditional homoskedasticity. Is the 2SLS as efficient as the two-step GMM (i.e., is its asymptotic variance as small as (3.5.13))? **Hint:** 2SLS is a GMM estimator with a choice of $\widehat{\mathbf{W}}$ that is not necessarily efficient without conditional homoskedasticity.

3. (GLS interpretation of 2SLS) Verify that the 2SLS estimator can be written as a GLS estimator if $\mathbf{S}_{\mathbf{xz}}$ and $\mathbf{s}_{\mathbf{xy}}$ are interpreted as the data matrix of regressors and the data vector of the dependent variable and $\mathbf{S}_{\mathbf{xx}}$ as the variance matrix of the error term.

4. Provide two cases in which $\hat{\boldsymbol{\delta}}_{2\text{SLS}}$ and $\hat{\boldsymbol{\delta}}(\widehat{\mathbf{S}}^{-1})$ are asymptotically equivalent in the sense that

$$\sqrt{n}\left[\hat{\boldsymbol{\delta}}_{2\text{SLS}} - \hat{\boldsymbol{\delta}}(\widehat{\mathbf{S}}^{-1})\right] \underset{\text{p}}{\to} \mathbf{0}.$$

Hint: Keywords are "conditional homoskedasticity" and "exactly identified."

5. Suppose the equation is just identified. Show that 2SLS (3.8.3) reduces to IV (3.4.4).

6. (Sargan as nR^2) Prove that Sargan's statistic (3.8.10′) equals nR_{uc}^2, where R_{uc}^2 is the uncentered R-squared from a regression of $\hat{\boldsymbol{\varepsilon}}$ on $\mathbf{X}$. **Hint:** Review Question 8 of Section 1.2.

7. (When $\mathbf{z}_i$ is a strict subset of $\mathbf{x}_i$) Suppose $\mathbf{z}_i$ is a strict subset of $\mathbf{x}_i$. So $\mathbf{x}_i$ includes, in addition to the regressors (which are all predetermined), some other predetermined variables. We have shown that the efficient GMM estimator is OLS under conditional homoskedasticity. Does the result remain true without conditional homoskedasticity? **Hint:** Review Question 5 of Section 3.5.

3.9 Application: Returns from Schooling

Since Mincer's (1958) pioneering study, the relationship between the wage rate and schooling has been the subject of a large number of empirical and theoretical investigations. You might find the amount of attention puzzling because the explanation of the positive relationship seems to be obvious: education enhances the individual's productivity. There are, however, other explanations. For example, in the Spencian job market signaling model, more educated individuals receive higher wages only because education is used as a signal of higher ability; although education does not increase the individual's earning capacity, there is a correlation between the wage rate and schooling because both variables are influenced by the third variable, ability. This section shows how to use the technique of this chapter to isolate the effect of education on the wage rate from that of ability. One of the earliest studies to address this issue is Griliches (1976).

The NLS-Y Data

The data used by Griliches are the Young Men's Cohort of the National Longitudinal Survey (NLS-Y). This cohort was first surveyed in 1966 at ages 14–24, with 5,225 respondents, and was resurveyed at one- or two-year intervals thereafter. By 1969, about a quarter of the original sample was lost, but there are 2,026 individuals who reported earnings in 1969 and whose records are complete enough to allow derivation of all the variables for analysis. A very attractive feature of the NLS-Y is its inclusion of two measures of ability. One of them is the score on the Knowledge of the World of Work (KWW) test administered by the NLS interviewers in 1966. The other measure is the IQ score. All youths in the survey who had completed ninth grade by 1966 were asked to sign waivers letting their school supply the survey administrator their scores on various tests and other background materials. The resulting School Survey, conducted in 1968, yielded data on different mental ability scores, which were combined into IQ equivalents. Of the 2,026 individuals with information about the 1969 wage rate and other variables, the IQ score is available for 1,362 individuals, reflecting the fact that the School Survey was able to cover only two-thirds of the original sample. Our discussion here concerns Griliches's results based on this smaller sample. Table 3.1 reports the means and standard deviation of key variables.

Table 3.1: Characteristics of Young Men from the National Longitudinal Survey

Means and Standard Deviations (in parentheses)

Variable	
Sample size	1,362
Age in 1969	22.3 (3.2)
Schooling in years in 1969 (S)	12.5 (1.9)
Logarithm of hourly wages (in cents) in 1969 (LW)	5.68 (0.40)
Score on the Knowledge of the World of Work test (KWW)	35.1 (7.9)
IQ score (IQ)	97.7 (15.3)
Experience in years in 1969	3.7 (2.8)

SOURCE: Griliches (1976, Table 1).

The Semi-Log Wage Equation

The typical wage equation estimated in the literature is the semi-log form:

$$LW = \alpha + \beta S + \gamma A + \boldsymbol{\delta}'\mathbf{h} + \varepsilon, \tag{3.9.1}$$

where LW is the log wage rate for the individual, S is schooling in years, A is a measure of ability, $\mathbf{h}$ is the vector of observable characteristics of the individual (such as experience and location dummies), $\boldsymbol{\delta}$ is the associated vector of coefficients, and ε is the unobservable error term with zero mean (in this section, the individual subscript i will be dropped for notational simplicity). The semi-log specification for schooling S is often justified by appealing to the well-established stylized fact from large cross-section data (such as the Current Population Survey) that the relationship between log wages and schooling is linear.[19]

The schooling coefficient β measures the percentage increase in the wage rate the individual would receive if she had one more year of education. It therefore

[19]For the functional form issue, see Card (1995).

represents the marginal return from investing in human capital, which should be in the same order of magnitude as the rate of return from financial assets. We assume that the nonconstant regressors, $(S, A, \mathbf{h})$, are uncorrelated with the error term ε so that the OLS is an appropriate estimation technique if ability A is included in the regression along with S and $\mathbf{h}$. In the rest of this section, we examine what Griliches called the "ability bias"—biases on the OLS estimate of β that would arise when ability A is not included in the regression and when its imperfect measure is included in its place.

Omitted Variable Bias

Sometimes the data set you work with has no measures of A (this is true for the Current Population Survey, for example). What is the consequence of ignoring ability by omitting A from the wage equation? We know from Section 2.9 that the regression of LW on a constant, S, and $\mathbf{h}$ provides a consistent estimator of the corresponding least squares projection, which can be written as

$$\begin{aligned}\widehat{\mathrm{E}}^*(LW \mid 1, S, \mathbf{h}) &= \widehat{\mathrm{E}}^*(\alpha + \beta S + \gamma A + \boldsymbol{\delta}'\mathbf{h} + \varepsilon \mid 1, S, \mathbf{h}) \quad \text{(by (3.9.1))} \\ &= \alpha + \beta S + \boldsymbol{\delta}'\mathbf{h} + \gamma\, \widehat{\mathrm{E}}^*(A \mid 1, S, \mathbf{h}) + \widehat{\mathrm{E}}^*(\varepsilon \mid 1, S, \mathbf{h}). \quad (3.9.2)\end{aligned}$$

Since the regressors in (3.9.1) are all predetermined, we have $\mathrm{E}(\varepsilon) = 0$, $\mathrm{E}(S\,\varepsilon) = 0$, and $\mathrm{E}(\mathbf{h}\cdot\varepsilon) = \mathbf{0}$. So $\widehat{\mathrm{E}}^*(\varepsilon \mid 1, S, \mathbf{h}) = 0$. Writing $\widehat{\mathrm{E}}^*(A \mid 1, S, \mathbf{h}) = \theta_1 + \theta_S\, S + \boldsymbol{\theta}_{\mathbf{h}}'\mathbf{h}$, (3.9.2) becomes

$$\widehat{\mathrm{E}}^*(LW \mid 1, S, \mathbf{h}) = (\alpha + \gamma\theta_1) + (\beta + \gamma\theta_S)S + (\boldsymbol{\delta} + \gamma\cdot\boldsymbol{\theta}_{\mathbf{h}})'\mathbf{h}.$$

Therefore, the OLS coefficient estimate can be asymptotically biased for *all* the included regressors. This phenomenon is called the **omitted variable bias**. In particular,

$$\operatorname{plim} \widehat{\beta}_{\mathrm{OLS}} = \beta + \gamma\theta_S.$$

That is, the OLS estimate of the schooling coefficient β includes the indirect effect of ability on log wages through schooling ($\gamma\theta_S$) as well as the direct effect of schooling (β). If θ_S is positive, then $\widehat{\beta}_{\mathrm{OLS}}$ is asymptotically biased upward.

Using the sample of 1,362 individuals from the NLS-Y described above, Griliches estimated the wage equation for 1969. The list of variables included in $\mathbf{h}$ will not be given here; suffice to say that it includes experience in years and some region and city-size dummies. Griliches's estimate of the schooling coefficient when ability is ignored in the wage equation is reproduced on line 1 of Table 3.2.

On the face of it, the estimate looks good: the point estimate resembles the rate of return one might get from financial assets, and it is sharply estimated as evidenced by the high t-value.

IQ as the Measure of Ability

As already mentioned, the NLS-Y has two measures of ability, KWW (the score on the Knowledge of the World of Work test) collected in 1966 and IQ (the IQ score). Since the NLS-Y respondents were at least fourteen years old in 1966, KWW would reflect the effect of schooling already undertaken, and so it cannot be a measure of raw ability. The IQ score does not have this problem. If IQ were a perfect measure of ability so that A can be equated with it, then the wage equation (3.9.1) could be estimated consistently with IQ substituting for A. Griliches's OLS estimates of β (schooling coefficient) and γ (ability coefficient) when IQ is included in the equation are reported in line 2 of Table 3.2. Now the estimated schooling coefficient is lower, confirming our prediction that the estimated schooling coefficient includes the effect of ability on the wage rate when ability is omitted from the regression.

Errors-in-Variables

Of course the IQ score may not be an error-free measure of ability. If η is the measurement error, IQ is related to A as

$$IQ = \phi + A + \eta, \tag{3.9.3}$$

with $\mathrm{E}(\eta) = 0$. The interpretation of η as measurement error makes it reasonable to assume that η is uncorrelated with A, S, $\mathbf{h}$, and the wage equation error term ε. Substituting (3.9.3) into (3.9.1), we obtain

$$LW = (\alpha - \gamma\phi) + \beta S + \gamma IQ + \boldsymbol{\delta}'\mathbf{h} + (\varepsilon - \gamma\eta). \tag{3.9.4}$$

We now illustrate for this example the general result that, if at least one of the regressors is measured with error, the OLS estimates of *all* the regression coefficients can be asymptotically biased.

To examine the consequence of using the error-ridden measure IQ for A, consider the corresponding least squares projection:

$$\begin{aligned}\widehat{\mathrm{E}}^*(LW \mid 1, S, IQ, \mathbf{h}) = (\alpha - \gamma\phi) + \beta S + \gamma IQ + \boldsymbol{\delta}'\mathbf{h} \\ + \widehat{\mathrm{E}}^*(\varepsilon \mid 1, S, IQ, \mathbf{h}) - \gamma\,\widehat{\mathrm{E}}^*(\eta \mid 1, S, IQ, \mathbf{h}).\end{aligned} \tag{3.9.5}$$

Table 3.2: Parameter Estimates

Estimation equation: $LW = \alpha + \beta S + \gamma IQ +$ other controls

Line no.	Estimation technique	Coefficient of *S*	Coefficient of *IQ*	*SER*	R^2	Which regressor is endogenous?	Excluded predetermined variables
1	OLS	0.065 (13.2)	—	0.332	0.309	none	—
2	OLS	0.059 (10.7)	0.0019 (2.8)	0.331	0.313	none	—
3	2SLS	0.052 (7.0)	0.0038 (2.4)	0.332	—	*IQ*	*MED*, *KWW*, age, age squared, background variables

SOURCE: Line 1: equation (B1) in Griliches (1976, Table 2). Line 2: equation (B3) in Griliches's Table 2. Line 3: line 3 in Griliches's Table 5. Figures in parentheses are t-values rather than standard errors.

Now consider $\widehat{\mathrm{E}}^*(\varepsilon \mid 1, S, IQ, \mathbf{h})$ in (3.9.5). Since $\mathrm{E}(\varepsilon) = 0$ and $(S, \mathbf{h})$ are uncorrelated with ε, $(1, S, \mathbf{h})$ are orthogonal to ε. IQ is also orthogonal to ε because

$$\begin{aligned} \mathrm{E}(IQ\,\varepsilon) &= \mathrm{E}[(\phi + A + \eta)\,\varepsilon] \quad \text{(by (3.9.3))} \\ &= \mathrm{E}(\eta\,\varepsilon) \quad (\text{since } \mathrm{E}(\varepsilon) = 0, \mathrm{Cov}(A, \varepsilon) = 0) \\ &= 0. \end{aligned}$$

Thus, $\widehat{\mathrm{E}}^*(\varepsilon \mid 1, S, IQ, \mathbf{h}) = 0$ in (3.9.5).

So the biases, if any, equal $-\gamma\,\widehat{\mathrm{E}}^*(\eta \mid 1, S, IQ, \mathbf{h})$ in (3.9.5). Let $(\theta_S, \theta_{IQ}, \theta_{\mathbf{h}})$ be the projection coefficients of $(S, IQ, \mathbf{h})$ in $\widehat{\mathrm{E}}^*(\eta \mid 1, S, IQ, \mathbf{h})$. By the formula (2.9.7) from Chapter 2,

$$\begin{bmatrix} \theta_S \\ \theta_{IQ} \\ \boldsymbol{\theta}_{\mathbf{h}} \end{bmatrix} = \begin{bmatrix} \mathrm{Var}(S) & \mathrm{Cov}(S, IQ) & \mathrm{Cov}(S, \mathbf{h}') \\ \mathrm{Cov}(IQ, S) & \mathrm{Var}(IQ) & \mathrm{Cov}(IQ, \mathbf{h}') \\ \mathrm{Cov}(\mathbf{h}, S) & \mathrm{Cov}(\mathbf{h}, IQ) & \mathrm{Var}(\mathbf{h}) \end{bmatrix}^{-1} \begin{bmatrix} \mathrm{Cov}(S, \eta) \\ \mathrm{Cov}(IQ, \eta) \\ \mathrm{Cov}(\mathbf{h}, \eta) \end{bmatrix}. \tag{3.9.6}$$

In this expression, $\mathrm{Cov}(S, \eta)$ and $\mathrm{Cov}(\mathbf{h}, \eta)$ are zero by assumption. $\mathrm{Cov}(IQ, \eta)$, however, is not zero because

$$\begin{aligned} \mathrm{Cov}(IQ, \eta) &= \mathrm{E}(IQ\,\eta) \quad (\text{since } \mathrm{E}(\eta) = 0) \\ &= \mathrm{E}[(\phi + A + \eta)\,\eta] \quad \text{(by (3.9.3))} \\ &= \phi\,\mathrm{E}(\eta) + \mathrm{E}(A\,\eta) + \mathrm{E}(\eta^2) \\ &= \mathrm{Var}(\eta) \quad (\text{since } \mathrm{E}(\eta) = 0 \text{ and } \mathrm{Cov}(A, \eta) = 0). \end{aligned}$$

That is, the measurement error, if uncorrelated with the true value, is necessarily correlated with the measured value. Using the fact that

$$\mathrm{Cov}(S, \eta) = 0, \quad \mathrm{Cov}(IQ, \eta) = \mathrm{Var}(\eta), \quad \text{and} \quad \mathrm{Cov}(\mathbf{h}, \eta) = \mathbf{0},$$

the projection coefficients can be rewritten as

$$\begin{bmatrix} \theta_S \\ \theta_{IQ} \\ \boldsymbol{\theta}_{\mathbf{h}} \end{bmatrix} = \mathrm{Var}(\eta)\cdot\mathbf{a},$$

where

$$\mathbf{a} \equiv \text{second column of} \begin{bmatrix} \mathrm{Var}(S) & \mathrm{Cov}(S, IQ) & \mathrm{Cov}(S, \mathbf{h}') \\ \mathrm{Cov}(IQ, S) & \mathrm{Var}(IQ) & \mathrm{Cov}(IQ, \mathbf{h}') \\ \mathrm{Cov}(\mathbf{h}, S) & \mathrm{Cov}(\mathbf{h}, IQ) & \mathrm{Var}(\mathbf{h}) \end{bmatrix}^{-1}.$$

Therefore, in the regression of *LW* on a constant, S, IQ, and $\mathbf{h}$,

$$\text{plim}\,\widehat{\beta}_{\text{OLS}} = \beta - \gamma \cdot \text{Var}(\eta) \cdot (\text{1st element of } \mathbf{a}), \tag{3.9.7a}$$

$$\text{plim}\,\hat{\gamma}_{\text{OLS}} = \gamma - \gamma \cdot \text{Var}(\eta) \cdot (\text{2nd element of } \mathbf{a}). \tag{3.9.7b}$$

Since the second element of **a** is positive (it is a diagonal element of the inverse of a variance-covariance matrix), the OLS estimate of the ability coefficient is biased downward. The direction of the asymptotic bias for the schooling coefficient, however, depends on the sign of the first element of **a**. Typically, $\text{Cov}(S, IQ)$ would be positive, so, barring unusually strong correlation of (S, IQ) with **h**, the first element of **a** would be negative. Thus, we conjecture that $\widehat{\beta}_{\text{OLS}}$ is biased upward for schooling.

2SLS to Correct for the Bias

To control for the bias, Griliches applies the 2SLS to the wage equation. To do so, the set of instruments needs to be specified. The predetermined regressors, $(1, S, \mathbf{h})$, can be included in the set. The additional variables included in the set to instrument *IQ* are age, age squared, *KWW*, mother's education, and some other background variables of the individual (such as father's occupation). Those variables are thus assumed to be predetermined. Griliches's 2SLS estimate for this specification is reproduced in line 3 of Table 3.2.[20] In accordance with our prediction that the OLS estimate of the ability coefficient is biased downward, the OLS estimate of the ability coefficient of 0.0019 in line 2 is lower than the 2SLS estimate of 0.0038 in line 3. Our conjecture that $\widehat{\beta}_{\text{OLS}}$ of the schooling coefficient when *IQ* is included in the regression is biased upward, too, is borne out by data because the estimate of β of 0.059 in line 2 is higher than the estimate of 0.052 in line 3.

To summarize, the "ability bias" studied by Griliches is that the schooling coefficient is biased upward if ability is ignored and is biased in an unknown direction (but perhaps upward) if an imperfect measure of ability (*IQ* in the present case) is included. The 2SLS provides a solution, but it is predicated on the assumption that the instruments used (such as *MED* and *KWW*) are uncorrelated with unobserved wage determinants ε and η. Those determinants would include personal characteristics like diligence. It seems not unreasonable to suppose that *KWW* depends on such characteristics. If so, *KWW* cannot serve as an instrument. One could go further and argue that *MED* is not predetermined either, because some

[20]The R^2 is not reported for the 2SLS estimate because, unlike in the OLS case, the sum of squared 2SLS residuals cannot be divided between the "explained variation" and the "unexplained variation."

of the mother's personal characteristics that influenced her education and that are valued in the marketplace would be inherited by the child. Whether those variables included in the set of instruments are predetermined can be tested by Sargan's statistic. But the statistic is not reported in Griliches's paper (which was written long before doing so became a standard practice).

Subsequent Developments

Perhaps because it is so difficult to come up with valid instruments that are uncorrelated with unobserved characteristics but correlated with IQ, controlling for the "ability bias" continued to attract much attention in the literature. There is a fairly large literature starting with Behrman et al. (1980), which compares identical twins with different levels of education to control for genetic characteristics and family background. One can also compare the same individual at two points in time. In either case, the appropriate estimation technique is what is called the fixed-effect estimator, to be covered in Chapter 5.

The endogeneity of schooling is another major issue. If one takes the view that the error term includes a host of unobservable individual characteristics that might affect the individual's choice of schooling, then schooling needs to be treated as an endogenous variable. But again, finding valid instruments uncorrelated with unobservable characteristics but correlated with schooling is extremely difficult. The recent literature can be viewed as a search for the determinants of schooling having little to do with the individual's unobserved characteristics. The variable used in Angrist and Krueger (1991), for example, is whether the individual is subject to compulsory schooling laws.

Finally, the literature on the relationship between school quality and earnings is attracting renewed attention. See Card and Krueger (1996) for a survey.

QUESTIONS FOR REVIEW

1. List all the assumptions made in this section about the means and covariances of $(S, A, IQ, KWW, \mathbf{h}, \varepsilon, \eta)$. Study how Griliches states those assumptions. Which ones are crucial for the 2SLS to be consistent?

2. Suppose the relationship between IQ and A is given not by (3.9.3) but by

$$IQ = \phi + \pi \cdot A + \eta.$$

Is the 2SLS estimator of β (the schooling coefficient) still consistent? [Answer: Yes.]

3. In the Spencian model of job market signaling, individuals are sorted into two groups, with low-ability individuals choosing a low level of education and high-ability ones choosing a high level of education. Education does not increase the earning capacity of individuals, so the individual's wage rate is determined by his or her ability. If we had data on the wage rate, ability, and schooling for a sample of individuals that includes both high- and low-ability individuals, can we test the hypothesis that education by itself does not contribute to higher wages? **Hint:** The data would have a multicollinearity problem.

PROBLEM SET FOR CHAPTER 3

ANALYTICAL EXERCISES

1. Prove: A symmetric and idempotent matrix is positive semidefinite.

2. We wish to prove Proposition 3.4. To avoid inessential complications, consider the case where $K = 1$ and $L = 1$ so that $\mathbf{x}_i$ and $\mathbf{z}_i$ are scalars. So (3.5.5) becomes

$$\hat{\varepsilon}_i^2 = \varepsilon_i^2 - 2(\hat{\delta} - \delta) z_i\, \varepsilon_i + (\hat{\delta} - \delta)^2 z_i^2,$$

and the $\widehat{\mathbf{S}}$ in (3.5.10) becomes

$$\frac{1}{n}\sum_{i=1}^{n} x_i^2\, \varepsilon_i^2 - 2(\hat{\delta} - \delta)\frac{1}{n}\sum_{i=1}^{n} z_i\, x_i^2\, \varepsilon_i + (\hat{\delta} - \delta)^2 \frac{1}{n}\sum_{i=1}^{n} z_i^2\, x_i^2. \qquad (*)$$

(a) Show: The first term on the RHS of $(*)$ converges in probability to S $(\equiv \mathrm{E}(x_i^2\, \varepsilon_i^2))$.

(b) Use the Cauchy-Schwartz inequality

$$\mathrm{E}(|X \cdot Y|) \le \sqrt{\mathrm{E}(X^2) \cdot \mathrm{E}(Y^2)}$$

to show that $\mathrm{E}(z_i x_i^2 \varepsilon_i)$ exists and is finite. **Hint:** $z_i x_i^2 \varepsilon_i$ is the product of $x_i \varepsilon_i$ and $x_i z_i$. Fact: $\mathrm{E}(x)$ exists and is finite if and only if $\mathrm{E}(|x|) < \infty$. Where do we use Assumption 3.6?

(c) Show that the second term on the RHS of $(*)$ converges to zero in probability.

(d) In a similar fashion, show that the third term on the RHS of $(*)$ converges to zero in probability.

3. We wish to prove the algebraic result (3.5.11). What needs to be proved is that $\mathbf{A} - \mathbf{B}$ is positive semidefinite where

$$\mathbf{A} \equiv (\boldsymbol{\Sigma}_{\mathbf{xz}}'\mathbf{W}\boldsymbol{\Sigma}_{\mathbf{xz}})^{-1}\boldsymbol{\Sigma}_{\mathbf{xz}}'\mathbf{WSW}\boldsymbol{\Sigma}_{\mathbf{xz}}(\boldsymbol{\Sigma}_{\mathbf{xz}}'\mathbf{W}\boldsymbol{\Sigma}_{\mathbf{xz}})^{-1}$$

and

$$\mathbf{B} \equiv (\boldsymbol{\Sigma}_{\mathbf{xz}}'\mathbf{S}^{-1}\boldsymbol{\Sigma}_{\mathbf{xz}})^{-1}.$$

A result from matrix algebra states:

> Let $\mathbf{A}$ and $\mathbf{B}$ be two positive definite and symmetric matrices. $\mathbf{A} - \mathbf{B}$ is positive semidefinite if and only if $\mathbf{B}^{-1} - \mathbf{A}^{-1}$ is positive semidefinite.

Therefore, what needs to be proved is that

$$\mathbf{Q} \equiv \boldsymbol{\Sigma}_{\mathbf{xz}}'\mathbf{S}^{-1}\boldsymbol{\Sigma}_{\mathbf{xz}} - \boldsymbol{\Sigma}_{\mathbf{xz}}'\mathbf{W}\boldsymbol{\Sigma}_{\mathbf{xz}}(\boldsymbol{\Sigma}_{\mathbf{xz}}'\mathbf{WSW}\boldsymbol{\Sigma}_{\mathbf{xz}})^{-1}\boldsymbol{\Sigma}_{\mathbf{xz}}'\mathbf{W}\boldsymbol{\Sigma}_{\mathbf{xz}}$$

is positive semidefinite.

(a) Since $\mathbf{S}$ $(K \times K)$ is positive definite, there exists a nonsingular $K \times K$ matrix $\mathbf{C}$ such that $\mathbf{C}'\mathbf{C} = \mathbf{S}^{-1}$. Verify that $\mathbf{Q}$ can be written as

$$\mathbf{Q} = \mathbf{H}'\mathbf{M}_{\mathbf{G}}\mathbf{H},$$

where

$$\mathbf{H} = \mathbf{C}\boldsymbol{\Sigma}_{\mathbf{xz}}, \quad \mathbf{M}_{\mathbf{G}} = \mathbf{I}_K - \mathbf{G}(\mathbf{G}'\mathbf{G})^{-1}\mathbf{G}', \quad \mathbf{G} = \mathbf{C}'^{-1}\mathbf{W}\boldsymbol{\Sigma}_{\mathbf{xz}}.$$

Hint: $\mathbf{C}^{-1}\mathbf{C}'^{-1} = \mathbf{S}$.

(b) Show that $\mathbf{Q}$ is positive semidefinite. **Hint:** First show that $\mathbf{M}_{\mathbf{G}}$ is symmetric and idempotent. As you showed in Exercise 1, a symmetric and idempotent matrix is positive semidefinite.

4. Suppose $\mathbf{z}_i$ is a strict subset of $\mathbf{x}_i$. Which one is smaller in the matrix sense, the asymptotic variance of the OLS estimator or the asymptotic variance of the efficient two-step GMM estimator? **Hint:** Without loss of generality, we can assume that the first L elements of the K-dimensional vector $\mathbf{x}_i$ are $\mathbf{z}_i$. If $K \times K$ matrix $\mathbf{W}$ is given by

$$\mathbf{W} = \begin{bmatrix} \mathbf{A}^{-1} & \mathbf{0} \\ \mathbf{0} & \mathbf{0} \end{bmatrix},$$

where

$$\underset{(L\times L)}{\mathbf{A}} \equiv \mathrm{E}(\varepsilon_i^2 \mathbf{z}_i \mathbf{z}_i') = \text{leading } (L \times L) \text{ submatrix of } \mathbf{S},$$

then the asymptotic variance of the OLS estimator can be written as (3.5.1). If you did Exercise 3, you can verify that the algebraic relation (3.5.11) does not require $\mathbf{W}$ to be positive definite, as long as $\mathbf{\Sigma}_{\mathbf{xz}}'\mathbf{WSW}\mathbf{\Sigma}_{\mathbf{xz}}$ is nonsingular.

5. (optional) Prove Proposition 3.6 by following the steps below.

   (a) Show: $\mathbf{g}_n(\hat{\boldsymbol{\delta}}(\widehat{\mathbf{S}}^{-1})) = \widehat{\mathbf{B}}\,\bar{\mathbf{g}}$ where $\widehat{\mathbf{B}} \equiv \mathbf{I}_K - \mathbf{S}_{\mathbf{xz}}(\mathbf{S}_{\mathbf{xz}}'\widehat{\mathbf{S}}^{-1}\mathbf{S}_{\mathbf{xz}})^{-1}\mathbf{S}_{\mathbf{xz}}'\widehat{\mathbf{S}}^{-1}$.

   (b) Since $\widehat{\mathbf{S}}$ is positive definite, there exists a nonsingular $K \times K$ matrix $\mathbf{C}$ such that $\mathbf{C}'\mathbf{C} = \widehat{\mathbf{S}}^{-1}$. Define $\mathbf{A} \equiv \mathbf{C}\mathbf{S}_{\mathbf{xz}}$. Show that $\widehat{\mathbf{B}}'\widehat{\mathbf{S}}^{-1}\widehat{\mathbf{B}} = \mathbf{C}'\mathbf{M}\mathbf{C}$, where $\mathbf{M} \equiv \mathbf{I}_K - \mathbf{A}(\mathbf{A}'\mathbf{A})^{-1}\mathbf{A}'$. What is the rank of $\mathbf{M}$? **Hint:** The rank of an idempotent matrix equals its trace.

   (c) Let $\mathbf{v} \equiv \sqrt{n}\,\mathbf{C}\,\bar{\mathbf{g}}$. Show that $\mathbf{v} \to_{\mathrm{d}} N(\mathbf{0}, \mathbf{I}_K)$.

   (d) Show that $J(\hat{\boldsymbol{\delta}}(\widehat{\mathbf{S}}^{-1}), \widehat{\mathbf{S}}^{-1}) = \mathbf{v}'\mathbf{M}\mathbf{v}$. What is its asymptotic distribution?

6. Show that the J statistic in Proposition 3.6 is numerically equal to

$$n\cdot \mathbf{s}_{\mathbf{xy}}'\widehat{\mathbf{B}}'\widehat{\mathbf{S}}^{-1}\widehat{\mathbf{B}}\mathbf{s}_{\mathbf{xy}},$$

   where $\widehat{\mathbf{B}}$ is defined in Exercise 5(a). **Hint:** From Exercise 5, $J = n\cdot\bar{\mathbf{g}}'\widehat{\mathbf{B}}'\widehat{\mathbf{S}}^{-1}\widehat{\mathbf{B}}\bar{\mathbf{g}}$. Show that $\widehat{\mathbf{B}}\bar{\mathbf{g}} = \widehat{\mathbf{B}}\mathbf{s}_{\mathbf{xy}}$.

7. (optional) Prove Proposition 3.7 by taking the following steps. The notation not introduced in this exercise is the same as in Exercise 5.

   (a) Prove:

$$\mathbf{g}_{1n}(\bar{\boldsymbol{\delta}}) = \widehat{\mathbf{B}}_1\bar{\mathbf{g}}_1 \quad \text{and} \quad \widehat{\mathbf{B}}_1'(\widehat{\mathbf{S}}_{11})^{-1}\widehat{\mathbf{B}}_1 = \mathbf{C}_1'\mathbf{M}_1\mathbf{C}_1,$$

   where

$$\bar{\mathbf{g}}_1 \equiv \frac{1}{n}\sum_{i=1}^{n} \mathbf{x}_{i1}\cdot\varepsilon_i,$$

$$\widehat{\mathbf{B}}_1 \equiv \mathbf{I}_{K_1} - \mathbf{S}_{\mathbf{x}_1\mathbf{z}}[\mathbf{S}_{\mathbf{x}_1\mathbf{z}}'(\widehat{\mathbf{S}}_{11})^{-1}\mathbf{S}_{\mathbf{x}_1\mathbf{z}}]^{-1}\mathbf{S}_{\mathbf{x}_1\mathbf{z}}'(\widehat{\mathbf{S}}_{11})^{-1},$$

$$\mathbf{C}_1'\mathbf{C}_1 \equiv (\widehat{\mathbf{S}}_{11})^{-1},$$

$$\mathbf{M}_1 \equiv \mathbf{I}_{K_1} - \mathbf{A}_1(\mathbf{A}_1'\mathbf{A}_1)^{-1}\mathbf{A}_1',$$
$$\mathbf{A}_1 \equiv \mathbf{C}_1\mathbf{S}_{\mathbf{x}_1\mathbf{z}}.$$

(b) Prove: $\text{rank}(\mathbf{M}) = K - L$, $\text{rank}(\mathbf{M}_1) = K_1 - L$.

(c) Prove: You have proved in the previous exercise that $J = \mathbf{v}'\mathbf{M}\mathbf{v}$, where $\mathbf{v} \equiv \sqrt{n}\,\mathbf{C}\,\bar{\mathbf{g}}$. Here, prove: $J_1 = \mathbf{v}_1'\mathbf{M}_1\mathbf{v}_1$, where $\mathbf{v}_1 \equiv \sqrt{n}\,\mathbf{C}_1\bar{\mathbf{g}}_1$.

To proceed further, define the $K \times K_1$ matrix $\mathbf{F}$ as

$$\underset{(K\times K_1)}{\mathbf{F}} = \begin{bmatrix} \mathbf{I}_{K_1} \\ \mathbf{0} \end{bmatrix} \begin{matrix} \}\quad K_1 \text{ rows}, \\ \}\quad K - K_1 \text{ rows}. \end{matrix}$$

Then: $\mathbf{x}_{i1} = \mathbf{F}'\mathbf{x}_i$, $\mathbf{S}_{\mathbf{x}_1\mathbf{z}} = \mathbf{F}'\mathbf{S}_{\mathbf{xz}}$, $\bar{\mathbf{g}}_1 = \mathbf{F}'\bar{\mathbf{g}}$.

(d) Prove $J - J_1 = \mathbf{v}'(\mathbf{M} - \mathbf{D})\mathbf{v}$ where $\mathbf{D} = \mathbf{C}'^{-1}\mathbf{F}\mathbf{C}_1'\mathbf{M}_1\mathbf{C}_1\mathbf{F}'\mathbf{C}^{-1}$.

(e) Prove that $\mathbf{D}$ is symmetric and idempotent, with rank $K_1 - L$. **Hint:**

$$\mathbf{F}'\mathbf{C}^{-1}\mathbf{C}'^{-1}\mathbf{F} = \mathbf{F}'(\mathbf{C}'\mathbf{C})^{-1}\mathbf{F} = \mathbf{F}'\widehat{\mathbf{S}}\mathbf{F} = \widehat{\mathbf{S}}_{11},$$
$$\mathbf{C}_1\widehat{\mathbf{S}}_{11}\mathbf{C}_1' = \mathbf{C}_1(\mathbf{C}_1'\mathbf{C}_1)^{-1}\mathbf{C}_1' = \mathbf{I}_{K_1}.$$

(f) Prove: $\mathbf{A}'\mathbf{D} = \mathbf{0}$. **Hint:**

$$\mathbf{A}'\mathbf{D} = (\mathbf{S}_{\mathbf{xz}}'\mathbf{C}')(\mathbf{C}'^{-1}\mathbf{F}\mathbf{C}_1'\mathbf{M}_1\mathbf{C}_1\mathbf{F}'\mathbf{C}^{-1}) = (\mathbf{S}_{\mathbf{xz}}'\mathbf{F}\mathbf{C}_1'\mathbf{M}_1)(\mathbf{C}_1\mathbf{F}'\mathbf{C}^{-1}),$$
$$\mathbf{S}_{\mathbf{xz}}'\mathbf{F}\mathbf{C}_1' = \mathbf{A}_1',$$

so

$$\mathbf{S}_{\mathbf{xz}}'\mathbf{F}\mathbf{C}_1'\mathbf{M}_1 = \mathbf{A}_1'\mathbf{M}_1.$$

(g) Prove: $\mathbf{M} - \mathbf{D}$ is symmetric and idempotent, with rank $K - K_1$.

(h) Prove the desired result: $J - J_1 \to_{\text{d}} \chi^2(K - K_1)$.

(i) Step (d) has established that $C = n{\cdot}\bar{\mathbf{g}}'\mathbf{C}'(\mathbf{M} - \mathbf{D})\mathbf{C}\,\bar{\mathbf{g}}$. Show that C can be written as

$$n{\cdot}\mathbf{s}_{\mathbf{xy}}'\mathbf{C}'(\mathbf{M} - \mathbf{D})\mathbf{C}\,\mathbf{s}_{\mathbf{xy}}.$$

Hint: $\mathbf{g}_n(\hat{\delta}) = \widehat{\mathbf{B}}\mathbf{s}_{\mathbf{xy}}$. So the numerical value of C would have been the same if we replaced $\bar{\mathbf{g}}$ by $\mathbf{s}_{\mathbf{xy}}$ from the beginning in (a).

(j) Show that $\mathbf{M} - \mathbf{D}$ is positive semidefinite. Thus, the quadratic form C is nonnegative for any sample.

8. (Optional, proof of numerical equivalence in Proposition 3.8) In the restricted efficient GMM, the J function is minimized subject to the restriction $\mathbf{R}\tilde{\boldsymbol{\delta}} = \mathbf{r}$. For the time being, do not restrict $\widehat{\mathbf{W}}$ to be equal to $\widehat{\mathbf{S}}^{-1}$ and form the Lagrangian as

$$\mathcal{L} = n\cdot(\mathbf{s_{xy}} - \mathbf{S_{xz}}\tilde{\boldsymbol{\delta}})'\widehat{\mathbf{W}}(\mathbf{s_{xy}} - \mathbf{S_{xz}}\tilde{\boldsymbol{\delta}}) + \boldsymbol{\lambda}'(\mathbf{R}\tilde{\boldsymbol{\delta}} - \mathbf{r}),$$

where $\boldsymbol{\lambda}$ is the #$\mathbf{r}$-dimensional Lagrange multipliers (recall: $\mathbf{r}$ is #$\mathbf{r} \times 1$, $\mathbf{R}$ is #$\mathbf{r} \times L$, and $\tilde{\boldsymbol{\delta}}$ is $L \times 1$). Let $\bar{\boldsymbol{\delta}}$ be the solution to the constrained minimization problem. (If $\widehat{\mathbf{W}} = \widehat{\mathbf{S}}^{-1}$, it is the restricted efficient GMM estimator of $\boldsymbol{\delta}$.)

(a) Let $\hat{\boldsymbol{\delta}}(\widehat{\mathbf{W}})$ be the unrestricted GMM estimator that minimizes $J(\tilde{\boldsymbol{\delta}}, \widehat{\mathbf{W}})$. Show:

$$\bar{\boldsymbol{\delta}} = \hat{\boldsymbol{\delta}}(\widehat{\mathbf{W}}) - (\mathbf{S}'_{\mathbf{xz}}\widehat{\mathbf{W}}\mathbf{S_{xz}})^{-1}\mathbf{R}'\left[\mathbf{R}(\mathbf{S}'_{\mathbf{xz}}\widehat{\mathbf{W}}\mathbf{S_{xz}})^{-1}\mathbf{R}'\right]^{-1}[\mathbf{R}\hat{\boldsymbol{\delta}}(\widehat{\mathbf{W}}) - \mathbf{r}],$$
$$\boldsymbol{\lambda} = 2n\cdot\left[\mathbf{R}(\mathbf{S}'_{\mathbf{xz}}\widehat{\mathbf{W}}\mathbf{S_{xz}})^{-1}\mathbf{R}'\right]^{-1}[\mathbf{R}\hat{\boldsymbol{\delta}}(\widehat{\mathbf{W}}) - \mathbf{r}].$$

Hint: The first-order conditions are

$$-2n\mathbf{S}'_{\mathbf{xz}}\widehat{\mathbf{W}}\mathbf{s_{xy}} + 2n(\mathbf{S}'_{\mathbf{xz}}\widehat{\mathbf{W}}\mathbf{S_{xz}})\bar{\boldsymbol{\delta}} + \mathbf{R}'\boldsymbol{\lambda} = \mathbf{0}.$$

Combine this with the constraint $\mathbf{R}\bar{\boldsymbol{\delta}} = \mathbf{r}$ to solve for $\boldsymbol{\lambda}$ and $\bar{\boldsymbol{\delta}}$.

(b) Show:

$$J(\bar{\boldsymbol{\delta}}, \widehat{\mathbf{W}}) = J(\hat{\boldsymbol{\delta}}(\widehat{\mathbf{W}}), \widehat{\mathbf{W}}) + n\cdot(\hat{\boldsymbol{\delta}}(\widehat{\mathbf{W}}) - \bar{\boldsymbol{\delta}})'(\mathbf{S}'_{\mathbf{xz}}\widehat{\mathbf{W}}\mathbf{S_{xz}})(\hat{\boldsymbol{\delta}}(\widehat{\mathbf{W}}) - \bar{\boldsymbol{\delta}}).$$

Hint:

$$\begin{aligned} J(\bar{\boldsymbol{\delta}}, \widehat{\mathbf{W}}) &= n\cdot(\mathbf{s_{xy}} - \mathbf{S_{xz}}\bar{\boldsymbol{\delta}})'\widehat{\mathbf{W}}(\mathbf{s_{xy}} - \mathbf{S_{xz}}\bar{\boldsymbol{\delta}}) \\ &= n\cdot[(\mathbf{s_{xy}} - \mathbf{S_{xz}}\hat{\boldsymbol{\delta}}(\widehat{\mathbf{W}})) + \mathbf{S_{xz}}(\hat{\boldsymbol{\delta}}(\widehat{\mathbf{W}}) - \bar{\boldsymbol{\delta}})]'\widehat{\mathbf{W}} \\ &\quad \cdot[(\mathbf{s_{xy}} - \mathbf{S_{xz}}\hat{\boldsymbol{\delta}}(\widehat{\mathbf{W}})) + \mathbf{S_{xz}}(\hat{\boldsymbol{\delta}}(\widehat{\mathbf{W}}) - \bar{\boldsymbol{\delta}})]. \end{aligned}$$

Use the first-order conditions for the unrestricted GMM:

$$\mathbf{S}'_{\mathbf{xz}}\widehat{\mathbf{W}}(\mathbf{s_{xy}} - \mathbf{S_{xz}}\hat{\boldsymbol{\delta}}(\widehat{\mathbf{W}})) = \mathbf{0}.$$

(c) Now set $\widehat{\mathbf{W}} = \widehat{\mathbf{S}}^{-1}$ and show that the Wald statistic W defined in (3.5.8) is numerically equal to LR in (3.7.2).

9. (GMM Hausman principle) Let $\hat{\boldsymbol{\delta}}_1 \equiv \hat{\boldsymbol{\delta}}(\widehat{\mathbf{W}}_1)$ and $\hat{\boldsymbol{\delta}}_2 \equiv \hat{\boldsymbol{\delta}}(\widehat{\mathbf{W}}_2)$ be two GMM estimators with two different choices of the weighting matrix, $\widehat{\mathbf{W}}_1$ and $\widehat{\mathbf{W}}_2$.

(a) Show:

$$\begin{bmatrix} \sqrt{n}(\hat{\boldsymbol{\delta}}_1 - \boldsymbol{\delta}) \\ \sqrt{n}(\hat{\boldsymbol{\delta}}_2 - \boldsymbol{\delta}) \end{bmatrix} \underset{\mathrm{d}}{\to} N\left(\mathbf{0}, \begin{bmatrix} \mathbf{A}_{11} & \mathbf{A}_{12} \\ \mathbf{A}_{21} & \mathbf{A}_{22} \end{bmatrix}\right),$$

where

$$\mathbf{A}_{11} = \mathbf{Q}_1^{-1}\boldsymbol{\Sigma}_{\mathbf{xz}}'\mathbf{W}_1\mathbf{S}\mathbf{W}_1\boldsymbol{\Sigma}_{\mathbf{xz}}\mathbf{Q}_1^{-1}, \quad \mathbf{A}_{12} = \mathbf{Q}_1^{-1}\boldsymbol{\Sigma}_{\mathbf{xz}}'\mathbf{W}_1\mathbf{S}\mathbf{W}_2\boldsymbol{\Sigma}_{\mathbf{xz}}\mathbf{Q}_2^{-1},$$
$$\mathbf{A}_{21} = \mathbf{Q}_2^{-1}\boldsymbol{\Sigma}_{\mathbf{xz}}'\mathbf{W}_2\mathbf{S}\mathbf{W}_1\boldsymbol{\Sigma}_{\mathbf{xz}}\mathbf{Q}_1^{-1}, \quad \mathbf{A}_{22} = \mathbf{Q}_2^{-1}\boldsymbol{\Sigma}_{\mathbf{xz}}'\mathbf{W}_2\mathbf{S}\mathbf{W}_2\boldsymbol{\Sigma}_{\mathbf{xz}}\mathbf{Q}_2^{-1}.$$
$$\mathbf{Q}_1 = \boldsymbol{\Sigma}_{\mathbf{xz}}'\mathbf{W}_1\boldsymbol{\Sigma}_{\mathbf{xz}}, \quad \mathbf{Q}_2 = \boldsymbol{\Sigma}_{\mathbf{xz}}'\mathbf{W}_2\boldsymbol{\Sigma}_{\mathbf{xz}}, \quad \operatorname*{plim}_{n\to\infty} \widehat{\mathbf{W}}_j = \mathbf{W}_j \quad (j = 1, 2).$$

(b) Let $\mathbf{q} \equiv \hat{\boldsymbol{\delta}}_1 - \hat{\boldsymbol{\delta}}_2$. Show that $\sqrt{n}\,\mathbf{q} \to_{\mathrm{d}} N(\mathbf{0}, \operatorname{Avar}(\mathbf{q}))$, where

$$\operatorname{Avar}(\mathbf{q}) = \mathbf{A}_{11} + \mathbf{A}_{22} - \mathbf{A}_{12} - \mathbf{A}_{21}.$$

(c) Set $\widehat{\mathbf{W}}_2 = \widehat{\mathbf{S}}^{-1}$ so that $\hat{\boldsymbol{\delta}}_2$ is efficient GMM. Show that

$$\operatorname{Avar}(\mathbf{q}) = \mathbf{A}_{11} - (\boldsymbol{\Sigma}_{\mathbf{xz}}'\mathbf{S}^{-1}\boldsymbol{\Sigma}_{\mathbf{xz}})^{-1} = \operatorname{Avar}(\hat{\boldsymbol{\delta}}(\widehat{\mathbf{W}}_1)) - \operatorname{Avar}(\hat{\boldsymbol{\delta}}(\widehat{\mathbf{S}}^{-1})).$$

10. (Weak instruments. This question is due to M. Watson.) Consider the following model:

$$y_i = z_i\delta + \varepsilon_i \quad (i = 1, 2, \dots, n),$$

where y_i, z_i, and ε_i are scalar random variables. Let x_i denote a scalar instrumental variable that is related to z_i via the equation:

$$z_i = x_i\beta + v_i.$$

Let

$$\boldsymbol{\eta}_i \equiv \begin{bmatrix} \varepsilon_i \\ v_i \end{bmatrix}, \quad \mathbf{g}_i \equiv \boldsymbol{\eta}_i \cdot x_i \equiv \begin{bmatrix} g_{1i} \\ g_{2i} \end{bmatrix} = \begin{bmatrix} x_i\varepsilon_i \\ x_i v_i \end{bmatrix}.$$

Assume that

(1) $\{x_i, \boldsymbol{\eta}_i\}$ follows a stationary and ergodic process.

(2) $\mathbf{g}_i$ is a martingale difference sequence with $\mathrm{E}(\mathbf{g}_i\mathbf{g}_i') = \mathbf{S}$, which is a positive definite matrix.

(3) $\mathrm{E}(x_i^2) = \sigma_x^2 > 0$.

(4) $\beta \neq 0$.

Let $\hat{\delta} \equiv s_{xz}^{-1} s_{xy}$ where

$$s_{xz} \equiv \frac{1}{n} \sum_{i=1}^{n} x_i z_i, \quad s_{xy} \equiv \frac{1}{n} \sum_{i=1}^{n} x_i y_i.$$

(a) Prove that $\sigma_{xz} \equiv \mathrm{E}(x_i z_i) \neq 0$ (so that the rank condition for identification is satisfied).

(b) Prove that $\hat{\delta} \to_{\mathrm{p}} \delta$.

We now want to consider a case in which the rank condition is just barely satisfied, that is, σ_{xz} is very close to zero. One way to do this is to replace Assumption (4) with

(4′) $\beta = 1/\sqrt{n}$.

For the remainder of the problem, assume that (1)–(3) and (4′) hold. (This assumption and the following questions are based on Staiger and Stock (1997).) Note that $\hat{\delta} - \delta = s_{xz}^{-1} \bar{g}_1$, where $\bar{g}_1$ is the sample mean of g_{1i} $(\equiv x_i \varepsilon_i)$.

(c) Show that $s_{xz} \to_{\mathrm{p}} 0$.

(d) Show that $\sqrt{n}\, s_{xz} \to_{\mathrm{d}} \sigma_x^2 + a$, where a is distributed $N(0, s_{22})$ and s_{22} is the (2, 2) element of $\mathbf{S}$.

(e) Show that $\hat{\delta} - \delta \to_{\mathrm{d}} (\sigma_x^2 + a)^{-1} b$, where (a, b) are jointly normally distributed with mean zero and covariance matrix $\mathbf{S}$.

(f) Is $\hat{\delta}$ consistent?

EMPIRICAL EXERCISES

Read Griliches (1976) before answering. We will estimate the type of the wage equation estimated by Griliches using an extract from the NLS-Y used by Blackburn and Neumark (1992).[21] The NLS-Y is **panel data**, with the same set of young men surveyed at several points in time (we will not exploit the panel feature of the data set in this exercise, though). The extract contains information about those individuals at two points in time: first, the earliest year in which wages and other variables are available, and second, in 1980. In a data file GRILIC.ASC, data are provided on *RNS*, *RNS80*, *MRT*, *MRT80*, *SMSA*, *SMSA80*, *MED*, *IQ*, *KWW*, *YEAR*, *AGE*, *AGE80*, *S*, *S80*, *EXPR*, *EXPR80*, *TENURE*, *TENURE80*, *LW*, and *LW80* (in this order, with the columns corresponding to the variables, as usual). The variable

[21] See Blackburn and Neumark (1992, Section III) for a more detailed description of the sample.

YEAR is the year of the first point in time. Variables without "*80*" are for the first point, and those with "*80*" are for 1980. The definition of the variables for the first point is:

$$\begin{aligned}
RNS &= \text{dummy for residency in the southern states} \\
MRT &= \text{dummy for marital status (1 if married)} \\
SMSA &= \text{dummy for residency in metropolitan areas} \\
MED &= \text{mother's education in years} \\
KWW &= \text{score on the ``Knowledge of the World of Work'' test} \\
IQ &= \text{IQ score} \\
AGE &= \text{age of the individual} \\
S &= \text{completed years of schooling} \\
EXPR &= \text{experience in years} \\
TENURE &= \text{tenure in years} \\
LW &= \text{log wage.}
\end{aligned}$$

The Blackburn-Neumark sample has 815 observations after deleting black individuals. Also deleted are cases with missing information on mother's education, reducing the sample size to 758.

(a) Calculate means and standard deviations of all the provided variables (including those for 1980) and prepare a table similar to Griliches's Table 1. Also, calculate the correlation between *IQ* and *S* (use the `MSD(CORR)` command for TSP, `CMOM(PRINT,CORR)` for RATS).

Since the year the wage rate is observed differs across individuals, the wage rate will have the year effect. Generate eight year dummies for $YEAR = 66, \ldots, 73$. (Note: There is no observation for 1972.) The year dummies will be included in the log wage equation to control for the year effect.

(b) Consider the wage equation (dropping the individual subscript i)

$$LW = \beta S + \gamma IQ + \boldsymbol{\delta}'\mathbf{h} + \varepsilon,$$

where *LW* is log wages, *S* is schooling, and

$$\mathbf{h} \equiv (EXPR, TENURE, RNS, SMSA, \text{year dummies})'.$$

(There is no need to include a constant because it is a linear combination of the year dummies.) Prepare a table similar to Table 3.2. In your 2SLS estimation of the wage equation, the set of instruments should consist of predetermined regressors (S and $\mathbf{h}$) and excluded predetermined variables (MED, KWW, MRT, AGE). Is the relative magnitude of the three different estimates of the schooling coefficient consistent with the prediction based on the omitted variable and errors-in-variables biases?

TSP Tip: To do 2SLS, use the `INST` or `2SLS` command.

RATS Tip: Use the `LINREG` command with the `INST` option. To define the instrument set, use the `INSTRUMENTS` command.

(c) For your 2SLS estimation of the wage equation in part (b), calculate Sargan's statistic (it should be 87.655). What should the degrees of freedom be? Calculate the p-value.

TSP Tip: Sargan's statistic can be calculated as `@phi/(@ssr/@nob)`, where the variables with "`@`" are outputs from TSP commands. `@nob` is sample size, `@phi` is $\hat{\boldsymbol{\varepsilon}}'\mathbf{X}(\mathbf{X}'\mathbf{X})^{-1}\mathbf{X}'\hat{\boldsymbol{\varepsilon}}$ where $\hat{\boldsymbol{\varepsilon}}$ is the 2SLS residual vector, and `@ssr` is $\hat{\boldsymbol{\varepsilon}}'\hat{\boldsymbol{\varepsilon}}$.

RATS Tip: Sargan's statistic is `%uzwzu/(%rss/%nobs)`, where variables with "`%`" are outputs from RATS commands. `%nobs` is sample size, `%uzwzu` is $\hat{\boldsymbol{\varepsilon}}'\mathbf{X}(\mathbf{X}'\mathbf{X})^{-1}\mathbf{X}'\hat{\boldsymbol{\varepsilon}}$, and `%rss` is $\hat{\boldsymbol{\varepsilon}}'\hat{\boldsymbol{\varepsilon}}$.

(d) Obtain the 2SLS estimate by actually running two regressions. Verify that the standard errors given by the second stage regression are *different* from those you obtained in (b).

(e) Griliches mentions that schooling, too, may be endogenous. What is his argument? Estimate by 2SLS the wage equation, treating both IQ and S as endogenous. What happens to the schooling coefficient? How would you explain the difference between your 2SLS estimate of the schooling coefficient here and your 2SLS estimate in (b)? Calculate Sargan's statistic (it should be 13.268) and its p-value.

(f) Estimate the wage equation by GMM, treating schooling as predetermined as in the 2SLS estimation in part (b). Are 2SLS standard errors smaller than GMM standard errors? Test whether schooling is predetermined by the C statistic. To calculate C, you need to do two GMMs with and without schooling as an instrument. Use the same $\widehat{\mathbf{S}}$ throughout. To calculate $\widehat{\mathbf{S}}$, use the 2SLS residual from part (b). The C statistic should be 58.168.

TSP Tip: It is a bit awkward to calculate $\widehat{\mathbf{S}}$ in TSP. The following codes, though not elegant, get the job done. Here, `res0` is the residuals from the 2SLS estimation in (b).

```
smpl 1 758;
x0=res0*s;
x1=res0*expr;
x2=res0*tenure;
x3=res0*rns;
x4=res0*smsa;
x5=res0*y66;
      ⋮
x11=res0*y73;
x12=res0*med;
x13=res0*kww;
x14=res0*mrt;
x15=res0*age;
msd(noprint,moment) x0-x15;
```

`@mom`, an output from the TSP command `MSD`, is $\widehat{\mathbf{S}}$. To do GMM, use TSP's `GMM` command. The GMM option `COVOC=matrix name` forces the GMM command to use the assigned matrix for $\widehat{\mathbf{S}}$. The J statistic is given by `@nob*@phi`.

RATS Tip: The `LINREG` with the `INST` and `ROBUSTERRORS` option does GMM for linear equations. The `WMATRIX=`*`matrix name`* option of `LINREG` accepts $\widehat{\mathbf{S}}^{-1}$, not $\widehat{\mathbf{S}}$. To calculate $\widehat{\mathbf{S}}^{-1}$ in RATS, do the following. Here, `res0` is the residuals from the 2SLS estimation in part (b).

```
mcov / res0
# s expr tenure rns smsa y66 ... y73
  med kww mrt age
compute sinv=inv(%cmom)
```

`sinv` is $\widehat{\mathbf{S}}^{-1}$. The J statistic is given by `%uzwzu`.

(g) Go back to the wage equation you estimated in (e) by 2SLS endogenous schooling. The large Sargan's statistic (and the large J statistic in part (f)) is a concern. So consider dropping both *MED* and *KWW* from the list of instruments. Is the order condition for identification still satisfied? What happens to the

2SLS estimates? (The schooling coefficient will be −529.3%!) What do you think is the problem? **Hint:** There are two endogenous regressors, S and IQ. MRT and AGE are the only excluded predetermined variables. If MRT and AGE do not have explanatory power in the first-stage regression of S and IQ on the instruments, then the fitted values of S and IQ will be very close to linear combinations of the included predetermined variables. This will lead to a near-multicollinearity problem in the second-stage regression. Make sure you examine the first-stage regressions to check the explanatory power of MRT and AGE.

ANSWERS TO SELECTED QUESTIONS

ANALYTICAL EXERCISES

4. The asymptotic variance of the OLS estimator is (by setting $\mathbf{x} = \mathbf{z}$ in (3.5.1))

$$\boldsymbol{\Sigma}_{\mathbf{zz}}^{-1}\mathbf{A}\boldsymbol{\Sigma}_{\mathbf{zz}}^{-1} = (\boldsymbol{\Sigma}_{\mathbf{zz}}\mathbf{A}^{-1}\boldsymbol{\Sigma}_{\mathbf{zz}})^{-1},$$

where $\mathbf{A} \equiv \mathrm{E}(\varepsilon_i^2 \mathbf{z}_i \mathbf{z}_i')$. The asymptotic variance of the two-step GMM is, by (3.5.13),

$$(\boldsymbol{\Sigma}_{\mathbf{xz}}' \mathbf{S}^{-1}\boldsymbol{\Sigma}_{\mathbf{xz}})^{-1},$$

where $\mathbf{S} \equiv \mathrm{E}(\varepsilon_i^2 \mathbf{x}_i \mathbf{x}_i')$. If $\mathbf{W}$ is as defined in the hint, then

$$\mathbf{WSW} = \mathbf{W} \quad \text{and} \quad \boldsymbol{\Sigma}_{\mathbf{xz}}'\mathbf{W}\boldsymbol{\Sigma}_{\mathbf{xz}} = \boldsymbol{\Sigma}_{\mathbf{zz}}\mathbf{A}^{-1}\boldsymbol{\Sigma}_{\mathbf{zz}}.$$

So (3.5.1) reduces to the asymptotic variance of the OLS estimator. By (3.5.11), it is no smaller than $(\boldsymbol{\Sigma}_{\mathbf{xz}}' \mathbf{S}^{-1}\boldsymbol{\Sigma}_{\mathbf{xz}})^{-1}$, which is the asymptotic variance of the two-step GMM estimator.

EMPIRICAL EXERCISES

(b) See Table 3.3, lines 1–5.

(e) He gives three reasons for the endogeneity of schooling. First, the measurement error η may be related to success in schooling. The second reason is the argument we made in the text: the choice of S is influenced by unobservable characteristics. Third, schooling may be measured with error. The general

Table 3.3: Parameter Estimates, Blackburn-Neumark Sample

Estimation equation: dependent variable = *LW*, regressors: *S*, *IQ*, *EXPR*, *TENURE*, and other controls

Line no.	Estimation technique	Coefficient of				*SEE*	R^2	Test of over-identifying restrictions	Which regressor is endogenous?	Excluded predetermined variables besides regional dummies
		S	*IQ*	*EXPR*	*TENURE*					
1	OLS	0.070 (0.0067)	—	0.030 (0.0065)	0.043 (0.0075)	0.328	0.425	—	none	—
2	OLS	0.062 (0.0073)	0.0027 (0.0010)	0.031 (0.0065)	0.042 (0.0075)	0.326	0.430	—	none	—
3	2SLS	0.069 (0.013)	0.0002 (0.0039)	0.030 (0.0066)	0.043 (0.0076)	0.328	—	87.6 ($p = 0.0000$)	*IQ*	*MED*, *KWW*, *AGE*, *MRT*
4	2SLS	0.172 (0.021)	−0.009 (0.0047)	0.049 (0.0082)	0.042 (0.0088)	0.380	—	13.3 ($p = 0.00131$)	*S*, *IQ*	*MED*, *KWW*, *AGE*, *MRT*
5	GMM	0.176 (0.021)	−0.009 (0.0049)	0.050 (0.0080)	0.043 (0.0095)	0.379	—	11.6 ($p = 0.00303$)	*S*, *IQ*	*MED*, *KWW*, *AGE*, *MRT*
6	2SLS	0.117 (0.027)	0.002 (0.0050)	0.033 (0.0052)	0.0051 (0.0029)	0.380	—	14.9 ($p = 0.00058$)	*S80*, *IQ*	*MED*, *KWW*, *AGE80*, *MRT80*

NOTE: Standard errors in parentheses. Line 6 is for 1980.

formula for the asymptotic bias for the 2SLS estimator is given by

$$\operatorname{plim} \hat{\boldsymbol{\delta}}_{2SLS} - \boldsymbol{\delta} = (\boldsymbol{\Sigma}'_{\mathbf{xz}} \boldsymbol{\Sigma}_{\mathbf{xx}}^{-1} \boldsymbol{\Sigma}_{\mathbf{xz}})^{-1} \boldsymbol{\Sigma}'_{\mathbf{xz}} \boldsymbol{\Sigma}_{\mathbf{xx}}^{-1} \mathrm{E}(\mathbf{x}_i \cdot \varepsilon_i).$$

If S is endogenous, the instrument set $\mathbf{x}_i$ for the 2SLS estimation in (b) erroneously includes a variable (which is S) that is not predetermined. So one of the elements of $\mathrm{E}(\mathbf{x}_i \cdot \varepsilon_i)$ is not zero. Then it is clear from the formula that asymptotic bias can exist at least for some coefficients.

(g) Without *MED* and *KWW* as instruments, the 2SLS estimator becomes imprecise. The order condition is satisfied with equality. The culprit is the low explanatory power of *MRT* (look at its t-value in the first-stage regressions for S and *IQ*).

References

Angrist, J., and A. Krueger, 1991, "Does Compulsory School Attendance Affect Schooling and Earnings?" *Quarterly Journal of Economics*, 106, 979–1014.

Behrman, J., Z. Hrubec, P. Taubman, and T. Wales, 1980, *Socioeconomic Success: A Study of the Effects of Genetic Endowments, Family Environment, and Schooling*, Amsterdam: North-Holland.

Blackburn, M., and D. Neumark, 1992, "Unobserved Ability, Efficiency Wages, and Interindustry Wage Differentials," *Quarterly Journal of Economics*, 107, 1421–1436.

Card, D., 1995, "Earnings, Schooling, and Ability Revisited," *Research in Labor Economics*, 14, 23–48.

Card, D., and A. Krueger, 1996, "Labor Market Effects of School Quality: Theory and Evidence," Working Paper 5450, NBER.

Eichenbaum, M., L. Hansen, and K. Singleton, 1985, "A Time Series Analysis of Representative Agent Models of Consumption and Leisure Choice under Uncertainty," *Quarterly Journal of Economics*, 103, 51–78.

Friedman, M., 1957, *A Theory of the Consumption Function*, Princeton: Princeton University Press.

Gallant, R., and D. Jorgenson, 1979, "Statistical Inference for a System of Simultaneous, Non-linear, Implicit Equations in the Context of Instrumental Variable Estimation," *Journal of Econometrics*, 11, 275–302.

Griliches, Z., 1976, "Wages of Very Young Men," *Journal of Political Economy*, 84, S69–S85.

Haavelmo, T., 1943, "The Statistical Implications of a System of Simultaneous Equations," *Econometrica*, 11, 1–12.

Hansen, L., 1982, "Large Sample Properties of Generalized Method of Moments Estimators," *Econometrica*, 50, 1029–1054.

Hausman, J., and W. Taylor, 1980, "Comparing Specification Tests and Classical Tests," MIT Working Paper No. 266.

Judge, G., W. Griffiths, R. Hill, H. Lütkepohl, and T. Lee, 1985, *The Theory and Practice of Econometrics* (2d ed.), New York: Wiley.

Mincer, J., 1958, "Investment in Human Capital and Personal Income Distribution," *Journal of Political Economy*, 66, 281–302.

Nelson, C., and R. Startz, 1990, "Some Further Results on the Exact Small Sample Properties of the Instrumental Variable Estimator," *Econometrica*, 58, 967–976.

Newey, W., 1985, "Generalized Method of Moments Specification Testing," *Journal of Econometrics*, 29, 229–256.

Newey, W., and D. McFadden, 1994, "Large Sample Estimation and Hypothesis Testing," Chapter 36 in R. Engle and D. McFadden (eds.), *Handbook of Econometrics*, Volume IV, New York: North-Holland.

Sargan, D., 1958, "The Estimation of Economic Relationships Using Instrumental Variables," *Econometrica*, 26, 393–415.

Searle, S., 1982, *Matrix Algebra Useful for Statistics*, New York: Wiley.

Staiger, D., and J. Stock, 1997, "Instrumental Variables Regression with Weak Instruments," *Econometrica*, 65, 557–586.

Theil, H., 1953, "Repeated Least-Squares Applied to Complete Equation Systems," MS., The Hague: Central Planning Bureau.

White, H., 1982, "Instrumental Variables Regression with Independent Observations," *Econometrica*, 50, 483–499.

———, 1984, *Asymptotic Theory for Econometricians*, Academic.

Working, E. J., 1927, "What Do 'Statistical Demand' Curves Show?" *Quarterly Journal of Economics*, 41, 212–235.

CHAPTER 4

Multiple-Equation GMM

ABSTRACT

This chapter is concerned about estimating more than one equation jointly by GMM. Having learned how to do the single-equation GMM, it is only a small step to get to a system of multiple equations, despite the seemingly complicated notation designed to keep tabs on individual equations. This is because the multiple-equation GMM estimator can be expressed as a single-equation GMM estimator by suitably specifying the matrices and vectors comprising the single-equation GMM formula. This being the case, we can develop large-sample theory of multiple-equation GMM almost off the shelf.

The payoff from mastering multiple-equation GMM is considerable. Under conditional homoskedasticity, it reduces to the full-information instrumental variable efficient (FIVE) estimator, which in turn reduces to three-stage least squares (3SLS) if the set of instrumental variables is common to all equations. If we further assume that all the regressors are predetermined, then 3SLS reduces to seemingly unrelated regressions (SUR), which in turn reduces to the multivariate regression when all the equations have the same regressors.

We will also show that the multiple-equation system can be written as an equation system with its coefficients constrained to be the same across equations. The GMM estimator for this system is again a special case of single-equation GMM. The GMM estimator when all the regressors are predetermined and errors are conditionally homoskedastic is called the random-effects (RE) estimator. Therefore, SUR and RE are equivalent estimators.

The application of this chapter is estimation of interrelated factor demands by SUR/RE. A system of factor demand functions is derived from a cost function called the translog cost function, which is a generalization of the linear logarithmic cost function considered in Chapter 1.

This chapter does not consider the maximum likelihood (ML) estimation of multiple-equation models. The ML counterpart of 3SLS is full-information maximum likelihood (FIML). For a full treatment of FIML, see Section 8.5.

If the complexity of this chapter's notation stands in your way, just set M (the number of equations) to two. Doing so does not impair the generality of any of the results of this chapter.

4.1 The Multiple-Equation Model

To be able to deal with more than one equation, we need to complicate the notation by introducing an additional subscript designating the equation. For example, the dependent variable of the m-th equation for observation i will be denoted y_{im}.

Linearity

There are M linear equations, each of which is a linear equation like the one in Assumption 3.1:

Assumption 4.1 (linearity): *There are M linear equations*

$$y_{im} = \mathbf{z}_{im}'\boldsymbol{\delta}_m + \varepsilon_{im} \quad (m = 1, 2, \ldots, M; i = 1, 2, \ldots, n), \tag{4.1.1}$$

where n is the sample size, $\mathbf{z}_{im}$ is the L_m-dimensional vector of regressors, $\boldsymbol{\delta}_m$ is the conformable coefficient vector, and ε_{im} is an unobservable error term in the m-th equation.

The model will make no assumptions about the **interequation** (or **contemporaneous) correlation** between the errors $(\varepsilon_{i1}, \ldots, \varepsilon_{iM})$. Also, no *a priori* restrictions are placed on the coefficients from different equations. That is, the model assumes no **cross-equation restrictions** on the coefficients. These points can be illustrated in

> **Example 4.1 (wage equation):** In the Griliches exercise of Chapter 3, we estimated the wage equation. In one specification, Griliches adds to it the equation for *KWW* (score on the "Knowledge of the World of Work" test):
>
> $$LW_i = \phi_1 + \beta_1 S_i + \gamma_1 IQ_i + \pi EXPR_i + \varepsilon_{i1},$$
> $$KWW_i = \phi_2 + \beta_2 S_i + \gamma_2 IQ_i + \varepsilon_{i2},$$
>
> where (to refresh your memory) LW_i is the log wage of the i-th individual in the first year of the survey, S_i is schooling in years, IQ_i is IQ, and $EXPR_i$ is experience in years. In this example, $M = 2$, $L_1 = 4$, $L_2 = 3$, $y_{i1} = LW_i$, $y_{i2} = KWW_i$, and

$$\mathbf{z}_{i1} = \begin{bmatrix} 1 \\ S_i \\ IQ_i \\ EXPR_i \end{bmatrix}, \quad \mathbf{z}_{i2} = \begin{bmatrix} 1 \\ S_i \\ IQ_i \end{bmatrix}, \quad \boldsymbol{\delta}_1 = \begin{bmatrix} \phi_1 \\ \beta_1 \\ \gamma_1 \\ \pi \end{bmatrix}, \quad \boldsymbol{\delta}_2 = \begin{bmatrix} \phi_2 \\ \beta_2 \\ \gamma_2 \end{bmatrix}. \tag{4.1.2}$$

The errors ε_{i1} and ε_{i2} can be correlated. The correlation arises if, for example, there is an unobservable individual characteristic that affects both the wage rate and the test score. There are no cross-equation restrictions such as $\beta_1 = \beta_2$.

Cross-equation restrictions naturally arise in **panel data** models where the same relationship can be estimated for different points in time.

Example 4.2 (wage equation for two years): The NLS-Y data we used for the Griliches exercise actually has information for 1980, so we can estimate two wage equations, one for the first point in time (say, 1969) and the other for 1980:

$$LW69_i = \phi_1 + \beta_1 S69_i + \gamma_1 IQ_i + \pi_1 EXPR69_i + \varepsilon_{i1},$$
$$LW80_i = \phi_2 + \beta_2 S80_i + \gamma_2 IQ_i + \pi_2 EXPR80_i + \varepsilon_{i2}.$$

In the language of multiple equations, $S69_i$ (education in 1969) and $S80_i$ (education in 1980) are two different variables. It would be natural to entertain the case where the coefficients remained unchanged over time, with $\phi_1 = \phi_2$, $\beta_1 = \beta_2$, $\gamma_1 = \gamma_2$, $\pi_1 = \pi_2$. This is a set of linear cross-equation restrictions.

As will be shown in Section 4.3 below, testing (linear or nonlinear) cross-equation restrictions is straightforward. Estimation while imposing the restriction that the coefficients are the same across equations will be considered in Section 4.6.

Stationarity and Ergodicity

Let $\mathbf{x}_{im}$ be the vector of K_m instruments for the m-th equation. Although not frequently the case in practice, the set of instruments can differ across equations, and so the number of instruments, K_m, can depend on the equation.

Example 4.1 (continued): Suppose that IQ_i is endogenous in both equations and that there is a variable, MED_i (mother's education), that is predetermined in the first equation (so $\mathrm{E}(MED_i\, \varepsilon_{i1}) = 0$). So the instruments for the LW

equation are $(1, S_i, EXPR_i, MED_i)$. If these instruments are also orthogonal to ε_{i2}, then the *KWW* equation can be estimated with the same set of instruments as the *LW* equation. In this example, $K_1 = K_2 = 4$, and

$$\mathbf{x}_{i1} = \mathbf{x}_{i2} = \begin{bmatrix} 1 \\ S_i \\ EXPR_i \\ MED_i \end{bmatrix}. \tag{4.1.3}$$

The multiple-equation version of Assumption 3.2 is

Assumption 4.2 (ergodic stationarity): *Let* $\mathbf{w}_i$ *be unique and nonconstant elements of* $(y_{i1}, \ldots, y_{iM}, \mathbf{z}_{i1}, \ldots, \mathbf{z}_{iM}, \mathbf{x}_{i1}, \ldots, \mathbf{x}_{iM})$. $\{\mathbf{w}_i\}$ *is jointly stationary and ergodic.*

This assumption is stronger than just assuming that ergodic stationarity is satisfied for each equation of the system. Even if $\{y_{im}, \mathbf{z}_{im}, \mathbf{x}_{im}\}$ is stationary and ergodic for each individual equation m, it does not necessarily follow, strictly speaking, that the larger process $\{\mathbf{w}_i\}$, which is the union of individual processes, is (jointly) stationary and ergodic (see Example 2.3 of Chapter 2 for an example of a vector nonstationary process whose components are univariate stationary processes). In practice, the distinction is somewhat blurred because the equations often share common variables.

Example 4.1 (continued): Because $\mathbf{z}_{i1}, \mathbf{z}_{i2}, \mathbf{x}_{i1}$, and $\mathbf{x}_{i2}$ for the example have some common elements, $\mathbf{w}_i$ has only six elements: $(LW_i, KWW_i, S_i, IQ_i, EXPR_i, MED_i)$. The ergodic stationarity assumption for the first equation of this example is that $\{LW_i, S_i, IQ_i, EXPR_i, MED_i\}$ is jointly stationary and ergodic. Assumption 4.2 requires that the joint process include KWW_i.

Orthogonality Conditions

The orthogonality conditions for the M-equation system are just a collection of the orthogonality conditions for individual equations.

Assumption 4.3 (orthogonality conditions): *For each equation* m, *the* K_m *variables in* $\mathbf{x}_{im}$ *are predetermined. That is, the following orthogonality conditions are satisfied:*

$$\mathrm{E}(\mathbf{x}_{im} \cdot \varepsilon_{im}) = \mathbf{0} \quad (m = 1, 2, \ldots, M).$$

So there are $\sum_m K_m$ orthogonality conditions in total. If we define

$$\underset{(\sum_{m=1}^{M} K_m \times 1)}{\mathbf{g}_i} \equiv \begin{bmatrix} \mathbf{x}_{i1} \cdot \varepsilon_{i1} \\ \vdots \\ \mathbf{x}_{iM} \cdot \varepsilon_{iM} \end{bmatrix}, \tag{4.1.4}$$

then all those orthogonality conditions can be written compactly as $\mathrm{E}(\mathbf{g}_i) = \mathbf{0}$. Note that we are not assuming "cross" orthogonalities; for example, $\mathbf{x}_{i1}$ does not have to be orthogonal to ε_{i2}, although it is required to be orthogonal to ε_{i1}. However, if a variable is included in both $\mathbf{x}_{i1}$ and $\mathbf{x}_{i2}$, then the assumption does imply that the variable is orthogonal to both ε_{i1} and ε_{i2}.

Example 4.1 (continued): $\sum_m K_m$ in the current example is 8 $(= 4 + 4)$ and $\mathbf{g}_i$ is

$$\mathbf{g}_i = \begin{bmatrix} \varepsilon_{i1} \\ S_i\, \varepsilon_{i1} \\ EXPR_i\, \varepsilon_{i1} \\ MED_i\, \varepsilon_{i1} \\ \varepsilon_{i2} \\ S_i\, \varepsilon_{i2} \\ EXPR_i\, \varepsilon_{i2} \\ MED_i\, \varepsilon_{i2} \end{bmatrix}.$$

Because $\mathbf{x}_{i1}$ and $\mathbf{x}_{i2}$ have the same set of instruments, each instrument is orthogonal to both ε_{i1} and ε_{i2}.

Identification

Having set up the orthogonality conditions for multiple equations, we can derive the identification condition in much the same way as in the single-equation case. The multiple-equation version of (3.3.1) is

$$\mathbf{g}(\mathbf{w}_i; \boldsymbol{\delta}) \equiv \begin{bmatrix} \mathbf{x}_{i1} \cdot (y_{i1} - \mathbf{z}_{i1}'\boldsymbol{\delta}_1) \\ \vdots \\ \mathbf{x}_{iM} \cdot (y_{iM} - \mathbf{z}_{iM}'\boldsymbol{\delta}_M) \end{bmatrix}, \tag{4.1.5}$$

where $\mathbf{w}_i$ is as in Assumption 4.2, and $\boldsymbol{\delta}$ without the subscript is a stacked vector of coefficients:

$$\underset{(\sum_{m=1}^{M} L_m \times 1)}{\boldsymbol{\delta}} = \begin{bmatrix} \boldsymbol{\delta}_1 \\ \vdots \\ \boldsymbol{\delta}_M \end{bmatrix}. \tag{4.1.6}$$

So the orthogonality conditions can be written as $\mathrm{E}[\mathbf{g}(\mathbf{w}_i; \boldsymbol{\delta})] = \mathbf{0}$. The coefficient vector is identified if $\tilde{\boldsymbol{\delta}} = \boldsymbol{\delta}$ is the only solution to the system of equations

$$\mathrm{E}[\mathbf{g}(\mathbf{w}_i; \tilde{\boldsymbol{\delta}})] = \mathbf{0}. \tag{4.1.7}$$

Using the definition (4.1.5), we can rewrite the left-hand side of this equation, $\mathrm{E}[\mathbf{g}(\mathbf{w}_i; \tilde{\boldsymbol{\delta}})]$, as

$$\begin{aligned}
\mathrm{E}[\mathbf{g}(\mathbf{w}_i; \tilde{\boldsymbol{\delta}})] &\equiv \begin{bmatrix} \mathrm{E}[\mathbf{x}_{i1} \cdot (y_{i1} - \mathbf{z}_{i1}'\tilde{\boldsymbol{\delta}}_1)] \\ \vdots \\ \mathrm{E}[\mathbf{x}_{iM} \cdot (y_{iM} - \mathbf{z}_{iM}'\tilde{\boldsymbol{\delta}}_M)] \end{bmatrix} \\
&= \begin{bmatrix} \mathrm{E}(\mathbf{x}_{i1} \cdot y_{i1}) \\ \vdots \\ \mathrm{E}(\mathbf{x}_{iM} \cdot y_{iM}) \end{bmatrix} - \begin{bmatrix} \mathrm{E}(\mathbf{x}_{i1}\mathbf{z}_{i1}')\tilde{\boldsymbol{\delta}}_1 \\ \vdots \\ \mathrm{E}(\mathbf{x}_{iM}\mathbf{z}_{iM}')\tilde{\boldsymbol{\delta}}_M \end{bmatrix} \\
&= \begin{bmatrix} \mathrm{E}(\mathbf{x}_{i1} \cdot y_{i1}) \\ \vdots \\ \mathrm{E}(\mathbf{x}_{iM} \cdot y_{iM}) \end{bmatrix} - \begin{bmatrix} \mathrm{E}(\mathbf{x}_{i1}\mathbf{z}_{i1}') & & \\ & \ddots & \\ & & \mathrm{E}(\mathbf{x}_{iM}\mathbf{z}_{iM}') \end{bmatrix} \begin{bmatrix} \tilde{\boldsymbol{\delta}}_1 \\ \vdots \\ \tilde{\boldsymbol{\delta}}_M \end{bmatrix} \\
&\equiv \boldsymbol{\sigma}_{\mathbf{xy}} - \boldsymbol{\Sigma}_{\mathbf{xz}}\tilde{\boldsymbol{\delta}},
\end{aligned} \tag{4.1.8}$$

where

$$\boldsymbol{\sigma}_{\mathbf{xy}} \equiv \begin{bmatrix} \mathrm{E}(\mathbf{x}_{i1} \cdot y_{i1}) \\ \vdots \\ \mathrm{E}(\mathbf{x}_{iM} \cdot y_{iM}) \end{bmatrix}, \quad \boldsymbol{\Sigma}_{\mathbf{xz}} \equiv \begin{bmatrix} \mathrm{E}(\mathbf{x}_{i1}\mathbf{z}_{i1}') & & \\ & \ddots & \\ & & \mathrm{E}(\mathbf{x}_{iM}\mathbf{z}_{iM}') \end{bmatrix}. \tag{4.1.9}$$

(The third equality in (4.1.8) is obtained by formula (A.4) of Appendix A for multiplication of partitioned matrices.) Therefore, the system of equations determining $\tilde{\boldsymbol{\delta}}$ can be written as

$$\boldsymbol{\Sigma}_{\mathbf{xz}}\tilde{\boldsymbol{\delta}} = \boldsymbol{\sigma}_{\mathbf{xy}}, \tag{4.1.10}$$

which is the *same* in form as (3.3.4), the system of equations determining $\tilde{\boldsymbol{\delta}}$ in the single-equation case!

It then follows from the discussion of identification for the single-equation case that a necessary and sufficient condition for identification is that $\mathbf{\Sigma}_{\mathbf{xz}}$ be of full column rank. But, since $\mathbf{\Sigma}_{\mathbf{xz}}$ is block diagonal, this condition is equivalent to

Assumption 4.4 (rank condition for identification): *For each* m $(= 1, 2, \dots, M)$, $\mathrm{E}(\mathbf{x}_{im}\mathbf{z}_{im}')$ $(K_m \times L_m)$ *is of full column rank.*

It should be clear why the identification condition becomes thus. We can uniquely determine all coefficient vectors $(\boldsymbol{\delta}_1, \dots, \boldsymbol{\delta}_M)$ if and only if each coefficient vector $\boldsymbol{\delta}_m$ is uniquely determined, which occurs if and only if Assumption 3.4 holds for each equation. The rank condition is this simple because there are no *a priori* cross-equation restrictions. Identification when the coefficients are assumed to be the same across equations will be covered in Section 4.6.

The Assumption for Asymptotic Normality

As in the single-equation estimation, the orthogonality conditions need to be strengthened for asymptotic normality:

Assumption 4.5 ($\mathbf{g}_i$ is a martingale difference sequence with finite second moments): $\{\mathbf{g}_i\}$ *is a joint martingale difference sequence.* $\mathrm{E}(\mathbf{g}_i\mathbf{g}_i')$ *is nonsingular.*

The same comment that we made above about joint ergodic stationarity applies here: the assumption is stronger than requiring the same for each equation. As in the previous chapters, we use the symbol $\mathbf{S}$ for $\mathrm{Avar}(\bar{\mathbf{g}})$, the asymptotic variance of $\bar{\mathbf{g}}$ (i.e., the variance of the limiting distribution of $\sqrt{n}\,\bar{\mathbf{g}}$). By the CLT for stationary and ergodic martingale difference sequences (see Section 2.2), it equals $\mathrm{E}(\mathbf{g}_i\mathbf{g}_i')$. It has the following partitioned structure:

$$\mathbf{S} = \underset{(\sum_{m=1}^M K_m \times \sum_{m=1}^M K_m)}{\mathrm{E}(\mathbf{g}_i\mathbf{g}_i')} = \begin{bmatrix} \mathrm{E}(\varepsilon_{i1}\varepsilon_{i1}\mathbf{x}_{i1}\mathbf{x}_{i1}') & \cdots & \mathrm{E}(\varepsilon_{i1}\varepsilon_{iM}\mathbf{x}_{i1}\mathbf{x}_{iM}') \\ \vdots & & \vdots \\ \mathrm{E}(\varepsilon_{iM}\varepsilon_{i1}\mathbf{x}_{iM}\mathbf{x}_{i1}') & \cdots & \mathrm{E}(\varepsilon_{iM}\varepsilon_{iM}\mathbf{x}_{iM}\mathbf{x}_{iM}') \end{bmatrix}. \tag{4.1.11}$$

That is, the (m, h) block of $\mathbf{S}$ is $\mathrm{E}(\varepsilon_{im}\varepsilon_{ih}\mathbf{x}_{im}\mathbf{x}_{ih}')$ $(m, h = 1, 2, \dots, M)$.

In sum, the multiple-equation model is a system of equations where the assumptions we made for the single-equation model apply to each equation, with the added requirement of jointness (such as joint stationarity) where applicable.

Connection to the "Complete" System of Simultaneous Equations

The multiple-equation model presented in most other textbooks, called the "complete" system of simultaneous equations, adds more assumptions to our model. Those additional assumptions are *not* needed for the development of multiple-equation GMM, but if you are curious about them, you can at this junction make a detour to the first two subsections of Section 8.5.

4.2 Multiple-Equation GMM Defined

Derivation of the GMM estimator for multiple equations, too, can be carried out in much the same way as in the single-equation case. Let $\tilde{\boldsymbol{\delta}}$ be a hypothetical value of the true parameter vector $\boldsymbol{\delta}$ and define $\mathbf{g}_n(\tilde{\boldsymbol{\delta}})$ by (3.4.1). The definition of the GMM estimator is the same as in (3.4.5), provided that the weighting matrix $\widehat{\mathbf{W}}$ is now $\sum_m K_m \times \sum_m K_m$. In the previous section, we were able to rewrite $\mathrm{E}[\mathbf{g}(\mathbf{w}_i; \tilde{\boldsymbol{\delta}})]$ for multiple equations as a linear function of $\tilde{\boldsymbol{\delta}}$ (see (4.1.8)). We can do the same for the sample analogue $\mathbf{g}_n(\tilde{\boldsymbol{\delta}})$:

$$
\underset{(\sum_{m=1}^{M} K_m \times 1)}{\mathbf{g}_n(\tilde{\boldsymbol{\delta}})} = \begin{bmatrix} \frac{1}{n}\sum_{i=1}^{n} \mathbf{x}_{i1} \cdot (y_{i1} - \mathbf{z}_{i1}'\tilde{\boldsymbol{\delta}}_1) \\ \vdots \\ \frac{1}{n}\sum_{i=1}^{n} \mathbf{x}_{iM} \cdot (y_{iM} - \mathbf{z}_{iM}'\tilde{\boldsymbol{\delta}}_M) \end{bmatrix}
$$

$$
= \begin{bmatrix} \frac{1}{n}\sum_{i=1}^{n} \mathbf{x}_{i1} \cdot y_{i1} \\ \vdots \\ \frac{1}{n}\sum_{i=1}^{n} \mathbf{x}_{iM} \cdot y_{iM} \end{bmatrix} - \begin{bmatrix} \frac{1}{n}\sum_{i=1}^{n} \mathbf{x}_{i1}\mathbf{z}_{i1}'\tilde{\boldsymbol{\delta}}_1 \\ \vdots \\ \frac{1}{n}\sum_{i=1}^{n} \mathbf{x}_{iM}\mathbf{z}_{iM}'\tilde{\boldsymbol{\delta}}_M \end{bmatrix}
$$

$$
= \begin{bmatrix} \frac{1}{n}\sum_{i=1}^{n} \mathbf{x}_{i1} \cdot y_{i1} \\ \vdots \\ \frac{1}{n}\sum_{i=1}^{n} \mathbf{x}_{iM} \cdot y_{iM} \end{bmatrix} - \begin{bmatrix} \frac{1}{n}\sum_{i=1}^{n} \mathbf{x}_{i1}\mathbf{z}_{i1}' & & \\ & \ddots & \\ & & \frac{1}{n}\sum_{i=1}^{n} \mathbf{x}_{iM}\mathbf{z}_{iM}' \end{bmatrix} \begin{bmatrix} \tilde{\boldsymbol{\delta}}_1 \\ \vdots \\ \tilde{\boldsymbol{\delta}}_M \end{bmatrix}
$$

$$
\equiv \mathbf{s}_{\mathbf{xy}} - \mathbf{S}_{\mathbf{xz}}\tilde{\boldsymbol{\delta}}, \tag{4.2.1}
$$

where

$$\mathbf{s}_{\mathbf{xy}} \equiv \begin{bmatrix} \frac{1}{n}\sum_{i=1}^{n}\mathbf{x}_{i1}\cdot y_{i1} \\ \vdots \\ \frac{1}{n}\sum_{i=1}^{n}\mathbf{x}_{iM}\cdot y_{iM} \end{bmatrix}, \quad \mathbf{S}_{\mathbf{xz}} \equiv \begin{bmatrix} \frac{1}{n}\sum_{i=1}^{n}\mathbf{x}_{i1}\mathbf{z}'_{i1} & & \\ & \ddots & \\ & & \frac{1}{n}\sum_{i=1}^{n}\mathbf{x}_{iM}\mathbf{z}'_{iM} \end{bmatrix}. \tag{4.2.2}$$

Again, this is the *same* in form as the expression for $\mathbf{g}_n(\tilde{\boldsymbol{\delta}})$ for the single-equation case.

It follows that the results of Section 3.4 about the derivation of the GMM estimator are applicable to the multiple-equation case. In particular, just reproducing (3.4.8) and (3.4.11),

$$\text{multiple-equation GMM estimator: } \hat{\boldsymbol{\delta}}(\widehat{\mathbf{W}}) = (\mathbf{S}'_{\mathbf{xz}}\widehat{\mathbf{W}}\mathbf{S}_{\mathbf{xz}})^{-1}\mathbf{S}'_{\mathbf{xz}}\widehat{\mathbf{W}}\mathbf{s}_{\mathbf{xy}}, \tag{4.2.3}$$

$$\text{its sampling error: } \hat{\boldsymbol{\delta}}(\widehat{\mathbf{W}}) - \boldsymbol{\delta} = (\mathbf{S}'_{\mathbf{xz}}\widehat{\mathbf{W}}\mathbf{S}_{\mathbf{xz}})^{-1}\mathbf{S}'_{\mathbf{xz}}\,\widehat{\mathbf{W}}\bar{\mathbf{g}}. \tag{4.2.4}$$

The features specific to the multiple-equation GMM formula are the following: (i) $\mathbf{s}_{\mathbf{xy}}$ is a stacked vector as in (4.2.2), (ii) $\mathbf{S}_{\mathbf{xz}}$ is a block diagonal matrix as in (4.2.2), (iii) accordingly, the size of the weighting matrix $\widehat{\mathbf{W}}$ is $\sum_m K_m \times \sum_m K_m$, and (iv) $\bar{\mathbf{g}}$ in (4.2.4), the sample mean of $\mathbf{g}_i$, is the stacked vector

$$\bar{\mathbf{g}} \equiv \frac{1}{n}\sum_{i=1}^{n}\mathbf{g}_i = \begin{bmatrix} \frac{1}{n}\sum_{i=1}^{n}\mathbf{x}_{i1}\cdot\varepsilon_{i1} \\ \vdots \\ \frac{1}{n}\sum_{i=1}^{n}\mathbf{x}_{iM}\cdot\varepsilon_{iM} \end{bmatrix} = \mathbf{g}_n(\boldsymbol{\delta}). \tag{4.2.5}$$

It will be necessary to rewrite the multiple-equation GMM formula (4.2.3) while explicitly taking account of those special features. If $\widehat{\mathbf{W}}_{mh}$ $(K_m \times K_h)$ is the (m, h) block of $\widehat{\mathbf{W}}$ $(m, h = 1, 2, \ldots, M)$, then (4.2.3) can be written out in full as

$$
\hat{\boldsymbol{\delta}}(\widehat{\mathbf{W}}) = \begin{bmatrix} \hat{\boldsymbol{\delta}}_1(\widehat{\mathbf{W}}) \\ \vdots \\ \hat{\boldsymbol{\delta}}_M(\widehat{\mathbf{W}}) \end{bmatrix} = \left(\begin{bmatrix} \frac{1}{n}\sum_{i=1}^{n}\mathbf{z}_{i1}\mathbf{x}_{i1}' & & \\ & \ddots & \\ & & \frac{1}{n}\sum_{i=1}^{n}\mathbf{z}_{iM}\mathbf{x}_{iM}' \end{bmatrix} \begin{bmatrix} \widehat{\mathbf{W}}_{11} \cdots \widehat{\mathbf{W}}_{1M} \\ \vdots \quad\quad \vdots \\ \widehat{\mathbf{W}}_{M1} \cdots \widehat{\mathbf{W}}_{MM} \end{bmatrix} \begin{bmatrix} \frac{1}{n}\sum_{i=1}^{n}\mathbf{x}_{i1}\mathbf{z}_{i1}' & & \\ & \ddots & \\ & & \frac{1}{n}\sum_{i=1}^{n}\mathbf{x}_{iM}\mathbf{z}_{iM}' \end{bmatrix} \right)^{-1}
$$

$$
\begin{bmatrix} \frac{1}{n}\sum_{i=1}^{n}\mathbf{z}_{i1}\mathbf{x}_{i1}' & & \\ & \ddots & \\ & & \frac{1}{n}\sum_{i=1}^{n}\mathbf{z}_{iM}\mathbf{x}_{iM}' \end{bmatrix} \begin{bmatrix} \widehat{\mathbf{W}}_{11} \cdots \widehat{\mathbf{W}}_{1M} \\ \vdots \quad\quad \vdots \\ \widehat{\mathbf{W}}_{M1} \cdots \widehat{\mathbf{W}}_{MM} \end{bmatrix} \begin{bmatrix} \frac{1}{n}\sum_{i=1}^{n}\mathbf{x}_{i1}\cdot y_{i1} \\ \vdots \\ \frac{1}{n}\sum_{i=1}^{n}\mathbf{x}_{iM}\cdot y_{iM} \end{bmatrix}
$$

$$
= \begin{bmatrix} \left(\frac{1}{n}\sum_{i=1}^{n}\mathbf{z}_{i1}\mathbf{x}_{i1}'\right)\widehat{\mathbf{W}}_{11}\left(\frac{1}{n}\sum_{i=1}^{n}\mathbf{x}_{i1}\mathbf{z}_{i1}'\right) & \cdots & \left(\frac{1}{n}\sum_{i=1}^{n}\mathbf{z}_{i1}\mathbf{x}_{i1}'\right)\widehat{\mathbf{W}}_{1M}\left(\frac{1}{n}\sum_{i=1}^{n}\mathbf{x}_{iM}\mathbf{z}_{iM}'\right) \\ \vdots & & \vdots \\ \left(\frac{1}{n}\sum_{i=1}^{n}\mathbf{z}_{iM}\mathbf{x}_{iM}'\right)\widehat{\mathbf{W}}_{M1}\left(\frac{1}{n}\sum_{i=1}^{n}\mathbf{x}_{i1}\mathbf{z}_{i1}'\right) & \cdots & \left(\frac{1}{n}\sum_{i=1}^{n}\mathbf{z}_{iM}\mathbf{x}_{iM}'\right)\widehat{\mathbf{W}}_{MM}\left(\frac{1}{n}\sum_{i=1}^{n}\mathbf{x}_{iM}\mathbf{z}_{iM}'\right) \end{bmatrix}^{-1}
$$

$$
\begin{bmatrix} \left(\frac{1}{n}\sum_{i=1}^{n}\mathbf{z}_{i1}\mathbf{x}_{i1}'\right)\widehat{\mathbf{W}}_{11}\left(\frac{1}{n}\sum_{i=1}^{n}\mathbf{x}_{i1}y_{i1}'\right) + \cdots + \left(\frac{1}{n}\sum_{i=1}^{n}\mathbf{z}_{i1}\mathbf{x}_{i1}'\right)\widehat{\mathbf{W}}_{1M}\left(\frac{1}{n}\sum_{i=1}^{n}\mathbf{x}_{iM}y_{iM}'\right) \\ \vdots \\ \left(\frac{1}{n}\sum_{i=1}^{n}\mathbf{z}_{iM}\mathbf{x}_{iM}'\right)\widehat{\mathbf{W}}_{M1}\left(\frac{1}{n}\sum_{i=1}^{n}\mathbf{x}_{i1}\,y_{i1}\right) + \cdots + \left(\frac{1}{n}\sum_{i=1}^{n}\mathbf{z}_{iM}\mathbf{x}_{iM}'\right)\widehat{\mathbf{W}}_{MM}\left(\frac{1}{n}\sum_{i=1}^{n}\mathbf{x}_{iM}\,y_{iM}\right) \end{bmatrix}. \tag{4.2.6}
$$

To go from the second-to-last to the last line, use formulas (A.6) and (A.7) of the appendix on partitioned matrices. If you find the operation too much, just set $M = 2$.

4.3 Large-Sample Theory

Large-sample theory for the single-equation GMM was stated in Propositions 3.1–3.8. It is just a matter of mechanical substitution to translate it to the multiple-equation model. Provided that $\boldsymbol{\delta}$, $\boldsymbol{\Sigma}_{\mathbf{xz}}$, $\mathbf{S}$, $\mathbf{g}_i$, $\mathbf{s}_{\mathbf{xy}}$, and $\mathbf{S}_{\mathbf{xz}}$ are as defined in the previous sections and that "Assumption 3.x" is replaced by "Assumption 4.x," Propositions 3.1, 3.3, and 3.5–3.8 are valid as stated for the multiple-equation model. Only a few comments about their interpretation are needed.

- (Hypothesis testing) In the present case of multiple equations, $\boldsymbol{\delta}$ is a stacked vector composed of coefficients from different equations. The import of Propositions 3.3 and 3.8 about hypothesis testing for multiple equations is that we can test cross-equation restrictions.

> **Example 4.2 (continued):** For the two-equation system of wage equations for two years, the stacked coefficient vector $\boldsymbol{\delta}$ is
>
> $$\boldsymbol{\delta} = (\phi_1, \beta_1, \gamma_1, \pi_1, \phi_2, \beta_2, \gamma_2, \pi_2)'.$$
>
> It would be interesting to test H_0: $\beta_1 = \beta_2$ and $\pi_1 = \pi_2$, namely, that the schooling and experience premia remained stable over time. The hypothesis can be written as $\mathbf{R}\boldsymbol{\delta} = \mathbf{r}$, where
>
> $$\mathbf{R} = \begin{bmatrix} 0 & 1 & 0 & 0 & 0 & -1 & 0 & 0 \\ 0 & 0 & 0 & 1 & 0 & 0 & 0 & -1 \end{bmatrix}, \quad \mathbf{r} = \begin{bmatrix} 0 \\ 0 \end{bmatrix}.$$
>
> Nonlinear cross equation restrictions, too, can be tested; just use part (c) of Proposition 3.3 or Proposition 3.8.

- (Test of overidentifying restrictions) The number of orthogonality conditions is $\sum_m K_m$ and the number of coefficients is $\sum_m L_m$. Accordingly, the degrees of freedom for the J statistic in Proposition 3.6 are $\sum_m K_m - \sum_m L_m$, and that for the C statistic in Proposition 3.7 is the total number of suspect instruments from different equations.

Proposition 3.2 does not apply to multiple equations as is, but it is obvious how it can be adapted.

Proposition 4.1 (consistent estimation of contemporaneous error cross-equation moments): *Let $\hat{\boldsymbol{\delta}}_m$ be a consistent estimator of $\boldsymbol{\delta}_m$, and let $\hat{\varepsilon}_{im} \equiv y_{im} - \mathbf{z}'_{im}\hat{\boldsymbol{\delta}}_m$ be* *the implied residual for* $m = 1, 2, \ldots, M$*. Under Assumptions 4.1 and 4.2, plus the assumption that* $\mathrm{E}(\mathbf{z}_{im}\mathbf{z}_{ih}')$ *exists and is finite for all* $m, h \; (= 1, 2, \ldots, M)$,

$$\hat{\sigma}_{mh} \underset{\mathrm{p}}{\rightarrow} \sigma_{mh}, \tag{4.3.1}$$

where

$$\hat{\sigma}_{mh} \equiv \frac{1}{n}\sum_{i=1}^{n} \hat{\varepsilon}_{im}\hat{\varepsilon}_{ih} \quad \text{and} \quad \sigma_{mh} \equiv \mathrm{E}(\varepsilon_{im}\varepsilon_{ih})$$

provided that $\mathrm{E}(\varepsilon_{im}\varepsilon_{ih})$ *exists and is finite.*

The proof, very similar to the proof of Proposition 3.2 and tedious, is left as an analytical exercise.

This leaves Proposition 3.4 about consistently estimating $\mathbf{S}$. The assumption corresponding to Assumption 3.6 (the finite fourth-moment assumption) is

Assumption 4.6 (finite fourth moments): $\mathrm{E}[(x_{imk} \cdot z_{ihj})^2]$ *exists and is finite for all* $k \; (= 1, 2, \ldots, K_m)$, $j \; (= 1, 2, \ldots, L_h)$, $m, h \; (= 1, 2, \ldots, M)$, *where* x_{imk} *is the* k*-th element of* $\mathbf{x}_{im}$ *and* z_{ihj} *is the* j*-th element of* $\mathbf{z}_{ih}$.

The multiple-equation version of the formula (3.5.10) for consistently estimating $\mathbf{S}$ is

$$\widehat{\mathbf{S}} = \begin{bmatrix} \frac{1}{n}\sum_{i=1}^{n} \hat{\varepsilon}_{i1}\hat{\varepsilon}_{i1}\mathbf{x}_{i1}\mathbf{x}_{i1}' & \cdots & \frac{1}{n}\sum_{i=1}^{n} \hat{\varepsilon}_{i1}\hat{\varepsilon}_{iM}\mathbf{x}_{i1}\mathbf{x}_{iM}' \\ \vdots & & \vdots \\ \frac{1}{n}\sum_{i=1}^{n} \hat{\varepsilon}_{iM}\hat{\varepsilon}_{i1}\mathbf{x}_{iM}\mathbf{x}_{i1}' & \cdots & \frac{1}{n}\sum_{i=1}^{n} \hat{\varepsilon}_{iM}\hat{\varepsilon}_{iM}\mathbf{x}_{iM}\mathbf{x}_{iM}' \end{bmatrix}, \tag{4.3.2}$$

for some consistent estimate $\hat{\varepsilon}_{im}$ of ε_{im}.

Proposition 4.2 (consistent estimation of S, the asymptotic variance of $\bar{\mathbf{g}}$): *Let* $\hat{\boldsymbol{\delta}}_m$ *be a consistent estimator of* $\boldsymbol{\delta}_m$*, and let* $\hat{\varepsilon}_{im} \equiv y_{im} - \mathbf{z}_{im}'\hat{\boldsymbol{\delta}}_m$ *be the implied residual for* $m = 1, 2, \ldots, M$*. Under Assumptions 4.1, 4.2, and 4.6,* $\widehat{\mathbf{S}}$ *given in (4.3.2) is consistent for* $\mathbf{S}$.

We will not give a proof; the technique is very similar to the one used in the proof of Proposition 2.4.

Table 4.1: Multiple-Equation GMM in the Single-Equation Format

Sample Analogue of Orthogonality Conditions: $\mathbf{g}_n(\tilde{\boldsymbol{\delta}}) = \mathbf{s_{xy}} - \mathbf{S_{xz}}\tilde{\boldsymbol{\delta}} = \mathbf{0}$

GMM Estimator: $\hat{\boldsymbol{\delta}}(\widehat{\mathbf{W}}) = (\mathbf{S}'_{\mathbf{xz}}\widehat{\mathbf{W}}\mathbf{S_{xz}})^{-1}\mathbf{S}'_{\mathbf{xz}}\widehat{\mathbf{W}}\mathbf{s_{xy}}$

Its Sampling Error: $\hat{\boldsymbol{\delta}}(\widehat{\mathbf{W}}) - \boldsymbol{\delta} = (\mathbf{S}'_{\mathbf{xz}}\widehat{\mathbf{W}}\mathbf{S_{xz}})^{-1}\mathbf{S}'_{\mathbf{xz}}\widehat{\mathbf{W}}\bar{\mathbf{g}}$

Asymptotic Variance of Optimal GMM: $\text{Avar}(\hat{\boldsymbol{\delta}}(\widehat{\mathbf{S}}^{-1})) = (\boldsymbol{\Sigma}'_{\mathbf{xz}}\mathbf{S}^{-1}\boldsymbol{\Sigma}_{\mathbf{xz}})^{-1}$

Its Estimator: $\widehat{\text{Avar}(\hat{\boldsymbol{\delta}}(\widehat{\mathbf{S}}^{-1}))} = (\mathbf{S}'_{\mathbf{xz}}\widehat{\mathbf{S}}^{-1}\mathbf{S_{xz}})^{-1}$

J Statistic: $J(\hat{\boldsymbol{\delta}}(\widehat{\mathbf{S}}^{-1}), \widehat{\mathbf{S}}^{-1}) \equiv n \cdot \mathbf{g}_n(\hat{\boldsymbol{\delta}}(\widehat{\mathbf{S}}^{-1}))'\widehat{\mathbf{S}}^{-1}\mathbf{g}_n(\hat{\boldsymbol{\delta}}(\widehat{\mathbf{S}}^{-1}))$

	Single-Equation GMM applied to the equation in question	Multiple-Equation GMM
$\mathbf{g}_i$	$\mathbf{x}_i \cdot \varepsilon_i$	(4.1.4)
$\boldsymbol{\delta}$	$\boldsymbol{\delta}$	(4.1.6)
$\mathbf{s_{xy}}$	$\frac{1}{n}\sum_{i=1}^{n}\mathbf{x}_i \cdot y_i$	(4.2.2)
$\mathbf{S_{xz}}$	$\frac{1}{n}\sum_{i=1}^{n}\mathbf{x}_i\mathbf{z}'_i$	(4.2.2)
Size of $\mathbf{W}$	$K \times K$	$\sum_m K_m \times \sum_m K_m$
$\boldsymbol{\Sigma}_{\mathbf{xz}}$	$\text{E}(\mathbf{x}_i\mathbf{z}'_i)$	(4.1.9)
$\mathbf{S}$ ($\equiv \text{Avar}(\bar{\mathbf{g}})$)	$\text{E}(\varepsilon_i^2\mathbf{x}_i\mathbf{x}'_i)$	(4.1.11)
$\widehat{\mathbf{S}}$	$\frac{1}{n}\sum_{i=1}^{n}\hat{\varepsilon}_i^2\mathbf{x}_i\mathbf{x}'_i$	(4.3.2)
Estimator consistent under which assumptions?	3.1–3.4	4.1–4.4
Estimator asymptotic normal under which assumptions?	3.1–3.5	4.1–4.5
$\widehat{\mathbf{S}} \to_{\text{p}} \mathbf{S}$ under which assumptions?	3.1, 3.2, 3.6, $\text{E}(\mathbf{g}_i\mathbf{g}'_i)$ finite	4.1, 4.2, 4.6, $\text{E}(\mathbf{g}_i\mathbf{g}'_i)$ finite
d.f. of J	$K - L$	$\sum_m(K_m - L_m)$

Since this $\widehat{\mathbf{S}}$ is consistent for $\mathbf{S}$, the multiple-equation GMM estimator, using $\widehat{\mathbf{S}}^{-1}$ as the weighting matrix, $\hat{\boldsymbol{\delta}}(\widehat{\mathbf{S}}^{-1})$, is an efficient multiple-equation GMM estimator with minimum asymptotic variance. The formulas for the asymptotic variance and its consistent estimator are (3.5.13) and (3.5.14), which are reproduced here for convenience:

$$\text{Avar}(\hat{\boldsymbol{\delta}}(\widehat{\mathbf{S}}^{-1})) = (\boldsymbol{\Sigma}'_{\mathbf{xz}}\mathbf{S}^{-1}\boldsymbol{\Sigma}_{\mathbf{xz}})^{-1}, \tag{4.3.3}$$

$$\widehat{\text{Avar}(\hat{\boldsymbol{\delta}}(\widehat{\mathbf{S}}^{-1}))} = (\mathbf{S}'_{\mathbf{xz}}\widehat{\mathbf{S}}^{-1}\mathbf{S}_{\mathbf{xz}})^{-1}. \tag{4.3.4}$$

To recapitulate, the features specific to the multiple-equation GMM are: $\boldsymbol{\Sigma}_{\mathbf{xz}}$ is a block diagonal matrix given by (4.1.9), $\mathbf{S}$ is given by (4.1.11), $\mathbf{s}_{\mathbf{xy}}$ and $\mathbf{S}_{\mathbf{xz}}$ by (4.2.2), and $\widehat{\mathbf{S}}$ by (4.3.2). For the initial estimator $\hat{\boldsymbol{\delta}}_m$ needed to calculate $\hat{\varepsilon}_{im}$ and $\widehat{\mathbf{S}}$, we can use the FIVE estimator (to be presented below) or the efficient single-equation GMM applied to each equation separately. Of course, as long as it is consistent, the choice of the initial estimator does not affect the asymptotic distribution of the efficient GMM estimator.

Table 4.1 summarizes the results of this chapter so far.

4.4 Single-Equation versus Multiple-Equation Estimation

An obvious alternative to multiple-equation GMM, which estimates the stacked coefficient vector $\boldsymbol{\delta}$ ($\sum_m L_m \times 1$) jointly, is to apply the single-equation GMM separately to each equation and then stack the estimated coefficients. If the weighting matrix in the single-equation GMM for the m-th equation is $\widehat{\mathbf{W}}_{mm}$ ($K_m \times K_m$), the resulting equation-by-equation GMM estimator of the stacked coefficient vector $\boldsymbol{\delta}$ can be written as the multiple-equation GMM estimator $\hat{\boldsymbol{\delta}}(\widehat{\mathbf{W}})$ given in (4.2.3), where the $\sum_m K_m \times \sum_m K_m$ weighting matrix $\widehat{\mathbf{W}}$ is a block diagonal matrix whose m-th block is $\widehat{\mathbf{W}}_{mm}$:

$$\widehat{\mathbf{W}} = \begin{bmatrix} \widehat{\mathbf{W}}_{11} & & \\ & \ddots & \\ & & \widehat{\mathbf{W}}_{MM} \end{bmatrix}. \tag{4.4.1}$$

This is because both $\mathbf{S}_{\mathbf{xz}}$ ($\sum_m K_m \times \sum_m L_m$) and $\widehat{\mathbf{W}}$ are block diagonal. (The reader should actually substitute the expressions (4.2.2) for $\mathbf{S}_{\mathbf{xz}}$ and (4.4.1) for $\widehat{\mathbf{W}}$ into (4.2.3) to verify that $\mathbf{S}'_{\mathbf{xz}}\widehat{\mathbf{W}}\mathbf{S}_{\mathbf{xz}}$ and hence $(\mathbf{S}'_{\mathbf{xz}}\widehat{\mathbf{W}}\mathbf{S}_{\mathbf{xz}})^{-1}\mathbf{S}'_{\mathbf{xz}}\widehat{\mathbf{W}}$ are block diagonal, using formulas (A.5) and (A.9) of Appendix A. Set $M = 2$ if it makes it easier.)

Therefore, the difference between the multiple-equation GMM and the equation-by-equation GMM estimation of the stacked coefficient vector $\boldsymbol{\delta}$ lies in the choice of the $\sum_m K_m \times \sum_m K_m$ weighting matrix $\widehat{\mathbf{W}}$. Put differently, the equation-by-equation GMM is a particular multiple-equation GMM.

When Are They "Equivalent"?

As seen in Chapter 3, if the equation is just identified, the choice of the weighting matrix $\widehat{\mathbf{W}}$ does not matter because the GMM estimator, regardless of the choice of $\widehat{\mathbf{W}}$, numerically equals the IV estimator. The same is true for multiple-equation GMM: if each equation of the system is exactly identified so that $L_m = K_m$ for all m, then $\mathbf{S_{xz}}$ in the GMM formula (4.2.3) is a square matrix and the GMM estimator for any choice of $\widehat{\mathbf{W}}$ becomes the multiple-equation IV estimator $\mathbf{S}_{\mathbf{xz}}^{-1}\mathbf{s_{xy}}$ (and, since $\mathbf{S_{xz}}$ is block diagonal, the estimator is just a collection of single-equation IV estimators).

On the other hand, if at least one of the M equations is overidentified, the choice of $\widehat{\mathbf{W}}$ ($\sum_m K_m \times \sum_m K_m$) does affect the numerical value of the GMM estimator. Consider the efficient equation-by-equation GMM estimator of $\boldsymbol{\delta}$ ($\sum_m L_m \times 1$), where each equation is estimated by the efficient single-equation GMM with an optimal choice of $\widehat{\mathbf{W}}_{mm}$ ($m = 1, 2, \dots, M$). Is it as efficient as the efficient multiple-equation GMM? The equation-by-equation estimator can be written as $\hat{\boldsymbol{\delta}}(\widehat{\mathbf{W}})$, where the $\sum_m K_m \times \sum_m K_m$ block diagonal weighting matrix $\widehat{\mathbf{W}}$ satisfies

$$\operatorname*{plim}_{n\to\infty} \widehat{\mathbf{W}} = \begin{bmatrix} \left(\mathrm{E}(\varepsilon_{i1}^2 \mathbf{x}_{i1}\mathbf{x}_{i1}')\right)^{-1} & & \\ & \ddots & \\ & & \left(\mathrm{E}(\varepsilon_{iM}^2 \mathbf{x}_{iM}\mathbf{x}_{iM}')\right)^{-1} \end{bmatrix}. \tag{4.4.2}$$

Because this plim is not necessarily equal to $\mathbf{S}^{-1}$ (unless (4.4.3) below holds), the estimator is generally less efficient than the efficient multiple-equation GMM estimator $\hat{\boldsymbol{\delta}}(\widehat{\mathbf{S}}^{-1})$, where $\widehat{\mathbf{S}}$ is a consistent estimator of $\mathbf{S}$. But if the equations are "unrelated"[1] in the sense that

$$\mathrm{E}(\varepsilon_{im}\varepsilon_{ih}\mathbf{x}_{im}\mathbf{x}_{ih}') = \mathbf{0} \quad \text{for all } m \neq h \ (= 1, 2, \dots, M), \tag{4.4.3}$$

then $\mathbf{S}$ becomes block diagonal and for the weighting matrix $\widehat{\mathbf{W}}$ defined above $\operatorname{plim} \widehat{\mathbf{W}} = \mathbf{S}^{-1}$. Since in this case $\widehat{\mathbf{W}} - \widehat{\mathbf{S}}^{-1} \to_{\mathrm{p}} \mathbf{0}$, we have (as we proved in Review Question 3 of Section 3.5)

[1]Under conditional homoskedasticity, this condition becomes the more familiar condition that $\mathrm{E}(\varepsilon_{im}\varepsilon_{ih}) = 0$. See the next section.

$$\sqrt{n}\,\hat{\boldsymbol{\delta}}(\widehat{\mathbf{W}}) - \sqrt{n}\,\hat{\boldsymbol{\delta}}(\widehat{\mathbf{S}}^{-1}) \underset{\mathrm{p}}{\to} \mathbf{0}.$$

It then follows from Lemma 2.4(a) that the asymptotic distribution of $\hat{\boldsymbol{\delta}}(\widehat{\mathbf{W}})$ is the same as that of $\hat{\boldsymbol{\delta}}(\widehat{\mathbf{S}}^{-1})$, so the efficient equation-by-equation GMM estimator is an efficient multiple-equation GMM estimator.

We summarize the discussion so far as

Proposition 4.3 (equivalence between single-equation and multiple-equation GMM):

(a) If all equations are just identified, then the equation-by-equation GMM and the multiple-equation GMM are numerically the same *and equal to the* IV *estimator.*

(b) If at least one equation is overidentified but the equations are "unrelated" in the sense of (4.4.3), then the efficient equation-by-equation GMM and the efficient multiple-equation GMM are asymptotically equivalent in that $\sqrt{n}$ times the difference converges to zero in probability.

For those two cases, there is no efficiency gain from joint estimation. Furthermore, if it is known *a priori* that the equations are "unrelated," then the equation-by-equation estimation should be preferred, because exploiting the *a priori* knowledge by requiring the off-diagonal blocks of $\widehat{\mathbf{W}}$ to be zeros (which is what the equation-by-equation estimation entails) will most likely improve the finite-sample properties of the estimator.

Joint Estimation Can Be Hazardous

Except for cases (a) and (b), joint estimation is asymptotically more efficient. Even if you are interested in estimating one particular equation (say, the *LW* equation in Example 4.1), you can generally gain asymptotic efficiency by combining it with some other equations (see, however, Analytical Exercise 10 for an example where joint estimation entails no efficiency gain even if the added equations are not unrelated).

There are caveats, however. First of all, the small-sample properties of the coefficient estimates of the equation in question might be better without joint estimation. Second, the asymptotic result presumes that the model is **correctly specified**, that is, all the model assumptions are satisfied. If the model is misspecified, neither the single-equation GMM nor the multiple-equation GMM is guaranteed even to be consistent. And chances of misspecification increase as you add equations to the system.

To illustrate this second point, suppose Assumption 4.3 does not hold because, only for the M-th equation, the orthogonality conditions do not hold: $\mathrm{E}(\mathbf{x}_{iM} \cdot \varepsilon_{iM}) \neq \mathbf{0}$. This may come about if, for example, the equation omits a variable that should have been included as a regressor. To see that this leads to possible inconsistency for *all* equations, examine the formula (4.2.4) for the sampling error where $\bar{\mathbf{g}}$ is given by (4.2.5). The M-th block of $\text{plim}_{n\to\infty} \bar{\mathbf{g}}$ is not zero. Since $\text{plim}\, \mathbf{S}_{\mathbf{xz}} = \boldsymbol{\Sigma}_{\mathbf{xz}}$ under ergodic stationarity and $\text{plim}\, \widehat{\mathbf{W}} = \mathbf{W}$ by assumption, the asymptotic bias is

$$\underset{n\to\infty}{\text{plim}}\, \hat{\boldsymbol{\delta}}(\widehat{\mathbf{W}}) - \boldsymbol{\delta} = (\boldsymbol{\Sigma}'_{\mathbf{xz}} \mathbf{W} \boldsymbol{\Sigma}_{\mathbf{xz}})^{-1} \boldsymbol{\Sigma}'_{\mathbf{xz}} \mathbf{W} \begin{bmatrix} \mathbf{0} \\ \vdots \\ \mathbf{0} \\ \mathrm{E}(\mathbf{x}_{iM} \cdot \varepsilon_{iM}) \end{bmatrix}. \tag{4.4.4}$$

In efficient multiple-equation GMM, $\mathbf{W}$—hence $(\boldsymbol{\Sigma}'_{\mathbf{xz}} \mathbf{W} \boldsymbol{\Sigma}_{\mathbf{xz}})^{-1} \boldsymbol{\Sigma}'_{\mathbf{xz}} \mathbf{W}$—are not generally block diagonal, so any element of $\text{plim}_{n\to\infty}\, \hat{\boldsymbol{\delta}}(\widehat{\mathbf{W}}) - \boldsymbol{\delta}$ can be different from zero. Even for the coefficients of the equations of interest involving no misspecification the asymptotic bias may not be zero. That is, in joint estimation, biases due to a local misspecification contaminate the rest of the system. This problem does not arise for the equation-by-equation GMM which constrains $\widehat{\mathbf{W}}$ to be block diagonal.

QUESTION FOR REVIEW

1. Express the equation-by-equation 2SLS estimator in the form (4.2.3) by suitably specifying $\widehat{\mathbf{W}}_{mm}$'s in (4.4.1). [Answer: $\widehat{\mathbf{W}}_{mm} = \left(\frac{1}{n} \sum_{i=1}^{n} \mathbf{x}_{im} \mathbf{x}'_{im}\right)^{-1}$.]

4.5 Special Cases of Multiple-Equation GMM: FIVE, 3SLS, and SUR

Conditional Homoskedasticity

Under conditional homoskedasticity, we can easily derive a number of prominent estimators as special cases of multiple-equation GMM. The multiple-equation version of conditional homoskedasticity is

Assumption 4.7 (conditional homoskedasticity):

$$\mathrm{E}(\varepsilon_{im}\, \varepsilon_{ih} \mid \mathbf{x}_{im}, \mathbf{x}_{ih}) = \sigma_{mh}$$

for all $m, h = 1, 2, \ldots, M$.

Then the unconditional cross moment $\mathrm{E}(\varepsilon_{im}\varepsilon_{ih})$ equals σ_{mh} by the Law of Total Expectations. You should have no trouble showing that

$$\begin{aligned}
&(m, h) \text{ block of } \mathrm{E}(\mathbf{g}_i\mathbf{g}_i') \text{ given in (4.1.11)} \\
&\quad = \mathrm{E}(\varepsilon_{im}\varepsilon_{ih}\mathbf{x}_{im}\mathbf{x}_{ih}') \\
&\quad = \mathrm{E}[\mathrm{E}(\varepsilon_{im}\varepsilon_{ih}\mathbf{x}_{im}\mathbf{x}_{ih}' \mid \mathbf{x}_{im}, \mathbf{x}_{ih})] \quad \text{(by the Law of Total Expectations)} \\
&\quad = \mathrm{E}[\mathrm{E}(\varepsilon_{im}\varepsilon_{ih} \mid \mathbf{x}_{im}, \mathbf{x}_{ih})\mathbf{x}_{im}\mathbf{x}_{ih}'] \quad \text{(by linearity of conditional expectations)} \\
&\quad = \mathrm{E}[\sigma_{mh}\mathbf{x}_{im}\mathbf{x}_{ih}'] \quad \text{(by conditional homoskedasticity)} \\
&\quad = \sigma_{mh}\,\mathrm{E}(\mathbf{x}_{im}\mathbf{x}_{ih}') \quad \text{(by linearity of expectations).} \qquad (4.5.1)
\end{aligned}$$

Thus, the $\mathbf{S}$ in (4.1.11) can be written as

$$\mathbf{S} = \begin{bmatrix} \sigma_{11}\,\mathrm{E}(\mathbf{x}_{i1}\mathbf{x}_{i1}') & \cdots & \sigma_{1M}\,\mathrm{E}(\mathbf{x}_{i1}\mathbf{x}_{iM}') \\ \vdots & & \vdots \\ \sigma_{M1}\,\mathrm{E}(\mathbf{x}_{iM}\mathbf{x}_{i1}') & \cdots & \sigma_{MM}\,\mathrm{E}(\mathbf{x}_{iM}\mathbf{x}_{iM}') \end{bmatrix}. \qquad (4.5.2)$$

Since by Assumption 4.5 $\mathbf{S}$ is finite, this decomposition implies that $\mathrm{E}(\mathbf{x}_{im}\mathbf{x}_{ih}')$ exists and is finite for all m, h $(= 1, 2, \dots, M)$.

Full-Information Instrumental Variables Efficient (FIVE)

An estimator of $\mathbf{S}$ exploiting the structure of fourth moments shown in (4.5.2) is

$$\widehat{\mathbf{S}} = \begin{bmatrix} \hat{\sigma}_{11}\cdot\left(\frac{1}{n}\sum_{i=1}^{n}\mathbf{x}_{i1}\mathbf{x}_{i1}'\right) & \cdots & \hat{\sigma}_{1M}\cdot\left(\frac{1}{n}\sum_{i=1}^{n}\mathbf{x}_{i1}\mathbf{x}_{iM}'\right) \\ \vdots & & \vdots \\ \hat{\sigma}_{M1}\cdot\left(\frac{1}{n}\sum_{i=1}^{n}\mathbf{x}_{iM}\mathbf{x}_{i1}'\right) & \cdots & \hat{\sigma}_{MM}\cdot\left(\frac{1}{n}\sum_{i=1}^{n}\mathbf{x}_{iM}\mathbf{x}_{iM}'\right) \end{bmatrix}, \qquad (4.5.3)$$

where, for some consistent estimator $\hat{\boldsymbol{\delta}}_m$ of $\boldsymbol{\delta}$,

$$\hat{\sigma}_{mh} \equiv \frac{1}{n}\sum_{i=1}^{n}\hat{\varepsilon}_{im}\,\hat{\varepsilon}_{ih},\ \hat{\varepsilon}_{im} \equiv y_{im} - \mathbf{z}_{im}'\hat{\boldsymbol{\delta}}_m \quad (m, h = 1, 2, \dots, M). \qquad (4.5.4)$$

By Proposition 4.1, $\hat{\sigma}_{mh} \to_{\mathrm{p}} \sigma_{mh}$ provided (in addition to Assumptions 4.1 and 4.2) that $\mathrm{E}(\mathbf{z}_{im}\mathbf{z}_{ih}')$ is finite. By ergodic stationarity, $\frac{1}{n}\sum_i \mathbf{x}_{im}\mathbf{x}_{ih}'$ converges in probability to $\mathrm{E}(\mathbf{x}_{im}\mathbf{x}_{ih}')$, which, as just noted, exists and is finite. Therefore, (4.5.3) is consistent for $\mathbf{S}$, without the fourth-moment assumption (Assumption 4.6).

The **FIVE estimator** of $\boldsymbol{\delta}$, denoted $\hat{\boldsymbol{\delta}}_{\text{FIVE}}$, is

$$\hat{\boldsymbol{\delta}}_{\text{FIVE}} \equiv \hat{\boldsymbol{\delta}}(\widehat{\mathbf{S}}^{-1})$$

with $\widehat{\mathbf{S}}$ given by (4.5.3) to exploit conditional homoskedasticity.[2] Being a multiple-equation GMM for some choice of $\widehat{\mathbf{W}}$, it is consistent and asymptotically normal by (the multiple-equation adaptation of) Proposition 3.1. Because $\widehat{\mathbf{S}}$ is consistent for $\mathbf{S}$, the estimator is efficient by Proposition 3.5. Thus, we have proved

Proposition 4.4 (large-sample properties of FIVE): *Suppose Assumptions 4.1–4.5 and 4.7 hold. Suppose, furthermore, that* $\text{E}(\mathbf{z}_{im}\mathbf{z}_{ih}')$ *exists and is finite for all* $m, h\ (= 1, 2, \ldots, M)$.[3] *Let* $\mathbf{S}$ *and* $\widehat{\mathbf{S}}$ *be as in (4.5.2) and (4.5.3), respectively. Then*

(a) $\widehat{\mathbf{S}} \to_{\text{p}} \mathbf{S}$;

(b) $\hat{\boldsymbol{\delta}}_{\text{FIVE}}$, *defined as* $\hat{\boldsymbol{\delta}}(\widehat{\mathbf{S}}^{-1})$, *is consistent, asymptotically normal, and efficient, with* $\text{Avar}(\hat{\boldsymbol{\delta}}_{\text{FIVE}})$ *given by (4.3.3);*

(c) The estimated asymptotic variance given in (4.3.4) is consistent for $\text{Avar}(\hat{\boldsymbol{\delta}}_{\text{FIVE}})$;

(d) (Sargan's statistic)

$$J(\hat{\boldsymbol{\delta}}_{\text{FIVE}}, \widehat{\mathbf{S}}^{-1}) \equiv n \cdot \mathbf{g}_n(\hat{\boldsymbol{\delta}}_{\text{FIVE}})' \widehat{\mathbf{S}}^{-1} \mathbf{g}_n(\hat{\boldsymbol{\delta}}_{\text{FIVE}}) \underset{\text{d}}{\to} \chi^2\Big(\sum_m (K_m - L_m)\Big),$$

where $\mathbf{g}_n(\cdot)$ *is given in (4.2.1).*

Usually, the initial estimator $\hat{\boldsymbol{\delta}}_m$ needed to calculate $\widehat{\mathbf{S}}$ is the 2SLS estimator.

Three-Stage Least Squares (3SLS)

When the set of instruments is the same across equations, the FIVE formula can be simplified somewhat. The simplified formula is the **3SLS estimator**, denoted $\hat{\boldsymbol{\delta}}_{\text{3SLS}}$.[4] To this end, let

$$\underset{(M\times 1)}{\boldsymbol{\varepsilon}_i} \equiv \begin{bmatrix} \varepsilon_{i1} \\ \vdots \\ \varepsilon_{iM} \end{bmatrix}. \tag{4.5.5}$$

[2]The estimator is due to Brundy and Jorgenson (1971).

[3]This assumption is needed for $\hat{\sigma}_{mh}$ to be consistent. See Proposition 4.1.

[4]The estimator is due to Zellner and Theil (1962).

Then the $M \times M$ matrix of cross moments of $\boldsymbol{\varepsilon}_i$, denoted $\boldsymbol{\Sigma}$, can be written as

$$\underset{(M\times M)}{\boldsymbol{\Sigma}} \equiv \begin{bmatrix} \sigma_{11} & \cdots & \sigma_{1M} \\ \vdots & & \vdots \\ \sigma_{M1} & \cdots & \sigma_{MM} \end{bmatrix} = \mathrm{E}(\boldsymbol{\varepsilon}_i \boldsymbol{\varepsilon}_i'). \tag{4.5.6}$$

To estimate $\boldsymbol{\Sigma}$ consistently, we need an initial consistent estimator of $\boldsymbol{\delta}_m$ for the purpose of calculating the residual $\hat{\varepsilon}_{im}$. The term 3SLS comes from the fact that the 2SLS estimator of $\boldsymbol{\delta}_m$ is used as the initial estimator. Given the residuals thus calculated, a natural estimator of $\boldsymbol{\Sigma}$ is

$$\widehat{\boldsymbol{\Sigma}} \equiv \begin{bmatrix} \hat{\sigma}_{11} & \cdots & \hat{\sigma}_{1M} \\ \vdots & & \vdots \\ \hat{\sigma}_{M1} & \cdots & \hat{\sigma}_{MM} \end{bmatrix} = \frac{1}{n}\sum_{i=1}^{n} \hat{\boldsymbol{\varepsilon}}_i \hat{\boldsymbol{\varepsilon}}_i', \tag{4.5.7}$$

which is a matrix whose (m, h) element is the estimated cross moment given in (4.5.4).

If $\mathbf{x}_i$ $(= \mathbf{x}_{i1} = \mathbf{x}_{i2} = \cdots = \mathbf{x}_{iM})$ is the common set of instruments with dimension K, then $\mathbf{g}_i$ in (4.1.4), $\mathbf{S}$ in (4.5.2), and $\widehat{\mathbf{S}}$ in (4.5.3) can be written compactly using the Kronecker product[5] as

$$\underset{(MK\times 1)}{\mathbf{g}_i} = \boldsymbol{\varepsilon}_i \otimes \mathbf{x}_i, \tag{4.5.8}$$

$$\underset{(MK\times MK)}{\mathbf{S}} = \underset{(M\times M)}{\boldsymbol{\Sigma}} \otimes \underset{(K\times K)}{\mathrm{E}(\mathbf{x}_i\mathbf{x}_i')}, \tag{4.5.9}$$

so $\mathbf{S}^{-1} = \boldsymbol{\Sigma}^{-1} \otimes \left[\mathrm{E}(\mathbf{x}_i\mathbf{x}_i')\right]^{-1}$,

$$\widehat{\mathbf{S}} = \widehat{\boldsymbol{\Sigma}} \otimes \left(\frac{1}{n}\sum_{i=1}^{n} \mathbf{x}_i\mathbf{x}_i'\right), \tag{4.5.10}$$

so $\widehat{\mathbf{S}}^{-1} = \widehat{\boldsymbol{\Sigma}}^{-1} \otimes (\frac{1}{n}\sum_{i=1}^{n} \mathbf{x}_i\mathbf{x}_i')^{-1}$. The Kronecker product decomposition (4.5.9) of $\mathbf{S}$ and the nonsingularity of $\mathbf{S}$ (by Assumption 4.5) imply that both $\boldsymbol{\Sigma}$ and $\mathrm{E}(\mathbf{x}_i\mathbf{x}_i')$ are nonsingular.

To achieve further rewriting of the 3SLS formulas, we need to go back to (4.2.6), which, with $\widehat{\mathbf{W}} = \widehat{\mathbf{S}}^{-1}$, writes out in full the efficient multiple-equation GMM estimator. The formula (4.5.10) implies that the $\widehat{\mathbf{W}}$ in (4.2.6) is such that

[5] See formulas (A.11) and (A.15) of the Appendix if you are not familiar with the Kronecker product notation.

$$\widehat{\mathbf{W}}_{mh} \; (\equiv (m,h) \text{ block of } \widehat{\mathbf{W}}) = \hat{\sigma}^{mh} \cdot \Bigl(\frac{1}{n}\sum_{i=1}^{n} \mathbf{x}_i \mathbf{x}_i'\Bigr)^{-1}, \tag{4.5.11}$$

where $\hat{\sigma}^{mh}$ is the (m, h) element of $\widehat{\mathbf{\Sigma}}^{-1}$. Substitute this into (4.2.6) to obtain

$$\hat{\boldsymbol{\delta}}_{3\text{SLS}} = \begin{bmatrix} \hat{\sigma}^{11}\widehat{\mathbf{A}}_{11} & \cdots & \hat{\sigma}^{1M}\widehat{\mathbf{A}}_{1M} \\ \vdots & & \vdots \\ \hat{\sigma}^{M1}\widehat{\mathbf{A}}_{M1} & \cdots & \hat{\sigma}^{MM}\widehat{\mathbf{A}}_{MM} \end{bmatrix}^{-1} \begin{bmatrix} \hat{\sigma}^{11}\hat{\mathbf{c}}_{11} & + \cdots + & \hat{\sigma}^{1M}\hat{\mathbf{c}}_{1M} \\ \vdots & & \vdots \\ \hat{\sigma}^{M1}\hat{\mathbf{c}}_{M1} & + \cdots + & \hat{\sigma}^{MM}\hat{\mathbf{c}}_{MM} \end{bmatrix}, \tag{4.5.12}$$

where

$$\widehat{\mathbf{A}}_{mh} \equiv \underset{(L_m \times K)}{\Bigl(\frac{1}{n}\sum_{i=1}^{n} \mathbf{z}_{im}\mathbf{x}_i'\Bigr)} \underset{(K \times K)}{\Bigl(\frac{1}{n}\sum_{i=1}^{n} \mathbf{x}_i\mathbf{x}_i'\Bigr)^{-1}} \underset{(K \times L_h)}{\Bigl(\frac{1}{n}\sum_{i=1}^{n} \mathbf{x}_i\mathbf{z}_{ih}'\Bigr)}, \tag{4.5.13}$$

$$\hat{\mathbf{c}}_{mh} \equiv \underset{(L_m \times K)}{\Bigl(\frac{1}{n}\sum_{i=1}^{n} \mathbf{z}_{im}\mathbf{x}_i'\Bigr)} \underset{(K \times K)}{\Bigl(\frac{1}{n}\sum_{i=1}^{n} \mathbf{x}_i\mathbf{x}_i'\Bigr)^{-1}} \underset{(K \times 1)}{\Bigl(\frac{1}{n}\sum_{i=1}^{n} \mathbf{x}_i \cdot y_{ih}\Bigr)}. \tag{4.5.14}$$

Similarly, substituting into (4.3.3) the expression for $\mathbf{\Sigma}_{\mathbf{xz}}$ in (4.1.9) and the expression for $\mathbf{S}$ in (4.5.9) and using formula (A.6) of the Appendix, we obtain the expressions for $\text{Avar}(\hat{\boldsymbol{\delta}}_{3\text{SLS}})$:

$$\text{Avar}(\hat{\boldsymbol{\delta}}_{3\text{SLS}}) = \begin{bmatrix} \sigma^{11}\mathbf{A}_{11} & \cdots & \sigma^{1M}\mathbf{A}_{1M} \\ \vdots & & \vdots \\ \sigma^{M1}\mathbf{A}_{M1} & \cdots & \sigma^{MM}\mathbf{A}_{MM} \end{bmatrix}^{-1} \tag{4.5.15}$$

where

$$\mathbf{A}_{mh} \equiv \text{E}(\mathbf{z}_{im}\mathbf{x}_i') \left[\text{E}(\mathbf{x}_i\mathbf{x}_i')\right]^{-1} \text{E}(\mathbf{x}_i\mathbf{z}_{ih}'), \tag{4.5.16}$$

and σ^{mh} is the (m, h) element of $\mathbf{\Sigma}^{-1}$. This is consistently estimated by

$$\widehat{\text{Avar}(\hat{\boldsymbol{\delta}}_{3\text{SLS}})} = \begin{bmatrix} \hat{\sigma}^{11}\widehat{\mathbf{A}}_{11} & \cdots & \hat{\sigma}^{1M}\widehat{\mathbf{A}}_{1M} \\ \vdots & & \vdots \\ \hat{\sigma}^{M1}\widehat{\mathbf{A}}_{M1} & \cdots & \hat{\sigma}^{MM}\widehat{\mathbf{A}}_{MM} \end{bmatrix}^{-1}. \tag{4.5.17}$$

(This sample version can also be obtained directly by substituting (4.2.2) and (4.5.10) into (4.3.4).)

Most textbooks give expressions even prettier than these by using data matrices (such as the $n \times K$ matrix $\mathbf{X}$). Deriving such expressions is an analytical exercise to this chapter. The preceding discussion can be summarized as

Proposition 4.5 (large-sample properties of 3SLS): *Suppose Assumptions 4.1–4.5 and 4.7 hold, and suppose $\mathbf{x}_{im} = \mathbf{x}_i$ (common set of instruments). Suppose, furthermore, that $\mathrm{E}(\mathbf{z}_{im}\mathbf{z}_{ih}')$ exists and is finite for all $m, h\ (= 1, 2, \ldots, M)$. Let $\widehat{\mathbf{\Sigma}}$ be the $M \times M$ matrix of estimated error cross moments calculated by (4.5.7) using the 2SLS residuals. Then*

(a) $\hat{\boldsymbol{\delta}}_{\text{3SLS}}$ *given by (4.5.12) is consistent, asymptotically normal, and efficient, with* $\mathrm{Avar}(\hat{\boldsymbol{\delta}}_{\text{3SLS}})$ *given by (4.5.15).*

(b) The estimated asymptotic variance (4.5.17) is consistent for $\mathrm{Avar}(\hat{\boldsymbol{\delta}}_{\text{3SLS}})$.

(c) (Sargan's statistic)

$$J(\hat{\boldsymbol{\delta}}_{\text{3SLS}}, \widehat{\mathbf{S}}^{-1}) \equiv n \cdot \mathbf{g}_n(\hat{\boldsymbol{\delta}}_{\text{3SLS}})' \widehat{\mathbf{S}}^{-1} \mathbf{g}_n(\hat{\boldsymbol{\delta}}_{\text{3SLS}}) \underset{\text{d}}{\to} \chi^2\Big(MK - \sum_m L_m\Big),$$

where $\widehat{\mathbf{S}} = \widehat{\mathbf{\Sigma}} \otimes \big(\frac{1}{n}\sum_i \mathbf{x}_i\mathbf{x}_i'\big)$, *$K$ is the number of common instruments, and* $\mathbf{g}_n(\cdot)$ *is given in (4.2.1).*

Seemingly Unrelated Regressions (SUR)

The 3SLS formula can further be simplified if

$$\mathbf{x}_i = \text{union of } (\mathbf{z}_{i1}, \ldots, \mathbf{z}_{iM}). \tag{4.5.18}$$

This is equivalent to the condition that

$$\mathrm{E}(\mathbf{z}_{im} \cdot \varepsilon_{ih}) = \mathbf{0} \quad (m, h = 1, 2, \ldots, M). \tag{4.5.18$'$}$$

That is, the predetermined regressors satisfy "cross" orthogonalities: not only are they predetermined in each equation (i.e., $\mathrm{E}(\mathbf{z}_{im} \cdot \varepsilon_{im}) = \mathbf{0}$), but also they are predetermined in the other equations (i.e., $\mathrm{E}(\mathbf{z}_{im} \cdot \varepsilon_{ih}) = \mathbf{0}$ for $m \neq h$). The simplified formula is called the **SUR estimator**, to be denoted $\hat{\boldsymbol{\delta}}_{\text{SUR}}$.[6]

[6]The estimator is due to Zellner (1962).

Example 4.3 (Example 4.1 with different specification for instruments): If (4.5.18) holds for the two-equation system of Example 4.1, $\mathbf{x}_i$ is the union of $\mathbf{z}_{i1}$ and $\mathbf{z}_{i2}$, so

$$\mathbf{x}_i = \begin{bmatrix} 1 \\ S_i \\ IQ_i \\ EXPR_i \end{bmatrix}. \tag{4.5.19}$$

The orthogonality conditions that $\text{E}(\mathbf{x}_i \cdot \varepsilon_{i1}) = \mathbf{0}$ and $\text{E}(\mathbf{x}_i \cdot \varepsilon_{i2}) = \mathbf{0}$ become

$$\text{E}\begin{bmatrix} \varepsilon_{i1} \\ S_i\,\varepsilon_{i1} \\ IQ_i\,\varepsilon_{i1} \\ EXPR_i\,\varepsilon_{i1} \end{bmatrix} = \mathbf{0} \quad \text{and} \quad \text{E}\begin{bmatrix} \varepsilon_{i2} \\ S_i\,\varepsilon_{i2} \\ IQ_i\,\varepsilon_{i2} \\ EXPR_i\,\varepsilon_{i2} \end{bmatrix} = \mathbf{0}, \tag{4.5.20}$$

which should be contrasted with the statement that the regressors are predetermined in each equation:

$$\text{E}\begin{bmatrix} \varepsilon_{i1} \\ S_i\,\varepsilon_{i1} \\ IQ_i\,\varepsilon_{i1} \\ EXPR_i\,\varepsilon_{i1} \end{bmatrix} = \mathbf{0} \quad \text{and} \quad \text{E}\begin{bmatrix} \varepsilon_{i2} \\ S_i\,\varepsilon_{i2} \\ IQ_i\,\varepsilon_{i2} \end{bmatrix} = \mathbf{0}. \tag{4.5.21}$$

The difference between (4.5.20) and (4.5.21) is that the *KWW* equation is overidentified with *EXPR* as the additional instrument.

Because SUR is a special case of 3SLS, formulas (4.5.12), (4.5.15), and (4.5.17) for $\hat{\boldsymbol{\delta}}_{\text{3SLS}}$ apply to $\hat{\boldsymbol{\delta}}_{\text{SUR}}$. The implication of the SUR assumption (4.5.18) is that, in the above expressions for $\widehat{\mathbf{A}}_{mh}$, $\hat{\mathbf{c}}_{mh}$, and $\mathbf{A}_{mh}$, $\mathbf{x}_i$ "disappears":

$$\widehat{\mathbf{A}}_{mh} = \frac{1}{n}\sum_{i=1}^{n} \mathbf{z}_{im}\mathbf{z}'_{ih}, \tag{4.5.13$'$}$$

$$\hat{\mathbf{c}}_{mh} = \frac{1}{n}\sum_{i=1}^{n} \mathbf{z}_{im} \cdot y_{ih}, \tag{4.5.14$'$}$$

$$\mathbf{A}_{mh} = \text{E}(\mathbf{z}_{im}\mathbf{z}'_{ih}). \tag{4.5.16$'$}$$

Here we give a proof of (4.5.16$'$). Without loss of generality, suppose $\mathbf{z}_{im}$ is the first L_m elements of the K elements of $\mathbf{x}_i$. Let $\mathbf{D}$ ($K \times L_m$) be the first L_m columns of $\mathbf{I}_K$. Then we have

$$\mathbf{z}_{im} = \mathbf{D}'\mathbf{x}_i, \ \mathrm{E}(\mathbf{z}_{im}\mathbf{x}_i') = \mathbf{D}'\,\mathrm{E}(\mathbf{x}_i\mathbf{x}_i'), \ \mathbf{D}\,\mathrm{E}(\mathbf{x}_i\mathbf{z}_{ih}') = \mathrm{E}(\mathbf{z}_{im}\mathbf{z}_{ih}').$$

Substituting these into (4.5.16) yields (4.5.16′). The proof of (4.5.13′) and (4.5.14′), which are about the sample moments, proceeds similarly, with $\mathbf{z}_{im} = \mathbf{D}'\mathbf{x}_i$. (You will be asked to provide an alternative proof by the use of the projection matrix in the problem set.)

In 3SLS, the initial consistent estimator for calculating $\widehat{\boldsymbol{\Sigma}}$ was 2SLS. But, 2SLS when the regressors are a subset of the instrument set is OLS (as you showed for Review Question 7 of Section 3.8). So, for SUR, the initial estimator is the OLS estimator. The preceding discussion can be summarized as

Proposition 4.6 (large-sample properties of SUR): *Suppose Assumptions 4.1–4.5 and 4.7 hold with* $\mathbf{x}_i$ = *union of* $(\mathbf{z}_{i1}, \dots, \mathbf{z}_{iM})$. *Let* $\widehat{\boldsymbol{\Sigma}}$ *be the* $M \times M$ *matrix of estimated error cross moments calculated by (4.5.7) using the OLS residuals. Then*

(a) $\hat{\boldsymbol{\delta}}_{\text{SUR}}$ *given by (4.5.12) with* $\widehat{\mathbf{A}}_{mh}$ *and* $\hat{\mathbf{c}}_{mh}$ *given by (4.5.13′) and (4.5.14′) for* $m, h = 1, \dots, M$ *is consistent, asymptotically normal, and efficient, with* $\text{Avar}(\hat{\boldsymbol{\delta}}_{\text{SUR}})$ *given by (4.5.15) where* $\mathbf{A}_{mh}$ *is given by (4.5.16′).*

(b) The estimated asymptotic variance (4.5.17) where $\widehat{\mathbf{A}}_{mh}$ *is given by (4.5.13′) is consistent for* $\text{Avar}(\hat{\boldsymbol{\delta}}_{\text{SUR}})$.

(c) (Sargan's statistic)

$$J(\hat{\boldsymbol{\delta}}_{\text{SUR}}, \widehat{\mathbf{S}}^{-1}) \equiv n \cdot \mathbf{g}_n(\hat{\boldsymbol{\delta}}_{\text{SUR}})' \widehat{\mathbf{S}}^{-1} \mathbf{g}_n(\hat{\boldsymbol{\delta}}_{\text{SUR}}) \underset{\text{d}}{\to} \chi^2\Big(MK - \sum_m L_m\Big),$$

where $\widehat{\mathbf{S}} = \widehat{\boldsymbol{\Sigma}} \otimes (\frac{1}{n}\sum_i \mathbf{x}_i\mathbf{x}_i')$, K *is the number of common instruments, and* $\mathbf{g}_n(\cdot)$ *is given in (4.2.1).*

(Unlike in Proposition 4.5, the condition that $\mathrm{E}(\mathbf{z}_{im}\mathbf{z}_{ih}')$ be finite is not needed because, thanks to (4.5.18), it is implied by the condition that $\mathrm{E}(\mathbf{x}_i\mathbf{x}_i')$ be nonsingular, which in turn is implied by the nonsingularity of $\mathbf{S}$ [from Assumption 4.5] and the fact that $\mathbf{S}$ can be written as $\boldsymbol{\Sigma} \otimes \mathrm{E}(\mathbf{x}_i\mathbf{x}_i')$.) Sargan's statistic for SUR is rarely reported in practice.

SUR versus OLS

Since the regressors are predetermined, the system can also be estimated by the equation-by-equation OLS. Then why SUR over OLS? As just seen, under conditional homoskedasticity, the efficient multiple-equation GMM is FIVE, which in turn is numerically equal to SUR under (4.5.18). As shown in Chapter 3, under conditional homoskedasticity, the efficient single-equation GMM is 2SLS, which in turn is numerically equal to OLS because the regressors are predetermined under (4.5.18). This interrelationship is shown in Figure 4.1. Therefore, the relation between SUR and equation-by-equation OLS is strictly analogous to the relation between the multiple-equation GMM and the equation-by-equation GMM. As discussed in Section 4.4, there are two cases to consider.

(a) Each equation is just identified. Because the common instrument set is the union of all the regressors, this is possible only if the regressors are the same for all equations, i.e., if $\mathbf{z}_{im} = \mathbf{x}_i$ for all m. The SUR for this case is called the **multivariate regression**. We observed in Section 4.4 that both the efficient multiple-equation GMM and the efficient single-equation GMM are numerically the same as the IV estimator for the just identified system. Because the regressors are predetermined, we conclude that the GMM estimator of the multivariate regression model is simply equation-by-equation OLS.[7] This can be verified directly by substituting (4.5.13′) and (4.5.14′) on page 280 (with $\mathbf{z}_{im} = \mathbf{x}_i$) into the expression for the point estimate (4.5.12). Also substituting (4.5.16′) and (4.5.13′) (again with $\mathbf{z}_{im} = \mathbf{x}_i$) into (4.5.15) and (4.5.17), we obtain, for multivariate regression,

$$\text{Avar}(\hat{\boldsymbol{\delta}}) = \boldsymbol{\Sigma} \otimes \left[\text{E}(\mathbf{x}_i \mathbf{x}_i')\right]^{-1}, \tag{4.5.22}$$

$$\widehat{\text{Avar}(\hat{\boldsymbol{\delta}})} = \widehat{\boldsymbol{\Sigma}} \otimes \left(\frac{1}{n} \sum_{i=1}^{n} \mathbf{x}_i \mathbf{x}_i'\right)^{-1}. \tag{4.5.23}$$

(b) At least one equation is overidentified. Then SUR is more efficient than equation-by-equation OLS, unless equations are "unrelated" to each other in the sense of (4.4.3). In the present case of conditional homoskedasticity and the common set of instruments, (4.4.3) becomes

$$\sigma_{mh}\, \text{E}(\mathbf{x}_i \mathbf{x}_i') = \mathbf{0} \quad \text{for all } m \neq h.$$

Since $\text{E}(\mathbf{x}_i \mathbf{x}_i')$ cannot be a zero matrix (it is assumed to be nonsingular), equations are "unrelated" to each other if and only if $\sigma_{mh} = 0$. Therefore, SUR is more efficient than OLS if $\sigma_{mh} \neq 0$ for some pair (m, h). If $\sigma_{mh} = 0$ for all (m, h), the two estimators are asymptotically equivalent (i.e., $\sqrt{n}$ times the difference vanishes).

[7] It will be shown in Chapter 8 that the estimator is also the maximum likelihood estimator.

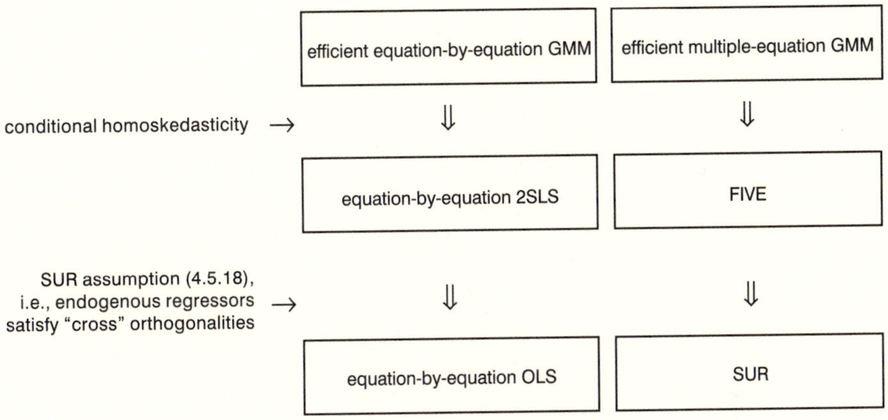

Figure 4.1: OLS and GMM

Another way to see the efficiency of SUR is to view the SUR model as a multivariate regression model with *a priori* exclusion restrictions. As an example, expand the two-equation system of Example 4.3 as

$$\begin{aligned} LW_i &= \phi_1 + \beta_1 S_i + \gamma_1 IQ_i + \pi_1 EXPR_i + \varepsilon_{i1}, \\ KWW_i &= \phi_2 + \beta_2 S_i + \gamma_2 IQ_i + \pi_2 EXPR_i + \varepsilon_{i2}. \end{aligned}$$

The common instrument set is $(1, S_i, IQ_i, EXPR_i)$. Then this two-equation system is a multivariate regression model with the same regressors in both equations. But if π_2 is *a priori* restricted to be 0 and thus $EXPR_i$ is excluded from the second equation, then the model becomes the SUR model. The SUR estimator is more efficient than the multivariate regression because it exploits exclusion restrictions.

The relationship among the estimators considered in this section is summarized in Table 4.2.

QUESTIONS FOR REVIEW

1. (FIVE without conditional homoskedasticity) Without conditional homoskedasticity, is the $\widehat{\mathbf{S}}$ in (4.5.3) consistent for $\mathbf{S}$ in (4.1.11)? [Answer: No. Why?] Under conditional homoskedasticity, is (4.3.2) consistent for (4.5.2)? [Answer: Yes. Why?]

2. (FIVE without conditional homoskedasticity) Without conditional homoskedasticity, is FIVE consistent and asymptotically normal? Efficient? **Hint:** The FIVE estimator is a multiple-equation GMM estimator (4.2.3) for some $\widehat{\mathbf{W}}$. Does the $\widehat{\mathbf{W}}$ satisfy the efficiency condition that $\operatorname{plim} \widehat{\mathbf{W}} = \mathbf{S}^{-1}$?

Table 4.2: Relationship between Multiple-Equation Estimators

	Multiple-equation GMM	FIVE	3SLS	SUR	Multivariate regression
The model	Assumptions 4.1–4.6	Assumptions 4.1–4.5, Assumption 4.7, $\mathrm{E}(\mathbf{z}_{im}\mathbf{z}_{ih}')$ finite	Assumptions 4.1–4.5, Assumption 4.7, $\mathrm{E}(\mathbf{z}_{im}\mathbf{z}_{ih}')$ finite, $\mathbf{x}_{im} = \mathbf{x}_i$ for all m	Assumptions 4.1–4.5, Assumption 4.7, $\mathbf{x}_{im} = \mathbf{x}_i$ for all m, $\mathbf{x}_i =$ union of $\mathbf{z}_{i1}, \dots, \mathbf{z}_{iM}$	Assumptions 4.1–4.5, Assumption 4.7, $\mathbf{x}_{im} = \mathbf{x}_i$ for all m, $\mathbf{z}_{im} = \mathbf{x}_i$ for all m
$\mathbf{S}\ (\equiv \mathrm{Avar}(\bar{\mathbf{g}}))$	(4.1.11)	(4.5.2)	$\mathbf{\Sigma} \otimes \mathrm{E}(\mathbf{x}_i\mathbf{x}_i')$	$\mathbf{\Sigma} \otimes \mathrm{E}(\mathbf{x}_i\mathbf{x}_i')$	irrelevant
$\widehat{\mathbf{S}}$	(4.3.2)	(4.5.3)	$\widehat{\mathbf{\Sigma}} \otimes (n^{-1}\Sigma_i \mathbf{x}_i\mathbf{x}_i')$ $\widehat{\mathbf{\Sigma}}$ from 2SLS residuals	$\widehat{\mathbf{\Sigma}} \otimes (n^{-1}\Sigma_i \mathbf{x}_i\mathbf{x}_i')$ $\widehat{\mathbf{\Sigma}}$ from OLS residuals	irrelevant
$\hat{\boldsymbol{\delta}}(\widehat{\mathbf{S}}^{-1})$	no simplification	no simplification	(4.5.12) with (4.5.13), (4.5.14)	(4.5.12) with (4.5.13′), (4.5.14′)	equation-by-equation OLS
$\mathrm{Avar}(\hat{\boldsymbol{\delta}}(\widehat{\mathbf{S}}^{-1}))$	(4.3.3)	(4.3.3)	(4.5.15) with (4.5.16)	(4.5.15) with (4.5.16′)	OLS formula
$\widehat{\mathrm{Avar}(\hat{\boldsymbol{\delta}}(\widehat{\mathbf{S}}^{-1}))}$	(4.3.4)	(4.3.4)	(4.5.17) with (4.5.13)	(4.5.17) with (4.5.13′)	OLS formula

3. (When FIVE and eq-by-eq 2SLS are numerically the same) Suppose each equation is just identified. Are the equation-by-equation 2SLS and FIVE estimators asymptotically equivalent (in that $\sqrt{n}$ times the difference vanishes)? Numerically the same? **Hint:** Both FIVE and 2SLS reduce to IV.

4. (When are FIVE and eq-by-eq 2SLS asymptotically equivalent) When the errors are orthogonal to each other (so $\sigma_{mh} = 0$ for $m \neq h$), the FIVE and equation-by-equation 2SLS estimators are asymptotically equivalent (in that $\sqrt{n}$ times the difference vanishes). Prove this. **Hint:** Superimpose conditional homoskedasticity on Proposition 4.3(b). Under conditional homoskedasticity, the efficient multiple-equation GMM reduces to the FIVE and the efficient single-equation GMM reduces to the equation-by-equation 2SLS. Also under conditional homoskedasticity, the equations are "unrelated" in the sense of (4.4.3) if $\sigma_{mh} = 0$.

5. (Conditional homoskedasticity under SUR assumptions) Verify that, under the SUR assumption (4.5.18), Assumption 4.7 becomes

$$\mathrm{E}(\varepsilon_{im}\,\varepsilon_{ih} \mid \mathbf{z}_{i1}, \ldots, \mathbf{z}_{iM}) = \sigma_{mh} \quad \text{for all } m, h = 1, 2, \ldots, M.$$

6. In Example 4.3, what happens to the SUR estimator when $\mathbf{x}_i$ includes MED_i also? **Hint:** $\mathbf{x}_i$ still "disappears" from (4.5.13), (4.5.14), and (4.5.16). To Sargan's statistic?

7. (Identification in SUR) In Proposition 4.6, the identification condition (Assumption 4.4) is actually not needed because it is implied by the other assumptions. Verify that Assumptions 4.5 and 4.7 imply Assumption 4.4. **Hint:** By Assumption 4.5 and the Kronecker decomposition (4.5.9) of $\mathbf{S}$, $\mathrm{E}(\mathbf{x}_i\mathbf{x}_i')$ is nonsingular. $\mathbf{z}_{im}$ is a subset of $\mathbf{x}_i$.

8. (SUR without conditional homoskedasticity)

   (a) Without conditional homoskedasticity, is SUR consistent and asymptotically normal? Efficient? **Hint:** The SUR estimator is still a multiple-equation GMM estimator, so Proposition 3.1 applies.

   (b) Without conditional homoskedasticity, does SUR still reduce to the multivariate regression when the system is just identified in that each equation is just identified (so $\mathbf{z}_{im} = \mathbf{x}_i$)? [Answer: Yes.]

9. (Role of "cross" orthogonalities) Suppose, instead of (4.5.18′) on page 279, the orthogonality conditions are that $\mathrm{E}(\mathbf{z}_{im} \cdot \varepsilon_{im}) = \mathbf{0}$ for $m = 1, 2, \ldots, M$. Is

SUR consistent? [Answer: Not necessarily.] Derive the efficient multiple-equation GMM estimator under conditional homoskedasticity. [Answer: It is OLS.]

10. Verify that Sargan's statistic for the multivariate regression model is zero.

4.6 Common Coefficients

In many applications, particularly in panel data contexts, you deal with a special case of the multiple-equation model where the number of regressors is the same across equations with the same coefficients. Such a model is a special case of the multiple-equation model of Section 4.1. This section shows how to apply GMM to multiple equations while imposing the common coefficient restriction. It will be shown at the end that the seemingly restrictive model actually includes as a special case the multiple-equation model *without* the common coefficient restriction.

The Model with Common Coefficients

With common coefficients, the multiple-equation system becomes

Assumption 4.1′ (linearity): *There are M linear equations to be estimated:*

$$y_{im} = \mathbf{z}'_{im}\boldsymbol{\delta} + \varepsilon_{im} \quad (m = 1, 2, \ldots, M; i = 1, 2, \ldots, n), \tag{4.6.1}$$

where n is the sample size, $\mathbf{z}_{im}$ is an L-dimensional vector of regressors, $\boldsymbol{\delta}$ is an L-dimensional coefficient vector common to all equations, and ε_{im} is an unobservable error term of the m-th equation.

Of the other assumptions of the multiple-equation model, Assumptions 4.2–4.6, only Assumption 4.4 (identification) needs to be modified to reflect the common coefficient restriction. The multiple-equation version of $\mathbf{g}(\mathbf{w}_i; \tilde{\boldsymbol{\delta}})$ is now

$$\mathbf{g}(\mathbf{w}_i; \tilde{\boldsymbol{\delta}}) \equiv \begin{bmatrix} \mathbf{x}_{i1} \cdot (y_{i1} - \mathbf{z}'_{i1}\tilde{\boldsymbol{\delta}}) \\ \vdots \\ \mathbf{x}_{iM} \cdot (y_{iM} - \mathbf{z}'_{iM}\tilde{\boldsymbol{\delta}}) \end{bmatrix}, \tag{4.6.2}$$

so that $\mathrm{E}[\mathbf{g}(\mathbf{w}_i; \tilde{\boldsymbol{\delta}})]$ becomes

$$\mathrm{E}[\mathbf{g}(\mathbf{w}_i;\tilde{\boldsymbol{\delta}})] = \begin{bmatrix} \mathrm{E}(\mathbf{x}_{i1}\cdot y_{i1}) \\ \vdots \\ \mathrm{E}(\mathbf{x}_{iM}\cdot y_{iM}) \end{bmatrix} - \begin{bmatrix} \mathrm{E}(\mathbf{x}_{i1}\cdot \mathbf{z}_{i1}')\tilde{\boldsymbol{\delta}} \\ \vdots \\ \mathrm{E}(\mathbf{x}_{iM}\cdot \mathbf{z}_{iM}')\tilde{\boldsymbol{\delta}} \end{bmatrix}$$

$$= \underset{(\sum_{m=1}^{M} K_m\times 1)}{\boldsymbol{\sigma}_{\mathbf{xy}}} - \underset{(\sum_{m=1}^{M} K_m\times L)}{\boldsymbol{\Sigma}_{\mathbf{xz}}} \underset{(L\times 1)}{\tilde{\boldsymbol{\delta}}}, \tag{4.6.3}$$

where

$$\boldsymbol{\sigma}_{\mathbf{xy}} \equiv \begin{bmatrix} \mathrm{E}(\mathbf{x}_{i1}\cdot y_{i1}) \\ \vdots \\ \mathrm{E}(\mathbf{x}_{iM}\cdot y_{iM}) \end{bmatrix}, \quad \boldsymbol{\Sigma}_{\mathbf{xz}} \equiv \begin{bmatrix} \mathrm{E}(\mathbf{x}_{i1}\mathbf{z}_{i1}') \\ \vdots \\ \mathrm{E}(\mathbf{x}_{iM}\mathbf{z}_{iM}') \end{bmatrix}. \tag{4.6.4}$$

So the implication of common coefficients is that $\boldsymbol{\Sigma}_{\mathbf{xz}}$ is now a stacked, not a block diagonal, matrix. With this change, the system of equations determining $\tilde{\boldsymbol{\delta}}$ is again (4.1.10), so the identification condition is

Assumption 4.4′ (identification with common coefficients): *The* $\sum_{m=1}^{M} K_m \times L$ *matrix* $\boldsymbol{\Sigma}_{\mathbf{xz}}$ *defined in (4.6.4) is of full column rank.*

This condition is weaker than Assumption 4.4, which requires that each equation of the system be identified. Indeed, a sufficient condition for identification is that $\mathrm{E}(\mathbf{x}_{im}\mathbf{z}_{im}')$ be of full column rank for *some* m.[8] This is thanks to the *a priori* restriction that the coefficients are the same across equations. It is possible that the system is identified even if none of the equations are identified individually.

The GMM Estimator

It is left to you to verify that $\mathbf{g}_n(\tilde{\boldsymbol{\delta}})$ can be written as $\mathbf{s}_{\mathbf{xy}} - \mathbf{S}_{\mathbf{xz}}\tilde{\boldsymbol{\delta}}$ with

$$\mathbf{s}_{\mathbf{xy}} \equiv \begin{bmatrix} \frac{1}{n}\sum_{i=1}^{n} \mathbf{x}_{i1}\cdot y_{i1} \\ \vdots \\ \frac{1}{n}\sum_{i=1}^{n} \mathbf{x}_{iM}\cdot y_{iM} \end{bmatrix}, \quad \mathbf{S}_{\mathbf{xz}} \equiv \begin{bmatrix} \frac{1}{n}\sum_{i=1}^{n} \mathbf{x}_{i1}\mathbf{z}_{i1}' \\ \vdots \\ \frac{1}{n}\sum_{i=1}^{n} \mathbf{x}_{iM}\mathbf{z}_{iM}' \end{bmatrix}, \tag{4.6.5}$$

[8]Proof: If $\mathrm{E}(\mathbf{x}_{im}\mathbf{z}_{im}')$ is of full column rank, its rank is L. Since the rank of a matrix is also equal to the number of linearly independent rows, $\mathrm{E}(\mathbf{x}_{im}\mathbf{z}_{im}')$ has L linearly independent rows. Thus, $\boldsymbol{\Sigma}_{\mathbf{xz}}$ has at least L linearly independent rows.

so that the GMM estimator with a $\sum_m K_m \times \sum_m K_m$ weighting matrix $\widehat{\mathbf{W}}$ is (4.2.3) with the sampling error given by (4.2.4). Provided that $\boldsymbol{\Sigma}_{\mathbf{xz}}$ and $\mathbf{S}_{\mathbf{xz}}$ are as just redefined and $\boldsymbol{\delta}$ is interpreted as the common coefficient, large-sample theory for the multiple-equation model with common coefficients is the same as that with separate coefficients developed in Section 4.3, with Assumption 4.1′ replacing Assumption 4.1, Assumption 4.4′ replacing Assumption 4.4, and the residual $\hat{\varepsilon}_i$ redefined to be $y_{im} - \mathbf{z}_{im}'\hat{\boldsymbol{\delta}}$ (not $y_{im} - \mathbf{z}_{im}'\hat{\boldsymbol{\delta}}_m$) for some consistent estimate of the L-dimensional common coefficient vector $\boldsymbol{\delta}$.

In order to relate this GMM estimator to popular estimators in the literature, it is necessary to write out the GMM formula in full. Substituting (4.6.5) into (4.2.3), we obtain

$$\hat{\boldsymbol{\delta}}(\widehat{\mathbf{W}}) = \left(\begin{bmatrix} \frac{1}{n}\sum_{i=1}^{n} \mathbf{z}_{i1}\mathbf{x}_{i1}' \cdots \frac{1}{n}\sum_{i=1}^{n} \mathbf{z}_{iM}\mathbf{x}_{iM}' \end{bmatrix} \begin{bmatrix} \widehat{\mathbf{W}}_{11} \cdots \widehat{\mathbf{W}}_{1M} \\ \vdots \quad\quad \vdots \\ \widehat{\mathbf{W}}_{M1} \cdots \widehat{\mathbf{W}}_{MM} \end{bmatrix} \begin{bmatrix} \frac{1}{n}\sum_{i=1}^{n} \mathbf{x}_{i1}\mathbf{z}_{i1}' \\ \vdots \\ \frac{1}{n}\sum_{i=1}^{n} \mathbf{x}_{iM}\mathbf{z}_{iM}' \end{bmatrix} \right)^{-1}$$

$$\begin{bmatrix} \frac{1}{n}\sum_{i=1}^{n} \mathbf{z}_{i1}\mathbf{x}_{i1}' \cdots \frac{1}{n}\sum_{i=1}^{n} \mathbf{z}_{iM}\mathbf{x}_{iM}' \end{bmatrix} \begin{bmatrix} \widehat{\mathbf{W}}_{11} \cdots \widehat{\mathbf{W}}_{1M} \\ \vdots \quad\quad \vdots \\ \widehat{\mathbf{W}}_{M1} \cdots \widehat{\mathbf{W}}_{MM} \end{bmatrix} \begin{bmatrix} \frac{1}{n}\sum_{i=1}^{n} \mathbf{x}_{i1} \cdot y_{i1} \\ \vdots \\ \frac{1}{n}\sum_{i=1}^{n} \mathbf{x}_{iM} \cdot y_{iM} \end{bmatrix}$$

$$= \left[\sum_{m=1}^{M}\sum_{h=1}^{M} \left\{ \left(\frac{1}{n}\sum_{i=1}^{n} \mathbf{z}_{im}\mathbf{x}_{im}' \right) \widehat{\mathbf{W}}_{mh} \left(\frac{1}{n}\sum_{i=1}^{n} \mathbf{x}_{ih}\mathbf{z}_{ih}' \right) \right\} \right]^{-1}$$

$$\left[\sum_{m=1}^{M}\sum_{h=1}^{M} \left\{ \left(\frac{1}{n}\sum_{i=1}^{n} \mathbf{z}_{im}\mathbf{x}_{im}' \right) \widehat{\mathbf{W}}_{mh} \left(\frac{1}{n}\sum_{i=1}^{n} \mathbf{x}_{ih} \cdot y_{ih} \right) \right\} \right], \tag{4.6.6}$$

where $\widehat{\mathbf{W}}_{mh}$ is the (m, h) block of $\widehat{\mathbf{W}}$. (For the second equality, use formula (A.8) of Appendix A.) The efficient GMM estimator obtains if the $\widehat{\mathbf{W}}$ in this expression is replaced by the inverse of $\widehat{\mathbf{S}}$ defined in (4.3.2).

Imposing Conditional Homoskedasticity

The efficient GMM estimator obtains when we set in (4.6.6) $\widehat{\mathbf{W}} = \widehat{\mathbf{S}}^{-1}$ where $\widehat{\mathbf{S}}$ is a consistent estimator of $\mathbf{S}$. As before, we can impose conditional homoskedasticity to reduce the efficient GMM estimator to popular estimators. The FIVE estimator obtains if $\widehat{\mathbf{S}}$ is given by (4.5.3).

If we further assume that the set of instruments is the same across equations, then, as before, this $\widehat{\mathbf{S}}$ has the Kronecker product structure

$$\widehat{\mathbf{S}} = \widehat{\boldsymbol{\Sigma}} \otimes \Big(\frac{1}{n}\sum_{i=1}^{n} \mathbf{x}_i \mathbf{x}_i'\Big),$$

so that $\widehat{\mathbf{W}}_{mh}$ in (4.6.6) is given by (4.5.11), resulting in what should be called the 3SLS estimator with common coefficients:

$$\Bigg[\sum_{m=1}^{M}\sum_{h=1}^{M}\Big\{\hat{\sigma}^{mh}\cdot\Big(\frac{1}{n}\sum_{i=1}^{n}\mathbf{z}_{im}\mathbf{x}_i'\Big)\Big(\frac{1}{n}\sum_{i=1}^{n}\mathbf{x}_i\mathbf{x}_i'\Big)^{-1}\Big(\frac{1}{n}\sum_{i=1}^{n}\mathbf{x}_i\mathbf{z}_{ih}'\Big)\Big\}\Bigg]^{-1}$$
$$\Bigg[\sum_{m=1}^{M}\sum_{h=1}^{M}\Big\{\hat{\sigma}^{mh}\cdot\Big(\frac{1}{n}\sum_{i=1}^{n}\mathbf{z}_{im}\mathbf{x}_i'\Big)\Big(\frac{1}{n}\sum_{i=1}^{n}\mathbf{x}_i\mathbf{x}_i'\Big)^{-1}\Big(\frac{1}{n}\sum_{i=1}^{n}\mathbf{x}_i\cdot y_{ih}\Big)\Big\}\Bigg], \tag{4.6.7}$$

where $\hat{\sigma}^{mh}$ is the (m, h) element of $\widehat{\boldsymbol{\Sigma}}^{-1}$. If, in addition, the SUR condition (4.5.18) is assumed, then the "disappearance of $\mathbf{x}$" occurs in (4.6.7) and the efficient GMM estimator becomes what is called (for historical reasons) the **random-effects estimator**:

$$\hat{\boldsymbol{\delta}}_{\text{RE}} = \Bigg[\sum_{m=1}^{M}\sum_{h=1}^{M}\hat{\sigma}^{mh}\Big(\frac{1}{n}\sum_{i=1}^{n}\mathbf{z}_{im}\mathbf{z}_{ih}'\Big)\Bigg]^{-1}\sum_{m=1}^{M}\sum_{h=1}^{M}\hat{\sigma}^{mh}\Big(\frac{1}{n}\sum_{i=1}^{n}\mathbf{z}_{im}\cdot y_{ih}\Big). \tag{4.6.8}$$

Its asymptotic variance is

$$\text{Avar}(\hat{\boldsymbol{\delta}}_{\text{RE}}) = \Bigg[\sum_{m=1}^{M}\sum_{h=1}^{M}\sigma^{mh}\,\text{E}(\mathbf{z}_{im}\mathbf{z}_{ih}')\Bigg]^{-1}. \tag{4.6.9}$$

(To derive this, go back to the general formula (4.3.3) for the Avar of efficient GMM. Set $\boldsymbol{\Sigma}_{\mathbf{xz}}$ as in (4.6.4), $\mathbf{S} = \boldsymbol{\Sigma} \otimes \text{E}(\mathbf{x}_i\mathbf{x}_i')$, use formula (A.8) of Appendix A to calculate the matrix product, and observe the "disappearance of $\mathbf{x}$" that (4.5.16) becomes (4.5.16′) on page 280 under the SUR assumption (4.5.18).) It is consistently estimated by

$$\widehat{\text{Avar}(\hat{\boldsymbol{\delta}}_{\text{RE}})} = \Bigg[\sum_{m=1}^{M}\sum_{h=1}^{M}\hat{\sigma}^{mh}\Big(\frac{1}{n}\sum_{i=1}^{n}\mathbf{z}_{im}\mathbf{z}_{ih}'\Big)\Bigg]^{-1}. \tag{4.6.10}$$

We summarize the result about the random-effects estimator as

Proposition 4.7 (large-sample properties of the random-effects estimator): *Suppose Assumptions 4.1′, 4.2, 4.3, 4.4′, 4.5, and 4.7 hold with* $\mathbf{x}_i$ = *union of* $(\mathbf{z}_{i1}, \dots, \mathbf{z}_{iM})$. *Let* $\boldsymbol{\Sigma}$ *be the* $M \times M$ *matrix whose* (m, h) *element is* $\text{E}(\varepsilon_{im}\,\varepsilon_{ih})$, *and let* $\widehat{\boldsymbol{\Sigma}}$ *be a consistent estimate of* $\boldsymbol{\Sigma}$. *Then*

(a) $\hat{\boldsymbol{\delta}}_{\text{RE}}$, *given by (4.6.8) is consistent, asymptotically normal, and efficient, with* $\text{Avar}(\hat{\boldsymbol{\delta}}_{\text{RE}})$ *given by (4.6.9).*

(b) The estimated asymptotic variance (4.6.10) is consistent for $\text{Avar}(\hat{\boldsymbol{\delta}}_{\text{RE}})$.

(c) (Sargan's statistic)

$$J(\hat{\boldsymbol{\delta}}_{\text{RE}}, \widehat{\mathbf{S}}^{-1}) \equiv n \cdot \mathbf{g}_n(\hat{\boldsymbol{\delta}}_{\text{RE}})' \widehat{\mathbf{S}}^{-1} \mathbf{g}_n(\hat{\boldsymbol{\delta}}_{\text{RE}}) \underset{\text{d}}{\to} \chi^2(MK - L),$$

where $\widehat{\mathbf{S}} = \widehat{\boldsymbol{\Sigma}} \otimes (\frac{1}{n}\sum \mathbf{x}_i\mathbf{x}_i')$, K *is the number of common instruments, and* $\mathbf{g}_n(\tilde{\boldsymbol{\delta}}) = \mathbf{s}_{\mathbf{xy}} - \mathbf{S}_{\mathbf{xz}}\tilde{\boldsymbol{\delta}}$ *with* $\mathbf{s}_{\mathbf{xy}}$ *and* $\mathbf{S}_{\mathbf{xz}}$ *given by (4.6.5).*

Below we will rewrite the formulas (4.6.8)–(4.6.10) in more elegant forms.

Pooled OLS

For the SUR of the previous section, we obtained $\widehat{\boldsymbol{\Sigma}}$ from the residuals from the equation-by-equation OLS. The consistency is all that is required for $\widehat{\boldsymbol{\Sigma}}$, so the same procedure for $\widehat{\boldsymbol{\Sigma}}$ works here just as well, but the finite sample distribution of $\hat{\boldsymbol{\delta}}_{\text{RE}}$ might be improved if we exploit the *a priori* restriction that the coefficients be the same across equations in the estimation of $\widehat{\boldsymbol{\Sigma}}$. So consider setting $\widehat{\mathbf{W}}$ to

$$\mathbf{I}_M \otimes \Big(\frac{1}{n}\sum_{i=1}^{n} \mathbf{x}_i\mathbf{x}_i'\Big)^{-1},$$

rather than

$$\widehat{\boldsymbol{\Sigma}}^{-1} \otimes \Big(\frac{1}{n}\sum_{i=1}^{n} \mathbf{x}_i\mathbf{x}_i'\Big)^{-1},$$

in the first-step GMM estimation for the purpose of obtaining an initial consistent estimate of $\boldsymbol{\delta}$. The estimator is (4.6.8) with $\hat{\sigma}^{mh} = 1$ for $m = h$ and 0 for $m \neq h$, which can be written as

$$
\begin{aligned}
\hat{\boldsymbol{\delta}}_{\text{pooled OLS}} &= \left[\sum_{m=1}^{M}\Big(\frac{1}{n}\sum_{i=1}^{n}\mathbf{z}_{im}\mathbf{z}_{im}'\Big)\right]^{-1}\sum_{m=1}^{M}\Big(\frac{1}{n}\sum_{i=1}^{n}\mathbf{z}_{im}\cdot y_{im}\Big) \\
&= \Big(\sum_{i=1}^{n}\sum_{m=1}^{M}\mathbf{z}_{im}\mathbf{z}_{im}'\Big)^{-1}\sum_{i=1}^{n}\sum_{m=1}^{M}\mathbf{z}_{im}\cdot y_{im},
\end{aligned}
\tag{4.6.11}
$$

which is simply the OLS estimator on the sample of size Mn where observations are pooled across equations. For this reason, the estimator is called the **pooled OLS** estimator. The expression suggests that the orthogonality conditions that are being exploited are

$$
\mathrm{E}(\mathbf{z}_{i1}\cdot\varepsilon_{i1}+\cdots+\mathbf{z}_{iM}\cdot\varepsilon_{iM})=\mathbf{0},
\tag{4.6.12}
$$

which does not involve the "cross" orthogonalities $\mathrm{E}(\mathbf{z}_{im}\cdot\varepsilon_{ih})=\mathbf{0}$ $(m\neq h)$. It is left as an analytical exercise to show that the pooled OLS is the GMM estimator exploiting (4.6.12).

Because it is so easy to calculate, pooled OLS is a popular option for those researchers who do not want to program estimators. The estimator is also robust to the failure of the "cross" orthogonalities. But it is important to keep in mind that the standard errors printed out by the OLS package, which do not take into account the interequation cross moments (σ_{mh}), are biased. For the pooled OLS estimator, which is a GMM estimator with a nonoptimal choice of $\widehat{\mathbf{W}}$, the correct formula for the asymptotic variance is (3.5.1) of Proposition 3.1. Setting $\mathbf{W}=\mathbf{I}_M\otimes[\mathrm{E}(\mathbf{x}_i\mathbf{x}_i')]^{-1}$, $\mathbf{S}=\boldsymbol{\Sigma}\otimes\mathrm{E}(\mathbf{x}_i\mathbf{x}_i')$, $\boldsymbol{\Sigma}_{\mathbf{xz}}$ as in (4.6.4), and again observing the disappearance of $\mathbf{x}$, we obtain

$$
\mathrm{Avar}(\hat{\boldsymbol{\delta}}_{\text{pooled OLS}}) = \left[\sum_{m=1}^{M}\mathrm{E}(\mathbf{z}_{im}\mathbf{z}_{im}')\right]^{-1}\sum_{m=1}^{M}\sum_{h=1}^{M}\sigma_{mh}\,\mathrm{E}(\mathbf{z}_{im}\mathbf{z}_{ih}')\left[\sum_{m=1}^{M}\mathrm{E}(\mathbf{z}_{im}\mathbf{z}_{im}')\right]^{-1},
\tag{4.6.13}
$$

which is consistently estimated by

$$
\Big(\sum_{m=1}^{M}\frac{1}{n}\sum_{i=1}^{n}\mathbf{z}_{im}\mathbf{z}_{im}'\Big)^{-1}\sum_{m=1}^{M}\sum_{h=1}^{M}\hat{\sigma}_{mh}\frac{1}{n}\sum_{i=1}^{n}\mathbf{z}_{im}\mathbf{z}_{ih}'\Big(\sum_{m=1}^{M}\frac{1}{n}\sum_{i=1}^{n}\mathbf{z}_{im}\mathbf{z}_{im}'\Big)^{-1}.
\tag{4.6.14}
$$

Since the pooled OLS estimator is consistent, the associated residual can be used to calculate $\hat{\sigma}_{mh}$ $(m,h=1,\ldots,M)$ in this expression. The correct standard errors of pooled OLS are the square roots of $(1/n$ times) the diagonal element of this matrix.

Beautifying the Formulas

These formulas for the random-effects and pooled OLS estimators are quite straightforward to derive but look complicated, with double and triple summations. They can, however, be beautified—and at the same time more useful for programming—if we introduce some new matrix notation. Let

$$\underset{(M\times 1)}{\mathbf{y}_i} = \begin{bmatrix} y_{i1} \\ \vdots \\ y_{iM} \end{bmatrix}, \quad \underset{(M\times L)}{\mathbf{Z}_i} = \begin{bmatrix} \mathbf{z}'_{i1} \\ \vdots \\ \mathbf{z}'_{iM} \end{bmatrix}, \quad \underset{(M\times 1)}{\boldsymbol{\varepsilon}_i} = \begin{bmatrix} \varepsilon_{i1} \\ \vdots \\ \varepsilon_{iM} \end{bmatrix}, \tag{4.6.15}$$

so that the M-equation system with common coefficients in Assumption 4.1′ can be written compactly as

$$\mathbf{y}_i = \mathbf{Z}_i\boldsymbol{\delta} + \boldsymbol{\varepsilon}_i \quad (i = 1, 2, \dots, n). \tag{4.6.1′}$$

The beautification of the complicated formulas utilizes the following algebraic results:

$$\sum_{m=1}^{M} \mathbf{z}_{im}\mathbf{z}'_{im} = \mathbf{Z}'_i\mathbf{Z}_i, \quad \sum_{m=1}^{M} \mathbf{z}_{im} \cdot y_{im} = \mathbf{Z}'_i\mathbf{y}_i, \tag{4.6.16a}$$

$$\sum_{m=1}^{M}\sum_{h=1}^{M} c_{mh} \cdot \mathbf{z}_{im} \cdot y_{ih} = \mathbf{Z}'_i\mathbf{C}\mathbf{y}_i, \quad \sum_{m=1}^{M}\sum_{h=1}^{M} c_{mh} \cdot \mathbf{z}_{im}\mathbf{z}'_{ih} = \mathbf{Z}'_i\mathbf{C}\mathbf{Z}_i \tag{4.6.16b}$$

for any $M \times M$ matrix $\mathbf{C} = (c_{mh})$. Now take the triple summation in (4.6.8)

$$\begin{aligned} &\sum_{m=1}^{M}\sum_{h=1}^{M} \hat{\sigma}^{mh} \cdot \Big(\frac{1}{n}\sum_{i=1}^{n} \mathbf{z}_{im} \cdot y_{ih}\Big) \\ &\quad = \frac{1}{n}\sum_{i=1}^{n}\Big(\sum_{m=1}^{M}\sum_{h=1}^{M} \hat{\sigma}^{mh} \cdot \mathbf{z}_{im} \cdot y_{ih}\Big) \quad \text{(by changing order of summations)} \\ &\quad = \frac{1}{n}\sum_{i=1}^{n} \mathbf{Z}'_i\widehat{\boldsymbol{\Sigma}}^{-1}\mathbf{y}_i \quad \text{(by (4.6.16b) with } \mathbf{C} = \widehat{\boldsymbol{\Sigma}}^{-1}\text{).} \end{aligned} \tag{4.6.17}$$

Similarly, by (4.6.16b) with $\mathbf{C} = \widehat{\boldsymbol{\Sigma}}^{-1}$, the other triple summation in (4.6.8) becomes

$$\sum_{m=1}^{M}\sum_{h=1}^{M} \hat{\sigma}^{mh} \frac{1}{n}\sum_{i=1}^{n} \mathbf{z}_{im}\mathbf{z}'_{ih} = \frac{1}{n}\sum_{i=1}^{n} \mathbf{Z}'_i\widehat{\boldsymbol{\Sigma}}^{-1}\mathbf{Z}_i. \tag{4.6.18}$$

The double and triple summations in (4.6.9) and (4.6.10) can be written similarly. We have thus rewritten the random-effects formulas as

$$\hat{\boldsymbol{\delta}}_{\text{RE}} = \Big(\frac{1}{n}\sum_{i=1}^{n}\mathbf{Z}_i'\widehat{\boldsymbol{\Sigma}}^{-1}\mathbf{Z}_i\Big)^{-1}\frac{1}{n}\sum_{i=1}^{n}\mathbf{Z}_i'\widehat{\boldsymbol{\Sigma}}^{-1}\mathbf{y}_i, \tag{4.6.8$'$}$$

$$\text{Avar}(\hat{\boldsymbol{\delta}}_{\text{RE}}) = \big(\text{E}(\mathbf{Z}_i'\boldsymbol{\Sigma}^{-1}\mathbf{Z}_i)\big)^{-1}, \tag{4.6.9$'$}$$

$$\widehat{\text{Avar}(\hat{\boldsymbol{\delta}}_{\text{RE}})} = \Big(\frac{1}{n}\sum_{i=1}^{n}\mathbf{Z}_i'\widehat{\boldsymbol{\Sigma}}^{-1}\mathbf{Z}_i\Big)^{-1}. \tag{4.6.10$'$}$$

Using (4.6.16a), the pooled OLS formulas can be written as

$$\hat{\boldsymbol{\delta}}_{\text{pooled OLS}} = \Big(\frac{1}{n}\sum_{i=1}^{n}\mathbf{Z}_i'\mathbf{Z}_i\Big)^{-1}\frac{1}{n}\sum_{i=1}^{n}\mathbf{Z}_i'\mathbf{y}_i, \tag{4.6.11$'$}$$

$$\text{Avar}(\hat{\boldsymbol{\delta}}_{\text{pooled OLS}}) = [\text{E}(\mathbf{Z}_i'\mathbf{Z}_i)]^{-1}\,\text{E}(\mathbf{Z}_i'\boldsymbol{\Sigma}\mathbf{Z}_i)[\text{E}(\mathbf{Z}_i'\mathbf{Z}_i)]^{-1}, \tag{4.6.13$'$}$$

$$\widehat{\text{Avar}(\hat{\boldsymbol{\delta}}_{\text{pooled OLS}})} = \Big(\frac{1}{n}\sum_{i=1}^{n}\mathbf{Z}_i'\mathbf{Z}_i\Big)^{-1}\Big(\frac{1}{n}\sum_{i=1}^{n}\mathbf{Z}_i'\widehat{\boldsymbol{\Sigma}}\mathbf{Z}_i\Big)\Big(\frac{1}{n}\sum_{i=1}^{n}\mathbf{Z}_i'\mathbf{Z}_i\Big)^{-1}. \tag{4.6.14$'$}$$

These formulas are not just pretty; as will be seen in the next section, they will be useful for handling certain classes of panel data (called **unbalanced panel** data).

The Restriction That Isn't

Although it appears that the model of this section, with the common coefficient assumption, is a special case of the model of Section 4.1, the latter can be cast in the format of the model of this section with a proper redefinition of regressors. For example, consider Example 4.1. Instead of defining $\mathbf{z}_{i1}$ and $\mathbf{z}_{i2}$ as in (4.1.2), define them as

$$\mathbf{z}_{i1} = \begin{bmatrix} 1 \\ S_i \\ IQ_i \\ EXPR_i \\ 0 \\ 0 \\ 0 \end{bmatrix}, \qquad \mathbf{z}_{i2} = \begin{bmatrix} 0 \\ 0 \\ 0 \\ 0 \\ 1 \\ S_i \\ IQ_i \end{bmatrix} \qquad \text{with} \quad \boldsymbol{\delta} = \begin{bmatrix} \phi_1 \\ \beta_1 \\ \gamma_1 \\ \pi \\ \phi_2 \\ \beta_2 \\ \gamma_2 \end{bmatrix}.$$

Then the two-equation system fits the format of Assumption 4.1$'$. (See Review Question 5 below for a demonstration of the same point more generally.)

Furthermore, a system in which only a subset of variables have common coefficients can be written in the form of Assumption 4.1′. Consider Example 4.2. Suppose we wish to assume *a priori* that the coefficients of schooling, IQ, and experience remain constant over time (so $\beta_1 = \beta_2 = \beta$, $\gamma_1 = \gamma_2 = \gamma$, $\pi_1 = \pi_2 = \pi$) but the intercept does not. The translation is accomplished by setting

$$\mathbf{z}_{i1} = \begin{bmatrix} 1 \\ 0 \\ S69_i \\ IQ_i \\ EXPR69_i \end{bmatrix}, \quad \mathbf{z}_{i2} = \begin{bmatrix} 0 \\ 1 \\ S80_i \\ IQ_i \\ EXPR80_i \end{bmatrix}, \quad \boldsymbol{\delta} = \begin{bmatrix} \phi_1 \\ \phi_2 \\ \beta \\ \gamma \\ \pi \end{bmatrix}. \tag{4.6.19}$$

Therefore, the common coefficient restriction is not restrictive. We could have derived the GMM estimator for the model of Section 4.1 as a special case of the GMM estimator with the common coefficient restriction. But the model without the restriction is perhaps an easier introduction to multiple equations.

QUESTIONS FOR REVIEW

1. (Identification with common coefficients) Let z_{imj} be the j-th element of $\mathbf{z}_{im}$. That is, z_{imj} is the j-th regressor in the m-th equation. Assume that $z_{im1} = 1$ for all i, m. Which of the assumptions made for the model is violated if $z_{im2} = 1$ for all i, m? **Hint:** Look at the rank condition. Would your answer change if $z_{im2} = m$ for all i, m? **Hint:** It should.

2. (Importance of "cross" orthogonalities) Suppose $\mathrm{E}(\mathbf{z}_{im} \cdot \varepsilon_{ih}) = \mathbf{0}$ for $m = h$ but not necessarily for $m \neq h$. Would the random-effects estimator be consistent? **Hint:** The sampling error of the random-effects estimator is

$$\hat{\boldsymbol{\delta}}_{\mathrm{RE}} - \boldsymbol{\delta} = \left[\sum_{m=1}^{M}\sum_{h=1}^{M} \hat{\sigma}^{mh}\Big(\frac{1}{n}\sum_{i=1}^{n} \mathbf{z}_{im}\mathbf{z}_{ih}'\Big)\right]^{-1} \sum_{m=1}^{M}\sum_{h=1}^{M} \hat{\sigma}^{mh}\Big(\frac{1}{n}\sum_{i=1}^{n} \mathbf{z}_{im} \cdot \varepsilon_{ih}\Big).$$

3. (Inefficiency of pooled OLS) Derive the efficient GMM estimator of $\boldsymbol{\delta}$ that exploits $\mathrm{E}(\mathbf{z}_{im} \cdot \varepsilon_{im}) = \mathbf{0}$ for all m. Is it the same as the pooled OLS? [Answer: No.] Is it the same as the random-effects estimator? [Answer: No.]

4. ($\boldsymbol{\Sigma}_{\mathbf{xz}}$, $\mathbf{s}_{\mathbf{xy}}$, $\mathbf{S}_{\mathbf{xz}}$ with common instruments in Kronecker products) Suppose the instruments are the same across equations: $\mathbf{x}_{im} = \mathbf{x}_i$. Show that $\boldsymbol{\Sigma}_{\mathbf{xz}}$ in (4.6.4)

can be written as $E(\mathbf{Z}_i \otimes \mathbf{x}_i)$, where $\mathbf{Z}_i$ is the $M \times L$ matrix defined in (4.6.15). Also, $\mathbf{s_{xy}} = \frac{1}{n}\sum_{i=1}^{n} \mathbf{y}_i \otimes \mathbf{x}_i$, $\mathbf{S_{xz}} = \frac{1}{n}\sum_{i=1}^{n} \mathbf{Z}_i \otimes \mathbf{x}_i$. **Hint:** $\mathbf{x}_i\mathbf{z}'_{im} = \mathbf{z}'_{im} \otimes \mathbf{x}_i$.

5. (The restriction that isn't) To avoid possible confusion arising from the fact that the $\mathbf{z}_{im}$ in Section 4.1 and the $\mathbf{z}_{im}$ in this section are different, write the M-equation system in (4.1.1) as

$$y_{im} = \mathbf{z}^{*\prime}_{im}\boldsymbol{\delta}^{*}_{m} + \varepsilon_{im} \quad (m = 1, 2, \ldots, M;\ i = 1, 2, \ldots, n), \tag{1}$$

where $\mathbf{z}^{*}_{im}$ and $\boldsymbol{\delta}^{*}_{m}$ are L_m-dimensional.

(a) (Assumption 4.1 as a special case of Assumption 4.1′) Verify that (1) can be written as (4.6.1) if we define

$$\underset{(\sum_{m=1}^{M} L_m \times 1)}{\mathbf{z}_{im}} = \begin{bmatrix} \mathbf{0} \\ \vdots \\ \mathbf{0} \\ \mathbf{z}^{*}_{im} \\ \mathbf{0} \\ \vdots \\ \mathbf{0} \end{bmatrix} \begin{matrix} \} \ L_1 \text{ rows} \\ \vdots \\ \} \ L_{m-1} \text{ rows} \\ \} \ L_m \text{ rows} \\ \} \ L_{m+1} \text{ rows} \\ \vdots \\ \} \ L_M \text{ rows} \end{matrix} \quad \text{and} \quad \underset{(\sum_{m=1}^{M} L_m \times 1)}{\boldsymbol{\delta}} = \begin{bmatrix} \boldsymbol{\delta}^{*}_{1} \\ \vdots \\ \boldsymbol{\delta}^{*}_{M} \end{bmatrix}. \tag{2}$$

(b) (Assumption 4.4 as a special case of Assumption 4.4′) Verify that, when $\mathbf{z}_{im}$ is defined as in (2) with $\mathbf{z}^{*}_{im}$ interpreted as the $\mathbf{z}_{im}$ of Section 4.1, Assumption 4.4′ becomes Assumption 4.4.

(c) (GMM formula) Under the same interpretation, verify that $\mathbf{S_{xz}}$ of (4.6.5) becomes a block diagonal matrix whose m-th block is $\frac{1}{n}\sum_i \mathbf{x}_{im}\mathbf{z}^{*\prime}_{im}$, so that (4.6.6) becomes (4.2.6) if the $\mathbf{z}_{im}$ in (4.2.6) is understood to mean $\mathbf{z}^{*}_{im}$.

6. (Identification in the RE model) Assumption 4.4′ in Proposition 4.7 is actually unnecessary. Verify that Assumptions 4.5 and 4.7 imply Assumption 4.4′. **Hint:** If $E(\mathbf{x}_i\mathbf{x}'_i)$ is nonsingular, then Assumption 4.4 holds, as shown in Review Question 7 to Section 4.5. Assumption 4.4′ is weaker than Assumption 4.4.

7. (Only for those who have become familiar with Kronecker products)

(a) Show that $E(\mathbf{Z}'_i\boldsymbol{\Sigma}^{-1}\mathbf{Z}_i)$ in (4.6.9′) on page 293 for the random-effects estimator is nonsingular if the assumptions of Proposition 4.7 hold. **Hint:**

$$\begin{aligned}
\mathrm{E}(\mathbf{Z}_i'\boldsymbol{\Sigma}^{-1}\mathbf{Z}_i) &= \sum_{m=1}^{M}\sum_{h=1}^{M}\sigma^{mh}\,\mathrm{E}(\mathbf{z}_{im}\mathbf{z}_{ih}') \\
&= \sum_{m=1}^{M}\sum_{h=1}^{M}\sigma^{mh}\,\mathrm{E}(\mathbf{z}_{im}\mathbf{x}_i')\left[\mathrm{E}(\mathbf{x}_i\mathbf{x}_i')\right]^{-1}\mathrm{E}(\mathbf{x}_i\mathbf{z}_{ih}')
\end{aligned}$$

($\mathbf{x}_i$ can reappear, since $\mathbf{x}_i$ includes $\mathbf{z}_{im}$ and $\mathbf{z}_{ih}$)

$$= \boldsymbol{\Sigma}_{\mathbf{xz}}'\left(\boldsymbol{\Sigma}^{-1}\otimes[\mathrm{E}(\mathbf{x}_i\mathbf{x}_i')]^{-1}\right)\boldsymbol{\Sigma}_{\mathbf{xz}}.$$

$\boldsymbol{\Sigma}_{\mathbf{xz}}$ is of full column rank by Assumption 4.4$'$.

(b) Show that $\mathrm{E}(\mathbf{Z}_i'\mathbf{Z}_i)$ in (4.6.13$'$) on page 293 for pooled OLS is invertible. **Hint:** Replace $\boldsymbol{\Sigma}^{-1}$ by $\mathbf{I}$.

4.7 Application: Interrelated Factor Demands

The **translog cost function** is a generalization of the Cobb-Douglas (log-linear) cost function introduced in Section 1.7. An attractive feature of the translog specification is that the cost-minimizing input demand equations, if transformed into cost share equations, are linear in the logs of output and factor prices, with the coefficients inheriting (a subset of) the cost function parameters characterizing the technology. Those technology parameters can be estimated from a system of equations for cost shares. Early applications of this idea include Berndt and Wood (1975) and Christensen and Greene (1976). This section reviews their basic methodology. The methodology is also applicable in the analysis of consumer demand.

To better focus on the issue at hand and to follow the practice of those original studies, we will proceed under the assumption of conditional homoskedasticity. Also, we will assume that the regressors in the system of share equations, which are log factor prices and log output, are predetermined. As we argued in Section 1.7, this assumption is not unreasonable for the U.S. electric power industry before the recent deregulation. Consequently, the appropriate multiple-equation estimation technique is the multivariate regression.

The Translog Cost Function

We have already made a partial transition from the log-linear to translog cost function: in the empirical exercise of Chapter 1, we entertained the idea of adding the square of log output to the log-linear cost function (see Model 4). If this idea is extended to the quadratic and cross terms in the logs of all the arguments, the log-linear cost function with three inputs (1.7.4) becomes the translog cost function:

$$\log(C) = \alpha_0 + \sum_{j=1}^{3} \alpha_j \log(p_j) + \frac{1}{2}\sum_{j=1}^{3}\sum_{k=1}^{3} \gamma_{jk} \log(p_j)\log(p_k)$$
$$+ \alpha_Q \log(Q) + \frac{1}{2}\gamma_{QQ}(\log(Q))^2 + \sum_{j=1}^{3} \gamma_{jQ} \log(p_j)\log(Q) + \varepsilon. \tag{4.7.1}$$

Here, and as in the rest of this section, the observation subscript "i" is dropped. In this expression, the term

$$\frac{1}{2}\sum_{j=1}^{3}\sum_{k=1}^{3} \gamma_{jk} \log(p_j)\log(p_k)$$

is a quadratic form representing the second-order effect of factor prices. We can assume, without loss of generality, that the 3×3 matrix of quadratic form coefficients, (γ_{jk}), is symmetric:[9]

$$\gamma_{jk} = \gamma_{kj} \quad (j, k = 1, 2, 3). \tag{4.7.2}$$

In the case of log-linear cost function examined in Section 1.7, the degree of returns to scale can be calculated as the reciprocal of the elasticity of costs with respect to output. If this definition is applied to the translog cost function, we have

$$\text{returns to scale} = \frac{1}{\partial \log(C)/\partial log(Q)}$$
$$= \frac{1}{\alpha_Q + \gamma_{QQ}\log(Q) + \sum_{j=1}^{3} \gamma_{jQ}\log(p_j)}. \tag{4.7.3}$$

Factor Shares

The link between the cost function parameters and factor demands is given by **Shephard's Lemma** from microeconomics. Let x_j be the cost-minimizing demand for factor input j given factor prices (p_1, p_2, p_3) and output Q. So $\sum_{j=1}^{3} p_j x_j = C$. The lemma states that

[9]Let $\mathbf{x}$ be an n-dimensional vector. The associated quadratic form is $\mathbf{x}'\mathbf{A}\mathbf{x}$. Since $\mathbf{x}'\mathbf{A}\mathbf{x} = \mathbf{x}'\mathbf{A}'\mathbf{x}$, we have $\mathbf{x}'\mathbf{A}\mathbf{x} = \mathbf{x}'[(\mathbf{A} + \mathbf{A}')/2]\mathbf{x}$. So if $\mathbf{A}$ is not symmetric, it can be replaced by the symmetric matrix $(\mathbf{A} + \mathbf{A}')/2$ without changing the value of the quadratic form.

$$\frac{\partial C}{\partial p_j} = x_j. \tag{4.7.4}$$

Noting that

$$\frac{\partial \log(C)}{\partial \log(p_j)} = \frac{p_j}{C} \cdot \frac{\partial C}{\partial p_j},$$

the lemma can also be written as stating that the logarithmic partial derivative of the cost function equals the factor share, namely,

$$\frac{\partial \log(C)}{\partial \log(p_j)} = \frac{p_j x_j}{C}. \tag{4.7.5}$$

For the case of translog cost function given in (4.7.1), the log partial derivative is easy to calculate:

$$\frac{\partial \log(C)}{\partial \log(p_j)} = \alpha_j + \sum_{k=1}^{3} \gamma_{jk} \log(p_k) + \gamma_{jQ} \log(Q) \quad (j = 1, 2, 3). \tag{4.7.6}$$

Combining this with (4.7.5) and defining the cost shares $s_j \equiv p_j x_j / C$, we obtain the following system of cost share equations associated with the translog cost function:

$$s_j = \alpha_j + \sum_{k=1}^{3} \gamma_{jk} \log(p_k) + \gamma_{jQ} \log(Q) \quad (j = 1, 2, 3). \tag{4.7.7}$$

This system of share equations is subject to the *cross-equation restrictions* that the coefficient of $\log(p_k)$ in the s_j equation equals the coefficient of $\log(p_j)$ in the s_k equation for $j \neq k$. In the rest of this section, these cross-equation restrictions will be called the symmetry restrictions, although they are *not* a consequence of the symmetry assumption (4.7.2). Those cross-equation restrictions are a consequence of calculus: you should verify that, if you did not assume symmetry, the coefficient of $\log(p_2)$ in the s_1 equation, for example, would be $(\gamma_{12} + \gamma_{21})/2$, which would equal the $\log(p_1)$ coefficient in the s_2 equation.

Substitution Elasticities

In the production function literature, a great deal of attention has been paid to estimating the elasticities of substitution (more precisely, the Hicks-Allen partial elasticities of substitution) between various inputs.[10] As shown in Uzawa (1962),

[10] See Section 9.2 of Berndt (1991) for a historical overview.

the substitution elasticity between inputs j and k, denoted η_{jk}, is related to the cost function C by the formula

$$\eta_{jk} = \frac{C \cdot \dfrac{\partial^2 C}{\partial p_j \partial p_k}}{\dfrac{\partial C}{\partial p_j} \cdot \dfrac{\partial C}{\partial p_k}}. \tag{4.7.8}$$

For the translog cost function, some routine calculus and Shephard's lemma show that

$$\eta_{jk} = \begin{cases} \dfrac{\gamma_{jk} + s_j s_k}{s_j s_k} & \text{for } j \neq k \\ \dfrac{\gamma_{jj} + s_j{}^2 - s_j}{s_j{}^2} & \text{for } j = k, \end{cases} \tag{4.7.9}$$

where s_j is the cost share of input j. In the special case of the log-linear cost function where $\gamma_{jk} = 0$ for all j, k, we have $\eta_{jk} = 1$ for $j \neq k$, verifying that the substitution elasticities are unity between any two factor inputs for the Cobb-Douglas technology.

Properties of Cost Functions

As is well known in microeconomics (see, e.g., Varian, 1992, Chapter 5), cost functions have the following properties.

1. (Homogeneity) Homogeneous of degree one in factor prices.
2. (Monotonicity) Nondecreasing in factor prices, which requires that $\partial C / \partial p_j \geq 0$ for all j.
3. (Concavity) Concave in factor prices, which requires that the Hessian (the matrix of second-order derivatives) of a cost function C, say

$$\mathbf{H} \equiv (\partial^2 C / \partial p_j \partial p_k),$$

be negative semidefinite. By (4.7.8), concavity is satisfied if and only if the matrix of substitution elasticities, (η_{jk}), is negative semidefinite.[11]

For the case of translog cost function, these properties take the following form.

[11] Let $\mathbf{H}$ be the Hessian of the cost function C and $\mathbf{V}$ be a diagonal matrix whose j-th diagonal is $\partial C / \partial p_j$. Then the matrix of substitution elasticities, (η_{jk}), given in (4.7.8) can be written compactly as: $(\eta_{jk}) = C \cdot \mathbf{V}^{-1} \mathbf{H} \mathbf{V}^{-1}$. Since $\mathbf{V}$ is a diagonal matrix, $\mathbf{V}^{-1} \mathbf{H} \mathbf{V}^{-1}$ is negative semidefinite if and only if $\mathbf{H}$ is.

1. *Homogeneity:* It is easy to verify (see a review question) that, with the symmetry restrictions imposed on (γ_{jk}), the homogeneity condition can be expressed as

$$\begin{cases} \alpha_1 + \alpha_2 + \alpha_3 = 1, \\ \gamma_{11} + \gamma_{12} + \gamma_{13} = 0, \\ \gamma_{12} + \gamma_{22} + \gamma_{23} = 0, \\ \gamma_{13} + \gamma_{23} + \gamma_{33} = 0, \\ \gamma_{1Q} + \gamma_{2Q} + \gamma_{3Q} = 0. \end{cases} \tag{4.7.10}$$

   Homogeneity will be imposed in our estimation of the share equations.

2. *Monotonicity:* Given Shephard's lemma, monotonicity is equivalent to requiring that the right-hand sides of the share equations (4.7.7) be nonnegative for any combinations of factor prices and output. For any values of coefficients, we can always choose factor prices and output so that this condition is violated. Accordingly, we cannot impose monotonicity on the share equations. It is possible, however, to check whether monotonicity is satisfied for the "relevant range," that is, if it is satisfied for all the combinations of factor prices and output found in the data at hand; we will do this for the estimated parameters below.

3. *Concavity:* Concavity requires that the matrix of substitution elasticities given by (4.7.9) be negative semidefinite for any combinations of cost shares. It is possible to show that a necessary and sufficient condition for concavity is that the 3×3 matrix (γ_{jk}) be negative semidefinite.[12] In particular, the diagonal elements, $(\gamma_{11}, \gamma_{22}, \gamma_{33})$, have to be nonpositive. The condition that the matrix (γ_{jk}) be negative semidefinite is a set of inequality conditions on its elements. Estimation while imposing inequality conditions is feasible (see Jorgenson, 1986, Section 2.4.5, for the required technique), but it will not be pursued here.

Stochastic Specifications

The translog cost function given in (4.7.1) has an (additive) error term, ε, while the share equations derived from it have none. On our data, the share equations do

[12] Proof: Let $\mathbf{s}$ here be a 3×1 vector whose j-th element is s_j and $\mathbf{S}$ here be a diagonal matrix whose j-th element is s_j. Then the matrix of substitution elasticities given in (4.7.9) can be written as $(\eta_{jk}) = \mathbf{S}^{-1}[(\gamma_{jk}) + \mathbf{ss}' - \mathbf{S}]\mathbf{S}^{-1}$. For some combination of cost shares, $\mathbf{ss}' - \mathbf{S}$ is zero (for example, set $\mathbf{s} = (1, 0, 0)'$). So a necessary condition for the matrix (η_{jk}) to be negative semidefinite is that the matrix (γ_{jk}) is negative semidefinite. This condition is also sufficient, because the matrix $\mathbf{ss}' - \mathbf{S}$ is negative semidefinite and the sum of two negative semidefinite matrices is negative semidefinite.

not hold exactly for each firm, so we need to allow for errors. The usual practice is to add a random disturbance term to each share equation. There are two ways to justify such a stochastic specification. One is optimization errors: firms make random errors in choosing their cost-minimizing input combinations. But then actual total costs will not be as low as what is indicated in the cost function, because there is no room for optimization errors in the derivation of the cost function. The other justification for errors is to allow α_j in the share equations to be stochastic and differ across firms. The intercept in the share equation for j would then be the mean of α_j, and the error term would be the deviation of α_j from its mean. But this also means that the α_j in the cost function has to be treated as random.

In either case, therefore, internal consistency would prevent us from adding the cost function to the share equations with additive errors to form a system of estimation equations. In the rest of this section, we will focus on a system that consists entirely of share equations. This, however, means that we can estimate only a subset of the cost function parameters. Two parameters, α_Q and γ_{QQ}, which are absent in factor demands, cannot be estimated. Since the degree of returns to scale depends on them (see (4.7.3)), it cannot be estimated either.

The Nature of Restrictions

With the additive errors appended, the system of share equations (4.7.7) is written out in full as

$$\begin{cases} s_1 = \alpha_1 + \gamma_{11}\log(p_1) + \gamma_{12}\log(p_2) + \gamma_{13}\log(p_3) + \gamma_{1Q}\log(Q) + \varepsilon_1, \\ s_2 = \alpha_2 + \gamma_{21}\log(p_1) + \gamma_{22}\log(p_2) + \gamma_{23}\log(p_3) + \gamma_{2Q}\log(Q) + \varepsilon_2, \\ s_3 = \alpha_3 + \gamma_{31}\log(p_1) + \gamma_{32}\log(p_2) + \gamma_{33}\log(p_3) + \gamma_{3Q}\log(Q) + \varepsilon_3. \end{cases} \tag{4.7.11}$$

This system has fifteen coefficients or parameters. The cross-equation restrictions (that the 3×3 matrix of log price coefficients, (γ_{jk}), be symmetric) and the homogeneity restrictions (4.7.10) form a set of eight restrictions, so that the fifteen parameters can be described by seven free parameters. To understand this, it is useful to decompose the restrictions into the following three groups.

$$\text{adding-up restrictions:} \quad \begin{cases} \alpha_1 + \alpha_2 + \alpha_3 = 1, \\ \gamma_{11} + \gamma_{21} + \gamma_{31} = 0, \\ \gamma_{12} + \gamma_{22} + \gamma_{32} = 0, \\ \gamma_{13} + \gamma_{23} + \gamma_{33} = 0, \\ \gamma_{1Q} + \gamma_{2Q} + \gamma_{3Q} = 0. \end{cases} \tag{4.7.12}$$

$$\text{homogeneity:} \quad \begin{cases} \gamma_{11} + \gamma_{12} + \gamma_{13} = 0, \\ \gamma_{21} + \gamma_{22} + \gamma_{23} = 0, \\ \gamma_{31} + \gamma_{32} + \gamma_{33} = 0, \end{cases} \tag{4.7.13}$$

$$\text{symmetry:} \quad \begin{cases} \gamma_{12} = \gamma_{21}, \\ \gamma_{13} = \gamma_{31}, \\ \gamma_{23} = \gamma_{32}. \end{cases} \tag{4.7.14}$$

These are eleven equations, but only eight of them are restrictive: given the adding-up restrictions, one of the three homogeneity restrictions is implied by the two others, and given the adding-up and homogeneity restrictions, two of the three symmetry restrictions are implied by the other (you should verify this).

Multivariate Regression Subject to Cross-Equation Restrictions

It is straightforward to impose the homogeneity restrictions, (4.7.13), because they are not cross-equation restrictions. We can eliminate three parameters, say $(\gamma_{13}, \gamma_{23}, \gamma_{33})$, from the system to obtain

$$\begin{cases} s_1 = \alpha_1 + \gamma_{11} \log(p_1/p_3) + \gamma_{12} \log(p_2/p_3) + \gamma_{1Q} \log(Q) + \varepsilon_1, \\ s_2 = \alpha_2 + \gamma_{21} \log(p_1/p_3) + \gamma_{22} \log(p_2/p_3) + \gamma_{2Q} \log(Q) + \varepsilon_2, \\ s_3 = \alpha_3 + \gamma_{31} \log(p_1/p_3) + \gamma_{32} \log(p_2/p_3) + \gamma_{3Q} \log(Q) + \varepsilon_3. \end{cases} \tag{4.7.15}$$

The system (with or without the imposition of homogeneity) has the special feature that the sum of the dependent variables, (s_1, s_2, s_3), adds up to unity for all observations. This feature and the adding-up restrictions imply that the sum of the error terms, $(\varepsilon_1, \varepsilon_2, \varepsilon_3)$, is zero for all observations, so the 3×3 error covariance matrix, $\mathbf{\Sigma} \equiv \text{Var}(\varepsilon_1, \varepsilon_2, \varepsilon_3)$, is singular. Recall that, in the multivariate regression model (which is the special case of the SUR model described in Proposition 4.6), the $\mathbf{S}$ matrix defined in (4.1.11) can be written as a Kronecker product: $\mathbf{S} = \mathbf{\Sigma} \otimes \text{E}(\mathbf{x}_i \mathbf{x}_i')$. Thus $\mathbf{S}$ becomes singular, in violation of Assumption 4.5. The common practice to deal with this singularity problem is to drop one equation from the system and estimate the system composed of the remaining equations (see below for more on this issue). The coefficients in the equation that was dropped can be calculated from the coefficient estimates for the included two equations by using the adding-up restrictions. The adding-up restrictions as well as homogeneity are thus incorporated.

As mentioned above, given the adding-up restrictions and homogeneity, there is effectively only one symmetry restriction. For example, if $(\gamma_{13}, \gamma_{23}, \gamma_{33})$ are eliminated from the system to incorporate homogeneity, as in (4.7.15), and if the third equation is dropped to incorporate the adding-up restrictions, then the unique symmetry restriction can be stated as $\gamma_{12} = \gamma_{21}$. If this cross-equation restriction is imposed, the system becomes

$$\begin{cases} s_1 = \alpha_1 + \gamma_{11}\log(p_1/p_3) + \gamma_{12}\log(p_2/p_3) + \gamma_{1Q}\log(Q) + \varepsilon_1, \\ s_2 = \alpha_2 + \gamma_{12}\log(p_1/p_3) + \gamma_{22}\log(p_2/p_3) + \gamma_{2Q}\log(Q) + \varepsilon_2. \end{cases} \tag{4.7.16}$$

Since the regressors are predetermined and since the equations have common regressors, the system can be estimated by the multivariate regression subject to the cross-equation restriction of symmetry. This constrained estimation, if it is cast in the "common coefficient" format explored in Section 4.6, can be transformed into an unconstrained estimation. That is, the system (4.7.16) can be written in the "common coefficient" format of $\mathbf{y}_i = \mathbf{Z}_i\boldsymbol{\delta} + \boldsymbol{\varepsilon}_i$ (see (4.6.1′) on page 292), if we set (while still dropping the "i" subscript from s_1, s_2, $\log(p_1/p_3)$, $\log(p_2/p_3)$, and $\log(Q)$)

$$\mathbf{y}_i = \begin{bmatrix} s_1 \\ s_2 \end{bmatrix},$$

$$\mathbf{Z}_i = \begin{bmatrix} 1 & 0 & \log(p_1/p_3) & \log(p_2/p_3) & 0 & \log(Q) & 0 \\ 0 & 1 & 0 & \log(p_1/p_3) & \log(p_2/p_3) & 0 & \log(Q) \end{bmatrix},$$

$$\boldsymbol{\delta}' = \begin{bmatrix} \alpha_1 & \alpha_2 & \gamma_{11} & \gamma_{12} & \gamma_{22} & \gamma_{1Q} & \gamma_{2Q} \end{bmatrix}. \tag{4.7.17}$$

So the multivariate regression subject to symmetry is equivalent to the (unconstrained) random-effects estimation.

This random-effects estimation of the two-equation system produces consistent estimates of the following seven parameters:

$$\alpha_1, \alpha_2, \gamma_{11}, \gamma_{12}, \gamma_{22}, \gamma_{1Q}, \gamma_{2Q}.$$

The rest of the fifteen share equation parameters,

$$\alpha_3, \gamma_{13}, \gamma_{21}, \gamma_{23}, \gamma_{31}, \gamma_{32}, \gamma_{33}, \gamma_{3Q},$$

can be calculated using the adding-up restrictions (4.7.12), homogeneity (4.7.13), and symmetry (4.7.14). For example, γ_{33} can be calculated as

$$\gamma_{33} = -\gamma_{31} - \gamma_{32} = -\gamma_{13} - \gamma_{23} = (\gamma_{11} + \gamma_{12}) + (\gamma_{12} + \gamma_{22}) = \gamma_{11} + 2\gamma_{12} + \gamma_{22}.$$

So the point estimate of γ_{33} is given by

$$\hat{\gamma}_{33} = \hat{\gamma}_{11} + 2\hat{\gamma}_{12} + \hat{\gamma}_{22},$$

where $(\hat{\gamma}_{11}, \hat{\gamma}_{12}, \hat{\gamma}_{22})$ are the random-effects estimates. The standard error of $\hat{\gamma}_{33}$ can be calculated by applying the "delta method" (see Lemma 2.5) to the consistent estimate of $\text{Avar}(\hat{\gamma}_{11}, \hat{\gamma}_{12}, \hat{\gamma}_{22})$ obtained from the random-effects estimation.

Which Equation to Delete?

Does it matter which equation is to be dropped from the system? It clearly would not if there were no cross-equation restrictions, because the multivariate regression is numerically equivalent to the equation-by-equation OLS. To see if the numerical invariance holds under the cross-equation restriction, let $\mathbf{\Sigma}^*$ be the 2×2 matrix of error covariances for the two-equation system obtained from dropping one equation from the three-equation system (4.7.15). It is the appropriate submatrix of the 3×3 error covariance matrix $\mathbf{\Sigma}$. (For example, if the third equation is dropped, then $\mathbf{\Sigma}^*$ is the leading 2×2 submatrix of the 3×3 matrix $\mathbf{\Sigma}$.) To implement the random-effects estimation, we need a consistent estimate, $\widehat{\mathbf{\Sigma}}^*$, of $\mathbf{\Sigma}^*$. Two ways for obtaining $\widehat{\mathbf{\Sigma}}^*$ are:

- (equation-by-equation OLS) Estimate the two equations separately, thus ignoring the cross-equation restriction, and then use the residuals to calculate $\widehat{\mathbf{\Sigma}}^*$. Equivalently, estimate the *three* equations separately by OLS, use the three-equation residuals to calculate $\widehat{\mathbf{\Sigma}}$ (an estimate of the 3×3 error covariance matrix $\mathbf{\Sigma}$), and then extract the appropriate submatrix from $\widehat{\mathbf{\Sigma}}$. If $\widehat{\mathbf{\Sigma}}^*$ is thus obtained, then (as you will verify in the empirical exercise) the numerical invariance is guaranteed; it does not matter which equation to drop.
- Obtain $\widehat{\mathbf{\Sigma}}^*$ from some technique that exploits the cross-equation restriction (such as the pooled OLS applied to the common coefficient format). The numerical invariance in this case is not guaranteed.

The numerical invariance holds under equation-by-equation OLS, because the 3×3 matrix $\widehat{\mathbf{\Sigma}}$, from which $\widehat{\mathbf{\Sigma}}^*$ is derived, is singular in finite samples. In large samples, as long as $\widehat{\mathbf{\Sigma}}^*$ is consistent, and even if $\widehat{\mathbf{\Sigma}}^*$ is not from equation-by-equation OLS, this relationship between $\widehat{\mathbf{\Sigma}}^*$ and $\widehat{\mathbf{\Sigma}}$ holds asymptotically because $\mathbf{\Sigma}$ is singular. So the invariance holds asymptotically if $\widehat{\mathbf{\Sigma}}^*$ is consistent. In particular, the asymptotic variance of parameter estimates does not depend on the choice of equation to drop.

Results

Nerlove's study examined in Chapter 1 was based on 1955 cross-section data for U.S. electric utility companies. Christensen and Greene (1976) updated Nerlove's data to 1970 for 99 firms, using data sources that allowed them to construct better measures of the wage rate and fuel prices (see their Section V for more details). Their data set includes information on factor shares, so the share equations can be estimated. The means and standard deviations for some of the variables in the data are reported in Table 4.3, which shows that fuel accounts for a very large share of the cost of electricity generation.

We use the equation-by-equation OLS residuals to calculate $\widehat{\mathbf{\Sigma}}^*$, so that the random-effects estimates are numerically invariant to the choice of equation to drop. The estimates are reported in Table 4.4, along with $\widehat{\mathbf{\Sigma}}$ derived from the equation-by-equation OLS. The factor input index j is 1 for labor, 2 for capital, and 3 for fuel. Some (actually all) of the diagonal elements of the matrix of estimated price coefficients, $(\hat{\gamma}_{jk})$, are positive. So the matrix is not negative semidefinite, in violation of concavity.[13]

Even if $(\widehat{\gamma}_{jk})$ is not negative semidefinite, the associated substitution elasticities given in the formula (4.7.9) may be negative semidefinite. Since the formula is derived assuming no optimization errors, fitted cost shares, rather than actual cost shares, should be used for the s_j and s_k in the formula. The elasticities averaged over firms are shown in Table 4.5. (They are the off-diagonal elements of the symmetric 3×3 substitution elasticity matrix thus calculated.) The three factor inputs are substitutes because the substitution elasticities are positive, but the degree of substitutability is far less than what is assumed in the log-linear technology. Concavity is violated even in the "relevant range": for 20 firms out of the 99 in the sample, the matrix of substitution elasticities is not negative semidefinite. Monotonicity, in contrast, is satisfied in the relevant range: fitted cost shares are nonnegative for all inputs for all firms in the sample.

[13]This "test" of concavity can be formalized. Using the delta method, we can calculate the asymptotic distribution of the characteristic roots of $(\hat{\gamma}_{jk})$. The null hypothesis of concavity is that those characteristic roots are all nonpositive.

Table 4.3: Simple Statistics (Sample Size = 99)

	Output in kilowatt hours	Labor share	Capital share	Fuel share
Mean	9.0	0.141	0.227	0.631
Std. deviation	10.3	0.059	0.062	0.095

Table 4.4: Random-Effects Estimates

Parameter	Point estimate	Standard error	t-value
α_1	−0.132	0.106	−1.25
α_2	0.318	0.085	3.75
α_3	0.813	0.094	8.69
γ_{11}	0.084	0.020	4.19
γ_{12}	−0.023	0.016	−1.46
γ_{13}	−0.060	0.015	−3.92
γ_{22}	0.122	0.020	6.19
γ_{23}	−0.099	0.017	−5.75
γ_{33}	0.159	0.023	6.90
γ_{1Q}	−0.0211	0.0025	−8.55
γ_{2Q}	−0.0086	0.0030	−2.87
γ_{3Q}	0.0297	0.0037	7.98

$$\widehat{\boldsymbol{\Sigma}} \text{ by pooled OLS} = \begin{bmatrix} 0.00173 & -0.000171 & -0.00156 \\ -0.000171 & 0.00253 & -0.00236 \\ -0.00156 & -0.00236 & 0.00391 \end{bmatrix}$$

Table 4.5: Substitution Elasticities

Labor-Capital	Capital-Fuel	Labor-Fuel
0.17	0.27	0.29

QUESTIONS FOR REVIEW

1. Derive (4.7.6). Verify that the symmetry of (γ_{jk}) is used in the derivation.

2. Derive the homogeneity restrictions (4.7.10). **Hint:** For the translog cost function (4.7.1) to be homogeneous of degree one in factor prices, it is necessary and sufficient that, for any scalar $\lambda \neq 0$,

$$\sum_{j=1}^{3} \alpha_j \log(\lambda \cdot p_j) + \frac{1}{2} \sum_{j=1}^{3} \sum_{k=1}^{3} \gamma_{jk} \log(\lambda \cdot p_j) \log(\lambda \cdot p_k)$$
$$+ \alpha_Q \log(Q) + \frac{1}{2} \gamma_{QQ} (\log(Q))^2 + \sum_{j=1}^{3} \gamma_{jQ} \log(\lambda \cdot p_j) \log(Q)$$
$$= \log(\lambda) + \sum_{j=1}^{3} \alpha_j \log(p_j) + \frac{1}{2} \sum_{j=1}^{3} \sum_{k=1}^{3} \gamma_{jk} \log(p_j) \log(p_k)$$
$$+ \alpha_Q \log(Q) + \frac{1}{2} \gamma_{QQ} (\log(Q))^2 + \sum_{j=1}^{3} \gamma_{jQ} \log(p_j) \log(Q).$$

3. (Counting restrictions) Using the adding-up restrictions (4.7.12), two of the three equations in (4.7.13), and one of the three equations in (4.7.14), derive the other two equations in (4.7.14).

4. (OLS respects singularity) Consider applying the equation-by-equation OLS to each of the three equations in (4.7.15). Show that the equation-by-equation OLS estimates of the coefficients satisfy the adding-up restrictions. Show that the 3×3 error covariance matrix calculated from the equation-by-equation OLS residuals is singular. **Hint:** Let $\mathbf{y}_1$, $\mathbf{y}_2$, $\mathbf{y}_3$ be n-dimensional vectors of the three dependent variables (where n is the sample size), and let $\mathbf{X}$ be the $n \times K$ data matrix of the common K regressors ($K = 4$ in (4.7.15)). Note that $\mathbf{y}_1 + \mathbf{y}_2 + \mathbf{y}_3 = \mathbf{0}$. The equation-by-equation OLS coefficient estimates are $(\mathbf{X}'\mathbf{X})^{-1}\mathbf{X}'\mathbf{y}_j$, $j = 1, 2, 3$. The three $n \times 1$ residual vectors are $\mathbf{M}\mathbf{y}_j$, $j = 1, 2, 3$, where $\mathbf{M} \equiv \mathbf{I}_n - \mathbf{X}(\mathbf{X}'\mathbf{X})^{-1}\mathbf{X}'$.

PROBLEM SET FOR CHAPTER 4

ANALYTICAL EXERCISES

1. (Data matrix representation of 3SLS) In the 3SLS model, the set of instruments is the same across equations. Let K be the number of common instruments. Define:

$$\underset{(n\times K)}{\mathbf{X}} = \begin{bmatrix} \mathbf{x}_1' \\ \vdots \\ \mathbf{x}_n' \end{bmatrix} = \begin{bmatrix} x_{11} & \cdots & x_{1K} \\ \vdots & & \vdots \\ x_{n1} & \cdots & x_{nK} \end{bmatrix},$$

$$\underset{(n\times L_m)}{\mathbf{Z}_m} = \begin{bmatrix} \mathbf{z}_{1m}' \\ \vdots \\ \mathbf{z}_{nm}' \end{bmatrix}, \quad \underset{(Mn\times\sum_{m=1}^{M} L_m)}{\mathbf{Z}} = \begin{bmatrix} \mathbf{Z}_1 & & \\ & \ddots & \\ & & \mathbf{Z}_M \end{bmatrix},$$

$$\underset{(\sum_{m=1}^{M} L_m\times 1)}{\boldsymbol{\delta}} = \begin{bmatrix} \boldsymbol{\delta}_1 \\ \vdots \\ \boldsymbol{\delta}_M \end{bmatrix},$$

$$\underset{(Mn\times 1)}{\mathbf{y}} = \begin{bmatrix} \mathbf{y}_1 \\ \vdots \\ \mathbf{y}_M \end{bmatrix}, \quad \underset{(n\times 1)}{\mathbf{y}_m} = \begin{bmatrix} y_{1m} \\ \vdots \\ y_{nm} \end{bmatrix},$$

$$\underset{(Mn\times 1)}{\boldsymbol{\varepsilon}} = \begin{bmatrix} \boldsymbol{\varepsilon}_1 \\ \vdots \\ \boldsymbol{\varepsilon}_M \end{bmatrix}, \quad \underset{(n\times 1)}{\boldsymbol{\varepsilon}_m} = \begin{bmatrix} \varepsilon_{1m} \\ \vdots \\ \varepsilon_{nm} \end{bmatrix}.$$

Show the following:

- Assumption 4.1 becomes $\mathbf{y} = \mathbf{Z}\boldsymbol{\delta} + \boldsymbol{\varepsilon}$,
- $\widehat{\mathbf{S}}$ in (4.5.10) becomes $\widehat{\mathbf{S}} = \widehat{\boldsymbol{\Sigma}} \otimes \frac{1}{n}\mathbf{X}'\mathbf{X}$,
- $\hat{\boldsymbol{\delta}}_{3\text{SLS}} = [\mathbf{Z}'(\widehat{\boldsymbol{\Sigma}}^{-1} \otimes \mathbf{P})\mathbf{Z}]^{-1}\mathbf{Z}'(\widehat{\boldsymbol{\Sigma}}^{-1} \otimes \mathbf{P})\mathbf{y}$, where $\mathbf{P} \equiv \mathbf{X}(\mathbf{X}'\mathbf{X})^{-1}\mathbf{X}'$,
- $\widehat{\text{Avar}(\hat{\boldsymbol{\delta}}_{3\text{SLS}})} = n \cdot [\mathbf{Z}'(\widehat{\boldsymbol{\Sigma}}^{-1} \otimes \mathbf{P})\mathbf{Z}]^{-1}$,
- $\widehat{\mathbf{A}}_{mh}$ in (4.5.13) becomes $\widehat{\mathbf{A}}_{mh} = \frac{1}{n}\mathbf{Z}_m'\mathbf{P}\mathbf{Z}_h$,
- $\hat{\mathbf{c}}_{mh}$ in (4.5.14) becomes $\hat{\mathbf{c}}_{mh} = \frac{1}{n}\mathbf{Z}_m'\mathbf{P}\mathbf{y}_h$.
- $J(\hat{\boldsymbol{\delta}}_{3\text{SLS}}, \widehat{\mathbf{S}}^{-1}) = (\mathbf{y} - \mathbf{Z}\hat{\boldsymbol{\delta}}_{3\text{SLS}})'(\widehat{\boldsymbol{\Sigma}}^{-1} \otimes \mathbf{P})(\mathbf{y} - \mathbf{Z}\hat{\boldsymbol{\delta}}_{3\text{SLS}})$.

Hint:

$$\frac{1}{n}\sum_{i=1}^{n}\mathbf{x}_i\mathbf{x}_i' = \frac{1}{n}\mathbf{X}'\mathbf{X},\quad \mathbf{s}_{\mathbf{xy}} = \frac{1}{n}(\mathbf{I}_M \otimes \mathbf{X})'\mathbf{y},\quad \mathbf{S}_{\mathbf{xz}} = \frac{1}{n}(\mathbf{I}_M \otimes \mathbf{X})'\mathbf{Z}.$$

Use formulas (A.11) and (A.13)–(A.15) of Appendix A.

2. (Data matrix representation of SUR, RE, and Pooled OLS)

(a) Prove that (4.5.13) reduces to (4.5.13$'$) (on page 280) and (4.5.14) to (4.5.14$'$), under the SUR assumption (4.5.18). **Hint:** If $\mathbf{P} \equiv \mathbf{X}(\mathbf{X}'\mathbf{X})^{-1}\mathbf{X}'$, then $\widehat{\mathbf{A}}_{mh} = \frac{1}{n}\mathbf{Z}_m'\mathbf{P}\mathbf{Z}_h$, $\hat{\mathbf{c}}_{mh} = \frac{1}{n}\mathbf{Z}_m'\mathbf{P}\mathbf{y}_h$. $\mathbf{P}\mathbf{Z}_m = \mathbf{Z}_m$ if the columns of $\mathbf{Z}_m$ are taken from the columns of $\mathbf{X}$.

(b) Show that, for SUR,

$$\text{the estimator} = [\mathbf{Z}'(\widehat{\boldsymbol{\Sigma}}^{-1} \otimes \mathbf{I}_n)\mathbf{Z}]^{-1}\mathbf{Z}'(\widehat{\boldsymbol{\Sigma}}^{-1} \otimes \mathbf{I}_n)\mathbf{y},$$
$$\text{its } \widehat{\text{Avar}} = n \cdot [\mathbf{Z}'(\widehat{\boldsymbol{\Sigma}}^{-1} \otimes \mathbf{I}_n)\mathbf{Z}]^{-1}.$$

(c) Suppose, just for this part of the question, that $\mathbf{z}_{im} = \mathbf{x}_i$ for all m. So $\mathbf{Z} = \mathbf{I}_M \otimes \mathbf{X}$. Show that SUR reduces to the multivariate regression estimator

$$[\mathbf{I}_M \otimes (\mathbf{X}'\mathbf{X})^{-1}\mathbf{X}']\mathbf{y}.$$

Verify that the m-th K-dimensional block of this MK-dimensional vector is $(\mathbf{X}'\mathbf{X})^{-1}\mathbf{X}'\mathbf{y}_m$.

Now redefine $\mathbf{Z}$ as

$$\underset{(Mn\times L)}{\mathbf{Z}} \equiv \begin{bmatrix} \mathbf{Z}_1 \\ \vdots \\ \mathbf{Z}_M \end{bmatrix}. \qquad (*)$$

So Assumption 4.1$'$ (linear equations with common coefficients) can be written as $\mathbf{y} = \mathbf{Z}\boldsymbol{\delta} + \boldsymbol{\varepsilon}$, where $\mathbf{y}$ and $\boldsymbol{\varepsilon}$ are as in Analytical Exercise 1 and $\boldsymbol{\delta}$ is the L-dimensional vector of common coefficients.

(d) Show that, for the random-effects estimator, the same formulas you derived in (b) for SUR hold with $\mathbf{Z}$ as just redefined as in $(*)$. **Hint:** The estimator is given in (4.6.8) and its $\widehat{\text{Avar}}$ is in (4.6.10). Use formula (A.8) of the Appendix.

(e) Show that

$$\hat{\boldsymbol{\delta}}_{\text{pooled OLS}} \text{ in (4.6.11)} = (\mathbf{Z}'\mathbf{Z})^{-1}\mathbf{Z}'\mathbf{y},$$

$$\widehat{\text{Avar}(\hat{\boldsymbol{\delta}}_{\text{pooled OLS}})} \text{ in (4.6.14)} = n \cdot (\mathbf{Z}'\mathbf{Z})^{-1}[\mathbf{Z}'(\widehat{\boldsymbol{\Sigma}} \otimes \mathbf{I}_n)\mathbf{Z}](\mathbf{Z}'\mathbf{Z})^{-1}.$$

(f) In the $Mn \times L$ matrix $\mathbf{Z}$ defined in $(*)$, its rows are ordered first by the equation (m) and then by observation (i). Now order the rows first by observation (i), which amounts to redefining $\mathbf{Z}$ as

$$\underset{(Mn\times L)}{\mathbf{Z}} \equiv \begin{bmatrix} \mathbf{Z}_1 \\ \vdots \\ \mathbf{Z}_n \end{bmatrix},$$

where $\mathbf{Z}_i$ $(i = 1, 2, \dots, n)$ is the $M \times L$ matrix defined in (4.6.15). Reorder rows of $\mathbf{y}$ and $\boldsymbol{\varepsilon}$ similarly:

$$\underset{(Mn\times 1)}{\mathbf{y}} = \begin{bmatrix} \mathbf{y}_1 \\ \vdots \\ \mathbf{y}_n \end{bmatrix}, \quad \underset{(Mn\times 1)}{\boldsymbol{\varepsilon}} = \begin{bmatrix} \boldsymbol{\varepsilon}_1 \\ \vdots \\ \boldsymbol{\varepsilon}_n \end{bmatrix}.$$

How would the formulas for RE and pooled OLS you derived in (d) and (e) change? **Hint:** Just replace "$\widehat{\boldsymbol{\Sigma}} \otimes \mathbf{I}_n$" by "$\mathbf{I}_n \otimes \widehat{\boldsymbol{\Sigma}}$". Set $M = 2$ if you find the translation too hard.

3. (GLS interpretation of SUR and RE) The SUR model consists of Assumptions 4.1–4.5, 4.7, and (4.5.18) (that $\mathbf{x}_i$ = union of $(\mathbf{z}_{i1}, \dots, \mathbf{z}_{iM})$). Specialize the model by strengthening Assumption 4.3 (orthogonality conditions) as

$$\text{E}(\varepsilon_{im} \mid \mathbf{z}_{i1}, \dots, \mathbf{z}_{iM}) = 0 \quad (m = 1, \dots, M),$$

and Assumption 4.2 (ergodic stationarity) as stating that

$$\{y_{i1}, \dots, y_{iM}, \mathbf{z}_{i1}, \dots, \mathbf{z}_{iM}\}$$

is i.i.d.

(a) (Easy) Explain why these are stronger assumptions.

(b) Let $\boldsymbol{\varepsilon}$ $(Mn \times 1)$ and $\mathbf{Z}$ $(Mn \times \sum_m L_m)$ be as in Analytical Exercise 1 above.

Show that the specialized model implies

$$\mathrm{E}(\boldsymbol{\varepsilon} \mid \mathbf{Z}) = \mathbf{0} \quad \text{and} \quad \mathrm{E}(\boldsymbol{\varepsilon}\boldsymbol{\varepsilon}' \mid \mathbf{Z}) = \boldsymbol{\Sigma} \otimes \mathbf{I}_n.$$

Hint: For the first, what needs to be shown is $\mathrm{E}(\varepsilon_{im} \mid \mathbf{Z}) = 0$. For the latter, the (m, h) block of $\mathrm{E}(\boldsymbol{\varepsilon}\boldsymbol{\varepsilon}' \mid \mathbf{Z})$ is $\mathrm{E}(\boldsymbol{\varepsilon}_m \boldsymbol{\varepsilon}_h' \mid \mathbf{Z})$, an $n \times n$ matrix. What needs to be shown is that this matrix is $\sigma_{mh}\mathbf{I}_n$.

(c) (Finite-sample properties of SUR) Suppose $\boldsymbol{\Sigma}$ is known so that the consistent estimates $\hat{\sigma}_{mh}$ in the SUR formulas in Proposition 4.6 can be equated with the true value σ_{mh}.

(i) Verify that the model satisfies the GLS assumptions of Section 1.6 (which are Assumptions 1.1–1.3 and (1.6.1)) with a sample size of Mn.

(ii) Verify that the SUR estimator is the GLS estimator. **Hint:** The $\mathbf{X}$ in Section 1.6 is $\mathbf{Z}$ here. Show that $\sigma^2 \mathbf{V}$ there is $\boldsymbol{\Sigma} \otimes \mathbf{I}_n$. Use your answer to 2(b).

(iii) Verify that SUR is unbiased in finite samples in that $\mathrm{E}(\hat{\boldsymbol{\delta}}_{\mathrm{SUR}} - \boldsymbol{\delta} \mid \mathbf{Z}) = \mathbf{0}$.

(iv) The expression for $\mathrm{Var}(\hat{\boldsymbol{\delta}}_{\mathrm{SUR}} \mid \mathbf{Z})$ is given in Proposition 1.7 of Section 1.6. Show that

$$\mathrm{Avar}(\hat{\boldsymbol{\delta}}_{\mathrm{SUR}}) = \operatorname*{plim}_{n \to \infty} n \cdot \mathrm{Var}(\hat{\boldsymbol{\delta}}_{\mathrm{SUR}} \mid \mathbf{Z}).$$

Hint: With $\mathrm{E}(\boldsymbol{\varepsilon}\boldsymbol{\varepsilon}' \mid \mathbf{Z}) = \boldsymbol{\Sigma} \otimes \mathbf{I}_n$, the matrix $\mathrm{Var}(\hat{\boldsymbol{\delta}}_{\mathrm{SUR}} \mid \mathbf{Z})$ is the inverse of a matrix whose (m, h) block is $\sigma^{mh}\mathbf{Z}_m'\mathbf{Z}_h$. $\mathbf{Z}_m'\mathbf{Z}_h = \sum_i \mathbf{z}_{im}\mathbf{z}_{ih}'$.

(d) (Finite-sample properties of RE) Now impose on the model the condition that the coefficient vector is the same across equations so that $\mathbf{Z}$ is as in $(*)$ of Analytical Exercise 2. As in (c), suppose $\boldsymbol{\Sigma}$ is known so that the consistent estimates $\hat{\sigma}_{mh}$ in the RE formulas in Proposition 4.7 can be equated with the true value σ_{mh}.

(i) Verify that this model with common coefficients satisfies the GLS assumptions of Section 1.6. In particular, Assumption 1.1 can be written as $\mathbf{y} = \mathbf{Z}\boldsymbol{\delta} + \boldsymbol{\varepsilon}$, where $\mathbf{y}$ and $\boldsymbol{\varepsilon}$ are as in Analytical Exercise 2.

(ii) Verify that the random-effects estimator is the GLS estimator.

(iii) Verify that the random-effects estimator is unbiased in finite samples.

(iv) Show that

$$\text{Avar}(\hat{\boldsymbol{\delta}}_{\text{RE}}) = \operatorname*{plim}_{n\to\infty} n \cdot \text{Var}(\hat{\boldsymbol{\delta}}_{\text{RE}} \mid \mathbf{Z}).$$

Hint: $\text{Var}(\hat{\boldsymbol{\delta}}_{\text{RE}} \mid \mathbf{Z})$ is the inverse of $\sum_m \sum_h \sigma^{mh} \mathbf{Z}'_m \mathbf{Z}_h$.

4. (Standard errors from equation-by-equation vs. multiple-equation GMM) We have shown in Section 4.4 that the Avar of the efficient equation-by-equation GMM estimator is no less (in matrix sense) than the Avar of the efficient multiple-equation GMM estimators. In this exercise we show that the same holds for $\widehat{\text{Avar}}$. Let $\widehat{\mathbf{S}}$ and $\mathbf{S_{xz}}$ be as in (4.3.2) and (4.2.2), respectively.

   (a) (Trivial) Verify that, under appropriate assumptions, $(\mathbf{S}'_{\mathbf{xz}}\widehat{\mathbf{S}}^{-1}\mathbf{S_{xz}})^{-1}$ is consistent for the asymptotic variance of the efficient multiple-equation GMM estimator. What are those appropriate assumptions?

   (b) Let $\tilde{\boldsymbol{\delta}}_m$ be the efficient single-equation GMM estimator of $\boldsymbol{\delta}_m$ and $\tilde{\boldsymbol{\delta}}$ be the stacked vector formed from $(\tilde{\boldsymbol{\delta}}_1, \ldots, \tilde{\boldsymbol{\delta}}_M)$. $\tilde{\boldsymbol{\delta}}$ is the efficient equation-by-equation GMM estimator of $\boldsymbol{\delta}$. Show that $\text{Avar}(\tilde{\boldsymbol{\delta}}_m)$ is consistently estimated by

$$\left(\frac{1}{n}\sum_{i=1}^{n} \mathbf{z}_{im}\mathbf{x}'_{im}\widehat{\mathbf{W}}_{mm}\frac{1}{n}\sum_{i=1}^{n}\mathbf{x}_{im}\mathbf{z}'_{im}\right)^{-1}, \tag{$*$}$$

   where

$$\widehat{\mathbf{W}}_{mm} = \left(\frac{1}{n}\sum_{i=1}^{n} \hat{\varepsilon}_{im}^2 \mathbf{x}_{im}\mathbf{x}'_{im}\right)^{-1}.$$

   (c) Verify that $(*)$ is the (m, m) block of

$$(\mathbf{S}'_{\mathbf{xz}}\widehat{\mathbf{W}}\mathbf{S_{xz}})^{-1}\mathbf{S}'_{\mathbf{xz}}\widehat{\mathbf{W}}\,\widehat{\mathbf{S}}\,\widehat{\mathbf{W}}\mathbf{S_{xz}}(\mathbf{S}'_{\mathbf{xz}}\widehat{\mathbf{W}}\mathbf{S_{xz}})^{-1}, \tag{$**$}$$

   where $\widehat{\mathbf{W}}$ is the block diagonal matrix whose m-th diagonal block is $\widehat{\mathbf{W}}_{mm}$.

   (d) Proposition 3.5 is an algebraic result applicable not just to population moments, so it implies that

$$(**) \geq (\mathbf{S}'_{\mathbf{xz}}\widehat{\mathbf{S}}^{-1}\mathbf{S_{xz}})^{-1}.$$

   Taking this for granted, show the following: If the same residuals are used to calculate $\widehat{\mathbf{W}}$ for the equation-by-equation GMM and $\widehat{\mathbf{S}}$ for the multiple-equation GMM, then, for each coefficient, the standard error from the efficient multiple-equation GMM is no larger than that from the efficient equation-by-equation GMM. **Hint:** The standard errors are the square roots of the diagonal elements of the estimated asymptotic variance divided by the sample size.

(e) Does the result you proved in (d) hold true if the model is misspecified in any way? **Hint:** What you have proved is an algebraic result.

(f) Go through steps (a)–(d) for the FIVE and equation-by-equation 2SLS. **Hint:** It's just a matter of redefining $\widehat{\mathbf{S}}$ and the m-th diagonal block, $\widehat{\mathbf{W}}_{mm}$, of $\widehat{\mathbf{W}}$. The $\widehat{\mathbf{W}}_{mm}$ for 2SLS is the inverse of

$$\frac{1}{n}\sum_{i=1}^{n}\hat{\varepsilon}_{im}^{2}\cdot\frac{1}{n}\sum_{i=1}^{n}\mathbf{x}_{im}\mathbf{x}_{im}'$$

and the $\widehat{\mathbf{S}}$ for FIVE is (4.5.3).

5. (Identification and cross-equation restrictions) Consider the wage equation for 1969 and 1980:

$$\begin{aligned}LW69_i &= \beta_0+\beta_1\cdot S69_i+\beta_2\cdot IQ_i+\varepsilon_{i1},\\ LW80_i &= \beta_0+\beta_1\cdot S80_i+\beta_2\cdot IQ_i+\varepsilon_{i2}.\end{aligned}$$

The orthogonality conditions are $\mathrm{E}(\varepsilon_{i1})=0$, $\mathrm{E}(\varepsilon_{i2})=0$, $\mathrm{E}(MED_i\,\varepsilon_{i1})=0$, $\mathrm{E}(MED_i\,\varepsilon_{i2})=0$. Assume we have a random sample on (*LW69*, *LW80*, *S69*, *S80*, *IQ*, *MED*).

(a) Is the *LW69* equation identified in isolation? **Hint:** Check the order condition for identification for the *LW69* equation.

(b) Write the four orthogonality conditions in terms of $(\beta_0,\beta_1,\beta_2)$ as a system of equations linear in β's. How many equations are there? State the rank condition for identification in terms of relevant cross moments. (This example shows that even if each equation of the system is not identified in isolation, the system can be identified thanks to the cross-equation restriction that β's are the same across equations.)

(c) Show that the system cannot be identified if *IQ* and *MED* are uncorrelated.

6. (Optional) Prove Proposition 4.1. **Hint:** Generalize the proof of Proposition 3.2.

7. (Numerical equivalence of 2SLS and 3SLS) In the system of equations $y_{im} = \mathbf{z}'_{im}\boldsymbol{\delta}_m + \varepsilon_{im}$ $(i = 1, \dots, n; m = 1, \dots, M)$, suppose all equations share the same set of instruments (so $\mathbf{x}_{im} = \mathbf{x}_i$). (In what follows, assume all the conditions for the 3SLS estimator are satisfied.)

   (a) When each equation has the same RHS variables (so $\mathbf{z}_{im} = \mathbf{z}_i$), the 2SLS and 3SLS estimators are numerically the same. Prove this. **Hint:** Let $\mathbf{B} \equiv \frac{1}{n}\sum_i \mathbf{x}_i\mathbf{z}'_i$. The 3SLS estimator is (4.2.3) with $\mathbf{S}_{\mathbf{xz}} = \mathbf{I}_M \otimes \mathbf{B}$, $\widehat{\mathbf{W}} = \widehat{\boldsymbol{\Sigma}}^{-1} \otimes \mathbf{S}_{\mathbf{xx}}^{-1}$ where $\mathbf{S}_{\mathbf{xx}} \equiv \frac{1}{n}\sum_i \mathbf{x}_i\mathbf{x}'_i$.

   (b) If the errors are not conditionally homoskedastic, does (a) remain true for the single-equation and multiple-equation GMM estimators? **Hint:** The answer is no. Why? Can you write $\widehat{\mathbf{S}}^{-1}$ as a Kronecker product without conditional homoskedasticy?

8. (SUR is more than assuming predetermined regressors in each equation) Consider estimating a system of M equations: $y_{im} = \mathbf{z}'_{im}\boldsymbol{\delta}_m + \varepsilon_{im}$ $(i = 1, \dots, n;$ $m = 1, \dots, M)$. The orthogonality conditions are $\mathrm{E}(\mathbf{z}_{im} \cdot \varepsilon_{im}) = \mathbf{0}$ $(m = 1, 2, \dots, M)$.

   (a) Does the efficient multiple-equation GMM estimator $\hat{\boldsymbol{\delta}}(\widehat{\mathbf{S}}^{-1})$ reduce to the equation-by-equation OLS? Does your conclusion change if the errors are conditionally homoskedastic? **Hint:** What's the size of $\mathbf{S}_{\mathbf{xz}}$? $\widehat{\mathbf{S}}$?

   (b) Explain why the efficient GMM you derived in (a) under conditional homoskedasticity differs from SUR. **Hint:** The difference is in the orthogonality conditions.

9. (Optional, peril of joint estimation) Taken from Greene (1997, p. 706). Consider the two-equation SUR model:

$$
\begin{aligned}
y_{i1} &= \beta_1 x_{i1} + \varepsilon_{i1}, \\
y_{i2} &= \beta_2 x_{i2} + \beta_3 x_{i3} + \varepsilon_{i2}.
\end{aligned}
$$

For simplicity, assume that $\mathrm{E}(\varepsilon_{i1}^2)$, $\mathrm{E}(\varepsilon_{i1}\,\varepsilon_{i2})$, and $\mathrm{E}(\varepsilon_{i2}^2)$ are known. Now suppose you apply SUR, but erroneously omit x_{i3} from the second equation. What effect does this have on the consistency of the estimator of β_1? **Hint:** Let $\mathbf{x}_1$, $\mathbf{x}_2$, $\mathbf{x}_3$, $\mathbf{y}_1$, $\mathbf{y}_2$, $\boldsymbol{\varepsilon}_1$, and $\boldsymbol{\varepsilon}_2$ be n-dimensional vectors of respective variables and

$$
\mathbf{y} = \begin{bmatrix} \mathbf{y}_1 \\ \mathbf{y}_2 \end{bmatrix}, \quad \boldsymbol{\varepsilon} = \begin{bmatrix} \boldsymbol{\varepsilon}_1 \\ \boldsymbol{\varepsilon}_2 \end{bmatrix}, \quad \overline{\mathbf{X}} = \begin{bmatrix} \mathbf{x}_1 & \mathbf{0} \\ \mathbf{0} & \mathbf{x}_2 \end{bmatrix},
$$

$$\mathbf{d} = \begin{bmatrix} \mathbf{0} \\ \mathbf{x}_3 \end{bmatrix}, \quad \boldsymbol{\beta} = \begin{bmatrix} \beta_1 \\ \beta_2 \end{bmatrix}, \quad \boldsymbol{\Sigma} = \begin{bmatrix} \mathrm{E}(\varepsilon_{i1}^2) & \mathrm{E}(\varepsilon_{i1}\,\varepsilon_{i2}) \\ \mathrm{E}(\varepsilon_{i2}\,\varepsilon_{i1}) & \mathrm{E}(\varepsilon_{i2}^2) \end{bmatrix}.$$

(So, for example, $\overline{\mathbf{X}}$ is $2n \times 2$ and $\boldsymbol{\beta}$ is 2×1.) Show that:

(a) The two-equation system can be written as $\mathbf{y} = \overline{\mathbf{X}}\boldsymbol{\beta} + \beta_3 \cdot \mathbf{d} + \boldsymbol{\varepsilon}$.

(b) The SUR estimator of $\boldsymbol{\beta}$ when x_{i3} is inadvertently left out is

$$\widehat{\boldsymbol{\beta}}_{\text{SUR}} = \left[\overline{\mathbf{X}}'(\boldsymbol{\Sigma}^{-1} \otimes \mathbf{I}_n)\overline{\mathbf{X}}\right]^{-1} \overline{\mathbf{X}}'(\boldsymbol{\Sigma}^{-1} \otimes \mathbf{I}_n)\mathbf{y}.$$

(c) Use formulas (A.6) and (A.7) of the Appendix to show

$$\widehat{\boldsymbol{\beta}}_{\text{SUR}} = \boldsymbol{\beta} + \beta_3 \cdot \mathbf{a} + \mathbf{b},$$

where

$$\mathbf{a} = \begin{bmatrix} \sigma^{11}\frac{1}{n}\sum_{i=1}^{n} x_{i1}^2 & \sigma^{12}\frac{1}{n}\sum_{i=1}^{n} x_{i1}x_{i2} \\ \sigma^{21}\frac{1}{n}\sum_{i=1}^{n} x_{i2}x_{i1} & \sigma^{22}\frac{1}{n}\sum_{i=1}^{n} x_{i2}^2 \end{bmatrix}^{-1} \begin{bmatrix} \sigma^{12}\frac{1}{n}\sum_{i=1}^{n} x_{i1}x_{i3} \\ \sigma^{22}\frac{1}{n}\sum_{i=1}^{n} x_{i2}x_{i3} \end{bmatrix},$$

$$\mathbf{b} = \begin{bmatrix} \sigma^{11}\frac{1}{n}\sum_{i=1}^{n} x_{i1}^2 & \sigma^{12}\frac{1}{n}\sum_{i=1}^{n} x_{i1}x_{i2} \\ \sigma^{21}\frac{1}{n}\sum_{i=1}^{n} x_{i2}x_{i1} & \sigma^{22}\frac{1}{n}\sum_{i=1}^{n} x_{i2}^2 \end{bmatrix}^{-1} \begin{bmatrix} \sigma^{11}\frac{1}{n}\sum_{i=1}^{n} x_{i1}\varepsilon_{i1} + \sigma^{12}\frac{1}{n}\sum_{i=1}^{n} x_{i1}\varepsilon_{i2} \\ \sigma^{21}\frac{1}{n}\sum_{i=1}^{n} x_{i2}\varepsilon_{i1} + \sigma^{22}\frac{1}{n}\sum_{i=1}^{n} x_{i2}\varepsilon_{i2} \end{bmatrix}.$$

(d) Argue that $\operatorname{plim} \mathbf{b} = \mathbf{0}$. Is $\operatorname{plim} \mathbf{a} = \mathbf{0}$?

10. (Optional, adding just-identified equations does not increase efficiency) Consider the 3SLS two-equation model where the second equation is just identified (so $L_2 = K$). Let $\hat{\boldsymbol{\delta}}_{1,\text{3SLS}}$ be the 3SLS estimator of the coefficients of the first equation and $\hat{\boldsymbol{\delta}}_{1,\text{2SLS}}$ be the 2SLS estimator of the same coefficients.

(a) Write down $\text{Avar}(\hat{\boldsymbol{\delta}}_{1,\text{2SLS}})$ in terms of σ_{11} and $\mathbf{A}_{11}$, which is defined in (4.5.16).

(b) Show that $\text{Avar}(\hat{\boldsymbol{\delta}}_{1,\text{3SLS}}) = \text{Avar}(\hat{\boldsymbol{\delta}}_{1,\text{2SLS}})$. **Hint:** Use the partitioned inverse formula (see formula (A.10) of the Appendix) to write the upper-left $(L_1 \times L_1)$ block of $\text{Avar}(\hat{\boldsymbol{\delta}}_{1,\text{3SLS}})$ as $\mathbf{G}^{-1}$ where

$$\mathbf{G} = \sigma^{11}\mathbf{A}_{11} - \left(\frac{\sigma^{12} \cdot \sigma^{21}}{\sigma^{22}}\right)\mathbf{A}_{12}\mathbf{A}_{22}^{-1}\mathbf{A}_{21}.$$

But by (4.5.16),

$$\begin{aligned}
&\mathbf{A}_{12}\mathbf{A}_{22}^{-1}\mathbf{A}_{21} \\
&= \text{E}(\mathbf{z}_{i1}\mathbf{x}_i')[\text{E}(\mathbf{x}_i\mathbf{x}_i')]^{-1}\,\text{E}(\mathbf{x}_i\mathbf{z}_{i2}') \\
&\qquad [\text{E}(\mathbf{z}_{i2}\mathbf{x}_i')[\text{E}(\mathbf{x}_i\mathbf{x}_i')]^{-1}\,\text{E}(\mathbf{x}_i\mathbf{z}_{i2}')]^{-1}\,\text{E}(\mathbf{z}_{i2}\mathbf{x}_i')[\text{E}(\mathbf{x}_i\mathbf{x}_i')]^{-1}\,\text{E}(\mathbf{x}_i\mathbf{z}_{i1}') \\
&= \text{E}(\mathbf{z}_{i1}\mathbf{x}_i')[\text{E}(\mathbf{x}_i\mathbf{x}_i')]^{-1}\,\text{E}(\mathbf{x}_i\mathbf{z}_{i1}') \quad \text{(since } \#\mathbf{z}_{i2}\ (= L_2) = \#\mathbf{x}_i\ (= K)) \\
&= \mathbf{A}_{11}.
\end{aligned}$$

So

$$\mathbf{G} = \left[\sigma^{11} - \left(\frac{\sigma^{12} \cdot \sigma^{21}}{\sigma^{22}}\right)\right]\mathbf{A}_{11} = \frac{\mathbf{A}_{11}}{\sigma_{11}}$$

$$\text{(since } \sigma^{11} - \left(\frac{\sigma^{12} \cdot \sigma^{21}}{\sigma^{22}}\right) = 1/\sigma_{11}).$$

11. (Linear combinations of orthogonality conditions) For the multiple-equation model of Proposition 4.7, derive the efficient GMM estimator that exploits the following orthogonality conditions:

$$\text{E}(\mathbf{z}_{i1} \cdot \varepsilon_{i1} + \cdots + \mathbf{z}_{iM} \cdot \varepsilon_{iM}) = \mathbf{0}. \tag{1}$$

Hint: The sample analogue of the left-hand side the orthogonality conditions is

$$\begin{aligned}
\mathbf{g}_n(\tilde{\boldsymbol{\delta}}) \equiv \frac{1}{n}\sum_{i=1}^{n}\mathbf{z}_{i1}\cdot y_{i1} + \cdots + \frac{1}{n}\sum_{i=1}^{n}\mathbf{z}_{iM}\cdot y_{iM} \\
- \left(\frac{1}{n}\sum_{i=1}^{n}\mathbf{z}_{i1}\mathbf{z}_{i1}' + \cdots + \frac{1}{n}\sum_{i=1}^{n}\mathbf{z}_{iM}\mathbf{z}_{iM}'\right)\tilde{\boldsymbol{\delta}}.
\end{aligned}$$

There are as many orthogonality conditions as there are coefficients. The efficient GMM estimator is the IV estimator that solves $\mathbf{g}_n(\tilde{\boldsymbol{\delta}}) = \mathbf{0}$.

EMPIRICAL EXERCISES

In data file GREENE.ASC, data are provided on the following variables.

Column 1: firm ID in Nerlove's 1955 sample
Column 2: costs in 1970 in millions of dollars
Column 3: output in millions of kilowatt hours
Column 4: price of labor
Column 5: price of capital
Column 6: price of fuel
Column 7: labor's cost share
Column 8: capital's cost share

The sample has 99 observations. Fuel's cost share can be calculated as one minus the sum of labor and capital cost shares. These data were used in Christensen and Greene (1976).

In the text, the third equation (for fuel share) of the system was dropped in the random-effects estimation. To verify the numerical invariance, drop the second equation (for capital share) and eliminate $(\gamma_{12}, \gamma_{22}, \gamma_{32})$ when imposing homogeneity. This produces the two-equation system:

$$\begin{cases} s_1 = \alpha_1 + \gamma_{11}\log(p_1/p_2) + \gamma_{13}\log(p_3/p_2) + \gamma_{1Q}\log(Q) + \varepsilon_1 & \text{(labor share)}, \\ s_3 = \alpha_3 + \gamma_{31}\log(p_1/p_2) + \gamma_{33}\log(p_3/p_2) + \gamma_{3Q}\log(Q) + \varepsilon_3 & \text{(fuel share)}. \end{cases}$$

Call this the *unconstrained system*. The *constrained system* imposes symmetry $\gamma_{13} = \gamma_{31}$ on the unconstrained system.

(a) Verify that the simple statistics of the sample shown in the text can be duplicated.

(b) (Numerical invariance) Apply the random-effects estimation (i.e., the multivariate regression subject to the cross-equation restriction) to the constrained system. Can you duplicate the coefficient estimates in the text? You should first apply equation-by-equation OLS to the unconstrained system to calculate $\widehat{\boldsymbol{\Sigma}}^*$. (Note on computation: Programming joint estimation is much easier with canned programs such as TSP and RATS. However, those canned programs will not print out Sargan's statistic for the SUR.)

Gauss Tip: The random-effects estimator could be calculated by operating on data matrices, but we recommend the use of do loops. Use (4.6.8′) on page 293.

RATS Tip: Use the `NLSYS` proc, which is designed for handling nonlinear equations but which can be used for linear equations. It can also be used for calculating $\widehat{\boldsymbol{\Sigma}}^*$, as done in the following codes:

```
* Estimation with capital share equation dropped
* Define parameters
nonlin al af gll glf gfl gff gly gfy
* Define two eq. system
frml labor sl = al+gll*log(pl/pk)+glf*log(pf/pk)
                +gly*log(kwh)
frml fuel sf = af+gfl*log(pl/pk)+gff*log(pf/pk)
               +gfy*log(kwh)
* Set starting values for the parameters
compute al=af=gll=glf=gfl=gff=gly=gfy=0
* Now do multivariate regression w/o cross-eq.
* restriction
nlsystem(outsigma=sigmahat) / labor fuel
```

Here, `sigmahat` is the 2×2 matrix $\widehat{\boldsymbol{\Sigma}}^*$. The random-effects estimation using this $\widehat{\boldsymbol{\Sigma}}^*$ is done by the following codes.

```
* Now impose cross-eq. restriction on fuel share
* eq. (set gfl=glf)
* Define parameters.
nonlin al af gll glf gff gly gfy
* Impose symmetry.
frml fuelb sf = af+glf*log(pl/pk)+gff*log(pf/pk)
                +gfy*log(kwh)
* Multivariate regression with covariance matrix
* calculated from equation-by-equation OLS
* residuals
nlsystem(isigma=sigmahat) / labor fuelb
```

TSP Tip: An example of TSP codes that accomplish the same thing as the RATS codes above is:

```
? Estimate the system with capital equation
? dropped.
frml labor sl=al+gll*log(pl/pk)+glf*log(pf/pk)
              +gly*log(kwh);
```

```
frml fuel sf=af+gfl*log(pl/pk)+gff*log(pf/pk)
             +gfy*log(kwh);
? Set parameter values to zero.
param al af gll glf gfl gff gly gfy;
? Multivariate regression without symmetry
sur labor fuel;
? Estimate error covariance matrix from residuals
mform sigmahat=@covu;
?
? Do multivariate regression with cross-equation
? restriction.
? Impose symmetry.
frml fuel sf=af+glf*log(pl/pk)+gff*log(pf/pk)
             +gfy*log(kwh);
? Multivariate regression subject to symmetry
lsq(maxitw=0,wname=sigmahat) labor fuel;
```

This gives the random-effects estimate of the seven free parameters,

$$\alpha_1, \alpha_3, \gamma_{11}, \gamma_{13}, \gamma_{33}, \gamma_{1Q}, \gamma_{3Q}.$$

As explained in the text, use the adding-up, homogeneity, and symmetry restrictions to calculate the point estimates and their standard errors of the remaining eight parameters. The TSP command ANALYZ should be useful here.

(c) (Optional, for Gauss users) Calculate Sargan's statistic. **Hint:** Use the formula in Proposition 4.7. The $\mathbf{x}_i$ vector should be: a constant, $\log(p_1/p_2)$, $\log(p_3/p_2)$, $\log(Q)$. For $\widehat{\boldsymbol{\Sigma}}^*$, use the one obtained from the unconstrained system. $\mathbf{s}_{\mathbf{xy}} = \frac{1}{n}\sum_{i=1}^n \mathbf{y}_i \otimes \mathbf{x}_i$ and $\mathbf{S}_{\mathbf{xz}} = \frac{1}{n}\sum_{i=1}^n \mathbf{Z}_i \otimes \mathbf{x}_i$. The statistic should be 0.63313 with a p-value of 0.42621.

(d) (Testing symmetry) Given that Sargan's statistic is 0.63313, perform the following hypothesis testing. Take the maintained hypothesis to be the unconstrained system. The null hypothesis is the symmetry restriction that $\gamma_{13} = \gamma_{31}$. **Hint:** By Proposition 3.8, the difference in the Sargan statistics with and without symmetry is asymptotically chi-squared. What is Sargan's statistic for the unconstrained system?

(e) (Wald test of symmetry) Test the same null hypothesis by the Wald principle. So you test the symmetry restriction in the unconstrained system. Verify that the test statistic is numerically equal to Sargan's statistic for the constrained system you estimated in (b).

TSP Tip: Just insert the line

```
analyz wald wald=glf-gfl;
```

right after the codes for the unconstrained estimation.

(f) Using the parameter estimates you obtained in (b), calculate the elasticity of substitution between labor and capital averaged over the 99 firms. Can you duplicate the result in the text?

ANSWERS TO SELECTED QUESTIONS

ANALYTICAL EXERCISES

3b. $\mathrm{E}(\varepsilon_{im} \mid \mathbf{Z})$

$= \mathrm{E}(\varepsilon_{im} \mid \mathbf{z}_{11}, \ldots, \mathbf{z}_{1M}, \mathbf{z}_{21}, \ldots \mathbf{z}_{2M}, \ldots, \mathbf{z}_{n1}, \ldots, \mathbf{z}_{nM})$ (by definition of $\mathbf{Z}$)

$= \mathrm{E}(\varepsilon_{im} \mid \mathbf{z}_{i1}, \ldots, \mathbf{z}_{iM})$ (by the i.i.d. assumption)

$= 0$ (by the strengthened orthogonality conditions).

The (i, j) element of the $n \times n$ matrix $\mathrm{E}(\boldsymbol{\varepsilon}_m \boldsymbol{\varepsilon}_h' \mid \mathbf{Z})$ is $\mathrm{E}(\varepsilon_{im}\, \varepsilon_{jh} \mid \mathbf{Z})$. By the i.i.d. assumption, this is zero for $j \neq i$. For $j = i$,

$$\begin{aligned}
&\mathrm{E}(\varepsilon_{im}\, \varepsilon_{ih} \mid \mathbf{Z})\\
&= \mathrm{E}(\varepsilon_{im}\, \varepsilon_{ih} \mid \mathbf{z}_{11}, \ldots, \mathbf{z}_{1M}, \mathbf{z}_{21}, \ldots \mathbf{z}_{2M}, \ldots, \mathbf{z}_{n1}, \ldots, \mathbf{z}_{nM})\\
&= \mathrm{E}(\varepsilon_{im}\, \varepsilon_{ih} \mid \mathbf{z}_{i1}, \ldots, \mathbf{z}_{iM}) \quad \text{(by the i.i.d. assumption).}
\end{aligned}$$

Since $\mathbf{x}_{im} = \mathbf{x}_i$ and $\mathbf{x}_i$ is the union of $(\mathbf{z}_{i1}, \ldots, \mathbf{z}_{iM})$ in the SUR model, the conditional homoskedasticity assumption, Assumption 4.7, states that $\mathrm{E}(\varepsilon_{im}\varepsilon_{ih} \mid \mathbf{z}_{i1}, \ldots, \mathbf{z}_{iM}) = \sigma_{mh}$.

5b.

$$\begin{bmatrix} 1 & \mathrm{E}(S69) & \mathrm{E}(IQ) \\ 1 & \mathrm{E}(S80) & \mathrm{E}(IQ) \\ \mathrm{E}(MED) & \mathrm{E}(S69 \cdot MED) & \mathrm{E}(IQ \cdot MED) \\ \mathrm{E}(MED) & \mathrm{E}(S80 \cdot MED) & \mathrm{E}(IQ \cdot MED) \end{bmatrix} \begin{bmatrix} \beta_0 \\ \beta_1 \\ \beta_2 \end{bmatrix} = \begin{bmatrix} \mathrm{E}(LW69) \\ \mathrm{E}(LW80) \\ \mathrm{E}(LW69 \cdot MED) \\ \mathrm{E}(LW80 \cdot MED) \end{bmatrix}.$$

The condition for the system to be identified is that the 4×3 coefficient matrix is of full column rank.

5c. If IQ and MED are uncorrelated, then $\mathrm{E}(IQ \cdot MED) = \mathrm{E}(IQ) \cdot \mathrm{E}(MED)$ and the third column of the coefficient matrix is $\mathrm{E}(IQ)$ times the first column. So the matrix cannot be of full column rank.

6. $\hat{\varepsilon}_{im} = y_{im} - \mathbf{z}_{im}'\hat{\boldsymbol{\delta}}_m = \varepsilon_{im} - \mathbf{z}_{im}'(\hat{\boldsymbol{\delta}}_m - \boldsymbol{\delta}_m)$. So

$$\frac{1}{n}\sum_{i=1}^{n}[\varepsilon_{im} - \mathbf{z}_{im}'(\hat{\boldsymbol{\delta}}_m - \boldsymbol{\delta}_m)][\varepsilon_{ih} - \mathbf{z}_{ih}'(\hat{\boldsymbol{\delta}}_h - \boldsymbol{\delta}_h)] = (1) + (2) + (3) + (4),$$

where

$$(1) = \frac{1}{n}\sum_{i=1}^{n}\varepsilon_{im}\,\varepsilon_{ih},$$

$$(2) = -(\hat{\boldsymbol{\delta}}_m - \boldsymbol{\delta}_m)'\frac{1}{n}\sum_{i=1}^{n}\mathbf{z}_{im}\cdot\varepsilon_{ih},$$

$$(3) = -(\hat{\boldsymbol{\delta}}_h - \boldsymbol{\delta}_h)'\frac{1}{n}\sum_{i=1}^{n}\mathbf{z}_{ih}\cdot\varepsilon_{im},$$

$$(4) = (\hat{\boldsymbol{\delta}}_m - \boldsymbol{\delta}_m)'\Big(\frac{1}{n}\sum_{i=1}^{n}\mathbf{z}_{im}\mathbf{z}_{ih}'\Big)(\hat{\boldsymbol{\delta}}_h - \boldsymbol{\delta}_h).$$

As usual, under Assumption 4.1 and 4.2, $(1) \to_{\mathrm{p}} \sigma_{mh}$ $(\equiv \mathrm{E}(\varepsilon_{im}\,\varepsilon_{ih}))$.

For (4), by Assumption 4.2 and the assumption that $\mathrm{E}(\mathbf{z}_{im}\mathbf{z}_{ih}')$ is finite, $\frac{1}{n}\sum_i \cdot \mathbf{z}_{im}\mathbf{z}_{ih}'$ converges in probability to a (finite) matrix. So $(4) \to_{\mathrm{p}} 0$.

Regarding (2), by Cauchy-Schwartz,

$$\mathrm{E}(|z_{imj}\cdot\varepsilon_{ih}|) \le \sqrt{\mathrm{E}(z_{imj}^2)\cdot\mathrm{E}(\varepsilon_{ih}^2)},$$

where z_{imj} is the j-th element of $\mathbf{z}_{im}$. So $\mathrm{E}(\mathbf{z}_{im}\cdot\varepsilon_{ih})$ is finite and $(2) \to_{\mathrm{p}} 0$ because $\hat{\boldsymbol{\delta}}_m - \boldsymbol{\delta}_m \to_{\mathrm{p}} \mathbf{0}$. Similarly, $(3) \to_{\mathrm{p}} 0$.

References

Berndt, E., 1991, *The Practice of Econometrics*, New York: Addison-Wesley.

Berndt, E., and D. Wood, 1975, "Technology, Prices, and the Derived Demand for Energy," *Review of Economics and Statistics*, 57, 259–268.

Brundy, J., and D. Jorgenson, 1971, "Efficient Estimation of Simultaneous Systems by Instrumental Variables," *Review of Economics and Statistics*, 53, 207–224.

Christensen, L., and W. Greene, 1976, "Economies of Scale in U.S. Electric Power Generation," *Journal of Political Economy*, 84, 655–676.

Greene, W., 1997, *Econometric Analysis* (3d ed.), New Jersey: Prentice Hall.

Jorgenson, D., 1986, "Econometric Methods for Modeling Producer Behavior," in Z. Griliches and M. Intriligator (eds.), *Handbook of Econometrics*, Volume III, Amsterdam: Elsevier Science Publishers, 1841–1915.

Uzawa, H., 1962, "Production Function with Constant Elasticities of Substitution," *Review of Economic Studies*, 29, 291–299.

Varian, H., 1992, *Microeconomic Analysis* (3d ed.), New York: Norton.

Zellner, A., 1962, "An Efficient Method of Estimating Seemingly Unrelated Regressions and Tests for Aggregation Bias," *Journal of the American Statistical Association*, 63, 502–511.

Zellner, A., and H. Theil, 1962, "Three-Stage Least Squares: Simultaneous Estimation of Simultaneous Equations," *Econometrica*, 30, 54–78.

CHAPTER 5

Panel Data

ABSTRACT

A **longitudinal** or **panel** data set has multiple observations for a number of cross-section units. As its name suggests, a panel has two dimensions, one for cross-section units and the other for observations. The latter dimension is usually time, but there are exceptions. A cross-section sample of twins, for example, is a panel where the second dimension is siblings. The distinction between cross-section units and observations, the two terms used interchangeably until now, should be kept in mind throughout this chapter. When it is apt to do so, we will use the term "group" for the cross-section unit.

In many applications, we encounter the **error-components model**. In such models, the error term of the equation has a component that is common to all observations (time-invariant if the second dimension of the panel is time) but that may not be orthogonal to regressors. There is available a technique, called the "fixed-effects estimator," which allows us to estimate the model without the help of instrumental variables. It and the random-effects estimator of the previous chapter are the two staple techniques in panel econometrics.

The optional section of this chapter, Section 5.3, shows how to modify the fixed-effects estimator when the number of observations varies across groups. The empirical section takes up growth empirics, a topic that has recently attracted a great deal of attention.

As it turns out, the fixed-effects and other estimators covered in this chapter are particular GMM estimators on a suitable transformation of the error-components model. The GMM interpretation of the fixed-effects estimator is pursued in an analytical exercise to this chapter, where you will be asked to find an estimator that is asymptotically more efficient than the fixed-effects estimator.

5.1 The Error-Components Model

Our point of departure is the multiple-equation model with common coefficients of Proposition 4.7. To simplify the discussion, we will assume that the sample is a random sample. This assumption is satisfied in most popular panels, such as the Panel Study of Income Dynamics (PSID) and the National Longitudinal Survey (NLS). In those panels, a large number — hundreds or even thousands — of cross-section units are randomly drawn from the population.

For this case of random samples, the assumptions of Proposition 4.7 can be restated as (see (4.6.15) for the definition of $\mathbf{y}_i$ $(M \times 1)$, $\mathbf{Z}_i$ $(M \times L)$, $\boldsymbol{\varepsilon}_i$ $(M \times 1)$):

$$\text{(system of } M \text{ linear equations)} \quad \mathbf{y}_i = \mathbf{Z}_i \boldsymbol{\delta} + \boldsymbol{\varepsilon}_i \tag{5.1.1}$$

$$\text{(random sample)} \quad \{\mathbf{y}_i, \mathbf{Z}_i\} \text{ is i.i.d.} \tag{5.1.2}$$

$$\text{(“SUR assumption”)} \quad \mathrm{E}(\mathbf{z}_{im} \cdot \varepsilon_{ih}) = \mathbf{0} \quad \text{for } m, h = 1, 2, \dots, M, \tag{5.1.3}$$

i.e., $\mathrm{E}(\boldsymbol{\varepsilon}_i \otimes \mathbf{x}_i) = \mathbf{0}$ where $\mathbf{x}_i$ = union of $(\mathbf{z}_{i1}, \dots, \mathbf{z}_{iM})$,

$$\text{(identification)} \quad \mathrm{E}(\mathbf{Z}_i \otimes \mathbf{x}_i) \text{ is of full column rank,}^1 \tag{5.1.4}$$

$$\text{(conditional homoskedasticity)} \quad \mathrm{E}(\boldsymbol{\varepsilon}_i \boldsymbol{\varepsilon}_i' \mid \mathbf{x}_i) = \mathrm{E}(\boldsymbol{\varepsilon}_i \boldsymbol{\varepsilon}_i') \equiv \boldsymbol{\Sigma} \tag{5.1.5}$$

$$\text{(nonsingularity of } \mathrm{E}(\mathbf{g}_i \mathbf{g}_i')) \quad \mathrm{E}(\mathbf{g}_i \mathbf{g}_i') \text{ is nonsingular, where } \mathbf{g}_i \equiv \boldsymbol{\varepsilon}_i \otimes \mathbf{x}_i. \tag{5.1.6}$$

As noted in Section 4.5, since $\mathrm{E}(\mathbf{g}_i \mathbf{g}_i') = \boldsymbol{\Sigma} \otimes \mathrm{E}(\mathbf{x}_i \mathbf{x}_i')$ under conditional homoskedasticity, (5.1.6) is equivalent to the condition

$$\boldsymbol{\Sigma} \text{ and } \mathrm{E}(\mathbf{x}_i \mathbf{x}_i') \text{ are nonsingular.} \tag{5.1.6$'$}$$

Under these assumptions, the random-effects estimator $\hat{\boldsymbol{\delta}}_{\mathrm{RE}}$, defined in (4.6.8′) on page 293, is the efficient GMM estimator.

Error Components

This model, very frequently used for panel data, is one where the unobservable error term ε_{im} is assumed to consist of two components:

$$\varepsilon_{im} = \alpha_i + \eta_{im}. \tag{5.1.7}$$

[1]The $\boldsymbol{\Sigma}_{\mathbf{xz}}$ in Assumption 4.4′ can be written as $\mathrm{E}(\mathbf{Z}_i \otimes \mathbf{x}_i)$; see Review Question 4 to Section 4.6.

The first unobservable component α_i, without the m subscript and hence common to all equations, is called the **individual effect**, the **individual heterogeneity**, or the **fixed effect**. If we define

$$\underset{(M\times 1)}{\boldsymbol{\eta}_i} \equiv \begin{bmatrix} \eta_{i1} \\ \vdots \\ \eta_{iM} \end{bmatrix},$$

the matrix representation of the M-equation system is

$$\begin{bmatrix} y_{i1} \\ \vdots \\ y_{iM} \end{bmatrix} = \begin{bmatrix} \mathbf{z}_{i1}'\boldsymbol{\delta} \\ \vdots \\ \mathbf{z}_{iM}'\boldsymbol{\delta} \end{bmatrix} + \begin{bmatrix} \alpha_i \\ \vdots \\ \alpha_i \end{bmatrix} + \begin{bmatrix} \eta_{i1} \\ \vdots \\ \eta_{iM} \end{bmatrix}$$

or

$$\mathbf{y}_i = \mathbf{Z}_i\boldsymbol{\delta} + \mathbf{1}_M \cdot \alpha_i + \boldsymbol{\eta}_i \quad (i = 1, 2, \ldots, n), \tag{5.1.1$'$}$$

where $\mathbf{1}_M$ is the M-dimensional vector of ones.

The orthogonality conditions (5.1.3) are satisfied if the regressors of the system are orthogonal to both error components, that is, if

$$\mathrm{E}(\mathbf{z}_{im} \cdot \alpha_i) = \mathbf{0} \quad \text{for } m = 1, 2, \ldots, M, \tag{5.1.8a}$$

and

$$\mathrm{E}(\mathbf{z}_{im} \cdot \eta_{ih}) = \mathbf{0} \quad \text{for } m, h = 1, 2, \ldots, M. \tag{5.1.8b}$$

However, in many applications that utilize panel data, (5.1.8a) is not a reasonable assumption to make. This is because the fixed effect represents some permanent characteristics of the individual economic unit, as illustrated by the following examples.

Example 5.1 (production function with firm heterogeneity): In the log-linear production function (3.2.13) of Section 3.2, suppose the firm's efficiency u_i stays constant over time. Then the equation for year m is

$$\log(Q_{im}) = \phi_0 + \phi_1 \log(L_{im}) + u_i + v_{im},$$

where Q_{im} is the output of firm i in year m, L_{im} is labor input in year m, and v_{im} is the technology shock in year m. The equation can be written as (5.1.1$'$) by setting

$$y_{im} = \log(Q_{im}),\ \mathbf{z}_{im} = (1, \log(L_{im}))',\ \boldsymbol{\delta} = (\phi_0, \phi_1)',\ \alpha_i = u_i,\ \eta_{im} = v_{im}.$$

Also,

$$\mathbf{x}_i = (1, \log(L_{i1}), \ldots, \log(L_{iM}))'.$$

Under perfect competition, the individual effect u_i would be positively correlated with labor input because efficient firms, whose u_i is higher than its mean value, would hire more labor to expand (see (3.2.14)). If v_{im} represents unexpected shocks that are unforeseen by the firm when input choices are made, it is reasonable to assume that v_{im} is uncorrelated with the regressors.

Example 5.2 (wage equation): For simplicity, drop experience from the wage equation of Example 4.2 but suppose data for 1982, in addition to 1969 and 1980, are available. Suppose also that the coefficient of schooling and that of IQ remain the same over time but that the intercept is time-dependent (due, for example, to business-cycle effects on wages). With the error decomposition (5.1.7), the three-equation system is

$$\begin{cases} LW69_i = \phi_1 + \beta S69_i + \gamma IQ_i + \alpha_i + \eta_{i1}, \\ LW80_i = \phi_2 + \beta S80_i + \gamma IQ_i + \alpha_i + \eta_{i2}, \\ LW82_i = \phi_3 + \beta S82_i + \gamma IQ_i + \alpha_i + \eta_{i3}. \end{cases}$$

As noted at the end of Section 4.6, even if a subset of the coefficients differs across equations, the system can be written as multiple equations with common coefficients. In this example, this is accomplished with

$$\mathbf{Z}_i = \begin{bmatrix} \mathbf{z}'_{i1} \\ \mathbf{z}'_{i2} \\ \mathbf{z}'_{i3} \end{bmatrix} = \begin{bmatrix} 1 & 0 & 0 & S69_i & IQ_i \\ 0 & 1 & 0 & S80_i & IQ_i \\ 0 & 0 & 1 & S82_i & IQ_i \end{bmatrix}, \quad \boldsymbol{\delta}' = (\phi_1, \phi_2, \phi_3, \beta, \gamma). \quad (5.1.9)$$

Also,

$$\mathbf{x}_i = (1, S69_i, S80_i, S82_i, IQ_i)'.$$

The error term includes the wage determinants not accounted for by schooling and IQ. It may be reasonable to assume that they are divided between the permanent individual traits (denoted α_i), which would affect the individual's choice of schooling, and other factors (denoted η_{im}) uncorrelated with the regressors, such as measurement error in the log wage rate.

Group Means

Fortunately, there is available a popular estimator, called the **fixed-effects estimator**, that is robust to the failure of (5.1.8a), i.e., that is consistent even when the regressors are not orthogonal to the fixed effect α_i. To anticipate the next section's discussion, the estimator is applied to an M-equation system transformed from the original system (5.1.1′). The matrix used for the transformation is the annihilator associated with $\mathbf{1}_M$:

$$\underset{(M\times M)}{\mathbf{Q}} \equiv \mathbf{I}_M - \mathbf{1}_M(\mathbf{1}_M'\mathbf{1}_M)^{-1}\mathbf{1}_M'$$
$$= \mathbf{I}_M - \frac{1}{M}\mathbf{1}_M\mathbf{1}_M'$$
$$= \mathbf{I}_M - \begin{bmatrix} 1/M & \cdots & 1/M \\ \vdots & & \vdots \\ 1/M & \cdots & 1/M \end{bmatrix}. \tag{5.1.10}$$

What this matrix does is to extract **deviations from group means**. For example, multiplying the M-dimensional vector $\mathbf{y}_i$ from left by $\mathbf{Q}$ results in

$$\tilde{\mathbf{y}}_i \equiv \mathbf{Q}\mathbf{y}_i = \begin{bmatrix} y_{i1} - \bar{y}_i \\ \vdots \\ y_{iM} - \bar{y}_i \end{bmatrix} = \mathbf{y}_i - \mathbf{1}_M \cdot \bar{y}_i, \tag{5.1.11}$$

where

$$\bar{y}_i = \frac{1}{M}\mathbf{1}_M'\mathbf{y}_i = \frac{1}{M}\sum_{m=1}^{M} y_{im}$$

is the **group mean** for the dependent variable. Note that this mean is over m, *not* over i; it is specific to each group (i). Similarly for the regressors, each column of $\mathbf{QZ}_i$ is the vector of deviations for the corresponding column of $\mathbf{Z}_i$.

A Reparameterization

Not surprisingly, however, robustness to the failure of (5.1.8a) comes at a price: some of the parameters of the model may no longer be identifiable after the transformation by $\mathbf{Q}$. To provide two examples,

- The obvious case is the coefficient of a variable common to all equations. For example, IQ_i in Example 5.2 is a common regressor (see (5.1.9)), so the column of $\mathbf{Z}_i$ corresponding to IQ_i (the fifth column) is $\mathbf{1}_M \cdot IQ_i$ and the fifth column of $\mathbf{QZ}_i$ is a vector of zeros. Consequently, the IQ coefficient, γ, cannot be identified after the transformation. To separate the coefficient of common regressors from the rest, let $\mathbf{b}_i$ be the vector of common regressors and write the $M \times L$ matrix of regressors, $\mathbf{Z}_i$, as

$$\mathbf{Z}_i = (\mathbf{F}_i \,\vdots\, \mathbf{1}_M \mathbf{b}_i') \tag{5.1.12}$$

and partition the coefficient vector $\boldsymbol{\delta}$ accordingly:

$$\boldsymbol{\delta} = \begin{bmatrix} \boldsymbol{\beta} \\ \boldsymbol{\gamma} \end{bmatrix}.$$

The coefficient vector $\boldsymbol{\gamma}$ cannot be identified after transformation.

- It may also be the case that, in addition to $\boldsymbol{\gamma}$, some of the coefficients in $\boldsymbol{\beta}$ are unidentifiable and a reparameterization is needed. Consider Example 5.2 where each equation has a different intercept. One of the intercepts needs to be dropped from $\mathbf{F}_i$ and included in $\mathbf{b}_i$, because a common intercept can be created by taking a linear combination of the equation-specific intercepts. One reparameterization is to define

$$\mathbf{F}_i = \begin{bmatrix} 1 & 0 & S69_i \\ 0 & 1 & S80_i \\ 0 & 0 & S82_i \end{bmatrix}, \quad \mathbf{b}_i = (1, IQ_i)', \tag{5.1.13}$$

so

$$\mathbf{Z}_i = \begin{bmatrix} 1 & 0 & S69_i & 1 & IQ_i \\ 0 & 1 & S80_i & 1 & IQ_i \\ 0 & 0 & S82_i & 1 & IQ_i \end{bmatrix}, \quad \boldsymbol{\beta} = (\phi_1 - \phi_3, \phi_2 - \phi_3, \beta)', \quad \boldsymbol{\gamma} = (\phi_3, \gamma)'. \tag{5.1.14}$$

More generally, the identification condition for fixed-effects estimation is that $\mathbf{F}_i$ and $\mathbf{b}_i$ are defined so that

$$\mathrm{E}(\mathbf{Q}\mathbf{F}_i \otimes \mathbf{x}_i) \text{ is of full column rank} \tag{5.1.15}$$

where $\mathbf{x}_i$ = union of $(\mathbf{z}_{i1}, \ldots, \mathbf{z}_{iM})$. Why is this an identification condition? Because (as you will see more clearly in Analytical Exercise 2), the fixed-effects estimator is a (specialization of the) random-effects estimator applied to the transformed regression of $\mathbf{Qy}$ on $\mathbf{QF}$. (5.1.15) is just the adaptation of the identification condition (5.1.4) to the transformed regression.

With $\mathbf{Z}_i$ thus divided between $\mathbf{F}_i$ and $\mathbf{b}_i$, the system of M-equations (5.1.1′) on page 325 can be rewritten as

$$\mathbf{y}_i = \mathbf{F}_i\boldsymbol{\beta} + \mathbf{1}_M \cdot \mathbf{b}_i'\boldsymbol{\gamma} + \mathbf{1}_M \cdot \alpha_i + \boldsymbol{\eta}_i \quad (i = 1, 2, \dots, n), \text{ or}$$
$$y_{im} = \mathbf{f}_{im}'\boldsymbol{\beta} + \mathbf{b}_i'\boldsymbol{\gamma} + \alpha_i + \eta_{im} \quad (i = 1, 2, \dots, n; m = 1, \dots, M), \tag{5.1.1″}$$

where $\mathbf{f}_{im}'$ is the m-th row of $\mathbf{F}_i$. The **error-components model** consists of assumptions (5.1.1″) (M linear equations), (5.1.2) (random samples), (5.1.8) (SUR assumption with two error components), (5.1.4) (identification), (5.1.5) (conditional homoskedasticity), (5.1.6) (nonsingular $\text{E}(\mathbf{g}_i\mathbf{g}_i')$), and (5.1.15) (fixed-effects identification). We include the additional identification condition (5.1.15) for fixed-effects estimation, so that both the random-effects estimator and the fixed-effects estimator are well-defined for the same model.

QUESTIONS FOR REVIEW

1. (Verification of Proposition 4.7 assumptions) Verify that the conditions of Proposition 4.7 are satisfied when (5.1.1)–(5.1.6) hold. Show that the identification condition (5.1.4) is satisfied when $\text{E}(\mathbf{x}_i\mathbf{x}_i')$ is nonsingular. **Hint:** $\mathbf{z}_{im}$ is a subset of $\mathbf{x}_i$. Thus, (5.1.4) is redundant.

2. (Nonuniqueness of reparameterization) (5.1.13) is not the only reparameterization for Example 5.2. If $\mathbf{F}_i$ is defined as

$$\mathbf{F}_i = \begin{bmatrix} 0 & 0 & S69_i \\ 1 & 0 & S80_i \\ 0 & 1 & S82_i \end{bmatrix},$$

how should $\mathbf{b}_i$ and $\boldsymbol{\delta}$ be defined?

3. Without reparameterization, the $\mathbf{F}_i$ for Example 5.2 is

$$\mathbf{F}_i = \begin{bmatrix} 1 & 0 & 0 & S69_i \\ 0 & 1 & 0 & S80_i \\ 0 & 0 & 1 & S82_i \end{bmatrix}$$

with $\mathbf{b}_i = IQ_i$. Verify that (5.1.15) is not satisfied.

5.2 The Fixed-Effects Estimator

The Formula

As already mentioned, the fixed-effects estimator is defined for the transformed system. Multiplying both sides of (5.1.1″) on page 329 from the left by $\mathbf{Q}$ and making use of the fact that $\mathbf{Q1}_M = \mathbf{0}$, we obtain

$$\mathbf{Qy}_i = \mathbf{QF}_i\boldsymbol{\beta} + \mathbf{Q}\boldsymbol{\eta}_i$$

or

$$\tilde{\mathbf{y}}_i = \widetilde{\mathbf{F}}_i\boldsymbol{\beta} + \tilde{\boldsymbol{\eta}}_i \quad (i = 1, 2, \ldots, n), \tag{5.2.1}$$

where

$$\underset{(M\times 1)}{\tilde{\mathbf{y}}_i} \equiv \mathbf{Qy}_i, \quad \underset{(M\times\#\boldsymbol{\beta})}{\widetilde{\mathbf{F}}_i} \equiv \mathbf{QF}_i, \quad \underset{(M\times 1)}{\tilde{\boldsymbol{\eta}}_i} \equiv \mathbf{Q}\boldsymbol{\eta}_i. \tag{5.2.2}$$

Thus, the fixed effect α_i and common regressors drop out in the transformed equations. Now form the pooled sample of transformed $\mathbf{y}_i$ and $\mathbf{F}_i$ as

$$\underset{(Mn\times 1)}{\tilde{\mathbf{y}}} \equiv \begin{bmatrix} \tilde{\mathbf{y}}_1 \\ \vdots \\ \tilde{\mathbf{y}}_n \end{bmatrix}, \quad \underset{(Mn\times\#\boldsymbol{\beta})}{\widetilde{\mathbf{F}}} \equiv \begin{bmatrix} \widetilde{\mathbf{F}}_1 \\ \vdots \\ \widetilde{\mathbf{F}}_n \end{bmatrix}. \tag{5.2.3}$$

The **fixed-effects estimator** of $\boldsymbol{\beta}$, denoted $\widehat{\boldsymbol{\beta}}_{\text{FE}}$, is the pooled OLS estimator, that is, the OLS estimator applied to the pooled sample $(\tilde{\mathbf{y}}, \widetilde{\mathbf{F}})$ of size Mn. Therefore,

$$\begin{aligned}
\widehat{\boldsymbol{\beta}}_{\text{FE}} &\equiv (\widetilde{\mathbf{F}}'\widetilde{\mathbf{F}})^{-1}\widetilde{\mathbf{F}}'\tilde{\mathbf{y}} \\
&= \Big(\frac{1}{n}\sum_{i=1}^{n}\widetilde{\mathbf{F}}_i'\widetilde{\mathbf{F}}_i\Big)^{-1}\frac{1}{n}\sum_{i=1}^{n}\widetilde{\mathbf{F}}_i'\tilde{\mathbf{y}}_i \\
&= \Big[\frac{1}{n}\sum_{i=1}^{n}(\mathbf{QF}_i)'(\mathbf{QF}_i)\Big]^{-1}\frac{1}{n}\sum_{i=1}^{n}(\mathbf{QF}_i)'(\mathbf{Qy}_i) \\
&= \Big(\frac{1}{n}\sum_{i=1}^{n}\mathbf{F}_i'\mathbf{QQF}_i\Big)^{-1}\frac{1}{n}\sum_{i=1}^{n}\mathbf{F}_i'\mathbf{QQy}_i \\
&= \Big(\frac{1}{n}\sum_{i=1}^{n}\mathbf{F}_i'\mathbf{QF}_i\Big)^{-1}\frac{1}{n}\sum_{i=1}^{n}\mathbf{F}_i'\mathbf{Qy}_i \quad \text{(since } \mathbf{Q} \text{ is symmetric and idempotent).}
\end{aligned} \tag{5.2.4}$$

Substituting (5.2.1) into (5.2.4), the sampling error can be obtained as

$$\begin{aligned}\widehat{\boldsymbol{\beta}}_{\text{FE}} - \boldsymbol{\beta} &= \Big(\frac{1}{n}\sum_{i=1}^{n} \widetilde{\mathbf{F}}_i'\widetilde{\mathbf{F}}_i\Big)^{-1} \frac{1}{n}\sum_{i=1}^{n} \widetilde{\mathbf{F}}_i'\tilde{\boldsymbol{\eta}}_i \\ &= \Big(\frac{1}{n}\sum_{i=1}^{n} \mathbf{F}_i'\mathbf{Q}\mathbf{F}_i\Big)^{-1} \frac{1}{n}\sum_{i=1}^{n} \mathbf{F}_i'\mathbf{Q}\boldsymbol{\eta}_i. \end{aligned} \tag{5.2.5}$$

Because it is based on deviations from group means, the fixed-effects estimator is also known as the **within estimator** or the **covariance estimator**. Another, and perhaps more popular, derivation is to apply OLS to levels, i.e., not in deviations but with group (i) specific dummies added to the list of regressors. For this reason the estimator is also called the **least squares dummy variables (LSDV)** estimator. The LSDV interpretation allows us to see what additional assumptions are needed for the error-components model in developing a finite-sample theory for the estimator. This is left as Analytical Exercise 1.

Large-Sample Properties

As you will prove in Analytical Exercise 2, the fixed-effects estimator can also be written as a GMM estimator, which lends itself to a straightforward development of large-sample theory for the fixed-effects estimator summarized in Proposition 5.1 below. Proving the proposition, however, can be accomplished more easily by inspecting the expression (5.2.5) for sampling error.

Proposition 5.1 (large-sample properties of the fixed-effects estimator): *Consider the error-components model (consisting of (5.1.1″) on page 329, (5.1.2), (5.1.8), (5.1.4)–(5.1.6), and (5.1.15)), but relax the SUR assumption (5.1.8b) by requiring only that*

$$\mathrm{E}(\mathbf{f}_{im}\cdot\eta_{ih}) = \mathbf{0} \quad \text{for all } m, h\ (= 1, 2, \ldots, M), \tag{5.2.6}$$

where $\mathbf{f}_{im}'$ is the m-th row of $\mathbf{F}_i$. Define $\tilde{\mathbf{y}}_i$, $\widetilde{\mathbf{F}}_i$, and $\tilde{\boldsymbol{\eta}}_i$ by (5.2.2). Then:

(a) the fixed-effects estimator (5.2.4) is consistent and asymptotically normal with

$$\mathrm{Avar}(\widehat{\boldsymbol{\beta}}_{\text{FE}}) = \big[\mathrm{E}(\widetilde{\mathbf{F}}_i'\widetilde{\mathbf{F}}_i)\big]^{-1}\,\mathrm{E}\big[\widetilde{\mathbf{F}}_i'\,\mathrm{E}(\tilde{\boldsymbol{\eta}}_i\tilde{\boldsymbol{\eta}}_i')\widetilde{\mathbf{F}}_i\big]\,\big[\mathrm{E}(\widetilde{\mathbf{F}}_i'\widetilde{\mathbf{F}}_i)\big]^{-1}. \tag{5.2.7}$$

(b) This asymptotic variance is consistently estimated by

$$\widehat{\mathrm{Avar}(\widehat{\boldsymbol{\beta}}_{\text{FE}})} = \Big(\frac{1}{n}\sum_{i=1}^{n} \widetilde{\mathbf{F}}_i'\widetilde{\mathbf{F}}_i\Big)^{-1}\Big(\frac{1}{n}\sum_{i=1}^{n} \widetilde{\mathbf{F}}_i'\widehat{\mathbf{V}}\widetilde{\mathbf{F}}_i\Big)\Big(\frac{1}{n}\sum_{i=1}^{n} \widetilde{\mathbf{F}}_i'\widetilde{\mathbf{F}}_i\Big)^{-1}, \tag{5.2.8}$$

where $\widehat{\mathbf{V}}$ is the sample cross-moment matrix of transformed residuals associated with the fixed-effects estimator:

$$\underset{(M\times M)}{\widehat{\mathbf{V}}} \equiv \frac{1}{n}\sum_{i=1}^{n}(\tilde{\mathbf{y}}_i - \widetilde{\mathbf{F}}_i\widehat{\boldsymbol{\beta}}_{\text{FE}})(\tilde{\mathbf{y}}_i - \widetilde{\mathbf{F}}_i\widehat{\boldsymbol{\beta}}_{\text{FE}})'. \tag{5.2.9}$$

The only nontrivial part of the proof is to show:

(1) $\mathrm{E}(\widetilde{\mathbf{F}}_i'\widetilde{\mathbf{F}}_i)$ is nonsingular (and hence invertible),

(2) $\mathrm{E}(\mathbf{F}_i'\mathbf{Q}\boldsymbol{\eta}_i) = \mathbf{0}$ (which is needed for consistency), and

(3) $\mathrm{E}(\widetilde{\mathbf{F}}_i'\tilde{\boldsymbol{\eta}}_i\tilde{\boldsymbol{\eta}}_i'\widetilde{\mathbf{F}}_i)$ (which is the Avar of $\frac{1}{n}\sum_{i=1}^{n}\widetilde{\mathbf{F}}_i'\tilde{\boldsymbol{\eta}}_i) = \mathrm{E}\big[\widetilde{\mathbf{F}}_i'\,\mathrm{E}(\tilde{\boldsymbol{\eta}}_i\tilde{\boldsymbol{\eta}}_i')\widetilde{\mathbf{F}}_i\big]$.

The rest of the proof is an easy application of Kolmogorov's LLN and the Lindeberg-Levy CLT.

Proving that (5.1.15) implies (1) is left as an optional analytical exercise.

To prove (2), use formula (4.6.16b) and rewrite the expectation as

$$\begin{aligned}\mathrm{E}(\mathbf{F}_i'\mathbf{Q}\boldsymbol{\eta}_i) &= \mathrm{E}\Big(\sum_{m=1}^{M}\sum_{h=1}^{M} q_{mh}\mathbf{f}_{im}\cdot\eta_{ih}\Big) \quad (q_{mh} \equiv (m,h) \text{ element of } \mathbf{Q})\\ &= \sum_{m=1}^{M}\sum_{h=1}^{M} q_{mh}\,\mathrm{E}(\mathbf{f}_{im}\cdot\eta_{ih}).\end{aligned} \tag{5.2.10}$$

This is zero by the orthogonality conditions (5.2.6).

Proof of (3) is as follows. First note that

$$\mathrm{E}(\widetilde{\mathbf{F}}_i'\tilde{\boldsymbol{\eta}}_i\tilde{\boldsymbol{\eta}}_i'\widetilde{\mathbf{F}}_i) = \mathrm{E}\big[\widetilde{\mathbf{F}}_i'\,\mathrm{E}(\tilde{\boldsymbol{\eta}}_i\tilde{\boldsymbol{\eta}}_i' \mid \mathbf{x}_i)\widetilde{\mathbf{F}}_i\big].$$

(This follows by the Law of Total Expectations and by the fact that $\mathbf{x}_i$ [= union of $(\mathbf{z}_{i1},\dots,\mathbf{z}_{iM})$] includes the elements of $\mathbf{F}_i$ and $\widetilde{\mathbf{F}}_i$ is a function of $\mathbf{F}_i$.) But $\mathrm{E}(\tilde{\boldsymbol{\eta}}_i\tilde{\boldsymbol{\eta}}_i' \mid \mathbf{x}_i)$ equals the unconditional mean $\mathrm{E}(\tilde{\boldsymbol{\eta}}_i\tilde{\boldsymbol{\eta}}_i')$ because

$$\begin{aligned}&\mathrm{E}(\tilde{\boldsymbol{\eta}}_i\tilde{\boldsymbol{\eta}}_i' \mid \mathbf{x}_i) = \mathrm{E}(\tilde{\boldsymbol{\varepsilon}}_i\tilde{\boldsymbol{\varepsilon}}_i' \mid \mathbf{x}_i) \quad (\text{since } \tilde{\boldsymbol{\varepsilon}}_i \equiv \mathbf{Q}\boldsymbol{\varepsilon}_i = \mathbf{Q}(\mathbf{1}_M\cdot\alpha_i + \boldsymbol{\eta}_i) = \mathbf{Q}\boldsymbol{\eta}_i = \tilde{\boldsymbol{\eta}}_i)\\ &= \mathbf{Q}\,\mathrm{E}(\boldsymbol{\varepsilon}_i\boldsymbol{\varepsilon}_i' \mid \mathbf{x}_i)\mathbf{Q}\\ &= \mathbf{Q}\,\mathrm{E}(\boldsymbol{\varepsilon}_i\boldsymbol{\varepsilon}_i')\mathbf{Q} \quad (\text{by (5.1.5)})\\ &= \mathrm{E}(\tilde{\boldsymbol{\varepsilon}}_i\tilde{\boldsymbol{\varepsilon}}_i')\\ &= \mathrm{E}(\tilde{\boldsymbol{\eta}}_i\tilde{\boldsymbol{\eta}}_i') \quad (\text{since } \tilde{\boldsymbol{\varepsilon}}_i = \tilde{\boldsymbol{\eta}}_i).\end{aligned} \tag{5.2.11}$$

A glance at the expression for the asymptotic variance should make you suspect that there must be some other estimator that is asymptotically more efficient, because the asymptotic variance of an efficient estimator can be written as the inverse of a matrix. Indeed, as you will prove in Analytical Exercise 2, there is available an estimator that is asymptotically more efficient than the fixed-effects estimator.

Digression: When $\boldsymbol{\eta}_i$ Is Spherical

The usual error-components model assumes, additionally, that the second error component $\boldsymbol{\eta}_i$ is spherical:

$$\mathrm{E}(\boldsymbol{\eta}_i \boldsymbol{\eta}_i') = \sigma_\eta^2 \mathbf{I}_M, \quad \text{so that } \mathrm{E}(\tilde{\boldsymbol{\eta}}_i \tilde{\boldsymbol{\eta}}_i') = \sigma_\eta^2 \mathbf{Q}. \tag{5.2.12}$$

If, as in many panel data sets, m is time, this assumption is often referred to as the assumption of no "serial correlation." The lack of serial correlation in this sense should not be confused with the condition that $\boldsymbol{\eta}_i$ be uncorrelated with $\boldsymbol{\eta}_j$ for $i \neq j$. The latter is a consequence of our maintained assumption that the sample is i.i.d.

Substituting this into (5.2.7) and noting that $\mathbf{Q}\widetilde{\mathbf{F}}_i = \widetilde{\mathbf{F}}_i$, we find that the expression for the asymptotic variance simplifies to

$$\mathrm{Avar}(\widehat{\boldsymbol{\beta}}_{\mathrm{FE}}) = \sigma_\eta^2 \cdot \left[\mathrm{E}(\widetilde{\mathbf{F}}_i' \widetilde{\mathbf{F}}_i)\right]^{-1}. \tag{5.2.13}$$

If there is a consistent estimate, $\hat{\sigma}_\eta^2$, of σ_η^2, then the asymptotic variance is consistently estimated by

$$\widehat{\mathrm{Avar}(\widehat{\boldsymbol{\beta}}_{\mathrm{FE}})} = \hat{\sigma}_\eta^2 \cdot \left(\frac{1}{n} \sum_{i=1}^{n} \widetilde{\mathbf{F}}_i' \widetilde{\mathbf{F}}_i\right)^{-1}, \tag{5.2.14}$$

which equals n times $\hat{\sigma}_\eta^2 \cdot (\widetilde{\mathbf{F}}'\widetilde{\mathbf{F}})^{-1}$, that is, n times the usual expression for the estimated variance matrix when OLS is applied to the pooled sample $(\tilde{\mathbf{y}}, \widetilde{\mathbf{F}})$ of size Mn.

To extend the OLS analogy, define SSR as

$$SSR = (\tilde{\mathbf{y}} - \widetilde{\mathbf{F}}\widehat{\boldsymbol{\beta}}_{\mathrm{FE}})'(\tilde{\mathbf{y}} - \widetilde{\mathbf{F}}\widehat{\boldsymbol{\beta}}_{\mathrm{FE}}) = \sum_{i=1}^{n} (\tilde{\mathbf{y}}_i - \widetilde{\mathbf{F}}_i\widehat{\boldsymbol{\beta}}_{\mathrm{FE}})'(\tilde{\mathbf{y}}_i - \widetilde{\mathbf{F}}_i\widehat{\boldsymbol{\beta}}_{\mathrm{FE}}). \tag{5.2.15}$$

In the pooled OLS on deviations from group means, there are $\#\boldsymbol{\beta}$ coefficients to be estimated. The usual OLS estimate of the error variance is

$$\frac{SSR}{Mn - \#\boldsymbol{\beta}}. \tag{5.2.16}$$

This, however, is *not* consistent for σ_η^2. You will be asked to show in Analytical Exercise 3 that a consistent estimator is

$$\frac{SSR}{Mn - n - \#\boldsymbol{\beta}}. \tag{5.2.17}$$

(For that matter, $SSR/(Mn - n)$ is also consistent.) The reason n has to be subtracted from the denominator of (5.2.16) is that M transformed equations are not linearly independent; for both sides of the M transformed equations, the sum is always zero, as you can see by multiplying both sides of (5.2.1) from left by $\mathbf{1}'_M$ and making use of $\mathbf{1}'_M\mathbf{Q} = \mathbf{0}'$. The effective sample size of the pooled sample is $Mn - n$, not Mn. Use of (5.2.16) instead of (5.2.17) is a very common mistake, which results in an underestimation of standard errors and an overestimation of t-values. For example, if $M = 3$, $n = 1{,}000$, and $\#\boldsymbol{\beta} = 5$, the t-values will be overestimated by about 23% (= square root of 2995/1995 minus one).

Random Effects versus Fixed Effects

Now get back to the general case of no restriction on $\mathrm{E}(\boldsymbol{\eta}_i\boldsymbol{\eta}_i')$, so the error term can have an arbitrary pattern of "serial correlation" across m. Comparing (5.2.6) with (5.1.8), we see that the orthogonality conditions *not* used by the fixed-effects estimator are

$$\mathrm{E}(\mathbf{f}_{im} \cdot \alpha_i) = \mathbf{0} \text{ for all } m, \quad \mathrm{E}(\mathbf{b}_i \cdot \alpha_i) = \mathbf{0}, \quad \mathrm{E}(\mathbf{b}_i \cdot \eta_{im}) = \mathbf{0} \text{ for all } m. \tag{5.2.18}$$

That is, the fixed-effects estimator is robust to the failure of (5.2.18). Let $\widehat{\boldsymbol{\beta}}_{\mathrm{RE}}$ be the elements of $\hat{\boldsymbol{\delta}}_{\mathrm{RE}}$ (the random-effects estimator applied to the original M-equation system (5.1.1″) on page 329) that correspond to $\boldsymbol{\beta}$:

$$\hat{\boldsymbol{\delta}}_{\mathrm{RE}} \equiv \begin{bmatrix} \widehat{\boldsymbol{\beta}}_{\mathrm{RE}} \\ \hat{\boldsymbol{\gamma}}_{\mathrm{RE}} \end{bmatrix}. \tag{5.2.19}$$

Also, let $\mathrm{Avar}(\widehat{\boldsymbol{\beta}}_{\mathrm{RE}})$ be the asymptotic variance of $\widehat{\boldsymbol{\beta}}_{\mathrm{RE}}$. It is the leading submatrix of $\mathrm{Avar}(\hat{\boldsymbol{\delta}}_{\mathrm{RE}})$ (given by (4.6.9′) on page 293) corresponding to $\boldsymbol{\beta}$.

The random-effects estimator $\widehat{\boldsymbol{\beta}}_{\mathrm{RE}}$ is an efficient estimator while $\widehat{\boldsymbol{\beta}}_{\mathrm{FE}}$ is consistent but not efficient. However, if (5.2.18) is violated, $\widehat{\boldsymbol{\beta}}_{\mathrm{RE}}$ is no longer guaranteed to be consistent, while $\widehat{\boldsymbol{\beta}}_{\mathrm{FE}}$ remains consistent. Thus, a natural test of (5.2.18) is to consider the difference between the two estimators,

$$\hat{\mathbf{q}} \equiv \widehat{\boldsymbol{\beta}}_{\mathrm{FE}} - \widehat{\boldsymbol{\beta}}_{\mathrm{RE}}. \tag{5.2.20}$$

It is easy to prove that $\sqrt{n}\,\hat{\mathbf{q}}$ is asymptotically normal. The Hausman principle (originally developed for ML estimators but proved to be applicable to GMM estimators in Analytical Exercise 9 to Chapter 3) implies that

$$\text{Avar}(\hat{\mathbf{q}}) = \text{Avar}(\widehat{\boldsymbol{\beta}}_{\text{FE}}) - \text{Avar}(\widehat{\boldsymbol{\beta}}_{\text{RE}}). \tag{5.2.21}$$

(So, there is no need to incorporate the asymptotic covariance between $\widehat{\boldsymbol{\beta}}_{\text{FE}}$ and $\widehat{\boldsymbol{\beta}}_{\text{RE}}$ because it is zero.) By Proposition 4.7, the leading submatrix of (4.6.9′) on page 293 provides a consistent estimator of $\text{Avar}(\widehat{\boldsymbol{\beta}}_{\text{RE}})$. By Proposition 5.1, $\text{Avar}(\widehat{\boldsymbol{\beta}}_{\text{FE}})$ is consistently estimated by (5.2.8). A consistent estimator of $\text{Avar}(\hat{\mathbf{q}})$, therefore, is the difference. Write this as $\widehat{\text{Avar}(\hat{\mathbf{q}})}$. It is proved in the appendix that (i) $\text{Avar}(\hat{\mathbf{q}})$ is nonsingular (and hence positive definite) and (ii) the Hausman statistic defined below is guaranteed to be nonnegative for any sample $\{\mathbf{y}_i, \mathbf{Z}_i\}$. To summarize,

Proposition 5.2 (Hausman specification test): *Suppose the assumptions of the error-components model ((5.1.1″) (on page 329), (5.1.2), (5.1.8), (5.1.4)–(5.1.6), and (5.1.15)) hold. Define $\hat{\mathbf{q}}$ and $\widehat{\text{Avar}(\hat{\mathbf{q}})}$ as just described. Then the Hausman statistic*

$$H \equiv n \cdot \hat{\mathbf{q}}' \left(\widehat{\text{Avar}(\hat{\mathbf{q}})}\right)^{-1} \hat{\mathbf{q}} \tag{5.2.22}$$

is distributed asymptotically chi-square with $\#\boldsymbol{\beta}$ degrees of freedom. It is nonnegative in finite samples.

This test is a specification test because it can detect a failure of (5.2.18) which is part of the maintained assumptions of the error-components model. More specifically, consider a sequence of local alternatives that satisfy all the assumptions of the error-components model except (5.2.18).[2] With some additional technical assumptions, it can be shown that the Hausman statistic converges to a noncentral χ^2 distribution with a noncentrality parameter along those sequences of local alternatives.[3] That is, the Hausman statistic has power against local alternatives under which the random-effects estimator is inconsistent.

Relaxing Conditional Homoskedasticity

It is straightforward to derive the large sample distribution of the fixed-effects estimator without conditional homoskedasticity. As will be seen in the next section,

[2]The notion of local alternatives was introduced in Section 2.4.

[3]See Newey (1985). The required technical assumption is Newey's Assumption 5.

extension of the large sample results to cover unbalanced panels is actually easier without conditional homoskedasticity.

Proposition 5.3 (fixed-effects estimator without conditional homoskedasticity): *Drop conditional homoskedasticity (5.1.5) from the hypothesis of Proposition 5.1. Define* $\tilde{\mathbf{y}}_i$, $\widetilde{\mathbf{F}}_i$, *and* $\tilde{\boldsymbol{\eta}}_i$ *by (5.2.2). Then:*

(a) the fixed-effects estimator (5.2.4) is consistent and asymptotically normal with

$$\text{Avar}(\widehat{\boldsymbol{\beta}}_{\text{FE}}) = \left[\text{E}(\widetilde{\mathbf{F}}_i'\widetilde{\mathbf{F}}_i)\right]^{-1} \text{E}(\widetilde{\mathbf{F}}_i'\tilde{\boldsymbol{\eta}}_i\tilde{\boldsymbol{\eta}}_i'\widetilde{\mathbf{F}}_i) \left[\text{E}(\widetilde{\mathbf{F}}_i'\widetilde{\mathbf{F}}_i)\right]^{-1}. \tag{5.2.23}$$

(b) If, furthermore, some appropriate finite fourth-moment assumption (which is an adaptation of Assumption 4.6) is satisfied, then the asymptotic variance is consistently estimated by

$$\widehat{\text{Avar}(\widehat{\boldsymbol{\beta}}_{\text{FE}})} = \left(\frac{1}{n}\sum_{i=1}^{n}\widetilde{\mathbf{F}}_i'\widetilde{\mathbf{F}}_i\right)^{-1}\left(\frac{1}{n}\sum_{i=1}^{n}(\widetilde{\mathbf{F}}_i'\breve{\boldsymbol{\eta}}_i\breve{\boldsymbol{\eta}}_i'\widetilde{\mathbf{F}}_i)\right)\left(\frac{1}{n}\sum_{i=1}^{n}\widetilde{\mathbf{F}}_i'\widetilde{\mathbf{F}}_i\right)^{-1}, \tag{5.2.24}$$

where $\breve{\boldsymbol{\eta}}_i \equiv \tilde{\mathbf{y}}_i - \widetilde{\mathbf{F}}_i\widehat{\boldsymbol{\beta}}_{\text{FE}}$ *(this* $\breve{\boldsymbol{\eta}}_i$ *should not be confused with* $\tilde{\boldsymbol{\eta}}_i$ *in (5.2.1)).*

Again, there are two ways to prove this. Write the fixed-effects estimator as a GMM estimator and then apply the large sample theory of GMM estimators. Or you can prove it directly by inspecting the expression (5.2.4) for the sampling error. The only non-trivial part of the proof is that the middle summation in the expression for $\widehat{\text{Avar}(\widehat{\boldsymbol{\beta}}_{\text{FE}})}$ converges in probability to its population counterpart, $\text{E}(\widetilde{\mathbf{F}}_i'\tilde{\boldsymbol{\eta}}_i\tilde{\boldsymbol{\eta}}_i'\widetilde{\mathbf{F}}_i)$. The required technique is very similar to the one used for proving Proposition 4.2 and so is not repeated here.

QUESTIONS FOR REVIEW

1. For the large sample results of this section to hold, do we have to assume that α_i and $\boldsymbol{\eta}_i$ are orthogonal to each other?

2. (Dropping redundant equations) As mentioned in the text, the M transformed equations are not linearly independent in the sense that any one of the M transformed equations is a linear combination of the remaining $M-1$ equations. So consider forming a pooled sample of size $Mn-n$ by dropping one transformed equation (say, the last equation) for each group (i). Is the OLS estimator on this smaller pooled sample the fixed-effects estimator? [Answer: No.]

3. (Importance of cross orthogonalities) Suppose (5.2.6) holds for $m = h$ but not necessarily for $m \neq h$. Would the fixed-effects estimator be necessarily consistent? [Answer: No.]

4. Verify that $\mathrm{E}(\tilde{\boldsymbol{\eta}}_i \tilde{\boldsymbol{\eta}}_i')$ is singular. (Nevertheless, $\mathrm{E}\big[\widetilde{\mathbf{F}}_i' \,\mathrm{E}(\tilde{\boldsymbol{\eta}}_i \tilde{\boldsymbol{\eta}}_i')\widetilde{\mathbf{F}}_i\big]$ in (5.2.7) and $\mathrm{E}(\widetilde{\mathbf{F}}_i' \tilde{\boldsymbol{\eta}}_i \tilde{\boldsymbol{\eta}}_i' \widetilde{\mathbf{F}}_i)$ in (5.2.23) are nonsingular, as an optional analytical exercise will ask you to show.)

5. (Consistent estimation of error covariances) To prove that (5.2.9) is consistent for $\mathrm{E}(\tilde{\boldsymbol{\eta}}_i \tilde{\boldsymbol{\eta}}_i')$, you would apply Proposition 4.1 to the transformed system of M equations. Verify that the conditions of the proposition are satisfied here. In particular, is the requirement that $\mathrm{E}(\tilde{\mathbf{f}}_{im}\tilde{\mathbf{f}}_{im}')$ (where $\tilde{\mathbf{f}}_{im}$ is the m-th row of $\widetilde{\mathbf{F}}_i$) be finite satisfied by the error-component model? **Hint:** $\tilde{\mathbf{f}}_{im}$ is a linear transformation of $\mathbf{x}_i$. (5.1.5) and (5.1.6) imply that $\mathrm{E}(\mathbf{x}_i \mathbf{x}_i')$ is nonsingular.

6. (What the Hausman statistic tests) For simplicity, assume $\boldsymbol{\Sigma}$ ($\equiv \mathrm{E}(\boldsymbol{\varepsilon}_i \boldsymbol{\varepsilon}_i')$) is known. Also for simplicity, assume that there are no common regressors, so $\mathbf{z}_{im} = \mathbf{f}_{im}$ and (5.2.18) reduces to (5.1.8a): $\mathrm{E}(\mathbf{z}_{im} \cdot \alpha_i) = \mathbf{0}$ for all m. This is the restriction *not* used by the fixed-effects estimator. Is the random-effects estimator necessarily inconsistent when (5.1.8a) fails but all the other assumptions of the error-components model (such as (5.1.8b)) are satisfied? **Hint:** Show that, without (5.1.8a),

$$\operatorname{plim} \hat{\boldsymbol{\delta}}_{\mathrm{RE}} - \boldsymbol{\delta} = \mathrm{E}(\mathbf{Z}_i' \boldsymbol{\Sigma}^{-1} \mathbf{Z}_i)^{-1}\, \mathrm{E}(\mathbf{Z}_i' \boldsymbol{\Sigma}^{-1} \boldsymbol{\varepsilon}_i),$$

where $\boldsymbol{\varepsilon}_i = \mathbf{1}\cdot\alpha_i + \boldsymbol{\eta}_i$. Provided (5.1.8b) holds, (5.1.8a) is *sufficient* for $\mathrm{E}(\mathbf{Z}_i' \boldsymbol{\Sigma}^{-1} \boldsymbol{\varepsilon}_i)$ to be zero. Is it necessary? Thus, strictly speaking, the Hausman test is not a test of (5.1.8a); it is a test of $\mathrm{E}(\mathbf{Z}_i' \boldsymbol{\Sigma}^{-1} \boldsymbol{\varepsilon}_i) = \mathbf{0}$.

5.3 Unbalanced Panels (optional)

In applying the multiple-equation model to panel data, we have been making an implicit but important assumption that the variables are observable for all m, so that the number of observations for each cross-section unit is the same (M). Such a panel is called a **balanced panel**. But no available panel data sets are balanced, thanks to exits from and entries to the survey. Inevitably, some firms disappear from the sample due to bankruptcies and mergers before the end year M of the survey, while those firms that did not exist at the start of the survey may be included later. Some of the households initially in the survey will not complete the spell of M periods due to household resolutions or because respondents get tired of being asked the same questions over and over again. The panel of identical siblings is unbalanced if it includes identical triplets (and even septuplets) as well as twins.

This section shows that the fixed-effects estimator easily extends to unbalanced panels. This sanguine conclusion, however, depends on the assumption that whether the cross-section unit stays in the sample does not depend on the error term. Without this assumption, the estimator is no longer consistent. This phenomenon is called the **selectivity bias**. A full discussion of why a selectivity bias arises and how it can be corrected for is relegated to Section 8.2, because the issue is not specific to panel data.

"Zeroing Out" Missing Observations

To handle missing observations, it is convenient to define a dummy variable, d_{im},

$$d_{im} = \begin{cases} 1 & \text{if observation } m \text{ is in the sample,} \\ 0 & \text{otherwise,} \end{cases} \tag{5.3.1}$$

and

$$\underset{(M\times 1)}{\mathbf{d}_i} = \begin{bmatrix} d_{i1} \\ \vdots \\ d_{iM} \end{bmatrix}, \quad M_i = \sum_{m=1}^{M} d_{im} = \#\,\text{observations from } i. \tag{5.3.2}$$

If observation m is missing for group i, fill the m-th rows of $\mathbf{y}_i$, $\mathbf{F}_i$, and $\boldsymbol{\eta}_i$ with zeros so that they continue to be of fixed size. That is,

$$\underset{(M\times 1)}{\mathbf{y}_i} = \begin{bmatrix} d_{i1}\cdot y_{i1} \\ \vdots \\ d_{iM}\cdot y_{iM} \end{bmatrix}, \quad \underset{(M\times \#\boldsymbol{\beta})}{\mathbf{F}_i} = \begin{bmatrix} d_{i1}\cdot \mathbf{f}'_{i1} \\ \vdots \\ d_{iM}\cdot \mathbf{f}'_{iM} \end{bmatrix}, \quad \underset{(M\times 1)}{\boldsymbol{\eta}_i} = \begin{bmatrix} d_{i1}\cdot \eta_{i1} \\ \vdots \\ d_{iM}\cdot \eta_{iM} \end{bmatrix}. \tag{5.3.3}$$

Thus, for each i and m, either all the elements of the vector $(y_{im}, \mathbf{f}_{im})$ are observable or none is observable. We will not consider the case where some, but not all, elements of $(y_{im}, \mathbf{f}_{im})$ are observable.

With this new notation, (5.1.1″) on page 329 becomes

$$\mathbf{y}_i = \mathbf{F}_i\boldsymbol{\beta} + \mathbf{d}_i\cdot \mathbf{b}'_i\boldsymbol{\gamma} + \mathbf{d}_i\cdot \alpha_i + \boldsymbol{\eta}_i \quad (i = 1, 2, \ldots, n). \tag{5.3.4}$$

In the case of balanced panels, where $\mathbf{d}_i = \mathbf{1}_M$, the transformation matrix $\mathbf{Q}$ in the fixed-effects formula (5.2.4) is the annihilator associated with $\mathbf{1}_M$ (see (5.1.10)).

With missing observations, we use as the transformation matrix the annihilator associated with $\mathbf{d}_i$:

$$\underset{(M\times M)}{\mathbf{Q}} = \mathbf{I}_M - \mathbf{d}_i(\mathbf{d}_i'\mathbf{d}_i)^{-1}\mathbf{d}_i'$$

$$= \mathbf{I}_M - \frac{1}{M_i}\mathbf{d}_i\mathbf{d}_i' \quad (\text{since } \mathbf{d}_i'\mathbf{d}_i = M_i). \tag{5.3.5}$$

This matrix depends on i because $\mathbf{d}_i$ differs across i. Nevertheless, we leave this dependence of $\mathbf{Q}$ on i implicit for economy of notation. With $\mathbf{y}_i$, $\mathbf{F}_i$, $\boldsymbol{\eta}_i$, and $\mathbf{Q}$ thus redefined, the formula for the fixed-effects estimator remains the same as (5.2.4). Substituting (5.3.4) into this formula and observing that $\mathbf{Q}\mathbf{d}_i = \mathbf{0}$, we see that the expression for the sampling error, too, is the same as (5.2.5).

Zeroing Out versus Compression

As seen in Section 5.2 for the case of balanced panels, the fixed-effects estimator can be calculated as the OLS estimator on the pooled sample (of size Mn) of deviations from group means. As before, let $\tilde{\mathbf{y}}_i$, $\widetilde{\mathbf{F}}_i$, and $\tilde{\boldsymbol{\eta}}_i$ be the transformations by $\mathbf{Q}$ of $\mathbf{y}_i$, $\mathbf{F}_i$, and $\boldsymbol{\eta}_i$, respectively. For example, $\tilde{\mathbf{y}}_i$ looks like

$$\underset{(M\times M)}{\tilde{\mathbf{y}}_i} \equiv \mathbf{Q}\mathbf{y}_i = \begin{bmatrix} d_{i1}\cdot y_{i1} - d_{i1}\cdot \bar{y}_i \\ \vdots \\ d_{iM}\cdot y_{iM} - d_{iM}\cdot \bar{y}_i \end{bmatrix},$$

where

$$\bar{y}_i \equiv \frac{1}{M_i}\mathbf{d}_i'\mathbf{y}_i = \frac{1}{M_i} \times (\text{sum of } y_{im} \text{ over } m \text{ for which data are available}). \tag{5.3.6}$$

Thus, if observation m for group i is available, the m-th element of $\tilde{\mathbf{y}}_i$ is still the deviation of y_{im} from the group mean, but the group mean is over available observations. Since $d_{im} = 0$ if observation m is not available, the rows corresponding to missing observations in $\tilde{\mathbf{y}}_i$ are zero. The same structure applies to columns of $\widetilde{\mathbf{F}}_i$. Therefore, the pooled sample of size Mn created from $(\tilde{\mathbf{y}}_i, \widetilde{\mathbf{F}}_i)$ $(i = 1, \dots, n)$ has a number of rows filled with zeros. Those rows can be dropped from the pooled sample without affecting the numerical value of the fixed-effects estimator. That is, we can "compress" $(\tilde{\mathbf{y}}_i, \widetilde{\mathbf{F}}_i)$ by dropping rows filled with zeros, before forming the pooled sample.

No Selectivity Bias

The fixed-effects estimator, thus adapted to unbalanced panels, remains consistent and asymptotically normal, if the orthogonality conditions (5.2.6) in Proposition 5.1 are modified to

$$\text{(no selectivity bias)}\quad \mathrm{E}(\mathbf{f}_{im} \cdot \eta_{ih} \mid \mathbf{d}_i) = \mathbf{0} \quad (m, h = 1, 2, \dots, M). \tag{5.3.7}$$

As shown in the next proposition, this condition is crucial for ensuring the consistency of the fixed-effects estimator. By the Law of Total Expectations, this condition is stronger than (5.2.6) that the *un*conditional expectation is zero. It is easy to construct an example where (5.3.7) does not hold because the pattern of selection $\mathbf{d}_i$ depends on the error term $\boldsymbol{\eta}_i$. Note that (5.3.7) does not involve the fixed effect α_i. Thus, if the dependence of sample selection on the error term is only through the fixed effect, the problem of sample selectivity bias does not occur.

If the orthogonality conditions (5.2.6) are strengthened as (5.3.7), the conclusions of Proposition 5.3 carry over:

Proposition 5.4 (large-sample properties of the fixed-effects estimator for unbalanced panels): *Consider the error-components model consisting of (5.3.4), (5.1.2), (5.1.4)–(5.1.6), (5.1.15), and (5.3.7), with* $(\mathbf{y}_i, \mathbf{F}_i, \boldsymbol{\eta}_i)$ *as in (5.3.3). As before, define* $(\tilde{\mathbf{y}}_i, \widetilde{\mathbf{F}}_i, \tilde{\boldsymbol{\eta}}_i)$ *by (5.2.2), but with* $\mathbf{Q}$ *given by (5.3.5). Then the conclusions of Proposition 5.3 hold.*

Here we show that $\mathrm{E}(\mathbf{F}_i'\mathbf{Q}\boldsymbol{\eta}_i) = \mathbf{0}$. (The other parts of the proof, which are applications of Kolmogorov's LLN and the Lindeberg-Levy CLT, are the same as in the proof of Proposition 5.3.) Since

$$\mathbf{F}_i'\mathbf{Q}\boldsymbol{\eta}_i = \sum_{m=1}^{M}\sum_{h=1}^{M} q_{mh}^{(i)} \cdot d_{im} \cdot d_{ih} \cdot \mathbf{f}_{im} \cdot \eta_{ih}, \tag{5.3.8}$$

where $q_{mh}^{(i)}$ is the (m, h) element of $\mathbf{Q}$ applied to the i-th equations, we have

$$\mathrm{E}(\mathbf{F}_i'\mathbf{Q}\boldsymbol{\eta}_i) = \sum_{m=1}^{M}\sum_{h=1}^{M} \mathrm{E}(q_{mh}^{(i)} \cdot d_{im} \cdot d_{ih} \cdot \mathbf{f}_{im} \cdot \eta_{ih}). \tag{5.3.9}$$

If there is no selectivity bias so that $\mathrm{E}(\mathbf{f}_{im} \cdot \eta_{ih} \mid \mathbf{d}_i) = \mathbf{0}$, then (5.3.9) equals zero because

$$\begin{aligned}&\mathrm{E}(q_{mh}^{(i)} \cdot d_{im} \cdot d_{ih} \cdot \mathbf{f}_{im} \cdot \eta_{ih})\\ &= \mathrm{E}\left[q_{mh}^{(i)} \cdot d_{im} \cdot d_{ih} \cdot \mathrm{E}(\mathbf{f}_{im} \cdot \eta_{ih} \mid \mathbf{d}_i)\right] \quad \text{(since } q_{mh}^{(i)} \text{ is a function of } \mathbf{d}_i\text{).}\end{aligned} \tag{5.3.10}$$

It is interesting that the extension to unbalanced panels is easier without conditional homoskedasticity. In order for (5.2.7) of Proposition 5.1 to be the asymptotic variance of the estimator under conditional homoskedasticity, we would have to assume that the second moment of $\tilde{\boldsymbol{\eta}}_i$ conditional on $\mathbf{x}_i$ *and* $\mathbf{d}_i$ equals the unconditional second moment, and consistent estimation of this second moment would be a bit complicated.

QUESTIONS FOR REVIEW

1. For $\mathbf{d}_i = (1, 0, 1)'$, write down $\mathbf{Q}$.

2. (Alternative derivation of the fixed-effects estimator for unbalanced panels) Let $\mathbf{y}_i^*$ be the M_i-dimensional vector created from the M-dimensional vector $\mathbf{y}_i$ by dropping rows for which there is no observation. Similarly, create $\mathbf{F}_i^*$ $(M_i \times \#\boldsymbol{\beta})$ from $\mathbf{F}_i$ and $\mathbf{d}_i^*$ from $\mathbf{d}_i$ (so $\mathbf{d}_i^*$ is the M_i-dimensional vector of ones). Let $\mathbf{Q}^*$ $(M_i \times M_i)$ be the annihilator associated with $\mathbf{d}_i^*$. Verify that the fixed-effects estimator can also be written as (5.2.4) in terms of those starred matrices and vectors.

3. Section 4.6 described the pooled OLS in levels for the system (4.6.1′) on page 292.

   (a) How would you modify the estimator (4.6.11′) on page 293 to accommodate unbalanced panels? **Hint:** Define $\mathbf{y}_i$ and $\mathbf{Z}_i$ $(M \times L)$ by "zeroing out."

   (b) Without conditional homoskedasticity, what is its asymptotic variance? [Answer: $\left[\mathrm{E}(\mathbf{Z}_i\mathbf{Z}_i')\right]^{-1} \mathrm{E}(\mathbf{Z}_i\boldsymbol{\varepsilon}_i\boldsymbol{\varepsilon}_i'\mathbf{Z}_i') \left[\mathrm{E}(\mathbf{Z}_i\mathbf{Z}_i')\right]^{-1}$.]

   (c) How would you estimate the asymptotic variance? **Hint:** Replace $\widetilde{\mathbf{F}}_i$ by $\mathbf{Z}_i$, $\mathbf{Q}$ by $\mathbf{I}_M$, and $\tilde{\boldsymbol{\eta}}_i$ by $\boldsymbol{\varepsilon}_i$ in Proposition 5.3.

5.4 Application: International Differences in Growth Rates

Do poor economies grow faster than rich economies? If so, how much faster? These are the questions addressed in the recent burgeoning literature of growth.[4] This section derives the key equation that has been used to explain economic growth of nations and discusses ways to estimate it. Actual estimation of several specifications of the equation is relegated to the empirical exercise.

Derivation of the Estimation Equation

In neoclassical growth theory, output per effective labor in period t, denoted $q(t)$ and to be defined more precisely in (5.4.4) below, converges to the steady-state level q^*. The log-linear approximation around the steady state gives

$$\frac{\mathrm{d}\log(q(t))}{\mathrm{d}t} = \lambda \cdot [\log(q^*) - \log(q(t))]. \tag{5.4.1}$$

Estimating λ, the **speed of convergence**, has been the objective of the recent growth literature. (5.4.1) implies that, for any two points, t_{m-1} and t_m in time,

$$\log(q(t_m)) = (1-\rho)\cdot\log(q^*) + \rho\cdot\log(q(t_{m-1})), \tag{5.4.2}$$

where

$$\rho \equiv \exp[-\lambda\cdot(t_m - t_{m-1})]. \tag{5.4.3}$$

(Since in our data t_m's are equally spaced in time, ρ will not depend on m.) Output per effective labor is defined as

$$q(t) \equiv \frac{Y(t)}{A(t)\,L(t)}, \tag{5.4.4}$$

where $Y(t)$ equals aggregate output, $L(t)$ equals aggregate hours worked, and $A(t)$ equals level of labor-augmenting technical progress. Assuming $A(t)$ grows at a constant rate g (so that $A(t) = A(0)\exp(gt)$), (5.4.4) implies

$$\log(q(t)) = \log\left(\frac{Y(t)}{L(t)}\right) - \log(A(0)) - g\cdot t. \tag{5.4.5}$$

Substituting this into (5.4.2), we obtain

[4] A very extensive survey of the literature is Barro and Sala-i-Martin (1995).

$$\log\left(\frac{Y(t_m)}{L(t_m)}\right) = \rho \cdot \log\left(\frac{Y(t_{m-1})}{L(t_{m-1})}\right) + (1-\rho) \cdot [\log(q^*) + \log(A(0))] + \phi_m, \tag{5.4.6}$$

where

$$\phi_m \equiv g \cdot (t_m - \rho \cdot t_{m-1}). \tag{5.4.7}$$

An equivalent form of equation (5.4.6) can be obtained by subtracting $\log \frac{Y(t_{m-1})}{L(t_{m-1})}$ from both sides:

$$\log\left(\frac{Y(t_m)}{L(t_m)}\right) - \log\left(\frac{Y(t_{m-1})}{L(t_{m-1})}\right)$$
$$= (\rho - 1)\log\left(\frac{Y(t_{m-1})}{L(t_{m-1})}\right) + (1-\rho) \cdot [\log(q^*) + \log(A(0))] + \phi_m. \tag{5.4.6$'$}$$

Since $\rho < 1$ as $\lambda > 0$, this equation says that the level of per capita output has a negative effect on subsequent growth. The country, when poor, should grow faster. This form of the equation is more intuitive, but for the purpose of choosing the correct estimation technique, (5.4.6) rather than (5.4.6′) is more instructive.

Equation (5.4.6) should hold for each country i.[5] For the rest of this section, we assume that the speed of convergence (λ) and the growth rate of labor-augmenting technical progress (g) are the same across countries. Then (5.4.6) for country i can be written as

$$y_{im} = \phi_m + \rho y_{i,m-1} + \alpha_i, \tag{5.4.8}$$

where

$$y_{im} = \log\left(\frac{Y(t_m)}{L(t_m)}\right) \text{ for country } i,$$
$$\alpha_i = (1-\rho) \times \{\log(q^*) + \log(A(0))\} \text{ for country } i. \tag{5.4.9}$$

Appending the Error Term

It is a fairly standard practice in applied econometrics to derive an equation without an error term from the theory and then append an error term for estimation. Growth empirics is not an exception; an error term η_{im} is added to (5.4.8) to obtain

$$y_{im} = \phi_m + \rho y_{i,m-1} + \alpha_i + \eta_{im}. \tag{5.4.10}$$

[5] We have derived the equation describing convergence assuming a closed economy. The assumption is hard to justify, but a similar equation can be derived under free mobility of physical capital if human capital is another factor of production and not freely mobile internationally. See, e.g., Barro and Sala-i-Martin (1995).

One natural interpretation of η_{im} is business cycles, which in macroeconomics are defined as the difference between actual output and potential output. Growth theory is about potential output. The discrepancy between potential output and actual output becomes the error term in the estimation equation derived from growth theory. But then there would be an errors-in-variables problem, which renders the regressors endogenous.[6] For the rest of this section, we follow the mainstream growth literature and ignore the endogeneity problem.

Another problem is the possible correlation in η_{im} between countries (i's). This spatial (or geographical) correlation would not arise if the sample were a random sample. But the sample of nations is not a random sample; it is the universe. The phenomenon known as international business cycles implies that the spatial correlation would be positive. Statistical inference treating countries as if they were independent data points would overstate statistical significance. This problem, too, is largely ignored in the literature and will be ignored in our discussion.

Treatment of α_i

As is clear from (5.4.9), the term α_i in equation (5.4.10) depends on the steady-state level q^* and the initial level of technology $A(0)$. How you treat α_i in the estimation depends on which version of neoclassical growth theory you subscribe to. According to the Cass-Koopmans optimal growth model, the sole determinant of the steady-state level q^* is the growth rate of labor. Thus, if technological knowledge freely flows internationally so that $A(0)$ is the same across countries, the international differences in α_i are completely explained by the labor growth rate. Therefore, leaving aside the endogeneity problem just mentioned, OLS estimation of (5.4.10) delivers consistency if the labor growth rate is included as the additional regressor to control for α_i. If you subscribe to the Solow-Swan growth theory, the saving rate is the other determinant of q^*, so the regression should include the saving rate along with the labor growth rate.

A large fraction of the recent growth literature under the rubric of "conditional convergence" includes these and other variables that might affect q^* or $A(0)$ — such as measures of political stability and the degree of financial intermediation — in order to control for α_i. In the empirical exercise, you will be asked to estimate ρ, and hence the speed of convergence λ, using this conditional convergence approach.

[6]Let x_{im} be the log potential output in year t_m for country i that growth theory is purported to explain, so that (5.4.8) holds for x_{im} rather than for y_{im}. Let log actual output y_{im} be related to x_{im} as $y_{im} = x_{im} + \eta_{im}$. Then (5.4.10) results, but with the error term $\eta_{im} - \rho\eta_{i,m-1}$. Not only would there be an errors-in-variables problem, but also the error term has a moving-average structure.

However, no matter how ingeniously the variables are selected to control for α_i, some component of α_i having to do with features unique to the country would remain unexplained and find its way in the error term. Being part of α_i, it is correlated with the regressor $y_{i,m-1}$ in (5.4.10). The OLS estimation, even if the equation includes a variety of variables to control for α_i, will not provide consistency. The alternative approach is to treat α_i as an unobservable fixed effect.

Consistent Estimation of Speed of Convergence

If output and other variables are observed at $M+1$ points in time, $t_0, t_1, t_2, \ldots, t_M$, equation (5.4.10) is available for $m = 1, \ldots, M$. The fixed-effects technique could be applied to this M-equation system, but it does not provide consistency. The reason is that the system is "dynamic" in that some of the regressors are the dependent variables for other equations of the system. To see this, look at the first two equations of the system:

$$y_{i1} = \phi_1 + \rho y_{i0} + \alpha_i + \eta_{i1},$$
$$y_{i2} = \phi_2 + \rho y_{i1} + \alpha_i + \eta_{i2}.$$

Suppose the error term η_{i1} is orthogonal to the regressors (which are a constant and y_{i0}) in the first equation, so that $\mathrm{E}(\eta_{i1}) = 0$ and $\mathrm{E}(y_{i0}\,\eta_{i1}) = 0$. If we further make the assumption that $\mathrm{E}(\alpha_i\,\eta_{i1}) = 0$, then from the first equation

$$\mathrm{E}(y_{i1}\,\eta_{i1}) = \mathrm{Var}(\eta_{i1}) \neq 0.$$

But y_{i1} is one of the regressors in the second equation. Therefore, if the error term η_{im} is orthogonal to the regressors for each equation, the "cross" orthogonalities are necessarily violated.[7] As emphasized in Section 5.2 (see Review Question 3), the fixed-effects estimator is not guaranteed to be consistent if the cross orthogonalities are not satisfied. For a precise expression for the bias, see Analytical Question 4 to this chapter.

One way to obtain consistency is the following. Take the first differences of the M-equations to obtain $M-1$ equations:

$$y_{i2} - y_{i1} = \mu_1 + (y_{i1} - y_{i0})\rho + (\eta_{i2} - \eta_{i1}),$$
$$y_{i3} - y_{i2} = \mu_2 + (y_{i2} - y_{i1})\rho + (\eta_{i3} - \eta_{i2}),$$
$$\cdots$$
$$y_{iM} - y_{i,M-1} = \mu_{M-1} + (y_{i,M-1} - y_{i,M-2})\rho + (\eta_{iM} - \eta_{i,M-1}), \quad (5.4.11)$$

[7]This was first pointed out by Nickell (1981).

where

$$\mu_m \equiv \phi_{m+1} - \phi_m.$$

The random-effects estimator and the equation-by-equation OLS do not provide consistency because the regressors are not orthogonal to the error term. For example in the first equation, $y_{i1} - y_{i0}$ is not orthogonal to $\eta_{i2} - \eta_{i1}$ because $\mathrm{E}(y_{i1} \cdot \eta_{i1}) \neq 0$ as just seen. Consistent estimation can be done by multiple-equation GMM, if there are valid instruments. In the optional empirical exercise to this chapter, you will be asked to use the saving rate as the instrument for the endogenous regressors. To the extent that the saving rate is uncorrelated with η_{im}, this estimator is robust to the endogeneity problem mentioned above.

QUESTIONS FOR REVIEW

1. The assumption that g (growth rate of technical progress) is common to all countries is needed to derive (5.4.8). Do we have to assume that g is constant over time? [Answer: No.]

2. (Identification) For simplicity, let $M = 3$ so that (5.4.11) is a two-equation system.

   (a) Write (5.4.11) as a multiple-equation system with common coefficients by properly defining the $y_{i1}, y_{i2}, \mathbf{z}_{i1}, \mathbf{z}_{i2}, \boldsymbol{\delta}$ in (4.6.1). **Hint:** $\mathbf{z}_{i2}$, for example, is $(0, 1, y_{i2} - y_{i1})'$.

   (b) If s_{im} is the instrument for $y_{im} - y_{i,m-1}$, the instrument vector for the m-th equation is $\mathbf{x}_{im} = (1, s_{im})'$ for $m = 1, 2$. Show that the system is not identified if $\mathrm{Cov}(s_{im}, y_{im} - y_{i,m-1}) = 0$ for all m. **Hint:**

$$\boldsymbol{\Sigma}_{\mathbf{xz}} = \begin{bmatrix} 1 & 0 & \mathrm{E}(y_{i1} - y_{i0}) \\ \mathrm{E}(s_{i1}) & 0 & \mathrm{E}[s_{i1}(y_{i1} - y_{i0})] \\ 0 & 1 & \mathrm{E}(y_{i2} - y_{i1}) \\ 0 & \mathrm{E}(s_{i1}) & \mathrm{E}[s_{i2}(y_{i2} - y_{i1})] \end{bmatrix}.$$

Appendix 5.A: Distribution of Hausman Statistic

This appendix proves that the $\mathrm{Avar}(\hat{\mathbf{q}})$ in (5.2.21) is positive definite and the Hausman statistic (5.2.22) is guaranteed to be nonnegative in any finite samples.

As shown in Section 4.6,

$$\hat{\boldsymbol{\delta}}_{\text{RE}} = (\mathbf{S}'_{\mathbf{xz}}\widehat{\mathbf{S}}^{-1}\mathbf{S}_{\mathbf{xz}})^{-1}\mathbf{S}'_{\mathbf{xz}}\widehat{\mathbf{S}}^{-1}\mathbf{s}_{\mathbf{xy}}, \tag{5.A.1}$$

where

$$\underset{(MK\times L)}{\mathbf{S}_{\mathbf{xz}}} \equiv \frac{1}{n}\sum_{i=1}^{n}\mathbf{Z}_i \otimes \mathbf{x}_i, \qquad \underset{(MK\times MK)}{\widehat{\mathbf{S}}} \equiv \widehat{\boldsymbol{\Sigma}} \otimes \mathbf{S}_{\mathbf{xx}},$$

$$\underset{(K\times K)}{\mathbf{S}_{\mathbf{xx}}} \equiv \frac{1}{n}\sum_{i=1}^{n}\mathbf{x}_i\mathbf{x}'_i, \qquad \mathbf{s}_{\mathbf{xy}} \equiv \frac{1}{n}\sum_{i=1}^{n}\mathbf{y}_i \otimes \mathbf{x}_i,$$

$$K \equiv \#\mathbf{x}_i,\; L \equiv \#\mathbf{z}_{im} \text{ (so } \mathbf{Z}_i \text{ is } M \times L\text{)}.$$

Let

$$\mathbf{Z}_i = (\mathbf{F}_i \,\vdots\, \mathbf{1b}'_i),\; p \equiv \#\boldsymbol{\beta},\; \underset{(L\times p)}{\mathbf{D}} = \begin{bmatrix}\mathbf{I}_p\\ \mathbf{0}\end{bmatrix},$$

so that $\mathbf{F}_i = \mathbf{Z}_i\mathbf{D}$. Then it can be shown fairly easily that

$$\widehat{\boldsymbol{\beta}}_{\text{FE}} = (\mathbf{D}'\mathbf{S}'_{\mathbf{xz}}\widehat{\mathbf{W}}\mathbf{S}_{\mathbf{xz}}\mathbf{D})^{-1}\mathbf{D}'\mathbf{S}'_{\mathbf{xz}}\widehat{\mathbf{W}}\mathbf{s}_{\mathbf{xy}}, \tag{5.A.2}$$

where

$$\widehat{\mathbf{W}} = \mathbf{Q} \otimes \mathbf{S}_{\mathbf{xx}}^{-1},\; \mathbf{Q} \equiv \text{annihilator associated with } \mathbf{1}_M.$$

From (5.A.1) and (5.A.2) it follows that

$$\hat{\mathbf{q}} = (\mathbf{D}'\mathbf{S}'_{\mathbf{xz}}\widehat{\mathbf{W}}\mathbf{S}_{\mathbf{xz}}\mathbf{D})^{-1}\mathbf{D}'\mathbf{S}'_{\mathbf{xz}}\widehat{\mathbf{W}}\mathbf{g}_n(\hat{\boldsymbol{\delta}}_{\text{RE}}),\; \mathbf{g}_n(\hat{\boldsymbol{\delta}}_{\text{RE}}) = \mathbf{s}_{\mathbf{xy}} - \mathbf{S}_{\mathbf{xz}}\hat{\boldsymbol{\delta}}_{\text{RE}}. \tag{5.A.3}$$

(To derive this, recall from Section 4.6 that

$$\mathbf{S}'_{\mathbf{xz}}\widehat{\mathbf{W}}\mathbf{S}_{\mathbf{xz}} = \frac{1}{n}\sum_{i=1}^{n}\mathbf{Z}'_i\mathbf{Q}\mathbf{Z}_i.$$

But since $\mathbf{Q}\mathbf{Z}_i = (\mathbf{Q}\mathbf{F}_i \,\vdots\, \mathbf{0})$, this equals

$$\begin{bmatrix}\frac{1}{n}\sum_{i=1}^{n}\mathbf{F}'_i\mathbf{Q}\mathbf{F}_i & \mathbf{0}\\ \mathbf{0} & \mathbf{0}\end{bmatrix} \tag{5.A.4}$$

so that $\mathbf{S}'_{\mathbf{xz}}\widehat{\mathbf{W}}\mathbf{S}_{\mathbf{xz}} = \mathbf{D}\mathbf{D}'\mathbf{S}'_{\mathbf{xz}}\widehat{\mathbf{W}}\mathbf{S}_{\mathbf{xz}} = \mathbf{S}'_{\mathbf{xz}}\widehat{\mathbf{W}}\mathbf{S}_{\mathbf{xz}}\mathbf{D}\mathbf{D}'$.)

As was shown in Analytical Exercise 5 of Chapter 3,

$$\mathbf{g}_n(\hat{\boldsymbol{\delta}}_{\text{RE}}) = \widehat{\mathbf{B}}\bar{\mathbf{g}},\; \widehat{\mathbf{B}} = \mathbf{I}_{MK} - \mathbf{S}_{\mathbf{xz}}(\mathbf{S}'_{\mathbf{xz}}\widehat{\mathbf{S}}^{-1}\mathbf{S}_{\mathbf{xz}})^{-1}\mathbf{S}'_{\mathbf{xz}}\widehat{\mathbf{S}}^{-1}. \tag{5.A.5}$$

Substituting this into (5.A.3), we obtain

$$\sqrt{n}\,\hat{\mathbf{q}} = (\mathbf{D}'\mathbf{S}'_{\mathbf{xz}}\widehat{\mathbf{W}}\mathbf{S}_{\mathbf{xz}}\mathbf{D})^{-1}\mathbf{D}'\mathbf{S}'_{\mathbf{xz}}\widehat{\mathbf{W}}\widehat{\mathbf{B}}\sqrt{n}\,\bar{\mathbf{g}}. \tag{5.A.6}$$

The asymptotic variance of this expression is

$$\text{Avar}(\hat{\mathbf{q}}) = (\mathbf{D}'\boldsymbol{\Sigma}'_{\mathbf{xz}}\mathbf{W}\boldsymbol{\Sigma}_{\mathbf{xz}}\mathbf{D})^{-1}\mathbf{D}'\boldsymbol{\Sigma}'_{\mathbf{xz}}\mathbf{W}\,\mathbf{B}\,\mathbf{S}\,\mathbf{B}\mathbf{W}\boldsymbol{\Sigma}_{\mathbf{xz}}\mathbf{D}(\mathbf{D}'\boldsymbol{\Sigma}'_{\mathbf{xz}}\mathbf{W}\boldsymbol{\Sigma}_{\mathbf{xz}}\mathbf{D})^{-1}, \tag{5.A.7}$$

where $\mathbf{B} = \text{plim}\,\widehat{\mathbf{B}}$, $\mathbf{W} = \text{plim}\,\widehat{\mathbf{W}} = \mathbf{Q}\otimes\boldsymbol{\Sigma}_{\mathbf{xx}}^{-1}$, and $\mathbf{S} \equiv \text{Avar}(\hat{\mathbf{g}})$. Here, $\mathbf{D}'\boldsymbol{\Sigma}'_{\mathbf{xz}}\mathbf{W}\cdot\boldsymbol{\Sigma}_{\mathbf{xz}}\mathbf{D}$ is invertible because it is easy to show that

$$\mathbf{D}'\boldsymbol{\Sigma}'_{\mathbf{xz}}\mathbf{W}\boldsymbol{\Sigma}_{\mathbf{xz}}\mathbf{D} = \text{E}(\mathbf{F}_i\mathbf{Q}\mathbf{F}_i'), \tag{5.A.8}$$

which, as proved in Analytical Exercise 5, is nonsingular. (5.A.7) is consistently estimated by

$$\widehat{\text{Avar}(\hat{\mathbf{q}})} = (\mathbf{D}'\mathbf{S}'_{\mathbf{xz}}\widehat{\mathbf{W}}\mathbf{S}_{\mathbf{xz}}\mathbf{D})^{-1}\mathbf{D}'\mathbf{S}'_{\mathbf{xz}}\widehat{\mathbf{W}}\,\widehat{\mathbf{B}}\,\widehat{\mathbf{S}}\,\widehat{\mathbf{B}}\,\widehat{\mathbf{W}}\mathbf{S}_{\mathbf{xz}}\mathbf{D}(\mathbf{D}'\mathbf{S}'_{\mathbf{xz}}\widehat{\mathbf{W}}\mathbf{S}_{\mathbf{xz}}\mathbf{D})^{-1}. \tag{5.A.9}$$

A straightforward but lengthy matrix calculation shows that (5.A.7) equals $\text{Avar}(\widehat{\boldsymbol{\beta}}_{\text{FE}}) - \mathbf{D}'\,\text{Avar}(\hat{\boldsymbol{\delta}}_{\text{RE}})\mathbf{D}$ and (5.A.9) equals $\widehat{\text{Avar}(\widehat{\boldsymbol{\beta}}_{\text{FE}})} - \mathbf{D}'\widehat{\text{Avar}(\hat{\boldsymbol{\delta}}_{\text{RE}})}\mathbf{D}$. In any finite sample, (5.A.9) is positive semidefinite. So the Hausman statistic is guaranteed to be nonnegative.

We now show that (5.A.7) is nonsingular. By (5.1.6), $\mathbf{S}$ is positive definite. Therefore, the rank of $\text{Avar}(\hat{\mathbf{q}})$ equals the rank of

$$\mathbf{B}(\mathbf{Q}\otimes\boldsymbol{\Sigma}_{\mathbf{xz}}^{-1})\boldsymbol{\Sigma}_{\mathbf{xz}}\mathbf{D}. \tag{5.A.10}$$

Since the columns of $\mathbf{S}^{-1}\boldsymbol{\Sigma}_{\mathbf{xz}}$ form a basis for the column null space of $\mathbf{B}$ and since $(\mathbf{Q}\otimes\boldsymbol{\Sigma}_{\mathbf{xz}}^{-1})\boldsymbol{\Sigma}_{\mathbf{xz}}\mathbf{D}$ is of full column rank by (5.1.15), by Lemma A.5 of Newey (1985),[8] the rank of (5.A.10) equals

$$\text{rank}[(\boldsymbol{\Sigma}^{-1}\otimes\boldsymbol{\Sigma}_{\mathbf{xx}}^{-1})\boldsymbol{\Sigma}_{\mathbf{xz}} \,\vdots\, (\mathbf{Q}\otimes\boldsymbol{\Sigma}_{\mathbf{xx}}^{-1})\boldsymbol{\Sigma}_{\mathbf{xz}}\mathbf{D}] - L, \tag{5.A.11}$$

where use has been made of the fact that $\mathbf{S} = \boldsymbol{\Sigma}\otimes\boldsymbol{\Sigma}_{\mathbf{xx}}$.

Now, $\mathbf{x}_i$ collects all the unique variables in $\mathbf{Z}_i$. Rearrange $\mathbf{x}_i$ as

$$\mathbf{x}_i = (\mathbf{z}_{i1}', \ldots, \mathbf{z}_{iM}', \mathbf{b}_i')'. \tag{5.A.12}$$

[8]The lemma states: Let $\mathbf{A}$ be a $k\times\ell$ matrix, $\mathbf{B}$ an $\ell\times m$ matrix, and $\mathbf{C}$ an $\ell\times n$ matrix. If the columns of $\mathbf{C}$ form a basis for the column null space of $\mathbf{A}$ and $\text{rank}(\mathbf{B}) = m$, then $\text{rank}(\mathbf{AB}) = \text{rank}(\mathbf{C}\,\vdots\,\mathbf{B}) - n$. Here, $k = \ell = MK$, $m = p$, and $n = L$.

Then

$$\mathbf{z}'_{im} = \mathbf{x}'_i \mathbf{H}_m, \ \mathbf{H}_m \equiv \begin{bmatrix} \mathbf{e}_m \otimes \mathbf{I}_p & \mathbf{0} \\ \mathbf{0} & \mathbf{I}_{L-p} \end{bmatrix}, \ \mathbf{e}_m = m\text{-th column of } \mathbf{I}_M, \quad (5.A.13)$$

so that $\boldsymbol{\Sigma}_{\mathbf{xz}}$ can be written as

$$\boldsymbol{\Sigma}_{\mathbf{xz}} = (\mathbf{I}_M \otimes \boldsymbol{\Sigma}_{\mathbf{xx}})\mathbf{H}, \quad (5.A.14)$$

where $\mathbf{H}' = (\mathbf{H}'_1, \dots, \mathbf{H}'_M)$. Substituting (5.A.14) into (5.A.11), the rank of $\text{Avar}(\hat{\mathbf{q}})$ is

$$\text{rank}[(\boldsymbol{\Sigma}^{-1} \otimes \mathbf{I}_K)\mathbf{H} \vdots (\mathbf{Q} \otimes \mathbf{I}_K)\mathbf{HD}] - L.$$

The m-th K rows of the $(MK \times (L+p))$ matrix $[(\boldsymbol{\Sigma}^{-1} \otimes \mathbf{I}_K)\mathbf{H} \vdots (\mathbf{Q} \otimes \mathbf{I}_K)\mathbf{HD}]$ are

$$\begin{bmatrix} \begin{pmatrix} \sigma^{m1} \\ \vdots \\ \sigma^{mM} \end{pmatrix} \otimes \mathbf{I}_p & \mathbf{0} & \begin{pmatrix} q_{m1} \\ \vdots \\ q_{mM} \end{pmatrix} \otimes \mathbf{I}_p \\ \mathbf{0} & \left(\sum_{h=1}^{M} \sigma^{mh}\right)\mathbf{I}_{L-p} & \mathbf{0} \end{bmatrix}. \quad (5.A.15)$$

Therefore, $\text{rank}[(\boldsymbol{\Sigma}^{-1} \otimes \mathbf{I}_K)\mathbf{H} \vdots (\mathbf{Q} \otimes \mathbf{I}_K)\mathbf{HD}] = L + p$ unless $\text{vec}(\boldsymbol{\Sigma}^{-1})$ and $\text{vec}(\mathbf{Q})$ are linearly dependent; that is, unless $\boldsymbol{\Sigma}^{-1}$ is proportional to $\mathbf{Q}$. But since $\text{rank}(\boldsymbol{\Sigma}^{-1}) = M \neq \text{rank}(\mathbf{Q}) = M - 1$, $\boldsymbol{\Sigma}^{-1}$ cannot be proportional to $\mathbf{Q}$. ■

PROBLEM SET FOR CHAPTER 5

ANALYTICAL EXERCISES

1. (Fixed-effects estimator as the LSDV estimator) In (5.1.1″) on page 329, redefine α_i to be the sum of old α_i and $\mathbf{b}'_i\boldsymbol{\gamma}$, so that (5.1.1″) becomes

$$\mathbf{y}_i = \mathbf{F}_i\boldsymbol{\beta} + \mathbf{1}_M \cdot \alpha_i + \boldsymbol{\eta}_i \quad (i = 1, 2, \dots, n). \quad (1)$$

Define the following stacked vectors and matrices:

$$\underset{(Mn\times 1)}{\mathbf{y}} = \begin{bmatrix} \mathbf{y}_1 \\ \vdots \\ \mathbf{y}_n \end{bmatrix}, \quad \underset{(Mn\times \#\boldsymbol{\beta})}{\mathbf{F}} = \begin{bmatrix} \mathbf{F}_1 \\ \vdots \\ \mathbf{F}_n \end{bmatrix}, \quad \underset{(Mn\times 1)}{\boldsymbol{\eta}} = \begin{bmatrix} \boldsymbol{\eta}_1 \\ \vdots \\ \boldsymbol{\eta}_n \end{bmatrix}, \quad \underset{(n\times 1)}{\boldsymbol{\alpha}} = \begin{bmatrix} \alpha_1 \\ \vdots \\ \alpha_n \end{bmatrix},$$

$$\underset{(Mn\times(n+\#\boldsymbol{\beta}))}{\mathbf{W}} = (\mathbf{D} \vdots \mathbf{F}), \quad \underset{((n+\#\boldsymbol{\beta})\times 1)}{\boldsymbol{\theta}} = \begin{bmatrix} \boldsymbol{\alpha} \\ \boldsymbol{\beta} \end{bmatrix},$$

$$\underset{(Mn\times n)}{\mathbf{D}} = \mathbf{I}_n \otimes \mathbf{1}_M = \begin{bmatrix} \mathbf{1}_M & & & \\ & \mathbf{1}_M & & \\ & & \ddots & \\ & & & \mathbf{1}_M \end{bmatrix}, \tag{2}$$

so that the M-equation system (1) for $i = 1, 2, \ldots, n$ can be written as

$$\begin{bmatrix} \mathbf{y}_1 \\ \mathbf{y}_2 \\ \vdots \\ \mathbf{y}_n \end{bmatrix} = \begin{bmatrix} \mathbf{1}_M \cdot \alpha_1 \\ \mathbf{1}_M \cdot \alpha_2 \\ \vdots \\ \mathbf{1}_M \cdot \alpha_n \end{bmatrix} + \begin{bmatrix} \mathbf{F}_1\boldsymbol{\beta} \\ \mathbf{F}_2\boldsymbol{\beta} \\ \vdots \\ \mathbf{F}_n\boldsymbol{\beta} \end{bmatrix} + \begin{bmatrix} \boldsymbol{\eta}_1 \\ \boldsymbol{\eta}_2 \\ \vdots \\ \boldsymbol{\eta}_n \end{bmatrix}$$

or

$$\begin{bmatrix} \mathbf{y}_1 \\ \mathbf{y}_2 \\ \vdots \\ \mathbf{y}_n \end{bmatrix} = \begin{bmatrix} \mathbf{1}_M & & & \\ & \mathbf{1}_M & & \\ & & \ddots & \\ & & & \mathbf{1}_M \end{bmatrix} \begin{bmatrix} \alpha_1 \\ \alpha_2 \\ \vdots \\ \alpha_n \end{bmatrix} + \begin{bmatrix} \mathbf{F}_1 \\ \mathbf{F}_2 \\ \vdots \\ \mathbf{F}_n \end{bmatrix} \boldsymbol{\beta} + \begin{bmatrix} \boldsymbol{\eta}_1 \\ \boldsymbol{\eta}_2 \\ \vdots \\ \boldsymbol{\eta}_n \end{bmatrix}$$

or

$$\mathbf{y} = \mathbf{D}\boldsymbol{\alpha} + \mathbf{F}\boldsymbol{\beta} + \boldsymbol{\eta} = \mathbf{W}\boldsymbol{\theta} + \boldsymbol{\eta}. \tag{3}$$

The OLS estimator of $\boldsymbol{\theta}$ on a pooled sample of size Mn, $(\mathbf{y}, \mathbf{W})$, is $(\mathbf{W}'\mathbf{W})^{-1} \cdot \mathbf{W}'\mathbf{y}$.

(a) Show that the fixed-effects estimator given in (5.2.4) is the last $\#\boldsymbol{\beta}$ elements of this vector. **Hint:** Use the Frisch-Waugh Theorem about partitioned regressions (see Analytical Exercise 4(c) of Chapter 1). The first step is to regress $\mathbf{y}$ on $\mathbf{D}$ and regress each column of $\mathbf{F}$ on $\mathbf{D}$. If we define the annihilator associated with $\mathbf{D}$ as

$$\underset{(Mn\times Mn)}{\mathbf{M}_{\mathbf{D}}} \equiv \mathbf{I}_{Mn} - \mathbf{D}(\mathbf{D}'\mathbf{D})^{-1}\mathbf{D}', \tag{4}$$

then the residual vectors can be written as $\mathbf{M_D y}$ and $\mathbf{M_D F}$. The second step is to regress $\mathbf{M_D y}$ on $\mathbf{M_D F}$. Show that the estimated regression coefficient can be written as

$$(\mathbf{F}'\mathbf{M_D}\mathbf{F})^{-1}\mathbf{F}'\mathbf{M_D}\mathbf{y}. \tag{5}$$

Show that $\mathbf{M_D} = \mathbf{I}_n \otimes \mathbf{Q}$ (where $\mathbf{Q}$ is the annihilator associated with $\mathbf{1}_M$, as in the text) and use this to show that (1) is indeed the fixed-effects estimator.

Alternatively, you can go all the way back to the normal equations. If $\mathbf{a}$ and $\mathbf{b}$ are the OLS estimators of $\boldsymbol{\alpha}$ and $\boldsymbol{\beta}$, then $(\mathbf{a}, \mathbf{b})$ satisfies the system of $n + \#\boldsymbol{\beta}$ linear simultaneous equations:

$$\begin{bmatrix} \mathbf{D}'\mathbf{D} & \mathbf{D}'\mathbf{F} \\ \mathbf{F}'\mathbf{D} & \mathbf{F}'\mathbf{F} \end{bmatrix} \begin{bmatrix} \mathbf{a} \\ \mathbf{b} \end{bmatrix} = \begin{bmatrix} \mathbf{D}'\mathbf{y} \\ \mathbf{F}'\mathbf{y} \end{bmatrix}. \tag{6}$$

Take the first n equations and solve for $\mathbf{a}$ taking $\mathbf{b}$ as given. This should yield: $\mathbf{a} = (\mathbf{D}'\mathbf{D})^{-1}(\mathbf{D}'\mathbf{y} - \mathbf{D}'\mathbf{F}\mathbf{b})$. Then substitute this into the rest of the equations to solve for $\mathbf{b}$. (You can accomplish the same thing by using the formula for inverting partitioned matrices.)

(b) Show:

$$a_i = \bar{y}_i - \Big(\frac{1}{M}\sum_{m=1}^{M} \mathbf{f}'_{im}\Big)\widehat{\boldsymbol{\beta}}_{\text{FE}},$$

where a_i is the OLS estimator of α_i, $\mathbf{f}'_{im}$ is the m-th row of $\mathbf{F}_i$, and $\bar{y}_i = \frac{1}{M}(y_{i1} + \cdots + y_{iM})$. **Hint:** Use the normal equations for $\boldsymbol{\alpha}$.

(c) Assume:

(i) $\{\mathbf{y}_i, \mathbf{F}_i\}$ is i.i.d.,

(ii) $\mathrm{E}(\boldsymbol{\eta}_i \mid \mathbf{F}_i) = \mathbf{0}$ (which is stronger than the orthogonality conditions (5.1.8b)),

(iii) $\mathrm{E}(\boldsymbol{\eta}_i\boldsymbol{\eta}'_i \mid \mathbf{F}_i) = \sigma_\eta^2 \mathbf{I}_M$ (the spherical error assumption), and

(iv) $\mathbf{W}$ is of full column rank.

Show that the assumptions of the Classical Regression Model are satisfied for the pooled regression (3). **Hint:** You have to show that $\mathbf{W}$ is *exogenous* in (3), that is,

$$\mathrm{E}(\boldsymbol{\eta} \mid \mathbf{W}) = \underset{(Mn\times 1)}{\mathbf{0}}.$$

Also show that $\mathrm{E}(\boldsymbol{\eta}\boldsymbol{\eta}' \mid \mathbf{W}) = \sigma_\eta^2 \mathbf{I}_{Mn}$. Develop the *small sample* theory for $\mathbf{a}$ and $\mathbf{b}$. For example, are they unbiased? Let *SSR* be the sum of squared residuals from the pooled regression (3). Is this *SSR* the same as the *SSR* from the "within" regression (5.2.15)?

2. (GMM interpretation of FE) It is fairly well known for the case of two equations ($M = 2$) that the fixed-effects estimator is the OLS estimator in the regression of first differences: $y_{i2} - y_{i1}$ on $\mathbf{z}_{i2} - \mathbf{z}_{i1}$. This question generalizes this argument to the case of arbitrary M.

   We wish to write the fixed-effects estimator (5.2.4) in the GMM format

$$(\mathbf{S}_{\mathbf{xz}}' \widehat{\mathbf{W}} \mathbf{S}_{\mathbf{xz}})^{-1} \mathbf{S}_{\mathbf{xz}}' \widehat{\mathbf{W}} \mathbf{s}_{\mathbf{xy}} \tag{7}$$

   for properly defined $\mathbf{S}_{\mathbf{xz}}$, $\widehat{\mathbf{W}}$, and $\mathbf{s}_{\mathbf{xy}}$. Let $\mathbf{C}$ be a matrix such that

$$\mathbf{C} \text{ is an } M \times (M-1) \text{ matrix of full column rank satisfying } \mathbf{C}'\mathbf{1}_M = \mathbf{0}. \tag{8}$$

   A prominent example of such a matrix $\mathbf{C}$ is the matrix of first differences:

$$\underset{(M\times(M-1))}{\mathbf{C}} = \begin{bmatrix} -1 & 0 & 0 & 0 & \dots & 0 \\ 1 & -1 & 0 & 0 & \dots & 0 \\ 0 & 1 & -1 & 0 & \dots & 0 \\ & & \ddots & \ddots & & \\ 0 & \dots & 0 & 1 & -1 & 0 \\ 0 & \dots & 0 & 0 & 1 & -1 \\ 0 & \dots & 0 & 0 & 0 & 1 \end{bmatrix}.$$

   Another example is an $M \times (M-1)$ matrix created by dropping one column, say the last, from $\mathbf{Q}$, the annihilator associated with $\mathbf{1}_M$.

   (a) Verify that these two matrices satisfy (8).

   (b) For any given choice of $\mathbf{C}$, verify that you can derive the following system of $M - 1$ transformed equations by multiplying both sides of the system of M equations (5.1.1″) (on page 329) from left by $\mathbf{C}'$:

$$\hat{\mathbf{y}}_i = \widehat{\mathbf{F}}_i \boldsymbol{\beta} + \hat{\boldsymbol{\eta}}_i \tag{9}$$

   where

$$\underset{((M-1)\times 1)}{\hat{\mathbf{y}}_i} \equiv \mathbf{C}'\mathbf{y}_i, \quad \underset{((M-1)\times \#\boldsymbol{\beta})}{\widehat{\mathbf{F}}_i} \equiv \mathbf{C}'\mathbf{F}_i, \quad \underset{((M-1)\times 1)}{\hat{\boldsymbol{\eta}}_i} \equiv \mathbf{C}'\boldsymbol{\eta}_i.$$

(c) (optional) Verify the following:

If $\{\mathbf{y}_i, \mathbf{Z}_i\}$ satisfies the assumptions of the error-components model (which are (5.1.1″), (5.1.2), (5.1.8), (5.1.4), (5.1.5), and (5.1.6) or (5.1.6′) on page 324), then $\{\hat{\mathbf{y}}_i, \widehat{\mathbf{F}}_i\}$ satisfies the assumptions of the random-effects model, i.e., for the $M-1$ equation system (9),

(random sample) $\{\hat{\mathbf{y}}_i, \widehat{\mathbf{F}}_i\}$ is i.i.d.,

(orthogonality conditions) $\mathrm{E}(\hat{\boldsymbol{\eta}}_i \otimes \mathbf{x}_i) = \mathbf{0}$ with $\mathbf{x}_i$ = union of $(\mathbf{z}_{i1}, \dots, \mathbf{z}_{iM})$ = unique elements of $(\mathbf{F}_i, \mathbf{b}_i)$,

(identification) $\mathrm{E}(\widehat{\mathbf{F}}_i \otimes \mathbf{x}_i)$ is of full column rank,

(conditional homoskedasticity) $\mathrm{E}(\hat{\boldsymbol{\eta}}_i \hat{\boldsymbol{\eta}}_i' \mid \mathbf{x}_i) = \mathrm{E}(\hat{\boldsymbol{\eta}}_i \hat{\boldsymbol{\eta}}_i')$ which is nonsingular,

(nonsingularity of $\mathrm{E}(\hat{\mathbf{g}}_i \hat{\mathbf{g}}_i')$) $\mathrm{E}(\hat{\mathbf{g}}_i \hat{\mathbf{g}}_i')$ is nonsingular, $\hat{\mathbf{g}}_i \equiv \hat{\boldsymbol{\eta}}_i \otimes \mathbf{x}_i$.

Hint: For the orthogonality conditions, note that (5.1.8b) can be written as $\mathrm{E}(\boldsymbol{\eta}_i \otimes \mathbf{x}_i) = \mathbf{0}$ and that $\hat{\boldsymbol{\eta}}_i \otimes \mathbf{x}_i = (\mathbf{C}' \otimes \mathbf{I}_K)(\boldsymbol{\eta}_i \otimes \mathbf{x}_i)$. The identification condition is equivalent to (5.1.15) (see the answer sheet for proof). To show that $\mathrm{E}(\hat{\boldsymbol{\eta}}_i \hat{\boldsymbol{\eta}}_i' \mid \mathbf{x}_i)$ does not depend on $\mathbf{x}_i$, use the fact that $\hat{\boldsymbol{\eta}}_i = \mathbf{C}'\boldsymbol{\eta}_i = \mathbf{C}'\boldsymbol{\varepsilon}_i$ since $\boldsymbol{\varepsilon}_i = \mathbf{1}_M \cdot \alpha_i + \boldsymbol{\eta}_i$. Given conditional homoskedasticity, we have

$$\mathrm{E}(\hat{\mathbf{g}}_i \hat{\mathbf{g}}_i') = \mathrm{E}(\hat{\boldsymbol{\eta}}_i \hat{\boldsymbol{\eta}}_i') \otimes \mathrm{E}(\mathbf{x}_i \mathbf{x}_i').$$

So the last condition (nonsingularity of $\mathrm{E}(\hat{\mathbf{g}}_i \hat{\mathbf{g}}_i')$) is simply that $\mathrm{E}(\mathbf{x}_i \mathbf{x}_i')$ be nonsingular.

(d) Show that the fixed-effects estimator (5.2.4) can be written in the GMM format (7) with

$$\mathbf{S}_{\mathbf{xz}} = \frac{1}{n}\sum_{i=1}^{n} \widehat{\mathbf{F}}_i \otimes \mathbf{x}_i, \quad \mathbf{s}_{\mathbf{xy}} = \frac{1}{n}\sum_{i=1}^{n} \hat{\mathbf{y}}_i \otimes \mathbf{x}_i,$$
$$\widehat{\mathbf{W}} = (\mathbf{C}'\mathbf{C})^{-1} \otimes \left(\frac{1}{n}\sum_{i=1}^{n} \mathbf{x}_i \mathbf{x}_i'\right)^{-1}. \tag{10}$$

Hint: Use the following result from matrix algebra: If $\mathbf{C}$ satisfies condition (8), then

$$\mathbf{C}(\mathbf{C}'\mathbf{C})^{-1}\mathbf{C}' = \mathbf{Q} \tag{11}$$

(the annihilator associated with $\mathbf{1}_M$). The elements of $\mathbf{f}_{im}$ are a subset of the elements of $\mathbf{x}_i$. Observe the "disappearance of $\mathbf{x}$." So, for example,

$$\frac{1}{n}\sum_{i=1}^{n}\mathbf{f}_{im}\mathbf{x}_i'\Big(\frac{1}{n}\sum_{i=1}^{n}\mathbf{x}_i\mathbf{x}_i'\Big)^{-1}\frac{1}{n}\sum_{i=1}^{n}\mathbf{x}_i\mathbf{f}_{ih}' = \frac{1}{n}\sum_{i=1}^{n}\mathbf{f}_{im}\mathbf{f}_{ih}'.$$

(e) Let $\widehat{\boldsymbol{\Psi}}$ $((M-1)\times(M-1))$ be a consistent estimate of $\boldsymbol{\Psi} \equiv \mathrm{E}(\hat{\boldsymbol{\eta}}_i\hat{\boldsymbol{\eta}}_i')$. Show that the efficient GMM estimator is given by

$$\widehat{\boldsymbol{\beta}} = \Big(\frac{1}{n}\sum_{i=1}^{n}\widehat{\mathbf{F}}_i'\widehat{\boldsymbol{\Psi}}^{-1}\widehat{\mathbf{F}}_i\Big)^{-1}\frac{1}{n}\sum_{i=1}^{n}\widehat{\mathbf{F}}_i'\widehat{\boldsymbol{\Psi}}^{-1}\hat{\mathbf{y}}_i. \tag{12}$$

Show that

$$\mathrm{Avar}(\widehat{\boldsymbol{\beta}}) = \left[\mathrm{E}\left(\widehat{\mathbf{F}}_i'\boldsymbol{\Psi}^{-1}\widehat{\mathbf{F}}_i\right)\right]^{-1}. \tag{13}$$

Hint: Apply Proposition 4.7 to the present system of $M-1$ equations.

(f) Show that the following is consistent for $\boldsymbol{\Psi}$:

$$\underset{((M-1)\times(M-1))}{\widehat{\boldsymbol{\Psi}}} = \frac{1}{n}\sum_{i=1}^{n}(\hat{\mathbf{y}}_i - \widehat{\mathbf{F}}_i\hat{\boldsymbol{\delta}}_{\mathrm{FE}})(\hat{\mathbf{y}}_i - \widehat{\mathbf{F}}_i\hat{\boldsymbol{\delta}}_{\mathrm{FE}})'. \tag{14}$$

Hint: Verify that all the assumptions of Proposition 4.1 are satisfied.

(g) (Sargan's statistic) Derive Sargan's statistic associated with the efficient GMM estimator. **Hint:** In Proposition 4.7(c), set

$$\widehat{\mathbf{S}} = \widehat{\boldsymbol{\Psi}} \otimes \Big(\frac{1}{n}\sum_{i=1}^{n}\mathbf{x}_i\mathbf{x}_i'\Big),\ \mathbf{g}_n(\widehat{\boldsymbol{\beta}}) = \mathbf{s}_{\mathbf{xy}} - \mathbf{S}_{\mathbf{xz}}\widehat{\boldsymbol{\beta}}.$$

(h) Suppose that $\boldsymbol{\eta}_i$ is spherical in that

$$\mathrm{E}(\boldsymbol{\eta}_i\boldsymbol{\eta}_i') = \sigma_\eta^2\,\mathbf{I}_M. \tag{15}$$

Verify that, if $\hat{\sigma}_\eta^2$ is a consistent estimator of σ_η^2, then

$$\widehat{\boldsymbol{\Psi}} = \hat{\sigma}_\eta^2\mathbf{C}'\mathbf{C} \tag{16}$$

is consistent for $\boldsymbol{\Psi}$. Verify that the efficient GMM estimator (12) with this choice of $\widehat{\boldsymbol{\Psi}}$ is numerically equal to the fixed-effects estimator.

(i) (Invariance to the choice of $\mathbf{C}$) Verify: if an $M \times (M-1)$ matrix $\mathbf{C}$ satisfies (8), so does $\mathbf{B} = \mathbf{CA}$ where $\mathbf{A}$ is an $(M-1) \times (M-1)$ nonsingular matrix. Replace $\mathbf{C}$ everywhere in this section by $\mathbf{B}$ and verify that the choice of $\mathbf{C}$ does not change any of the results of this question.

3. Let SSR be the sum of squared residuals defined in (5.2.15). For the error-component model with the spherical assumption that $\mathrm{E}(\boldsymbol{\eta}_i \boldsymbol{\eta}_i') = \sigma_\eta^2 \mathbf{I}_M$, prove

$$\operatorname*{plim}_{n\to\infty} \frac{SSR}{n} = (M-1)\cdot \sigma_\eta^2.$$

Hint:

$$SSR = \sum_{i=1}^{n} [\mathbf{Q}(\mathbf{y}_i - \mathbf{F}_i \widehat{\boldsymbol{\beta}}_{\mathrm{FE}})]'[\mathbf{Q}(\mathbf{y}_i - \mathbf{F}_i \widehat{\boldsymbol{\beta}}_{\mathrm{FE}})]$$

$$= \sum_{i=1}^{n} (\mathbf{y}_i - \mathbf{F}_i \widehat{\boldsymbol{\beta}}_{\mathrm{FE}})'\mathbf{Q}(\mathbf{y}_i - \mathbf{F}_i \widehat{\boldsymbol{\beta}}_{\mathrm{FE}})$$

(since $\mathbf{Q}$ is symmetric and idempotent)

$$= \sum_{i=1}^{n} (\mathbf{y}_i - \mathbf{F}_i \widehat{\boldsymbol{\beta}}_{\mathrm{FE}})'\mathbf{C}(\mathbf{C}'\mathbf{C})^{-1}\mathbf{C}'(\mathbf{y}_i - \mathbf{F}_i \widehat{\boldsymbol{\beta}}_{\mathrm{FE}}) \quad \text{(by (11))}$$

$$= \sum_{i=1}^{n} \hat{\mathbf{v}}_i'(\mathbf{C}'\mathbf{C})^{-1}\hat{\mathbf{v}}_i \quad (\hat{\mathbf{v}}_i \equiv \mathbf{C}'\mathbf{y}_i - \mathbf{C}'\mathbf{F}_i \widehat{\boldsymbol{\beta}}_{\mathrm{FE}})$$

$$= \sum_{i=1}^{n} \operatorname{trace}[\hat{\mathbf{v}}_i'(\mathbf{C}'\mathbf{C})^{-1}\hat{\mathbf{v}}_i]$$

$$= \sum_{i=1}^{n} \operatorname{trace}[(\mathbf{C}'\mathbf{C})^{-1}\hat{\mathbf{v}}_i\hat{\mathbf{v}}_i']$$

$$= n \cdot \operatorname{trace}\left[(\mathbf{C}'\mathbf{C})^{-1}\frac{1}{n}\sum_{i=1}^{n}\hat{\mathbf{v}}_i\hat{\mathbf{v}}_i'\right] \quad \text{(since the trace operator is linear).}$$

With the usual technical condition (that $\mathrm{E}(\mathbf{f}_{im}\,\mathbf{f}_{ih}')$ exists and is finite for all m, h, which obtains if $\mathrm{E}(\mathbf{x}_i\mathbf{x}_i')$ exists and is finite), it should now be routine to show that

$$\frac{1}{n}\sum_{i=1}^{n}\hat{\mathbf{v}}_i\hat{\mathbf{v}}_i' \underset{\mathrm{p}}{\to} \mathrm{E}(\mathbf{v}_i\mathbf{v}_i') \quad \text{as } n \to \infty,$$

where $\mathbf{v}_i \equiv \mathbf{C}'\mathbf{y}_i - \mathbf{C}'\mathbf{F}_i\boldsymbol{\beta}$. Show that $\mathrm{E}(\mathbf{v}_i\mathbf{v}_i') = \sigma_\eta^2 \cdot \mathbf{C}'\mathbf{C}$.

4. (Inconsistency of the fixed-effects estimator for dynamic models) Consider a "dynamic" model

$$y_{im} = \alpha_i + \rho \cdot y_{i,m-1} + \eta_{im} \quad (m = 1, 2, \dots, M; i = 1, 2, \dots, n).$$

Suppose we have a random sample on $(y_{i0}, y_{i1}, \dots, y_{iM})$. We assume that $\mathrm{E}(\alpha_i\, \eta_{im}) = 0$, and $\mathrm{E}(y_{i0}\, \eta_{im}) = 0$ for all m. Also assume there is no cross-equation correlation: $\mathrm{E}(\eta_{im}\, \eta_{ih}) = 0$ for $m \neq h$, and that the second moment is the same across equations: $\mathrm{E}(\eta_{im}^2) = \sigma_\eta^2$.

(a) Write this system of M equations as (5.1.1″) on page 329 by properly defining $\mathbf{y}_i$, $\mathbf{F}_i$, and $\mathbf{b}_i$.

(b) Show: $\mathrm{E}(y_{im} \cdot \eta_{ih}) = 0$ if $m < h$. **Hint:**

$$y_{im} = \eta_{im} + \rho\eta_{i,m-1} + \cdots + \rho^{m-1}\eta_{i1} + \frac{1-\rho^m}{1-\rho}\,\alpha_i + \rho^m y_{i0}.$$

(c) Verify that $\mathrm{E}(y_{im} \cdot \eta_{ih}) = \rho^{m-h}\sigma_\eta^2$ for $m \geq h$. (optional) Show that

$$\mathrm{E}(\mathbf{F}_i'\mathbf{Q}\boldsymbol{\eta}_i) = -\frac{\sigma_\eta^2}{M}\,\frac{(M-1) - M\rho + \rho^M}{(1-\rho)^2}.$$

(d) Therefore, if $\mathrm{E}(\mathbf{F}_i'\mathbf{Q}\mathbf{F}_i)$ is nonsingular and if $(M-1) - M\rho + \rho^M \neq 0$, then the fixed-effects estimator for this dynamic model is *inconsistent*. Which assumption of Proposition 5.1 guaranteeing the consistency of the fixed-effects estimator is violated?

5. (Optional, identification ensures nonsingularity)

(a) Show that $\mathrm{E}(\widetilde{\mathbf{F}}_i'\widetilde{\mathbf{F}}_i)$ in (5.2.7) is invertible under assumption (5.1.15), that $\mathrm{E}(\mathbf{Q}\mathbf{F}_i \otimes \mathbf{x}_i)$ is of full column rank. **Hint:**

$$\mathrm{E}(\widetilde{\mathbf{F}}_i'\widetilde{\mathbf{F}}_i) = \mathrm{E}(\mathbf{F}_i'\mathbf{Q}\mathbf{F}_i) = \sum_{m=1}^{M}\sum_{h=1}^{M} q_{mh}\,\mathrm{E}(\mathbf{f}_{im}\,\mathbf{f}_{ih}')$$

where $q_{mh} = (m, h)$ element of $\mathbf{Q}$. Show that

$$\mathrm{E}(\mathbf{f}_{im}\,\mathbf{f}_{ih}') = \mathrm{E}(\mathbf{f}_{im}\mathbf{x}_i')\left[\mathrm{E}(\mathbf{x}_i\mathbf{x}_i')\right]^{-1}\mathrm{E}(\mathbf{x}_i\mathbf{f}_{ih}').$$

(Recall that the elements of $\mathbf{f}_{im}$ are included in $\mathbf{x}_i$.) Finally, show that

$\mathbf{x}_i\mathbf{f}'_{im} = \mathbf{f}'_{im} \otimes \mathbf{x}_i$, $(\mathbf{F}_i \otimes \mathbf{x}_i)' = (\mathbf{f}_{i1} \otimes \mathbf{x}'_i, \ldots, \mathbf{f}_{iM} \otimes \mathbf{x}'_i)$, and

$$\begin{aligned}\mathrm{E}(\widetilde{\mathbf{F}}'_i\widetilde{\mathbf{F}}_i) &= \mathrm{E}(\mathbf{F}_i \otimes \mathbf{x}_i)'\big[\mathbf{Q} \otimes \big[\mathrm{E}(\mathbf{x}_i\mathbf{x}'_i)\big]^{-1}\big]\,\mathrm{E}(\mathbf{F}_i \otimes \mathbf{x}_i)\\ &= \mathrm{E}(\mathbf{QF}_i \otimes \mathbf{x}_i)'\big(\mathbf{I}_M \otimes \big[\mathrm{E}(\mathbf{x}_i\mathbf{x}'_i)\big]^{-1}\big)\,\mathrm{E}(\mathbf{QF}_i \otimes \mathbf{x}_i).\end{aligned}$$

(b) Use a similar argument to show that $\mathrm{E}\big[\widetilde{\mathbf{F}}'_i\,\mathrm{E}(\tilde{\boldsymbol{\eta}}_i\tilde{\boldsymbol{\eta}}'_i)\widetilde{\mathbf{F}}_i\big]$ in (5.2.7) is nonsingular. **Hint:** Since

$$\tilde{\boldsymbol{\eta}}_i = \mathbf{Q}\boldsymbol{\eta}_i = \mathbf{Q}\boldsymbol{\varepsilon}_i,$$

we have

$$\widetilde{\mathbf{F}}'_i\,\mathrm{E}(\tilde{\boldsymbol{\eta}}_i\tilde{\boldsymbol{\eta}}'_i)\widetilde{\mathbf{F}}_i = \widetilde{\mathbf{F}}'_i\mathbf{Q}\,\mathrm{E}(\boldsymbol{\varepsilon}_i\boldsymbol{\varepsilon}'_i)\mathbf{Q}\widetilde{\mathbf{F}}_i = \widetilde{\mathbf{F}}'_i\,\mathrm{E}(\boldsymbol{\varepsilon}_i\boldsymbol{\varepsilon}'_i)\widetilde{\mathbf{F}}_i.$$

Also,

$$\mathrm{E}\big[\widetilde{\mathbf{F}}'_i\,\mathrm{E}(\boldsymbol{\varepsilon}_i\boldsymbol{\varepsilon}'_i)\widetilde{\mathbf{F}}_i\big] = \mathrm{E}(\mathbf{QF}_i \otimes \mathbf{x}_i)'\big(\mathrm{E}(\boldsymbol{\varepsilon}_i\boldsymbol{\varepsilon}'_i) \otimes \big[\mathrm{E}(\mathbf{x}_i\mathbf{x}'_i)\big]^{-1}\big)\,\mathrm{E}(\mathbf{QF}_i \otimes \mathbf{x}_i).$$

(c) Show that $\mathrm{E}(\widehat{\mathbf{F}}'_i\boldsymbol{\Psi}^{-1}\widehat{\mathbf{F}}_i)$ in (13) of Analytical Exercise 2 is nonsingular. **Hint:** As shown in Analytical Exercise 2(c), $\mathrm{E}(\mathbf{QF}_i \otimes \mathbf{x}_i)$ is of full column rank if and only if $\mathrm{E}(\mathbf{C}'\mathbf{F}_i \otimes \mathbf{x}_i)$ is of full column rank.

6. (Optional, alternative identification condition) Consider the error-component model (5.1.1″) on page 329. Let $p \equiv \#\boldsymbol{\beta}$. If $\mathbf{A}_m$ is the matrix that picks up $\mathbf{f}_{im}$ from $\mathbf{x}_i$, it can be written as

$$\underset{(K\times p)}{\mathbf{A}_m} = \begin{bmatrix}\mathbf{e}_m \otimes \mathbf{I}_p\\ \mathbf{0}\end{bmatrix},$$

where $\mathbf{e}_m$ is the m-th row of $\mathbf{I}_M$.

(a) Let $\mathbf{A}$ $(KM \times p)$ be the matrix obtained from stacking $(\mathbf{A}_1, \ldots, \mathbf{A}_M)$. Show that $\mathbf{F}_i = (\mathbf{I}_M \otimes \mathbf{x}'_i)\mathbf{A}$.

(b) Show that the rank condition (5.1.15), combined with the condition that $\mathrm{E}(\mathbf{x}_i\mathbf{x}'_i)$ be nonsingular (which is implied by (5.1.5) and (5.1.6)), can be written as

$$\mathrm{rank}[(\mathbf{Q} \otimes \mathbf{I}_K)\mathbf{A}] = p \quad (\equiv \#\boldsymbol{\beta}).$$

(This result will be used in the next exercise.) **Hint:**

$$\begin{aligned}\mathbf{F}_i \otimes \mathbf{x}_i &= \big([(\mathbf{I}_M \otimes \mathbf{x}_i')\mathbf{A}]\big) \otimes \mathbf{x}_i \\ &= [(\mathbf{I}_M \otimes \mathbf{x}_i') \otimes \mathbf{x}_i](\mathbf{A} \otimes 1) \\ &= (\mathbf{I}_M \otimes \mathbf{x}_i' \otimes \mathbf{x}_i)\mathbf{A} \\ &= [\mathbf{I}_M \otimes (\mathbf{x}_i\mathbf{x}_i')]\mathbf{A}.\end{aligned}$$

So

$$\begin{aligned}\widetilde{\mathbf{F}}_i \otimes \mathbf{x}_i &= (\mathbf{Q} \otimes \mathbf{I}_K)(\mathbf{F}_i \otimes \mathbf{x}_i) \\ &= [\mathbf{Q} \otimes (\mathbf{x}_i\mathbf{x}_i')]\mathbf{A} \\ &= (\mathbf{I}_M \otimes \mathbf{x}_i\mathbf{x}_i')(\mathbf{Q} \otimes \mathbf{I}_K)\mathbf{A}.\end{aligned}$$

So $\mathrm{E}(\widetilde{\mathbf{F}}_i \otimes \mathbf{x}_i) = [\mathbf{I}_M \otimes \mathrm{E}(\mathbf{x}_i\mathbf{x}_i')](\mathbf{Q} \otimes \mathbf{I}_K)\mathbf{A}$.

7. (Optional, checking nonsingularity) Prove that $\mathrm{E}(\widetilde{\mathbf{F}}_i'\tilde{\boldsymbol{\eta}}_i\tilde{\boldsymbol{\eta}}_i'\widetilde{\mathbf{F}}_i)$ in (5.2.23) is nonsingular, by taking the following steps.

   (a) Write $\widetilde{\mathbf{F}}_i'\tilde{\boldsymbol{\eta}}_i$ as a linear function of $\mathbf{g}_i \equiv \boldsymbol{\varepsilon}_i \otimes \mathbf{x}_i$. **Hint:** Let $\mathbf{A}$ be as in the previous exercise.

$$\begin{aligned}\widetilde{\mathbf{F}}_i'\tilde{\boldsymbol{\eta}}_i &= \mathbf{A}'(\mathbf{I}_M \otimes \mathbf{x}_i)\mathbf{Q}\boldsymbol{\eta}_i \\ &= \mathbf{A}'(\mathbf{I}_M \otimes \mathbf{x}_i)\mathbf{Q}\boldsymbol{\varepsilon}_i \quad (\text{since } \boldsymbol{\varepsilon}_i = \mathbf{1}_M \cdot \alpha_i + \boldsymbol{\eta}_i) \\ &= \mathbf{A}'(\mathbf{I}_M \otimes \mathbf{x}_i)(\mathbf{Q}\boldsymbol{\varepsilon}_i \otimes 1) \\ &= \mathbf{A}'(\mathbf{Q}\boldsymbol{\varepsilon}_i \otimes \mathbf{x}_i) \\ &= \mathbf{A}'(\mathbf{Q} \otimes \mathbf{I}_K)(\boldsymbol{\varepsilon}_i \otimes \mathbf{x}_i) \\ &= \mathbf{A}'(\mathbf{Q} \otimes \mathbf{I}_K)\mathbf{g}_i.\end{aligned}$$

   (b) Prove the desired result. **Hint:** $\mathrm{E}(\mathbf{g}_i\mathbf{g}_i')$ is positive definite by (5.1.6).

EMPIRICAL EXERCISES

In this exercise, you will estimate the speed of convergence using several different estimation techniques. We use the international panel constructed by Summers and Heston (1991), which has become the standard data set for studying the growth of nations. The Summers-Heston panel (also called the Penn World Table) includes major macro variables measured in a consistent basis for virtually all the countries of the world.

The file `SUM_HES.ASC` is an extract for 1960–1985 from version 5.6 of the Penn World Table downloaded from the NBER's home page (www.nber.org). The file is organized as follows. For each country, information on the country is contained in multiple records (rows). The first record has the country's identification code and two dummies, one for a communist regime (referred to as *COM* below) and the other for the Organization of Petroleum Exporting Countries (referred to as *OPEC* below). The second record has the year, the population (in thousands), real GDP per capita (in 1985 U.S. dollars), and the saving rate (in percent) for 1960. The third record has the same for 1961, and so forth. The twenty-seventh record of the country is for 1985. The first few records of the file look like:

```
  1 0 0
1960    10800    1723   19.9
1961    11016    1599   21.1
                  ⋮
1984    21173    2962   26.4
1985    21848    2988   26.0

  2 0 0
1960     4816     931    3.3
1961     4918     976    2.9
```

The file contains all 125 countries for which the data are available. (The mapping between the country ID and the country name is in `country.asc`. Country 1 is Algeria, 2 is Angola, etc. Note that the mapping in Penn World Table version 5.6 is different from that in Summers and Heston (1991).) GDP per capita is the country's real GDP converted into U.S. dollars using the purchasing power parity of the country's currency against the dollar for 1985 (the variable "RGDPCH" in the Penn World Table). The saving rate is measured as the ratio of real investment to real GDP ("I" in the Penn World Table). See Sections II and III (particularly III.D) of Summers and Heston (1991) for how the variables are constructed.

The first issue we examine empirically is conditional convergence. (At this juncture it would be useful to skim Mankiw, Romer, and Weil (1992).) Let s_i be the saving rate of country i and n_i be the country's population growth rate (which we take to be the growth rate of labor). In the Solow-Swan growth model with a Cobb-Douglas production function, the steady-state level of output per effective labor, denoted q^* in the text, is a linear function of $\log(s_i) - \log(n_i + g + \delta)$, where g is the rate of labor-augmenting technical progress and δ is the depreciation rate of the capital stock. Then, assuming $A(0)$, the initial level of technology, to be the same across countries, equation (5.4.10) can be written as

$$y_{im} = \phi_m + \rho y_{i,m-1} + \gamma_1 \log(s_i) + \gamma_2 \log(n_i + g + \delta) + \eta_{im}. \tag{1}$$

The growth model implies that $\gamma_1 = -\gamma_2$, but we will not impose this restriction. This is the specification estimated in Table IV of Mankiw et al. (1992). As in Mankiw et al., assume $g + \delta$ to be 5 percent for all countries, and take s_i to be the saving rate averaged over the 1960–1985 period. We measure n_i as the average annual population growth rate over the same period (Mankiw et al. uses the average growth rate of the working-age population). Because our sample of 125 countries includes (former) communist countries and OPEC, we add *COM* (= 1 if communist, 0 otherwise) and *OPEC* (= 1 if OPEC, 0 otherwise) to the equation:

$$\begin{aligned} y_{im} = \phi_m + \rho y_{i,m-1} + \gamma_1 \log(s_i) + \gamma_2 \log(n_i + g + \delta) \\ + \gamma_3 COM_i + \gamma_4 OPEC_i + \eta_{im}. \end{aligned} \tag{2}$$

(a) By subtracting $y_{i,m-1}$ from both sides, we can rewrite (2) as

$$\begin{aligned} y_{im} - y_{i,m-1} = \phi_m + (\rho - 1) y_{i,m-1} + \gamma_1 \log(s_i) + \gamma_2 \log(n_i + g + \delta) \\ + \gamma_3 COM_i + \gamma_4 OPEC_i + \eta_{im}. \end{aligned} \tag{2$'$}$$

For this specification, set $M = 1$ (just one equation to estimate) and take $t_0 =$ 1960 and $t_1 = 1985$, so the dependent variable, $y_{i1} - y_{i0}$, is the cumulative growth between 1960 and 1985. Plot $y_{i1} - y_{i0}$ against y_{i0} for the 125 countries included in the sample. Is there any relation between the initial GDP (y_{i0}) and the subsequent growth ($y_{i1} - y_{i0}$)? Assuming outright that the error term is orthogonal to the regressors, estimate equation (2′) by OLS. Calculate the value of λ (speed of convergence) implied by the OLS estimate of ρ. (It should be less than 1 percent per year.) Calculate the asymptotic standard error (i.e., $1/n$ times the square root of the asymptotic variance) of your estimate of λ. **Hint:** By (5.4.3), $\hat{\lambda} = -\log(\hat{\rho})/25$. By the delta method (Lemma 2.5 of Section 2.1),

$$\text{Avar}(\hat{\lambda}) = \frac{\text{Avar}(\hat{\rho})}{(25\rho)^2}$$

(since the derivative of $\log(\rho)$ is $1/\rho$). So a consistent estimate of $\text{Avar}(\hat{\lambda})$ is $\widehat{\text{Avar}(\hat{\rho})}/(25\hat{\rho})^2$. The standard error of $\hat{\lambda}$ is $1/n$ times the square root of this. So: the standard error of $\hat{\lambda}$ = (standard error of $\hat{\rho}$)/$(25\hat{\rho})$. Can you confirm the finding that "if countries did not vary in their investment and population growth rates, there would be a strong tendency for poor countries to grow faster than rich ones" (Mankiw et al., 1992, p. 428).

(b) (Fixed-effects estimation) By setting $M = 25$, $t_0 = 1960$, $t_1 = 1961, \ldots,$ $t_{25} = 1985$, we can form a system of 25 equations, with (5.4.10) as the m-th equation. Estimate the system by the fixed-effect technique, assuming that the error is spherical in the sense of (5.2.12). What is the implied value of λ? (It should be about 6.4 percent per year.) (Optional: Calculate the standard errors without the spherical error assumption. As emphasized in the text, the fixed-effects estimator is *not* consistent. We nevertheless apply blindly the fixed-effect technique just to gain programming experience.)

TSP Tip: TSP's command for the fixed-effects estimator (with the spherical error assumption) is `PANEL`. It, however, does not accept the data organization of `SUM_HES.ASC`. It requires that the group (country) ID and the year be included in the rows containing information on group-years. The data file that `PANEL` can accept is `FIXED.ASC`. Its first few records are:

```
1 0 0  1961   1599   1723
1 0 0  1962   1275   1599
              ⋮
1 0 0  1984   2962   2903
1 0 0  1985   2988   2962
2 0 0  1961    976    931
2 0 0  1962    984    976
              ⋮
```

Here, the first variable is the country ID, followed by *COM*, *OPEC*, year, real per capita GDP for the year, and real per capita GDP for the previous year.

RATS Tip: RATS does not have a command specifically for the fixed-effects estimator, but there is a command called `PANEL` (not to be confused with TSP's `PANEL`) that calculates deviations from group means. The RATS codes for doing this part of the exercise are shown here:

```
*
* (b) fixed-effects estimation.
*
calendar(panelobs=25)
allocate 0 125//25
```

```
open data fixed.asc
data(org=obs) / id com opec year rgdp rgdpl
* generate year dummies (only 24 dummies are
* enough)
dec vector[series] dummies(24)
do i=1,24
 set dummies(i) = (year==i+1960)
end do i
* log transformation
set y = log(rgdp);
set ylag = log(rgdpl);
* simple statistics
table
* calculate deviations from group means
panel y / yw 1 entry 1.0 indiv -1.0
dec vector[series] dumw(24)
panel ylag / ylagw 1 entry 1.0 indiv -1.0
do i=1,24
 panel  dummies(i) / dumw(i) 1 entry 1.0
                     indiv -1.0
end do i
* Within regression, with degrees of freedom
* correction
linreg(dfc=125) yw;# dumw ylagw
```

(c) (optional) As in the previous question, take $M = 25$ and $t_0 = 1960$, $t_1 = 1961$, $t_2 = 1962, \ldots, t_{25} = 1985$. Then (5.4.11) is a system of 24 equations if written as the model of Section 4.6:

$$y_{im} = \mathbf{z}_{im}'\boldsymbol{\delta} + \varepsilon_{im} \quad (i = 1, 2, \ldots, 125;\, m = 1, 2, \ldots, 24), \tag{3}$$

where the y_{im} in (3) equals $y_{i,m+1} - y_{im}$ in (5.4.11),

$$\mathbf{z}_{im} = (0, \ldots, 0, 1, 0, \ldots, 0, y_{im} - y_{i,m-1})',$$

a 25-dimensional vector whose m-th element is 1,

$$\boldsymbol{\delta} = (\mu_1, \ldots, \mu_{24}, \rho)'.$$

If s_{im} is country i's saving rate (investment/GDP ratio) in year m, use a constant and $s_{i,m-1}$ as the instrument in the m-th equation (so, for example, in the first equation where the nonconstant regressor is $y_{i,1961} - y_{i,1960}$, the vector of instruments is $(1, s_{i,1960})'$). Apply the multiple-equation GMM technique to (3) assuming conditional homoskedasticity. (It will be very clumsy to use TSP or RATS; use GAUSS. The estimator is (4.6.6) with $\widehat{\mathbf{W}}$ set to the inverse of (4.5.3).) The implied value of λ should be about 36 percent per year!

ANSWERS TO SELECTED QUESTIONS

ANALYTICAL EXERCISES

1c. $\mathrm{E}(\boldsymbol{\eta}_i \mid \mathbf{W})$

$= \mathrm{E}(\boldsymbol{\eta}_i \mid \mathbf{F})$ (since $\mathbf{D}$ is a matrix of constants)

$= \mathrm{E}(\boldsymbol{\eta}_i \mid \mathbf{F}_1, \dots, \mathbf{F}_n)$

$= \mathrm{E}(\boldsymbol{\eta}_i \mid \mathbf{F}_i)$

(since $\boldsymbol{\eta}_i$ is indep. of $(\mathbf{F}_1, \dots, \mathbf{F}_{i-1}, \mathbf{F}_{i+1}, \dots, \mathbf{F}_n)$ by i.i.d. assumption)

$= \mathbf{0}.$

Therefore, the regressors are exogenous. Also,

$$\begin{aligned}\mathrm{E}(\boldsymbol{\eta}_i\boldsymbol{\eta}_i' \mid \mathbf{W}) &= \mathrm{E}(\boldsymbol{\eta}_i\boldsymbol{\eta}_i' \mid \mathbf{F}) \\ &= \mathrm{E}(\boldsymbol{\eta}_i\boldsymbol{\eta}_i' \mid \mathbf{F}_i) \\ &= \sigma_\eta^2 \mathbf{I}_M \quad \text{(by the spherical error assumption).}\end{aligned}$$

By the i.i.d. assumption, $\mathrm{E}(\boldsymbol{\eta}_i\boldsymbol{\eta}_j' \mid \mathbf{W}) = \mathbf{0}$ for $i \neq j$. So $\mathrm{E}(\boldsymbol{\eta}\boldsymbol{\eta}' \mid \mathbf{W}) = \sigma_\eta^2 \mathbf{I}_{Mn}$.

2c. Proof that "$\mathrm{E}(\mathbf{QF}_i \otimes \mathbf{x}_i)$ is of full column rank" $\Leftrightarrow$ "$\mathrm{E}(\mathbf{C}'\mathbf{F}_i \otimes \mathbf{x}_i)$ is of full column rank":

Let $\mathbf{A} \equiv \mathrm{E}(\mathbf{QF}_i \otimes \mathbf{x}_i)$ and $\mathbf{B} \equiv \mathrm{E}(\mathbf{C}'\mathbf{F}_i \otimes \mathbf{x}_i)$. There exists an $M \times (M-1)$ matrix $\mathbf{L}$ of full column rank such that $\mathbf{Q} = \mathbf{LC}'$ (it is actually $\mathbf{C}(\mathbf{C}'\mathbf{C})^{-1}$ by (11)). Let $\mathbf{D} \equiv \mathbf{L} \otimes \mathbf{I}_K$. Then $\mathbf{A} = \mathbf{DB}$. Since the rank of a product of two matrices is less than or equal to the rank of either of the two matrices,

$$\operatorname{rank}(\mathbf{A}) \leq \operatorname{rank}(\mathbf{B}). \tag{1}$$

Next consider a product $\mathbf{D}'\mathbf{A} = \mathbf{D}'\mathbf{D}\mathbf{B}$.

$$\text{rank}(\mathbf{D}'\mathbf{D}\mathbf{B}) \leq \text{rank}(\mathbf{D}'\mathbf{A}) \leq \text{rank}(\mathbf{A}). \tag{2}$$

But since $\mathbf{L}$ is of full column rank, $\mathbf{D}'\mathbf{D}$ is nonsingular. Since multiplication by a nonsingular matrix does not alter rank,

$$\text{rank}(\mathbf{D}'\mathbf{D}\mathbf{B}) = \text{rank}(\mathbf{B}). \tag{3}$$

From (1)–(3) it follows that $\text{rank}(\mathbf{A}) = \text{rank}(\mathbf{B})$. Since $\mathbf{A}$ and $\mathbf{B}$ have the same number of columns, the desired conclusion follows.

4a.

$$\mathbf{y}_i = \begin{bmatrix} y_{i1} \\ \vdots \\ y_{iM} \end{bmatrix}, \quad \mathbf{F}_i = \begin{bmatrix} y_{i0} \\ \vdots \\ y_{i,M-1} \end{bmatrix}.$$

There is no $\mathbf{b}_i$.

4d. Since $\text{E}(\eta_{ih} \cdot y_{im}) \neq 0$ for $m \geq h$, some of the "cross" orthogonalities are not satisfied.

References

Barro, R., and X. Sala-i-Martin, 1995, *Economic Growth*, New York: McGraw-Hill.

Mankiw, G., D. Romer, and D. Weil, 1992, "A Contribution to the Empirics of Economic Growth," *Quarterly Journal of Economics*, 107, 407–437.

Newey, W., 1985, "Generalized Method of Moments Specification Testing," *Journal of Econometrics*, 29, 229–256.

Nickell, S., 1981, "Biases in Dynamic Models with Fixed Effects," *Econometrica*, 49, 1417–1426.

Summers, R., and A. Heston, 1991, "The Penn World Table (Mark 5): An Expanded Set of International Comparisons, 1950–1988," *Quarterly Journal of Economics*, 106, 327–368.

CHAPTER 6

Serial Correlation

ABSTRACT

This chapter extends the GMM model of Chapter 3 to incorporate serial correlation in the product of the vector of instruments and the error term. To do so, we need to generalize the Central Limit Theorems of Chapter 2 to serially correlated processes. The generalization is possible under certain conditions restricting the degree of serial correlation. The condition is transparent for the stochastic processes called linear processes. Linear processes are important in their own right, and this chapter devotes four sections to covering them. In the application section, the extended GMM model is used to test the efficient market hypothesis, this time for the foreign exchange market.

A Note on Notation: Because the issues treated here are specific to time-series data, we use the subscript "t" instead of "i" in this chapter.

6.1 Modeling Serial Correlation: Linear Processes

Section 2.2 introduced covariance-stationary processes and their autocovariances. In particular, a (scalar or univariate) **white noise process** $\{\varepsilon_t\}$ is a zero-mean covariance-stationary process with no serial correlation:

$$\mathrm{E}(\varepsilon_t) = 0, \ \ \mathrm{E}(\varepsilon_t^2) = \sigma^2 > 0, \ \ \mathrm{E}(\varepsilon_t \varepsilon_{t-j}) = 0 \quad \text{for } j \neq 0.$$

A very important class of covariance-stationary processes, called **linear processes**, can be created by taking a moving average of a white noise process. This section studies general properties of linear processes using an apparatus called the **filter**.

Because the current value of a linear process can depend on possibly infinite past values of a white noise process, it is convenient to have the white noise process and the linear process it generates defined for $t = 0, -1, -2, \ldots$ as well as for $t = 1, 2, \ldots$. Intuitively, a covariance-stationary process defined for all integers ($t = 0, \pm 1, \pm 2, \ldots$) is a process that started so long ago that its mean and autocovariances have stabilized to time-invariant constants.

MA(q)

The simplest example of linear processes that exhibit serial correlation is a finite-order moving average process. A process $\{y_t\}$ is called the **q-th order moving average process** (MA(q)) if it can be written as a weighted average of the current and most recent q values of a white noise process:

$$y_t = \mu + \theta_0 \varepsilon_t + \theta_1 \varepsilon_{t-1} + \cdots + \theta_q \varepsilon_{t-q} \quad \text{with } \theta_0 = 1. \tag{6.1.1}$$

Evidently, a moving average process is covariance-stationary with mean μ. It is easy to verify that the j-th order autocovariance, γ_j ($\equiv \mathrm{E}[(y_t - \mu)(y_{t-j} - \mu)]$), is

$$\gamma_j = (\theta_j \theta_0 + \theta_{j+1}\theta_1 + \cdots + \theta_q \theta_{q-j})\sigma^2 = \sigma^2 \sum_{k=0}^{q-j} \theta_{j+k}\theta_k \quad \text{for } j = 0, 1, \ldots, q, \tag{6.1.2a}$$

$$\gamma_j = 0 \quad \text{for } j > q, \tag{6.1.2b}$$

where $\sigma^2 \equiv \mathrm{E}(\varepsilon_t^2)$. (This formula also covers γ_{-j} because $\gamma_j = \gamma_{-j}$.) For example, for $q = 1$, we have

$$\begin{aligned}
\gamma_0 &= (\theta_0^2 + \theta_1^2)\sigma^2 = (1 + \theta_1^2)\sigma^2 \\
&\qquad \text{(by setting } j = 0 \text{ and } q = 1 \text{ in (6.1.2a) and noting } \theta_0 = 1), \\
\gamma_1 &= \gamma_{-1} = (\theta_1 \theta_0)\sigma^2 = \theta_1 \sigma^2 \\
&\qquad \text{(by setting } j = 1 \text{ and } q = 1 \text{ in (6.1.2a) and noting } \theta_0 = 1), \\
\gamma_j &= 0 \quad \text{for } j = \pm 2, \pm 3, \ldots.
\end{aligned}$$

The whole profile of autocovariances, $\{\gamma_j\}$, is described by just $q + 1$ parameters ($\theta_1, \theta_2, \ldots, \theta_q$, and σ^2), and the correlogram $\{\rho_j\}$ (where $\rho_j \equiv \gamma_j / \gamma_0$) by q parameters ($\theta_1, \theta_2, \ldots, \theta_q$).

MA(∞) as a Mean Square Limit

As illustrated in the above example, serial correlation in MA(q) processes dies out completely after q lags. Although some time series have this property (we will see an example in the application below), it is certainly desirable to be able to model serial correlation that does not have this property. An obvious idea is to have y_t

depend on the infinite past by replacing the sum of finitely many terms in (6.1.1),

$$\theta_0 \varepsilon_t + \theta_1 \varepsilon_{t-1} + \cdots + \theta_q \varepsilon_{t-q},$$

by an infinite sum

$$\psi_0 \varepsilon_t + \psi_1 \varepsilon_{t-1} + \cdots = \sum_{j=0}^{\infty} \psi_j \varepsilon_{t-j} \tag{6.1.3}$$

where $\{\psi_j\}$ is a sequence of real numbers.

For this idea to work, we must make sure that this sum of infinitely many random variables is well defined, namely, that the partial sum

$$\sum_{j=0}^{n} \psi_j \varepsilon_{t-j} \tag{6.1.4}$$

converges (in some appropriate sense) to a random variable as $n \to \infty$. One popular condition under which this happens is that the sequence of real numbers $\{\psi_j\}$ be **absolutely summable**:

$$\sum_{j=0}^{\infty} |\psi_j| < \infty. \tag{6.1.5}$$

(This is a standard short-hand expression in calculus. Equation (6.1.5) reads: the partial sum $\sum_{j=0}^{n} |\psi_j|$ converges to a real number [i.e., a finite limit] as $n \to \infty$ and the infinite sum in (6.1.5) is *defined* to be this real number.) For the sequence $\{\psi_j\}$ to be absolutely summable, it is necessary (but certainly not sufficient) that $\psi_j \to 0$ as $j \to \infty$. Thus, absolute summability requires that the effect of the past shocks represented by ψ_j eventually die away.

As claimed in the next proposition, the partial sum (6.1.4) converges in mean square to some random variable for any given t. The mean square limit is unique in the following sense. If there exists another random variable to which the partial sum converges in mean square, then (as you will show in Analytical Exercise 1) the two mean square limits are equal with probability one. We *define* the infinite sum (6.1.3) to be the unique mean square limit of the partial sum (6.1.4) and say "the infinite sum converges in mean square."

Proposition 6.1 (MA(∞) with absolutely summable coefficients): *Let $\{\varepsilon_t\}$ be white noise and $\{\psi_j\}$ be a sequence of real numbers that is absolutely summable. Then*

(a) For each t,

$$y_t = \mu + \sum_{j=0}^{\infty} \psi_j \varepsilon_{t-j} \tag{6.1.6}$$

converges in mean square. $\{y_t\}$ is covariance-stationary. (The process $\{y_t\}$ is called the **infinite-order moving-average process** (MA(∞)).*)*

(b) The mean of y_t is μ. The autocovariances $\{\gamma_j\}$ are given by

$$\begin{aligned}\gamma_j &= (\psi_j\psi_0 + \psi_{j+1}\psi_1 + \psi_{j+2}\psi_2 + \cdots)\sigma^2 \\ &= \sigma^2 \sum_{k=0}^{\infty} \psi_{j+k}\psi_k \quad (j = 0, 1, 2, \dots).\end{aligned} \tag{6.1.7}$$

(c) The autocovariances are absolutely summable:

$$\sum_{j=0}^{\infty} |\gamma_j| < \infty. \tag{6.1.8}$$

(d) If, in addition, $\{\varepsilon_t\}$ is i.i.d, then the process $\{y_t\}$ is (strictly) stationary and ergodic.

This result includes MA(q) processes as a special case with $\psi_j = \theta_j$ for $j = 0, 1, \dots, q$ and $\psi_j = 0$ for $j > q$. Evidently, this sequence $\{\psi_j\}$ is absolutely summable. Proving parts (a)–(c) is Analytical Exercise 2. Proving (a) would use the fact from calculus that Cauchy sequences converge (see Review Question 1 about Cauchy sequences). Part (b) is an obvious extrapolation to infinity of the corresponding results on the mean and autocovariances of finite-order MA processes, but the extrapolation involves interchanging the order of expectations and summations. For example, to prove that the mean of the MA(∞) process is μ, you would have to show that the expected value of the mean square limit of (6.1.3) is the limit of the expected value of (6.1.4). The fact that this operation is legitimate under mean square convergence would be used in the proof of part (b). Part (c) says, intuitively, that if the effect of past shocks represented by ψ_j dies out fast enough to make $\{\psi_j\}$ absolutely summable, then serial correlation dies out just as fast. Absolute summability of autocovariances will play a key role in the theory of covariance-stationary processes to be developed in this chapter. For a proof of (d), see, e.g., Hannan (1970, p. 204, Theorem 3).[1]

[1] Absolute summability of $\{\psi_j\}$ is more than enough for part (a) to hold. As shown in Analytical Exercise 2, square summability, which is weaker than absolute summability, is enough to ensure that the infinite sum is well defined as a mean square limit. However, for the other parts of this proposition to hold, absolute summability is needed.

The MA(∞) process in (6.1.6) is said to be **one-sided** because the moving average does not include future values of ε_t. It is a special case of a **linear process**, which is defined to be two-sided moving averages of the form:

$$y_t = \mu + \sum_{j=-\infty}^{\infty} \psi_j \varepsilon_{t-j} \text{ with } \sum_{j=-\infty}^{\infty} |\psi_j| < \infty.$$

The proposition (and all the results in this section) can easily be extended to general linear processes. We nevertheless focus on one-sided moving averages, only because two-sided moving averages are very rarely encountered in economics.

Proposition 6.1 can be generalized to the case where the process $\{y_t\}$ is a moving average of a general covariance-stationary process rather than of a white noise process. In particular, absolute summability of autocovariances survives the operation of taking an absolutely summable weighted average.

Proposition 6.2 (Filtering covariance-stationary processes): *Let $\{x_t\}$ be a covariance-stationary process and $\{h_j\}$ be a sequence of real numbers that is absolutely summable. Then*

(a) For each t, the infinite sum

$$y_t = \sum_{j=0}^{\infty} h_j x_{t-j} \tag{6.1.9}$$

converges in mean square. The process $\{y_t\}$ is covariance-stationary.

(b) If, furthermore, the autocovariances of $\{x_t\}$ are absolutely summable, then so are the autocovariances of $\{y_t\}$.

We defer to, e.g., Fuller (1996, Theorem 4.3.1) for a proof, but the basic technique is the same as in the proof of Proposition 6.1. Deriving the autocovariances of $\{y_t\}$, which would generalize (6.1.7), is Analytical Exercise 3.

Filters

The operation of taking a weighted average of (possibly infinitely many) successive values of a process, as in (6.1.6) and (6.1.9), is called **filtering**. It can be expressed compactly if we use the device called the **lag operator** L, defined by the relation $L^j x_t = x_{t-j}$. We now introduce some concepts associated with the lag operator that will be useful in time-series analysis.[2]

[2]For a fuller treatment of filters, see, e.g., Gourieroux and Monfort (1997, Sections 5.2 and 7.4).

Filters Defined

For a given arbitrary sequence of real numbers, $(\alpha_0, \alpha_1, \alpha_2, \dots)$, define a **filter** by

$$\alpha(L) \equiv \alpha_0 + \alpha_1 L + \alpha_2 L^2 + \cdots . \tag{6.1.10}$$

If we just mechanically and mindlessly apply the definition of the lag operator to an input process $\{x_t\}$, we get

$$\begin{aligned}\alpha(L)x_t &= \alpha_0 x_t + \alpha_1 L x_t + \alpha_2 L^2 x_t + \cdots \\ &= \alpha_0 x_t + \alpha_1 x_{t-1} + \alpha_2 x_{t-2} + \cdots \\ &= \sum_{j=0}^{\infty} \alpha_j x_{t-j}.\end{aligned} \tag{6.1.11}$$

This is indeed the definition of $\alpha(L)x_t$. If $x_t = c$ (a constant), $\alpha(L)c = \alpha(1)c = c\sum_{j=0}^{\infty} \alpha_j$. If $\alpha_j \neq 0$ for $j = p$ and $\alpha_j = 0$ for $j > p$, the filter reduces to a ***p*-th degree lag polynomial**:

$$\alpha(L) = \alpha_0 + \alpha_1 L + \cdots + \alpha_p L^p.$$

When applied to an input process, it creates a weighted average of the current and p most recent values of the process. Proposition 6.2 assures us that the object $\alpha(L)x_t$ defined by (6.1.11) is a well-defined random variable forming a covariance-stationary process if the sequence $\{\alpha_j\}$ is absolutely summable and if the input process $\{x_t\}$ is covariance-stationary. A filter with absolutely summable coefficients will be referred to (in this book) as an **absolutely summable filter**. To use some fancy set theory language, an absolutely summable filter is a mapping from the set of covariance-stationary processes to itself.

Products of Filters

Let $\{\alpha_j\}$ and $\{\beta_j\}$ be two arbitrary sequences of real numbers and define the sequence $\{\delta_j\}$ by the relation

$$\begin{gathered}\alpha_0\beta_0 = \delta_0, \\ \alpha_0\beta_1 + \alpha_1\beta_0 = \delta_1, \\ \alpha_0\beta_2 + \alpha_1\beta_1 + \alpha_2\beta_0 = \delta_2, \\ \dots, \\ \alpha_0\beta_j + \alpha_1\beta_{j-1} + \alpha_2\beta_{j-2} + \cdots + \alpha_{j-1}\beta_1 + \alpha_j\beta_0 = \delta_j, \\ \dots .\end{gathered} \tag{6.1.12}$$

The sequence $\{\delta_j\}$ created from this convoluted formula is called the **convolution** of $\{\alpha_j\}$ and $\{\beta_j\}$. Let $\alpha(L) \equiv \alpha_0+\alpha_1 L+\alpha_2 L^2+\cdots$, $\beta(L) \equiv \beta_0+\beta_1 L+\beta_2 L^2+\cdots$, and $\delta(L) = \delta_0+\delta_1 L+\delta_2 L^2+\cdots$ be the associated filters. We define the **product** of two filters $\alpha(L)$ and $\beta(L)$ to be this filter $\delta(L)$ and write it as

$$\delta(L) = \alpha(L)\,\beta(L).$$

For example, for $\alpha(L) = 1+\alpha_1 L$ and $\beta(L) = 1+\beta_1 L$, the convolution formula yields

$$(1+\alpha_1 L)(1+\beta_1 L) = 1+(\alpha_1+\beta_1)L+\alpha_1\beta_1 L^2.$$

(If you are familiar with the product of two polynomials of the usual sort from calculus, you can immediately see that this definition for filters is strictly analogous.) As is clear from the definition, filters are **commutative**:

$$\alpha(L)\,\beta(L) = \beta(L)\,\alpha(L).$$

Commutativity, however, will not carry over to matrix filters (see Section 6.3 below).

If the two sequences $\{\alpha_j\}$ and $\{\beta_j\}$ are absolutely summable and if $\{x_t\}$ is covariance-stationary, then Proposition 6.2 assures us that $\{\beta(L)x_t\}$ is covariance-stationary and so $\alpha(L)\beta(L)x_t$ is a well-defined random variable, equal to $\delta(L)x_t$. Thus, if $\alpha(L)$ and $\beta(L)$ are absolutely summable and $\{x_t\}$ is covariance-stationary, then

$$\text{“}\alpha(L)\,\beta(L) = \delta(L)\text{”} \Rightarrow \text{“}\alpha(L)\,\beta(L)x_t = \delta(L)x_t.\text{”} \tag{6.1.13}$$

(Incidentally, $\{\delta_j\}$ is absolutely summable [see, e.g., Fuller, 1996, p. 30].)

Inverses

Of particular interest is the case when $\delta(L) = 1$ (a very special filter) so that the two filters $\alpha(L)$ and $\beta(L)$ satisfy $\alpha(L)\,\beta(L) = 1$. We say that $\beta(L)$ is the **inverse** of $\alpha(L)$ and denote it as $\alpha(L)^{-1}$ or $1/\alpha(L)$. That is,

$$\alpha(L)^{-1} \text{ is a filter satisfying } \alpha(L)\,\alpha(L)^{-1} = 1. \tag{6.1.14}$$

As long as $\alpha_0 \neq 0$ in $\alpha(L) = \alpha_0+\alpha_1 L+\cdots$, the inverse of $\alpha(L)$ can be defined for any arbitrary sequence $\{\alpha_j\}$ because the set of equations (6.1.12) with $\delta_0 = 1$,

$\delta_j = 0\ (j = 1, 2, \dots)$ can be solved successively for $\{\beta_j\}$:

$$\beta_0 = \frac{1}{\alpha_0}, \quad \beta_1 = -\frac{\alpha_1 \beta_0}{\alpha_0} = -\frac{\alpha_1}{\alpha_0^2}, \quad \text{etc.}$$

For example, consider the filter $1 - L$. Its inverse is given by

$$(1 - L)^{-1} = 1 + L + L^2 + L^3 + \cdots .$$

The coefficient sequence is obviously not absolutely summable. This example illustrates the point that an inverse filter may not be absolutely summable.

It is left as Review Question 3 to show that

$$\alpha(L)\,\alpha(L)^{-1} = \alpha(L)^{-1}\alpha(L) \quad \text{(so inverses are commutative)}, \tag{6.1.15a}$$

$$\text{“}\alpha(L)\,\beta(L) = \delta(L)\text{”} \Leftrightarrow \text{“}\beta(L) = \alpha(L)^{-1}\delta(L)\text{”} \Leftrightarrow \text{“}\alpha(L) = \delta(L)\,\beta(L)^{-1}\text{,”} \tag{6.1.15b}$$

provided $\alpha_0 \neq 0$ and $\beta_0 \neq 0$. Therefore, for example, to solve $\alpha(L)\,\beta(L) = \delta(L)$ for $\beta(L)$, you “multiply from the left” by the inverse of $\alpha(L)$. We have noted above that commutativity does not necessarily hold for matrix filters. As will be shown in Section 6.3, for inverses, commutativity does generalize to matrix filters.

Inverting Lag Polynomials

In the next section on ARMA processes, it will become necessary to calculate the inverse of a p-th degree lag polynomial $\phi(L)$

$$\phi(L) = 1 - \phi_1 L - \phi_2 L^2 - \cdots - \phi_p L^p.$$

Since $\phi_0 = 1 \neq 0$, the inverse can be defined. Let $\psi(L) \equiv \phi(L)^{-1}$. By definition, it satisfies

$$\phi(L)\,\psi(L) = 1.$$

The convolution formula (6.1.12) provides an algorithm for solving this for $\psi(L)$. Setting $\alpha(L) = \phi(L)$, $\beta(L) = \psi(L)$, and $\delta(L) = 1$ in the formula yields

$$
\begin{array}{rlr}
\text{constant:} & \psi_0 & = 1, \\
L: & \psi_1 \quad - \phi_1\psi_0 & = 0, \\
L^2: & \psi_2 \quad - \phi_1\psi_1 \quad - \phi_2\psi_0 & = 0, \\
\cdots & \qquad\qquad \cdots & \\
L^{p-1}: & \psi_{p-1} - \phi_1\psi_{p-2} - \phi_2\psi_{p-3} - \cdots - \phi_{p-1}\psi_0 & = 0, \\
L^p: & \psi_p \quad - \phi_1\psi_{p-1} - \phi_2\psi_{p-2} - \cdots - \phi_{p-1}\psi_1 - \phi_p\psi_0 & = 0, \\
L^{p+1}: & \psi_{p+1} - \phi_1\psi_p \quad - \phi_2\psi_{p-1} - \cdots - \phi_{p-1}\psi_2 - \phi_p\psi_1 & = 0, \\
L^{p+2}: & \psi_{p+2} - \phi_1\psi_{p+1} - \phi_2\psi_p \quad - \cdots - \phi_{p-1}\psi_3 - \phi_p\psi_2 & = 0, \\
 & \qquad\qquad \cdots & .
\end{array} \quad (6.1.16)
$$

These equations can easily be solved successively for $(\psi_0, \psi_1, \psi_2, \dots)$ as

$$\psi_0 = 1, \quad \psi_1 = \phi_1, \quad \psi_2 = \phi_2 + \phi_1^2, \quad \text{etc.}$$

Also, notice that for sufficiently large j (actually for $j \geq p$), $\{\psi_j\}$ follows the p-th order homogeneous difference equation

$$\psi_j - \phi_1\psi_{j-1} - \phi_2\psi_{j-2} - \cdots - \phi_{p-1}\psi_{j-p+1} - \phi_p\psi_{j-p} = 0. \quad (6.1.17)$$

So, once the first p coefficients $(\psi_0, \psi_1, \dots, \psi_{p-1})$ are calculated, we can use this homogeneous p-th order difference equation to generate the rest of the coefficients $(\psi_j, j \geq p)$ with those first p coefficients as the initial condition.

As we know from the theory of homogeneous difference equations (summarized in Analytical Exercise 4), the solution sequence $\{\psi_j\}$ to (6.1.17) eventually starts declining at a geometric rate if what is known as the **stability condition** holds. The condition states:

All the roots of the p-th degree polynomial equation in z

$$\phi(z) = 0 \text{ where } \phi(z) \equiv 1 - \phi_1 z - \phi_2 z^2 - \cdots - \phi_p z^p \quad (6.1.18)$$

are greater than 1 in absolute value.

The roots of the polynomial equation $\phi(z) = 0$ can be complex numbers. If your command of complex numbers is rusty, a complex number z can be written as

$$z = a + bi,$$

where a and b are two real numbers and $i = \sqrt{-1}$. So a complex number can be represented as a point in a two-dimensional diagram with the horizontal axis measuring a (the real part) and the vertical axis measuring b (the imaginary part).

Its absolute value is $|z| = \sqrt{a^2 + b^2}$, which is the distance between the origin and the point representing z. We say that z lies outside the unit circle when $|z| > 1$. So the stability condition above can be restated as requiring that the roots lie outside the unit circle. Because $z = \lambda$ solves $\phi(z) = 0$ whenever $z = 1/\lambda$ solves $z^p - \phi_1 z^{p-1} - \phi_2 z^{p-2} - \cdots - \phi_{p-1} z - \phi_p = 0$, the stability condition can be equivalently stated as

All the roots of the p-th order polynomial equation

$$z^p - \phi_1 z^{p-1} - \phi_2 z^{p-2} - \cdots - \phi_{p-1} z - \phi_p = 0 \tag{6.1.18$'$}$$

are *less* than 1 in absolute value (i.e., lie *inside* the unit circle).

Under this condition, as you will be asked to prove (Analytical Exercise 4), there exist two real numbers, $A > 0$ and $0 < b < 1$, such that

$$|\psi_j| < Ab^j \quad \text{for all } j. \tag{6.1.19}$$

Given (6.1.19), the absolute summability of $\{\psi_j\}$ follows because

$$\sum_{j=0}^{\infty} |\psi_j| < \sum_{j=0}^{\infty} Ab^j = \frac{A}{1-b} < \infty.$$

Thus, we have proved

Proposition 6.3 (Absolutely summable inverses of lag polynomials): *Consider a p-th degree lag polynomial $\phi(L) = 1 - \phi_1 L - \phi_2 L^2 - \cdots - \phi_p L^p$, and let $\psi(L) \equiv \phi(L)^{-1}$. If the associated p-th degree polynomial equation $\phi(z) = 0$ satisfies the stability condition (6.1.18) or (6.1.18$'$), then the coefficient sequence $\{\psi_j\}$ of $\psi(L)$ is bounded in absolute value by a geometrically declining sequence (as in (6.1.19)) and hence is absolutely summable.*

To illustrate, consider a lag polynomial of degree one, $1 - \phi L$. The root of the associated polynomial equation $1 - \phi z = 0$ is $1/\phi$. The stability condition is that $|1/\phi| > 1$ or $|\phi| < 1$. The filter

$$1 + \phi L + \phi^2 L^2 + \cdots \tag{6.1.20}$$

is evidently its inverse. The coefficient sequence $\{\phi^j\}$ is indeed bounded in absolute value by a geometrically declining sequence (for example, set $A = 1.1$ and $b = \phi$).

QUESTIONS FOR REVIEW

1. (Cauchy sequences) A sequence of real numbers, $\{\alpha_n\}$, is said to be a **Cauchy sequence** if $|\alpha_m - \alpha_n| \to 0$ as $m, n \to \infty$. An important result from calculus is that α_n converges to a real number if and only if the sequence is Cauchy. Taking this as given, show that $\{\gamma_j\}$ is absolutely summable if and only if $\sum_{j=n+1}^{m} |\gamma_j| \to 0$ as $m, n \to \infty$. (You can assume, without loss of generality, that $m > n$.)

2. (How filtering alters autocovariances) Let $h(L) = h_0 + h_1 L$ and $y_t = h(L)x_t$ where $\{x_t\}$ is covariance-stationary. Verify that (with $\{\gamma_j^x\}$ being the autocovariance of $\{x_t\}$) the autocovariances of $\{y_t\}$ are given by

$$\gamma_j^y = \sum_{k=0}^{1} \sum_{\ell=0}^{1} h_k \, h_\ell \, \gamma_{j-k+\ell}^x .$$

3. Prove (6.1.15b). **Hint:** Here is a proof that "$\alpha(L)\,\beta(L) = \delta(L)$" $\Rightarrow$ "$\beta(L) = \alpha(L)^{-1}\delta(L)$":

$$\alpha(L)^{-1}\delta(L) = \alpha(L)^{-1}\alpha(L)\,\beta(L) = \alpha(L)\,\alpha(L)^{-1}\beta(L) = \beta(L).$$

4. Does $\phi(z) = 1 - \frac{3}{4}z + \frac{9}{16}z^2$ satisfy the stability condition? **Hint:** The roots of $\phi(z) = 0$ are $2(1 \pm \sqrt{3}\,i)/3$.

5. (Coefficients of polynomial equations) Consider a polynomial equation $\phi(z) = 0$ where $\phi(z) = 1 - \phi_1 z - \phi_2 z^2$ and let (λ_1, λ_2) be the two roots. Verify that $\phi_1 = 1/\lambda_1 + 1/\lambda_2$, $\phi_2 = -1/(\lambda_1 \cdot \lambda_2)$. **Hint:** If λ_1 and λ_2 are the two roots of $\phi(z) = 0$, $\phi(z)$ can be written as $\phi(z) = (1 - \frac{1}{\lambda_1}z)(1 - \frac{1}{\lambda_2}z)$.

6. (Inverting $1 - \phi L$) Verify that (6.1.20) is the inverse of $1 - \phi L$ by checking the convolution formula (6.1.12) with $\delta_0 = 1$, $\delta_j = 0$ for $j \geq 1$.

6.2 ARMA Processes

Having introduced the concept of filters, we can study with ease and grace a class of linear processes called ARMA processes, which are a parameterization of the coefficients of MA(∞) processes.

AR(1) and Its MA(∞) Representation

A **first-order autoregressive process** (**AR(1)**) satisfies the following stochastic difference equation:

$$y_t = c + \phi y_{t-1} + \varepsilon_t \quad \text{or} \quad y_t - \phi y_{t-1} = c + \varepsilon_t \quad \text{or} \quad (1 - \phi L)y_t = c + \varepsilon_t, \tag{6.2.1}$$

where $\{\varepsilon_t\}$ is white noise. If $\phi \neq 1$, let $\mu \equiv c/(1-\phi)$ and rewrite this equation as

$$(y_t - \mu) - \phi \cdot (y_{t-1} - \mu) = \varepsilon_t \quad \text{or} \quad (1 - \phi L)(y_t - \mu) = \varepsilon_t. \tag{6.2.1$'$}$$

As will be seen in a moment, μ, not c, is the mean of y_t if y_t is covariance-stationary. For this reason, we will call (6.2.1$'$) a deviation-from-the-mean form. The moving average is on the successive values of $\{y_t\}$, not on $\{\varepsilon_t\}$. The difference equation is called stochastic because of the presence of the random variable ε_t.

We seek a covariance-stationary solution $\{y_t\}$ to this stochastic difference equation. The solution depends on whether $|\phi|$ is less than, equal to, or greater than 1.

Case 1: $|\phi| < 1$

The solution can be obtained easily by the use of the inverse $(1 - \phi L)^{-1}$ given by (6.1.20). Since this filter is absolutely summable when $|\phi| < 1$, we can apply it to both sides of the AR(1) equation (6.2.1$'$) to obtain

$$(1 - \phi L)^{-1}(1 - \phi L)(y_t - \mu) = (1 - \phi L)^{-1}\varepsilon_t.$$

This operation is legitimate because, thanks to Proposition 6.2, both sides of this equation are well defined as mean square limits. By the definition (6.1.14) of inverses, $(1-\phi L)(1-\phi L)^{-1} = 1$, and by commutativity of inverses $(1-\phi L)^{-1}(1-\phi L) = 1$. Therefore, if $\{y_t\}$ is covariance-stationary, the left-hand side equals $y_t - \mu$ by (6.1.13). So

$$y_t - \mu = (1 - \phi L)^{-1}\varepsilon_t = (1 + \phi L + \phi^2 L^2 + \cdots)\varepsilon_t = \sum_{j=0}^{\infty} \phi^j \varepsilon_{t-j}$$

$$\text{or} \quad y_t = \mu + \sum_{j=0}^{\infty} \phi^j \varepsilon_{t-j}. \tag{6.2.2}$$

What we have shown is that, if $\{y_t\}$ is a covariance-stationary solution to the stochastic difference equation (6.2.1) or (6.2.1$'$), then y_t has the **moving-average representation** as in (6.2.2). Conversely, if y_t has the representation (6.2.2), then it satisfies the difference equation. This can be derived easily by substitution of (6.2.2) into (6.2.1′):

$$\begin{aligned}(1-\phi L)(y_t-\mu) &= (1-\phi L)(1-\phi L)^{-1}\varepsilon_t \\ &= \varepsilon_t \quad \text{(since } (1-\phi L)(1-\phi L)^{-1}=1 \text{ by definition of inverses).}\end{aligned}$$

Thus, the process $\{y_t\}$ given by (6.2.2) is the *unique* covariance-stationary solution to the first-order stochastic difference equation if $|\phi| < 1$. The mean of this process is μ by Proposition 6.1(b).

The condition $|\phi| < 1$, which is the stability condition (6.1.18) associated with the first-degree polynomial equation $1 - \phi z = 0$, is called the **stationarity condition** in the present context of autoregressive processes. Intuitively, this result says that the process, if it started a long time ago, "settles down," provided that $|\phi| < 1$ so that the effect of the past dies out geometrically as time progresses.

Case 2: $|\phi| > 1$

By shifting time forward by one period (i.e., by replacing "t" by "$t+1$"), multiplying both sides by ϕ^{-1}, and rearranging, the stochastic difference equation (6.2.1′) can be written as

$$y_t - \mu = \phi^{-1}(y_{t+1} - \mu) - \phi^{-1}\varepsilon_{t+1}. \tag{6.2.3}$$

Applying the above argument but this time moving in the opposite direction in time shows that the unique covariance-stationary solution is

$$y_t = \mu - \sum_{j=1}^{\infty} \phi^{-j}\varepsilon_{t+j}. \tag{6.2.4}$$

That is, the current value of y is a moving average of *future* values of ε. The infinite sum is well defined because the sequence $\{\phi^{-j}\}$ is absolutely summable if $|\phi| > 1$.

Case 3: $|\phi| = 1$

The stochastic difference equation has no covariance-stationary solution. For example, if $\phi = 1$, the stochastic difference equation becomes

$$\begin{aligned}y_t &= c + y_{t-1} + \varepsilon_t \\ &= c + (c + y_{t-2} + \varepsilon_{t-1}) + \varepsilon_t \qquad (\text{since } y_{t-1} = c + y_{t-2} + \varepsilon_{t-1}) \\ &= c + \big(c + (c + y_{t-3} + \varepsilon_{t-2}) + \varepsilon_{t-1}\big) + \varepsilon_t, \quad \text{etc.}\end{aligned}$$

Repeating this type of successive substitution j times, we obtain

$$y_t - y_{t-j} = c \cdot j + (\varepsilon_t + \varepsilon_{t-1} + \cdots + \varepsilon_{t-j+1}).$$

(If $\{\varepsilon_t\}$ is independent white noise, this process is a **random walk with drift c**.) Suppose, contrary to our claim, that the process is covariance-stationary. Then the variance of $y_t - y_{t-j}$ is $2(\gamma_0 - \gamma_j)$. The variance of the right-hand side is $\sigma^2 \cdot j$. So

$$2 \cdot (\gamma_0 - \gamma_j) = \sigma^2 \cdot j \quad \text{or}$$

$$\rho_j = 1 - \frac{\sigma^2}{2\gamma_0} \cdot j < -1 \quad \text{for } j \text{ large enough (recall: } \rho_j = \gamma_j/\gamma_0).$$

This is a contradiction since autocorrelation coefficients cannot be greater than one in absolute value. So $\{y_t\}$ cannot be covariance-stationary. Processes with $\phi = 1$ are examples of "unit-root processes" and will be studied in Chapter 9.

The solution (6.2.4) for the case of $|\phi| > 1$, with the current value of y linked to the future values of the forcing process $\{\varepsilon_t\}$, is not useful in economics, which does not confer perfect foresight on economic agents. In what follows, unless otherwise stated, we will use the term "an AR(1) process" as the unique covariance-stationary solution to an AR(1) equation (6.2.1) or (6.2.1′) when the stationarity condition holds.

Autocovariances of AR(1)

The autocovariances $\{\gamma_j\}$ of AR(1) (for the case of $|\phi| < 1$) can be calculated in two ways. The first method is to represent AR(1) as MA(∞) as in (6.2.2) and use (6.1.7). Since $\psi_j = \phi^j$ for AR(1), we have

$$\gamma_j = (\phi^j + \phi^{j+2} + \phi^{j+4} + \cdots)\sigma^2 = \frac{\phi^j \sigma^2}{1 - \phi^2} \tag{6.2.5}$$

$$\text{and} \quad \rho_j \; (\equiv \gamma_j/\gamma_0) = \phi^j \qquad (j = 0, 1, \ldots).$$

So the correlogram of an AR(1) process is very simple: it declines with j at a constant geometric rate.

The second method bases the calculation on what is called the **Yule-Walker equations**; see Analytical Exercise 5 for the use of the Yule-Walker equations in the calculation of autocovariances.

AR(p) and Its MA(∞) Representation

All the results just derived for AR(1) can be generalized to AR(p), the ***p*-th order autoregressive process**, which satisfies the p-th order stochastic difference equation:

$$y_t = c + \phi_1 y_{t-1} + \cdots + \phi_p y_{t-p} + \varepsilon_t \quad \text{or}$$
$$y_t - \phi_1 y_{t-1} - \cdots - \phi_p y_{t-p} = c + \varepsilon_t \quad \text{or}$$
$$\phi(L)y_t = c + \varepsilon_t \quad \text{with } \phi(L) = 1 - \phi_1 L - \phi_2 L^2 - \cdots - \phi_p L^p, \tag{6.2.6}$$

where $\{\varepsilon_t\}$ is white noise and $\phi_p \neq 0$. Evidently, $\phi(1) = 1 - \phi_1 - \cdots - \phi_p$. If $\phi(1) \neq 0$, let $\mu \equiv c/(1 - \phi_1 - \cdots - \phi_p) = c/\phi(1)$. As shown below, μ is the mean of y_t if y_t is covariance-stationary. Substituting for c, the AR(p) equation (6.2.6) can be written equivalently in deviation-from-the-mean form:

$$(y_t - \mu) - \phi_1 \cdot (y_{t-1} - \mu) - \cdots - \phi_p \cdot (y_{t-p} - \mu) = \varepsilon_t$$
$$\text{or} \quad \phi(L)(y_t - \mu) = \varepsilon_t. \tag{6.2.6$'$}$$

The generalization to AR(p) of what we have derived for AR(1) is

Proposition 6.4 (AR(p) as MA(∞) with absolutely summable coefficients): *Suppose the p-th degree polynomial $\phi(z)$ satisfies the stationarity (stability) condition (6.1.18) or (6.1.18′). Then*

(a) The unique covariance-stationary solution to the p-th order stochastic difference equation (6.2.6) or (6.2.6′) has the MA(∞) *representation*

$$y_t = \mu + \psi(L)\varepsilon_t, \quad \psi(L) = \psi_0 + \psi_1 L + \psi_2 L^2 + \psi_3 L^3 + \cdots, \tag{6.2.7}$$

where $\psi(L) = \phi(L)^{-1}$. The coefficient sequence $\{\psi_j\}$ is bounded in absolute value by a geometrically declining sequence and hence is absolutely summable.

(b) The mean μ of the process is given by

$$\mu = \phi(1)^{-1}c \quad \text{where } c \text{ is the constant in (6.2.6).} \tag{6.2.8}$$

(c) $\{\gamma_j\}$ is bounded in absolute value by a sequence that declines geometrically with j. Hence, the autocovariances are absolutely summable.

Unless otherwise stated, we will use the term "an AR(p) process" as the unique covariance-stationary solution (6.2.7) to an AR(p) equation (6.2.6) that satisfies the stationarity condition. The absolute summability of the inverse $\phi(L)^{-1}$ in part (a) of this proposition is immediate from Proposition 6.3. Given absolute summability, the first part of (a) can be proved by the same argument we used for AR(1); just multiply both sides of (6.2.6′) by $\phi(L)^{-1}$ and observe that

$$\phi(L)^{-1}\phi(L) = \phi(L)\,\phi(L)^{-1} = 1.$$

Part (b) is immediate from Proposition 6.1(b). Part (c) can easily be proved by combining (a) and Proposition 6.1(b). Analytical Exercise 7 will ask you to give an alternative proof of the proposition without using filters but using the apparatus called the **companion form**.

As in AR(1), autocovariances can be obtained in two ways. The first method utilizes the MA(∞) representation. The coefficients $\{\psi_j\}$ in the MA representation are the coefficients in the inverse of the lag polynomial $\phi(L)$, and the algorithm for calculating the inverse coefficients has already been presented (see (6.1.16)). Given $\{\psi_j\}$, use (6.1.7) to calculate the autocovariances $\{\gamma_j\}$. The second method uses the Yule-Walker equations.

ARMA(p, q)

An ARMA(p, q) process combines AR(p) and MA(q):

$$\begin{aligned} y_t = c + \phi_1 y_{t-1} + \phi_2 y_{t-2} + \cdots + \phi_p y_{t-p} \\ + \theta_0 \varepsilon_t + \theta_1 \varepsilon_{t-1} + \theta_2 \varepsilon_{t-2} + \cdots + \theta_q \varepsilon_{t-q} \end{aligned}$$

or

$$\begin{aligned} y_t - \phi_1 y_{t-1} - \phi_2 y_{t-2} - \cdots - \phi_p y_{t-p} \\ = c + \theta_0 \varepsilon_t + \theta_1 \varepsilon_{t-1} + \theta_2 \varepsilon_{t-2} + \cdots + \theta_q \varepsilon_{t-q} \end{aligned}$$

or

$$\begin{aligned} \phi(L) y_t = c + \theta(L)\varepsilon_t,\ \ \phi(L) = 1 - \phi_1 L - \cdots - \phi_p L^p, \\ \theta(L) = \theta_0 + \theta_1 L + \cdots + \theta_q L^q, \end{aligned} \tag{6.2.9}$$

where $\{\varepsilon_t\}$ is white noise. If $\phi(1) \neq 1$, set $\mu = c/\phi(1)$. The deviation-from-the-mean form is

$$\begin{aligned} (y_t - \mu) - \phi_1 \cdot (y_{t-1} - \mu) - \cdots - \phi_p \cdot (y_{t-p} - \mu) \\ = \theta_0 \varepsilon_t + \theta_1 \varepsilon_{t-1} + \cdots + \theta_q \varepsilon_{t-q} \end{aligned}$$

or

$$\phi(L)(y_t - \mu) = \theta(L)\varepsilon_t. \tag{6.2.9′}$$

This is still a stochastic p-th order difference equation but with a serially correlated forcing process $\{\theta(L)\varepsilon_t\}$ instead of a white noise process $\{\varepsilon_t\}$. Proposition 6.4 generalizes easily to

Proposition 6.5 (ARMA(p, q) as MA(∞) with absolutely summable coefficients): *Suppose the p-th degree polynomial $\phi(z)$ satisfies stationarity (stability) condition (6.1.18) or (6.1.18′). Then*

(a) The unique covariance-stationary solution to the p-th order stochastic difference equation (6.2.9) or (6.2.9′) has the MA(∞) *representation*

$$y_t = \mu + \psi(L)\varepsilon_t, \quad \psi(L) = \psi_0 + \psi_1 L + \psi_2 L^2 + \psi_3 L^3 + \cdots, \tag{6.2.10}$$

where $\psi(L) \equiv \phi(L)^{-1}\theta(L)$. The coefficient sequence $\{\psi_j\}$ is bounded in absolute value by a geometrically declining sequence and hence is absolutely summable.

(b) The mean μ of the process is given by

$$\mu = \phi(1)^{-1}c \quad \text{where } c \text{ is the constant in (6.2.9).} \tag{6.2.11}$$

(c) $\{\gamma_j\}$ is bounded in absolute value by a sequence that declines geometrically with j. Hence, the autocovariances are absolutely summable.

Unless otherwise stated, we will use the term "an ARMA process" as the unique solution (6.2.10) to an ARMA equation (6.2.9) or (6.2.9′) that satisfies the stationarity condition. The MA(∞) representation can be derived easily by multiplying both sides of (6.2.9′) by the inverse $\phi(L)^{-1}$ and observing that $\phi(L)^{-1}\phi(L) = \phi(L)\,\phi(L)^{-1} = 1$. For the rest of part (a) and part (b), the only nontrivial part of the proof is to show that $\{\psi_j\}$ is bounded in absolute value by a geometrically declining sequence. For AR(p) we used the algorithm based on the set of equations (6.1.16) to solve $\phi(L)\,\psi(L) = 1$ for $\psi(L)$. This algorithm can easily be generalized. This time $\psi(L) \equiv \phi(L)^{-1}\theta(L)$ or

$$\phi(L)\,\psi(L) = \theta(L).$$

To solve this for $\psi(L)$, apply the convolution formula (6.1.12) with $\alpha(L) = \phi(L)$, $\beta(L) = \psi(L)$, and $\delta(L) = \theta(L)$ (instead of 1). The resulting set of equations is the same as (6.1.16), except that the right-hand side of the equation for the constant is θ_0 rather than 1, that of the equation for L is θ_1 rather than 0, that of L^2 is θ_2, and so forth, until the equation for L^q, whose right-hand side is θ_q. The right-hand side of the rest of the equations is 0. As in AR(p), these equations can easily be solved successively for $(\psi_0, \psi_1, \psi_2, \dots)$ as

$$\psi_0 = \theta_0 = 1, \quad \psi_1 = \theta_1 + \phi_1, \quad \psi_2 = \theta_2 + \phi_2 + \theta_1\phi_1 + \phi_1^2, \quad \text{etc.}$$

Again, as in the AR(p) case, for sufficiently large j (actually, for $j \geq \max(p, q+1)$, as you will verify in Review Question 5), $\{\psi_j\}$ follows the same p-th order homogeneous difference equation (6.1.17). So $\{\psi_j\}$ is bounded in absolute value by a geometrically declining sequence and hence is absolutely summable.

Again there are two ways to derive the expression for autocovariances in terms of $(\phi_1, \dots, \phi_p, \theta_1, \dots, \theta_q, \sigma^2)$. You can calculate the coefficients $\{\psi_j\}$ in the MA representation as just described and then use (6.1.7). The other method is based on the Yule-Walker equations.

ARMA(p, q) with Common Roots

In the ARMA(p, q) equation (6.2.9′), suppose $\phi(L)$ satisfies the stationarity condition as in Proposition 6.5, but suppose that one of the roots of $\phi(z) = 0$ is also a root of $\theta(z) = 0$. If that root is λ, the polynomials $\phi(z)$ and $\theta(z)$ have a factorization

$$\phi(z) = \alpha(z)\,\phi^*(z), \quad \theta(z) = \alpha(z)\,\theta^*(z) \quad \text{with } \alpha(z) = 1 - \lambda^{-1}z.$$

The inverse of $\phi(L)$ is $\phi^*(L)^{-1}\alpha(L)^{-1}$. So the $\psi(L)$ in Proposition 6.5 can be written as

$$\psi(L) = \phi(L)^{-1}\theta(L) = \phi^*(L)^{-1}\alpha(L)^{-1}\alpha(L)\,\theta^*(L) = \phi^*(L)^{-1}\theta^*(L), \quad (6.2.12)$$

which shows that the ARMA(p, q) equation (6.2.9′) and the simpler ARMA($p - 1, q - 1$) equation

$$\phi^*(L)(y_t - \mu) = \theta^*(L)\varepsilon_t$$

share the same process as the unique covariance-stationary solution.[3] For reasons of parsimony, ARMA equations with common roots are rarely used to parameterize covariance-stationary processes.

[3] Since we defined filters for sequences of real numbers, the discussion in the text presumes that the root λ is real. If λ is complex, then there must be another common root which is the complex conjugate of λ. Let $\lambda_1 = a + bi$ and $\lambda_2 = a - bi$ be the pair of complex roots. Then if we define

$$\alpha(z) = 1 - (\lambda_1^{-1} + \lambda_2^{-1})z + \frac{1}{(\lambda_1 \cdot \lambda_2)}z^2 = 1 - \frac{2a}{(a^2 + b^2)}z + \frac{1}{(a^2 + b^2)}z^2,$$

the discussion in the text carries over.

Invertibility

For the ARMA(p, q) equation (6.2.9), if $\phi(z) = 0$ and $\theta(z) = 0$ have no common roots and if $\theta(z)$ satisfies the stability condition (6.1.18) or (6.1.18′), then the ARMA process is said to be **invertible** and the stability condition on $\theta(z)$ is called the **invertibility condition.**[4] Since $\theta(L)^{-1}$ is absolutely summable if $\theta(z)$ satisfies the invertibility (stability) condition, we can multiply both sides of the ARMA equation (6.2.9) by $\theta(L)^{-1}$ and use the relation $\theta(L)^{-1}c = c\,\theta(1)^{-1} = c/\theta(1)$ to obtain

$$\theta(L)^{-1}\phi(L)y_t = \frac{c}{\theta(1)} + \varepsilon_t. \tag{6.2.13}$$

So, the process has the infinite-order autoregressive (AR(∞)) representation. The derivation does not require the stationarity condition (that $\phi(z)$ satisfies the stability condition). If both $\phi(z)$ and $\theta(z)$ satisfy the stability condition, then the ARMA(p, q) process has both the MA(∞) and AR(∞) representations.

Autocovariance-Generating Function and the Spectrum

A particularly useful way to summarize the whole profile of autocovariances, $\{\gamma_j\}$, of a covariance-stationary process $\{y_t\}$ is the **autocovariance-generating function**:

$$\begin{aligned} g_Y(z) &\equiv \sum_{j=-\infty}^{\infty} \gamma_j z^j \\ &= \gamma_0 + \sum_{j=1}^{\infty} \gamma_j \cdot (z^j + z^{-j}) \quad (\text{since } \gamma_{-j} = \gamma_j). \end{aligned} \tag{6.2.14}$$

The argument of this function (z) is a complex scalar. Because the summation involves infinitely many terms, there arises a question as to whether the function is well defined. A familiar result from calculus says that the infinite sum is well defined at least for $|z| = 1$ (the unit circle) if $\{\gamma_j\}$ is absolutely summable. For example, for $z = 1$,

$$g_Y(1) = \sum_{j=-\infty}^{\infty} \gamma_j = \gamma_0 + 2\sum_{j=1}^{\infty} \gamma_j. \tag{6.2.15}$$

[4]It is easy to confuse invertibility and the existence of an inverse. Since $\theta_0 = 1 \neq 0$, $\theta(L)$ does have an inverse without the invertibility condition. The inverse, however, may not be absolutely summable unless the invertibility condition is satisfied.

This is indeed well defined because the infinite sum converges.[5]

Any complex number on the unit circle can be represented as

$$z = \cos(\omega) - i\,\sin(\omega) = e^{-i\omega}, \tag{6.2.16}$$

where $i = \sqrt{-1}$ and ω is the negative of the radian angle that z makes with the real axis. If the autocovariance-generating function is evaluated at this z and divided by 2π, the resulting function of ω,

$$s_Y(\omega) \equiv \frac{1}{2\pi}\, g_Y\big(\cos(\omega) - i\,\sin(\omega)\big) = \frac{1}{2\pi}\, g_Y(e^{-i\omega}) \tag{6.2.17}$$

is called the **(power) spectrum** or the **spectral density (function)** of $\{y_t\}$, and ω is referred to as the **frequency**.

It can be shown that for absolutely summable autocovariances, all of the autocovariances can be calculated from the spectrum (hence the term autocovariance-generating function). So there is a one-to-one mapping between the $\{\gamma_j\}$ sequence and $g_Y(z)$ or $s_Y(\omega)$. The **time domain approach**, which concentrates on $\{\gamma_j\}$ and which is what we have been doing, and the **frequency domain approach**, which is based on the interpretation of the spectrum, are therefore *equivalent*, although some results can be more easily stated in one approach than in the other. This book will not cover the frequency domain approach any further than this.

If $\{y_t\}$ is white noise, then evidently $g_Y(z)$ is constant and equal to the variance. For MA(1), $g_Y(z)$ is obtained by simple substitution of (6.1.2) for $q = 1$ into the definition (6.2.14):

$$\begin{aligned} g_Y(z) &= \gamma_{-1} z^{-1} + \gamma_0 + \gamma_1 z \\ &= (\theta_1\sigma^2) z^{-1} + (1+\theta_1^2)\sigma^2 + (\theta_1\sigma^2) z \\ &= \sigma^2 \cdot [\theta_1 z^{-1} + (1+\theta_1^2) + \theta_1 z] \\ &= \sigma^2 \cdot (1+\theta_1 z)(1+\theta_1 z^{-1}). \end{aligned}$$

So

$$g_Y(z) = \sigma^2 \theta(z)\,\theta(z^{-1}), \tag{6.2.18}$$

where $\theta(z) = 1 + \theta_1 z$. This last expression generalizes to the MA(q) case where $\theta(z) = 1 + \theta_1 z + \theta_2 z^2 + \cdots + \theta_q z^q$. (You should verify this by carrying out the multiplication in this expression for $g_Y(z)$ for MA(q), collecting terms by powers of z, and looking at the coefficient of z^j or z^{-j}.) The expression is also good for

[5]Fact: If $\{\gamma_j\}$ is absolutely summable, then it is summable (i.e., the partial sum of $\{\gamma_j\}$ converges to a finite limit).

MA(∞) processes if the coefficients are absolutely summable, as the following result assures us.

Proposition 6.6 (Autocovariance-generating function for filtered processes): *Let $\{\varepsilon_t\}$ be white noise and let $\psi(L) = \psi_0 + \psi_1 L + \psi_2 L^2 + \cdots$ be an absolutely summable filter (i.e., with $\{\psi_j\}$ absolutely summable). Then the autocovariance-generating function of the* MA(∞) *process $\{y_t\}$ where $y_t = \mu + \psi(L)\varepsilon_t$ is*

$$g_Y(z) = \sigma^2\, \psi(z)\, \psi(z^{-1}). \tag{6.2.19}$$

More generally, let $\{x_t\}$ be covariance-stationary with absolutely summable autocovariances and $g_X(z)$ be the autocovariance-generating function of $\{x_t\}$. The autocovariance-generating function of the filtered series $\{y_t\}$ where $y_t = h(L)x_t$ (with absolutely summable $\{h_j\}$) is

$$g_Y(z) = h(z)\, g_X(z)\, h(z^{-1}). \tag{6.2.20}$$

We will not prove this result; see, e.g., Theorem 4.3.1 of Fuller (1996).

Because AR(p) and ARMA(p, q) processes have the MA(∞) representations, their autocovariance-generating functions can be derived easily from (6.2.19). Since $\psi(L) = 1/\phi(L)$ for AR(p), and $\psi(L) = \theta(L)/\phi(L)$ for ARMA(p, q), we have

$$\text{AR}(p)\colon\ g_Y(z) = \sigma^2 \frac{1}{\phi(z)\,\phi(z^{-1})}, \tag{6.2.21}$$

$$\text{ARMA}(p, q)\colon\ g_Y(z) = \sigma^2 \frac{\theta(z)\,\theta(z^{-1})}{\phi(z)\,\phi(z^{-1})}. \tag{6.2.22}$$

QUESTIONS FOR REVIEW

1. If $\{y_t\}$ is the covariance-stationary solution to the AR(1) equation (6.2.1) with $|\phi| < 1$, what is

$$\widehat{\text{E}}^*(y_t \mid 1, y_{t-1})$$

(the least squares projection)? **Hint:** $\text{E}(y_{t-1}\varepsilon_t) = 0$. Do the projection coefficients depend on t? Is $\widehat{\text{E}}^*(y_t \mid 1, y_{t-1}) = \text{E}(y_t \mid y_{t-1})$? **Hint:** $\text{E}(y_{t-1}\varepsilon_t) = 0$ but does it mean $\text{E}(\varepsilon_t \mid y_{t-1}) = 0$? What is $\widehat{\text{E}}^*(y_t \mid 1, y_{t-1}, y_{t-2})$? Now suppose that $\{y_t\}$ is the covariance-stationary solution to the AR(1) equation when $|\phi| > 1$. Is it true that $\text{E}(y_{t-1}\varepsilon_t) = 0$? [Answer: No.] Does $\widehat{\text{E}}^*(y_t \mid 1, y_{t-1}) = c + \phi y_{t-1}$ as was the case when $|\phi| < 1$?

2. (AR(1) with $\phi = -1$) For simplicity, set $c = 0$ in the AR(1) equation (6.2.1). Show that the AR(1) equation with $\phi = -1$ has no covariance-stationary solution. **Hint:** The same sort of successive substitution we did for the case $\phi = 1$ yields

$$y_t - (-1)^j y_{t-j} = \varepsilon_t - \varepsilon_{t-1} + \cdots + (-1)^{j-1}\varepsilon_{t-j+1}.$$

From this, derive

$$(-1)^j \rho_j = 1 - \frac{\sigma^2}{2\gamma_0} \cdot j.$$

3. (About Proposition 6.4) How do we know that $\phi(1) \neq 0$ in (6.2.8)? **Hint:** Use the stationarity condition. Prove (b) of Proposition 6.4. **Hint:** Take the expectation of both sides of (6.2.6) and exploit the covariance-stationarity of $\{y_t\}$.

4. (About Proposition 6.5) Verify that $y_t - \mu = \phi(L)^{-1}\,\theta(L)\varepsilon_t$ is a solution to the ARMA(p, q) equation.

5. ($\{\psi_j\}$ for ARMA(p, q)) For AR(p), we used the equations (6.1.12) to calculate the MA coefficients $\{\psi_j\}$. For ARMA(3, 1), write down the corresponding equations. From which lag j does $\{\psi_j\}$ start following

$$\psi_j - \phi_1 \psi_{j-1} - \phi_2\, \psi_{j-2} - \phi_3\, \psi_{j-3} = 0,$$

which is (6.1.17) for $p = 3$? Do the same for ARMA$(1, 2)$. From which j does $\{\psi_j\}$ start following (6.1.17) for $p = 1$? [Answer: $j = 3$.]

6. (How filtering alters the spectrum) Let $h(L)$ be absolutely summable. By Proposition 6.2, if $\{x_t\}$ is covariance-stationary with absolutely summable autocovariances, then so is $\{y_t\}$ where $y_t = h(L)x_t$. Using (6.2.20), verify that

$$s_Y(\omega) = h(e^{-i\omega})\, s_X(\omega)\, h(e^{i\omega}).$$

7. (The spectrum is real valued) Show that the spectrum is real valued. **Hint:** Substitute (6.2.16) into (6.2.14). Use the following facts from complex analysis: $[\cos(\omega) - i\,\sin(\omega)]^j = \cos(j\omega) - i\,\sin(j\omega)$; $\sin(-\omega) = -\sin(\omega)$.

6.3 Vector Processes

It is straightforward to extend all the concepts introduced so far to vector processes.

A **vector white noise process** $\{\boldsymbol{\varepsilon}_t\}$ is a jointly covariance-stationary process satisfying

$$\mathrm{E}(\boldsymbol{\varepsilon}_t) = \mathbf{0}, \quad \mathrm{E}(\boldsymbol{\varepsilon}_t\boldsymbol{\varepsilon}_t') = \boldsymbol{\Omega} \text{ (positive definite)}, \quad \text{and}$$
$$\mathrm{E}(\boldsymbol{\varepsilon}_t\boldsymbol{\varepsilon}_{t-j}') = \mathbf{0} \quad \text{for } j \neq 0. \tag{6.3.1}$$

Since $\boldsymbol{\Omega}$ is not restricted to being diagonal, there can be contemporaneous correlation between the elements of $\boldsymbol{\varepsilon}_t$. Perfect correlation among the elements of $\boldsymbol{\varepsilon}_t$ is ruled out because $\boldsymbol{\Omega}$ is required to be positive definite.

A **vector MA(∞) process** is the obvious vector version of (6.1.6):

$$\mathbf{y}_t = \boldsymbol{\mu} + \sum_{j=0}^{\infty} \boldsymbol{\Psi}_j \boldsymbol{\varepsilon}_{t-j} \quad \text{with } \boldsymbol{\Psi}_0 = \mathbf{I}, \tag{6.3.2}$$

where $\{\boldsymbol{\Psi}_j\}$ are square matrices. The sequence of coefficient matrices is said to be absolutely summable if each element is absolutely summable. That is, if $\psi_{k\ell j}$ is the (k, ℓ) element of $\boldsymbol{\Psi}_j$,

$$\text{“}\{\boldsymbol{\Psi}_j\} \text{ is absolutely summable”} \Leftrightarrow \text{“}\sum_{j=0}^{\infty} |\psi_{k\ell j}| < \infty \text{ for all } (k, \ell).\text{”} \tag{6.3.3}$$

With this definition, Proposition 6.1 generalizes to the multivariate case in an obvious way. In particular, if $\boldsymbol{\Gamma}_j$ $(\equiv \mathrm{E}[(\mathbf{y}_t - \boldsymbol{\mu})(\mathbf{y}_{t-j} - \boldsymbol{\mu})'])$ is the j-th order autocovariance matrix, then the expression for autocovariances in part (b) of Proposition 6.1 becomes

$$\boldsymbol{\Gamma}_j = \sum_{k=0}^{\infty} \boldsymbol{\Psi}_{j+k}\, \boldsymbol{\Omega}\, \boldsymbol{\Psi}_k' \quad (j = 0, 1, 2, \dots). \tag{6.3.4}$$

(This formula also covers $j = -1, -2, \dots$ because $\boldsymbol{\Gamma}_{-j} = \boldsymbol{\Gamma}_j'$.)

A **multivariate filter** can be written as

$$\mathbf{H}(L) = \mathbf{H}_0 + \mathbf{H}_1 L + \mathbf{H}_2 L^2 + \cdots,$$

where $\{\mathbf{H}_j\}$ is a sequence of (not necessarily square) matrices. So if $H_{k\ell j}$ is the

(k, ℓ) element of $\mathbf{H}_j$, the (k, ℓ) element of $\mathbf{H}(L)$ is

$$H_{k\ell 0} + H_{k\ell 1} L + H_{k\ell 2} L^2 + \cdots .$$

The multivariate version of Proposition 6.2 is obvious, with $\mathbf{y}_t = \mathbf{H}(L)\, \mathbf{x}_t$.

Product of Filters

Let $\mathbf{A}(L)$ and $\mathbf{B}(L)$ be two filters where $\{\mathbf{A}_j\}$ is $m \times r$ and $\{\mathbf{B}_j\}$ is $r \times s$ so that the matrix product $\mathbf{A}_j \mathbf{B}_k$ can be defined. The product of two filters, $\mathbf{D}(L) = \mathbf{A}(L)\, \mathbf{B}(L)$ is an $m \times s$ filter whose coefficient matrix sequence $\{\mathbf{D}_j\}$ is given by the multivariate version of the convolution formula (6.1.12):

$$\begin{gathered} \mathbf{A}_0\, \mathbf{B}_0 = \mathbf{D}_0, \\ \mathbf{A}_0\, \mathbf{B}_1 + \mathbf{A}_1\, \mathbf{B}_0 = \mathbf{D}_1, \\ \mathbf{A}_0\, \mathbf{B}_2 + \mathbf{A}_1\, \mathbf{B}_1 + \mathbf{A}_2\, \mathbf{B}_0 = \mathbf{D}_2, \\ \cdots, \\ \mathbf{A}_0\, \mathbf{B}_j + \mathbf{A}_1\, \mathbf{B}_{j-1} + \mathbf{A}_2\, \mathbf{B}_{j-2} + \cdots + \mathbf{A}_{j-1}\, \mathbf{B}_1 + \mathbf{A}_j\, \mathbf{B}_0 = \mathbf{D}_j, \\ \cdots . \end{gathered} \tag{6.3.5}$$

Inverses

Let $\mathbf{A}(L)$ and $\mathbf{B}(L)$ be two filters whose coefficient matrices are square. $\mathbf{B}(L)$ is said to be the **inverse** of $\mathbf{A}(L)$ and is denoted $\mathbf{A}(L)^{-1}$ if

$$\mathbf{A}(L)\, \mathbf{B}(L) = \mathbf{I}. \tag{6.3.6}$$

For any arbitrary sequence of square matrices $\{\mathbf{A}_j\}$, the inverse of $\mathbf{A}(L)$ exists if $\mathbf{A}_0$ is nonsingular. It is easy to show that inverses are commutative (see Review Question 2), so

$$\mathbf{A}(L)\, \mathbf{A}(L)^{-1} = \mathbf{A}(L)^{-1} \mathbf{A}(L).$$

Absolutely Summable Inverses of Lag Polynomials

A ***p*-th degree lag matrix polynomial** is

$$\mathbf{\Phi}(L) = \mathbf{I}_r - \mathbf{\Phi}_1 L - \mathbf{\Phi}_2 L^2 - \cdots - \mathbf{\Phi}_p L^p, \tag{6.3.7}$$

where $\{\mathbf{\Phi}_j\}$ is a sequence of $r \times r$ matrices with $\mathbf{\Phi}_p \neq \mathbf{0}$. From the theory of homogeneous difference equations, the stability condition for the multivariate case is as follows:

All the roots of the determinantal equation

$$|\mathbf{I} - \mathbf{\Phi}_1 z - \cdots - \mathbf{\Phi}_p z^p| = 0 \tag{6.3.8}$$

are greater than 1 in absolute value (i.e., lie outside the unit circle).

Or, equivalently,

All the roots of the determinantal equation

$$|\mathbf{I}z^p - \mathbf{\Phi}_1 z^{p-1} - \cdots - \mathbf{\Phi}_p| = 0 \tag{6.3.8$'$}$$

are less than 1 in absolute value (i.e., lie inside the unit circle).

As an example, consider a first-degree lag polynomial $\mathbf{\Phi}(L) = \mathbf{I} - \mathbf{\Phi}_1 L$ where $\mathbf{\Phi}_1 = (\phi_{k\ell})$ is 2×2. Equation (6.3.8) can be written as

$$\begin{vmatrix} 1 - \phi_{11}z & -\phi_{12}z \\ -\phi_{21}z & 1 - \phi_{22}z \end{vmatrix} = 1 - (\phi_{11} + \phi_{22})z + (\phi_{11}\phi_{22} - \phi_{21}\phi_{12})z^2 = 0.$$

With the stability condition thus generalized, Proposition 6.3 generalizes in an obvious way. Let $\mathbf{\Psi}(L) = \mathbf{\Phi}(L)^{-1}$. Each component of the coefficient matrix sequence $\{\mathbf{\Psi}_j\}$ will be bounded in absolute value by a geometrically declining sequence.

The multivariate analogue of an AR(p) is a **vector autoregressive process of *p*-th order (VAR(*p*))**. It is the unique covariance-stationary solution under stationarity condition (6.3.8) to the following vector stochastic difference equation:

$$\mathbf{y}_t - \mathbf{\Phi}_1 \mathbf{y}_{t-1} - \cdots - \mathbf{\Phi}_p \mathbf{y}_{t-p} = \mathbf{c} + \boldsymbol{\varepsilon}_t \quad \text{or} \quad \mathbf{\Phi}(L)(\mathbf{y}_t - \boldsymbol{\mu}) = \boldsymbol{\varepsilon}_t$$
$$\text{where} \quad \mathbf{\Phi}(L) = \mathbf{I}_r - \mathbf{\Phi}_1 L - \mathbf{\Phi}_2 L^2 - \cdots - \mathbf{\Phi}_p L^p \quad \text{and} \quad \boldsymbol{\mu} = \mathbf{\Phi}(1)^{-1}\mathbf{c}, \tag{6.3.9}$$

where $\mathbf{\Phi}_p \neq \mathbf{0}$. For example, a bivariate VAR(1) can be written out in full as a two-equation system with common regressors:

$$y_{1t} = c_1 + \phi_{11} y_{1,t-1} + \phi_{12} y_{2,t-1} + \varepsilon_{1t},$$
$$y_{2t} = c_2 + \phi_{21} y_{1,t-1} + \phi_{22} y_{2,t-1} + \varepsilon_{2t}, \quad \text{where } \mathbf{\Phi}_1 = \begin{bmatrix} \phi_{11} & \phi_{12} \\ \phi_{21} & \phi_{22} \end{bmatrix}.$$

More generally, an M-variate VAR(p) is a set of M equations with $Mp+1$ common regressors. Proposition 6.4 generalizes straightforwardly to the multivariate case.

In particular, each element of $\mathbf{\Gamma}_j$ is bounded in absolute value by a geometrically declining sequence.

Vector autoregressions are a very popular tool for analyzing the dynamic interrelationship between key macro variables. A thorough treatment can be found in Hamilton (1994, Chapter 11).

The multivariate analogue of an ARMA(p, q) is a **vector ARMA(p, q) (VARMA(p, q))**. It is the unique covariance-stationary solution under the stationarity condition to the following vector stochastic difference equation:

$$\begin{aligned}\mathbf{y}_t &= \mathbf{c} + \mathbf{\Phi}_1 \mathbf{y}_{t-1} + \mathbf{\Phi}_2 \mathbf{y}_{t-2} + \cdots + \mathbf{\Phi}_p \mathbf{y}_{t-p} + \boldsymbol{\varepsilon}_t \\ &\quad + \mathbf{\Theta}_1 \boldsymbol{\varepsilon}_{t-1} + \mathbf{\Theta}_2 \boldsymbol{\varepsilon}_{t-2} + \cdots + \mathbf{\Theta}_q \boldsymbol{\varepsilon}_{t-q} \quad \text{or} \\ \mathbf{\Phi}(L)(\mathbf{y}_t - \boldsymbol{\mu}) &= \mathbf{\Theta}(L)\boldsymbol{\varepsilon}_t,\end{aligned}$$

where

$$\mathbf{\Phi}(L) = \mathbf{I} - \mathbf{\Phi}_1 L - \cdots - \mathbf{\Phi}_p L^p, \quad \mathbf{\Theta}(L) = \mathbf{I} + \mathbf{\Theta}_1 L + \cdots + \mathbf{\Theta}_q L^q,$$
$$\boldsymbol{\mu} = \mathbf{\Phi}(1)^{-1}\mathbf{c}, \tag{6.3.10}$$

where $\mathbf{\Phi}_p \neq \mathbf{0}$ and $\mathbf{\Theta}_q \neq \mathbf{0}$. Proposition 6.5 generalizes in an obvious way.

Autocovariance Generating Function

The multivariate version of the autocovariance-generating function for a vector covariance-stationary process $\{\mathbf{y}_t\}$ is

$$\mathbf{G_Y}(z) = \sum_{j=-\infty}^{\infty} \mathbf{\Gamma}_j z^j = \mathbf{\Gamma}_0 + \sum_{j=1}^{\infty} (\mathbf{\Gamma}_j z^j + \mathbf{\Gamma}_j' z^{-j}) \quad (\text{since } \mathbf{\Gamma}_{-j} = \mathbf{\Gamma}_j'). \tag{6.3.11}$$

The spectrum of a vector process $\{\mathbf{y}_t\}$ is defined as

$$\mathbf{s_Y}(\omega) = \frac{1}{2\pi} \mathbf{G_Y}(e^{-i\omega}). \tag{6.3.12}$$

Proposition 6.6 generalizes easily. In particular, if $\mathbf{H}(L)$ is an $r \times s$ absolutely summable filter and $\mathbf{G_X}(z)$ is the autocovariance-generating function of an s-dimensional covariance-stationary process $\{\mathbf{x}_t\}$ with absolutely summable autocovariances, then the autocovariance-generating function of $\mathbf{y}_t = \mathbf{H}(L)\mathbf{x}_t$ is given by

$$\underset{(r\times r)}{\mathbf{G_Y}(z)} = \underset{(r\times s)}{\mathbf{H}(z)}\, \underset{(s\times s)}{\mathbf{G_x}(z)}\, \underset{(s\times r)}{\mathbf{H}(z^{-1})'}. \tag{6.3.13}$$

As special cases of this, we have

$$\text{vector white noise}: \mathbf{G_Y}(z) = \boldsymbol{\Omega}, \tag{6.3.14}$$

$$\text{VMA}(\infty): \mathbf{G_Y}(z) = \boldsymbol{\Psi}(z)\,\boldsymbol{\Omega}\,\boldsymbol{\Psi}(z^{-1})', \tag{6.3.15}$$

$$\text{VAR}(p): \mathbf{G_Y}(z) = [\boldsymbol{\Phi}(z)^{-1}]\,\boldsymbol{\Omega}\,[\boldsymbol{\Phi}(z^{-1})^{-1}]', \tag{6.3.16}$$

$$\text{VARMA}(p,q): \mathbf{G_Y}(z) = [\boldsymbol{\Phi}(z)^{-1}]\,[\boldsymbol{\Theta}(z)]\,\boldsymbol{\Omega}\,[\boldsymbol{\Theta}(z^{-1})]'\,[\boldsymbol{\Phi}(z^{-1})^{-1}]'. \tag{6.3.17}$$

For example, if $\mathbf{y}_t = \boldsymbol{\varepsilon}_t + \boldsymbol{\Theta}_1\boldsymbol{\varepsilon}_{t-1}$,

$$\mathbf{G_Y}(z) = (\mathbf{I} + \boldsymbol{\Theta}_1 z)\boldsymbol{\Omega}(\mathbf{I} + \boldsymbol{\Theta}_1' z^{-1}).$$

QUESTIONS FOR REVIEW

1. Verify (6.3.4) for vector MA(1).

2. (Commutativity of inverses) Verify the commutativity of inverses, that is, "$\mathbf{A}(L)\,\mathbf{B}(L) = \mathbf{I}$" $\Leftrightarrow$ "$\mathbf{B}(L)\,\mathbf{A}(L) = \mathbf{I}$" for two square filters of dimension r with $|\mathbf{A}_0| \neq 0$ and $|\mathbf{B}_0| \neq 0$. **Hint:** Set $\mathbf{D}_0 = \mathbf{I}$, $\mathbf{D}_j = \mathbf{0}$ ($j \geq 1$) in (6.3.5) and solve for $\mathbf{B}$'s. Show that this $\mathbf{B}(L)$ satisfies $\mathbf{B}(L)\,\mathbf{A}(L) = \mathbf{I}$.

3. (Lack of commutativity for multivariate filters) Provide an example where $\mathbf{A}(L)$ and $\mathbf{B}(L)$ are 2×2 but $\mathbf{A}(L)\,\mathbf{B}(L) \neq \mathbf{B}(L)\,\mathbf{A}(L)$. **Hint:** How about $\mathbf{A}(L) = \mathbf{I} + \mathbf{A}_1 L$ and $\mathbf{B}(L) = \mathbf{I} + \mathbf{B}_1 L$? Find two square matrices $\mathbf{A}_1$ and $\mathbf{B}_1$ such that $\mathbf{A}_1\,\mathbf{B}_1 \neq \mathbf{B}_1\,\mathbf{A}_1$.

4. Verify the multivariate version of (6.1.15b), namely,

$$\text{“}\mathbf{A}(L)\,\mathbf{B}(L) = \mathbf{D}(L)\text{”} \Leftrightarrow \text{“}\mathbf{B}(L) = \mathbf{A}(L)^{-1}\mathbf{D}(L)\text{”}$$
$$\Leftrightarrow \text{“}\mathbf{A}(L) = \mathbf{D}(L)\,\mathbf{B}(L)^{-1}\text{,”}$$

provided $\mathbf{A}_0$ and $\mathbf{B}_0$ are nonsingular.

So, to solve $\mathbf{A}(L)\,\mathbf{B}(L) = \mathbf{D}(L)$ for $\mathbf{B}(L)$, "multiply both sides from the left" by $\mathbf{A}(L)^{-1}$.

5. Show that $[\mathbf{A}(L)\,\mathbf{B}(L)]^{-1} = \mathbf{B}(L)^{-1}\mathbf{A}(L)^{-1}$, provided that $\mathbf{A}_0$ and $\mathbf{B}_0$ are nonsingular. **Hint:** By definition, $\mathbf{A}(L)\mathbf{B}(L)[\mathbf{A}(L)\mathbf{B}(L)]^{-1} = \mathbf{I}$.

6.4 Estimating Autoregressions

Autoregressive processes (autoregressions) are popular in econometrics, not only because they have a natural interpretation but also because they are easy to estimate. This section considers the estimation of autoregressions. Estimation of ARMA processes will be touched upon at the end.

Estimation of AR(1)

Recall that an AR(1) is an MA(∞) with absolutely summable coefficients. So if $\{\varepsilon_t\}$ is independent white noise (an i.i.d. sequence with zero mean and finite variance), it is strictly stationary and ergodic (Proposition 6.1(d)). Letting $\mathbf{x}_t = (1, y_{t-1})'$ and $\boldsymbol{\beta} = (c, \phi)'$, the AR(1) equation (6.2.1) can be written as a regression equation

$$y_t = \mathbf{x}_t'\boldsymbol{\beta} + \varepsilon_t. \tag{6.4.1}$$

We assume the sample is $(y_0, y_1, y_2, \ldots, y_n)$, y_0 inclusive, so that (6.4.1) for $t = 1$ (which has y_0 on the right-hand side) can be included in the estimation. So the sample period is from $t = 1$ to n.

We now show that all the conditions of Proposition 2.5 about the asymptotic properties of the OLS estimator of $\boldsymbol{\beta}$ with conditional homoskedasticity are satisfied here. First, obviously, linearity (Assumption 2.1) is satisfied. Second, as just noted, $\{y_t, \mathbf{x}_t\}$ is jointly stationary and ergodic (Assumption 2.2). Third, since y_{t-1} (the nonconstant regressor in $\mathbf{x}_t$) is a function of $\{\varepsilon_{t-1}, \varepsilon_{t-2}, \ldots\}$, it is independent of the error term ε_t by the i.i.d. assumption for $\{\varepsilon_t\}$. Thus

$$\mathrm{E}(\varepsilon_t^2 \mid \mathbf{x}_t) = \sigma^2, \tag{6.4.2}$$

that is, the error is conditionally homoskedastic (Assumption 2.7). Fourth, if $\mathbf{g}_t \equiv \mathbf{x}_t \cdot \varepsilon_t = (\varepsilon_t, y_{t-1}\varepsilon_t)'$, $\{\mathbf{g}_t\}$ is a martingale difference sequence, as required in Assumption 2.5, because

$$\begin{aligned}
&\text{first element of } \mathrm{E}(\mathbf{g}_t \mid \mathbf{g}_{t-1}, \mathbf{g}_{t-2}, \ldots) \\
&= \mathrm{E}(\varepsilon_t \mid \mathbf{g}_{t-1}, \mathbf{g}_{t-2}, \ldots) \\
&= \mathrm{E}(\varepsilon_t \mid \varepsilon_{t-1}, \varepsilon_{t-2}, \ldots, y_{t-2}\varepsilon_{t-1}, y_{t-3}\varepsilon_{t-2}, \ldots) \\
&= 0 \quad (\text{since } \{\varepsilon_t\} \text{ is i.i.d. and } y_{t-j} \text{ is a function of } (\varepsilon_{t-j}, \varepsilon_{t-j-1}, \ldots))
\end{aligned}$$

and

$$\begin{aligned}
&\text{second element of } \mathrm{E}(\mathbf{g}_t \mid \mathbf{g}_{t-1}, \mathbf{g}_{t-2}, \dots) \\
&= \mathrm{E}(\varepsilon_t y_{t-1} \mid \mathbf{g}_{t-1}, \mathbf{g}_{t-2}, \dots) \\
&= \mathrm{E}[\mathrm{E}(\varepsilon_t y_{t-1} \mid y_{t-1}, \mathbf{g}_{t-1}, \mathbf{g}_{t-2}, \dots) \mid \mathbf{g}_{t-1}, \mathbf{g}_{t-2}, \dots] \\
&\qquad\qquad\qquad\qquad \text{(by the Law of Iterated Expectations)} \\
&= \mathrm{E}[y_{t-1}\, \mathrm{E}(\varepsilon_t \mid y_{t-1}, \mathbf{g}_{t-1}, \mathbf{g}_{t-2}, \dots) \mid \mathbf{g}_{t-1}, \mathbf{g}_{t-2}, \dots] \\
&= 0 \quad (\text{since } \mathrm{E}(\varepsilon_t \mid y_{t-1}, \varepsilon_{t-1}, \varepsilon_{t-2}, \dots, y_{t-2}\varepsilon_{t-1}, y_{t-3}\varepsilon_{t-2}, \dots) = 0). \qquad (6.4.3)
\end{aligned}$$

In particular, $\mathrm{E}(\varepsilon_t y_{t-1}) = 0$, so $\mathbf{x}_t$ is orthogonal to the error term (Assumption 2.3). Finally, the rank condition about the moment matrix $\mathrm{E}(\mathbf{x}_t\mathbf{x}_t')$ (Assumption 2.4) is satisfied because the determinant of

$$\mathrm{E}(\mathbf{x}_t\mathbf{x}_t') = \begin{bmatrix} 1 & \mu \\ \mu & \gamma_0 + \mu^2 \end{bmatrix} \qquad (6.4.4)$$

is $\gamma_0 > 0$. This also means that $\mathrm{E}(\mathbf{g}_t\mathbf{g}_t')$ is nonsingular because under conditional homoskedasticity $\mathrm{E}(\mathbf{g}_t\mathbf{g}_t') = \sigma^2\mathrm{E}(\mathbf{x}_t\mathbf{x}_t')$. So the nonsingularity condition in Assumption 2.5 is met.

Thus the AR(1) with an independent white noise process satisfies all the assumptions of Proposition 2.5, so parts (a)–(c) of the propositions hold true here, with $(c, \phi)'$ as $\boldsymbol{\beta}$, $(1, y_{t-1})'$ as $\mathbf{x}_t$, and σ^2 as the error variance. In particular, the OLS estimate of the error variance,

$$s^2 = \frac{1}{n-2}\sum_{t=1}^{n} e_t^2, \quad e_t \equiv y_t - \hat{c} - \hat{\phi} y_{t-1} \text{ where } (\hat{c}, \hat{\phi}) \text{ are OLS estimates,}$$

is consistent for σ^2.

Estimation of AR(p)

Similarly for AR(p), the autoregressive coefficients $(\phi_1, \dots, \phi_p)$ can be consistently estimated by regressing y_t on the constant and lagged y's, $(y_{t-1}, \dots, y_{t-p})$. We assume the sample is $(y_{-p+1}, y_{-p+2}, \dots, y_0, y_1, \dots, y_n)$, inclusive of p lagged values prior to y_1, so that the AR(p) equation for $t = 1$ can be included and the sample period is from $t = 1$ to n.

Proposition 6.7 (Estimation of AR coefficients): *Let $\{y_t\}$ be the AR(p) process following (6.2.6) with the stationarity condition (6.1.18). Suppose further that $\{\varepsilon_t\}$ is independent white noise. Then the OLS estimator of $(c, \phi_1, \phi_2, \dots, \phi_p)$*

obtained by regressing y_t on the constant and p lagged values of y for the sample period of $t = 1, 2, \ldots, n$ is consistent and asymptotically normal. Letting $\boldsymbol{\beta} = (c, \phi_1, \phi_2, \ldots, \phi_p)'$ and $\mathbf{x}_t = (1, y_{t-1}, \ldots, y_{t-p})'$, and $\widehat{\boldsymbol{\beta}}$ = OLS estimate of $\boldsymbol{\beta}$, we have

$$\text{Avar}(\widehat{\boldsymbol{\beta}}) = \sigma^2 \, \text{E}(\mathbf{x}_t \mathbf{x}_t')^{-1},$$

which is consistently estimated by

$$\widehat{\text{Avar}(\widehat{\boldsymbol{\beta}})} = s^2 \cdot \Big(\frac{1}{n}\sum_{t=1}^{n} \mathbf{x}_t \mathbf{x}_t'\Big)^{-1},$$

where s^2 is the OLS estimate of the error variance given by

$$s^2 = \frac{1}{n-p-1}\sum_{t=1}^{n}(y_t - \hat{c} - \hat{\phi}_1 y_{t-1} - \cdots - \hat{\phi}_p y_{t-p})^2. \tag{6.4.5}$$

The proof is to verify the assumptions of Proposition 2.5, which can be done in the same way as we did for AR(1). The only difficult part is to show that $\text{E}(\mathbf{x}_t \mathbf{x}_t')$ is nonsingular (Assumption 2.4), which is equivalent to requiring the $p \times p$ autocovariance matrix $\text{Var}(y_t, \ldots, y_{t-p+1})$ to be nonsingular (see Review Question 1(b) below). It can be shown that the autocovariance matrix of a covariance-stationary process is nonsingular for any p if $\gamma_0 > 0$ and $\gamma_j \to 0$ as $j \to \infty$.[6] So Assumption 2.4, too, is met.

We have not covered the maximum likelihood estimation of AR(p), but for those of you who are curious about the connection to ML, the OLS estimator is numerically the same as the conditional Gaussian ML estimator and asymptotically equivalent to the exact Gaussian ML estimator. See Section 8.7.

Choice of Lag Length

All these nice results about estimation of autoregressions assume that the order (the lag length) of autoregression, p, is known. How should we proceed if the order p is unknown? First of all, it is clear that Proposition 6.7, which is about p-th order autoregressions, is applicable to autoregressions of lower order, say $r < p$. That is, even if $\phi_r \neq 0$ but $\phi_{r+1} = \phi_{r+2} = \cdots = \phi_p = 0$, the proposition remains applicable as long as $(\phi_1, \phi_2, \ldots, \phi_r)$ satisfies the stationarity condition. In particular, the OLS estimates of $(\phi_{r+1}, \phi_{r+2}, \ldots, \phi_p)$ will converge to the true value of zero. To put the same argument differently, suppose that the true order of

[6]See, e.g., Proposition 5.1.1 of Brockwell and Davis (1991).

the autoregression is p (so $\phi_p \neq 0$) and suppose that all we know about p is that it is less than or equal to some known integer p_{max}. By setting the r in the argument just given to p and the p to p_{max}, we see that Proposition 6.7 is applicable to autoregressions with p_{max} lags: if the $\{y_t\}$ is stationary AR(p) and if we regress y_t on the constant and p_{max} lags of y, then the OLS coefficient estimates will be consistent and asymptotically normal.

It is natural to think that the true lag length may be estimated from this OLS estimate of $(\phi_1, \ldots, \phi_{p_{max}})$. We consider two classes of rules for determining the lag length. The first is the

General-to-specific sequential *t* rule: Start with an autoregression of p_{max} lags. If the last lag is significant at some prespecified significance level (say, 10 percent), then end the procedure and set the lag length to p_{max}. Otherwise drop the last lag, reestimate the autoregression with one fewer lag, and repeat the same test. If this process continues until there is only one lag in the autoregression and if that lag is insignificant, then set the lag length to 0 (no lags).

This rule has the following properties, to be illustrated in a moment. Since the t-test is consistent, the lag length thus chosen will never be less than p (the true lag length) in large samples. However, the probability of overfitting (that the lag length chosen is greater than the true lag length p) is not zero, even in large samples. That is, if $\hat{p}$ is the lag length chosen by the sequential t rule,

$$\lim_{n\to\infty} \text{Prob}(\hat{p} < p) = 0 \quad \text{and} \quad \lim_{n\to\infty} \text{Prob}(\hat{p} > p) > 0. \tag{6.4.6}$$

To illustrate, suppose $p = 2$ and $p_{max} = 3$. The sequential t rule starts out with three lags in the autoregression:

$$y_t = c + \phi_1 y_{t-1} + \phi_2 y_{t-2} + \phi_3 y_{t-3} + \varepsilon_t.$$

We test the null hypothesis that $\phi_3 = 0$ at the 10 percent significance level. With a probability of 10 percent, we reject the (true) null and set the lag length to 3, or accept the null with a probability of 90 percent, in large samples. In the event of accepting the null, we set $\phi_3 = 0$, estimate an autoregression with two lags, and test the hypothesis that $\phi_2 = 0$. Since $\phi_2 \neq 0$ in truth (i.e., since $p = 2$), the absolute value of the t-value on the OLS estimate of ϕ_2 would be very large in large samples, so we would never accept the (false) null that the second lag is zero. Therefore, in this example, $\text{Prob}(\hat{p} = 2) = 90\%$ and $\text{Prob}(\hat{p} = 3) = 10\%$ in large samples.

There are two minor variations in the choice of the sample period with data $(y_1, \ldots, y_n)$. One is to use the same sample period of $t = p_{max}+1, p_{max}+2, \ldots, n$

throughout. The other is to let the sample period be "elastic" by expanding it as fewer and fewer lags are included. That is, when the autoregression being estimated has j lags, the sample period is $t = j+1, j+2, \ldots, n$.

The second rule for selecting the lag length uses either the **Akaike information criterion** (AIC) or the **Schwartz information criterion** (SIC), also called the **Bayesian information criterion** (BIC). This procedure sets the lag length to the j that minimizes

$$\log(SSR_j/n) + (j+1)C(n)/n, \tag{6.4.7}$$

over $j = 0, 1, 2, \ldots, p_{max}$, where SSR_j is the sum of squared residuals for the autoregression with j lags. In this formula, "$j+1$" enters as the number of parameters (the coefficients of the constant and j lags). For the AIC, $C(n) = 2$ while for the BIC, $C(n) = \log(n)$. A few comments about this information-criterion-based rule:

- As the number of parameters increases with j, the first term of the objective function (6.4.7) declines because the fit of the equation gets better, but the second term increases. The information criterion strikes a balance between a better fit and model parsimony.

- Without an upper bound p_{max}, a ridiculously large value of j might be chosen (indeed, the information criterion achieves a minimum of $-\infty$ at $j+1 = n$ because $SSR_j = 0$ for $j = n-1$). In the present context where the true DGP is a finite-order autoregression, a reasonable upper bound is the maximum possible lag length.

- Again there can be two ways to set the sample period. You can use the fixed sample period of $t = p_{max}+1, p_{max}+2, \ldots, n$ throughout, in which case SSR_j is the sum of $n - p_{max}$ squared residuals. Or you can use the "elastic" sample period, in which case SSR_j is the sum of $n - j$ squared residuals. In either case, there is yet another variation, which is to replace the n in the information criterion (6.4.7) by the actual sample size. So you replace the n by $n - p_{max}$ if the fixed sample is to be used. Based on simulations and some theoretical considerations, Ng and Perron (2000) recommend the use of a fixed, rather than an "elastic," sample period, with $n - p_{max}$ replacing n in the information criterion.

Let $\hat{p}_{\text{AIC}}$ and $\hat{p}_{\text{BIC}}$ be the lag lengths chosen by the AIC and BIC, respectively. Like the lag length selected by the general-to-specific t rule, they are functions of data, and hence are random variables. For them it is possible to show the following (see, e.g., Lütkepohl, 1993, Section 4.3):

(1) $\hat{p}_{\text{BIC}} \leq \hat{p}_{\text{AIC}}$ unless the sample size is very small. (If the fixed sample of $t = p_{max} + 1, \ldots, n$ is used and "$n - p_{max}$" replaces n in (6.4.7), this is true for any finite sample with $n \geq p_{max} + 8$.) This is an algebraic result and holds for any sample on y.

(2) Suppose that $\{y_t\}$ is stationary AR(p) and $\{\varepsilon_t\}$ is independent white noise with a finite fourth moment. Then

$$\lim_{n\to\infty} \hat{p}_{\text{BIC}} = p, \quad \lim_{n\to\infty} \text{Prob}(\hat{p}_{\text{AIC}} < p) = 0, \quad \lim_{n\to\infty} \text{Prob}(\hat{p}_{\text{AIC}} > p) > 0. \tag{6.4.8}$$

That is, just like the general-to-specific sequential t rule, the AIC rule has a positive probability of overfitting. In contrast, the BIC rule is consistent. Furthermore, Hannan and Deistler (1988, Theorem 5.4.1(c) and its Remark 1) have shown that the consistency of $\hat{p}_{\text{BIC}}$ holds when the upper bound p_{max} is made to increase at a rate of $\log(n)$ (i.e., when it is set to $[c\log(n)]$ [the integer part of $c\log(n)$] for any given $c > 0$). This means that you do not need to know an upper bound in the consistent estimation by BIC of the order of an autoregression.

Estimation of VARs

Estimation of VAR coefficients is equally easy. If $\mathbf{y}_t$ is M-dimensional, the VAR(p) (6.3.9) is an M-equation system and can be written as

$$y_{tm} = \mathbf{x}_t'\boldsymbol{\delta}_m + \varepsilon_{tm} \quad (m = 1, 2, \ldots, M), \tag{6.4.9}$$

where y_{tm} is the m-th element of $\mathbf{y}_t$, ε_{tm} is the m-th element of $\boldsymbol{\varepsilon}_t$, and

$$\underset{(Mp+1)\times 1}{\mathbf{x}_t} = \begin{bmatrix} 1 \\ \mathbf{y}_{t-1} \\ \mathbf{y}_{t-2} \\ \vdots \\ \mathbf{y}_{t-p} \end{bmatrix}, \quad \boldsymbol{\delta}_m = \begin{bmatrix} c_m \\ \boldsymbol{\phi}_{1m} \\ \boldsymbol{\phi}_{2m} \\ \vdots \\ \boldsymbol{\phi}_{pm} \end{bmatrix},$$

$$c_m = m\text{-th element of } \mathbf{c}, \quad \boldsymbol{\phi}_{jm}' = m\text{-th row of } \boldsymbol{\Phi}_j.$$

So the M equations share the same set of regressors. It is easy to verify that $\mathbf{x}_t$ is orthogonal to the error term in each equation and that the error is conditionally homoskedastic (the proof is very similar to the proof for AR(p)). So the M-equation system with i.i.d. $\{\boldsymbol{\varepsilon}_t\}$ satisfies all the conditions for the multivariate regression model of Section 4.5. Thus, efficient GMM estimation is very easy:

just do equation-by-equation OLS. The expressions for the asymptotic variance and its consistent estimate can be obtained from Proposition 4.6 with $\mathbf{z}_{im} = \mathbf{x}_t$ (so (4.5.13′) on page 280 becomes $\frac{1}{n}\sum_t \mathbf{x}_t\mathbf{x}_t'$). If $\boldsymbol{\delta}$ is the $(Mp+1)M$-dimensional stacked vector created from $(\boldsymbol{\delta}_1, \dots, \boldsymbol{\delta}_M)$ and if $\hat{\boldsymbol{\delta}}$ is the equation-by-equation OLS estimate of $\boldsymbol{\delta}$, we have from (4.5.17)

$$\widehat{\text{Avar}(\hat{\boldsymbol{\delta}})} = \widehat{\boldsymbol{\Omega}} \otimes \left(\frac{1}{n}\sum_{t=1}^{n} \mathbf{x}_t\mathbf{x}_t'\right)^{-1}, \tag{6.4.10}$$

where

$$\widehat{\boldsymbol{\Omega}} \equiv \frac{1}{n - Mp - 1}\sum_{t=1}^{n} \hat{\boldsymbol{\varepsilon}}_t\hat{\boldsymbol{\varepsilon}}_t', \quad \hat{\boldsymbol{\varepsilon}}_t = \mathbf{y}_t - \hat{\mathbf{c}} - \widehat{\boldsymbol{\Phi}}_1\mathbf{y}_{t-1} - \cdots - \widehat{\boldsymbol{\Phi}}_p\mathbf{y}_{t-p}. \tag{6.4.11}$$

If we do not know the lag length p, we estimate it from data. In the information-criteria-based rule, the lag length we choose is the k that minimizes

$$\log\left(\left|\frac{1}{n}\sum_{t=1}^{n} \hat{\boldsymbol{\varepsilon}}_t\hat{\boldsymbol{\varepsilon}}_t'\right|\right) + (kM^2 + M)\cdot\frac{C(n)}{n}, \tag{6.4.12}$$

over $k = 0, 1, \dots, p_{max}$. Here, as in the univariate case, $C(n) = 2$ for the AIC and $\log(n)$ for the BIC. Exactly the same results, listed as (1) and (2) above for the univariate case, hold for the multivariate case (see, e.g, Lütkepohl, 1993, Section 4.3).

Estimation of ARMA(p, q)

Letting

$$u_t \equiv \varepsilon_t + \theta_1\varepsilon_{t-1} + \theta_2\varepsilon_{t-2} + \cdots + \theta_q\varepsilon_{t-q},$$
$$\mathbf{z}_t = (1, y_{t-1}, y_{t-2}, \dots, y_{t-p})', \quad \boldsymbol{\delta} = (c, \phi_1, \phi_2, \dots, \phi_p)',$$

the univariate ARMA(p, q) equation (6.2.9) can be written as

$$y_t = \mathbf{z}_t'\boldsymbol{\delta} + u_t. \tag{6.4.13}$$

The moving-average component of ARMA creates two problems. First, obviously, the error term u_t is serially correlated (in fact, it is MA(q)). Second, since the lagged dependent variables included in $\mathbf{z}_t$ are correlated with lags of ε included in the error term, the regressors $\mathbf{z}_t$ are not orthogonal to the error term u_t. That is, serial correlation in the presence of lagged dependent variables results in biased estimation. The second problem could be dealt with by using suitably lagged dependent variables $(y_{t-q-1}, y_{t-q-2}, \dots)$ as instruments. Regarding the first problem, the method to be developed later in this chapter provides consistent estimates of the coefficient vector in the presence of serial correlation. Given a consistent estimate of $\boldsymbol{\delta}$, the MA parameters (θ's) can be estimated from the residuals. This procedure, however, is not efficient.[7] We will not cover the topic of efficient estimation of ARMA(p, q) processes with Gaussian errors. Interested readers are referred to, e.g., Fuller (1996, Chapter 8) or Hamilton (1994, Chapter 5).

QUESTIONS FOR REVIEW

1. (Avar of AR coefficients)

   (a) For AR(1), show that

$$\text{Avar}(\hat{\phi}) = \frac{\sigma^2}{\gamma_0} = 1 - \phi^2,$$

   where $\hat{\phi}$ is the OLS estimator of ϕ. **Hint:** It is σ^2 times the (2, 2) element of the inverse of (6.4.4).

   (b) For AR(p), let $\hat{\boldsymbol{\phi}}$ be the OLS estimate of $(\phi_1, \phi_2, \dots, \phi_p)'$. Show that

$$\text{Avar}(\hat{\boldsymbol{\phi}}) = \sigma^2 \mathbf{V}^{-1},$$

   where $\mathbf{V}$ is the $p \times p$ autocovariance matrix

$$\mathbf{V} = \text{Var}(y_t, \dots, y_{t-p+1}) = \begin{bmatrix} \gamma_0 & \gamma_1 & \gamma_2 & \cdots & \gamma_{p-1} \\ \gamma_1 & \gamma_0 & \gamma_1 & \cdots & \gamma_{p-2} \\ \vdots & \ddots & \ddots & \ddots & \vdots \\ \gamma_{p-2} & \cdots & \gamma_1 & \gamma_0 & \gamma_1 \\ \gamma_{p-1} & \cdots & \gamma_2 & \gamma_1 & \gamma_0 \end{bmatrix}.$$

   Hint: If $\mathbf{x}_t$ is as in Proposition 6.7, then

$$\text{E}(\mathbf{x}_t \mathbf{x}_t') = \begin{bmatrix} 1 & \mu \mathbf{1}' \\ \mu \mathbf{1} & \mathbf{V} + \mu^2 \mathbf{1}\mathbf{1}' \end{bmatrix},$$

   where $\mathbf{1}$ is a $p \times 1$ vector of ones. Show that the inverse of this matrix is

[7] The model yields infinitely many orthogonality conditions, $\text{E}(u_t \cdot y_s) = 0$ for all $s \le t - q - 1$. The GMM procedure can exploit only finitely many orthogonality conditions.

given by

$$\mathbf{A} \equiv \begin{bmatrix} a & \mathbf{c}' \\ \mathbf{c} & \mathbf{V}^{-1} \end{bmatrix} \quad \text{where } a \equiv 1 + \mu^2 \mathbf{1}'\mathbf{V}^{-1}\mathbf{1},\ \mathbf{c} \equiv -\mu\mathbf{V}^{-1}\mathbf{1}.$$

This also shows that $\mathrm{E}(\mathbf{x}_t\mathbf{x}_t')$ is nonsingular if and only if $\mathbf{V}$ is. (If $\mathbf{V}$ is nonsingular, then $\mathrm{E}(\mathbf{x}_t\mathbf{x}_t')$ is nonsingular because it is invertible. If $\mathbf{V}$ is singular, then there exists a p-dimensional vector $\mathbf{d} \neq \mathbf{0}$ such that $\mathbf{V}\mathbf{d} = \mathbf{0}$ and $\mathrm{E}(\mathbf{x}_t\mathbf{x}_t')\mathbf{f} = \mathbf{0}$ where $\mathbf{f}' = (-\mu\mathbf{1}'\mathbf{d}, \mathbf{d}')$.)

2. (Estimated VAR(1) coefficients) Consider a VAR(1) without the intercept: $\mathbf{y}_t = \mathbf{A}\mathbf{y}_{t-1} + \boldsymbol{\varepsilon}_t$. Verify that the estimate of $\mathbf{A}$ by multivariate regression using the sample $(\mathbf{y}_1, \mathbf{y}_2, \ldots, \mathbf{y}_n)$ (so the sample period is $t = 2, 3, \ldots, n$) is

$$\widehat{\mathbf{A}} = \Big(\sum_{t=2}^{n} \mathbf{y}_t\mathbf{y}_{t-1}'\Big)\Big(\sum_{t=2}^{n} \mathbf{y}_{t-1}\mathbf{y}_{t-1}'\Big)^{-1}.$$

Hint: The coefficient vector in the m-th equation is the m-th *row* of $\mathbf{A}$.

6.5 Asymptotics for Sample Means of Serially Correlated Processes

This section studies the asymptotic properties of the sample mean

$$\bar{y} \equiv \frac{1}{n}\sum_{t=1}^{n} y_t$$

for serially correlated processes. (It should be kept in mind that $\bar{y}$ depends on n, although the notation does not make it explicit.) For the consistency of the sample mean, we already have a sufficient condition in the Ergodic Theorem of Chapter 2. The first proposition of this section provides another sufficient condition in the form of restrictions on covariance-stationary processes. We also provide two CLTs for serially correlated processes, one for linear processes and the other for ergodic stationary processes. Chapter 2 includes a CLT for ergodic stationary processes, but it rules out serial correlation because the process is assumed to be a martingale difference sequence. The CLT for ergodic stationary processes of this section generalizes it by allowing for serial correlation.

LLN for Covariance-Stationary Processes

Proposition 6.8 (LLN for covariance-stationary processes with vanishing autocovariances): *Let $\{y_t\}$ be covariance-stationary with mean μ and $\{\gamma_j\}$ be the autocovariances of $\{y_t\}$. Then*

(a) $\bar{y} \to_{\text{m.s.}} \mu$ *as* $n \to \infty$ *if* $\lim_{j\to\infty} \gamma_j = 0$.

(b)
$$\lim_{n\to\infty} \text{Var}(\sqrt{n}\,\bar{y}) = \sum_{j=-\infty}^{\infty} \gamma_j < \infty \quad \textit{if } \{\gamma_j\} \textit{ is summable.}^8 \tag{6.5.1}$$

Since a mean square convergence implies a convergence in probability, part (a) shows that a very mild condition on covariance-stationary processes suffices for the sample mean to be consistent for μ. To prove part (a), by Chebychev's LLN (see Section 2.1), it suffices to show that $\lim_{n\to\infty} \text{Var}(\bar{y}) = 0$, which is fairly easy (Analytical Exercise 9) once the expression for $\text{Var}(\bar{y})$ is derived. Unlike in the case without serial correlation in $\{y_t\}$, calculating the variance of $\bar{y}$ is more cumbersome because covariances between two different terms have to be taken into account:

$$\begin{aligned}
n \cdot \text{Var}(\bar{y}) &= \text{Var}(\sqrt{n}\,\bar{y}) \\
&= \frac{1}{n}[\text{Cov}(y_1, y_1 + \cdots + y_n) + \cdots + \text{Cov}(y_n, y_1 + \cdots + y_n)] \\
&= \frac{1}{n}\,[(\gamma_0 + \gamma_1 + \cdots + \gamma_{n-2} + \gamma_{n-1}) + (\gamma_1 + \gamma_0 + \gamma_1 + \cdots + \gamma_{n-2}) \\
&\qquad + \cdots + (\gamma_{n-1} + \gamma_{n-2} + \cdots + \gamma_1 + \gamma_0)] \\
&= \frac{1}{n}\,[n\gamma_0 + 2(n-1)\gamma_1 + \cdots + 2(n-j)\gamma_j + \cdots + 2\gamma_{n-1}] \\
&= \gamma_0 + 2\sum_{j=1}^{n-1}\Big(1 - \frac{j}{n}\Big)\gamma_j.
\end{aligned} \tag{6.5.2}$$

(If you have difficulty deriving this, set n to, say, 3 to verify.) For each fixed $j \geq 1$, the coefficient of γ_j in (6.5.2) goes to 1 as $n \to \infty$, so that all the autocovariances eventually enter the sum with a coefficient of one. This is not enough to show the desired result (6.5.1). Filling in the rest of the proof of (b) is Analytical Exercise 10.

For a covariance-stationary process $\{y_t\}$, we define the **long-run variance** to be the limit as $n \to \infty$ of $\text{Var}(\sqrt{n}\,\bar{y})$ (if it exists). So part (b) of the proposition says that the long-run variance equals $\sum_{j=-\infty}^{\infty} \gamma_j$, which in turn equals the value of

[8] Anderson (1971, Lemma 8.3.1, p. 460). Absolute summability of $\{\gamma_j\}$ is not needed.

the autocovariance-generating function $g_Y(z)$ at $z = 1$ (see (6.2.15)) or 2π times the spectrum at frequency zero (see (6.2.17)).

Two Central Limit Theorems

We present two CLTs to cover serial correlation. The first is a generalization of Lindeberg-Levy.

Proposition 6.9 (CLT for MA(∞)): *Let* $y_t = \mu + \sum_{j=0}^{\infty} \psi_j \varepsilon_{t-j}$ *where* $\{\varepsilon_t\}$ *is independent white noise and* $\sum_{j=0}^{n} |\psi_j| < \infty$. *Then*

$$\sqrt{n}\,(\bar{y} - \mu) \underset{d}{\rightarrow} N\Big(0, \sum_{j=-\infty}^{\infty} \gamma_j\Big). \tag{6.5.3}$$

We will not prove this result (see Anderson, 1971, Theorem 7.7.8 or Brockwell and Davis, 1991, Theorem 7.1.2 for a proof), but we should not be surprised to see that $\text{Avar}(\bar{y})$ (the variance of the limiting distribution of $\sqrt{n}\,(\bar{y} - \mu)$) equals the long-run variance $\sum_{j=-\infty}^{\infty} \gamma_j$. We know from Lemma 2.1 that "$x_n \rightarrow_d x$," "$\text{Var}(x_n) \rightarrow c < \infty$" $\Rightarrow$ "$\text{Var}(x) = c$." Here, set $x_n = \sqrt{n}\,(\bar{y} - \mu)$. By (6.5.1), $\text{Var}(x_n)$ converges to a finite limit $\sum \gamma_j$. So the variance of the limiting distribution of $\sqrt{n}\,(\bar{y} - \mu)$ is $\sum \gamma_j$.

By Proposition 6.1(d), the process in Proposition 6.9 is (stationary and) ergodic. Remember that ergodicity limits serial correlation by requiring that two random variables sufficiently far apart in the sequence be almost independent. But ergodic stationarity alone is not sufficient to ensure the asymptotic normality of $\bar{y}$. A natural question arises: is there a further restriction on ergodicity, short of requiring the process to be linear as in Proposition 6.9, that delivers asymptotic normality? The restriction that has become increasingly popular is what this book calls **Gordin's condition** for ergodic stationary processes. It has three parts. The first two parts follow:

(a) $\text{E}(y_t^2) < \infty$. (This is a restriction on [strictly] stationary processes because, strictly speaking, a stationary process might not have finite second moments.)

(b) $\text{E}(y_t \mid y_{t-j}, y_{t-j-1}, \ldots) \rightarrow_{\text{m.s.}} 0$ as $j \rightarrow \infty$. (Since $\{y_t\}$ is stationary, this condition is equivalent to $\text{E}(y_0 \mid y_{-j}, y_{-j-1}, \ldots) \rightarrow_{\text{m.s.}} 0$ as $j \rightarrow \infty$. Because $\text{E}(y_t \mid y_{t-j}, y_{t-j-1}, \ldots)$ is a random variable, the convergence cannot be the usual convergence for real numbers.)

This condition implies that the unconditional mean is zero, $\mathrm{E}(y_t) = 0$.[9] As the forecast (the conditional expectation) is based on less and less information, it should approach the forecast based on no information, i.e., the unconditional expectation. To prepare for the third part, let $I_t \equiv (y_t, y_{t-1}, y_{t-2}, \dots)$ and write y_t as

$$\begin{aligned} y_t &= y_t - [\mathrm{E}(y_t \mid I_{t-1}) - \mathrm{E}(y_t \mid I_{t-1})] - [\mathrm{E}(y_t \mid I_{t-2}) - \mathrm{E}(y_t \mid I_{t-2})] - \cdots \\ &\qquad - [\mathrm{E}(y_t \mid I_{t-j}) - \mathrm{E}(y_t \mid I_{t-j})] \\ &= [y_t - \mathrm{E}(y_t \mid I_{t-1})] + [\mathrm{E}(y_t \mid I_{t-1}) - \mathrm{E}(y_t \mid I_{t-2})] + \cdots \\ &\qquad + [\mathrm{E}(y_t \mid I_{t-j+1}) - \mathrm{E}(y_t \mid I_{t-j})] + \mathrm{E}(y_t \mid I_{t-j}) \\ &= (r_{t0} + r_{t1} + \cdots + r_{t,j-1}) + \mathrm{E}(y_t \mid y_{t-j}, y_{t-j-1}, \dots) \end{aligned}$$

where

$$r_{tk} \equiv \mathrm{E}(y_t \mid I_{t-k}) - \mathrm{E}(y_t \mid I_{t-k-1}).$$

This r_{tk} is the revision of expectations about y_t as the information set increases from I_{t-k-1} to I_{t-k}. By (b), $y_t - (r_{t0} + r_{t1} + \cdots + r_{t,j-1})$ converges in mean square to zero as $j \to \infty$ for each t. So y_t can be written as

$$y_t = \sum_{j=0}^{\infty} r_{tj}.$$

This sum is called the **telescoping sum**. The third part of Gordin's condition is

(c) $\displaystyle\sum_{j=0}^{\infty} [\mathrm{E}(r_{tj}^2)]^{1/2} < \infty.$

The telescoping sum indicates how the "shocks" represented by $(r_{t0}, r_{t1}, \dots)$ influence the current value of y. Condition (c) says, roughly speaking, that shocks that occurred a long time ago do not have disproportionately large influence. As such, the condition restricts the extent of serial correlation in $\{y_t\}$.

To understand the condition, take for example a zero-mean AR(1) with independent errors:

$$y_t = \phi y_{t-1} + \varepsilon_t, \quad |\phi| < 1, \quad \{\varepsilon_t\} \text{ independent white noise with } \sigma^2 = \mathrm{Var}(\varepsilon_t).$$

Evidently, Gordin's condition (a) is satisfied. Condition (b) too is satisfied because

[9] See Lemma 5.14 of White (1984) for a proof.

$$\mathrm{E}(y_t \mid y_{t-j}, y_{t-j-1}, \dots) = \phi^j y_{t-j} \tag{6.5.4}$$

and $\mathrm{E}[(\phi^j y_{t-j})^2] \to 0$ as $j \to \infty$. The expectation revision r_{tj} can be written as

$$r_{tj} = \phi^j y_{t-j} - \phi^{j+1} y_{t-j-1} = \phi^j (y_{t-j} - \phi y_{t-j-1}) = \phi^j \varepsilon_{t-j}. \tag{6.5.5}$$

So the telescoping sum for AR(1) is the MA(∞) representation. Condition (c) is satisfied because $[\mathrm{E}(r_{tj}^2)]^{1/2} = |\phi|^j \sigma$ and

$$\sum_{j=0}^{\infty} |\phi|^j \sigma = \frac{\sigma}{1 - |\phi|} < \infty.$$

The CLT we have been seeking is

Proposition 6.10 (Gordin's CLT for zero-mean ergodic stationary processes):[10] *Suppose $\{y_t\}$ is stationary and ergodic and suppose Gordin's condition is satisfied. Then $\mathrm{E}(y_t) = 0$, the autocovariances $\{\gamma_j\}$ are absolutely summable, and*

$$\sqrt{n}\,\bar{y} \underset{\mathrm{d}}{\to} N\Big(0, \sum_{j=-\infty}^{\infty} \gamma_j\Big).$$

Since Gordin's condition is satisfied if $\{y_t\}$ is a martingale difference sequence, which exhibits no serial correlation, Proposition 6.10 is a generalization of the ergodic stationary Martingale Difference Sequence CLT of Chapter 2.

Multivariate Extension

Extension of the above results to the multivariate case is straightforward. Let

$$\bar{\mathbf{y}} \equiv \frac{1}{n} \sum_{t=1}^{n} \mathbf{y}_t$$

be the sample mean of a vector process $\{\mathbf{y}_t\}$.

- The multivariate version of Proposition 6.8 is that
  (a) $\bar{\mathbf{y}} \to_{\text{m.s.}} \boldsymbol{\mu}$ if each diagonal element of $\boldsymbol{\Gamma}_j$ goes to zero as $j \to \infty$, and
  (b) $\lim_{n\to\infty} \mathrm{Var}(\sqrt{n}\,\bar{\mathbf{y}})$ (which is the **long-run covariance matrix** of $\{\mathbf{y}_t\}$) equals $\sum_{j=-\infty}^{\infty} \boldsymbol{\Gamma}_j$ if $\{\boldsymbol{\Gamma}_j\}$ is summable (i.e., if each component of $\boldsymbol{\Gamma}_j$ is summable).

[10] This result is due to Gordin (1969), restated as Theorem 5.15 of White (1984). The claim about the absolute summability of autocovariances is noted in footnote 19 of Hansen (1982).

- Therefore, the long-run covariance matrix of $\{\mathbf{y}_t\}$ can be written as

$$\mathbf{G_Y}(1) = 2\pi \mathbf{s}_Y(0) = \sum_{j=-\infty}^{\infty} \mathbf{\Gamma}_j = \mathbf{\Gamma}_0 + \sum_{j=1}^{\infty}(\mathbf{\Gamma}_j + \mathbf{\Gamma}'_j), \tag{6.5.6}$$

where $\mathbf{G_Y}(z)$ (the autocovariance-generating function) and $\mathbf{s}_Y(\omega)$ (the spectrum) for the vector process $\{\mathbf{y}_t\}$ are defined in Section 6.3.

- The multivariate version of Proposition 6.9 is that

$$\sqrt{n}\,(\bar{\mathbf{y}} - \boldsymbol{\mu}) \underset{\text{d}}{\to} N\Big(\mathbf{0}, \sum_{j=-\infty}^{\infty} \mathbf{\Gamma}_j\Big) \tag{6.5.7}$$

if $\{\mathbf{y}_t\}$ is vector MA(∞) with absolutely summable coefficients and $\{\boldsymbol{\varepsilon}_t\}$ is vector independent white noise.

- The multivariate extension of Gordin's condition on ergodic stationary processes is obvious:[11]

Gordin's condition on ergodic stationary processes

(a) $\mathrm{E}(\mathbf{y}_t\mathbf{y}'_t)$ *exists and is finite.*

(b) $\mathrm{E}(\mathbf{y}_t \mid \mathbf{y}_{t-j}, \mathbf{y}_{t-j-1}, \dots) \to_{\text{m.s.}} \mathbf{0}$ *as* $j \to \infty$.

(c) $\sum_{j=0}^{\infty} [\mathrm{E}(\mathbf{r}'_{tj}\mathbf{r}_{tj})]^{1/2}$ *is finite, where*

$$\mathbf{r}_{tj} \equiv \mathrm{E}(\mathbf{y}_t \mid \mathbf{y}_{t-j}, \mathbf{y}_{t-j-1}, \dots) - \mathrm{E}(\mathbf{y}_t \mid \mathbf{y}_{t-j-1}, \mathbf{y}_{t-j-2}, \dots).$$

- The multivariate version of Proposition 6.10 is obvious: Suppose Gordin's condition holds for vector ergodic stationary process $\{\mathbf{y}_t\}$. Then $\mathrm{E}(\mathbf{y}_t) = \mathbf{0}$, $\{\mathbf{\Gamma}_j\}$ is absolutely summable, and

$$\sqrt{n}\,\bar{\mathbf{y}} \underset{\text{d}}{\to} N\Big(\mathbf{0}, \sum_{j=-\infty}^{\infty} \mathbf{\Gamma}_j\Big). \tag{6.5.8}$$

QUESTIONS FOR REVIEW

1. Show that $\mathrm{Var}(\sqrt{n}\,\bar{y}) = \mathbf{1}'\,\mathrm{Var}(y_t, y_{t-1}, \dots, y_{t-n+1})\mathbf{1}/n$, where $\mathrm{Var}(y_t, y_{t-1}, \dots, y_{t-n+1})$ is the $n \times n$ autocovariance matrix of a covariance-stationary process $\{y_t\}$.

[11] Stated as Assumption 3.5 in Hansen (1982).

2. (Avar($\bar{y}$) for MA(∞)) Verify that Avar($\bar{y}$) for the MA(∞) process in Proposition 6.9 equals

$$\sigma^2 \cdot \Big(\sum_{j=0}^{\infty} \psi_j\Big)^2.$$

Hint: It should equal $g_Y(1)$ for MA(∞).

3. (Asymptotics of $\bar{y}$ for AR(1)) Consider the AR(1) process $y_t = c + \phi y_{t-1} + \varepsilon_t$ with $|\phi| < 1$. Does $\bar{y} \to_{\text{p}} \mu$? Add the assumption that $\{\varepsilon_t\}$ is an independent white noise process. Calculate Avar($\bar{y}$). [Answer: $[(1+\phi)/(1-\phi)]\gamma_0$.]

4. (Long-run covariance matrix of filtered series) Let $\mathbf{H}(L) = \mathbf{H}_0 + \mathbf{H}_1 L$ and $\{\mathbf{x}_t\}$ be covariance-stationary with absolutely summable autocovariances. Verify that the long-run covariance matrix of $\mathbf{y}_t = \mathbf{H}(L)\,\mathbf{x}_t$ is given by

$$(\mathbf{H}_0 + \mathbf{H}_1)\,\mathbf{G}_{\mathbf{x}}(1)\,(\mathbf{H}_0' + \mathbf{H}_1').$$

Hint: Use (6.3.13) and (6.5.6).

5. (Long-run variance of "unit-root MA" processes) What is the long-run variance of $y_t = \varepsilon_t - \varepsilon_{t-1}$, where ε_t is white noise? [Answer: zero.]

6.6 Incorporating Serial Correlation in GMM

The Model and Asymptotic Results

We have now all the tools needed to introduce serial correlation in the single-equation GMM model of Chapter 3. Recall that $\mathbf{g}_t$ in Chapter 3 (with the subscript "i" replaced by "t") is a K-dimensional vector defined as $\mathbf{x}_t \cdot \varepsilon_t$, the product of the K-dimensional vector of instruments $\mathbf{x}_t$ and the scalar error term ε_t. By Assumption 3.3 (orthogonality conditions), the mean of $\mathbf{g}_t$ is zero. We assumed in Assumption 3.5 that $\{\mathbf{g}_t\}$ was a martingale difference sequence. Since no serial correlation is allowed under this assumption, the matrix $\mathbf{S}$, defined to be the asymptotic variance of $\bar{\mathbf{g}}$ ($\equiv \frac{1}{n}\sum_{t=1}^{n} \mathbf{g}_t$), was simply the variance of $\mathbf{g}_t$. We can now allow for serial correlation in $\{\mathbf{g}_t\}$ by relaxing Assumption 3.5 as

Assumption 3.5′ (Gordin's condition restricting the degree of serial correlation): $\{\mathbf{g}_t\}$ *satisfies Gordin's condition. Its long-run covariance matrix is nonsingular.*

Then by the multivariate version of Proposition 6.10, $\sqrt{n}\,\bar{\mathbf{g}}$ converges to a normal distribution. The variance of this limiting distribution (namely, Avar($\bar{\mathbf{g}}$)), denoted $\mathbf{S}$, equals the long-run covariance matrix,

$$\mathbf{S} = \sum_{j=-\infty}^{\infty} \boldsymbol{\Gamma}_j = \boldsymbol{\Gamma}_0 + \sum_{j=1}^{\infty} (\boldsymbol{\Gamma}_j + \boldsymbol{\Gamma}_j'), \tag{6.6.1}$$

where $\boldsymbol{\Gamma}_j$ is the j-th order autocovariance matrix

$$\boldsymbol{\Gamma}_j = \mathrm{E}(\mathbf{g}_t \mathbf{g}_{t-j}') \quad (j = 0, \pm 1, \pm 2, \dots). \tag{6.6.2}$$

(Since $\mathrm{E}(\mathbf{g}_t) = \mathbf{0}$ by the orthogonality conditions, there is no need to subtract the mean from $\mathbf{g}_t$.)

That is, $\mathbf{S}$ ($\equiv$ Avar($\bar{\mathbf{g}}$)) equals $\boldsymbol{\Gamma}_0$ under Assumption 3.5 and $\sum_{j=-\infty}^{\infty} \boldsymbol{\Gamma}_j$ under Assumption 3.5′. This is the *only* difference between the GMM model with and without serial correlation. Accordingly, all the results we developed in Sections 3.5–3.7 carry over, provided that $\mathbf{S}$ is now given by (6.6.1) and $\widehat{\mathbf{S}}$, some consistent estimation of $\mathbf{S}$, is redefined to take into account serial correlation. More specifically:

- The GMM estimator $\hat{\boldsymbol{\delta}}(\widehat{\mathbf{W}})$ remains consistent and asymptotically normal. Its asymptotic variance is consistently estimated by (3.5.2), provided that the $\widehat{\mathbf{S}}$ there is consistent for $\mathbf{S}$ defined in (6.6.1). This estimated asymptotic variance sometimes gets the adjective heteroskedasticity and autocorrelation consistent (**HAC**).

- The GMM estimator achieves the minimum variance when $\text{plim}_{n\to\infty} \widehat{\mathbf{W}} = \mathbf{S}^{-1}$ where $\mathbf{S}$ is given by (6.6.1).

- The two-step procedure described in Section 3.5 still provides an efficient GMM estimator, provided that $\widehat{\mathbf{S}}$ calculated in *Step 1* is consistent for $\mathbf{S}$.

- With $\widehat{\mathbf{S}}$ thus properly defined, the expressions for the t, W, J, C, and LR statistics of Sections 3.5–3.7 remain valid; those statistics retain the same asymptotic distributions in the presence of serial correlation.

Estimating S When Autocovariances Vanish after Finite Lags

All these results assume that you have a consistent estimate, $\widehat{\mathbf{S}}$, of the long-run variance matrix $\mathbf{S}$. Obtaining such an estimate takes some intellectual effort, particularly when autocovariances do not vanish after finite lags.

We start our quest with consistent estimation of individual autocovariances. The natural estimator is

$$\widehat{\mathbf{\Gamma}}_j = \frac{1}{n} \sum_{t=j+1}^{n} \hat{\mathbf{g}}_t \hat{\mathbf{g}}'_{t-j} \quad (j = 0, 1, \ldots, n-1) \tag{6.6.3}$$

where

$$\hat{\mathbf{g}}_t \equiv \mathbf{x}_t \cdot \hat{\varepsilon}_t, \quad \hat{\varepsilon}_t = y_t - \mathbf{z}_t' \hat{\boldsymbol{\delta}}, \quad \hat{\boldsymbol{\delta}} \text{ consistent for } \boldsymbol{\delta}.$$

If we had the true value $\mathbf{g}_t$ in place of the estimated value $\hat{\mathbf{g}}_t$ in this formula, then $\widehat{\mathbf{\Gamma}}_j$ would be consistent for $\mathbf{\Gamma}_j$ under Assumptions 3.1 and 3.2, the assumptions implying ergodic stationarity for $\{\mathbf{g}_t\}$. But we have to use the estimated series $\{\hat{\mathbf{g}}_t\}$ rather than the true series to calculate autocovariances. For this reason we need some suitable fourth-moment condition (which we will not bother to state) for the estimated autocovariances to be consistent. The proof of consistency is not given here because it is very similar to the proof of Proposition 3.4.

Given the estimated autocovariances, there are two cases to consider for the calculation of $\widehat{\mathbf{S}}$. If we know *a priori* that $\mathbf{\Gamma}_j = \mathbf{0}$ for $j > q$ where q is known and finite, then clearly $\mathbf{S}$ can be consistently estimated by

$$\widehat{\mathbf{S}} = \widehat{\mathbf{\Gamma}}_0 + \sum_{j=1}^{q} (\widehat{\mathbf{\Gamma}}_j + \widehat{\mathbf{\Gamma}}_j') = \sum_{j=-q}^{q} \widehat{\mathbf{\Gamma}}_j \quad (\text{recall: } \widehat{\mathbf{\Gamma}}_{-j} = \widehat{\mathbf{\Gamma}}_j'). \tag{6.6.4}$$

More difficult is the other case where we do not know q (which may or may not be infinite). How can we estimate the long-run variance matrix, which involves possibly infinitely many parameters? There are two approaches.

Using Kernels to Estimate S

Recently, several procedures have been proposed to estimate the long-run variance matrix $\mathbf{S}$.[12] A class of estimators, called the **kernel-based** (or "nonparametric") **estimators**, can be expressed as a weighted average of estimated autocovariances:

$$\widehat{\mathbf{S}} = \sum_{j=-n+1}^{n-1} k\left(\frac{j}{q(n)}\right) \cdot \widehat{\mathbf{\Gamma}}_j. \tag{6.6.5}$$

[12]For the results to be stated in this and the next subsection to hold, we need to impose a set of technical conditions (in addition to Gordin's condition above) that further restrict the nature of serial correlation. For a statement of those conditions and a more detailed discussion of the subject treated in this and the next subsection, see Den Haan and Levin (1996b).

Here, the function $k(\cdot)$, which gives weights for autocovariances, is called a **kernel** and $q(n)$ is called the **bandwidth**. The bandwidth can depend on the sample size n. The estimator (6.6.4) above is a special kernel-based estimator with $q(n) = q$ and

$$k(x) = \begin{cases} 1 & \text{for } |x| \leq 1, \\ 0 & \text{for } |x| > 1. \end{cases} \tag{6.6.6}$$

This kernel is called the **truncated kernel**. In the present case of unknown q, we could use the truncated kernel with a bandwidth $q(n)$ that increases with the sample size. As $q(n)$ increases to infinity, more and more (and ultimately all) autocovariances can be included in the calculation of $\widehat{\mathbf{S}}$. This truncated kernel-based $\widehat{\mathbf{S}}$, however, is not guaranteed to be positive semidefinite in finite samples. This is a problem because then the estimated asymptotic variance of the GMM estimator may not be positive semidefinite.

Newey and West (1987) noted that the kernel-based estimator can be made nonnegative definite in finite samples if the kernel is the **Bartlett kernel**:

$$k(x) = \begin{cases} 1 - |x| & \text{for } |x| \leq 1, \\ 0 & \text{for } |x| > 1. \end{cases} \tag{6.6.7}$$

The Bartlett kernel-based estimator of $\mathbf{S}$ is called (in econometrics) the **Newey-West estimator**. For example, for $q(n) = 3$, the kernel-based estimator includes autocovariances up to two (*not* three) lags:

$$\widehat{\mathbf{S}} = \widehat{\mathbf{\Gamma}}_0 + \left(\frac{2}{3}\right)(\widehat{\mathbf{\Gamma}}_1 + \widehat{\mathbf{\Gamma}}_1') + \left(\frac{1}{3}\right)(\widehat{\mathbf{\Gamma}}_2 + \widehat{\mathbf{\Gamma}}_2'). \tag{6.6.8}$$

In his definitive treatment of kernel-based estimation of the long-run variance, Andrews (1991) has examined positive semidefinite kernels, namely, the class of kernels (including Bartlett's) that yield a positive semidefinite $\widehat{\mathbf{S}}$. He shows, under some suitable regularity conditions, how the speed at which $\widehat{\mathbf{S}}$ converges (in mean square) to $\mathbf{S}$ depends on the kernel and $q(n)$. The most rapid possible rate is $n^{2/5}$ (i.e., $n^{2/5} \cdot (\widehat{\mathbf{S}} - \mathbf{S})$ remains stochastically bounded),[13] which occurs when $q(n)$ grows at rate $n^{1/5}$ (i.e., $q(n)/n^{1/5}$ remains bounded) and the kernel is a member of a certain subset of positive semidefinite kernels. The Bartlett kernel is not in this subset. For Bartlett, the most rapid possible rate is $n^{1/3}$ which occurs when $q(n)$ grows at rate $n^{1/3}$. Therefore, at least on asymptotic grounds, positive semidefinite

[13] A sequence of random variables $\{x_n\}$ is said to be **stochastically bounded** and written $x_n = O_p$ if for any ε there exists an $M > 0$ such that $\text{Prob}(|x_n| > M) < \varepsilon$ for all n. If a sequence converges in distribution to a random variable, then the sequence is stochastically bounded.

kernels in this subset should be preferred to Bartlett. An example of such kernels is the **quadratic spectral (QS)** kernel:

$$k(x) = \frac{25}{12\pi^2 x^2}\left(\frac{\sin(6\pi x/5)}{6\pi x/5} - \cos(6\pi x/5)\right). \tag{6.6.9}$$

Since $k(x) \neq 0$ for $|x| > 1$ in the QS kernel, all the estimated autocovariances $\widehat{\mathbf{\Gamma}}_j$ ($j = 0, 1, \dots, n-1$) enter the calculation of $\widehat{\mathbf{S}}$ even if $q(n) < n - 1$.

To be sure, the knowledge of the growth rate is not enough to determine the value of the bandwidth for any particular data of finite length. Andrews (1991) also considered a data-dependent formula for determining the bandwidth that not only grows at the optimal rate but also minimizes some appropriate criterion (the asymptotic mean square error). But even in this formula, some parameter values need to be provided by the user, so the formula does not really provide automatic data-based selection of the bandwidth.

VARHAC

The other procedure for estimating **S**, called the VAR Heteroskedasticity and Autocorrelation Consistent (**VARHAC**) estimator, was proposed by Den Haan and Levin (1996a). The idea is to fit a finite-order VAR to the K-dimensional series $\{\hat{\mathbf{g}}_t\}$ and then construct the long-run covariance matrix implied by the estimated VAR. This is not to say that $\mathbf{g}_t$ is assumed to be a finite-order VAR. In fact, in this procedure (and also in the kernel-based procedure), $\mathbf{g}_t$ does not even have to be a linear process, let alone a finite-order autoregression. The VARHAC procedure consists of two steps.

Step 1: ***Lag length selection for each VAR equation.*** In this step, for each VAR equation, you determine the lag length by the Bayesian information criterion (BIC). Let $\hat{g}_{kt}$ be the k-th element of the K-dimensional vector $\hat{\mathbf{g}}_t$. The k-th VAR equation can be written as

$$\begin{aligned}
\hat{g}_{kt} &= \phi_{11}^{(k)}\hat{g}_{1,t-1} + \phi_{12}^{(k)}\hat{g}_{1,t-2} + \cdots + \phi_{1p}^{(k)}\hat{g}_{1,t-p} \\
&\quad + \phi_{21}^{(k)}\hat{g}_{2,t-1} + \phi_{22}^{(k)}\hat{g}_{2,t-2} + \cdots + \phi_{2p}^{(k)}\hat{g}_{2,t-p} \\
&\quad \dots \\
&\quad + \phi_{K1}^{(k)}\hat{g}_{K,t-1} + \phi_{K2}^{(k)}\hat{g}_{K,t-2} + \cdots + \phi_{Kp}^{(k)}\hat{g}_{K,t-p} + e_{kt} \\
&= \boldsymbol{\phi}_1^{(k)}\hat{\mathbf{g}}_{t-1} + \cdots + \boldsymbol{\phi}_p^{(k)}\hat{\mathbf{g}}_{t-p} + e_{kt},
\end{aligned} \tag{6.6.10}$$

where

$$\underset{(1\times K)}{\boldsymbol{\phi}_j^{(k)}} = (\phi_{1j}^{(k)}, \dots, \phi_{Kj}^{(k)}) \quad (j = 1, 2, \dots, p).$$

In picking the lag length by the BIC, the maximum lag length p_{max} needs to be specified. In Section 6.4, when the BIC was introduced in the context of estimating the true order (lag length) of a finite-order autoregression, p_{max} was set to some integer known to be greater than or equal to the true lag length. In the present case where $\mathbf{g}_t$ is not necessarily a finite-order VAR, Den Haan and Levin (1996a, Theorem 2(c)) show that the VARHAC estimator is consistent for $\mathbf{S}$ when p_{max} grows at rate $n^{1/3}$ and recommend setting p_{max} to $[n^{1/3}]$ (the integer part of $n^{1/3}$). To emphasize its dependence on the sample size, we denote the maximum lag length by $p_{max}(n)$. Let $SSR_p^{(k)}$ be the sum of squared residuals (SSR) from the OLS estimation of (6.6.10) (the k-th equation in the VAR) for $t = p_{max}(n) + 1, p_{max}(n) + 2, \dots, n$.[14] For $p = 0$, $SSR_p^{(k)} = \sum_{t=p_{max}(n)+1}^{n} (\hat{g}_{kt})^2$, the SSR from the regression of $\hat{g}_{kt}$ on no regressors. Since there are pK coefficients in the k-th equation, the BIC criterion is

$$\log(SSR_p^{(k)}/n) + pK \cdot \log(n)/n. \tag{6.6.11}$$

(The n in this expression could be replaced by the actual sample size $n - p_{max}$ with no asymptotic consequences.) Let $p(k)$ be the p that minimizes the information criterion over $p = 0, 1, \dots, p_{max}(n)$ for the k-th VAR equation. Also let $\hat{\boldsymbol{\phi}}_j^{(k)}$ $(j = 1, 2, \dots, p(k))$ be the OLS estimate of the VAR coefficients $\boldsymbol{\phi}_j^{(k)}$ $(j = 1, 2, \dots, p(k))$ when (6.6.10) is estimated by OLS for $p = p(k)$.

Step 2:* *Calculating the implied long-run variance. Let

$$P \equiv \max\{p(1), p(2), \dots, p(K)\},$$

the largest lag length in the K equations. By construction, $P \le p_{max}(n)$. *Step 1* produces an estimated VAR which can be written as

$$\underset{(K\times 1)}{\hat{\mathbf{g}}_t} = \underset{(K\times K)}{\widehat{\boldsymbol{\Phi}}_1}\underset{(K\times 1)}{\hat{\mathbf{g}}_{t-1}} + \cdots + \underset{(K\times K)}{\widehat{\boldsymbol{\Phi}}_P}\underset{(K\times 1)}{\hat{\mathbf{g}}_{t-P}} + \underset{(K\times 1)}{\hat{\mathbf{e}}_t}$$

$$(t = p_{max}(n) + 1, p_{max}(n) + 2, \dots, n). \tag{6.6.12}$$

[14] So the sample period is fixed throughout the process of picking the lag length.

Since the lag length differs across equations, some rows of $\widehat{\mathbf{\Phi}}_p$ ($p = 1, 2, \ldots, P$) may be zero. The rows of $\widehat{\mathbf{\Phi}}_p$ are related to $\hat{\boldsymbol{\phi}}_j^{(k)}$ ($j = 1, 2, \ldots, p(k)$) obtained in *Step 1* as

$$k\text{-th row of } \underset{(K\times K)}{\widehat{\mathbf{\Phi}}_p} = \begin{cases} \hat{\boldsymbol{\phi}}_p^{(k)} & \text{for } 1 \le p \le p(k), \\ \mathbf{0} & \text{for } p(k) < p \le P. \end{cases} \tag{6.6.13}$$

Let $\widehat{\mathbf{\Omega}}$ be the VAR residual variance matrix:

$$\underset{(K\times K)}{\widehat{\mathbf{\Omega}}} \equiv \frac{1}{n} \sum_{t=p_{max}(n)+1}^{n} \hat{\mathbf{e}}_t \hat{\mathbf{e}}_t'. \tag{6.6.14}$$

Recall that the long-run variance matrix of a VAR is given by (6.3.16) for $z = 1$. The estimator of $\mathbf{S}$ implied by the estimated VAR (6.6.12) is then

$$\widehat{\mathbf{S}} = \left[\mathbf{I}_K - \sum_{p=1}^{P} \widehat{\mathbf{\Phi}}_p\right]^{-1} \widehat{\mathbf{\Omega}} \left[\mathbf{I}_K - \sum_{p=1}^{P} \widehat{\mathbf{\Phi}}_p'\right]^{-1}. \tag{6.6.15}$$

This VARHAC estimator is positive semidefinite by construction. Den Haan and Levin (1996a) show that (under suitable regularity conditions) the estimator converges to $\mathbf{S}$ at a faster rate than any positive semidefinite kernel-based estimator for almost all autocovariance structures of $\mathbf{g}_t$ (which is not necessarily a finite-order VAR). In particular, if $\mathbf{g}_t$ is finite-order VARMA, then the lag order chosen by the BIC grows at a logarithmic rate and the VARHAC estimator converges at a rate arbitrarily close to $n^{1/2}$, which is faster than the maximum rate $n^{2/5}$ achieved by positive semidefinite kernel-based estimators.

QUESTIONS FOR REVIEW

1. When $\mathbf{x}_t = \mathbf{z}_t$, what is the efficient GMM estimator?

2. (Consequence of ignoring serial correlation) Consider the efficient GMM estimator that presumes $\{\mathbf{g}_t\}$ to be serially *un*correlated. If $\{\mathbf{g}_t\}$ is in fact serially correlated, is the estimator consistent? Efficient?

6.7 Estimation under Conditional Homoskedasticity (Optional)

We saw in Section 3.8 that the GMM estimator reduced to the 2SLS estimator under conditional homoskedasticity. This section shows how the 2SLS can be generalized to incorporate serial correlation. It will then become clear that the GLS estimator is not a GMM estimator with serial correlation. The latter half of this section examines the relationship between the GLS and GMM.

Kernel-Based Estimation of S under Conditional Homoskedasticity

The relationship between serial correlation in $\mathbf{g}_t \equiv \mathbf{x}_t \cdot \varepsilon_t$ and serial correlation in the error term ε_t becomes clearer under conditional homoskedasticity. Let

$$\omega_j \equiv \mathrm{E}(\varepsilon_t \varepsilon_{t-j}) \quad \text{for all } j. \tag{6.7.1}$$

Since $\{\varepsilon_t\}$ is stationary by Assumptions 3.1 and 3.2, ω_j does not depend on t. If $\mathrm{E}(\varepsilon_t) = 0$ (which is the case if $\mathbf{x}_t$ includes the constant), then ω_j equals the j-th order autocovariance of $\{\varepsilon_t\}$. Suppose the error term is conditionally homoskedastic:

conditional homoskedasticity:

$$\mathrm{E}(\varepsilon_t \varepsilon_{t-j} \mid \mathbf{x}_t, \mathbf{x}_{t-j}) = \omega_j \quad (j = 0, \pm 1, \pm 2, \dots). \tag{6.7.2}$$

Under this additional condition, the usual argument utilizing the Law of Total Expectations can be applied to $\mathbf{\Gamma}_j$:

$$\begin{aligned}
\mathbf{\Gamma}_j &= \mathrm{E}(\mathbf{g}_t \mathbf{g}_{t-j}') \quad (\text{since } \mathrm{E}(\mathbf{g}_t) = \mathbf{0}) \\
&= \mathrm{E}(\varepsilon_t \varepsilon_{t-j} \mathbf{x}_t \mathbf{x}_{t-j}') \\
&= \mathrm{E}[\mathrm{E}(\varepsilon_t \varepsilon_{t-j} \mid \mathbf{x}_t, \mathbf{x}_{t-j}) \mathbf{x}_t \mathbf{x}_{t-j}'] \quad (\text{by the Law of Total Expectations}) \\
&= \omega_j \, \mathrm{E}(\mathbf{x}_t \mathbf{x}_{t-j}').
\end{aligned} \tag{6.7.3}$$

Thus, unless $\mathrm{E}(\mathbf{x}_t \mathbf{x}_{t-j}')$ is zero, $\{\mathbf{g}_t\}$ is serially correlated if and only if $\{\varepsilon_t\}$ is.

To estimate $\mathbf{\Gamma}_j$, we exploit the fact that $\mathbf{\Gamma}_j$ is a product of two second moments, $\mathrm{E}(\mathbf{x}_t \mathbf{x}_{t-j}')$ and $\mathrm{E}(\varepsilon_t \varepsilon_{t-j})$. A natural estimator of $\mathrm{E}(\mathbf{x}_t \mathbf{x}_{t-j}')$ is $\frac{1}{n}\sum_{t=j+1}^{n} \mathbf{x}_t \mathbf{x}_{t-j}'$. It is easy to show that ω_j is consistently estimated by $\frac{1}{n}\sum_{t=j+1}^{n} \hat{\varepsilon}_t \hat{\varepsilon}_{t-j}$ where $\hat{\varepsilon}_t$ is the residual from some consistent estimator (the proof is almost the same as in the case with no serial correlation, see Proposition 3.2). Thus, a natural estimate of $\mathbf{\Gamma}_j$

under conditional homoskedasticity is

$$\widehat{\boldsymbol{\Gamma}}_j = \left(\frac{1}{n}\sum_{t=j+1}^{n} \hat{\varepsilon}_t\hat{\varepsilon}_{t-j}\right)\left(\frac{1}{n}\sum_{t=j+1}^{n} \mathbf{x}_t\mathbf{x}_{t-j}'\right). \tag{6.7.4}$$

Given these estimated autocovariances, the kernel-based estimation of $\widehat{\mathbf{S}}$ is exactly the same as in the case without conditional homoskedasticity described in the previous section.

Data Matrix Representation of Estimated Long-Run Variance

For the purpose of relating the GMM estimator with serial correlation but with conditional homoskedasticity to conventional estimators, the data matrix representation of $\widehat{\mathbf{S}}$ is useful. By defining an $n \times n$ matrix $\widehat{\boldsymbol{\Omega}}$ suitably, we can write $\widehat{\mathbf{S}}$ as

$$\widehat{\mathbf{S}} = \frac{1}{n}\mathbf{X}'\widehat{\boldsymbol{\Omega}}\mathbf{X}, \tag{6.7.5}$$

where $\mathbf{X}$ is the $n \times K$ data matrix whose t-th row is $\mathbf{x}_t'$. The matrix $\widehat{\boldsymbol{\Omega}}$ looks much like the autocovariance matrix of $\{\varepsilon_t\}$:

$$\underset{(n\times n)}{\widehat{\boldsymbol{\Omega}}} = \begin{bmatrix} \hat{\omega}_0 & \hat{\omega}_1 & \hat{\omega}_2 & \cdots & \hat{\omega}_{n-1} \\ \hat{\omega}_1 & \hat{\omega}_0 & \hat{\omega}_1 & \cdots & \hat{\omega}_{n-2} \\ \vdots & \ddots & \ddots & \ddots & \vdots \\ \hat{\omega}_{n-2} & \cdots & \hat{\omega}_1 & \hat{\omega}_0 & \hat{\omega}_1 \\ \hat{\omega}_{n-1} & \cdots & \hat{\omega}_2 & \hat{\omega}_1 & \hat{\omega}_0 \end{bmatrix}. \tag{6.7.6}$$

If we know *a priori* that $\text{Cov}(\varepsilon_t, \varepsilon_{t-j}) = 0$ (so that $\boldsymbol{\Gamma}_j = \mathbf{0}$) for $j > q$, specify the elements of this $\widehat{\boldsymbol{\Omega}}$ as

$$\hat{\omega}_j = \begin{cases} \dfrac{1}{n}\displaystyle\sum_{t=j+1}^{n} \hat{\varepsilon}_t\hat{\varepsilon}_{t-j} & \text{if } 0 \le j \le q, \\ 0 & \text{if } j > q. \end{cases} \tag{6.7.7}$$

Then the $\widehat{\mathbf{S}}$ in (6.6.4) can be written as (6.7.5). If we do not know that there is such a q, then use the kernel-based estimator of $\mathbf{S}$. For the Bartlett kernel, let

$$\hat{\omega}_j = \begin{cases} \left[1 - \dfrac{j}{q(n)}\right]\dfrac{1}{n}\displaystyle\sum_{t=j+1}^{n} \hat{\varepsilon}_t\hat{\varepsilon}_{t-j} & \text{if } 0 \le j \le q(n) - 1, \\ 0 & \text{if } j > q(n) - 1. \end{cases} \tag{6.7.8}$$

Then the consistent estimator (6.6.3) with (6.6.4) equals (6.7.5).

It is now easy to show the following extension of the 2SLS estimator to encompass serial correlation:

- The efficient GMM estimator under conditional homoskedasticity can be written as

$$\hat{\boldsymbol{\delta}}(\widehat{\mathbf{S}}^{-1}) = [\mathbf{Z}'\mathbf{X}(\mathbf{X}'\widehat{\boldsymbol{\Omega}}\mathbf{X})^{-1}\mathbf{X}'\mathbf{Z}]^{-1}\mathbf{Z}'\mathbf{X}(\mathbf{X}'\widehat{\boldsymbol{\Omega}}\mathbf{X})^{-1}\mathbf{X}'\mathbf{y}, \qquad (6.7.9)$$

  where $\mathbf{Z}$ and $\mathbf{y}$ are the data matrices of the regressors and the dependent variable. This generalizes (3.8.3′) on page 230.

- The consistent estimator of $\text{Avar}\big(\hat{\boldsymbol{\delta}}(\widehat{\mathbf{S}}^{-1})\big)$ reduces to

$$\begin{aligned}\widehat{\text{Avar}\big(\hat{\boldsymbol{\delta}}(\widehat{\mathbf{S}}^{-1})\big)} &= \left[\frac{1}{n}\mathbf{Z}'\mathbf{X}\Big(\frac{1}{n}\mathbf{X}'\widehat{\boldsymbol{\Omega}}\mathbf{X}\Big)^{-1}\frac{1}{n}\mathbf{X}'\mathbf{Z}\right]^{-1} \\ &= n\cdot\big[\mathbf{Z}'\mathbf{X}(\mathbf{X}'\widehat{\boldsymbol{\Omega}}\mathbf{X})^{-1}\mathbf{X}'\mathbf{Z}\big]^{-1}. \qquad (6.7.10)\end{aligned}$$

So the square roots of the diagonal elements of $[\mathbf{Z}'\mathbf{X}(\mathbf{X}'\widehat{\boldsymbol{\Omega}}\mathbf{X})^{-1}\mathbf{X}'\mathbf{Z}]^{-1}$ are the standard errors. This generalizes (3.8.5′) on page 230.

Relation to GLS

The procedure for incorporating serial correlation into the GMM estimation we have described is different from the GLS procedure. To see the difference most clearly, consider the case where $\mathbf{x}_t = \mathbf{z}_t$. If there are L regressors, $\mathbf{X}'\mathbf{Z}$ and $\mathbf{X}'\widehat{\boldsymbol{\Omega}}\mathbf{X}$ in (6.7.9) are all $L \times L$ matrices, so the efficient GMM estimator that exploits the orthogonality conditions $\text{E}(\mathbf{z}_t \cdot \varepsilon_t) = \mathbf{0}$ is the OLS estimator $\hat{\boldsymbol{\delta}}_{\text{OLS}} = (\mathbf{Z}'\mathbf{Z})^{-1}\mathbf{Z}'\mathbf{y}$. The consistent estimate of its asymptotic variance is obtained by setting $\mathbf{X} = \mathbf{Z}$ in (6.7.10):

$$\widehat{\text{Avar}(\hat{\boldsymbol{\delta}}_{\text{OLS}})} = n\cdot(\mathbf{Z}'\mathbf{Z})^{-1}(\mathbf{Z}'\widehat{\boldsymbol{\Omega}}\mathbf{Z})(\mathbf{Z}'\mathbf{Z})^{-1}. \qquad (6.7.11)$$

This may seem strange because we know from Section 1.6 that the GLS estimator is more efficient than OLS when the error is serially correlated. This is a finite sample result, but, given that we have a consistent estimator $\widehat{\boldsymbol{\Omega}}$ of $\boldsymbol{\Omega}$, we could take the GLS formula and estimate $\boldsymbol{\delta}$ as

$$\hat{\boldsymbol{\delta}}_{\text{GLS}} = (\mathbf{Z}'\widehat{\boldsymbol{\Omega}}^{-1}\mathbf{Z})^{-1}\mathbf{Z}'\widehat{\boldsymbol{\Omega}}^{-1}\mathbf{y}.$$

Is not this estimator asymptotically more efficient than OLS in that its asymptotic variance is smaller? The problem with GLS is that consistency is *not* guaranteed, if the regressors are merely predetermined, as shown below. As we emphasized in Chapter 2, the regressors are not strictly exogenous in most time series models. It follows that *GLS should not be used to correct for serial correlation in the error term for models lacking strict exogeneity.* In particular, for the $\mathbf{x}_t = \mathbf{z}_t$ case, the correct procedure to adjust for serial correlation is to leave the point estimate unchanged while incorporating serial correlation in the estimate of the asymptotic variance.

That the GLS estimator is generally inconsistent can be seen as follows. To focus on the problem at hand, assume that the true autocovariance matrix is proportional to some known $n \times n$ matrix $\mathbf{V}$:

$$\text{Var}(\varepsilon_1, \varepsilon_2, \ldots, \varepsilon_n) = \sigma^2 \cdot \mathbf{V}.$$

As shown in Section 1.6, the GLS estimator of the coefficient $\boldsymbol{\delta}$ in the regression model $\mathbf{y} = \mathbf{Z}\boldsymbol{\delta} + \boldsymbol{\varepsilon}$ can be calculated as the OLS estimator on the transformed model $\mathbf{Cy} = \mathbf{CZ}\boldsymbol{\delta} + \mathbf{C}\boldsymbol{\varepsilon}$, where $\mathbf{C}$ is the "square root" of $\mathbf{V}^{-1}$ such that $\mathbf{C}'\mathbf{C} = \mathbf{V}^{-1}$. But look at the t-th observation of the transformed model, which can be written as

$$\tilde{y}_t = \tilde{\mathbf{z}}_t'\boldsymbol{\delta} + \tilde{\varepsilon}_t, \tag{6.7.12}$$

where

$$\begin{aligned} \tilde{y}_t &= c_{t1}y_1 + \cdots + c_{tn}y_n, \\ \tilde{\mathbf{z}}_t &= c_{t1}\mathbf{z}_1 + \cdots + c_{tn}\mathbf{z}_n, \\ \tilde{\varepsilon}_t &= c_{t1}\varepsilon_1 + \cdots + c_{tn}\varepsilon_n, \\ (c_{t1}, \ldots, c_{tn}) &\text{ is the } t\text{-th row of } \mathbf{C}. \end{aligned}$$

For the GLS estimator to be consistent, it is necessary that $\text{E}(\tilde{\mathbf{z}}_t \cdot \tilde{\varepsilon}_t) = \mathbf{0}$. The left-hand side of this condition can be written as

$$\text{E}(\tilde{\mathbf{z}}_t \cdot \tilde{\varepsilon}_t) = \text{(a)} + \text{(b)},$$
$$\text{(a)} = \sum_{s=1}^{n} c_{ts}^2 \, \text{E}(\mathbf{z}_s \cdot \varepsilon_s), \quad \text{(b)} = \sum_{s \neq v} c_{ts} \cdot c_{tv} \, \text{E}(\mathbf{z}_s \cdot \varepsilon_v).$$

By the orthogonality condition $\text{E}(\mathbf{z}_t \cdot \varepsilon_t) = \mathbf{0}$, (a) is zero. For (b), because the regressors are merely predetermined and not assumed to be strictly exogenous, $\text{E}(\mathbf{z}_s \cdot \varepsilon_v)$ is not guaranteed to be zero for $s \neq v$. So (b) is not zero, unless the c's take particular values to offset the nonzero terms.

There is one important special case where GLS is consistent, and that is when the error is a finite-order autoregressive process. To take the simplest case, suppose that $\{\varepsilon_t\}$ is AR(1): $\varepsilon_t = \phi\varepsilon_{t-1} + \eta_t$. Its autocovariance matrix is

$$\text{Var}(\varepsilon_1, \varepsilon_2, \dots, \varepsilon_n) = \sigma^2 \cdot \mathbf{V}, \quad \mathbf{V} = \frac{1}{1-\phi^2}\begin{bmatrix} 1 & \phi & \phi^2 & \cdots & \phi^{n-1} \\ \phi & 1 & \phi & \cdots & \phi^{n-2} \\ & & \ddots & & \\ \phi^{n-2} & \cdots & \phi & 1 & \phi \\ \phi^{n-1} & \cdots & \phi^2 & \phi & 1 \end{bmatrix}.$$

It is easy to verify that the square root, $\mathbf{C}$, of $\mathbf{V}^{-1}$ (satisfying $\mathbf{C}'\mathbf{C} = \mathbf{V}$) is given by

$$\mathbf{C} = \begin{bmatrix} \sqrt{1-\phi^2} & 0 & 0 & \cdots & 0 & 0 \\ -\phi & 1 & 0 & \cdots & 0 & 0 \\ 0 & -\phi & 1 & \cdots & 0 & 0 \\ \vdots & \vdots & \vdots & \cdots & \vdots & \vdots \\ 0 & 0 & 0 & \cdots & -\phi & 1 \end{bmatrix}. \tag{6.7.13}$$

So the t-th transformed equation is

$$y_t - \phi y_{t-1} = (\mathbf{z}_t - \phi\mathbf{z}_{t-1})'\boldsymbol{\delta} + \eta_t. \tag{6.7.14}$$

The GLS estimate of $\boldsymbol{\delta}$, which is the OLS estimate in the regression of $y_t - \phi y_{t-1}$ on $\mathbf{z}_t - \phi\mathbf{z}_{t-1}$ is consistent if η_t is orthogonal to *both* $\mathbf{z}_t$ *and* $\mathbf{z}_{t-1}$. However, those orthogonality conditions are different from the orthogonality conditions for the untransformed model, which are that $\text{E}(\mathbf{z}_t \cdot \varepsilon_t) = \mathbf{0}$.

QUESTIONS FOR REVIEW

1. Verify (6.7.5) for $n = 3$, $q = 1$.
2. (Sargan's statistic) Derive the generalization of Sargan's statistic (3.8.10′) on page 230 to the case of serially correlated errors.
3. Suppose that $\mathbf{z}_t$ is a strict subset of $\mathbf{x}_t$. We have seen in Section 3.8 that the 2SLS estimator reduces to the OLS estimator. Is this true here as well? That is, does (6.7.9) reduce to $(\mathbf{Z}'\mathbf{Z})^{-1}\mathbf{Z}'\mathbf{y}$? [Answer: No.]
4. (Data matrix representation of $\widehat{\mathbf{S}}$ without conditional homoskedasticity) Define $\widehat{\boldsymbol{\Omega}}$ suitably so that (6.7.5) equals the Bartlett kernel-based estimator of $\widehat{\mathbf{S}}$ without conditional homoskedasticity, namely, (6.6.5) with (6.6.7). **Hint:** Write $\widehat{\boldsymbol{\Omega}}$ as (6.7.6). If the lag length q is known, $\hat{\omega}_j = \hat{\varepsilon}_j\hat{\varepsilon}_{t-j}$ for $0 \le j \le q$ and 0 for $j > q$. How would you define $\hat{\omega}_j$ for the Bartlett kernel-based estimator?

5. Consider the simple regression model: $y_t = \beta z_t + \varepsilon_t$, where $\{\varepsilon_t\}$ is AR(1), $\varepsilon_t = \phi\varepsilon_{t-1} + \eta_t$ with known ϕ. Assume $\mathrm{E}(z_t\varepsilon_t) = 0$, $\mathrm{E}(z_t\eta_t) = 0$, $\mathrm{E}(z_{t-1}\eta_t) = 0$, and conditional homoskedasticity. Also, to simplify, assume $\mathrm{E}(z_t) = 0$. Show that

$$\mathrm{Avar}(\widehat{\beta}_{\mathrm{OLS}}) = \frac{\sigma_\eta^2}{\sigma_z^2}\,\frac{1 + 2\sum_{j=1}^{\infty}\phi^j\rho_j}{1-\phi^2}, \quad \mathrm{Avar}(\widehat{\beta}_{\mathrm{GLS}}) = \frac{\sigma_\eta^2}{\sigma_z^2}\,\frac{1}{(1+\phi^2) - 2\phi\rho_1},$$

where $\sigma_z^2 \equiv \mathrm{Var}(z_t)$, $\sigma_\eta^2 \equiv \mathrm{Var}(\eta_t)$, $\rho_j \equiv \mathrm{Corr}(z_t, z_{t-j})$. Find a configuration of $(\phi, \{\gamma_j\})$ such that $\mathrm{Avar}(\widehat{\beta}_{\mathrm{OLS}}) > \mathrm{Avar}(\widehat{\beta}_{\mathrm{GLS}})$. Explain why this is consistent with the fact that β_{OLS} is an efficient GMM estimator.

6.8 Application: Forward Exchange Rates as Optimal Predictors

In foreign exchange markets, the percentage difference between the forward exchange rate and the spot exchange rate is called the **forward premium**. The relation between the forward premium and the expected rate of currency appreciation/depreciation over the life of the forward contract has been the subject of a large number of empirical studies. The simplest hypothesis about the relationship is that the two are the same. In this section, we test this hypothesis using the same weekly data set used by Bekaert and Hodrick (1993).

The data cover the period of 1975–1989 and include the following variables:

S_t = spot exchange rate, stated in units of the foreign currency per dollar (e.g., 125 yen per dollar) on the Friday of week t,

F_t = 30-day forward exchange rate on Friday of week t, namely, the price in foreign currency units of the dollar deliverable 30 days from Friday of week t,

$S30_t$ = the spot rate on the delivery date on a 30-day forward contract made on Friday of week t.

The important feature of the data is that the maturity of the contract covers several sampling intervals; the delivery date is after the Friday of week $t+4$ but before the Friday of week $t+5$.

The Market Efficiency Hypothesis

To indicate the assumptions underlying the hypothesis, consider three strategies for investing dollar funds for 30 days at date t. The first is to invest in a domestic money market instrument (e.g., U.S. Treasury bills) whose maturity is 30 days. Let i_t be the rate of return over the 30-day period. The second investment strategy is to convert dollars into foreign currency units, buy a 30-day money market instrument denominated in the foreign currency whose interest rate is denoted i_t^*, and convert back to dollars at maturity. The rate of return from this investment strategy is

$$S_t \cdot (1 + i_t^*)/S30_t.$$

This strategy involves foreign exchange risk because at time t of investing you do not know $S30_t$ which is the spot rate 30 days hence. The third investment strategy differs from the second in that it hedges against exchange risk by buying dollars forward at price F_t at the same time the dollar fund is converted into foreign currency units. This hedged foreign investment provides a sure return equal to

$$S_t \cdot (1 + i_t^*)/F_t.$$

Because the first and the third strategies involve no risk, arbitrage requires that the rates of return be the same:

$$1 + i_t = S_t \cdot (1 + i_t^*)/F_t.$$

Taking logs of both sides and using the approximation $\log(1 + x) \approx x$, we obtain the **covered interest parity** equation:

$$i_t = s_t - f_t + i_t^* \quad \text{or} \quad f_t - s_t = i_t^* - i_t, \tag{6.8.1}$$

where lower case letters for S and F are natural logs. That is, the forward premium, $f_t - s_t$, equals the interest rate differential. This relationship holds almost exactly in real data. In fact, people routinely calculate the forward premium as the interest rate differential.

The rate of return from the second investment strategy is uncertain, but if investors are risk-neutral, its expected return is equal to the sure rate of return. Furthermore, if their expectations are rational, the expected return is the conditional expectation based on the information currently available, so

$$\mathrm{E}[S_t \cdot (1 + i_t^*)/S30_t \mid I_t] = S_t \cdot (1 + i_t^*)/F_t, \tag{6.8.2}$$

where $E(\cdot \mid I_t)$ is the expectations operator and I_t is the information set as of date t. Since S_t, F_t, and i_t^* are known at date t, this equality reduces to

$$E(F_t/S30_t \mid I_t) = 1.$$

Again, by log approximation, $F_t/S30_t \approx 1 + f_t - s30_t$. Therefore,

$$E(s30_t \mid I_t) = f_t \text{ or } E(\varepsilon_t \mid I_t) = 0 \quad \text{where } \varepsilon_t \equiv s30_t - f_t. \tag{6.8.3}$$

This is the market efficiency hypothesis. As is clear from the derivation, the hypothesis assumes risk-neutrality and rational expectations. The hypothesis is sometimes described as the forward rate being the optimal forecast of future spot rates, because the conditional expectation is the optimal forecast in that it minimizes the mean square error (see Proposition 2.7).

Testing Whether the Unconditional Mean Is Zero

Taking the unconditional expectation of both sides of (6.8.3), we obtain the unconditional relationship:

$$E(s30_t) = E(f_t) \quad \text{or} \quad E(\varepsilon_t) = 0. \tag{6.8.4}$$

That is, the forecast must be correct on average. Figure 6.1 is a plot of the forecast error ε_t for the yen/dollar exchange rate. It looks like a stationary series, and we proceed under the assumption that it is.[15] Because the forecast error is observable, we can test the hypothesis that its unconditional mean is zero. This is in contrast to the Fama exercise, where the forecast error (about future inflation) is observable only up to a constant.

To test the hypothesis of market efficiency, we need to derive the asymptotic distribution of the sample mean, $\bar{\varepsilon}$, under the hypothesis. The task is somewhat involved because $\{\varepsilon_t\}$ is serially correlated. To see why the forecast error has serial correlation, note that I_t, while including $\{\varepsilon_{t-5}, \varepsilon_{t-6}, \dots\}$, does not include $\{\varepsilon_t, \dots, \varepsilon_{t-4}\}$ because ε_t, which depends on $s30_t$, cannot be observed until after $t+4$. Therefore,

$$E(\varepsilon_t \mid \varepsilon_{t-5}, \varepsilon_{t-6}, \dots) = 0. \tag{6.8.5}$$

It follows that $\text{Cov}(\varepsilon_t, \varepsilon_{t-j}) = 0$ for $j \geq 5$ but not necessarily for $j \leq 4$. In

[15] Using covered interest rate parity, $\varepsilon_t = (s30_t - s_t) - (i_t^* - i_t)$. If you believe that both the 30-day rate of change $s30_t - s_t$ and the interest rate differential $i_t^* - i_t$ are stationary, you have to believe that the forecast error is stationary.

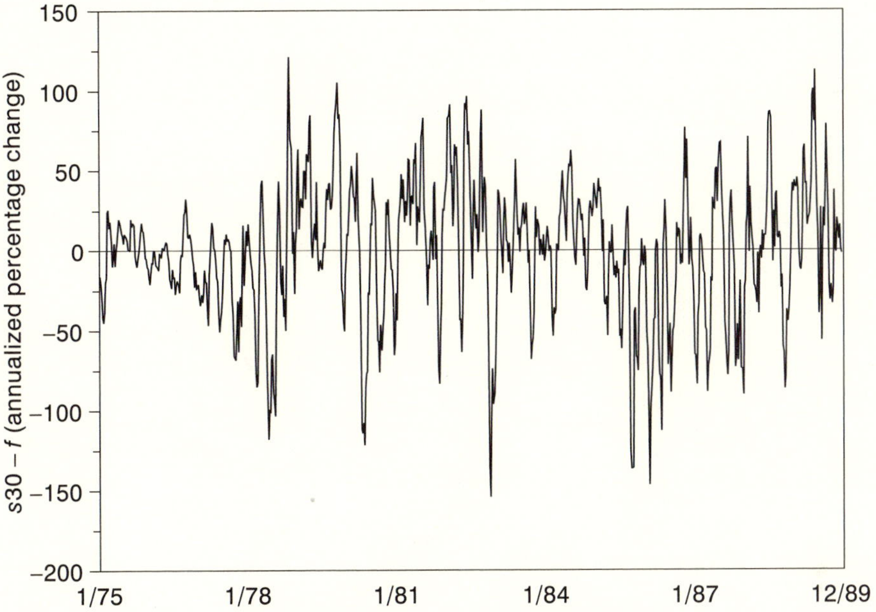

Figure 6.1: Forecast Error, Yen/Dollar

the Fama exercise, the ex-post real interest rate (which is the inflation forecast error plus a constant) was serially uncorrelated because the maturity for the interest rate and the sampling interval were the same. Here, the forecast error has serial correlation because the maturity of the forward contract (30 days) is longer than the sampling interval (a week). The estimated correlogram is displayed along with the two-standard error band in Figure 6.2.[16] The standard error is calculated under the assumption that the forecast error is i.i.d. So it equals $1/\sqrt{n}$, as in Table 2.1. The pattern of autocorrelation is broadly consistent with the hypothesis: it stays well above two standard errors for the first four lags and generally lies within the band thereafter.

Under the null of market efficiency, since serial correlation vanishes after a finite lag, it is easy to see that $\{\varepsilon_t\}$ satisfies the essential part of Gordin's condition restricting serial correlation. By the Law of Iterated Expectations, (6.8.5) implies $\mathrm{E}(\varepsilon_t \mid \varepsilon_{t-j}, \varepsilon_{t-j-1}, \dots) = 0$ for $j \geq 5$, which immediately implies part (b) of Gordin's condition. Since the revision of expectations, r_{tj}, is zero for $j \geq 5$, part (c) is satisfied, provided that r_{tj} $(0 \leq j \leq 4)$ have finite second moments. It then

[16] Although theory implies that the population mean is zero, I subtracted the sample mean in the calculation of sample autocorrelations.

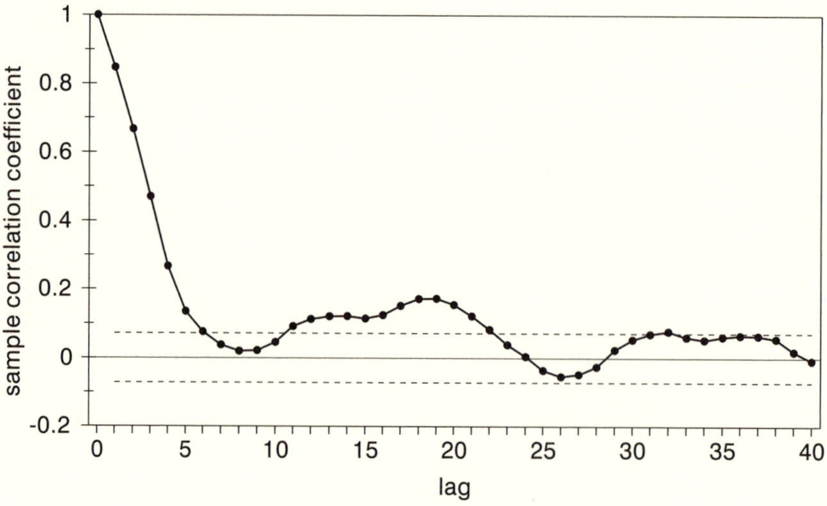

Figure 6.2: Correlogram of $s30 - f$, Yen/Dollar

follows from Proposition 6.10 that

$$\frac{\sqrt{n}\,\bar{\varepsilon}}{\sqrt{\gamma_0 + 2\sum_{j=1}^{4}\gamma_j}} = \frac{\bar{\varepsilon}}{\sqrt{\left(\gamma_0 + 2\sum_{j=1}^{4}\gamma_j\right)/n}} \underset{d}{\to} N(0, 1). \tag{6.8.6}$$

Furthermore, the denominator is consistently estimated by replacing γ_j by its sample counterpart $\hat{\gamma}_j$. So the ratio

$$\frac{\bar{\varepsilon}}{\sqrt{\left(\hat{\gamma}_0 + 2\sum_{j=1}^{4}\hat{\gamma}_j\right)/n}} \tag{6.8.7}$$

is also asymptotically standard normal. The denominator of this expression will be called the standard error of the sample mean.

Table 6.1 reports results for testing the implication of the hypothesis that the unconditional mean of the forecast error is zero, for three foreign exchange rates against the dollar. The three currencies are the Deutsche mark, the British pound, and the Japanese yen. Columns 1 and 2 of the table report the mean and the standard deviation of the actual rate of change of the spot rate, $s30_t - s_t$, and the forward premium, $f_t - s_t$. (Because the spot rate is per dollar, a positive rate of change means that the dollar strengthened.) The monthly rates of change and the

Table 6.1: Means of Rates of Change, Forward Premiums, and Differences between the Two: 1975–1989

	Means and Standard Deviations		
Exchange rate	$s30 - s$ (actual rate of change)	$f - s$ (expected rate of change)	Difference (unexpected rate of change)
¥/$	−4.98	−3.74	−1.25
	(41.6)	(3.65)	(42.4)
			standard error = 3.56
DM/$	−1.78	−3.91	2.13
	(40.6)	(2.17)	(41.1)
			standard error = 3.26
£/$	3.59	2.16	1.43
	(39.2)	(3.49)	(39.9)
			standard error = 3.29

NOTE: $s30 - s$ is the rate of change over 30 days and $f - s$ is the forward premium, expressed as annualized percentage changes. Standard deviations are in parentheses. The standard errors are the values of the denominator of (6.8.7). The data are weekly, from 1975 to 1989. The sample size is 778.

forward premium have been multiplied by 1,200 to express the rates in annualized percentages. The market efficiency hypothesis is that the forward premium is the expected rate of change of the spot rate. It is evident that the actual rate of change is much more volatile than the forward premium. The third column reports the sample mean of ε_t, which equals the difference between the first two columns for the sample mean. The numbers in parentheses below the sample mean are the standard errors calculated as described above. In no case is there significant evidence against the null hypothesis of zero mean.

Regression Tests

The unconditional test, however, does not exploit the implication of market efficiency that the forecast error is orthogonal to conditioning information I_t. Probably the most important variable in the information set I_t for future spot rates is the forward rate f_t. We can test whether the forecast error is uncorrelated with the forward rate by regressing ε_t on the constant and f_t. This is equivalent to running

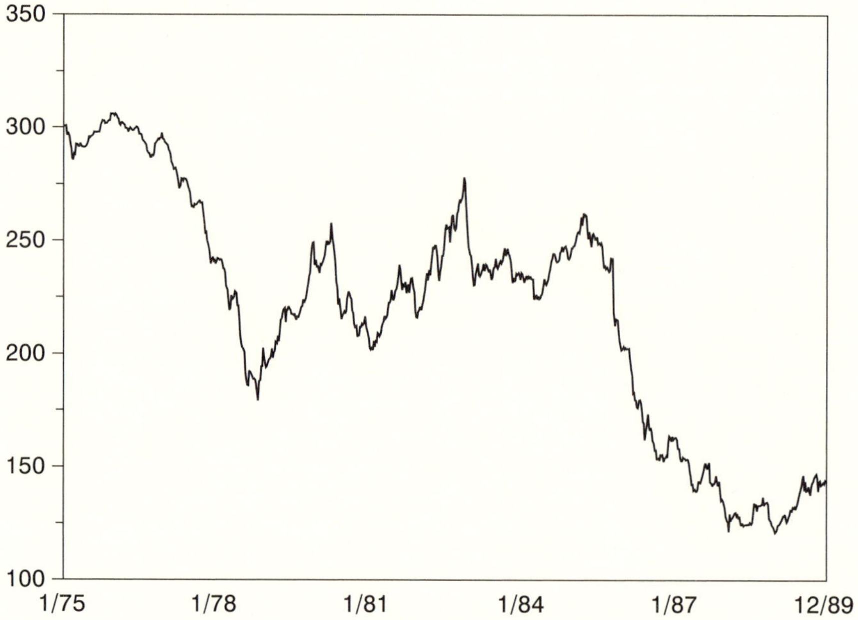

Figure 6.3: Yen/Dollar Spot Rate, Jan. 1975–Dec. 1989

the following regression

$$s30_t = \beta_0 + \beta_1 f_t + \varepsilon_t, \tag{6.8.8}$$

and testing whether $\beta_0 = 0$ and $\beta_1 = 1$. Because the error term is the forecast error orthogonal to anything known at date t including f_t, the regressors are guaranteed to be orthogonal to the error term. So it might appear that we can estimate (6.8.8) by OLS and adjust for serial correlation in the error term as indicated in Section 6.6 for correct inference.

However, as the graph in Figure 6.3 suggests, the spot exchange rate looks like a process with increasing variance. As we will verify in Chapter 9, we cannot reject the hypothesis that the process has a unit root. The forward rate has the same property. (Its plot is not shown here because it is indistinguishable from the plot of the spot rate.) Thus, Assumption 3.2, which requires the regressor (f_t) and the dependent variable ($s30_t$) to be stationary, is not satisfied. The problem actually runs deeper. We have observed in Figure 6.1 that the *difference* between $s30_t$ and f_t looked like a stationary series. In the language to be introduced in Chapter 10, $s30_t$ and f_t are "cointegrated" with a cointegrating vector of $(1, -1)$, in which case the OLS estimate of β_1 in (6.8.8) converges quickly to 1. This can be verified in Figure 6.4 where $s30_t$ is plotted against f_t. If a regression line is fitted, its slope

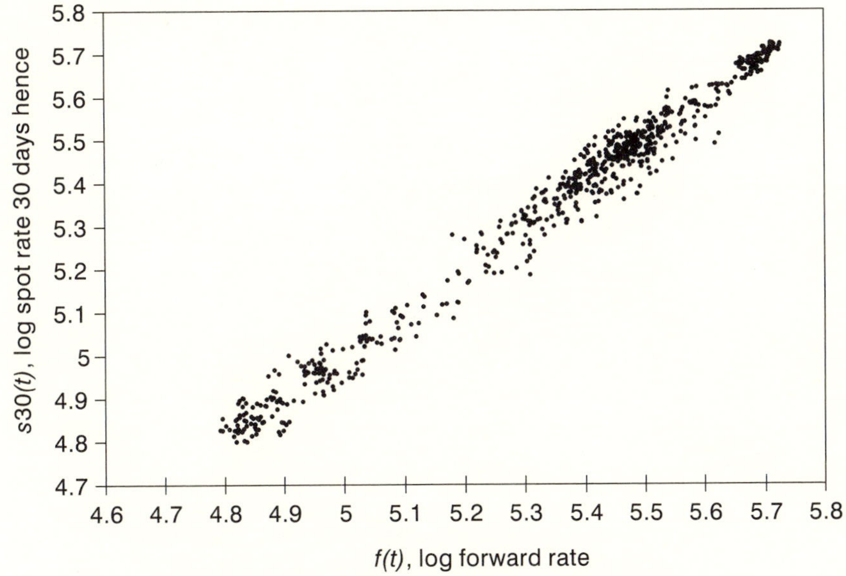

Figure 6.4: Plot of $s30$ against f, Yen/Dollar

is 0.99. The problem from the point of view of testing market efficiency is that the OLS estimate converges to 1 *regardless* of whether or not the hypothesis is true. Therefore, the test has no power.

The problem can be dealt with by estimating a different regression,

$$s30_t - s_t = \beta_0 + \beta_1(f_t - s_t) + \varepsilon_t. \tag{6.8.9}$$

Judging from the plot of $s30_t - s_t$ and $f_t - s_t$ (not shown), it is reasonable to assume that they are stationary, which is consistent with Assumption 3.2 (ergodic stationarity). That the equation satisfies other GMM assumptions under market efficiency can be verified as follows. For $\beta_0 = 0$ and $\beta_1 = 1$, the error term ε_t equals the forecast error $s30_t - f_t$ and so the orthogonality conditions $\mathrm{E}(\varepsilon_t) = 0$ and $\mathrm{E}[(f_t - s_t) \cdot \varepsilon_t] = 0$ (Assumption 3.3 with $\mathbf{z}_t = \mathbf{x}_t$) are satisfied. The identification condition is that the second moment of $(1, f_t - s_t)$ be nonsingular, which is true if and only if $\mathrm{Var}(f_t - s_t) > 0$. This is evidently satisfied; if the population variance were zero, we would not observe any variations in $f_t - s_t$. This leaves us with Assumption 3.5′, which requires that there is not too much serial correlation in

$$\mathbf{g}_t \equiv \mathbf{x}_t \cdot \varepsilon_t = \begin{bmatrix} \varepsilon_t \\ (f_t - s_t)\,\varepsilon_t \end{bmatrix}.$$

Table 6.2: Regression Tests of Market Efficiency: 1975–1989

$$s30_t - s_t = \beta_0 + \beta_1(f_t - s_t) + \varepsilon_t$$

Currency	Regression Coefficients: Constant	Regression Coefficients: Forward premium	R^2	Wald Statistic for H_0: $\beta_0 = 0, \beta_1 = 1$
¥/$	−12.8	−2.10	0.034	18.6
	(4.01)	(0.738)		($p = 0.009\%$)
DM/$	−13.6	−3.01	0.026	8.7
	(5.72)	(1.37)		($p = 1.312\%$)
£/$	7.96	−2.02	0.033	12.9
	(3.54)	(0.85)		($p = 0.156\%$)

NOTE: Standard errors are in parentheses. They are heteroskedasticity-robust and allow for serial correlation up to four lags calculated by the formula (6.8.11). The sample size is 778. Our results differ slightly from those in Bekaert and Hodrick (1993) because they used the Bartlett kernel-based estimator with $q(n) = 4$ to estimate $\mathbf{S}$.

As already noted, since I_t includes $\{\varepsilon_{t-5}, \varepsilon_{t-6}, \dots\}$, the forecast error satisfies (6.8.5). Review Question 3 will ask you to show that $\{\mathbf{g}_t\}$ inherits the same property, namely,

$$\mathrm{E}(\mathbf{g}_t \mid \mathbf{g}_{t-5}, \mathbf{g}_{t-6}, \dots) = \mathbf{0}. \tag{6.8.10}$$

So, as in the unconditional test, Gordin's condition is satisfied, provided that the relevant second moments are finite. Since $\mathrm{E}(\mathbf{g}_t \mathbf{g}_{t-j}') = \mathbf{0}$ for $j \geq 5$, the long-run covariance matrix $\mathbf{S}$ can be estimated as in (6.6.4) with $q = 4$. (In the empirical exercise, you will be asked to estimate $\widehat{\mathbf{S}}$ by the Bartlett kernel and also by VARHAC.)

To summarize, the efficient GMM estimator of $\boldsymbol{\beta} = (\beta_0, \beta_1)'$ in (6.8.9) is OLS and the consistent estimator of its asymptotic variance is given by

$$\widehat{\mathrm{Avar}(\widehat{\boldsymbol{\beta}}_{\mathrm{OLS}})} = \mathbf{S}_{\mathbf{xx}}^{-1}\,\widehat{\mathbf{S}}\,\mathbf{S}_{\mathbf{xx}}^{-1}, \tag{6.8.11}$$

where $\widehat{\mathbf{S}}$ is given in (6.6.4) with $q = 4$. Table 6.2 reports the regression test results for the three currencies. The corresponding plot for the yen/$ exchange rate is in Figure 6.5. Notice that the estimated slope coefficient is not only significantly different from 1 but also negative, for all three currencies. The null hypothesis

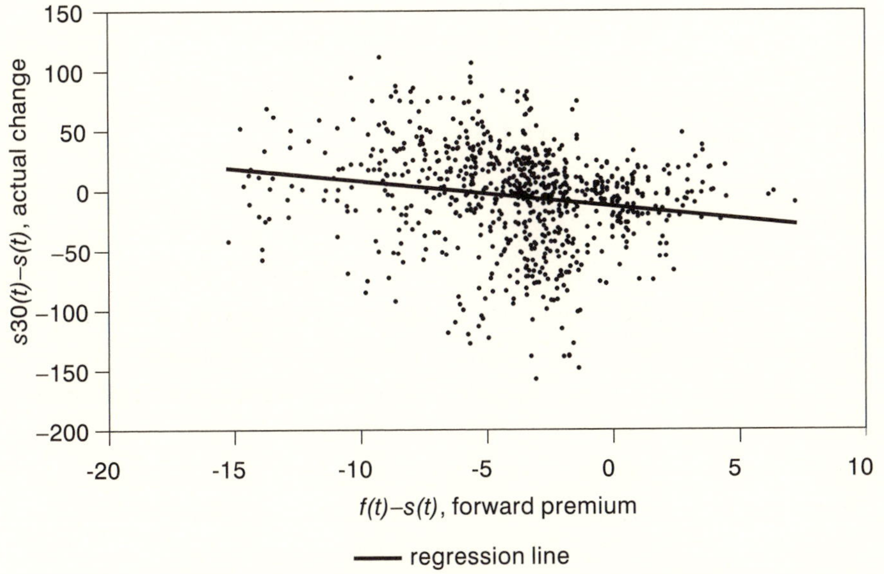

Figure 6.5: Plot of $s30 - s$ against $f - s$, Yen/Dollar

implied by market efficiency that $\beta_0 = 0$ and $\beta_1 = 1$ can be rejected decisively. This is reflected in the too many observations in the north-west quadrant of Figure 6.5; too often expected dollar depreciation (negative $f_t - s_t$) is associated with actual dollar *appreciation* (positive $s30_t - s_t$).

QUESTIONS FOR REVIEW

1. (The standard error in the unconditional test) Let $\varepsilon_t = s30_t - f_t$ and consider a regression of ε_t on the constant. To account for serial correlation, use (6.6.4) with $q = 4$ for $\widehat{\mathbf{S}}$. Verify that the t-value for the hypothesis that the intercept is zero is given by (6.8.7).

2. (Lack of identification) For simplicity suppose F_t is the two-week forward exchange rate so that the $s30_t$ in (6.8.9) can be replaced by s_{t+2}. Suppose that the spot exchange rate is a random walk and $I_t = \{s_t, s_{t-1}, \dots\}$. What should f_t be under the hypothesis? Which of the required assumptions are violated? [Answer: The identification condition.] Suppose, instead, that s_t is AR(1) satisfying $s_t = c + \phi s_{t-1} + \eta_t$ where $\{\eta_t\}$ is i.i.d. and $|\phi| < 1$. Verify that $f_t = (1+\phi)c + \phi^2 s_t$. **Hint:** $s_{t+2} = (1+\phi)c + \phi^2 s_t + (\eta_{t+2} + \phi\eta_{t+1})$. Verify that $\varepsilon_t = \eta_{t+2} + \phi\eta_{t+1}$.

3. Prove (6.8.10). **Hint:** $\mathrm{E}(\varepsilon_t \mid I_t) = 0$. Verify that I_t includes $s_t - f_t$ and $\{\mathbf{g}_{t-5}, \mathbf{g}_{t-6}, \dots\}$. Use the Law of Iterated Expectations.

PROBLEM SET FOR CHAPTER 6

ANALYTICAL EXERCISES

1. (Mean square limits and their uniqueness) In Chapter 2, we defined the mean square convergence of a sequence of random variables $\{z_n\}$ to a random variable z. In this and other questions, we will deal with sequences of random variables with finite second moments. For those sequences, the definition of mean square convergence is

DEFINITION. Let $\{z_n\}$ be a sequence of random variables with $\mathrm{E}(z_n^2) < \infty$. We say that $\{z_n\}$ converges in mean square to a random variable z with $\mathrm{E}(z^2) < \infty$, written $z_n \to_{\text{m.s.}} z$, if $\mathrm{E}[(z_n - z)^2] \to 0$ as $n \to \infty$.

(a) Show that, if $z_n \to_{\text{m.s.}} z$ and $z_n \to_{\text{m.s.}} z'$, then $\mathrm{E}[(z - z')^2] = 0$. **Hint:** $z - z' = (z - z_n) + (z_n - z')$. Define $\|x\| = \sqrt{\mathrm{E}(x^2)}$. Then

$$\begin{aligned}\|z - z'\|^2 &= \|z - z_n\|^2 + 2\,\mathrm{E}[(z - z_n)(z_n - z')] + \|z_n - z'\|^2 \\ &\le \|z - z_n\|^2 + 2\sqrt{\mathrm{E}[(z - z_n)^2]}\,\sqrt{\mathrm{E}[(z_n - z')^2]} + \|z_n - z'\|^2 \\ &\qquad \text{(by Cauchy-Schwartz inequality that } \mathrm{E}(xy) \le \sqrt{\mathrm{E}(x^2)}\,\sqrt{\mathrm{E}(y^2)}) \\ &= (\|z - z_n\| + \|z_n - z'\|)^2.\end{aligned}$$

So $\|z - z'\| \le \|z - z_n\| + \|z_n - z'\|$. This is called the **triangle inequality**.

(b) Show that $\mathrm{Prob}(z = z') = 1$. **Hint:** Use Chebychev's inequality:

$$\mathrm{Prob}\big(|z - z'| > \varepsilon\big) \le \frac{1}{\varepsilon^2}\,\mathrm{E}\big[\|z - z'\|^2\big].$$

2. (Proof of Proposition 6.1) A well-known result about mean square convergence (see, e.g., Brockwell and Davis, 1991, Proposition 2.7.1) is

(i) $\{z_n\}$ converges in mean square if and only if $\mathrm{E}[(z_m - z_n)^2] \to 0$ as $m, n \to \infty$.

(ii) If $x_n \to_{\text{m.s.}} x$ and $z_n \to_{\text{m.s.}} z$, then

$$\lim_{n\to\infty} \mathrm{E}(x_n) = \mathrm{E}(x) \quad \text{and} \quad \lim_{n\to\infty} \mathrm{E}(x_n z_n) = \mathrm{E}(xz).$$

Take this result for granted in answering.

(a) Prove that (6.1.6) converges in mean square as $n \to \infty$ under the hypothesis of Proposition 6.1. **Hint:** Let

$$y_{t,n} = \mu + \sum_{j=0}^{n} \psi_j \varepsilon_{t-j}.$$

What needs to be proved is that $\{y_{t,n}\}$ converges in mean square as $n \to \infty$ for each t. Given (i) above, it is sufficient to prove that (assuming $m > n$ without loss of generality)

$$\mathrm{E}\Big[\Big(\sum_{j=n+1}^{m} \psi_j \varepsilon_{t-j}\Big)^2\Big] = \sigma^2 \sum_{j=n+1}^{m} \psi_j^2 \to 0 \quad \text{as } m, n \to \infty.$$

Use the fact that an absolutely summable sequence is **square summable**, i.e.,

$$\sum_{j=0}^{\infty} |\psi_j| < \infty \Rightarrow \sum_{j=0}^{\infty} \psi_j^2 < \infty,$$

and the fact that a sequence of real numbers $\{\alpha_n\}$ converges (to a finite limit) if and only if α_n is a Cauchy sequence:

$$\alpha_n \to \alpha \Leftrightarrow |\alpha_m - \alpha_n| \to 0 \quad \text{as } m, n \to \infty.$$

Set $\alpha_n = \sum_{j=0}^{n} \psi_j^2$.

(b) Prove that $\mathrm{E}(y_t) = \mu$. **Hint:** Let $y_{t,n} = \mu + \sum_{j=0}^{n} \psi_j \varepsilon_{t-j}$ as in (a). It was shown in (a) that $y_{t,n} \to_{\text{m.s.}} y_t$.

(c) (Proof of part (b) of Proposition 6.1) Show that

$$\mathrm{E}[(y_t - \mu)(y_{t-j} - \mu)] = \lim_{n \to \infty} \mathrm{E}[(y_{t,n} - \mu)(y_{t-j,n} - \mu)].$$

Have we shown that $\{y_t\}$ is covariance-stationary? [Answer: Yes.]

(d) (Optional) Prove part (c) of Proposition 6.1, taking the following facts from calculus for granted.

(i) If $\{a_j\}$ is absolutely summable, then $\{a_j\}$ is summable (i.e., $-\infty < \sum_{j=0}^{\infty} a_j < \infty$) and

$$\left|\sum_{j=0}^{\infty} a_j\right| \le \sum_{j=0}^{\infty} |a_j|.$$

(ii) Consider a sequence with two subscripts, $\{a_{jk}\}$ $(j, k = 0, 1, 2, \dots)$. Suppose $\sum_{j=0}^{\infty} |a_{jk}| < \infty$ for each k and let $s_k \equiv \sum_{j=0}^{\infty} |a_{jk}|$. Suppose $\{s_k\}$ is summable. Then

$$\left|\sum_{j=0}^{\infty}\Big(\sum_{k=0}^{\infty} a_{jk}\Big)\right| < \infty \quad \text{and} \quad \sum_{j=0}^{\infty}\Big(\sum_{k=0}^{\infty} a_{jk}\Big) = \sum_{k=0}^{\infty}\Big(\sum_{j=0}^{\infty} a_{jk}\Big) < \infty.$$

Hint: Derive

$$\sum_{j=0}^{\infty} |\gamma_j| \le \sigma^2 \sum_{j=0}^{\infty}\Big(\sum_{k=0}^{\infty} |\psi_{j+k}| \cdot |\psi_k|\Big) < \infty.$$

3. (Autocovariances of $h(L)x_t$) We wish to derive the autocovariances of $\{y_t\}$ of Proposition 6.2. As in Proposition 6.2, assume throughout this question that $\{x_t\}$ is covariance-stationary. First consider a weighted average of finitely many terms:

$$y_{t,n} = h_0 x_t + h_1 x_{t-1} + \cdots + h_n x_{t-n}.$$

(a) Show that for this $\{y_{t,n}\}$,

$$\gamma_j = \sum_{k=0}^{n}\sum_{\ell=0}^{n} h_k h_\ell \gamma^x_{j-k+\ell}$$

where γ^x_j is the j-th order autocovariance of $\{x_t\}$.
Verify that this reduces to (6.1.2) if $\{x_t\}$ is white noise. **Hint:** If you find this difficult, first set $n = 1$, and then increase n to establish the pattern.

(b) Now consider a weighted average of possibly infinitely many terms:

$$y_t = h_0 x_t + h_1 x_{t-1} + \cdots.$$

Taking Proposition 6.2(a) for granted, show that

$$\gamma_j = \sum_{k=0}^{\infty}\sum_{\ell=0}^{\infty} h_k h_\ell \gamma^x_{j-k+\ell} \quad \text{if } \{h_j\} \text{ is absolutely summable.}$$

Hint: $y_{t,n} \to_{\text{m.s.}} y_t$ as $n \to \infty$ by Proposition 6.2. Proceed as in 2(c).

4. (Homogeneous linear difference equations) Consider a p-th order homogeneous linear difference equation:

$$y_j - \phi_1 y_{j-1} - \phi_2 y_{j-2} - \cdots - \phi_p y_{j-p} = 0 \quad (j = p, p+1, \ldots), \qquad (1)$$

where $(\phi_1, \phi_2, \ldots, \phi_p)$ are real constants with $\phi_p \neq 0$, with the initial condition that $(y_0, y_1, \ldots, y_{p-1})$ are given. The associated polynomial equation is

$$1 - \phi_1 z - \phi_2 z^2 - \cdots - \phi_{p-1} z^{p-1} - \phi_p z^p = 0. \qquad (2)$$

Let λ_k $(k = 1, 2, \ldots, K)$ be the distinct roots of this equation (they can be complex numbers) and r_k be the multiplicity of λ_k. So $r_1 + r_2 + \cdots + r_K = p$. The polynomial equation can be written as

$$\prod_{k=1}^{K} (1 - \lambda_k^{-1} z)^{r_k} = 0. \qquad (3)$$

For example, consider the second degree polynomial equation

$$1 - z + \tfrac{1}{4} z^2 = 0. \qquad (4)$$

Its root is 2 with the multiplicity of 2 because

$$1 - z + \tfrac{1}{4} z^2 = (1 - \tfrac{1}{2} z)^2.$$

So $K = 1$ and $r_1 = 2$ and $\lambda_1 = 2$ in this example.

As you verify below, the solution to the p-th order homogeneous equation can be written as

$$y_j = \sum_{k=1}^{K} \sum_{n=0}^{r_k - 1} c_{kn} \cdot (j)^n \lambda_k^{-j}. \qquad (5)$$

The coefficients c_{kn} (there are p of those because $r_1 + \cdots + r_K = p$) can be determined from the initial conditions which specify the values for $(y_0, y_1, \ldots, y_{p-1})$. In the above example of (4),

$$y_j = c_{10} \cdot 2^{-j} + c_{11} \cdot j \cdot 2^{-j}. \qquad (6)$$

In the important special case where all the roots are distinct, $K = p$ and $r_k = 1$

for all k, and (5) becomes

$$y_j = \sum_{k=1}^{p} c_{k0}\, \lambda_k^{-j}. \tag{7}$$

(a) For the special case of $p = 2$ and distinct roots, (7) is

$$y_j = c_{10}\, \lambda_1^{-j} + c_{20}\, \lambda_2^{-j}. \tag{8}$$

Verify that this solves the homogeneous difference equation (1) with $p = 2$ for any given (c_{10}, c_{20}). To determine (c_{10}, c_{20}), write down (8) for $j = 0$ and $j = 1$, and solve for c's as a function of $(y_0, y_1, \lambda_1, \lambda_2)$.

(b) To learn (remember) how to deal with multiple roots, consider example (4) above. Verify that (6) solves the second-order homogeneous difference equation

$$y_j - y_{j-1} + \tfrac{1}{4} y_{j-2} = 0.$$

(c) (Optional) Prove the following lemma.

Lemma. *Let $0 \le \xi < 1$ and let n be a non-negative integer. Then there exist two real numbers, A and b, such that $\xi < b < 1$ and $(j)^n \xi^j < A b^j$ for $j = 0, 1, 2, \ldots$.*

Hint: Pick any b such that $\xi < b < 1$. Because b^j eventually gets larger than $(j)^n \xi^j$ as j increases, there exists some j, call it J, such that $(j)^n \xi^j < b^j$ for all $j \ge J$.

(d) Suppose the stability condition holds for the p-th order homogeneous linear difference equation. Prove that there exist two numbers, A and b, such that $0 < b < 1$ and

$$|y_j| < A b^j \quad \text{for } j = 0, 1, 2, \ldots.$$

Hint:

$$|y_j| = \left| \sum_{k=1}^{K} \sum_{n=0}^{r_k - 1} c_{kn} \cdot (j)^n \lambda_k^{-j} \right|$$

$$\leq \sum_{k=1}^{K} \sum_{n=0}^{r_k-1} |c_{kn}| \cdot (j)^n \cdot |\lambda_k^{-1}|^j$$

$$\leq c \sum_{k=1}^{K} \sum_{n=0}^{r_k-1} (j)^n |\lambda_k^{-1}|^j,$$

where $c = \max\{|c_{kn}|\}$. Since $|\lambda_k^{-1}| < 1$ by the stability condition, we can apply the lemma with $\xi = |\lambda_k^{-1}|$ and claim

$$(j)^n |\lambda_k^{-1}|^j < A_k (b_k)^j \quad \text{for all } j$$

for some $A_k > 0$ and $|\lambda_k^{-1}| < b_k < 1$. Set $A^* = \max\{A_k\}$ and $b = \max\{b_k\}$, so that $A_k (b_k)^j \leq A^* b^j$ for all k. So

$$|y_j| < c \sum_{k=1}^{K} \sum_{n=0}^{r_k-1} A^* b^j = cpA^* b^j.$$

(Recall that $p = r_1 + \cdots + r_K$.) Then define A to be cpA^*. You may find this sort of argument using inequalities hard to follow. If so, set p, K, and $(r_1, \ldots, r_K)$ to some specific numbers (e.g., $p = 3$, $K = 2$, $r_1 = 1$, $r_2 = 2$).

5. (Yule-Walker equations) In the text, the autocovariances of an AR(1) process were calculated from the MA(∞) representation. Here, we use the Yule-Walker equations.

   (a) From (6.2.1′) on page 376, derive

   $$\gamma_j - \phi \gamma_{j-1} = \mathrm{E}[\varepsilon_t \cdot (y_{t-j} - \mu)] \quad (j = 0, 1, 2, \ldots).$$

   (b) (Easy) From the MA representation, show that

   $$\mathrm{E}[\varepsilon_t \cdot (y_{t-j} - \mu)] = \begin{cases} \sigma^2 & (j = 0) \\ 0 & (j = 1, 2, \ldots). \end{cases}$$

   (c) Derive the Yule-Walker equations:

   $$\gamma_0 - \phi \gamma_1 = \sigma^2, \tag{9}$$

   $$\gamma_j - \phi \gamma_{j-1} = 0 \quad (j = 1, 2, \ldots). \tag{10}$$

(d) Calculate $(\gamma_0, \gamma_1, \dots)$ from (9) and (10). **Hint:** First set $j = 1$ in (10) to obtain $\gamma_1 = \phi\gamma_0$. This and (9) can be solved for (γ_0, γ_1).

6. (AR(1) without using filters) We wish to prove, without the help of Proposition 6.2, that $\{y_t\}$ following the AR(1) equation (6.2.1), with the stationarity condition $|\phi| < 1$, must have an MA(∞) representation if it is covariance-stationary.

 (a) Let $x_t \equiv y_t - \mu$ so that $\mathrm{E}(x_t) = 0$. By successive substitution, derive from (6.2.1′) (on page 376)

$$x_t = x_{t,n} + \phi^n x_{t-n}$$

 where

$$x_{t,n} = \varepsilon_t + \phi\varepsilon_{t-1} + \phi^2\varepsilon_{t-2} + \cdots + \phi^{n-1}\varepsilon_{t-n+1}.$$

 (b) Show that $x_{t,n} \to_{\text{m.s.}} x_t$. **Hint:** What needs to be shown is that $\mathrm{E}[(x_{t,n} - x_t)^2] \to 0$ as $n \to \infty$. $(x_{t,n} - x_t)^2 = \phi^{2n} x_{t-n}^2$. Because $\{y_t\}$ is assumed to be covariance-stationary, $\mathrm{E}(x_{t-n}^2) < \infty$.

 (c) (Trivial) Recalling that the infinite sum

$$\sum_{j=0}^{\infty} \phi^j \varepsilon_{t-j}$$

 is *defined* to be the mean square limit of the partial sum $x_{t,n}$, show that y_t can be written as

$$y_t = \mu + \sum_{j=0}^{\infty} \phi^j \varepsilon_{t-j}.$$

7. (Companion form) We wish to generalize the argument just developed in question 6 to AR(p). Without loss of generality, we can assume that $\mu = 0$ (or redefine y_t to be the deviation from the mean of y_t). Define

$$\underset{(p\times 1)}{\boldsymbol{\xi}_t} = \begin{bmatrix} y_t \\ y_{t-1} \\ y_{t-2} \\ \vdots \\ y_{t-p+1} \end{bmatrix}, \quad \underset{(p\times 1)}{\mathbf{v}_t} = \begin{bmatrix} \varepsilon_t \\ 0 \\ 0 \\ \vdots \\ 0 \end{bmatrix},$$

$$\underset{(p\times p)}{\mathbf{F}} = \begin{bmatrix} \phi_1 & \phi_2 & \phi_3 & \cdots & \phi_{p-1} & \phi_p \\ 1 & 0 & 0 & \cdots & 0 & 0 \\ 0 & 1 & 0 & \cdots & 0 & 0 \\ \vdots & \vdots & \vdots & \cdots & \vdots & \vdots \\ 0 & 0 & 0 & \cdots & 1 & 0 \end{bmatrix}.$$

Consider the following first-order vector stochastic difference equation:

$$\boldsymbol{\xi}_t = \mathbf{F}\boldsymbol{\xi}_{t-1} + \mathbf{v}_t. \tag{11}$$

In this system of p equations, called the **companion form**, the first equation is the same as the AR(p) equation (6.2.6′) on page 379 and the rest are just identities about y_{t-j} ($j = 1, 2, \ldots, p-1$).

(a) By successive substitution, show that

$$\begin{gathered} \boldsymbol{\xi}_t = \boldsymbol{\xi}_{t,n} + (\mathbf{F})^n \boldsymbol{\xi}_{t-n}, \\ \boldsymbol{\xi}_{t,n} \equiv \mathbf{v}_t + \mathbf{F}\mathbf{v}_{t-1} + \mathbf{F}^2\mathbf{v}_{t-2} + \cdots + (\mathbf{F})^{n-1}\mathbf{v}_{t-n+1}. \end{gathered} \tag{12}$$

The **eigenvalues** or **characteristic roots** of a $p \times p$ matrix $\mathbf{F}$ are the roots of the determinantal equation

$$|\mathbf{F} - \lambda \mathbf{I}_p| = 0. \tag{13}$$

It can be shown that the left-hand side of this is $\lambda^p - \phi_1\lambda^{p-1} - \cdots - \phi_{p-1}\lambda - \phi_p$. So the determinantal equation becomes the p-th order polynomial equation:

$$\lambda^p - \phi_1\lambda^{p-1} - \cdots - \phi_{p-1}\lambda - \phi_p = 0. \tag{14}$$

(b) Verify this for $p = 2$.

In the rest of this question, assume that all the roots of the p-th order polynomial equation (which, as just seen, are the eigenvalues of $\mathbf{F}$) are distinct. Let $(\lambda_1, \lambda_2, \ldots, \lambda_p)$ be those distinct eigenvalues. We have from matrix algebra that there exists a nonsingular $p \times p$ matrix $\mathbf{T}$ such that

$$\mathbf{F} = \mathbf{T}\boldsymbol{\Lambda}\mathbf{T}^{-1}, \quad \underset{(p\times p)}{\boldsymbol{\Lambda}} = \begin{bmatrix} \lambda_1 & 0 & 0 & \cdots & 0 \\ 0 & \lambda_2 & 0 & \cdots & 0 \\ \vdots & & \ddots & & \vdots \\ 0 & \cdots & 0 & \lambda_{p-1} & 0 \\ 0 & \cdots & 0 & 0 & \lambda_p \end{bmatrix}. \tag{15}$$

(This fact does not depend on the special form of the matrix $\mathbf{F}$; all that is needed for (15) is that the λ's are distinct eigenvalues of $\mathbf{F}$.) From (15) it follows that

$$(\mathbf{F})^n = \mathbf{T}(\mathbf{\Lambda})^n\mathbf{T}^{-1}.$$

(c) (Very easy) Prove this for $n = 3$.

(d) Show that $\boldsymbol{\xi}_{t,n} \rightarrow_{\text{m.s.}} \boldsymbol{\xi}_t$ as $n \to \infty$ if the stationarity condition about the AR(p) equation is satisfied and if $\{y_t\}$ is covariance-stationary. **Hint:** The stationarity condition requires that all the roots of (13) be less than 1 in absolute value. By (12) what needs to be shown is that $(\mathbf{F})^n\boldsymbol{\xi}_{t-n} \rightarrow_{\text{m.s.}} \mathbf{0}$. Recall that $\mathbf{z}_n \rightarrow_{\text{m.s.}} \boldsymbol{\alpha}$ if the mean square convergence occurs component-wise.

(e) Show that y_t has the MA(∞) representation

$$y_t = \psi_0\varepsilon_t + \psi_1\varepsilon_{t-1} + \psi_2\varepsilon_{t-2} + \cdots.$$

How is ψ_j related to the characteristic roots? **Hint:** From (d) it immediately follows that

$$\boldsymbol{\xi}_t = \mathbf{v}_t + \mathbf{F}\mathbf{v}_{t-1} + (\mathbf{F})^2\mathbf{v}_{t-2} + \cdots.$$

The top equation of this is the MA(∞) representation for y_t.

(If all the eigenvalues are not distinct, we need what is called the "Jordan decomposition" of $\mathbf{F}$ in place of (15).)

8. (AR(1) that started at $t = 0$) In the text, the MA(∞) representation (6.2.2) of an AR(1) process following $y_t = c + \phi y_{t-1} + \varepsilon_t$ assumes that the process is defined for $t = -1, -2, \ldots$ as well as for $t = 0, 1, 2, \ldots$. Instead, consider an AR(1) process that started at $t = 0$ with the initial value of y_0. Suppose that $|\phi| < 1$ and that y_0 is uncorrelated with the subsequent white noise process $(\varepsilon_1, \varepsilon_2, \ldots)$.

(a) Write the variance of y_t as a function of σ^2 ($\equiv \text{Var}(\varepsilon_t)$), $\text{Var}(y_0)$, and ϕ. **Hint:** By successive substitution,

$$\begin{aligned} y_t =& (1 + \phi + \phi^2 + \cdots + \phi^{t-1})c \\ &+ \varepsilon_t + \phi\varepsilon_{t-1} + \phi^2\varepsilon_{t-2} + \cdots + \phi^{t-1}\varepsilon_1 + \phi^t y_0. \end{aligned}$$

Let μ and $\{\gamma_j\}$ be the mean and autocovariances of the covariance-stationary AR(1) process, so $\mu = c/(1 - \phi)$ and $\{\gamma_j\}$ are as in (6.2.5).

Show that

$$\lim_{t\to\infty} \mathrm{E}(y_t) = \mu, \quad \lim_{t\to\infty} \mathrm{Var}(y_t) = \gamma_0, \quad \text{and} \quad \lim_{t\to\infty} \mathrm{Cov}(y_t, y_{t-j}) = \gamma_j.$$

(b) Show that $\{y_t\}$ is covariance-stationary if $\mathrm{E}(y_0) = \mu$ and $\mathrm{Var}(y_0) = \gamma_0$.

9. (Proof of Proposition 6.8(a)) We wish to prove Proposition 6.8(a). By Chebychev's inequality, it suffices to show that $\lim_{n\to\infty} \mathrm{Var}(\bar{y}) = 0$. From (6.5.2),

$$\begin{aligned}
\mathrm{Var}(\bar{y}) &= \frac{\gamma_0}{n} + \frac{2}{n}\sum_{j=1}^{n-1}\left(1 - \frac{j}{n}\right)\gamma_j \\
&= \frac{\gamma_0}{n} + \frac{2}{n}\sum_{j=1}^{n}\left(1 - \frac{j}{n}\right)\gamma_j \quad \left(\text{since } 1 - \frac{j}{n} = 0 \text{ for } j = n\right) \\
&\le \frac{\gamma_0}{n} + \frac{2}{n}\sum_{j=1}^{n}\left(1 - \frac{j}{n}\right)|\gamma_j| \\
&\le \frac{\gamma_0}{n} + \frac{2}{n}\sum_{j=1}^{n}|\gamma_j|.
\end{aligned}$$

(a) (Optional) Prove the following result:

$$\lim_{j\to\infty} a_j = 0 \Rightarrow \lim_{n\to\infty} \frac{1}{n}\sum_{j=1}^{n} a_j = 0.$$

Hint: $\{a_j\}$ converges to 0. So (i) $|a_j| < M$ for all j, and (ii) for any given $\varepsilon > 0$ there exists a positive integer N such that $|a_j| < \varepsilon/2$ for all $j > N$. So

$$\begin{aligned}
\left|\frac{1}{n}\sum_{j=1}^{n} a_j\right| &\le \frac{1}{n}\sum_{j=1}^{n}|a_j| \\
&= \frac{1}{n}\sum_{j=1}^{N}|a_j| + \frac{1}{n}\sum_{j=N+1}^{n}|a_j| < \frac{1}{n}\sum_{j=1}^{N} M + \frac{1}{n}\sum_{j=N+1}^{n}\frac{\varepsilon}{2} \\
&= \frac{NM}{n} + \frac{(n-N)}{n}\frac{\varepsilon}{2} < \frac{NM}{n} + \frac{\varepsilon}{2}.
\end{aligned}$$

By taking n large enough, NM/n can be made less than $\varepsilon/2$.

(b) Taking the result in (a) as given, prove that $\mathrm{Var}(\bar{y}) \to 0$ as $n \to \infty$.

10. (Proof of Proposition 6.8(b))

(a) (optional) Prove the following result:

$$\sum_{j=1}^{\infty} a_j < \infty \Rightarrow \lim_{n\to\infty} \frac{1}{n} \sum_{j=1}^{n} j a_j = 0.$$

Hint:

$$\begin{aligned}
\sum_{j=1}^{n} j a_j &= a_1 + 2a_2 + 3a_3 + \cdots + n a_n \\
&= (a_1 + a_2 + \cdots + a_n) + (a_2 + a_3 + \cdots + a_n) + \cdots \\
&\quad + (a_{n-1} + a_n) + a_n \\
&= \sum_{j=1}^{n} \sum_{k=j}^{n} a_k \le \sum_{j=1}^{n} \left| \sum_{k=j}^{n} a_k \right| \\
&= \sum_{j=1}^{N} \left| \sum_{k=j}^{n} a_k \right| + \sum_{j=N+1}^{n} \left| \sum_{k=j}^{n} a_k \right|.
\end{aligned}$$

Since $\{a_j\}$ is summable, (i) $|\sum_{k=j}^{n} a_k| < M$ for all j, n, and (ii) there exists a positive integer N such that $|\sum_{k=j}^{n} a_k| < \varepsilon/2$ for any given $\varepsilon > 0$ for all $j, n > N$ (this follows because $\{\sum_{j=1}^{n} a_j\}$ is Cauchy).

(b) Taking this result as given, prove Proposition 6.8(b).

EMPIRICAL EXERCISES

1. Read at least pp. 115–119 (except the last two paragraphs of p. 119) of Bekaert and Hodrick (1993) before answering. Data files DM.ASC (for the Deutsche Mark), POUND.ASC (British Pound), and YEN.ASC (Japanese Yen) contain weekly data on the following items:

Column 1: the date of the observation (e.g., "19850104" is January 4, 1985)
Column 2: the ask price of the dollar in units of the foreign currency in the spot market on Friday of the current week (S_t)
Column 3: the ask price of the dollar in units of the foreign currency in the 30-day forward market on Friday of the current week (F_t)
Column 4: the bid price of the dollar in units of the foreign currency in the spot market on the delivery date on a current forward contract ($S30_t$).

The sample period is the first week of 1975 through the last week of 1989. The sample size is 778. As in the text, define $s_t \equiv \log(S_t)$, $f_t \equiv \log(F_t)$, $s30_t \equiv \log(S30_t)$. If I_t is the information available on the Friday of week t, it includes $\{s_t, s_{t-1}, \dots, f_t, f_{t-1}, \dots, s30_{t-5}, s30_{t-6}, \dots\}$. Note that $s30_t$ is not observed until after the Friday of week $t+4$. Define $\varepsilon_t \equiv s30_t - f_t$.

Pick your favorite currency to answer the following questions.

(a) (Library/internet work) For the foreign currency of your choice, identify the week when the absolute value of the forward premium is largest. For that week, find some measure of the domestic one-month interest rate (e.g., the one-month CD rate) for the United States and the currency's home country, to verify that the interest rate differential is as large as is indicated in the forward premium.

(b) (Correlogram of $\{\varepsilon_t\}$) Draw the sample correlogram of ε_t with 40 lags. Does the autocorrelation appear to vanish after 4 lags? (It is up to you to decide whether to subtract the sample mean in the calculation of sample correlations. Theory says the population mean is zero, which you might want to impose in the calculation. In the calculation of the correlogram for the yen/$ exchange rate shown in Figure 6.2, the sample mean was subtracted.)

(c) (Is the log spot rate a random walk?) Draw the sample correlogram of $s_{t+1} - s_t$ with 40 lags. For those 40 autocorrelations, use the Box-Ljung statistic to test for serial correlation. Can you reject the hypothesis that $\{s_t\}$ is a random walk with drift?

(d) (Unconditional test) Carry out the unconditional test. Can you replicate the results of Table 6.1 for the currency?

(e) (Optional, regression test with truncated kernel) Carry out the regression test. Can you replicate the results of Table 6.2 for the currency?

RATS Tip: Use `LINREG` with the `ROBUSTERRORS` option. To include autocorrelations up to the fourth, set `LAGS = 4` in `LINREG`. The `DAMP = 0` option instructs `LINREG` to use the truncated kernel.

TSP Tip: TSP's `GMM` procedure has the `KERNEL` option, but the choice is limited to Bartlett and the kernel called Parzen. You would have to use TSP's matrix commands to do the truncated kernel estimation.

(f) (Bartlett kernel) Use the Bartlett kernel-based estimator of $\mathbf{S}$ to do the regression test. Newey and West (1994) provide a data-dependent automatic bandwidth selection procedure. Take for granted that the autocovariance lag length determined by this procedure is 12 for yen/$ (so autocovariances up to the twelfth are included in the calculation of $\widehat{\mathbf{S}}$), 8 for DM/$, and 16 for Pound/$.

RATS Tip: The `ROBUSTERRORS, DAMP = 1` option instructs `LINREG` to use Bartlett. For yen/$, for example, set `LAGS = 12`.

TSP Tip: Set `het, kernel = bartlett` in the `GMM` procedure. Set `NMA = 12` for yen/$.

The standard error for the $f - s$ coefficient for yen/$ should be 0.6815.

(g) (Optional, VARHAC) Use the VARHAC estimator for $\widehat{\mathbf{S}}$ in the regression test. Set p_{max} to the integer part of $n^{1/3}$. In Step 1 of the VARHAC, you would estimate a bivariate VAR, and for each of the two VAR equations, you would pick the lag length p by BIC on the fixed sample of $t = p_{max} + 1, \ldots, T$. The information criterion could be (6.6.11) or, alternatively,

$$\log\left(SSR_p^{(k)}/(n - p_{max})\right) + pK \cdot \log(n - p_{max})/(n - p_{max}). \qquad (16)$$

Just to be clear about how you picked p in your answer, use this latter objective function in selecting p by BIC. For the case of yen/$, the lag length selected should be 4 for the first VAR equation and 6 for the second equation. For yen/$, the standard error for the $f - s$ coefficient should be 0.8027.

2. (Continuation of the Fama exercise of Chapter 2) Now we know how to use the three-month T-bill rate to test the efficiency of the U.S. Treasury bills market using monthly data. Let

π_t = inflation rate (in percent, annual rate) over the three-month period ending in month $t - 1$,

R_t = three-month T-bill rate (in percent, annual rate) at the beginning of month t.

Consider the Fama regression for testing market efficiency:

$$\pi_{t+3} = \beta_0 + \beta_1 R_t + \varepsilon_t.$$

(a) (Trivial) Why is the dependent variable π_{t+3} rather than, say, π_t?

(b) Show that, under the efficient market hypothesis, $\beta_1 = 1$ and the autocovariance of $\{\varepsilon_t\}$ vanishes after the second lag (i.e., $\gamma_j = 0$ for $j > 2$).

(c) Let $r_{t+3} \equiv R_t - \pi_{t+3}$ be the ex-post real rate on the three-month T-bill. Use *PAI3* in MISHKIN.ASC as the measure of the three-month inflation rate to calculate the ex-post real rate. (The timing of the variables in MISHKIN.ASC is such that a January interest rate observation uses end-of-December bill rate data and a January observation for a three-month inflation rate is from the December to March CPI data. So *PAI3* and *TB3* (three-month T-bill rate) for the same month can be paired in the regression.) Draw the sample correlogram for the sample period of 1/53–7/71. What is the prediction of the efficient market hypothesis about the correlogram?

(d) Test market efficiency by estimating the Fama regression for the sample period of 1/53–7/71. (The sample size should be 223; do not throw away two-thirds of the observations, as Fama did in his Tables 6–8.) Use (6.6.4) with $q = 2$ for $\widehat{\mathbf{S}}$.

ANSWERS TO SELECTED QUESTIONS

ANALYTICAL EXERCISES

2d. Since $\{\psi_j\}$ is absolutely summable, $\psi_j \to 0$ as $j \to \infty$. So for any j, there exists an $A > 0$ such that $|\psi_{j+k}| \leq A$ for all j, k. So $|\psi_{j+k} \cdot \psi_k| \leq A|\psi_k|$. Since $\{\psi_k\}$ (and hence $\{A\psi_k\}$) is absolutely summable, so is $\{\psi_{j+k} \cdot \psi_k\}$ ($k = 0, 1, 2, \ldots$) for any given j. Thus by (i),

$$|\gamma_j| = \sigma^2 \left| \sum_{k=0}^{\infty} \psi_{j+k}\psi_k \right| \leq \sigma^2 \sum_{k=0}^{\infty} |\psi_{j+k}\psi_k| = \sigma^2 \sum_{k=0}^{\infty} |\psi_{j+k}|\,|\psi_k| < \infty.$$

Now set a_{jk} in (ii) to $|\psi_{j+k}| \cdot |\psi_k|$. Then

$$\sum_{j=0}^{\infty} |a_{jk}| = \sum_{j=0}^{\infty} |\psi_k|\,|\psi_{j+k}| \leq |\psi_k| \sum_{j=0}^{\infty} |\psi_j| < \infty.$$

Let

$$M \equiv \sum_{j=0}^{\infty} |\psi_j| \quad \text{and} \quad s_k \equiv |\psi_k| \sum_{j=0}^{\infty} |\psi_{j+k}|.$$

Then $\{s_k\}$ is summable because $|s_k| \leq |\psi_k| \cdot M$ and $\{\psi_k\}$ is absolutely summable. Therefore, by (ii),

$$\sum_{j=0}^{\infty}\Big(\sum_{k=0}^{\infty} |\psi_{j+k}| \cdot |\psi_k|\Big) < \infty.$$

This times σ^2 is $\sum_{j=0}^{\infty} |\gamma_j|$. So $\{\gamma_j\}$ is absolutely summable.

7e. ψ_j is the (1, 1) element of $\mathbf{T}(\mathbf{\Lambda})^j\mathbf{T}^{-1}$.

8a.

$$\begin{aligned}
\mathrm{E}(y_t) &= \frac{1-\phi^t}{1-\phi} c + \phi^t \,\mathrm{E}(y_0) \\
&= (1-\phi^t)\mu + \phi^t \,\mathrm{E}(y_0) \quad (\text{since } \mu = c/(1-\phi)) \\
&= \mu + \phi^t \cdot [\mathrm{E}(y_0) - \mu],
\end{aligned}$$

$$\begin{aligned}
\mathrm{Var}(y_t) &= (1 + \phi^2 + \phi^4 + \cdots + \phi^{2t-2})\sigma^2 \\
&\quad + \phi^{2t}\,\mathrm{Var}(y_0) \quad (\text{since } \mathrm{Cov}(\varepsilon_t, y_0) = 0) \\
&= \frac{1-\phi^{2t}}{1-\phi^2}\sigma^2 + \phi^{2t}\,\mathrm{Var}(y_0) \\
&= (1-\phi^{2t})\gamma_0 + \phi^{2t}\,\mathrm{Var}(y_0) \quad (\text{since } \gamma_0 \equiv \sigma^2/(1-\phi^2)), \\
&= \gamma_0 + \phi^{2t} \cdot [\mathrm{Var}(y_0) - \gamma_0],
\end{aligned}$$

$$\begin{aligned}
\mathrm{Cov}(y_t, y_{t-j}) &= (\phi^j + \phi^{j+2} + \cdots + \phi^{2t-j-2})\sigma^2 + \phi^{2t-j}\,\mathrm{Var}(y_0) \\
&= \phi^j \cdot (1 + \phi^2 + \cdots + \phi^{2t-2j-2})\sigma^2 + \phi^{2t-j}\,\mathrm{Var}(y_0) \\
&= \phi^j \cdot \frac{1-\phi^{2(t-j)}}{1-\phi^2}\sigma^2 + \phi^{2t-j}\,\mathrm{Var}(y_0) \\
&= \phi^j \cdot (1-\phi^{2(t-j)})\gamma_0 + \phi^{2t-j}\,\mathrm{Var}(y_0) \\
&= \gamma_0\phi^j + \phi^{2t-j} \cdot [\mathrm{Var}(y_0) - \gamma_0] \\
&= \gamma_j + \phi^{2t-j} \cdot [\mathrm{Var}(y_0) - \gamma_0].
\end{aligned}$$

EMPIRICAL EXERCISES

1c. The Ljung-Box statistic with 40 lags is 84.0 with a p-value of 0.0058%. So the hypothesis that the spot rate is a random walk with drift can be rejected. See Figure 6.6 for the correlogram for yen/\$.

1f. For the yen/\$ exchange rate, the standard errors are 3.72 for the constant and 0.68 for the $f - s$ coefficient. The Wald statistic for the hypothesis that $\beta_0 = 0$ and $\beta_1 = 1$ is 21.85 ($p = 0.002\%$).

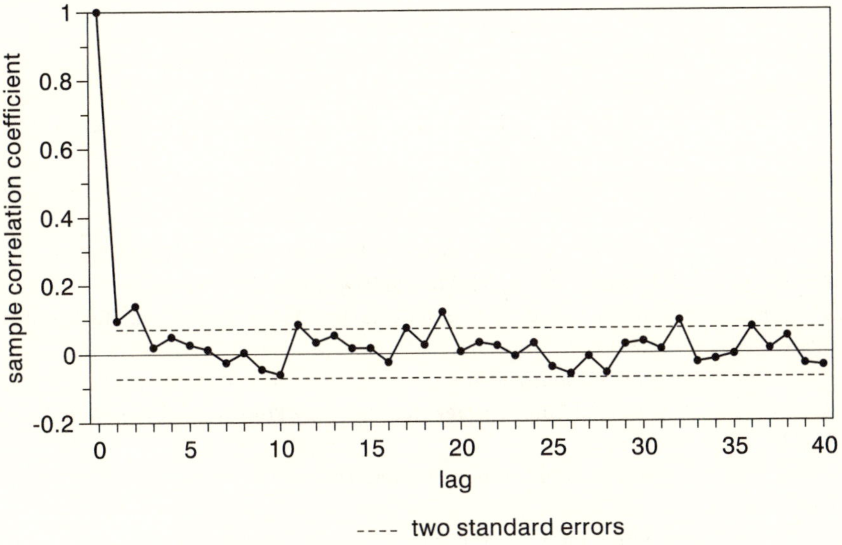

Figure 6.6: Correlogram of $s_{t+1} - s_t$, Yen/Dollar

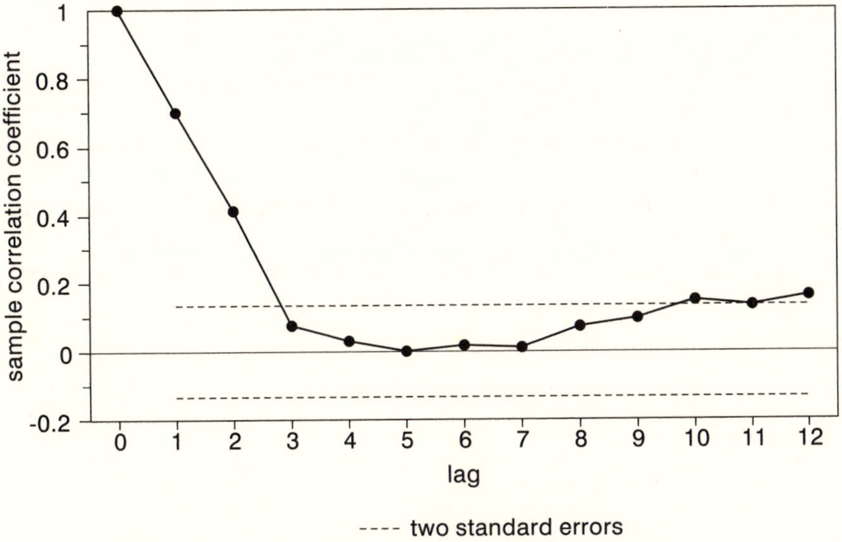

Figure 6.7: Correlogram of Three-Month Ex-Post Real Rate

2c. The correlogram for the three-month ex-post real rate is shown above (Figure 6.7). Theory predicts that serial correlation vanishes after the second lag. The correlogram is mostly consistent with this prediction.

References

Anderson, T. W., 1971, *The Statistical Analysis of Time Series*, New York: Wiley.

Andrews, D., 1991, "Heteroskedasticity and Autocorrelation Consistent Covariance Matrix Estimation," *Econometrica*, 59, 817–858.

Bekaert, G., and R. Hodrick, 1993, "On Biases in the Measurement of Foreign Exchange Risk Premiums," *Journal of International Money and Finance*, 12, 115–138.

Brockwell, P., and R. Davis, 1991, *Time Series: Theory and Methods* (2d ed.), Berlin: Springer-Verlag.

Den Haan, W., and A. Levin, 1996a, "Inferences from Parametric and Non-Parametric Covariance Matrix Estimation Procedures," Technical Working Paper Series 195, NBER.

______, 1996b, "A Practitioner's Guide to Robust Covariance Matrix Estimation," Technical Working Paper Series 197, NBER.

Fuller, W., 1996, *Introduction to Statistical Time Series* (2d ed.), New York: Wiley.

Gordin, M. I., 1969, "The Central Limit Theorem for Stationary Processes," *Soviet Math. Dokl.*, 10, 1174–1176.

Gourieroux, C., and A. Monfort, 1997, *Time Series and Dynamic Models*, Cambridge: Cambridge University Press.

Hamilton, J., 1994, *Time Series Analysis*, Princeton: Princeton University Press.

Hannan, E. J., 1970, *Multiple Time Series*, New York: Wiley.

Hannan, E. J., and M. Deistler, 1988, *The Statistical Theory of Linear Systems*, New York: Wiley.

Hansen, L., 1982, "Large Sample Properties of Generalized Method of Moments Estimators," *Econometrica*, 50, 1029–1054.

Lütkepohl, H., 1993, *Introduction to Multiple Time Series Analysis* (2d ed.), New York: Springer-Verlag.

Newey, W., and K. West, 1987, "Hypothesis Testing with Efficient Method of Moments Estimation," *International Economic Review*, 28, 777–787.

______, 1994, "Automatic Lag Selection in Covariance Matrix Estimation," *Review of Economic Studies*, 61, 631–653.

Ng, S., and P. Perron, 2000, "A Note on Model Selection in Time Series Analysis," mimeo., Boston: Boston College.

White, H., 1984, *Asymptotic Theory for Econometricians*, New York: Academic.

CHAPTER 7

Extremum Estimators

ABSTRACT

In the previous chapters, the generalized method of moments (GMM) has been our choice for estimating the various models we have considered. The method of maximum likelihood (ML) has been discussed, but only in passing. In this chapter, we expand our repertoire of estimation techniques by examining a class of estimators called "extremum estimators," which includes (linear and nonlinear) least squares, (linear and nonlinear) GMM, and ML as special cases. As has been emphasized by Amemiya (1985) and others, this unified approach is useful for bringing out the common structure that underlies those apparently diverse estimation principles.

Section 7.1 introduces extremum estimators. The two sections that follow develop the asymptotic properties of extremum estimators. Section 7.4 defines the trio of test statistics — the Wald, Langrange multipler, and likelihood-ratio statistics — for extremum estimators in general, and shows how they can be specialized to individual cases. Section 7.5 is a brief discussion of the computational aspects of extremum estimators.

The discussion of this chapter may appear daunting, as it combines a heavy use of asymptotic theory with calculus. The essence, however, is really straightforward. If you can read graduate textbooks on micro and macroeconomics without too much difficulty, you should be able to understand most of the discussion on the second (if not the first) reading.

If you are not interested in the asymptotics of extremum estimators *per se* but plan to study Chapter 8, there is no need to read this chapter in its entirety. Just read Section 7.1 and then try to understand the statements in Propositions 7.5, 7.6, 7.8, 7.9, and 7.11.

A Note on Notation: Unlike in the previous chapters, we use the parameter vector with subscript 0 for its true value. So $\boldsymbol{\theta}_0$ is the true parameter value, while $\boldsymbol{\theta}$ represents a hypothetical parameter value. This notation is standard in the "high-brow" literature on nonlinear estimation. Also, we will use "t" rather than "i" for the observation index.

7.1 Extremum Estimators

An estimator $\hat{\boldsymbol{\theta}}$ is called an **extremum estimator** if there is a scalar objective function $Q_n(\boldsymbol{\theta})$ such that

$$\hat{\boldsymbol{\theta}} \text{ maximizes } Q_n(\boldsymbol{\theta}) \text{ subject to } \boldsymbol{\theta} \in \Theta \subset \mathbb{R}^p, \tag{7.1.1}$$

where Θ, called the **parameter space**, is the set of possible parameter values. In this book, we restrict our attention to the case where Θ is a subset of the finite dimensional Euclidean space $\mathbb{R}^p$. The objective function $Q_n(\boldsymbol{\theta})$ depends not only on $\boldsymbol{\theta}$ but also on the sample or the data, $(\mathbf{w}_1, \mathbf{w}_2, \dots, \mathbf{w}_n)$, where $\mathbf{w}_t$ is the t-th observation and n is the sample size. In our notation the dependence of the objective function on the sample of size n is signalled by the subscript n. The maximum likelihood (ML) and the linear and nonlinear generalized method of moments (GMM) estimators are particular extremum estimators. This section presents these and other extremum estimators and indicates how they are related to each other.

"Measurability" of $\hat{\boldsymbol{\theta}}$

To be sure, the maximization problem (7.1.1) may not necessarily have a solution. But recall from calculus the following fact:

> Let $h : \mathbb{R}^p \to \mathbb{R}$ be continuous and $A \subset \mathbb{R}^p$ be a compact (closed and bounded) set. Then h has a maximum on the set A. That is, there exists an $\mathbf{x}^* \in A$ such that $h(\mathbf{x}^*) \geq h(\mathbf{x})$ for all $\mathbf{x}$ in A.

Therefore, if $Q_n(\boldsymbol{\theta})$ is continuous in $\boldsymbol{\theta}$ for any data $(\mathbf{w}_1, \mathbf{w}_2, \dots, \mathbf{w}_n)$ and Θ is compact, then there exists a $\boldsymbol{\theta}$ that solves the maximization problem in (7.1.1) for any given data $(\mathbf{w}_1, \dots, \mathbf{w}_n)$. In the event of multiple solutions, we would choose one from them. So $\hat{\boldsymbol{\theta}}$, thus uniquely determined for any data $(\mathbf{w}_1, \dots, \mathbf{w}_n)$, is a function of the data. Strictly speaking, however, being a function of the vector of random variables $(\mathbf{w}_1, \dots, \mathbf{w}_n)$ is not enough to make $\hat{\boldsymbol{\theta}}$ a well-defined random variable; $\hat{\boldsymbol{\theta}}$ needs to be a "measurable" function of $(\mathbf{w}_1, \dots, \mathbf{w}_n)$. (If a function is continuous, it is measurable.) The following lemma shows that $\hat{\boldsymbol{\theta}}$ is measurable if $Q_n(\boldsymbol{\theta})$ is

Lemma 7.1 (Existence of extremum estimators): *Suppose that (i) the parameter space Θ is a compact subset of $\mathbb{R}^p$, (ii) $Q_n(\boldsymbol{\theta})$ is continuous in $\boldsymbol{\theta}$ for any data $(\mathbf{w}_1, \dots, \mathbf{w}_n)$, and (iii) $Q_n(\boldsymbol{\theta})$ is a measurable function of the data for all $\boldsymbol{\theta}$ in Θ. Then there exists a measurable function $\hat{\boldsymbol{\theta}}$ of the data that solves (7.1.1).*

See, e.g., Gourieroux and Monfort (1995, Property 24.1) for a proof. In all the examples of this chapter, $Q_n(\boldsymbol{\theta})$ is measurable.

In most applications, we do not know the upper or lower bound for the true parameter vector. Even if we do, those bounds are not included in the parameter space, so the parameter space is not closed (see the CES example below for an example). So the compactness assumption for Θ is something we wish to avoid. In some of the asymptotic results of this chapter, we will replace the compactness assumption by some other conditions that are satisfied in many applications.

Two Classes of Extremum Estimators

In the next two sections, we will develop asymptotic results for extremum estimators and then specialize those results to the following two classes of extremum estimators.

1. **M-Estimators**. An extremum estimator is an **M-estimator** if the objective function is a sample average:

$$Q_n(\boldsymbol{\theta}) = \frac{1}{n}\sum_{t=1}^{n} m(\mathbf{w}_t; \boldsymbol{\theta}), \tag{7.1.2}$$

where m is a real-valued function of $(\mathbf{w}_t, \boldsymbol{\theta})$. Two examples of an M-estimator we study are the **maximum likelihood (ML)** and the **nonlinear least squares (NLS)**.

2. **GMM**. An extremum estimator is a **GMM estimator** if the objective function can be written as

$$Q_n(\boldsymbol{\theta}) = -\frac{1}{2}\mathbf{g}_n(\boldsymbol{\theta})'\widehat{\mathbf{W}}\mathbf{g}_n(\boldsymbol{\theta}) \text{ with } \underset{(K\times 1)}{\mathbf{g}_n(\boldsymbol{\theta})} \equiv \frac{1}{n}\sum_{t=1}^{n} \mathbf{g}(\mathbf{w}_t; \boldsymbol{\theta}), \tag{7.1.3}$$

where $\widehat{\mathbf{W}}$ is a $K \times K$ symmetric and positive definite matrix that defines the distance of $\mathbf{g}_n(\boldsymbol{\theta})$ from zero. It can depend on the data. Maximizing this objective function is equivalent to minimizing the distance $\mathbf{g}_n(\boldsymbol{\theta})'\widehat{\mathbf{W}}\mathbf{g}_n(\boldsymbol{\theta})$, which is how we defined GMM in Chapter 3. As will become clear, the deflation of the distance by 2 simplifies the expression for the derivative of the objective function. We have introduced GMM estimation for linear models where $\mathbf{g}(\mathbf{w}_t; \boldsymbol{\theta})$ is linear in $\boldsymbol{\theta}$. Below we will show that GMM estimation can be extended easily to nonlinear models.

There are extremum estimators that do not fall into either class. A prominent example is **classical minimum distance estimators**. Their objective function can be written as $-\mathbf{g}_n(\boldsymbol{\theta})'\widehat{\mathbf{W}}\mathbf{g}_n(\boldsymbol{\theta})$ but $\mathbf{g}_n(\boldsymbol{\theta})$ is not necessarily a sample mean. The consistency theorem of the next section is general enough to cover this class as well.

In the rest of this section, we present examples of M-estimators and GMM estimators. Each example is a combination of the *model* (a set of data generating processes [DGPs]) and the *estimation method.*

Maximum Likelihood (ML)

A prime example of an M-estimator is the maximum likelihood for the case where $\{\mathbf{w}_t\}$ is i.i.d. The model here is a set of i.i.d. sequences $\{\mathbf{w}_t\}$ where the density of $\mathbf{w}_t$ is a member of the family of densities indexed by a finite-dimensional vector $\boldsymbol{\theta}$: $f(\mathbf{w}_t; \boldsymbol{\theta})$, $\boldsymbol{\theta} \in \Theta$. (Since $\{\mathbf{w}_t\}$ is identically distributed, the functional form of $f(\cdot;\cdot)$ does not depend on t.) The functional form of $f(\cdot;\cdot)$ is known. The model is **parametric** because the parameter vector $\boldsymbol{\theta}$ is finite dimensional. At the true parameter value $\boldsymbol{\theta}_0$, the density of the true DGP (the DGP that actually generated the data) is $f(\mathbf{w}_t; \boldsymbol{\theta}_0)$.[1] We say that the model is **correctly specified** if $\boldsymbol{\theta}_0 \in \Theta$.

Since $\{\mathbf{w}_t\}$ is independently distributed, the joint density of the data $(\mathbf{w}_1, \mathbf{w}_2, \ldots, \mathbf{w}_n)$ is

$$f(\mathbf{w}_1, \mathbf{w}_2, \ldots, \mathbf{w}_n; \boldsymbol{\theta}_0) = \prod_{t=1}^{n} f(\mathbf{w}_t; \boldsymbol{\theta}_0). \tag{7.1.4}$$

With the distribution of the data thus completely specified, the natural estimation method is maximum likelihood, which proceeds as follows. With the true parameter vector $\boldsymbol{\theta}_0$ replaced by its hypothetical value $\boldsymbol{\theta}$, this density, viewed as a function of $\boldsymbol{\theta}$, is called the **likelihood function**. The maximum likelihood (ML) estimator of $\boldsymbol{\theta}_0$ is the $\boldsymbol{\theta}$ that maximizes the likelihood function. Since the log transformation is a monotone transformation, maximizing the likelihood function is equivalent to maximizing the **log likelihood function**:[2]

$$\log f(\mathbf{w}_1, \mathbf{w}_2, \ldots, \mathbf{w}_n; \boldsymbol{\theta}) = \log\left[\prod_{t=1}^{n} f(\mathbf{w}_t; \boldsymbol{\theta})\right] = \sum_{t=1}^{n} \log f(\mathbf{w}_t; \boldsymbol{\theta}). \tag{7.1.5}$$

The ML estimator of $\boldsymbol{\theta}_0$, therefore, is an M-estimator with

[1] Had we adhered to the notational convention of the previous sections, the true parameter value would be denoted by $\boldsymbol{\theta}$ and a hypothetical value by $\tilde{\boldsymbol{\theta}}$. In this chapter, we use $\boldsymbol{\theta}_0$ for the true value and $\boldsymbol{\theta}$ for a hypothetical value of the parameter vector.

[2] For $\boldsymbol{\theta}$ such that $f(\mathbf{w}_t; \boldsymbol{\theta}) = 0$, the log cannot be taken. This does not present a problem because such $\boldsymbol{\theta}$ never maximizes the (level) likelihood function $f(\mathbf{w}_1, \ldots, \mathbf{w}_n; \boldsymbol{\theta})$. For such $\boldsymbol{\theta}$ we can assign an arbitrarily small number to $\log f(\mathbf{w}_t; \boldsymbol{\theta})$ so that the maximizer of the level likelihood is also the maximization of the log likelihood. See White (1994, p. 15) for a more formal treatment of this issue.

$$m(\mathbf{w}_t;\boldsymbol{\theta}) = \log f(\mathbf{w}_t;\boldsymbol{\theta}), \quad \text{that is,} \quad Q_n(\boldsymbol{\theta}) = \frac{1}{n}\sum_{t=1}^{n} \log f(\mathbf{w}_t;\boldsymbol{\theta}). \tag{7.1.6}$$

Before illustrating ML by an example, it is useful to make three remarks.

- (Serially correlated observations) The average log likelihood would not take a form as simple as this if $\{\mathbf{w}_t\}$ were serially correlated. Examples of ML for serially correlated observations will be studied in the next chapter.
- (Alternative estimators) Maximum likelihood is not the only way to estimate the parameter vector. For example, let $\boldsymbol{\mu}(\boldsymbol{\theta})$ be the expectation of $\mathbf{w}_t$ implied by the density function $f(\mathbf{w}_t;\boldsymbol{\theta})$. It is a known function of $\boldsymbol{\theta}$. By construction, the following zero-mean condition holds:

$$\mathrm{E}[\mathbf{w}_t - \boldsymbol{\mu}(\boldsymbol{\theta}_0)] = \mathbf{0}. \tag{7.1.7}$$

The parameter vector $\boldsymbol{\theta}_0$ could be estimated by GMM with $\mathbf{g}(\mathbf{w}_t;\boldsymbol{\theta}) = \mathbf{w}_t - \boldsymbol{\mu}(\boldsymbol{\theta})$ in the GMM objective function (7.1.3).

- (Efficiency of ML) As will be shown in the next two sections, ML is consistent and asymptotically normal under suitable conditions. It was widely believed that ML is efficient (i.e., achieves minimum asymptotic variance) in the class of all consistent and asymptotically normal estimators. This belief was shown to be wrong by a counterexample (described, for example, in Amemiya, 1985, Example 4.2.4). Nevertheless, ML is efficient in quite general classes of asymptotically normal estimators. One such general class is GMM estimators. In Section 7.3, we will note that the asymptotic variance of any GMM estimator of $\boldsymbol{\theta}_0$ is no smaller than that of the ML estimator.

Example 7.1 (Estimating the mean of a normal distribution): Let the data $(w_1, \ldots, w_n)$ be a scalar i.i.d. sequence with the distribution of w_t given by $N(\mu, \sigma^2)$. So $\boldsymbol{\theta} = (\mu, \sigma^2)'$ and

$$f(w_t;\mu,\sigma^2) = \frac{1}{\sqrt{2\pi\sigma^2}} \exp\left[-\frac{(w_t-\mu)^2}{2\sigma^2}\right].$$

The average log likelihood of the data $(w_1, \ldots, w_n)$ is

$$\frac{1}{n}\sum_{t=1}^{n} \log f(w_t;\mu,\sigma^2) = -\frac{1}{2}\log(2\pi) - \frac{1}{2}\log(\sigma^2) - \frac{1}{n}\sum_{t=1}^{n}\left[\frac{(w_t-\mu)^2}{2\sigma^2}\right]. \tag{7.1.8}$$

The ML estimator of (μ_0, σ_0^2) is an extremum estimator with $Q_n(\boldsymbol{\theta})$ taken to be this average log likelihood. Suppose that the variance is assumed to be positive but that there is no *a priori* restriction on μ_0, so the parameter space Θ is $\mathbb{R} \times \mathbb{R}_{++}$, where $\mathbb{R}_{++}$ is the set of positive real numbers. It is easy to check that the ML estimator of μ_0 is the sample mean of w_t. The GMM estimator of μ_0 based on the zero-mean condition $\mathrm{E}(w_t - \mu_0) = 0$, too, is the sample mean of w_t.

Conditional Maximum Likelihood

In most applications, the vector $\mathbf{w}_t$ is partitioned into two groups, y_t and $\mathbf{x}_t$, and the researcher's interest is to examine how $\mathbf{x}_t$ influences the conditional distribution of y_t given $\mathbf{x}_t$. We have been calling the variable y_t the **dependent variable** and $\mathbf{x}_t$ **regressors**. None of the results of this chapter depends on y_t being a scalar; y_t can be a vector and still all the results will remain valid with the scalar "y_t" replaced by a vector "$\mathbf{y}_t$." We nevertheless use the scalar notation, simply because in all the examples we consider in this chapter, there is only one dependent variable.

Let $f(y_t \mid \mathbf{x}_t; \boldsymbol{\theta}_0)$ be the conditional density of y_t given $\mathbf{x}_t$, and let $f(\mathbf{x}_t; \boldsymbol{\psi}_0)$ be the marginal density of $\mathbf{x}_t$. Then

$$f(y_t, \mathbf{x}_t; \boldsymbol{\theta}_0, \boldsymbol{\psi}_0) = f(y_t \mid \mathbf{x}_t; \boldsymbol{\theta}_0) f(\mathbf{x}_t; \boldsymbol{\psi}_0) \tag{7.1.9}$$

is the joint density of $\mathbf{w}_t = (y_t, \mathbf{x}_t')'$. Suppose, for now, that $\boldsymbol{\theta}_0$ and $\boldsymbol{\psi}_0$ are not functionally related (see the next paragraph for an example of a functional relationship). The average log likelihood of the data $(\mathbf{w}_1, \ldots, \mathbf{w}_n)$ is

$$\frac{1}{n}\sum_{t=1}^{n} \log f(\mathbf{w}_t; \boldsymbol{\theta}, \boldsymbol{\psi}) = \frac{1}{n}\sum_{t=1}^{n} \log f(y_t \mid \mathbf{x}_t; \boldsymbol{\theta}) + \frac{1}{n}\sum_{t=1}^{n} \log f(\mathbf{x}_t; \boldsymbol{\psi}). \tag{7.1.10}$$

The first term on the right-hand side is the average **log conditional likelihood**. The **conditional ML estimator** of $\boldsymbol{\theta}_0$ maximizes this first term, thus ignoring the second term. It is an M-estimator with

$$m(\mathbf{w}_t; \boldsymbol{\theta}) = \log f(y_t \mid \mathbf{x}_t; \boldsymbol{\theta}), \quad \text{that is,} \quad Q_n(\boldsymbol{\theta}) = \frac{1}{n}\sum_{t=1}^{n} \log f(y_t \mid \mathbf{x}_t; \boldsymbol{\theta}). \tag{7.1.11}$$

The second term on the right-hand side of (7.1.10) is the average log marginal likelihood. It does not depend on $\boldsymbol{\theta}$, so the conditional ML estimator of $\boldsymbol{\theta}_0$ is numerically the same as the (joint or full) ML estimator that maximizes the average joint likelihood (7.1.10).

Now suppose that $\boldsymbol{\theta}_0$ and $\boldsymbol{\psi}_0$ are functionally related. For example, $\boldsymbol{\theta}_0$ and $\boldsymbol{\psi}_0$ might be partitioned as $\boldsymbol{\theta}_0 = (\boldsymbol{\alpha}_0', \boldsymbol{\beta}_0')'$, $\boldsymbol{\psi}_0 = (\boldsymbol{\beta}_0', \boldsymbol{\gamma}_0')'$. Then the full (i.e., unconditional) ML and conditional ML estimators are no longer numerically equal. It is intuitively clear that the conditional ML misses information that could have been obtained from the marginal likelihood. Indeed it can be shown that the conditional ML estimator of $\boldsymbol{\theta}_0$ is less efficient than the full ML estimator obtained from maximizing the joint log likelihood (7.1.10) (see, e.g., Gourieroux and Monfort, 1995, Section 7.5.3). In most applications, this loss of efficiency is unavoidable because we do not know, or do not wish to specify, the parametric form, $f(\mathbf{x}_t; \boldsymbol{\psi})$, of the marginal distribution.

Here are two examples of conditional ML (other examples will be in the next chapter).

Example 7.2 (Linear regression model with normal errors): In Chapter 2, we considered the linear regression model with conditional homoskedasticity. Assume further that the error term is normally distributed, so

$$\{y_t, \mathbf{x}_t\} \text{ is i.i.d.}, \quad y_t = \mathbf{x}_t'\boldsymbol{\beta}_0 + \varepsilon_t, \quad \varepsilon_t \mid \mathbf{x}_t \sim N(0, \sigma_0^2). \tag{7.1.12}$$

The conditional likelihood of y_t given $\mathbf{x}_t$, $f(\mathbf{y}_t \mid \mathbf{x}_t; \boldsymbol{\theta})$, is the density function of $N(\mathbf{x}_t'\boldsymbol{\beta}, \sigma^2)$. So, with $\boldsymbol{\theta} = (\boldsymbol{\beta}', \sigma^2)'$ and $\mathbf{w}_t = (y_t, \mathbf{x}_t')'$, the m function is

$$\begin{aligned} m(\mathbf{w}_t; \boldsymbol{\theta}) &= \log f(y_t \mid \mathbf{x}_t; \boldsymbol{\beta}, \sigma^2) \\ &= \log\left(\frac{1}{\sqrt{2\pi\sigma^2}} \exp\left[-\frac{(y_t - \mathbf{x}_t'\boldsymbol{\beta})^2}{2\sigma^2}\right]\right) \\ &= -\frac{1}{2}\log(2\pi) - \log(\sigma) - \frac{1}{2}\left(\frac{y_t - \mathbf{x}_t'\boldsymbol{\beta}}{\sigma}\right)^2. \end{aligned} \tag{7.1.13}$$

The parameter space Θ is $\mathbb{R}^K \times \mathbb{R}_{++}$, where K is the dimension of $\boldsymbol{\beta}$ and $\mathbb{R}_{++}$ is the set of positive real numbers reflecting the *a priori* restriction that $\sigma_0^2 > 0$. As was verified in Chapter 1, the ML estimator of $\boldsymbol{\beta}_0$ is the OLS estimator and the ML estimator of σ_0^2 is the sum of squared residuals divided by the sample size n.

Example 7.3 (Probit): In the **probit model**, a scalar dependent variable y_t is a binary variable, $y_t \in \{0, 1\}$. For example, $y_t = 1$ if the wife chooses to enter the labor force and $y_t = 0$ otherwise, and $\mathbf{x}_t$ might include the husband's income. The conditional probability of y_t given a vector of regressors $\mathbf{x}_t$ is given by

$$\begin{cases} f(y_t = 1 \mid \mathbf{x}_t; \boldsymbol{\theta}_0) = \Phi(\mathbf{x}_t'\boldsymbol{\theta}_0), \\ f(y_t = 0 \mid \mathbf{x}_t; \boldsymbol{\theta}_0) = 1 - \Phi(\mathbf{x}_t'\boldsymbol{\theta}_0), \end{cases} \tag{7.1.14}$$

where $\Phi(\cdot)$ is the cumulative density function of the standard normal distribution. This can be written compactly as

$$f(y_t \mid \mathbf{x}_t; \boldsymbol{\theta}_0) = \Phi(\mathbf{x}_t'\boldsymbol{\theta}_0)^{y_t}[1 - \Phi(\mathbf{x}_t'\boldsymbol{\theta}_0)]^{1-y_t}.$$

If there is no *a priori* restriction on $\boldsymbol{\theta}_0$, the parameter space Θ is $\mathbb{R}^p$. The ML estimator of $\boldsymbol{\theta}_0$ is an M-estimator with the m function given by

$$m(\mathbf{w}_t; \boldsymbol{\theta}) = \log f(y_t \mid \mathbf{x}_t; \boldsymbol{\theta}) = y_t \log \Phi(\mathbf{x}_t'\boldsymbol{\theta}) + (1 - y_t) \log[1 - \Phi(\mathbf{x}_t'\boldsymbol{\theta})]. \tag{7.1.15}$$

Invariance of ML

The joint ML and conditional ML estimators have a number of desirable properties. One of them, which holds true in finite samples, is **invariance**. To describe invariance for an extremum estimator in general, consider **reparameterizing** the model by a mapping or function $\boldsymbol{\lambda} = \boldsymbol{\tau}(\boldsymbol{\theta})$ defined on Θ. Let Λ be the range of the mapping:

$$\Lambda \equiv \boldsymbol{\tau}(\Theta) \equiv \{\boldsymbol{\lambda} \mid \boldsymbol{\lambda} = \boldsymbol{\tau}(\boldsymbol{\theta}) \text{ for some } \boldsymbol{\theta} \in \Theta\}. \tag{7.1.16}$$

By definition, for every $\boldsymbol{\lambda}$ in Λ, there exists at least one $\boldsymbol{\theta}$ such that $\boldsymbol{\lambda} = \boldsymbol{\tau}(\boldsymbol{\theta})$. The mapping $\boldsymbol{\tau} : \Theta \to \Lambda$ is called a reparameterization if it is one-to-one; namely, for every $\boldsymbol{\lambda}$ in Λ, there is only one $\boldsymbol{\theta}$ in Θ such that $\boldsymbol{\lambda} = \boldsymbol{\tau}(\boldsymbol{\theta})$. This unique $\boldsymbol{\theta}$ is therefore a function of $\boldsymbol{\lambda}$. This mapping from Λ to Θ is called the **inverse** of $\boldsymbol{\tau}$ and denoted $\boldsymbol{\tau}^{-1}$. We say that an extremum estimator $\hat{\boldsymbol{\theta}}$ is **invariant** to reparameterization $\boldsymbol{\tau}$ if the extremum estimator for the reparameterized model is $\boldsymbol{\tau}(\hat{\boldsymbol{\theta}})$. Let $\widetilde{Q}_n(\boldsymbol{\lambda})$ be the objective function associated with the reparameterized model. An extremum estimator is invariant if and only if

$$\widetilde{Q}_n(\boldsymbol{\lambda}) = Q_n(\boldsymbol{\tau}^{-1}(\boldsymbol{\lambda})) \quad \text{for all} \quad \boldsymbol{\lambda} \in \Lambda. \tag{7.1.17}$$

To see this, let $\hat{\boldsymbol{\lambda}} \equiv \boldsymbol{\tau}(\hat{\boldsymbol{\theta}})$. For any $\boldsymbol{\lambda} \in \Lambda$, we have $\widetilde{Q}_n(\boldsymbol{\lambda}) = Q_n(\boldsymbol{\tau}^{-1}(\boldsymbol{\lambda})) \leq Q_n(\hat{\boldsymbol{\theta}})$ because $\hat{\boldsymbol{\theta}}$ maximizes $Q_n(\boldsymbol{\theta})$ on Θ and $\boldsymbol{\tau}^{-1}(\boldsymbol{\lambda})$ is in Θ. But $Q_n(\hat{\boldsymbol{\theta}}) = Q_n(\boldsymbol{\tau}^{-1}(\hat{\boldsymbol{\lambda}})) = \widetilde{Q}_n(\hat{\boldsymbol{\lambda}})$. So $\widetilde{Q}_n(\boldsymbol{\lambda}) \leq \widetilde{Q}_n(\hat{\boldsymbol{\lambda}})$ for all $\boldsymbol{\lambda} \in \Lambda$.

ML (be it conditional or joint) is invariant to reparameterization because the likelihood after reparameterization is $\tilde{f}(.; \boldsymbol{\lambda}) = f(.; \boldsymbol{\tau}^{-1}(\boldsymbol{\lambda}))$, which produces the objective functions that satisfy (7.1.17). Can there be an estimator that is *not* invariant? The answer is yes; Review Question 5 will ask you to verify that GMM is not invariant.

Nonlinear Least Squares (NLS)

In NLS, as in conditional ML, the observation vector $\mathbf{w}_t$ is partitioned into two groups, y_t and $\mathbf{x}_t$: $\mathbf{w}_t = (y_t, \mathbf{x}_t')'$. The model in NLS is a set of stochastic processes $\{y_t, \mathbf{x}_t\}$ such that the conditional mean $\mathrm{E}(y_t \mid \mathbf{x}_t)$, which is a function of $\mathbf{x}_t$, is a member of the parametric family of functions $\varphi(\mathbf{x}_t; \boldsymbol{\theta}), \boldsymbol{\theta} \in \Theta$. The functional form of $\varphi(\cdot; \cdot)$ is known. If $\boldsymbol{\theta}_0$ is the true parameter value, then $\mathrm{E}(y_t \mid \mathbf{x}_t) = \varphi(\mathbf{x}_t; \boldsymbol{\theta}_0)$ for the true DGP $\{y_t, \mathbf{x}_t\}$. If we define $\varepsilon_t \equiv y_t - \mathrm{E}(y_t \mid \mathbf{x}_t)$, then the correctly specified model can be written as

$$y_t = \varphi(\mathbf{x}_t; \boldsymbol{\theta}_0) + \varepsilon_t, \quad \mathrm{E}(\varepsilon_t \mid \mathbf{x}_t) = 0, \quad \boldsymbol{\theta}_0 \in \Theta. \tag{7.1.18}$$

The most widely used estimation method to estimate $\boldsymbol{\theta}_0$ here is **least squares**, which is to minimize the sum of squared residuals. Therefore, an NLS estimator, which is least squares applied to the model just described, is an M-estimator with

$$m(\mathbf{w}_t; \boldsymbol{\theta}) = -[y_t - \varphi(\mathbf{x}_t; \boldsymbol{\theta})]^2, \quad \text{that is,} \quad Q_n(\boldsymbol{\theta}) = -\frac{1}{n}\sum_{t=1}^{n} [y_t - \varphi(\mathbf{x}_t; \boldsymbol{\theta})]^2. \tag{7.1.19}$$

Here maximization of $Q_n(\boldsymbol{\theta})$ is the same as *minimization* of the sum of squared residuals.

Example 7.4 (CES production function with additive errors): As an illustration, consider the CES production function

$$Q_t = A_0 \cdot \left[\delta_0 K_t^{-\rho_0} + (1-\delta_0) L_t^{-\rho_0}\right]^{-1/\rho_0} + \varepsilon_t, \tag{7.1.20}$$

where Q_t is output in period t, K_t is the capital stock, L_t is labor input, and ε_t is an additive shock to the production function with $\mathrm{E}(\varepsilon_t \mid K_t, L_t) = 0$. This is a conditional mean model (7.1.18) with $y_t = Q_t$, $\mathbf{x}_t = (K_t, L_t)'$, $\boldsymbol{\theta}_0 = (A_0, \delta_0, \rho_0)'$, $\varphi(\mathbf{x}_t; \boldsymbol{\theta}) = A \cdot \left[\delta K_t^{-\rho} + (1-\delta) L_t^{-\rho}\right]^{-1/\rho}$. The usual properties for production functions (of monotonicity and concavity) are satisfied if $A > 0$, $0 < \delta < 1$, $-1 < \rho$, which determines the parameter space Θ.

Linear and Nonlinear GMM

In Chapter 3, we applied GMM to linear equations. The linear equation to be estimated was

$$y_t = \mathbf{z}_t'\boldsymbol{\theta}_0 + \varepsilon_t. \tag{7.1.21}$$

With $\mathbf{x}_t$ as the vector of instruments, the orthogonality (zero-mean) conditions were

$$\mathrm{E}[\mathbf{x}_t \cdot (y_t - \mathbf{z}_t'\boldsymbol{\theta}_0)] = \mathbf{0}. \tag{7.1.22}$$

The correctly specified model here is a set of ergodic stationary processes $\mathbf{w}_t = (y_t, \mathbf{z}_t', \mathbf{x}_t')'$ such that these zero-mean conditions hold for $\boldsymbol{\theta}_0$ in Θ. The linear GMM estimator of $\boldsymbol{\theta}_0$ is a GMM estimator with the $\mathbf{g}$ function in the GMM objective function (7.1.3) given by

$$\mathbf{g}(\mathbf{w}_t; \boldsymbol{\theta}) \equiv \mathbf{x}_t \cdot (y_t - \mathbf{z}_t'\boldsymbol{\theta}) = \mathbf{x}_t \cdot y_t - \mathbf{x}_t\mathbf{z}_t'\boldsymbol{\theta}. \tag{7.1.23}$$

GMM can be readily applied to nonlinear equations. Suppose that the estimation equation is nonlinear and also implicit in y_t:

$$a(y_t, \mathbf{z}_t; \boldsymbol{\theta}_0) = \varepsilon_t. \tag{7.1.24}$$

Just set $\mathbf{g}(\mathbf{w}_t; \boldsymbol{\theta}) = \mathbf{x}_t \cdot a(y_t, \mathbf{z}_t; \boldsymbol{\theta})$. This estimator is called a **generalized nonlinear instrumental variables estimator**.[3] It is still a special case of GMM because the $\mathbf{g}$ function here can be written as a product of the vector of instruments and the error term. The properties of GMM estimators to be developed in this chapter do not rely on this special structure.

As an example of nonlinear GMM, consider the nonlinear Euler equation of Hansen and Singleton (1982).

Example 7.5 (Nonlinear consumption Euler equation): The Euler equation for the household optimization problem, standard in macroeconomics, is

$$\mathrm{E}\left[R_{t+1}\frac{\beta_0 u'(c_{t+1})}{u'(c_t)} \;\middle|\; I_t\right] = 1, \tag{7.1.25}$$

where R_{t+1} is the gross ex-post rate of return (1 plus the rate of return) from the asset in question, c_t is consumption, β_0 is the discounting factor, $u'(c)$ is the marginal utility, and I_t is the information available at date t. Assume for

[3] It is more general than the usual nonlinear instrumental variables estimator because conditional homoskedasticity is not assumed.

the utility function that $u(c) = c^{1-\alpha_0}/(1-\alpha_0)$. Then $u'(c) = c^{-\alpha_0}$ and the Euler equation becomes

$$\mathrm{E}\Big[a\Big(\frac{c_{t+1}}{c_t}, R_{t+1}; \alpha_0, \beta_0\Big) \,\Big|\, I_t\Big] = 0$$

$$\text{with } a\Big(\frac{c_{t+1}}{c_t}, R_{t+1}; \alpha_0, \beta_0\Big) \equiv R_{t+1} \cdot \beta_0 \cdot \Big(\frac{c_{t+1}}{c_t}\Big)^{-\alpha_0} - 1. \quad (7.1.26)$$

If $\mathbf{x}_t$ is a vector of variables whose values are known at date t, then $\mathbf{x}_t \in I_t$ and it follows from (7.1.26) that

$$\mathrm{E}\Big[\mathbf{x}_t \cdot a\Big(\frac{c_{t+1}}{c_t}, R_{t+1}; \alpha_0, \beta_0\Big) \,\Big|\, I_t\Big] = \mathbf{0}. \quad (7.1.27)$$

Taking the unconditional expectation of both sides and using the Law of Total Expectations (that $\mathrm{E}[\mathrm{E}(x \mid I_t)] = \mathrm{E}(x)$), we obtain the orthogonality (zero-mean) conditions $\mathrm{E}[\mathbf{g}(\mathbf{w}_t; \boldsymbol{\theta}_0)] = \mathbf{0}$ where

$$\mathbf{g}(\mathbf{w}_t; \boldsymbol{\theta}_0) = \mathbf{x}_t \cdot a\Big(\frac{c_{t+1}}{c_t}, R_{t+1}; \alpha_0, \beta_0\Big) \text{ with } \mathbf{w}_t = \begin{bmatrix} \mathbf{x}_t \\ c_{t+1}/c_t \\ R_{t+1} \end{bmatrix}, \ \boldsymbol{\theta}_0 = \begin{bmatrix} \beta_0 \\ \alpha_0 \end{bmatrix}. \quad (7.1.28)$$

QUESTIONS FOR REVIEW

1. (Estimating probit model by NLS) For the probit model, verify that $\mathrm{E}(y_t \mid \mathbf{x}_t) = \Phi(\mathbf{x}_t'\boldsymbol{\theta}_0)$. Consider applying least squares to this model. Specify the m function in the M-estimator objective function (7.1.2).

2. (Estimating probit model by GMM) For the probit model, verify that the orthogonality conditions $\mathrm{E}[\mathbf{x}_t \cdot (y_t - \Phi(\mathbf{x}_t'\boldsymbol{\theta}_0))] = \mathbf{0}$ hold. Specify the $\mathbf{g}$ function in the GMM objective function (7.1.3).

3. (Estimation by ML of a GMM model?) Suppose that $\{y_t, \mathbf{z}_t, \mathbf{x}_t\}$ is i.i.d. in the correctly specified linear model described in the last subsection. Can you estimate $\boldsymbol{\theta}_0$ by ML? [Answer: No, because the model does not specify the parametric form for the density of $\mathbf{w}_t$.]

4. ($\mathrm{E}(\varepsilon_t \mid \mathbf{x}_t) = 0$ vs. $\mathrm{E}(\varepsilon_t \cdot \mathbf{x}_t) = \mathbf{0}$ in NLS) Consider the quadratic NLS model where $\varphi(x_t; \boldsymbol{\theta}) = \theta_0 + \theta_1 x_t + \theta_2 x_t^2$. Suppose that $\mathrm{E}(\varepsilon_t x_t) = 0$ but $\mathrm{E}(\varepsilon_t x_t^2) \neq 0$. Does $\mathrm{E}(\varepsilon_t \mid x_t) = 0$ hold? [Answer: No. If $\mathrm{E}(\varepsilon_t \mid x_t) = 0$, then $\mathrm{E}(\varepsilon_t h(x_t)) = 0$

for any (measurable) function h.] Would the NLS estimator of $\boldsymbol{\theta}_0$ be consistent? [Answer: No.]

5. (Lack of invariance in GMM) Consider the linear model $y_t = \theta_0 z_t + \varepsilon_t$ where θ_0 and z_t are scalars. The orthogonality conditions are $\mathrm{E}[\mathbf{x}_t \cdot (y_t - \theta_0 z_t)] = \mathbf{0}$. Write down the GMM objective function $Q_n(\theta)$. Assume that $\Theta = \mathbb{R}_{++}$ (i.e., $\theta_0 > 0$) and consider the reparameterization $\lambda = 1/\theta$. With this reparameterization, the linear equation can be rewritten as $z_t = \lambda_0 y_t - \lambda_0 \varepsilon_t$ and the orthogonality conditions can be rewritten as $\mathrm{E}[\mathbf{x}_t \cdot (z_t - \lambda_0 y_t)] = \mathbf{0}$. Let $\widetilde{Q}_n(\lambda)$ be the GMM objective functions associated with this set of orthogonality conditions. Is it the case that $Q_n(\theta) = \widetilde{Q}_n(1/\theta)$ or $\widetilde{Q}_n(\lambda) = Q_n(1/\lambda)$ when $\widehat{\mathbf{W}}$ is the same in the two objective functions? [Answer: No.]

7.2 Consistency

In this section, we first present a set of sufficient conditions under which an extremum estimator is consistent. Those conditions will then be specialized to NLS, ML, and GMM.

Two Consistency Theorems for Extremum Estimators

The objective function $Q_n(\cdot)$ is a random function because for each $\boldsymbol{\theta}$ its value $Q_n(\boldsymbol{\theta})$, being dependent on the data $(\mathbf{w}_1, \ldots, \mathbf{w}_n)$, is a random variable. The basic idea for the consistency of an extremum estimator is that if $Q_n(\boldsymbol{\theta})$ converges in probability to $Q_0(\boldsymbol{\theta})$, and the true parameter $\boldsymbol{\theta}_0$ solves the "limit problem" of maximizing the limit function $Q_0(\boldsymbol{\theta})$, then the limit of the maximum $\hat{\boldsymbol{\theta}}$ should be $\boldsymbol{\theta}_0$. Sufficient conditions for the maximum of the limit to be the limit of the maximum are that the convergence in probability be "uniform" (in the sense made precise in a moment) and that the parameter space Θ be compact. As already mentioned, the parameter space is not compact in most applications. We therefore provide an alternative set of consistency conditions, which does not require Θ to be compact.

To state the first consistency theorem for extremum estimators, we need to make precise what we mean by convergence being "uniform." If you are already familiar from calculus with the notion of uniform convergence of a sequence of *functions*, you will recognize that the definition about to be given is a natural extension to a sequence of random functions, $Q_n(\cdot)$ $(n = 1, 2, \ldots)$. **Pointwise convergence in probability** of $Q_n(\cdot)$ to some nonrandom function $Q_0(\cdot)$ simply means $\operatorname{plim}_{n\to\infty} Q_n(\boldsymbol{\theta}) = Q_0(\boldsymbol{\theta})$ for all $\boldsymbol{\theta}$, namely, that the sequence of random variables $|Q_n(\boldsymbol{\theta}) - Q_0(\boldsymbol{\theta})|$ $(n = 1, 2, \dots)$ converges in probability to 0 for each $\boldsymbol{\theta}$. **Uniform convergence in probability** is stronger. The convergence has to occur "uniformly" over the parameter space Θ in the following sense:

$$\sup_{\boldsymbol{\theta} \in \Theta} |Q_n(\boldsymbol{\theta}) - Q_0(\boldsymbol{\theta})| \underset{\text{p}}{\rightarrow} 0 \text{ as } n \to \infty. \tag{7.2.1}$$

As in the case of convergence in probability, uniform convergence in probability can be extended readily to sequences of *vector* random functions or matrix random functions (by viewing a matrix as a vector whose elements have been rearranged), by requiring uniform convergence for each element: a sequence of vector random functions $\{\mathbf{h}_n(\cdot)\}$ converges uniformly in probability to a nonrandom function $\mathbf{h}_0(\cdot)$ if each element converges uniformly. This element-by-element convergence is equivalent to convergence in the norm:

$$\sup_{\boldsymbol{\theta} \in \Theta} \|\mathbf{h}_n(\boldsymbol{\theta}) - \mathbf{h}_0(\boldsymbol{\theta})\| \underset{\text{p}}{\rightarrow} 0 \text{ as } n \to \infty, \tag{7.2.2}$$

where $\|.\|$ is the usual Euclidean norm.[4]

In the following statement of our first consistency theorem, the conditions ensuring that $\hat{\boldsymbol{\theta}}$ is well defined are labeled (i)–(iii), while those ensuring consistency are (a) and (b).

Proposition 7.1 (Consistency with compact parameter space): *Suppose that (i) Θ is a compact subset of $\mathbb{R}^p$, (ii) $Q_n(\boldsymbol{\theta})$ is continuous in $\boldsymbol{\theta}$ for any data $(\mathbf{w}_1, \dots, \mathbf{w}_n)$, and (iii) $Q_n(\boldsymbol{\theta})$ is a measurable function of the data for all $\boldsymbol{\theta}$ in Θ (so by Lemma 7.1 the extremum estimator $\hat{\boldsymbol{\theta}}$ defined in (7.1.1) is a well-defined random variable). If there is a function $Q_0(\boldsymbol{\theta})$ such that*

(a) (identification) $Q_0(\boldsymbol{\theta})$ is uniquely maximized on Θ at $\boldsymbol{\theta}_0 \in \Theta$,

(b) (uniform convergence) $Q_n(\cdot)$ converges uniformly in probability to $Q_0(\cdot)$,

then $\hat{\boldsymbol{\theta}} \to_{\text{p}} \boldsymbol{\theta}_0$.

We will not prove this result; see, e.g., Amemiya (1985, Theorem 4.1.1) for a proof. For estimates such as ML, NLS, and GMM, we will state later the identification condition (a) in more primitive terms so that the condition can be interpreted more intuitively.

[4]The Euclidean norm of a p-dimensional vector $\mathbf{x} = (x_1, x_2, \dots, x_p)'$, denoted $\|\mathbf{x}\|$, is defined as $\sqrt{x_1^2 + x_2^2 + \dots + x_p^2}$.

The theorem that does away with the compactness of Θ is

Proposition 7.2 (Consistency without compactness): *Suppose that (i) the true parameter vector $\boldsymbol{\theta}_0$ is an element of the interior of a convex parameter space Θ ($\subset \mathbb{R}^p$), (ii) $Q_n(\boldsymbol{\theta})$ is concave*[5] *over the parameter space for any data $(\mathbf{w}_1, \ldots, \mathbf{w}_n)$, and (iii) $Q_n(\boldsymbol{\theta})$ is a measurable function of the data for all $\boldsymbol{\theta}$ in Θ. Let $\hat{\boldsymbol{\theta}}$ be the extremum estimator defined by (7.1.1) (wait for a moment to learn about its existence). If there is a function $Q_0(\boldsymbol{\theta})$ such that*

(a) (identification) $Q_0(\boldsymbol{\theta})$ is uniquely maximized on Θ at $\boldsymbol{\theta}_0 \in \Theta$,

(b) (pointwise convergence) $Q_n(\boldsymbol{\theta})$ converges in probability to $Q_0(\boldsymbol{\theta})$ for all $\boldsymbol{\theta} \in \Theta$,

then, as $n \to \infty$, $\hat{\boldsymbol{\theta}}$ exists with probability approaching 1 and $\hat{\boldsymbol{\theta}} \to_{\mathrm{p}} \boldsymbol{\theta}_0$.

See Newey and McFadden (1994, pp. 2133–2134) for a proof. In most applications, Θ is an open convex set (as in Examples 7.1–7.4), so condition (i) is satisfied. The convergence of $Q_n(\boldsymbol{\theta})$ to $Q_0(\boldsymbol{\theta})$ is required to be only pointwise, which is easier to verify in applications. The price of these niceties is the requirement that the objective function $Q_n(\boldsymbol{\theta})$ be concave for any data (under which pointwise convergence implies uniform convergence), but in many applications this condition is satisfied. Below we will verify that concavity is satisfied for ML for the linear regression model (after a reparameterization), probit ML, and linear GMM.

Consistency of M-Estimators

For an M-estimator, the objective function is given by (7.1.2). If $\{\mathbf{w}_t\}$ is ergodic stationary, the Ergodic Theorem implies pointwise convergence for $Q_n(\boldsymbol{\theta})$: $Q_n(\boldsymbol{\theta})$ converges in probability pointwise for each $\boldsymbol{\theta} \in \Theta$ to $Q_0(\boldsymbol{\theta})$ given by

$$Q_0(\boldsymbol{\theta}) = \mathrm{E}[m(\mathbf{w}_t; \boldsymbol{\theta})] \tag{7.2.3}$$

(provided, of course, that $\mathrm{E}[m(\mathbf{w}_t; \boldsymbol{\theta})]$ exists and is finite). To apply the first consistency result (Proposition 7.1) to M-estimators, we need to show that the convergence of $\frac{1}{n}\sum_{t=1}^{n} m(\mathbf{w}_t; .)$ to $\mathrm{E}[m(\mathbf{w}_t; .)]$ is uniform. A standard method to prove uniform convergence in probability, which exploits the fact that the expression is

[5] A scalar function $h(\mathbf{x})$ is said to be **concave** if $\alpha h(\mathbf{x}_1) + (1-\alpha)h(\mathbf{x}_2) \le h(\alpha\mathbf{x}_1 + (1-\alpha)\mathbf{x}_2)$ for all $\mathbf{x}_1, \mathbf{x}_2, 0 \le \alpha \le 1$. So a linear function is concave. Some authors use the term "globally concave" to distinguish it from the concept of "local concavity" that the Hessian evaluated at the parameter vector in question is negative semidefinite. If a function is concave, then it is continuous. So condition (ii) in this proposition is stronger than condition (ii) in the previous proposition.

a sample mean, is the **uniform law of large numbers**. Its version for ergodic stationary processes (stated as Lemma 2.4 in Newey and McFadden, 1994, and as Theorem A.2.2 in White, 1994) is

Lemma 7.2 (Uniform law of large numbers): *Let* $\{\mathbf{w}_t\}$ *be an ergodic stationary process. Suppose that (i) the set* Θ *is compact, (ii)* $m(\mathbf{w}_t;\boldsymbol{\theta})$ *is continuous in* $\boldsymbol{\theta}$ *for all* $\mathbf{w}_t$*, and (iii)* $m(\mathbf{w}_t;\boldsymbol{\theta})$ *is measurable in* $\mathbf{w}_t$ *for all* $\boldsymbol{\theta}$ *in* Θ*. Suppose, in addition, the*

> **dominance condition:** *there exists a function* $d(\mathbf{w}_t)$ *(sometimes called the "dominating function") such that* $|m(\mathbf{w}_t;\boldsymbol{\theta})| \leq d(\mathbf{w}_t)$ *for all* $\boldsymbol{\theta} \in \Theta$ *and* $\mathrm{E}[d(\mathbf{w}_t)] < \infty$.

Then $\frac{1}{n}\sum_{t=1}^{n} m(\mathbf{w}_t;.)$ *converges uniformly in probability to* $\mathrm{E}[m(\mathbf{w}_t;.)]$ *over* Θ*. Moreover,* $\mathrm{E}[m(\mathbf{w}_t;\boldsymbol{\theta})]$ *is a continuous function of* $\boldsymbol{\theta}$*.*

Since by construction $|m(\mathbf{w}_t;\boldsymbol{\theta})| \leq \sup_{\boldsymbol{\theta}\in\Theta}|m(\mathbf{w}_t;\boldsymbol{\theta})|$ for all $\boldsymbol{\theta} \in \Theta$, we can use $\sup_{\boldsymbol{\theta}\in\Theta}|m(\mathbf{w}_t;\boldsymbol{\theta})|$ for $d(\mathbf{w}_t)$, so the above dominance condition can be stated simply as $\mathrm{E}[\sup_{\boldsymbol{\theta}\in\Theta}|m(\mathbf{w}_t;\boldsymbol{\theta})|] < \infty$. The Uniform Law of Large Numbers can be extended immediately to vector random functions as follows:

> Let $\{\mathbf{w}_t\}$ be an ergodic stationary process. Suppose that (i) the parameter space Θ is compact, (ii) $\mathbf{h}(\mathbf{w}_t;\boldsymbol{\theta})$ is continuous in $\boldsymbol{\theta}$ for all $\mathbf{w}_t$, and (iii) $\mathbf{h}(\mathbf{w}_t;\boldsymbol{\theta})$ is measurable in $\mathbf{w}_t$ for all $\boldsymbol{\theta}$ in Θ. Suppose, in addition, the
>
> ***dominance condition:*** $\mathrm{E}[\sup_{\boldsymbol{\theta}\in\Theta}\|\mathbf{h}(\mathbf{w}_t;\boldsymbol{\theta})\|] < \infty.$
>
> Then $\mathrm{E}[\mathbf{h}(\mathbf{w}_t;\boldsymbol{\theta})]$ is a continuous function of $\boldsymbol{\theta}$ and $\frac{1}{n}\sum_{t=1}^{n}\mathbf{h}(\mathbf{w}_t;.)$ converges uniformly in probability to $\mathrm{E}[\mathbf{h}(\mathbf{w}_t;.)]$ over Θ.

Just by combining this lemma with the first consistency theorem for extremum estimators, and noting that $Q_n(\boldsymbol{\theta})$ is continuous if $m(\mathbf{w}_t;\boldsymbol{\theta})$ is continuous in $\boldsymbol{\theta}$ and that $Q_n(\boldsymbol{\theta})$ is a measurable function of the data if $m(\mathbf{w}_t;\boldsymbol{\theta})$ is measurable in $\mathbf{w}_t$, we obtain

Proposition 7.3 (Consistency of M-estimators with compact parameter space): *Let* $\{\mathbf{w}_t\}$ *be ergodic stationary. Suppose that (i) the parameter space* Θ *is a compact subset of* $\mathbb{R}^p$*, (ii)* $m(\mathbf{w}_t;\boldsymbol{\theta})$ *is continuous in* $\boldsymbol{\theta}$ *for all* $\mathbf{w}_t$*, and (iii)* $m(\mathbf{w}_t;\boldsymbol{\theta})$ *is measurable in* $\mathbf{w}_t$ *for all* $\boldsymbol{\theta}$ *in* Θ*. Let* $\hat{\boldsymbol{\theta}}$ *be the M-estimator defined by (7.1.1) and (7.1.2). Suppose, further, that*

(a) (identification) $\mathrm{E}[m(\mathbf{w}_t;\boldsymbol{\theta})]$ *is uniquely maximized on* Θ *at* $\boldsymbol{\theta}_0 \in \Theta$,

(b) (dominance) $\mathrm{E}[\sup_{\boldsymbol{\theta}\in\Theta} |m(\mathbf{w}_t;\boldsymbol{\theta})|] < \infty$.

Then $\hat{\boldsymbol{\theta}} \to_{\mathrm{p}} \boldsymbol{\theta}_0$.

It is even more straightforward to specialize the second consistency theorem for extremum estimators to M-estimators. The objective function $Q_n(\boldsymbol{\theta})$ is concave if $m(\mathbf{w}_t;\boldsymbol{\theta})$ is concave in $\boldsymbol{\theta}$.[6] As noted above, the pointwise convergence of $Q_n(\boldsymbol{\theta})$ to $Q_0(\boldsymbol{\theta})$ $(= \mathrm{E}[m(\mathbf{w}_t;\boldsymbol{\theta})])$ is assured by the Ergodic Theorem if $\mathrm{E}[m(\mathbf{w}_t;\boldsymbol{\theta})]$ exists and is finite for all $\boldsymbol{\theta}$. Thus

Proposition 7.4 (Consistency of M-estimators without compactness): *Let* $\{\mathbf{w}_t\}$ *be ergodic stationary. Suppose that (i) the true parameter vector* $\boldsymbol{\theta}_0$ *is an element of the interior of a convex parameter space* Θ $(\subset \mathbb{R}^p)$, *(ii)* $m(\mathbf{w}_t;\boldsymbol{\theta})$ *is concave over the parameter space for all* $\mathbf{w}_t$, *and (iii)* $m(\mathbf{w}_t;\boldsymbol{\theta})$ *is measurable in* $\mathbf{w}_t$ *for all* $\boldsymbol{\theta}$ *in* Θ. *Let* $\hat{\boldsymbol{\theta}}$ *be the M-estimator defined by (7.1.1) and (7.1.2). Suppose, further, that*

(a) (identification) $\mathrm{E}[m(\mathbf{w}_t;\boldsymbol{\theta})]$ *is uniquely maximized on* Θ *at* $\boldsymbol{\theta}_0 \in \Theta$,

(b) $\mathrm{E}[|m(\mathbf{w}_t;\boldsymbol{\theta})|] < \infty$ *(i.e.,* $\mathrm{E}[m(\mathbf{w}_t;\boldsymbol{\theta})]$ *exists and is finite) for all* $\boldsymbol{\theta} \in \Theta$.

Then, as $n \to \infty$, $\hat{\boldsymbol{\theta}}$ *exists with probability approaching 1 and* $\hat{\boldsymbol{\theta}} \to_{\mathrm{p}} \boldsymbol{\theta}_0$.

The following example shows that probit conditional ML satisfies the concavity condition.

Example 7.6 (Concavity of the probit likelihood function): The m function for probit is given in (7.1.15) where $\Phi(\cdot)$ is the cumulative density function of the standard normal distribution. Since the normal distribution is symmetric, $\Phi(-v) = 1 - \Phi(v)$ and the m function can be rewritten as

$$m(\mathbf{w}_t;\boldsymbol{\theta}) = y_t \log \Phi(\mathbf{x}_t'\boldsymbol{\theta}) + (1 - y_t) \log \Phi(-\mathbf{x}_t'\boldsymbol{\theta}). \tag{7.2.4}$$

Concavity of m is implied if both $\log \Phi(\mathbf{x}_t'\boldsymbol{\theta})$ and $\log \Phi(-\mathbf{x}_t'\boldsymbol{\theta})$ are concave in $\boldsymbol{\theta}$. Since $\mathbf{x}_t'\boldsymbol{\theta}$ is linear in $\boldsymbol{\theta}$, it suffices to show concavity of $\log \Phi(v)$. The first derivative of $\log \Phi(v)$ is

$$\frac{\mathrm{d} \log \Phi(v)}{\mathrm{d}v} = \frac{\phi(v)}{\Phi(v)}, \tag{7.2.5}$$

[6] A fact from calculus: if $f(\mathbf{x})$ and $g(\mathbf{x})$ are concave functions, then so is $f(\mathbf{x}) + g(\mathbf{x})$.

where $\phi(v)$ $(= \Phi'(v))$ is the density function of $N(0, 1)$. It is well known that $\phi(v)/\Phi(v)$ is a decreasing function. So $\log \Phi(v)$ is (strictly) concave.

Concavity after Reparameterization

Proposition 7.4 can be extended easily to estimators for objective functions that are concave after reparameterization. Suppose that all the conditions of the proposition except concavity are satisfied and that there is a continuous one-to-one mapping $\boldsymbol{\tau}(\boldsymbol{\theta}) : \Theta \to \Lambda \equiv \boldsymbol{\tau}(\Theta)$ such that

$$\widetilde{m}(\mathbf{w}_t; \boldsymbol{\lambda}) \equiv m(\mathbf{w}_t; \boldsymbol{\tau}^{-1}(\boldsymbol{\lambda}))$$

is concave in $\boldsymbol{\lambda}$ and $\Lambda = \boldsymbol{\tau}(\Theta)$ is a convex set. Let

$$\widetilde{Q}_n(\boldsymbol{\lambda}) \equiv \frac{1}{n} \sum_{t=1}^{n} \widetilde{m}(\mathbf{w}_t; \boldsymbol{\lambda})$$

be the objective function after this reparameterization. Clearly, all the assumptions of Proposition 7.4 are satisfied for $\boldsymbol{\lambda}$, Λ, and $\widetilde{m}(\mathbf{w}_t; \boldsymbol{\lambda})$: $\boldsymbol{\lambda}_0 \equiv \boldsymbol{\tau}(\boldsymbol{\theta}_0)$ is an interior point of Λ, $\mathrm{E}[\widetilde{m}(\mathbf{w}_t; \boldsymbol{\lambda})]$ is uniquely maximized at $\boldsymbol{\lambda}_0$, and $\mathrm{E}[\,|\widetilde{m}(\mathbf{w}_t; \boldsymbol{\lambda})|\,] < \infty$ for all $\boldsymbol{\lambda}$ in Λ. Thus for sufficiently large n, there exists an M-estimator $\hat{\boldsymbol{\lambda}}$ such that $\operatorname{plim}_{n\to\infty} \hat{\boldsymbol{\lambda}} = \boldsymbol{\lambda}_0$. Since $\widetilde{Q}_n(\boldsymbol{\lambda})$ satisfies (7.1.17) for the one-to-one mapping $\boldsymbol{\tau}$, $\hat{\boldsymbol{\theta}} \equiv \boldsymbol{\tau}^{-1}(\hat{\boldsymbol{\lambda}})$ maximizes the original objective function $Q_n(\boldsymbol{\theta})$. The estimator $\hat{\boldsymbol{\theta}}$ is consistent because

$$\begin{aligned} \operatorname*{plim}_{n\to\infty} \hat{\boldsymbol{\theta}} &= \operatorname*{plim}_{n\to\infty} \boldsymbol{\tau}^{-1}(\hat{\boldsymbol{\lambda}}) \\ &= \boldsymbol{\tau}^{-1}(\operatorname*{plim}_{n\to\infty} \hat{\boldsymbol{\lambda}}) \quad \text{(since } \boldsymbol{\tau}^{-1} \text{ is continuous)} \\ &= \boldsymbol{\tau}^{-1}(\boldsymbol{\lambda}_0) = \boldsymbol{\theta}_0. \end{aligned} \tag{7.2.6}$$

Example 7.7 (Concavity of linear regression likelihood function): In the conditional ML estimation of the linear regression model, $m(\mathbf{w}_t; \boldsymbol{\theta})$ is given in (7.1.13) with $\boldsymbol{\theta} = (\boldsymbol{\beta}', \sigma^2)'$ and $\mathbf{w}_t = (y_t, \mathbf{x}_t')'$. This function is not necessarily concave,[7] but consider a reparameterization: $\gamma = 1/\sigma$ and $\boldsymbol{\delta} = \boldsymbol{\beta}/\sigma$. It is a continuous one-to-one mapping between $\Theta = \mathbb{R}^K \times \mathbb{R}_{++}$ and $\Lambda = \mathbb{R}^K \times \mathbb{R}_{++}$. The new parameter space Λ is convex. With $\boldsymbol{\lambda} = (\boldsymbol{\delta}', \gamma)'$,

[7] For example, the second partial derivative of m with respect to σ^2 may or may not be non-negative depending on the value of $y_t - \mathbf{x}_t'\boldsymbol{\beta}$. Recall that a necessary condition for a twice differentiable function $h(x_1, \dots, x_p)$ to be concave is that $\partial^2 h/(\partial x_j)^2$ be non-negative for all $j = 1, 2, \dots, p$.

the m function after reparameterization becomes

$$\widetilde{m}(\mathbf{w}_t; \boldsymbol{\lambda}) = -\frac{1}{2}\log(2\pi) + \log(\gamma) - \frac{1}{2}(\gamma y_t - \mathbf{x}_t'\boldsymbol{\delta})^2. \tag{7.2.7}$$

Since $\log(\gamma)$ is concave in γ, it is concave in $\boldsymbol{\lambda}$. Since $v \equiv \gamma y_t - \mathbf{x}_t'\boldsymbol{\delta}$ is linear in $\boldsymbol{\lambda}$ and $-\frac{1}{2}v^2$ is concave, $-\frac{1}{2}(\gamma y_t - \mathbf{x}_t'\boldsymbol{\delta})^2$ is concave in $\boldsymbol{\lambda}$. So $\widetilde{m}$ above, which is the sum of two concave functions (plus a constant), is concave in $\boldsymbol{\lambda}$ for any $\mathbf{w}_t$. Therefore, provided that all the conditions of Proposition 7.4 besides concavity are satisfied for $\boldsymbol{\theta}$, Θ, and $m(\mathbf{w}_t; \boldsymbol{\theta})$, the conditional ML estimator $\hat{\boldsymbol{\theta}}$ is consistent.

Identification in NLS and ML

The identification condition (a) (that $\mathrm{E}[m(\mathbf{w}_t; \boldsymbol{\theta})]$ be uniquely maximized at $\boldsymbol{\theta}_0$) in these consistency theorems for M-estimators can be stated in more primitive terms for NLS and ML.

NLS

Consider first NLS, where $m(\mathbf{w}_t; \boldsymbol{\theta}) = -(y_t - \varphi(\mathbf{x}_t; \boldsymbol{\theta}))^2$ and $\mathrm{E}(y_t \mid \mathbf{x}_t) = \varphi(\mathbf{x}_t; \boldsymbol{\theta}_0)$. We have shown in Section 2.9 that the conditional expectation minimizes the mean squared error, that is, for any (measurable) function $h(\mathbf{x}_t)$,

$$\begin{aligned}
\text{mean squared error } &\equiv \mathrm{E}\big[\{y_t - h(\mathbf{x}_t)\}^2\big] \\
&= \mathrm{E}\big[\{y_t - \mathrm{E}(y_t \mid \mathbf{x}_t)\}^2\big] + \mathrm{E}\big[\{\mathrm{E}(y_t \mid \mathbf{x}_t) - h(\mathbf{x}_t)\}^2\big] \\
&\geq \mathrm{E}\big[\{y_t - \mathrm{E}(y_t \mid \mathbf{x}_t)\}^2\big].
\end{aligned} \tag{7.2.8}$$

This is just reproducing (2.9.4) in the current notation. Furthermore, the conditional expectation is essentially the unique minimizer in the following sense.

Being functions of $\mathbf{x}_t$, $h(\mathbf{x}_t)$ and $\mathrm{E}(y_t \mid \mathbf{x}_t)$ are random variables. For two random variables X and Y, let $X \neq Y$ mean $\mathrm{Prob}(X \neq Y) > 0$ (i.e., $\mathrm{Prob}(X = Y) < 1$) and let $X = Y$ mean $\mathrm{Prob}(X \neq Y) = 0$. (If X and Y differ only for events whose probability is zero, we do not need to care about the difference.) Therefore, $h(\mathbf{x}_t) \neq \mathrm{E}(y_t \mid \mathbf{x}_t)$ means $\mathrm{Prob}(h(\mathbf{x}_t) \neq \mathrm{E}(y_t \mid \mathbf{x}_t)) > 0$. If $h(\mathbf{x}_t) \neq \mathrm{E}(y_t \mid \mathbf{x}_t)$ in this sense, then $\{\mathrm{E}(y_t \mid \mathbf{x}_t) - h(\mathbf{x}_t)\}^2 > 0$ with positive probability. Consequently, $\mathrm{E}\big[\{\mathrm{E}(y_t \mid \mathbf{x}_t) - h(\mathbf{x}_t)\}^2\big]$ in (7.2.8) is positive and the mean squared error is strictly greater than $\mathrm{E}\big[\{y_t - \mathrm{E}(y_t \mid \mathbf{x}_t)\}^2\big]$.

Just setting $h(\mathbf{x}_t) = \varphi(\mathbf{x}_t; \boldsymbol{\theta})$ and noting that $\varphi(\mathbf{x}_t; \boldsymbol{\theta}_0) = \mathrm{E}(y_t \mid \mathbf{x}_t)$, we conclude that

$$\begin{cases} \mathrm{E}\big[\{y_t - \varphi(\mathbf{x}_t; \boldsymbol{\theta})\}^2\big] > \mathrm{E}\big[\{y_t - \varphi(\mathbf{x}_t; \boldsymbol{\theta}_0)\}^2\big] & \text{if } \varphi(\mathbf{x}_t; \boldsymbol{\theta}) \neq \varphi(\mathbf{x}_t; \boldsymbol{\theta}_0), \\ \mathrm{E}\big[\{y_t - \varphi(\mathbf{x}_t; \boldsymbol{\theta})\}^2\big] = \mathrm{E}\big[\{y_t - \varphi(\mathbf{x}_t; \boldsymbol{\theta}_0)\}^2\big] & \text{if } \varphi(\mathbf{x}_t; \boldsymbol{\theta}) = \varphi(\mathbf{x}_t; \boldsymbol{\theta}_0). \end{cases} \tag{7.2.9}$$

Therefore, the identification condition — that $\mathrm{E}\big[m(\mathbf{x}_t; \boldsymbol{\theta})\big] = -\mathrm{E}\big[\{y_t - \varphi(\mathbf{x}_t; \boldsymbol{\theta})\}^2\big]$ be maximized (i.e., $\mathrm{E}\big[\{y_t - \varphi(\mathbf{x}_t; \boldsymbol{\theta})\}^2\big]$ be minimized) uniquely at $\boldsymbol{\theta}_0$ — holds if

$$\textbf{\textit{conditional mean identification:}} \quad \varphi(\mathbf{x}_t; \boldsymbol{\theta}) \neq \varphi(\mathbf{x}_t; \boldsymbol{\theta}_0) \quad \text{for all } \boldsymbol{\theta} \neq \boldsymbol{\theta}_0. \tag{7.2.10}$$

ML

For ML, the role played by (7.2.8) for NLS is played by the **Kullback-Leibler information inequality**. Here we examine identification for conditional ML (doing the same for unconditional or joint ML is more straightforward). The hypothetical conditional density $f(y_t \mid \mathbf{x}_t; \boldsymbol{\theta})$, being a function of $(y_t, \mathbf{x}_t)$, is a random variable for any $\boldsymbol{\theta}$. The expected value of the random variable $\log f(y_t \mid \mathbf{x}_t; \boldsymbol{\theta})$ can be written as[8]

$$\mathrm{E}[\log f(y_t \mid \mathbf{x}_t; \boldsymbol{\theta})] = \int \log f(y_t \mid \mathbf{x}_t; \boldsymbol{\theta}) f(y_t, \mathbf{x}_t; \boldsymbol{\theta}_0, \boldsymbol{\psi}_0) \mathrm{d}y_t \mathrm{d}\mathbf{x}_t. \tag{7.2.11}$$

Note well that the expected value is with respect to the *true* joint density $f(y_t, \mathbf{x}_t; \boldsymbol{\theta}_0, \boldsymbol{\psi}_0)$. The Kullback-Leibler information inequality about density functions (adapted to conditional densities) states that

$$\begin{cases} \mathrm{E}[\log f(y_t \mid \mathbf{x}_t; \boldsymbol{\theta})] < \mathrm{E}[\log f(y_t \mid \mathbf{x}_t; \boldsymbol{\theta}_0)] & \text{if } f(y_t \mid \mathbf{x}_t; \boldsymbol{\theta}) \neq f(y_t \mid \mathbf{x}_t; \boldsymbol{\theta}_0), \\ \mathrm{E}[\log f(y_t \mid \mathbf{x}_t; \boldsymbol{\theta})] = \mathrm{E}[\log f(y_t \mid \mathbf{x}_t; \boldsymbol{\theta}_0)] & \text{if } f(y_t \mid \mathbf{x}_t; \boldsymbol{\theta}) = f(y_t \mid \mathbf{x}_t; \boldsymbol{\theta}_0) \end{cases} \tag{7.2.12}$$

(provided, of course, that $\mathrm{E}[\log f(y_t \mid \mathbf{x}_t; \boldsymbol{\theta})]$ exists and is finite). (See Analytical Exercise 1 for derivation.) It immediately follows that the identification condition (that $\mathrm{E}[\log f(y_t \mid \mathbf{x}_t; \boldsymbol{\theta})]$ be maximized uniquely at $\boldsymbol{\theta}_0$) is satisfied if

$$\textbf{\textit{conditional density identification:}} \quad f(y_t \mid \mathbf{x}_t; \boldsymbol{\theta}) \neq f(y_t \mid \mathbf{x}_t; \boldsymbol{\theta}_0) \quad \text{for all } \boldsymbol{\theta} \neq \boldsymbol{\theta}_0. \tag{7.2.13}$$

[8] If $f(y_t \mid \mathbf{x}_t; \boldsymbol{\theta}) = 0$, then its log cannot be defined. If this bothers you, assume $f(y_t \mid \mathbf{x}_t; \boldsymbol{\theta})$ is positive for all $y_t, \mathbf{x}_t$, and $\boldsymbol{\theta}$. See White (1994, p. 9) for an argument that avoids such a simplifying assumption.

We can turn the two consistency theorems for M-estimators, Propositions 7.3 and 7.4, into ones for conditional ML, with $\mathbf{w}_t = (y_t, \mathbf{x}_t')'$ and $m(\mathbf{w}_t; \boldsymbol{\theta}) = \log f \cdot (y_t \mid \mathbf{x}_t; \boldsymbol{\theta})$. Replacing the identification condition for M-estimators by conditional density identification, we obtain the following two self-contained statements about consistency of ML.

Proposition 7.5 (Consistency of conditional ML with compact parameter space): *Let $\{y_t, \mathbf{x}_t\}$ be ergodic stationary with conditional density $f(y_t \mid \mathbf{x}_t; \boldsymbol{\theta}_0)$ and let $\hat{\boldsymbol{\theta}}$ be the conditional ML estimator, which maximizes the average log conditional likelihood (derived under the assumption that $\{y_t, \mathbf{x}_t\}$ is i.i.d.):*

$$\hat{\boldsymbol{\theta}} = \underset{\boldsymbol{\theta} \in \Theta}{\operatorname{argmax}} \frac{1}{n} \sum_{t=1}^{n} \log f(y_t \mid \mathbf{x}_t; \boldsymbol{\theta}).$$

Suppose the model is correctly specified so that $\boldsymbol{\theta}_0$ is in Θ. Suppose that (i) the parameter space Θ is a compact subset of $\mathbb{R}^p$, (ii) $f(y_t \mid \mathbf{x}_t; \boldsymbol{\theta})$ is continuous in $\boldsymbol{\theta}$ for all $(y_t, \mathbf{x}_t)$, and (iii) $f(y_t \mid \mathbf{x}_t; \boldsymbol{\theta})$ is measurable in $(y_t, \mathbf{x}_t)$ for all $\boldsymbol{\theta} \in \Theta$ (so by Lemma 7.1 $\hat{\boldsymbol{\theta}}$ is a well-defined random variable). Suppose, further, that

(a) (identification) $\text{Prob}[f(y_t \mid \mathbf{x}_t; \boldsymbol{\theta}) \neq f(y_t \mid \mathbf{x}_t; \boldsymbol{\theta}_0)] > 0$ *for all* $\boldsymbol{\theta} \neq \boldsymbol{\theta}_0$ *in* Θ,

(b) (dominance) $\text{E}[\sup_{\boldsymbol{\theta} \in \Theta} |\log f(y_t \mid \mathbf{x}_t; \boldsymbol{\theta})|] < \infty$ *(note: the expectation is over y_t* and *$\mathbf{x}_t$).*

Then $\hat{\boldsymbol{\theta}} \rightarrow_{\text{p}} \boldsymbol{\theta}_0$.

Proposition 7.6 (Consistency of conditional ML without compactness): *Let $\{y_t, \mathbf{x}_t\}$ be ergodic stationary with conditional density $f(y_t \mid \mathbf{x}_t; \boldsymbol{\theta}_0)$ and let $\hat{\boldsymbol{\theta}}$ be the conditional ML estimator, which maximizes the average log conditional likelihood (derived under the assumption that $\{y_t, \mathbf{x}_t\}$ is i.i.d.):*

$$\hat{\boldsymbol{\theta}} = \underset{\boldsymbol{\theta} \in \Theta}{\operatorname{argmax}} \frac{1}{n} \sum_{t=1}^{n} \log f(y_t \mid \mathbf{x}_t; \boldsymbol{\theta}).$$

Suppose the model is correctly specified so that $\boldsymbol{\theta}_0$ is in Θ. Suppose that (i) the true parameter vector $\boldsymbol{\theta}_0$ is an element of the interior of a convex parameter space Θ $(\subset \mathbb{R}^p)$, (ii) $\log f(y_t \mid \mathbf{x}_t; \boldsymbol{\theta})$ *is concave in $\boldsymbol{\theta}$ for all $(y_t, \mathbf{x}_t)$, and (iii)* $\log f(y_t \mid \mathbf{x}_t; \boldsymbol{\theta})$ *is measurable in $(y_t, \mathbf{x}_t)$ for all $\boldsymbol{\theta}$ in Θ. (For sufficiently large n, $\hat{\boldsymbol{\theta}}$ is well defined; see a few lines below.) Suppose, further, that*

(a) (identification) $\text{Prob}[f(y_t \mid \mathbf{x}_t; \boldsymbol{\theta}) \neq f(y_t \mid \mathbf{x}_t; \boldsymbol{\theta}_0)] > 0$ *for all* $\boldsymbol{\theta} \neq \boldsymbol{\theta}_0$ *in* Θ,

(b) $\mathrm{E}[\,|\log f(y_t \mid \mathbf{x}_t; \boldsymbol{\theta})|\,] < \infty$ *(i.e.,* $\mathrm{E}[\log f(y_t \mid \mathbf{x}_t; \boldsymbol{\theta})]$ *exists and is finite) for all* $\boldsymbol{\theta} \in \Theta$ *(note: the expectation is over* y_t and $\mathbf{x}_t$*).*

Then, as $n \to \infty$, $\hat{\boldsymbol{\theta}}$ *exists with probability approaching 1 and* $\hat{\boldsymbol{\theta}} \to_{\mathrm{p}} \boldsymbol{\theta}_0$.

There are two remarks worth making.

- The Kullback-Leibler information inequality (7.2.12) holds for unconditional densities as well (the proof is easier for unconditional densities). Therefore, Propositions 7.5 and 7.6 hold for unconditional ML; just replace $f(y_t \mid \mathbf{x}_t; \boldsymbol{\theta})$ by $f(\mathbf{w}_t; \boldsymbol{\theta})$.
- The noteworthy feature of these two ML consistency theorems is that, *despite* the fact that the log likelihood is derived under the i.i.d. assumption for $\{y_t, \mathbf{x}_t\}$, consistency is assured even if $\{y_t, \mathbf{x}_t\}$ is not i.i.d. but merely ergodic stationary. This is because the ML estimator is an M-estimator. An ML estimator that maximizes a likelihood function different from the model's likelihood function is called a **quasi-ML estimator** or **QML estimator**. Put differently, a QML estimator maximizes the likelihood function of a misspecified model. Therefore, the "maximum likelihood" estimators in Propositions 7.5 and 7.6 are QML estimators if $\{y_t, \mathbf{x}_t\}$ is ergodic stationary but not i.i.d. The propositions say that those particular QML estimators are consistent.

The identification condition in conditional ML can be stated in even more primitive terms for specific examples.

Example 7.8 (Identification in linear regression model): For the linear regression model with normal errors, the log conditional likelihood for observation t is

$$\log f(y_t \mid \mathbf{x}_t; \boldsymbol{\theta}) = -\frac{1}{2}\log(2\pi) - \frac{1}{2}\log(\sigma^2) - \frac{1}{2\sigma^2}(y_t - \mathbf{x}_t'\boldsymbol{\beta})^2.$$

Since the log function is strictly monotonic, conditional density identification is equivalent to the condition that $\log f(y_t \mid \mathbf{x}_t; \boldsymbol{\theta}) \neq \log f(y_t \mid \mathbf{x}_t; \boldsymbol{\theta}_0)$ with positive probability if $\boldsymbol{\theta} \neq \boldsymbol{\theta}_0$. This condition is satisfied if $\mathrm{E}(\mathbf{x}_t\mathbf{x}_t')$ is nonsingular (and hence positive definite). To see why, let $\boldsymbol{\theta} = (\boldsymbol{\beta}', \sigma^2)'$ and $\boldsymbol{\theta}_0 = (\boldsymbol{\beta}_0', \sigma_0^2)'$. Clearly, $\log f(y_t \mid \mathbf{x}_t; \boldsymbol{\theta}) \neq \log f(y_t \mid \mathbf{x}_t; \boldsymbol{\theta}_0)$ with positive probability if $\sigma^2 \neq \sigma_0^2$. So consider the case where $\sigma^2 = \sigma_0^2$ but $\boldsymbol{\beta} \neq \boldsymbol{\beta}_0$. Then

$$\mathrm{E}\big[\{\mathbf{x}_t'\boldsymbol{\beta} - \mathbf{x}_t'\boldsymbol{\beta}_0\}^2\big] = \mathrm{E}\big[\{\mathbf{x}_t'(\boldsymbol{\beta} - \boldsymbol{\beta}_0)\}^2\big] = (\boldsymbol{\beta} - \boldsymbol{\beta}_0)'\,\mathrm{E}(\mathbf{x}_t\mathbf{x}_t')(\boldsymbol{\beta} - \boldsymbol{\beta}_0) > 0.$$

Hence, $\mathbf{x}_t'\boldsymbol{\beta} \neq \mathbf{x}_t'\boldsymbol{\beta}_0$ with positive probability; if $\mathbf{x}_t'\boldsymbol{\beta} = \mathbf{x}_t'\boldsymbol{\beta}_0$ with probability 1 (i.e., if $\mathbf{x}_t'\boldsymbol{\beta} \neq \mathbf{x}_t'\boldsymbol{\beta}_0$ with probability zero), then $\mathrm{E}\big[\{\mathbf{x}_t'\boldsymbol{\beta} - \mathbf{x}_t'\boldsymbol{\beta}_0\}^2\big]$ will be zero. Thus, $y_t - \mathbf{x}_t'\boldsymbol{\beta} \neq y_t - \mathbf{x}_t'\boldsymbol{\beta}_0$ with positive probability, implying that the identification condition is satisfied. The same condition about $\mathrm{E}(\mathbf{x}_t\mathbf{x}_t')$ also implies condition (b) in Proposition 7.6 because

$$\begin{aligned}\mathrm{E}[(y_t - \mathbf{x}_t'\boldsymbol{\beta})^2] &= \mathrm{E}\big[\{\varepsilon_t + \mathbf{x}_t'(\boldsymbol{\beta}_0 - \boldsymbol{\beta})\}^2\big] \quad (\text{since } \ y_t = \mathbf{x}_t'\boldsymbol{\beta}_0 + \varepsilon_t)\\ &= \mathrm{E}(\varepsilon_t^2) + (\boldsymbol{\beta}_0 - \boldsymbol{\beta})'\,\mathrm{E}(\mathbf{x}_t\mathbf{x}_t')(\boldsymbol{\beta}_0 - \boldsymbol{\beta})\\ &\qquad (\text{since } \ \mathrm{E}(\varepsilon_t \cdot \mathbf{x}_t) = \mathbf{0}).\end{aligned}$$

The last term is finite if $\mathrm{E}(\mathbf{x}_t\mathbf{x}_t')$ is. These results, together with the fact noted earlier that the log likelihood is concave after reparameterization, imply that the conditional ML estimator of the linear regression model with normal errors (derived under the i.i.d. assumption for $\{y_t, \mathbf{x}_t\}$) is consistent if $\{y_t, \mathbf{x}_t\}$ is ergodic stationary and $\mathrm{E}(\mathbf{x}_t\mathbf{x}_t')$ is nonsingular.

Example 7.9 (Identification in probit): The same conclusion just derived in the previous example for the linear model also holds for the probit model, whose conditional likelihood for observation t is

$$f(y_t \mid \mathbf{x}_t; \boldsymbol{\theta}) = \Phi(\mathbf{x}_t'\boldsymbol{\theta})^{y_t}\,\Phi(-\mathbf{x}_t'\boldsymbol{\theta})^{1-y_t}.$$

The same argument used in Example 7.8 implies that, under the nonsingularity of $\mathrm{E}(\mathbf{x}_t\mathbf{x}_t')$, $\mathbf{x}_t'\boldsymbol{\theta} \neq \mathbf{x}_t'\boldsymbol{\theta}_0$ with positive probability if $\boldsymbol{\theta} \neq \boldsymbol{\theta}_0$. But since $\Phi(v)$ is strictly monotonic, $\mathbf{x}_t'\boldsymbol{\theta} \neq \mathbf{x}_t'\boldsymbol{\theta}_0$ with positive probability implies $\Phi(\mathbf{x}_t'\boldsymbol{\theta}) \neq \Phi(\mathbf{x}_t'\boldsymbol{\theta}_0)$ and $\Phi(-\mathbf{x}_t'\boldsymbol{\theta}) \neq \Phi(-\mathbf{x}_t'\boldsymbol{\theta}_0)$ with positive probability. Hence, the identification condition (a) in Proposition 7.6 is satisfied if $\mathrm{E}(\mathbf{x}_t\mathbf{x}_t')$ is nonsingular.

The nonsingularity of $\mathrm{E}(\mathbf{x}_t\mathbf{x}_t')$ also implies that condition (b) of Proposition 7.6 is satisfied for probit. It is easy to verify that

$$|\log\Phi(v)| \leq |\log\Phi(0)| + |v| + |v|^2 \ \text{ for all } \ v. \tag{7.2.14}$$

Combining this bound for $|\log\Phi(v)|$ and the fact that y_t and $1 - y_t$ are less than or equal to 1 in absolute value, it is easy to show that $\mathrm{E}[\,|\log f(y_t \mid \mathbf{x}_t; \boldsymbol{\theta})|\,] < \infty$ if $\mathrm{E}(\mathbf{x}_t\mathbf{x}_t')$ exists and is finite (a condition implied by the nonsingularity of $\mathrm{E}(\mathbf{x}_t\mathbf{x}_t')$).[9] We therefore conclude that the probit ML estimator (whose log likelihood is derived under the i.i.d. assumption for $\{y_t, \mathbf{x}_t\}$) is consistent if $\{y_t, \mathbf{x}_t\}$ is ergodic stationary and $\mathrm{E}(\mathbf{x}_t\mathbf{x}_t')$ is nonsingular.

Consistency of GMM

We now turn to GMM and specialize Proposition 7.1 to GMM by verifying the conditions of the proposition under a set of appropriate sufficient conditions. The GMM objective function is given by (7.1.3). Clearly, the continuity of $Q_n(\boldsymbol{\theta})$ in $\boldsymbol{\theta}$ is satisfied if $\mathbf{g}(\mathbf{w}_t; \boldsymbol{\theta})$ is continuous in $\boldsymbol{\theta}$ for all $\mathbf{w}_t$. If $\{\mathbf{w}_t\}$ is ergodic stationary, then $\mathbf{g}_n(\boldsymbol{\theta})$ $(\equiv \frac{1}{n}\sum_{t=1}^{n}\mathbf{g}(\mathbf{w}_t; \boldsymbol{\theta})) \to_{\mathrm{p}} \mathrm{E}[\mathbf{g}(\mathbf{w}_t; \boldsymbol{\theta})]$. So the limit function $Q_0(\boldsymbol{\theta})$ is

$$Q_0(\boldsymbol{\theta}) = -\frac{1}{2}\,\mathrm{E}[\mathbf{g}(\mathbf{w}_t; \boldsymbol{\theta})]'\,\mathbf{W}\,\mathrm{E}[\mathbf{g}(\mathbf{w}_t; \boldsymbol{\theta})]. \tag{7.2.15}$$

This function is nonpositive if $\mathbf{W}$ $(\equiv \operatorname{plim}\widehat{\mathbf{W}})$ is positive definite. It has a maximum of zero at $\boldsymbol{\theta}_0$ because $\mathrm{E}[\mathbf{g}(\mathbf{w}_t; \boldsymbol{\theta}_0)] = \mathbf{0}$ by the orthogonality conditions. Thus, the identification condition (that $Q_0(\boldsymbol{\theta})$ be uniquely maximized at $\boldsymbol{\theta}_0$) in Proposition 7.1 is satisfied if $\mathrm{E}[\mathbf{g}(\mathbf{w}_t; \boldsymbol{\theta})] \neq \mathbf{0}$ for $\boldsymbol{\theta} \neq \boldsymbol{\theta}_0$. Regarding the uniform convergence of $Q_n(\boldsymbol{\theta})$ to $Q_0(\boldsymbol{\theta})$, it is not hard to show that the condition is satisfied if $\mathbf{g}_n(\cdot)$ converges uniformly to $\mathrm{E}[\mathbf{g}(\mathbf{w}_t; \cdot)]$ (see Newey and McFadden, 1994, p. 2132). The multivariate version of the Uniform Law of Large Numbers stated right below Lemma 7.2, in turn, provides a sufficient condition for the uniform convergence. So we have proved

Proposition 7.7 (Consistency of GMM with compact parameter space): *Let $\{\mathbf{w}_t\}$ be ergodic stationary and let $\hat{\boldsymbol{\theta}}$ be the GMM estimator defined by*

$$\hat{\boldsymbol{\theta}} = \underset{\boldsymbol{\theta}\in\Theta}{\operatorname{argmin}}\left[\frac{1}{n}\sum_{t=1}^{n}\mathbf{g}(\mathbf{w}_t; \boldsymbol{\theta})\right]'\widehat{\mathbf{W}}\left[\frac{1}{n}\sum_{t=1}^{n}\mathbf{g}(\mathbf{w}_t; \boldsymbol{\theta})\right],$$

where the symmetric matrix $\widehat{\mathbf{W}}$ is assumed to converge in probability to some

[9] Only for interested readers, here is a proof:

$$\begin{aligned}
|\log f(y_t \mid \mathbf{x}_t; \boldsymbol{\theta})| &\le |y_t|\,|\log\Phi(\mathbf{x}_t'\boldsymbol{\theta})| + |1-y_t|\,|\log\Phi(-\mathbf{x}_t'\boldsymbol{\theta})| \\
&\le |\log\Phi(\mathbf{x}_t'\boldsymbol{\theta})| + |\log\Phi(-\mathbf{x}_t'\boldsymbol{\theta})| \quad (\text{since } |y_t|\le 1 \text{ and } |1-y_t|\le 1) \\
&\le 2\times\big[\,|\log\Phi(0)| + |\mathbf{x}_t'\boldsymbol{\theta}| + |\mathbf{x}_t'\boldsymbol{\theta}|^2\big] \quad (\text{by } (7.2.14)) \\
&\le 2\times\big[\,|\log\Phi(0)| + \|\mathbf{x}_t\|\cdot\|\boldsymbol{\theta}\| + \|\mathbf{x}_t\|^2\cdot\|\boldsymbol{\theta}\|^2\big].
\end{aligned}$$

The last inequality is due to the Cauchy-Schwartz inequality that $|\mathbf{x}'\mathbf{y}| \le \|\mathbf{x}\|\,\|\mathbf{y}\|$ for any two conformable vectors $\mathbf{x}$ and $\mathbf{y}$. Also, $\mathrm{E}(\|\mathbf{x}_t\|^2)$, which is the sum of $\mathrm{E}(x_{it}^2)$ over i, is finite because the nonsingularity of $\mathrm{E}(\mathbf{x}_t\mathbf{x}_t')$ implies $\mathrm{E}(x_{it}^2) < \infty$ for all i. If $\mathrm{E}(\|\mathbf{x}_t\|^2) < \infty$, then $\mathrm{E}(\|\mathbf{x}_t\|) < \infty$.

symmetric positive definite matrix $\mathbf{W}$. *Suppose that the model is correctly specified in that* $\mathrm{E}[\mathbf{g}(\mathbf{w}_t; \boldsymbol{\theta}_0)] = \mathbf{0}$ *(i.e., the orthogonality conditions hold) for* $\boldsymbol{\theta}_0 \in \Theta$. *Suppose that (i) the parameter space* Θ *is a compact subset of* $\mathbb{R}^p$, *(ii)* $\mathbf{g}(\mathbf{w}_t; \boldsymbol{\theta})$ *is continuous in* $\boldsymbol{\theta}$ *for all* $\mathbf{w}_t$, *and (iii)* $\mathbf{g}(\mathbf{w}_t; \boldsymbol{\theta})$ *is measurable in* $\mathbf{w}_t$ *for all* $\boldsymbol{\theta}$ *in* Θ *(so* $\hat{\boldsymbol{\theta}}$ *is a well-defined random variable by Lemma 7.1). Suppose, further, that*

(a) (identification) $\mathrm{E}[\mathbf{g}(\mathbf{w}_t; \boldsymbol{\theta})] \neq \mathbf{0}$ *for all* $\boldsymbol{\theta} \neq \boldsymbol{\theta}_0$ *in* Θ,

(b) (dominance) $\mathrm{E}[\sup_{\boldsymbol{\theta}\in\Theta} \|\mathbf{g}(\mathbf{w}_t; \boldsymbol{\theta})\|] < \infty$.

Then $\hat{\boldsymbol{\theta}} \to_{\mathrm{p}} \boldsymbol{\theta}_0$.

If $Q_n(\boldsymbol{\theta})$ is concave, then the compactness of Θ, the continuity of $\mathbf{g}(\mathbf{w}_t; \boldsymbol{\theta})$, and the dominance condition can be replaced by the condition that $\mathrm{E}[\mathbf{g}(\mathbf{w}_t; \boldsymbol{\theta})]$ exist and be finite for all $\boldsymbol{\theta}$. We will not state this result as a proposition because there are very few applications in which $Q_n(\boldsymbol{\theta})$ is concave. For example, the GMM objective function for the Euler equation model in Example 7.5 is not concave. Just about the only well-known case is one in which $\mathbf{g}(\mathbf{w}_t; \boldsymbol{\theta})$ is linear in $\boldsymbol{\theta}$, but the linear case has been treated rather thoroughly in Chapter 3. When $\mathbf{g}(\mathbf{w}_t; \boldsymbol{\theta})$ is nonlinear in $\boldsymbol{\theta}$, specifying primitive conditions for (a) (identification) and (b) (dominance) in Proposition 7.7 is generally quite difficult. So in most applications those conditions are simply assumed.

QUESTIONS FOR REVIEW

1. (Necessity of density identification) We have shown for conditional ML that the conditional density identification (7.2.13) is sufficient for condition (a) (that $\mathrm{E}[\log f(y_t \mid \mathbf{x}_t; \boldsymbol{\theta})]$ be maximized uniquely at $\boldsymbol{\theta}_0$). That it is also a necessary condition is clear from the Kullback-Leibler information inequality. Without using this inequality, show the necessity of conditional mean identification. **Hint:** Show that, if (7.2.13) were false, then (a) would not hold. Suppose that there exists a $\boldsymbol{\theta}_1 \neq \boldsymbol{\theta}_0$ such that $\boldsymbol{\theta}_1 \in \Theta$ and $f(y_t \mid \mathbf{x}_t; \boldsymbol{\theta}_1) = f(y_t \mid \mathbf{x}_t; \boldsymbol{\theta}_0)$. Then $\mathrm{E}[\log f(y_t \mid \mathbf{x}_t; \boldsymbol{\theta}_1)] = \mathrm{E}[\log f(y_t \mid \mathbf{x}_t; \boldsymbol{\theta}_0)]$.
2. (Necessity of conditional mean identification) Without using (7.2.8), show that conditional mean identification is necessary as well as sufficient for identification in NLS.
3. (Identification in NLS) Suppose that the φ function in NLS is linear: $\varphi(\mathbf{x}_t; \boldsymbol{\theta}) = \mathbf{x}_t'\boldsymbol{\theta}$. Verify that identification is satisfied if $\mathrm{E}(\mathbf{x}_t\mathbf{x}_t')$ is nonsingular.

4. (Identification in NLS estimation of probit) In the probit model, $\mathrm{E}(y_t \mid \mathbf{x}_t) = \Phi(\mathbf{x}_t'\boldsymbol{\theta}_0)$. Consider estimating $\boldsymbol{\theta}_0$ by least squares. Verify that conditional mean identification is satisfied if $\mathrm{E}(\mathbf{x}_t\mathbf{x}_t')$ is nonsingular.

5. (Quasi-ML) Suppose in Proposition 7.5 that $\{y_t, \mathbf{x}_t\}$ is i.i.d., so the likelihood function itself is not misspecified. But suppose that the true parameter vector $\boldsymbol{\theta}_0$ is *not* included in the assumed parameter space Θ. So in this sense the estimator $\hat{\boldsymbol{\theta}}$ is a quasi-ML estimator. Drop condition (a), and suppose instead that there is a unique $\boldsymbol{\theta}^*$ in Θ that maximizes $\mathrm{E}[\log f(y_t \mid \mathbf{x}_t; \boldsymbol{\theta})]$. Show that the QML estimator $\hat{\boldsymbol{\theta}}$ is consistent for $\boldsymbol{\theta}^*$. **Hint:** Replace the $\boldsymbol{\theta}_0$ in Proposition 7.3 by $\boldsymbol{\theta}^*$. In Propositions 7.1–7.4, $\boldsymbol{\theta}_0$ does not need to be the "true" parameter vector.

6. (Identification in linear GMM) Consider the linear GMM model of Chapter 3. Verify that the rank condition for identification derived in Chapter 3 is equivalent to the identification condition in Proposition 7.7.

7. (Concavity of the objective function in linear GMM) Verify that the GMM objective function in linear GMM is concave in $\boldsymbol{\theta}$. **Hint:** The Hessian (the matrix of second derivatives) of $Q_n(\boldsymbol{\theta})$ is $-\mathbf{S}_{\mathbf{xz}}'\widehat{\mathbf{W}}\mathbf{S}_{\mathbf{xz}}$ where $\mathbf{S}_{\mathbf{xz}} \equiv \frac{1}{n}\sum_{t=1}^{n}\mathbf{x}_t\mathbf{z}_t'$. A twice continuously differentiable function is concave if and only if its Hessian is everywhere negative semidefinite.

8. (GMM identification with singular $\mathbf{W}$) For $\mathbf{W}$, if we require it to be merely positive semidefinite, not necessarily positive definite, what would be the identification condition in Proposition 7.7? **Hint:** Suppose $\mathbf{W}$ is positive semidefinite. Show that if $\mathrm{E}[\mathbf{g}(\mathbf{w}_t; \boldsymbol{\theta}_0)] = \mathbf{0}$ and $\mathbf{W}\,\mathrm{E}[\mathbf{g}(\mathbf{w}_t; \boldsymbol{\theta})] \neq \mathbf{0}$ for $\boldsymbol{\theta} \neq \boldsymbol{\theta}_0$, then $Q_0(\boldsymbol{\theta}) = -\frac{1}{2}\mathrm{E}[\mathbf{g}(\mathbf{w}_t; \boldsymbol{\theta})]'\mathbf{W}\,\mathrm{E}[\mathbf{g}(\mathbf{w}_t; \boldsymbol{\theta})]$ has a unique maximum at $\boldsymbol{\theta}_0$.

7.3 Asymptotic Normality

The basic tool in deriving the asymptotic distribution of an extremum estimator is the Mean Value Theorem from calculus. How it is used depends on whether the estimator is an M-estimator or a GMM estimator. Therefore, the proof of asymptotic normality will be done separately for M-estimators (including ML as a special case) and GMM estimators. This is followed by a brief remark on the relative efficiency of GMM and ML. By way of summing up, we will point out at the end of the section that the Taylor expansion for the sampling error has a structure shared by both M-estimators and GMM.

Asymptotic Normality of M-Estimators

Reproducing (7.1.2), the objective function for M-estimators is

$$Q_n(\boldsymbol{\theta}) = \frac{1}{n}\sum_{t=1}^{n} m(\mathbf{w}_t; \boldsymbol{\theta}). \tag{7.3.1}$$

It will be convenient to give symbols to the gradient (vector of first derivatives) and the Hessian (matrix of second derivatives) of the m function as

$$\underset{(p\times 1)}{\mathbf{s}(\mathbf{w}_t; \boldsymbol{\theta})} = \frac{\partial m(\mathbf{w}_t; \boldsymbol{\theta})}{\partial \boldsymbol{\theta}}, \tag{7.3.2}$$

$$\underset{(p\times p)}{\mathbf{H}(\mathbf{w}_t; \boldsymbol{\theta})} = \frac{\partial \mathbf{s}(\mathbf{w}_t; \boldsymbol{\theta})}{\partial \boldsymbol{\theta}'} = \frac{\partial^2 m(\mathbf{w}_t; \boldsymbol{\theta})}{\partial \boldsymbol{\theta}\, \partial \boldsymbol{\theta}'}. \tag{7.3.3}$$

In analogy to ML, $\mathbf{s}(\mathbf{w}_t; \boldsymbol{\theta})$ will be referred to as the **score vector for observation t**. This $\mathbf{s}(\mathbf{w}_t; \boldsymbol{\theta})$ should not be confused with the score in the usual sense, which is the gradient of the objective function $Q_n(\boldsymbol{\theta})$. The score in the latter sense will be denoted $\mathbf{s}_n(\boldsymbol{\theta})$ later in this chapter. The same applies to the Hessian: $\mathbf{H}(\mathbf{w}_t; \boldsymbol{\theta})$ will be referred to as the **Hessian for observation** t, and the Hessian of $Q_n(\boldsymbol{\theta})$ will be denoted $\mathbf{H}_n(\boldsymbol{\theta})$.

The goal of this subsection is the asymptotic normality of $\hat{\boldsymbol{\theta}}$ described in (7.3.10) below. In the process of deriving it, we will make a number of assumptions, which will be collected in Proposition 7.8 below. Assume that $m(\mathbf{w}_t; \boldsymbol{\theta})$ is differentiable in $\boldsymbol{\theta}$ and that $\hat{\boldsymbol{\theta}}$ is in the interior of Θ. So $\hat{\boldsymbol{\theta}}$, being the interior solution to the problem of maximizing $Q_n(\boldsymbol{\theta})$, satisfies the first-order conditions

$$\begin{aligned}\underset{(p\times 1)}{\mathbf{0}} &= \frac{\partial Q_n(\hat{\boldsymbol{\theta}})}{\partial \boldsymbol{\theta}} \\ &= \frac{1}{n}\sum_{t=1}^{n} \mathbf{s}(\mathbf{w}_t; \hat{\boldsymbol{\theta}}) \quad \text{(by (7.3.1) and (7.3.2))}.\end{aligned} \tag{7.3.4}$$

We now use the following result from calculus:

Mean Value Theorem: *Let $\mathbf{h} : \mathbb{R}^p \to \mathbb{R}^q$ be continuously differentiable. Then $\mathbf{h}(\mathbf{x})$ admits the* ***mean value expansion***

$$\underset{(q\times 1)}{\mathbf{h}(\mathbf{x})} = \underset{(q\times 1)}{\mathbf{h}(\mathbf{x}_0)} + \underset{(q\times p)}{\frac{\partial \mathbf{h}(\bar{\mathbf{x}})}{\partial \mathbf{x}'}} \underset{(p\times 1)}{(\mathbf{x} - \mathbf{x}_0)},$$

where $\bar{\mathbf{x}}$ is a mean value lying between $\mathbf{x}$ and $\mathbf{x}_0$.[10]

Setting $q = p$, $\mathbf{x} = \hat{\boldsymbol{\theta}}$, $\mathbf{x}_0 = \boldsymbol{\theta}_0$, and $\mathbf{h}(\cdot) = \frac{\partial Q_n(\cdot)}{\partial \boldsymbol{\theta}}$ in the Mean Value Theorem, we obtain the following mean value expansion:

$$\begin{aligned}\underset{(p\times 1)}{\frac{\partial Q_n(\hat{\boldsymbol{\theta}})}{\partial \boldsymbol{\theta}}} &= \underset{(p\times 1)}{\frac{\partial Q_n(\boldsymbol{\theta}_0)}{\partial \boldsymbol{\theta}}} + \underset{(p\times p)}{\frac{\partial^2 Q_n(\bar{\boldsymbol{\theta}})}{\partial \boldsymbol{\theta}\,\partial \boldsymbol{\theta}'}} \underset{(p\times 1)}{(\hat{\boldsymbol{\theta}} - \boldsymbol{\theta}_0)} \\ &= \underset{(p\times 1)}{\frac{1}{n}\sum_{t=1}^{n} \mathbf{s}(\mathbf{w}_t; \boldsymbol{\theta}_0)} + \underset{(p\times p)}{\left[\frac{1}{n}\sum_{t=1}^{n} \mathbf{H}(\mathbf{w}_t; \bar{\boldsymbol{\theta}})\right]} \underset{(p\times 1)}{(\hat{\boldsymbol{\theta}} - \boldsymbol{\theta}_0)} \quad \text{(by (7.3.1)–(7.3.3))},\end{aligned} \tag{7.3.5}$$

where $\bar{\boldsymbol{\theta}}$ is a mean value that lies between $\hat{\boldsymbol{\theta}}$ and $\boldsymbol{\theta}_0$. The continuous differentiability requirement of the Mean Value Theorem is satisfied if $m(\mathbf{w}_t; \boldsymbol{\theta})$ is *twice* continuously differentiable with respect to $\boldsymbol{\theta}$. Combining this equation with the first-order condition above, we obtain

$$\underset{(p\times 1)}{\mathbf{0}} = \frac{1}{n}\sum_{t=1}^{n} \mathbf{s}(\mathbf{w}_t; \boldsymbol{\theta}_0) + \left[\frac{1}{n}\sum_{t=1}^{n} \mathbf{H}(\mathbf{w}_t; \bar{\boldsymbol{\theta}})\right](\hat{\boldsymbol{\theta}} - \boldsymbol{\theta}_0). \tag{7.3.6}$$

Assuming that $\frac{1}{n}\sum_{t=1}^{n} \mathbf{H}(\mathbf{w}_t; \bar{\boldsymbol{\theta}})$ is nonsingular, this equation can be solved for $\hat{\boldsymbol{\theta}} - \boldsymbol{\theta}_0$ to yield

$$\sqrt{n}(\hat{\boldsymbol{\theta}} - \boldsymbol{\theta}_0) = -\left[\frac{1}{n}\sum_{t=1}^{n} \mathbf{H}(\mathbf{w}_t; \bar{\boldsymbol{\theta}})\right]^{-1} \frac{1}{\sqrt{n}}\sum_{t=1}^{n} \mathbf{s}(\mathbf{w}_t; \boldsymbol{\theta}_0). \tag{7.3.7}$$

This expression for ($\sqrt{n}$ times) the sampling error will be referred to as the **mean value expansion for the sampling error**. Note that the score vector $\mathbf{s}(\mathbf{w}_t; \boldsymbol{\theta})$ is evaluated at the true parameter value $\boldsymbol{\theta}_0$.

Now, since $\bar{\boldsymbol{\theta}}$ lies between $\boldsymbol{\theta}_0$ and $\hat{\boldsymbol{\theta}}$, $\bar{\boldsymbol{\theta}}$ is consistent for $\boldsymbol{\theta}_0$ if $\hat{\boldsymbol{\theta}}$ is. If $\{\mathbf{w}_t\}$ is ergodic stationary, it is natural to conjecture that

$$\frac{1}{n}\sum_{t=1}^{n} \mathbf{H}(\mathbf{w}_t; \bar{\boldsymbol{\theta}}) \underset{\text{p}}{\to} \mathrm{E}\big[\mathbf{H}(\mathbf{w}_t; \boldsymbol{\theta}_0)\big]. \tag{7.3.8}$$

[10]The Mean Value Theorem only applies to individual elements of $\mathbf{h}$, so that $\bar{\mathbf{x}}$ actually differs from element to element of the vector equation. This complication does not affect the discussion in the text.

The ergodic stationarity of $\mathbf{w}_t$ and consistency of $\bar{\boldsymbol{\theta}}$ alone, however, are not enough to ensure this; some technical condition needs to be assumed. One such technical condition is the uniform convergence of $\frac{1}{n}\sum_{t=1}^{n}\mathbf{H}(\mathbf{w}_t;\cdot)$ to $\mathrm{E}\big[\mathbf{H}(\mathbf{w}_t;\cdot)\big]$ in a neighborhood of $\boldsymbol{\theta}_0$.[11] But by the Uniform Convergence Theorem, the uniform convergence of $\frac{1}{n}\sum_{t=1}^{n}\mathbf{H}(\mathbf{w}_t;\cdot)$ is satisfied if the following dominance condition is satisfied for the Hessian: for some neighborhood $\mathcal{N}$ of $\boldsymbol{\theta}_0$, $\mathrm{E}[\sup_{\boldsymbol{\theta}\in\mathcal{N}}\|\mathbf{H}(\mathbf{w}_t;\boldsymbol{\theta})\|]<\infty$ (this is condition (4) below).[12] This is a sufficient condition for (7.3.8); if you can directly verify (7.3.8), then there is no need to verify the dominance condition for asymptotic normality.

Finally, if (7.3.8) holds and if

$$\frac{1}{\sqrt{n}}\sum_{t=1}^{n}\mathbf{s}(\mathbf{w}_t;\boldsymbol{\theta}_0)\underset{\mathrm{d}}{\to}N(\mathbf{0},\boldsymbol{\Sigma}), \tag{7.3.9}$$

then by the Slutzky theorem (see Lemma 2.4(c)) we have

$$\sqrt{n}(\hat{\boldsymbol{\theta}}-\boldsymbol{\theta}_0)\underset{\mathrm{d}}{\to}N\Big(\mathbf{0},\big(\mathrm{E}\big[\mathbf{H}(\mathbf{w}_t;\boldsymbol{\theta}_0)\big]\big)^{-1}\boldsymbol{\Sigma}\big(\mathrm{E}\big[\mathbf{H}(\mathbf{w}_t;\boldsymbol{\theta}_0)\big]\big)^{-1}\Big). \tag{7.3.10}$$

Collecting the assumptions we have made so far, we have

Proposition 7.8 (Asymptotic normality of M-estimators): *Suppose that the conditions of either Proposition 7.3 or Proposition 7.4 are satisfied, so that $\{\mathbf{w}_t\}$ is ergodic stationary and the M-estimator $\hat{\boldsymbol{\theta}}$ defined by (7.1.1) and (7.1.2) is consistent. Suppose, further, that*

(1) $\boldsymbol{\theta}_0$ is in the interior of Θ,

(2) $m(\mathbf{w}_t;\boldsymbol{\theta})$ is twice continuously differentiable in $\boldsymbol{\theta}$ for any $\mathbf{w}_t$,

(3) $\frac{1}{\sqrt{n}}\sum_{t=1}^{n}\mathbf{s}(\mathbf{w}_t;\boldsymbol{\theta}_0)\to_{\mathrm{d}}N(\mathbf{0},\boldsymbol{\Sigma})$, $\boldsymbol{\Sigma}$ positive definite, where $\mathbf{s}(\mathbf{w}_t;\boldsymbol{\theta})$ is defined in (7.3.2),

[11] This is a consequence of the following result (see, e.g., Theorem 4.1.5 of Amemiya, 1985):

> Suppose a sequence of random functions $h_n(\boldsymbol{\theta})$ converges to a nonstochastic function $h_0(\boldsymbol{\theta})$ uniformly in $\boldsymbol{\theta}$ over an open neighborhood of $\boldsymbol{\theta}_0$. Then $\operatorname{plim}_{n\to\infty}h_n(\tilde{\boldsymbol{\theta}})=h_0(\boldsymbol{\theta}_0)$ if $\operatorname{plim}\tilde{\boldsymbol{\theta}}=\boldsymbol{\theta}_0$ and $h_0(\boldsymbol{\theta})$ is continuous at $\boldsymbol{\theta}_0$.

Set $h_n(\boldsymbol{\theta})$ to $\frac{1}{n}\sum_{t=1}^{n}\mathbf{H}(\mathbf{w}_t;\cdot)$ and $h_0(\boldsymbol{\theta})$ to $\mathrm{E}\big[\mathbf{H}(\mathbf{w}_t;\boldsymbol{\theta})\big]$. Continuity of $\mathrm{E}[\mathbf{H}(\mathbf{w}_t;\boldsymbol{\theta})]$ will be assured by the Uniform Convergence Theorem. The uniform convergence needs to be only over a neighborhood of $\boldsymbol{\theta}_0$, not over the entire parameter space, because $\tilde{\boldsymbol{\theta}}$ is close to $\boldsymbol{\theta}_0$ for n sufficiently large.

[12] A matrix can be viewed as a vector whose elements have been rearranged. So the Euclidean norm of a matrix, such as $\|\mathbf{H}(\mathbf{w}_t;\boldsymbol{\theta})\|$, is the square root of the sum of squares of all its elements.

(4) (local dominance condition on the Hessian) for some neighborhood $\mathcal{N}$ of $\boldsymbol{\theta}_0$,

$$\mathrm{E}[\sup_{\boldsymbol{\theta}\in\mathcal{N}} \|\mathbf{H}(\mathbf{w}_t;\boldsymbol{\theta})\|\,] < \infty,$$

so that for any consistent estimator $\tilde{\boldsymbol{\theta}}$, $\frac{1}{n}\sum_{t=1}^{n}\mathbf{H}(\mathbf{w}_t;\tilde{\boldsymbol{\theta}}) \to_{\mathrm{p}} \mathrm{E}\big[\mathbf{H}(\mathbf{w}_t;\boldsymbol{\theta}_0)\big]$, where $\mathbf{H}(\mathbf{w}_t;\boldsymbol{\theta})$ is defined in (7.3.3),

(5) $\mathrm{E}\big[\mathbf{H}(\mathbf{w}_t,\boldsymbol{\theta}_0)\big]$ is nonsingular.

Then $\hat{\boldsymbol{\theta}}$ is asymptotically normal with

$$\mathrm{Avar}(\hat{\boldsymbol{\theta}}) = \big(\mathrm{E}\big[\mathbf{H}(\mathbf{w}_t;\boldsymbol{\theta}_0)\big]\big)^{-1}\,\boldsymbol{\Sigma}\big(\mathrm{E}\big[\mathbf{H}(\mathbf{w}_t;\boldsymbol{\theta}_0)\big]\big)^{-1}.$$

(This is Theorem 4.1.3 of Amemiya (1985) adapted to M-estimators.) Two remarks are in order.

- Of the assumptions we have made in the derivation of asymptotic normality, the following are not listed in the proposition: (i) $\hat{\boldsymbol{\theta}}$ is an interior point, and (ii) $\frac{1}{n}\sum_{t=1}^{n}\mathbf{H}(\mathbf{w}_t;\bar{\boldsymbol{\theta}})$ is nonsingular. It is intuitively clear that these conditions hold because $\hat{\boldsymbol{\theta}}$ converges in probability to an interior point $\boldsymbol{\theta}_0$, and $\frac{1}{n}\sum_{t=1}^{n}\mathbf{H}(\mathbf{w}_t;\bar{\boldsymbol{\theta}})$ converges in probability to a nonsingular matrix $\mathrm{E}\big[\mathbf{H}(\mathbf{w}_t;\boldsymbol{\theta}_0)\big]$. See Newey and McFadden (1994, p. 2152) for a rigorous proof. This sort of technicality will be ignored in the rest of this chapter.
- If $\mathbf{w}_t$ is ergodic stationary, then so is $\mathbf{s}(\mathbf{w}_t;\boldsymbol{\theta}_0)$ and the matrix $\boldsymbol{\Sigma}$ is the long run variance matrix of $\{\mathbf{s}(\mathbf{w}_t;\boldsymbol{\theta}_0)\}$.[13] A sufficient condition for (3) is Gordin's condition introduced in Section 6.5. So condition (3) in the proposition can be replaced by Gordin's condition on $\{\mathbf{s}(\mathbf{w}_t;\boldsymbol{\theta}_0)\}$. It is satisfied, for example, if $\mathbf{w}_t$ is i.i.d. and $\mathrm{E}[\mathbf{s}(\mathbf{w}_t;\boldsymbol{\theta}_0)] = \mathbf{0}$. The assumption that $\boldsymbol{\Sigma}$ is positive definite is not really needed for the conclusion of the proposition, but we might as well assume it here because in virtually all applications it is satisfied (or assumed) and also because it will be required in the discussion of hypothesis testing later in this chapter.

Consistent Asymptotic Variance Estimation

To use this asymptotic result for hypothesis testing, we need a consistent estimate of

$$\mathrm{Avar}(\hat{\boldsymbol{\theta}}) = \big(\mathrm{E}\big[\mathbf{H}(\mathbf{w}_t;\boldsymbol{\theta}_0)\big]\big)^{-1}\,\boldsymbol{\Sigma}\big(\mathrm{E}\big[\mathbf{H}(\mathbf{w}_t;\boldsymbol{\theta}_0)\big]\big)^{-1}.$$

[13] The long-run variance was introduced in Section 6.5.

Since $\hat{\boldsymbol{\theta}} \to_{\text{p}} \boldsymbol{\theta}_0$, condition (4) of Proposition 7.8 implies that

$$\frac{1}{n}\sum_{t=1}^{n} \mathbf{H}(\mathbf{w}_t; \hat{\boldsymbol{\theta}}) \underset{\text{p}}{\to} \text{E}\big[\mathbf{H}(\mathbf{w}_t; \boldsymbol{\theta}_0)\big].$$

Therefore, provided that there is available a consistent estimator $\widehat{\boldsymbol{\Sigma}}$ of $\boldsymbol{\Sigma}$,

$$\widehat{\text{Avar}(\hat{\boldsymbol{\theta}})} = \left\{\frac{1}{n}\sum_{t=1}^{n} \mathbf{H}(\mathbf{w}_t; \hat{\boldsymbol{\theta}})\right\}^{-1} \widehat{\boldsymbol{\Sigma}} \left\{\frac{1}{n}\sum_{t=1}^{n} \mathbf{H}(\mathbf{w}_t; \hat{\boldsymbol{\theta}})\right\}^{-1} \tag{7.3.11}$$

is a consistent estimator of the asymptotic variance matrix. To obtain $\widehat{\boldsymbol{\Sigma}}$, the methods introduced in Section 6.6, such as the VARHAC, can be applied to the estimated series $\{\mathbf{s}(\mathbf{w}_t; \hat{\boldsymbol{\theta}})\}$ under some suitable technical conditions.

Asymptotic Normality of Conditional ML

We now specialize this asymptotic normality result to ML for the case of i.i.d. data. In ML, where the m function is a log (conditional) likelihood, the first-order conditions (7.3.4) are called the **likelihood equations**. The fact that the m function is a log (conditional) likelihood leads to a simplification of the asymptotic variance matrix of $\hat{\boldsymbol{\theta}}$. We show this for conditional ML; doing the same for unconditional or joint ML is easier.

Consider the two equalities in condition (3) of Proposition 7.9 below. The second equality is called the **information matrix equality** (not to be confused with the Kullback-Leibler information *in*equality). It is so called because $\text{E}\big[\mathbf{s}(\mathbf{w}_t; \boldsymbol{\theta}_0)\,\mathbf{s}(\mathbf{w}_t; \boldsymbol{\theta}_0)'\big]$ is the **information matrix for observation t**. It is left as Analytical Exercise 2 to derive these two equalities under some technical conditions permitting the interchange of differentiation and integration. Here, we just note the implication of these two equalities for Proposition 7.8. If $\mathbf{w}_t$ is i.i.d., the Lindeberg-Levy CLT and the first equality (that $\text{E}[\mathbf{s}(\mathbf{w}_t; \boldsymbol{\theta}_0)] = \mathbf{0}$) imply

$$\frac{1}{\sqrt{n}}\sum_{t=1}^{n} \mathbf{s}(\mathbf{w}_t; \boldsymbol{\theta}_0) \underset{\text{d}}{\to} N(\mathbf{0}, \boldsymbol{\Sigma}) \;\text{ where }\; \boldsymbol{\Sigma} = \text{E}\big[\mathbf{s}(\mathbf{w}_t; \boldsymbol{\theta}_0)\,\mathbf{s}(\mathbf{w}_t; \boldsymbol{\theta}_0)'\big]. \tag{7.3.12}$$

This and the information matrix equality imply that $\text{Avar}(\hat{\boldsymbol{\theta}})$ in Proposition 7.8 is simplified in two ways as

$$\text{Avar}(\hat{\boldsymbol{\theta}}) = -\big\{\text{E}\big[\mathbf{H}(\mathbf{w}_t; \boldsymbol{\theta}_0)\big]\big\}^{-1} = \big\{\text{E}\big[\mathbf{s}(\mathbf{w}_t; \boldsymbol{\theta}_0)\,\mathbf{s}(\mathbf{w}_t; \boldsymbol{\theta}_0)'\big]\big\}^{-1}. \tag{7.3.13}$$

Thus, we have proved

Proposition 7.9 (Asymptotic normality of conditional ML): *Let* $\mathbf{w}_t$ ($\equiv (y_t, \mathbf{x}_t')'$) *be i.i.d. Suppose the conditions of either Proposition 7.5 or Proposition 7.6 are satisfied, so that* $\hat{\boldsymbol{\theta}} \to_{\mathrm{p}} \boldsymbol{\theta}_0$. *Suppose, in addition, that*

(1) $\boldsymbol{\theta}_0$ *is in the interior of* Θ,

(2) $f(y_t \mid \mathbf{x}_t; \boldsymbol{\theta})$ *is twice continuously differentiable in* $\boldsymbol{\theta}$ *for all* $(y_t, \mathbf{x}_t)$,

(3) $\mathrm{E}[\mathbf{s}(\mathbf{w}_t; \boldsymbol{\theta}_0)] = \mathbf{0}$ *and* $-\mathrm{E}\big[\mathbf{H}(\mathbf{w}_t; \boldsymbol{\theta}_0)\big] = \mathrm{E}\big[\mathbf{s}(\mathbf{w}_t; \boldsymbol{\theta}_0)\,\mathbf{s}(\mathbf{w}_t; \boldsymbol{\theta}_0)'\big]$, *where* $\mathbf{s}$ *and* $\mathbf{H}$ *functions are defined in (7.3.2) and (7.3.3),*

(4) (local dominance condition on the Hessian) for some neighborhood $\mathcal{N}$ *of* $\boldsymbol{\theta}_0$,

$$\mathrm{E}[\sup_{\boldsymbol{\theta}\in\mathcal{N}} \|\mathbf{H}(\mathbf{w}_t; \boldsymbol{\theta})\|\,] < \infty,$$

so that for any consistent estimator $\tilde{\boldsymbol{\theta}}$, $\frac{1}{n}\sum_{t=1}^{n} \mathbf{H}(\mathbf{w}_t; \tilde{\boldsymbol{\theta}}) \to_{\mathrm{p}} \mathrm{E}\big[\mathbf{H}(\mathbf{w}_t; \boldsymbol{\theta}_0)\big]$,

(5) $\mathrm{E}\big[\mathbf{H}(\mathbf{w}_t; \boldsymbol{\theta}_0)\big]$ *is nonsingular.*

Then $\hat{\boldsymbol{\theta}}$ *is asymptotically normal with* $\mathrm{Avar}(\hat{\boldsymbol{\theta}})$ *given by (7.3.13).*

Two remarks about the proposition:

- Condition (3) is stated as an assumption here because its derivation requires interchange of integration and differentiation (see Analytical Exercise 2). A technical condition under which the interchange is legal is readily available from calculus (see, e.g., Lemma 3.6 of Newey and McFadden, 1994). So condition (3) could be replaced by such a technical condition on $f(y_t \mid \mathbf{x}_t; \boldsymbol{\theta})$. We do not do it here because in most applications condition (3) can be verified directly.
- It should be clear from the above discussion how this proposition can be adapted to unconditional ML: simply replace $f(y_t \mid \mathbf{x}_t; \boldsymbol{\theta})$ by $f(\mathbf{w}_t; \boldsymbol{\theta})$.

To use this asymptotic result for hypothesis testing, we need a consistent estimate of $\mathrm{Avar}(\hat{\boldsymbol{\theta}})$. Noting that it can be written as $-\big\{\mathrm{E}\big[\mathbf{H}(\mathbf{w}_t; \boldsymbol{\theta}_0)\big]\big\}^{-1}$, a natural estimator is

$$\text{first estimator of } \mathrm{Avar}(\hat{\boldsymbol{\theta}}) = -\left\{\frac{1}{n}\sum_{t=1}^{n} \mathbf{H}(\mathbf{w}_t; \hat{\boldsymbol{\theta}})\right\}^{-1}. \tag{7.3.14}$$

Since $\hat{\boldsymbol{\theta}} \to_{\mathrm{p}} \boldsymbol{\theta}_0$, this estimator is consistent by condition (4) of Proposition 7.9.

Another estimator, based on the relation $\text{Avar}(\hat{\boldsymbol{\theta}}) = \big\{\text{E}\big[\mathbf{s}(\mathbf{w}_t;\boldsymbol{\theta}_0)\,\mathbf{s}(\mathbf{w}_t;\boldsymbol{\theta}_0)'\big]\big\}^{-1}$, is

$$\text{second estimator of Avar}(\hat{\boldsymbol{\theta}}) = \left\{\frac{1}{n}\sum_{t=1}^{n}\mathbf{s}(\mathbf{w}_t;\hat{\boldsymbol{\theta}})\,\mathbf{s}(\mathbf{w}_t;\hat{\boldsymbol{\theta}})'\right\}^{-1}. \tag{7.3.15}$$

To insure consistency for this estimator, we need to make an assumption in addition to the hypothesis of Proposition 7.9 (see, e.g., Theorem 4.4 of Newey and McFadden, 1994). We will not show it here because in many applications the consistency of this second estimator can be verified directly.

There is no compelling reason for preferring one estimator of $\text{Avar}(\hat{\boldsymbol{\theta}})$ over the other. The second estimator, which requires only the first derivative of the log likelihood, is easier to compute than the first. This can be an important consideration when it is impossible to calculate the derivatives of the density function analytically and some numerical method must be used. On the other hand, in at least some cases the first provides a better finite-sample approximation of the asymptotic distribution (see, e.g., Davidson and MacKinnon, 1993).

Two Examples

To get a better grasp of the asymptotic normality results about conditional ML, it is useful to see how the results can be applied to familiar examples. We consider two such examples.

Example 7.10 (Asymptotic normality in linear regression model): To reproduce the log conditional density for observation t for the linear regression model with normal errors,

$$\log f(y_t \mid \mathbf{x}_t;\boldsymbol{\beta},\sigma^2) = -\frac{1}{2}\log(2\pi) - \frac{1}{2}\log(\sigma^2) - \frac{(y_t - \mathbf{x}_t'\boldsymbol{\beta})^2}{2\sigma^2}. \tag{7.3.16}$$

With $\Theta = \mathbb{R}^K \times \mathbb{R}_{++}$ (where K is the dimension of $\boldsymbol{\beta}$), condition (1) of Proposition 7.9 is satisfied. Condition (2) is obviously satisfied. To verify (3), a routine calculation yields:[14]

$$\mathbf{s}(\mathbf{w}_t;\boldsymbol{\theta}) = \begin{bmatrix} \frac{1}{\sigma^2}\mathbf{x}_t\cdot\hat{\varepsilon}_t \\ -\frac{1}{2\sigma^2} + \frac{1}{2\sigma^4}\hat{\varepsilon}_t^2 \end{bmatrix},\quad \mathbf{H}(\mathbf{w}_t;\boldsymbol{\theta}) = \begin{bmatrix} -\frac{1}{\sigma^2}\mathbf{x}_t\mathbf{x}_t' & -\frac{1}{\sigma^4}\mathbf{x}_t\cdot\hat{\varepsilon}_t \\ -\frac{1}{\sigma^4}\mathbf{x}_t'\cdot\hat{\varepsilon}_t & \frac{1}{2\sigma^4} - \frac{1}{\sigma^6}\hat{\varepsilon}_t^2 \end{bmatrix},$$

$$\mathbf{s}(\mathbf{w}_t;\boldsymbol{\theta})\,\mathbf{s}(\mathbf{w}_t;\boldsymbol{\theta})' = \begin{bmatrix} \frac{1}{\sigma^4}\mathbf{x}_t\mathbf{x}_t'\hat{\varepsilon}_t^2 & -\frac{1}{2\sigma^4}\mathbf{x}_t\cdot\hat{\varepsilon}_t + \frac{1}{2\sigma^6}\mathbf{x}_t\cdot\hat{\varepsilon}_t^3 \\ -\frac{1}{2\sigma^4}\mathbf{x}_t'\cdot\hat{\varepsilon}_t + \frac{1}{2\sigma^6}\mathbf{x}_t'\cdot\hat{\varepsilon}_t^3 & \frac{1}{4\sigma^4} - \frac{1}{2\sigma^6}\hat{\varepsilon}_t^2 + \frac{1}{4\sigma^8}\hat{\varepsilon}_t^4 \end{bmatrix}, \tag{7.3.17}$$

[14]For the parameter σ^2 the differentiation is with respect to σ^2 rather than σ.

where $\mathbf{w}_t = (y_t, \mathbf{x}_t')'$, $\boldsymbol{\theta} = (\boldsymbol{\beta}', \sigma^2)'$ and $\hat{\varepsilon}_t \equiv y_t - \mathbf{x}_t'\boldsymbol{\beta}$ (which should be distinguished from $\varepsilon_t \equiv y_t - \mathbf{x}_t'\boldsymbol{\beta}_0$). So for $\boldsymbol{\theta} = \boldsymbol{\theta}_0$ the $\hat{\varepsilon}_t$ in these expressions can be replaced by ε_t. In the linear regression model, $\mathrm{E}(\varepsilon_t \mid \mathbf{x}_t) = 0$. Also, since ε_t is $N(0, \sigma_0^2)$, we have $\mathrm{E}(\varepsilon_t^3) = 0$ and $\mathrm{E}(\varepsilon_t^4) = 3\sigma_0^4$. Using these relations, it is easy to verify (3). In particular,

$$-\mathrm{E}\big[\mathbf{H}(\mathbf{w}_t; \boldsymbol{\theta}_0)\big] = \mathrm{E}\big[\mathbf{s}(\mathbf{w}_t; \boldsymbol{\theta}_0)\, \mathbf{s}(\mathbf{w}_t; \boldsymbol{\theta}_0)'\big] = \begin{bmatrix} \frac{1}{\sigma_0^2}\mathrm{E}(\mathbf{x}_t\mathbf{x}_t') & \mathbf{0} \\ \mathbf{0}' & \frac{1}{2\sigma_0^4} \end{bmatrix}. \tag{7.3.18}$$

If $\mathrm{E}(\mathbf{x}_t\mathbf{x}_t')$ is nonsingular, then $\mathrm{E}\big[\mathbf{H}(\mathbf{w}_t; \boldsymbol{\theta}_0)\big]$ is nonsingular and (5) is satisfied. Regarding condition (4), let $\tilde{\varepsilon}_t \equiv y_t - \mathbf{x}_t'\widetilde{\boldsymbol{\beta}}$ for some consistent estimator $\widetilde{\boldsymbol{\beta}}$ and $\tilde{\sigma}^2$. Condition (7.3.8) in this example is

$$\begin{bmatrix} -\frac{1}{\tilde{\sigma}^2}\frac{1}{n}\sum_{t=1}^n \mathbf{x}_t\mathbf{x}_t' & -\frac{1}{(\tilde{\sigma}^2)^2}\frac{1}{n}\sum_{t=1}^n \mathbf{x}_t \cdot \tilde{\varepsilon}_t \\ -\frac{1}{(\tilde{\sigma}^2)^2}\frac{1}{n}\sum_{t=1}^n \mathbf{x}_t' \cdot \tilde{\varepsilon}_t & \frac{1}{2(\tilde{\sigma}^2)^2} - \frac{1}{(\tilde{\sigma}^2)^3}\frac{1}{n}\sum_{t=1}^n \tilde{\varepsilon}_t^2 \end{bmatrix}$$
$$\underset{\mathrm{p}}{\to} \begin{bmatrix} -\frac{1}{\sigma_0^2}\mathrm{E}(\mathbf{x}_t\mathbf{x}_t') & \mathbf{0} \\ \mathbf{0}' & -\frac{1}{2\sigma_0^4} \end{bmatrix}. \tag{7.3.19}$$

It is straightforward to show this, given that $\tilde{\varepsilon}_t = \varepsilon_t - \mathbf{x}_t'(\widetilde{\boldsymbol{\beta}} - \boldsymbol{\beta}_0)$. We conclude that all the conditions of Proposition 7.9 are satisfied if $\mathrm{E}(\mathbf{x}_t\mathbf{x}_t')$ is nonsingular.

Example 7.11 (Asymptotic normality of probit ML): To reproduce the log conditional likelihood of the probit model,

$$\log f(y_t \mid \mathbf{x}_t; \boldsymbol{\theta}) = y_t \log \Phi(\mathbf{x}_t'\boldsymbol{\theta}) + (1 - y_t) \log[1 - \Phi(\mathbf{x}_t'\boldsymbol{\theta})]. \tag{7.3.20}$$

With $\Theta = \mathbb{R}^p$, condition (1) of Proposition 7.9 is satisfied. Condition (2) is obviously satisfied. To verify (3), a tedious calculation yields

$$\mathbf{s}(\mathbf{w}_t; \boldsymbol{\theta}) = \frac{(y_t - \Phi(\mathbf{x}_t'\boldsymbol{\theta}))\phi(\mathbf{x}_t'\boldsymbol{\theta})}{(1 - \Phi(\mathbf{x}_t'\boldsymbol{\theta}))\Phi(\mathbf{x}_t'\boldsymbol{\theta})}\mathbf{x}_t, \tag{7.3.21}$$

$$\mathbf{H}(\mathbf{w}_t; \boldsymbol{\theta}) = \Bigg\{-\left[\frac{y_t - \Phi(\mathbf{x}_t'\boldsymbol{\theta})}{\Phi(\mathbf{x}_t'\boldsymbol{\theta})(1 - \Phi(\mathbf{x}_t'\boldsymbol{\theta}))}\right]^2 [\phi(\mathbf{x}_t'\boldsymbol{\theta})]^2 + \left[\frac{y_t - \Phi(\mathbf{x}_t'\boldsymbol{\theta})}{\Phi(\mathbf{x}_t'\boldsymbol{\theta})(1 - \Phi(\mathbf{x}_t'\boldsymbol{\theta}))}\right] \phi'(\mathbf{x}_t'\boldsymbol{\theta})\Bigg\}\mathbf{x}_t\mathbf{x}_t'. \tag{7.3.22}$$

(To derive (7.3.22), use the fact that $y_t^2 = y_t$.) Here, $\Phi(\cdot)$ is the cumulative density function of $N(0, 1)$ and $\phi(\cdot) \equiv \Phi'(\cdot)$ is its density function. It is then easy to prove the conditional version of (3):

$$\mathrm{E}[\mathbf{s}(\mathbf{w}_t; \boldsymbol{\theta}_0) \mid \mathbf{x}_t] = \mathbf{0} \text{ and}$$
$$-\mathrm{E}\big[\mathbf{H}(\mathbf{w}_t; \boldsymbol{\theta}_0) \mid \mathbf{x}_t\big] = \mathrm{E}\big[\mathbf{s}(\mathbf{w}_t; \boldsymbol{\theta}_0)\, \mathbf{s}(\mathbf{w}_t; \boldsymbol{\theta}_0)' \mid \mathbf{x}_t\big]. \qquad (7.3.23)$$

So (3) is satisfied by the Law of Total Expectations. In particular, for probit, it is easy to show that

$$-\mathrm{E}\big[\mathbf{H}(\mathbf{w}_t; \boldsymbol{\theta}_0)\big] = \mathrm{E}\big[\mathbf{s}(\mathbf{w}_t; \boldsymbol{\theta}_0)\, \mathbf{s}(\mathbf{w}_t; \boldsymbol{\theta}_0)'\big] = \mathrm{E}\big[\lambda(\mathbf{x}_t'\boldsymbol{\theta}_0)\lambda(-\mathbf{x}_t'\boldsymbol{\theta}_0)\mathbf{x}_t\mathbf{x}_t'\big], \qquad (7.3.24)$$

where

$$\lambda(v) \equiv \frac{\phi(v)}{1 - \Phi(v)} \qquad (7.3.25)$$

is called the **inverse Mill's ratio** or the **hazard** for $N(0, 1)$. It can be shown that the term in braces in (7.3.22) is between 0 and 2 (see Newey and McFadden, 1994, p. 2147). So

$$\|\mathbf{H}(\mathbf{w}_t; \boldsymbol{\theta})\| \le 2\|\mathbf{x}_t\mathbf{x}_t'\|. \qquad (7.3.26)$$

The Euclidean norm $\|\mathbf{x}_t\mathbf{x}_t'\|$ is the square root of the sum of squares of the elements of $\mathbf{x}_t\mathbf{x}_t'$. Therefore, the expectation of $\|\mathbf{x}_t\mathbf{x}_t'\|^2$ and hence that of $\|\mathbf{x}_t\mathbf{x}_t'\|$ are finite if $\mathrm{E}(\mathbf{x}_t\mathbf{x}_t')$ (exists and) is finite. So the local dominance condition on the Hessian (condition (4)) is satisfied if $\mathrm{E}(\mathbf{x}_t\mathbf{x}_t')$ is nonsingular. It can be shown that condition (5) is satisfied if $\mathrm{E}(\mathbf{x}_t\mathbf{x}_t')$ is nonsingular (see footnote 29 on p. 2147 of Newey and McFadden, 1994). We conclude, again, that all the conditions of Proposition 7.9 are satisfied if $\mathrm{E}(\mathbf{x}_t\mathbf{x}_t')$ is nonsingular.

Asymptotic Normality of GMM

Now turn to GMM. The GMM objective function is

$$Q_n(\boldsymbol{\theta}) = -\frac{1}{2}\mathbf{g}_n(\boldsymbol{\theta})'\,\widehat{\mathbf{W}}\mathbf{g}_n(\boldsymbol{\theta}) \text{ with } \underset{(K\times 1)}{\mathbf{g}_n(\boldsymbol{\theta})} \equiv \frac{1}{n}\sum_{t=1}^{n}\mathbf{g}(\mathbf{w}_t; \boldsymbol{\theta}). \qquad (7.3.27)$$

As in the case of M-estimators, we apply the Mean Value Theorem to the first-order condition for maximization, but the theorem will be applied to $\mathbf{g}_n(\boldsymbol{\theta})$, not its first derivative. Thus, unlike in the case of M-estimators, the objective function needs to be continuously differentiable only once, not twice. This reflects the fact that the sample average enters the objective function differently for the case of GMM.

Assuming that $\hat{\boldsymbol{\theta}}$ is an interior point, the first-order condition for maximization of the objective function is

$$\underset{(p\times 1)}{\mathbf{0}} = \underset{(p\times 1)}{\frac{\partial Q_n(\hat{\boldsymbol{\theta}})}{\partial \boldsymbol{\theta}}} = -\underset{(p\times K)}{\mathbf{G}_n(\hat{\boldsymbol{\theta}})'}\ \underset{(K\times K)}{\widehat{\mathbf{W}}}\ \underset{(K\times 1)}{\mathbf{g}_n(\hat{\boldsymbol{\theta}})}, \tag{7.3.28}$$

where $\mathbf{G}_n(\boldsymbol{\theta})$ is the Jacobian of $\mathbf{g}_n(\boldsymbol{\theta})$:

$$\underset{(K\times p)}{\mathbf{G}_n(\boldsymbol{\theta})} \equiv \frac{\partial \mathbf{g}_n(\boldsymbol{\theta})}{\partial \boldsymbol{\theta}'}. \tag{7.3.29}$$

Now apply the Mean Value Theorem to $\mathbf{g}_n(\boldsymbol{\theta})$, not to $\partial Q_n(\boldsymbol{\theta})/\partial\boldsymbol{\theta}$ as in M-estimation, to obtain the mean value expansion

$$\underset{(K\times 1)}{\mathbf{g}_n(\hat{\boldsymbol{\theta}})} = \underset{(K\times 1)}{\mathbf{g}_n(\boldsymbol{\theta}_0)} + \underset{(K\times p)}{\mathbf{G}_n(\bar{\boldsymbol{\theta}})}\ \underset{(p\times 1)}{(\hat{\boldsymbol{\theta}} - \boldsymbol{\theta}_0)}. \tag{7.3.30}$$

Substituting this into the first-order condition above, we obtain

$$\underset{(p\times 1)}{\mathbf{0}} = -\underset{(p\times K)}{\mathbf{G}_n(\hat{\boldsymbol{\theta}})'}\ \underset{(K\times K)}{\widehat{\mathbf{W}}}\ \underset{(K\times 1)}{\mathbf{g}_n(\boldsymbol{\theta}_0)} - \underset{(p\times K)}{\mathbf{G}_n(\hat{\boldsymbol{\theta}})'}\ \underset{(K\times K)}{\widehat{\mathbf{W}}}\ \underset{(K\times p)}{\mathbf{G}_n(\bar{\boldsymbol{\theta}})}\ \underset{(p\times 1)}{(\hat{\boldsymbol{\theta}} - \boldsymbol{\theta}_0)}. \tag{7.3.31}$$

Solving this for $(\hat{\boldsymbol{\theta}} - \boldsymbol{\theta}_0)$ and noting that $\mathbf{g}_n(\boldsymbol{\theta}) = \frac{1}{n}\sum_{t=1}^{n} \mathbf{g}(\mathbf{w}_t; \boldsymbol{\theta})$, we obtain

$$\underset{(p\times 1)}{\sqrt{n}(\hat{\boldsymbol{\theta}} - \boldsymbol{\theta}_0)} = -\left[\underset{(p\times K)}{\mathbf{G}_n(\hat{\boldsymbol{\theta}})'}\ \underset{(K\times K)}{\widehat{\mathbf{W}}}\ \underset{(K\times p)}{\mathbf{G}_n(\bar{\boldsymbol{\theta}})}\right]^{-1} \underset{(p\times K)}{\mathbf{G}_n(\hat{\boldsymbol{\theta}})'}\ \underset{(K\times K)}{\widehat{\mathbf{W}}}\ \underset{(K\times 1)}{\frac{1}{\sqrt{n}}\sum_{t=1}^{n} \mathbf{g}(\mathbf{w}_t; \boldsymbol{\theta}_0)}. \tag{7.3.32}$$

In this expression, the Jacobian $\mathbf{G}_n(\boldsymbol{\theta})$ of $\mathbf{g}_n(\boldsymbol{\theta})$ is evaluated at two different points, $\hat{\boldsymbol{\theta}}$ and $\bar{\boldsymbol{\theta}}$. Since $\mathbf{g}_n(\boldsymbol{\theta}) = \frac{1}{n}\sum_{t=1}^{n} \mathbf{g}(\mathbf{w}_t; \boldsymbol{\theta})$, the Jacobian at any given estimator $\tilde{\boldsymbol{\theta}}$ can be written as

$$\mathbf{G}_n(\tilde{\boldsymbol{\theta}}) = \frac{1}{n}\sum_{t=1}^{n} \frac{\partial \mathbf{g}(\mathbf{w}_t; \tilde{\boldsymbol{\theta}})}{\partial \boldsymbol{\theta}'}. \tag{7.3.33}$$

If $\mathbf{w}_t$ is ergodic stationary and $\tilde{\boldsymbol{\theta}}$ is consistent, it is natural to conjecture that this expression converges to $\mathrm{E}\big[\partial \mathbf{g}(\mathbf{w}_t; \boldsymbol{\theta}_0)/\partial \boldsymbol{\theta}'\big]$. As was true for M-estimators, this conjecture is true if $\partial \mathbf{g}(\mathbf{w}_t; \boldsymbol{\theta})/\partial \boldsymbol{\theta}'$ satisfies the suitable dominance condition specified in condition (4) below. It should now be clear that the GMM equivalent of Proposition 7.8 is

Proposition 7.10 (Asymptotic normality of GMM): *Suppose that the conditions of Proposition 7.7 are satisfied, so that* $\{\mathbf{w}_t\}$ *is ergodic stationary,* $\widehat{\mathbf{W}}$ $(K \times K)$ *converges in probability to a symmetric positive definite matrix* $\mathbf{W}$*, and the* p*-dimensional GMM estimator* $\hat{\boldsymbol{\theta}}$ *is consistent. Suppose, further, that*

(1) $\boldsymbol{\theta}_0$ *is in the interior of* Θ,

(2) $\underset{(K\times 1)}{\mathbf{g}(\mathbf{w}_t;\boldsymbol{\theta})}$ *is continuously differentiable in* $\boldsymbol{\theta}$ *for any* $\mathbf{w}_t$,

(3) $\frac{1}{\sqrt{n}}\sum_{t=1}^{n}\mathbf{g}(\mathbf{w}_t;\boldsymbol{\theta}_0) \to_{\mathrm{d}} N(\mathbf{0}, \underset{(K\times K)}{\mathbf{S}})$, $\mathbf{S}$ *positive definite,*

(4) (local dominance condition on $\frac{\partial \mathbf{g}(\mathbf{w}_t;\boldsymbol{\theta})}{\partial \boldsymbol{\theta}'}$*) for some neighborhood* $\mathcal{N}$ *of* $\boldsymbol{\theta}_0$,

$$\mathrm{E}\left[\sup_{\boldsymbol{\theta}\in\mathcal{N}}\left\|\frac{\partial \mathbf{g}(\mathbf{w}_t;\boldsymbol{\theta})}{\partial \boldsymbol{\theta}'}\right\|\right] < \infty,$$

so that for any consistent estimator $\tilde{\boldsymbol{\theta}}$, $\frac{1}{n}\sum_{t=1}^{n}\underset{(K\times p)}{\frac{\partial \mathbf{g}(\mathbf{w}_t;\tilde{\boldsymbol{\theta}})}{\partial \boldsymbol{\theta}'}} \to_{\mathrm{p}} \mathrm{E}\left[\frac{\partial \mathbf{g}(\mathbf{w}_t;\boldsymbol{\theta}_0)}{\partial \boldsymbol{\theta}'}\right]$,

(5) $\underset{(K\times p)}{\mathrm{E}\left[\frac{\partial \mathbf{g}(\mathbf{w}_t;\boldsymbol{\theta}_0)}{\partial \boldsymbol{\theta}'}\right]}$ *is of full column rank.*

Then the following results hold:

(a) (asymptotic normality) $\hat{\boldsymbol{\theta}}$ *is asymptotically normal with*

$$\underset{(p\times p)}{\mathrm{Avar}(\hat{\boldsymbol{\theta}})} = (\mathbf{G}'\mathbf{W}\mathbf{G})^{-1}\mathbf{G}'\mathbf{W}\mathbf{S}\mathbf{W}\mathbf{G}(\mathbf{G}'\mathbf{W}\mathbf{G})^{-1},$$

where $\underset{(K\times p)}{\mathbf{G}} \equiv \mathrm{E}\left[\frac{\partial \mathbf{g}(\mathbf{w}_t;\boldsymbol{\theta}_0)}{\partial \boldsymbol{\theta}'}\right]$,

(b) (consistent asymptotic variance estimation) Suppose there is available a consistent estimate $\widehat{\mathbf{S}}$ *of* $\mathbf{S}$*. The asymptotic variance is consistently estimated by*

$$\widehat{\mathrm{Avar}(\hat{\boldsymbol{\theta}})} = (\widehat{\mathbf{G}}'\widehat{\mathbf{W}}\widehat{\mathbf{G}})^{-1}\widehat{\mathbf{G}}'\widehat{\mathbf{W}}\widehat{\mathbf{S}}\widehat{\mathbf{W}}\widehat{\mathbf{G}}(\widehat{\mathbf{G}}'\widehat{\mathbf{W}}\widehat{\mathbf{G}})^{-1}, \tag{7.3.34}$$

where $\underset{(K\times p)}{\widehat{\mathbf{G}}} \equiv \mathbf{G}_n(\hat{\boldsymbol{\theta}}) = \frac{1}{n}\sum_{t=1}^{n}\frac{\partial \mathbf{g}(\mathbf{w}_t;\hat{\boldsymbol{\theta}})}{\partial \boldsymbol{\theta}'}$.

The assumption that $\mathbf{S}$ is positive definite is not really needed for the conclusion of the proposition, but we might as well assume it here because in virtually all applications it is satisfied (or assumed) and also because it will be required in the discussion of hypothesis testing later in this chapter.

It is useful to note the analogy between linear and nonlinear GMM by comparing this proposition to Proposition 3.1. In linear GMM, $\mathbf{g}_n(\boldsymbol{\theta})$ is given by

$$\mathbf{g}_n(\boldsymbol{\theta}) = \Big(\frac{1}{n}\sum_{t=1}^{n} \mathbf{x}_t \cdot y_t\Big) - \Big(\frac{1}{n}\sum_{t=1}^{n} \mathbf{x}_t \mathbf{z}_t'\Big)\boldsymbol{\theta}. \tag{7.3.35}$$

So $\widehat{\mathbf{G}} \equiv \mathbf{G}_n(\hat{\boldsymbol{\theta}})$ in Proposition 7.10 reduces to $-(\frac{1}{n}\sum \mathbf{x}_t\mathbf{z}_t')$, and $\mathbf{G}$ reduces to $-\operatorname{E}(\mathbf{x}_t\mathbf{z}_t')$. The thrust of Proposition 7.10 is that the asymptotic distribution of the nonlinear GMM estimator can be obtained by taking the linear approximation of $\mathbf{g}_n(\boldsymbol{\theta})$ around the true parameter value.

The analogy to linear GMM extends further:

- (Efficient nonlinear GMM) Using the current notation, the matrix inequality (3.5.11) in Section 3.5 is

$$(\mathbf{G}'\mathbf{W}\mathbf{G})^{-1}\mathbf{G}'\mathbf{W}\mathbf{S}\mathbf{W}\mathbf{G}(\mathbf{G}'\mathbf{W}\mathbf{G})^{-1} \geq (\mathbf{G}'\mathbf{S}^{-1}\mathbf{G})^{-1}, \tag{7.3.36}$$

  which says that the lower bound for $\operatorname{Avar}(\hat{\boldsymbol{\theta}})$ is $(\mathbf{G}'\mathbf{S}^{-1}\mathbf{G})^{-1}$. The lower bound is achieved if $\widehat{\mathbf{W}}$ satisfies the efficiency condition that $\operatorname{plim}_{n\to\infty} \widehat{\mathbf{W}} = \mathbf{S}^{-1}$, namely, that $\widehat{\mathbf{W}} = \widehat{\mathbf{S}}^{-1}$ for some consistent estimator of $\mathbf{S}$.

- (J statistic for testing overidentifying restrictions) Suppose that the conditions of Proposition 7.10 are satisfied and that $\widehat{\mathbf{W}} = \widehat{\mathbf{S}}^{-1}$ so that $\widehat{\mathbf{W}}$ satisfies the efficiency condition: $\operatorname{plim} \widehat{\mathbf{W}} = \mathbf{S}^{-1}$. Then the minimized distance $J \equiv n\mathbf{g}_n(\hat{\boldsymbol{\theta}})'\widehat{\mathbf{S}}^{-1}\mathbf{g}_n(\hat{\boldsymbol{\theta}})$ $(= -2nQ_n(\hat{\boldsymbol{\theta}}))$ is asymptotically chi-squared with $K - p$ degrees of freedom. The proof of this result is essentially the same as in the linear case; see Newey and McFadden (1994, Section 9.5) for a proof.

- (Estimation of $\mathbf{S}$) $\mathbf{S}$ is the long-run variance of $\{\mathbf{g}(\mathbf{w}_t; \boldsymbol{\theta}_0)\}$. Under some suitable technical conditions, the methods introduced in Section 6.6—such as the VARHAC—can be applied to the estimated series $\{\mathbf{g}(\mathbf{w}_t; \hat{\boldsymbol{\theta}})\}$ to obtain $\widehat{\mathbf{S}}$. In particular, if $\mathbf{w}_t$ is i.i.d., then $\mathbf{S} = \operatorname{E}\big[\mathbf{g}(\mathbf{w}_t; \boldsymbol{\theta}_0)\mathbf{g}(\mathbf{w}_t; \boldsymbol{\theta}_0)'\big]$ and the sample second moment of $\mathbf{g}(\mathbf{w}_t; \hat{\boldsymbol{\theta}})$ can serve as $\widehat{\mathbf{S}}$.

GMM versus ML

The question we have just answered is: taking the orthogonality conditions as given, what is the optimal choice of the weighting matrix $\mathbf{W}$? A related, but distinct, question is: what is the optimal choice of orthogonality conditions?[15] This question, too, has a clear answer, provided that the parametric form of the density of the data $(\mathbf{w}_1, \dots, \mathbf{w}_n)$ is known. Here, we focus on the i.i.d. case with the

[15] Yet another efficiency question concerns the optimal choice of instruments in generalized nonlinear instrumental estimation (a special case of GMM where the $\mathbf{g}$ function is a product of the vector of instruments and the error term for an estimation equation). See Newey and McFadden (1994, Section 5.4) for a discussion of optimal instruments.

density of $\mathbf{w}_t$ given by $f(\mathbf{w}_t; \boldsymbol{\theta})$. Let $\hat{\boldsymbol{\theta}}$ be the GMM estimator associated with the orthogonality conditions $\mathrm{E}[\mathbf{g}(\mathbf{w}_t; \boldsymbol{\theta}_0)] = \mathbf{0}$. Its asymptotic variance $\mathrm{Avar}(\hat{\boldsymbol{\theta}})$ is given in Proposition 7.10. It is not hard to show that

$$\mathrm{Avar}(\hat{\boldsymbol{\theta}}) \geq \mathrm{E}\big[\mathbf{s}(\mathbf{w}_t; \boldsymbol{\theta}_0)\, \mathbf{s}(\mathbf{w}_t; \boldsymbol{\theta}_0)'\big]^{-1} \text{ where } \underset{(p\times 1)}{\mathbf{s}(\mathbf{w}_t; \boldsymbol{\theta}_0)} \equiv \frac{\partial \log f(\mathbf{w}_t; \boldsymbol{\theta}_0)}{\partial \boldsymbol{\theta}}. \tag{7.3.37}$$

That is, the inverse of the information matrix $\mathrm{E}(\mathbf{ss}')$ is the lower bound for the asymptotic variance of GMM estimators. This matrix inequality holds under the conditions of Proposition 7.10 plus some technical condition on $f(\mathbf{w}_t; \boldsymbol{\theta})$ which allows the interchange of differentiation and integration. See Newey and McFadden (1994, Theorem 5.1) for a statement of those conditions and a proof. Asymptotic efficiency of ML over GMM estimators then follows from this result because the lower bound $[\mathrm{E}(\mathbf{ss}')]^{-1}$ is the asymptotic variance of the ML estimator. The superiority of ML, however, is not very surprising, given that ML exploits the knowledge of the parametric form $f(\mathbf{w}_t; \boldsymbol{\theta})$ of the density function while GMM does not.

As you will show in Review Question 4 below, GMM achieves this lower bound when the $\mathbf{g}$ function in the orthogonality conditions is the score for observation t:

$$\underset{(K\times 1)}{\mathbf{g}(\mathbf{w}_t; \boldsymbol{\theta})} = \underset{(p\times 1)}{\mathbf{s}(\mathbf{w}_t; \boldsymbol{\theta})} \equiv \frac{\partial \log f(\mathbf{w}_t; \boldsymbol{\theta})}{\partial \boldsymbol{\theta}}. \tag{7.3.38}$$

Therefore, the GMM estimator with optimal orthogonality conditions is asymptotically equivalent to ML. Actually, they are numerically equivalent, which can be shown as follows. Since K (the number of orthogonality conditions) equals p (the number of parameters) when $\mathbf{g}$ is chosen optimally as in (7.3.38), the GMM estimator $\hat{\boldsymbol{\theta}}$ should satisfy $\mathbf{g}_n(\hat{\boldsymbol{\theta}}) = \mathbf{0}$, which under (7.3.38) can be written as

$$\frac{1}{n}\sum_{t=1}^{n} \mathbf{s}(\mathbf{w}_t; \hat{\boldsymbol{\theta}}) = \mathbf{0}. \tag{7.3.39}$$

This is none other than the likelihood equations (i.e., the first-order condition for ML). They have at least one solution because the ML estimator satisfies them. If they have only one solution, then $\hat{\boldsymbol{\theta}}$ is the ML estimator as well as the GMM estimator. If they have more than one solution, we need to choose one from them as the GMM estimator. Since one of the solutions is the ML estimator, we can simply choose it as the GMM estimator.

Expressing the Sampling Error in a Common Format

To prepare for the next section's discussion, it is useful to develop a slightly different proof of asymptotic normality. We have used the Mean Value Theorem to derive the mean value expansion for the sampling error, which is (7.3.7) for M-estimators and (7.3.32) for GMM. We show in this subsection that they can be written in a common format, (7.3.43) below.

Consider M-estimators first. Noting that $\frac{\partial Q_n(\boldsymbol{\theta}_0)}{\partial \boldsymbol{\theta}} = \frac{1}{n}\sum_{t=1}^{n} \mathbf{s}(\mathbf{w}_t; \boldsymbol{\theta}_0)$, the mean value expansion (7.3.7) can be written as

$$\sqrt{n}\,(\hat{\boldsymbol{\theta}} - \boldsymbol{\theta}_0) = -\left[\frac{1}{n}\sum_{t=1}^{n} \mathbf{H}(\mathbf{w}_t; \bar{\boldsymbol{\theta}})\right]^{-1} \sqrt{n}\,\frac{\partial Q_n(\boldsymbol{\theta}_0)}{\partial \boldsymbol{\theta}}. \tag{7.3.40}$$

By condition (4) of Proposition 7.8, $\frac{1}{n}\sum_{t=1}^{n} \mathbf{H}(\mathbf{w}_t; \bar{\boldsymbol{\theta}})$ converges in probability to some $p \times p$ symmetric matrix $\boldsymbol{\Psi}$ given by

$$\underset{(p\times p)}{\boldsymbol{\Psi}} = \mathrm{E}\big[\mathbf{H}(\mathbf{w}_t; \boldsymbol{\theta}_0)\big]. \tag{7.3.41}$$

So rewrite (7.3.40) as

$$\begin{aligned}\sqrt{n}(\hat{\boldsymbol{\theta}} - \boldsymbol{\theta}_0) = &- \boldsymbol{\Psi}^{-1}\sqrt{n}\,\frac{\partial Q_n(\boldsymbol{\theta}_0)}{\partial \boldsymbol{\theta}} \\ &- \left\{\left[\frac{1}{n}\sum_{t=1}^{n} \mathbf{H}(\mathbf{w}_t; \bar{\boldsymbol{\theta}})\right]^{-1} - \boldsymbol{\Psi}^{-1}\right\}\sqrt{n}\,\frac{\partial Q_n(\boldsymbol{\theta}_0)}{\partial \boldsymbol{\theta}}.\end{aligned} \tag{7.3.42}$$

By construction, the term in braces converges in probability to zero. By condition (3) of Proposition 7.8, $\sqrt{n}\,\frac{\partial Q_n(\boldsymbol{\theta}_0)}{\partial \boldsymbol{\theta}}$ $(= \frac{1}{\sqrt{n}}\sum_{t=1}^{n} \mathbf{s}(\mathbf{w}_t; \boldsymbol{\theta}_0))$ converges to a random variable. So the last term, which is the product of the term in braces and $\sqrt{n}\,\frac{\partial Q_n(\boldsymbol{\theta}_0)}{\partial \boldsymbol{\theta}}$, converges to zero in probability by Lemma 2.4(b). This fact can be written compactly as a **Taylor expansion**:[16]

$$\underset{(p\times 1)}{\sqrt{n}(\hat{\boldsymbol{\theta}} - \boldsymbol{\theta}_0)} = -\underset{(p\times p)}{\boldsymbol{\Psi}^{-1}}\,\sqrt{n}\,\underset{(p\times 1)}{\frac{\partial Q_n(\boldsymbol{\theta}_0)}{\partial \boldsymbol{\theta}}} + \underset{(p\times 1)}{o_p}, \tag{7.3.43}$$

where the term "o_p" means "some random variable that converges to zero in probability."[17] The exact expression for the o_p term will depend on the context. Here, it equals the last term in (7.3.42). As you will see, all that matters for our argument

[16]It is apt to call this equation a Taylor expansion rather than a mean value expansion because the matrix that multiplies $\sqrt{n}\,\frac{\partial Q_n(\boldsymbol{\theta}_0)}{\partial \boldsymbol{\theta}}$ is evaluated at $\boldsymbol{\theta}_0$ rather than at $\bar{\boldsymbol{\theta}}$ as in the mean value expansion.

[17]The "o_p" notation was introduced in Section 2.1.

is that the o_p term vanishes (converges to zero in probability), not its expression. Since the difference between $\sqrt{n}(\hat{\boldsymbol{\theta}} - \boldsymbol{\theta}_0)$ and $-\boldsymbol{\Psi}^{-1}\sqrt{n}\,\frac{\partial Q_n(\boldsymbol{\theta}_0)}{\partial \boldsymbol{\theta}}$ vanishes, the asymptotic distribution of $\sqrt{n}(\hat{\boldsymbol{\theta}} - \boldsymbol{\theta}_0)$ is the same as that of $-\boldsymbol{\Psi}^{-1}\sqrt{n}\,\frac{\partial Q_n(\boldsymbol{\theta}_0)}{\partial \boldsymbol{\theta}}$ by Lemma 2.4(a). It then follows that $\sqrt{n}(\hat{\boldsymbol{\theta}} - \boldsymbol{\theta}_0)$ converges to a normal distribution with mean zero and asymptotic variance given by

$$\text{Avar}(\hat{\boldsymbol{\theta}}) = \boldsymbol{\Psi}^{-1}\boldsymbol{\Sigma}\boldsymbol{\Psi}^{-1} \text{ where } \underset{(p\times p)}{\boldsymbol{\Sigma}} \equiv \text{Avar}\Big(\frac{\partial Q_n(\boldsymbol{\theta}_0)}{\partial \boldsymbol{\theta}}\Big). \tag{7.3.44}$$

For M-estimators, $\sqrt{n}\,\frac{\partial Q_n(\boldsymbol{\theta}_0)}{\partial \boldsymbol{\theta}} = \frac{1}{\sqrt{n}}\sum_{t=1}^{n}\mathbf{s}(\mathbf{w}_t;\boldsymbol{\theta}_0)$ and $\boldsymbol{\Sigma}$ is the long-run variance of $\mathbf{s}(\mathbf{w}_t;\boldsymbol{\theta}_0)$. Setting $\boldsymbol{\Psi} = \text{E}\big[\mathbf{H}(\mathbf{w}_t;\boldsymbol{\theta}_0)\big]$ gives the expression for $\text{Avar}(\hat{\boldsymbol{\theta}})$ in Proposition 7.8.

Next turn to GMM. The expression for $\sqrt{n}\,\frac{\partial Q_n(\boldsymbol{\theta}_0)}{\partial \boldsymbol{\theta}}$ is

$$\sqrt{n}\,\frac{\partial Q_n(\boldsymbol{\theta}_0)}{\partial \boldsymbol{\theta}} = -[\mathbf{G}_n(\boldsymbol{\theta}_0)]'\,\widehat{\mathbf{W}}\frac{1}{\sqrt{n}}\sum_{t=1}^{n}\mathbf{g}(\mathbf{w}_t;\boldsymbol{\theta}_0). \tag{7.3.45}$$

(Recall that $\mathbf{G}_n(\boldsymbol{\theta}) \equiv \frac{\partial \mathbf{g}_n(\boldsymbol{\theta})}{\partial \boldsymbol{\theta}'}$.) Since $\mathbf{G}_n(\boldsymbol{\theta}_0) = \frac{1}{n}\sum \frac{\partial \mathbf{g}(\mathbf{w}_t;\boldsymbol{\theta}_0)}{\partial \boldsymbol{\theta}'} \to_{\text{p}} \mathbf{G}\ (\equiv \text{E}[\frac{\partial \mathbf{g}(\mathbf{w}_t;\boldsymbol{\theta}_0)}{\partial \boldsymbol{\theta}'}])$, $\widehat{\mathbf{W}} \to_{\text{p}} \mathbf{W}$, and $\frac{1}{\sqrt{n}}\sum_{t=1}^{n}\mathbf{g}(\mathbf{w}_t;\boldsymbol{\theta}_0) \to_{\text{d}} N(\mathbf{0},\mathbf{S})$ under the conditions of Proposition 7.10, we have $\sqrt{n}\,\frac{\partial Q_n(\boldsymbol{\theta}_0)}{\partial \boldsymbol{\theta}}$ converging to a normal distribution with mean zero and

$$\underset{(p\times p)}{\boldsymbol{\Sigma}} \equiv \text{Avar}\Big(\frac{\partial Q_n(\boldsymbol{\theta}_0)}{\partial \boldsymbol{\theta}}\Big) = \underset{(p\times K)}{\mathbf{G}'}\ \underset{(K\times K)}{\mathbf{W}}\ \underset{(K\times K)}{\mathbf{S}}\ \underset{(K\times K)}{\mathbf{W}}\ \underset{(K\times p)}{\mathbf{G}}. \tag{7.3.46}$$

Now rewrite the mean value expansion for the sampling error for GMM (7.3.32) as

$$\sqrt{n}(\hat{\boldsymbol{\theta}} - \boldsymbol{\theta}_0) = -\mathbf{B}^{-1}\mathbf{c},\ \ \mathbf{B} \equiv -\mathbf{G}_n(\hat{\boldsymbol{\theta}})'\,\widehat{\mathbf{W}}\mathbf{G}_n(\bar{\boldsymbol{\theta}}),$$
$$\mathbf{c} \equiv -\mathbf{G}_n(\hat{\boldsymbol{\theta}})'\,\widehat{\mathbf{W}}\frac{1}{\sqrt{n}}\sum_{t=1}^{n}\mathbf{g}(\mathbf{w}_t;\boldsymbol{\theta}_0). \tag{7.3.47}$$

It is left as Review Question 5 below to show that this can be written as the Taylor expansion (7.3.43), with the symmetric matrix $\boldsymbol{\Psi}$ given by

$$\underset{(p\times p)}{\boldsymbol{\Psi}} = -\underset{(p\times K)}{\mathbf{G}'}\ \underset{(K\times K)}{\mathbf{W}}\ \underset{(K\times p)}{\mathbf{G}}. \tag{7.3.48}$$

Substituting (7.3.48) and (7.3.46) into (7.3.44), we obtain the GMM asymptotic variance indicated in Proposition 7.10.

Table 7.1 summarizes the discussion of this subsection by indicating how the substitution should be done to make the common formulas applicable to M-estimators and GMM.

Table 7.1: Taylor Expansion for the Sampling Error

$$\sqrt{n}(\hat{\boldsymbol{\theta}} - \boldsymbol{\theta}_0) = -\boldsymbol{\Psi}^{-1}\sqrt{n}\,\frac{\partial Q_n(\boldsymbol{\theta}_0)}{\partial \boldsymbol{\theta}} + o_p,\ \sqrt{n}\,\frac{\partial Q_n(\boldsymbol{\theta}_0)}{\partial \boldsymbol{\theta}} \underset{d}{\to} N(\mathbf{0}, \boldsymbol{\Sigma}),\ \text{Avar}(\hat{\boldsymbol{\theta}}) = \boldsymbol{\Psi}^{-1}\boldsymbol{\Sigma}\boldsymbol{\Psi}^{-1}$$

Terms for substitution	M-estimators	GMM
$Q_n(\boldsymbol{\theta})$	$\frac{1}{n}\sum_{t=1}^{n} m(\mathbf{w}_t; \boldsymbol{\theta})$	$-\frac{1}{2}\mathbf{g}_n(\boldsymbol{\theta})'\widehat{\mathbf{W}}\mathbf{g}_n(\boldsymbol{\theta})$
$\sqrt{n}\,\frac{\partial Q_n(\boldsymbol{\theta}_0)}{\partial \boldsymbol{\theta}}$	$\frac{1}{\sqrt{n}}\sum_{t=1}^{n} \mathbf{s}(\mathbf{w}_t; \boldsymbol{\theta}_0)$	$-\big[\mathbf{G}_n(\boldsymbol{\theta}_0)\big]'\widehat{\mathbf{W}}\frac{1}{\sqrt{n}}\sum_{t=1}^{n}\mathbf{g}(\mathbf{w}_t; \boldsymbol{\theta}_0)$
$\boldsymbol{\Psi}$	$\text{E}\big[\mathbf{H}(\mathbf{w}_t; \boldsymbol{\theta}_0)\big]$	$-\mathbf{G}'\mathbf{W}\mathbf{G}$
$\boldsymbol{\Sigma}$	long-run variance of $\mathbf{s}(\mathbf{w}_t; \boldsymbol{\theta}_0)$	$\mathbf{G}'\mathbf{W}\mathbf{S}\mathbf{W}\mathbf{G}$

NOTE: See (7.3.2) and (7.3.3) for definition of $\mathbf{s}(\mathbf{w}_t; \boldsymbol{\theta})$ and $\mathbf{H}(\mathbf{w}_t; \boldsymbol{\theta})$. Also,

$$\mathbf{g}_n(\boldsymbol{\theta}) \equiv \frac{1}{n}\sum_{t=1}^{n}\mathbf{g}(\mathbf{w}_t; \boldsymbol{\theta}) \quad \text{and} \quad \mathbf{G} \equiv \text{E}\left[\frac{\partial \mathbf{g}(\mathbf{w}_t; \boldsymbol{\theta}_0)}{\partial \boldsymbol{\theta}'}\right].$$

In passing, it is useful for the next section's discussion to note that $\mathbf{\Sigma} = -\mathbf{\Psi}$ for ML with i.i.d. observations and efficient GMM (the GMM with $\mathbf{W} = \mathbf{S}^{-1}$). For ML, $\mathbf{\Sigma} = \mathrm{E}\big[\mathbf{s}(\mathbf{w}_t; \boldsymbol{\theta}_0)\, \mathbf{s}(\mathbf{w}_t; \boldsymbol{\theta}_0)'\big]$, which equals the negative of the $\mathbf{\Psi}$ given in (7.3.41) thanks to the information matrix equality. For efficient GMM, setting $\mathbf{W} = \mathbf{S}^{-1}$ in (7.3.46) gives

$$\mathbf{\Sigma} = \mathbf{G}'\mathbf{S}^{-1}\mathbf{G}, \tag{7.3.49}$$

which is the negative of the $\mathbf{\Psi}$ in (7.3.48).

QUESTIONS FOR REVIEW

1. (Score and Hessian of objective function) For M-estimators and ML in particular, we defined the score for observation t, $\mathbf{s}(\mathbf{w}_t; \boldsymbol{\theta})$, to be the gradient (vector of first derivatives) of $m(\mathbf{w}_t; \boldsymbol{\theta})$ and the Hessian for observation t, $\mathbf{H}(\mathbf{w}_t; \boldsymbol{\theta})$, to be the Hessian of $m(\mathbf{w}_t; \boldsymbol{\theta})$. Let the score (without the qualifier "for observation t") be the gradient of the objective function $Q_n(\boldsymbol{\theta})$ and denote it as $\mathbf{s}_n(\boldsymbol{\theta})$. Let the Hessian (without the qualifier "for observation t") be the Hessian of $Q_n(\boldsymbol{\theta})$ and denote it as $\mathbf{H}_n(\boldsymbol{\theta})$. Under the conditions of Proposition 7.9, show that

$$\mathrm{E}\big[\mathbf{s}_n(\boldsymbol{\theta}_0)\big] = \mathbf{0}, \quad -\frac{1}{n}\,\mathrm{E}\big[\mathbf{H}_n(\boldsymbol{\theta}_0)\big] = \mathrm{E}\big[\mathbf{s}_n(\boldsymbol{\theta}_0)\, \mathbf{s}_n(\boldsymbol{\theta}_0)'\big].$$

   Hint: $\{\mathbf{s}(\mathbf{w}_t; \boldsymbol{\theta}_0)\}$ is i.i.d.

2. (Conditional information matrix equality for the linear regression model) For the linear regression model of Example 7.10, verify that

$$\mathrm{E}\big[\mathbf{s}(\mathbf{w}_t; \boldsymbol{\theta}_0) \mid \mathbf{x}_t\big] = \mathbf{0} \;\text{ and }\; -\mathrm{E}\big[\mathbf{H}(\mathbf{w}_t; \boldsymbol{\theta}_0) \mid \mathbf{x}_t\big] = \mathrm{E}\big[\mathbf{s}(\mathbf{w}_t; \boldsymbol{\theta}_0)\, \mathbf{s}(\mathbf{w}_t; \boldsymbol{\theta}_0)' \mid \mathbf{x}_t\big].$$

3. (Avar for the linear regression model) For the linear regression model of Example 7.10, let $(\widehat{\boldsymbol{\beta}}, \hat{\sigma}^2)$ be the ML estimate of $(\boldsymbol{\beta}, \sigma^2)$. Write down the first estimator of $\mathrm{Avar}(\hat{\boldsymbol{\theta}})$ defined in (7.3.14). Does $\widehat{\mathrm{Avar}(\widehat{\boldsymbol{\beta}})}$ equal $\hat{\sigma}^2(\frac{1}{n}\sum \mathbf{x}_t\mathbf{x}_t')^{-1}$? [Answer: No.]

4. (GMM with optimal orthogonality conditions) Assume that the relevant technical conditions are satisfied for the hypothetical density $f(\mathbf{w}_t; \boldsymbol{\theta})$ so that the information matrix equality holds. Using Proposition 7.10, show that when the $\mathbf{g}$ function in the orthogonality conditions is given as in (7.3.38), the asymptotic variance matrix of the GMM estimator equals the inverse of the information matrix for observation t (which is the lower bound in (7.3.37)). **Hint:** Since K equals p, $\mathbf{G}$ is a square matrix and the expression for $\mathrm{Avar}(\hat{\boldsymbol{\theta}})$ in

Proposition 7.10 reduces to $\text{Avar}(\hat{\boldsymbol{\theta}}) = \mathbf{G}^{-1}\mathbf{S}\mathbf{G}'^{-1}$. The choice of $\mathbf{g}$ implies $\mathbf{G} = \mathrm{E}\big[\mathbf{H}(\mathbf{w}_t; \boldsymbol{\theta}_0)\big]$ and $\mathbf{S} = \mathrm{E}\big[\mathbf{s}(\mathbf{w}_t; \boldsymbol{\theta}_0)\, \mathbf{s}(\mathbf{w}_t; \boldsymbol{\theta}_0)'\big]$.

5. (Taylor expansion of the sampling error for GMM) Show that (7.3.47) can be written as the Taylor expansion (7.3.43) under the conditions of Proposition 7.10, by taking the following steps.

   (a) Show that $\mathbf{B}^{-1} = \boldsymbol{\Psi}^{-1} + \mathbf{Y}_n$ where $\mathbf{Y}_n \to_{\mathrm{p}} \mathbf{0}$.

   (b) Show that $\mathbf{c} = \sqrt{n}\,\frac{\partial Q_n(\boldsymbol{\theta}_0)}{\partial \boldsymbol{\theta}} + \mathbf{y}_n$ where $\mathbf{y}_n \to_{\mathrm{p}} \mathbf{0}$. **Hint:** $\mathbf{G}_n(\hat{\boldsymbol{\theta}}) - \mathbf{G}_n(\boldsymbol{\theta}_0) = (\mathbf{G}_n(\hat{\boldsymbol{\theta}}) - \mathbf{G}) - (\mathbf{G}_n(\boldsymbol{\theta}_0) - \mathbf{G}) \to_{\mathrm{p}} \mathbf{0}$ and $\widehat{\mathbf{W}}\frac{1}{\sqrt{n}}\sum_{t=1}^{n} \mathbf{g}(\mathbf{w}_t; \boldsymbol{\theta}_0)$ converges in distribution to a random variable.

   (c) Show that $-\mathbf{B}^{-1}\mathbf{c} = -\boldsymbol{\Psi}^{-1}\sqrt{n}\,\frac{\partial Q_n(\boldsymbol{\theta}_0)}{\partial \boldsymbol{\theta}} + \mathbf{x}_n$, where $\mathbf{x}_n \equiv -\big[\mathbf{Y}_n\sqrt{n}\,\frac{\partial Q_n(\boldsymbol{\theta}_0)}{\partial \boldsymbol{\theta}} + \boldsymbol{\Psi}^{-1}\mathbf{y}_n + \mathbf{Y}_n\mathbf{y}_n\big]$.

   (d) Show that $\mathbf{x}_n \to_{\mathrm{p}} \mathbf{0}$.

6. (Why the GMM distance is deflated by 2) Verify that, if the negative of the distance $\mathbf{g}_n(\boldsymbol{\theta})'\widehat{\mathbf{S}}^{-1}\mathbf{g}_n(\boldsymbol{\theta})$ were not divided by 2 in the definition of the efficient GMM objective function, then we would not have $\boldsymbol{\Sigma} = -\boldsymbol{\Psi}$.

7.4 Hypothesis Testing

As is well known for ML, there is a trio of statistics—the Wald, Lagrange multiplier (LM), and likelihood ratio (LR) statistics—that can be used for testing the null hypothesis. The three statistics are asymptotically equivalent in that they share the same asymptotic distribution (of χ^2). In this section we show that the asymptotic equivalence of the trinity can be extended to GMM by developing an argument applicable to both ML and GMM. The key to the argument is the common format for the sampling error derived at the end of the previous section. On the first reading, you may wish to read the next subsection and then jump to the last subsection.

The Null Hypothesis

We have already considered, in the context of the linear regression model, the problem of testing a set of r possibly nonlinear restrictions (see Section 2.4). To recapitulate, let $\boldsymbol{\theta}_0$ be the p-dimensional model parameter. The null hypothesis can be expressed as

$$\mathrm{H}_0: \underset{(r\times 1)}{\mathbf{a}(\boldsymbol{\theta}_0)} = \mathbf{0}. \tag{7.4.1}$$

We assume that $\mathbf{a}(\cdot)$ is continuously differentiable. Also, let

$$\underset{(r\times p)}{\mathbf{A}(\boldsymbol{\theta})} \equiv \frac{\partial \mathbf{a}(\boldsymbol{\theta})}{\partial \boldsymbol{\theta}'} \tag{7.4.2}$$

be the Jacobian of $\mathbf{a}(\boldsymbol{\theta})$. We assume that

$$\underset{(r\times p)}{\mathbf{A}_0} \equiv \mathbf{A}(\boldsymbol{\theta}_0) \text{ is of full row rank.} \tag{7.4.3}$$

This ensures that the r restrictions are not redundant. This rank condition implies that $r \leq p$.

Let $\hat{\boldsymbol{\theta}}$ be the extremum estimator in question. It is either ML or GMM. It solves the unconstrained optimization problem (7.1.1). The Wald statistic for testing the null hypothesis utilizes the unconstrained estimator. The LM statistic, in contrast, utilizes the **constrained estimator**, denoted $\tilde{\boldsymbol{\theta}}$, which solves

$$\max_{\boldsymbol{\theta}\in\Theta} Q_n(\boldsymbol{\theta}) \text{ s.t. } \mathbf{a}(\boldsymbol{\theta}) = \mathbf{0}. \tag{7.4.4}$$

As was shown in Section 7.2, the true parameter value $\boldsymbol{\theta}_0$ solves the "limit unconstrained problem" where Q_n in the unconstrained optimization problem (7.1.1) is replaced by the limit function Q_0. It also solves the "limit constrained problem" where Q_n in the above constrained optimization problem is replaced by Q_0, because $\boldsymbol{\theta}_0$ satisfies the constraint. It turns out that the uniform convergence in probability of $Q_n(\cdot)$ to $Q_0(\cdot)$ assures that the limit of the constrained estimator $\tilde{\boldsymbol{\theta}}$ is the solution to the limit constrained problem, which is $\boldsymbol{\theta}_0$. For a proof, see Newey and McFadden (1994, Theorem 9.1) for GMM and Gallant and White (1988, Lemma 7.3(b)) for general extremum estimators. It is also possible to show that, if all the conditions ensuring the asymptotic normality of the unconstrained estimator are satisfied, then $\tilde{\boldsymbol{\theta}}$, too, is asymptotically normal under the null. For a proof for GMM, see Newey and McFadden (1994, Theorem 9.2); for ML, see, e.g., Amemiya (1985, Section 4.5).[18]

[18] If you are interested in the proof, it is just the mean value version of the discussion in the subsection on the LM statistic below, which is based on Taylor expansions.

The Working Assumptions

The argument for showing that the Wald, LM, and LR statistics are all asymptotically $\chi^2(r)$ is based on the truth of the following conditions.

(A) $\sqrt{n}(\hat{\boldsymbol{\theta}} - \boldsymbol{\theta}_0)$ admits the Taylor expansion (7.3.43), which is reproduced here

$$\sqrt{n}(\hat{\boldsymbol{\theta}} - \boldsymbol{\theta}_0) = -\boldsymbol{\Psi}^{-1}\sqrt{n}\,\frac{\partial Q_n(\boldsymbol{\theta}_0)}{\partial \boldsymbol{\theta}} + o_p. \tag{7.4.5}$$

(B) $\sqrt{n}\,\frac{\partial Q_n(\boldsymbol{\theta}_0)}{\partial \boldsymbol{\theta}} \to_{\mathrm{d}} N(\mathbf{0}, \boldsymbol{\Sigma})$, $\boldsymbol{\Sigma}$ positive definite.

(C) $\sqrt{n}(\tilde{\boldsymbol{\theta}} - \boldsymbol{\theta}_0)$ converges in distribution to a random variable.

(D) $\boldsymbol{\Sigma} = -\boldsymbol{\Psi}$.

We have shown in the previous section that the first two conditions are satisfied for conditional ML under the hypothesis of Proposition 7.9, for unconditional ML under the hypothesis suitably modified, and for GMM under the hypothesis of Proposition 7.10. As just noted, under the same hypothesis, the constrained estimator $\tilde{\boldsymbol{\theta}}$ is consistent and asymptotically normal, ensuring condition (C). So conditions (A)–(C) are implied by the hypothesis assuring the asymptotic normality of the extremum estimator.

The Wald and LM statistics, if defined appropriately so as not to depend on condition (D), are asymptotically $\chi^2(r)$. But their expressions can be simplified if condition (D) is invoked. Furthermore, without the condition, the LR statistic would *not* be asymptotically χ^2. As was noted at the end of the previous section, condition (D) is satisfied for ML and also for efficient GMM with $\mathbf{W} = \mathbf{S}^{-1}$. Therefore, the part of the discussion that relies on condition (D) is not applicable to nonefficient GMM.

The Wald Statistic

Throughout the book we have had several occasions to derive the Wald statistic using the "delta method" of Lemma 2.5. Here, we provide a slightly different derivation based on the Taylor expansion. Applying the Mean Value Theorem to $\mathbf{a}(\hat{\boldsymbol{\theta}})$ around $\boldsymbol{\theta}_0$ and noting that $\mathbf{a}(\boldsymbol{\theta}_0) = \mathbf{0}$ under the null, the mean value expansion of $\sqrt{n}\,\mathbf{a}(\hat{\boldsymbol{\theta}})$ is

$$\underset{(r\times 1)}{\sqrt{n}\,\mathbf{a}(\hat{\boldsymbol{\theta}})} = \underset{(r\times p)}{\mathbf{A}(\bar{\boldsymbol{\theta}})}\,\underset{(p\times 1)}{\sqrt{n}(\hat{\boldsymbol{\theta}} - \boldsymbol{\theta}_0)}. \tag{7.4.6}$$

Derivation of the Taylor expansion from the mean value expansion is more transparent than in the previous section and proceeds as follows. Since $\bar{\boldsymbol{\theta}}$, lying between

$\boldsymbol{\theta}_0$ and $\hat{\boldsymbol{\theta}}$, is consistent and since $\mathbf{A}(\cdot)$ is continuous, $\mathbf{A}(\bar{\boldsymbol{\theta}})$ converges in probability to $\mathbf{A}_0$ ($\equiv \mathbf{A}(\boldsymbol{\theta}_0)$). Furthermore, the term multiplying $\mathbf{A}(\bar{\boldsymbol{\theta}})$, $\sqrt{n}(\hat{\boldsymbol{\theta}} - \boldsymbol{\theta}_0)$, converges to a random variable. So $(\mathbf{A}(\bar{\boldsymbol{\theta}}) - \mathbf{A}_0)\sqrt{n}(\hat{\boldsymbol{\theta}} - \boldsymbol{\theta}_0)$ vanishes (converges to zero in probability) by Lemma 2.4(b). Denoting this term by o_p, the mean value expansion can be rewritten as a Taylor expansion:

$$\underset{(r\times 1)}{\sqrt{n}\,\mathbf{a}(\hat{\boldsymbol{\theta}})} = \underset{(r\times p)}{\mathbf{A}_0}\ \underset{(p\times 1)}{\sqrt{n}(\hat{\boldsymbol{\theta}} - \boldsymbol{\theta}_0)} + \underset{(r\times 1)}{o_p}\ . \tag{7.4.7}$$

(Note that this argument would not be valid if $\sqrt{n}(\hat{\boldsymbol{\theta}} - \boldsymbol{\theta}_0)$ did not converge to a random variable.)

Substituting the Taylor expansion (7.4.5) into this, we obtain an equation linking $\sqrt{n}\,\mathbf{a}(\hat{\boldsymbol{\theta}})$ to $\sqrt{n}\,\frac{\partial Q_n(\boldsymbol{\theta}_0)}{\partial \boldsymbol{\theta}}$:

$$\underset{(r\times 1)}{\sqrt{n}\,\mathbf{a}(\hat{\boldsymbol{\theta}})} = -\underset{(r\times p)}{\mathbf{A}_0}\ \underset{(p\times p)}{\boldsymbol{\Psi}^{-1}}\ \underset{(p\times 1)}{\sqrt{n}\,\frac{\partial Q_n(\boldsymbol{\theta}_0)}{\partial \boldsymbol{\theta}}} + o_p. \tag{7.4.8}$$

(The o_p here is $\mathbf{A}_0$ times the o_p in (7.4.5) plus the o_p in (7.4.7), but it still converges to zero in probability.) It immediately follows from this expression and the asymptotic normality of $\sqrt{n}\,\frac{\partial Q_n(\boldsymbol{\theta}_0)}{\partial \boldsymbol{\theta}}$ (condition (B)) that $\sqrt{n}\,\mathbf{a}(\hat{\boldsymbol{\theta}})$ converges to a normal distribution with mean zero and

$$\begin{aligned}\underset{(r\times r)}{\text{Avar}(\mathbf{a}(\hat{\boldsymbol{\theta}}))} &= \mathbf{A}_0\boldsymbol{\Psi}^{-1}\boldsymbol{\Sigma}\boldsymbol{\Psi}^{-1}\mathbf{A}_0' \\ &= \underset{(r\times p)}{\mathbf{A}_0}\ \underset{(p\times p)}{\boldsymbol{\Sigma}^{-1}}\ \underset{(p\times r)}{\mathbf{A}_0'} \quad \text{(if condition (D) is invoked).}\end{aligned} \tag{7.4.9}$$

Since the $r \times p$ matrix $\mathbf{A}_0$ is of full row rank and $\boldsymbol{\Sigma}$ is positive definite (by condition (B)), this $r \times r$ matrix is positive definite. Therefore, the associated quadratic form

$$n\mathbf{a}(\hat{\boldsymbol{\theta}})'\big[\mathbf{A}_0\boldsymbol{\Sigma}^{-1}\mathbf{A}_0'\big]^{-1}\mathbf{a}(\hat{\boldsymbol{\theta}}) \tag{7.4.10}$$

is asymptotically $\chi^2(r)$ under the null. As noted above, $\mathbf{A}(\hat{\boldsymbol{\theta}}) \to_{\mathrm{p}} \mathbf{A}_0$. So if there is available a consistent estimator $\widehat{\boldsymbol{\Sigma}}$ of $\boldsymbol{\Sigma}$, then $\mathbf{A}(\hat{\boldsymbol{\theta}})\widehat{\boldsymbol{\Sigma}}^{-1}\mathbf{A}(\hat{\boldsymbol{\theta}})'$ is consistent for $\mathbf{A}_0\boldsymbol{\Sigma}^{-1}\mathbf{A}_0'$, which implies by Lemma 2.4(d) that the Wald statistic defined by

$$W \equiv n\mathbf{a}(\hat{\boldsymbol{\theta}})'\big[\mathbf{A}(\hat{\boldsymbol{\theta}})\widehat{\boldsymbol{\Sigma}}^{-1}\mathbf{A}(\hat{\boldsymbol{\theta}})'\big]^{-1}\mathbf{a}(\hat{\boldsymbol{\theta}}) \tag{7.4.11}$$

too is asymptotically $\chi^2(r)$ under the null.

How the consistent estimator $\widehat{\boldsymbol{\Sigma}}$ of $\boldsymbol{\Sigma}$ ($= -\boldsymbol{\Psi}$) is obtained depends on whether the extremum estimator is ML or efficient GMM. For ML, it is given by a consistent estimate of $-\boldsymbol{\Psi} = -\operatorname{E}\big[\mathbf{H}(\mathbf{w}_t; \boldsymbol{\theta}_0)\big]$:

$$-\frac{\partial^2 Q_n(\hat{\boldsymbol{\theta}})}{\partial \boldsymbol{\theta}\, \partial \boldsymbol{\theta}'} = -\frac{1}{n}\sum_{t=1}^{n} \mathbf{H}(\mathbf{w}_t; \hat{\boldsymbol{\theta}}), \tag{7.4.12}$$

or by a consistent estimate of $\boldsymbol{\Sigma} = \operatorname{E}\big[\mathbf{s}(\mathbf{w}_t; \boldsymbol{\theta}_0)\, \mathbf{s}(\mathbf{w}_t; \boldsymbol{\theta}_0)'\big]$:

$$\frac{1}{n}\sum \mathbf{s}(\mathbf{w}_t; \hat{\boldsymbol{\theta}})\, \mathbf{s}(\mathbf{w}_t; \hat{\boldsymbol{\theta}})'. \tag{7.4.13}$$

For efficient GMM, $\boldsymbol{\Sigma} = \mathbf{G}'\mathbf{S}^{-1}\mathbf{G}$ (see (7.3.49)), which is consistently estimated by

$$\widehat{\boldsymbol{\Sigma}} = \widehat{\mathbf{G}}'\widehat{\mathbf{S}}^{-1}\widehat{\mathbf{G}} \quad \text{with} \quad \underset{(K\times p)}{\widehat{\mathbf{G}}} \equiv \mathbf{G}_n(\hat{\boldsymbol{\theta}}) = \frac{1}{n}\sum_{t=1}^{n} \frac{\partial \mathbf{g}(\mathbf{w}_t; \hat{\boldsymbol{\theta}})}{\partial \boldsymbol{\theta}'}. \tag{7.4.14}$$

As already mentioned, $\widehat{\mathbf{S}}$ is an estimate of the long-run variance matrix constructed from the estimated series $\{\mathbf{g}(\mathbf{w}_t; \hat{\boldsymbol{\theta}})\}$.

The Lagrange Multiplier (LM) Statistic

Let $\boldsymbol{\gamma}_n$ $(r \times 1)$ be the Lagrange multiplier for the constrained problem (7.4.4). The constrained estimator $\tilde{\boldsymbol{\theta}}$ satisfies the first-order conditions

$$\sqrt{n}\,\frac{\partial Q_n(\tilde{\boldsymbol{\theta}})}{\partial \boldsymbol{\theta}} + \mathbf{A}(\tilde{\boldsymbol{\theta}})'\sqrt{n}\,\boldsymbol{\gamma}_n = \underset{(p\times 1)}{\mathbf{0}}, \tag{7.4.15}$$

$$\sqrt{n}\,\mathbf{a}(\tilde{\boldsymbol{\theta}}) = \underset{(r\times 1)}{\mathbf{0}}. \tag{7.4.16}$$

We seek the Taylor expansion of these first-order conditions. By condition (C), $\sqrt{n}(\tilde{\boldsymbol{\theta}} - \boldsymbol{\theta}_0)$ converges to a random variable. So $\sqrt{n}\,\mathbf{a}(\tilde{\boldsymbol{\theta}})$ admits the Taylor expansion

$$\sqrt{n}\,\mathbf{a}(\tilde{\boldsymbol{\theta}}) = \mathbf{A}_0\,\sqrt{n}(\tilde{\boldsymbol{\theta}} - \boldsymbol{\theta}_0) + o_p. \tag{7.4.17}$$

It is left as Review Question 2 to show that the following Taylor expansion holds for both ML and GMM:

$$\sqrt{n}\,\frac{\partial Q_n(\tilde{\boldsymbol{\theta}})}{\partial \boldsymbol{\theta}} = \sqrt{n}\,\frac{\partial Q_n(\boldsymbol{\theta}_0)}{\partial \boldsymbol{\theta}} + \boldsymbol{\Psi}\sqrt{n}(\tilde{\boldsymbol{\theta}} - \boldsymbol{\theta}_0) + o_p. \tag{7.4.18}$$

An implication of this equation is that $\sqrt{n}\,\frac{\partial Q_n(\tilde{\boldsymbol{\theta}})}{\partial \boldsymbol{\theta}}$ converges to a random variable. So $\sqrt{n}\,\boldsymbol{\gamma}_n$, satisfying (7.4.15), converges to a random variable. Consequently, since

$\mathbf{A}(\tilde{\boldsymbol{\theta}}) \to_{\mathrm{p}} \mathbf{A}_0$, we obtain

$$\mathbf{A}(\tilde{\boldsymbol{\theta}})'\sqrt{n}\,\boldsymbol{\gamma}_n = \mathbf{A}_0'\sqrt{n}\,\boldsymbol{\gamma}_n + (\mathbf{A}(\tilde{\boldsymbol{\theta}}) - \mathbf{A}_0)'\sqrt{n}\,\boldsymbol{\gamma}_n = \mathbf{A}_0'\sqrt{n}\,\boldsymbol{\gamma}_n + o_p. \tag{7.4.19}$$

Substituting these three equations into the first-order conditions, we obtain

$$\begin{bmatrix} \underset{(p\times p)}{\boldsymbol{\Psi}} & \underset{(p\times r)}{\mathbf{A}_0'} \\ \underset{(r\times p)}{\mathbf{A}_0} & \underset{(r\times r)}{\mathbf{0}} \end{bmatrix} \begin{bmatrix} \underset{(p\times 1)}{\sqrt{n}(\tilde{\boldsymbol{\theta}} - \boldsymbol{\theta}_0)} \\ \underset{(r\times 1)}{\sqrt{n}\,\boldsymbol{\gamma}_n} \end{bmatrix} = \begin{bmatrix} \underset{(p\times 1)}{-\sqrt{n}\,\frac{\partial Q_n(\boldsymbol{\theta}_0)}{\partial \boldsymbol{\theta}}} \\ \underset{(r\times 1)}{\mathbf{0}} \end{bmatrix} + o_p. \tag{7.4.20}$$

Using the formula for partitioned inverses, this can be solved to yield

$$\sqrt{n}\,\boldsymbol{\gamma}_n = -(\mathbf{A}_0\boldsymbol{\Psi}^{-1}\mathbf{A}_0')^{-1}\mathbf{A}_0\boldsymbol{\Psi}^{-1}\sqrt{n}\,\frac{\partial Q_n(\boldsymbol{\theta}_0)}{\partial \boldsymbol{\theta}} + o_p, \tag{7.4.21}$$

$$\sqrt{n}(\tilde{\boldsymbol{\theta}} - \boldsymbol{\theta}_0) = -\big[\boldsymbol{\Psi}^{-1} - \boldsymbol{\Psi}^{-1}\mathbf{A}_0'(\mathbf{A}_0\boldsymbol{\Psi}^{-1}\mathbf{A}_0')^{-1}\mathbf{A}_0\boldsymbol{\Psi}^{-1}\big]\sqrt{n}\,\frac{\partial Q_n(\boldsymbol{\theta}_0)}{\partial \boldsymbol{\theta}} + o_p. \tag{7.4.22}$$

The rest is the same as in the derivation of the Wald statistic. From (7.4.21), $\sqrt{n}\,\boldsymbol{\gamma}_n$ converges to a normal distribution with mean zero and variance given by

$$\begin{aligned} \underset{(r\times r)}{\text{Avar}(\boldsymbol{\gamma}_n)} &= (\mathbf{A}_0\boldsymbol{\Psi}^{-1}\mathbf{A}_0')^{-1}\mathbf{A}_0\boldsymbol{\Psi}^{-1}\boldsymbol{\Sigma}\boldsymbol{\Psi}^{-1}\mathbf{A}_0'(\mathbf{A}_0\boldsymbol{\Psi}^{-1}\mathbf{A}_0')^{-1} \\ &= (\mathbf{A}_0\boldsymbol{\Sigma}^{-1}\mathbf{A}_0')^{-1} \quad \text{(if condition (D) is invoked).} \end{aligned} \tag{7.4.23}$$

Since this $r \times r$ matrix is positive definite, the associated quadratic form

$$n\boldsymbol{\gamma}_n'(\mathbf{A}_0\boldsymbol{\Sigma}^{-1}\mathbf{A}_0')\boldsymbol{\gamma}_n \tag{7.4.24}$$

is asymptotically $\chi^2(r)$ under the null. If there is available a consistent estimator, denoted $\widetilde{\boldsymbol{\Sigma}}$, of $\boldsymbol{\Sigma}$, then $\mathbf{A}(\tilde{\boldsymbol{\theta}})\widetilde{\boldsymbol{\Sigma}}^{-1}\mathbf{A}(\tilde{\boldsymbol{\theta}})'$ is consistent for $\mathbf{A}_0\boldsymbol{\Sigma}^{-1}\mathbf{A}_0'$. So the LM statistic defined by the first line below is asymptotically $\chi^2(r)$ under the null. This statistic can be beautified by the first-order conditions (7.4.15):

$$\begin{aligned} LM &\equiv n \underset{(1\times r)}{\boldsymbol{\gamma}_n'} \underbrace{\big[\mathbf{A}(\tilde{\boldsymbol{\theta}})\widetilde{\boldsymbol{\Sigma}}^{-1}\mathbf{A}(\tilde{\boldsymbol{\theta}})'\big]}_{(r\times r)} \underset{(r\times 1)}{\boldsymbol{\gamma}_n} \\ &= n\big(\mathbf{A}(\tilde{\boldsymbol{\theta}})'\boldsymbol{\gamma}_n\big)'\widetilde{\boldsymbol{\Sigma}}^{-1}\big(\mathbf{A}(\tilde{\boldsymbol{\theta}})'\boldsymbol{\gamma}_n\big) \\ &= n\underset{(1\times p)}{\Big(\frac{\partial Q_n(\tilde{\boldsymbol{\theta}})}{\partial \boldsymbol{\theta}}\Big)'} \underset{(p\times p)}{\widetilde{\boldsymbol{\Sigma}}}^{-1} \underset{(p\times 1)}{\Big(\frac{\partial Q_n(\tilde{\boldsymbol{\theta}})}{\partial \boldsymbol{\theta}}\Big)} \quad \Big(\text{since } \mathbf{A}(\tilde{\boldsymbol{\theta}})'\boldsymbol{\gamma}_n = -\tfrac{\partial Q_n(\tilde{\boldsymbol{\theta}})}{\partial \boldsymbol{\theta}} \text{ by (7.4.15)}\Big). \end{aligned} \tag{7.4.25}$$

The last expression for the LM statistic is the reason why the statistic is also called the **score test statistic**. It is the distance from zero of the score evaluated at the constrained estimate $\tilde{\boldsymbol{\theta}}$. You should not be fooled by its beauty, however: despite being a quadratic form associated with a p-dimensional vector, the degrees of freedom of its χ^2 asymptotic distribution are r, not p, as is clear from the derivation.

For ML, $\widetilde{\boldsymbol{\Sigma}}$ is given by (7.4.12) or (7.4.13), evaluated at $\tilde{\boldsymbol{\theta}}$. For GMM, $\boldsymbol{\Sigma}$ is consistently estimated by

$$\widetilde{\boldsymbol{\Sigma}} = \widetilde{\mathbf{G}}'\widetilde{\mathbf{S}}^{-1}\widetilde{\mathbf{G}} \text{ with } \underset{(K\times p)}{\widetilde{\mathbf{G}}} \equiv \mathbf{G}_n(\tilde{\boldsymbol{\theta}}) = \frac{1}{n}\sum_{t=1}^{n}\frac{\partial \mathbf{g}(\mathbf{w}_t;\tilde{\boldsymbol{\theta}})}{\partial \boldsymbol{\theta}'}. \tag{7.4.26}$$

Here, $\widetilde{\mathbf{S}}$ is an estimate of the long-run variance matrix constructed from the estimated series $\{\mathbf{g}(\mathbf{w}_t;\tilde{\boldsymbol{\theta}})\}$.

The Likelihood Ratio (LR) Statistic

The LR statistic is defined as $2n$ times $Q_n(\hat{\boldsymbol{\theta}}) - Q_n(\tilde{\boldsymbol{\theta}})$. (For efficient GMM, calling this the likelihood ratio statistic is a slight abuse of the language because Q_n for GMM is not the likelihood function, but we will continue to use the term for both ML and GMM.) It is not hard to show for ML and GMM (see Review Questions 6 and 7) that

$$LR \equiv 2n\cdot[Q_n(\hat{\boldsymbol{\theta}}) - Q_n(\tilde{\boldsymbol{\theta}})] = -n(\hat{\boldsymbol{\theta}} - \tilde{\boldsymbol{\theta}})'\boldsymbol{\Psi}(\hat{\boldsymbol{\theta}} - \tilde{\boldsymbol{\theta}}) + o_p. \tag{7.4.27}$$

The validity of this expression does not depend on condition (D).

From this expression, it is easy to derive the asymptotic distribution of the LR statistic. Subtracting (7.4.22) from (7.4.5), we obtain

$$\sqrt{n}(\hat{\boldsymbol{\theta}} - \tilde{\boldsymbol{\theta}}) = -\boldsymbol{\Psi}^{-1}\mathbf{A}_0'(\mathbf{A}_0\boldsymbol{\Psi}^{-1}\mathbf{A}_0')^{-1}\mathbf{A}_0\boldsymbol{\Psi}^{-1}\sqrt{n}\,\frac{\partial Q_n(\boldsymbol{\theta}_0)}{\partial \boldsymbol{\theta}} + o_p. \tag{7.4.28}$$

Substituting this into (7.4.27), the LR statistic can be written as

$$LR = -\Big(\sqrt{n}\,\frac{\partial Q_n(\boldsymbol{\theta}_0)}{\partial \boldsymbol{\theta}}\Big)'\boldsymbol{\Psi}^{-1}\mathbf{A}_0'(\mathbf{A}_0\boldsymbol{\Psi}^{-1}\mathbf{A}_0')^{-1}\mathbf{A}_0\boldsymbol{\Psi}^{-1}\Big(\sqrt{n}\,\frac{\partial Q_n(\boldsymbol{\theta}_0)}{\partial \boldsymbol{\theta}}\Big) + o_p. \tag{7.4.29}$$

Now invoke assumption (D). The LR statistic becomes

$$LR = \Big(\sqrt{n}\,\frac{\partial Q_n(\boldsymbol{\theta}_0)}{\partial \boldsymbol{\theta}}\Big)'\boldsymbol{\Sigma}^{-1}\mathbf{A}_0'\left[\mathbf{A}_0\boldsymbol{\Sigma}^{-1}\mathbf{A}_0'\right]^{-1}\mathbf{A}_0\boldsymbol{\Sigma}^{-1}\Big(\sqrt{n}\,\frac{\partial Q_n(\boldsymbol{\theta}_0)}{\partial \boldsymbol{\theta}}\Big) + o_p. \tag{7.4.30}$$

This is asymptotically $\chi^2(r)$ because the variance of the limiting distribution of $\mathbf{A}_0\mathbf{\Sigma}^{-1}(\sqrt{n}\,\frac{\partial Q_n(\boldsymbol{\theta}_0)}{\partial \boldsymbol{\theta}})$ is the positive definite matrix in brackets.

This completes the proof of the asymptotic equivalence of the trio of statistics. But it should be clear from the proof that something stronger than asymptotic equivalence (that the three statistics share the same asymptotic distribution) holds. We have shown in the proof that the difference between the Wald statistic and (7.4.10) is o_p. But by (7.4.8) the difference between the latter and the quadratic form in the expression for the LR statistic (7.4.30) is o_p when $\mathbf{\Sigma} = -\mathbf{\Psi}$. So the numerical difference between the Wald statistic and the LR statistic is o_p when $\mathbf{\Sigma} = -\mathbf{\Psi}$. The same applies to the LM statistic. The difference between it and (7.4.24) is o_p. But the difference between the latter and the quadratic form in (7.4.30) is again o_p when $\mathbf{\Sigma} = -\mathbf{\Psi}$.

Summary of the Trinity

To summarize the rather lengthy discussion of this section,

Proposition 7.11 (The trinity): *Let $\hat{\boldsymbol{\theta}}$ the extremum estimator defined in (7.1.1). Consider the null hypothesis (7.4.1) where $\mathbf{a}(\cdot)$ is continuously differentiable (so the Jacobian $\mathbf{A}(\boldsymbol{\theta}) \equiv \frac{\partial \mathbf{a}(\boldsymbol{\theta})}{\partial \boldsymbol{\theta}'}$ is continuous) and the rank condition (7.4.3) is satisfied. Let $\tilde{\boldsymbol{\theta}}$ be the constrained extremum estimator defined in (7.4.4). Assume:*

- *the hypothesis of Proposition 7.9, if the extremum estimator is conditional ML,*
- *the hypothesis appropriately modified as indicated right below Proposition 7.9, in the case of unconditional ML,*
- *the hypothesis of Proposition 7.10 with $\mathbf{W} = \mathbf{S}^{-1}$ and that there is available a consistent estimator $\widehat{\mathbf{S}}$ of $\mathbf{S}$ constructed from $\hat{\boldsymbol{\theta}}$ and $\widetilde{\mathbf{S}}$ constructed from $\tilde{\boldsymbol{\theta}}$, in the case of efficient GMM.*

Define the Wald, LM, and LR statistics as in Table 7.2. Then

(a) the constrained extremum estimator $\tilde{\boldsymbol{\theta}}$ is consistent and asymptotically normal,

(b) the three statistics all converge in distribution to $\chi^2(r)$ under the null where r is the number of restrictions in the null,

(c) moreover, the numerical difference between the three statistics converges in probability to zero under the null.

Table 7.2: Trinity

$$\text{Wald: } n\underset{(1\times r)}{\mathbf{a}(\hat{\boldsymbol{\theta}})'}\Big[\underset{(r\times p)}{\mathbf{A}(\hat{\boldsymbol{\theta}})}\,\underset{(p\times p)}{\widehat{\boldsymbol{\Sigma}}^{-1}}\,\underset{(p\times r)}{\mathbf{A}(\hat{\boldsymbol{\theta}})'}\Big]^{-1}\underset{(r\times 1)}{\mathbf{a}(\hat{\boldsymbol{\theta}})}$$

$$\text{LM: } n\underset{(1\times p)}{\left(\frac{\partial Q_n(\tilde{\boldsymbol{\theta}})}{\partial\boldsymbol{\theta}}\right)'}\,\underset{(p\times p)}{\widetilde{\boldsymbol{\Sigma}}^{-1}}\,\underset{(p\times 1)}{\left(\frac{\partial Q_n(\tilde{\boldsymbol{\theta}})}{\partial\boldsymbol{\theta}}\right)}$$

$$\text{LR: } 2n\cdot[Q_n(\hat{\boldsymbol{\theta}})-Q_n(\tilde{\boldsymbol{\theta}})]$$

Terms for substitution	Conditional ML	Efficient GMM
$Q_n(\boldsymbol{\theta})$	$\frac{1}{n}\sum_{t=1}^{n}\log f(y_t \mid \mathbf{x}_t;\boldsymbol{\theta})$	$-\frac{1}{2}\mathbf{g}_n(\boldsymbol{\theta})'\widehat{\mathbf{S}}^{-1}\mathbf{g}_n(\boldsymbol{\theta})$
$\widehat{\boldsymbol{\Sigma}}$	$-\frac{\partial^2 Q_n(\hat{\boldsymbol{\theta}})}{\partial\boldsymbol{\theta}\,\partial\boldsymbol{\theta}'}$ or $\frac{1}{n}\sum \mathbf{s}(\mathbf{w}_t;\hat{\boldsymbol{\theta}})\,\mathbf{s}(\mathbf{w}_t;\hat{\boldsymbol{\theta}})'$	$\widehat{\mathbf{G}}'\widehat{\mathbf{S}}^{-1}\widehat{\mathbf{G}},\quad \underset{(K\times p)}{\widehat{\mathbf{G}}} \equiv \mathbf{G}_n(\hat{\boldsymbol{\theta}})$
$\widetilde{\boldsymbol{\Sigma}}$	replace $\hat{\boldsymbol{\theta}}$ by $\tilde{\boldsymbol{\theta}}$ in above	$\widetilde{\mathbf{G}}'\widetilde{\mathbf{S}}^{-1}\widetilde{\mathbf{G}},\quad \underset{(K\times p)}{\widetilde{\mathbf{G}}} \equiv \mathbf{G}_n(\tilde{\boldsymbol{\theta}})$

NOTE: See (7.3.2) and (7.3.3) for definitions of $\mathbf{s}(\mathbf{w}_t;\boldsymbol{\theta})$ and $\mathbf{H}(\mathbf{w}_t;\boldsymbol{\theta})$. Also,

$$\mathbf{g}_n(\boldsymbol{\theta}) \equiv \frac{1}{n}\sum_{t=1}^{n}\mathbf{g}(\mathbf{w}_t;\boldsymbol{\theta}),\quad \mathbf{G}_n(\boldsymbol{\theta}) \equiv \frac{\partial \mathbf{g}_n(\boldsymbol{\theta})}{\partial\boldsymbol{\theta}'},\quad \text{and}\quad \mathbf{G} \equiv \mathrm{E}\left[\frac{\partial \mathbf{g}(\mathbf{w}_t;\boldsymbol{\theta}_0)}{\partial\boldsymbol{\theta}'}\right].$$

The same middle matrix is used in $Q_n(\hat{\boldsymbol{\theta}})$ and $Q_n(\tilde{\boldsymbol{\theta}})$ for GMM.

QUESTIONS FOR REVIEW

1. Verify that the LM statistic for ML can be written as

$$n\Big(\frac{1}{n}\sum_{t=1}^{n}\mathbf{s}(\mathbf{w}_t;\tilde{\boldsymbol\theta})\Big)'\Big\{\frac{1}{n}\sum\mathbf{s}(\mathbf{w}_t;\tilde{\boldsymbol\theta})\mathbf{s}(\mathbf{w}_t;\tilde{\boldsymbol\theta})'\Big\}^{-1}\Big(\frac{1}{n}\sum_{t=1}^{n}\mathbf{s}(\mathbf{w}_t;\tilde{\boldsymbol\theta})\Big).$$

2. Derive (7.4.18). **Hint:** For ML, replace $\hat{\boldsymbol\theta}$ by $\tilde{\boldsymbol\theta}$ in (7.3.5). For GMM, derive

$$\sqrt{n}\,\frac{\partial Q_n(\tilde{\boldsymbol\theta})}{\partial\boldsymbol\theta} = -\mathbf{G}_n(\tilde{\boldsymbol\theta})'\widehat{\mathbf{W}}\frac{1}{\sqrt{n}}\sum_{t=1}^{n}\mathbf{g}(\mathbf{w}_t;\boldsymbol\theta_0) - \mathbf{G}_n(\tilde{\boldsymbol\theta})'\,\widehat{\mathbf{W}}\mathbf{G}_n(\bar{\boldsymbol\theta})\sqrt{n}(\tilde{\boldsymbol\theta}-\boldsymbol\theta_0),$$

where $\bar{\boldsymbol\theta}$ lies between $\boldsymbol\theta_0$ and $\tilde{\boldsymbol\theta}$. The derivation of this should be as easy as the derivation of (7.3.31).

3. Explain why the LR statistic would not be asymptotically χ^2 if $\boldsymbol\Sigma = -\boldsymbol\Psi$ did not hold.

4. For ML, suppose the trio of statistics are calculated as indicated in Table 7.2, but suppose $\mathbf{w}_t$ is actually serially correlated. Which one is still asymptotically χ^2? [Answer: None.]

5. Suppose $\boldsymbol\Sigma = -\boldsymbol\Psi$ does not hold but suppose that a consistent estimate $\widetilde{\boldsymbol\Psi}$ of $\boldsymbol\Psi$ is available along with the consistent estimate $\widetilde{\boldsymbol\Sigma}$ of $\boldsymbol\Sigma$. Propose an LM statistic that is asymptotically $\chi^2(r)$. **Hint:** Use the first equality in (7.4.23), which is valid without $\boldsymbol\Sigma = -\boldsymbol\Psi$. The answer is

$$n\Big(\frac{\partial Q_n(\tilde{\boldsymbol\theta})}{\partial\boldsymbol\theta}\Big)'\widetilde{\boldsymbol\Psi}^{-1}\mathbf{A}(\tilde{\boldsymbol\theta})'\big[\mathbf{A}(\tilde{\boldsymbol\theta})\widetilde{\boldsymbol\Psi}^{-1}\widetilde{\boldsymbol\Sigma}\widetilde{\boldsymbol\Psi}^{-1}\mathbf{A}(\tilde{\boldsymbol\theta})'\big]^{-1}\mathbf{A}(\tilde{\boldsymbol\theta})\widetilde{\boldsymbol\Psi}^{-1}\Big(\frac{\partial Q_n(\tilde{\boldsymbol\theta})}{\partial\boldsymbol\theta}\Big). \tag{7.4.31}$$

6. (Optional, proof of (7.4.27)) Prove (7.4.27) for M-estimators. **Hint:** Take for granted the "second-order" mean value expansion around $\hat{\boldsymbol\theta}$,

$$Q_n(\tilde{\boldsymbol\theta}) = Q_n(\hat{\boldsymbol\theta}) + \frac{\partial Q_n(\hat{\boldsymbol\theta})}{\partial\boldsymbol\theta'}(\tilde{\boldsymbol\theta}-\hat{\boldsymbol\theta}) + \frac{1}{2}(\tilde{\boldsymbol\theta}-\hat{\boldsymbol\theta})'\frac{\partial^2 Q_n(\bar{\boldsymbol\theta})}{\partial\boldsymbol\theta\,\partial\boldsymbol\theta'}(\tilde{\boldsymbol\theta}-\hat{\boldsymbol\theta}), \tag{7.4.32}$$

where $\bar{\boldsymbol\theta}$ lies between $\hat{\boldsymbol\theta}$ and $\tilde{\boldsymbol\theta}$. By the first-order condition, $\frac{\partial Q_n(\hat{\boldsymbol\theta})}{\partial\boldsymbol\theta'} = \mathbf{0}$. Also, $\frac{\partial^2 Q_n(\bar{\boldsymbol\theta})}{\partial\boldsymbol\theta\,\partial\boldsymbol\theta'} \to_{\mathrm{p}} \mathrm{E}\big[\mathbf{H}(\mathbf{w}_t;\boldsymbol\theta_0)\big]$.

7. (Optional, proof of (7.4.27) for GMM) Prove (7.4.27) for GMM. **Hint:** From the mean value expansion of $\mathbf{g}_n(\boldsymbol{\theta})$ around $\hat{\boldsymbol{\theta}}$, derive the Taylor expansion

$$\mathbf{g}_n(\tilde{\boldsymbol{\theta}}) = \mathbf{g}_n(\hat{\boldsymbol{\theta}}) + \mathbf{G}_n(\hat{\boldsymbol{\theta}})(\tilde{\boldsymbol{\theta}} - \hat{\boldsymbol{\theta}}) + o_p. \tag{7.4.33}$$

Substitute this into $Q_n(\tilde{\boldsymbol{\theta}}) = -\frac{1}{2}\mathbf{g}_n(\tilde{\boldsymbol{\theta}})' \widehat{\mathbf{W}} \mathbf{g}_n(\tilde{\boldsymbol{\theta}})$. Then use the first-order condition that $\mathbf{G}_n(\hat{\boldsymbol{\theta}})' \widehat{\mathbf{W}} \mathbf{g}_n(\hat{\boldsymbol{\theta}}) = \mathbf{0}$.

7.5 Numerical Optimization

So far, we have not been concerned about the computational aspect of extremum estimators. In the ML estimation of the linear regression model, for example, the objective function $Q_n(\boldsymbol{\theta})$ is quadratic in $\boldsymbol{\theta}$, so there is a closed-form formula for the maximizer, which is the OLS estimator. The objective function is quadratic for linear GMM also, with the linear GMM estimator being the closed-form formula. In most other cases, however, no such closed-form formulas are available, and some numerical algorithm must be employed to locate the maximum. A number of algorithms are available, but this section covers only the two most important ones. More details can be found in, e.g., Judge et al. (1985, Appendix B). The first is used for calculating M-estimators, while the second is used for GMM.

Newton-Raphson

We first consider M-estimators, whose objective function $Q_n(\boldsymbol{\theta})$ is (7.1.2). Since $Q_n(\boldsymbol{\theta})$ is twice continuously differentiable for M-estimators, there is a second-order Taylor expansion

$$Q_n(\boldsymbol{\theta}) \cong Q_n(\hat{\boldsymbol{\theta}}_j) + \mathbf{s}_n(\hat{\boldsymbol{\theta}}_j)'(\boldsymbol{\theta} - \hat{\boldsymbol{\theta}}_j) + \frac{1}{2}(\boldsymbol{\theta} - \hat{\boldsymbol{\theta}}_j)' \mathbf{H}_n(\hat{\boldsymbol{\theta}}_j)(\boldsymbol{\theta} - \hat{\boldsymbol{\theta}}_j), \tag{7.5.1}$$

where $\hat{\boldsymbol{\theta}}_j$ is the estimate in the j-th round of the iterative procedure to be described in a moment, and $\mathbf{s}_n$ and $\mathbf{H}_n$ are the gradient and the Hessian of the objective function:

$$\mathbf{s}_n(\boldsymbol{\theta}) \equiv \frac{\partial Q_n(\boldsymbol{\theta})}{\partial \boldsymbol{\theta}'}, \quad \mathbf{H}_n(\boldsymbol{\theta}) \equiv \frac{\partial^2 Q_n(\boldsymbol{\theta})}{\partial \boldsymbol{\theta} \partial \boldsymbol{\theta}'}. \tag{7.5.2}$$

The $(j+1)$-th round estimator $\hat{\boldsymbol{\theta}}_{j+1}$ is the maximizer of the quadratic function on the right-hand side of (7.5.1). It is given by

$$\hat{\boldsymbol{\theta}}_{j+1} = \hat{\boldsymbol{\theta}}_j - \left[\mathbf{H}_n(\hat{\boldsymbol{\theta}}_j)\right]^{-1}\mathbf{s}_n(\hat{\boldsymbol{\theta}}_j). \tag{7.5.3}$$

This iterative procedure is called the **Newton-Raphson algorithm**. If the objective function is concave, the algorithm often converges quickly to the global maximum.

For ML estimators, when the global maximum $\hat{\boldsymbol{\theta}}$ is thus obtained, the estimate of Avar$(\hat{\boldsymbol{\theta}})$ is obtained as $-\mathbf{H}_n(\hat{\boldsymbol{\theta}})^{-1}$ (recall that $\mathbf{H}_n(\boldsymbol{\theta}) \equiv \frac{1}{n}\sum \mathbf{H}(\mathbf{w}_t;\boldsymbol{\theta})$).

Gauss-Newton

Now turn to GMM, whose objective function is $Q_n(\boldsymbol{\theta}) = -\frac{1}{2}\mathbf{g}_n(\boldsymbol{\theta})'\widehat{\mathbf{W}}\mathbf{g}_n(\boldsymbol{\theta})$ (see (7.1.3)). As in the derivation of the asymptotic distribution, we work with a linearization of the $\mathbf{g}_n(\boldsymbol{\theta})$ function. The first-order Taylor expansion of $\mathbf{g}_n(\boldsymbol{\theta})$ around $\hat{\boldsymbol{\theta}}_j$ is

$$\begin{aligned}\underset{(K\times 1)}{\mathbf{g}_n(\boldsymbol{\theta})} &\cong \mathbf{g}_n(\hat{\boldsymbol{\theta}}_j) + \underset{(K\times p)}{\mathbf{G}_n(\hat{\boldsymbol{\theta}}_j)}\underset{(p\times 1)}{(\boldsymbol{\theta} - \hat{\boldsymbol{\theta}}_j)} \\ &= \left[\mathbf{g}_n(\hat{\boldsymbol{\theta}}_j) - \mathbf{G}_n(\hat{\boldsymbol{\theta}}_j)\hat{\boldsymbol{\theta}}_j\right] - \left[-\mathbf{G}_n(\hat{\boldsymbol{\theta}}_j)\right]\boldsymbol{\theta} \\ &= \mathbf{v}_j - \mathbf{G}_j\boldsymbol{\theta},\end{aligned} \tag{7.5.4}$$

where

$$\mathbf{v}_j \equiv \mathbf{g}_n(\hat{\boldsymbol{\theta}}_j) - \mathbf{G}_n(\hat{\boldsymbol{\theta}}_j)\hat{\boldsymbol{\theta}}_j, \quad \mathbf{G}_j \equiv -\mathbf{G}_n(\hat{\boldsymbol{\theta}}_j). \tag{7.5.5}$$

(Recall that $\mathbf{G}_n(\boldsymbol{\theta}) \equiv \frac{\partial \mathbf{g}_n(\boldsymbol{\theta})}{\partial \boldsymbol{\theta}'}$.) If the $\mathbf{g}_n(\boldsymbol{\theta})$ function in the expression for the GMM objective function were this linear function $\mathbf{v}_j - \mathbf{G}_j\boldsymbol{\theta}$, then the objective function would be quadratic in $\boldsymbol{\theta}$ and the maximizer (or the minimizer of the GMM distance) would be the linear GMM estimator:

$$\hat{\boldsymbol{\theta}}_{j+1} = (\mathbf{G}_j'\widehat{\mathbf{W}}\mathbf{G}_j)^{-1}\mathbf{G}_j'\widehat{\mathbf{W}}\mathbf{v}_j. \tag{7.5.6}$$

This is the $(j+1)$-th round estimate in the **Gauss-Newton algorithm**.[19] Unlike in Newton-Raphson, there is no need to calculate second-order derivatives.

Writing Newton-Raphson and Gauss-Newton in a Common Format

There are also similarities between Gauss-Newton and Newton-Raphson. Substituting (7.5.5) into (7.5.6) and rearranging, we obtain

[19] The Gauss-Newton algorithm was originally developed for nonlinear least squares. See Review Question 2 for how Gauss-Newton is applied to NLS. The algorithm presented here is therefore its GMM adaptation.

$$\hat{\boldsymbol{\theta}}_{j+1} = \hat{\boldsymbol{\theta}}_j - \left[-\mathbf{G}_n(\hat{\boldsymbol{\theta}}_j)' \widehat{\mathbf{W}} \mathbf{G}_n(\hat{\boldsymbol{\theta}}_j)\right]^{-1} \left[-\mathbf{G}_n(\hat{\boldsymbol{\theta}}_j)' \widehat{\mathbf{W}} \mathbf{g}_n(\hat{\boldsymbol{\theta}}_j)\right]. \tag{7.5.7}$$

The second bracketed term is none other than the gradient evaluated at $\hat{\boldsymbol{\theta}}_j$ for the GMM objective function $Q_n(\boldsymbol{\theta}) = -\frac{1}{2}\mathbf{g}_n(\boldsymbol{\theta})' \widehat{\mathbf{W}} \mathbf{g}_n(\boldsymbol{\theta})$. The role played by the Hessian of the objective function in (7.5.3) is played here by the first bracketed term, which is the estimate based on $\hat{\boldsymbol{\theta}}_j$ of the $-\mathbf{G}'\mathbf{W}\mathbf{G}$ in Table 7.1. Therefore, the analogy between M-estimators and GMM noted in Table 7.1 also holds here. Furthermore, if $\mathbf{g}_n$ is linear, then the Hessian equivalent (the first bracketed term in (7.5.7)) *is* the Hessian of the GMM objective function. So the analogy is exact: the Gauss-Newton algorithm coincides with the Newton-Raphson algorithm.

Equations Nonlinear in Parameters Only

In the Gauss-Newton algorithm (7.5.7), when $\mathbf{g}_n(\boldsymbol{\theta})$ $(\equiv \frac{1}{n}\sum \mathbf{g}(\mathbf{w}_t; \boldsymbol{\theta}))$ is not linear in $\boldsymbol{\theta}$, it is generally necessary to take averages over observations to evaluate the gradient and the Hessian equivalent in each iteration. (This is also generally true in Newton-Raphson if the objective function is not quadratic in $\boldsymbol{\theta}$.) For large data sets it is a very CPU time-intensive operation. There is, however, one case where the averaging over observations in each iteration is not needed. That occurs in a class of generalized nonlinear instrumental variable estimation (a special case of nonlinear GMM where $\mathbf{g}(y_t, \mathbf{z}_t, \boldsymbol{\theta})$ can be written as $a(y_t, \mathbf{z}_t; \boldsymbol{\theta})\mathbf{x}_t$). Suppose that the equation $a(y_t, \mathbf{z}_t; \boldsymbol{\theta})$ takes the form

$$a(y_t, \mathbf{z}_t; \boldsymbol{\theta}) = a_0(y_t, \mathbf{z}_t) + \underset{(1\times q)}{\mathbf{a}_1(y_t, \mathbf{z}_t)'} \underset{(q\times 1)}{\boldsymbol{\alpha}(\boldsymbol{\theta})}, \tag{7.5.8}$$

where $a_0(\cdot)$ and $\mathbf{a}_1(\cdot)$ are known functions of $(y_t, \mathbf{z}_t)$ (but not functions of $\boldsymbol{\theta}$). A function of this form is said to be **nonlinear in parameters only** or **linear in variables**. It can be easily seen that

$$\begin{aligned} \mathbf{g}_n(\boldsymbol{\theta}) &\equiv \frac{1}{n}\sum_{t=1}^{n} \mathbf{g}(y_t, \mathbf{z}_t; \boldsymbol{\theta}) = \frac{1}{n}\sum_{t=1}^{n} a(y_t, \mathbf{z}_t; \boldsymbol{\theta}) \cdot \mathbf{x}_t \\ &= \underset{(K\times 1)}{\left(\frac{1}{n}\sum_{t=1}^{n} a_0(y_t, \mathbf{z}_t) \cdot \mathbf{x}_t\right)} + \underset{(K\times q)}{\left(\frac{1}{n}\sum_{t=1}^{n} \mathbf{x}_t \mathbf{a}_1(y_t, \mathbf{z}_t)'\right)} \underset{(q\times 1)}{\boldsymbol{\alpha}(\boldsymbol{\theta})}, \end{aligned} \tag{7.5.9}$$

$$\mathbf{G}_n(\boldsymbol{\theta}) = \frac{\partial \mathbf{g}_n(\boldsymbol{\theta})}{\partial \boldsymbol{\theta}'} = \underset{(K\times q)}{\left(\frac{1}{n}\sum_{t=1}^{n} \mathbf{x}_t \mathbf{a}_1(y_t, \mathbf{z}_t)'\right)} \underset{(q\times p)}{\frac{\partial \boldsymbol{\alpha}(\boldsymbol{\theta})}{\partial \boldsymbol{\theta}'}}. \tag{7.5.10}$$

These equations make it clear that the sample averages need to be calculated just once, before the start of iterations.

QUESTIONS FOR REVIEW

1. (Does Q_n increase during iterations?) Set $\boldsymbol{\theta} = \hat{\boldsymbol{\theta}}_{j+1}$ in (7.5.1) and rewrite it as

$$Q_n(\hat{\boldsymbol{\theta}}_{j+1}) - Q_n(\hat{\boldsymbol{\theta}}_j) \cong \mathbf{s}_n(\hat{\boldsymbol{\theta}}_j)'(\hat{\boldsymbol{\theta}}_{j+1} - \hat{\boldsymbol{\theta}}_j) + \frac{1}{2}(\hat{\boldsymbol{\theta}}_{j+1} - \hat{\boldsymbol{\theta}}_j)'\,\mathbf{H}_n(\hat{\boldsymbol{\theta}}_j)(\hat{\boldsymbol{\theta}}_{j+1} - \hat{\boldsymbol{\theta}}_j).$$

Consider the Newton-Raphson algorithm (7.5.3). Suppose that $\hat{\boldsymbol{\theta}}_{j+1}$ is sufficiently close to $\hat{\boldsymbol{\theta}}_j$ so that the sign of $Q_n(\hat{\boldsymbol{\theta}}_{j+1}) - Q_n(\hat{\boldsymbol{\theta}}_j)$ is the same as that of the right hand side of the equation. Show that $Q_n(\hat{\boldsymbol{\theta}}_{j+1}) \geq Q_n(\hat{\boldsymbol{\theta}}_j)$ if $Q_n(\boldsymbol{\theta})$ is concave. **Hint:** Using (7.5.3), the right-hand side can be written as

$$-\frac{1}{2}(\hat{\boldsymbol{\theta}}_{j+1} - \hat{\boldsymbol{\theta}}_j)'\,\mathbf{H}_n(\hat{\boldsymbol{\theta}}_j)(\hat{\boldsymbol{\theta}}_{j+1} - \hat{\boldsymbol{\theta}}_j).$$

2. (Gauss-Newton for NLS) In NLS (nonlinear least squares), the objective function is given by (7.1.19). Let $\hat{\boldsymbol{\theta}}_j$ be the estimate in the j-th round and consider the linear approximation

$$\begin{aligned}\varphi(\mathbf{x}_t;\boldsymbol{\theta}) &\cong \varphi(\mathbf{x}_t;\hat{\boldsymbol{\theta}}_j) + \Big(\underset{(p\times 1)}{\frac{\partial\varphi(\mathbf{x}_t;\hat{\boldsymbol{\theta}}_j)}{\partial\boldsymbol{\theta}}}\Big)' \underset{(p\times 1)}{(\boldsymbol{\theta} - \hat{\boldsymbol{\theta}}_j)} \\ &= \Big[\varphi(\mathbf{x}_t;\hat{\boldsymbol{\theta}}_j) - \Big(\frac{\partial\varphi(\mathbf{x}_t;\hat{\boldsymbol{\theta}}_j)}{\partial\boldsymbol{\theta}}\Big)'\hat{\boldsymbol{\theta}}_j\Big] + \Big(\frac{\partial\varphi(\mathbf{x}_t;\hat{\boldsymbol{\theta}}_j)}{\partial\boldsymbol{\theta}}\Big)'\boldsymbol{\theta}. \end{aligned} \tag{7.5.11}$$

Replace $\varphi(\mathbf{x}_t;\boldsymbol{\theta})$ in the m function by this linear function in $\boldsymbol{\theta}$. Show that the maximizer of this linearized problem is

$$\begin{aligned}\hat{\boldsymbol{\theta}}_{j+1} = \hat{\boldsymbol{\theta}}_j + &\Big[\frac{1}{n}\sum_{t=1}^{n}\Big(\frac{\partial\varphi(\mathbf{x}_t;\hat{\boldsymbol{\theta}}_j)}{\partial\boldsymbol{\theta}}\Big)\Big(\frac{\partial\varphi(\mathbf{x}_t;\hat{\boldsymbol{\theta}}_j)}{\partial\boldsymbol{\theta}}\Big)'\Big]^{-1} \\ &\Big\{\frac{1}{n}\sum_{t=1}^{n}\underset{(p\times 1)}{\Big(\frac{\partial\varphi(\mathbf{x}_t;\hat{\boldsymbol{\theta}}_j)}{\partial\boldsymbol{\theta}}\Big)}\cdot[y_t - \varphi(\mathbf{x}_t;\hat{\boldsymbol{\theta}}_j)]\Big\}. \end{aligned} \tag{7.5.12}$$

PROBLEM SET FOR CHAPTER 7

ANALYTICAL EXERCISES

1. (Kullback-Leibler information inequality) Let $f(y \mid \mathbf{x}; \boldsymbol{\theta})$ be a parametric family of hypothetical conditional density functions, with the true density function given by $f(y \mid \mathbf{x}; \boldsymbol{\theta}_0)$. Suppose $\mathrm{E}[\log f(y \mid \mathbf{x}; \boldsymbol{\theta})]$ exists and is finite for all $\boldsymbol{\theta}$. The Kullback-Leibler information inequality states that

$$\begin{aligned}&\text{Prob}[f(y \mid \mathbf{x}; \boldsymbol{\theta}) \neq f(y \mid \mathbf{x}; \boldsymbol{\theta}_0)] > 0\\ &\qquad \Rightarrow \mathrm{E}[\log f(y \mid \mathbf{x}; \boldsymbol{\theta})] < \mathrm{E}[\log f(y \mid \mathbf{x}; \boldsymbol{\theta}_0)].\end{aligned}$$

Prove this by taking the following steps. In the proof, for simplicity only, assume that $f(y \mid \mathbf{x}; \boldsymbol{\theta}) > 0$ for all $(y, \mathbf{x})$ and $\boldsymbol{\theta}$, so that it is legitimate to take logs of the density $f(y \mid \mathbf{x}; \boldsymbol{\theta})$.

(a) Suppose $\text{Prob}[f(y \mid \mathbf{x}; \boldsymbol{\theta}) \neq f(y \mid \mathbf{x}; \boldsymbol{\theta}_0)] > 0$. Let $\mathbf{w} = (y, \mathbf{x}')'$ and define

$$a(\mathbf{w}) \equiv f(y \mid \mathbf{x}; \boldsymbol{\theta})/f(y \mid \mathbf{x}; \boldsymbol{\theta}_0).$$

Verify that $a(\mathbf{w}) \neq 1$ with positive probability, so that $a(\mathbf{w})$ is a nonconstant random variable.

(b) The strict version of **Jensen's inequality** states that

> if $c(x)$ is a strictly concave function and x is a nonconstant random variable, then $\mathrm{E}[c(x)] < c(\mathrm{E}(x))$.

Using this fact, show that

$$\mathrm{E}[\log a(\mathbf{w})] < \log\{\mathrm{E}[a(\mathbf{w})]\}.$$

Hint: $\log(x)$ is strictly concave.

(c) Show that $\mathrm{E}[a(\mathbf{w})] = 1$. **Hint:** The conditional mean of $a(\mathbf{w})$ equals 1 because

$$\begin{aligned}\mathrm{E}[a(\mathbf{w}) \mid \mathbf{x}] &= \int a(\mathbf{w}) f(y \mid \mathbf{x}; \boldsymbol{\theta}_0) \mathrm{d}y \\ &= \int \frac{f(y \mid \mathbf{x}; \boldsymbol{\theta})}{f(y \mid \mathbf{x}; \boldsymbol{\theta}_0)} f(y \mid \mathbf{x}; \boldsymbol{\theta}_0) \mathrm{d}y \\ &= \int f(y \mid \mathbf{x}; \boldsymbol{\theta}) \mathrm{d}y \\ &= 1.\end{aligned}$$

The last equality holds because $f(y \mid \mathbf{x}; \boldsymbol{\theta})$ is a density function for any $\mathbf{x}$ and $\boldsymbol{\theta}$. Note well that the conditional expectation is taken with respect to the true conditional density $f(y \mid \mathbf{x}; \boldsymbol{\theta}_0)$.

(d) Finally, show the desired result.

2. (Information matrix equality) For ML, the score vector and the Hessian for observation $(y, \mathbf{x})$ can be rewritten (with $\mathbf{w} \equiv (y, \mathbf{x}')'$) as:

$$\underset{(p\times 1)}{\mathbf{s}(\mathbf{w}; \boldsymbol{\theta})} = \frac{\partial \log f(y \mid \mathbf{x}; \boldsymbol{\theta})}{\partial \boldsymbol{\theta}},$$

$$\underset{(p\times p)}{\mathbf{H}(\mathbf{w}; \boldsymbol{\theta})} = \frac{\partial s(\mathbf{w}; \boldsymbol{\theta})}{\partial \boldsymbol{\theta}'} = \frac{\partial^2 \log f(y \mid \mathbf{x}; \boldsymbol{\theta})}{\partial \boldsymbol{\theta} \partial \boldsymbol{\theta}'}.$$

As usual, for simplicity, assume $f(y \mid \mathbf{x}, \boldsymbol{\theta}) > 0$ for all $(y, \mathbf{x})$ and $\boldsymbol{\theta}$, so it is legitimate to take logs of the density function.

(a) Assuming that integration (i.e., taking expectations) and differentiation can be interchanged, show that $\mathrm{E}[\mathbf{s}(\mathbf{w}; \boldsymbol{\theta}_0)] = \mathbf{0}$. **Hint:** Since $f(y \mid \mathbf{x}; \boldsymbol{\theta})$ is a hypothetical density, its integral is unity:

$$\int f(y \mid \mathbf{x}; \boldsymbol{\theta}) \mathrm{d}y = 1.$$

Differentiate both sides of this equation with respect to $\boldsymbol{\theta}$ and then change the order of differentiation and integration to obtain the identity

$$\int \mathbf{s}(\mathbf{w}; \boldsymbol{\theta}) f(y \mid \mathbf{x}; \boldsymbol{\theta}) \mathrm{d}y = \underset{(p\times 1)}{\mathbf{0}}.$$

Set $\boldsymbol{\theta} = \boldsymbol{\theta}_0$ and obtain $\mathrm{E}[\mathbf{s}(\mathbf{w}; \boldsymbol{\theta}_0) \mid \mathbf{x}] = \mathbf{0}$.

(b) Show the information matrix equality:

$$-\mathrm{E}\big[\mathbf{H}(\mathbf{w}; \boldsymbol{\theta}_0)\big] = \mathrm{E}\big[\mathbf{s}(\mathbf{w}; \boldsymbol{\theta}_0)\, \mathbf{s}(\mathbf{w}; \boldsymbol{\theta}_0)'\big].$$

Hint: Differentiating both sides of the above identity in the previous hint and assuming that the order of differentiation and integration can be interchanged, we obtain

$$\int \frac{\partial}{\partial \boldsymbol{\theta}'} \underbrace{\left[\mathbf{s}(\mathbf{w};\boldsymbol{\theta}) f(y \mid \mathbf{x};\boldsymbol{\theta})\right]}_{(p\times 1)} \mathrm{d}y = \underset{(p\times p)}{\mathbf{0}}.$$

Show that the integrand can be written as

$$\begin{aligned}&\frac{\partial}{\partial \boldsymbol{\theta}'}\left[\mathbf{s}(\mathbf{w};\boldsymbol{\theta}) f(y \mid \mathbf{x};\boldsymbol{\theta})\right]\\ &\qquad = \mathbf{H}(\mathbf{w};\boldsymbol{\theta}) f(y \mid \mathbf{x};\boldsymbol{\theta}) + \mathbf{s}(\mathbf{w};\boldsymbol{\theta})\,\mathbf{s}(\mathbf{w};\boldsymbol{\theta})' f(y \mid \mathbf{x};\boldsymbol{\theta}).\end{aligned}$$

3. (Trinity for linear regression model) Consider the linear regression model with normal errors, whose conditional density for observation t is

$$\log f(y_t \mid \mathbf{x}_t; \boldsymbol{\beta}, \sigma^2) = -\frac{1}{2}\log(2\pi) - \frac{1}{2}\log(\sigma^2) - \frac{(y_t - \mathbf{x}_t'\boldsymbol{\beta})^2}{2\sigma^2}.$$

Let $(\widehat{\boldsymbol{\beta}}, \hat{\sigma}^2)$ be the unrestricted ML estimate of $\boldsymbol{\theta} = (\boldsymbol{\beta}'\sigma^2)'$ and let $(\widetilde{\boldsymbol{\beta}}, \tilde{\sigma}^2)$ be the restricted ML estimate subject to the constraint $\mathbf{R}\boldsymbol{\beta} = \mathbf{c}$ where $\mathbf{R}$ is an $r \times K$ matrix of known constants. Assume that $\Theta = \mathbb{R}^K \times \mathbb{R}_{++}$ and that $\mathrm{E}(\mathbf{x}_t\mathbf{x}_t')$ is nonsingular. Also, let

$$\widehat{\boldsymbol{\Sigma}} = \begin{bmatrix} \frac{1}{\hat{\sigma}^2}\frac{1}{n}\sum_{t=1}^{n}\mathbf{x}_t\mathbf{x}_t' & \mathbf{0} \\ \mathbf{0}' & \frac{1}{2(\hat{\sigma}^2)^2}\end{bmatrix}, \quad \widetilde{\boldsymbol{\Sigma}} = \begin{bmatrix} \frac{1}{\tilde{\sigma}^2}\frac{1}{n}\sum_{t=1}^{n}\mathbf{x}_t\mathbf{x}_t' & \mathbf{0} \\ \mathbf{0}' & \frac{1}{2(\tilde{\sigma}^2)^2}\end{bmatrix}.$$

(a) Verify that $\widehat{\boldsymbol{\beta}}$ minimizes the sum of squared residuals. So it is the OLS estimator. Verify that $\widetilde{\beta}$ minimizes the sum of squared residuals subject to the constraint $\mathbf{R}\boldsymbol{\beta} = \mathbf{c}$. So it is the restricted least squares estimator.

(b) Let $Q_n(\boldsymbol{\theta}) = \frac{1}{n}\sum_{t=1}^{n}\log f(y_t \mid \mathbf{x}_t; \boldsymbol{\beta}, \sigma^2)$. Show that

$$\begin{aligned} Q_n(\hat{\boldsymbol{\theta}}) &= -\frac{1}{2}\log(2\pi) - \frac{1}{2} - \frac{1}{2}\log\left(\frac{SSR_U}{n}\right),\\ Q_n(\tilde{\boldsymbol{\theta}}) &= -\frac{1}{2}\log(2\pi) - \frac{1}{2} - \frac{1}{2}\log\left(\frac{SSR_R}{n}\right),\end{aligned}$$

where SSR_U ($\equiv \sum(y_t - \mathbf{x}_t'\widehat{\boldsymbol{\beta}})^2$) is the unrestricted sum of squared residuals and SSR_R ($\equiv \sum(y_t - \mathbf{x}_t'\widetilde{\boldsymbol{\beta}})^2$) is the restricted sum of squared residuals. **Hint:** Show that $\hat{\sigma}^2 = SSR_U/n$ and $\tilde{\sigma}^2 = SSR_R/n$.

(c) Verify that the $\widehat{\boldsymbol{\Sigma}}$ given here, although not the same as $-\frac{1}{n}\sum_{t=1}^{n}\mathbf{H}(\mathbf{w}_t;\hat{\boldsymbol{\theta}})$, is consistent for $-\mathrm{E}\big[\mathbf{H}(\mathbf{w}_t;\boldsymbol{\theta}_0)\big]$. Verify that the $\widetilde{\boldsymbol{\Sigma}}$ given here, although not the same as $-\frac{1}{n}\sum_{t=1}^{n}\mathbf{H}(\mathbf{w}_t;\tilde{\boldsymbol{\theta}})$, is consistent for $-\mathrm{E}\big[\mathbf{H}(\mathbf{w}_t;\boldsymbol{\theta}_0)\big]$. **Hint:** From the discussion in Example 7.8, $\hat{\boldsymbol{\theta}}$ is consistent. As mentioned in Section 7.4, $\tilde{\boldsymbol{\theta}}$ too is consistent under the null. Given the consistency of $\hat{\boldsymbol{\theta}}$ and $\tilde{\boldsymbol{\theta}}$, it should be easy to show that $\hat{\sigma}^2$ and $\tilde{\sigma}^2$ are consistent for σ^2.

(d) Show that the Wald, LM, and LR statistics using $\widehat{\boldsymbol{\Sigma}}$ and $\widetilde{\boldsymbol{\Sigma}}$ given here in the formulas in Table 7.2 can be written as

$$W = n \cdot \frac{(\mathbf{R}\widehat{\boldsymbol{\beta}} - \mathbf{c})'\big[\mathbf{R}(\mathbf{X}'\mathbf{X})^{-1}\mathbf{R}'\big]^{-1}(\mathbf{R}\widehat{\boldsymbol{\beta}} - \mathbf{c})}{SSR_U},$$

$$LM = n \cdot \frac{(\mathbf{y} - \mathbf{X}\widetilde{\boldsymbol{\beta}})'\mathbf{P}(\mathbf{y} - \mathbf{X}\widetilde{\boldsymbol{\beta}})}{SSR_R},$$

$$LR = n \cdot \left\{\log\left(\frac{SSR_R}{n}\right) - \log\left(\frac{SSR_U}{n}\right)\right\},$$

where $\mathbf{y}$ $(n \times 1)$ and $\mathbf{X}$ $(n \times K)$ are the data vector and matrix associated with y_t and $\mathbf{x}_t$, and $\mathbf{P} = \mathbf{X}(\mathbf{X}'\mathbf{X})^{-1}\mathbf{X}'$. **Hint:** The $\mathbf{A}(\boldsymbol{\theta})$ $(r \times (K+1))$ in Table 7.2 is

$$\Big(\underset{(r\times K)}{\mathbf{R}} \;\vdots\; \underset{(r\times 1)}{\mathbf{0}}\Big).$$

(e) Show that the three statistics can also be written as

$$W = n \cdot \frac{SSR_R - SSR_U}{SSR_U},$$

$$LM = n \cdot \frac{SSR_R - SSR_U}{SSR_R},$$

$$LR = n \cdot \log\left(\frac{SSR_R}{SSR_U}\right).$$

Hint: As we have shown in an analytical exercise of Chapter 1,

$$\begin{aligned} SSR_R - SSR_U &= (\widehat{\boldsymbol{\beta}} - \widetilde{\boldsymbol{\beta}})'(\mathbf{X}'\mathbf{X})(\widehat{\boldsymbol{\beta}} - \widetilde{\boldsymbol{\beta}}) \\ &= (\mathbf{R}\widehat{\boldsymbol{\beta}} - \mathbf{c})'\big[\mathbf{R}(\mathbf{X}'\mathbf{X})^{-1}\mathbf{R}'\big]^{-1}(\mathbf{R}\widehat{\boldsymbol{\beta}} - \mathbf{c}) \\ &= (\mathbf{y} - \mathbf{X}\widetilde{\boldsymbol{\beta}})'\mathbf{P}(\mathbf{y} - \mathbf{X}\widetilde{\boldsymbol{\beta}}). \end{aligned}$$

(f) Show that $W \geq LR \geq LM$. (These inequalities do not always hold in nonlinear regression models.)

ANSWERS TO SELECTED QUESTIONS

2a. Since $f(y \mid \mathbf{x}; \boldsymbol{\theta})$ is a hypothetical density, its integral is unity:

$$\int f(y \mid \mathbf{x}; \boldsymbol{\theta}) \mathrm{d}y = 1. \tag{1}$$

This is an identity, valid for any $\boldsymbol{\theta} \in \Theta$. Differentiating both sides of this identity with respect to $\boldsymbol{\theta}$, we obtain

$$\frac{\partial}{\partial \boldsymbol{\theta}} \int f(y \mid \mathbf{x}; \boldsymbol{\theta}) \mathrm{d}y = \underset{(p\times 1)}{\mathbf{0}}. \tag{2}$$

If the order of differentiation and integration can be interchanged, then

$$\frac{\partial}{\partial \boldsymbol{\theta}} \int f(y \mid \mathbf{x}; \boldsymbol{\theta}) \mathrm{d}y = \int \frac{\partial}{\partial \boldsymbol{\theta}} f(y \mid \mathbf{x}; \boldsymbol{\theta}) \mathrm{d}y. \tag{3}$$

But by the definition of the score, $\mathbf{s}(\mathbf{w}; \boldsymbol{\theta}) f(y \mid \mathbf{x}; \boldsymbol{\theta}) = \frac{\partial}{\partial \boldsymbol{\theta}} f(y \mid \mathbf{x}; \boldsymbol{\theta})$. Substituting this into (3), we obtain

$$\int \mathbf{s}(\mathbf{w}; \boldsymbol{\theta}) f(y \mid \mathbf{x}; \boldsymbol{\theta}) \mathrm{d}y = \underset{(p\times 1)}{\mathbf{0}}. \tag{4}$$

This holds for any $\boldsymbol{\theta} \in \Theta$, in particular, for $\boldsymbol{\theta}_0$. Setting $\boldsymbol{\theta} = \boldsymbol{\theta}_0$, we obtain

$$\int \mathbf{s}(\mathbf{w}; \boldsymbol{\theta}_0) f(y \mid \mathbf{x}; \boldsymbol{\theta}_0) \mathrm{d}y = \mathrm{E}[\mathbf{s}(\mathbf{w}; \boldsymbol{\theta}_0) \mid \mathbf{x}] = \underset{(p\times 1)}{\mathbf{0}}. \tag{5}$$

Then, by the Law of Total Expectations, we obtain the desired result.

References

Amemiya, T., 1985, *Advanced Econometrics*, Cambridge: Harvard University Press.

Davidson, R., and J. MacKinnon, 1993, *Estimation and Inference in Econometrics*, New York: Oxford University Press.

Gallant, R., and H. White, 1988, *A Unified Theory of Estimation and Inference for Nonlinear Dynamic Models*, New York: Basil Blackwell.

Gourieroux, C., and A. Monfort, 1995, *Statistics and Econometric Models*, New York: Cambridge University Press.

Hansen, L. P., and K. Singleton, 1982, "Generalized Instrumental Variables Estimation of Nonlinear Rational Expectations Models," *Econometrica*, 50, 1269–1286.

Judge, G., W. Griffiths, R. Hill, H. Lütkepohl, and T, Lee, 1985, *The Theory and Practice of Econometrics* (2d ed.), New York: Wiley.

Newey, W., and D. McFadden, 1994, "Large Sample Estimation and Hypothesis Testing," Chapter 36 in R. Engle and D. McFadden (eds.), *Handbook of Econometrics*, Volume IV, New York: North-Holland.

White, H., 1994, *Estimation, Inference, and Specification Analysis*, New York: Cambridge University Press.

CHAPTER 8

Examples of Maximum Likelihood

ABSTRACT

The method of maximum likelihood (ML) was developed in the previous chapter as a special case of extremum estimators. In view of its importance in econometrics, this chapter considers applications of ML to some prominent models. We have already seen some of those models in Chapters 3 and 4 in the context of GMM estimation.

In deriving the asymptotic properties of ML estimators for the models considered here, the general results for ML developed in Chapter 7 will be utilized. Before proceeding, you should review Section 7.1, Propositions 7.5, 7.6, 7.8, 7.9, and 7.11.

A Note on Notation: We will maintain the notation, introduced in the previous chapter, of indicating the true parameter value by subscript 0. So $\boldsymbol{\theta}$ is a hypothetical parameter value, while $\boldsymbol{\theta}_0$ is the true parameter value.

8.1 Qualitative Response (QR) Models

In many applications in economics and other sciences, the dependent variable is a categorical variable. For example, a person may be in the labor force or not; a commuter chooses a particular mode of transportation; a patient may die or not; and so on. Regression models in which the dependent variable takes on discrete values are called **qualitative response (QR) models**. A QR model is described by a parameterized density function $f(y_t \mid \mathbf{x}_t; \boldsymbol{\theta})$ representing a family of *discrete* probability distributions of y_t given $\mathbf{x}_t$, indexed by $\boldsymbol{\theta}$.

A QR model is called a **binary response model** if the dependent variable can take on only two values (which can be taken to be 0 and 1 without loss of generality) and is called a **multinomial response model** if the dependent variable can take on more than two values. Only binary models are treated in this subsection. For a thorough treatment of binary and multinomial models, see Amemiya (1985, Chapter 9).

The most popular binary response model is the probit model, which has already been presented in Example 7.3. Another popular binary model is the **logit model**:

$$\begin{cases} f(y_t = 1 \mid \mathbf{x}_t; \boldsymbol{\theta}_0) = \Lambda(\mathbf{x}_t'\boldsymbol{\theta}_0), \\ f(y_t = 0 \mid \mathbf{x}_t; \boldsymbol{\theta}_0) = 1 - \Lambda(\mathbf{x}_t'\boldsymbol{\theta}_0), \end{cases} \tag{8.1.1}$$

where Λ is the cumulative density function of the logistic distribution:

$$\Lambda(v) \equiv \frac{\exp(v)}{1 + \exp(v)}. \tag{8.1.2}$$

This density $f(y_t \mid \mathbf{x}_t; \boldsymbol{\theta}_0)$ can be written as

$$f(y_t \mid \mathbf{x}_t; \boldsymbol{\theta}_0) = \Lambda(\mathbf{x}_t'\boldsymbol{\theta}_0)^{y_t} \times [1 - \Lambda(\mathbf{x}_t'\boldsymbol{\theta}_0)]^{1-y_t}. \tag{8.1.3}$$

Taking logs of both sides and replacing the true parameter value $\boldsymbol{\theta}_0$ by its hypothetical value $\boldsymbol{\theta}$, we obtain the log likelihood for observation t:

$$\log f(y_t \mid \mathbf{x}_t; \boldsymbol{\theta}) = y_t \log \Lambda(\mathbf{x}_t'\boldsymbol{\theta}) + (1 - y_t) \log[1 - \Lambda(\mathbf{x}_t'\boldsymbol{\theta})]. \tag{8.1.4}$$

The logit objective function $Q_n(\boldsymbol{\theta})$ is $1/n$ times the log likelihood of the sample $(y_1, \mathbf{x}_1, y_2, \mathbf{x}_2, \ldots, y_n, \mathbf{x}_n)$. Under the assumption that $\{y_t, \mathbf{x}_t\}$ is i.i.d., the log likelihood of the sample is the sum of the log likelihood for observation t over t. Therefore,

$$Q_n(\boldsymbol{\theta}) = \frac{1}{n} \sum_{t=1}^{n} \big\{ y_t \log \Lambda(\mathbf{x}_t'\boldsymbol{\theta}) + (1 - y_t) \log[1 - \Lambda(\mathbf{x}_t'\boldsymbol{\theta})] \big\}. \tag{8.1.5}$$

For probit, we have proved that its log likelihood function is concave (Example 7.6), and that the ML estimator is consistent (Example 7.9) and asymptotically normal (Example 7.11) under the assumption that $\mathrm{E}(\mathbf{x}_t\mathbf{x}_t')$ is nonsingular. You are about to find out that doing the same for logit is easier. (On the first reading, however, you may wish to skip the discussion on consistency and asymptotic normality.)

Score and Hessian for Observation *t*

The logistic cumulative density function has the convenient property that

$$\Lambda'(v) = \Lambda(v)(1 - \Lambda(v)), \quad \Lambda''(v) = [1 - 2\Lambda(v)]\Lambda(v)[1 - \Lambda(v)]. \tag{8.1.6}$$

Using this, it is easy to derive (see Review Question 1(a)) the following expressions for the score and the Hessian for observation t:

$$\mathbf{s}(\mathbf{w}_t;\boldsymbol{\theta})\left(\equiv\frac{\partial\log f(y_t\mid\mathbf{x}_t;\boldsymbol{\theta})}{\partial\boldsymbol{\theta}}\right)=[y_t-\Lambda(\mathbf{x}_t'\boldsymbol{\theta})]\mathbf{x}_t, \tag{8.1.7}$$

$$\mathbf{H}(\mathbf{w}_t;\boldsymbol{\theta})\left(\equiv\frac{\partial\mathbf{s}(\mathbf{w}_t;\boldsymbol{\theta})}{\partial\boldsymbol{\theta}'}\right)=-\Lambda(\mathbf{x}_t'\boldsymbol{\theta})[1-\Lambda(\mathbf{x}_t'\boldsymbol{\theta})]\mathbf{x}_t\mathbf{x}_t', \tag{8.1.8}$$

where $\mathbf{w}_t=(y_t,\mathbf{x}_t')'$.

Consistency

Since $\mathbf{x}_t\mathbf{x}_t'$ is positive semidefinite, it immediately follows from its expression that $\mathbf{H}(\mathbf{w}_t;\boldsymbol{\theta})$ is negative semidefinite and hence $Q_n(\boldsymbol{\theta})$ is concave. The relevant consistency theorem, therefore, is Proposition 7.6. We show here that the conditions of the proposition are satisfied under the nonsingularity of $\mathrm{E}(\mathbf{x}_t\mathbf{x}_t')$. Condition (a) of the proposition is the (conditional) density identification: $f(y_t\mid\mathbf{x}_t;\boldsymbol{\theta})\neq f(y_t\mid\mathbf{x}_t;\boldsymbol{\theta}_0)$ with positive probability for $\boldsymbol{\theta}\neq\boldsymbol{\theta}_0$.[1] Since a logarithm is a strictly monotone transformation, this condition is equivalent to

$$\log f(y_t\mid\mathbf{x}_t;\boldsymbol{\theta})\neq\log f(y_t\mid\mathbf{x}_t;\boldsymbol{\theta}_0)\text{ with positive probability for }\boldsymbol{\theta}\neq\boldsymbol{\theta}_0, \tag{8.1.9}$$

where $\boldsymbol{\theta}_0$ is the true parameter value and the density f is given in (8.1.3). Verification of this condition is the same as in the probit example in Example 7.9 and proceeds as follows. The discussion in Example 7.8 has established that

$$\mathrm{E}(\mathbf{x}_t\mathbf{x}_t')\text{ nonsingular }\Rightarrow\ \mathbf{x}_t'\boldsymbol{\theta}\neq\mathbf{x}_t'\boldsymbol{\theta}_0\text{ with positive probability for }\boldsymbol{\theta}\neq\boldsymbol{\theta}_0. \tag{8.1.10}$$

Since the logit function $\Lambda(v)$ is a strictly monotone function of v, we have $\Lambda(\mathbf{x}_t'\boldsymbol{\theta})\neq\Lambda(\mathbf{x}_t'\boldsymbol{\theta}_0)$ when $\mathbf{x}_t'\boldsymbol{\theta}\neq\mathbf{x}_t'\boldsymbol{\theta}_0$. Thus, condition (a) is implied by the nonsingularity of $\mathrm{E}(\mathbf{x}_t\mathbf{x}_t')$. Turning to condition (b) (that $\mathrm{E}\big[|\log f(y_t|\mathbf{x}_t;\boldsymbol{\theta})|\big]<\infty$ for all $\boldsymbol{\theta}$), it is easy to show that

$$|\log\Lambda(v)|\leq|\log\Lambda(0)|+|v|. \tag{8.1.11}$$

Condition (b) can then be verified in a way analogous to the verification of the same condition for probit in Example 7.9. Thus, as in probit, the nonsingularity of $\mathrm{E}(\mathbf{x}_t\mathbf{x}_t')$ ensures that logit ML is consistent.

[1] In other words, let $X\equiv f(y_t\mid\mathbf{x}_t;\boldsymbol{\theta})$ and $Y\equiv f(y_t\mid\mathbf{x}_t;\boldsymbol{\theta}_0)$. X and Y are random variables because they are functions of $\mathbf{w}_t\equiv(y_t,\mathbf{x}_t')'$. The condition can be stated simply as $\mathrm{Prob}(X\neq Y)>0$ for $\boldsymbol{\theta}\neq\boldsymbol{\theta}_0$.

Asymptotic Normality

To prove asymptotic normality under the same condition, we verify the conditions of Proposition 7.9. Condition (1) of the proposition is satisfied if the parameter space Θ is taken to be $\mathbb{R}^p$. Condition (2) is obviously satisfied. Condition (3) can be checked easily as follows. Since $\mathrm{E}(y_t \mid \mathbf{x}_t) = \Lambda(\mathbf{x}_t'\boldsymbol{\theta})$, we have $\mathrm{E}[\mathbf{s}(\mathbf{w}_t; \boldsymbol{\theta}_0) \mid \mathbf{x}_t] = \mathbf{0}$ from (8.1.7). Hence, $\mathrm{E}[\mathbf{s}(\mathbf{w}_t; \boldsymbol{\theta}_0)] = \mathbf{0}$ by the Law of Total Expectations. It is left as Review Question 1(b) to derive the conditional information matrix equality

$$\mathrm{E}\big[\mathbf{s}(\mathbf{w}_t; \boldsymbol{\theta}_0)\, \mathbf{s}(\mathbf{w}_t; \boldsymbol{\theta}_0)' \mid \mathbf{x}_t\big] = -\,\mathrm{E}\big[\mathbf{H}(\mathbf{w}_t; \boldsymbol{\theta}_0) \mid \mathbf{x}_t\big]. \tag{8.1.12}$$

Hence, (3) is satisfied by the Law of Total Expectations. The local dominance condition (condition (4)) is easy to verify for logit because, since $|\Lambda(\mathbf{x}_t'\boldsymbol{\theta})[1 - \Lambda(\mathbf{x}_t'\boldsymbol{\theta})]| < 1$, we have: $\|\mathbf{H}_t(\mathbf{w}_t; \boldsymbol{\theta})\| \leq \|\mathbf{x}_t\mathbf{x}_t'\|$ for all $\boldsymbol{\theta}$. The expectation of $\|\mathbf{x}_t\mathbf{x}_t'\|^2$ (the sum of squares of the elements of $\mathbf{x}_t\mathbf{x}_t'$) is finite if $\mathrm{E}(\mathbf{x}_t\mathbf{x}_t')$ is nonsingular (and hence finite). So $\mathrm{E}(\|\mathbf{x}_t\mathbf{x}_t'\|)$ is finite. Regarding condition (5), the argument in footnote 29 of Newey and McFadden (1994) used for verifying the same condition for probit can be used for logit as well.[2]

Thus, we conclude that if $\{y_t, \mathbf{x}_t\}$ is i.i.d. and $\mathrm{E}(\mathbf{x}_t\mathbf{x}_t')$ is nonsingular, then the logit ML estimator $\hat{\boldsymbol{\theta}}$ of $\boldsymbol{\theta}_0$ is consistent and asymptotically normal, with the asymptotic variance consistently estimated by

$$\widehat{\mathrm{Avar}(\hat{\boldsymbol{\theta}})} = -\left[\frac{1}{n}\sum_{t=1}^{n} \mathbf{H}(\mathbf{w}_t; \hat{\boldsymbol{\theta}})\right]^{-1}, \tag{8.1.13}$$

where $\mathbf{w}_t = (y_t, \mathbf{x}_t')'$ and $\mathbf{H}(\mathbf{w}_t; \boldsymbol{\theta})$ is given in (8.1.8).

QUESTIONS FOR REVIEW

1. (Score and Hessian for observation t for general densities) In (8.1.1), replace the logit cumulative density function (c.d.f.) $\Lambda(\mathbf{x}_t'\boldsymbol{\theta}_0)$ by a general c.d.f. $F(\mathbf{x}_t'\boldsymbol{\theta}_0)$.

   (a) Verify that the score and Hessian for observation t are given by

$$\mathbf{s}(\mathbf{w}_t; \boldsymbol{\theta}) = \frac{y_t - F_t}{F_t \cdot (1 - F_t)} f_t \mathbf{x}_t,$$

[2]Only for interested readers, here's the argument. For any $\bar{v} > 0$, there exists a C such that $\Lambda(v)[1 - \Lambda(v)] \geq C > 0$ for $|v| \leq \bar{v}$. So $\mathrm{E}\big[\Lambda(\mathbf{x}'\boldsymbol{\theta})[1 - \Lambda(\mathbf{x}'\boldsymbol{\theta})]\mathbf{x}\mathbf{x}'\big] \geq \mathrm{E}\big[1(|\mathbf{x}'\boldsymbol{\theta}| \leq \bar{v})\Lambda(\mathbf{x}'\boldsymbol{\theta})[1 - \Lambda(\mathbf{x}'\boldsymbol{\theta})]\mathbf{x}\mathbf{x}'\big] \geq C\,\mathrm{E}\big[1(|\mathbf{x}'\boldsymbol{\theta}| \leq \bar{v})\mathbf{x}\mathbf{x}'\big]$ in the matrix inequality sense, where $1(|v| \leq \bar{v})$ is the indicator function. The last term is positive definite (not just positive semi-definite) for large enough $\bar{v}$ by non-singularity of $\mathrm{E}(\mathbf{x}\mathbf{x}')$.

$$\mathbf{H}(\mathbf{w}_t;\boldsymbol{\theta}) = -\left[\frac{y_t - F_t}{F_t\cdot(1-F_t)}\right]^2 f_t^2\mathbf{x}_t\mathbf{x}_t' + \left[\frac{y_t - F_t}{F_t\cdot(1-F_t)}\right] f_t'\mathbf{x}_t\mathbf{x}_t',$$

where $F_t = F(\mathbf{x}_t'\boldsymbol{\theta})$, $f_t = f(\mathbf{x}_t'\boldsymbol{\theta})$, and $f(\cdot) = F'(\cdot)$ is the density function.

(b) Verify the conditional information matrix equality (8.1.12) for the general c.d.f. F. **Hint:** Show that the expected value of the second term in the expression for the Hessian in the previous question is zero.

2. Verify (8.1.7) and (8.1.8).

3. (Logit for serially correlated observations) Suppose $\{y_t, \mathbf{x}_t\}$ is ergodic stationary but not necessarily i.i.d. Is the logit ML estimator described in the text consistent? [Answer: Yes, because the relevant consistency theorem, Proposition 7.6, does not require a random sample. However, the expression for $\text{Avar}(\hat{\boldsymbol{\theta}})$ is not given by the negative of the inverse of the sample Hessian.]

8.2 Truncated Regression Models

A **limited dependent variable (LDV) model** is a regression model in which either the dependent variable y_t is constrained in some way or the observations for which y_t does not meet some prespecified criterion are excluded from the sample. The LDV model of the former sort is called a **censored regression model**, while the latter is called a **truncated regression model**. This section presents truncated regression models; censored regression models are presented in the next section.

The Model

Suppose that $\{y_t, \mathbf{x}_t\}$ is i.i.d. satisfying

$$y_t = \mathbf{x}_t'\boldsymbol{\beta}_0 + \varepsilon_t, \quad \varepsilon_t \mid \mathbf{x}_t \sim N(0, \sigma_0^2). \tag{8.2.1}$$

The model would be just the standard linear regression model with normal errors, were it not for the following feature: only those observations that meet some prespecified rule for y_t are included in the sample. We will consider only the simplest truncation rule: $y_t > c$ where c is a known constant. This rule is sometimes called a "truncation from below." Once this case is worked out, it should not be hard to consider more general truncation rules.

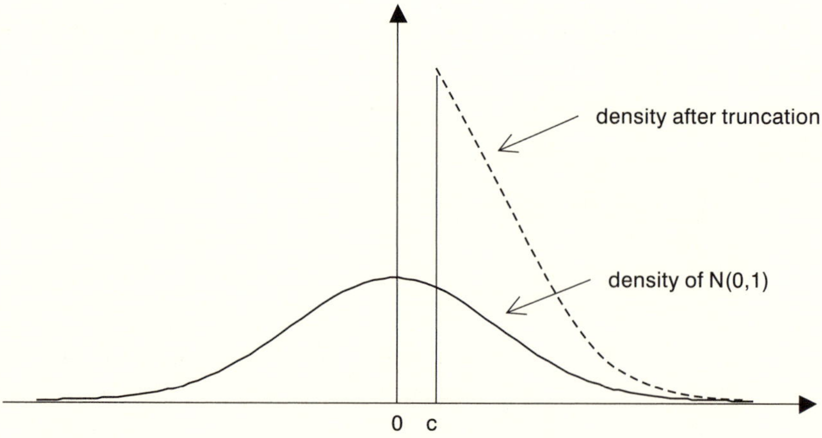

Figure 8.1: Effect of Truncation

Truncated Distributions

To proceed, we need two results from probability theory.

Density of a Truncated Random Variable: If a continuous random variable y has a density function $f(y)$ and c is a constant, then its distribution after the truncation $y > c$ is defined over the interval (c, ∞) and is given by

$$f(y \mid y > c) = \frac{f(y)}{\text{Prob}(y > c)}. \tag{8.2.2}$$

Figure 8.1 illustrates how truncation alters the distribution for $N(0, 1)$. The solid curve is the density of $N(0, 1)$. Because it is a density, the area under the curve is unity. The dotted curve is the distribution after truncation, which is defined over the interval (c, ∞). It lies above the solid curve over this interval so that the area under the dotted curve is unity.

The second result follows.

Moments of the Truncated Normal Distribution: If $y \sim N(\mu_0, \sigma_0^2)$ and c is a constant, then the mean and the variance of the truncated distribution are

$$\text{E}(y \mid y > c) = \mu_0 + \sigma_0 \lambda(v), \tag{8.2.3}$$

$$\text{Var}(y \mid y > c) = \sigma_0^2\{1 - \lambda(v)[\lambda(v) - v]\}, \tag{8.2.4}$$

where $v = (c - \mu_0)/\sigma_0$ and $\lambda(v) \equiv \frac{\phi(v)}{1-\Phi(v)}$.

This formula for the mean clearly shows that the sample mean of draws from the truncated distribution is not consistent for μ_0. This is an example of the **sample selection bias**. The bias equals $\sigma_0\lambda(v)$. The function $\lambda(v)$ is called the **inverse Mill's ratio** or the **hazard function**. The function $\lambda(v)$ is convex and asymptotes to v as $v \to \infty$ and to zero as $v \to -\infty$. So its derivative $\lambda'(v)$ is between 0 and 1. It is easy to show that

$$\lambda'(v) = \lambda(v)(\lambda(v) - v). \tag{8.2.5}$$

Using (8.2.3) and (8.2.4), we can show how truncation alters the form of the regression of y_t on $\mathbf{x}_t$. By (8.2.1), the distribution of y_t conditional on $\mathbf{x}_t$ *before* truncation is $N(\mathbf{x}_t'\boldsymbol{\beta}_0, \sigma_0^2)$. Observation t is in the sample if and only if $y_t > c$. So

$$\mathrm{E}(y_t \mid \mathbf{x}_t, t \text{ in the sample}) = \mathbf{x}_t'\boldsymbol{\beta}_0 + \sigma_0\lambda\left(\tfrac{c-\mathbf{x}_t'\boldsymbol{\beta}_0}{\sigma_0}\right), \tag{8.2.6}$$

$$\mathrm{Var}(y_t \mid \mathbf{x}_t, t \text{ in the sample}) = \sigma_0^2\left\{1 - \lambda\left(\tfrac{c-\mathbf{x}_t'\boldsymbol{\beta}_0}{\sigma_0}\right)\left[\lambda\left(\tfrac{c-\mathbf{x}_t'\boldsymbol{\beta}_0}{\sigma_0}\right) - \tfrac{c-\mathbf{x}_t'\boldsymbol{\beta}_0}{\sigma_0}\right]\right\}. \tag{8.2.7}$$

This formula shows that the OLS estimate of the $\mathbf{x}_t$ coefficient from the linear regression of y_t on $\mathbf{x}_t$ is not consistent because the correction term $\sigma_0\lambda\left(\tfrac{c-\mathbf{x}_t'\boldsymbol{\beta}_0}{\sigma_0}\right)$, which is correlated with $\mathbf{x}_t$, would be included in the error term in the linear regression. Since the functional form of the hazard function $\lambda(v)$ is known (under the normality assumption for ε_t), we could avoid the sample selection bias by applying nonlinear least squares to estimate $(\boldsymbol{\beta}_0, \sigma_0^2)$, but maximum likelihood should be the preferred estimation method because it is asymptotically more efficient.

In passing, we note that the sample selection bias does not arise if selection is based on the regressors, not on the dependent variable. Suppose that observation t is in the sample if $\phi(\mathbf{x}_t) \geq 0$. Then

$$\begin{aligned}\mathrm{E}(y_t \mid \mathbf{x}_t, t \text{ in the sample}) &= \mathrm{E}[\mathbf{x}_t'\boldsymbol{\beta}_0 + \varepsilon_t \mid \mathbf{x}_t, \phi(\mathbf{x}_t) \geq 0] \\ &= \mathbf{x}_t'\boldsymbol{\beta}_0 + \mathrm{E}\,[\varepsilon_t \mid \mathbf{x}_t, \phi(\mathbf{x}_t) \geq 0] \\ &= \mathbf{x}_t'\boldsymbol{\beta}_0.\end{aligned} \tag{8.2.8}$$

The last equality holds since $\mathrm{E}\,[\varepsilon_t \mid \mathbf{x}_t, \phi(\mathbf{x}_t) \geq 0] = \mathrm{E}(\varepsilon_t \mid \mathbf{x}_t) = 0$ if $\phi(\mathbf{x}_t) \geq 0$.

The Likelihood Function

Derivation of the likelihood function utilizes (8.2.2). As just noted, the pretruncation distribution of $y_t \mid \mathbf{x}_t$ is $N(\mathbf{x}_t'\boldsymbol{\beta}_0, \sigma_0^2)$, whose density function is

$$\frac{1}{\sqrt{2\pi\sigma_0^2}}\exp\left[-\frac{1}{2}\left(\frac{y_t-\mathbf{x}_t'\boldsymbol{\beta}_0}{\sigma_0}\right)^2\right]=\frac{1}{\sigma_0}\phi\left(\frac{y_t-\mathbf{x}_t'\boldsymbol{\beta}_0}{\sigma_0}\right), \tag{8.2.9}$$

where $\phi(\cdot)$ is the density of $N(0, 1)$. The probability that observation t is in the sample is given by

$$\begin{aligned}\text{Prob}(y_t > c \mid \mathbf{x}_t) &= 1 - \text{Prob}(y_t \le c \mid \mathbf{x}_t)\\ &= 1 - \text{Prob}\left(\frac{y_t-\mathbf{x}_t'\boldsymbol{\beta}_0}{\sigma_0} \le \frac{c-\mathbf{x}_t'\boldsymbol{\beta}_0}{\sigma_0} \,\Big|\, \mathbf{x}_t\right)\\ &= 1 - \Phi\left(\frac{c-\mathbf{x}_t'\boldsymbol{\beta}_0}{\sigma_0}\right) \quad \left(\text{since } \tfrac{y_t-\mathbf{x}_t'\boldsymbol{\beta}_0}{\sigma_0} \mid \mathbf{x}_t \sim N(0,1)\right). \end{aligned} \tag{8.2.10}$$

Therefore, by (8.2.2), the post-truncation density, defined over (c, ∞), is

$$f(y_t \mid \mathbf{x}_t, t \text{ in the sample}; \boldsymbol{\beta}_0, \sigma_0^2) = \frac{\frac{1}{\sigma_0}\phi\left(\frac{y_t-\mathbf{x}_t'\boldsymbol{\beta}_0}{\sigma_0}\right)}{1-\Phi\left(\frac{c-\mathbf{x}_t'\boldsymbol{\beta}_0}{\sigma_0}\right)}. \tag{8.2.11}$$

This is the density (conditional on $\mathbf{x}_t$) of observation t *in the sample*. Taking logs and replacing $(\boldsymbol{\beta}_0, \sigma_0^2)$ by their hypothetical values $(\boldsymbol{\beta}, \sigma^2)$, we obtain the log conditional likelihood for observation t:

$$\begin{aligned}&\log f(y_t \mid \mathbf{x}_t; \boldsymbol{\beta}, \sigma^2)\\ &= \left\{-\frac{1}{2}\log(2\pi) - \frac{1}{2}\log(\sigma^2) - \frac{1}{2}\left(\frac{y_t-\mathbf{x}_t'\boldsymbol{\beta}}{\sigma}\right)^2\right\} - \log\left[1-\Phi\left(\frac{c-\mathbf{x}_t'\boldsymbol{\beta}}{\sigma}\right)\right].\end{aligned} \tag{8.2.12}$$

Were it not for the last term, this would be the log likelihood (conditional on $\mathbf{x}_t$) for the usual linear regression model. The last term is needed because the value of the dependent variable for observation t, having passed the test $y_t > c$ and thus being in the sample, is never less than or equal to c.

Reparameterizing the Likelihood Function

This log likelihood function can be made easier to analyze if we introduce the following reparameterization:

$$\boldsymbol{\delta} = \boldsymbol{\beta}/\sigma, \quad \gamma = 1/\sigma. \tag{8.2.13}$$

(We have considered this reparameterization in Example 7.7 for the linear regression model.) This is a one-to-one mapping between $(\boldsymbol{\beta}, \sigma^2)$ and $(\boldsymbol{\delta}, \gamma)$, with the inverse mapping given by $\boldsymbol{\beta} = \boldsymbol{\delta}/\gamma, \sigma^2 = 1/\gamma^2$. The reparameterized log conditional likelihood is

$$\log \tilde{f}(y_t \mid \mathbf{x}_t; \boldsymbol{\lambda})$$
$$= \left[-\frac{1}{2}\log(2\pi) + \log(\gamma) - \frac{1}{2}(\gamma y_t - \mathbf{x}_t'\boldsymbol{\delta})^2\right] - \log[1 - \Phi(\gamma c - \mathbf{x}_t'\boldsymbol{\delta})]. \tag{8.2.14}$$

The objective function in ML estimation is $1/n$ times the log likelihood of the sample. For a random sample, the log likelihood of the sample is the sum over t of the log likelihood for observation t. Thus, the objective function in the ML estimation of the reparameterized truncated regression model, denoted $\widetilde{Q}_n(\boldsymbol{\delta}, \gamma)$, is the average over t of (8.2.14). The ML estimator $(\hat{\boldsymbol{\delta}}, \hat{\gamma})$ of $(\boldsymbol{\delta}_0, \gamma_0)$ is the $(\boldsymbol{\delta}, \gamma)$ that maximizes this objective function.

Verifying Consistency and Asymptotic Normality

The next task is to derive the score and the Hessian and check the conditions for consistency and asymptotic normality for the reparameterized log likelihood (8.2.14). (On the first reading, you may wish to skip the discussion on consistency and asymptotic normality.)

Score and Hessian for Observation t

A tedious calculation yields

$$\underset{((K+1)\times 1)}{\mathbf{s}(\mathbf{w}_t; \boldsymbol{\delta}, \gamma)} = \begin{bmatrix} (\gamma y_t - \mathbf{x}_t'\boldsymbol{\delta})\mathbf{x}_t \\ \frac{1}{\gamma} - (\gamma y_t - \mathbf{x}_t'\boldsymbol{\delta})y_t \end{bmatrix} + \lambda(v_t)\begin{bmatrix} -\mathbf{x}_t \\ c \end{bmatrix}, \tag{8.2.15}$$

$$\underset{((K+1)\times(K+1))}{\mathbf{H}(\mathbf{w}_t; \boldsymbol{\delta}, \gamma)} = -\begin{bmatrix} \mathbf{x}_t\mathbf{x}_t' & -y_t\mathbf{x}_t \\ -y_t\mathbf{x}_t' & \frac{1}{\gamma^2} + y_t^2 \end{bmatrix} + \lambda(v_t)[\lambda(v_t) - v_t]\begin{bmatrix} \mathbf{x}_t\mathbf{x}_t' & -c\mathbf{x}_t \\ -c\mathbf{x}_t' & c^2 \end{bmatrix}, \tag{8.2.16}$$

where K is the number of regressors, $\mathbf{w}_t = (y_t, \mathbf{x}_t')'$, and $v_t \equiv \gamma c - \mathbf{x}_t'\boldsymbol{\delta}$ $(= \frac{c - \mathbf{x}_t'\boldsymbol{\beta}}{\sigma})$. The Hessian is *not* everywhere negative semidefinite even after the reparameterization. So the objective function $\widetilde{Q}_n(\boldsymbol{\delta}, \gamma)$ is not concave.[3] The relevant consistency theorem, therefore, is Proposition 7.5, not Proposition 7.6, while the relevant asymptotic normality theorem remains Proposition 7.9.

[3]However, it can be shown that the Hessian of the objective function $Q_n(\boldsymbol{\theta})$ is negative semidefinite at any solution to the likelihood equations (see Orme, 1989). Since this rules out any saddle points or local minima, having more than two local maxima is impossible. Therefore, provided that the maximum of $\widetilde{Q}_n(\boldsymbol{\delta}, \gamma)$ occurs at a point interior to the parameter space, the first-order condition is necessary and sufficient for a *global* maximum. If an algorithm such as Newton-Raphson produces convergence, the point of convergence is the global maximum.

Consistency

Condition (a) of Proposition 7.5 is the (conditional) density identification

$$\tilde{f}(y_t \mid \mathbf{x}_t; \boldsymbol{\delta}, \gamma) \neq \tilde{f}(y_t \mid \mathbf{x}_t; \boldsymbol{\delta}_0, \gamma_0)$$
$$\text{with positive probability for } (\boldsymbol{\delta}, \gamma) \neq (\boldsymbol{\delta}_0, \gamma_0),$$

where $(\boldsymbol{\delta}_0, \gamma_0)$ is the true parameter value and the parameterized log density $\tilde{f}(y_t \mid \mathbf{x}_t; \boldsymbol{\delta}, \gamma)$ is given in (8.2.14). Clearly, given $(y_t, \mathbf{x}_t)$, the value of $\tilde{f}(y_t \mid \mathbf{x}_t; \boldsymbol{\delta}, \gamma)$ is different for different values of γ. So identification boils down to the condition that $\mathbf{x}_t'\boldsymbol{\delta} \neq \mathbf{x}_t'\boldsymbol{\delta}_0$ with positive probability for $\boldsymbol{\delta} \neq \boldsymbol{\delta}_0$. But (8.1.10) indicates that this condition is satisfied if $\mathrm{E}(\mathbf{x}_t\mathbf{x}_t')$ is nonsingular. Turning to condition (b) of the proposition (the dominance condition for $\tilde{f}(y_t \mid \mathbf{x}_t; \boldsymbol{\delta}, \gamma)$), it is easy to show that the condition is satisfied under the nonsingularity of $\mathrm{E}(\mathbf{x}_t\mathbf{x}_t')$.[4] Therefore, the ML estimator $(\hat{\boldsymbol{\delta}}, \hat{\gamma})$ of $(\boldsymbol{\delta}_0, \gamma_0)$ is consistent under the nonsingularity of $\mathrm{E}(\mathbf{x}_t\mathbf{x}_t')$.

Asymptotic Normality

A rather tedious calculation using (8.2.6), (8.2.7), and (8.2.13) shows that $\mathrm{E}[\mathbf{s} \mid \mathbf{x}_t] = \mathbf{0}$. An extremely tedious calculation yields the conditional information matrix equality: $\mathrm{E}[\mathbf{s}\mathbf{s}' \mid \mathbf{x}_t] = -\mathrm{E}[\mathbf{H} \mid \mathbf{x}_t]$. Therefore, condition (3) of Proposition 7.9 is satisfied. We will not discuss verification of conditions (4) and (5) of the proposition.[5]

Thus, we conclude: if $\{y_t, \mathbf{x}_t\}$ is i.i.d. and $\mathrm{E}(\mathbf{x}_t\mathbf{x}_t')$ is nonsingular, then the ML estimator $(\hat{\boldsymbol{\delta}}, \hat{\gamma})$ of the truncated regression model is consistent and asymptotically normal with the asymptotic variance consistently estimated by

$$\widehat{\mathrm{Avar}(\hat{\boldsymbol{\delta}}, \hat{\gamma})} = -\left[\frac{1}{n}\sum_{t=1}^{n} \mathbf{H}(\mathbf{w}_t; \hat{\boldsymbol{\delta}}, \hat{\gamma})\right]^{-1}, \tag{8.2.17}$$

where $\mathbf{w}_t = (y_t, \mathbf{x}_t')'$ and $\mathbf{H}(\mathbf{w}_t; \boldsymbol{\theta})$ is given in (8.2.16).

[4] Only for interested readers, what needs to be shown is $\mathrm{E}\big[\sup_{\boldsymbol{\theta}\in\Theta} |\log \tilde{f}(y_t \mid \mathbf{x}_t; \boldsymbol{\theta})|\big] < \infty$, where $\boldsymbol{\theta} = (\boldsymbol{\delta}', \gamma)'$ and Θ is a compact set. An extension of the argument in Example 7.8 shows that there is a dominating function for the bracketed term in (8.2.14). The inequality (7.2.14) can be used to show that there is a dominating function for $\log[1 - \Phi(c\gamma - \mathbf{x}_t'\boldsymbol{\delta})]$.

[5] There seems to be no published work that verifies conditions (4) and (5). For the case where $\{\mathbf{x}_t\}$ is a sequence of fixed constants, Sapra (1992) proved asymptotic normality under the assumption that $\mathbf{x}_t$ is bounded and $\lim_{n\to\infty} \frac{1}{n}\sum_{t=1}^{n} \mathbf{x}_t\mathbf{x}_t'$ is nonsingular. (His proof is for the more general setting of serially correlated observations.) It would seem reasonable to conjecture that for the case where $\mathbf{x}_t$ is random (as here), a sufficient condition for consistency and asymptotic normality is the nonsingularity of $\mathrm{E}(\mathbf{x}_t\mathbf{x}_t')$.

Recovering Original Parameters

By the invariance property of ML (see Section 7.1), the ML estimate of $(\boldsymbol{\beta}_0, \sigma_0^2)$ is $\widehat{\boldsymbol{\beta}} = \hat{\boldsymbol{\delta}}/\hat{\gamma}$ and $\hat{\sigma}^2 = 1/\hat{\gamma}^2$, the value of the inverse mapping. Clearly, if the ML estimate of the reparameterized model, $(\hat{\boldsymbol{\delta}}, \hat{\gamma})$, is consistent, then so is the ML estimate $(\widehat{\boldsymbol{\beta}}, \hat{\sigma}^2)$ thus recovered. The asymptotic variance of $(\widehat{\boldsymbol{\beta}}, \hat{\sigma}^2)$ can be obtained by the delta method (see Lemma 2.5) as $\widehat{\mathbf{J}}\widehat{\text{Avar}(\hat{\boldsymbol{\delta}}, \hat{\gamma})}\widehat{\mathbf{J}}'$, where $\widehat{\mathbf{J}}$ is the estimate of the Jacobian matrix for the inverse mapping $(\boldsymbol{\beta} = \boldsymbol{\delta}/\gamma,\ \sigma^2 = 1/\gamma^2)$ evaluated at $(\hat{\boldsymbol{\delta}}, \hat{\gamma})$:

$$\widehat{\mathbf{J}} = \begin{bmatrix} \frac{1}{\hat{\gamma}}\mathbf{I} & -\frac{\hat{\boldsymbol{\delta}}}{\hat{\gamma}^2} \\ \mathbf{0}' & -\frac{2}{\hat{\gamma}^3} \end{bmatrix}. \tag{8.2.18}$$

QUESTIONS FOR REVIEW

1. (Second moment of y_t) From (8.2.6) and (8.2.7), derive:

$$\text{E}(y_t^2 \mid \mathbf{x}_t, t \text{ in sample}) = \frac{1}{\gamma^2}\big[1 + \lambda(v_t)\gamma c + (\mathbf{x}_t'\boldsymbol{\delta})^2 + \lambda(v_t)\mathbf{x}_t'\boldsymbol{\delta}\big],$$

where $v_t \equiv \gamma c - \mathbf{x}_t'\boldsymbol{\delta}$.

2. (Estimation of truncated regression model by GMM) The truncated regression model can also be estimated by GMM. Consider the following $K+1$ orthogonality conditions. The first K of them are

$$\underset{(K\times 1)}{\mathbf{g}_1}(\mathbf{w}_t; \boldsymbol{\delta}, \gamma) = \left(y_t - \frac{1}{\gamma}\mathbf{x}_t'\boldsymbol{\delta} - \frac{\lambda(v_t)}{\gamma}\right) \cdot \mathbf{x}_t, \tag{8.2.19}$$

where $\mathbf{w}_t = (y_t, \mathbf{x}_t')'$ and $v_t \equiv \gamma c - \mathbf{x}_t'\boldsymbol{\delta}$. The $(K+1)$-th orthogonality condition is

$$g_2(\mathbf{w}_t; \boldsymbol{\delta}, \gamma) = y_t^2 - \frac{1}{\gamma^2}\big[1 + \lambda(v_t)\gamma c + (\mathbf{x}_t'\boldsymbol{\delta})^2 + \lambda(v_t)\mathbf{x}_t'\boldsymbol{\delta}\big]. \tag{8.2.20}$$

(a) Verify that $\text{E}[\mathbf{g}_1(\mathbf{w}_t; \boldsymbol{\delta}_0, \gamma_0)] = \mathbf{0}$ and $\text{E}[g_2(\mathbf{w}_t; \boldsymbol{\delta}_0, \gamma_0)] = 0$. **Hint:** Use the Law of Total Expectations. v_t is a function of $\mathbf{x}_t$.

(b) Show that $(\boldsymbol{\delta}^*, \gamma^*)$ satisfies the likelihood equations if and only if it satisfies the $K+1$ orthogonality conditions. **Hint:** Let $s_2(\mathbf{w}_t; \boldsymbol{\delta}, \gamma)$ be the $(K+1)$-th element of $\mathbf{s}(\mathbf{w}_t; \boldsymbol{\delta}, \gamma)$ in (8.2.15). Then

$$s_2(\mathbf{w}_t; \boldsymbol{\delta}, \gamma) + \gamma g_2(\mathbf{w}_t; \boldsymbol{\delta}, \gamma) = (\mathbf{x}_t'\boldsymbol{\delta})\Big(y_t - \frac{1}{\gamma}\mathbf{x}_t'\boldsymbol{\delta} - \frac{\lambda(v_t)}{\gamma}\Big).$$

8.3 Censored Regression (Tobit) Models

The censored regression model is also called the **Tobit model** to pay respect to Tobin (1958), who was the first to introduce censoring in economics. The simplest Tobit model can be written as follows:

$$y_t^* = \mathbf{x}_t'\boldsymbol{\beta}_0 + \varepsilon_t, \quad t = 1, 2, \ldots, n, \tag{8.3.1}$$

$$y_t = \begin{cases} y_t^* & \text{if } y_t^* > c, \\ c & \text{if } y_t^* \leq c. \end{cases} \tag{8.3.2}$$

Here, $\varepsilon_t \mid \mathbf{x}_t$ is $N(0, \sigma_0^2)$ and $\{y_t, \mathbf{x}_t\}$ $(t = 1, 2, \ldots, n)$ is i.i.d. The threshold value c is known. Unlike in the truncated regression model, there is no truncation here: observations for which the value of the dependent variable y_t^* fails to pass the test $y_t^* > c$ *are* in the sample. The feature that distinguishes the censored regression model from the usual regression model is that the dependent variable is censored, that is, constrained to lie in a certain range, which necessitates a distinction between the observable dependent variable y_t and the unobservable or latent variable y_t^*. The former is the censored value of the latter. An equivalent way to write the model is

$$y_t = \max\{\mathbf{x}_t'\boldsymbol{\beta}_0 + \varepsilon_t, c\}. \tag{8.3.3}$$

Tobit Likelihood Function

For those observations that remain intact after censoring (Tobin (1958) called those observations **nonlimit observations**), the density of y_t (conditional on $\mathbf{x}_t$) is

$$\frac{1}{\sigma_0}\phi\Big(\frac{y_t - \mathbf{x}_t'\boldsymbol{\beta}_0}{\sigma_0}\Big). \tag{8.3.4}$$

This differs from the density for the truncated model (8.2.11) simply because there is no truncation. For those observations, called **limit observations**, for which the value of the dependent variable is altered by censoring, all we know is that $y_t^* \leq c$, the probability of which is given by

$$\begin{aligned}\text{Prob}(y_t^* \le c \mid \mathbf{x}_t) &= \text{Prob}\Big(\frac{y_t^* - \mathbf{x}_t'\boldsymbol{\beta}_0}{\sigma_0} \le \frac{c - \mathbf{x}_t'\boldsymbol{\beta}_0}{\sigma_0} \mid \mathbf{x}_t\Big) \\ &= \Phi\Big(\frac{c - \mathbf{x}_t'\boldsymbol{\beta}_0}{\sigma_0}\Big) \quad \Big(\text{since } \tfrac{y_t^* - \mathbf{x}_t'\boldsymbol{\beta}_0}{\sigma_0} \mid \mathbf{x}_t \sim N(0,1)\Big). \qquad (8.3.5)\end{aligned}$$

Therefore, the density of y_t, defined over the interval $[c, \infty)$, is (8.3.4) for $y_t > c$ and a probability mass of size $\Phi(\frac{c - \mathbf{x}_t'\boldsymbol{\beta}_0}{\sigma_0})$ at $y_t = c$. This density can be written as

$$\Big[\frac{1}{\sigma_0}\phi\Big(\frac{y_t - \mathbf{x}_t'\boldsymbol{\beta}_0}{\sigma_0}\Big)\Big]^{1-D_t} \times \Big[\Phi\Big(\frac{c - \mathbf{x}_t'\boldsymbol{\beta}_0}{\sigma_0}\Big)\Big]^{D_t}, \qquad (8.3.6)$$

where the dummy variable D_t is a function of y_t defined as

$$D_t = \begin{cases} 0 & \text{if } y_t > c \text{ (i.e., } y_t^* > c), \\ 1 & \text{if } y_t = c \text{ (i.e., } y_t^* \le c). \end{cases} \qquad (8.3.7)$$

Taking logs and replacing $(\boldsymbol{\beta}_0, \sigma_0^2)$ by their hypothetical values $(\boldsymbol{\beta}, \sigma^2)$, we obtain the log conditional likelihood for observation t:

$$\log f(y_t \mid \mathbf{x}_t; \boldsymbol{\beta}, \sigma^2) = (1 - D_t)\log\Big[\frac{1}{\sigma}\phi\Big(\frac{y_t - \mathbf{x}_t'\boldsymbol{\beta}}{\sigma}\Big)\Big] + D_t \log \Phi\Big(\frac{c - \mathbf{x}_t'\boldsymbol{\beta}}{\sigma}\Big). \qquad (8.3.8)$$

Thus, the Tobit average log likelihood for a random sample can be written as

$$\begin{aligned} Q_n(\boldsymbol{\theta}) &= \frac{1}{n}\sum_{t=1}^{n}\Big\{(1 - D_t)\log\Big[\frac{1}{\sigma}\phi\Big(\frac{y_t - \mathbf{x}_t'\boldsymbol{\beta}}{\sigma}\Big)\Big] + D_t \log \Phi\Big(\frac{c - \mathbf{x}_t'\boldsymbol{\beta}}{\sigma}\Big)\Big\} \\ &= \frac{1}{n}\sum_{y_t > c}\Big\{\log\Big[\frac{1}{\sigma}\phi\Big(\frac{y_t - \mathbf{x}_t'\boldsymbol{\beta}}{\sigma}\Big)\Big]\Big\} + \frac{1}{n}\sum_{y_t = c}\Big\{\log \Phi\Big(\frac{c - \mathbf{x}_t'\boldsymbol{\beta}}{\sigma}\Big)\Big\}. \qquad (8.3.9)\end{aligned}$$

Reparameterization

As in the truncated regression model, the discussion is simplified if we introduce the reparameterization (8.2.13). The reparameterized log conditional likelihood is

$$\begin{aligned}\log \tilde{f}(y_t \mid \mathbf{x}_t; \boldsymbol{\delta}, \gamma) = (1 - D_t)\Big\{-\frac{1}{2}\log(2\pi) + \log(\gamma) - \frac{1}{2}(\gamma y_t - \mathbf{x}_t'\boldsymbol{\delta})^2\Big\} \\ + D_t \log \Phi(\gamma c - \mathbf{x}_t'\boldsymbol{\delta}). \qquad (8.3.10)\end{aligned}$$

We have seen that the term in braces is concave in $(\boldsymbol{\delta}, \gamma)$ (see Example 7.7). We have also seen that $\log \Phi(v)$ is concave (see Example 7.6), which implies that $\log \Phi(\gamma c - \mathbf{x}_t'\boldsymbol{\delta})$ is concave in $(\boldsymbol{\delta}, \gamma)$. It follows that the reparameterized Tobit average log likelihood for observation t, being a non-negative weighted average of two concave functions, *is* concave in the parameters (this finding is due to Olsen, 1978). Accordingly, as in probit and logit, the relevant consistency theorem for Tobit is Proposition 7.6.

The remaining task is to write down the score and the Hessian and check the conditions for consistency and asymptotic normality for the reparameterized log likelihood (8.3.10).

Score and Hessian for Observation *t*

A straightforward calculation utilizing the fact that $\lambda(-v) = \frac{\phi(-v)}{1-\Phi(-v)} = \frac{\phi(v)}{\Phi(v)}$ and (8.2.5) produces

$$\underset{((K+1)\times 1)}{\mathbf{s}(\mathbf{w}_t; \boldsymbol{\delta}, \gamma)} = (1 - D_t) \cdot \begin{bmatrix} (\gamma y_t - \mathbf{x}_t'\boldsymbol{\delta})\mathbf{x}_t \\ \frac{1}{\gamma} - (\gamma y_t - \mathbf{x}_t'\boldsymbol{\delta}) y_t \end{bmatrix} + D_t \cdot \lambda(-v_t) \begin{bmatrix} -\mathbf{x}_t \\ c \end{bmatrix}, \tag{8.3.11}$$

$$\begin{aligned} \underset{((K+1)\times(K+1))}{\mathbf{H}(\mathbf{w}_t; \boldsymbol{\delta}, \gamma)} &= -(1 - D_t) \cdot \begin{bmatrix} \mathbf{x}_t\mathbf{x}_t' & -y_t\mathbf{x}_t \\ -y_t\mathbf{x}_t' & \frac{1}{\gamma^2} + y_t^2 \end{bmatrix} \\ &\quad - D_t \cdot \lambda(-v_t)[\lambda(-v_t) + v_t] \begin{bmatrix} \mathbf{x}_t\mathbf{x}_t' & -c\mathbf{x}_t \\ -c\mathbf{x}_t' & c^2 \end{bmatrix}, \end{aligned} \tag{8.3.12}$$

where $v_t \equiv \gamma c - \mathbf{x}_t'\boldsymbol{\delta}$ $(= \frac{c - \mathbf{x}_t'\boldsymbol{\beta}}{\sigma})$.

Consistency and Asymptotic Normality

For Tobit, we will not verify the conditions for consistency and asymptotic normality. For the case where $\{\mathbf{x}_t\}$ is a sequence of fixed constants, Amemiya (1973) has proved the consistency and asymptotic normality of Tobit ML under the assumption that $\mathbf{x}_t$ is bounded and $\lim \frac{1}{n}\sum_{t=1}^{n} \mathbf{x}_t\mathbf{x}_t'$ is nonsingular. It seems a reasonable guess that for the case where $\mathbf{x}_t$ is stochastic (as here), a sufficient condition for consistency and asymptotic normality is the nonsingularity of $\mathrm{E}(\mathbf{x}_t\mathbf{x}_t')$.

Recovering Original Parameters

As in the truncated regression model, the ML estimate of $(\boldsymbol{\beta}_0, \sigma_0^2)$ can be recovered as $\widehat{\boldsymbol{\beta}} = \hat{\boldsymbol{\delta}}/\hat{\gamma}$ and $\hat{\sigma}^2 = 1/\hat{\gamma}^2$. The asymptotic variance of $(\widehat{\boldsymbol{\beta}}, \hat{\sigma}^2)$ can be obtained by the delta method as $\widehat{\mathbf{J}}\widehat{\text{Avar}(\hat{\boldsymbol{\delta}}, \hat{\gamma})}\widehat{\mathbf{J}}'$, where $\widehat{\mathbf{J}}$ is as in (8.2.18) and $\widehat{\text{Avar}(\hat{\boldsymbol{\delta}}, \hat{\gamma})}$ is $-\left[\frac{1}{n}\sum_{t=1}^{n} \mathbf{H}(\mathbf{w}_t; \hat{\boldsymbol{\delta}}, \hat{\gamma})\right]^{-1}$.

QUESTIONS FOR REVIEW

1. (Censored vs. truncated regression) One way to see the difference between truncation and censoring is to calculate $\text{E}(y_t \mid \mathbf{x}_t)$ for the censored regression model. Show that

$$\text{E}(y_t \mid \mathbf{x}_t) = \left[1 - \Phi\left(\tfrac{c-\mathbf{x}_t'\boldsymbol{\beta}_0}{\sigma_0}\right)\right] \times \left[\mathbf{x}_t'\boldsymbol{\beta}_0 + \sigma_0 \lambda\left(\tfrac{c-\mathbf{x}_t'\boldsymbol{\beta}_0}{\sigma_0}\right)\right] + \Phi\left(\tfrac{c-\mathbf{x}_t'\boldsymbol{\beta}_0}{\sigma_0}\right)c.$$

Hint: Conditional on $y_t > c$, the distribution of y_t (conditional on $\mathbf{x}_t$) is none other than the truncated distribution derived in the previous section, whose expectation is given in (8.2.6). The probability that $y_t > c$ is given in (8.2.10).

2. Show that the Hessian given in (8.3.12) is negative semidefinite. **Hint:**

$$\begin{bmatrix} \mathbf{x}_t\mathbf{x}_t' & -y_t\mathbf{x}_t \\ -y_t\mathbf{x}_t' & \frac{1}{\gamma^2} + y_t^2 \end{bmatrix} = \begin{bmatrix} \mathbf{x}_t \\ -y_t \end{bmatrix} \begin{bmatrix} \mathbf{x}_t' & -y_t \end{bmatrix} + \begin{bmatrix} \mathbf{0} & \mathbf{0} \\ \mathbf{0}' & \frac{1}{\gamma^2} \end{bmatrix},$$
$$\begin{bmatrix} \mathbf{x}_t\mathbf{x}_t' & -c\mathbf{x}_t \\ -c\mathbf{x}_t' & c^2 \end{bmatrix} = \begin{bmatrix} \mathbf{x}_t \\ -c \end{bmatrix} \begin{bmatrix} \mathbf{x}_t' & -c \end{bmatrix}.$$

Also, $\lambda(v) \geq v$ for all v (i.e., $\lambda(-v) + v \geq 0$ for all $-v$).

3. (Tobit for serially correlated observations) Suppose $\{y_t, \mathbf{x}_t\}$ is ergodic stationary but not necessarily i.i.d. Is the Tobit ML estimator described in the text consistent? [Answer: Yes.]

8.4 Multivariate Regressions

In Section 1.5 and also in Example 7.2 of Chapter 7, we pointed out that the OLS estimator of the linear regression model is numerically the same as the ML estimator of the same model with normal errors. We have derived the GMM estimators for the single-equation models with endogenous regressors in Chapter 3 and for their multiple-equation versions in Chapter 4, but we have not indicated what the ML estimators for those models are. In this section and the next, we derive those ML counterparts. This section examines the ML estimation of the multivariate regression model, which is the simplest multiple-equation model.

The Multivariate Regression Model Restated

The multivariate regression model is described by Assumptions 4.1–4.5 and 4.7, with $\mathbf{z}_{tm} = \mathbf{x}_{tm} = \mathbf{x}_t$ for all $m = 1, 2, \ldots, M$. To change the notation of Chapter 4, the system of M equations can be written as

$$y_{tm} = \underset{(1\times K)}{\mathbf{x}_t'} \underset{(K\times 1)}{\boldsymbol{\pi}_{0m}} + v_{tm} \quad (m = 1, 2, \ldots, M; t = 1, 2, \ldots, n). \tag{8.4.1}$$

Here, we maintain the convention of designating the true parameter vector by subscript 0. If we define

$$\underset{(M\times 1)}{\mathbf{y}_t} = \begin{bmatrix} y_{t1} \\ y_{t2} \\ \vdots \\ y_{tM} \end{bmatrix}, \quad \underset{(M\times 1)}{\mathbf{v}_t} = \begin{bmatrix} v_{t1} \\ v_{t2} \\ \vdots \\ v_{tM} \end{bmatrix}, \quad \underset{(K\times M)}{\boldsymbol{\Pi}_0} = \begin{bmatrix} \boldsymbol{\pi}_{01} & \boldsymbol{\pi}_{02} & \cdots & \boldsymbol{\pi}_{0M} \end{bmatrix}, \tag{8.4.2}$$

then the M-equation system can be written compactly as

$$\mathbf{y}_t = \boldsymbol{\Pi}_0'\mathbf{x}_t + \mathbf{v}_t \quad (t = 1, 2, \ldots, n). \tag{8.4.3}$$

The model has the following features.

- $\{y_t, \mathbf{x}_t\}$ is ergodic stationary (Assumption 4.2).
- The common regressors $\mathbf{x}_t$ are predetermined in that $\mathrm{E}(\mathbf{x}_t \cdot v_{tm}) = \mathbf{0}$ for all m (Assumption 4.3).
- The rank condition for identification (Assumption 4.4) reduces to the familiar condition that $\mathrm{E}(\mathbf{x}_t\mathbf{x}_t')$ be nonsingular.
- The error vector is conditionally homoskedastic in that $\mathrm{E}(\mathbf{v}_t\mathbf{v}_t' \mid \mathbf{x}_t) = \boldsymbol{\Omega}_0$, and $\boldsymbol{\Omega}_0$ is positive definite (Assumption 4.7).

The GMM estimator of $\boldsymbol{\pi}_{0m}$ is the OLS estimator:

$$\widehat{\boldsymbol{\pi}}_m = \Big(\frac{1}{n}\sum_{t=1}^{n}\mathbf{x}_t\mathbf{x}_t'\Big)^{-1}\Big(\frac{1}{n}\sum_{t=1}^{n}\mathbf{x}_t \cdot y_{tm}\Big). \tag{8.4.4}$$

So the GMM (OLS) estimate of $\boldsymbol{\Pi}_0$ is given by

$$\underset{(K\times M)}{\widehat{\boldsymbol{\Pi}}} = \Big(\underset{(K\times K)}{\frac{1}{n}\sum_{t=1}^{n}\mathbf{x}_t\mathbf{x}_t'}\Big)^{-1}\Big(\underset{(K\times M)}{\frac{1}{n}\sum_{t=1}^{n}\mathbf{x}_t\mathbf{y}_t'}\Big). \tag{8.4.5}$$

The Likelihood Function

The model is not yet specific enough to lend itself to ML estimation. We make the supplementary assumptions that (1) $\mathbf{v}_t \mid \mathbf{x}_t \sim N(\mathbf{0}, \mathbf{\Omega}_0)$, and (2) $\{\mathbf{y}_t, \mathbf{x}_t\}$ is i.i.d. (This assumption strengthens Assumptions 4.2 and 4.5.)

The multivariate regression model with the normality assumption (1) implies that $\mathbf{y}_t \mid \mathbf{x}_t \sim N(\mathbf{\Pi}_0'\mathbf{x}_t, \mathbf{\Omega}_0)$. The density of this multivariate normal distribution is

$$(2\pi)^{-M/2}|\mathbf{\Omega}_0|^{-1/2}\exp\Big[-\frac{1}{2}(\mathbf{y}_t - \mathbf{\Pi}_0'\mathbf{x}_t)'\mathbf{\Omega}_0^{-1}(\mathbf{y}_t - \mathbf{\Pi}_0'\mathbf{x}_t)\Big]. \tag{8.4.6}$$

Replacing the true parameter values $(\mathbf{\Pi}_0, \mathbf{\Omega}_0)$ by their hypothetical values $(\mathbf{\Pi}, \mathbf{\Omega})$ and taking logs, we obtain the log conditional likelihood for observation t:

$$\begin{aligned}\log f(\mathbf{y}_t \mid \mathbf{x}_t; \mathbf{\Pi}, \mathbf{\Omega})\\ = -\frac{M}{2}\log(2\pi) + \frac{1}{2}\log(|\mathbf{\Omega}^{-1}|) - \frac{1}{2}(\mathbf{y}_t - \mathbf{\Pi}'\mathbf{x}_t)'\mathbf{\Omega}^{-1}(\mathbf{y}_t - \mathbf{\Pi}'\mathbf{x}_t),\end{aligned} \tag{8.4.7}$$

where use has been made of the fact that $-\log(|\mathbf{\Omega}|) = \log(|\mathbf{\Omega}^{-1}|)$.

For a random sample, $1/n$ times the log conditional likelihood of the sample is the average over t of the log conditional likelihood for observation t. So the objective function $Q_n(\mathbf{\Pi}, \mathbf{\Omega})$ is

$$Q_n(\mathbf{\Pi}, \mathbf{\Omega}) = -\frac{M}{2}\log(2\pi) + \frac{1}{2}\log(|\mathbf{\Omega}^{-1}|) - \frac{1}{2n}\sum_{t=1}^{n}(\mathbf{y}_t - \mathbf{\Pi}'\mathbf{x}_t)'\mathbf{\Omega}^{-1}(\mathbf{y}_t - \mathbf{\Pi}'\mathbf{x}_t). \tag{8.4.8}$$

It is left as Review Question 2 to show that the last term can be written as

$$\frac{1}{2n}\sum_{t=1}^{n}(\mathbf{y}_t - \mathbf{\Pi}'\mathbf{x}_t)'\mathbf{\Omega}^{-1}(\mathbf{y}_t - \mathbf{\Pi}'\mathbf{x}_t) = \frac{1}{2}\operatorname{trace}[\mathbf{\Omega}^{-1}\widehat{\mathbf{\Omega}}(\mathbf{\Pi})], \tag{8.4.9}$$

where $\widehat{\mathbf{\Omega}}(\mathbf{\Pi})$ is defined as

$$\underset{(M\times M)}{\widehat{\mathbf{\Omega}}(\mathbf{\Pi})} \equiv \frac{1}{n}\sum_{t=1}^{n}(\mathbf{y}_t - \mathbf{\Pi}'\mathbf{x}_t)(\mathbf{y}_t - \mathbf{\Pi}'\mathbf{x}_t)'. \tag{8.4.10}$$

So the objective function can be rewritten as

$$Q_n(\mathbf{\Pi}, \mathbf{\Omega}) = -\frac{M}{2}\log(2\pi) + \frac{1}{2}\log(|\mathbf{\Omega}^{-1}|) - \frac{1}{2}\operatorname{trace}[\mathbf{\Omega}^{-1}\widehat{\mathbf{\Omega}}(\mathbf{\Pi})]. \tag{8.4.11}$$

The ML estimate of $(\mathbf{\Pi}_0, \mathbf{\Omega}_0)$ is the $(\mathbf{\Pi}, \mathbf{\Omega})$ that maximizes this objective function.

The parameter space for $(\mathbf{\Pi}_0, \mathbf{\Omega}_0)$ is

$$\{(\mathbf{\Pi}, \mathbf{\Omega}) \mid \mathbf{\Omega} \text{ is symmetric and positive definite}\}.$$

Maximizing the Likelihood Function

We now prove that the solution to the maximization problem is numerically the same as the GMM estimator. That is, the ML estimator of $\mathbf{\Pi}_0$ is given by the GMM/OLS estimator $\widehat{\mathbf{\Pi}}$ in (8.4.5) and the ML estimate of $\mathbf{\Omega}_0$ is given by

$$\widehat{\mathbf{\Omega}} = \frac{1}{n}\sum_{t=1}^{n} \hat{\mathbf{v}}_t \hat{\mathbf{v}}_t' = \widehat{\mathbf{\Omega}}(\widehat{\mathbf{\Pi}}), \tag{8.4.12}$$

where $\hat{\mathbf{v}}_t \equiv \mathbf{y}_t - \widehat{\mathbf{\Pi}}'\mathbf{x}_t$.

It is left as Analytical Exercise 2 to show that, under the assumptions of the multivariate regression model stated above, $\widehat{\mathbf{\Omega}}(\mathbf{\Pi})$ is positive definite with probability one for any given $\mathbf{\Pi}$ for sufficiently large n. So we can assume that $\widehat{\mathbf{\Omega}}(\mathbf{\Pi})$ is positive definite, not just positive semidefinite. The proof that the GMM estimator is numerically the same as the ML estimator is based on the following two-step maximization of the objective function.

Step 1: The first step is to maximize $Q_n(\mathbf{\Pi}, \mathbf{\Omega})$ with respect to $\mathbf{\Omega}$, taking $\mathbf{\Pi}$ as given. For this purpose, the following fact from matrix algebra is useful.

> ***An Inequality Involving Trace and Determinant:***[6] Let $\mathbf{A}$ and $\mathbf{B}$ be two symmetric and positive definite matrices of the same size. Then the function
>
> $$f(\mathbf{A}) \equiv \log(|\mathbf{A}|) - \text{trace}(\mathbf{AB})$$
>
> is maximized uniquely by $\mathbf{A} = \mathbf{B}^{-1}$.

This result, with $\mathbf{A} = \mathbf{\Omega}^{-1}$ and $\mathbf{B} = \widehat{\mathbf{\Omega}}(\mathbf{\Pi})$, immediately implies that the objective function (8.4.11) is maximized uniquely by $\mathbf{\Omega} = \widehat{\mathbf{\Omega}}(\mathbf{\Pi})$, given $\mathbf{\Pi}$. Substituting this $\mathbf{\Omega}$ into (8.4.11) gives ($1/n$ times) the **concentrated log likelihood function** (concentrated with respect to $\mathbf{\Omega}$):

[6]This result is implied by Lemma A.6 of Johansen (1995). The uniqueness of the minimizer is due to the linearity of the trace operator and the strict concavity of $\log(|\mathbf{A}|)$ noted in Magnus and Neudecker (1988, p. 222).

$$
\begin{aligned}
Q_n^*(\mathbf{\Pi}) &\equiv Q_n(\mathbf{\Pi}, \widehat{\mathbf{\Omega}}(\mathbf{\Pi})) \\
&= -\frac{M}{2}\log(2\pi) + \frac{1}{2}\log(|\widehat{\mathbf{\Omega}}(\mathbf{\Pi})^{-1}|) - \frac{1}{2}\operatorname{trace}[\widehat{\mathbf{\Omega}}(\mathbf{\Pi})^{-1}\widehat{\mathbf{\Omega}}(\mathbf{\Pi})] \\
&= -\frac{M}{2}\log(2\pi) - \frac{1}{2}\log(|\widehat{\mathbf{\Omega}}(\mathbf{\Pi})|) - \frac{M}{2}. \qquad (8.4.13)
\end{aligned}
$$

Step 2: Looking at the concentrated log likelihood function $Q_n^*(\mathbf{\Pi})$, we see that the ML estimator of $\mathbf{\Pi}_0$ should minimize

$$
|\widehat{\mathbf{\Omega}}(\mathbf{\Pi})| = \left|\frac{1}{n}\sum_{t=1}^{n}(\mathbf{y}_t - \mathbf{\Pi}'\mathbf{x}_t)(\mathbf{y}_t - \mathbf{\Pi}'\mathbf{x}_t)'\right|. \qquad (8.4.14)
$$

It is left as Analytical Exercise 1 to show that this is minimized by the OLS estimator $\widehat{\mathbf{\Pi}}$ given in (8.4.5). Finally, setting $\mathbf{\Pi} = \widehat{\mathbf{\Pi}}$ in (8.4.10) gives (8.4.12).

Consistency and Asymptotic Normality

We have shown in Chapter 4, without the normality assumption (that $\boldsymbol{\varepsilon}_t \mid \mathbf{x}_t$ is normal) or the i.i.d. assumption for $\{y_t, \mathbf{x}_t\}$, that the GMM/OLS estimator $\widehat{\mathbf{\Pi}}$ in (8.4.5) is consistent and asymptotically normal and that $\widehat{\mathbf{\Omega}}$ in (8.4.12) is consistent. It then follows, trivially, that the ML estimator of $\mathbf{\Pi}_0$ is consistent and asymptotically normal and the ML estimator of $\mathbf{\Omega}_0$ is consistent. It is worth emphasizing that the ML estimator of $\mathbf{\Pi}_0$ based on the likelihood function that assumes normality is consistent and asymptotically normal even if the error term is not normally distributed.

We will not be concerned with the asymptotic normality of the ML estimator of $\mathbf{\Omega}_0$, $\widehat{\mathbf{\Omega}}(\widehat{\mathbf{\Pi}})$. One way to demonstrate the asymptotic normality would be to verify the conditions of the relevant asymptotic normality theorem of the previous chapter.

QUESTION FOR REVIEW

1. Prove (8.4.9). **Hint:** Use the following properties of the trace operator. (1) $\operatorname{trace}(x) = x$ if x is a scalar, (2) $\operatorname{trace}(\mathbf{A}+\mathbf{B}) = \operatorname{trace}(\mathbf{A}) + \operatorname{trace}(\mathbf{B})$, and (3) $\operatorname{trace}(\mathbf{AB}) = \operatorname{trace}(\mathbf{BA})$ provided $\mathbf{AB}$ and $\mathbf{BA}$ are well defined. The answer is

$$
\begin{aligned}
&\frac{1}{n}\sum_{t=1}^{n}(\mathbf{y}_t - \mathbf{\Pi}'\mathbf{x}_t)'\mathbf{\Omega}^{-1}(\mathbf{y}_t - \mathbf{\Pi}'\mathbf{x}_t) \\
&= \operatorname{trace}\left[\frac{1}{n}\sum_{t=1}^{n}(\mathbf{y}_t - \mathbf{\Pi}'\mathbf{x}_t)'\mathbf{\Omega}^{-1}(\mathbf{y}_t - \mathbf{\Pi}'\mathbf{x}_t)\right]
\end{aligned}
$$

$$= \frac{1}{n}\sum_{t=1}^{n} \text{trace}\big[(\mathbf{y}_t - \boldsymbol{\Pi}'\mathbf{x}_t)'\boldsymbol{\Omega}^{-1}(\mathbf{y}_t - \boldsymbol{\Pi}'\mathbf{x}_t)\big]$$

$$= \frac{1}{n}\sum_{t=1}^{n} \text{trace}\big[\boldsymbol{\Omega}^{-1}(\mathbf{y}_t - \boldsymbol{\Pi}'\mathbf{x}_t)(\mathbf{y}_t - \boldsymbol{\Pi}'\mathbf{x}_t)'\big]$$

$$= \text{trace}\left[\frac{1}{n}\sum_{t=1}^{n} \boldsymbol{\Omega}^{-1}(\mathbf{y}_t - \boldsymbol{\Pi}'\mathbf{x}_t)(\mathbf{y}_t - \boldsymbol{\Pi}'\mathbf{x}_t)'\right]$$

$$= \text{trace}\left[\boldsymbol{\Omega}^{-1}\frac{1}{n}\sum_{t=1}^{n} (\mathbf{y}_t - \boldsymbol{\Pi}'\mathbf{x}_t)(\mathbf{y}_t - \boldsymbol{\Pi}'\mathbf{x}_t)'\right].$$

8.5 FIML

As seen in Chapter 4, the multivariate regression model is a specialization of the seemingly unrelated regression (SUR) model, which in turn is a specialization of the multiple-equation system to which three-stage least squares (3SLS) is applicable. The two-stage least squares (2SLS) estimator is the GMM estimator when each equation of the system is estimated separately, while 3SLS is the GMM estimator when the system as a whole is estimated. This section presents the ML counterparts of 2SLS and 3SLS.

The Multiple-Equation Model with Common Instruments Restated

To refresh your memory, the model is an M-equation system described by Assumptions 4.1–4.5 and 4.7, with $\mathbf{x}_{tm} = \mathbf{x}_t$ for all $m = 1, 2, \ldots, M$ (so the set of instruments is the same across equations). Still maintaining the convention of denoting the true parameter value by subscript 0, we can write the M equations of the system as

$$y_{tm} = \underset{(1\times L_m)}{\mathbf{z}'_{tm}} \underset{(L_m\times 1)}{\boldsymbol{\delta}_{0m}} + \varepsilon_{tm} \quad (m = 1, 2, \ldots, M;\, t = 1, 2, \ldots, n). \tag{8.5.1}$$

The model has the following features.

- Unlike in the multivariate regression model, for each equation m, the regressors $\mathbf{z}_{tm}$ may not be orthogonal to the error term, but there are available K predetermined variables $\mathbf{x}_t$ that are known to satisfy the orthogonality conditions $\mathrm{E}(\mathbf{x}_t \cdot \varepsilon_{tm}) = \mathbf{0}$ for all m (this is Assumption 4.3). Defining the $M \times 1$ vector $\boldsymbol{\varepsilon}_t$ as

$$\underset{(M\times 1)}{\boldsymbol{\varepsilon}_t} = \begin{bmatrix} \varepsilon_{t1} \\ \varepsilon_{t2} \\ \vdots \\ \varepsilon_{tM} \end{bmatrix}, \tag{8.5.2}$$

the orthogonality conditions can be expressed as

$$\mathrm{E}(\mathbf{x}_t \boldsymbol{\varepsilon}_t') = \underset{(K\times M)}{\mathbf{0}}. \tag{8.5.3}$$

These K predetermined variables serve as the common set of instruments in the GMM estimation.

- The **endogenous variables** of the system are those variables (apart from the errors) in the system that are not included in $\mathbf{x}_t$.
- The rank condition for identification (Assumption 4.4) is that the $K \times L_m$ matrix $\mathrm{E}(\mathbf{x}_t \mathbf{z}_{tm}')$ be of full column rank for all m. Equation m is said to be **overidentified** if the rank condition is satisfied and $L_m < K$.
- The error vector is conditionally homoskedastic in that $\mathrm{E}(\boldsymbol{\varepsilon}_t \boldsymbol{\varepsilon}_t' \mid \mathbf{x}_t) = \boldsymbol{\Sigma}_0$, and $\boldsymbol{\Sigma}_0$ is positive definite (Assumption 4.7).
- $\mathrm{E}(\mathbf{x}_t \mathbf{x}_t')$ is nonsingular (a consequence of conditional homoskedasticity and the nonsingularity requirement in Assumption 4.5).

The GMM estimator for this system as a whole is the 3SLS estimator given in (4.5.12), while the single-equation GMM estimator of each equation in isolation is 2SLS given in (3.8.3).

The following examples will be used to illustrate the concepts to be introduced shortly.

Example 8.1 (A model of market equilibrium): An expanded version of Working's example considered in Section 3.1 is a two-equation system:

$$q_t = \gamma_{11} p_t + \beta_{11} + \beta_{12} a_t + \varepsilon_{t1} \quad \text{(demand)}, \tag{8.5.4}$$

$$q_t = \gamma_{21} p_t + \beta_{21} + \beta_{22} w_t + \varepsilon_{t2} \quad \text{(supply)}. \tag{8.5.5}$$

In this system, q_t is the amount of coffee transacted and p_t is the coffee price. The variable a_t appearing in the demand equation is a taste shifter, while the variable w_t is the amount of rainfall that affects the supply of coffee. The system can be cast in the general format by setting

$$y_{t1} = q_t,\ y_{t2} = q_t,\ \mathbf{z}_{t1} = \begin{bmatrix} p_t \\ 1 \\ a_t \end{bmatrix},\ \mathbf{z}_{t2} = \begin{bmatrix} p_t \\ 1 \\ w_t \end{bmatrix},$$

$$\boldsymbol{\delta}_{01} = \begin{bmatrix} \gamma_{11} \\ \beta_{11} \\ \beta_{12} \end{bmatrix},\ \boldsymbol{\delta}_{02} = \begin{bmatrix} \gamma_{21} \\ \beta_{21} \\ \beta_{22} \end{bmatrix}.$$

(Note that y_{t1} and y_{t2} are the same variable.) If $\mathrm{E}(\varepsilon_{tj}) = 0$, $\mathrm{E}(a_t \varepsilon_{tj}) = 0$, and $\mathrm{E}(w_t \varepsilon_{tj}) = 0$ for $j = 1, 2$, then $(1, a_t, w_t)$ can be included in the common set of instruments. So

$$\mathbf{x}_t = \begin{bmatrix} 1 \\ a_t \\ w_t \end{bmatrix}.$$

The other nonerror variables in the system, p_t and q_t, are endogenous variables. Provided that the rank condition for identification is satisfied, each equation is just identified because the number of right-hand side variables equals that of instruments.

Example 8.2 (Wage equation): In the empirical exercise of Chapter 3, we estimated a standard wage equation. Consider supplementing the wage equation by an equation explaining *KWW* (the score on the "Knowledge of the World of Work" test):

$$LW_t = \gamma_{11} S_t + \beta_{11} + \beta_{12} IQ_t + \varepsilon_{t1}, \tag{8.5.6}$$

$$KWW_t = \gamma_{21} S_t + \beta_{21} + \varepsilon_{t2}, \tag{8.5.7}$$

where S_t, for example, is years in schooling for individual t. Assume that $\mathrm{E}(\varepsilon_{tj}) = 0$ and $\mathrm{E}(IQ_t \varepsilon_{tj}) = 0$ for $j = 1, 2$. Assume also that there is a variable *MED* (mother's education), which does not appear in either equation but which is predetermined in that $\mathrm{E}(MED_t \varepsilon_{tj}) = 0$ for $j = 1, 2$. So the common set of instruments is $\mathbf{x}_t = (1, IQ_t, MED_t)'$. The rest of the nonerror variables in the system are endogenous variables. This two-equation system has *three* endogenous variables, *LW*, *S*, and *KWW*. Provided that the rank condition is satisfied, the first equation is just identified because the number of right-hand side variables equals the number of instruments, while the second equation is overidentified.

The Complete System of Simultaneous Equations

The ML counterpart of 3SLS is called the **full-information maximum likelihood (FIML) estimator**. If it is to be estimated by FIML, the multiple-equation model needs to be further specialized *before* introducing the normality and i.i.d. assumptions. The required specialization is that those M equations form a "complete" system of simultaneous equations. Completeness requires two things.

1. There are as many endogenous variables as there are equations. This condition implies that, if $\mathbf{y}_t$ is an M-dimensional vector collecting those M endogenous variables, then $(y_{t1}, \dots, y_{tM}, \mathbf{z}_{t1}, \dots, \mathbf{z}_{tM})$ are all elements of $(\mathbf{y}_t, \mathbf{x}_t)$, which allows one to write the M-equation system (8.5.1) as

$$\underset{(M\times M)}{\mathbf{\Gamma}_0}\underset{(M\times 1)}{\mathbf{y}_t} + \underset{(M\times K)}{\mathbf{B}_0}\underset{(K\times 1)}{\mathbf{x}_t} = \underset{(M\times 1)}{\boldsymbol{\varepsilon}_t} \quad (t = 1, 2, \dots, n), \tag{8.5.8}$$

   with the m-th equation being $y_{tm} = \mathbf{z}'_{tm}\boldsymbol{\delta}_{0m} + \varepsilon_{tm}$. (This is illustrated for Example 8.1 below.) The equation system written in this way is called the **structural form**, and $(\mathbf{\Gamma}_0, \mathbf{B}_0)$ are called the **structural form parameters**. As will be illustrated below, each of the structural form parameters is a function of $(\boldsymbol{\delta}_{01}, \dots, \boldsymbol{\delta}_{0M})$.

   The system in Example 8.1 satisfies this first requirement. The system in Example 8.2 is not a complete system because the number of endogenous variables is greater than the number of equations. It is not possible to estimate incomplete systems by FIML (unless we complete the system by adding appropriate equations, see the discussion about LIML below). This is in contrast to GMM; incomplete systems can be estimated by 3SLS (or more generally by multiple-equation GMM if conditional homoskedasticity is not assumed), as long as they satisfy the rank condition for identification.

2. The square matrix $\mathbf{\Gamma}_0$ is nonsingular. This implies that the structural form can be solved for the endogenous variables $\mathbf{y}_t$ as

$$\mathbf{y}_t = -\mathbf{\Gamma}_0^{-1}\mathbf{B}_0\mathbf{x}_t + \mathbf{\Gamma}_0^{-1}\boldsymbol{\varepsilon}_t \equiv \mathbf{\Pi}'_0\mathbf{x}_t + \mathbf{v}_t, \tag{8.5.9}$$

   where

$$\underset{(M\times K)}{\mathbf{\Pi}'_0} \equiv - \underset{(M\times M)}{\mathbf{\Gamma}_0}{}^{-1} \underset{(M\times K)}{\mathbf{B}_0}, \tag{8.5.10}$$

$$\underset{(M\times 1)}{\mathbf{v}_t} \equiv \underset{(M\times M)}{\mathbf{\Gamma}_0}{}^{-1} \underset{(M\times 1)}{\boldsymbol{\varepsilon}_t}. \tag{8.5.11}$$

   Expression (8.5.9) is known as the **reduced-form** representation of the structural form, and the elements of $\mathbf{\Pi}_0$ are called the **reduced-form coefficients**. In each equation of the reduced form, the regressors are the same set of variables, $\mathbf{x}_t$. From (8.5.3) and (8.5.11), it follows that $\mathrm{E}(\mathbf{x}_t \mathbf{v}_t') = \mathbf{0}$, namely, that all the regressors are predetermined. The reduced form, therefore, is a multivariate regression model.

Relationship between $(\boldsymbol{\Gamma}_0, \mathbf{B}_0)$ and $\boldsymbol{\delta}_0$

Let $\boldsymbol{\delta}_0$ be the stacked vector collecting all the coefficients in the M-equation system (8.5.1):

$$\underset{(\sum_{m=1}^{M} L_m \times 1)}{\boldsymbol{\delta}_0} = \begin{bmatrix} \boldsymbol{\delta}_{01} \\ \boldsymbol{\delta}_{02} \\ \vdots \\ \boldsymbol{\delta}_{0M} \end{bmatrix}. \tag{8.5.12}$$

For understanding the mechanics of FIML, it is important to see how the coefficient matrices $(\boldsymbol{\Gamma}_0, \mathbf{B}_0)$ depend on $\boldsymbol{\delta}_0$. To illustrate, consider Example 8.1. The $\boldsymbol{\delta}_0$ vector is

$$\underset{(6\times 1)}{\boldsymbol{\delta}_0} = \begin{bmatrix} \gamma_{11} \\ \beta_{11} \\ \beta_{12} \\ \gamma_{21} \\ \beta_{21} \\ \beta_{22} \end{bmatrix}. \tag{8.5.13}$$

The two endogenous variables are (p_t, q_t). It does not matter how the endogenous variables are ordered, so arbitrarily put p_t first in $\mathbf{y}_t$: $\mathbf{y}_t = (p_t, q_t)'$. The structural form parameters can be written as

$$\underset{(2\times 2)}{\boldsymbol{\Gamma}_0} = \begin{bmatrix} -\gamma_{11} & 1 \\ -\gamma_{21} & 1 \end{bmatrix}, \quad \underset{(2\times 3)}{\mathbf{B}_0} = \begin{bmatrix} -\beta_{11} & -\beta_{12} & 0 \\ -\beta_{21} & 0 & -\beta_{22} \end{bmatrix}. \tag{8.5.14}$$

This example serves to illustrate three points. First, each row of $\boldsymbol{\Gamma}_0$ has an element of unity, reflecting the fact that the coefficient of the dependent variable in each of the M equations (8.5.1) is unity. In this sense $\boldsymbol{\Gamma}_0$ is already normalized. Second, some elements of $\boldsymbol{\Gamma}_0$ and $\mathbf{B}_0$ are zeros, reflecting the fact that some endogenous or predetermined variables do not appear in certain equations of the M-equation system. This feature of the structural form coefficient matrices is called the **exclusion restrictions**. (In Example 8.1, no elements of $\boldsymbol{\Gamma}_0$ happen to be zero because the two endogenous variables appear in both equations.) Third, the system involves no cross-equation restrictions, so each element of δ_0 appears in $(\boldsymbol{\Gamma}_0, \mathbf{B}_0)$ just once.

The FIML Likelihood Function

To make the complete system of simultaneous equations estimable by FIML, we assume (1) that the structural error vector $\boldsymbol{\varepsilon}_t$ is jointly normal conditional on $\mathbf{x}_t$, i.e., $\boldsymbol{\varepsilon}_t \mid \mathbf{x}_t \sim N(\mathbf{0}, \boldsymbol{\Sigma}_0)$, and (2) that $\{\mathbf{y}_t, \mathbf{x}_t\}$ is i.i.d., not just ergodic stationary martingale differences (this assumption strengthens Assumptions 4.2 and 4.5).

By the normality assumption (1) about the structural errors $\boldsymbol{\varepsilon}_t$ and (8.5.11), we have $\mathbf{v}_t \mid \mathbf{x}_t \sim N(\mathbf{0}, \boldsymbol{\Gamma}_0^{-1}\boldsymbol{\Sigma}_0(\boldsymbol{\Gamma}_0^{-1})')$. Combining this and the reduced form $\mathbf{y}_t = \boldsymbol{\Pi}_0'\mathbf{x}_t + \mathbf{v}_t$ with (8.5.10) produces

$$\mathbf{y}_t \mid \mathbf{x}_t \sim N(-\boldsymbol{\Gamma}_0^{-1}\mathbf{B}_0\mathbf{x}_t, \boldsymbol{\Gamma}_0^{-1}\boldsymbol{\Sigma}_0(\boldsymbol{\Gamma}_0^{-1})'). \tag{8.5.15}$$

So the log conditional likelihood for observation t is

$$\begin{aligned}\log f(\mathbf{y}_t \mid \mathbf{x}_t; \boldsymbol{\delta}, \boldsymbol{\Sigma}) &= -\frac{M}{2}\log(2\pi) - \frac{1}{2}\log(|\boldsymbol{\Gamma}^{-1}\boldsymbol{\Sigma}(\boldsymbol{\Gamma}^{-1})'|) \\ &\quad - \frac{1}{2}[\mathbf{y}_t + \boldsymbol{\Gamma}^{-1}\mathbf{B}\mathbf{x}_t]'\big[\boldsymbol{\Gamma}^{-1}\boldsymbol{\Sigma}(\boldsymbol{\Gamma}^{-1})'\big]^{-1}[\mathbf{y}_t + \boldsymbol{\Gamma}^{-1}\mathbf{B}\mathbf{x}_t]. \end{aligned} \tag{8.5.16}$$

The likelihood is a function of $(\boldsymbol{\delta}, \boldsymbol{\Sigma})$ because, as illustrated in (8.5.14), the structural form coefficients $(\boldsymbol{\Gamma}, \mathbf{B})$ are functions of $\boldsymbol{\delta}$. Now

$$\begin{aligned}&[\mathbf{y}_t + \boldsymbol{\Gamma}^{-1}\mathbf{B}\mathbf{x}_t]'\big[\boldsymbol{\Gamma}^{-1}\boldsymbol{\Sigma}(\boldsymbol{\Gamma}^{-1})'\big]^{-1}[\mathbf{y}_t + \boldsymbol{\Gamma}^{-1}\mathbf{B}\mathbf{x}_t] \\ &= [\mathbf{y}_t + \boldsymbol{\Gamma}^{-1}\mathbf{B}\mathbf{x}_t]'\big[\boldsymbol{\Gamma}'\boldsymbol{\Sigma}^{-1}\boldsymbol{\Gamma}\big][\mathbf{y}_t + \boldsymbol{\Gamma}^{-1}\mathbf{B}\mathbf{x}_t] \\ &= \big[\boldsymbol{\Gamma}\mathbf{y}_t + \mathbf{B}\mathbf{x}_t\big]'\boldsymbol{\Sigma}^{-1}\big[\boldsymbol{\Gamma}\mathbf{y}_t + \mathbf{B}\mathbf{x}_t\big]\end{aligned} \tag{8.5.17}$$

and

$$|\boldsymbol{\Gamma}^{-1}\boldsymbol{\Sigma}(\boldsymbol{\Gamma}^{-1})'| = |\boldsymbol{\Gamma}^{-1}||\boldsymbol{\Sigma}||(\boldsymbol{\Gamma}^{-1})'| = |\boldsymbol{\Sigma}|/|\boldsymbol{\Gamma}|^2. \tag{8.5.18}$$

Substituting these into (8.5.16),

$$\begin{aligned}\log f(\mathbf{y}_t \mid \mathbf{x}_t; \boldsymbol{\delta}, \boldsymbol{\Sigma}) &= -\frac{M}{2}\log(2\pi) + \frac{1}{2}\log(|\boldsymbol{\Gamma}|^2) - \frac{1}{2}\log(|\boldsymbol{\Sigma}|) \\ &\quad - \frac{1}{2}\big[\boldsymbol{\Gamma}\mathbf{y}_t + \mathbf{B}\mathbf{x}_t\big]'\boldsymbol{\Sigma}^{-1}\big[\boldsymbol{\Gamma}\mathbf{y}_t + \mathbf{B}\mathbf{x}_t\big].\end{aligned} \tag{8.5.19}$$

Taking the average over t, we obtain the FIML objective function for a random sample:

$$Q_n(\boldsymbol{\delta}, \boldsymbol{\Sigma}) = -\frac{M}{2}\log(2\pi) + \frac{1}{2}\log(|\boldsymbol{\Gamma}|^2) - \frac{1}{2}\log(|\boldsymbol{\Sigma}|) - \frac{1}{2n}\sum_{t=1}^{n}\big[\boldsymbol{\Gamma}\mathbf{y}_t + \mathbf{B}\mathbf{x}_t\big]'\boldsymbol{\Sigma}^{-1}\big[\boldsymbol{\Gamma}\mathbf{y}_t + \mathbf{B}\mathbf{x}_t\big]. \quad (8.5.20)$$

The FIML estimate of $(\boldsymbol{\delta}_0, \boldsymbol{\Sigma}_0)$ is the $(\boldsymbol{\delta}, \boldsymbol{\Sigma})$ that maximizes this objective function.

The FIML Concentrated Likelihood Function

As in the maximization of the objective function of the multivariate regression model, we can proceed in two steps. The first step is to maximize $Q_n(\boldsymbol{\delta}, \boldsymbol{\Sigma})$ with respect to $\boldsymbol{\Sigma}$ given $\boldsymbol{\delta}$. This yields

$$\underset{(M\times M)}{\widehat{\boldsymbol{\Sigma}}(\boldsymbol{\delta})} = \frac{1}{n}\sum_{t=1}^{n}(\boldsymbol{\Gamma}\mathbf{y}_t + \mathbf{B}\mathbf{x}_t)(\boldsymbol{\Gamma}\mathbf{y}_t + \mathbf{B}\mathbf{x}_t)'. \quad (8.5.21)$$

Its (m, h) element can be written as

$$\hat{\sigma}_{mh} = \frac{1}{n}\sum_{t=1}^{n}(y_{tm} - \mathbf{z}_{tm}'\boldsymbol{\delta}_m)(y_{th} - \mathbf{z}_{th}'\boldsymbol{\delta}_h). \quad (8.5.22)$$

By substituting (8.5.21) back into the objective function (8.5.20), ($1/n$ times) the FIML concentrated likelihood function can be derived as

$$\begin{aligned} Q_n^*(\boldsymbol{\delta}) &\equiv Q_n(\boldsymbol{\delta}, \widehat{\boldsymbol{\Sigma}}(\boldsymbol{\delta})) \\ &= -\frac{M}{2}\log(2\pi) - \frac{M}{2} + \frac{1}{2}\log(|\boldsymbol{\Gamma}|^2) - \frac{1}{2}\log(|\widehat{\boldsymbol{\Sigma}}(\boldsymbol{\delta})|) \\ &= -\frac{M}{2}\log(2\pi) - \frac{M}{2} - \frac{1}{2}\log\left|\frac{1}{n}\sum_{t=1}^{n}(\mathbf{y}_t + \boldsymbol{\Gamma}^{-1}\mathbf{B}\mathbf{x}_t)(\mathbf{y}_t + \boldsymbol{\Gamma}^{-1}\mathbf{B}\mathbf{x}_t)'\right|. \end{aligned} \quad (8.5.23)$$

The second step is to maximize this FIML concentrated likelihood with respect to $\boldsymbol{\delta}$. The FIML estimator $\hat{\boldsymbol{\delta}}$ of $\boldsymbol{\delta}_0$ is the $\boldsymbol{\delta}$ that maximizes this function.[7] The FIML estimator of $\boldsymbol{\Sigma}_0$ is $\widehat{\boldsymbol{\Sigma}}(\hat{\boldsymbol{\delta}})$.

[7] So the FIML estimator $\hat{\boldsymbol{\delta}}$ is an extremum estimator that maximizes

$$-\left|\frac{1}{n}\sum_{t=1}^{n}(\mathbf{y}_t + \boldsymbol{\Gamma}^{-1}\mathbf{B}\mathbf{x}_t)(\mathbf{y}_t + \boldsymbol{\Gamma}^{-1}\mathbf{B}\mathbf{x}_t)'\right|.$$

Some aspects of this extremum estimator are explored in an optional analytical exercise (see Analytical Exercise 3).

Testing Overidentifying Restrictions

Now compare this FIML concentrated likelihood $Q_n^*(\boldsymbol{\delta})$ given in (8.5.23) with that for the multivariate regression model, $Q_n^*(\boldsymbol{\Pi})$ given in (8.4.13). The FIML concentrated likelihood $Q_n^*(\boldsymbol{\delta})$ is what obtains when we impose on $Q_n^*(\boldsymbol{\Pi})$ the restrictions implied by the null hypothesis that

$$\mathrm{H}_0: \boldsymbol{\Pi}_0' = -\boldsymbol{\Gamma}_0^{-1}\mathbf{B}_0 \text{ or } \boldsymbol{\Gamma}_0\boldsymbol{\Pi}_0' + \mathbf{B}_0 = \mathbf{0}. \tag{8.5.24}$$

Put differently, FIML estimation of $\boldsymbol{\delta}_0$ is a constrained multivariate regression. Therefore, the truth of the null hypothesis can be tested by the likelihood ratio principle. Since the OLS estimator $\widehat{\boldsymbol{\Pi}}$ given in (8.4.5) maximizes the multivariate regression concentrated likelihood function $Q_n^*(\boldsymbol{\Pi})$ given in (8.4.13) and the FIML estimator $\hat{\boldsymbol{\delta}}$ maximizes the FIML concentrated likelihood function $Q_n^*(\hat{\boldsymbol{\delta}})$ given in (8.5.23), the likelihood ratio test statistic is

$$\begin{aligned} LR &= 2n \cdot (Q_n^*(\widehat{\boldsymbol{\Pi}}) - Q_n^*(\hat{\boldsymbol{\delta}})) \\ &= n \times \left(\log\left|\widehat{\boldsymbol{\Omega}}(-(\widehat{\boldsymbol{\Gamma}}^{-1}\widehat{\mathbf{B}})')\right| - \log|\widehat{\boldsymbol{\Omega}}(\widehat{\boldsymbol{\Pi}})|\right), \end{aligned} \tag{8.5.25}$$

where $\widehat{\boldsymbol{\Omega}}(\boldsymbol{\Pi})$ is defined in (8.4.10) and $(\widehat{\boldsymbol{\Gamma}}, \widehat{\mathbf{B}})$ is the value of $(\boldsymbol{\Gamma}, \mathbf{B})$ implied by $\hat{\boldsymbol{\delta}}$. Since the dimension of $\boldsymbol{\delta}$ equals $\sum_{m=1}^{M} L_m$, the number of restrictions implied by the null hypothesis H_0 above is

$$KM - \sum_{m=1}^{M} L_m = \sum_{m=1}^{M}(K - L_m), \tag{8.5.26}$$

which is the total number of overidentifying restrictions of the system. Therefore, the likelihood ratio test based on the *LR* statistic (8.5.25) is a **test of overidentifying restrictions**. It is a specification test because the restriction being tested is a condition assumed in the model.

Properties of the FIML Estimator

There is no closed-form solution to the FIML estimator. So, in order to establish the consistency and asymptotic normality, we would have to verify the conditions of relevant theorems of the previous chapter. We summarize here, without proof, the main properties of the FIML estimator.

Identification

Stating the identification condition in various forms for complete simultaneous equations systems is a major topic in most textbooks. Here it is left as an optional analytical exercise (Analytical Exercise 3) to show that the identification condition for FIML as an extremum estimator is equivalent to the rank condition for identification (that $E(\mathbf{x}_t \mathbf{z}'_{tm})$ be of full column rank for all $m = 1, 2, \dots, M$).

Asymptotic Properties

Although the FIML objective function (8.5.20) is derived under the normality of $\boldsymbol{\varepsilon}_t \mid \mathbf{x}_t$, the FIML estimator of $\boldsymbol{\delta}_0$ is consistent and asymptotically normal without the normality assumption. For a proof of consistency without normality, see, e.g., Amemiya (1985, pp. 232–233). There is a nice proof of asymptotic normality of $\hat{\boldsymbol{\delta}}$ due to Hausman (1975), which shows that an iterative instrumental variable estimation can be viewed as an algorithm for solving the first-order conditions for the maximization of $Q_n(\boldsymbol{\delta}, \boldsymbol{\Sigma})$.[8] This argument shows that the FIML estimator of $\boldsymbol{\delta}_0$ is asymptotically equivalent to the 3SLS estimator.[9] Therefore, its asymptotic variance is given by (4.5.15), and a consistent estimator of the asymptotic variance is (4.5.17).

Invariance

Since the FIML estimator is an ML estimator, it has the invariance property discussed in Section 7.1. To illustrate, consider Example 8.1 and suppose you wish to reparameterize the supply equation as

$$p_t = \tilde{\gamma}_{21} q_t + \widetilde{\beta}_{21} + \widetilde{\beta}_{22} w_t + \tilde{\varepsilon}_{t2} \quad \text{(supply)}. \tag{8.5.27}$$

The old supply parameters $(\gamma_{21}, \beta_{21}, \beta_{22})$ and the new supply parameters $(\tilde{\gamma}_{21}, \widetilde{\beta}_{21}, \widetilde{\beta}_{22})$ are connected by the one-to-one mapping

$$\tilde{\gamma}_{21} = 1/\gamma_{21}, \widetilde{\beta}_{21} = -\beta_{21}/\gamma_{21}, \widetilde{\beta}_{22} = -\beta_{22}/\gamma_{21}. \tag{8.5.28}$$

If $(\hat{\gamma}_{21}, \widehat{\beta}_{21}, \widehat{\beta}_{22})$ is the FIML estimator of $(\gamma_{21}, \beta_{21}, \beta_{22})$ for the system consisting of the demand equation (8.5.4) and the old supply equation (8.5.5), then the FIML estimator based on the system consisting of (8.5.4) and the new supply equation is numerically the same as the value of the above mapping at $(\hat{\gamma}_{21}, \widehat{\beta}_{21}, \widehat{\beta}_{22})$. The 3SLS estimator (and 2SLS for that matter) does not have this invariance property.

[8] We will not display the first-order conditions (the likelihood equations) for FIML because it requires some cumbersome matrix notation. See Amemiya (1985, pp. 233–234) or Davidson and MacKinnon (1993, pp. 658–660) for more details. For the SUR model, the likelihood equations and the iterative procedure are much easier to describe; see the next subsection.

[9] This asymptotic equivalence does not carry over to nonlinear equation systems; nonlinear FIML is more efficient than nonlinear 3SLS. See Amemiya (1985, Section 8.2).

The foregoing discussion about FIML can be summarized as

Proposition 8.1 (Asymptotic properties of FIML): *Consider the M-equation system (8.5.1) and let $\boldsymbol{\delta}_0$ be the stacked vector collecting all the coefficients in the M-equation system. Make the following assumptions.*

- *the rank condition for identification (that* $\mathrm{E}(\mathbf{x}_t \mathbf{z}'_{tm})$ *be of full column rank for all* $m = 1, 2, \dots, M$*) is satisfied,*
- $\mathrm{E}(\mathbf{x}_t \mathbf{x}'_t)$ *is nonsingular,*
- *the M-equation system can be written as a complete system of simultaneous equations (8.5.8) with* $\boldsymbol{\Gamma}_0$ *nonsingular,*
- $\boldsymbol{\varepsilon}_t \mid \mathbf{x}_t \sim N(\mathbf{0}, \boldsymbol{\Sigma}_0)$, $\boldsymbol{\Sigma}_0$ *positive definite,*
- $\{\mathbf{y}_t, \mathbf{x}_t\}$ *is i.i.d.,*
- *the parameter space for* $(\boldsymbol{\delta}_0, \boldsymbol{\Sigma}_0)$ *is compact with the true parameter vector* $(\boldsymbol{\delta}_0, \boldsymbol{\Sigma}_0)$ *included as an interior point.*

Then

(a) the FIML estimator $(\hat{\boldsymbol{\delta}}, \widehat{\boldsymbol{\Sigma}})$*, which maximizes (8.5.20), is consistent and asymptotically normal,*

(b) the asymptotic variance of $\hat{\boldsymbol{\delta}}$ *is given by (4.5.15), and a consistent estimator of the asymptotic variance is (4.5.17) where* $\hat{\sigma}^{mh}$ *is the* (m, h) *element of* $\widehat{\boldsymbol{\Sigma}}^{-1}$*,*

(c) the likelihood ratio statistic (8.5.25) for testing overidentifying restrictions is asymptotically χ^2 *with* $KM - \sum_{m=1}^{M} L_m$ *degrees of freedom.*

Furthermore, these asymptotic results about $\hat{\boldsymbol{\delta}}$ *hold even if* $\boldsymbol{\varepsilon}_t \mid \mathbf{x}_t$ *is not normal.*

ML Estimation of the SUR Model

The SUR model is a specialization of the FIML model with $\mathbf{z}_{tm}$ being a subvector of $\mathbf{x}_t$. It is therefore an M-equation system (8.5.1) where the regressors $\mathbf{z}_{tm}$ are predetermined. Unlike in the multivariate regression model, the set of regressors could differ across equations. It is easy to show (see Review Question 3) that no two dependent variables can be the same variable, so $\mathbf{y}_t$ $(M \times 1)$ in the structural form (8.5.8) simply collects the M dependent variables. Furthermore, since $\mathbf{z}_{tm}$ includes no endogenous variables, $\boldsymbol{\Gamma}_0$ in the structural form is the identity matrix. Thus, the FIML objective function (8.5.20) becomes

$$Q_n(\boldsymbol{\delta}, \boldsymbol{\Sigma}) = -\frac{M}{2}\log(2\pi) - \frac{1}{2}\log(|\boldsymbol{\Sigma}|) - \frac{1}{2n}\sum_{t=1}^{n}[\boldsymbol{\Gamma}\mathbf{y}_t + \mathbf{B}\mathbf{x}_t]'\boldsymbol{\Sigma}^{-1}[\boldsymbol{\Gamma}\mathbf{y}_t + \mathbf{B}\mathbf{x}_t], \tag{8.5.29}$$

where $\boldsymbol{\Gamma}$ is understood to be the identity matrix. (We continue to carry $\boldsymbol{\Gamma}$ around in order to facilitate the comparison to the objective function for LIML to be introduced in the next subsection.) As in FIML, the $\boldsymbol{\Sigma}$ that maximizes the objective function given $\boldsymbol{\delta}$ is given by $\widehat{\boldsymbol{\Sigma}}(\boldsymbol{\delta})$ in (8.5.21).

For the SUR model, the score with respect to $\boldsymbol{\delta}$ can be written down rather easily. The m-th row of $\boldsymbol{\Gamma}\mathbf{y}_t + \mathbf{B}\mathbf{x}_t$ is $y_{tm} - \mathbf{z}'_{tm}\boldsymbol{\delta}_m$. Define $\mathbf{y}$ ($Mn \times 1$) and $\mathbf{Z}$ ($Mn \times \sum_{m=1}^{M} L_m$) as in the first analytical exercise to Chapter 4. Then

$$\sum_{t=1}^{n}[\boldsymbol{\Gamma}\mathbf{y}_t + \mathbf{B}\mathbf{x}_t]'\boldsymbol{\Sigma}^{-1}[\boldsymbol{\Gamma}\mathbf{y}_t + \mathbf{B}\mathbf{x}_t] = (\mathbf{y} - \mathbf{Z}\boldsymbol{\delta})'(\boldsymbol{\Sigma}^{-1} \otimes \mathbf{I}_n)(\mathbf{y} - \mathbf{Z}\boldsymbol{\delta}). \tag{8.5.30}$$

Therefore,

$$\frac{\partial Q_n(\boldsymbol{\delta}, \boldsymbol{\Sigma})}{\partial \boldsymbol{\delta}} = \frac{1}{n}\mathbf{Z}'(\boldsymbol{\Sigma}^{-1} \otimes \mathbf{I}_n)(\mathbf{y} - \mathbf{Z}\boldsymbol{\delta}). \tag{8.5.31}$$

(Doing the same for the more general case of FIML is not as easy because, although (8.5.30) holds for FIML as well, the score $\frac{\partial Q_n}{\partial \boldsymbol{\delta}}$ is more complicated thanks to the term $\log(|\boldsymbol{\Gamma}|^2)$ in the FIML likelihood function. Put differently, if $|\boldsymbol{\Gamma}|$ is a constant (i.e., independent of $\boldsymbol{\delta}$), then $\frac{\partial Q_n}{\partial \boldsymbol{\delta}}$ for FIML is the same as (8.5.31).) Setting this equal to zero and solving for $\boldsymbol{\delta}$, we obtain

$$\hat{\boldsymbol{\delta}}(\boldsymbol{\Sigma}) \equiv \left[\mathbf{Z}'(\boldsymbol{\Sigma}^{-1} \otimes \mathbf{I}_n)\mathbf{Z}\right]^{-1}\mathbf{Z}'(\boldsymbol{\Sigma}^{-1} \otimes \mathbf{I}_n)\mathbf{y}. \tag{8.5.32}$$

Given some consistent estimator $\widehat{\boldsymbol{\Sigma}}$ of $\boldsymbol{\Sigma}_0$, $\hat{\boldsymbol{\delta}}(\widehat{\boldsymbol{\Sigma}})$ is the SUR estimator of $\boldsymbol{\delta}_0$ derived in Chapter 4.

These two functions $(\hat{\boldsymbol{\delta}}(\boldsymbol{\Sigma}), \widehat{\boldsymbol{\Sigma}}(\boldsymbol{\delta}))$ define a mapping from the parameter space for $(\boldsymbol{\delta}, \boldsymbol{\Sigma})$ to itself, and a solution to the first-order conditions for the maximization of $Q_n(\boldsymbol{\delta}, \boldsymbol{\Sigma})$ is a fixed point in this mapping. Such a fixed point can be calculated by the following **iterative SUR**. Let $(\hat{\boldsymbol{\delta}}^{(j)}, \widehat{\boldsymbol{\Sigma}}^{(j)})$ be the estimate of $(\boldsymbol{\delta}_0, \boldsymbol{\Sigma}_0)$ in the j-th iteration. The estimate in the next iteration is

$$\hat{\boldsymbol{\delta}}^{(j+1)} = \hat{\boldsymbol{\delta}}(\widehat{\boldsymbol{\Sigma}}^{(j)}),\ \widehat{\boldsymbol{\Sigma}}^{(j+1)} = \widehat{\boldsymbol{\Sigma}}(\hat{\boldsymbol{\delta}}^{(j+1)}). \tag{8.5.33}$$

The first part of this iteration is the SUR estimation given $\widehat{\boldsymbol{\Sigma}}^{(j)}$, while the latter part updates the estimate of $\mathbf{\Sigma}_0$ using the current estimate of $\boldsymbol{\delta}_0$. If this process converges, then the limit is a solution to the first-order conditions.

QUESTIONS FOR REVIEW

1. (Deriving $f(\mathbf{y}_t \mid \mathbf{x}_t)$ from $f(\boldsymbol{\varepsilon}_t \mid \mathbf{x}_t)$) In this exercise, we wish to derive the likelihood for observation t for the FIML model by the following fact from probability theory:

   Change of Variable Formula: Suppose $\boldsymbol{\varepsilon}$ is a continuous M-dimensional random vector with density $f_{\boldsymbol{\varepsilon}}(\boldsymbol{\varepsilon})$ and $\mathbf{g} : \mathbb{R}^M \to \mathbb{R}^M$ is a one-to-one and differentiable mapping on an open set S, with the inverse mapping denoted as $\mathbf{g}^{-1}(\cdot)$. Let the $M \times M$ matrix $\mathbf{J}(\varepsilon)$ be the Jacobian matrix $\frac{\partial \mathbf{g}(\boldsymbol{\varepsilon})}{\partial \boldsymbol{\varepsilon}'}$ (the $M \times M$ matrix of partial derivatives, whose (i, j) element is $\frac{\partial g_i(\boldsymbol{\varepsilon})}{\partial \varepsilon_j}$). Assume that $|\mathbf{J}(\boldsymbol{\varepsilon})|$ is not zero at any point in S. Then the density of $\mathbf{y} = \mathbf{g}(\boldsymbol{\varepsilon})$ is given by

   $$f(\mathbf{y}) = \frac{f_{\boldsymbol{\varepsilon}}(\mathbf{g}^{-1}(\mathbf{y}))}{\text{abs}(|\mathbf{J}(\mathbf{g}^{-1}(\mathbf{y}))|)}.$$

   (Note that $|\mathbf{J}(\mathbf{g}^{-1}(\mathbf{y}))|$ is a determinant, which may or may not be positive.) Using this fact, derive the density of $\mathbf{y}_t \mid \mathbf{x}_t$ from the density of $\boldsymbol{\varepsilon}_t \mid \mathbf{x}_t$ and verify that the associated log likelihood is given by (8.5.16). **Hint:** The inverse mapping $\mathbf{g}^{-1}(\mathbf{y}_t)$ is the left-hand side of (8.5.8). So $\mathbf{J}(\boldsymbol{\varepsilon}_t) = \mathbf{\Gamma}_0^{-1}$. Also, $\log(\text{abs}(|\mathbf{\Gamma}|)) = \frac{1}{2}\log(|\mathbf{\Gamma}|^2)$.

2. (Instruments outside the system) Consider the complete system of simultaneous equations (8.5.8) with $|\mathbf{\Gamma}_0| \neq 0$. Suppose that one of the K predetermined variables, say x_{tK}, does not appear in any of the M-equations. Let $\widehat{\text{E}}^*(y \mid \mathbf{x})$ be the least squares projection of y on $\mathbf{x}$. Show that $\widehat{\text{E}}^*(y_{tm} \mid \mathbf{x}_t) = \widehat{\text{E}}^*(y_{tm} \mid \tilde{\mathbf{x}}_t)$, where $\tilde{\mathbf{x}}_t = (x_{t1}, \dots, x_{t,K-1})'$ (so $\mathbf{x}_t = (\tilde{\mathbf{x}}_t', x_{tK})'$). (As you will show in Analytical Exercise 4, including x_{tK} in the list of instruments in addition to $\tilde{\mathbf{x}}_t$ will not change the asymptotic variance of the FIML estimator of $\boldsymbol{\delta}_0$; it probably makes the small sample properties only worse.)

3. Recall that in Example 8.1 y_{t1} and y_{t2} are the same variable. In the SUR model, this cannot happen; that is, no two elements of $(y_{t1}, y_{t2}, \dots, y_{tM})$ are the same variable if the assumptions describing the model are satisfied. Prove this. **Hint:** Suppose y_{t1} and y_{t2} are the same variable. Then

   $$\varepsilon_{t1} - \varepsilon_{t2} = \mathbf{z}_{t1}'\boldsymbol{\delta}_{0,1} - \mathbf{z}_{t2}'\boldsymbol{\delta}_{0,2}.$$

Since $\mathbf{z}_{t1}$ and $\mathbf{z}_{t2}$ are subvectors of $\mathbf{x}_t$, the right-hand side can be written as $\mathbf{x}_t'\boldsymbol{\alpha}$ for some K-dimensional vector $\boldsymbol{\alpha}$. Use the orthogonality conditions that $\mathrm{E}(\mathbf{x}_t\boldsymbol{\varepsilon}_t') = \mathbf{0}$ and the nonsingularity of $\mathrm{E}(\mathbf{x}_t\mathbf{x}_t')$ to show that $\boldsymbol{\alpha} = \mathbf{0}$.

8.6 LIML

LIML Defined

The advantage of the FIML estimator is that it allows you to exploit all the information afforded by the complete system of simultaneous equations. This, however, is also a weakness because, as is true with any other system or joint estimation procedure, the estimator is not consistent if any part of the system is misspecified. If you are confident that the equation in question is correctly specified but not so sure about the rest of the system, you may well prefer to employ single-equation methods such as 2SLS. The rest of this section derives the ML estimator called the **limited-information maximum likelihood (LIML) estimator**, which is the ML counterpart of 2SLS.

Let the m-th equation of the M-equation system be the equation of interest. The L_m regressors, $\mathbf{z}_{tm}$, are either endogenous or predetermined. Let $\tilde{\mathbf{y}}_t$ be the vector of M_m endogenous variables and $\tilde{\mathbf{x}}_t$ be the vector of K_m predetermined variables, with $M_m + K_m = L_m$. Partition $\boldsymbol{\delta}_{0m}$ conformably as $\boldsymbol{\delta}_{0m} = (\boldsymbol{\gamma}_{0m}', \boldsymbol{\beta}_{0m}')'$. Then the m-th equation can be written as

$$y_{tm} = \underset{(1\times L_m)}{\mathbf{z}_{tm}'}\underset{(L_m\times 1)}{\boldsymbol{\delta}_{0m}} + \varepsilon_{tm} = \underset{(1\times M_m)}{\tilde{\mathbf{y}}_t'}\underset{(M_m\times 1)}{\boldsymbol{\gamma}_{0m}} + \underset{(1\times K_m)}{\tilde{\mathbf{x}}_t'}\underset{(K_m\times 1)}{\boldsymbol{\beta}_{0m}} + \varepsilon_{tm}. \tag{8.6.1}$$

Obviously, this single equation in isolation is an incomplete system because of the existence of the M_m included endogenous variables $\tilde{\mathbf{y}}_t$. However, if this equation is supplemented by the M_m reduced-form equations for $\tilde{\mathbf{y}}_t$ taken from (8.5.9), then the system of $1 + M_m$ equations thus formed is a complete system of simultaneous equations. To describe this idea more fully, let $\boldsymbol{\Pi}_0$ be the associated reduced-form coefficient matrix and collect appropriate M_m columns from $\boldsymbol{\Pi}_0$ and write the reduced-form equations for the M_m included endogenous variables as

$$\underset{(M_m\times 1)}{\tilde{\mathbf{y}}_t} = \underset{(M_m\times K)}{\tilde{\boldsymbol{\Pi}}_0'}\underset{(K\times 1)}{\mathbf{x}_t} + \underset{(M_m\times 1)}{\tilde{\mathbf{v}}_t}. \tag{8.6.2}$$

Combining (8.6.1) and (8.6.2), we obtain the system of $1 + M_m$ equations:

$$\underset{((1+M_m)\times(1+M_m))}{\overline{\boldsymbol{\Gamma}}_0} \underset{((1+M_m)\times 1)}{\bar{\mathbf{y}}_t} + \underset{((1+M_m)\times K)}{\overline{\mathbf{B}}_0} \underset{(K\times 1)}{\mathbf{x}_t} = \underset{((1+M_m)\times 1)}{\bar{\boldsymbol{\varepsilon}}_t}, \tag{8.6.3}$$

where

$$\bar{\mathbf{y}}_t \equiv \begin{bmatrix} y_{tm} \\ \underset{(M_m\times 1)}{\tilde{\mathbf{y}}_t} \end{bmatrix}, \quad \bar{\boldsymbol{\varepsilon}}_t \equiv \begin{bmatrix} \varepsilon_{tm} \\ \underset{(M_m\times 1)}{\tilde{\mathbf{v}}_t} \end{bmatrix},$$

$$\overline{\boldsymbol{\Gamma}}_0 \equiv \begin{bmatrix} 1 & -\underset{(1\times M_m)}{\boldsymbol{\gamma}'_{0m}} \\ \underset{(M_m\times 1)}{\mathbf{0}} & \mathbf{I}_{M_m} \end{bmatrix}, \quad \overline{\mathbf{B}}_0 \equiv \begin{bmatrix} -\underset{(1\times K_m)}{\boldsymbol{\beta}'_{0m}} & \underset{(1\times(K-K_m))}{\mathbf{0}'} \\ -\underset{(M_m\times K)}{\widetilde{\boldsymbol{\Pi}}'_0} & \end{bmatrix}. \tag{8.6.4}$$

Here, we have assumed, without loss of generality, that the included predetermined variables $\tilde{\mathbf{x}}_t$ are the first K_m elements of $\mathbf{x}_t$. The equation system (8.6.3) is a complete system of $1 + M_m$ simultaneous equations because

$$|\overline{\boldsymbol{\Gamma}}_0| = 1 \neq 0. \tag{8.6.5}$$

For example, consider Example 8.2. The included endogenous variable in the wage equation is S_t. Supplement the wage equation by a reduced-form equation for S_t, a regression of S_t on a constant, IQ_t, and MED_t. The $\overline{\boldsymbol{\Gamma}}_0$ matrix for the two-equation system that results is

$$\overline{\boldsymbol{\Gamma}}_0 = \begin{bmatrix} 1 & -\gamma_{11} \\ 0 & 1 \end{bmatrix}.$$

The hypothetical value $\overline{\boldsymbol{\Gamma}}$ of $\overline{\boldsymbol{\Gamma}}_0$ has the same structure shown in (8.6.4) for $\overline{\boldsymbol{\Gamma}}_0$. So $|\overline{\boldsymbol{\Gamma}}| = 1$. Replacing in the FIML objective function (8.5.20) $(\boldsymbol{\delta}, \mathbf{B})$ by $(\boldsymbol{\gamma}_m, \boldsymbol{\beta}_m, \overline{\boldsymbol{\Pi}})$, $\boldsymbol{\Gamma}$ by $\overline{\boldsymbol{\Gamma}}$, and $\boldsymbol{\Sigma}$ by $\overline{\boldsymbol{\Sigma}}$, and noting that $|\overline{\boldsymbol{\Gamma}}| = 1$, we obtain the LIML objective function:

$$\begin{aligned} Q_n(\boldsymbol{\gamma}_m, \boldsymbol{\beta}_m, \overline{\boldsymbol{\Pi}}, \overline{\boldsymbol{\Sigma}}) = &-\frac{M_m}{2}\log(2\pi) - \frac{1}{2}\log(|\overline{\boldsymbol{\Sigma}}|) \\ &- \frac{1}{2n}\sum_{t=1}^{n}\left[\overline{\boldsymbol{\Gamma}}\bar{\mathbf{y}}_t + \overline{\mathbf{B}}\mathbf{x}_t\right]'\overline{\boldsymbol{\Sigma}}^{-1}\left[\overline{\boldsymbol{\Gamma}}\bar{\mathbf{y}}_t + \overline{\mathbf{B}}\mathbf{x}_t\right], \end{aligned} \tag{8.6.6}$$

where $\overline{\boldsymbol{\Sigma}}$ is the $(1 + M_m) \times (1 + M_m)$ variance matrix of $\bar{\boldsymbol{\varepsilon}}_t$. Let $(\hat{\boldsymbol{\gamma}}_m, \widehat{\boldsymbol{\beta}}_m, \widehat{\overline{\boldsymbol{\Pi}}}, \widehat{\overline{\boldsymbol{\Sigma}}})$ be the FIML estimator of this system. The **LIML estimator** of $\boldsymbol{\delta}_{0m} = (\boldsymbol{\gamma}'_{0m}, \boldsymbol{\beta}'_{0m})'$ is $(\hat{\boldsymbol{\gamma}}'_m, \widehat{\boldsymbol{\beta}}'_m)'$. This derivation of the LIML estimator, which is different from the original derivation by Anderson and Rubin (1949), is due to Pagan (1979). Since LIML is a FIML estimator, Proposition 8.1 assures us that the LIML estimator is consistent and asymptotically normal even if the error is not normally distributed.

Computation of LIML

For the SUR model, we have shown that the ML estimator can be obtained from the iterative SUR procedure. If you reexamine the argument, you should see that it does not depend on $\mathbf{\Gamma}$ in the SUR objective function (8.5.29) being the identity matrix; all that is needed is that the determinant of $\mathbf{\Gamma}$ is a constant. Therefore, the same argument also applies to the LIML objective function (8.6.6). That is, we can obtain the LIML estimator of $\boldsymbol{\delta}_{0m}$ by applying the iterative SUR procedure to the $(1+M_m)$-equation system (8.6.3). In particular, if $\mathbf{\Sigma}_0$ is known, the LIML estimator is the SUR estimator. On the face of it, this conclusion — that SUR can be used to estimate the coefficients of included *endogenous* variables — is surprising, but it is true. The essential reason is this: the sampling error $\hat{\boldsymbol{\delta}}_m - \boldsymbol{\delta}_{0m}$ depends not only on the correlation between the included endogenous variables $\tilde{\mathbf{y}}_t$ and the error term ε_{tm} but also on the correlation between $\tilde{\mathbf{y}}_t$ and $\tilde{\mathbf{v}}_t$. Those two correlations cancel each other out. Review Question 1 verifies this for a simple example.

The iterative SUR procedure, however, is not how the LIML estimator is usually calculated, because there is a closed-form expression for the estimator. The simultaneous equation system (8.6.3) has two special features. One is the special structure of $\overline{\mathbf{\Gamma}}$, which we have noted, and the other is the fact that there are no exclusion restrictions in the rows of $\overline{\mathbf{B}}$ corresponding to the included endogenous variables $\tilde{\mathbf{y}}_t$. Thanks to these features, the LIML estimator $\hat{\boldsymbol{\delta}}_m = (\hat{\boldsymbol{\gamma}}'_m, \widehat{\boldsymbol{\beta}}'_m)'$ and also the likelihood ratio statistic (8.5.25) can be calculated explicitly.

To write down the closed-form expressions for the LIML estimator and the likelihood ratio statistic, we need to introduce some more notation. Let $\mathbf{Z}_m$, $\widetilde{\mathbf{Y}}$, $\widetilde{\mathbf{X}}$, $\mathbf{X}$, and $\mathbf{y}_m$ be the data matrices and the data vector associated with $\mathbf{z}_{tm}$, $\tilde{\mathbf{y}}_t$, $\tilde{\mathbf{x}}_t$, $\mathbf{x}_t$, and y_{tm}, respectively:

$$\underset{(n\times L_m)}{\mathbf{Z}_m} \equiv \begin{bmatrix} \mathbf{z}'_{1m} \\ \vdots \\ \mathbf{z}'_{nm} \end{bmatrix}, \quad \underset{(n\times M_m)}{\widetilde{\mathbf{Y}}} \equiv \begin{bmatrix} \tilde{\mathbf{y}}'_1 \\ \vdots \\ \tilde{\mathbf{y}}'_n \end{bmatrix}, \quad \underset{(n\times K_m)}{\widetilde{\mathbf{X}}} \equiv \begin{bmatrix} \tilde{\mathbf{x}}'_1 \\ \vdots \\ \tilde{\mathbf{x}}'_n \end{bmatrix},$$

$$\underset{(n\times K)}{\mathbf{X}} \equiv \begin{bmatrix} \mathbf{x}'_1 \\ \vdots \\ \mathbf{x}'_n \end{bmatrix}, \quad \underset{(n\times 1)}{\mathbf{y}_m} \equiv \begin{bmatrix} y_{1m} \\ \vdots \\ y_{nm} \end{bmatrix}, \tag{8.6.7}$$

and let $\mathbf{M}$ and $\widetilde{\mathbf{M}}$ be the annihilators based on $\mathbf{X}$ and $\widetilde{\mathbf{X}}$, respectively:

$$\underset{(n\times n)}{\mathbf{M}} \equiv \mathbf{I}_n - \mathbf{X}(\mathbf{X}'\mathbf{X})^{-1}\mathbf{X}', \quad \underset{(n\times n)}{\widetilde{\mathbf{M}}} \equiv \mathbf{I}_n - \widetilde{\mathbf{X}}(\widetilde{\mathbf{X}}'\widetilde{\mathbf{X}})^{-1}\widetilde{\mathbf{X}}'. \tag{8.6.8}$$

Then the LIML estimator $\hat{\boldsymbol{\delta}}_m$ can be written as

$$\hat{\boldsymbol{\delta}}_m \equiv \left[\mathbf{Z}_m'(\mathbf{I}_n - k\mathbf{M})\mathbf{Z}_m\right]^{-1}\mathbf{Z}_m'(\mathbf{I}_n - k\mathbf{M})\mathbf{y}_m, \tag{8.6.9}$$

where k is the smallest characteristic root of

$$\widetilde{\mathbf{W}}\mathbf{W}^{-1}, \tag{8.6.10}$$

with $(1 + M_m) \times (1 + M_m)$ matrices $\widetilde{\mathbf{W}}$ and $\mathbf{W}$ defined by

$$\widetilde{\mathbf{W}} \equiv \left[\mathbf{y}_m \,\vdots\, \widetilde{\mathbf{Y}}\right]'\widetilde{\mathbf{M}}\left[\mathbf{y}_m \,\vdots\, \widetilde{\mathbf{Y}}\right], \quad \mathbf{W} \equiv \left[\mathbf{y}_m \,\vdots\, \widetilde{\mathbf{Y}}\right]'\mathbf{M}\left[\mathbf{y}_m \,\vdots\, \widetilde{\mathbf{Y}}\right]. \tag{8.6.11}$$

(See, e.g., Davidson and MacKinnon, 1993, pp. 645–649, for a derivation.) The likelihood ratio statistic (8.5.25) for testing overidentifying restrictions reduces to

$$LR = n \log k. \tag{8.6.12}$$

Since there are no overidentifying restrictions in the supplementary M_m equations (8.6.2), the equation of interest is the only source of overidentifying restrictions, which are $K - L_m$ in number. Therefore, by Proposition 8.1, this statistic for testing overidentifying restrictions is asymptotically $\chi^2(K - L_m)$. When the equation is just identified so that $K = L_m$, then the LR statistic should be zero. Indeed, it can be shown that $k = 1$ in this case (see, e.g., p. 647 of Davidson and MacKinnon, 1993).

If we do not necessarily require k to be as just defined, the estimator (8.6.9) is called a ***k*-class estimator**. The LIML estimator is thus a k-class estimator with k defined above. Inspection of the 2SLS formula in terms of data matrices (see (3.8.3′) on page 230) immediately shows that the 2SLS estimator is a k-class estimator with $k = 1$, and the OLS estimator is a k-class estimator with $k = 0$. It follows that LIML and 2SLS are numerically the same when the equation is just identified (so that $k = 1$).

We have already shown that LIML is consistent and asymptotically normal. Moreover, using the explicit formula (8.6.9), it can be shown that the LIML estimator of $\boldsymbol{\delta}_{0m}$ has the same asymptotic distribution as 2SLS (see, e.g., Amemiya, 1985, Section 7.3.4). So the formula for the asymptotic variance of LIML is given by (3.8.4) and its consistent estimate by (3.8.5).

LIML versus 2SLS

Since LIML and 2SLS share the same asymptotic distribution, you cannot prefer one over the other on asymptotic grounds. For any finite sample, LIML has the invariance property, while 2SLS is not invariant. Furthermore, the conclusion one could draw from the large literature on finite-sample properties (see, e.g., Judge et al., 1985, Section 15.4) is that LIML should be preferred to 2SLS. Major conclusions from the literature are listed below. They assume that the predetermined variables $\mathbf{x}_t$ are fixed constants, however.

- Suppose errors are normally distributed. The p-th moment of the 2SLS estimator exists if and only if $p < K - L_m + 1$, where K is the number of predetermined variables and L_m is the number of regressors in the m-th equation. Thus, 2SLS does not even have a mean if the equation is just identified (i.e., if $K = L_m$), and this is true even if the distribution of errors is a normal distribution, whose moments are all finite.
- The LIML estimator has no finite moments even if errors are normally distributed.
- However, in most Monte Carlo simulations (see, e.g., Anderson, Kunitomo, and Sawa, 1982), LIML approaches its asymptotic normal distribution much more rapidly than does 2SLS.

QUESTIONS FOR REVIEW

1. (Why SUR can be used for a structural equation) To see why SUR can be used to estimate the coefficients of included endogenous variables, consider the following simple example:

$$\begin{cases} y_{t1} = \gamma_0 y_{t2} + \varepsilon_{t1}, \\ y_{t2} = \beta_0 x_t + v_t, \end{cases}$$

where x_t is predetermined. Suppose for simplicity that

$$\underset{(2\times 2)}{\mathbf{\Sigma}_0} \equiv \mathrm{E}\left(\begin{bmatrix} \varepsilon_{t1} \\ v_t \end{bmatrix} \begin{bmatrix} \varepsilon_{t1} & v_t \end{bmatrix}\right)$$

is known. Let $(\hat{\gamma}, \widehat{\beta})$ be the SUR estimator of (γ_0, β_0).

(a) Show that

$$\begin{bmatrix} \hat{\gamma} \\ \widehat{\beta} \end{bmatrix} - \begin{bmatrix} \gamma_0 \\ \beta_0 \end{bmatrix}$$
$$= \begin{bmatrix} \sigma^{11}\frac{1}{n}\sum y_{t2}^2 & \sigma^{12}\frac{1}{n}\sum y_{t2}x_t \\ \sigma^{21}\frac{1}{n}\sum x_t y_{t2} & \sigma^{22}\frac{1}{n}\sum x_t^2 \end{bmatrix}^{-1} \begin{bmatrix} \sigma^{11}\frac{1}{n}\sum y_{t2}\varepsilon_{t1} + \sigma^{12}\frac{1}{n}\sum y_{t2}v_t \\ \sigma^{21}\frac{1}{n}\sum x_t\varepsilon_{t1} + \sigma^{22}\frac{1}{n}\sum x_t v_t \end{bmatrix},$$

where σ^{mh} is the (m, h) element of $\mathbf{\Sigma}_0^{-1}$. **Hint:** The formula for the SUR estimator is given by (4.5.12) with (4.5.13′) and (4.5.14′) on page 280.

(b) Show that

$$\sigma^{11}\frac{1}{n}\sum_{t=1}^{n} y_{t2}\varepsilon_{t1} + \sigma^{12}\frac{1}{n}\sum_{t=1}^{n} y_{t2}v_t$$

converges to zero in probability. **Hint:**

$$\mathrm{E}(y_{t2}\varepsilon_{t1}) = \mathrm{E}(\varepsilon_{t1}v_t) = \sigma_{12},\ \ \mathrm{E}(y_{t2}v_t) = \mathrm{E}(v_t^2) = \sigma_{22}.$$

8.7 Serially Correlated Observations

So far, we have assumed i.i.d. observations in deriving the asymptotic variance of ML estimators. This section is concerned with ML estimation when observations are serially correlated.

Two Questions

When observations are serially correlated, there arise two distinct questions. The first is whether the ML estimator that maximizes a likelihood function derived from the assumption of i.i.d. observations is consistent and asymptotically normal when indeed the observations are serially correlated. More precisely, suppose that the observation vector $\mathbf{w}_t$ is ergodic stationary but not necessarily i.i.d., and consider the ML estimator that maximizes

$$Q_n(\boldsymbol{\theta}) = \frac{1}{n}\sum_{t=1}^{n} \log f(\mathbf{w}_t; \boldsymbol{\theta}), \tag{8.7.1}$$

where $\log f(\mathbf{w}_t; \boldsymbol{\theta})$ is the log likelihood for observation t. This objective function would be ($1/n$ times) the log likelihood of the sample $(\mathbf{w}_1, \dots, \mathbf{w}_n)$ if the observations were i.i.d. Even though the log likelihood for observation t, $\log f(\mathbf{w}_t; \boldsymbol{\theta})$, is correctly specified, this objective function is misspecified because it assumes, incorrectly, that $\{\mathbf{w}_t\}$ is i.i.d. The ML estimator that maximizes this objective function is a quasi-ML estimator because the likelihood function is misspecified. Is a quasi-ML estimator that incorrectly assumes no serial correlation consistent and asymptotically normal?

We have actually answered this first question in the previous chapter. By Propositions 7.5 and 7.6, the quasi-ML estimator is consistent because it is an M-estimator, with $m(\mathbf{w}_t; \boldsymbol{\theta})$ given by the log likelihood for observation t. For asymptotic normality, the relevant theorem is Proposition 7.8, which spells out conditions under which an M-estimator is asymptotically normal. Just reproducing the conclusion of Proposition 7.8, the expression for the asymptotic variance is given by

$$\text{Avar}(\hat{\boldsymbol{\theta}}) = \big(\text{E}\big[\mathbf{H}(\mathbf{w}_t; \boldsymbol{\theta}_0)\big]\big)^{-1} \boldsymbol{\Sigma} \big(\text{E}\big[\mathbf{H}(\mathbf{w}_t; \boldsymbol{\theta}_0)\big]\big)^{-1}, \tag{8.7.2}$$

where $\boldsymbol{\theta}_0$ is the true value of $\boldsymbol{\theta}$, $\mathbf{H}(\mathbf{w}_t; \boldsymbol{\theta})$ is the Hessian for observation t, and $\boldsymbol{\Sigma}$ is the long-run variance of the score for observation t evaluated at $\boldsymbol{\theta}_0$, $\mathbf{s}(\mathbf{w}_t; \boldsymbol{\theta}_0)$. This asymptotic variance can be consistently estimated by

$$\widehat{\text{Avar}(\hat{\boldsymbol{\theta}})} = \left\{\frac{1}{n}\sum_{t=1}^{n} \mathbf{H}(\mathbf{w}_t; \hat{\boldsymbol{\theta}})\right\}^{-1} \widehat{\boldsymbol{\Sigma}} \left\{\frac{1}{n}\sum_{t=1}^{n} \mathbf{H}(\mathbf{w}_t; \hat{\boldsymbol{\theta}})\right\}^{-1}, \tag{8.7.3}$$

where $\widehat{\boldsymbol{\Sigma}}$ is a consistent estimate of $\boldsymbol{\Sigma}$. Any of the "nonparametric" methods discussed in Chapter 6 (such as the VARHAC) can be used to calculate $\widehat{\boldsymbol{\Sigma}}$ from the estimated series $\{\mathbf{s}(\mathbf{w}_t; \hat{\boldsymbol{\theta}})\}$; there is no need to parameterize the serial correlation in $\{\mathbf{s}(\mathbf{w}_t; \boldsymbol{\theta}_0)\}$.

The second question is what is the likelihood function that properly accounts for serial correlation in observations and what are the properties of the "genuine" ML estimator that maximizes it. The question can be posed for conditional ML as well as unconditional ML. In conditional ML, we divide the observation vector $\mathbf{w}_t$ into two groups, the dependent variable y_t and the regressors $\mathbf{x}_t$, and examine the conditional distribution of $(y_1, \dots, y_n)$ conditional on $(\mathbf{x}_1, \dots, \mathbf{x}_n)$. Parameterizing this conditional distribution is relatively straightforward when $\{\mathbf{w}_t\}$ is i.i.d., because it can be written as a product over t of the conditional distribution of y_t given $\mathbf{x}_t$. In fact, this i.i.d. case is what we have examined in this and previous chapters. If $\{\mathbf{w}_t\}$ is serially correlated, however, the researcher does not know the dynamic interaction between y_t and $\mathbf{x}_t$ well enough to be able to write down the conditional distribution.[10] In the rest of this section, we deal only with examples of unconditional ML estimation with serially correlated observations.

Unconditional ML for Dependent Observations

We start out with the simplest case of a univariate series. Let $(y_0, y_1, \ldots, y_n)$ be the sample. (For notational convenience, we assume that the sample includes observation for $t = 0$.) When the observations are serially correlated, the density function of the sample can no longer be expressed as a product of individual densities. However, it can be written down in terms of a series of conditional probability density functions. The joint density function of (y_0, y_1) can be written as

$$f(y_0, y_1) = f(y_1 \mid y_0) f(y_0). \tag{8.7.4}$$

Similarly, for (y_0, y_1, y_2),

$$f(y_0, y_1, y_2) = f(y_2 \mid y_1, y_0) f(y_0, y_1). \tag{8.7.5}$$

Substituting (8.7.4) into this, we obtain

$$f(y_0, y_1, y_2) = f(y_2 \mid y_1, y_0) f(y_1 \mid y_0) f(y_0). \tag{8.7.6}$$

A repeated use of this sort of sequential substitution produces

$$f(y_0, y_1, \ldots, y_n) = \prod_{t=1}^{n} f(y_t \mid y_{t-1}, \ldots, y_1, y_0) f(y_0). \tag{8.7.7}$$

If the conditional density $f(y_t \mid y_{t-1}, \ldots, y_1, y_0)$ and the unconditional density $f(y_0)$ are parameterized by a finite-dimensional parameter vector $\boldsymbol{\theta}$, then ($1/n$ times) the log likelihood of the sample $(y_0, y_1, \ldots, y_n)$ can be written as

$$\frac{1}{n} \sum_{t=1}^{n} \log f(y_t \mid y_{t-1}, \ldots, y_1, y_0; \boldsymbol{\theta}) + \frac{1}{n} \log f(y_0; \boldsymbol{\theta}). \tag{8.7.8}$$

The ML estimator $\tilde{\boldsymbol{\theta}}$ of the true parameter value $\boldsymbol{\theta}_0$ is the $\boldsymbol{\theta}$ that maximizes this log likelihood function. We will call this ML estimator the **exact ML estimator**.

[10]For a discussion of conditional ML when the complete specification of the dynamic interaction is not possible or undesirable, see Wooldridge (1994, Section 5). For a discussion of possible restrictions on the dynamic interaction (such as "Granger causality" and "weak exogeneity"), see, e.g., Davidson and MacKinnon (1993, Section 18.2).

ML Estimation of AR(1) Processes

In Section 6.2, we considered in some detail first-order autoregressive (AR(1)) processes. If we assume for an AR(1) process that the error term is normally distributed, we obtain a **Gaussian AR(1) process**:

$$y_t = c_0 + \phi_0 y_{t-1} + \varepsilon_t, \tag{8.7.9}$$

with $\varepsilon_t \sim$ i.i.d. $N(0, \sigma_0^2)$. We assume the stationarity condition that $|\phi_0| < 1$. So $\{y_t\}$ is ergodic stationary by Proposition 6.1(d). From Section 6.2, we know that the unconditional mean of y_t is $c_0/(1-\phi_0)$ and the unconditional variance is $\sigma_0^2/(1-\phi_0^2)$. Furthermore, since y_t can be written as a weighted average of $(\varepsilon_t, \varepsilon_{t-1}, \dots)$, its distribution is normal when ε_t is normal. Therefore,

$$y_0 \sim N\left(\frac{c_0}{1-\phi_0}, \frac{\sigma_0^2}{1-\phi_0^2}\right). \tag{8.7.10}$$

Also, it follows directly from (8.7.9) and the normality assumption that

$$y_t \mid (y_{t-1}, \dots, y_1, y_0) \sim N(c_0 + \phi_0 y_{t-1}, \sigma_0^2). \tag{8.7.11}$$

Therefore, using the formula (8.7.7), the joint density of $(y_0, y_1, \dots, y_n)$ for a hypothetical parameter value $\boldsymbol{\theta} \equiv (c, \phi, \sigma^2)'$ can be written as

$$f(y_0, y_1, \dots, y_n; \boldsymbol{\theta}) = \prod_{t=1}^{n} \left\{ \frac{1}{\sqrt{2\pi\sigma^2}} \exp\left[-\frac{1}{2\sigma^2}(y_t - c - \phi y_{t-1})^2\right]\right\}$$
$$\times \frac{1}{\sqrt{2\pi \frac{\sigma^2}{1-\phi^2}}} \exp\left[\frac{-\left(y_0 - \frac{c}{1-\phi}\right)^2}{2\frac{\sigma^2}{1-\phi^2}}\right]. \tag{8.7.12}$$

Taking logs and dividing both sides by n, we obtain the objective function for exact ML:

$$\widetilde{Q}_n(\boldsymbol{\theta}) = \frac{1}{n}\sum_{t=1}^{n}\left\{-\frac{1}{2}\log(2\pi) - \frac{1}{2}\log(\sigma^2) - \frac{1}{2\sigma^2}(y_t - c - \phi y_{t-1})^2\right\}$$
$$+ \frac{1}{n}\left\{-\frac{1}{2}\log(2\pi) - \frac{1}{2}\log\left(\frac{\sigma^2}{1-\phi^2}\right) - \left[\frac{\left(y_0 - \frac{c}{1-\phi}\right)^2}{2\frac{\sigma^2}{1-\phi^2}}\right]\right\}. \tag{8.7.13}$$

The exact ML estimator $\tilde{\boldsymbol{\theta}}$ of the AR(1) process is the $\boldsymbol{\theta}$ that maximizes this objective function. Assuming an interior solution, the estimator solves the first-order conditions (the likelihood equations) obtained by setting $\frac{\partial \widetilde{Q}_n}{\partial \boldsymbol{\theta}}$ to zero. They are a system of equations that are nonlinear in $\boldsymbol{\theta}$, so finding $\tilde{\boldsymbol{\theta}}$ requires iterative algorithms such as those described in Section 7.5.

Conditional ML Estimation of AR(1) Processes

The source of the nonlinearity in the likelihood equations is the log likelihood of y_0. As an alternative, consider dropping this term and maximizing

$$Q_n(\boldsymbol{\theta}) = \frac{1}{n}\sum_{t=1}^{n}\Big\{-\frac{1}{2}\log(2\pi) - \frac{1}{2}\log(\sigma^2) - \frac{1}{2\sigma^2}(y_t - c - \phi y_{t-1})^2\Big\}. \quad (8.7.14)$$

Using the relation $f(y_0, y_1, \ldots, y_n) = f(y_1, \ldots, y_n \mid y_0) f(y_0)$ and (8.7.12), we see that this objective function is ($1/n$ times) the log of the likelihood conditional on the first observation y_0,

$$f(y_1, y_2, \ldots, y_n \mid y_0; \boldsymbol{\theta}) = \prod_{t=1}^{n}\Big\{\frac{1}{\sqrt{2\pi\sigma^2}}\exp\Big[-\frac{1}{2\sigma^2}(y_t - c - \phi y_{t-1})^2\Big]\Big\}. \quad (8.7.15)$$

Let $\hat{\boldsymbol{\theta}}$ be the $\boldsymbol{\theta}$ that maximizes the log conditional likelihood (8.7.14) (conditional on y_0). This ML estimator will henceforth be called the **y_0-conditional ML estimator**. Here, conditioning is on y_0, which makes the estimator here conceptually different from the conditional ML estimators of the previous sections where conditioning is on $\mathbf{x}_t$.

Before examining the relationship between the two ML estimators, the exact ML estimator $\tilde{\boldsymbol{\theta}}$ and the y_0-conditional ML estimator $\hat{\boldsymbol{\theta}}$, we give two derivations of the asymptotic properties of the latter. The first derivation is based on the explicit solution for the estimator. Recall from Section 1.5 and Example 7.2 that the objective function in the ML estimation of the linear regression model $y_t = \mathbf{x}_t'\boldsymbol{\beta}_0 + \varepsilon_t$ for i.i.d. observations is

$$\frac{1}{n}\sum_{t=1}^{n}\Big\{-\frac{1}{2}\log(2\pi) - \frac{1}{2}\log(\sigma^2) - \frac{1}{2\sigma^2}(y_t - \mathbf{x}_t'\boldsymbol{\beta})^2\Big\}. \quad (8.7.16)$$

It was shown in Section 1.5, and is very easy to show, that the ML estimator of $\boldsymbol{\beta}_0$ is the OLS coefficient estimator and the ML estimator of σ_0^2 equals the sum of squared residuals divided by the sample size. Now, with $\mathbf{x}_t = (1, y_{t-1})'$ and $\boldsymbol{\beta}_0 = (c_0, \phi_0)'$, the objective function for the linear regression model reduces to $Q_n(\boldsymbol{\theta})$ in (8.7.14), the conditional log likelihood for the AR(1) process. Therefore, algebraically, the conditional ML estimator $(\hat{c}, \hat{\phi})$ of (c_0, ϕ_0) is numerically the same as the OLS coefficient estimator in the regression of y_t on a constant and y_{t-1}, and the conditional ML estimator $\hat{\sigma}^2$ of σ_0^2 is the sum of squared residuals divided by n. Regarding the asymptotic properties of the estimator, we have shown in Section 6.4 that $(\hat{c}, \hat{\phi})$ is consistent and asymptotically normal with the asymptotic variance indicated in Proposition 6.7 for $p = 1$ and that $\hat{\sigma}_2$ is consistent for σ_0^2. Therefore, for the asymptotic normality of the conditional ML estimator $(\hat{c}, \hat{\phi})$, which maximizes the y_0-conditional likelihood for normal errors, the normality assumption is not needed.

The second derivation is more indirect but nevertheless more instructive. As just noted, the objective function $Q_n(\boldsymbol{\theta})$ coincides with (8.7.16) with $\mathbf{x}_t = (1, y_{t-1})'$ and $\boldsymbol{\beta}_0 = (c_0, \phi_0)'$. Since $\{y_t, \mathbf{x}_t\}$ is merely ergodic stationary and not necessarily i.i.d., the conditional ML estimator $(\hat{c}, \hat{\phi}, \hat{\sigma}^2)$ can be viewed as the quasi-ML estimator considered in Proposition 7.6. It has been verified in Example 7.8 that the objective function satisfies all the conditions of Proposition 7.6 if $\mathrm{E}(\mathbf{x}_t\mathbf{x}_t')$ where $\mathbf{x}_t = (1, y_{t-1})'$ is nonsingular. We have shown in Section 6.4 that this nonsingularity condition is satisfied for AR(1) processes if $\sigma_0^2 > 0$. Thus, the conditional ML is consistent. To prove asymptotic normality, view the conditional ML estimator as an M-estimator with $\mathbf{w}_t = (y_t, y_{t-1})'$ and

$$m(\mathbf{w}_t; \boldsymbol{\theta}) = -\frac{1}{2}\log(2\pi) - \frac{1}{2}\log(\sigma^2) - \frac{1}{2\sigma^2}(y_t - c - \phi y_{t-1})^2. \quad (8.7.17)$$

The relevant theorem, therefore, is Proposition 7.8. Let $\mathbf{s}(\mathbf{w}_t; \boldsymbol{\theta})$ be the score for observation t and let $\mathbf{H}(\mathbf{w}_t; \boldsymbol{\theta})$ be the Hessian for observation t associated with this m function, and consider the conditions (1)–(5) of Proposition 7.8. The discussion in Example 7.10 implies that all the conditions except for (3) hold if $\mathrm{E}(\mathbf{x}_t\mathbf{x}_t')$ where $\mathbf{x}_t = (1, y_{t-1})'$ is nonsingular, which as just noted is satisfied if $\sigma_0^2 > 0$. This leaves condition (3) that $\frac{1}{\sqrt{n}}\sum_{t=1}^{n} \mathbf{s}(\mathbf{w}_t; \boldsymbol{\theta}_0) \to_{\mathrm{d}} N(\mathbf{0}, \boldsymbol{\Sigma})$. In the AR(1) model, $f(y_t \mid y_{t-1}, \ldots, y_1, y_0) = f(y_t \mid y_{t-1})$. As you will show in Review Question 1, this special feature of the joint density function implies that the sequence $\{\mathbf{s}(\mathbf{w}_t; \boldsymbol{\theta}_0)\}$ is a martingale difference sequence. Since $\mathbf{s}(\mathbf{w}_t; \boldsymbol{\theta}_0)$ is a function of $\mathbf{w}_t = (y_t, y_{t-1})'$ and $\{y_t\}$ is ergodic stationary, the sequence $\{\mathbf{s}(\mathbf{w}_t; \boldsymbol{\theta}_0)\}$ also is ergodic stationary. So by the ergodic stationary martingale difference CLT of Chapter 2, we can claim that condition (3) is satisfied with

$$\boldsymbol{\Sigma} = \mathrm{E}\big[\mathbf{s}(\mathbf{w}_t; \boldsymbol{\theta}_0)\, \mathbf{s}(\mathbf{w}_t; \boldsymbol{\theta}_0)'\big]. \quad (8.7.18)$$

Finally, it is easy to show the information matrix equality for observation t that $-\mathrm{E}\big[\mathbf{H}(\mathbf{w}_t; \boldsymbol{\theta}_0)\big] = \mathrm{E}\big[\mathbf{s}(\mathbf{w}_t; \boldsymbol{\theta}_0)\, \mathbf{s}(\mathbf{w}_t; \boldsymbol{\theta}_0)'\big]$ (a proof is in Example 7.10). Substituting this and (8.7.18) into (8.7.2), we conclude that the asymptotic variance of the

y_0-conditional ML estimator $\hat{\boldsymbol{\theta}}$ of $\boldsymbol{\theta}_0$ is given by

$$\text{Avar}(\hat{\boldsymbol{\theta}}) = -\big(\text{E}\big[\mathbf{H}(\mathbf{w}_t; \boldsymbol{\theta}_0)\big]\big)^{-1} = \big(\text{E}\big[\mathbf{s}(\mathbf{w}_t; \boldsymbol{\theta}_0)\,\mathbf{s}(\mathbf{w}_t; \boldsymbol{\theta}_0)'\big]\big)^{-1}. \quad (8.7.19)$$

That is, the usual conclusion for a correctly specified ML estimator for i.i.d. observations is applicable to the y_0-conditional ML estimator that maximizes the correctly specified conditional likelihood (8.7.14) for dependent observations.[11]

The difference between (8.7.13) and (8.7.14) is the log likelihood of y_0 divided by n. If the sample size n is sufficiently large, then the first observation y_0 makes a negligible contribution to the likelihood of the sample. The exact ML estimator and the y_0-conditional ML estimator turn out to have the same asymptotic distribution, provided that $|\phi| < 1$ (see, e.g., Fuller, 1996, Sections 8.1 and 8.4). For this reason, in most applications the parameters of an autoregression are estimated by OLS (y_0-conditional ML) rather than exact ML.

Conditional ML Estimation of AR(p) and VAR(p) Processes

A **Gaussian AR(p) process** can be written as

$$y_t = c_0 + \phi_{01} y_{t-1} + \phi_{02} y_{t-2} + \cdots + \phi_{0p} y_{t-p} + \varepsilon_t, \quad (8.7.20)$$

with $\varepsilon_t \sim$ i.i.d. $N(0, \sigma_0^2)$. The conditional ML estimation of the AR(p) process is completely analogous to the AR(1) case. If the sample is $(y_{-p+1}, y_{-p+2}, \ldots, y_0, y_1, \ldots, y_n)$, then ($1/n$ times) the log likelihood of the sample conditional on $(y_{-p+1}, \ldots, y_0)$ is (8.7.16) with

$$\mathbf{x}_t = (1, y_{t-1}, \ldots, y_{t-p})' \quad \text{and} \quad \boldsymbol{\beta}_0 = (c_0, \phi_{01}, \phi_{02}, \ldots, \phi_{0p})'.$$

Therefore, the conditional ML (conditional on $(y_{-p+1}, y_{-p+2}, \ldots, y_0)$) estimator of $(c_0, \phi_{01}, \ldots, \phi_{0p})$ is numerically the same as the OLS coefficient estimator in the regression of y_t on a constant and p lagged values of y_t. The conditional ML estimate of σ_0^2 is the sum of squared residuals divided by the sample size. By Proposition 6.7, the conditional ML estimator of the coefficients is consistent and asymptotically normal if the stationarity condition (that the roots of $1 - \phi_{01} z - \cdots - \phi_{0p} z^p = 0$ be greater than 1 in absolute value) is satisfied. Again as in the AR(1) case, the error term does not need to be normal for consistency and asymptotic normality. The exact ML estimates and the conditional ML estimates have the same asymptotic distribution if the stationarity condition is satisfied.

[11] This argument can be applied to models more general than autoregressive processes. See Lemma 5.2 of Wooldridge (1994).

These results generalize readily to vector processes. A **Gaussian VAR(p)** (p-th order vector autoregression) can be written as

$$\underset{(M\times 1)}{\mathbf{y}_t} = \mathbf{c}_0 + \mathbf{\Phi}_{01}\mathbf{y}_{t-1} + \cdots + \mathbf{\Phi}_{0p}\mathbf{y}_{t-p} + \boldsymbol{\varepsilon}_t, \tag{8.7.21}$$

with $\boldsymbol{\varepsilon}_t \sim$ i.i.d. $N(\mathbf{0}, \mathbf{\Omega}_0)$. The objective function in the conditional ML estimation is ($1/n$ times) the log conditional likelihood:

$$Q_n(\boldsymbol{\theta}) = -\frac{M}{2}\log(2\pi) + \frac{1}{2}\log(|\mathbf{\Omega}^{-1}|) - \frac{1}{2n}\sum_{t=1}^{n}\{(\mathbf{y}_t - \mathbf{\Pi}'\mathbf{x}_t)'\mathbf{\Omega}^{-1}(\mathbf{y}_t - \mathbf{\Pi}'\mathbf{x}_t)\}, \tag{8.7.22}$$

where

$$\mathbf{\Pi}' \equiv \begin{bmatrix} \mathbf{c} & \mathbf{\Phi}_1 & \mathbf{\Phi}_2 & \cdots & \mathbf{\Phi}_p \end{bmatrix}, \quad \mathbf{x}_t \equiv \begin{bmatrix} 1 \\ \mathbf{y}_{t-1} \\ \mathbf{y}_{t-2} \\ \vdots \\ \mathbf{y}_{t-p} \end{bmatrix}. \tag{8.7.23}$$

This coincides with the objective function in the ML estimation of the multivariate regression model considered in Section 8.4. Therefore, the conditional ML estimate of $(\mathbf{c}_0, \mathbf{\Pi}_0)$ is numerically the same as the equation-by-equation OLS estimator. It is consistent and asymptotically normal if the coefficient matrices satisfy the stationarity condition (that all the roots of $|\mathbf{I}_M - \mathbf{\Phi}_{01}z - \cdots - \mathbf{\Phi}_{0p}z^p| = 0$ be greater than 1 in absolute value). This result does not require the error vector $\boldsymbol{\varepsilon}_t$ to be normally distributed.

QUESTIONS FOR REVIEW

1. (Score is m.d.s.) Consider the Gaussian AR(1) process (8.7.9) and let $\mathbf{s}(\mathbf{w}_t; \boldsymbol{\theta})$ be the score for observation t (the gradient of (8.7.17)) with $\mathbf{w}_t = (y_t, y_{t-1})'$ and $\boldsymbol{\theta} = (c, \phi, \sigma^2)'$.

   (a) Show that

   $$\mathbf{s}(\mathbf{w}_t; \boldsymbol{\theta}) = \begin{bmatrix} \frac{1}{\sigma^2}\mathbf{x}_t \cdot (y_t - \mathbf{x}_t'\boldsymbol{\beta}) \\ -\frac{1}{2\sigma^2} + \frac{1}{2\sigma^4}(y_t - \mathbf{x}_t'\boldsymbol{\beta})^2 \end{bmatrix},$$

   where $\boldsymbol{\beta} = (c, \phi)'$ and $\mathbf{x}_t = (1, y_{t-1})'$.

(b) Show that

$$\mathrm{E}[\mathbf{s}(\mathbf{w}_t;\boldsymbol{\theta}_0) \mid y_{t-1}, y_{t-2}, \ldots] = \mathbf{0}.$$

Hint: At $\boldsymbol{\theta} = \boldsymbol{\theta}_0$, $y_t - \mathbf{x}_t'\boldsymbol{\beta} = \varepsilon_t$.

(c) Show that $\{\mathbf{s}(\mathbf{w}_t;\boldsymbol{\theta}_0)\}$ is a martingale difference sequence. **Hint:** $\mathbf{s}(\mathbf{w}_t;\boldsymbol{\theta}_0)$ is a (measurable) function of (y_t, y_{t-1}). So $\mathbf{s}(\mathbf{w}_{t-j};\boldsymbol{\theta}_0)$ $(j \geq 1)$ can be calculated from $(y_{t-1}, y_{t-2}, \ldots)$.

(d) Does this result in (c) carry over to Gaussian AR(p)? [Answer: Yes.]

PROBLEM SET FOR CHAPTER 8

ANALYTICAL EXERCISES

1. Show that

$$\left|\frac{1}{n}\sum_{t=1}^{n}(\mathbf{y}_t - \boldsymbol{\Pi}'\mathbf{x}_t)(\mathbf{y}_t - \boldsymbol{\Pi}'\mathbf{x}_t)'\right| \geq \left|\frac{1}{n}\sum_{t=1}^{n}\hat{\mathbf{v}}_t\hat{\mathbf{v}}_t'\right|, \tag{1}$$

where $\hat{\mathbf{v}}_t \equiv \mathbf{y}_t - \widehat{\boldsymbol{\Pi}}'\mathbf{x}_t$ and $\widehat{\boldsymbol{\Pi}}$ is given in (8.4.5). (Since $\hat{\mathbf{v}}_t$ does not depend on $\boldsymbol{\Pi}$ by construction, this inequality shows that the left-hand side is minimized at $\boldsymbol{\Pi} = \widehat{\boldsymbol{\Pi}}$.) **Hint:** Use the "add-and-subtract" strategy to derive

$$\mathbf{y}_t - \boldsymbol{\Pi}'\mathbf{x}_t = \hat{\mathbf{v}}_t + (\widehat{\boldsymbol{\Pi}} - \boldsymbol{\Pi})'\mathbf{x}_t.$$

So

$$\begin{aligned}
&\sum_{t=1}^{n}(\mathbf{y}_t - \boldsymbol{\Pi}'\mathbf{x}_t)(\mathbf{y}_t - \boldsymbol{\Pi}'\mathbf{x}_t)' \\
&= \sum_{t=1}^{n}\hat{\mathbf{v}}_t\hat{\mathbf{v}}_t' + (\widehat{\boldsymbol{\Pi}} - \boldsymbol{\Pi})'\sum_{t=1}^{n}\mathbf{x}_t\hat{\mathbf{v}}_t' + \sum_{t=1}^{n}\hat{\mathbf{v}}_t\mathbf{x}_t'(\widehat{\boldsymbol{\Pi}} - \boldsymbol{\Pi}) \\
&\quad + (\widehat{\boldsymbol{\Pi}} - \boldsymbol{\Pi})'\Big(\sum_{t=1}^{n}\mathbf{x}_t\mathbf{x}_t'\Big)(\widehat{\boldsymbol{\Pi}} - \boldsymbol{\Pi}) \\
&= \sum_{t=1}^{n}\hat{\mathbf{v}}_t\hat{\mathbf{v}}_t' + (\widehat{\boldsymbol{\Pi}} - \boldsymbol{\Pi})'\Big(\sum_{t=1}^{n}\mathbf{x}_t\mathbf{x}_t'\Big)(\widehat{\boldsymbol{\Pi}} - \boldsymbol{\Pi}) \quad \text{(since } \sum_{t=1}^{n}\mathbf{x}_t\hat{\mathbf{v}}_t' = \mathbf{0}\text{).}
\end{aligned}$$

Then use the following result from matrix algebra:

> Let $\mathbf{A}$ and $\mathbf{B}$ be two positive semidefinite matrices of the same size. Then $|\mathbf{A}+\mathbf{B}| \geq |\mathbf{A}|$.

2. ($\widehat{\boldsymbol{\Omega}}(\boldsymbol{\Pi})$ is positive definite.) Under the conditions of the multivariate regression model, show that $\widehat{\boldsymbol{\Omega}}(\boldsymbol{\Pi})$ defined in (8.4.10) is positive definite for any given $\boldsymbol{\Pi}$. **Hint:** Derive $\mathbf{y}_t - \boldsymbol{\Pi}'\mathbf{x}_t = \mathbf{v}_t + (\boldsymbol{\Pi}_0 - \boldsymbol{\Pi})'\mathbf{x}_t$. Since $\{y_t, \mathbf{x}_t\}$ is i.i.d., $\widehat{\boldsymbol{\Omega}}(\boldsymbol{\Pi})$ converges almost surely to $\mathrm{E}\big[(\mathbf{y}_t - \boldsymbol{\Pi}'\mathbf{x}_t)(\mathbf{y}_t - \boldsymbol{\Pi}'\mathbf{x}_t)'\big]$. Show that

$$\mathrm{E}\big[(\mathbf{y}_t - \boldsymbol{\Pi}'\mathbf{x}_t)(\mathbf{y}_t - \boldsymbol{\Pi}'\mathbf{x}_t)'\big] = \boldsymbol{\Omega}_0 + (\boldsymbol{\Pi}_0 - \boldsymbol{\Pi})'\,\mathrm{E}(\mathbf{x}_t\mathbf{x}_t')(\boldsymbol{\Pi}_0 - \boldsymbol{\Pi}).$$

Then use the matrix inequaltiy mentioned in the previous exercise. $\boldsymbol{\Omega}_0$ is positive definite by assumption.

3. (Optional, identification of $\boldsymbol{\delta}$ in FIML) As noted in footnote 7 of Section 8.5, the FIML estimator of $\boldsymbol{\delta}_0$ is an extremum estimator whose objective function is

$$Q_n(\boldsymbol{\delta}) = -|\widehat{\boldsymbol{\Omega}}(\boldsymbol{\delta})|, \tag{2}$$

where

$$\widehat{\boldsymbol{\Omega}}(\boldsymbol{\delta}) \equiv \frac{1}{n}\sum_{t=1}^{n}(\mathbf{y}_t + \boldsymbol{\Gamma}^{-1}\mathbf{B}\mathbf{x}_t)(\mathbf{y}_t + \boldsymbol{\Gamma}^{-1}\mathbf{B}\mathbf{x}_t)'. \tag{3}$$

Let

$$Q_0(\boldsymbol{\delta}) \equiv \operatorname*{plim}_{n\to\infty} Q_n(\boldsymbol{\delta}). \tag{4}$$

To show the consistency of this extremum estimator, we would verify the two conditions of Proposition 7.1 of the previous chapter. Reproducing these two conditions in the current notation:

identification: $Q_0(\boldsymbol{\delta})$ is uniquely maximized on the compact parameter space at $\boldsymbol{\delta}_0$,

uniform convergence: $Q_n(\cdot)$ converges uniformly in probability to $Q_0(\cdot)$.

In this exercise we prove that the rank condition for identification (that $\mathrm{E}(\mathbf{x}_t\mathbf{z}_{tm}')$ be of full column rank for all m) is equivalent to the above extremum estimator identification condition. In the proof, take for granted all the assumptions we made about FIML in the text.

To set up the discussion, we need to introduce some new notation. Reproducing the m-th equation of the structural form from the text:

$$y_{tm} = \underset{(1\times L_m)}{\mathbf{z}'_{tm}} \underset{(L_m\times 1)}{\boldsymbol{\delta}_{0m}} + \varepsilon_{tm}. \tag{5}$$

The regressors $\mathbf{z}_{tm}$ consist of M_m endogenous variables and K_m predetermined variables with $M_m + K_m = L_m$. Define

$\underset{(M_m\times M)}{\mathbf{S}_m}$: a matrix that selects those M_m endogenous regressors from $\mathbf{y}_t$,

$\underset{(K_m\times K)}{\mathbf{C}_m}$: a matrix that selects those K_m predetermined regressors from $\mathbf{x}_t$.

To illustrate, $\mathbf{S}_1$ and $\mathbf{C}_1$ for Example 8.1 with $\mathbf{y}_t = (p_t, q_t)'$ and $\mathbf{x}_t = (1, a_t, w_t)'$ is

$$\mathbf{S}_1 = \begin{bmatrix} 1 & 0 \end{bmatrix}, \mathbf{C}_1 = \begin{bmatrix} 1 & 0 & 0 \\ 0 & 1 & 0 \end{bmatrix}.$$

So the regressors in the m-th equation can be written as

$$\mathbf{z}'_{tm} = (\mathbf{y}'_t\mathbf{S}'_m \vdots \mathbf{x}'_t\mathbf{C}'_m).$$

(a) Show that

$$\underset{(K\times L_m)}{\mathrm{E}(\mathbf{x}_t\mathbf{z}'_{tm})} = \underset{(K\times K)}{\mathrm{E}(\mathbf{x}_t\mathbf{x}'_t)} \underbrace{\left[\underset{(K\times M)}{\boldsymbol{\Pi}_0} \underset{(M\times M_m)}{\mathbf{S}'_m} \vdots \underset{(K\times K_m)}{\mathbf{C}'_m} \right]}_{(K\times L_m)}. \tag{6}$$

Hint: Use the reduced form (8.5.9) and the fact that $\mathrm{E}(\mathbf{x}_t\mathbf{v}'_t) = \mathbf{0}$.

Since multiplication by a nonsingular matrix ($\mathrm{E}(\mathbf{x}_t\mathbf{x}'_t)$ here) does not alter rank, equation (6) implies that the rank condition for identification is equivalent to the condition that the rank of $\left[\boldsymbol{\Pi}_0\mathbf{S}'_m \vdots \mathbf{C}'_m\right]$ be L_m.

(b) Show that

$$\underset{n\to\infty}{\text{plim}}\ \widehat{\boldsymbol{\Omega}}(\boldsymbol{\delta}) = \boldsymbol{\Gamma}_0^{-1}\boldsymbol{\Sigma}_0(\boldsymbol{\Gamma}_0^{-1})' + \left[\boldsymbol{\Pi}'_0 + \boldsymbol{\Gamma}^{-1}\mathbf{B}\right]\mathrm{E}(\mathbf{x}_t\mathbf{x}'_t)\left[\boldsymbol{\Pi}'_0 + \boldsymbol{\Gamma}^{-1}\mathbf{B}\right]', \tag{7}$$

where $\boldsymbol{\Pi}'_0 \equiv -\boldsymbol{\Gamma}_0^{-1}\mathbf{B}_0$. **Hint:** Since $\{\mathbf{y}_t, \mathbf{x}_t\}$ is i.i.d., the probability limit is given by $\mathrm{E}\left[(\mathbf{y}_t + \boldsymbol{\Gamma}^{-1}\mathbf{B}\mathbf{x}_t)(\mathbf{y}_t + \boldsymbol{\Gamma}^{-1}\mathbf{B}\mathbf{x}_t)'\right]$. Also,

$$\mathbf{y}_t + \boldsymbol{\Gamma}^{-1}\mathbf{B}\mathbf{x}_t = \mathbf{v}_t + (\boldsymbol{\Pi}'_0 + \boldsymbol{\Gamma}^{-1}\mathbf{B})\mathbf{x}_t.$$

(c) Show that $|\widehat{\boldsymbol{\Omega}}(\boldsymbol{\delta})|$ is minimized only if $\boldsymbol{\Gamma}\boldsymbol{\Pi}_0' + \mathbf{B} = \mathbf{0}$. **Hint:** Since $\mathrm{E}(\mathbf{x}_t\mathbf{x}_t')$ is positive definite, the second term on the right-hand side of (7) is zero only if $\boldsymbol{\Pi}_0 + \mathbf{B}'(\boldsymbol{\Gamma}^{-1})' = \mathbf{0}$. Use the fact from matrix algebra noted in Exercise 1 above.

Therefore, the extremum estimator identification condition (that $Q_0(\boldsymbol{\delta})$ be maximized uniquely at $\boldsymbol{\delta}_0$) holds if and only if $(\boldsymbol{\Gamma}, \mathbf{B}) = (\boldsymbol{\Gamma}_0, \mathbf{B}_0)$ is the only solution to $\boldsymbol{\Gamma}\boldsymbol{\Pi}_0' + \mathbf{B} = \mathbf{0}$ viewed as a system of simultaneous equations for $(\boldsymbol{\Gamma}, \mathbf{B})$.

(d) Let $\boldsymbol{\alpha}_m'$ $(1 \times (M+K))$ be the m-th row of $\left[\boldsymbol{\Gamma} \vdots \mathbf{B}\right]$, and let $\mathbf{e}_m'$ be a $(1 \times (M+K))$ vector whose element corresponding to y_{tm} is one and whose other elements are zero. To illustrate, $\mathbf{e}_1'$ for Example 8.1 with $\mathbf{y}_t = (p_t, q_t)'$ and $\mathbf{x}_t = (1, a_t, w_t)'$ is $(0, 1, 0, 0, 0)$. Verify for Example 8.1 the general result that

$$\underset{(1\times(M+K))}{\boldsymbol{\alpha}_m'} = \mathbf{e}_m' - \underset{(1\times(M_m+K_m))}{\boldsymbol{\delta}_m'} \begin{bmatrix} \underset{(M_m\times M)}{\mathbf{S}_m} & \underset{(M_m\times K)}{\mathbf{0}} \\ \underset{(K_m\times M)}{\mathbf{0}} & \underset{(K_m\times K)}{\mathbf{C}_m} \end{bmatrix}. \tag{8}$$

(e) Rewrite $\boldsymbol{\Gamma}\boldsymbol{\Pi}_0' + \mathbf{B} = \mathbf{0}$ as

$$\left[\boldsymbol{\Gamma} \vdots \mathbf{B}\right] \begin{bmatrix} \boldsymbol{\Pi}_0' \\ \mathbf{I}_K \end{bmatrix} = \mathbf{0}. \tag{9}$$

Show that the m-th row of $\boldsymbol{\Gamma}\boldsymbol{\Pi}_0' + \mathbf{B} = \mathbf{0}$ can be written as

$$\boldsymbol{\delta}_m' \begin{bmatrix} \mathbf{S}_m\boldsymbol{\Pi}_0' \\ \mathbf{C}_m \end{bmatrix} = \boldsymbol{\pi}_{0m}', \tag{10}$$

where

$$\boldsymbol{\pi}_{0m} \equiv \left[\boldsymbol{\Pi}_0 \vdots \mathbf{I}_K\right]\mathbf{e}_m. \tag{11}$$

(f) Verify that $\boldsymbol{\delta}_m = \boldsymbol{\delta}_{0m}$ is *a* solution to (10). Show that a necessary and sufficient condition that $\boldsymbol{\delta}_m = \boldsymbol{\delta}_{0m}$ is the only solution to (10) is the rank condition for identification for equation m. **Hint:** Recall the following fact from linear algebra: Suppose $\mathbf{A}\mathbf{x} = \mathbf{y}$ has a solution $\mathbf{x}_0$. A necessary and sufficient condition that it is the only solution is that $\mathbf{A}$ is of full column rank.

(g) Explain why we can conclude that the only solution to $\boldsymbol{\Gamma}\boldsymbol{\Pi}_0 + \mathbf{B} = \mathbf{0}$ is $(\boldsymbol{\Gamma}, \mathbf{B}) = (\boldsymbol{\Gamma}_0, \mathbf{B}_0)$. **Hint:** Each element of $\boldsymbol{\delta}$ appears in either $\boldsymbol{\Gamma}$ or $\mathbf{B}$ only once.

4. (Optional, instruments that do not show up in the system) Consider the complete system of simultaneous equations discussed in Section 8.5. Let

$$\underset{(K\times 1)}{\mathbf{x}_t} = \begin{bmatrix} \underset{((K-1)\times 1)}{\tilde{\mathbf{x}}_t} \\ x_{tK} \end{bmatrix}.$$

Suppose that x_{tK} does not appear in any of the M structural equations. Show that dropping x_{tK} from the list of instruments changes neither the rank condition for identification nor the asymptotic variance of the FIML estimator of δ_0. **Hint:** Define the two matrices, $\mathbf{S}_m$ and $\mathbf{C}_m$ as in Exercise 3, so that $\mathbf{z}'_{tm} = (\mathbf{y}'_t\mathbf{S}'_m \vdots \mathbf{x}'_t\mathbf{C}'_m)$ and (6) holds. FIML is asymptotically equivalent to 3SLS, so its asymptotic variance is given in (4.5.15). The last row of $\mathbf{C}'_m$ is a vector of zeros. Let $\widetilde{\mathbf{\Pi}}_0$ $((K-1)\times M)$ be the matrix of reduced-form coefficients when x_{tK} is dropped from the system. Then

$$\mathbf{\Pi}_0 = \begin{bmatrix} \underset{((K-1)\times M)}{\widetilde{\mathbf{\Pi}}_0} \\ \underset{(1\times M)}{\mathbf{0}'} \end{bmatrix}.$$

References

Amemiya, T., 1973, "Regression Analysis When the Dependent Variable is Truncated Normal," *Econometrica*, 41, 997–1016.

———, 1985, *Advanced Econometrics*, Cambridge: Harvard University Press.

Anderson, T. W., and H. Rubin, 1949, "Estimator of the Parameters of a Single Equation in a Complete System of Stochastic Equations," *Annals of Mathematical Statistics*, 20, 46–63.

Anderson, T. W., N. Kunitomo, and T. Sawa, 1982, "Evaluation of the Distribution Function of the Limited Information Maximum Likelihood Estimator," *Econometrica*, 50, 1009–1027.

Davidson, R., and J. MacKinnon, 1993, *Estimation and Inference in Econometrics*, New York: Oxford University Press.

Fuller, W., 1996, *Introduction to Statistical Time Series* (2d ed.), New York: Wiley.

Hausman, J., 1975, "An Instrumental Variable Approach to Full Information Estimators for Linear and Certain Nonlinear Econometric Models," *Econometrica*, 43, 727–738.

Johansen, S., 1995, *Likelihood-Based Inference in Cointegrated Vector Auto-Regressive Models*, New York: Oxford University Press.

Judge, G., W. Griffiths, R. Hill, H. Lütkepohl, and T, Lee, 1985, *The Theory and Practice of Econometrics* (2d ed.), New York: Wiley.

Magnus, J., and H. Neudecker, 1988, *Matrix Differential Calculus with Applications in Statistics and Econometrics*, New York: Wiley.

Newey, W., and D. McFadden, 1994, "Large Sample Estimation and Hypothesis Testing," Chapter 36 in R. Engle and D. McFadden (eds.), *Handbook of Econometrics*, Volume IV, New York: North-Holland.

Olsen, R. J., 1978, "Note on the Uniqueness of the Maximum Likelihood Estimator for the Tobit Model," *Econometrica*, 46, 1211–1215.

Orme, C., 1989, "On the Uniqueness of the Maximum Likelihood Estimator in Truncated Regression Models," *Econometric Reviews*, 8, 217–222.

Pagan, A., 1979, "Some Consequences of Viewing LIML As an Iterated Aitken Estimator," *Economics Letters*, 3, 369–372.

Sapra, S. K., 1992, "Asymptotic Properties of a Quasi-Maximum Likelihood Estimator in Truncated Regression Model with Serial Correlation," *Econometric Reviews*, 11, 253–260.

Tobin, J., 1958, "Estimation of Relationships for Limited Dependent Variables," *Econometrica*, 26, 24–36.

Wooldridge, J., 1994, "Estimation and Inference for Dependent Processes," Chapter 45 in R. Engle and D. McFadden (eds.), *Handbook of Econometrics*, Volume IV, New York: North-Holland.

CHAPTER 9

Unit-Root Econometrics

ABSTRACT

Up to this point our analysis has been confined to stationary processes. Section 9.1 introduces two classes of processes with trends: trend-stationary processes and unit-root processes. A unit-root process is also called difference-stationary or integrated of order 1 (I(1)) because its first difference is a stationary, or I(0), process. The technical tools for deriving the limiting distributions of statistics involving I(0) and I(1) processes are collected in Section 9.2. Using these tools, we will derive some unit-root tests of the null hypothesis that the process in question is I(1). Those tests not only are popular but also have better finite-sample properties than most other existing tests. In Section 9.3, we cover the Dickey-Fuller tests, which were developed to test the null that the process is a random walk, a prototypical I(1) process whose first difference is serially uncorrelated. Section 9.4 shows that these tests can be generalized to cover I(1) processes with serially correlated first differences. These and other unit-root tests are compared briefly in Section 9.5. Section 9.6, the application of this chapter, utilizes the unit-root tests to test purchasing power parity (PPP), the fundamental proposition in international economics that exchange rates adjust to national price levels.

9.1 Modeling Trends

There is no shortage of examples of time series with what could be reasonably described as trends in economics. Figure 9.1 displays the log of U.S. real GDP. The log GDP clearly has an upward trend in that its mean, instead of being constant as with stationary processes, increases steadily over time. The trend in the mean is called a **deterministic trend** or **time trend**. For the case of log U.S. GDP, the deterministic trend appears to be linear. Another kind of trend can be seen from Figure 6.3 on page 424, which graphs the log yen/dollar exchange rate. The log exchange rate does not have a trend in the mean, but its every change seems to have a permanent effect on its future values so that the best predictor of future values is

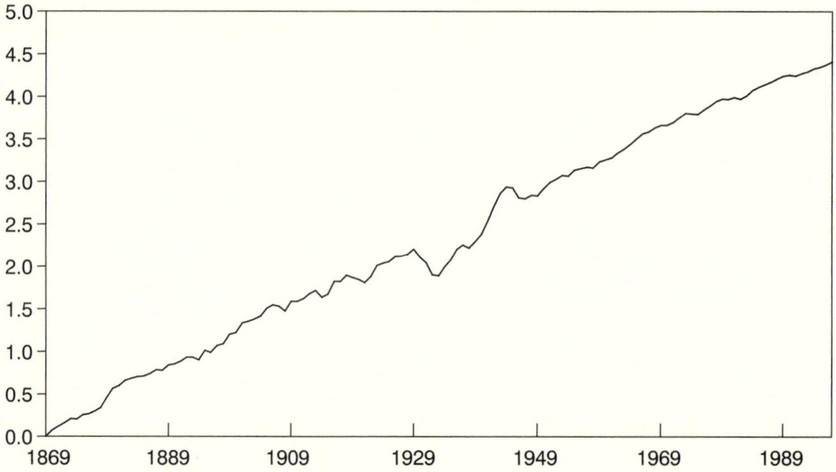

Figure 9.1: Log U.S. Real GDP, Value for 1869 Set to 0

its current value. A process with this property, which is not shared by stationary processes, is called a **stochastic trend**. If you recall the definition of a martingale, it fits this description of a stochastic trend. Stochastic trends and martingales are synonymous.

The basic premise of this chapter and the next is that economic time series can be represented as the sum of a linear time trend, a stochastic trend, and a stationary process.[1]

Integrated Processes

A random walk is an example of a class of trending processes known as **integrated processes**. To give a precise definition of integrated processes, we first define I(0) processes. An **I(0) process** is a (strictly) stationary process whose **long-run variance** (defined in the discussion following Proposition 6.8 of Section 6.5) is finite and positive. (We will explain why the long-run variance is required to be positive in a moment.) Following, e.g., Hamilton (1994, p. 435), we allow I(0) processes to have possibly nonzero means (some authors, e.g., Stock, 1994, require I(0) processes to have zero mean). Therefore, an I(0) process can be written as

$$\delta + u_t, \tag{9.1.1}$$

where $\{u_t\}$ is zero-mean stationary with positive long-run variance.

[1]A note on semantics. Processes with trends are often called "nonstationary processes." We will not use this term in the rest of this book because a process can be not stationary without containing a trend. For example, let ε_t be an i.i.d. process with unit variance and let d_t take a value of 1 for t odd and 2 for t even. Then a process $\{u_t\}$ defined by $u_t = d_t \cdot \varepsilon_t$ is not stationary because its variance depends on t. Yet the process cannot be reasonably described as a process with a trend.

The definition of integrated processes follows from the definition of I(0) processes. Let Δ be the difference operator, so, for a sequence $\{\xi_t\}$,

$$\begin{aligned} \Delta\xi_t &\equiv (1-L)\xi_t \;\; = \xi_t - \xi_{t-1}, \\ \Delta^2\xi_t &= (1-L)^2\xi_t = (\xi_t - \xi_{t-1}) - (\xi_{t-1} - \xi_{t-2}), \;\; \text{etc.} \end{aligned} \tag{9.1.2}$$

Definition 9.1 (I(d) processes): A process is said to be integrated of order d (**I(d)**) ($d = 1, 2, \dots$) if its d-th difference $\Delta^d\xi_t$ is I(0). In particular, a process $\{\xi_t\}$ is integrated of order 1 (**I(1)**) if the first difference, $\Delta\xi_t$, is I(0).

The reason the long-run variance of an I(0) process is required to be positive is to rule out the following definitional anomaly. Consider the process $\{v_t\}$ defined by

$$v_t \equiv \varepsilon_t - \varepsilon_{t-1}, \tag{9.1.3}$$

where $\{\varepsilon_t\}$ is independent white noise. As we verified in Review Question 5 of Section 6.5, the long-run variance of $\{v_t\}$ is zero. If it were not for the requirement for the long-run variance, $\{v_t\}$ would be I(0). But then, since $\Delta\varepsilon_t = v_t$, the independent white noise process $\{\varepsilon_t\}$ would have to be I(1)! If a process $\{v_t\}$ is written as the first difference of an I(0) process, it is called an I(-1) process. The long-run variance of an I(-1) process is zero (proving this is Review Question 1).

For the rest of this chapter, the integrated processes we deal with are of order 1. A few comments about I(1) processes follow.

- (When did it start?) As is clear with random walks, the variance of an I(1) process increases linearly with time. Thus if the process had started in the infinite past, the variance would be infinite. To focus on I(1) processes with finite variance, we assume that the process began in the finite past, and without loss of generality we can assume that the starting date is $t = 0$. Since an I(0) process can be written as (9.1.1) and since by definition an I(1) process $\{\xi_t\}$ satisfies the relation $\Delta\xi_t = \delta + u_t$, we can write ξ_t in levels as

$$\xi_t = \xi_0 + \delta \cdot t + (u_1 + u_2 + \cdots + u_t), \tag{9.1.4}$$

  where $\{u_t\}$ is zero-mean I(0). So the specification of the levels process $\{\xi_t\}$ must include an assumption about the initial condition. Unless otherwise stated, we assume throughout that $\mathrm{E}(\xi_0^2) < \infty$. So ξ_0 can be random.

- (The mean in I(0) is the trend in I(1)) As is clear from (9.1.4), an I(1) process can have a linear trend, $\delta \cdot t$. This is a consequence of having allowed I(0) processes to have a nonzero mean δ. If $\delta = 0$, then the I(1) process has no trend and is called a **driftless I(1) process**, while if $\delta \neq 0$, the process is called an **I(1) process with drift**. Evidently, an I(1) process with drift can be written as the sum of a linear trend and a driftless I(1) process.

- (Two other names of I(1) processes) An I(1) process has two other names. It is called a **difference-stationary process** because the first difference is stationary. It is also called a **unit-root process**. To see why it is so called, consider a model

$$(1 - \rho L)y_t = \delta + u_t, \tag{9.1.5}$$

where u_t is zero-mean I(0). It is an autoregressive model with possibly serially correlated errors represented by u_t. If the autoregressive root ρ is unity, then the first difference of y_t is I(0), so $\{y_t\}$ is I(1).

Why Is It Important to Know if the Process Is I(1)?

For the rest of this chapter, we will be concerned with distinguishing between **trend-stationary processes**, which can be written as the sum of a linear time trend (if there is one) and a stationary process, on one hand, and difference-stationary processes (i.e., I(1) processes with or without drift) on the other. As will be shown in Proposition 9.1, an I(1) process can be written as the sum of a linear trend (if any), a stationary process, and a stochastic trend. Therefore, the difference between the two classes of processes is the existence of a stochastic trend. There are at least two reasons why the distinction is important.

1. First, it matters a great deal in forecasting. To make the point, consider the following simple AR(1) process with trend:

$$\begin{aligned} y_t &= \alpha + \delta \cdot t + z_t, \\ z_t &= \rho z_{t-1} + \varepsilon_t, \end{aligned} \tag{9.1.6}$$

where $\{\varepsilon_t\}$ is independent white noise. The s-period-ahead forecast of y_{t+s} conditional on $(y_t, y_{t-1}, \dots)$ can be written as

$$\begin{aligned} &\mathrm{E}(y_{t+s} \mid y_t, y_{t-1}, \dots) \\ &\quad = \mathrm{E}[\alpha + \delta \cdot (t+s) \mid y_t, y_{t-1}, \dots] + \mathrm{E}(z_{t+s} \mid y_t, y_{t-1}, \dots) \\ &\quad = \alpha + \delta \cdot (t+s) + \mathrm{E}(z_{t+s} \mid y_t, y_{t-1}, \dots). \end{aligned} \tag{9.1.7}$$

Both $(y_t, y_{t-1}, \dots)$ and $(z_t, z_{t-1}, \dots)$ contain the same information because there is a one-to-one mapping between the two. So the last term can be written as

$$\mathrm{E}(z_{t+s} \mid y_t, y_{t-1}, \dots) = \mathrm{E}(z_{t+s} \mid z_t, z_{t-1}, \dots) = \rho^s z_t \tag{9.1.8}$$

since $z_{t+s} = \varepsilon_{t+s} + \rho\varepsilon_{t+s-1} + \cdots + \rho^{s-1}\varepsilon_{t+1} + \rho^s z_t$. Substituting (9.1.8) into (9.1.7), we obtain the following expression for the s-period-ahead forecast:

$$\begin{aligned} \mathrm{E}(y_{t+s} \mid y_t, y_{t-1}, \dots) &= \alpha + \delta \cdot (t+s) + \rho^s z_t \\ &= \alpha + \delta \cdot (t+s) + \rho^s \cdot (y_t - \alpha - \delta \cdot t). \end{aligned} \tag{9.1.9}$$

There are two cases to consider.

Case $|\rho| < 1$. Now if $|\rho| < 1$, then $\{z_t\}$ is a stationary AR(1) process and thus is zero-mean I(0). So $\{y_t\}$ is trend stationary. In this case, since $\mathrm{E}(z_t^2) < \infty$, we have

$$\mathrm{E}[(\rho^s z_t)^2] = \rho^{2s}\,\mathrm{E}(z_t^2) \to 0 \text{ as } s \to \infty.$$

Therefore, the s-period-ahead forecast $\mathrm{E}(y_{t+s} \mid y_t, y_{t-1}, \dots)$ converges in mean square to the linear time trend $\alpha + \delta \cdot (t+s)$ as $s \to \infty$. More precisely,

$$\mathrm{E}\big\{[\mathrm{E}(y_{t+s} \mid y_t, y_{t-1}, \dots) - \alpha - \delta \cdot (t+s)]^2\big\} \to 0 \text{ as } s \to \infty. \tag{9.1.10}$$

That is, the current and past values of y do not affect the forecast if the forecasting horizon s is sufficiently long. In particular, if $\delta = 0$, then

$$\mathrm{E}(y_{t+s} \mid y_t, y_{t-1}, \dots) \underset{\text{m.s.}}{\to} \mathrm{E}(y_t) \text{ as } s \to \infty. \tag{9.1.11}$$

That is, a long-run forecast is the unconditional mean. This property, called **mean reversion**, holds for any linear stationary processes, not just for stationary AR(1) processes.[2] For this reason, a linear stationary process is sometimes called a **transitory component**.

Case $\rho = 1$. Suppose, instead, that $\rho = 1$. Then $\{z_t\}$ is a driftless random walk (a particular stochastic trend), and y_t can be written as

$$y_t = (\alpha + z_0) + \delta \cdot t + \varepsilon_1 + \varepsilon_2 + \cdots + \varepsilon_t, \tag{9.1.12}$$

which shows that $\{y_t\}$ is a random walk with drift with the initial value of $z_0 + \alpha$ (a particular I(1) or difference-stationary process). Setting $\rho = 1$ in (9.1.9), we obtain

$$\mathrm{E}(y_{t+s} \mid y_t, y_{t-1}, \dots) = \delta \cdot s + y_t. \tag{9.1.13}$$

[2] See, e.g., Hamilton (1994, p. 439) for a proof.

That is, a random walk with drift δ is expected to grow at a constant rate of δ per period from whatever its current value y_t happens to be. Unlike in the trend-stationary case, the current value has a permanent effect on the forecast for all forecast horizons. This is because of the presence of a stochastic trend z_t. A stochastic trend is also called a **permanent component**.

2. The second reason for distinguishing between trend-stationary and difference-stationary processes arises in the context of inference. For example, suppose you are interested in testing a hypothesis about β in a regression equation

$$y_t = x_t\beta + u_t, \tag{9.1.14}$$

where u_t is a stationary error term. If the regressor x_t is trend stationary, then, as was shown in Section 2.12, the t-value on the OLS estimate of β is asymptotically standard normal. On the other hand, if x_t is difference stationary, that is, if it has a stochastic trend, then the t-value has a nonstandard limiting distribution, so inference about β cannot be made in the usual way. The regression in this case is called a "cointegrating regression." Inference about a cointegrating regression will be studied in the next chapter.

Which Should Be Taken as the Null, I(0) or I(1)?

To distinguish between trend-stationary processes and difference-stationary, or I(1), processes, the usual practice in the literature is to test the null hypothesis that the process is I(1), rather than taking the hypothesis of trend stationarity as the null. Presumably there are two reasons for this. One is that the researcher believes the variables of the equation of interest to be I(1) and wishes to control type I error with respect to the I(1) null. This, however, is not ultimately convincing because usually the researcher does not have a strong prior belief as to whether the variables are I(0) or I(1). For a concise statement of the problem this poses for inference, see Watson (1994, pp. 2867–2870). The other reason is simply that the literature on tests of the trend-stationary null against the I(1) alternative is still relatively underdeveloped. There are available several tests of the null hypothesis that the process is I(0) or more generally trend stationary; see contributions by Tanaka (1990), Kwiatkowski et al. (1992), and Leybourne and McCabe (1994), and surveys by Stock (1994, Section 4) and Maddala and Kim (1998, Section 4.5). As of this writing, there is no single I(0) test commonly used by the majority of researchers that has good finite-sample properties. In this book, therefore, we will concentrate on tests of the I(1) null.

Other Approaches to Modeling Trends

In addition to stochastic trends and time trends, there are two other popular approaches to modeling trends: fractionally integration and broken trends with an unknown break date. They will not be covered in this book. For a survey of the former approach, see Baillie (1996). The literature on trend breaks is growing rapidly. Surveys can be found in Stock (1994, Section 5) and Maddala and Kim (1998, Chapter 13).

QUESTION FOR REVIEW

1. (Long-run variance of differences of I(0) processes) Let $\{u_t\}$ be I(0) with $\text{Var}(u_t) < \infty$. Verify that $\{\Delta u_t\}$ is covariance stationary and that the long-run variance of $\{\Delta u_t\}$ is zero. **Hint:** The long-run variance of $\{v_t\}$ (where $v_t \equiv \Delta u_t$) is defined to be the limit as $T \to \infty$ of $\text{Var}(\sqrt{T}\bar{v})$. $\sqrt{T}\bar{v} = (v_1 + v_2 + \cdots + v_T)/\sqrt{T} = (u_T - u_0)/\sqrt{T}$.

9.2 Tools for Unit-Root Econometrics

The basic tool in unit-root econometrics is what is called the "functional central limit theorem" (FCLT). For the FCLT to be applicable, we need to specialize I(1) processes by placing restrictions on the associated I(0) processes. Which restrictions to place, that is, which class of I(0) processes to focus on, differs from author to author, depending on the version of the FCLT in use. In this book, following the practice in the literature, we focus on linear I(0) processes. After defining linear I(0) processes, this section introduces some concepts and results that will be used repeatedly in the rest of this chapter.

Linear I(0) Processes

Our definition of linear I(0) processes is as follows.

Definition 9.2 (Linear I(0) processes): A linear I(0) process can be written as a constant plus a zero-mean linear process $\{u_t\}$ such that

$$u_t = \psi(L)\varepsilon_t,\ \psi(L) \equiv \psi_0 + \psi_1 L + \psi_2 L^2 + \cdots \text{ for } t = 0, \pm 1, \pm 2, \ldots. \tag{9.2.1}$$

$$\{\varepsilon_t\} \text{ is independent white noise (i.i.d. with mean 0 and } \text{E}(\varepsilon_t^2) \equiv \sigma^2 > 0), \tag{9.2.2}$$

$$\sum_{j=0}^{\infty} j|\psi_j| < \infty, \tag{9.2.3a}$$

$$\psi(1) \neq 0. \tag{9.2.3b}$$

The innovation process $\{\varepsilon_t\}$ is assumed to be white noise i.i.d. This requirement is for simplifying the exposition and can be relaxed substantially.[3] In the rest of this chapter, we will refer to linear I(0) processes as simply I(0) processes, without the qualifier "linear." Also, unless otherwise stated, $\{\varepsilon_t\}$ will be an independent white noise process and $\{u_t\}$ a zero-mean I(0) process.

Condition (9.2.3a) (sometimes called the **one-summability** condition) is stronger than the more familiar condition of absolute summability. This stronger assumption will make it easier to prove large sample results of the next section, with the help of the Beveridge-Nelson decomposition to be introduced shortly. Since $\{\psi_j\}$ is absolutely summable, the linear process $\{u_t\}$ is strictly stationary and ergodic by Proposition 6.1(d). The j-th order autocovariance of $\{u_t\}$ will be denoted γ_j. Since $\mathrm{E}(u_t) = 0$, $\gamma_j = \mathrm{E}(u_t u_{t-j})$. By Proposition 6.1(c) the autocovariances are absolutely summable.

To understand condition (9.2.3b), recall that the long-run variance (which we denote λ^2 in this chapter) equals the value of the autocovariance-generating function at $z = 1$ by Proposition 6.8(b). By Proposition 6.6 it is given by

$$\lambda^2 \equiv \text{long-run variance of } \{u_t\} = \gamma_0 + 2\sum_{j=1}^{\infty} \gamma_j = \sigma^2 \cdot [\psi(1)]^2. \tag{9.2.4}$$

The condition (9.2.3b) thus ensures the long-run variance to be positive.

Approximating I(1) by a Random Walk

Let $\{\xi_t\}$ be I(1) so that $\Delta\xi_t = \delta + u_t$ where $u_t \equiv \psi(L)\varepsilon_t$ is a zero-mean I(0) process satisfying (9.2.1)–(9.2.3) with $\mathrm{E}(\xi_0^2) < \infty$. Using the following identity (to be verified in Review Question 1):

$$\psi(L) = \psi(1) + \Delta\alpha(L), \quad \Delta \equiv 1 - L,$$

$$\alpha(L) \equiv \sum_{j=0}^{\infty} \alpha_j L^j, \quad \alpha_j = -(\psi_{j+1} + \psi_{j+2} + \cdots) \quad (j = 0, 1, 2, \ldots), \tag{9.2.5}$$

[3] For example, the innovation process can be stationary martingale differences. See, e.g., Theorem 3.8 of Tanaka (1996, p. 80).

we can write u_t as

$$u_t \equiv \psi(L)\varepsilon_t = \psi(1) \cdot \varepsilon_t + \eta_t - \eta_{t-1} \text{ with } \eta_t \equiv \alpha(L)\varepsilon_t. \tag{9.2.6}$$

It can be shown (see Analytical Exercise 7) that $\alpha(L)$ is absolutely summable. So, by Proposition 6.1(a), $\{\eta_t\}$ is a well-defined zero-mean covariance-stationary process (it is actually ergodic stationary by Proposition 6.1(d)). Substituting (9.2.6) into (9.1.4), we obtain (what is known in econometrics as) the **Beveridge-Nelson decomposition**:

$$\begin{aligned}\xi_t &= \delta \cdot t + \sum_{s=1}^{t}[\psi(1) \cdot \varepsilon_s + \eta_s - \eta_{s-1}] + \xi_0 \\ &= \delta \cdot t + \psi(1) \sum_{s=1}^{t} \varepsilon_s + \eta_t + (\xi_0 - \eta_0) \ \left(\text{since } \sum_{s=1}^{t}(\eta_s - \eta_{s-1}) = \eta_t - \eta_0\right).\end{aligned} \tag{9.2.7}$$

Thus, any linear I(1) process can be written as the sum of a linear time trend $(\delta \cdot t)$, a driftless random walk or a stochastic trend $(\psi(1)(\varepsilon_1 + \varepsilon_2 + \cdots + \varepsilon_t))$, a stationary process (η_t), and an initial condition $(\xi_0 - \eta_0)$. Stated somewhat differently, we have

Proposition 9.1 (Beveridge-Nelson decomposition): *Let $\{u_t\}$ be a zero-mean I(0) process satisfying (9.2.1)–(9.2.3). Then*

$$u_1 + u_2 + \cdots + u_t = \psi(1)(\varepsilon_1 + \varepsilon_2 + \cdots + \varepsilon_t) + \eta_t - \eta_0,$$

where $\eta_t \equiv \alpha(L)\varepsilon_t$, $\alpha_j = -(\psi_{j+1} + \psi_{j+2} + \cdots)$. $\{\eta_t\}$ is zero-mean ergodic stationary.[4]

For a moment set $\delta = 0$ in (9.2.7) so that $\{\xi_t\}$ is driftless I(1). An important implication of the decomposition is that any driftless I(1) process is dominated by the stochastic trend $\psi(1)\sum_{s=1}^{t}\varepsilon_s$ in the following sense. Divide both sides of the decomposition (9.2.7) (with $\delta = 0$) by $\sqrt{t}$ to obtain

$$\frac{\xi_t}{\sqrt{t}} = \psi(1) \cdot \frac{1}{\sqrt{t}} \sum_{s=1}^{t} \varepsilon_s + \left[\frac{\xi_0}{\sqrt{t}} + \frac{\eta_t}{\sqrt{t}} - \frac{\eta_0}{\sqrt{t}}\right]. \tag{9.2.8}$$

[4]For a more general condition, which does not require the I(0) process $\{u_t\}$ to be linear, under which $u_1 + \cdots + u_t$ is decomposed as shown here, see Theorem 5.4 of Hall and Heyde (1980). In that theorem, $\{\varepsilon_t\}$ is a stationary martingale difference sequence, so the stochastic trend is a martingale.

Since $\mathrm{E}(\xi_0^2) < \infty$ by assumption, $\mathrm{E}[(\xi_0/\sqrt{t})^2] \to 0$ as $t \to \infty$. So $\xi_0/\sqrt{t}$ converges in mean square (and hence in probability) to zero. The same applies to $\eta_t/\sqrt{t}$ and $\eta_0/\sqrt{t}$. So the terms in the brackets on the right-hand side of (9.2.8) can be ignored asymptotically. In contrast, the first term has a limiting distribution of $N(0, \sigma^2 \cdot [\psi(1)]^2)$ by the Lindeberg-Levy CLT of Section 2.1. In this sense, the stochastic trend grows at rate $\sqrt{t}$. Using (9.2.4), the stochastic trend can be written as

$$\psi(1)(\varepsilon_1 + \varepsilon_2 + \cdots + \varepsilon_t) = \lambda \cdot \left(\frac{\varepsilon_1}{\sigma} + \frac{\varepsilon_2}{\sigma} + \cdots + \frac{\varepsilon_t}{\sigma}\right), \tag{9.2.9}$$

which shows that changes in the stochastic trend in ξ_t have a variance of λ^2, the long-run variance of $\{\Delta\xi_t\}$.

Now suppose $\delta \neq 0$ so that $\{\xi_t\}$ is I(1) with drift. As is clear from dividing both sides of (9.2.7) by t rather than $\sqrt{t}$ and applying the same argument just given for the $\delta = 0$ case, the stochastic trend as well as the stationary component can be ignored asymptotically, with ξ_t/t converging in probability to δ. In this sense the time trend dominates the I(1) process in large samples.

Relation to ARMA Models

In Section 6.2, we defined a zero-mean stationary ARMA process $\{u_t\}$ as the unique covariance-stationary process satisfying the stationary ARMA(p, q) equation

$$\phi(L)u_t = \theta(L)\varepsilon_t, \tag{9.2.10}$$

where $\phi(L)$ satisfies the stationarity condition. If $\{\varepsilon_t\}$ is independent white noise and if $\theta(1) \neq 0$, then the ARMA(p, q) process is zero-mean I(0). To see this, note from Proposition 6.5(a) that u_t can be written as (9.2.1) with

$$\psi(L) = \phi(L)^{-1}\theta(L). \tag{9.2.11}$$

Since $\phi(1) \neq 0$ by the stationarity condition and $\theta(1) \neq 0$ by assumption, condition (9.2.3b) (that $\psi(1) \neq 0$) is satisfied. By Proposition 6.4(a), the coefficient sequence $\{\psi_j\}$ is bounded in absolute value by a geometrically declining sequence, which ensures that (9.2.3a) is satisfied.

Given the zero-mean stationary ARMA(p, q) process $\{u_t\}$ just described, the associated I(1) process $\{\xi_t\}$ defined by the relation $\Delta\xi_t = u_t$ is called an **autoregressive integrated moving average (ARIMA$(p, 1, q)$)** process. Substituting the relation $u_t = (1 - L)\xi_t$ into (9.2.10), we obtain

$$\phi^*(L)\xi_t = \theta(L)\varepsilon_t, \tag{9.2.12}$$

with $\phi^*(L) \equiv \phi(L)(1-L)$, $\phi(L)$ stationary, and $\theta(1) \neq 0$. One of the roots of the associated autoregressive polynomial equation $\phi^*(z) = 0$ is unity and all other roots lie outside the unit circle. More generally, a class of I(d) processes can be represented as satisfying (9.2.12) where $\phi^*(L)$ is now defined as

$$\phi^*(L) = \phi(L)(1-L)^d. \tag{9.2.13}$$

So $\phi^*(z) = 0$ now has a root of unity with a multiplicity of d (i.e., d unit roots) and all other roots lie outside the unit circle. This class of I(d) processes is called autoregressive integrated moving average (**ARIMA(p, d, q)**) processes. The first parameter (p) refers to the order of autoregressive lags (not counting the unit roots), the second parameter (d) refers to the order of integration, and the third parameter (q) is the number of moving average lags. Since $\phi(L)$ satisfies the stationarity condition, taking d-th differences of an ARIMA(p, d, q) produces a zero-mean stationary ARMA(p, q) process. So an ARIMA(p, d, q) process is I(d).

The Wiener Process

The next two sections will present a variety of unit-root tests. The limiting distributions of their test statistics will be written in terms of **Wiener processes** (also called **Brownian motion processes**). Some of you may already be familiar with this from continuous-time finance, but to refresh your memory,

Definition 9.3 (Standard Wiener processes): A standard Wiener (Brownian motion) process $W(\cdot)$ is a continuous-time stochastic process, associating each date $t \in [0, 1]$ with the scalar random variable $W(t)$, such that

(1) $W(0) = 0$;

(2) for any dates $0 \leq t_1 < t_2 < \cdots < t_k \leq 1$, the changes

$$W(t_2) - W(t_1), W(t_3) - W(t_2), \ldots, W(t_k) - W(t_{k-1})$$

are independent multivariate normal with $W(s) - W(t) \sim N(0, (s-t))$ (so in particular $W(1) \sim N(0, 1)$);

(3) for any realization, $W(t)$ is continuous in t with probability 1.

Roughly speaking, the **functional central limit theorem (FCLT)**, also called the **invariance principle**, states that a Wiener process is a continuous-time analogue of a driftless random walk. Imagine that you generate a realization of a standard random walk (whose changes have a unit variance) of length T, scale the graph vertically by deflating all its values by $\sqrt{T}$, and then horizontally compress this normalized graph so that it fits the unit interval [0, 1]. In Panel (a) of Figure 9.2, that is done for a sample size of $T = 10$. The sample size is increased to 100 in Panel (b), and then to 1,000 in Panel (c). As the figure shows, the graph becomes increasingly dense over the unit interval. The FCLT assures us that there exists a well-defined limit as $T \to \infty$ and that the limiting process is the Wiener process. Property (2) of Definition 9.3 is a mathematical formulation of the property that the sequence of instantaneous changes of a Wiener process is i.i.d. The continuous-time analogue of a driftless random walk whose changes have a variance of σ^2, rather than unity, can be written as $\sigma W(r)$.

To pursue the analogy between a driftless random walk and a Wiener process a bit further, consider a "demeaned standard random walk" which is constructed from a standard driftless random walk by subtracting the sample mean. That is, let $\{\xi_t\}$ be a driftless random walk with $\text{Var}(\Delta\xi_t) = 1$ and define

$$\xi_t^\mu \equiv \xi_t - \frac{\xi_0 + \xi_1 + \cdots + \xi_{T-1}}{T} \quad (t = 0, 1, \ldots, T-1). \tag{9.2.14}$$

The continuous-time analogue of this demeaned random walk is a **demeaned standard Wiener process** defined as

$$W^\mu(r) \equiv W(r) - \int_0^1 W(s)\,\mathrm{d}s. \tag{9.2.15}$$

(We defined the demeaned series for $t = 0, 1, \ldots, T-1$, to match the dating convention of Proposition 9.2 below. If the demeaned series is defined for $t = 1, 2, \ldots, T$, then its continuous-time analogue, too, is (9.2.15).)

We can also create from the standard random walk $\{\xi_t\}$ a detrended series:

$$\xi_t^\tau \equiv \xi_t - \hat{\alpha} - \hat{\delta} \cdot t \quad (t = 0, 1, \ldots, T-1), \tag{9.2.16}$$

where $\hat{\alpha}$ and $\hat{\delta}$ are the OLS estimates of the intercept and the time coefficient in the regression of ξ_t on $(1, t)$ $(t = 0, 1, \ldots, T-1)$. The continuous-time analogue of

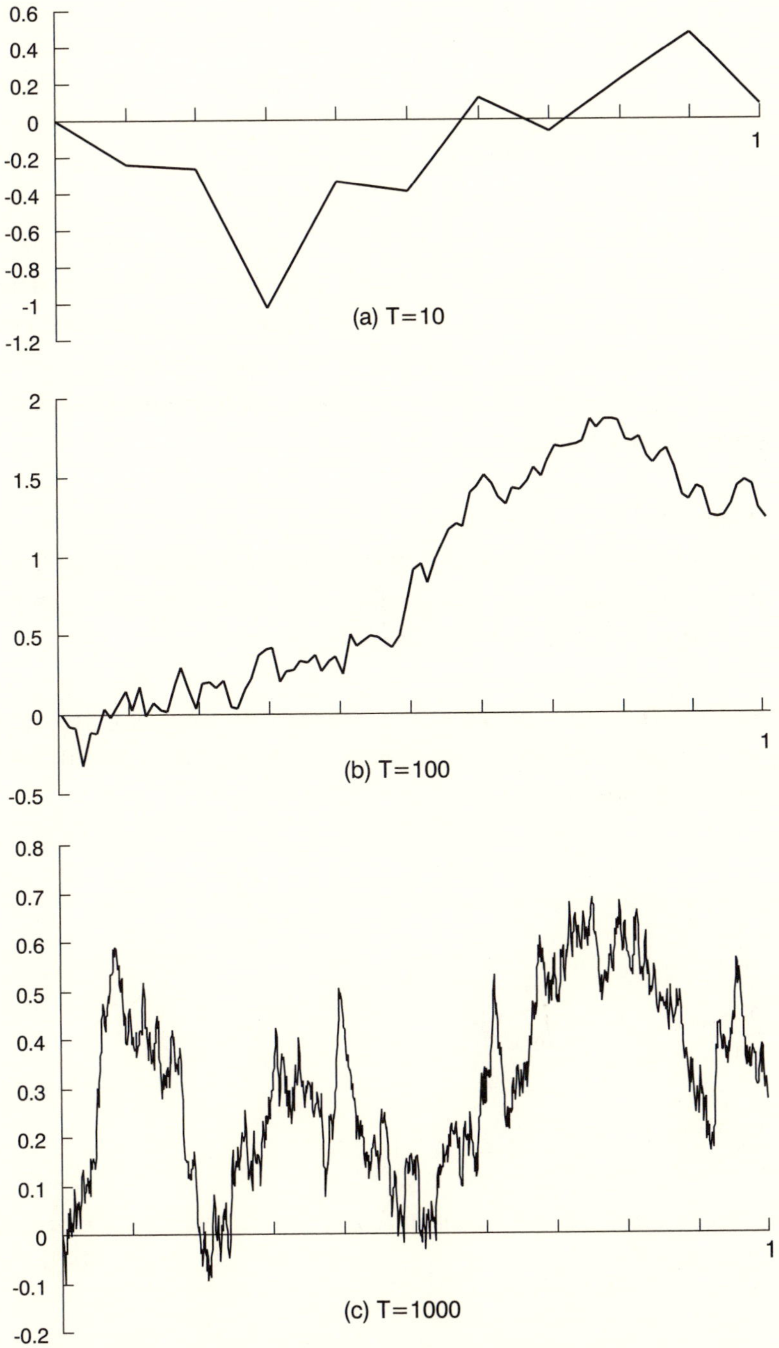

Figure 9.2: Illustration of the Functional Central Limit Theorem

the detrended random walk is a **detrended standard Wiener process** defined as

$$W^{\tau}(r) \equiv W(r) - a - d \cdot r,$$
$$a \equiv \int_0^1 (4 - 6s)W(s)\,\mathrm{d}s,$$
$$d \equiv \int_0^1 (-6 + 12s)W(s)\,\mathrm{d}s. \tag{9.2.17}$$

The coefficients a and d are the limiting random variables of $\hat{\alpha}$ and $\hat{\delta}$, respectively, as $T \to \infty$ (see, e.g., Phillips and Durlauf, 1986, for a derivation). Therefore, if a linear time trend is fitted to a *driftless* random walk by OLS, the estimated linear time trend $\hat{\delta}$ converges in distribution to a random variable d; even in large samples $\hat{\delta}$ will never be zero unless by accident. This phenomenon is sometimes called **spurious detrending**.

A Useful Lemma

Unit-root tests utilize statistics involving I(0) and I(1) processes. The key results collected in the following proposition will be used to derive the limiting distributions of the test statistics of the unit-root tests of Sections 9.3–9.4.

Proposition 9.2 (Limiting distributions of statistics involving I(0) and I(1) variables): *Let $\{\xi_t\}$ be driftless* I(1) *so that $\Delta\xi_t$ is zero-mean* I(0) *satisfying (9.2.1)–(9.2.3) and* $\mathrm{E}(\xi_0^2) < \infty$. *Let*

$$\lambda^2 \equiv \textit{long-run variance of } \{\Delta\xi_t\} \textit{ and } \gamma_0 \equiv \mathrm{Var}(\Delta\xi_t).$$

Then

(a) $\displaystyle \frac{1}{T^2}\sum_{t=1}^{T}(\xi_{t-1})^2 \underset{\mathrm{d}}{\to} \lambda^2 \cdot \int_0^1 W(r)^2\,\mathrm{d}r,$

(b) $\displaystyle \frac{1}{T}\sum_{t=1}^{T}\Delta\xi_t\,\xi_{t-1} \underset{\mathrm{d}}{\to} \frac{\lambda^2}{2}W(1)^2 - \frac{\gamma_0}{2}.$

Let $\{\xi_t^{\mu}\}$ be the demeaned series created from $\{\xi_t\}$ by the formula (9.2.14). Then

(c) $\displaystyle \frac{1}{T^2}\sum_{t=1}^{T}(\xi_{t-1}^{\mu})^2 \underset{\mathrm{d}}{\to} \lambda^2 \cdot \int_0^1 [W^{\mu}(r)]^2\,\mathrm{d}r,$

(d) $\displaystyle \frac{1}{T}\sum_{t=1}^{T}\Delta\xi_t\,\xi_{t-1}^{\mu} \underset{\mathrm{d}}{\to} \frac{\lambda^2}{2}\{[W^{\mu}(1)]^2 - [W^{\mu}(0)]^2\} - \frac{\gamma_0}{2}.$

Let $\{\xi_t^\tau\}$ be the detrended series created from $\{\xi_t\}$ by the formula (9.2.16). Then

(e) $\frac{1}{T^2}\sum_{t=1}^{T}(\xi_{t-1}^\tau)^2 \underset{d}{\to} \lambda^2 \cdot \int_0^1 [W^\tau(r)]^2\, dr,$

(f) $\frac{1}{T}\sum_{t=1}^{T}\Delta\xi_t\, \xi_{t-1}^\tau \underset{d}{\to} \frac{\lambda^2}{2}\{[W^\tau(1)]^2 - [W^\tau(0)]^2\} - \frac{\gamma_0}{2}.$

The convergence is joint. That is, a vector consisting of the statistics indicated in (a)–(f) converges to a random vector whose elements are the corresponding random variables also indicated in (a)–(f).

Part (a), for example, reads as follows: the sequence of random variables $\{(1/T)^2 \sum_{t=1}^{T}(\xi_{t-1})^2\}$ indexed by T converges in distribution to a random variable $\lambda^2 \int W^2 dr$. The limiting random variables in the proposition are all written in terms of standard Wiener processes. Note that the *same* Wiener process $W(\cdot)$ appears in (a) and (b) and that the demeaned and detrended Wiener processes in (c)–(f) are derived from the Wiener process appearing in (a) and (b). So the limiting random variables in (a)–(f) can be correlated.

To gain some understanding of this result, suppose temporarily that $\{\xi_t\}$ is a driftless random walk with $\text{Var}(\Delta\xi_t) = \sigma^2$. Given that a Wiener process is the continuous-time analogue, it is not surprising that "$\sum_{t=1}^{T}(\xi_{t-1})^2$" suitably normalized by a power of T becomes "$\sigma^2 \int W^2$." Perhaps what you might not have guessed is the normalization by T^2. One way to see why the square of T provides the right normalization, is to recall that $\text{E}[(\xi_t)^2] = \text{Var}(\xi_t) = \sigma^2 \cdot t$. Thus,

$$\text{E}\left[\sum_{t=1}^{T}(\xi_{t-1})^2\right] = \sigma^2\sum_{t=1}^{T}(t-1) = \sigma^2 \cdot (T-1)\frac{T}{2}. \tag{9.2.18}$$

So the mean of $\sum_{t=1}^{T}(\xi_{t-1})^2$ grows at rate T^2. In order to construct a random variable that could have a limiting distribution, $\sum_{t=1}^{T}(\xi_{t-1})^2$ will have to be divided by T^2.

Now suppose that $\{\xi_t\}$ is a general driftless I(1) process whose first difference is a zero-mean I(0) process satisfying (9.2.1)–(9.2.3). Then serial correlation in $\Delta\xi_t$ can be taken into account by replacing σ^2 by λ^2 (the long-run variance of $\{\Delta\xi_t\}$). This is due to implication (9.2.9) of the Beveridge-Nelson decomposition that a driftless I(1) process is dominated in large samples by a random walk whose changes have a variance of λ^2. Put differently, the limiting distribution of $\sum_{t=1}^{T}(\xi_{t-1})^2/T^2$ would be the same if $\{\xi_t\}$, instead of being a general driftless

I(1) process with serially correlated first differences, were a driftless random walk whose changes have a variance of λ^2.

For a proof of Proposition 9.2, see, e.g., Stock (1994, pp. 2751–2753). It is a rather mechanical application of the FCLT and a theorem called the "continuous mapping theorem." Since $W(1) \sim N(0, 1)$, the limiting random variable in (b) is

$$\left(\frac{\lambda^2}{2}\right)X - \frac{\gamma_0}{2} \tag{9.2.19}$$

where $X \sim \chi^2(1)$ (chi-squared with 1 degree of freedom). Proof of (b) can be done without the fancy apparatus of the FCLT and the continuous mapping theorem and is left as Analytical Exercise 1.

QUESTIONS FOR REVIEW

1. (Verifying Beveridge-Nelson for simple cases) Verify (9.2.5) for $\psi(L) = 1 + \psi_1 L$. Do the same for $\psi(L) = (1 - \phi L)^{-1}$ where $|\phi| < 1$.

2. (A CLT for I(0)) Proposition 6.9 is about the asymptotics of the sample mean of a linear process. Verify that the paragraph right below Proposition 9.1 is a proof of Proposition 6.9 with the added assumption of one-summability.

3. (Is the stationary component in Beveridge-Nelson I(0)?) Consider a zero-mean I(0) process

$$u_t = \psi_0 \varepsilon_t - 2\varepsilon_{t-1} + \varepsilon_{t-2}.$$

Verify that the long-run variance of $\{\eta_t\}$ defined in (9.2.6) is zero.

4. (Initial values and demeaned values) Let $\{\xi_t\}$ be driftless I(1) so that ξ_t can be written as $\xi_t = \xi_0 + u_1 + u_2 + \cdots + u_t$. Does the value of ξ_0 affect the value of ξ_t^μ where $\{\xi_t^\mu\}$ is the demeaned series created from $\{\xi_t\}$ by the formula (9.2.14)? [Answer: No.]

5. (Linear trends and detrended values) Let ξ_t be I(1) with drift, so it can be written as the sum of a linear time trend $\alpha + \delta \cdot t$ and a driftless I(1) process. Do the values of α and δ affect the value of ξ_t^τ where $\{\xi_t^\tau\}$ is the detrended series created from $\{\xi_t\}$ by the formula (9.2.16)? [Answer: No.]

9.3 Dickey-Fuller Tests

In this and the following section, we will present several tests of the null hypothesis that the data generating process (DGP) is I(1). In this section, the I(1) process is a random walk with or without drift, and the tests are based on the OLS estimation of appropriate AR(1) equations. Those tests were developed by Dickey (1976) and Fuller (1976) and are referred to as **Dickey-Fuller tests** or **DF tests**. We take the convention that the sample has $T+1$ observations $(y_0, y_1, \dots, y_T)$, so that the AR(1) equation can be estimated for $t = 1, 2, \dots, T$.

The AR(1) Model

The Dickey-Fuller test statistics are derived from the estimation of the first-order autoregressive model:

$$y_t = \rho y_{t-1} + \varepsilon_t, \ \{\varepsilon_t\} \text{ independent white noise.} \tag{9.3.1}$$

(The case with intercept will be studied in a moment.) This model includes both I(1) and I(0) processes: if $\rho = 1$, that is, if the associated polynomial equation $1 - \rho z = 0$ has a unit root, then $\Delta y_t = \varepsilon_t$ and $\{y_t\}$ is a driftless random walk, whereas if $|\rho| < 1$, the process is zero-mean stationary AR(1). Thus, the hypothesis that the data are generated by a driftless random walk can be formulated as the null hypothesis that $\rho = 1$. If we take the position that the DGP is either I(0) or I(1), then $-1 < \rho \leq 1$. Given this *a priori* restriction on ρ, the I(0) alternative can be expressed as $\rho < 1$. So one-tailed tests will be used to test the null of $\rho = 1$ against the I(0) alternative.

The tests will be based on $\hat{\rho}$, the OLS estimate of ρ in the AR(1) equation (9.3.1). Under the I(1) null of $\rho = 1$, the sampling error is $\hat{\rho} - 1$, whose expression is given by

$$\hat{\rho} - 1 \equiv \frac{\sum_{t=1}^{T} y_t\, y_{t-1}}{\sum_{t=1}^{T} (y_{t-1})^2} - 1 = \frac{\sum_{t=1}^{T} \Delta y_t\, y_{t-1}}{\sum_{t=1}^{T} (y_{t-1})^2}. \tag{9.3.2}$$

As will be verified in a moment, the numerator has a limiting distribution if divided by T and the denominator has one if divided by T^2. So consider the sampling error magnified by T:

$$T \cdot (\hat{\rho} - 1) = T \cdot \frac{\sum_{t=1}^{T} \Delta y_t\, y_{t-1}}{\sum_{t=1}^{T} (y_{t-1})^2} = \frac{\frac{1}{T} \sum_{t=1}^{T} \Delta y_t\, y_{t-1}}{\frac{1}{T^2} \sum_{t=1}^{T} (y_{t-1})^2}. \tag{9.3.3}$$

Deriving the Limiting Distribution under the I(1) Null

Deriving the limiting distribution of $T \cdot (\hat{\rho} - 1)$ under the I(1) null (a driftless random walk) is very straightforward. Since $\{y_t\}$ is driftless I(1), parts (a) and (b) of Proposition 9.2 are applicable with $\xi_t = y_t$. Furthermore, since Δy_t is independent white noise, λ^2 (the long-run variance of $\{\Delta y_t\}$) equals γ_0 (the variance of Δy_t). Thus,

$$w_{1T} \equiv \frac{1}{T}\sum_{t=1}^{T} \Delta y_t \, y_{t-1} \underset{d}{\to} \frac{\gamma_0}{2} W(1)^2 - \frac{\gamma_0}{2} \equiv w_1, \tag{9.3.4}$$

$$w_{2T} \equiv \frac{1}{T^2}\sum_{t=1}^{T} (y_{t-1})^2 \underset{d}{\to} \gamma_0 \int_0^1 W(r)^2 \, dr \equiv w_2. \tag{9.3.5}$$

As noted in the Proposition, the convergence is *joint*, so $\mathbf{w}_T \equiv (w_{1T}, w_{2T})'$ as a vector converges to a 2×1 random vector, $\mathbf{w} \equiv (w_1, w_2)'$. Since (9.3.3) is a continuous function of $\mathbf{w}_T$ (it equals w_{1T}/w_{2T}), it follows from Lemma 2.3(b) that

$$T \cdot (\hat{\rho} - 1) = \frac{\frac{1}{T}\sum_{t=1}^{T} \Delta y_t \, y_{t-1}}{\frac{1}{T^2}\sum_{t=1}^{T} (y_{t-1})^2} = \frac{w_{1T}}{w_{2T}}$$

$$\underset{d}{\to} \frac{w_1}{w_2} = \frac{\frac{\gamma_0}{2} W(1)^2 - \frac{\gamma_0}{2}}{\gamma_0 \cdot \int_0^1 W(r)^2 \, dr} = \frac{\frac{1}{2}(W(1)^2 - 1)}{\int_0^1 W(r)^2 \, dr} \equiv DF_\rho. \tag{9.3.6}$$

The test statistic $T \cdot (\hat{\rho} - 1)$ is called the **Dickey-Fuller**, or **DF, ρ statistic**. Several points are worth noting:

- $T \cdot (\hat{\rho} - 1)$, rather than the usual $\sqrt{T} \cdot (\hat{\rho} - 1)$, has a nondegenerate limiting distribution. The estimator $\hat{\rho}$ is said to be **superconsistent** because it converges to the true value of unity at a faster rate (T).

- The null hypothesis does not specify the values of $\text{Var}(\varepsilon_t)$ and y_0 (the initial value) of the DGP, yet they do not affect the limiting distribution, the distribution of the random variable DF_ρ. That is, the limiting distribution does not involve those **nuisance parameters**. So we can use $T \cdot (\hat{\rho} - 1)$ as the test statistic. This test of a driftless random walk is called the **Dickey-Fuller ρ test**.

- Note that both the numerator and the denominator involve the *same* Wiener process, so they are correlated. Since $W(1)$ is distributed as standard normal, the numerator of the expression for DF_ρ could be written as $(\chi^2(1) - 1)/2$. But this would obscure the point being made here.

The usual t-test for the null of $\rho = 1$, too, has a limiting distribution. It is just a matter of simple algebra to show that the t-value for the null of $\rho = 1$ can be written as

$$t = \frac{\hat{\rho} - 1}{s \div \sqrt{\sum_{t=1}^{T} (y_{t-1})^2}} = \frac{\frac{1}{T} \sum_{t=1}^{T} \Delta y_t \, y_{t-1}}{s \cdot \sqrt{\frac{1}{T^2} \sum_{t=1}^{T} (y_{t-1})^2}}, \tag{9.3.7}$$

where s is the standard error of regression:

$$s \equiv \sqrt{\frac{1}{T-1} \sum_{t=1}^{T} (y_t - \hat{\rho} y_{t-1})^2}. \tag{9.3.8}$$

It is easy to prove (see Review Question 3) that s^2 is consistent for γ_0 ($\equiv \text{Var}(\Delta y_t)$). It is then immediate from this and (9.3.4) and (9.3.5) that

$$t \underset{\text{d}}{\rightarrow} \frac{\frac{1}{2}(W(1)^2 - 1)}{\sqrt{\int_0^1 W(r)^2 \, \text{d}r}} \equiv DF_t. \tag{9.3.9}$$

This limiting distribution, too, is free from nuisance parameters. So the t-value can be used for testing, but the critical values for the standard normal distribution cannot be used; they have to come from a tabulation (provided below) of DF_t. This test is called the **DF t test**.

We summarize the discussion so far as

Proposition 9.3 (Dickey-Fuller tests of a driftless random walk, the case without intercept): *Suppose that $\{y_t\}$ is a driftless random walk (so $\{\Delta y_t\}$ is independent white noise) with $\text{E}(y_0^2) < \infty$. Consider the regression of y_t on y_{t-1} (without intercept) for $t = 1, 2, \ldots, T$. Then*

$$DF\rho \text{ statistic: } T \cdot (\hat{\rho} - 1) \underset{\text{d}}{\rightarrow} DF_\rho,$$

$$DF t \text{ statistic: } t \underset{\text{d}}{\rightarrow} DF_t,$$

where $\hat{\rho}$ is the OLS estimate of the y_{t-1} coefficient, t is the t-value for the hypothesis that the y_{t-1} coefficient is 1, and DF_ρ and DF_t are the random variables defined in (9.3.6) and (9.3.9).

Thus, we have two test statistics, $T \cdot (\hat{\rho} - 1)$ and the t-value, for the same I(1) null. Comparison of the (generalizations of) these DF tests will be discussed in the next section.

Table 9.1: Critical Values for the Dickey-Fuller ρ Test

Sample size (T)	Probability that the statistic is less than entry 0.01	0.025	0.05	0.10	0.90	0.95	0.975	0.99
	Panel (a): $T \cdot (\hat{\rho} - 1)$							
25	−11.8	−9.3	−7.3	−5.3	1.01	1.41	1.78	2.28
50	−12.8	−9.9	−7.7	−5.5	0.97	1.34	1.69	2.16
100	−13.3	−10.2	−7.9	−5.6	0.95	1.31	1.65	2.09
250	−13.6	−10.4	−8.0	−5.7	0.94	1.29	1.62	2.05
500	−13.7	−10.4	−8.0	−5.7	0.93	1.28	1.61	2.04
∞	−13.8	−10.5	−8.1	−5.7	0.93	1.28	1.60	2.03
	Panel (b): $T \cdot (\hat{\rho}^{\mu} - 1)$							
25	−17.2	−14.6	−12.5	−10.2	−0.76	0.00	0.65	1.39
50	−18.9	−15.7	−13.3	−10.7	−0.81	−0.07	0.53	1.22
100	−19.8	−16.3	−13.7	−11.0	−0.83	−0.11	0.47	1.14
250	−20.3	−16.7	−13.9	−11.1	−0.84	−0.13	0.44	1.08
500	−20.5	−16.8	−14.0	−11.2	−0.85	−0.14	0.42	1.07
∞	−20.7	−16.9	−14.1	−11.3	−0.85	−0.14	0.41	1.05
	Panel (c): $T \cdot (\hat{\rho}^{\tau} - 1)$							
25	−22.5	−20.0	−17.9	−15.6	−3.65	−2.51	−1.53	−0.46
50	−25.8	−22.4	−19.7	−16.8	−3.71	−2.60	−1.67	−0.67
100	−27.4	−23.7	−20.6	−17.5	−3.74	−2.63	−1.74	−0.76
250	−28.5	−24.4	−21.3	−17.9	−3.76	−2.65	−1.79	−0.83
500	−28.9	−24.7	−21.5	−18.1	−3.76	−2.66	−1.80	−0.86
∞	−29.4	−25.0	−21.7	−18.3	−3.77	−2.67	−1.81	−0.88

SOURCE: Fuller (1976, Table 8.5.1), corrected in Fuller (1996, Table 10.A.1).

Panel (a) of Table 9.1 has critical values for the finite-sample distribution of the random variable $T \cdot (\hat{\rho} - 1)$ for various sample sizes. The solid curve in Figure 9.3 graphs the finite-sample distribution of $\hat{\rho}$ for $T = 100$, which shows that the OLS estimate of ρ is biased downward (i.e., the mean of $\hat{\rho}$ is less than 1). These are obtained by Monte Carlo assuming that ε_t is Gaussian and $y_0 = 0$. By Proposition 9.3, as the sample size T increases, those critical values converge to the critical values for the distribution of DF_ρ, reported in the row for $T = \infty$. (Since y_0 does not have to be zero and ε_t does not have to be Gaussian for the asymptotic results in Proposition 9.3 to hold, we should obtain the same limiting critical values if the finite-sample critical values were calculated with a different assumption about the initial value y_0 and the distribution of ε_t.) From the critical values for $T = \infty$,

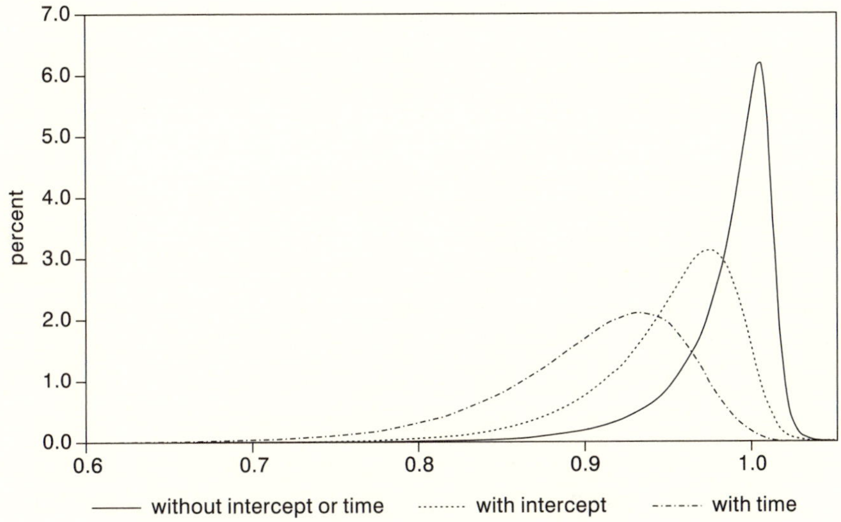

Figure 9.3: Finite-Sample Distribution of OLS Estimate of AR(1) Coefficient, $T = 100$

we can see that the DF_ρ distribution, too, is skewed to the left, with the 5 percent lower tail critical value of -8.1 (so $\text{Prob}(DF_\rho < -8.1) = 5\%$) and the 5 percent upper tail critical value of 1.28. The small-sample bias in $\hat{\rho}$ is reflected in the skewness in the limiting distribution of $T \cdot (\hat{\rho} - 1)$.

Critical values for DF_t (the limiting distribution of the t-value) are in the row for $T = \infty$ of Table 9.2, Panel (a). Like DF_ρ, it is skewed to the left. The table also has critical values for finite-sample sizes. Again, they assume that $y_0 = 0$ and ε_t is normally distributed.

Incorporating the Intercept

A shortcoming of the tests based on the AR(1) equation without intercept is its lack of invariance to an addition of a constant to the series. If the test is performed on a series of logarithms (as in Example 9.1 below), then a change in units of measurement of the series results in an addition of a constant to the series, which affects the value of the test statistic. To make the test statistic invariant to an addition of a constant, we generalize the model from which the statistic is derived. Consider the model

$$y_t = \alpha + z_t, \ z_t = \rho z_{t-1} + \varepsilon_t, \ \{\varepsilon_t\} \text{ independent white noise.} \tag{9.3.10}$$

Table 9.2: Critical Values for the Dickey-Fuller t-Test

Sample size (T)	Probability that the statistic is less than entry 0.01	0.025	0.05	0.10	0.90	0.95	0.975	0.99
				Panel (a): t				
25	−2.65	−2.26	−1.95	−1.60	0.92	1.33	1.70	2.15
50	−2.62	−2.25	−1.95	−1.61	0.91	1.31	1.66	2.08
100	−2.60	−2.24	−1.95	−1.61	0.90	1.29	1.64	2.04
250	−2.58	−2.24	−1.95	−1.62	0.89	1.28	1.63	2.02
500	−2.58	−2.23	−1.95	−1.62	0.89	1.28	1.62	2.01
∞	−2.58	−2.23	−1.95	−1.62	0.89	1.28	1.62	2.01
				Panel (b): t^{μ}				
25	−3.75	−3.33	−2.99	−2.64	−0.37	0.00	0.34	0.71
50	−3.59	−3.23	−2.93	−2.60	−0.41	−0.04	0.28	0.66
100	−3.50	−3.17	−2.90	−2.59	−0.42	−0.06	0.26	0.63
250	−3.45	−3.14	−2.88	−2.58	−0.42	−0.07	0.24	0.62
500	−3.44	−3.13	−2.87	−2.57	−0.44	−0.07	0.24	0.61
∞	−3.42	−3.12	−2.86	−2.57	−0.44	−0.08	0.23	0.60
				Panel (c): t^{τ}				
25	−4.38	−3.95	−3.60	−3.24	−1.14	−0.81	−0.50	−0.15
50	−4.16	−3.80	−3.50	−3.18	−1.19	−0.87	−0.58	−0.24
100	−4.05	−3.73	−3.45	−3.15	−1.22	−0.90	−0.62	−0.28
250	−3.98	−3.69	−3.42	−3.13	−1.23	−0.92	−0.64	−0.31
500	−3.97	−3.67	−3.42	−3.13	−1.24	−0.93	−0.65	−0.32
∞	−3.96	−3.67	−3.41	−3.13	−1.25	−0.94	−0.66	−0.32

SOURCE: Fuller (1976, Table 8.5.2), corrected in Fuller (1996, Table 10.A.2).

The process $\{y_t\}$ obtains when a constant α is added to a process satisfying (9.3.1). Under the null of $\rho = 1$, $\{z_t\}$ is a driftless random walk. Since y_t can be written as

$$y_t = \alpha + z_0 + \varepsilon_1 + \varepsilon_2 + \cdots + \varepsilon_t,$$

$\{y_t\}$ too is a driftless random walk with the initial value of $y_0 \equiv \alpha + z_0$. Under the alternative of $\rho < 1$, $\{y_t\}$ is stationary AR(1) with mean α. Thus, the class of I(0) processes included in (9.3.10) is larger than that in (9.3.1).

By eliminating $\{z_t\}$ from (9.3.10), we obtain an AR(1) equation with intercept

$$y_t = \alpha^* + \rho y_{t-1} + \varepsilon_t, \tag{9.3.11}$$

where

$$\alpha^* = (1 - \rho)\alpha. \tag{9.3.12}$$

Since $\alpha^* = 0$ when $\rho = 1$, the I(1) null (that the DGP is a driftless random walk) is the joint hypothesis that $\rho = 1$ *and* $\alpha^* = 0$ in terms of the coefficients of regression (9.3.11). Without the restriction $\alpha^* = 0$, $\{y_t\}$ could be a random walk *with* drift. We will develop tests of a random walk with drift in a moment. Until then, we continue to take the null to be a random walk without drift.

Let $\hat{\rho}^\mu$ here be the OLS estimate of ρ in (9.3.11) and t^μ be the t-value for the null of $\rho = 1$. It should be clear that α would not affect the value of $\hat{\rho}^\mu$ or its OLS standard error; adding the same constant to y_t for all t merely changes the estimated intercept. Therefore, the finite-sample as well as large-sample distributions of the **DF ρ^μ statistic**, $T \cdot (\hat{\rho}^\mu - 1)$, and the **DF t^μ statistic**, t^μ, will not depend on α regardless of the value of ρ.

As you will be asked to prove in Analytical Exercise 2, $T \cdot (\hat{\rho}^\mu - 1)$ converges in distribution to a random variable represented as

$$DF_\rho^\mu \equiv \frac{\frac{1}{2}\left([W^\mu(1)]^2 - [W^\mu(0)]^2 - 1\right)}{\int_0^1 [W^\mu(r)]^2 \, dr}, \tag{9.3.13}$$

and t^μ converges in distribution to

$$DF_t^\mu \equiv \frac{\frac{1}{2}\left([W^\mu(1)]^2 - [W^\mu(0)]^2 - 1\right)}{\sqrt{\int_0^1 [W^\mu(r)]^2 \, dr}}. \tag{9.3.14}$$

Here, $W^\mu(\cdot)$ is a demeaned standard Wiener process introduced in Section 9.2. These limiting distributions are free from nuisance parameters such as α. The basic idea of the proof is the following. First, obtain a demeaned series by subtracting the sample mean from $\{y_t\}$ (or equivalently, as the OLS residuals from the regression of $\{y_t\}$ on a constant). Second, use the Frisch-Waugh Theorem (introduced in Analytical Exercise 4 of Chapter 1) to write $T \cdot (\hat{\rho}^\mu - 1)$ and the t-value in formulas involving the demeaned series. Finally, use Proposition 9.2(c) and (d). Summarizing the discussion, we have

Proposition 9.4 (Dickey-Fuller tests of a driftless random walk, the case with intercept): *Suppose that $\{y_t\}$ is a driftless random walk (so $\{\Delta y_t\}$ is independent white noise) with $\mathrm{E}(y_0^2) < \infty$. Consider the regression of y_t on $(1, y_{t-1})$ for $t = 1, 2, \ldots, T$. Then*

$$DF\ \rho^\mu \text{ statistic: } T \cdot (\hat{\rho}^\mu - 1) \underset{d}{\rightarrow} DF_\rho^\mu,$$

$$DF\, t^{\mu} \text{ statistic: } t^{\mu} \underset{d}{\to} DF_t^{\mu},$$

where $\hat{\rho}^{\mu}$ is the OLS estimate of the y_{t-1} coefficient, t^{μ} is the t-value for the hypothesis that the y_{t-1} coefficient is 1, and DF_{ρ}^{μ} and DF_t^{μ} are the two random variables defined in (9.3.13) and (9.3.14).

Critical values for DF_{ρ}^{μ} are in Table 9.1, Panel (b), and those for DF_t^{μ} are in Table 9.2, Panel (b), in rows for $T = \infty$. The distribution is more strongly skewed to the left than in the case without intercept. The table also has critical values for finite-sample sizes based on the assumption that ε_t is normal. The finite-sample distribution of $\hat{\rho}^{\mu}$ for $T = 100$ is graphed in Figure 9.3. It shows a greater bias for $\hat{\rho}^{\mu}$ than for $\hat{\rho}$ (the OLS estimate without intercept). Unlike in the case without intercept, the finite-sample critical values do not depend on y_0. This is because, when $\rho = 1$, a change in the initial value y_0 only adds the same constant to y_t for all t, so the values of the DF ρ^{μ} and t^{μ} statistics are invariant to y_0.

We started out this subsection by saying that the I(1) null is the joint hypothesis that $\rho = 1$ *and* $\alpha^* = 0$. Yet the test statistics are for the hypothesis that $\rho = 1$. For the unit-root tests, this is the practice in the profession; test statistics for the joint hypothesis are rarely used.

Example 9.1 (Are the exchange rates a random walk?): Let y_t be the log of the spot yen/\$ exchange rate. To make the tests invariant to the choice of units (e.g., yen/\$ vs. yen/¢), we fit the AR(1) model with intercept, so Proposition 9.4 is applicable. For the weekly exchange rate data used in the empirical application of Chapter 6 and graphed in Figure 6.3 on page 424, the AR(1) equation estimated by OLS is

$$\underset{}{y_t =} \underset{(0.435)}{0.162} + \underset{(0.0019285)}{0.9983376}\, y_{t-1}, \quad R^2 = 0.997, \quad SER = 2.824.$$

Standard errors are in parentheses. Because of the lagged variable y_{t-1}, the actual sample period is from the second week rather than the first week of 1975. So $T = 777$ and

$$T \cdot (\hat{\rho}^{\mu} - 1) = 777 \cdot (0.9983376 - 1) = -1.29,$$

$$t^{\mu} = \frac{0.9983376 - 1}{0.0019285} = -0.86.$$

Since the alternative hypothesis is that $\rho < 1$, a one-tailed test is called for. (If you think that the process might be an explosive AR(1) with $\rho > 1$, you should perform a two-tailed test.) From Table 9.1, Panel (b), for DF_ρ^μ, the (asymptotic) critical value that gives 5 percent to the lower tail is -14.1. That is,

$$\text{Prob}(DF_\rho^\mu < -14.1) = 0.05.$$

The test statistic of -1.29 is well above this critical value, so the null is easily accepted at the 5 percent significance level. Turning to the DF t test, from Table 9.2, Panel (b), the 5 percent critical value is -2.86. The t-value of -0.86 is greater, so the null hypothesis is easily accepted.

Incorporating Time Trend

As was mentioned in Section 9.1, most economic time series appear to have linear time trends. To make the DF tests applicable to time series with trend, we generalize the model once again, this time by adding a linear time trend:

$$y_t = \alpha + \delta \cdot t + z_t,\ z_t = \rho z_{t-1} + \varepsilon_t,\ \{\varepsilon_t\} \text{ independent white noise.} \tag{9.3.15}$$

Here, δ is the slope of the linear trend which may or may not be zero. Under the null of $\rho = 1$, $\{z_t\}$ is a driftless random walk, and y_t can be written as

$$\begin{aligned} y_t &= \alpha + \delta \cdot t + z_0 + \varepsilon_1 + \varepsilon_2 + \cdots + \varepsilon_t \\ &= y_0 + \delta \cdot t + (\varepsilon_1 + \cdots + \varepsilon_t) \end{aligned} \tag{9.3.16}$$

with $y_0 \equiv \alpha + z_0$. So $\{y_t\}$ is a random walk with drift if $\delta \neq 0$ and without drift if $\delta = 0$. Under the alternative that $\rho < 1$, the process, being the sum of a linear trend and a zero-mean stationary AR(1) process, is trend stationary.

By eliminating $\{z_t\}$ from (9.3.15) we obtain

$$y_t = \alpha^* + \delta^* \cdot t + \rho y_{t-1} + \varepsilon_t, \tag{9.3.17}$$

where

$$\alpha^* = (1-\rho)\alpha + \rho\delta,\ \delta^* = (1-\rho)\delta. \tag{9.3.18}$$

Since $\delta^* = 0$ when $\rho = 1$, the I(1) null (that the DGP is a random walk with or without drift) is the joint hypothesis that $\rho = 1$ *and* $\delta^* = 0$ in terms of the regression coefficients. In practice, however, unit-root tests usually focus on the single restriction $\rho = 1$.

As in the AR(1) model with intercept, the statement of Proposition 9.3 can be readily modified to the AR(1) model with trend. Let $\hat{\rho}^\tau$ be the OLS estimate of the ρ in (9.3.17) and t^τ be the t-value for the null of $\rho = 1$. As you will be asked to prove in Analytical Exercise 3, $T \cdot (\hat{\rho}^\tau - 1)$ converges in distribution to

$$DF_\rho^\tau \equiv \frac{\frac{1}{2}\left([W^\tau(1)]^2 - [W^\tau(0)]^2 - 1\right)}{\int_0^1 [W^\tau(r)]^2 \, \mathrm{d}r}, \tag{9.3.19}$$

and t^τ converges in distribution to

$$DF_t^\tau \equiv \frac{\frac{1}{2}\left([W^\tau(1)]^2 - [W^\tau(0)]^2 - 1\right)}{\sqrt{\int_0^1 [W^\tau(r)]^2 \, \mathrm{d}r}}. \tag{9.3.20}$$

Here, $W^\tau(\cdot)$ is a detrended standard Wiener process introduced in Section 9.2. The basic idea of the proof is to use the Frisch-Waugh Theorem to write $T \cdot (\hat{\rho}^\tau - 1)$ and t^τ in formulas involving detrended series and then apply Proposition 9.2(e) and (f). Summarizing the discussion, we have

Proposition 9.5 (Dickey-Fuller tests of a random walk with or without drift): *Suppose that $\{y_t\}$ is a random walk with or without drift with $\mathrm{E}(y_0^2) < \infty$. Consider the regression of y_t on $(1, t, y_{t-1})$ for $t = 1, 2, \ldots, T$. Then*

$$DF\ \rho^\tau \text{ statistic: } T \cdot (\hat{\rho}^\tau - 1) \underset{\mathrm{d}}{\to} DF_\rho^\tau, \tag{9.3.21}$$

$$DF\ t^\tau \text{ statistic: } t^\tau \underset{\mathrm{d}}{\to} DF_t^\tau, \tag{9.3.22}$$

where $\hat{\rho}^\tau$ is the OLS estimate of the y_{t-1} coefficient, t^τ is the t-value for the hypothesis that the y_{t-1} coefficient is 1, and DF_ρ^τ and DF_t^τ are the two random variables defined in (9.3.19) and (9.3.20).

Critical values for DF_ρ^τ are in Table 9.1, Panel (c), and those for DF_t^τ are in Table 9.2, Panel (c). The table also has critical values for finite sample sizes based on the assumption that ε_t is normal (the initial value y_0 as well as the trend parameters α and δ need not be specified to calculate the finite-sample distributions because they do not affect the numerical values of the test statistics under the null of $\rho = 1$). For both the DF ρ^τ and t^τ statistics, the distribution is even more strongly skewed to the left than that for the case with intercept. Now for all sample sizes displayed in the tables, the 99 percent critical value is negative, meaning that more than 99 percent of the time $\hat{\rho}^\tau$ is less than unity when in fact the true value of ρ is unity! This is illustrated by the chained curve in Figure 9.3, which graphs the finite-sample distribution of $\hat{\rho}^\tau$ for $T = 100$.

Two comments are in order about Proposition 9.5.

- (Numerical invariance) The test statistics $\hat{\rho}^{\tau}$ and t^{τ} are invariant to (α, δ) regardless of the value of ρ; adding $\alpha + \delta \cdot t$ to the series $\{y_t\}$ merely changes the OLS estimates of α^* and δ^* but not $\hat{\rho}^{\tau}$ or its t-value. Therefore, the finite-sample as well as large-sample distributions of $T \cdot (\hat{\rho}^{\tau} - 1)$ and t^{τ} will not depend on (α, δ), regardless of the value of ρ.
- (Should the regression include time?) Since the test statistics are invariant to the value δ in the DGP, Proposition 9.5 is applicable even when $\delta = 0$. That is, the $\hat{\rho}^{\tau}$ and t^{τ} statistics can be used to test the null of a *driftless* random walk. However, if you are confident that the null process has no trend, then the DF ρ^{μ} and t^{μ} tests of Proposition 9.4 should be used, with the regression not including time, because the finite-sample power against stationary alternatives is generally greater with $\hat{\rho}^{\mu}$ and t^{μ} than with $\hat{\rho}^{\tau}$ and t^{τ} (you will be asked to verify this in Monte Carlo Exercise 1). On the other hand, if you think that the process might have a trend, then you should use $\hat{\rho}^{\tau}$ and t^{τ}, with time in the regression. If you fail to include time in the regression and use critical values from Table 9.1, Panel (b), and Table 9.2, Panel (b), when indeed the DGP has a trend, then the test will not be correctly sized in large samples (i.e., the probability of rejecting the null when the null is true will not approach the prespecified significance level (the nominal size) as the sample size goes to infinity). This is simply because the limiting distributions of $\hat{\rho}^{\mu}$ or t^{μ} when the DGP has a trend are not DF^{μ}_{ρ} or DF^{μ}_{t}.

QUESTIONS FOR REVIEW

1. (Superconsistency) Let $\hat{\rho}$ be the OLS coefficient estimate as in (9.3.2). Verify that $T^{1-\eta} \cdot (\hat{\rho} - 1) \to_{\text{p}} 0$ for $0 < \eta < 1$ if $\rho = 1$.
2. (Limiting distribution under general driftless I(1)) In the AR(1) model (9.3.1), drop the assumption that the error term is independent white noise by replacing ε_t by u_t and assuming that $\{u_t\}$ is a general zero-mean I(0) process satisfying (9.2.1)–(9.2.3). So the process under the null of $\rho = 1$ is a general driftless I(1) process. Show that $T \cdot (\hat{\rho} - 1)$ converges in distribution to

$$\frac{\frac{1}{2}\left(W(1)^2 - \frac{\gamma_0}{\lambda^2}\right)}{\int_0^1 W(r)^2 \, dr}$$

where $\lambda^2 \equiv$ long-run variance of $\{\Delta y_t\}$ and $\gamma_0 \equiv \text{Var}(\Delta y_t)$.

3. (Consistency of s^2) The usual OLS standard error of regression for the AR(1) equation, s, is defined in (9.3.8). If $|\rho| < 1$, we know from Section 6.4 that s^2 is consistent for $\text{Var}(\varepsilon_t)$. Show that, under the null of $\rho = 1$, s^2 remains consistent for $\text{Var}(\varepsilon_t)$. Since $\Delta y_t = \varepsilon_t$ when $\rho = 1$, s^2 is consistent for γ_0 ($\equiv \text{Var}(\Delta y_t)$) as well. **Hint:** Rewrite s^2 as

$$s^2 \equiv \frac{1}{T-1}\sum_{t=1}^{T}(\Delta y_t - (\hat{\rho}-1)y_{t-1})^2$$
$$= \frac{1}{T-1}\sum_{t=1}^{T}(\Delta y_t)^2 - \frac{2}{T-1}\cdot[T\cdot(\hat{\rho}-1)]\cdot\frac{1}{T}\sum_{t=1}^{T}\Delta y_t\, y_{t-1}$$
$$+ \frac{1}{T-1}\cdot[T\cdot(\hat{\rho}-1)]^2\cdot\frac{1}{T^2}\sum_{t=1}^{T}(y_{t-1})^2.$$

Also, $\text{E}[(\Delta y_t)^2] = \gamma_0$. Use the result we have used repeatedly: if $x_T \to_{\text{p}} 0$ and $y_T \to_{\text{d}} y$, then $x_T \cdot y_T \to_{\text{p}} 0$.

4. (Two tests for a random walk) Consider two regressions. One is to regress Δy_t on Δy_{t-1}, and the other is to regress Δy_t on y_{t-1}. To test the null that $\{y_t\}$ is a driftless random walk, which distribution should be used, the t-value from the first regression or the t-value from the second regression?

5. (Consistency of DF tests) Recall that a test is said to be **consistent** against a set of alternatives if the probability of rejecting a false null hypothesis when the true DGP is any of the alternatives approaches unity as the sample size increases. Let $T \cdot (\hat{\rho} - 1)$ be as defined in (9.3.3).

   (a) Suppose that $\{y_t\}$ is a zero-mean I(0) process and that its first-order autocorrelation coefficient is less than 1 (so $\text{E}(y_t^2) > \text{E}(y_t\, y_{t-1})$). Show that

   $$\underset{T\to\infty}{\text{plim}}\; T\cdot(\hat{\rho}-1) = -\infty.$$

   Thus, the DF ρ test is consistent against general I(0) alternatives. **Hint:** Show that, if $\{y_t\}$ is I(0),

   $$\underset{T\to\infty}{\text{plim}}\; \hat{\rho} = \frac{\text{E}(y_t\, y_{t-1})}{\text{E}(y_{t-1})^2}.$$

   (b) Show that the DF t test is consistent against general zero-mean I(0) alternatives. **Hint:** s converges in probability to some positive number when $\{y_t\}$ is zero-mean I(0).

6. (Effect of y_0 on test statistics) For $\hat{\rho}^{\mu}$ and t^{μ}, verify that the initial value y_0 does not affect their values in finite samples when $\rho = 1$. Does this hold true when $\rho < 1$? [Answer: No, because the effect of a change in y_0 on y_t depends on t.] Does the finite-sample power against the alternative of $\rho < 1$ depend on y_0? [Answer: Yes.]

7. (Sargan-Bhargava, 1983, statistic) Basing the test statistic on the OLS coefficient estimator is not the only way to derive a unit-root test. For a sample of $(y_0, y_1, \ldots, y_T)$, the **Sargan-Bhargava statistic** is defined as

$$SB = \frac{\frac{1}{T^2}\sum_{t=0}^{T}(y_t)^2}{\frac{1}{T}\sum_{t=1}^{T}(\Delta y_t)^2}.$$

   (a) Verify that it is the reciprocal of the Durbin-Watson statistic.

   (b) Show that, if $\{y_t\}$ is a driftless random walk, then

$$SB \underset{\text{d}}{\rightarrow} \int_0^1 [W(r)]^2 \, dr.$$

   Hint: $\sum_{t=0}^{T} y_t^2 = \sum_{t=1}^{T} y_{t-1}^2 + y_T^2$. Also, $y_T^2/T^2 \to_{\text{p}} 0$.

   (c) Verify that, under an I(0) alternative with $\mathrm{E}[(\Delta y_t)^2] \neq 0$, $SB \to_{\text{p}} 0$. (So the test rejects the I(1) null for *small* values of SB.)

9.4 Augmented Dickey-Fuller Tests

The I(1) null process in the previous section was a random walk, which does not allow for serial correlation in first differences. The tests of this section control for serial correlation by adding lagged first differences to the autoregressive equation. They are due to Dickey and Fuller (1979) and came to be known as the **Augmented Dickey-Fuller (ADF) tests.**

The Augmented Autoregression

The I(1) null in the simplest ADF tests is that $\{y_t\}$ is ARIMA$(p, 1, 0)$, that is, $\{\Delta y_t\}$ is a zero-mean stationary AR(p) process:

$$\Delta y_t = \zeta_1 \, \Delta y_{t-1} + \zeta_2 \, \Delta y_{t-2} + \cdots + \zeta_p \, \Delta y_{t-p} + \varepsilon_t, \quad \mathrm{E}(\varepsilon_t^2) \equiv \sigma^2, \quad (9.4.1)$$

where $\{\varepsilon_t\}$ is independent white noise and where the associated polynomial equation, $1-\zeta_1 z-\zeta_2 z^2-\cdots-\zeta_p z^p=0$, has all the roots outside the unit circle. (Later on we will allow $\{\Delta y_t\}$ to be stationary ARMA(p,q).) The first difference process $\{\Delta y_t\}$ is thus an I(0) process because it can be written as $\Delta y_t=\psi(L)\varepsilon_t$ where

$$\psi(L)=(1-\zeta_1 L-\zeta_2 L^2-\cdots-\zeta_p L^p)^{-1}. \tag{9.4.2}$$

The model used to derive the test statistics includes this process as a special case:

$$y_t=\rho y_{t-1}+\zeta_1\,\Delta y_{t-1}+\zeta_2\,\Delta y_{t-2}+\cdots+\zeta_p\,\Delta y_{t-p}+\varepsilon_t. \tag{9.4.3}$$

Indeed, (9.4.3) reduces to (9.4.1) when $\rho=1$.

Equation (9.4.3) can also be written as an AR$(p+1)$:

$$y_t=\phi_1 y_{t-1}+\phi_2 y_{t-2}+\cdots+\phi_{p+1}y_{t-p-1}+\varepsilon_t, \tag{9.4.4}$$

where the ϕ's are related to $(\rho,\zeta_1,\ldots,\zeta_p)$ by

$$\begin{aligned}\rho &\equiv \phi_1+\phi_2+\cdots+\phi_{p+1},\\ \zeta_j &\equiv -(\phi_{j+1}+\phi_{j+2}+\cdots+\phi_{p+1})\quad (j=1,2,\ldots,p).\end{aligned} \tag{9.4.5}$$

Conversely, any $(p+1)$-th order autoregression can be written in the form (9.4.3). This form (9.4.3) was originally proposed by Fuller (1976, p. 374). It is called the **augmented autoregression** because it can be obtained by adding lagged changes to the level AR(1) equation (9.3.1).

It is easy to show (Review Question 2) that the polynomial equation associated with (9.4.4) has a root inside the unit circle if $\rho>1$. Thus, if we take the position that the DGP is either I(1) or I(0), then ρ cannot be greater than 1 and the I(0) alternative is that $\rho<1$.

Limiting Distribution of the OLS Estimator

Having set up the model, we now turn to the task of deriving the limiting distribution of the OLS estimate of ρ in the augmented autoregression (9.4.3) under the I(1) null. Numerically the same estimate of ρ can be obtained from the AR$(p+1)$ equation (9.4.4) by calculating the sum of the OLS estimates of $(\phi_1,\phi_2,\ldots,\phi_{p+1})$ (recall that $\rho=\phi_1+\cdots+\phi_{p+1}$). For the purpose of deriving the limiting distribution, however, the augmented autoregression is more convenient. Under the I(1) null, all the $p+1$ regressors in (9.4.4) are driftless I(1), but it masks the fact, to be exploited below and clear from (9.4.3), that p linear combinations of them are zero-mean I(0).

To simplify the calculation, consider the special case of $p = 1$ (one lagged change in y_t or AR(2)), so that the augmented autoregression is

$$y_t = \rho y_{t-1} + \zeta_1 \, \Delta y_{t-1} + \varepsilon_t. \tag{9.4.6}$$

We assume that the sample is $(y_{-1}, y_0, \dots, y_T)$ so that the augmented autoregression can be estimated for $t = 1, 2, \dots, T$ (or alternatively, the sample is $(y_1, y_2, \dots, y_T)$ but the summations in what follows are from $t = 3$ to $t = T$ rather than from $t = 1$ to $t = T$). Write this as

$$y_t = \mathbf{x}_t' \boldsymbol{\beta} + \varepsilon_t$$

with

$$\underset{(2\times 1)}{\mathbf{x}_t} = \begin{bmatrix} y_{t-1} \\ \Delta y_{t-1} \end{bmatrix}, \qquad \underset{(2\times 1)}{\boldsymbol{\beta}} = \begin{bmatrix} \rho \\ \zeta_1 \end{bmatrix}. \tag{9.4.7}$$

If $\mathbf{b} \equiv (\hat{\rho}, \hat{\zeta}_1)'$ is the OLS estimator of the augmented autoregression coefficients $\boldsymbol{\beta}$ $(\equiv (\rho, \zeta_1)')$, the sampling error is given by

$$\mathbf{b} - \boldsymbol{\beta} = \Big(\sum_{t=1}^{T} \mathbf{x}_t \mathbf{x}_t'\Big)^{-1} \sum_{t=1}^{T} \mathbf{x}_t \cdot \varepsilon_t. \tag{9.4.8}$$

The individual terms in (9.4.8) are given by

$$\underset{(2\times 2)}{\mathbf{X}'\mathbf{X} \equiv \sum_{t=1}^{T} \mathbf{x}_t \mathbf{x}_t'} = \begin{bmatrix} \sum_{t=1}^{T} (y_{t-1})^2 & \sum_{t=1}^{T} y_{t-1} \, \Delta y_{t-1} \\ \sum_{t=1}^{T} \Delta y_{t-1} \, y_{t-1} & \sum_{t=1}^{T} (\Delta y_{t-1})^2 \end{bmatrix},$$

$$\underset{(2\times 1)}{\sum_{t=1}^{T} \mathbf{x}_t \cdot \varepsilon_t} = \begin{bmatrix} \sum_{t=1}^{T} y_{t-1} \, \varepsilon_t \\ \sum_{t=1}^{T} \Delta y_{t-1} \, \varepsilon_t \end{bmatrix}. \tag{9.4.9}$$

We can now apply the same trick we used for the time regression of Section 2.12. For some nonsingular matrix $\boldsymbol{\Upsilon}_T$ to be specified below, rewrite (9.4.8) as

$$\boldsymbol{\Upsilon}_T \cdot (\mathbf{b} - \boldsymbol{\beta}) = \boldsymbol{\Upsilon}_T \begin{bmatrix} \hat{\rho} - \rho \\ \hat{\zeta}_1 - \zeta_1 \end{bmatrix} = \mathbf{A}_T^{-1} \mathbf{c}_T, \tag{9.4.10}$$

where

$$\mathbf{A}_T \equiv \boldsymbol{\Upsilon}_T^{-1} \Bigg[\sum_{t=1}^{T} \mathbf{x}_t \, \mathbf{x}_t'\Bigg] \boldsymbol{\Upsilon}_T^{-1}, \quad \mathbf{c}_T \equiv \boldsymbol{\Upsilon}_T^{-1} \sum_{t=1}^{T} \mathbf{x}_t \cdot \varepsilon_t. \tag{9.4.11}$$

We seek a matrix $\boldsymbol{\Upsilon}_T$ such that $\boldsymbol{\Upsilon}_T \cdot (\mathbf{b} - \boldsymbol{\beta})$ has a nondegenerate limiting distribution under the I(1) null. This is accomplished by setting

$$\boldsymbol{\Upsilon}_T = \begin{bmatrix} T & 0 \\ 0 & \sqrt{T} \end{bmatrix}. \tag{9.4.12}$$

With this choice of the scaling matrix $\boldsymbol{\Upsilon}_T$, it follows from (9.4.9) and (9.4.11) that

$$\mathbf{A}_T = \begin{bmatrix} \frac{1}{T^2}\sum_{t=1}^T (y_{t-1})^2 & \frac{1}{\sqrt{T}}\frac{1}{T}\sum_{t=1}^T y_{t-1}\,\Delta y_{t-1} \\ \frac{1}{\sqrt{T}}\frac{1}{T}\sum_{t=1}^T \Delta y_{t-1}\,y_{t-1} & \frac{1}{T}\sum_{t=1}^T (\Delta y_{t-1})^2 \end{bmatrix},$$

$$\mathbf{c}_T = \begin{bmatrix} \frac{1}{T}\sum_{t=1}^T y_{t-1}\,\varepsilon_t \\ \frac{1}{\sqrt{T}}\sum_{t=1}^T \Delta y_{t-1}\,\varepsilon_t \end{bmatrix}. \tag{9.4.13}$$

Let us examine the elements of $\mathbf{A}_T$ and $\mathbf{c}_T$ and derive their limiting distributions under the null of $\rho = 1$.

The (1, 1) element of $\mathbf{A}_T$. Since $\{y_t\}$ is I(1) without drift, it converges in distribution to $\lambda^2 \cdot \int W^2\, dr$ by Proposition 9.2(a) where $\lambda^2 \equiv$ long-run variance of $\{\Delta y_t\}$.

The (2, 2) element of $\mathbf{A}_T$. It converges in probability (and hence in distribution) to γ_0 ($\equiv \text{Var}(\Delta y_t)$) because $\{\Delta y_t\}$, being stationary AR(1), is ergodic stationary with mean zero.

The off-diagonal elements of $\mathbf{A}_T$. They are $1/\sqrt{T}$ times

$$\frac{1}{T}\sum_{t=1}^T \Delta y_{t-1}\,y_{t-1}, \tag{9.4.14}$$

which is the average of the product of zero-mean I(0) and driftless I(1) variables. By Proposition 9.2(b), the similar product $(1/T)\sum_{t=1}^T \Delta y_t\, y_{t-1}$ converges in distribution to a random variable. It is easy to show (Review Question 3) that (9.4.14), too, converges to a random variable. So $1/\sqrt{T}$ times (9.4.14), which is the off-diagonal elements of $\mathbf{A}_T$, converges in probability (hence in distribution) to 0.

Therefore, $\mathbf{A}_T$, the properly rescaled $\mathbf{X}'\mathbf{X}$ matrix, is asymptotically diagonal:

$$\mathbf{A}_T \underset{d}{\rightarrow} \begin{bmatrix} \lambda^2 \cdot \int_0^1 W(r)^2\, dr & 0 \\ 0 & \gamma_0 \end{bmatrix},$$

so

$$(\mathbf{A}_T)^{-1} \underset{d}{\to} \begin{bmatrix} \left(\lambda^2 \cdot \int_0^1 W(r)^2 \, dr\right)^{-1} & 0 \\ 0 & \gamma_0^{-1} \end{bmatrix}. \tag{9.4.15}$$

We now turn to the elements of $\mathbf{c}_T$.

The first element of $\mathbf{c}_T$. Using the Beveridge-Nelson decomposition, it can be shown (Analytical Exercise 4) that

$$\frac{1}{T}\sum_{t=1}^{T} y_{t-1}\,\varepsilon_t \underset{d}{\to} c_1 \equiv \tfrac{1}{2}\sigma^2 \cdot \psi(1) \cdot [W(1)^2 - 1], \tag{9.4.16}$$

for a general zero-mean I(0) process

$$\Delta y_t = \psi(L)\varepsilon_t. \tag{9.4.17}$$

In the present case, $\Delta y_t = \zeta_1 \Delta y_{t-1} + \varepsilon_t$ under the null, so $\psi(L) = (1 - \zeta_1 L)^{-1}$ and

$$\psi(1) = \frac{1}{1 - \zeta_1}. \tag{9.4.18}$$

Second element of $\mathbf{c}_T$. It is easy to show (Review Question 4) that $\{\Delta y_{t-1}\,\varepsilon_t\}$ is a stationary and ergodic martingale difference sequence, so

$$\text{second element of } \mathbf{c}_T = \frac{1}{\sqrt{T}}\sum_{t=1}^{T} \Delta y_{t-1}\,\varepsilon_t \underset{d}{\to} c_2 \sim N(0, \gamma_0 \cdot \sigma^2), \tag{9.4.19}$$

where $\gamma_0 \equiv \text{Var}(\Delta y_t)$ and $\sigma^2 \equiv \text{Var}(\varepsilon_t)$.

Substituting (9.4.15)–(9.4.19) into (9.4.10) and noting that the true value of ρ is unity under the I(1) null, we obtain, for the OLS estimate of the augmented autoregression,[5]

[5] Here, we are using Lemma 2.3(b) to claim that $\mathbf{A}_T^{-1}\mathbf{c}_T$ converges in distribution to $\mathbf{A}^{-1}\mathbf{c}$ where $\mathbf{A}$ and $\mathbf{c}$ are the limiting random variables of $\mathbf{A}_T$ and $\mathbf{c}_T$, respectively. Note that, unlike in situations encountered for the stationary case, the convergence of $\mathbf{A}_T$ to $\mathbf{A}$ is in distribution, not in probability. We have proved in the text that $\mathbf{A}_T$ converges in distribution to $\mathbf{A}$ and $\mathbf{c}_T$ to $\mathbf{c}$, but we have not shown that $(\mathbf{A}_T, \mathbf{c}_T)$ converges in distribution jointly to $(\mathbf{A}, \mathbf{c})$, which is needed when using Lemma 2.3(b). However, by, e.g., Theorem 2.2 of Chan and Wei (1988), the convergence is joint.

$$\boldsymbol{\Upsilon}_T \cdot (\mathbf{b} - \boldsymbol{\beta}) = \begin{bmatrix} T \cdot (\hat{\rho} - 1) \\ \sqrt{T}(\hat{\zeta}_1 - \zeta_1) \end{bmatrix} \underset{d}{\rightarrow} \begin{bmatrix} \left(\lambda^2 \cdot \int_0^1 W(r)^2 \, dr\right)^{-1} & 0 \\ 0 & \gamma_0^{-1} \end{bmatrix} \begin{bmatrix} c_1 \\ c_2 \end{bmatrix}$$
$$= \begin{bmatrix} \left(\lambda^2 \cdot \int_0^1 W(r)^2 \, dr\right)^{-1} c_1 \\ \gamma_0^{-1} c_2 \end{bmatrix}.$$

Thus,

$$T \cdot (\hat{\rho} - 1) \underset{d}{\rightarrow} \frac{\sigma^2 \psi(1)}{\lambda^2} \cdot \frac{\frac{1}{2}[W(1)^2 - 1]}{\int_0^1 W(r)^2 \, dr} \quad \text{or} \quad \frac{\lambda^2}{\sigma^2 \psi(1)} \cdot T \cdot (\hat{\rho} - 1) \underset{d}{\rightarrow} DF_\rho, \tag{9.4.20}$$

$$\sqrt{T} \cdot (\hat{\zeta}_1 - \zeta_1) \underset{d}{\rightarrow} N\left(0, \frac{\sigma^2}{\gamma_0}\right), \tag{9.4.21}$$

where DF_ρ is none other than the DF ρ distribution defined in (9.3.6). Note that the estimated coefficient of the zero-mean I(0) variable (Δy_{t-1}) has the usual $\sqrt{T}$ asymptotics, while that of the driftless I(1) variable (y_{t-1}) has a nonstandard limiting distribution.

Deriving Test Statistics

There are no nuisance parameters entering the limiting distribution of the statistic $\frac{\lambda^2}{\sigma^2 \psi(1)} \cdot T \cdot (\hat{\rho} - 1)$ in (9.4.20), but the statistic itself involves nuisance parameters through $\frac{\lambda^2}{\sigma^2 \psi(1)}$. By the formula (9.2.4) for the long-run variance λ^2 of $\{\Delta y_t\}$, this ratio equals $\psi(1)$, which in turn equals $\frac{1}{1-\zeta_1}$ by (9.4.18) under the null. Now go back to the augmented autoregression (9.4.6). Since $\hat{\zeta}_1$, the OLS estimate of ζ_1, is consistent by (9.4.21), a consistent estimator of $\frac{1}{1-\zeta_1}$ is $(1 - \hat{\zeta}_1)^{-1}$. It then follows from (9.4.20) that

$$\frac{T \cdot (\hat{\rho} - 1)}{1 - \hat{\zeta}_1} \underset{d}{\rightarrow} DF_\rho. \tag{9.4.22}$$

That is, the required correction on $T \cdot (\hat{\rho} - 1)$ is done through the estimated coefficient of lagged Δy in the augmented autoregression. After the correction is made, the limiting distribution of the statistic does not depend on nuisance parameters controlling serial correlation of $\{\Delta y_t\}$ such as λ^2 and γ_0.

The OLS t-value for the hypothesis that $\rho = 1$, too, has a limiting distribution. It can be written as

$$t = \frac{\hat{\rho} - 1}{s \cdot \sqrt{(1,1) \text{ element of } \left(\sum_{t=1}^{T} \mathbf{x}_t \mathbf{x}_t'\right)^{-1}}}$$
$$= \frac{T \cdot (\hat{\rho} - 1)}{s \cdot \sqrt{(1,1) \text{ element of } (\mathbf{A}_T)^{-1}}}, \tag{9.4.23}$$

where s is the usual OLS standard error of regression. It follows easily from (9.4.15), (9.4.20), the consistency of s^2 for σ^2, and Proposition 9.2(a) and (b) for $\xi_t = y_t$ that

$$t \underset{\mathrm{d}}{\rightarrow} DF_t, \tag{9.4.24}$$

where DF_t is the DF t distribution defined in (9.3.9). Therefore, for the t-value, there is no need to correct for the fact that lagged Δy is included in the augmented autoregression.

All these results for $p = 1$ can be generalized easily:

Proposition 9.6 (Augmented Dickey-Fuller test of a unit root without intercept): *Suppose that $\{y_t\}$ is ARIMA$(p, 1, 0)$ so that $\{\Delta y_t\}$ is a zero-mean stationary AR(p) process following (9.4.1). Consider estimating the augmented autoregression, (9.4.3), and let $(\hat{\rho}, \hat{\zeta}_1, \hat{\zeta}_2, \ldots, \hat{\zeta}_p)$ be the OLS coefficient estimates. Also let t be the t-value for the hypothesis that $\rho = 1$. Then*

$$\text{ADF } \rho \text{ statistic: } \frac{T \cdot (\hat{\rho} - 1)}{1 - \hat{\zeta}_1 - \hat{\zeta}_2 - \cdots - \hat{\zeta}_p} \underset{\mathrm{d}}{\rightarrow} DF_\rho, \tag{9.4.25}$$

$$\text{ADF } t \text{ statistic: } t \underset{\mathrm{d}}{\rightarrow} DF_t, \tag{9.4.26}$$

where DF_ρ and DF_t are the two random variables defined in (9.3.6) and (9.3.9).

Testing Hypotheses about ζ

The argument leading to this surprisingly simple result is lengthy, but it has a by-product. The obvious generalization of (9.4.21) to the p-th order autoregression is

$$\sqrt{T} \cdot \begin{bmatrix} \hat{\zeta}_1 - \zeta_1 \\ \hat{\zeta}_2 - \zeta_2 \\ \vdots \\ \hat{\zeta}_p - \zeta_p \end{bmatrix} \underset{\mathrm{d}}{\rightarrow} N\left(\begin{bmatrix} 0 \\ 0 \\ \vdots \\ 0 \end{bmatrix}, \sigma^2 \cdot \begin{bmatrix} \gamma_0 & \gamma_1 & \cdots & \gamma_{p-1} \\ \gamma_1 & \gamma_0 & \cdots & \gamma_{p-2} \\ \vdots & \vdots & \cdots & \vdots \\ \gamma_{p-1} & \gamma_{p-2} & \cdots & \gamma_0 \end{bmatrix}^{-1} \right), \tag{9.4.27}$$

where γ_j is the j-th order autocovariance of $\{\Delta y_t\}$. By Proposition 6.7, this is the same asymptotic distribution you would get if the augmented autoregression (9.4.3) were estimated by OLS with the restriction $\rho = 1$, that is, if (9.4.1) is estimated by OLS. It is easy to show (Review Question 6) that hypotheses involving only the coefficients of the zero-mean I(0) regressors $(\zeta_1, \zeta_2, \dots, \zeta_p)$ can be tested in the usual way, with the usual t and F statistics asymptotically valid.

In deriving the limiting distributions of the regression coefficients, we have exploited the fact that one of the regressors is zero-mean I(0) while the other is driftless I(1). A systematic treatment of more general cases can be found in Sims, Stock, and Watson (1990) and Watson (1994, Section 2).

What to Do When p Is Unknown?

Proposition 9.6 assumes that the order of autoregression, p, for Δy_t is known. What can we do when the order p is unknown? To distinguish between the true order p and the number of lagged changes included in the augmented autoregression, we denote the latter by $\hat{p}$ in this section. We have considered a similar problem in Section 6.4. The difference is that the DGP here is a stationary process in first differences, not in levels as in Section 6.4, and that the estimation equation is an augmented autoregression with ρ freely estimated. We display below, without proof, three large-sample results about the choice of $\hat{p}$ under which the conclusion of Proposition 9.6 remains valid. These results are applicable to a class of processes more general than is assumed in Proposition 9.6: $\{\Delta y_t\}$ is zero-mean stationary and invertible ARMA(p, q) of unknown order (albeit with an additional assumption on ε_t that its fourth moment is finite).[6]

So, written as an autoregression, the order of autoregression for Δy_t can be infinite, as when $q > 0$, or finite, as when $q = 0$.

The first result is that the conclusion of Proposition 9.6 continues to hold when $\hat{p}$, the number of lagged first differences in the augmented autoregression, is increased with the sample size at an appropriate rate.

(1) (Said and Dickey, 1984, generalization of Proposition 9.6) Suppose that $\hat{p}$ satisfies

$$\hat{p} \to \infty \text{ but } \frac{\hat{p}}{T^{1/3}} \to 0 \text{ as } T \to \infty. \tag{9.4.28}$$

(That is, $\hat{p}$ goes to infinity but at a rate slower than $T^{1/3}$.) Then the two statistics, the ADF ρ and ADF t, based on the augmented autoregression with

[6]See Section 6.2 for the definition of invertible ARMA(p, q) processes. If an ARMA(p, q) process is invertible, then it can be written as an infinite-order autoregression.

$\hat{p}$ lagged changes, have the same limiting distributions as those indicated in Proposition 9.6.

This result, however, does not give us a practical guide for the lag length selection because there are infinitely many rules for $\hat{p}$ satisfying (9.4.28). A natural question is whether any of the rules for selecting the lag length considered in Section 6.4 — the general-to-specific sequential t rule or the information-criterion-based rules — can be used in the present context. To refresh your memory, the information-criterion-based rule is to set $\hat{p}$ to the j that minimizes

$$\log\left(\frac{SSR_j}{T}\right) + (j+1) \times \frac{C(T)}{T}, \tag{9.4.29}$$

where SSR_j is the sum of squared residuals from the autoregression with j lags:

$$\Delta y_t = \rho\, y_{t-1} + \zeta_1\, \Delta y_{t-1} + \zeta_2\, \Delta y_{t-2} + \cdots + \zeta_j\, \Delta y_{t-j} + \varepsilon_t. \tag{9.4.30}$$

The term $C(T)/T$ is multiplied by $j+1$, because the equation has $j+1$ coefficients including the lagged y_t coefficient. For the Akaike information criterion (AIC), $C(T) = 2$, while for the Bayesian information criterion (BIC), also called Schwartz information criterion (SIC), $C(T) = \log(T)$. In either rule, $\hat{p}$ is selected from the set $j = 0, 1, 2, \ldots, p_{max}$. In Section 6.4, this upper bound p_{max} was set to some known integer greater than or equal to the true order of the finite-order autoregressive process. The $\hat{p}$ selected by either of these rules is a function of data (not just a function of T), and hence is a random variable.

To be sure, when $\{\Delta y_t\}$ is stationary and invertible ARMA(p, q), the autoregressive order is infinite when $q > 0$ and the upper bound p_{max} obviously cannot be set to the true order. But it can be made to increase with the sample size T. To emphasize the dependence of p_{max} on T, write it as $p_{max}(T)$. If the rules are thus modified, does the Said-Dickey extension of Proposition 9.6 remain valid when $\hat{p}$ is chosen by either of the rules? The answer obtained by Ng and Perron (1995) is yes. More specifically,

(2) Suppose that $\hat{p}$ is selected by the general-to-specific t rule with $p_{max}(T)$ satisfying condition (9.4.28) (which in the Said-Dickey extension above was a condition for $\hat{p}$, not for $p_{max}(T)$) and $p_{max}(T) > c \cdot T^g$ for some $c > 0$ and $0 < g < 1/3$. Then the limiting distributions of the ADF ρ and ADF t statistics are as indicated in Proposition 9.6.[7]

[7] This is Theorem 5.3 of Ng and Perron (1995). Their condition A1 is (9.4.28) here. Their condition A2$''$ is implied by the second condition indicated here.

(3) Suppose that $\hat{p}$ is selected by AIC or by BIC with $p_{max}(T)$ satisfying condition (9.4.28). Then the same conclusion holds.[8]

Thus, no matter which rule — the sequential t, AIC, or BIC — for selecting $\hat{p}$ you employ, the large-sample distributions of the ADF statistics are the same as in Proposition 9.6.

A Suggestion for the Choice of $p_{max}(T)$

The finite-sample distribution, however, depends on which rule you use and also on the choice of the upper bound $p_{max}(T)$, and there are infinitely many valid choices for the function $p_{max}(T)$. For example, $p_{max}(T) = [T^{1/4}]$ (the integer part of $T^{1/4}$) satisfies the conditions in result (2) for the sequential t-test. So does $p_{max}(T) = [100T^{3/10}]$. It is important, therefore, that researchers use the same $p_{max}(T)$ when deciding the order of the augmented autoregression. In this context, the Monte Carlo literature examining the small-sample properties of various unit-root tests is relevant. Simulations run by Schwert (1989) show that in small and moderately large samples (from $T = 25$ to 1,000), including enough lags in the autoregression is important to minimize size distortions.[9] The choice of $\hat{p}$ (the number of lags included in the autoregression) that was more or less successful in controlling the actual size in Schwert's study is $\left[12 \cdot \left(\frac{T}{100}\right)^{1/4}\right]$. The upper bound $p_{max}(T)$ should therefore give lag selection rules a chance of selecting a $\hat{p}$ as large as this. Therefore, in the examples and application of this chapter, we use the function

$$p_{max}(T) = \left[12 \cdot \left(\frac{T}{100}\right)^{1/4}\right] \quad \text{(integer part of } 12 \cdot \left(\frac{T}{100}\right)^{1/4}\text{)} \tag{9.4.31}$$

in any of the rules for selecting the lag length. This function satisfies the conditions of results (2) and (3) above.

The sample period when selecting $\hat{p}$ is $t = p_{max}(T) + 2, p_{max}(T) + 3, \ldots, T$. The first t is $p_{max}(T) + 2$ because $p_{max}(T) + 1$ observations are needed to calculate $p_{max}(T)$ lagged changes in the augmented autoregression. Since only $T - p_{max}(T) - 1$ observations are used to estimate the autoregression (9.4.30) for $j = 1, 2, \ldots, p_{max}(T)$, the sample size in the objective function in (9.4.29) should be

[8]This is Theorem 4.3 of Ng and Perron (1995). The theorem does not indicate the upper bound $p_{max}(T)$, but (as pointed out by Pierre Perron in private communications with the author) Hannan and Deistler (1988, Section 7.4 (ii)) implies that (9.4.28) can be an upper bound.

[9]Recall that a size distortion refers to the difference between the actual or exact size (the finite-sample probability of rejecting a true null) and the nominal size (the probability of rejecting a true null when the sample size is infinite).

$T - p_{max}(T) - 1$ rather than T:

$$\log\Big(\frac{SSR_j}{T - p_{max}(T) - 1}\Big) + (j+1) \times \frac{C(T - p_{max}(T) - 1)}{T - p_{max}(T) - 1}. \qquad (9.4.32)$$

Including the Intercept in the Regression

As in the DF tests, we can modify the ADF tests so that they are invariant to an addition of a constant to the series. We allow $\{y_t\}$ to differ by an unspecified constant from the process that follows augmented autoregression without intercept (9.4.3). This amounts to replacing the y_t in (9.4.3) by $y_t - \alpha$, which yields

$$y_t = \alpha^* + \rho y_{t-1} + \zeta_1 \,\Delta y_{t-1} + \zeta_2 \,\Delta y_{t-2} + \cdots + \zeta_p \,\Delta y_{t-p} + \varepsilon_t, \quad (9.4.33)$$

where $\alpha^* = (1-\rho)\alpha$. As in the AR(1) model with intercept, the I(1) null is the joint hypothesis that $\rho = 1$ *and* $\alpha^* = 0$. Nevertheless, unit-root tests usually focus on the single restriction $\rho = 1$.

It is left as an analytical exercise to prove

Proposition 9.7 (Augmented Dickey-Fuller test of a unit root with intercept): *Suppose that $\{y_t\}$ is an ARIMA$(p, 1, 0)$ process so that $\{\Delta y_t\}$ is a zero-mean stationary AR(p) process following (9.4.1). Consider estimating the augmented autoregression with intercept, (9.4.33), and let $(\hat{\alpha}, \hat{\rho}^{\mu}, \hat{\zeta}_1, \hat{\zeta}_2, \ldots, \hat{\zeta}_p)$ be the OLS coefficient estimates. Also let t^{μ} be the t-value for the hypothesis that $\rho = 1$. Then*

$$\text{ADF } \rho^{\mu} \text{ statistic: } \frac{T \cdot (\hat{\rho}^{\mu} - 1)}{1 - \hat{\zeta}_1 - \hat{\zeta}_2 - \cdots - \hat{\zeta}_p} \underset{d}{\to} DF_{\rho}^{\mu}, \qquad (9.4.34)$$

$$\text{ADF } t^{\mu} \text{ statistic: } t^{\mu} \underset{d}{\to} DF_t^{\mu}, \qquad (9.4.35)$$

where the random variables DF_{ρ}^{μ} and DF_t^{μ} are defined in (9.3.13) and (9.3.14).

The basic idea of the proof is to use the Frisch-Waugh Theorem to write $\hat{\rho}^{\mu}$ and the t-value in formulas involving the demeaned series created from $\{y_t\}$.

Before turning to an example, two comments about Proposition 9.7 are in order.

- (Numerical invariance) As was true in Proposition 9.4, since the regression includes a constant, the test statistics are invariant to an addition of a constant to the series.

- (Said-Dickey extension) The Said-Dickey-Ng-Perron extension is also applicable here: if $\{\Delta y_t\}$ is stationary and invertible ARMA(p, q) (so Δy_t can be written as a possibly infinite-order autoregression), then the ADF ρ^{μ} and t^{μ} statistics have the limiting distributions indicated in Proposition 9.7, provided that $\hat{p}$ (the number of lagged changes to be included in the autoregression) is set by the sequential t rule or the AIC or BIC rules.[10]

Example 9.2 (ADF on T-bill rate): In the empirical exercise of Chapter 2, we remarked rather casually that the nominal interest rate R_t might have a trend for the sample period studied by Fama (1975). Here we test whether it has a stochastic trend (i.e., whether it is driftless I(1)). The data set we used in the empirical application of Chapter 2 was monthly observations on the U.S. one-month Treasury bill rate. We take the sample period to be from January 1953 to July 1971 ($T = 223$ observations), the sample period of Fama's (1975) study. The interest rate series does not exhibit time trend. So we include a constant but not time in the autoregression.

The maximum lag length $p_{max}(T)$ is set equal to 14 according to the function (9.4.31). In the process of choosing the actual lag length $\hat{p}$, we fix the sample period from $t = p_{max}(T) + 2 = 16$ (April 1954) to $t = 223$ (July 1971), with a sample size of 208 ($= T - p_{max}(T) - 1$). The sequential t rule picks a $\hat{p}$ of 14. The objective function in the information-criterion-based rule when the sample size is fixed is (9.4.32). The AIC picks $\hat{p} = 14$, while the BIC picks $\hat{p} = 1$. Given $\hat{p} = 1$, we estimate the augmented autoregression on the maximum sample period, which is $t = \hat{p}+2, \ldots, T$ (from March 1953 to July 1971) with 221 observations. The estimated regression is

$$R_t = \underset{(0.057)}{0.088} + \underset{(0.0162)}{0.97705}\, R_{t-1} - \underset{(0.067)}{0.20}\, \Delta R_{t-1},$$

$$R^2 = 0.944, \ \text{sample size} = 221.$$

From this estimated regression, we can calculate

$$\text{ADF } \hat{\rho}^{\mu} = 221 \times \frac{0.97705 - 1}{1 + 0.20} = -4.22, \quad t^{\mu} = \frac{0.97705 - 1}{0.0162} = -1.42.$$

From Table 9.1, Panel (b), the 5 percent critical value for the ADF ρ^{μ} statistic is -14.1. The 5 percent critical value for the ADF t^{μ} statistic is -2.86 from Table 9.2, Panel (b). For either statistic, the I(1) null is easily accepted.

[10]Ng and Perron (1995) proved this result about the selection of lag length only for the case without intercept. That it can be extended to the case with intercept and also to the case with trend was confirmed in a private communication with one of the authors of the paper.

Incorporating Time Trend

Allowing for a linear time trend, too, can be done as in the DF tests. Replacing the y_t in augmented autoregression (9.4.3) by $y_t - \alpha - \delta \cdot t$, we obtain the following augmented autoregression with time trend:

$$y_t = \alpha^* + \delta^* \cdot t + \rho y_{t-1} + \zeta_1 \, \Delta y_{t-1} + \zeta_2 \, \Delta y_{t-2} + \cdots + \zeta_p \, \Delta y_{t-p} + \varepsilon_t, \tag{9.4.36}$$

where

$$\alpha^* = (1-\rho)\alpha + (\rho - \zeta_1 - \zeta_2 - \cdots - \zeta_p)\delta, \;\; \delta^* = (1-\rho)\delta. \tag{9.4.37}$$

Since $\delta^* = 0$ when $\rho = 1$, the I(1) null (that the process is I(1) with or without drift) implies that $\rho = 1$ *and* $\delta^* = 0$ in (9.4.36), but, as usual, we focus on the single restriction $\rho = 1$.

Combining the techniques used for proving Propositions 9.5 and 9.7, it is easy to prove

Proposition 9.8 (Augmented Dickey-Fuller Test of a unit root with linear time trend): *Suppose that $\{y_t\}$ is the sum of a linear time trend and an* ARIMA$(p, 1, 0)$ *process so that $\{\Delta y_t\}$ is a stationary* AR(p) *process whose mean may or may not be zero. Consider estimating the augmented autoregression with trend, (9.4.36), and let $(\hat{\alpha}, \hat{\delta}, \hat{\rho}^\tau, \hat{\zeta}_1, \hat{\zeta}_2, \ldots, \hat{\zeta}_p)$ be the OLS coefficient estimates. Also let t^τ be the t-value for the hypothesis that $\rho = 1$. Then*

$$\text{ADF } \rho^\tau \text{ statistic: } \frac{T \cdot (\hat{\rho}^\tau - 1)}{1 - \hat{\zeta}_1 - \widehat{\zeta_2} - \cdots - \hat{\zeta}_p} \underset{d}{\to} DF_\rho^\tau, \tag{9.4.38}$$

$$\text{ADF } t^\tau \text{ statistic: } t^\tau \underset{d}{\to} DF_t^\tau, \tag{9.4.39}$$

where the random variables DF_ρ^τ and DF_t^τ are defined in (9.3.19) and (9.3.20).

Before turning to an example, three comments are in order.

- (Numerical invariance to trend parameters) As in Proposition 9.5, since the regression includes a constant and time, neither α nor δ affects the OLS estimates of $(\rho, \zeta_1, \ldots, \zeta_p)$ and their standard errors, so the finite-sample as well as large-sample distribution of the ADF statistics will not be affected by (α, δ).
- (Said-Dickey extension) Again, the Said-Dickey-Ng-Perron extension is applicable here: if $\{\Delta y_t\}$ is stationary and invertible ARMA(p, q) with possibly a nonzero mean, then the ADF ρ^τ and t^τ statistics have the limiting distributions

indicated in Proposition 9.8, provided that $\hat{p}$ is set by the sequential t-rule or the AIC or BIC rules.

- (Should the regression include time?) The same comment we made about the choice between the DF tests with or without trend is applicable to the ADF tests. If you are confident that the null process has no trend, then the ADF ρ^{μ} and t^{μ} tests of Proposition 9.7 should be used, with the augmented autoregression not including time, because the finite-sample power of the ADF tests is generally greater without time in the augmented autoregression. On the other hand, if you think that the process might have a trend, then you should use the ADF ρ^{τ} and t^{τ} tests of Proposition 9.8 with time in the augmented autoregression.

Example 9.3 (Does GDP have a unit root?): As was shown in Figure 9.1, the log of U.S. GDP clearly has a linear time trend, so we include time in the augmented autoregression. Using the logarithm of U.S. real GDP quarterly data from 1947:Q1 to 1998:Q1 (205 observations), we estimate the augmented autoregression (9.4.36). As in Example 9.2, we set $p_{max}(T) = [12 \cdot (205/100)^{1/4}]$ (which is 14). Also as in Example 9.2, the sample period is fixed ($t = p_{max}(T) + 2, \ldots, T$) in the process of selecting the number of lagged changes. The sequential t picks $\hat{p} = 12$, while both AIC and BIC pick $\hat{p} = 1$. Given $\hat{p} = 1$, the augmented autoregression estimated on the maximal sample of $t = \hat{p} + 2, \ldots, T$ (1947:Q3 to 1998:Q1) is

$$\underset{}{y_t} = \underset{(0.10)}{0.22} + \underset{(0.00011)}{0.00022 \cdot t} + \underset{(0.0137)}{0.9707\, y_{t-1}} + \underset{(0.066)}{0.348\, \Delta y_{t-1}},$$

$$R^2 = 0.999, \quad \text{sample size} = 203.$$

From this estimated regression, we can calculate

$$\text{ADF } \rho^{\tau} = 203 \times \frac{0.9707388 - 1}{1 - 0.348} = -9.11,$$

$$t^{\tau} = \frac{0.9707388 - 1}{0.0137104} = -2.13.$$

From Table 9.1, Panel (c), the 5 percent critical value for the ADF ρ^{τ} statistic is -21.7. The 5 percent critical value for the ADF t^{τ} statistic is -3.41 from Table 9.2, Panel (c). For either statistic, the I(1) null is easily accepted.

A little over 50 years of data may not be enough to discriminate between the I(1) and I(0) alternatives. (As noted by Perron (1991), among others, the span of the data rather than the sampling frequency, e.g., quarterly vs.

annual, is more important for the power of unit-root tests, because $1 - \hat{\rho}$ is much smaller on quarterly data than on annual data.) We now use annual GDP data from 1869 to 1997 for the ADF tests.[11] So $T = 129$. As before, we set $p_{max}(T) = [12 \cdot (129/100)^{1/4}]$ (which is 12) and fix the sample period in the process of choosing the lag length. The sequential t picks 9 for $\hat{p}$, while the value chosen by AIC and BIC is 1. When $\hat{p} = 1$, the regression estimated on the maximum sample of $t = \hat{p} + 2, \ldots, T$ (from 1871 to 1997, 127 observations) is

$$\begin{aligned} y_t = \underset{(0.18)}{0.67} + \underset{(0.0014)}{0.0048} \cdot t + \underset{(0.03989)}{0.85886}\, y_{t-1} + \underset{(0.086)}{0.32}\, \Delta y_{t-1}, \end{aligned}$$

$$R^2 = 0.999, \quad \text{sample size} = 127.$$

The ADF ρ^{τ} and t^{τ} statistics are -26.2 and -3.53, respectively, which are less (greater in absolute value) than their respective 5 percent critical values of -21.7 and -3.41. With the annual data covering a much longer span of time, we can reject the I(1) null that GDP has a stochastic trend.

The impression one gets from Examples 9.1–9.3 is the ease with which the I(1) null is accepted, which leads to the suspicion that the DF and ADF tests may have low power in finite samples. The power issue will be examined in the next section.

Summary of the DF and ADF Tests and Other Unit-Root Tests

The various I(1) processes we have considered in this and the previous section satisfy the model (a set of DGPs)

$$y_t = d_t + z_t, \quad z_t = \rho z_{t-1} + u_t, \quad \{u_t\} \sim \text{zero-mean I(0)}. \qquad (9.4.40)$$

The restrictions on (9.4.40), besides the restriction that $\rho = 1$, that characterize the I(1) null for each of the cases considered are the following.

(1) Proposition 9.3: $d_t = 0$, $\{u_t\}$ independent white noise,

(2) Proposition 9.4: $d_t = \alpha$, $\{u_t\}$ independent white noise,

(3) Proposition 9.5: $d_t = \alpha + \delta \cdot t$, $\{u_t\}$ independent white noise,

(4) Said-Dickey extension of Proposition 9.6: $d_t = 0$, $\{u_t\}$ is zero-mean ARMA(p, q),

[11] Annual GDP data from 1929 are available from the Bureau of Economic Analysis web site. The Balke-Gordon GNP data (Balke and Gordon, 1989) were used to extrapolate GDP back to 1869.

(5) Said-Dickey extension of Proposition 9.7: $d_t = \alpha$, $\{u_t\}$ is zero-mean ARMA(p, q),

(6) Said-Dickey extension of Proposition 9.8: $d_t = \alpha + \delta \cdot t$, $\{u_t\}$ is zero-mean ARMA(p, q).

QUESTIONS FOR REVIEW

1. (Non-uniqueness of the decomposition between zero-mean I(0) and driftless I(1)) Assume $p = 2$ in (9.4.4). Show that the third-order autoregression can be written equivalently as

$$y_t = a_1 \cdot y_{t-1} + a_2 \cdot (y_{t-1} - y_{t-2}) + a_3 \cdot (y_{t-1} - y_{t-3}) + \varepsilon_t.$$

How are (a_1, a_2, a_3) related to (ϕ_1, ϕ_2, ϕ_3)? Which regressor is zero-mean I(0) and which one is driftless I(1)? Verify that the OLS estimate of the y_{t-1} coefficient from this equation is numerically the same as the OLS estimate of ρ from (9.4.3) with $p = 2$.

2. Let $\phi(z) = 1 - \phi_1 z - \cdots - \phi_{p+1} z^{p+1}$ be the polynomial associated with the AR$(p+1)$ process (9.4.4). Show that $\phi(z) = 0$ has a real root inside the unit circle if $\rho > 1$. **Hint:** $\phi(1) = 1 - (\phi_1 + \cdots + \phi_{p+1}) = 1 - \rho < 0$ if $\rho > 1$. $\phi(0) = 1 > 0$.

3. Prove that (9.4.14) $\to_{\text{d}} \frac{\lambda^2}{2} W(1)^2 + \frac{\gamma_0}{2}$. **Hint:** The asymptotic distribution of $\frac{1}{T}\sum_{t=1}^{T} \Delta y_{t-1}\, y_{t-1}$ is the same as that of $\frac{1}{T}\sum_{t=1}^{T} \Delta y_t\, y_t$. Also, $\Delta y_t\, y_t = \Delta y_t\, y_{t-1} + (\Delta y_t)^2$. Use Proposition 9.2(b).

4. Let $\{\Delta y_t\}$ be a zero-mean I(0) process satisfying (9.2.1)–(9.2.3). (The zero-mean stationary AR(p) process for $\{\Delta y_t\}$ considered in Proposition 9.6 is a special case of this.)

   (a) Show that $\{\Delta y_{t-1} \varepsilon_t\}$ is a stationary and ergodic martingale difference sequence. **Hint:** Since $\{\varepsilon_t\}$ and $\{\Delta y_t\}$ are jointly ergodic stationary, $\{\Delta y_{t-1} \cdot \varepsilon_t\}$ is ergodic stationary. To show that $\{\Delta y_{t-1} \varepsilon_t\}$ is a martingale difference sequence, use the Law of Iterated Expectations. $\{\varepsilon_{t-1}, \varepsilon_{t-2}, \ldots\}$ has more information than $\{\Delta y_{t-2}\, \varepsilon_{t-1}, \Delta y_{t-3}\, \varepsilon_{t-2}, \ldots\}$.

   (b) Prove (9.4.19). **Hint:** You need to show that $\text{E}[(\Delta y_{t-1}\, \varepsilon_t)^2] = \gamma_0 \cdot \sigma^2$.

5. Verify (9.4.24). **Hint:** From (9.4.20) and (9.2.4),

$$T \cdot (\hat{\rho} - 1) \underset{d}{\rightarrow} \frac{1}{\psi(1)} \frac{\frac{1}{2}\left(W(1)^2 - 1\right)}{\int_0^1 W^2 dr}.$$

Also, by (9.4.15) and (9.2.4),

$$s \cdot \sqrt{(1, 1) \text{ element of } (\mathbf{A}_T)^{-1}} \underset{d}{\rightarrow} 1 \Big/ \sqrt{\psi(1)^2 \int_0^1 W^2 dr}. \qquad (9.4.41)$$

Since $\psi(1) > 0$ by the stationarity condition, $\sqrt{\psi(1)^2} = \psi(1)$.

6. (t-test on ζ) It is claimed in the text (right below (9.4.27)) that the usual t-value for each ζ is asymptotically standard normal. Verify this for the case of $p = 1$. **Hint:** (9.4.27) for $p = 1$ is

$$\sqrt{T} \cdot (\hat{\zeta}_1 - \zeta_1) \underset{d}{\rightarrow} N(0, \sigma^2/\gamma_0).$$

You need to show that $\sqrt{T}$ times the standard error of $\hat{\zeta}_1$ converges in probability to the square root of σ^2/γ_0. $\sqrt{T}$ times the standard error of $\hat{\zeta}_1$ is $s \cdot \sqrt{(2, 2) \text{ element of } (\mathbf{A}_T)^{-1}}$.

9.5 Which Unit-Root Test to Use?

Besides the DF and ADF tests, a number of other unit-root tests are available (see Maddala and Kim, 1998, Chapter 3, for a catalogue). The most prominent among them are the Phillips (1987) test for case (4) (mentioned at the end of the previous section) and the Phillips-Perron (1988) test, a generalization of the Phillips test to cover cases (5) and (6). (The Phillips tests are derived in Analytical Exercise 6.) Their tests are based on the OLS estimate of the y_{t-1} coefficient in an AR(1) equation, rather than an augmented autoregression, with the long-run variance of $\{\Delta y_t\}$ estimated from the residuals of the AR(1) equation. We did not present them in the text because the finite-sample properties of the tests are rather poor (see below). There is a new generation of unit-root tests with reasonably low size distortions and good power. They include the ADF-GLS test of Elliott, Rothenberg, and Stock (1996) and the M-tests of Perron and Ng (1996).

Local-to-Unity Asymptotics

These and most other unit-root tests are consistent against all fixed I(0) alternatives.[12] Which consistent test should be chosen over the other? Recall that in Section 2.4 we defined the asymptotic power against a sequence of local alternatives that drift toward the null at rate $\sqrt{T}$. It turns out that in the unit-root context the appropriate rate is T rather than $\sqrt{T}$ (see, e.g., Stock, 1994, pp. 2772–2773). That is, the probability of rejecting the null of $\rho = 1$ when the true DGP is

$$\rho = 1 + \frac{c}{T} \tag{9.5.1}$$

has a limit between 0 and 1 as T goes to infinity. This limit is the asymptotic power. The sequence of alternatives described by (9.5.1) is called **local-to-unity alternatives**. By definition, the asymptotic power equals the nominal size when $c = 0$. It can be shown that the DF or ADF ρ tests are more powerful than the DF or ADF t tests against local-to-unity alternatives (see Stock, 1994, pp. 2774–2776). That is, for any nominal size and c, the asymptotic power of the DF or ADF ρ statistic is greater than that of the DF or ADF t-statistic. On this score, we should prefer the ρ-based test to the t-based test, but the verdict gets overturned when we examine their finite-sample properties.

Small-Sample Properties

Turning to the issue of testing an I(1) null against a fixed, rather than drifting, I(0) alternative, the two desirable finite-sample properties of a test are a reasonably low size distortion and high power against I(0) alternatives. There is a large body of Monte Carlo evidence on the finite-sample properties of the DF, ADF, and other unit-root tests (for a reference, see the papers cited on p. 2777 of Stock, 1994, and see Ng and Perron, 1998, for a comparison of the ADF-GLS and the M-tests). Major findings are the following.

- Virtually all tests suffer from size distortions, particularly when the null is in a sense close to being I(0). The M-test generally has the smallest size distortion, followed by the ADF t. The size distortion of the ADF ρ is much larger than that of the ADF t. For example, the I(1) null considered by Schwert (1989) is

$$y_t - y_{t-1} = \varepsilon_t + \theta\varepsilon_{t-1},\ \{\varepsilon_t\} \text{ Gaussian i.i.d.} \tag{9.5.2}$$

When θ is close to -1, this I(1) process is very close to a white noise process,

[12]That the DF tests are consistent against general I(0) alternatives was verified in Review Question 5 to Section 9.3. For the consistency of the ADF tests, see, e.g., Stock (1994, p. 2770).

because the AR root of unity nearly equals the MA root of $-\theta$. Simulations by Schwert (1989) show that the ADF ρ and Phillips-Perron Z_ρ and Z_t tests (see Analytical Exercise 6) reject the I(1) null far too often in finite samples when θ is close to -1. In particular, for the Phillips-Perron tests, the actual size when the nominal size is 5 percent is more than 90 percent even for sample sizes as large as 1,000 when $\theta = -0.8$.

- In the case of ADF tests, how the lag length $\hat{p}$ is selected affects the finite-sample size and power. For a given rule for choosing $\hat{p}$, the power is generally higher for the ADF ρ-test than for the ADF t-test.
- The power is generally much higher for the ADF-GLS and the M-tests than for the ADF t- and ρ-tests.

Unlike the M-statistic, the ADF-GLS statistic can be calculated easily by standard regression packages. In the empirical exercise of this chapter, you will be asked to use the ADF-GLS to test an I(1) null.

9.6 Application: Purchasing Power Parity

The theory of **purchasing power parity** (PPP) states that, for any two countries, the currency exchange rate equals the ratio of the price levels of the two countries. Put differently, once converted to a common currency, national price levels should be equal. Let P_t be the price index for the United States, P_t^* be the price index for the foreign country in question (say, the United Kingdom), and S_t be the exchange rate in dollars per unit of the foreign currency. PPP states that

$$P_t = S_t \cdot P_t^*, \tag{9.6.1}$$

or taking logs and using lower-case letters for them,[13]

$$p_t = s_t + p_t^*. \tag{9.6.2}$$

PPP is related to but different from the **law of one price**, which states that (9.6.1) holds for any good, with P_t representing the dollar price of the good in question

[13]Equation (9.6.1) or (9.6.2) is a statement of "absolute PPP." What is called relative PPP requires only that the first difference of (9.6.2) hold, that is, the rate of growth of the exchange rate should offset the differential between the rate of growth in home and foreign price indexes. Relative PPP should not be confused with the weaker version of PPP to be introduced below.

and P_t^* the foreign currency price of the good. If international price arbitrage works smoothly, the law of one price should hold at every date t. If the law of one price holds for all goods and if the basket of goods for the price index is the same between two countries, then PPP should hold.

Due to a variety of factors limiting international price arbitrage, PPP does not hold exactly at every date t.[14] A weaker version of PPP is that the deviation from PPP

$$z_t \equiv s_t - p_t + p_t^*, \tag{9.6.3}$$

which is the real exchange rate, is stationary. Even if it does not enforce the law of one price in the short run, international arbitrage should have an effect in the long run.

The Embarrassing Resiliency of the Random Walk Model?

For many years researchers found it difficult to reject the hypothesis that real exchange rates follow a random walk under floating exchange regimes. As Rogoff (1996) notes, this was somewhat of an embarrassment because every reasonable theoretical model suggests the weaker version of PPP. However, studies since the mid 1980s looking at longer spans of data have been able to reject the random walk null. Recent work by Lothian and Taylor (1996) is a good example. It uses annual data spanning two centuries from 1791 to 1990 for dollar/sterling and franc/sterling real exchange rates to find that the random walk null can be rejected. In what follows, we apply the ADF t-test to their data on the dollar/sterling (dollars per pound) exchange rate.

The dollar/sterling real exchange rate, calculated as (9.6.3) and plotted in Figure 9.4, exhibits no time trend. We therefore do not include time in the augmented autoregression. If we were dealing with the weak version of the law of one price, with P_t and P_t^* denoting the home and foreign prices of a particular good, then we could exclude the intercept from the augmented autoregression because a change in units of measuring the good does not affect z_t. But P_t and P_t^* here are price indexes, and a change in the base year leads to adding a constant to z_t. To make the test invariant to such changes, a constant is included in the augmented autoregression. By applying the ADF test, rather than the DF test, we can allow for serial correlation in the first differences of z_t under the null, but the lag length chosen by BIC (with $p_{max}(T) = \left[12 \cdot (200/100)^{1/4}\right] = 14$) turned out to be 0, so the ADF t-test reduces to the DF t-test and an augmented autoregression reduces to an AR(1) equation. The estimated AR(1) equation is

[14] See, e.g., Section 4 of Rogoff (1996) for a list of factors that prevent PPP from holding.

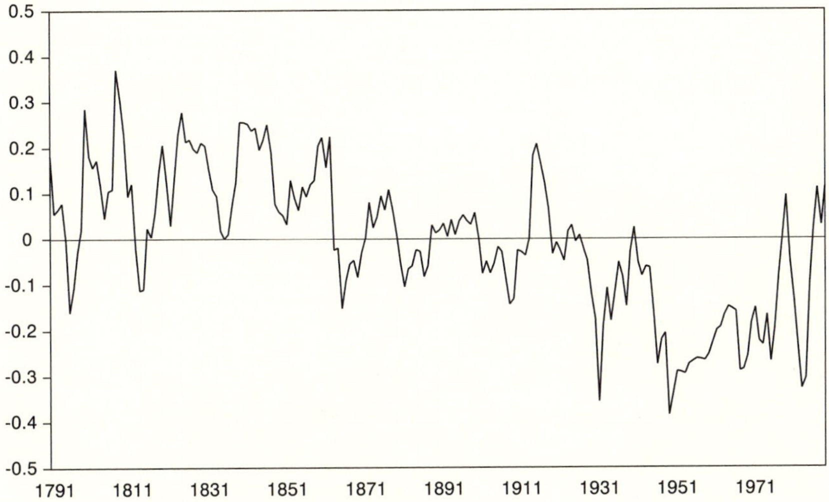

Figure 9.4: Dollar/Sterling Real Exchange Rate, 1791–1990, 1914 Value Set to 0

$$z_t = \underset{(0.052)}{0.179} + \underset{(0.0326)}{0.8869}\, z_{t-1}, \quad SER = 0.071, \quad R^2 = 0.790, \quad t = 1792, \ldots, 1990.$$

The DF t-statistic (t^μ) is -3.5 ($= (0.8869 - 1)/0.0326$), which is significant at 1 percent. Thus, we can indeed reject the hypothesis that the sterling/dollar real exchange rate is a random walk.

An obvious caveat to this result is that the sample period of 1791–1990 includes fixed and floating rate periods. It might be that international price arbitrage works more effectively under fixed exchange rate regimes. If so, the z_{t-1} coefficient should be closer to 0 during fixed rate periods. Lothian and Taylor (1996) report that if one uses a simple Chow test, one cannot reject the hypothesis that the z_{t-1} coefficient is the same before and after floating began in 1973. In the empirical exercise of this chapter, you will be asked to verify their finding and also use the ADF-GLS to test the same hypothesis.

PROBLEM SET FOR CHAPTER 9

ANALYTICAL EXERCISES

1. Prove Proposition 9.2(b). **Hint:** By the definition of $\Delta\xi_t$, we have $\xi_t = \xi_{t-1} + \Delta\xi_t$. So

$$(\xi_t)^2 = (\xi_{t-1} + \Delta\xi_t)^2.$$

From this, derive

$$\Delta\xi_t \cdot \xi_{t-1} = \left(\tfrac{1}{2}\right)\left[(\xi_t)^2 - (\xi_{t-1})^2 - (\Delta\xi_t)^2\right].$$

Sum this over $t = 1, 2, \dots, T$ to obtain

$$\sum_{t=1}^{T} \Delta\xi_t \cdot \xi_{t-1} = \left(\tfrac{1}{2}\right)\left[(\xi_T)^2 - (\xi_0)^2\right] - \left(\tfrac{1}{2}\right)\sum_{t=1}^{T}(\Delta\xi_t)^2.$$

Divide both sides by T to obtain

$$\frac{1}{T}\sum_{t=1}^{T} \Delta\xi_t \cdot \xi_{t-1} = \frac{1}{2}\left(\frac{\xi_T}{\sqrt{T}}\right)^2 - \frac{1}{2}\left(\frac{\xi_0}{\sqrt{T}}\right)^2 - \frac{1}{2T}\sum_{t=1}^{T}(\Delta\xi_t)^2. \qquad (*)$$

Apply Proposition 6.9 and the Ergodic Theorem to the terms on the right-hand side of $(*)$.

2. (Proof of Proposition 9.4) Let $\hat{\rho}^{\mu}$ be the OLS estimate of ρ in the AR(1) equation with intercept, (9.3.11), and define the demeaned series $\{y_{t-1}^{\mu}\}$ $(t = 1, 2, \dots, T)$ by

$$y_{t-1}^{\mu} \equiv y_{t-1} - \bar{y}, \quad \bar{y} \equiv \frac{y_0 + y_1 + \cdots + y_{T-1}}{T} \quad (t = 1, 2, \dots, T). \qquad (1)$$

This y_{t-1}^{μ} equals the OLS residual from the regression of y_{t-1} on a constant for $t = 1, 2, \dots, T$.

(a) Derive

$$\hat{\rho}^{\mu} - 1 = \frac{\sum_{t=1}^{T} \Delta y_t \, y_{t-1}^{\mu}}{\sum_{t=1}^{T}(y_{t-1}^{\mu})^2}. \qquad (2)$$

Hint: By the Frisch-Waugh Theorem, $\hat{\rho}^{\mu}$ is numerically equal to the OLS coefficient estimate in the regression of y_t on y_{t-1}^{μ} (*without* intercept). Thus,

$$\hat{\rho}^{\mu} = \frac{\sum_{t=1}^{T} y_t \, y_{t-1}^{\mu}}{\sum_{t=1}^{T}(y_{t-1}^{\mu})^2} \quad \text{or} \quad \hat{\rho}^{\mu} - 1 = \frac{\sum_{t=1}^{T}(y_t - y_{t-1}^{\mu}) \cdot y_{t-1}^{\mu}}{\sum_{t=1}^{T}(y_{t-1}^{\mu})^2}. \qquad (3)$$

Use the fact that $\sum_{t=1}^{T} y_{t-1}^{\mu} = 0$ to show that $\sum_{t=1}^{T}(y_t - y_{t-1}^{\mu}) \cdot y_{t-1}^{\mu} = \sum_{t=1}^{T}(y_t - y_{t-1}) \cdot y_{t-1}^{\mu}$.

(b) (Easy) Show that, under the null hypothesis that $\{y_t\}$ is driftless I(1) (not necessarily driftless random walk),

$$T \cdot (\hat{\rho}^{\mu} - 1) \underset{\mathrm{d}}{\rightarrow} \frac{\frac{\lambda^2}{2}\left([W^{\mu}(1)]^2 - [W^{\mu}(0)]^2\right) - \frac{\gamma_0}{2}}{\lambda^2 \cdot \int_0^1 [W^{\mu}(r)]^2 \, dr}, \tag{4}$$

where γ_0 is the variance of Δy_t, λ^2 is the long-run variance of Δy_t, and $W^{\mu}(\cdot)$ is a demeaned standard Brownian motion introduced in Section 9.2. **Hint:** Use Proposition 9.2(c) and (d) with $\xi_t = y_t$.

(c) (Trivial) Verify that $T \cdot (\hat{\rho}^{\mu} - 1)$ converges to DF^{μ}_{ρ} (defined in (9.3.13)) if $\{y_t\}$ is a driftless random walk. **Hint:** If y_t is a random walk, then $\lambda^2 = \gamma_0$.

(d) (Optional) Let s be the standard error of regression for the AR(1) equation with intercept, (9.3.11). Show that s^2 is consistent for γ_0 ($\equiv \mathrm{Var}(\Delta y_t)$) under the null that $\{y_t\}$ is driftless I(1) (so Δy_t is zero-mean I(0) satisfying (9.2.1)–(9.2.3)). **Hint:** Let $(\hat{\alpha}^*, \hat{\rho}^{\mu})$ be the OLS estimates of (α^*, ρ). Show that $\hat{\alpha}^*$ converges to zero in probability. Write s^2 as

$$\begin{aligned} s^2 &= \frac{1}{T-1}\sum_{t=1}^{T}[(\Delta y_t - \hat{\alpha}^*) - (\hat{\rho}^{\mu} - 1)y_{t-1}]^2 \\ &= \frac{1}{T-1}\sum_{t=1}^{T}(\Delta y_t - \hat{\alpha}^*)^2 \\ &\quad - \frac{2}{T-1} \cdot [T \cdot (\hat{\rho}^{\mu} - 1)] \cdot \frac{1}{T}\sum_{t=1}^{T}(\Delta y_t - \hat{\alpha}^*) \cdot y_{t-1} \\ &\quad + \frac{1}{T-1} \cdot [T \cdot (\hat{\rho}^{\mu} - 1)]^2 \cdot \frac{1}{T^2}\sum_{t=1}^{T}(y_{t-1})^2. \end{aligned} \tag{5}$$

Since $\operatorname{plim} \hat{\alpha}^* = 0$, it should be easy to show that the first term on the right-hand side of (5) converges in probability to $\gamma_0 = \mathrm{E}\big[(\Delta y_t)^2\big]$. To prove that the second term converges to zero in probability, take for granted that

$$\frac{1}{\sqrt{T}} \frac{1}{T} \sum_{t=1}^{T} y_{t-1} \underset{\mathrm{d}}{\rightarrow} \lambda \int_0^1 W(r) \, dr. \tag{6}$$

(e) Show that $t^{\mu} \to_{\mathrm{d}} DF^{\mu}_{t}$ if $\{y_t\}$ is a driftless random walk. **Hint:** Since $\{y_t\}$ is a driftless random walk, $\lambda^2 = \gamma_0 = \sigma^2$ ($\equiv$ variance of ε_t). So s is consistent for σ.

$$t^{\mu} = \frac{\hat{\rho}^{\mu} - 1}{s \times \sqrt{(2,2) \text{ element of } (\mathbf{X}'\mathbf{X})^{-1}}}. \tag{7}$$

Show that the square root of the (2, 2) element of $\left(\sum_{t=1}^{T} \mathbf{x}_t \mathbf{x}_t'\right)^{-1}$ is

$$\frac{1}{\sqrt{\sum_{t=1}^{T} (y_{t-1}^{\mu})^2}},$$

where $\mathbf{x}_t \equiv [1, y_{t-1}]'$.

3. (Proof of Proposition 9.5) Let $\hat{\rho}^{\tau}$ be the OLS estimate of ρ in the AR(1) equation with time trend, (9.3.17), and define the detrended series $\{y_{t-1}^{\tau}\}$ ($t = 1, 2, \ldots, T$) by

$$y_{t-1}^{\tau} \equiv y_{t-1} - \hat{\alpha} - \hat{\delta} \cdot t, \tag{8}$$

where $(\hat{\alpha}, \hat{\delta})$ are the OLS coefficient estimates for the regression of y_{t-1} on $(1, t)$ for $t = 1, 2, \ldots, T$.

(a) Derive

$$\hat{\rho}^{\tau} - 1 = \frac{\sum_{t=1}^{T} \Delta y_t \, y_{t-1}^{\tau}}{\sum_{t=1}^{T} (y_{t-1}^{\tau})^2}. \tag{9}$$

Hint: By the Frisch-Waugh Theorem, $\hat{\rho}^{\tau}$ is numerically equal to the OLS estimate of the y_{t-1}^{τ} coefficient in the regression of y_t on y_{t-1}^{τ} (*without* intercept or time). Thus,

$$\hat{\rho}^{\tau} = \frac{\sum_{t=1}^{T} y_t \, y_{t-1}^{\tau}}{\sum_{t=1}^{T} (y_{t-1}^{\tau})^2} \quad \text{or} \quad \hat{\rho}^{\tau} - 1 = \frac{\sum_{t=1}^{T} (y_t - y_{t-1}^{\tau}) \cdot y_{t-1}^{\tau}}{\sum_{t=1}^{T} (y_{t-1}^{\tau})^2}. \tag{10}$$

Show that $\sum_{t=1}^{T} (y_t - y_{t-1}^{\tau}) \cdot y_{t-1}^{\tau} = \sum_{t=1}^{T} (y_t - y_{t-1}) \cdot y_{t-1}^{\tau}$. (By construction, $\sum_{t=1}^{T} y_{t-1}^{\tau} = 0$ and $\sum_{t=1}^{T} t \cdot y_{t-1}^{\tau} = 0$ (these are the normal equations).)

(b) (Easy) Show that, under the assumption that $y_t = \alpha + \delta \cdot t + \xi_t$ where $\{\xi_t\}$ is driftless I(1),

$$T \cdot (\hat{\rho}^{\tau} - 1) \underset{d}{\rightarrow} \frac{\frac{\lambda^2}{2}\left([W^{\tau}(1)]^2 - [W^{\tau}(0)]^2\right) - \frac{\gamma_0}{2}}{\lambda^2 \int_0^1 [W^{\tau}(r)]^2 \, dr}, \tag{11}$$

where γ_0 is the variance of Δy_t, λ^2 is the long-run variance of Δy_t, and $W^\tau(\cdot)$ is a detrended standard Brownian motion introduced in Section 9.2. **Hint:** Let ξ_{t-1}^τ be the residual from the hypothetical regression of ξ_{t-1} on $(1, t)$ for $t = 1, 2, \ldots, T$ where $\xi_t \equiv y_t - \alpha - \delta \cdot t$ (this regression is hypothetical because we do not observe $\{\xi_t\}$). Then $\xi_{t-1}^\tau = y_{t-1}^\tau$ for $t = 1, 2, \ldots, T$, because ξ_t differs from y_t only by a linear trend $\alpha + \delta \cdot t$. Use Proposition 9.2(e) and (f). Since $\Delta y_t = \delta + \Delta\xi_t$ under the null, the variance of $\Delta\xi_t$ equals that of Δy_t and the long-run variance of $\Delta\xi_t$ equals that of Δy_t.

(c) (Trivial) Verify that $T \cdot (\hat{\rho}^\tau - 1)$ converges to DF_ρ^τ (defined in (9.3.19)) if $\{y_t\}$ is a random walk with or without drift.

4. (Proof of (9.4.16)) In the text,

$$\frac{1}{T}\sum_{t=1}^{T} y_{t-1}\,\varepsilon_t \underset{d}{\rightarrow} c_1 \equiv \frac{1}{2}\sigma^2 \cdot \psi(1) \cdot [W(1)^2 - 1] \tag{9.4.16}$$

was left unproved. Prove this under the condition that $\{y_t\}$ is driftless I(1) so that $\{\Delta y_t\}$ is zero-mean I(0) satisfying (9.2.1)–(9.2.3). **Hint:** The ε_t in (9.4.16) is the innovation process in the MA representation of $\{\Delta y_t\}$. Using the Beveridge-Nelson decomposition, we have

$$y_t = \psi(1)w_t + \eta_t + (y_0 - \eta_0), \quad w_t \equiv \varepsilon_1 + \varepsilon_2 + \cdots + \varepsilon_t.$$

So

$$\frac{1}{T}\sum_{t=1}^{T} y_{t-1}\,\varepsilon_t = \psi(1)\frac{1}{T}\sum_{t=1}^{T} w_{t-1}\,\varepsilon_t + \frac{1}{T}\sum_{t=1}^{T} \eta_{t-1}\,\varepsilon_t + (y_0 - \eta_0)\frac{1}{T}\sum_{t=1}^{T} \varepsilon_t. \tag{$*$}$$

Show that the second and the third term on the right-hand side of this equation converge in probability to zero. Once you have done Analytical Exercise 1 above, it should be easy to show that

$$\frac{1}{T}\sum_{t=1}^{T} w_{t-1}\,\varepsilon_t \underset{d}{\rightarrow} \left(\frac{\sigma^2}{2}\right)[W(1)^2 - 1].$$

5. (Optional, proof of Proposition 9.7) To simplify the calculation, set $p = 1$, so the augmented autoregression is

$$y_t = \alpha^* + \rho y_{t-1} + \zeta_1 \, \Delta y_{t-1} + \varepsilon_t.$$

Let $(\hat{\alpha}^*, \hat{\rho}^\mu, \hat{\zeta}_1)$ be the OLS coefficient estimates. Show that

$$\frac{T \cdot (\hat{\rho}^\mu - 1)}{1 - \hat{\zeta}_1} \underset{\text{d}}{\to} DF_\rho^\mu.$$

Hint: By the Frisch-Waugh Theorem, $(\hat{\rho}^\mu, \hat{\zeta}_1)$ are numerically the same as the OLS coefficient estimates from the regression of y_t on $(y_{t-1}^\mu, (\Delta y_{t-1})^{(\mu)})$, where y_{t-1}^μ is the residual from the regression of y_{t-1} on a constant and $(\Delta y_{t-1})^{(\mu)}$ is the residual from the regression of Δy_{t-1} on a constant for $t = 1, 2 \dots, T$. Therefore, if $\mathbf{b} = (\hat{\rho}^\mu, \hat{\zeta}_1)'$, $\boldsymbol{\beta} = (\rho, \zeta_1)'$, and $\mathbf{x}_t = (y_{t-1}^\mu, (\Delta y_{t-1})^{(\mu)})'$, then they satisfy (9.4.8). So

$$(1, 1) \text{ element of } \mathbf{A}_T = \frac{1}{T^2} \sum_{t=1}^{T} (y_{t-1}^\mu)^2,$$

$$\text{1st element of } \mathbf{c}_T = \frac{1}{T} \sum_{t=1}^{T} y_{t-1}^\mu \cdot \varepsilon_t.$$

Apply Proposition 9.2(c) and (d) with $\xi_t = y_t$ to these expressions.

6. (Phillips tests) Suppose that $\{y_t\}$ is driftless I(1), so Δy_t can be serially correlated. Nevertheless, estimate the AR(1) equation without intercept, rather than the augmented autoregression without intercept, on $\{y_t\}$. Let $\hat{\rho}$ be the OLS estimate of the y_{t-1} coefficient. Define

$$Z_\rho \equiv T \cdot (\hat{\rho} - 1) - \frac{1}{2} \cdot \left(\frac{T^2 \cdot \hat{\sigma}_{\hat{\rho}}^2}{s^2} \right) \cdot (\hat{\lambda}^2 - \hat{\gamma}_0),$$

$$Z_t \equiv \frac{s}{\hat{\lambda}} \cdot t - \frac{1}{2} \cdot \left(\frac{T \cdot \hat{\sigma}_{\hat{\rho}}}{s \cdot \hat{\lambda}} \right) \cdot (\hat{\lambda}^2 - \hat{\gamma}_0),$$

where $\hat{\sigma}_{\hat{\rho}}$ is the standard error of $\hat{\rho}$, s is the OLS standard error of regression, $\hat{\lambda}^2$ is a consistent estimate of λ^2, $\hat{\gamma}_0$ is a consistent estimate of γ_0, and t is the t-value for the hypothesis that $\rho = 1$.

(a) Show that Z_ρ and Z_t can be written as

$$Z_\rho = \frac{\frac{1}{T}\sum_{t=1}^{T}\Delta y_t\, y_{t-1} - \frac{1}{2}(\hat{\lambda}^2 - \hat{\gamma}_0)}{\frac{1}{T^2}\sum_{t=1}^{T}(y_{t-1})^2},$$

$$Z_t = \frac{s}{\hat{\lambda}}\cdot t - \frac{\frac{1}{2}(\hat{\lambda}^2 - \hat{\gamma}_0)}{\hat{\lambda}\times\sqrt{\frac{1}{T^2}\sum_{t=1}^{T}y_{t-1}^2}}.$$

Hint: By the algebra of least squares,

$$\frac{\hat{\sigma}_{\hat{\rho}}}{s} = \frac{1}{\sqrt{\sum_{t=1}^{T}(y_{t-1})^2}}.$$

(b) Show that

$$Z_\rho \underset{d}{\rightarrow} DF_\rho \text{ and } Z_t \underset{d}{\rightarrow} DF_t.$$

Hint: Use Proposition 9.2(a) and (b) with $\xi_t = y_t$.

7. (Optional) Show that $\alpha(L)$ in (9.2.5) is absolutely summable. **Hint:** A one-line proof is

$$\sum_{j=0}^{\infty}|\alpha_j| = \sum_{j=0}^{\infty}\left|-\sum_{i=j+1}^{\infty}\psi_i\right| \le \sum_{j=0}^{\infty}\sum_{i=j+1}^{\infty}|\psi_i| = \sum_{i=0}^{\infty}i|\psi_i| < \infty.$$

Justify each of the equalities and inequalities.

MONTE CARLO EXERCISES

1. (You have less power with time) In this simulation, we wish to verify that the finite-sample power against stationary alternatives is greater with the DF t^μ-test than with the DF t^τ-test, that is, inclusion of time in the AR(1) equation reduces power. The DGP we examine as the stationary alternative is a stationary AR(1) process:

$$y_t = \rho y_{t-1} + \varepsilon_t,\quad \rho = 0.95,\quad \varepsilon_t \sim \text{i.i.d. } N(0,1),\quad y_0 = 0.$$

Choose the sample size T to be 100 and the nominal size to be 5 percent. Your computer program for calculating the finite-sample power should have the following steps.

(1) Set counters to zero. There should be two counters, one for the DF t^μ and the other for t^τ. They will record the number of times the (false) null gets rejected.

(2) Start a do loop of a large number of replications (1 million, say). In each replication, do the following.

(i) Generate the data vector $(y_0, y_1, \ldots, y_T)$.

Gauss Tip: As was mentioned in the Monte Carlo exercise for Chapter 1, to generate $(y_1, y_2, \ldots, y_T)$, avoid creating a do loop within the current do loop; use the matrix operators. The matrix formula is

$$\underset{(T\times 1)}{\mathbf{y}} = \underset{(T\times 1)}{\mathbf{r}} \cdot y_0 + \underset{(T\times T)}{\mathbf{A}} \underset{(T\times 1)}{\boldsymbol{\varepsilon}}$$

where

$$\mathbf{y} = \begin{bmatrix} y_1 \\ y_2 \\ \vdots \\ y_T \end{bmatrix}, \quad \mathbf{r} = \begin{bmatrix} \rho \\ \rho^2 \\ \vdots \\ \rho^T \end{bmatrix},$$

$$\mathbf{A} = \begin{bmatrix} 1 & 0 & \cdots & \cdots & 0 \\ \rho & 1 & 0 & \cdots & 0 \\ \rho^2 & \rho & 1 & \ddots & 0 \\ \vdots & \vdots & \ddots & \ddots & \vdots \\ \rho^{T-1} & \rho^{T-2} & \cdots & \rho & 1 \end{bmatrix}, \quad \boldsymbol{\varepsilon} = \begin{bmatrix} \varepsilon_1 \\ \varepsilon_2 \\ \vdots \\ \varepsilon_T \end{bmatrix}.$$

To define **r**, use the Gauss command `seqm`. To define **A**, use `toeplitz` and `lowmat`. **r** and **A** should be defined in step (1), outside the current do loop.

(ii) Calculate t^μ and t^τ from $(y_0, y_1, \ldots, y_T)$. (So the sample size is actually $T + 1$.)

(iii) Increase the counter for t^μ by 1 if $t^\mu < -2.86$ (the 5 percent critical value for DF_t^μ). Increase the counter for t^τ by 1 if $t^\tau < -3.41$ (the 5 percent critical value for DF_t^τ).

(3) After the do loop, for each statistic, divide the counter by the number of replications to calculate the frequency of rejecting the null. This frequency converges to the finite-sample power as the number of Monte Carlo replications goes to infinity.

Power should be about 0.124 for the DF t^{μ}-test (so only about 12 percent of the time can we reject the false null!) and 0.092 for the DF t^{τ}-test. So indeed, power is less when time is included in the regression, at least against this particular DGP.

2. (Size distortions) In this Monte Carlo simulation, we calculate the size distortions for the ADF ρ^{μ}- and t^{μ}-tests. Our null DGP is the one examined by Schwert (1989):

$$y_t = \rho y_{t-1} + \varepsilon_t + \theta \varepsilon_{t-1}, \quad \rho = 1, \quad \theta = -0.8,$$
$$\varepsilon_t \sim \text{i.i.d. } N(0, 1), \quad y_0 = 0, \quad \varepsilon_0 = 0.$$

For $T = 100$ and the nominal size of 5 percent, calculate the finite-sample or exact size for $\hat{\rho}^{\mu}$ and t^{μ}. It would be useful to select the number of lagged changes in the augmented autoregression by one of the data-dependent methods (the sequential t, the AIC, or the BIC), but to keep the computer program simple and also to save CPU time, set it equal to 4. Thus, the regression equation, as opposed to the DGP, is

$$y_t = \text{const.} + \rho y_{t-1} + \zeta_1 \cdot (y_{t-1} - y_{t-2}) + \zeta_2 \cdot (y_{t-2} - y_{t-3})$$
$$+ \zeta_3 \cdot (y_{t-3} - y_{t-4}) + \zeta_4 \cdot (y_{t-4} - y_{t-5}) + \text{error}.$$

Since the sample includes y_0, the sample period that can accommodate four lagged changes is from $t = 5$ (not $p + 2 = 6$) to $t = T$ and the actual sample size is $T - 4$. Verify that the size distortion is less for the ADF t^{μ}- than for the ADF ρ^{μ}-test. (The size should be about 0.496 for the ADF ρ^{μ} and 0.290 for the ADF t^{μ}.)

EMPIRICAL EXERCISES

Read Lothian and Taylor (1996, pp. 488–509) (but skip over their discussion of the Phillips-Perron tests) before answering. The file LT.ASC has annual data on the following:

Column 1: year
Column 2: dollar/sterling exchange rate (call it S_t)
Column 3: U.S. WPI (wholesale price index), normalized to 100 for 1914 (P_t)
Column 4: U.K. WPI, normalized to 100 for 1914 (P_t^*).

The sample period is 1791 to 1990 (200 observations). These are the same data used by Lothian and Taylor (1996) and were made available to us. For data sources and how the authors combined them to construct consistent time series, see the Appendix of Lothian and Taylor (1996). (According to the Appendix, the exchange rate (and probably WPIs) are annual averages. This is rather unfortunate and point-in-time data should have been used, because of the time aggregation problem: if a variable follows a random walk on a daily basis, the annual averages of the variable do not follow a random walk. See part (f) below for more on this.)

Calculate the dollar/sterling real exchange rate as

$$z_t \equiv \ln(S_t) - \ln(P_t) + \ln(P_t^*). \tag{1}$$

Since S_t is in dollars per pound, an increase means sterling appreciation. The plot of the real exchange rate in Figure 9.4 shows no clear time trend, so we apply the ADF t^{μ}-test. Therefore, the augmented autoregression to be estimated is

$$z_t = \text{const.} + \rho z_{t-1} + \zeta_1 \cdot (z_{t-1} - z_{t-2}) + \cdots + \zeta_p \cdot (z_{t-p} - z_{t-p-1}) + \text{error}, \tag{2}$$

where p is the number of lagged changes included in the augmented autoregression (which was denoted $\hat{p}$ in the text).

(a) (ADF with automatic lag selection) For the entire sample period of 1791–1990, apply the sequential t-rule, the AIC, and the BIC to select p (the number of lagged changes to be included). Set p_{max} (the maximum number of lagged changes in the augmented autoregression, denoted $p_{max}(T)$ in the text) by (9.4.31) (so $p_{max} = 14$). For the sequential t test, use the significance level of 10 percent. (You should find $p = 14$ by the sequential t, 14 by AIC, and 0 by BIC.) Verify that the value of the t^{μ}-statistic for $p = 0$ (if estimated on the maximum sample) matches the value reported in Table 1 of Lothian and Taylor (1996) as τ_{μ}.

RATS Tip: RATS allows you to change the number of regressors in a do loop. Since the RATS OLS procedure `LINREG` does not allow the standard errors to be retrieved, the DF t^{μ} cannot be calculated in the program. So calculate the DF t^{μ}-statistic as the t-value on the z_{t-1} coefficient in the regression of $z_t - z_{t-1}$. Also, neither the AIC nor the BIC is calculated by `LINREG`. So use `COMPUTE`. In the RATS codes below, `z` is the log real exchange rate and `dz` is its first difference. In applying the sequential t, AIC, and BIC rules, fix the sample period to be 1806 to 1990 (which corresponds to $p_{max} + 2, \ldots, T$). The RATS codes for AIC and BIC are

```
linreg dz 1806:1 1990:1;# constant z{1}
```

```
compute ssrr=%rss
compute akaike = log(%rss/%nobs)+%nreg*2.0/%nobs
compute schwarz = log(%rss/%nobs)+%nreg*log(%nobs)
                 /%nobs
display akaike schwarz
* run ADF with 1 through 14 lagged changes
do p=1,14
 linreg dz 1806:1 1990:1;# constant z{1} dz{1 to p}
 compute akaike = log(%rss/%nobs)+%nreg*2.0/%nobs
 compute schwarz = log(%rss/%nobs)+%nreg
                  *log(%nobs)/%nobs
 display akaike schwarz
end do
```

TSP Tip: Unlike RATS, it appears that TSP does not allow you to change the sample period and the number of regressors in a do loop. The `OLSQ` procedure prints out the BIC, but not the AIC, so the AIC must be calculated using the `SET` command.

(b) (DF test on the floating period) Apply the DF t^{μ}-test to the floating exchange rate period of 1974–1990. Because of the lagged dependent variable z_{t-1}, the first equation is for $t = 1975$:

$$z_{1975} = \text{const.} + \rho z_{1974} + \text{error}.$$

So the sample size is 16. Can you reject the random walk null at 5 percent?

(c) (DF test on the gold standard period) Apply the DF t^{μ}-test to the gold standard period of 1870–1913. Take $t = 1$ for 1871, so the sample size is 43. Can you reject the random walk null at 5 percent? Is the estimate of ρ (the z_{t-1} coefficient in the regression of z_t on a constant and z_{t-1}) closer to zero than in (b)?

(d) (Chow test) Having rejected the I(1) null, we proceed under the maintained assumption that the log real exchange rate z_t follows a stationary AR(1) process. To test the null hypothesis that there is no structural change in the AR(1) equation, split the sample into two subsamples, 1791–1973 and 1974–1990, and apply the Chow test. You may recall that the Chow test was originally developed for models with strictly exogenous regressors. If K is the number of regressors including a constant (2 in the present case), it is an F-test with $(K, T - 2K)$ degrees of freedom. This result is not directly applicable here, because in the AR(1) equation the regressor is the lagged dependent variable which is not strictly exogenous. However, as you verified in Analytical Exercise 12 of Chapter 2, if the variables (the regressors and the dependent variable) are ergodic stationary (which is the case here because $\{z_t\}$ is ergodic stationary when $|\rho| < 1$), then in large samples, with the sizes of both subsamples increasing, $K \cdot F$ is asymptotically $\chi^2(K)$. This result does not require the regressors to be strictly exogenous. Calculate $K \cdot F$ and verify the claim (see pp. 498–502 of Lothian and Taylor, 1996) that "there is no sign of a structural shift in the parameters during the floating period." In the present case of a lagged dependent variable, there is an issue of whether the equation for 1974,

$$z_{1974} = \text{const.} + \rho z_{1973} + \text{error},$$

should be included in the first subsample or in the second. It does not matter in large samples; include the equation in the first subsample (so the sample size of the first subsample is 183). (Note: $K \cdot F$ should be about 1.26.)

(e) (The ADF-GLS) As was mentioned in Section 9.5, the ADF-GLS test achieves substantially higher power at a cost of only slightly higher size distortions. The ADF-GLS t^μ- and t^τ-statistics are calculated as follows. As in the ADF t^μ- and t^τ-tests, the null process is

$$y_t = d_t + z_t,\ z_t = \rho z_{t-1} + u_t,\ \rho = 1,\ \{u_t\} \text{ zero-mean I(0) process.} \quad (3)$$

Write $d_t = \mathbf{x}_t'\boldsymbol{\beta}$. For the case where d_t is a constant, $\mathbf{x}_t = 1$ and $\boldsymbol{\beta} = \alpha$, while for the case where d_t is a linear time trend, $\mathbf{x}_t = (1, t)'$ and $\boldsymbol{\beta} = (\alpha, \delta)'$. We assume the sample is of size T with $(y_1, y_2, \dots, y_T)$.

(i) (GLS estimation of $\boldsymbol{\beta}$) In estimating the regression equation

$$y_t = \mathbf{x}_t'\boldsymbol{\beta} + \text{error}, \quad (t = 1, 2, \dots, T), \quad (4)$$

do GLS assuming that the error process is AR(1) with the autoregressive coefficient of $\bar{\rho} = 1 + \bar{c}/T$. (The value of $\bar{c}$ will be specified in a moment.) That is, estimate $\boldsymbol{\beta}$ by OLS by regressing

$$y_1,\ y_2 - \bar{\rho} y_1,\ y_3 - \bar{\rho} y_2,\ \dots,\ y_T - \bar{\rho} y_{T-1}$$

on

$$\mathbf{x}_1,\ \mathbf{x}_2 - \bar{\rho}\mathbf{x}_1,\ \mathbf{x}_3 - \bar{\rho}\mathbf{x}_2,\ \dots,\ \mathbf{x}_T - \bar{\rho}\mathbf{x}_{T-1}.$$

(Unlike in the genuine GLS, the first observations, y_1 and $\mathbf{x}_1$, are not weighted by $\sqrt{1-\bar{\rho}^2}$, but this should not matter in large samples.) Set $\bar{c}$ according to

$$\bar{c} = -7$$

in the demeaned case (with $\mathbf{x}_t = 1$),

$$\bar{c} = -13.5$$

in the detrended case. (Roughly speaking, this choice of $\bar{c}$ ensures that the asymptotic power at $c = \bar{c}$ where $\rho = 1 + c/T$ is nearly 50 percent which is the asymptotic power achieved by an ideal test specifically tailored to this alternative of $c = \bar{c}$.) Call the resulting estimator $\widehat{\boldsymbol{\beta}}_{\text{GLS}}$ and define $\tilde{y}_t \equiv y_t - \mathbf{x}_t'\widehat{\boldsymbol{\beta}}_{\text{GLS}}$. (This should *not* be confused with the GLS residual, which is $(y_t - \bar{\rho}y_{t-1}) - (\mathbf{x}_t - \bar{\rho}\mathbf{x}_{t-1})'\widehat{\boldsymbol{\beta}}_{\text{GLS}}$.)

(ii) (ADF without intercept on the residuals) Estimate the augmented autoregression *without* intercept using $\tilde{y}_t$ instead of y_t:

$$\tilde{y}_t = \rho\tilde{y}_{t-1} + \zeta_1 \cdot (\tilde{y}_{t-1} - \tilde{y}_{t-2}) + \cdots + \zeta_p \cdot (\tilde{y}_{t-p} - \tilde{y}_{t-p-1}) + \text{error.}$$

The t-value for $\rho = 1$ is the ADF-GLS t-statistic; call it the ADF-GLS t^{μ} if $\mathbf{x}_t = 1$ and the ADF-GLS t^{τ} if $\mathbf{x}_t = (1, t)'$. The limiting distribution of the ADF-GLS t^{μ} is that of DF_t (which is tabulated in Table 9.2, Panel (a)), while that of the ADF-GLS t^{τ} is tabulated in Table I.C. of Elliott et al. (1996). Reproducing their lower tail critical values

$$-3.48 \text{ for } 1\%, -3.15 \text{ for } 2.5\%, -2.89 \text{ for } 5\%, \text{ and } -2.57 \text{ for } 10\%.$$

Elliott et al. (1996) show for the ADF-GLS test that the asymptotic power is higher than those of the ADF ρ- and t-tests, and that compared with the ADF tests, the finite-sample power is substantially higher with only a minor deterioration in size distortions.

Apply the ADF-GLS t^{μ}-test to the gold standard subsample 1870–1913. Choose the lag length by BIC with p_{max} (the maximum number of lagged changes in the augmented autoregression, denoted $p_{max}(T)$ in the text) by (9.4.31) (so $p_{max} = 9$). Can you reject the null that the real exchange rate is driftless I(1)? (Note: The BIC will pick 0 for p. The statistic should be -2.24. You should be able to reject the I(1) null at 5 percent.)

TSP Tip: An example of TSP codes assuming $p = 0$ for this part is the following.

```
?
? (e) ADF-GLS
?
? Step 1: GLS demeaning
?
set rhobar=1-7/(1913-1870+1);
smpl 1870 1913;
const=1;
ct=1;
zt=z;   ? z is the log real exchange rate
smpl 1871 1913;
zt=z-rhobar*z(-1);
ct=const-rhobar*const(-1);
smpl 1870 1913;
olsq zt ct;
z=z-@coef(1);
? @coef(1) is the GLS estimate of the mean
?
? Step 2: DF with demeaned variable
?
smpl 1871 1913;
olsq z z(-1);
set t=(@coef(1)-1)/@ses(1);print t;
```

(f) (Optional analytical exercise on time aggregation) Suppose y_t is a random walk without drift. Create from this time-averaged series by the formula

$$\bar{y}_1 = \frac{y_1 + y_2 + \cdots + y_n}{n}, \quad \bar{y}_2 = \frac{y_{n+1} + y_{n+2} + \cdots + y_{2n}}{n}, \ldots .$$

(Think of y_t as the exchange rate on day t and $\bar{y}_j$ as an annual average of daily exchange rates for year j.) Show that $\{\bar{y}_j\}$ is not a random walk. More specifically, show that

$$\text{Corr}(\bar{y}_{j+1} - \bar{y}_j, \bar{y}_{j+2} - \bar{y}_{j+1}) \underset{d}{\rightarrow} 0.25 \text{ as } n \rightarrow \infty.$$

ANSWERS TO SELECTED QUESTIONS

ANALYTICAL EXERCISES

1. Since $\mathrm{E}(\xi_0^2) < \infty$, $\xi_0/\sqrt{T}$ converges in mean square (and hence in probability) to 0 as $T \to \infty$. Thus, the second term on the right-hand side of $(*)$ in the hint can be ignored. Regarding the first term, we have

$$\frac{\xi_T}{\sqrt{T}} = \frac{\xi_0}{\sqrt{T}} + \frac{\Delta\xi_1 + \Delta\xi_2 + \cdots + \Delta\xi_T}{\sqrt{T}}.$$

The first term on the right-hand side of this equation can be ignored. By Proposition 6.9, the second term converges to $N(0, \lambda^2)$ because $\Delta\xi_t$ is a linear process with absolutely summable MA coefficients. So the first term on the right-hand side of $(*)$ converges in distribution to $(\lambda^2/2)X$ where $X \sim \chi^2(1)$. Since $\{\Delta\xi_t\}$ is ergodic stationary, the last term on the right-hand side of $(*)$ converges in probability to $\frac{1}{2}\,\mathrm{E}[(\Delta\xi_t)^2]$ by the Ergodic Theorem.

5. The (1, 1) element of $\mathbf{A}_T$ converges to the random variable indicated in Proposition 9.2(c). Regarding the first element of $\mathbf{c}_T$, by Beveridge-Nelson,

$$y_t = \psi(1)w_t + \eta_t + (y_0 - \eta_0), \quad w_t \equiv \varepsilon_1 + \varepsilon_2 + \cdots + \varepsilon_t. \tag{1}$$

Therefore,

$$y_{t-1}^{\mu} = \psi(1)w_{t-1}^{\mu} + \eta_{t-1}^{\mu}, \tag{2}$$

where

$$x_{t-1}^{\mu} = x_{t-1} - \bar{x}, \quad \bar{x} = \frac{x_0 + \cdots + x_{T-1}}{T} \quad \text{for } x = w, \eta,$$

and

$$\frac{1}{T}\sum_{t=1}^{T} y_{t-1}^{\mu} \cdot \varepsilon_t = \psi(1)\frac{1}{T}\sum_{t=1}^{T} w_{t-1}^{\mu} \cdot \varepsilon_t + \frac{1}{T}\sum_{t=1}^{T} \eta_{t-1}^{\mu} \cdot \varepsilon_t. \tag{3}$$

The second term on the right-hand side of this equation can be ignored asymptotically. By Proposition 9.2(d) for $\xi_t = w_t$ (a driftless random walk), the first term on the right-hand side converges to

$$\psi(1)\left(\frac{\sigma^2}{2}\right)\left\{[W^{\mu}(1)]^2 - [W^{\mu}(0)]^2 - 1\right\}.$$

From this, we have

$$\frac{1}{T}\sum_{t=1}^{T} y_{t-1}^{\mu}\cdot\varepsilon_t \underset{d}{\to} \frac{1}{2}\cdot\sigma^2\cdot\psi(1)\cdot\left\{[W^{\mu}(1)]^2-[W^{\mu}(0)]^2-1\right\}. \tag{4}$$

The $\mathbf{A}_T$ matrix is asymptotically diagonal for the demeaned case too. The off-diagonal elements of $\mathbf{A}_T$ are equal to $1/\sqrt{T}$ times

$$\frac{1}{T}\sum_{t=1}^{T}(\Delta y_{t-1})^{(\mu)}\, y_{t-1}^{\mu}. \tag{5}$$

Since $\sum_{t=1}^{T} y_{t-1}^{\mu}=0$, this equals

$$\frac{1}{T}\sum_{t=1}^{T}\Delta y_{t-1}\, y_{t-1}^{\mu}. \tag{6}$$

It is easy to show, by a little bit of algebra analogous to that in Review Question 3 of Section 9.4 and Proposition 9.2(d), that (6) has a limiting distribution. So $1/\sqrt{T}$ times (6), which is the off-diagonal elements of $\mathbf{A}_T$, converges to zero in probability. Then, using the same argument we used in the text for the case without intercept, it is easy to show that $\hat{\zeta}_1$ is consistent for ζ_1. So $\psi(1)$ is consistently estimated by $1/(1-\hat{\zeta}_1)$. Taken together,

$$\frac{T\cdot(\hat{\rho}^{\mu}-1)}{1-\hat{\zeta}_1}\underset{d}{\to} DF_{\rho}^{\mu}.$$

EMPIRICAL EXERCISES

(a) With $p=0$, the estimated AR(1) equation is

$$z_t = \text{const.} + \underset{(0.0326)}{0.8869}\, z_{t-1},\quad SSR=0.995135,\quad R^2=0.790,\quad T=199.$$

The value of t^{μ} is -3.47, which matches the value in Table 1 of Lothian and Taylor (1996). The 5 percent critical value is -2.86 from Table 9.2, Panel (b).

(b) The estimated AR(1) equation for 1974–1990 is

$$z_t = \text{const.} + \underset{(0.1904)}{0.7704}\, z_{t-1},\quad SSR=0.150964,\quad R^2=0.539,\quad T=16.$$

$t^{\mu}=-1.21>-2.86$. We fail to reject the null at 5 percent.

(c) The estimated AR(1) equation for 1870–1913 is

$$z_t = \text{const.} + \underset{(0.1045)}{0.7222}\, z_{t-1}, \quad SSR = 0.069429, \quad R^2 = 0.538, \quad T = 43.$$

$t^{\mu} = -2.66 > -2.86$. We fail to reject the null at 5 percent.

(d) The estimated AR(1) equation for 1791–1974 is

$$z_t = \text{const.} + \underset{(0.0329)}{0.8993}\, z_{t-1}, \quad SSR = 0.837772, \quad R^2 = 0.805, \quad T = 183.$$

From this and the results in (a) and (b),

$$K \cdot F = \frac{0.995135 - (0.837772 + 0.150964)}{\frac{0.837772+0.150964}{(199-4)}} = 1.26.$$

The 5 percent critical value for $\chi^2(2)$ is 5.99. So we accept the null hypothesis of parameter stability.

(e) The ADF-GLS $t^{\mu} = -2.24$. The 5 percent critical value is -1.95 from Table 9.2, Panel (a). So we *can* reject the I(1) null.

References

Baillie, R., 1996, "Long Memory Processes and Fractional Integration in Econometrics," *Journal of Econometrics*, 73, 5–59.

Balke, N., and R. Gordon, 1989, "The Estimation of Prewar Gross National Product: Methodology and New Evidence," *Journal of Political Economy*, 97, 39–92.

Chan, N., and C. Wei, 1988, "Limiting Distributions of Least Squares Estimates of Unstable Autoregressive Processes," *Annals of Statistics*, 16, 367–401.

Dickey, D., 1976, "Estimation and Hypothesis Testing in Nonstationary Time Series," Ph.D. dissertation, Iowa State University.

Dickey, D., and W. Fuller, 1979, "Distribtion of the Estimators for Autoregressive Time Series with a Unit Root," *Journal of the American Statistical Association*, 74, 427–431.

Elliott, G., T. Rothenberg, and J. Stock, 1996, "Efficient Tests for an Autoregressive Unit Root," *Econometrica*, 64, 813–836.

Fama, E., 1975, "Short-Term Interest Rates as Predictors of Inflation," *American Economic Review*, 65, 269–282.

Fuller, W., 1976, *Introduction to Statistical Time Series*, New York: Wiley.

———, 1996, *Introduction to Statistical Time Series* (2d ed.), New York: Wiley.

Hall, P., and C. Heyde, 1980, *Martingale Limit Theory and Its Application*, New York: Academic.

Hamilton, J., 1994, *Time Series Analysis*, Princeton: Princeton University Press.

Hannan, E. J., and M. Deistler, 1988, *The Statistical Theory of Linear Systems*, New York: Wiley.

Kwiatkowski, D., P. Phillips, P. Schmidt, and Y. Shin, 1992, "Testing the Null Hypothesis of Stationarity against the Alternative of a Unit Root," *Journal of Econometrics*, 54, 159–178.

Leybourne, S., and B. McCabe, 1994, "A Consistent Test for a Unit Root," *Journal of Business and Economic Statistics*, 12, 157–166.

Lothian, J., and M. Taylor, 1996, "Real Exchange Rate Behavior: The Recent Float from the Perspective of the Past Two Centuries," *Journal of Political Economy*, 104, 488–509.

Maddala, G. S., and In-Moo Kim, 1998, *Unit Roots, Cointegration, and Structural Change*, New York: Cambridge University Press.

Ng, S., and P. Perron, 1995, "Unit Root Tests in ARMA Models with Data-Dependent Methods for the Selection of the Truncation Lag," *Journal of the American Statistical Association*, 90, 268–281.

———, 1998, "Lag Length Selection and the Construction of Unit Root Tests with Good Size and Power," working paper, mimeo.

Perron, P., 1991, "Test Consistency with Varying Sampling Frequency," *Econometric Theory*, 7, 341–368.

Perron, P., and S. Ng, 1996, "Useful Modifications to Unit Root Tests with Dependent Errors and Their Local Asymptotic Properties," *Review of Economic Studies*, 63, 435–463.

Phillips, P., 1987, "Time Series Regression with a Unit Root," *Econometrica*, 55, 277–301.

Phillips, P., and S. Durlauf, 1986, "Multiple Time Series Regression with Integrated Processes," *Review of Economic Studies*, 53, 473–496.

Phillips, P., and P. Perron, 1988, "Testing for a Unit Root in Time Series Regression," *Biometrika*, 75, 335–346.

Rogoff, K., 1996, "The Purchasing Power Parity Puzzle," *Journal of Economic Literature*, 34, 647–668.

Said, S., and D. Dickey, 1984, "Testing for Unit Roots in Autoregressive-Moving Average Models of Unknown Order," *Biometrika*, 71, 599–607.

Sargan, D., and A. Bhargava, 1983, "Testing Residuals from Least Squares Regression for Being Generated by the Gaussian Random Walk," *Econometrica*, 51, 153–174.

Schwert, G., 1989, "Tests for Unit Roots: A Monte Carlo Investigation," *Journal of Business and Economic Statistics*, 7, 147–159.

Sims, C., J. Stock, and M. Watson, 1990, "Inference in Linear Time Series Models with Some Unit Roots," *Econometrica*, 58, 113–144.

Stock, J., 1994, "Unit Roots, Structural Breaks and Trends," Chapter 46 in R. Engle and D. McFadden (eds.), *Handbook of Econometrics*, Volume IV, New York: North Holland.

Tanaka, K., 1990, "Testing for a Moving Average Unit Root," *Econometric Theory*, 6, 433–444.

———, 1996, *Time Series Analysis*, New York: Wiley.

Watson, M., 1994, "Vector Autoregressions and Cointegration," Chapter 47 in R. Engle and D. McFadden (eds.), *Handbook of Econometrics*, Volume IV, New York: North Holland.

CHAPTER 10

Cointegration

ABSTRACT

As the examples of the previous section amply illustrate, many economic time series can be characterized as being I(1). But very often their linear combinations appear to be stationary. Those variables are said to be **cointegrated** and the weights in the linear combination are called a **cointegrating vector**. This chapter studies cointegrated systems, namely, vector I(1) processes whose elements are cointegrated.

In the previous chapter, we have defined univariate I(0) and I(1) processes. The first section of this chapter presents their generalization to vector processes and defines cointegration for vector I(1) processes. Section 10.2 presents alternative representations of a cointegrated system. Section 10.3 examines in some detail a test of whether a vector I(1) process is cointegrated. Techniques for estimating cointegrating vectors and making inferences about them are developed in Section 10.4.

As an application, Section 10.5 takes up the money demand function. The log real money supply, the nominal interest rate, and the log real income appear to be I(1), but the existence of a stable money demand function implies that those variables are cointegrated, with the coefficients in the money demand function forming a cointegrating vector. The techniques of Section 10.4 are utilized to estimate the cointegrating vector.

Unlike in other chapters, we will not present results in a series of propositions, because the level of the subject matter is such that it is difficult to state assumptions without introducing further technical concepts. However, for technically oriented readers, we indicate in the text references where the assumptions are formally stated.

A Note on Notation: Unlike in other chapters, the symbol "n" is used for the dimension of the vector processes, and as in the previous chapter, the symbol "T" is used for the sample size and "t" is the observation index. Also, if $\mathbf{y}_t$ is the t-th observation of an n-dimensional vector process, its j-th element will be denoted y_{jt} instead of y_{tj}. We make these changes to be consistent with the notation used in the majority of original papers on cointegration.

10.1 Cointegrated Systems

Figure 10.1(a) plots the logs of quarterly real per capita aggregate personal disposable income and personal consumption expenditure for the United States from 1947:Q1 to 1998:Q1. Both series have linear trends and—as will be verified in an example below—stochastic trends. However, these two I(1) series tend to move together, suggesting that the difference is stationary. This is an example of **cointegration**. Cointegration relations abound in economics. In fact, many of the variables we have examined in the book are cointegrated: prices of the same commodity in two different countries (the difference should be stationary under the weaker version of Purchasing Power Parity), long- and short-term interest rates (even though they have trends, yield differential may be stationary), forward and spot exchange rates, and so forth. Cointegration may characterize more than two variables. For example, the existence of a stable money demand function implies that a linear combination of the log of real money stock, the nominal interest rate, and log aggregate income may be stationary even though each of the three variables is I(1).

We start out this section by extending the definitions of univariate I(0) and I(1) processes of the previous chapter to vector processes. The concept of cointegration for multivariate I(1) processes will then be introduced formally.

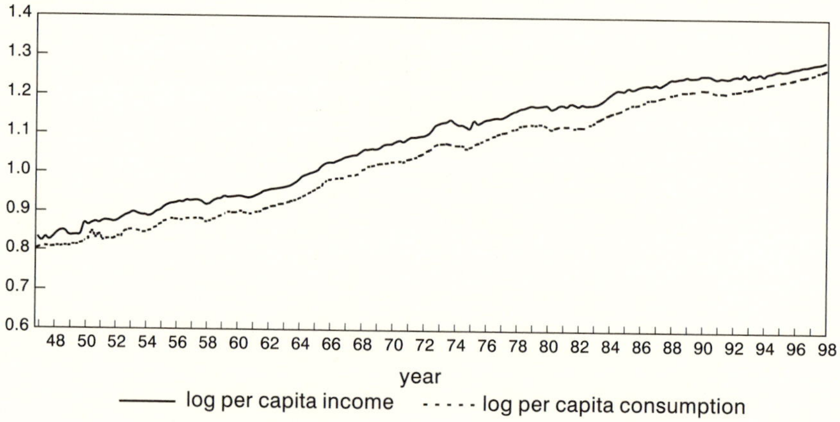

Figure 10.1(a): Log Income and Consumption

Linear Vector I(0) and I(1) Processes

Our definition of vector I(0) and I(1) processes follows Hamilton (1994) and Johansen (1995). To introduce the multivariate extension of a zero-mean linear univariate I(0) process, consider a zero-mean n-dimensional VMA (vector moving average) process:

$$\underset{(n\times 1)}{\mathbf{u}_t} = \underset{(n\times n)}{\boldsymbol{\Psi}(L)}\ \underset{(n\times 1)}{\boldsymbol{\varepsilon}_t}\ ,\quad \boldsymbol{\Psi}(L) \equiv \mathbf{I}_n + \boldsymbol{\Psi}_1 L + \boldsymbol{\Psi}_2 L^2 + \cdots\ , \tag{10.1.1}$$

where $\boldsymbol{\varepsilon}_t$ is i.i.d. with

$$\mathrm{E}(\boldsymbol{\varepsilon}_t) = \mathbf{0},\ \ \mathrm{E}(\boldsymbol{\varepsilon}_t\boldsymbol{\varepsilon}_t') = \underset{(n\times n)}{\boldsymbol{\Omega}}\ ,\quad \boldsymbol{\Omega} \text{ positive definite.} \tag{10.1.2}$$

(The error process $\boldsymbol{\varepsilon}_t$ could be a vector Martingale Difference Sequence satisfying certain properties, but we will not allow for this degree of generality.) As in the univariate case, we impose two restrictions. The first is one-summability:[1]

$$\{\boldsymbol{\Psi}_j\} \text{ is one-summable.} \tag{10.1.3}$$

Since $\{\boldsymbol{\Psi}_j\}$ is absolutely summable when one-summability holds, the multivariate version of Proposition 6.1(d) means that $\mathbf{u}_t$ is (strictly) stationary and ergodic. The second restriction on the zero-mean VMA process is

$$\boldsymbol{\Psi}(1) \neq \underset{(n\times n)}{\mathbf{0}} \quad (n \times n \text{ matrix of zeros}). \tag{10.1.4}$$

That is, at least one element of the $n \times n$ matrix $\boldsymbol{\Psi}(1)$ is not zero. This is a natural multivariate extension of condition (9.2.3b) in the definition of univariate I(0) processes on page 564.

A **(linear) zero-mean n-dimensional vector I(0) process** or a **(linear) zero-mean I(0) system** is a VMA process satisfying (10.1.1)–(10.1.4). Given a zero-mean I(0) system $\mathbf{u}_t$, a **(linear) vector I(0) process** or a **(linear) I(0) system** can be written as

$$\boldsymbol{\delta} + \mathbf{u}_t,$$

where $\boldsymbol{\delta}$ is an n-dimensional vector representing the mean of the stationary process. Using the formula (6.5.6) with (6.3.15), the long-run covariance matrix of the I(0) system is

$$\boldsymbol{\Psi}(1)\boldsymbol{\Omega}\boldsymbol{\Psi}(1)'. \tag{10.1.5}$$

Since $\boldsymbol{\Omega}$ is positive definite and $\boldsymbol{\Psi}(1)$ satisfies (10.1.4), at least one of the diagonal

[1]A sequence of matrices $\{\boldsymbol{\Psi}_j\}$ is said to be one-summable if $\{\Psi_{j,k\ell}\}$ is one-summable (i.e., $\sum_{j=0}^{\infty} j|\Psi_{j,k\ell}| < \infty$) for all $k, \ell = 1, 2, \ldots, n$, where $\Psi_{j,k\ell}$ is the (k, ℓ) element of the $n \times n$ matrix $\boldsymbol{\Psi}_j$.

elements of this long-run variance matrix is positive, implying that at least one of the elements of an I(0) system is individually I(0) (i.e., I(0) as a univariate process). We do not necessarily require $\boldsymbol{\Psi}(1)$ to be nonsingular. In fact, accommodating its singularity is the whole point of the theory of cointegration. Consequently, the long-run variance matrix, too, can be singular.

Example 10.1 (A bivariate I(0) system): Consider the following bivariate first-order VMA process:

$$\begin{cases} u_{1t} = \varepsilon_{1t} - \varepsilon_{1,t-1} + \gamma\varepsilon_{2,t-1}, \\ u_{2t} = \varepsilon_{2t}, \end{cases} \quad \text{or } \mathbf{u}_t = \boldsymbol{\varepsilon}_t + \boldsymbol{\Psi}_1\boldsymbol{\varepsilon}_{t-1}, \tag{10.1.6}$$

where

$$\boldsymbol{\varepsilon}_t = \begin{bmatrix} \varepsilon_{1t} \\ \varepsilon_{2t} \end{bmatrix}, \quad \boldsymbol{\Psi}_1 = \begin{bmatrix} -1 & \gamma \\ 0 & 0 \end{bmatrix}. \tag{10.1.7}$$

Since this is a finite-order VMA, the one-summability condition is trivially satisfied. Requirement (10.1.4) is satisfied because

$$\boldsymbol{\Psi}(1) = \mathbf{I}_2 + \boldsymbol{\Psi}_1 = \begin{bmatrix} 0 & \gamma \\ 0 & 1 \end{bmatrix} \neq \underset{(2\times 2)}{\mathbf{0}}. \tag{10.1.8}$$

So this example fits our definition of I(0) systems. If $\gamma = 0$, then the first element, u_{1t}, is actually I(-1) as a univariate process.

The ***n*-dimensional I(1) system $\mathbf{y}_t$** associated with a zero-mean I(0) system $\mathbf{u}_t$ can be defined by the relation

$$\Delta\mathbf{y}_t = \boldsymbol{\delta} + \mathbf{u}_t. \tag{10.1.9}$$

So the mean of $\Delta\mathbf{y}_t$ is $\boldsymbol{\delta}$. Since not every element of the associated zero-mean I(0) process $\mathbf{u}_t$ is required to be individually I(0), some of the elements of the I(1) system $\mathbf{y}_t$ may not be individually I(1).[2] Substituting (10.1.1) into this, we obtain

$$\Delta\mathbf{y}_t = \boldsymbol{\delta} + \boldsymbol{\Psi}(L)\boldsymbol{\varepsilon}_t. \tag{10.1.10}$$

This is called the **vector moving average (VMA) representation** of an I(1)

[2] In many textbooks and also in Engle and Granger (1987), all elements of an I(1) system are assumed to be individually I(1), but that assumption is not needed for the development of cointegration theory. This point is emphasized in, e.g., Lütkepohl (1993, pp. 352–353) and Johansen (1995, Chapter 3).

system. In levels, $\mathbf{y}_t$ can be written as

$$\mathbf{y}_t = \mathbf{y}_0 + \boldsymbol{\delta} \cdot t + \mathbf{u}_1 + \mathbf{u}_2 + \cdots + \mathbf{u}_t, \tag{10.1.11}$$

or, written out in full,

$$\begin{bmatrix} y_{1t} \\ y_{2t} \\ \vdots \\ y_{nt} \end{bmatrix} = \begin{bmatrix} y_{1,0} \\ y_{2,0} \\ \vdots \\ y_{n,0} \end{bmatrix} + \begin{bmatrix} \delta_1 \cdot t \\ \delta_2 \cdot t \\ \vdots \\ \delta_n \cdot t \end{bmatrix} + \begin{bmatrix} u_{1,1} \\ u_{2,1} \\ \vdots \\ u_{n,1} \end{bmatrix} + \begin{bmatrix} u_{1,2} \\ u_{2,2} \\ \vdots \\ u_{n,2} \end{bmatrix} + \cdots + \begin{bmatrix} u_{1t} \\ u_{2t} \\ \vdots \\ u_{nt} \end{bmatrix}.$$

Regarding the initial value $\mathbf{y}_0$, we assume either that it is a vector of fixed constants or that it is random but independent of $\boldsymbol{\varepsilon}_t$ for all t.

Example 10.2 (A bivariate I(1) system): An I(1) system whose associated zero-mean I(0) process is the bivariate process in Example 10.1 is

$$\begin{cases} \Delta y_{1t} = \delta_1 + \varepsilon_{1t} - \varepsilon_{1,t-1} + \gamma \varepsilon_{2,t-1}, \\ \Delta y_{2t} = \delta_2 + \varepsilon_{2t}, \end{cases} \quad \text{or } \Delta \mathbf{y}_t = \boldsymbol{\delta} + \boldsymbol{\varepsilon}_t + \boldsymbol{\Psi}_1 \boldsymbol{\varepsilon}_{t-1}, \tag{10.1.12}$$

where $\boldsymbol{\Psi}_1$ is given in (10.1.7). In levels,

$$\begin{cases} y_{1t} = y_{1,0} + \delta_1 \cdot t + (\varepsilon_{1t} - \varepsilon_{1,0}) + \gamma \cdot (\varepsilon_{2,0} + \varepsilon_{2,1} + \cdots + \varepsilon_{2,t-1}), \\ y_{2t} = y_{2,0} + \delta_2 \cdot t + (\varepsilon_{2,1} + \varepsilon_{2,2} + \cdots + \varepsilon_{2t}). \end{cases} \tag{10.1.13}$$

The second element of $\mathbf{y}_t$ is I(1) as a univariate process. If $\gamma = 0$, then the first element y_{1t} is trend stationary because the deviation from the trend function $(y_{1,0} - \varepsilon_{1,0}) + \delta_1 \cdot t$ is stationary (actually i.i.d.). Otherwise y_{1t} is I(1).

The Beveridge-Nelson Decomposition

For an I(1) system whose associated zero-mean I(0) process is $\mathbf{u}_t$ satisfying (10.1.1)–(10.1.4), it is easy to obtain the Beveridge-Nelson (BN) decomposition. Recall from Section 9.2 that the univariate BN decomposition is based on the rewriting of the MA filter as (9.2.5) on page 564. The obvious multivariate version of it is

$$\underset{(n\times n)}{\boldsymbol{\Psi}(L)} = \underset{(n\times n)}{\boldsymbol{\Psi}(1)} + (1-L)\underset{(n\times n)}{\boldsymbol{\alpha}(L)}, \quad \boldsymbol{\alpha}(L) = \sum_{j=0}^{\infty} \boldsymbol{\alpha}_j L^j,$$

$$\underset{(n\times n)}{\boldsymbol{\alpha}_j} = -(\boldsymbol{\Psi}_{j+1} + \boldsymbol{\Psi}_{j+2} + \cdots). \tag{10.1.14}$$

So the multivariate analogue of (9.2.6) on page 565 is

$$\mathbf{u}_t = \boldsymbol{\Psi}(1)\boldsymbol{\varepsilon}_t + \boldsymbol{\eta}_t - \boldsymbol{\eta}_{t-1}, \quad \underset{(n\times 1)}{\boldsymbol{\eta}_t} \equiv \boldsymbol{\alpha}(L)\boldsymbol{\varepsilon}_t. \tag{10.1.15}$$

Since $\boldsymbol{\Psi}(L)$ is one-summable, $\boldsymbol{\alpha}(L)$ is absolutely summable and $\boldsymbol{\eta}_t$ is a well-defined covariance-stationary process. Substituting this into (10.1.11), we obtain the multivariate version of the BN decomposition:

$$\mathbf{y}_t = \boldsymbol{\delta}\cdot t + \boldsymbol{\Psi}(1)(\boldsymbol{\varepsilon}_1 + \boldsymbol{\varepsilon}_2 + \cdots + \boldsymbol{\varepsilon}_t) + \boldsymbol{\eta}_t + (\mathbf{y}_0 - \boldsymbol{\eta}_0). \tag{10.1.16}$$

As in the univariate case, the I(1) system $\mathbf{y}_t$ is decomposed into a linear trend $\boldsymbol{\delta}\cdot t$, a stochastic trend $\boldsymbol{\Psi}(1)(\boldsymbol{\varepsilon}_1 + \boldsymbol{\varepsilon}_2 + \cdots + \boldsymbol{\varepsilon}_t)$, a stationary component $\boldsymbol{\eta}_t$, and the initial condition $\mathbf{y}_0 - \boldsymbol{\eta}_0$. By construction, $\boldsymbol{\eta}_0$ is a random variable. So unless $\mathbf{y}_0$ is perfectly correlated with $\boldsymbol{\eta}_0$, the initial condition is random.

Example 10.2 (continued): For the bivariate I(1) system in Example 10.2, the matrix version of $\boldsymbol{\alpha}(L)$ equals $-\boldsymbol{\Psi}_1$ so that the stationary component $\boldsymbol{\eta}_t$ in the BN decomposition is

$$\boldsymbol{\eta}_t = \begin{bmatrix} \varepsilon_{1t} - \gamma\varepsilon_{2t} \\ 0 \end{bmatrix}. \tag{10.1.17}$$

(It should be easy for you to verify this from the matrix version of (9.2.5).) The two-dimensional stochastic trend is written as

$$\boldsymbol{\Psi}(1)(\boldsymbol{\varepsilon}_1 + \boldsymbol{\varepsilon}_2 + \cdots + \boldsymbol{\varepsilon}_t) = \begin{bmatrix} 0 & \gamma \\ 0 & 1 \end{bmatrix} \begin{bmatrix} \sum_{s=1}^t \varepsilon_{1s} \\ \sum_{s=1}^t \varepsilon_{2s} \end{bmatrix} = \begin{bmatrix} \gamma\cdot\sum_{s=1}^t \varepsilon_{2s} \\ \sum_{s=1}^t \varepsilon_{2s} \end{bmatrix}. \tag{10.1.18}$$

Thus, the two-dimensional stochastic trend is driven by one common stochastic trend, $\sum_{s=1}^t \varepsilon_{2s}$. This is an example of the "common trend" representation of Stock and Watson (1993) (see Review Question 2 below).

Cointegration Defined

The I(1) system $\mathbf{y}_t$ is not stationary because it contains a stochastic trend $\boldsymbol{\Psi}(1) \cdot (\boldsymbol{\varepsilon}_1 + \cdots + \boldsymbol{\varepsilon}_t)$, and, if $\boldsymbol{\delta} \neq \mathbf{0}$, a deterministic trend $\boldsymbol{\delta} \cdot t$. The deterministic and stochastic trends, however, may disappear if we take a suitable linear combination of the elements of $\mathbf{y}_t$. To pursue this idea,[3] premultiply both sides of the BN decomposition (10.1.16) by some conformable vector $\mathbf{a}$ to obtain

$$\mathbf{a}'\mathbf{y}_t = \mathbf{a}'\boldsymbol{\delta} \cdot t + \mathbf{a}'\boldsymbol{\Psi}(1)(\boldsymbol{\varepsilon}_1 + \boldsymbol{\varepsilon}_2 + \cdots + \boldsymbol{\varepsilon}_t) + \mathbf{a}'\boldsymbol{\eta}_t + \mathbf{a}'(\mathbf{y}_0 - \boldsymbol{\eta}_0). \quad (10.1.19)$$

If $\mathbf{a}$ satisfies

$$\mathbf{a}'\boldsymbol{\Psi}(1) = \underset{(1\times n)}{\mathbf{0}'}, \quad (10.1.20)$$

then the stochastic trend is eliminated and $\mathbf{a}'\mathbf{y}_t$ becomes

$$\mathbf{a}'\mathbf{y}_t = \mathbf{a}'\boldsymbol{\delta} \cdot t + \mathbf{a}'\boldsymbol{\eta}_t + \mathbf{a}'(\mathbf{y}_0 - \boldsymbol{\eta}_0). \quad (10.1.21)$$

Strictly speaking, this process is not trend stationary because the initial condition $\mathbf{a}'(\mathbf{y}_0 - \boldsymbol{\eta}_0)$ can be correlated with the subsequent values of $\mathbf{a}'\boldsymbol{\eta}_t$ (see Review Question 3 below for an illustration). The process would be trend stationary if, for example, the initial value $\mathbf{y}_0$ were such that $\mathbf{a}'(\mathbf{y}_0 - \boldsymbol{\eta}_0) = 0$.

We are now ready to define cointegration.[4]

Definition 10.1 (Cointegration): Let $\mathbf{y}_t$ be an n-dimensional I(1) system whose associated zero-mean I(0) system $\mathbf{u}_t$ satisfies (10.1.1)–(10.1.4). We say that $\mathbf{y}_t$ is **cointegrated** with an n-dimensional **cointegrating vector a** if $\mathbf{a} \neq \mathbf{0}$ and $\mathbf{a}'\mathbf{y}_t$ can be made trend stationary by a suitable choice of its initial value $\mathbf{y}_0$.

Defining cointegration in this way, although dictated by logical consistency, does *not* necessarily mean that the theory of cointegration requires that the initial condition $\mathbf{y}_0$ be chosen as indicated in the definition. The process in (10.1.21) is not stationary because $\boldsymbol{\eta}_t$ and $\boldsymbol{\eta}_0$ are correlated. However, since $\boldsymbol{\eta}_t = \boldsymbol{\alpha}(L)\boldsymbol{\varepsilon}_t$ and $\boldsymbol{\alpha}(L)$ is absolutely summable, $\boldsymbol{\eta}_t$ and $\boldsymbol{\eta}_0$ will become asymptotically independent as t increases. In this sense, the process in (10.1.21) is "asymptotically stationary," and asymptotic stationarity is all that is needed for estimation and inference for cointegrated I(1) systems.[5]

[3]The idea was originally suggested by Granger (1981). See also Aoki (1968) and Box and Tiao (1977).

[4]Our definition is the same as Definition 3.4 in Johansen (1995).

[5]The distinction between stationarity and asymptotic stationarity is discussed in Lütkepohl (1993, pp. 348–349).

With cointegration thus defined, we can define the following related concepts.

- (Cointegration rank) The **cointegrating rank** is the number of linearly independent cointegrating vectors, and the **cointegrating space** is the space spanned by the cointegrating vectors. As the preceding discussion shows, an n-dimensional vector $\mathbf{a}$ is a cointegrating vector if and only if (10.1.20) holds. Since there are h linearly independent such vectors if the cointegration rank is h, it follows that

$$\operatorname{rank} \underset{(n \times n)}{[\boldsymbol{\Psi}(1)]} = n - h. \tag{10.1.22}$$

Put differently, the cointegration rank h equals $n - \operatorname{rank}[\boldsymbol{\Psi}(1)]$.

- (Cointegration among subsets of $\mathbf{y}_t$) At least one of the elements of a cointegrating vector is not zero. Suppose, without loss of generality, that the first element of the cointegrating vector is not zero. Then we say that y_{1t} (the first element of $\mathbf{y}_t$) is **cointegrated with** $\mathbf{y}_{2t}$ (the remaining $n - 1$ elements of $\mathbf{y}_t$) or that y_{1t} is **part of a cointegrating relationship**. We can also define cointegration for a subset of $\mathbf{y}_t$. For example, the $n-1$ variables in $\mathbf{y}_{2t}$ are not cointegrated if there does not exist an $(n - 1)$-dimensional vector $\mathbf{b} \neq \mathbf{0}$ such that (10.1.20) holds with $\mathbf{a}' = (0, \mathbf{b}')$. Therefore, $\mathbf{y}_{2t}$ is not cointegrated if and only if the last $n - 1$ rows of $\boldsymbol{\Psi}(1)$ are linearly independent.

- (Stochastic cointegration) Note that the deterministic trend $\mathbf{a}'\boldsymbol{\delta} \cdot t$ is not eliminated from $\mathbf{a}'\mathbf{y}_t$ unless the cointegrating vector also satisfies

$$\mathbf{a}'\boldsymbol{\delta} = 0. \tag{10.1.23}$$

In most applications, a cointegrating vector eliminates both the stochastic and deterministic trends in (10.1.19). That is, a vector $\mathbf{a}$ that satisfies (10.1.20) necessarily satisfies (10.1.23), so that $\mathbf{a}'\mathbf{y}_t$, which can now be written as

$$\mathbf{a}'\mathbf{y}_t = \mathbf{a}'\boldsymbol{\eta}_t + \mathbf{a}'(\mathbf{y}_0 - \boldsymbol{\eta}_0), \tag{10.1.24}$$

is stationary (not just trend stationary) for a suitable choice of $\mathbf{y}_0$. This implies that $\boldsymbol{\delta}$ is a linear combination of the columns of $\boldsymbol{\Psi}(1)$, so

$$\operatorname{rank} \underset{(n \times (n+1))}{\left[\boldsymbol{\delta} \ \vdots \ \boldsymbol{\Psi}(1)\right]} = n - h. \tag{10.1.25}$$

Unless otherwise noted, we will assume that (10.1.25) as well as (10.1.22) are satisfied when the cointegration rank is h. If we wish to describe the case where a cointegrating vector eliminates the stochastic trend but not necessarily the deterministic trend, we will use the term **stochastic cointegration**. Of course, if $\mathbf{y}_t$ does not contain a deterministic trend (i.e., if $\boldsymbol{\delta} = \mathbf{0}$), then there is no difference between cointegration and stochastic cointegration.

Example 10.2 (continued): In the bivariate I(1) system (10.1.12) in Example 10.2, the matrix $\boldsymbol{\Psi}(1)$ is given in (10.1.8), so

$$\left[\boldsymbol{\delta} \;\vdots\; \boldsymbol{\Psi}(1)\right] = \begin{bmatrix} \delta_1 & 0 & \gamma \\ \delta_2 & 0 & 1 \end{bmatrix}.$$

The rank of $\boldsymbol{\Psi}(1)$ is 1, so the cointegration rank is $1\ (= 2 - 1)$. All cointegrating vectors can be written as $(c, -c\gamma)'$, $c \neq 0$. The assumption that the cointegration vector also eliminates the deterministic trend can be written as $c\delta_1 - c\gamma\delta_2 = 0$ or $\delta_1 = \gamma\delta_2$, which implies that the rank of $[\boldsymbol{\delta} \vdots \boldsymbol{\Psi}(1)]$ shown above is one.

Quite a few implications for I(1) systems follow from the definition of cointegration. For example,

- $(h < n)$ For an n-dimensional I(1) system, the cointegration rank cannot be as large as n. If it were n, then $\text{rank}[\boldsymbol{\Psi}(1)] = 0$ and $\boldsymbol{\Psi}(1)$ would have to be a matrix of zeros, which is ruled out by requirement (10.1.4).
- (Implications of the positive definiteness of the long-run variance of $\Delta\mathbf{y}_t$) The long-run variance matrix of $\Delta\mathbf{y}_t$ is given by $\boldsymbol{\Psi}(1)\boldsymbol{\Omega}\boldsymbol{\Psi}(1)'$ (see (10.1.5)), which is positive definite if and only if $\boldsymbol{\Psi}(1)$ is nonsingular. Therefore, $\mathbf{y}_t$ is not cointegrated if and only if the long-run variance matrix of $\Delta\mathbf{y}_t$ is positive definite.[6] Since the long-run variance of each element of $\Delta\mathbf{y}_t$ is positive if the long-run variance matrix of $\Delta\mathbf{y}_t$ is positive definite, it follows that each element of $\mathbf{y}_t$ is individually I(1) (i.e., I(1) as a univariate process) if $\mathbf{y}_t$ is not cointegrated. The same is true for a subset of $\mathbf{y}_t$. For example, consider $\mathbf{y}_{2t}$, the last $n-1$ elements of $\mathbf{y}_t$. The long-run variance matrix of $\Delta\mathbf{y}_{2t}$ is given by $\boldsymbol{\Psi}_2(1)\boldsymbol{\Omega}\boldsymbol{\Psi}_2(1)'$ where $\boldsymbol{\Psi}_2(1)$ is the last $n-1$ rows of $\boldsymbol{\Psi}(1)$. It is positive definite if and only if the rows of $\boldsymbol{\Psi}_2(1)$ are linearly independent or $\mathbf{y}_{2t}$ is not cointegrated. In particular, each element of $\mathbf{y}_{2t}$ is individually I(1) if $\mathbf{y}_{2t}$ is not cointegrated.

[6] This equivalence is specific to linear processes. In general, the positive definiteness of the long-run variance matrix of $\Delta\mathbf{y}_t$ is sufficient, but not always necessary, for $\mathbf{y}_t$ to be not cointegrated. See Phillips (1986, p. 321).

- Suppose that y_{1t} is cointegrated with $\mathbf{y}_{2t}$. Then $\mathbf{y}_{2t}$ is not cointegrated if $h = 1$ and cointegrated if $h > 1$. The reason is as follows. Cointegration of y_{1t} with $\mathbf{y}_{2t}$ implies that there exists a cointegrating vector, call it $\mathbf{a}_1$, whose first element is not zero. If $h = 1$, then there should not exist an $(n-1)$-dimensional vector $\mathbf{b} \neq \mathbf{0}$ such that $\mathbf{a}_2' = (0, \mathbf{b}')$ is a cointegrating vector, because $\mathbf{a}_1$ and $\mathbf{a}_2$ are linearly independent. A vector such as $\mathbf{a}_2$ can be found if $h > 1$.

- (VAR in first differences?) If $\mathbf{y}_t$ is difference stationary (without drift), it is tempting to model it as a stationary finite-order VAR $\mathbf{\Phi}(L)\Delta\mathbf{y}_t = \boldsymbol{\varepsilon}_t$ where $\mathbf{\Phi}(L)$ is a matrix polynomial of degree p such that all the roots of $|\mathbf{\Phi}(z)| = 0$ are outside the unit circle. But then $\mathbf{y}_t$ cannot be cointegrated. The reason is as follows. If $\mathbf{\Phi}(L)$ satisfies the stationarity condition, the coefficient matrix sequence $\{\mathbf{\Psi}_j\}$ of its inverse $\mathbf{\Psi}(L) = \mathbf{\Phi}(L)^{-1}$ is bounded by a geometrically declining sequence (see Section 6.3). So $\mathbf{\Psi}(L)$ is one-summable and $\Delta\mathbf{y}_t = \mathbf{\Psi}(L)\boldsymbol{\varepsilon}_t$ is a VMA process satisfying (10.1.2) and (10.1.3). Furthermore,

$$|\mathbf{\Psi}(1)| = |\mathbf{\Phi}(1)^{-1}| = |\mathbf{\Phi}(1)|^{-1} \neq 0.$$

So $\mathbf{\Psi}(1)$ is nonsingular and the long-run variance matrix of $\Delta\mathbf{y}_t$ is positive definite.

QUESTIONS FOR REVIEW

1. Let (y_{1t}, y_{2t}) be as in Example 10.2 with $\gamma = 0$. Show that $\{y_{1t} + y_{2t}\}$ is I(1). **Hint:** You need to show that the long-run variance of $\{\Delta y_{1t} + \Delta y_{2t}\}$ is positive.

2. (Stock and Watson (1988) common-trend representation) Let $\mathbf{w}_t \equiv \boldsymbol{\varepsilon}_1 + \boldsymbol{\varepsilon}_2 + \cdots + \boldsymbol{\varepsilon}_t$ so that the BN decomposition is

$$\mathbf{y}_t = \boldsymbol{\delta} \cdot t + \mathbf{\Psi}(1)\mathbf{w}_t + \boldsymbol{\eta}_t + (\mathbf{y}_0 - \boldsymbol{\eta}_0).$$

A result from linear algebra states that

> if $\mathbf{C}$ is an $n \times n$ matrix of rank $n - h$, then there exists an $n \times n$ nonsingular matrix $\mathbf{G}$ and an $n \times (n-h)$ matrix $\mathbf{F}$ of full column rank such that

$$\underset{(n\times n)}{\mathbf{C}}\underset{(n\times n)}{\mathbf{G}} = \begin{bmatrix} \underset{(n\times(n-h))}{\mathbf{F}} & \vdots & \underset{(n\times h)}{\mathbf{0}} \end{bmatrix}.$$

Show that the permanent component $\mathbf{\Psi}(1)\mathbf{w}_t$ can be written as $\mathbf{F}\boldsymbol{\tau}_t$, where $\mathbf{F}$ is an $n \times (n-h)$ matrix of full column rank and $\boldsymbol{\tau}_t$ is an $(n-h)$-dimensional random walk with $\text{Var}(\Delta\boldsymbol{\tau}_t)$ positive definite. **Hint:** $\boldsymbol{\Psi}(1)\mathbf{w}_t = \boldsymbol{\Psi}(1)\mathbf{G}\mathbf{G}^{-1}\mathbf{w}_t$. Let $\boldsymbol{\tau}_t$ be the first $n-h$ elements of $\mathbf{G}^{-1}\mathbf{w}_t$. This representation makes clear that an I(1) system with a cointegrating rank of h has $n-h$ common stochastic trends.

3. ($\mathbf{a}'\mathbf{y}_t$ is not quite stationary) To show that the process in (10.1.21) is not quite stationary, consider the simple case where $\boldsymbol{\eta}_t = \boldsymbol{\varepsilon}_t - \boldsymbol{\varepsilon}_{t-1}$, $\boldsymbol{\delta} = \mathbf{0}$, and $\mathbf{y}_0 = \mathbf{0}$. Verify that

$$\text{Cov}(\boldsymbol{\eta}_t, \boldsymbol{\eta}_0) = \begin{cases} 2\boldsymbol{\Omega} & \text{for } t = 0, \\ -\boldsymbol{\Omega} & \text{for } t = 1, \\ \mathbf{0} & \text{for } t > 1, \end{cases} \quad \text{Var}(\mathbf{a}'\mathbf{y}_t) = \begin{cases} \mathbf{0} & \text{for } t = 0, \\ 6\mathbf{a}'\boldsymbol{\Omega}\mathbf{a} & \text{for } t = 1, \\ 4\mathbf{a}'\boldsymbol{\Omega}\mathbf{a} & \text{for } t > 1, \end{cases}$$

where $\boldsymbol{\Omega} = \text{Var}(\boldsymbol{\varepsilon}_t)$. Verify that $\{\mathbf{a}'\mathbf{y}_t\}$ is stationary for $t = 2, 3, \ldots$.

4. (What if some elements are stationary?) Let $\mathbf{y}_t$ be an I(1) system and suppose that the first element of $\mathbf{y}_t$ is stationary. Show that the cointegrating rank is at least 1.

5. (Matrix of cointegrating vectors) Suppose that the cointegration rank of an n dimensional I(1) system $\mathbf{y}_t$ is h and let $\mathbf{A}$ be an $n \times h$ matrix collecting h linearly independent cointegrating vectors. Let $\mathbf{F}$ be any $h \times h$ nonsingular matrix. Show that columns of $\mathbf{AF}$ are h linearly independent cointegrating vectors. **Hint:** Multiplication by a nonsingular matrix does not alter rank.

10.2 Alternative Representations of Cointegrated Systems

In addition to the common trend representation (see Review Question 2 of the previous section), there are three other useful representations of cointegrated vector I(1) processes: the triangular representation of Phillips (1991), the VAR representation, and the VECM (vector error-correction model) of Davidson et al. (1978). This section introduces these representations.

Phillips's Triangular Representation

This representation is convenient for the purpose of estimating cointegrating vectors. The representation is valid for any cointegration rank, but we initially assume that the cointegrating rank h is 1. Let $\mathbf{a}$ be a cointegrating vector, and suppose, without loss of generality, that the first element of $\mathbf{a}$ is not zero (if it is zero, change the ordering of the variables of the system so that the first element after reordering is not zero). Partition $\mathbf{y}_t$ accordingly:

$$\underset{(n\times 1)}{\mathbf{y}_t} \equiv \begin{bmatrix} y_{1t} \\ \underset{((n-1)\times 1)}{\mathbf{y}_{2t}} \end{bmatrix}. \tag{10.2.1}$$

Thus, y_{1t} is cointegrated with $\mathbf{y}_{2t}$. Since a scalar multiple of a cointegrating vector, too, is a cointegrating vector, we can normalize the cointegrating vector $\mathbf{a}$ so that its first element is unity:

$$\mathbf{a} = \begin{bmatrix} a_1 \\ a_2 \\ \vdots \\ a_n \end{bmatrix} = \begin{bmatrix} 1 \\ \underset{((n-1)\times 1)}{-\boldsymbol{\gamma}} \end{bmatrix}. \tag{10.2.2}$$

We have seen in the previous section that if a cointegrating vector $\mathbf{a}$ eliminates not only the stochastic trend (i.e., $\mathbf{a}'\boldsymbol{\Psi}(1) = \mathbf{0}'$) but also the deterministic trend (i.e., $\mathbf{a}'\boldsymbol{\delta} = 0$), then $\mathbf{a}'\mathbf{y}_t$ can be written as (10.1.24). Setting the $\mathbf{a}$ in (10.1.24) to the cointegrating vector in (10.2.2), we obtain

$$y_{1t} = \boldsymbol{\gamma}'\mathbf{y}_{2t} + z_t^* + \mu, \tag{10.2.3}$$

where

$$z_t^* \equiv (1, -\boldsymbol{\gamma}')\boldsymbol{\eta}_t, \quad \mu \equiv (1, -\boldsymbol{\gamma}')(\mathbf{y}_0 - \boldsymbol{\eta}_0). \tag{10.2.4}$$

Since $\boldsymbol{\eta}_t$ is jointly stationary, z_t^* is stationary. This equation, with z_t^* viewed as an error term and μ as an intercept, is called a **cointegrating regression**. Its regression coefficients $\boldsymbol{\gamma}$, relating the permanent component in y_{1t} to those in $\mathbf{y}_{2t}$, can be interpreted as describing the long-run relationship between y_{1t} and $\mathbf{y}_{2t}$. The cointegrating regression will have the trend term $\mathbf{a}'\boldsymbol{\delta}\cdot t$ as an additional regressor if the cointegrating vector does not eliminate the deterministic trend in $\mathbf{a}'\mathbf{y}_t$. The **triangular representation** is an n-equation system consisting of this cointegrating regression and the last $n-1$ rows of (10.1.9):

$$\Delta\mathbf{y}_{2t} = \boldsymbol{\delta}_2 + \mathbf{u}_{2t} = \underset{((n-1)\times 1)}{\boldsymbol{\delta}_2} + \underset{((n-1)\times n)}{\boldsymbol{\Psi}_2(L)} \underset{(n\times 1)}{\boldsymbol{\varepsilon}_t}, \tag{10.2.5}$$

where $\boldsymbol{\delta}_2$ and $\mathbf{u}_{2t}$ are the last $n-1$ elements of the n-dimensional vectors $\boldsymbol{\delta}$ and $\mathbf{u}_t$, respectively, and $\boldsymbol{\Psi}_2(L)$ is the last $n-1$ rows of the $\boldsymbol{\Psi}(L)$ in the VMA representation (10.1.10). The implication of the $h=1$ assumption is that, as noted in the previous section, $\mathbf{y}_{2t}$ is not cointegrated (it would be cointegrated if $h > 1$). In particular, each element of $\mathbf{y}_{2t}$ is individually I(1).

More generally, consider the case where the cointegration rank h is not necessarily 1. By changing the order of the elements of $\mathbf{y}_t$ if necessary, it is possible (see, e.g., Hamilton, 1994, pp. 576–577) to select h linearly independent cointegrating vectors, $\mathbf{a}_1, \mathbf{a}_2, \ldots, \mathbf{a}_h$, such that

$$\underset{(n\times h)}{\mathbf{A}} \equiv \begin{bmatrix} \mathbf{a}_1 & \cdots & \mathbf{a}_h \end{bmatrix} = \begin{bmatrix} \underset{(h\times h)}{\mathbf{I}_h} \\ \underset{((n-h)\times h)}{-\boldsymbol{\Gamma}} \end{bmatrix}. \tag{10.2.6}$$

Partition $\mathbf{y}_t$ conformably as

$$\underset{(n\times 1)}{\mathbf{y}_t} \equiv \begin{bmatrix} \underset{(h\times 1)}{\mathbf{y}_{1t}} \\ \underset{((n-h)\times 1)}{\mathbf{y}_{2t}} \end{bmatrix}. \tag{10.2.7}$$

Multiplying both sides of the BN decomposition (10.1.16) by this $\mathbf{A}'$ and noting that $\mathbf{A}'\boldsymbol{\Psi}(1) = \mathbf{0}$ (since the columns of $\mathbf{A}$ are cointegrating vectors), $\mathbf{A}'\boldsymbol{\delta} = \mathbf{0}$ (if those cointegrating vectors also eliminate the deterministic trend), and $\mathbf{A}'\mathbf{y}_t = \mathbf{y}_{1t} - \boldsymbol{\Gamma}'\mathbf{y}_{2t}$, we obtain the following h cointegrating regressions:

$$\underset{(h\times 1)}{\mathbf{y}_{1t}} = \underset{(h\times(n-h))}{\boldsymbol{\Gamma}'} \underset{((n-h)\times 1)}{\mathbf{y}_{2t}} + \underset{(h\times 1)}{\boldsymbol{\mu}} + \underset{(h\times 1)}{\mathbf{z}_t^*}, \tag{10.2.8}$$

where $\boldsymbol{\mu} \equiv \mathbf{A}'(\mathbf{y}_0 - \boldsymbol{\eta}_0)$ and $\mathbf{z}_t^* \equiv \mathbf{A}'\boldsymbol{\eta}_t$. Since $\boldsymbol{\eta}_t$ is jointly stationary, so is $\mathbf{z}_t^*$. The triangular representation is these h cointegrating regressions, supplemented by the rest of the VMA representation:

$$\underset{((n-h)\times 1)}{\Delta\mathbf{y}_{2t}} = \underset{((n-h)\times 1)}{\boldsymbol{\delta}_2} + \underset{((n-h)\times 1)}{\mathbf{u}_{2t}} = \underset{((n-h)\times 1)}{\boldsymbol{\delta}_2} + \underset{((n-h)\times n)}{\boldsymbol{\Psi}_2(L)} \underset{(n\times 1)}{\boldsymbol{\varepsilon}_t}. \tag{10.2.9}$$

Here, $\boldsymbol{\Psi}_2(L)$ is the last $n-h$ rows of the $\boldsymbol{\Psi}(L)$ in the VMA representation (10.1.10). It is easy to show (see Review Question 1) that $\mathbf{y}_{2t}$ is not cointegrated.

To illustrate the triangular representation and how it can be derived from the VMA representation, consider

Example 10.3 (From VMA to triangular): In the bivariate system (10.1.12) of Example 10.2, the cointegration rank is 1. The cointegrating vector whose first element is unity is $(1, -\gamma)'$. So the z_t^* and μ in (10.2.3) are

$$z_t^* = (1, -\gamma)\boldsymbol{\eta}_t = \varepsilon_{1t} - \gamma\varepsilon_{2t},$$
$$\mu = (1, -\gamma)(\mathbf{y}_0 - \boldsymbol{\eta}_0) = (y_{1,0} - \gamma y_{2,0}) - (\varepsilon_{1,0} - \gamma\varepsilon_{2,0}), \tag{10.2.10}$$

and the triangular representation is

$$\begin{cases} y_{1t} = \mu + \gamma y_{2t} + (\varepsilon_{1t} - \gamma\varepsilon_{2t}), \\ \Delta y_{2t} = \delta_2 + \varepsilon_{2t}. \end{cases} \tag{10.2.11}$$

VAR and Cointegration

For the stationary case, we found it useful and convenient to model a vector process as a finite-order VAR. Although, as seen above, no cointegrated I(1) system can be represented as a finite-order VAR in first differences, some cointegrated systems may admit a finite-order VAR representation in *levels*. So suppose a cointegrated I(1) system $\mathbf{y}_t$ can be written as

$$\underset{(n\times1)}{\mathbf{y}_t} = \boldsymbol{\alpha} + \boldsymbol{\delta}\cdot t + \boldsymbol{\xi}_t, \quad \boldsymbol{\Phi}(L)\boldsymbol{\xi}_t = \boldsymbol{\varepsilon}_t,$$
$$\underset{(n\times n)}{\boldsymbol{\Phi}(L)} \equiv \mathbf{I}_n - \boldsymbol{\Phi}_1 L - \boldsymbol{\Phi}_2 L^2 - \cdots - \boldsymbol{\Phi}_p L^p. \tag{10.2.12}$$

For later reference, we eliminate $\boldsymbol{\xi}$ from this to obtain

$$\mathbf{y}_t = \boldsymbol{\alpha}^* + \boldsymbol{\delta}^*\cdot t + \boldsymbol{\Phi}_1\mathbf{y}_{t-1} + \boldsymbol{\Phi}_2\mathbf{y}_{t-2} + \cdots + \boldsymbol{\Phi}_p\mathbf{y}_{t-p} + \boldsymbol{\varepsilon}_t, \tag{10.2.13}$$

where

$$\underset{(n\times1)}{\boldsymbol{\alpha}^*} \equiv (\boldsymbol{\Phi}_1 + 2\boldsymbol{\Phi}_2 + \cdots + p\boldsymbol{\Phi}_p)\boldsymbol{\delta} + \boldsymbol{\Phi}(1)\,\boldsymbol{\alpha}, \quad \underset{(n\times1)}{\boldsymbol{\delta}^*} \equiv \boldsymbol{\Phi}(1)\,\boldsymbol{\delta}. \tag{10.2.14}$$

How do we know that this finite-order VAR in levels is a cointegrated I(1) system? An obvious way to find out is to derive the VMA representation, $\Delta\boldsymbol{\xi}_t = \boldsymbol{\Psi}(L)\boldsymbol{\varepsilon}_t$, from the VAR representation, $\boldsymbol{\Phi}(L)\boldsymbol{\xi}_t = \boldsymbol{\varepsilon}_t$, and see if $\boldsymbol{\Psi}(L)$ satisfies the definition of a cointegrated system. The derivation is a bit tricky because the VMA representation is in first differences, but it can be done fairly easily as follows. Taking the first difference of both sides of $\boldsymbol{\Phi}(L)\boldsymbol{\xi}_t = \boldsymbol{\varepsilon}_t$ and noting that $\Delta = 1 - L$ and $(1 - L)\boldsymbol{\Phi}(L) = \boldsymbol{\Phi}(L)(1 - L)$, we obtain

$$\boldsymbol{\Phi}(L)\Delta\boldsymbol{\xi}_t = (1 - L)\boldsymbol{\varepsilon}_t. \tag{10.2.15}$$

Substitute $\Delta\boldsymbol{\xi}_t = \boldsymbol{\Psi}(L)\boldsymbol{\varepsilon}_t$ into this to obtain

$$\boldsymbol{\Phi}(L)\boldsymbol{\Psi}(L)\boldsymbol{\varepsilon}_t = (1-L)\boldsymbol{\varepsilon}_t. \tag{10.2.16}$$

This equation has to hold for any realization of $\boldsymbol{\varepsilon}_t$, so

$$\boldsymbol{\Phi}(L)\boldsymbol{\Psi}(L) = (1-L)\mathbf{I}_n. \tag{10.2.17}$$

This can be solved for $\boldsymbol{\Psi}(L)$ by multiplying both sides from the left by $\boldsymbol{\Phi}(L)^{-1}$, the inverse of $\boldsymbol{\Phi}(L)$.[7] This produces: $\boldsymbol{\Psi}(L) = \boldsymbol{\Phi}(L)^{-1}(1-L)$. The question is, under what conditions on $\boldsymbol{\Phi}(L)$ is this $\boldsymbol{\Psi}(L)$ one-summable and rank$[\boldsymbol{\Psi}(1)] = n-h$?

We can easily derive a necessary condition. Setting $L = 1$ in (10.2.17), we obtain

$$\underset{(n\times n)}{\boldsymbol{\Phi}(1)}\ \underset{(n\times n)}{\boldsymbol{\Psi}(1)} = \underset{(n\times n)}{\mathbf{0}}. \tag{10.2.18}$$

Since the rank of $\boldsymbol{\Psi}(1)$ equals $n-h$ when the cointegration rank of $\boldsymbol{\xi}_t$ is h, the rank of $\boldsymbol{\Phi}(1)$ is at most h. As shown below, the rank is actually h. To state a necessary and sufficient condition, let $\mathbf{U}(L)$ and $\mathbf{V}(L)$ be $n \times n$ matrix lag polynomials with all their roots outside the unit circle and let $\mathbf{M}(L)$ be a matrix polynomial satisfying

$$\mathbf{M}(L) = \begin{bmatrix} (1-L)\mathbf{I}_{n-h} & \underset{((n-h)\times h)}{\mathbf{0}} \\ \underset{(h\times(n-h))}{\mathbf{0}} & \mathbf{I}_h \end{bmatrix}. \tag{10.2.19}$$

That is, the first $n-h$ diagonal elements of the diagonal matrix $\mathbf{M}(L)$ are $1-L$ and the remaining h diagonal elements are unity. A necessary and sufficient condition for a finite-order VAR process $\{\boldsymbol{\xi}_t\}$ following $\boldsymbol{\Phi}(L)\boldsymbol{\xi}_t = \boldsymbol{\varepsilon}_t$ to be a cointegrated I(1) system with rank h is that $\boldsymbol{\Phi}(L)$ can be factored as $\boldsymbol{\Phi}(L) = \mathbf{U}(L)\mathbf{M}(L)\mathbf{V}(L)$.[8] Therefore, all the roots of $|\boldsymbol{\Phi}(z)| = 0$ are on or outside the unit circle and those that are on the unit circle are all unit roots ($z = 1$). It is not sufficient that $\boldsymbol{\Phi}(L)$ has $n-h$ unit roots with the other roots outside the unit circle; see an example in Review Question 4 where $\boldsymbol{\Phi}(z)$ has two unit roots and one root outside the unit circle yet the system is not I(1). The $n-h$ unit roots have to be located in the system in the particular way indicated by the factorization $\boldsymbol{\Phi}(z) = \mathbf{U}(z)\mathbf{M}(z)\mathbf{V}(z)$.

Setting $z = 1$ in this factorization, we obtain $\boldsymbol{\Phi}(1) = \mathbf{U}(1)\mathbf{M}(1)\mathbf{V}(1)$. Since the roots of $\mathbf{U}(z)$ and $\mathbf{V}(z)$ are all outside the unit circle, $\mathbf{U}(1)$ and $\mathbf{V}(1)$ are nonsingular

[7]The inverse exists because $\boldsymbol{\Phi}_0 = \mathbf{I}_n$ is nonsingular; see Section 6.3. Since we are not assuming the stationarity condition for $\boldsymbol{\Phi}(L)$, the inverse filter may not be absolutely summable.

[8]This result is an implication of the lemma due to Sam Yoo, cited in Engle and Yoo (1991). See Watson (1994, pp. 2870–2873) for an accessible exposition.

and the rank of $\mathbf{\Phi}(1)$ equals the rank of $\mathbf{M}(1)$, which is h. That is,

$$\operatorname{rank}[\mathbf{\Phi}(1)] = h. \qquad (10.2.20)$$

Then it follows from basic linear algebra that there exist two $n \times h$ matrices of full column rank, $\mathbf{B}$ and $\mathbf{A}$, such that

$$\underset{(n\times n)}{\mathbf{\Phi}(1)} = \underset{(n\times h)}{\mathbf{B}}\ \underset{(h\times n)}{\mathbf{A}'}. \qquad (10.2.21)$$

This is sometimes called the **reduced rank condition**. The choice of $\mathbf{B}$ and $\mathbf{A}$ is not unique; if $\mathbf{F}$ is an $h \times h$ nonsingular matrix, then $\mathbf{B}(\mathbf{F}')^{-1}$ and $\mathbf{AF}$ in place of $\mathbf{B}$ and $\mathbf{A}$ also satisfy (10.2.21). Substituting (10.2.21) into (10.2.18), we obtain $\mathbf{BA}'\mathbf{\Psi}(1) = \mathbf{0}$. Since $\mathbf{B}$ is of full column rank, this equation implies $\mathbf{A}'\mathbf{\Psi}(1) = \mathbf{0}$. So the columns of the $n \times h$ matrix $\mathbf{A}$ are cointegrating vectors.

The Vector Error-Correction Model (VECM)

For the univariate case, we derived the augmented autoregression (9.4.3) on page 586 from an AR equation. The same idea can be applied to the VAR here. It is a matter of simple algebra to show that the VAR representation $\mathbf{\Phi}(L)\boldsymbol{\xi}_t = \boldsymbol{\varepsilon}_t$ in (10.2.12) can be written equivalently as

$$\boldsymbol{\xi}_t = \boldsymbol{\rho}\,\boldsymbol{\xi}_{t-1} + \boldsymbol{\zeta}_1\Delta\boldsymbol{\xi}_{t-1} + \boldsymbol{\zeta}_2\Delta\boldsymbol{\xi}_{t-2} + \cdots + \boldsymbol{\zeta}_{p-1}\Delta\boldsymbol{\xi}_{t-p+1} + \boldsymbol{\varepsilon}_t, \qquad (10.2.22)$$

where

$$\underset{(n\times n)}{\boldsymbol{\rho}} \equiv \mathbf{\Phi}_1 + \mathbf{\Phi}_2 + \cdots + \mathbf{\Phi}_p, \qquad (10.2.23)$$

$$\underset{(n\times n)}{\boldsymbol{\zeta}_s} \equiv -(\mathbf{\Phi}_{s+1} + \mathbf{\Phi}_{s+2} + \cdots + \mathbf{\Phi}_p) \text{ for } s = 1, 2, \ldots, p-1. \qquad (10.2.24)$$

Subtracting $\boldsymbol{\xi}_{t-1}$ from both sides of (10.2.22) and noting that $\boldsymbol{\rho} - \mathbf{I}_n = -(\mathbf{I}_n - \mathbf{\Phi}_1 - \mathbf{\Phi}_2 - \cdots - \mathbf{\Phi}_p) = -\mathbf{\Phi}(1)$, we can rewrite (10.2.22) as

$$\begin{aligned}\Delta\boldsymbol{\xi}_t &= -\mathbf{\Phi}(1)\boldsymbol{\xi}_{t-1} + \boldsymbol{\zeta}_1\Delta\boldsymbol{\xi}_{t-1} + \boldsymbol{\zeta}_2\Delta\boldsymbol{\xi}_{t-2} + \cdots + \boldsymbol{\zeta}_{p-1}\Delta\boldsymbol{\xi}_{t-p+1} + \boldsymbol{\varepsilon}_t \\ &= -\mathbf{BA}'\boldsymbol{\xi}_{t-1} + \boldsymbol{\zeta}_1\Delta\boldsymbol{\xi}_{t-1} + \boldsymbol{\zeta}_2\Delta\boldsymbol{\xi}_{t-2} + \cdots + \boldsymbol{\zeta}_{p-1}\Delta\boldsymbol{\xi}_{t-p+1} + \boldsymbol{\varepsilon}_t. \qquad (10.2.25)\end{aligned}$$

Using the relation $\mathbf{y}_t = \boldsymbol{\alpha} + \boldsymbol{\delta} \cdot t + \boldsymbol{\xi}_t$, this can be translated into an equation in $\mathbf{y}_t$:

$$\begin{aligned}\Delta\mathbf{y}_t &= \boldsymbol{\alpha}^* + \boldsymbol{\delta}^* \cdot t - \mathbf{\Phi}(1)\,\mathbf{y}_{t-1} + \boldsymbol{\zeta}_1\Delta\mathbf{y}_{t-1} + \cdots + \boldsymbol{\zeta}_{p-1}\Delta\mathbf{y}_{t-p+1} + \boldsymbol{\varepsilon}_t \qquad (10.2.26)\\ &= \boldsymbol{\alpha}^* + \boldsymbol{\delta}^* \cdot t - \underset{(n\times h)}{\mathbf{B}}\ \underset{(h\times 1)}{\mathbf{z}_{t-1}} + \boldsymbol{\zeta}_1\Delta\mathbf{y}_{t-1} + \cdots + \boldsymbol{\zeta}_{p-1}\Delta\mathbf{y}_{t-p+1} + \boldsymbol{\varepsilon}_t, \qquad (10.2.27)\end{aligned}$$

where $\boldsymbol{\alpha}^*$ and $\boldsymbol{\delta}^*$ are as in (10.2.14) and $\mathbf{z}_t$ is given by

$$\underset{(h\times 1)}{\mathbf{z}_t} \equiv \underset{(h\times n)}{\mathbf{A}'}\ \underset{(n\times 1)}{\mathbf{y}_t}\ . \tag{10.2.28}$$

Since, as noted above, the $n \times h$ matrix $\mathbf{A}$ collects h cointegrating vectors, $\mathbf{z}_t$ is trend stationary (with a suitable choice of the initial value $\mathbf{y}_0$).[9] This representation is called the **vector error-correction model (VECM)** or the **error-correction representation**. If it were not for the term $\mathbf{B}\mathbf{z}_{t-1}$ in the VECM, the process, expressed as a VAR in first differences, could not be cointegrated. The VECM accommodates h cointegrating relationships by including h linear combinations of levels of the variables. If there are no time trends in the cointegrating relations, that is, if $\mathbf{A}'\boldsymbol{\delta} = \mathbf{0}$, then $\boldsymbol{\delta}^* = \boldsymbol{\Phi}(1)\boldsymbol{\delta} = \mathbf{B}\mathbf{A}'\boldsymbol{\delta} = \mathbf{0}$. So the VAR and the VECM representations do not involve time trends despite the possible existence of time trends in the elements of $\mathbf{y}_t$.

That the same I(0) process has the VMA, VAR, and VECM representations is known as the **Granger Representation Theorem**.

Example 10.4 (From VMA to VAR/VECM): In the previous example, we derived the triangular representation from the VMA representation (10.1.12). In this example, we derive the VAR and VECM representations from the same VMA representation. For the $\boldsymbol{\Psi}(L)$ in (10.1.12), it is easy to verify that (10.2.17) is satisfied with

$$\boldsymbol{\Phi}(L) = \mathbf{I}_2 - \boldsymbol{\Phi}_1 L,\quad \boldsymbol{\Phi}_1 = \begin{bmatrix} 0 & \gamma \\ 0 & 1 \end{bmatrix}. \tag{10.2.29}$$

So the VMA can be represented by a finite-order VAR. For this VAR, we have

$$\boldsymbol{\Phi}(1) = \mathbf{I}_2 - \boldsymbol{\Phi}_1 = \begin{bmatrix} 1 & -\gamma \\ 0 & 0 \end{bmatrix}, \tag{10.2.30}$$

which can be written as (10.2.21) with

[9] Just in case you are wondering why $\mathbf{y}_0$ is relevant. It is true that you can solve (10.2.27) for $\mathbf{z}_t$ as

$$\mathbf{z}_{t-1} = (\mathbf{B}'\mathbf{B})^{-1}\mathbf{B}'[\boldsymbol{\alpha}^* + \boldsymbol{\delta}^* \cdot t - \Delta\mathbf{y}_t + \boldsymbol{\zeta}_1 \Delta\mathbf{y}_{t-1} + \cdots + \boldsymbol{\zeta}_{p-1}\Delta\mathbf{y}_{t-p+1} + \boldsymbol{\varepsilon}_t].$$

So you might think that $\mathbf{z}_t$ is trend stationary regardless of the choice of $\mathbf{y}_0$. This is not true, strictly speaking, because, unlike in the VMA representation, $\Delta\mathbf{y}_t$ in the VAR/VECM representation is not defined for $t = -1, -2, \ldots$. Only with a judicious choice of $\mathbf{y}_0$ can one make $\Delta\mathbf{y}_t$ $(t = 1, 2, \ldots)$ stationary. This point is mentioned in Johansen (1995, Theorem 4.2).

$$\mathbf{B} = \begin{bmatrix} 1 \\ 0 \end{bmatrix} \quad \text{and } \mathbf{A} = \begin{bmatrix} 1 \\ -\gamma \end{bmatrix} \quad \text{(for example).} \tag{10.2.31}$$

By (10.2.27) and (10.2.28), the VECM for this choice of **B** and **A** is

$$\begin{bmatrix} \Delta y_{1t} \\ \Delta y_{2t} \end{bmatrix} = \begin{bmatrix} \gamma\delta_2 + \alpha_1 - \gamma\alpha_2 \\ \delta_2 \end{bmatrix} + \begin{bmatrix} \delta_1 - \gamma\delta_2 \\ 0 \end{bmatrix} \cdot t - \begin{bmatrix} 1 \\ 0 \end{bmatrix} z_{t-1} + \boldsymbol{\varepsilon}_t,$$
$$z_t \equiv \mathbf{A}'\mathbf{y}_t = y_{1t} - \gamma y_{2t}. \tag{10.2.32}$$

The deterministic trend disappears if $\delta_1 = \gamma\delta_2$, that is, if the cointegrating vector also eliminates the deterministic trend.

Johansen's ML Procedure

In closing this section, having introduced the VECM representation, we here provide an executive summary of the maximum likelihood (ML) estimation of cointegrated systems proposed by Johansen (1988). Go back to the VAR representation (10.2.13). For simplicity, we assume that there is no trend in the cointegrating relations, so that $\boldsymbol{\delta}^* = \mathbf{0}$.[10] We have considered the conditional ML estimation (conditional on the initial values of $\mathbf{y}$) of a VAR in Section 8.7. If the error vector $\boldsymbol{\varepsilon}_t$ is jointly normal $N(\mathbf{0}, \boldsymbol{\Omega})$ and if we have a sample of $T + p$ observations $(\mathbf{y}_{-p+1}, \mathbf{y}_{-p+2}, \ldots, \mathbf{y}_T)$, then the (average) log likelihood of $(\mathbf{y}_1, \ldots, \mathbf{y}_T)$ conditional on the initial values $(\mathbf{y}_{-p+1}, \mathbf{y}_{-p+2}, \ldots, \mathbf{y}_0)$ is given by

$$Q_T(\boldsymbol{\theta}) = -\frac{n}{2}\log(2\pi) + \frac{1}{2}\log(|\boldsymbol{\Omega}^{-1}|) - \frac{1}{2T}\sum_{t=1}^{T}\{(\mathbf{y}_t - \boldsymbol{\Pi}'\mathbf{x}_t)'\boldsymbol{\Omega}^{-1}(\mathbf{y}_t - \boldsymbol{\Pi}'\mathbf{x}_t)\}, \tag{10.2.33}$$

where n is the dimension of the system (not the sample size), $\boldsymbol{\theta} = (\boldsymbol{\Pi}, \boldsymbol{\Omega})$, and

$$\underset{}{\boldsymbol{\Pi}'} \equiv \begin{bmatrix} \underset{(n\times 1)}{\boldsymbol{\alpha}^*} & \underset{(n\times n)}{\boldsymbol{\Phi}_1} & \underset{(n\times n)}{\boldsymbol{\Phi}_2} & \cdots & \underset{(n\times n)}{\boldsymbol{\Phi}_p} \end{bmatrix}, \quad \underset{((1+np)\times 1)}{\mathbf{x}_t} \equiv \begin{bmatrix} 1 \\ \mathbf{y}_{t-1} \\ \mathbf{y}_{t-2} \\ \vdots \\ \mathbf{y}_{t-p} \end{bmatrix}. \tag{10.2.34}$$

[10] For a thorough treatment of time trends in the VECM, see Johansen (1995, Sections 5.7 and 6.2).

Let

$$\underset{(n\times n)}{\boldsymbol{\zeta}_0} \equiv -\boldsymbol{\Phi}(1) = -\big[\mathbf{I}_n - (\boldsymbol{\Phi}_1 + \cdots + \boldsymbol{\Phi}_p)\big]. \tag{10.2.35}$$

Then the reduced rank condition is that $\boldsymbol{\zeta}_0 = -\mathbf{BA}'$ and the VECM (10.2.26) can be written as

$$\Delta\mathbf{y}_t = \boldsymbol{\alpha}^* + \boldsymbol{\zeta}_0\mathbf{y}_{t-1} + \boldsymbol{\zeta}_1\Delta\mathbf{y}_{t-1} + \cdots + \boldsymbol{\zeta}_{p-1}\Delta\mathbf{y}_{t-p+1} + \boldsymbol{\varepsilon}_t. \tag{10.2.36}$$

Equations (10.2.35) and (10.2.24) provide a one-to-one mapping between ($\boldsymbol{\Phi}_1, \dots,$ $\boldsymbol{\Phi}_p$) and $(\boldsymbol{\zeta}_0, \dots, \boldsymbol{\zeta}_{p-1})$. Thus the same average log likelihood $Q_T(\boldsymbol{\theta})$ can be rewritten in terms of the VECM parameters as

$$-\frac{n}{2}\log(2\pi) + \frac{1}{2}\log(|\boldsymbol{\Omega}^{-1}|) - \frac{1}{2T}\sum_{t=1}^{T}\big\{(\Delta\mathbf{y}_t - \widetilde{\boldsymbol{\Pi}}'\tilde{\mathbf{x}}_t)'\boldsymbol{\Omega}^{-1}(\Delta\mathbf{y}_t - \widetilde{\boldsymbol{\Pi}}'\tilde{\mathbf{x}}_t)\big\}, \tag{10.2.37}$$

where

$$\widetilde{\boldsymbol{\Pi}}' \equiv \Big[\underset{(n\times 1)}{\boldsymbol{\alpha}^*} \quad \underset{(n\times n)}{\boldsymbol{\zeta}_0} \quad \underset{(n\times n)}{\boldsymbol{\zeta}_1} \quad \cdots \quad \underset{(n\times n)}{\boldsymbol{\zeta}_{p-1}}\Big], \quad \underset{((1+np)\times 1)}{\tilde{\mathbf{x}}_t} \equiv \begin{bmatrix} 1 \\ \mathbf{y}_{t-1} \\ \Delta\mathbf{y}_{t-1} \\ \vdots \\ \Delta\mathbf{y}_{t-p+1} \end{bmatrix}. \tag{10.2.38}$$

The ML estimate of the VECM parameters is the $(\boldsymbol{\alpha}^*, \boldsymbol{\zeta}_0, \dots, \boldsymbol{\zeta}_{p-1}, \boldsymbol{\Omega})$ that maximizes this objective function, subject to the reduced rank constraint that $\boldsymbol{\zeta}_0 = -\mathbf{BA}'$ for some $n \times h$ full rank matrices $\mathbf{A}$ and $\mathbf{B}$. This constraint accommodates h cointegrating relationships on the I(1) system. Obviously, the maximized log likelihood is higher the higher the assumed cointegration rank h. Thus, we can use the likelihood ratio statistic to test the null hypothesis that $h = h_0$ against the alternative hypothesis of *more* cointegration. Unlike in the stationary VAR case, the limiting distribution of the likelihood ratio statistic is nonstandard. Given the cointegration rank h thus determined, the ML estimate of h cointegrating vectors can be obtained as the estimate of $\mathbf{A}$. For a more detailed exposition of this procedure, see Hamilton (1994, Chapter 20) and also Johansen (1995, Chapter 6).

QUESTIONS FOR REVIEW

1. (Error vector in the triangular representation) Consider the error vector $(\mathbf{z}_t^*, \mathbf{u}_{2t})$ in the triangular representation (10.2.8) and (10.2.9). It can be written as

$$\begin{bmatrix} \underset{(h\times 1)}{\mathbf{z}_t^*} \\ \underset{((n-h)\times 1)}{\mathbf{u}_{2t}} \end{bmatrix} = \boldsymbol{\Psi}^*(L)\boldsymbol{\varepsilon}_t \equiv \begin{bmatrix} \underset{(h\times n)}{\boldsymbol{\Psi}_1^*(L)} \\ \underset{((n-h)\times n)}{\boldsymbol{\Psi}_2(L)} \end{bmatrix} \boldsymbol{\varepsilon}_t. \tag{10.2.39}$$

Here,

$$\boldsymbol{\Psi}_1^*(L) = \underset{(h\times n)}{(\mathbf{I}, -\boldsymbol{\Gamma}')}\, \underset{(n\times n)}{\boldsymbol{\alpha}(L)}, \tag{10.2.40}$$

where $\boldsymbol{\alpha}(L)$ is from the BN decomposition and $\boldsymbol{\Psi}_2(L)$ is the last $n-h$ rows of $\boldsymbol{\Psi}(L)$ in the VMA representation

(a) Show that $\boldsymbol{\Psi}_2(1)$ is of full row rank (i.e., the $n-h$ rows of $\boldsymbol{\Psi}_2(1)$ are linearly independent). **Hint:** Suppose, contrary to the claim, that there exists an $(n-h)$-dimensional vector $\mathbf{b} \neq \mathbf{0}$ such that $\mathbf{b}'\boldsymbol{\Psi}_2(1) = \mathbf{0}'$. Show that $(\mathbf{0}', \mathbf{b}')$ would be an (n-dimensional) cointegrating vector and the cointegration rank would be at least $h+1$.

(b) Verify that $\boldsymbol{\Psi}^*(L)$ is absolutely summable.

(c) Write $\boldsymbol{\Psi}^*(L) = \boldsymbol{\Psi}_0^* + \boldsymbol{\Psi}_1^* L + \boldsymbol{\Psi}_2^* L^2 + \cdots$. For the bivariate process of Example 10.3, verify that $\boldsymbol{\Psi}_0^*$ is not diagonal. (Therefore, even if the elements of $\boldsymbol{\varepsilon}_t$ are uncorrelated, $\mathbf{z}_t^*$ and $\mathbf{u}_{2t}$ can be correlated.)

2. (From triangular to VMA representations) For Example 10.3, start from the triangular representation (10.2.11) and recover the VMA representation. **Hint:** Take the first difference of the cointegrating regression.

3. (An alternative decomposition of $\boldsymbol{\Phi}(1)$) For the bivariate system of Example 10.4, verify that

$$\mathbf{B} = (\gamma, 0)', \quad \mathbf{A} = (1/\gamma, -1)'$$

is an alternative decomposition of $\boldsymbol{\Phi}(1)$. Write down the VECM corresponding to this choice of $\mathbf{B}$ and $\mathbf{A}$.

4. (A trivariate VAR that is I(2)) Consider a trivariate VAR given by

$$\begin{cases} y_{1t} = 2y_{1,t-1} - y_{1,t-2} + \varepsilon_{1t} & \text{(i.e., } \Delta^2 y_{1t} = \varepsilon_{1t}\text{),} \\ y_{2t} = \rho y_{2,t-1} + \varepsilon_{2t} & \text{with } |\rho| < 1, \text{ and} \\ y_{3t} = \varepsilon_{3t}. \end{cases}$$

Verify that this is an I(2) system by writing $\Delta^2 \mathbf{y}_t$ as a vector moving average process. Write down $\mathbf{\Phi}(L)$ for this system and show that $\mathbf{\Phi}(z)$ has three roots, two unit roots and one that is outside the unit circle.

10.3 Testing the Null of No Cointegration

Having introduced the notion of cointegration, we need to deal with two issues. The first is how to determine the cointegration rank, and the second is how to estimate and do inference on cointegrating vectors. The first will be discussed in this section, and the second will be the topic of the next section. There are several procedures for determining the cointegration rank. Among them are Johansen's (1988) likelihood ratio test derived from the maximum likelihood estimation of the VECM (briefly covered at the end of previous section) and the common trend procedure of Stock and Watson (1988). These procedures allow us to test the null of $h = h_0$ where h_0 is some arbitrary integer between 0 and $n - 1$. We will not cover these procedures.[11] Here, we cover only the simple test suggested by Engle and Granger (1987) and extended by Phillips and Ouliaris (1990). In that test, the null hypothesis is that $h = 0$ (no cointegration) and the alternative is that $h \geq 1$.

Spurious Regressions

The test of Engle and Granger (1987) is based on OLS estimation of the regression

$$y_{1t} = \mu + \boldsymbol{\gamma}'\mathbf{y}_{2t} + z_t^*, \tag{10.3.1}$$

where y_{1t} is the first element of $\mathbf{y}_t$, $\mathbf{y}_{2t}$ is the vector of the remaining $n - 1$ elements, and z_t^* is an error term. This regression would be a cointegrating regression if $h = 1$ and y_{1t} were part of the cointegrating relationship. Under the null of $h = 0$ (no cointegration), however, this regression does not represent a cointegrating relationship. Let $(\hat{\mu}, \hat{\boldsymbol{\gamma}})$ be the OLS coefficient estimates of $(\mu, \boldsymbol{\gamma})$. It turns out that $\hat{\boldsymbol{\gamma}}$

[11] See Maddala and Kim (1998, Section 7) for a catalogue of available procedures.

does not provide consistent estimates of any population parameters of the system! For example, even if y_{1t} is unrelated to $\mathbf{y}_{2t}$ (in that Δy_{1t} and $\Delta \mathbf{y}_{2s}$ are independent for all s, t), the t- and F-statistics associated with the OLS estimates become arbitrarily large as the sample size increases, giving a false impression that there is a close connection between y_{1t} and $\mathbf{y}_{2t}$. This phenomenon, called the **spurious regression**, was first discovered in Monte Carlo experiments by Granger and Newbold (1974). Phillips (1986) theoretically derived the large-sample distributions of the statistics for spurious regressions. For example, the t-value, if divided by $\sqrt{T}$, converges to a nondegenerate distribution.

The Residual-Based Test for Cointegration

The regression (10.3.1) nevertheless provides a useful device for testing the null of no cointegration, because the OLS residuals, $y_{1t} - \hat{\mu} - \hat{\boldsymbol{\gamma}}'\mathbf{y}_{2t}$, should appear to have a stochastic trend if $\mathbf{y}_t$ is not cointegrated and be stationary otherwise. Engle and Granger (1987) suggested applying the ADF t-test to the residuals in order to test the null of no cointegration. Because of the use of the residuals, the test is called the **residual-based test for cointegration**. The asymptotic distributions of the test statistic for some leading unit-root tests were derived theoretically and the (asymptotic) critical values tabulated by Phillips and Ouliaris (1990) and Hansen (1992a).

In contrast to the univariate unit-root tests, the asymptotic distributions (and hence the asymptotic critical values) depend on the dimension n of the system. This is because the residuals depend on $(\hat{\mu}, \hat{\boldsymbol{\gamma}})$, which, being estimates based on data, are random variables. Here we indicate the appropriate asymptotic critical values when the unit-root test applied to the residuals is the ADF t-test of Proposition 9.6 for autoregressions without a constant or time. That is, the ADF t-statistic is the t-value on the x_{t-1} coefficient in the following augmented autoregression estimated on residuals:

$$\Delta x_t = (\rho - 1)x_{t-1} + \zeta_1 \Delta x_{t-1} + \cdots + \zeta_p \Delta x_{t-p} + \text{error}, \qquad (10.3.2)$$

where x_t here is the residual from regression (10.3.1). There is no need to include a constant in this augmented autoregression because, with the regression already including a constant, the sample mean of the residuals is guaranteed to be zero. There is no need to include time either, because the variables of the regression (10.3.1) implicitly or explicitly include time trends (see below for more on this). The number of lagged changes, p, needs to be increased to infinity with the sample size T, but at a rate slower than $T^{1/3}$. More precisely,[12]

$$p \to \infty \text{ but } \frac{p}{T^{1/3}} \underset{\text{p}}{\to} 0 \text{ as } T \to \infty. \tag{10.3.3}$$

The critical values are the same if Phillips' Z_t-test (see Analytical Exercise 6 of the previous chapter) is used instead of the ADF t. There are three cases to consider.

1. $\mathrm{E}(\Delta \mathbf{y}_{2t}) = \mathbf{0}$ and $\mathrm{E}(\Delta y_{1t}) = 0$, so no elements of the I(1) system have drift. The appropriate critical values are in Table 10.1(a), which reproduces Table IIb of Phillips and Ouliaris (1990). For a statement of the conditions on the VMA representation under which the asymptotic distribution is derived, see Hamilton (1994, Proposition 19.4).

2. $\mathrm{E}(\Delta \mathbf{y}_{2t}) \neq \mathbf{0}$ but $\mathrm{E}(\Delta y_{1t})$ may or may not be zero. This case was discussed by Hansen (1992a). Let g ($\equiv n - 1$) be the number of regressors besides a constant in the regression (10.3.1). Some of the g regressors have drift. Since linear trends from different regressors can be combined into one,[13] the regression (10.3.1) can be rewritten as a regression of y_{1t} on a constant, $g - 1$ I(1) regressors without drift, and one I(1) regressor with drift. Now, since linear trends dominate stochastic trends (in the sense made precise in the discussion of the BN decomposition in the previous chapter), the I(1) regressor with a trend behaves very much like time in large samples. So the residuals are "asymptotically the same" as the residuals from a regression with a constant, $g - 1$ driftless I(1) variables, and time as regressors, in the sense that the limiting distribution of a statistic based on the residuals from the former regression is the same as that from the latter regression.

   The critical values for the ADF t test based on the latter regression are tabulated in Table IIc of Phillips and Ouliaris (1990). Therefore, to find the appropriate critical value when the regression (10.3.1) has a constant and g regressors but not time, turn to this table for $g - 1$ regressors. If the regression has only one regressor besides the constant (i.e., if $g = 1$), then the regression is asymptotically equivalent to a regression of y_{1t} on a constant and time. For this case, the limiting distribution of the ADF t-statistic calculated from the residuals turns out to be the Dickey-Fuller distribution (DF_t^{τ}) of Proposition 9.8. Table 10.1(b) combines these distributions: for the case of one I(1)

[12] See Phillips and Ouliaris (1990, Theorem 4.2). The lag length p can be a random variable because it can be data-dependent. This condition is the same as in the Said-Dickey extension of the ADF tests in the previous chapter (see Section 9.4), except that p here can be a random variable.

[13] For example, let $n = 3$ so that there are two regressors, y_{2t} and y_{3t} with coefficients γ_1 and γ_2, respectively. If δ_2 and δ_3 are the drifts in y_{2t} and y_{3t}, respectively, then the linear trends in regression (10.3.1) are $\gamma_1\delta_2 t$ and $\gamma_2\delta_3 t$, which can be combined into a single time trend $(\gamma_1\delta_2 + \gamma_2\delta_3)t$.

Table 10.1: Critical Values for the ADF t-Statistic Applied to Residuals

Estimated Regression: $y_{1t} = \mu + \gamma' \mathbf{y}_{2t}$				
Number of regressors, excluding constant	1%	2.5%	5%	10%
(a) Regressors have no drift				
1	−3.96	−3.64	−3.37	−3.07
2	−4.31	−4.02	−3.77	−3.45
3	−4.73	−4.37	−4.11	−3.83
4	−5.07	−4.71	−4.45	−4.16
5	−5.28	−4.98	−4.71	−4.43
(b) Some regressors have drift				
1	−3.96	−3.67	−3.41	−3.13
2	−4.36	−4.07	−3.80	−3.52
3	−4.65	−4.39	−4.16	−3.84
4	−5.04	−4.77	−4.49	−4.20
5	−5.36	−5.02	−4.74	−4.46

SOURCE: For panel (a), Phillips and Ouliaris (1990, Table IIb). For panel (b), the first row is from Fuller (1996, Table 10.A.2), and the other rows are from Phillips and Ouliaris (1990, Table IIc).

regressor ($g = 1$), it shows the ADF t^{τ}-distribution, and for the case of g (> 1) regressors, it shows the critical values from Table IIc of Phillips and Ouliaris (1990) for $g - 1$ regressors. For example, if $g = 2$, the 5 percent critical value is -3.80, which is the 5 percent critical value in Table IIc in Phillips and Ouliaris (1990) for one regressor.

3. This leaves the case where $\mathrm{E}(\Delta \mathbf{y}_{2t}) = \mathbf{0}$ and $\mathrm{E}(\Delta y_{1t}) \neq 0$. Since y_{1t} has drift and $\mathbf{y}_{2t}$ does not, we need to include time in the regression (10.3.1) in order to remove a linear trend from the residuals. The discussion for the previous case makes it clear that the ADF t-statistic calculated using the residuals from a regression of y_{1t} on a constant, g driftless I(1) regressors $\mathbf{y}_{2t}$, *and* time has the asymptotic distribution tabulated in Table 10.1(b) for $g + 1$ regressors (or Table IIc of Phillips and Ouliaris, 1990, for g regressors). For example, if $g = 2$, the regressor (10.3.1) has a constant, two I(1) regressors, and time; the critical values can be found from Table 10.1(b) for *three* regressors.

Several comments are in order about the residual-based test for cointegration.

- (Test consistency) The alternative hypothesis is that $\mathbf{y}_t$ is cointegrated (i.e., $h \geq 1$). The test is consistent against the alternative as long as y_{1t} is cointegrated with $\mathbf{y}_{2t}$.[14] The reason (we will discuss it in more detail below for the case with $h = 1$) is that the OLS residuals from the regression (10.3.1) will converge to a stationary process. However, if y_{1t} is I(1) and not part of the cointegration relationship, then the test may have no power against the alternative of cointegration because the OLS residuals, $y_{1t} - \boldsymbol{\gamma}'\mathbf{y}_{2t}$, with a nonzero coefficient (of unity) on the I(1) variable y_{1t}, will not converge to a stationary process. Thus, the choice of normalization (of which variable should be used as the dependent variable) matters for the consistency of the test.

- (Should time be included in the regression?) If time is included in the regression (10.3.1), then the drift in y_{1t}, $\mathrm{E}(\Delta y_{1t})$, affects only the time coefficient, making the numerical value of the residuals (and hence the ADF t-value) invariant to $\mathrm{E}(\Delta y_{1t})$. This means that the case 3 procedure, which adds time to the regressors, can be used for case 1, where $\mathrm{E}(\Delta y_{1t})$ happens to be zero. That is, if you include time in the regression (10.3.1), then the appropriate critical value for case 1 is given from Table 10.1(b) for $g + 1$ regressors. The procedure is also valid for case 2, because if time is included in addition to a constant and g I(1) regressors with drift, then the regression can be rewritten as a regression with a constant, g driftless I(1) regressors, and time that combines the drifts in the g I(1) regressors. This regression falls under case 3 and the critical values provided by Table 10.1(b) for $g + 1$ regressors apply. Therefore, when time is included in the regression (10.3.1), the same critical values can be used, regardless of the location of drifts. A possible disadvantage is reduced power in finite samples. The finite-sample power is indeed lower at least for the DGPs examined by Hansen (1992a) in his simulations.

- (Choice of lag length) The requirement (10.3.3) does not provide a practical rule in finite samples for selecting the lag length p in the augmented autoregression to be estimated on the residuals. There seems to be no work in the context of the residual-based test comparable to that of Ng and Perron (1995) for univariate I(1) processes. The usual practice is to proceed as in the univariate context, which is to use the Akaike information criterion (AIC) or the Bayesian information criterion (BIC), also called the Schwartz information criterion (SIC), to determine the number of lagged changes.

[14] For the case of $h = 1$, this is an implication of Theorem 5.1 of Phillips and Ouliaris (1990). Their remark (d) to this theorem shows that the test is consistent when $h > 1$ and hence $\mathbf{y}_{2t}$ is cointegrated.

- (Finite-sample considerations) Besides the residual-based ADF t-test, a number of tests are available for testing the null of no cointegration. They include tests proposed by Phillips and Ouliaris (1990), Stock and Watson (1988), and Johansen (1988). Haug (1996) reports a recent Monte Carlo study examining the finite-sample performance of these and other tests. It reveals a tradeoff between power and size distortions (that is, tests with the least size distortion tend to have low power). The residual-based ADF t-test with the lag length chosen by AIC, although less powerful than some other tests, has the least size distortion for the DGPs examined.

The following example applies the residual-based test with the ADF t-statistic to the consumption-income relationship.

Example 10.5 (Are consumption and income cointegrated?): As was already mentioned in connection with Figure 10.1(a), log income (y_t) and log consumption (c_t) appear to be cointegrated with a cointegrating vector of $(1, -1)$. This figure, however, is rather deceiving. The plot of $y_t - c_t$ (which is the log of the saving rate) in Figure 10.1(b) shows an upward drift right after the war and a downward drift since the mid 1980s. (The latter is the well-publicized fact that the U.S. personal saving rate has been declining.) As seen below, the test results depend on whether to include these periods or not. We initially focus on the sample period of 1950:Q1 to 1986:Q4 (148 obervations).

We first test whether the two series are individually I(1), by conducting the ADF t-test with a constant and time trend in the augmented autoregression. In applying the BIC to select the number of lagged changes in the augmented augoregression, we follow the same practice of the previous chapter: the maximum length (p_{max}) is $\left[12 \cdot (T/100)^{1/4}\right]$ (the integer part of $\left[12 \cdot (T/100)^{1/4}\right]$), the sample period is fixed at $t = p_{max}+2, p_{max}+3, \ldots, T$ in the process of choosing the lag length p, and, given p, the maximum sample of $t = p+2, p+3, \ldots, T$ is used to estimate the augmented autoregression with p lagged changes. For the present sample size, p_{max} is 13.

For disposable income, the BIC selects the lag length of 0 and the ADF t-statistic (t^{τ}) is -1.80. The 5 percent critical value from Table 9.2 (c) is -3.41, so we accept the hypothesis that y_t is I(1). For consumption, the lag length by the BIC is 1 and the ADF t statistic is -2.07. So we accept the I(1) null at 5 percent. Thus, both series might well be described as I(1) with drift.

Turning to the residual-based test for cointegration, the OLS estimate of the static regression is

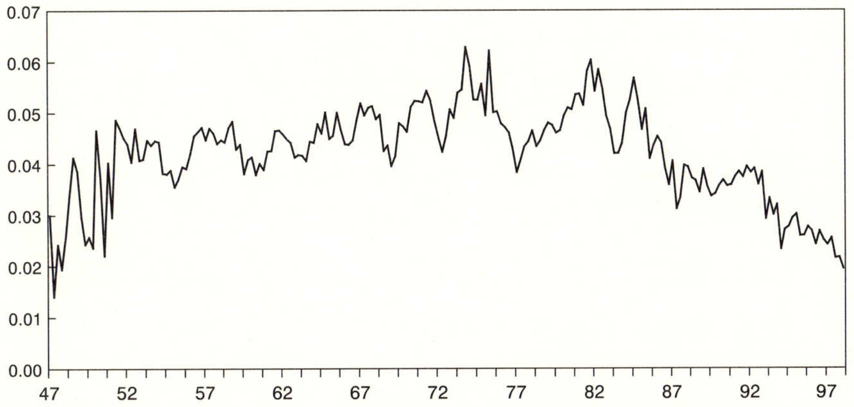

Figure 10.1(b): Log Income Minus Log Consumption

$$c_t = \underset{(0.009)}{-0.046} + \underset{(0.0037)}{0.975}\, y_t, \quad R^2 = 0.998, \quad t = \text{1950:Q1 to 1986:Q4.} \tag{10.3.4}$$

To conduct the residual-based ADF t test, an augmented autoregression without constant or time is estimated on the residuals with the lag length of 0 selected by the BIC. The ADF t statistic is -5.49. Since the series have time trends, we turn to Table 10.1(b), rather than Table 10.1(a), to find critical values. For $g = 1$, the 5 percent critical value is -3.41, so we can reject the null of no cointegration.

If the residual-based test is conducted on the entire sample of 47:Q1 to 98:Q1, the ADF t statistic is -2.94 with the lag length of 1 determined by BIC, and thus, we cannot reject the hypothesis that the consumption-on-income regression is spurious!

Testing the Null of Cointegration

In the above test, cointegration is taken as the alternative hypothesis rather than the null. But very often in economics the hypothesis of economic interest is whether the variables in question are cointegrated, so it would be desirable to develop tests where the null hypothesis is that $h = 1$ rather than that $h = 0$. Very recently, several tests of the null of cointegration have been proposed. For a catalogue of such tests, see Maddala and Kim (1998, Section 4.5). As was true in the testing of the null that a univariate process is I(0), there is no single test of cointegration used by the majority of researchers yet.[15]

QUESTION FOR REVIEW

1. For the residual-based test for cointegration with the regression (10.3.1) not including time as a regressor, verify that there is very little difference in the critical value between case 1 and case 2.

10.4 Inference on Cointegrating Vectors

In the previous section, we examined whether an I(1) system is cointegrated. In this section, we assume that the system is known to be cointegrated and that the cointegration rank and the associated triangular representation are known.[16] Our interest is to estimate the cointegrating vectors in the triangular representation and to make inference about them. For the most part, we focus on the special case where the cointegration rank is 1; the general case is briefly discussed at the end of the section.

The SOLS Estimator

For the $h = 1$ case, the triangular representation is

$$\begin{cases} y_{1t} = \mu + \boldsymbol{\gamma}'\mathbf{y}_{2t} + z_t^* \\ \underset{((n-1)\times 1)}{\Delta \mathbf{y}_{2t}} = \boldsymbol{\delta}_2 + \mathbf{u}_{2t} \end{cases}, \quad \begin{bmatrix} \underset{(1\times 1)}{z_t^*} \\ \underset{((n-1)\times 1)}{\mathbf{u}_{2t}} \end{bmatrix} = \underset{(n\times n)}{\boldsymbol{\Psi}^*(L)} \underset{(n\times 1)}{\boldsymbol{\varepsilon}_t}, \tag{10.4.1}$$

where $\mathbf{y}_{2t}$ is not cointegrated. (This is just reproducing (10.2.3) and (10.2.5) with (10.2.39) for $h = 1$.) So the regression (10.3.1) is now the cointegrating regression. Therefore, there exists a unique $(n-1)$-dimensional vector $\boldsymbol{\gamma}$ such that $y_{1t} - \tilde{\boldsymbol{\gamma}}'\mathbf{y}_{2t}$ is a stationary process (z_t^*) plus some time-invariant random variable (μ) when $\tilde{\boldsymbol{\gamma}} = \boldsymbol{\gamma}$ and has a stochastic trend when $\tilde{\boldsymbol{\gamma}} \neq \boldsymbol{\gamma}$. This suggests that the OLS estimate

[15] The procedures of Johansen (1988) and Stock and Watson (1988) cannot be used for testing the null of cointegration against the alternative of no cointegration, because in their tests the alternative hypothesis specifies *more* cointegration than the null.

[16] In practice, we rarely have such knowledge, and the decision to entertain a system with h cointegrating relationships is usually based on the outcome of prior tests (such as those mentioned in the previous section) designed for determining the cointegration rank. This creates a **pretest problem**, because the distribution of the estimated cointegrating vectors does not take into account the uncertainty about the cointegration rank. This issue has not been studied extensively.

$(\hat{\mu}, \hat{\gamma})$ of the coefficient vector, which minimizes the sum of squared residuals, is consistent. In fact, as was shown by Phillips and Durlauf (1986) and Stock (1987) for the case where $\boldsymbol{\delta}_2$ in (10.4.1) ($= \mathrm{E}(\Delta \mathbf{y}_{2t})$) is zero and by Hansen (1992a, Theorem 1(b)) for the $\boldsymbol{\delta}_2 \neq \mathbf{0}$ case, the OLS estimate $\hat{\gamma}$ is superconsistent for the cointegrating vector $\boldsymbol{\gamma}$, with the sampling error converging to 0 at a rate faster than the usual rate of $\sqrt{T}$.[17] Also, the R^2 converges to unity.[18] The OLS estimator of $\boldsymbol{\gamma}$ from the cointegrating regression will be referred to as the **"static" OLS (SOLS)** estimator of the cointegrating vector. Since the SOLS estimator is consistent, the residuals converge to a zero-mean stationary process. Thus, if a univariate unit-root test such as the ADF test is applied to the residuals, the test will reject the I(1) null in large samples. This is why the residual-based test of the previous section is consistent against cointegration.

This fact — that the OLS coefficient estimates are consistent when the regressors are I(1) and not cointegrated — is a remarkable result, in sharp contrast to the case of stationary regressors. To appreciate the contrast, remember from Chapter 3 what it takes to obtain a consistent estimator of $\boldsymbol{\gamma}$ when the regressors $\mathbf{y}_{2t}$ are stationary: for the OLS estimator to be consistent, the error term z_t^* has to be uncorrelated with $\mathbf{y}_{2t}$; otherwise we need instrumental variables for $\mathbf{y}_{2t}$. In contrast, if y_{1t} is cointegrated with $\mathbf{y}_{2t}$ and if the I(1) regressors $\mathbf{y}_{2t}$ are not cointegrated, as here, then we do not have to worry about the simultaneity bias, at least in large samples, even though the error term z_t^* and the I(1) regressors are correlated.[19]

In finite samples, however, the bias of the SOLS estimator (the difference between the expected value of the estimator and the true value) can be large, as noted by Banerjee et al. (1986) and Stock (1987). Another shortcoming of SOLS is that the asymptotic distribution of the associated t value depends on nuisance parameters (which are the coefficients in $\boldsymbol{\Psi}^*(L)$ in (10.4.1)), so it is difficult to do inference. Later in this section we will introduce another estimator (to be referred to as the "DOLS" estimator) which is efficient and whose associated test statistics (such as the t- and Wald statistics) have conventional asymptotic distributions.

[17] The speed of convergence is T if $\boldsymbol{\delta}_2 = \mathbf{0}$, and $T^{3/2}$ if $\boldsymbol{\delta}_2 \neq \mathbf{0}$. All the studies cited here assume that μ is a fixed constant. The same conclusion should hold even if μ is treated as random. As mentioned in Section 10.1 (see the paragraph right below (10.1.21)), strictly speaking, $\mu + z_t^*$ is not stationary even if z_t^* is stationary. However, since μ and z_t^* are asymptotically independent as $t \to \infty$, $\mu + z_t^*$ is asymptotically stationary, which is all that is needed for the asymptotic results here.

[18] For a statement of the conditions under which these results hold, see Hamilton (1994, Proposition 19.2). Those conditions are restrictions on $\boldsymbol{\Psi}^*(L)\boldsymbol{\varepsilon}_t$ in (10.4.1).

[19] If $\mathbf{y}_{2t}$ is cointegrated, then $h \geq 2$ and the regression (10.3.1) — with $n - 1$ regressors — is no longer a cointegrating regression (a cointegrating regression should have $n - h$ regressors, see the triangular representation (10.2.8)). This case can be handled by the general methodology presented by Sims, Stock, and Watson (1990). See Hamilton (1994, Chapter 18) or Watson (1994, Section 2) for an accessible exposition of the methodology.

The Bivariate Example

To be clear about the source and nature of the correlation between the error term and the I(1) regressors and also to pave the way for the introduction of the DOLS estimator, consider the bivariate version of (10.4.1). For the time being, assume $\boldsymbol{\Psi}^*(L) = \boldsymbol{\Psi}_0^*$ (so there is no serial correlation in (z_t^*, u_{2t})), $\delta_2 = 0$, and $\mu = 0$. The triangular representation can be written as

$$\begin{cases} y_{1t} = \gamma y_{2t} + z_t^* \\ \Delta y_{2t} = u_{2t}. \end{cases}, \quad \begin{bmatrix} z_t^* \\ u_{2t} \end{bmatrix} = \boldsymbol{\Psi}_0^* \boldsymbol{\varepsilon}_t. \tag{10.4.2}$$

The error term z_t^* and the I(1) regressor y_{2t} in the cointegrating regression in (10.4.2) can be correlated because

$$\begin{aligned} \text{Cov}(y_{2t}, z_t^*) &= \text{Cov}(y_{2,0} + \Delta y_{2,1} + \Delta y_{2,2} + \cdots + \Delta y_{2t}, z_t^*) \\ &= \text{Cov}(\Delta y_{2,1} + \Delta y_{2,2} + \cdots + \Delta y_{2t}, z_t^*) \quad (\text{since } \text{Cov}(y_{2,0}, z_t^*) = 0) \\ &= \text{Cov}(u_{2,1} + u_{2,2} + \cdots + u_{2t}, z_t^*) \quad (\text{since } \Delta y_{2t} = u_{2t}) \\ &= \text{Cov}(u_{2t}, z_t^*) \quad (\text{since } (u_{2t}, z_t^*) \text{ is i.i.d.}). \end{aligned} \tag{10.4.3}$$

Since $\boldsymbol{\Psi}_0^*$ and $\boldsymbol{\Omega}$ are not restricted to be diagonal, z_t^* and u_{2t} can be contemporaneously correlated.

To isolate this possible correlation, consider the least squares projection of z_t^* on a constant and u_{2t} $(= \Delta y_{2t})$. Recall from Section 2.9 that $\widehat{\text{E}}^*(y \mid 1, x) = [\text{E}(y) - \beta_0 \text{E}(x)] + \beta_0 x$ where $\beta_0 = \text{Cov}(x, y)/\text{Var}(x)$ and that the least squares projection error, $y - \widehat{\text{E}}^*(y \mid 1, x)$, has mean zero and is uncorrelated with x. Here, the mean is zero for both z_t^* and u_{2t}. So $\widehat{\text{E}}^*(z_t^* \mid 1, u_{2t}) = \beta_0 u_{2t}$ and, if we denote the least squares projection error by $v_t \equiv z_t^* - \widehat{\text{E}}^*(z_t^* \mid 1, u_{2t})$, we have

$$\begin{gathered} z_t^* = \beta_0 u_{2t} + v_t = \beta_0 \Delta y_{2t} + v_t, \\ \text{E}(v_t) = 0, \quad \text{Cov}(u_{2t}, v_t) = \text{Cov}(\Delta y_{2t}, v_t) = 0. \end{gathered} \tag{10.4.4}$$

Substituting this into the cointegrating regression, we obtain

$$y_{1t} = \gamma y_{2t} + \beta_0 \Delta y_{2t} + v_t. \tag{10.4.5}$$

This regression will be referred to as the **augmented cointegrating regression**. Now we show that the I(1) regressor y_{2t} is *strictly exogenous* in that $\text{Cov}(y_{2s}, v_t) = 0$ for all t, s. By construction, $\text{Cov}(\Delta y_{2t}, v_t) = 0$. For $\text{Cov}(\Delta y_{2s}, v_t)$ for $t \neq s$,

$$\begin{aligned} \text{Cov}(\Delta y_{2s}, v_t) &= \text{Cov}(u_{2s}, v_t) = \text{Cov}(u_{2s}, z_t^* - \beta_0 u_{2t}) \\ &= \text{Cov}(u_{2s}, z_t^*) - \beta_0 \text{Cov}(u_{2s}, u_{2t}) = 0, \end{aligned} \tag{10.4.6}$$

because (z_t^*, u_{2t}) is i.i.d. So Δy_{2t} is strictly exogenous. The strict exogeneity of Δy_{2t} implies the same for y_{2t}, because

$$\begin{aligned}\text{Cov}(y_{2s}, v_t) &= \text{Cov}(y_{2,0} + \Delta y_{2,1} + \Delta y_{2,2} + \cdots + \Delta y_{2s}, v_t) \\ &= \text{Cov}(\Delta y_{2,1} + \Delta y_{2,2} + \cdots + \Delta y_{2s}, v_t) \quad (\text{since } \text{Cov}(y_{2,0}, v_t) = 0) \\ &= 0 \quad \text{for all } t, s \text{ by (10.4.6).} \qquad (10.4.7)\end{aligned}$$

Continuing with the Bivariate Example

To recapitulate, we have shown that, in the augmented cointegrating regression (10.4.5), the I(1) regressor is strictly exogenous if $\boldsymbol{\Psi}^*(L) = \boldsymbol{\Psi}_0^*$. Let $(\hat{\gamma}, \widehat{\beta_0})$ be the OLS coefficient estimate of (γ, β_0) from the augmented cointegrating regression. (This $\hat{\gamma}$ should be distinguished from the SOLS estimator of γ in the cointegrating regression in (10.4.2).) This regression, (10.4.5), is very similar to the augmented autoregression (9.4.6) in that one of the two regressors is zero-mean I(0) and the other is driftless I(1). We have shown for the augmented autoregression that the "$\mathbf{X}'\mathbf{X}$" matrix, if properly scaled by T and $\sqrt{T}$, is asymptotically diagonal, so the existence of I(0) regressors can be ignored for the purpose of deriving the limiting distribution of $\hat{\gamma}$, the OLS estimator of the coefficient of the I(1) regressor. The same is true here, and the same argument exploiting the asymptotic diagonality of the suitably scaled "$\mathbf{X}'\mathbf{X}$" matrix shows that the usual t-value for the hypothesis that $\gamma = \gamma_0$ is asymptotically equivalent to

$$\tilde{t} = \frac{\dfrac{1}{T}\displaystyle\sum_{t=1}^{T} y_{2t} v_t}{\sqrt{\dfrac{\sigma_v^2}{T^2}\displaystyle\sum_{t=1}^{T}(y_{2t})^2}}, \qquad (10.4.8)$$

where σ_v^2 is the variance of v_t. That is, the difference between the usual t-value and $\tilde{t}$ in (10.4.8) converges to zero in probability, so the limiting distribution of t and that of $\tilde{t}$ are the same.

In the augmented autoregression used for the ADF test, the limiting distribution of the ADF t-statistic was nonstandard (it is the Dickey-Fuller t-distribution). In contrast, the asymptotic distribution of $\tilde{t}$ (and hence that of the usual t-value) is *standard normal.* To see why, first recall that the I(1) regressor y_{2t} is strictly exogenous in that $\text{Cov}(y_{2s}, v_t) = 0$ for all t, s. To develop intuition, *temporarily* assume that (z_t^*, u_{2t}) is jointly normal. Then y_{2s} and v_t are independent for all (s, t), not just uncorrelated. Consequently, the distribution of v_t conditional on $(y_{2,1}, y_{2,2}, \ldots, y_{2T})$ is the same as its unconditional distribution,which is $N(0, \sigma_v^2)$.

So the distribution of the numerator of (10.4.8) conditional on $(y_{2,1}, y_{2,2}, \ldots, y_{2T})$ is

$$N\left(0, \frac{\sigma_v^2}{T^2}\sum_{t=1}^{T}(y_{2t})^2\right).$$

But the standard deviation of this normal distribution equals the denominator of $\tilde{t}$, so

$$\tilde{t} \mid (y_{2,1}, y_{2,2}, \ldots, y_{2T}) \sim N(0, 1).$$

Since this conditional distribution of $\tilde{t}$ does not depend on $(y_{2,1}, y_{2,2}, \ldots, y_{2T})$, the *un*conditional distribution of $\tilde{t}$, too, is $N(0, 1)$. (This type of argument is not new to you; see the paragraph containing (1.4.3) of Chapter 1.) Recall from Chapter 2 that, even if the normality assumption is dropped, the distribution of the usual t-value is standard normal, albeit asymptotically, in large samples. The same conclusion is true here: the limiting distribution of $\tilde{t}$ is $N(0, 1)$ even if (z_t^*, u_{2t}) is not jointly normal. Proving this requires an argument different from the type used in Chapter 2, because y_{2t} here has a stochastic trend. We will not give a formal proof here; just an executive summary. It consists of two parts. The first is to derive the limiting distribution of the numerator of (10.4.8) (which can be done using a result stated in, e.g., Proposition 18.1(e) of Hamilton, 1994, or Lemma 2.3(c) of Watson, 1994). This distribution is nonstandard. The second is to show that normalization (10.4.8) converts the nonstandard distribution into a normal distribution (Lemma 5.1 of Park and Phillips, 1988).

This example of a bivariate I(1) system is special in several respects: (a) there is no serial correlation in the error process (z_t^*, u_{2t}), (b) the I(1) regressor y_{2t} is a scalar, (c) y_{2t} has no drift, and (d) $\mu = 0$. Of these, relaxing (a) requires some thoughts.

Allowing for Serial Correlation

If it is not the case that $\mathbf{\Psi}^*(L) = \mathbf{\Psi}_0^*$ as in (10.4.2), then (z_t^*, u_{2t}) is serially correlated. Consequently, the I(1) regressor y_{2t} in the augmented cointegrating regression (10.4.5) is no longer strictly exogenous because $\text{Cov}(\Delta y_{2s}, v_t)$, while still zero for $t = s$, is no longer guaranteed to be zero for $t \neq s$. To remove this correlation, consider the least squares projection of z_t^* on the current, past, and future values of u_2, not just on the current value of u_2. Noting that $\Delta y_{2t} = u_{2t}$, the projection can be written as

$$z_t^* = \beta(L)\Delta y_{2t} + v_t, \quad \beta(L) \equiv \sum_{j=-\infty}^{\infty} \beta_j L^j. \tag{10.4.9}$$

(This v_t is different from the v_t in (10.4.5).) By construction, $\mathrm{E}(v_t) = 0$ and $\mathrm{Cov}(\Delta y_{2s}, v_t) = 0$ for all t, s. The two-sided filter $\beta(L)$ can be of infinite order, but suppose — for now — that it is not and $\beta_j = 0$ for $|j| > p$. Thus,

$$\begin{aligned} z_t^* &= \beta_0 \Delta y_{2t} + \beta_{-1}\Delta y_{2,t+1} + \cdots + \beta_{-p}\Delta y_{2,t+p} \\ &\quad + \beta_1 \Delta y_{2,t-1} + \cdots + \beta_p \Delta y_{2,t-p} + v_t. \end{aligned} \tag{10.4.10}$$

Substituting this into the cointegrating regression in (10.4.2), we obtain the (vastly) augmented cointegrating regression

$$\begin{aligned} y_{1t} &= \gamma y_{2t} + \beta_0 \Delta y_{2t} + \beta_{-1}\Delta y_{2,t+1} + \cdots + \beta_{-p}\Delta y_{2,t+p} \\ &\quad + \beta_1 \Delta y_{2,t-1} + \cdots + \beta_p \Delta y_{2,t-p} + v_t. \end{aligned} \tag{10.4.11}$$

Since $\mathrm{Cov}(\Delta y_{2s}, v_t) = 0$ for all t and s, Δy_{2t} is strictly exogenous, which means (as seen above) that the level regressor y_{2t} too is strictly exogenous. Thus, by including not just the current change but also past and future changes of the I(1) regressor in the augmented cointegrating regression, we are able to maintain the strict exogeneity of y_{2t}. The OLS estimator of the cointegrating vector γ based on this augmented cointegrating regression is referred to as the **"dynamic" OLS** (**DOLS**), to distinguish it from the SOLS estimator based on the cointegrating regression without changes in y_2.

There are $2 + 2p$ regressors, the first of which is driftless I(1) and the rest zero-mean I(0). As before, with suitable scaling by T and $\sqrt{T}$, the I(1) regressor is asymptotically uncorrelated with the $2p + 1$ zero-mean I(0) regressors, so that the suitably scaled $\mathbf{X}'\mathbf{X}$ matrix is again block diagonal and the zero-mean I(0) regressors can be ignored for the purpose of deriving the limiting distribution of the DOLS estimate of γ. Therefore, the expression for the random variable that is asymptotically equivalent to the t-value for $\gamma = \gamma_0$ is again given by (10.4.8), the expression derived for the case where (z_t^*, u_{2t}) is serially uncorrelated.

However, when (z_t^*, u_{2t}) is serially correlated, the derivation of the asymptotic distribution of (10.4.8) is not the same as when (z_t^*, u_{2t}) is serially uncorrelated, because the error term v_t can now be serially correlated; the projection (10.4.9), while eliminating the correlation between Δy_{2s} and v_t for all s, t, does not remove its own serial correlation in v_t. To examine the asymptotic distribution, let $\mathbf{V}$ $(T \times T)$ be the autocovariance matrix of T successive values of v_t and λ_v^2 be the long-run variance of v_t. Also, let $\mathbf{X}$ in the rest of this subsection be the $T \times 1$ matrix $(y_{2,1}, y_{2,2}, \ldots, y_{2T})'$. Again, to develop intuition, temporarily assume that (z_t^*, u_{2t}) are jointly normal. Then, since y_{2t} is strictly exogenous, the distribution of the numerator of (10.4.8) conditional on $\mathbf{X}$ is normal with mean zero and the conditional variance

$$\frac{1}{T^2}\mathbf{X}'\mathbf{V}\mathbf{X}. \tag{10.4.12}$$

The square root of this would have to replace the denominator of (10.4.8) to make the ratio standard normal in finite samples. Fortunately, it turns out (see Corollary 2.7 of Phillips, 1988) that, in large samples, the distribution of the numerator is the same as the distribution you would get if v_t were serially uncorrelated but with the variance of λ_v^2 rather than σ_v^2.

Therefore, all that is required to modify the ratio (10.4.8) to accommodate serial correlation in v_t is to replace σ_v^2 $(\equiv \text{Var}(v_t))$ by λ_v^2 (the long-run variance of v_t), namely, if $\tilde{t}$ is given by (10.4.8) with σ_v^2 still in the denominator, its rescaled value

$$\left(\frac{\sigma_v}{\lambda_v}\right) \cdot \tilde{t} \tag{10.4.13}$$

is asymptotically $N(0, 1)$! Since the OLS t-value for γ is asymptotically equivalent to $\tilde{t}$, it follows that

$$\left(\frac{s}{\hat{\lambda}_v}\right) \cdot t \underset{\text{d}}{\to} N(0, 1), \tag{10.4.14}$$

where $\hat{\lambda}_v$ is some consistent estimator of λ_v and s is the usual OLS standard error of regression (it is easy to show that s is consistent for σ_v). Put differently, if we rescale the usual standard error of $\hat{\gamma}$ (the OLS estimate of the y_{2t} coefficient in (10.4.11)) as

$$\text{rescaled standard error} = \left(\frac{\hat{\lambda}_v}{s}\right) \times \text{usual standard error}, \tag{10.4.15}$$

then the t-value based on this rescaled standard error is asymptotically $N(0, 1)$.

The foregoing argument is applicable only to the coefficient of the I(1) regressor, so the t-values for β's in (10.4.11), even when their standard errors are rescaled as just described, are not necessarily $N(0, 1)$ in large samples.

Since the regressors are strictly exogenous, the discussion in Sections 1.6 and 6.7 suggests that the GLS might be applicable. However, the fact noted above that $\mathbf{X}'\mathbf{V}\mathbf{X}$ behaves asymptotically like $\lambda_v \mathbf{X}'\mathbf{X}$ implies that the GLS estimator of γ (to be referred to as the **DGLS** estimator) is asymptotically equivalent to the DOLS estimator (or more precisely, T times the difference converges to 0 in probability) (see Phillips, 1988, and Phillips and Park, 1988). Therefore, there is no efficiency gain from correcting for the serial correlation in the error term v_t by GLS.

A consistent estimate of λ_v is easy to obtain. Recall that in Section 6.6 we used the VARHAC procedure to estimate the long-run variance matrix of a vector process. The same procedure can be applied to the present case of a scalar error process. Consider fitting an AR(p) process to the residuals, $\hat{v}_t$, from the augmented cointegrating regression

$$\hat{v}_t = \phi_1 \hat{v}_{t-1} + \phi_2 \hat{v}_{t-2} + \cdots + \phi_p \hat{v}_{t-p} + e_t \quad (t = p+1, \ldots, T). \tag{10.4.16}$$

(This p should not be confused with the p in the augmented cointegrating regression.) Use the BIC to pick the lag length by searching over the possible lag lengths of $0, 1, \ldots, T^{1/3}$. Using the relation (6.2.21) on page 385 and noting that the long-run variance is the value at $z = 1$ of the autocovariance-generating function, the long-run variance λ_v^2 of v_t can be estimated by

$$\hat{\lambda}_v^2 = \frac{\hat{\sigma}_e^2}{(1 - \hat{\phi}_1 - \cdots - \hat{\phi}_p)^2}, \quad \hat{\sigma}_e^2 = \frac{1}{T-p} \sum_{t=p+1}^{T} \hat{e}_t^2, \tag{10.4.17}$$

where $\hat{\phi}_j$ $(j = 1, 2, \ldots, p)$ are the estimated AR(p) coefficients and $\hat{e}_t$ is the residual from the AR(p) equation (10.4.16).

General Case

We now turn to the general case of an n-dimensional cointegrated system with possibly nonzero drift. We focus on the $h = 1$ case because extending it to the case where $h > 1$ is straightforward. So the triangular representation is (10.4.1) and the augmented cointegrating regression is

$$\begin{aligned} y_{1t} = \mu + \boldsymbol{\gamma}'\mathbf{y}_{2t} + \boldsymbol{\beta}_0'\Delta\mathbf{y}_{2t} + \boldsymbol{\beta}_{-1}'\Delta\mathbf{y}_{2,t+1} + \cdots + \boldsymbol{\beta}_{-p}'\Delta\mathbf{y}_{2,t+p} \\ + \boldsymbol{\beta}_1'\Delta\mathbf{y}_{2,t-1} + \cdots + \boldsymbol{\beta}_p'\Delta\mathbf{y}_{2,t-p} + v_t. \end{aligned} \tag{10.4.18}$$

Here, $\boldsymbol{\beta}_j$ $(j = 0, 1, 2, \ldots, p, -1, -2, \ldots, -p)$ are the least squares projection coefficients in the projection of z_t^* (the error in the cointegrating regression) on the current, past, and future values of $\Delta\mathbf{y}_2$. The DOLS estimator of the cointegrating vector $\boldsymbol{\gamma}$ is simply the OLS estimator of $\boldsymbol{\gamma}$ from this augmented cointegrating regression.

The following results are proved in Saikkonen (1991) and Stock and Watson (1993).[20]

1. The bivariate results derived above carry over. That is, the DOLS estimator of $\boldsymbol{\gamma}$ is superconsistent and the properly rescaled t- and Wald statistics for hypotheses about $\boldsymbol{\gamma}$ have the conventional asymptotic distributions (standard normal and chi squared). The proper rescaling is to multiply the usual t-value by $(s/\hat{\lambda}_v)$ and the Wald statistics by the square of $(s/\hat{\lambda}_v)$. This simple rescaling, however, does not work for the t-value and the Wald statistic for hypotheses involving μ or $\boldsymbol{\beta}_j$.

2. If the two-sided filter $\boldsymbol{\beta}(L)$ in the projection of z_t^* on the leads and lags of $\Delta\mathbf{y}_{2t}$ is infinite order, then the error term v_t includes the truncation remainder,

$$\sum_{j=p+1}^{\infty} \boldsymbol{\beta}'_{-j}\Delta\mathbf{y}_{2,t+j} + \sum_{j=p+1}^{\infty} \boldsymbol{\beta}'_j\Delta\mathbf{y}_{2,t-j}.$$

   All the results just mentioned above carry over, provided that p in (10.4.18) is made to increase with the sample size T at a rate slower than $T^{1/3}$. See Saikkonen (1991, Section 4) for a statement of required regularity conditions.

3. The estimator is efficient in some precise sense.[21] The estimator is asymptotically equivalent to other efficient estimators such as Johansen's maximum likelihood procedure based on the VECM, the Fully Modified estimator of Phillips and Hansen (1990), and a nonlinear least squares estimator of Phillips and Loretan (1991) (and also to the DGLS, as mentioned above). For all these efficient estimators, the t- and Wald statistics for hypotheses about $\boldsymbol{\gamma}$, correctly rescaled if necessary, have standard asymptotic distributions (see Watson, 1994, Section 3.4.3, for more details).

Other Estimators and Finite-Sample Properties

Stock and Watson (1993) examined the finite-sample performance of these estimators just mentioned (excluding the Phillips-Loretan estimator). For the DGPs and the sample sizes ($T = 100$ and 300) they examined, the following results emerged.

[20] These authors assume that μ is a fixed constant. However, the same conclusions would hold even if μ were a time-invariant random variable.

[21] The t-value is asymptotically $N(0, 1)$, but the DOLS estimator itself is not asymptotically normal. So the usual criterion of comparing the variances of the asymptotic distributions among asymptotically normal estimators is not applicable here. See Saikkonen (1991, Section 3) for an appropriate definition of efficiency.

(1) The bias is smallest for the Johansen estimator and largest for SOLS. (2) However, the variance of the Johansen estimator is much larger than those for the other efficient estimators, and DOLS has the smallest root mean square error (RMSE). (3) For all estimators examined, the distribution of the t-values (correctly rescaled if necessary) tends to be spread out relative to $N(0, 1)$, suggesting that the null will be rejected too often. These conclusions are broadly consistent with the assessment of Monte Carlo studies found in Maddala and Kim (1998, Section 5.7).

QUESTION FOR REVIEW

1. As we have emphasized, there is a similarity between augmented autoregression (9.4.6) on page 587 and augmented cointegrating regression (10.4.5). Then why is the t-value on the I(1) regressor in the augmented cointegrating regression (10.4.5) asymptotically $N(0, 1)$ while that in (9.4.6) is not?

10.5 Application: The Demand for Money in the United States

The literature on the estimation of the money demand function is very large (see Goldfeld and Sichel, 1990, for a review). The money demand equation typically estimated in the literature is

$$m_t - p_t = \mu + \gamma_y y_t + \gamma_R R_t + z_t^*, \tag{10.5.1}$$

where m_t is the log of money stock in period t, p_t is the log of price level, y_t is log income, R_t is the nominal interest rate, and z_t^* is some error term. γ_y is the income elasticity and γ_R is the interest semielasticity of money demand (it is a semielasticity because the interest rate enters the money demand equation in levels, not in logs). Most empirical analyses that predate the literature on unit roots and cointegration suffer from two drawbacks. First, as will be verified below, all the variables involved, $m_t - p_t$, y_t, and R_t, appear to contain stochastic trends. If the variables have trends, conventional inference under the stationarity assumption is not valid. Second, the regressors may be endogenous. This is likely to be a serious problem in the case of money demand, because in virtually all macro models a shift in money demand represented by the error term z_t^* affects the nominal interest rate and perhaps income. A resolution of both problems is provided by the econometric technique for estimating cointegrating regressions presented in the previous section.

Another issue addressed in this section is the stability of the money demand function. The consensus in the literature is that money demand is unstable. This is challenged by Lucas (1988) who, using annual data since 1900, argues that the interest semielasticity is stable if the income elasticity is constrained to be unity. We will examine Lucas' claim by applying the state-of-the-art econometric techniques developed in this chapter.

The Data

We base our analysis on the annual data studied by Lucas (1988), extended by Stock and Watson (1993) to cover 1900–1989. Their measures of the money stock, income, and the nominal interest rate are M1, net national product (NNP), and the six-month commercial paper rate (in percent at an annual rate), respectively. The use of *net* national product — rather than gross national product — follows the tradition since Friedman (1959) that the scale variable (y_t) in the money demand equation should be a measure of wealth rather than a measure of transaction volume. There are no official statistics on M1 that date back to as early as 1900, so one needs to do some splicing on series from multiple sources. For the money stock and the interest rate, monthly data were averaged to obtain annual observations. See Appendix B of Stock and Watson (1993) for more details on data construction.

$(m - p, y, R)$ as a Cointegrated System

Figures 10.2 and 10.3 plot $m - p$, y, and R. The three series have clear trends. Log real money stock ($m - p$) grew rapidly over the first half of the century, but experienced almost no growth thereafter until 1981. Log income (y), on the other hand, grew steadily over the entire sample period with a major interruption from 1930 to the early 1940s, so M1 velocity ($y - (m - p)$), also plotted in Figure 10.3, dropped during that period and then grew steadily until 1981. This movement in M1 velocity is fairly closely followed by the nominal interest rate, which suggests that $m - p$, y, and R are cointegrated, with a cointegrating vector whose element corresponding to y is about 1.

Inspection of these figures suggests that the three variables, $m - p$, y, and R, might be well described as being individually I(1). In fact, Stock and Watson (1993), based on the ADF tests, report that $m - p$ and y are individually I(1) with drift, while R is I(1) with no drift. They also report, based on the Stock-Watson (1988) common trend test, that the three-variable system is cointegrated with a cointegrating rank of 1. In what follows, we proceed under the assumption that $m - p$ is cointegrated with y and R. (In the empirical exercise, you will be asked to check the validity of this premise.)

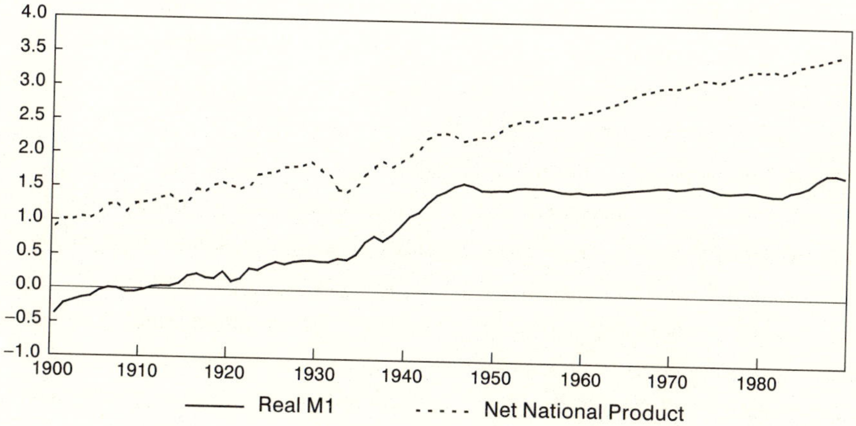

Figure 10.2: U.S. Real NNP and Real M1, in Logs

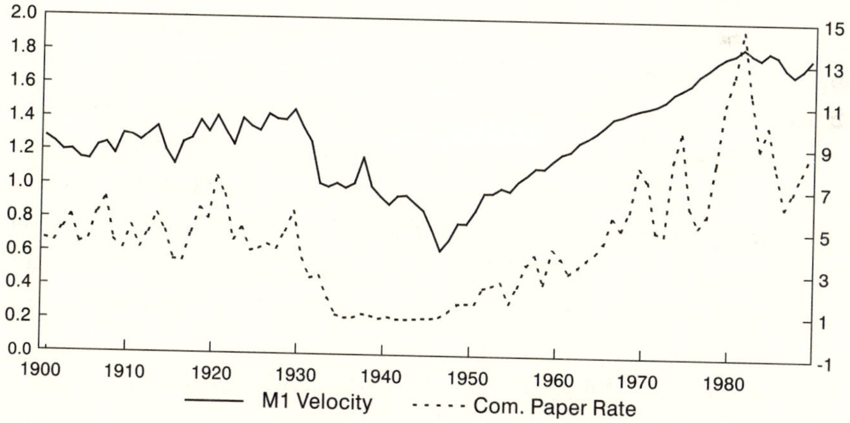

Figure 10.3: Log M1 Velocity (left scale) and Short-Term Commercial Paper Rate (right scale)

DOLS

The first line of Table 10.2 reports the SOLS estimate of the cointegrating regression (10.5.1). (The sample period is 1903–1987 because in the DOLS estimation below two lead and lagged changes will be included in the augmented cointegrating regression.) The standard errors are not reported because the asymptotic distribution of the associated t-ratio, being dependent on nuisance parameters, is unknown. The SOLS estimate of the income elasticity of 0.943 is close to unity, but we cannot tell whether it is insignificantly different from unity. To be able to do inference, we turn to the DOLS estimation of the cointegrating vector, which is to estimate the parameters $(\mu, \gamma_y, \gamma_R)$ in the cointegrating regression (10.5.1) by adding Δy_t, ΔR_t, and their leads and lags. Following Stock and Watson (1993), the number of leads and lags is (arbitrarily) chosen to be 2, so the augmented cointegrating regression associated with (10.5.1) is

$$\begin{aligned} m_t - p_t & \\ &= \mu + \gamma_y y_t + \gamma_R R_t \\ &\quad + \beta_{y0}\Delta y_t + \beta_{y,-1}\Delta y_{t+1} + \beta_{y,-2}\Delta y_{t+2} + \beta_{y1}\Delta y_{t-1} + \beta_{y2}\Delta y_{t-2} \\ &\quad + \beta_{R0}\Delta R_t + \beta_{R,-1}\Delta R_{t+1} + \beta_{R,-2}\Delta R_{t+2} + \beta_{R1}\Delta R_{t-1} + \beta_{R2}\Delta R_{t-2} + v_t. \end{aligned} \tag{10.5.2}$$

This dictates the sample period to be $t = 1903, \dots, 1987$. The DOLS point estimate of (γ_y, γ_R), reported in the second line of Table 10.2, is obtained from estimating this equation by OLS.

To calculate appropriate standard errors, the long-run variance of the error term v_t needs to be estimated. For this purpose we fit an autoregressive process to the DOLS residuals. The order of the autoregression is (again arbitrarily) set to 2. With the DOLS residuals calculated for $t = 1903, \dots, 1987$, the sample period for the AR(2) estimation is for $t = 1905, \dots, 1987$ (sample size = 83). The estimated autoregression is

$$\hat{v}_t = 0.93806\, \hat{v}_{t-1} - 0.13341\, \hat{v}_{t-2}, \quad SSR = 0.19843. \tag{10.5.3}$$

We then use the formula (10.4.17), but to be able to replicate the DOLS estimates by Stock and Watson (1993, Table III), we divide the SSR by $T - p - K$ rather than by $T - p$ to calculate $\hat{\sigma}_e^2$, where K here is the number of regressors in the augmented cointegrating regression (which is 13 here). Thus $\hat{\sigma}_e^2 = 0.19843/(83 - 2 - 13) = 0.0029181$ and

$$\hat{\lambda}_v^2 = \frac{0.0029181}{(1 - 0.93806 + 0.13341)^2} = 0.07647. \tag{10.5.4}$$

Table 10.2: SOLS and DOLS Estimates, 1903–1987

	γ_y	γ_R	R^2	Std. error of regression
SOLS estimates	0.943	−0.082	0.959	0.135
DOLS estimates	0.970	−0.101	0.982	0.096
(Rescaled standard errors)	(0.046)	(0.013)		

SOURCE: The point estimates and standard errors are from Table III of Stock and Watson (1993). The R^2 and standard error of regression are by author's calculation.

Table 10.3: Money Demand in Two Subsamples

	1903–1945		1946–1987	
	γ_y	γ_R	γ_y	γ_R
SOLS estimates	0.919	−0.085	0.192	−0.016
DOLS estimates	0.887	−0.104	0.269	−0.027
(Rescaled standard errors)	(0.197)	(0.038)	(0.213)	(0.025)

SOURCE: Table III of Stock and Watson (1993).

The estimate $\hat{\lambda}_v$ is the square root of this, which is 0.277. Since the standard error of the DOLS regression is 0.096, the factor in the formula (10.4.15) for rescaling the usual OLS standard errors from the augmented cointegrating regression is $0.277/0.096 = 2.89$. The numbers in parentheses in Table 10.2 are the adjusted standard errors thus calculated. Now we can see that the estimated income elasticity is not significantly different from unity.

Unstable Money Demand?

Table 10.3 reports the parameter estimates by SOLS and DOLS for two subsamples, 1903–1945 and 1946–1987. (Following Stock and Watson (1993), the break date of 1946 was chosen both because of the natural break at the end of World War II and because it divides the full sample nearly in two.) In sharp contrast to the estimates based on the first-half of the sample, the postwar estimates are very different from those based on the full sample.

Lucas (1988) argues that estimates like these are consistent with a stable demand for money with a unitary income elasticity. To support this view, he points

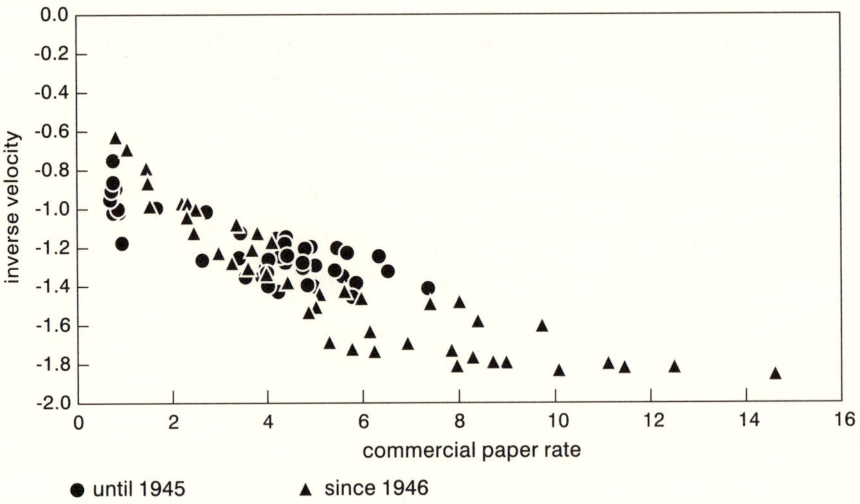

Figure 10.4: Plot of $m - p - y$ against R

to the evidence depicted in Figure 10.4. It plots $m_t - p_t - y_t$ (the log inverse velocity, which would be the dependent variable in the money demand equation (10.5.1) if the income elasticity γ_y were set to unity) against the interest rate, with the postwar observations indicated by a different set of symbols from the prewar observations. The striking feature is that, although postwar interest rates are substantially higher, postwar observations lie on the line defined by the prewar observations.[22]

This finding suggests that the postwar estimates suffer from the near multicollinearity problem: because of the similar trends in y and R in the postwar period (shown in Figures 10.2 and 10.3), γ_y and γ_R estimated on postwar data are strongly correlated. Even though for each element the postwar estimate of (γ_y, γ_R) is different from the prewar estimate, they may not be jointly significantly different. This possibility could be easily checked by the Chow test of structural change, at least if the regressors were stationary. In the Chow test, you would estimate

$$m_t - p_t = \mu + \gamma_y y_t + \gamma_R R_t + \delta_0 D_t + \delta_y y_t D_t + \delta_R R_t D_t + z_t^*, \quad (10.5.5)$$

where D_t is a dummy variable whose value is 1 if $t \geq 1946$ and 0 otherwise. Thus, the coefficients of the constant, y_t, and R_t are $(\mu, \gamma_y, \gamma_R)$ until 1945 and $(\mu + \delta_0, \gamma_y + \delta_y, \gamma_R + \delta_R)$ thereafter. If the regressors are stationary, the Wald statistic for the null hypothesis that $\delta_0 = 0, \delta_y = 0, \delta_R = 0$ is asymptotically $\chi^2(3)$ as both subsamples grow larger with the relative size held constant (see

[22]In Lucas' (1988) original plot, the sample period is 1900–1985 and the break date is 1957, but the message of the figure is essentially the same.

Analytical Exercise 12 in Chapter 2). Now in the present case where regressors are I(1) and not cointegrated, it has been shown by Hansen (1992b, Theorem 3(a)) that the Wald statistic (properly rescaled if necessary) has the same asymptotic distribution (of χ^2) if the parameters of the cointegration regression are estimated by an efficient method such as DOLS (which adds Δy_t, ΔR_t, and their leads and lags to the cointegrating regression (10.5.5)), the Fully Modified estimation, or the Johansen ML.[23] The DOLS estimates of (10.5.5) augmented with two leads and two lags of Δy and ΔR are shown in Table 10.4. The insignificant Wald statistic supports Lucas' view that the money demand in the United States has been stable in the twentieth century.

PROBLEM SET FOR CHAPTER 10

EMPIRICAL EXERCISES

(Skim Stock and Watson, 1993, Section 7 and Appendix B, before answering.) The file MPYR.ASC has annual data on the following:

Column 1: natural log of M1 (to be referred to as m)
Column 2: natural log of the NNP price deflator (p)
Column 3: natural log of NNP (y)
Column 4: the commercial paper rate in percent at an annual rate (R).

The sample period is 1900 to 1989. This is the same data used by Stock and Watson (1993) in their study of the U.S. money demand. See their Appendix B for data sources.

Questions (a) and (b) are for verifying the presumption that $m - p$ is cointegrated with (y, R). The rest of the questions are about estimating the cointegrating vector.

(a) (Univariate unit-root tests) Stock and Watson (1993, Appendix B) report that the ADF t^{μ} and t^{τ} statistics, computed with 2 and 4 lagged first differences, fail to reject a unit root in each of $m - p$ and R at the 10 percent level and that the unit root hypothesis is not rejected for y with 4 lags, but is rejected at the 10 percent (but not 5 percent) level with 2 lags. Verify these findings. In your tests, use the t^{μ} test for R, and t^{τ} for $m - p$ and y, and use asymptotic critical values (those critical values for $T = \infty$).

[23] We noted in the previous section that the Wald statistic is not asymptotically chi squared even after rescaling if the hypothesis involves μ. Hansen's (1992b) result, however, shows that the Wald statistic for the hypothesis about the *difference* in μ is asymptotically chi squared. Hansen (1992b) also develops tests for structural change at unknown break dates.

Table 10.4: Test for Structural Change

	γ_y	γ_R	δ_0	δ_y	δ_R	Wald statistic
DOLS estimates	0.925	−0.090	1.36	−0.52	0.048	1.85
(Rescaled standard errors)	(0.142)	(0.026)	(0.72)	(0.31)	(0.034)	(p-value = 0.60)

SOURCE: Author's calculation, to be verified in the empirical exercise.

(b) (Residual-based tests) Conduct the Engle-Granger test of the null that $m - p$ is not cointegrated with y and R. Set $p = 1$ (which is what is selected by BIC). (If you do not include time in the regression, the ADF t-statistic derived from the residuals should be about -4.7. Case 2 discussed in Section 10.3 should apply. So the 5 percent critical value should be -3.80.)

(c) (DOLS) Reproduce the SOLS and DOLS estimates of the cointegrating vector reported in Table 10.2.

(d) (Chow test) Reproduce the DOLS estimates reported in Table 10.4. They are based on the following augmented cointegrating regression:

$$\begin{aligned} m_t - p_t \\ &= \mu + \gamma_y y_t + \gamma_R R_t + \delta_0 D_t + \delta_y y_t D_t + \delta_R R_t D_t \\ &\quad + \beta_{y0}\Delta y_t + \beta_{y,-1}\Delta y_{t+1} + \beta_{y,-2}\Delta y_{t+2} + \beta_{y1}\Delta y_{t-1} + \beta_{y2}\Delta y_{t-2} \\ &\quad + \beta_{R0}\Delta R_t + \beta_{R,-1}\Delta R_{t+1} + \beta_{R,-2}\Delta R_{t+2} + \beta_{R1}\Delta R_{t-1} + \beta_{R2}\Delta R_{t-2} + v_t. \end{aligned}$$

The null hypothesis is that $\delta_0 = \delta_y = \delta_R = 0$. Set the p in (10.4.16) to 2. Calculate the Wald statistic for the null hypothesis of no structural change.

References

Aoki, Masanao, 1968, "Control of Large-Scale Dynamic Systems by Aggregation," *IEEE Transactions on Automatic Control*, AC-13, 246–253.

Banerjee, A., J. Dolado, D. Hendry, and G. Smith, 1986, "Exploring Equilibrium Relationships in Econometrics through Static Models: Some Monte Carlo Evidence," *Oxford Bulletin of Economics and Statistics*, 48, 253–277.

Box, G., and G. Tiao, 1977, "A Canonical Analysis of Multiple Time Series," *Biometrika*, 64, 355–365.

Davidson, J., D. Hendry, F. Srba, and S. Yeo, 1978, "Econometric Modelling of the Aggregate Time-Series Relationships between Consumers' Expenditure and Income in the United Kingdom," *Economic Journal*, 88, 661–692.

Engle, R., and C. Granger, 1987, "Co-Integration and Error Correction: Representation, Estimation, and Testing," *Econometrica*, 55, 251–276.

Engle, R., and S. Yoo, 1991, "Cointegrated Economic Time Series: An Overview with New Results," in R. Engle and C. Granger (eds.), *Long-Run Economic Relations: Readings in Cointegration*, New York: Oxford University Press.

Friedman, M., 1959, "The Demand for Money: Some Theoretical and Empirical Results," *Journal of Political Economy*, 67, 327–351.

Fuller, W., 1996, *Introduction to Statistical Time Series* (2d ed.), New York: Wiley.

Goldfeld, S., and D. Sichel, 1990, "The Demand for Money," Chapter 8 in B. Friedman and F. Hahn (eds.), *Handbook of Monetary Economics*, Volume I, New York: North-Holland.

Granger, C., 1981, "Some Properties of Time Series Data and Their Use in Econometric Model Specification," *Journal of Econometrics*, 16, 121–130.

Granger, C., and P. Newbold, 1974, "Spurious Regressions in Econometrics," *Journal of Econometrics*, 2, 111–120.

Hamilton, J., 1994, *Time Series Analysis*, Princeton: Princeton University Press.

Hansen, B., 1992a, "Efficient Estimation and Testing of Cointegrating Vectors in the Presence of Deterministic Trends," *Journal of Econometrics*, 53, 87–121.

———, 1992b, "Tests for Parameter Instability in Regressions with I(1) Processes," *Journal of Business and Economic Statistics*, 10, 321–335.

Haug, A., 1996, "Tests for Cointegration: A Monte Carlo Comparison," *Journal of Econometrics*, 71, 89–115.

Johansen, S., 1988, "Statistical Analysis of Cointegrated Vectors," *Journal of Economic Dyamics and Control*, 12, 231–254.

———, 1995, *Likelihood-Based Inference in Cointegrated Vector Auto-Regressive Models*, New York: Oxford University Press.

Lucas, R., 1988, *Money Demand in the United States: A Quantitative Review, Carnegie-Rochester Conference Series on Public Policy*, Volume 29, 137–168.

Lütkepohl, H., 1993, *Introduction to Multiple Time Series Analysis* (2d ed.), New York: Springer-Verlag.

Maddala, G. S., and In-Moo Kim, 1998, *Unit Roots, Cointegration, and Structural Change*, New York: Cambridge University Press.

Ng, S., and P. Perron, 1995, "Unit Root Tests in ARMA Models with Data-Dependent Methods for the Selection of the Truncated Lag," *Journal of the American Statistical Association*, 90, 268–281.

Park, J., and P. Phillips, 1988, "Statistical Inference in Regressions with Integrated Processes: Part 1," *Econometric Theory*, 4, 468–497.

Phillips, P., 1986, "Understanding Spurious Regressions in Econometrics," *Journal of Econometrics*, 33, 311–340.

———, 1988, "Weak Convergence to the Matrix Stochastic Integral $\int_0^1 BdB'$," *Journal of Multivariate Analysis*, 24, 252–264.

———, 1991, "Optimal Inference in Cointegrated Systems," *Econometrica*, 59, 283–306.

Phillips, P., and S. Durlauf, 1986, "Multiple Time Series Regression with Integrated Processes," *Review of Economic Studies*, 53, 473–495.

Phillips, P., and B. Hansen, 1990, "Statistical Inference in Instrumental Variables Regression with I(1) Processes," *Review of Economic Studies*, 57, 99–125.

Phillips, P., and M. Loretan, 1991, "Estimating Long-Run Economic Equilibria," *Review of Economic Studies*, 58, 407–436.

Phillips, P., and S. Ouliaris, 1990, "Asymptotic Properties of Residual Based Tests for Cointegration," *Econometrica*, 58, 165–193.

Phillips, P., and J. Park, 1988, "Asymptotic Equivalence of OLS and GLS in Regressions with Integrated Regressors," *Journal of the American Statistical Association*, 83, 111–115.

Saikkonen, P., 1991, "Asymptotically Efficient Estimation of Cointegration Regressions," *Econometric Theory*, 7, 1–21.

Sims, C., J. Stock, and M. Watson, 1990, "Inference in Linear Time Series Models with Some Unit Roots," *Econometrica*, 58, 113–144.

Stock, J., 1987, "Asymptotic Properties of Least Squares Estimators of Cointegrating Vectors," *Econometrica*, 55, 1035–1056.

Stock, J., and M. Watson, 1988, "Testing for Common Trends," *Journal of the American Statistical Association*, 83, 1097–1107.

———, 1993, "A Simple Estimator of Cointegrating Vectors in Higher Order Integrated Systems," *Econometrica*, 61, 783–820.

Watson, M., 1994, "Vector Autoregressions and Cointegration," Chapter 47 in R. Engle, and D. McFadden (eds.), *Handbook of Econometrics*, Volume IV, New York: North Holland.

APPENDIX A

Partitioned Matrices and Kronecker Products

Partitioned Matrices

It is sometimes useful to partition the elements of a matrix into MN submatrices as

$$\mathbf{A} = \begin{bmatrix} \mathbf{A}_{11} & \cdots & \mathbf{A}_{1N} \\ \vdots & & \vdots \\ \mathbf{A}_{M1} & \cdots & \mathbf{A}_{MN} \end{bmatrix}.$$

This is a **partitioned matrix**. The subscript of the submatrices are defined in the same fashion as those for the elements of a matrix. For example, we might write

$$\mathbf{A} = \begin{bmatrix} 1 & 4 & 7 \\ 2 & 5 & 8 \\ 3 & 6 & 9 \end{bmatrix} = \begin{bmatrix} \mathbf{A}_{11} & \mathbf{A}_{12} \\ \mathbf{A}_{21} & \mathbf{A}_{22} \end{bmatrix},$$

with

$$\mathbf{A}_{11} = \begin{bmatrix} 1 & 4 \\ 2 & 5 \end{bmatrix}, \quad \mathbf{A}_{12} = \begin{bmatrix} 7 \\ 8 \end{bmatrix}, \quad \mathbf{A}_{21} = [3 \quad 6], \quad \mathbf{A}_{22} = 9.$$

A common special case is where $M = N$ and the off-diagonal blocks ($\mathbf{A}_{mn}$ for $m \neq n$) are all zero matrices:

$$\mathbf{A} = \begin{bmatrix} \mathbf{A}_{11} & & \\ & \ddots & \\ & & \mathbf{A}_{MM} \end{bmatrix}.$$

This is a **block diagonal matrix**.

Addition and Multiplication of Partitioned Matrices

Matrix addition and multiplication extend to partitioned matrices. Therefore,

$$\mathbf{A}+\mathbf{B}=\begin{bmatrix}\mathbf{A}_{11}+\mathbf{B}_{11} & \cdots & \mathbf{A}_{1N}+\mathbf{B}_{1N}\\ \vdots & & \vdots\\ \mathbf{A}_{M1}+\mathbf{B}_{M1} & \cdots & \mathbf{A}_{MN}+\mathbf{B}_{MN}\end{bmatrix}, \tag{A.1}$$

$$\begin{aligned}\mathbf{AB}&=\begin{bmatrix}\mathbf{A}_{11} & \cdots & \mathbf{A}_{1N}\\ \vdots & & \vdots\\ \mathbf{A}_{M1} & \cdots & \mathbf{A}_{MN}\end{bmatrix}\begin{bmatrix}\mathbf{B}_{11} & \cdots & \mathbf{B}_{1L}\\ \vdots & & \vdots\\ \mathbf{B}_{N1} & \cdots & \mathbf{B}_{NL}\end{bmatrix}\\ &=\begin{bmatrix}\sum_{n=1}^{N}\mathbf{A}_{1n}\mathbf{B}_{n1} & \cdots & \sum_{n=1}^{N}\mathbf{A}_{1n}\mathbf{B}_{nL}\\ \vdots & & \vdots\\ \sum_{n=1}^{N}\mathbf{A}_{Mn}\mathbf{B}_{n1} & \cdots & \sum_{n=1}^{N}\mathbf{A}_{Mn}\mathbf{B}_{nL}\end{bmatrix}.\end{aligned} \tag{A.2}$$

In all these expressions, the matrices must be conformable for the operations involved. With respect to addition, the dimension of $\mathbf{A}_{mn}$ and $\mathbf{B}_{mn}$ must be the same for all m $(= 1, 2, \ldots, M)$ and n $(= 1, 2, \ldots, N)$. For multiplication, the number of columns in $\mathbf{A}_{mn}$ must equal the number of rows in $\mathbf{B}_{n\ell}$ for all m $(= 1, 2, \ldots, M)$, n $(= 1, 2, \ldots, N)$, and ℓ $(= 1, 2, \ldots, L)$. A special case of multiplication is when **B** is a **stacked vector c**:

$$\mathbf{Ac}=\begin{bmatrix}\mathbf{A}_{11} & \cdots & \mathbf{A}_{1N}\\ \vdots & & \vdots\\ \mathbf{A}_{M1} & \cdots & \mathbf{A}_{MN}\end{bmatrix}\begin{bmatrix}\mathbf{c}_{1}\\ \vdots\\ \mathbf{c}_{N}\end{bmatrix}=\begin{bmatrix}\sum_{n=1}^{N}\mathbf{A}_{1n}\mathbf{c}_{n}\\ \vdots\\ \sum_{n=1}^{N}\mathbf{A}_{Mn}\mathbf{c}_{n}\end{bmatrix}. \tag{A.3}$$

Several cases frequently encountered are of the form

$$\begin{bmatrix}\mathbf{A}_{11} & & \\ & \ddots & \\ & & \mathbf{A}_{MM}\end{bmatrix}\begin{bmatrix}\mathbf{c}_{1}\\ \vdots\\ \mathbf{c}_{M}\end{bmatrix}=\begin{bmatrix}\mathbf{A}_{11}\mathbf{c}_{1}\\ \vdots\\ \mathbf{A}_{MM}\mathbf{c}_{M}\end{bmatrix}, \tag{A.4}$$

$$\begin{bmatrix} \mathbf{A}_{11} & & \\ & \ddots & \\ & & \mathbf{A}_{MM} \end{bmatrix} \begin{bmatrix} \mathbf{B}_{11} & & \\ & \ddots & \\ & & \mathbf{B}_{MM} \end{bmatrix} = \begin{bmatrix} \mathbf{A}_{11}\mathbf{B}_{11} & & \\ & \ddots & \\ & & \mathbf{A}_{MM}\mathbf{B}_{MM} \end{bmatrix}, \tag{A.5}$$

$$\begin{bmatrix} \mathbf{A}'_{11} & & \\ & \ddots & \\ & & \mathbf{A}'_{MM} \end{bmatrix} \begin{bmatrix} \mathbf{B}_{11} & \cdots & \mathbf{B}_{1M} \\ \vdots & & \vdots \\ \mathbf{B}_{M1} & \cdots & \mathbf{B}_{MM} \end{bmatrix} \begin{bmatrix} \mathbf{A}_{11} & & \\ & \ddots & \\ & & \mathbf{A}_{MM} \end{bmatrix} = \begin{bmatrix} \mathbf{A}'_{11}\mathbf{B}_{11}\mathbf{A}_{11} & \cdots & \mathbf{A}'_{11}\mathbf{B}_{1M}\mathbf{A}_{MM} \\ \vdots & & \vdots \\ \mathbf{A}'_{MM}\mathbf{B}_{M1}\mathbf{A}_{11} & \cdots & \mathbf{A}'_{MM}\mathbf{B}_{MM}\mathbf{A}_{MM} \end{bmatrix}, \tag{A.6}$$

$$\begin{bmatrix} \mathbf{A}'_{11} & & \\ & \ddots & \\ & & \mathbf{A}'_{MM} \end{bmatrix} \begin{bmatrix} \mathbf{B}_{11} & \cdots & \mathbf{B}_{1M} \\ \vdots & & \vdots \\ \mathbf{B}_{M1} & \cdots & \mathbf{B}_{MM} \end{bmatrix} \begin{bmatrix} \mathbf{c}_1 \\ \vdots \\ \mathbf{c}_M \end{bmatrix} = \begin{bmatrix} \mathbf{A}'_{11}\mathbf{B}_{11}\mathbf{c}_1 & + \cdots + & \mathbf{A}'_{11}\mathbf{B}_{1M}\mathbf{c}_M \\ & \vdots & \\ \mathbf{A}'_{MM}\mathbf{B}_{M1}\mathbf{c}_1 & + \cdots + & \mathbf{A}'_{MM}\mathbf{B}_{MM}\mathbf{c}_M \end{bmatrix}, \tag{A.7}$$

$$\begin{bmatrix} \mathbf{A}'_{11} & \cdots & \mathbf{A}'_{MM} \end{bmatrix} \begin{bmatrix} \mathbf{B}_{11} & \cdots & \mathbf{B}_{1M} \\ \vdots & & \vdots \\ \mathbf{B}_{M1} & \cdots & \mathbf{B}_{MM} \end{bmatrix} \begin{bmatrix} \mathbf{A}_{11} \\ \vdots \\ \mathbf{A}_{MM} \end{bmatrix} = \sum_{m=1}^{M} \sum_{h=1}^{M} \mathbf{A}'_{mm}\mathbf{B}_{mh}\mathbf{A}_{hh}, \tag{A.8}$$

where $\mathbf{c}_m$ $(m = 1, 2, \ldots, M)$ are column vectors.

Inverting Partitioned Matrices

The inverse of a block diagonal matrix is

$$\begin{bmatrix} \mathbf{A}_{11} & & \\ & \ddots & \\ & & \mathbf{A}_{MM} \end{bmatrix}^{-1} = \begin{bmatrix} \mathbf{A}_{11}^{-1} & & \\ & \ddots & \\ & & \mathbf{A}_{MM}^{-1} \end{bmatrix}, \tag{A.9}$$

provided $\mathbf{A}_{mm}$ $(m = 1, 2, \ldots, M)$ are invertible. This can be verified by direct multiplication.

For the general 2×2 partitioned matrix, one form of the **partitioned inverse** is

$$\begin{bmatrix} \mathbf{A}_{11} & \mathbf{A}_{12} \\ \mathbf{A}_{21} & \mathbf{A}_{22} \end{bmatrix}^{-1} = \begin{bmatrix} \mathbf{A}_{11}^{-1} + \mathbf{A}_{11}^{-1}\mathbf{A}_{12}\mathbf{F}_2\mathbf{A}_{21}\mathbf{A}_{11}^{-1} & -\mathbf{A}_{11}^{-1}\mathbf{A}_{12}\mathbf{F}_2 \\ -\mathbf{F}_2\mathbf{A}_{21}\mathbf{A}_{11}^{-1} & \mathbf{F}_2 \end{bmatrix}, \tag{A.10}$$

where $\mathbf{F}_2 = (\mathbf{A}_{22} - \mathbf{A}_{21}\mathbf{A}_{11}^{-1}\mathbf{A}_{12})^{-1}$. This can be verified easily by multiplying $\mathbf{A}$ by the inverse. In view of the symmetry of the calculation, the upper left block can also be written as

$$\mathbf{F}_1 = (\mathbf{A}_{11} - \mathbf{A}_{12}\mathbf{A}_{22}^{-1}\mathbf{A}_{21})^{-1}.$$

Kronecker Products

For general matrices $\mathbf{A}$ $(M \times N)$ and $\mathbf{B}$ $(K \times L)$, the **Kronecker product** is defined as

$$\mathbf{A} \otimes \mathbf{B} = \begin{bmatrix} a_{11}\mathbf{B} & \cdots & a_{1N}\mathbf{B} \\ \vdots & & \vdots \\ a_{M1}\mathbf{B} & \cdots & a_{MN}\mathbf{B} \end{bmatrix}. \tag{A.11}$$

This is an $MK \times NL$ matrix. A special case is when both $\mathbf{A}$ and $\mathbf{B}$ are vectors:

$$\mathbf{a} \otimes \mathbf{b} = \begin{bmatrix} a_1 \\ \vdots \\ a_M \end{bmatrix} \otimes \begin{bmatrix} b_1 \\ \vdots \\ b_N \end{bmatrix} = \begin{bmatrix} a_1\mathbf{b} \\ \vdots \\ a_M\mathbf{b} \end{bmatrix}. \tag{A.12}$$

It is straightforward but cumbersome to verify the following:

$$(\mathbf{A} \otimes \mathbf{B})(\mathbf{C} \otimes \mathbf{D}) = \mathbf{AC} \otimes \mathbf{BD}, \tag{A.13}$$

provided $\mathbf{A}$ and $\mathbf{C}$ are conformable and $\mathbf{B}$ and $\mathbf{D}$ are conformable, and

$$(\mathbf{A} \otimes \mathbf{B})' = \mathbf{A}' \otimes \mathbf{B}', \tag{A.14}$$

$$(\mathbf{A} \otimes \mathbf{B})^{-1} = \mathbf{A}^{-1} \otimes \mathbf{B}^{-1}, \tag{A.15}$$

provided $\mathbf{A}$ and $\mathbf{B}$ are invertible.

Index